SYLVIA PANKHURST

ALSO BY RACHEL HOLMES

The Secret Life of Dr James Barry
The Hottentot Venus: The Life and Death of Sarah Baartman
Eleanor Marx: A Life

SYLVIA
PANKHURST

Natural Born Rebel

RACHEL HOLMES

BLOOMSBURY PUBLISHING
LONDON · OXFORD · NEW YORK · NEW DELHI · SYDNEY

BLOOMSBURY PUBLISHING
Bloomsbury Publishing Plc
50 Bedford Square, London, WC1B 3DP, UK

BLOOMSBURY, BLOOMSBURY PUBLISHING and the Diana logo are trademarks
of Bloomsbury Publishing Plc

First published in Great Britain 2020

Image credits: Part One: International Institute of Social History; Part Two: International Institute of
Social History; Part Three: Getty Images; Part Four: International Institute of Social History;
Part Five: International Institute of Social History; Part 6: Getty Images

A catalogue record for this book is available from the British Library

ISBN: HB: 978-1-4088-8041-8; TPB: 978-1-4088-8042-5; EBOOK: 978-1-4088-8043-2

2 4 6 8 10 9 7 5 3 1

Typeset by Newgen KnowledgeWorks Pvt. Ltd., Chennai, India
Printed and bound in Great Britain by CPI Group (UK) Ltd, Croydon CR0 4YY

MIX
Paper from
responsible sources
FSC® C019777

To find out more about our authors and books visit www.bloomsbury.com
and sign up for our newsletters

For Sarah and Ann

'Accepting equality takes courage'

Jodi Dean

'the demanding, brilliant art of peace'

Toni Morrison

'she stares at the world,
takes it to the edge of
all the words
men weren't able to invent'

Nathalie Handal

Contents

Preface

'Love and enthusiasm are the two great moving factors which make life worth living. This I aver in spite of all the materialists.'[1] A free spirit and a visionary, Estelle Sylvia Pankhurst was by nature an artist. Yet she became one of the greatest unsung political figures of the twentieth century.

She fulfilled the luminary and radical promise of her name. Estelle, for the stars. Sylvia, for the spirits of the wild forests and woodland of ancient Britain, whose folklore sylvan groves are the home of astonishing beings who delight gods and startle mortals. Her father nicknamed her Miss Woody Way. It was apparent from the very beginning that she would never settle for the easy path of least resistance.

Her surname placed her as a daughter of Britain's best-known feminist family, leading from the front in the history of the struggle for Votes for Women. Sylvia's mother Emmeline was Britain's most famous suffragette. Her barrister father Richard – known to all as the 'Red Doctor' – had drafted the 1870 Married Women's Property Act with his friend John Stuart Mill. Richard adored Emmeline and called her his queen. They had two sons and – as is proper to a dynastic saga – three daughters: first Christabel, next Sylvia and finally Adela.

The eldest Christabel intended to be the first woman lawyer in the land. Sylvia's vocation was to be an artist. Little Adela just wanted her older siblings to notice her. In order to follow their dreams, the sisters had first to fight for their rights to them. Like Malala Yousafzai and Greta Thunberg, the Pankhurst girls became teen radicals recognized by millions as icons of their cause. Under Emmeline's matriarchal leadership, they were educated in the activist school of 'Deeds, not words' and were taught that their mother's exhortation to fight for 'Freedom or Death' was not a rhetorical instruction.

They founded the Women's Social and Political Union in the cramped front parlour of their Manchester home at 62 Nelson Street in 1903. Within months of its formation the WSPU became known in the women's movement as 'the family party'. Two years after Queen Victoria's funeral the Pankhurst women crashed into national consciousness by creating a mass political movement on a scale unseen in Britain since the days of the Chartists. 'The Pankhursts' political views are a subject for controversy,' wrote a contemporary journalist, 'but we can surely all agree with regard to this remarkable family, that they are a British institution and a fine example of all that has been said or sung of British pluck.'[2]

Sylvia inherited her convictions via the cultural chromosomes of generations of her radical family who did not hold that social inequality was natural or human subjection inevitable. She inherited many -isms and -ists from her ancestors, political and philosophical tools for building equality and democracy in a Britain that at the time of her birth was deeply undemocratic. All women and the majority of working men were denied the right to vote and so prevented from enjoying full citizenship in their homeland.

Never baptized, Sylvia was instead plunged in infancy into a distinctively British secular home brew fermented from radical liberalism, Mancunian socialism and materialist Marxism, diluted with a trace of incorporeal Methodism whispering the possibility of transcendence for the perpetually struggling soul. Her mother was an atheist, her father agnostic. The Pankhursts were not Christian Socialists, radical reformist Jews, Hindu nationalists or secular cultural Muslims, but many of their friends and in their milieu were, and these strongly influenced the family.

Hers was in many ways an eccentric childhood, though with a Victorian domestic regimen built on large daily doses of character-building discipline and porridge. Self-mastery, mental toughness and fearsome physical and intellectual courage featured among Sylvia's defining adult characteristics. Porridge she abhorred for life – an unfortunate aversion, since she was to serve more sentences in Holloway Prison than any other suffragette.

The bestselling Australian writer Stella Miles Franklin, author of the international feminist hit *My Brilliant Career*, understood her friend's popular appeal. 'Sylvia Pankhurst is slender and girlish in appearance, just the sort of typical English girl that one sees reading a love story on the Underground, or riding a wheel [bicycle] about the suburbs.'[3] In her youth, Sylvia's big blue eyes, clear skin and abundant fair hair gave the misleading impression of blonde ethereality. Stella Franklin knew like many others that this belied the steely mettle that lay within the five-foot-four frame of her friend. Though she was of average height, many people perceived Sylvia as being much taller.

Judging by the voluminous number of descriptions they inspired, it was Sylvia's large and expressive blue eyes, framed by luxuriant eyebrows, and her voice that most compelled. Her eyes were described as, at times, soulful and compassionate, at others fierce, flashing and piercing. Adela, who thought Sylvia had a horse face, regarded all this attention to her charisma as ridiculous guff. She wrote, with eye-rolling contempt, about her sister's 'long face' and 'sharp shrill voice'.[4]

Interestingly, Sylvia's youthful self-portraits capture something of the otherworldliness that people said they saw in her. By her mid-fifties, she had become notably striking. Howard Coster's 1938 photographic portraits show her with an androgynous bobbed crop and the much lived-in face of an authoritative international stateswoman.

Sylvia was an extraordinarily gifted speaker. Above all else, it was her voice that persuaded, intrigued or infuriated. From tentative beginnings when she stood on a chair in the pouring rain nervously addressing a handful of stragglers, her voice grew to become an instrument of activism as vital as her pen and the printing presses of her newspapers. Radio recordings of her speaking sound to us now not like archaic communications from a different world, but modern, grounded and true. Her accents and tones connect us to her story. A history of British class is in Sylvia's voice. It tells the techniques of a woman who has learned to command public space. Her voice makes you listen, not only because of her skills, but also because it isn't always clear where it might go. Between the layers of her original Mancunian accent and the Received Pronunciation drilled into her at the aspirational Manchester Girls' School, there is a musicality that is all her own. Sylvia's friend Nellie Cressall recalled, 'Of course we had a lot to put up with to begin with. We had everything thrown at us. Rotten eggs, tomatoes ... But

Sylvia just went on speaking. "You see, dear, when you know you're right, you can't be turned aside." And it soon stopped. People came to respect us. After a while you could hear a pin drop at our meetings.'[5]

In 1896, when she was thirteen, Sylvia was taken by her father to the Mosley Hotel in Manchester to meet Eleanor Marx, Karl's youngest daughter, at an event held in honour of Wilhelm Liebknecht, leader of the German Social Democratic Party (SPD). At forty-one, Marx, leader of the National Union of Gas Workers and General Labourers, and fondly nicknamed 'Our Old Stoker', was at the height of her political career, and she profoundly impressed the adolescent Pankhurst. Like Sylvia's parents, she played a key role in the emergence of the Independent Labour Party. Decades later, Sylvia would in turn be claimed as 'Our Sylvia' by British workers.

At the reception, Sylvia's father introduced his daughter to the seasoned feminist elder. She was a hugely popular icon on the left. Marking the handing on of the torch from one generation of rebel feminist women to the next, this meeting is a significant moment in British history. Sylvia Pankhurst's story is the sequel to the life of Eleanor Marx. The flame passes from Marx to Pankhurst, blazing the radical trail of an unbroken British political and intellectual tradition that for too long lay dormant, shunted into the historical sidings. As Sheila Rowbotham observes, 'Socialist feminism hangs, suspended and fragile, in half forgotten memories.'[6]

Eleanor Marx validated something else for the youthful Sylvia: her impatience with feminine fashion. Marx wore comfortable, unconventional clothes, but clearly no corset. When asked in her seventies how she would like to be remembered, Sylvia, who never wore a slick of lipstick in her life, suggested, 'I think you could well save space by omitting your remarks on dress … It is in my opinion long past time for women who have done important public work to be … estimated on that basis. Who cares – for example – how Churchill dresses or whether he has a handsome nose or lovely complexion?'[7]

Sylvia grew up to embody what Melissa Benn calls 'the enduring principle of agitation',[8] the belief in principled and powerful collective protest as the only channel available to those systematically excluded from power or as the best tool available to promote unpopular causes. The test of democracy in early twentieth-century Britain was the ability of existing institutions of power to include and represent those outside.

Keir Hardie, the first leader of the Labour Party and also Sylvia's first great love, wrote, 'The agitator who has a touch of the seer in him is a far more valuable asset than the politician. Both are necessary, but if one must be sacrificed let it not be the agitator.'[9] George Bernard Shaw declared Sylvia a modern-day British Joan of Arc. He warned that 'the historian must understand that visionaries are neither imposters nor lunatics'. In the words Shaw used of St Joan, Sylvia had 'an unbounded and quite unconcealed contempt for official opinion, judgment, and authority ... there were only two opinions about her. One was that she was miraculous: the other that she was unbearable.'[10] Lenin applauded her for representing 'the interests of hundreds of thousands of people'.[11] The world's best-known revolutionary praised and promoted Comrade Pankhurst as Britain's most significant socialist until she disagreed with him and publicly took him to task. Sylvia so thoroughly stymied Lenin's attempts to discipline her, first with carrot and then with big stick, that he was forced to devise a new political concept in her honour and write a treatise about it in order to try and get her under control. He failed.

Sylvia tested the limits of tolerance in a nation that regarded toleration as one of its defining characteristics. To anyone who feared change, she was appalling. By the misogynistic standards of the time, she was considered insufferable, egotistic and presumptuous. Some regarded her as an over-zealous proselytizer, a hectoring busybody constantly badgering people into becoming better and developing a social conscience even if they really didn't want to. She was branded a wild, unconventional, obdurate, upstart ultra-lefty feminist nightmare.

The day after a political meeting at which a very young Sylvia and parliamentary hopeful Winston Churchill got into a skirmish on the platform, Churchill, who nearly broke Sylvia's arm before having her dragged off the stage and locked in a room, complained to the national press that he would not be 'henpecked' into supporting the women's vote. Later, when Sylvia became Britain's leading, and loudest, anti-fascist, Churchill directed the besieged Foreign Office to create a dedicated file entitled 'How to answer letters from Miss Sylvia Pankhurst'. What delicious irony to everyone except himself that, having been returned to parliament as the member for Epping at the 1924 general election, Churchill discovered that he was now Sylvia's MP, condemned to countless mailbags bulging with her unceasing battery of correspondence. Public enemies for decades, they finally made common cause over the Second World War.

Sylvia was a survivor. Over eighteen months in 1913 and 1914, the Liberal government imprisoned her thirteen times and subjected her to a regime of torture by force-feeding. For maximum physical and psychological torment, Herbert Asquith's cabinet authorized the abuse to be administered twice daily. Sylvia endured solitary confinement, hunger striking and thirst and sleep strikes.

Her explicit personal accounts of force-feeding, vividly showing its brutality, were the first to be published in Britain and the international press. She described her torture, and later that of her sister suffragettes, in harrowing detail. Her testimony, printed by the *Manchester Guardian* in 1913, reappeared on global social media a century later in order to draw attention to the experiences of prisoners subjected to force-feeding in Guantánamo Bay.

Later, she became one of a small group of courageous women who were the first to make public the fact that forcible-feeding torture had not only been administered orally. They bore witness also to the rape and other forms of physical sexual violence, harassment, police brutality and assault the suffragettes experienced, in street protests, in prison and in their own homes.

These experiences could have killed her or have dramatically abbreviated her life, as they did so many others. Members of her extended family were killed or permanently damaged by the suffragette struggle, shot during the Irish rebellion and murdered during anti-fascist campaigns. Her close friends James Connolly and Rosa Luxemburg were well-known casualties of freedom fighting. Her own experiences of imprisonment and life-threatening situations did not end with the struggle for the vote. Journeying to Bolshevik Russia by a clandestine route while under a travel ban, she narrowly escaped drowning in the Arctic Circle. In 1921 she served another six-month sentence in solitary confinement for being a communist, convicted of sedition.

Sylvia knew intimately the price to be paid for taking sides.

Her sustained and reluctant militance was motivated by rational pragmatism, not impulsive passion. In matters that were beyond even the best attempts at resolution by democratic consensus, such as achieving equality for women and fighting the ascendant forces of fascism, there was, as Orwell put it, 'no strong reason for thinking that any really fundamental change can ever be achieved peacefully'.[12]

In Elizabeth Robins' bestselling 1913 novel *The Convert*, the lead characters are modelled on the Pankhursts. Jean Dumbarton asks Vida Levering (Sylvia) where she is in her reading of Dante. Jean opens Vida's copy, 'Oh, the Inferno.' 'No, I'm in a worse place,' replies Vida, 'with the Vigliacchi.' 'I forget, were they Guelf or Ghibelline?' asks Jean. Vida says:

> They weren't either, and that was why Dante couldn't stand them. He said there was no place in Heaven nor in Purgatory – not even a corner in Hell, for the souls who had stood aloof from strife … He called them 'wretches who never lived,' Dante did, because they'd never felt the pangs of partisanship. And so they wander homeless on the skirts of limbo …[13]

Sylvia's life offers a voyage through the question of what makes a partisan, with what consequences. Asked how she would like to be remembered, she answered, 'As a citizen of the world.' This passport required the constant taking of sides, active reassessment after experience and the guts to stand out against dominant opinion. Sylvia held consistent values: and she constantly changed and evolved in order to protect and maintain them. It was not intransigence but continuous adjustment that enabled her to hold a steady course. As any mathematician of rocket propulsion knows, the only way to reach a goal is through constant and continuous course correction.

All civil wars begin in the family. Personal political tragedy sits at the centre of Sylvia's story.

Privately argued differences between Sylvia, Christabel and their mother developed into public battles. Then full-scale sex and class war broke out between them. Her mother sided with her elder sister and, more than once, expressed her regret that Sylvia continued to carry the family name. When Mrs Pankhurst heard in 1916 that her anti-war socialist daughter had organized a peace demonstration in Trafalgar Square, she sent Christabel a telegram, 'Strongly repudiate and condemn Sylvia's foolish and unpatriotic conduct. Regret I cannot prevent use of name. Make this public.'[14]

As Labour's Barbara Castle observed in the 1980s, the bitter rift
between the Pankhurst sisters would come 'to represent the two strands
of the development of feminism'.[15] At the time Castle wrote this, the
Conservative Margaret Thatcher, Britain's first female Prime Minister,
a self-proclaimed anti-feminist, had just been re-elected for a third
successive term.

The greatest tragedy was not, however, the largely inevitable ideological
fault line that broke the family's political unity. In 1928 the forty-five-
year-old Sylvia gave birth to her first and only child Richard. From the
beginning of their relationship, Emmeline had disapproved of Richard's
father Silvio Corio, a brilliant Italian anarchist exiled to London who
became Sylvia's life partner of thirty years and who, as she told the *News
of the World*, 'she was very much in love with'.[16] 'My parents,' Richard
explained, 'were old-style libertarian socialists ... Following the practice
of many who shared their political and philosophical point of view ...
they never married.'[17] Emmeline found this unacceptable. When she
heard that Sylvia was pregnant by Corio with no intention of marrying
him, she refused to speak to her ever again.

Born in the Victorian age, Sylvia lived until the advent of the Swinging
Sixties. Her life could be used as the definition of indefatigable. In her
seventies, she became a European migrant to Africa, emigrating with
her son and her Persian cat to Addis Ababa, where eventually she was
to be buried in a full state funeral in an Ethiopian Patriot's grave on the
instructions of her friend the Emperor Haile Selassie. The seven ages
of Sylvia, beginning in Victorian Britain and ending in the modern
transnational African Renaissance in Ethiopia, are an odyssey through
the key events and epochs of twentieth-century history. Sylvia's epic
journey was undertaken through the diverse idioms of modern struggle
in all its grand successes and dismal failures. A scholarship student at
the prestigious Royal College of Art, she was also a prolific writer, of
political and economic journalism, fiction, poetry and plays. She was
the author of a library of books and a phenomenally effective newspaper
editor for half a century. She wrote about the need for public maternal
health care in Britain and designed a blueprint for a national health
service; about anti-Semitism in Britain and Hitler's anti-Jewish laws in
Germany; about apartheid in South Africa; about the capitalist oil wars
in the Middle East and about the Israel–Palestine conflict, which she
believed might determine the political future of humanity.

Adolescent feminist militant, student extremist, hunger striker, street fighter, sometime communist, anti-fascist, champion of the Bolsheviks and African liberation movements, opponent of all forms of racism, and an Ethiopian patriot, her life spans decades of the world at war. From the reform of trade unionism to the founding of the Labour Party and of the modern feminist and anti-colonial movements; from fighting fascism to the social transformations and new artistic practices they brought about, Sylvia was a shaper of the modern world. Pick any year and you will find Sylvia at the heart of the fray, writing it all up inexhaustibly as she goes.

In *Natural Born Rebel* I reveal some new discoveries from the archive and living sources, but the book is built on the pioneering work of others. To Sylvia's son the late Richard Pankhurst and her daughter-in-law Rita Pankhurst, the world owes its thanks for securing her legacy. This torch is now carried by her granddaughter Helen Pankhurst, whose book *Deeds Not Words: The Story of Women's Rights, Then and Now*, published in 2018, exemplifies the Pankhurst spirit, past, present and future. Feminists owe a great debt of gratitude to the labours of David Mitchell, whose extraordinary archive is held at the Museum of London Library. During the pre-digital age of the 1960s and 1970s, Mitchell undertook prodigious research. He wrote thousands of letters to people all over the world, and conducted extensive interviews in person and on the telephone, many with by-then elderly suffragettes. The scholarship of June Purvis, biographer of both Emmeline and Christabel, has built the foundations of Pankhurst studies for a generation and is unrivalled in relation to the other wing of the family. Shirley Harrison is Sylvia's most reliable twentieth-century biographer. Sheila Rowbotham pointed us all in the right direction. Barbara Winslow, Mary Davis and Katherine Connelly lead the political and academic scholarship. Morag Shiach and Neelam Srivastava have broken new ground in the study of Sylvia's literary and political writings as campaigner and propagandist. Sylvia Pankhurst scholarship progresses. Katherine Connelly, young scholar, socialist activist and writer, has exponentially advanced our understanding of Sylvia's suffragette archive in recent years in a manner that secures her subject's legacy for the next generation.

Sylvia Pankhurst is a key protagonist in the development of British democracy, which has existed in an advanced form for less than a hundred years. Sharing her life is an immersive journey through the twentieth century. In the 1930s she restated the 'priorities for socialists': 'perhaps the most important point of all, we have in the world today the Fascist menace which stands against democracy – democracy in the large sense of the common people and their rights'.[18]

In the summer of 1919 Sylvia experienced her first bitter taste of emerging fascism in Italy. She was at a socialist conference in Bologna. Rumour held that Mussolini was hiding in the city, for the moment 'a discredited chauvinist'.[19] The Mayor of Bologna, Francesco Zanardi, invited the British conference delegates to a reception held in the town hall, the Palazzo d'Accursio in the main square, the Piazza Maggiore. As they entered, they were attacked by fascist blackshirts. The following year, fascists stormed the building and shot socialist representatives during a council in session.

In November 2019 anti-fascist activists launched the Sardines movement – *Sardine contro Salvini* – to organize against the rise of the far right in Italy and the hate-filled rhetoric of the former Deputy Prime Minister. Their founding protest took place outside the Palazzo d'Accursio in the Piazza Maggiore. Sylvia is most popularly associated with the suffragette cause. But by far the larger part of her life was dedicated to fighting the evils of racism, fascism and imperialism. She raised her voice long before others, and at a time when many in Britain's comfortable classes were wining and dining Mussolini, praising him for making the trains run on time and supporting his invasion of Ethiopia.

'Solidarity, Welcome, Respect, Rights, Inclusion, Non-Violence, Anti-Fascism' were the calls to arms written on the banners and placards in Bologna's protests in November 2019: the same watchwords that Sylvia printed on the placards that she held aloft when leading demonstrations against fascism in Parliament Square a century ago.

Sylvia's struggle was against the reduction of human life to anything less than its full potential and always in favour of the equality and democracy she cherished as 'the dream of many generations'.[20] This book is the story of how she pursued that dream.

PART ONE

How to Make a Feminist 1882–1898

Why are women so patient? Why don't you force us to give you the vote? ... Why don't you scratch our eyes out?

Dr Richard Pankhurst

I

Authority

All Sylvia's world crashed around her when her father died exactly two months after her sixteenth birthday. Shouting for help, she ran from his deathbed out into the blazing summer morning, across the scorched strip of front lawn to the street. She cried out to a man driving by in a trap, 'Bring a doctor! Bring a doctor!'[21] Two men passing by heard her and ran swiftly away for assistance. Then she fainted into darkness.

When she came to, vehicles blocked the drive. Four sombre men, including his doctor, filled her father's room. Her mother wasn't there.

The nursemaid led her younger siblings Adela and Harry silently away. Ellen the cook looked stricken. A few days earlier, on Saturday, Sylvia had burst into the kitchen, disturbing her lunch.

'Father is ill!'

'I suppose he thinks he's dying,'[22] Ellen snapped at the vexing child. Sylvia was sensitive and prone to agitation, unlike the more placid Christabel. Rebuffed by the only other adult authority in the house, Sylvia crept away, back to her father huddled around the hot-water bottle she had persuaded him to take to bed, a remedy learned from Mother. Her mind attached itself to a single thought: Mother must not see him like this. He must get better before she returned home. She wouldn't bear it.

Mrs Pankhurst was in Geneva with Christabel. Her parents were trying to steer their firstborn favourite towards some purposeful direction in life. When she turned sixteen, her father had raised the question of her future: 'Christabel has a good head ... I'll have her coached; she shall matriculate'[23] According to Sylvia, this prompted her mother to an outburst of tears and to protest that she did not want her daughters brought up to be high-school teachers. From childhood, Christabel went along with her mother's passionate wish that she become a dancer. But now she was seventeen, she had finally rejected as preposterous her mother's dream that she become a prima ballerina. As she explained to Sylvia, the thought suddenly occurred to her, 'People will think my brains are in my feet!'[24] Years later the composer and suffragette Ethel Smyth remarked, 'In her early youth there was a very charming witchery about Christabel, and it was Mrs Pankhurst's conviction that the Suffrage Movement had robbed the world of a great dancer – a second Génée.'[25]

As yet Christabel demonstrated no alternative ambitions aside from holding court with her friends at the Clarion Cycling Club and failing assiduously to apply herself to her studies. Naturally clever, she was a lazy student. Emmeline took charge and arranged with her best friend Noémie Rochefort, now Madame Dufaux, to swap daughters for a year: Christabel to perfect her French in Geneva and Lillie Dufaux her English in Manchester.

'Look after Father!'[26] Emmeline instructed Sylvia as they set off. 'I took the charge very seriously,' she wrote later.[27] Sylvia's father was preoccupied and irritated by his brief for the Manchester Corporation, representing the council on an inquiry into alleged fraud by the superintendent of cleaning services. It was petty work that exacerbated his illness, but it paid the urgent bills. The previous year Richard's suffering from his gastric ulcers had so dramatically increased that Emmeline packed up all the family and moved them for the summer months to Mobberley, a village within railway-commuting distance of Manchester. The children noticed for the first time their father's pain, but of course he said not a word about it to them. Out on one of their purposeful afternoon walks, breathlessness broke her father's stride. Sylvia watched, puzzled, as he drove his graceful hands forcibly into the thorny hedgerows. He did this in the hope that the thorns would counteract the gastric pain. Long afterwards, into her adulthood, Sylvia's visual memory retained this image of her father as hedgerow Messiah.

Richard was always sad and restless when Emmeline went away, even if it was just for the evening when she was out for a few hours at meetings. At the last moment before she left for Switzerland with Christabel, he hugged her tight, reluctant to let her go.

Norbury Williams, the city auditor who had instructed Dr Pankhurst in the case, took spiteful pleasure in chasing down the petty misdoings of the accused 'with a hunter's zest'.[28] Seeing her father's strained face when Williams arrived for unnecessarily lengthy meetings, Sylvia longed for the power to run him out of their home, devising ruses to interrupt them. When Williams eventually left on Friday night, her father had seemed forlorn and lonely. He took her on his knee and spoke to her, as he always did, of life and its work in an earnest grown-up way, repeating his mantra, 'Life is valueless without enthusiasms.'[29] Since infancy she had learned this Pankhurst family prayer.

As usual on Saturdays, Sylvia met her father at his chambers at noon. Habitually, he grasped her upper arm as they walked together, an awkward and outdated habit from his straitlaced youth when walking arm in arm was frowned upon. Sylvia had repeatedly told him she disliked being gripped like this. It made her feel as if she was under compulsion, on a sort of paternal forced march. This Saturday, to counter it she did what she always did, gently drawing his hand down to her wrist so that their arms were comfortably enfolded as they walked and talked their way home for lunch.

It was just the four of them for that last meal. Adela, who was thirteen, eight-year-old Harry, Father and Sylvia. Ellen produced an unexpected treat to offset the fierce summer heatwave: a bowl of strawberries and a dish of cream sat on the table for pudding. Yet halfway through the meal Father rose abruptly, plucked a strawberry from the bowl and left the dining room. Sylvia went to look for him in his library. He wasn't there. Instead she found him in her mother's buttercup-papered drawing room, crammed uncomfortably into her yellow upholstered lady's armchair, as Sylvia's artist's eye saw it, 'his every line denoting agony'.[30]

He refused her pleas to let her get the doctor. She went to the kitchen, where Ellen rebuffed her for being over-anxious – Sylvia so often was, as everyone in the household knew. A strange child, earnest and ethereal, sometimes hard to love. By the following morning Father was too weak to argue, and Sylvia rushed on foot for the doctor, who came round to the Pankhursts' house and examined him. The doctor assured her, 'He will soon be better; do not worry.'[31] He wouldn't answer her questions and tell her precisely what was wrong – treating her like a child. She allowed him to fob her off with the assurance that the oxygen cylinders he had sent for would bring Father relief. The doctor suggested a nurse, but Richard refused, telling him curtly that Sylvia and the servants were perfectly able to look after him. He feared the expense more than the illness. It was a tough responsibility to place on the distressed and inexperienced Sylvia, floundering without her mother and her big sister, to whom she was so close.

Uneasy sweats and spine chills passed swiftly into fever and dark delirium. Father struggled to breathe. The heatwave made it worse. Confused, he waved away the red india-rubber tube of oxygen Sylvia held towards him, 'No, not that.' And then, 'I am sorry, I thought you were offering me a cherry.'[32]

He seemed as helpless as a child. Her world contracted to the space around his sickbed.

On Monday, the doctor told Richard to send for his wife. He dictated a telegram to Sylvia, 'I am not well, please come home.'[33] She stayed with him, holding out the oxygen tube. The doctor seemed never to be there when needed. Her father pleaded with her constantly to call him to visit again through all those long slow hours of agony: 'No delay; no delay.'[34] On Tuesday morning he turned his gaze away. Leaning over him, awkwardly gripping the rubber tube, Sylvia saw him fade away. It seemed impossible. Then she was running down the stairs and out into the street shouting. 'No delay! No delay!'[35]

When she came to after fainting in the street, she returned to Father's room, where several men who had responded to her call now gathered around his bed. A flood of joy burst over her. She thought she saw Father move. But no, one of the men had touched him. Her mind was seized by self-recrimination: 'You did not get a doctor immediately. You did not send for Mother. If she had been here he might not have died.'[36] In her memoirs, Sylvia reconstructed her dialogue with the doctor, berating him for not telling her to send for her mother when he had visited on Sunday. Instead, he had waited until Monday night, by which time it was too late.

'Why did you not tell me to send for my mother?'

'I did not think he would last the night when I saw him on Sunday. I did not think she could arrive on time.'

'You said he would soon be better.'

'I could not tell the truth …'

'What was the matter with him?'[37]

The ulcer had perforated his stomach. Her father had known of his illness for some time, but not taken it sufficiently seriously and, the doctor added with a sniff, Dr Pankhurst thought eating green vegetables and fresh fruit would be cure enough.

'Did you tell him his stomach was ulcerated?' Sylvia asked.

'I did not want to worry him.'

Before she could utter any reproach, her rage and guilt were already redoubled against herself: 'You did not send for Mother.'[38]

From ten o'clock in the morning when he died till the small hours of the next day, Sylvia awaited her mother's return.[39] Stunned, Adela and Harry slept. Sylvia kept vigil, her natural tendency always to be on watch. She sat overwhelmed by panic at the thought of her mother on the night train with no idea that Father was dead. Why had she not insisted on calling for help sooner? Why hadn't she telegraphed her mother to come home immediately? Why had she not understood that Father was dying and how could Mother ever forgive her?

To all these questions the whisper of an answer formed. Father had died because she yielded to people in authority over her. She gave way first to his natural parental authority; then to Ellen's as surrogate matriarch of the household in her mother's absence; and finally to the professional obfuscations of the doctor. If only she had listened to her inner promptings, spoken up, challenged all the adults and acted sooner. Things might have been different. Father might still be alive.

Emmeline travelled back alone. She left Christabel in Geneva, believing that Richard's urgent message referred to Harry. She misunderstood his telegram, thinking it her husband's code to protect her from the blow she feared most. Ever since the death of their first son Frank, aged four, Richard understood his wife's mortal terror of losing their remaining son, sickly from childhood.

In the early hours of Wednesday morning Emmeline's train approached Manchester. She caught sight of the black-bordered headline on the newspaper in the hands of a fellow traveller: 'Dr Pankhurst Dead'. As she cried out in shock, the other passengers asked her, 'Are you Mrs Pankhurst?'[40] In just a few years Emmeline would be one of the most recognized public figures in Britain, forced to hide or disguise herself every time she went out.

Emmeline had told all her children that *Uncle Tom's Cabin* was one of her favourite childhood books. Published in 1852, Harriet Beecher Stowe's instant bestseller sold a million copies in Britain. Recalling her mother Jane reading this epic tale – a hymn to the cause of liberation – as a bedtime story, Emmeline told her own children, 'Young as I was – I could not have been older than five years – I knew perfectly well the meaning of the words slavery and emancipation.'[41] She used the novel as a source of stories for Sylvia and her siblings just as her own mother had done for her and her many brothers and sisters. Mrs Harriet Beecher Stowe, Mother explained, had a brother called Henry Ward Beecher, who visited Britain to give his first lecture tour opposing slavery. Their grandfather, Robert Goulden, an ardent abolitionist, was on the committee to meet and welcome Henry Ward Beecher when he arrived in Manchester, introducing him to their circle of abolitionist family friends.

Emmeline was five when her father met Henry Ward Beecher in 1863. Cotton manufacturing was the economic lifeblood of Lancashire, which therefore might have had good reason to support the South in the American Civil War. But Lancashire steadfastly upheld Lincoln and the North, suffering an economic crash in consequence of the North's blockade of Southern ports. Her mother dedicated as much energy to fundraising activities for newly emancipated slaves as she did to women's suffrage, and tiny Emmeline was given a special 'lucky bag' to collect pennies for the cause wherever she went.

The stories Emmeline's mother read from *Uncle Tom's Cabin* made a deep impression on her, far more vivid and longer lasting, she recalled, than the events detailed in the morning newspapers that it was her daily duty to read to her father at breakfast. Emmeline remembered the thrilled dread she experienced every time her mother related the tale of Eliza's race for freedom over the broken ice of the Ohio River, the agonizing pursuit and the final rescue at the hands of the determined old Quaker.

Another breathtaking tale from the novel was the story of a boy's brave and hazardous flight from the plantation of his cruel master. Staggering along the unfamiliar railroad track, the roar of an approaching engine seems to announce an awful threat to capture him. 'This was a terrible story,' Emmeline told her wide-eyed offspring, 'and throughout my childhood, whenever I rode in a train, I thought of that poor runaway slave escaping from the pursuing monster.'[42]

Of all the Pankhurst children Sylvia was the most impressionable in response to stories. Her mother's appalled coupling of train journeys with the spectre of racist cruelty, foreboding pursuit and the nightmare of outrunning monsters lodged itself firmly in her imagination. Fearful in her soulful night vigil with her dead father, she despaired at the thought of her mother hurtling through the dark on the night train, oblivious to the approaching disaster.

The newspaper announcement brutally informing Emmeline of her husband's death was the last line to a great love story. The final letter she received from Richard in Geneva – he wrote daily – spilled over with loving anticipation: 'When you return we will have a new honeymoon and reconsecrate each to the other in unity of heart. Be happy. Love and love, Your husband. R. M. Pankhurst'.[43]

'Where's my lady?' were always Dr Pankhurst's first words when he arrived home. He adored her. The children only ever heard him address their mother with terms of endearment, never by her name. 'Mother was queen,'[44] Christabel said, demonstrating a typically tin ear for working-class irony when she added, 'Some of the poor people took to calling her Lady Pankhurst with a vague idea that this must be her title.'[45] Yet the nuptials of Richard Pankhurst and Emmeline Goulden on 18 December 1879 were a far from grand affair. Richard's beloved seventy-five-year-old mother Margaret had died on 6 December, so sadly funeral and wedding were a mere week apart. The style-conscious twenty-one-year-old bride had longed for a white gown and veil, and the ceremonial conventions to go with it, but this was not a time for fuss and furbelows. With tact and compassion, Emmeline wore a ready-made brown velvet dress from Kendal Milne's department store. Burdened by grief for his mother, Richard, now in his mid-forties, insisted on a quick and low-key ceremony so that Emmeline could move into his family home immediately. All his life he had lived with his parents, apart from a period studying in London.

Having only months before declared to her parents that she proposed to ignore the stuffy conventions of the antiquated marriage institution altogether and enter into a free-love union with Richard, Emmeline wasn't in a position to voice her acute disappointment that the white wedding with orange blossom, four bridesmaids and elaborate reception she had planned had been scrapped in favour of Richard's preference for a simple ceremony at St Luke's parish church in Eccles attended by a handful of people.

In fact, this is the Jane Austenized version of the story which squints in order to blur less romantic but more interesting truths. Brainy intellectual political activist, legal whizz and civic hero, Richard had successfully avoided bending himself and his progressive convictions to the conventions of middle-class professional Victorian masculinity by evading marriage and continuing to live with his parents until he became an orphaned adult and middle-aged. Seamlessly, he substituted a marital household for his parental home. In this, he was highly conventional.

Richard's move from dead mother straight into marriage, for which he was roundly teased in the Manchester Brasenose Club, was characteristic. Dr Pankhurst maintained an unbroken feminine continuity in his life that ran parallel with his active engagement in the rights of women, feminist politics and philosophy in general.

Emmeline, on the other hand, had already for several years lived away from her parents, from her home and from England before she met Richard. She was in that sense more worldly. Taking as she did both her newfound soulmate and the politics of the moment seriously, it's unsurprising that she suggested they explore their independence of spirit and demonstrate their solidarity with unhappy wives by dispensing with a legal church ceremony and entering a free-love union. As Sylvia observed, Richard had spoken to Emmeline about the unconventional love matches of Mary Wollstonecraft and her daughter Mary Shelley, and so had led her to this thought.[46] 'Wouldn't you have liked to try first how we should get on?'[47] Emmeline suggested.

Richard quickly countered, very uncharacteristically, by putting political realities before social ideals. However orthodox their behaviour might be, public sentiment discriminated against people who challenged the marriage institution. A free-love union would expose her to slander and was a barrier in public life. 'I have often heard him say, in later years,' Sylvia said, 'that people who have displayed unconventionality in that direction, had usually been prevented from doing effective public work in any other.' Emmeline's anxious parents, naturally, enforced this view.[48]

Long after his death, Richard Pankhurst's views on the price of unconventionality for women when it came to marriage and childbirth returned to haunt Sylvia.

During the autumn of 1879, leading up to Emmeline and Richard's December wedding, the agitation for marriage reform reached new heights. Reformers argued that married women should enjoy the same rights as single women and that wives as well as husbands should be entitled to separate property interests.[49] Richard continued to be a member of the original Manchester Married Women's Property Committee founded in 1868 to campaign for the rights of wives.

Christabel frankly regarded their mother as the ingénue in the love match and was dismissive of her youthful attempt to try and think about her union in an unconventional and progressive way: 'Mother was no revolutionary in her views of marriage.'[50] It was Sylvia who identified the ambivalence and noticed the significance of the discussions, during her parents' courtship days, about Wollstonecraft; her lover, the philosopher William Godwin; and their daughter Mary, who married Percy Bysshe Shelley. On the subject of their romantic history, there was one aspect on which both sisters agreed: to their father their mother was the very perfection of womankind. He was besotted. After four decades of comfortable bachelorhood, Richard could not wait to tie the knot. 'It is only a few brief hours,' he wrote the night before their wedding, 'that separate us from that oneness of life which ought, which will, hold for us an existence of joyous love.'[51]

Richard and Emmeline's marriage was based on firm foundations: mutual working interests and needs, deep curiosity about what an unconventional intimate partner might emotionally deliver and shared political values. Emmeline's talents had been underdeveloped and frustrated by the feminine social constraint expected by her family. The worldly power of a charismatic, intelligent, educated, professional older man attracted her. Richard, in turn, had the opportunity of a second adulthood, with the compensations of intimacy and children he'd missed out on so far. Strikingly beautiful and poised, Emmeline was a young woman whose combination of determination, passionate force of nature, natural quickness and explicitly political disposition signalled that she was not going to trap him into a conventional Victorian marriage. His marriage and household could provide an opportunity for him to encourage his wife and children in the pursuit of freedom. The Pankhursts were a living experiment in how to make a feminist family.

Rebecca West remarked that Emmeline Pankhurst's burning fervour for the oppressed came to her much against the grain. 'What she would have preferred, could her social conscience have been quieted, was to live in a pleasant suburban house and give her cronies tea with very thin bread-and-butter, and sit about in the garden in a deck chair.'⁵² But Emmeline's conscience could not be quieted. And Dr Richard Pankhurst, barrister and socialist agitator, could never have married a woman who lounged about the garden in a deckchair. What did rub easily with the Goulden grain was Emmeline's instinctive flair for political theatre. Emmeline Pethick-Lawrence observed that Mrs Pankhurst 'could have been a Queen on the Stage or the Salon'.⁵³ From her amateur-dramatics-loving, civic-minded, liberal father and literature-and-liberty-loving, radical mother, she inherited an aptitude for political stunt that developed into a form of pioneering genius.

According to her birth certificate, Emmeline Goulden was born on 15 July 1858, in Moss Side, Manchester. Yet Emmeline maintained that she was born on Bastille Day, and celebrated her birthday always on 14 July. Perhaps her first-time parents muddled the date when they registered it four months after her birth; or perhaps it suited Emmeline to nudge her nativity to such a symbolic date, encapsulating the twin passions that shaped and drove her from her earliest days: France and female resistance to tyranny.

Emmeline revelled in sharing her birthday with the anniversary of the storming of the Bastille in 1789, the event that sparked the first French Revolution. 'I have always thought that the fact that I was born on that day had some kind of influence over my life … it was women who gave the signal to spur on the crowd, and led to the final taking of that monument of tyranny, the Bastille, in Paris.'⁵⁴ She appeared to have forgotten this fact by 1917 when women sparked the first Russian Revolution, which she vehemently opposed.

Emmeline was the first in a line of ten children. One of her earliest childhood memories was overhearing her father say about her to her mother, 'She should have been born a lad!'⁵⁵ Tasked with looking after each of her siblings as they arrived, Emmeline experienced from an early age the hierarchy in which privilege and comfort was prioritized for the boys, service and the cultivation of femininity for the girls.

Sylvia's paternal great-grandparents were Irish mill workers active in the early suffrage agitation. They took part in the great franchise meeting held in St Peter's Fields in 1819 that ended in the Peterloo

Massacre. Later, in the 1840s, when protest arose against the starvation caused by the Corn Laws, the Gouldens joined Cobden's Anti-Corn Law League. Their membership cards, with the inscription 'Give us this day our daily bread', passed into Emmeline's possession and were always on display in her homes. Many years later, they inspired Sylvia's iconic design for the membership cards of the Women's Social and Political Union (WSPU).

Their son Robert Goulden, Emmeline's father, was a self-made man who began his working life as an office boy and ended as partner in a textile factory that printed and bleached printing and bleaching cotton in Seedley, on the outskirts of Salford. A romantic Liberal and a keen amateur actor, Robert chaired the Athenaeum Dramatic Society in Manchester and enjoyed the praise he received for performing the big Shakespeare roles. He married Jane Quine, from Douglas, Isle of Man, the only daughter of a Manx farmer. Together they produced five sons and five daughters. They did well enough to buy a holiday home in Douglas Bay. Here the children went rowing and swimming, lost themselves in adventures in the lanes and glens and ate large quantities of their grandmother's soda cakes, presumably with lashings of ginger beer.

From a young age Emmeline was a precocious reader and had a quick ear for music and languages. John Bunyan's *The Pilgrim's Progress* and *The Holy War*, and Thomas Carlyle's *History of the French Revolution* were always more interesting to her than learning verbs or practising her scales. Reading was her most treasured way of passing the time when she was not, as the eldest girl in a large family, carrying considerable responsibilities for looking after her sisters and brothers. Her brothers nicknamed her 'the dictionary' for her eloquence and accuracy of spelling. She liked novels too.

At about nine-years-old, Emmeline was sent to a small boarding school for girls offering a curriculum of reading, writing, arithmetic, grammar, French, history and geography. But it was all delivered in a haphazard and unacademic way, aimed purely at cultivating social skills in the girls to make them attractive to potential husbands. She recalled, later in life, being puzzled by 'why I was under such a particular obligation to make home attractive to my brothers. We were on excellent terms of friendship, but it was never suggested to them as a duty that they make home attractive to me. Why not? Nobody seemed to know.'[56]

Emmeline's daily task of reading the newspapers to her father at breakfast sparked her interest in politics. An incident when Emmeline was ten years old points in the direction of her talent for the political stunt. The general election of 1868 was the first since the passage of the Reform Act the previous year. Emmeline and her favourite sister Mary had new green frocks worn over red-flannel petticoats – the colours of the party. They walked the mile to the nearest polling booth and earned themselves a severe telling-off from their nanny who caught them encouraging Liberal voters by cheekily lifting the hems of their dresses to reveal the red petticoats.

In 1872, when she was fourteen, Emmeline begged her mother to take her with her to a women's suffrage meeting. As a result of the long-standing agitation for the women's vote in the Isle of Man, Jane Goulden had been shaped by feminism. She attended women's suffrage meetings regularly and signed a petition to the Liberal Prime Minister William Gladstone on women's rights. She subscribed to the monthly *Women's Suffrage Journal*, edited by Lydia Becker and read eagerly by her daughters, though not by her sons. A leading figure in the Victorian women's rights movement, the severely tight-bunned and bespectacled Becker was secretary of the Manchester National Society for Women's Suffrage.

Reflecting on her famous mother's early years, Sylvia reminds us that Manchester was then the centre of the British women's movement. In 1866 when John Stuart Mill presented to parliament his historic petition for women's citizenship, the Suffrage Committee was already well established in the city. Among its founders were friends, neighbours and political colleagues of the Gouldens. These included Elizabeth Wolstenholme Elmy, Ursula and Jacob Bright and the radical barrister Dr Richard Pankhurst, well known as a far-left-leaning Liberal Party activist of extreme radical views.

Lydia Becker and Dr Pankhurst were close allies, at that time working together on a bill to secure votes for women on the same terms as men. John Stuart Mill's amendment to secure women's suffrage under the Reform Act of 1867 by substituting the word 'person' for the word 'man' had been defeated; but Mill still succeeded in opening up the possibility for a shift in principle. A subsequent amendment to substitute 'male person' for 'man' was also crushed, but under the provision of the Act 'words of the masculine gender legally included women unless the contrary were expressly provided'.[57]

Richard Pankhurst seized this as an opportunity to launch a campaign to get women's names on the electoral register, an effort that motivated 92 per cent of Manchester women to send in claims to be registered. A legal scuffle ensued, resulting in two test cases that found in favour of the so-called revising barristers who, tasked with reviewing the registers, had struck the women's names off on the grounds that under the British constitution women were not entitled to exercise any right or privilege unless an act of Parliament expressly conferred it on them. Tellingly, only in the case of punishments and obligations could the term 'person' be taken to include women.

Spurred by these setbacks, resistance grew. Meetings and demonstrations sprang up all over the city, and the Mayor of Manchester agreed to grant the Suffrage Society the open use of the town hall. Richard Pankhurst drafted the bill to secure votes for women and in 1870 the Liberal MP Jacob Bright introduced it in parliament where it passed its second reading amid cheers from the Liberal benches. When the bill went into committee, Gladstone spoke to oppose it, on the grounds that 'it would be a very great mistake to carry this Bill into law'. He offered no good reason for this other than it went against the 'opinion prevailing among' his colleagues, but the majority melted away nonetheless. Jacob Bright reintroduced the Women's Suffrage Bill the following year. Once again Gladstone ensured its defeat, this time clarifying his position. He protested that the physical participation and 'intervention' of women in parliamentary election proceedings would be 'a practical evil of an intolerable character'.[58]

It was in the context of these events that in 1872 schoolgirl Emmeline went to her first meeting with her mother. Like all the adults around her she was incensed by Gladstone's betrayal. Despite Lydia Becker's stern, buttoned-down demeanour, Emmeline was fascinated by the power and persuasiveness of her famed oratory and claimed that she left the meeting 'a conscious and confirmed' suffragist.[59] Little could she imagine that she would later become the older woman's resented love rival. Lydia Becker had long carried a torch for the unsuspecting bachelor Richard Pankhurst, and 'as rumour persistently declared' had suffered a great disappointment when he took a young wife. In an argument years later with Emmeline, by then mother of two children, Lydia Becker exclaimed, 'Married women have all the plums of life!'[60]

The same year, Emmeline's father took her to France and installed her at the École Normale in Neuilly, a leafy suburb of Paris. Her parents wanted to equip her with the accomplishments of a young lady. However, the École Normale was far from a stereotypical finishing school, and had a reputation among European radicals for the progressive education of girls.

So that he could get back to the demands of his business Robert needed to deposit Emmeline at Neuilly during the holidays. The school was empty, except for the motherless Noémie Rochefort. She couldn't go home for the vacation because her father, hero of the Paris Commune of the previous year, was imprisoned in the French colony New Caledonia in the south-west Pacific, east of Australia. Emmeline and Noémie struck up a friendship during that school holiday that endured without interruption until the end of their lives.

Noémie's father, Victor Henri Rochefort, Marquis de Rochefort-Luçay, a communist who refused to use his title, was a politician, journalist and playwright, ever eager to attack Napoleon III's empire with both pen and sword. Noémie's stories about her father – his fights on the barricades, his duels, repeated arrests, exile and imprisonment – enchanted Emmeline. In May 1871 Henri escaped Paris in disguise, but was captured. His friend Victor Hugo, the novelist, tried to prevent his deportation. Without success – Henri was transported. Two years later, he escaped in a rowing boat and was picked up by an American liner bound for San Francisco. From there he fled to London and Geneva until the 1880 amnesty permitted his return to France.

Believing that the education of girls should be equal to that of boys, the École Normale offered a curriculum that included chemistry, book-keeping, languages and sciences alongside the obligatory needlepoint and social skills. The school encouraged the latter by presenting the pupils at the salons of its founder, Madame Juliette Adam, editor of the *Nouvelle Revue*. Emmeline became a particular favourite with Madame Adam and met many Parisian notables, politicos and renegades at her soirées.

Together, the inseparable Emmeline and Noémie explored post-war Paris, still reeling from defeat in the recently ended Franco-Prussian War and suffering under the German army of occupation and the crushing reparations exacted by Bismarck. It was less than a year since the bloody end of the Paris Commune, the radical socialist, revolutionary government that ran the capital for three months until its

brutal suppression by the regular French army which then capitulated
to Bismarck's empire.

Emmeline's romantic revolutionary spirit was kindled in a decidedly
French fashion, informed and inspired by Noémie and her guardian,
Edmond Adam. It was a thorough grounding in French revolutionary
politics, its daring, violence and enmities. It was also a finishing school
in Parisian fashion and style.

It was Sylvia who pinpointed the significance of her mother's arrival
in Paris in the immediate wake of the Paris Commune, combined with
the influence of her fascinating, beautiful young friend and her family.
Emmeline imbibed the romantic revolutionary values of the Commune
in which women played a leading, defining role. However, her
perceptions of the defeat of that radical moment were tied uncritically
to the dangerous simplifications of nationalism: 'She conceived a
lifelong prejudice against all things German, a lasting enthusiasm for
France.'[61] This early chauvinism never left her and its implications were
to prove utterly disastrous for the suffragette movement. Rebecca West,
as a young adolescent suffragette lost in admiration for her leader,
was equally astute about the consequences of Emmeline's early anti-
German feeling for her later jingoism: 'This astonishing trace of the
influence of French politics on Mrs Pankhurst, so little modified by
time, makes us realize that the Suffragette Movement had been the
copy of a French model executed with North-Country persistence. We
had been watching a female General Boulanger with *nous*.'[62]

Her schooling over, the young female General Boulanger persuaded
her father to let her stay on with Noémie in Paris – as she could not
bear to be parted from either. Noémie married and the girls agreed
that Emmeline should quickly do the same, so that she could move in
next door and they could bring up their babies together as neighbours.
Clearly having mistaken herself for the heroine of one of her favourite
schlock novels, Emmeline accepted Noémie's recommendation of the
next available suitor and wrote to her well-to-do father to ask him to
settle her with the necessary dowry.

Young Emmeline's romantic Liberalism did not extend at this stage
of her life to challenging the conventions of transactional marriage.
Fortunately for her, her father's did. Goulden, enraged by the suggestion
that he should purchase Emmeline a French husband, ordered her to
pack up and come home immediately. Emmeline persisted in a furious

sulk with her father that didn't end until he made accidental amends by introducing her to the love of her life. Two decades later, she had further cause to be grateful for this patriarchal intervention. When on a visit to France she met again her old suitor, now 'a dreadful creature', a middle-aged, corpulent, crashing bore who, if rumour were true, abused his wife.[63]

It is unsurprising that Emmeline, at this age, had a pragmatic view of marriage as an opportunity for escape. Her objective was to be Parisian and to live next door to her best friend. The purchased husband was to have been a means to this end. As Emmeline understood very well, wives were not paid for their reproductive, domestic and social labour. She needed the dowry as a way to bank some economic security and relative autonomy. What her longer-toothed father understood better was that once her husband had the purse, she would have no control over that money. It's often claimed that Emmeline read a lot of French novels. If true, she missed the warnings to young modern women that were to be garnered from their plots.

Emmeline returned home unwillingly in 1878, furious with her obstructive father but having learned to wear her hair and clothes like a Parisian. Sylvia, who was generally unconcerned about her own appearance and never wore make-up, admired her mother's elegance and beauty, though she worried that Emmeline's use of cosmetics leaned towards artifice. Writing her biography later in life, Sylvia paid tribute to her mother's youthful grace and style and to her subtle, adept use of make-up and fashion. She painted a word portrait of Emmeline's svelte figure, raven black hair, olive skin with a slight flush of natural red, delicately pencilled black eyebrows, beautifully expressive deep violet-blue eyes and above all 'magnificent carriage and voice of remarkable melody'.[64]

Back in the Goulden family home in Manchester where her chief responsibilities were domestic, Emmeline became constrained and dejected. She looked after her younger siblings, redecorated the living room and did light housework and flower arranging while she watched her brothers go out with her father to the factory to learn the family business. For all his radicalism, Robert Goulden set clear limits on what he considered the proper expectations for his daughters. One of Emmeline's sisters longed to be an actress, a desire Goulden stamped out, despite the fact that he had inspired it in her by his own love of acting and theatre. Mary, who showed talent as an artist, was similarly thwarted when she tried to display and sell some of her paintings in a local shop. Observing the struggles of her sisters and considering her own options, Emmeline came rapidly to the conclusion that women needed work and ought to have the opportunity of being trained to some profession or business that would enable them to be self-supporting.

2

Red Doctor

The Britain Emmeline Goulden returned to in 1878 was split over the question of whether it should ally itself with Turkey in its war with Russia. In Manchester, the pacifists opposing entry into the conflict were led by Dr Richard Pankhurst, who persuaded the north country Liberal Associations to demand Gladstone's return to the Liberal leadership, 'to save the peace of Europe'.[65] Gladstone had resigned after losing the 1874 general election to Disraeli's Conservatives.

Emmeline's parents, supporters of the anti-war cause and great admirers of Dr Pankhurst, took their eldest daughter along to a huge public meeting in Manchester where they were going to hear him speak, denouncing Disraeli's imperialism and supporting Gladstone. The Gouldens stood on the steps when the Red Doctor's cab drew up. The roar of welcoming cheers, wildly waving hats and handkerchiefs that greeted him impressed Emmeline. From her vantage position, the twenty-year-old saw what she described as 'a beautiful hand' emerging to open the cab door.[66] When he appeared, upright, energetic, radiating the fervour of his convictions, Emmeline was captivated. She told Sylvia many years later that she was utterly astonished when Richard appeared to notice her at the crowded reception after the meeting. She thought he would pass over her as the uninteresting offspring of his political friends. But notice her he did. Her apparently artless little bonnet, pretending to be staid and matronly, gave her an air of propriety, offsetting the bold knot of scarlet ribbon tied in her hair from enthusiasm for the Liberal cause.

Instantaneous recognition sprang between Emmeline and Richard. Emmeline's mother Jane, completely unaware of the current that passed between them at their first meeting, waxed lyrical to her daughter about Dr Pankhurst, declaring herself 'charmed with him; he was so eloquent'.[67] To Emmeline's delight, shortly after the meeting she received a letter from him:

> Dear Miss Goulden,
> There is, as you know, now in action an important movement for the higher education of women. As one of the party of progress, you must be interested in this. I have much considered the subject and sought to frame a scheme for making such education as real and efficient as possible ...[68]

Such were Richard's cautious initial overtures to love. Resolved to stay single for the sake of his public crusades, unpractised in courtship, he began by speaking to Emmeline in the language of his deepest passions: justice, equality, education for working people, women's rights, anti-imperialism, republicanism. Within a fortnight, he cast aside this lofty formal style for more tender, fervent missives. Emmeline sent him a small photograph of herself known as a *carte de visite*:

> Dearest Treasure,
> I received with greatest joy your charming likeness (sent with too few words). The Carte itself has honestly tried to express you as you are, but of course it could not. The fire and soul of the original can never consent to enter a copy. Still, when the original is absent, the copy consoles and animates.[69]

Where his earnestness and radicalism might have deterred other fun-loving twenty-year-olds, for Emmeline this was the food of love. His idealism enchanted her. She longed to explore beyond the constraints of her narrowly defined family-focused life. With no hope of learning the family business and with no other profession in sight, Richard held out the promise of a life beyond the boundaries of bonded domesticity. He offered these enticements in terms of a radical idealism with missionary fervour that stirred her heart:

In all my happiness with you, I feel most deeply the responsibilities that are gathering round us ... Every struggling cause shall be ours ... So living, we even in the present enter, as it were, by inspiration into the good time yet far away and something of its morning glow touches our foreheads, or ever it is, by the many, even so much as dreamt of. Help me in this in the future, unceasingly. Herein is the strength – with bliss added – of two lives made one by that love which seeks more the other than self. How I long and yearn to have all this shared to the full between us in equal measure![70]

Emmeline's mother, initially pleased that Dr Pankhurst had taken notice of her eldest daughter, changed her tune when she realized the extent of the mutual infatuation. Jane accused Emmeline of throwing herself at Dr Pankhurst and failing to maintain properly maidenly reserve with studied rebuffs and persistent coldness. These, she advised her daughter, were the proper methods by which she had received her own future husband's attentions.

Emmeline was having none of it. Instinctively she understood that playing the hard-to-get ingénue would not work with this single-minded bachelor who was perfectly comfortable living with his aged parents, as he had done for nearly all of his life.

By the time Emmeline's enchanted gaze first met his, Richard was long equipped with academic and professional distinction and an unbroken record of sturdy public service. One of the most visible personalities of his native city, Pankhurst was nevertheless a controversial figure. 'Our father,' Sylvia wrote, 'vilified and boycotted, yet beloved by a multitude of people in many walks of life, was a standard-bearer of every forlorn hope, every unpopular yet worthy cause then conceived for the uplifting of oppressed and suffering humanity.'[71]

Sylvia captured him rather nicely when she said that in appearance her father both charmed and challenged, but her posthumous eulogy smoothed out his idiosyncratic wrinkles. Describing him as younger in looks than his years, graceful and vivacious in bearing, wearing his beard pointed like a Frenchman, she cast him as a heroic, romantic figure. In fact, Pankhurst was on the short side and possessed of an overlarge forehead that made the proportions of his facial hair eccentric rather than dashing. His unwaxed reddish beard was wispy rather than pointed, but either way it was resolutely unfashionable. The fashion of the time was for a meticulously smooth clean shave. His dress was also unconventional for his profession. His coats, made shapeless by huge pockets stuffed with papers, notebooks and his beloved little red-bound copy of Milton, gave him more the air of the philosopher-poet and romantic revolutionary than the slickly suited and booted Victorian barrister.

Pankhurst's beard and fulsomely crimson politics earned him the affectionate monikers of the 'Red Doctor' and 'Pankhurski' from the press, picked up by his friends and opponents, all of whom regarded him as an extremist. But for all that he was a firebrand, he was indisputably learned, committed and a fine orator much in demand at important civic occasions or when dignitaries visited Manchester.

As Sylvia admitted – for there was no getting round it – her father's voice was one of his most remarkable features. Considerably higher pitched than most men's, it startled people the first time they heard him speaking in public. Pankhurst's pitch descended the scale as he aged, but in his youthful heyday it was described as 'weird and wonderful' and was often the subject of press comment and ridicule. Sylvia heard admiring women tell him he would have made a glorious tenor singer, 'but, so far as I know, he never sang a note'.[72] She meant this quite literally. Her father sang all the time, but always off key. He trilled around the house, in the bathroom and to his children. When the family clustered around the piano, he wisely asked his wife to sing. His favourite ballad, Sylvia recalled, was 'The Bailiff's Daughter of Islington', the much loved eighteenth-century radical English folk air about a heroine's brave fighting spirit on behalf of her love – a tribute to his own adored Emmeline.

Richard Marsden Pankhurst was born in May 1836 at Stoke-on-Trent to Henry Francis Pankhurst and Margaret Marsden from Wigan, the youngest of four children. The Pankhurst family name, which seems to have originated as Pentecost or Pinkhurst, is associated with Sussex and Surrey.[73] Richard speculated that the family tree took root from a Norman ancestor. His paternal grandfather was a Staffordshire teacher and eventually headmaster at a school in Cheshire, where he remained for forty years, supporting a family of thirteen children. Richard's father started out as an auctioneer and ended up a Manchester stockbroker. Laying the foundations for his youngest son's rather puritanical brand of radicalism, Henry Francis broke with the Conservative and churchgoing tradition of the family and became a Liberal and Baptist dissenter. Henry and Margaret produced four children – two girls and two boys.

Richard grew up closer to his two sisters, Bess and Harriette, than to his elder brother John, who fell out with his parents and set sail to try his luck in America, never to return. Many years later Sylvia met her Uncle John in Chicago and discovered a resentful soul, bitter about the privation and hardships he'd endured as an immigrant. His penury cost him the life of his little daughter, from whose death he never recovered.

Both of Richard's sisters suffered from their marriages in ways that clearly influenced their younger brother's view of the challenges facing even comfortably off young middle-class women. Bess ran away from home to take up with an impecunious actor noted chiefly for the swan-like neck he displayed when appearing in women's roles at the Manchester Athenaeum Dramatic Society. Despite his elegant neck, her stage-struck husband never made it on the boards and the Pankhurst family set him up with a hat shop to try and help him put a roof over Bess's head. The millinery enterprise failed miserably, but in time Bess's husband became the manager of a theatre in Aberdeen and settled down into a position he enjoyed, ultimately proving himself a reliable spouse who, according to the family, deferred to the determined Bess in all things.

Richard's other sister Harriette endured a more tragic life. She married a peripatetic, addictive musician who beat her up. Nominally, he was editor of a music magazine, but in fact it was Harriette who ghost-edited the paper while simultaneously maintaining the home and raising the family. She died of a slow cancer caused, it was believed, by her husband's violence.

So it was on his younger son Richard that Henry Pankhurst focused his hopes. Richard went to the Manchester Grammar School, founded in 1519 by the progressive Hugh Oldham, Bishop of Exeter, 'to teach freely every child and scholar coming to the school', with the refreshing proviso that no member of the religious orders should ever be headmaster. Previous pupils included Thomas de Quincey and Harrison Ainsworth.

Manchester had no university of its own, but, by the bequest of a successful local merchant John Owens, a college was founded in 1851 to give an education equal to that of the universities, without religious tests for either students or teachers. The older universities barred entrance to dissenters. Richard was a dissenter. He studied at Owens College, and took his degrees at London University, established for nonconformists under the enlightened influence of Lord Brougham, the historian George Grote, the Scottish philosopher, historian and economist James Mill, father of John Stuart Mill, and others. His was a solidly progressive, dissenting middle-class education. He graduated in 1858, LLB, and began his professional life in 1859 with his appointment as Associate of Owens College, and later a governor, while he completed his MA Honours in principles of legislation and, finally, his LLD with a gold medal from the university in 1863.

After practising as a solicitor for a while, he was called to the Bar at Lincoln's Inn in 1867 and joined the Northern Circuit and Bar of the County Palatine of Lancashire Chancery Court. In 1862, he became a member of the Manchester Chamber of Commerce, and was praised for his proposals to amend the bankruptcy laws. Pankhurst immersed himself in the improvement of patent law and in securing better arrangements for litigation in Manchester, especially for commercial cases, which were costly and subject to appalling delays. All of this made him very popular with business clients. He worked also with George Odger for the repeal of iniquitous labour laws, which did not.

Author of many important legal papers dealing with both national and international law, Richard Pankhurst was one of the earliest advocates of a Court of Criminal Appeal and of an International Tribunal and League of Nations. The hardy roots of Sylvia's internationalism and predisposition to human rights lie here. In a legal system that carried the death penalty, Pankhurst argued that the treatment of law breakers should be designed not to punish but to reclaim and rehabilitate. This resonated with Emmeline's revulsion at capital punishment, discovered as a young girl when, walking home from school one afternoon, she passed the prison and saw a gallows through a gap in the wall. The three men hanged, she knew, were wrongly convicted of murder. Horrified by the sight and by the miscarriage of justice, Emmeline was convinced in that moment that the death penalty was a mistake – worse, a crime. 'It was my awakening to one of the most terrible facts of life – that justice and judgment lie often a world apart.'[74] The coalescence of values like this later drew Richard and Emmeline into intimacy and mutual understanding.

There was nothing unusual about the age difference between them, but Richard was far from a conventional middle-class Victorian bachelor. His progressive views were ahead of their time. It made sense that Emmeline, a beacon of new values, would appeal.

Richard became a member of the Royal Statistical Society and of the Society for the Reform and Codification of the Law of Nations. To this body he presented a pioneering scheme for international arbitration. He served as an original member of the council of the National Association for the promotion of Social Science, out of which arose many reform movements, and which substantially assisted the early campaigns for women's emancipation.

A close friend and supporter of the Chartist Ernest Jones, and of the civil servant, economist and philosopher John Stuart Mill, Richard Pankhurst was known for being as ardent for the liberty of women as he was for that of men. In the 1860s and 1870s he worked tirelessly for the causes of mass education and the right of married women to their own property and earnings. He drafted the first bill for women's parliamentary enfranchisement, the amendment to a government bill which secured women the municipal vote and famously the Married Women's Property Act of 1870. While Emmeline was pregnant with Sylvia, he continued to redraft this legislation. Her parents remembered 1882 as much for marking the extension of the original Married Women's Property Act as for their daughter's arrival. The outcome of nearly a century of campaigning, this law enabled women to buy, own and sell property and to keep their own earnings. Because Richard Pankhurst had drafted the legislation, this victory was a family matter.

Pankhurst's commitment to education made him more popular among working people in northern England than his support for women's suffrage. In 1858, he was one of the pioneers who initiated evening classes at Owens College for working people. He served as an unpaid member of the teaching staff, running courses both at the college itself and throughout Lancashire for people who could not afford to travel to Manchester. For thirteen years from 1863 he was honorary secretary of the prominent Union of Lancashire and Cheshire Institutes, established in 1839 as one of the Mechanics Institutes, which continued into the twentieth century.

All of these organizations, whose names might today sound like so many cumbersome Victorian institutions, were pioneering progressive teaching programmes that formed the foundations of public education for working people in Britain who had no access to regular schooling or the old universities. All her life, Sylvia argued relentlessly against the deeply held prejudice of the British ruling classes that the so-called masses (whoever they were supposed to be) could not be educated. It was one of the subjects on which she took no prisoners, ever. The consistency with which she upheld this belief, in thought and practice, was rooted in her father's philosophical and practical example that education was essential to liberation for working-class men and to women of all classes.

In sum, Richard Pankhurst was the living incarnation of every pioneering, radical Victorian cause. The enfranchisement of women stood at the pinnacle of his interests. Equally controversially, he was an outspoken republican, confronting what was a burning question in the 1870s. The struggle in France to overthrow the Second Empire at the end of the Franco-Prussian War had great influence in Britain, not least in the way it informed the young Emmeline Goulden's Francophilia. Dr Pankhurst was for the abolition of what he regarded as the parasitical monarchy and the scrapping of the House of Lords in favour of a more representative revising chamber.

He was also at the centre of middle-class Manchester's intellectual and cultural life: the Brasenose and the Arts Clubs, the Literary and Philosophic Society and the Law Students' Society. Strongly community spirited, he embraced social and public life with gusto and enjoyed being part of civic functions and institutions. He loved speechifying. A fellow member of the Brasenose Club, Edwin Waugh, the Lancashire poet who wrote always in dialect, chuckled of the humorous and entertaining, but loquacious, Pankhurst, 'The doctor's gradely a-gate this evening: he is, by gum!'[75] – teasing him for being garrulous. Founded in 1869, originally for the promotion of the arts, the Manchester Brasenose Club became a congenial gathering place for a diverse male fellowship – expanding to include men from business and the professions. The club became Manchester's artistic and cultural hub, where members came into contact with an array of local and travelling artists, musicians and literary men.[76]

The daily press frequently reported Dr Pankhurst's talks and speeches, citing, for example, his address to the Arts Club comparing characterization in the works of Shakespeare and Sophocles. He left one club, the press revealed, because it abandoned its more bohemian, relaxed, high-thinking style for opulent decor and flat conventionality.

In truth, he left in protest because the club blackballed a potential
member for being the son of a butcher.

As a legal expert, Pankhurst's expertise was wide-ranging. The journal
of the Manchester Literary and Philosophic Association, of which he
was a leading member, provides an insightful pen portrait of the man
who was to father the rebel daughters who, above all others, challenged
and defied the British rule of law:

> As a jurist Dr Pankhurst took a high place, and had not politics
> occupied his time to such a considerable extent, he would
> undoubtedly have achieved the highest distinction in the theoretical
> branches of legal science. As it was, he had a large share in the
> scheme for the reform of the Patent Laws in 1866, and published
> various addresses and essays of importance on questions of scientific
> jurisprudence and legal reform.[77]

Richard began his career during a key transition period in the English
law when it was re-examining historical methods and ideas so long
in vogue that they had ceased to be relevant to the times. He knew
the danger that such transitions risk compromising the move from
old to new law, leading to fudges, confusion and complications. 'Dr
Pankhurst, who was ever among the extreme reformers, was sure
to attract attention at such a time, and by the boldness of his ideas
and the clearness of his views had a very great influence on current
thought.'[78]

There was strong affection, mutual intellectual respect and a good
rapport between Henry Pankhurst and his younger son. Although he
worried about the impact of Richard's politics on his professional life,
he never disparaged or undermined his ideals, even when he was 'vilified
as an Atheist and a Communist'.[79] Henry would merely shake his head
and warn him, 'You are making the steep road harder.'[80]

From their swift marriage in 1879 to Richard's untimely death in
1898, Emmeline travelled that steep road alongside him. Straight after
the wedding she moved into Richard's family home, 1 Drayton Terrace,
Old Trafford, where he had lived with his parents until their deaths.
September 1880 heralded the arrival of their firstborn, named for Samuel
Taylor Coleridge's poem about 'The lovely lady, Christabel / Whom her
father loves so well'. Their second child, Estelle Sylvia, arrived less than

two years later, on 5 May 1882,[81] born at Drayton Terrace. Of that house
she had no recollection. But of the two years they spent at Seedley
Cottage, Pembleton, on the outskirts of Salford, she had many clear
memories. Seedley Cottage, the home of her maternal grandparents,
with whom they lived, was deceptively named.

Far from being a cottage, Seedley was a large white house surrounded
by gardens that to Sylvia seemed enormous. The property was set
adjacent to Robert Goulden's textile printing works and the several
reservoirs that serviced the factory. Her aspirational grandparents
bought the property and built the factory on land surrounded by the
estates of conservative landed gentry who disapproved of having as their
neighbours the former master cotton spinner and bleacher turned self-
made man and his opinionated wife. By the time Sylvia lived there, the
old estates had given way to rows of terraced houses forming an ever-
expanding residential district.

Grandma Goulden's gardens seemed of great size, many groved
and easy to get lost in. Everything appeared on a large scale: Sylvia
herself was small. Of Seedley, she most strongly remembered the shade
of green leaves in the summer gardens; the sniff of polish on heavy
Victorian furniture; the feeling of light kisses and heavy words from
adults; delight in play, upsets and accidents.

The Pankhursts, together with Susannah Jones, the children's Welsh
nurse and nanny, moved into this roomy house of Emmeline's parents
shortly before the birth of their third child in February 1884, Henry
Francis Robert, known as Frank. Emmeline reacted to the birth of their
first son, her husband noticed, with an unprecedented happiness.

Sylvia associated her grandmother with the sound of bustling in the
kitchen and laundry smells and the hardworking efficiency of what
she described as a typical old-fashioned housewife.[82] The household
was largely self-sufficient, growing its own vegetables and fruit. Jane
Goulden worked alongside her housemaids producing butter, bread,
jams and pickles. Laundering was an art and a seamstress came in for
weeks at a time at the turn of seasons to make and mend. Manx-born
Granny Goulden was a dissenter of agricultural stock who had educated
her children in women's rights, universal suffrage, free thought and
opposition to racism and slavery. Sylvia's childhood notion of a typical
old-fashioned housewife was steeped in a long and deep tradition of
British radicalism where strong, hard-working women participated as

agents of change in the family and on the streets beyond their laboriously managed households.

Jane Goulden's influence on her eldest daughter Emmeline and in turn on her granddaughters is unmistakable. The Isle of Man was the first place in the British Isles to give the vote to women, thirty-seven years before the opportunity was given to women in the rest of the kingdom. In 1881, the year before Sylvia's birth, the Isle of Man extended the right to vote to unmarried women and widows who owned property on the island. As a result 700 women received the vote, comprising about 10 per cent of the Manx electorate. It was a small seed but tellingly planted in the minds of the women in the family.

In the Christmas pantomime staged in the front parlour at Seedley Cottage, Sylvia played a tiny Cinderella whose party gown of stiff pink tulle emerged out of a giant cracker. She rode to the ball on an elephant composed of two uncles and a damask tablecloth, and Christabel performed the role of Prince Charming, adored by all.

Susannah took Sylvia and Christabel on a long-promised visit to see their twelve-year-old Aunt Ada's much talked-about doll's house and meet its diverse family. The Scotsman, Aunt Ada's favourite, was placed carefully in Sylvia's hands. She studied him critically, disappointed by the ugliness of the limp white calico stuffed with sawdust and clumsily daubed with gaudy paint. When Christabel reached out to take him from Sylvia, Aunt Ada looked alarmed, afraid that the favoured Scotsman might be dismembered in a sisterly tug of war. But the uninterested Sylvia readily handed him over, mystified that a little girl could care so much for such a lifeless and unbeautiful object.

The thud of her head on a big black block of coal and the burning of her hand and arm in the glowing fireplace were further imprints in Sylvia's memories of Seedley. Left alone, she and Christabel had been chasing each other round the great dining table until Sylvia, dizzy, tripped over its great claw foot and fell headlong into the fireplace. Later in life she observed that it was only the lavishness of old-fashioned Lancashire fire-making that placed there the extra coal block that saved her. Thanks to that lump of coal, she didn't catch fire.

The accident made her the pet of her four young aunts and five young uncles, her mother being the second of the ten surviving Goulden siblings. Sylvia wore her arm in a sling, her nails came off and her uncles nicknamed her 'Little Briton' for her stoicism in not screaming when the burns were dressed. To console her she was given a small black rabbit – or wabbit, as Sylvia pronounced it – doubtless chosen for its witty likeness to the coal block that broke her fall. The rabbit soon died and was buried in the garden with a little gravestone to mark the spot. The loss of her first pet upset Sylvia.

When they were a bit older, the three sisters dramatized Heinrich Hoffmann's wildly popular poem *Struwwelpeter*, with Christabel and Adela playing the cats and Sylvia Harriet, even though Harriette was Christabel's second name, after her paternal aunt. To play the part, Sylvia wore her hair in plaits,[83] a rare moment of attention to coiffure.

Left alone by her mother and nurse, Harriet's foolish disobedience in playing with matches causes her death. Her action as she lights the match is in imitation of her domesticated mother, who so often does the same. Hoffmann wrote his gory black-humoured stories (published in 1845) for his son and illustrated them himself, an early example of a hugely successful children's picture book. Sylvia loved the images and the menace lurking within the home, represented by the conflagration that engulfs Harriet when, mimicking her mother's domesticity, she lights a match to cook over a stove and is distracted by the 'pretty' flames, which set her apron strings alight. Christabel and Adela performed the cat chorus:

> The cats saw this
> And said: 'Oh, naughty, naughty Miss!'
> And stretched their claws,
> And raised their paws:
> ''Tis very, very wrong you know,
> Me-ow, me-o, me-ow, me-o!
> You will be burnt, if you do so.'
>
> And see! What dreadful thing!
> The fire has caught her apron string;
> Her apron burns, her arms, her hair;
> She burns all over, everywhere.

Burning all over everywhere held another strong association for Sylvia. Emmeline introduced her little girls to the story of Joan of Arc, whom she'd learned about at school in Paris. Later in life Christabel remarked that those who really wanted to know what Emmeline was like, in form and spirit, should go to the Place Saint-Augustin in Paris and look at the Joan of Arc statue there: 'It is exactly Mother!'[84] Radical Francophile republican to her core, there was nothing cautionary in the way Emmeline told her daughters the tale of the Maid of Orleans.

Little could they envisage the future when a young militant Sylvia would find herself heckled by an agent provocateur suggesting that she share the same fate as Joan and Hoffmann's hapless Harriet. Addressing a crowded meeting in Limehouse town hall in London's East End, Sylvia asked the audience what means they should resort to in order to get the government's attention. 'Burn you,' came a voice from the of the hall.

While all instances of conflagration prefigured the symbolic role of Jean d'Arc in their lives, cats were a reminder of what Sylvia later described as her own and Christabel's 'stumbling dullness'.[85] She recognized their over-earnestness. Barely nine and eleven respectively, Sylvia and Christabel decided to give a series of public lectures to the family, Christabel on the subject of coal, Sylvia on tea. For several days they researched and wrote their lectures. Adela, age six, as yet unable to read, watched them miserably, feeling the pinch of exclusion. It never occurred to her elder sisters that she would try and copy them.

An hour before their family guests assembled for their edifying lectures, Adela announced that she too was going to speak, on the subject of the family cat. Puss was duly laid on the hearthrug and solemnly examined. Furious at Adela's levity and concerned that she was going to make their event seem ridiculous, her two sisters urged her to stop making fools of all of them. It was too late. Adela was determined to take her turn and their father was already calling to order the assembly of adults that included two aunts, a second cousin and family friends.

Christabel stumbled apprehensively through her notes, struggling to read her own handwriting and almost inaudible. Father made matters worse by interjecting 'Speak up!' and 'Don't be self-conscious!'[86] Wishing to run away but realizing it would be very mean to desert her elder sister, Sylvia grimly plodded through what she admitted was her own even worse performance. Barely had she reached the end of her economic and political survey of the history of tea when, to the immense relief of the adults, Adela powered forward, 'unencumbered by notes, brisk and clear of voice', issuing animated and utterly obvious physical descriptions of the family mog.[87] She was, of course, rewarded with enthusiastic rounds of applause.

Christabel was disgusted, Sylvia deflated. They had worked so hard on their *facts*, many of which they knew for certain to be new to their browbeaten audience. Adela, conversely, had taken no trouble at all and pursued not a single fact, to great acclaim. Brooding over this event, Sylvia realized that the applause for Adela was a delighted mockery of her own and Christabel's earnest efforts – and an outburst of relief from the adults thus saved from their terrible dullness. Aunt Mary was the only grown-up who tried to console the older girls, assuring them that she had learned a great deal from their presentations. This acute consciousness of being overly serious and therefore perhaps less lovable permeated Sylvia's early years.

It wasn't until she was older that Sylvia knew why they'd moved away from Grandmother and Grandfather Goulden's great house, but even before she understood the reason she sensed the differences between Mother and Grandmother Goulden. There was none of the old-fashioned managerial housewife about Emmeline – no pickle making or successful baking, and no make-do-and-mend efficient running of the family resources. Emmeline had learned a great deal during her years of education in Paris, but the principles of domestic economy were not among them. When she and Richard moved the family to Green Hayes in Old Trafford, Emmeline handed over the management of the household budget to Susannah Jones, the children's Welsh nanny, on the very sound basis that she could make it stretch much further.

From when they were small children at Green Hayes, their father maintained a never-ending improvised story cycle about the startling and absurd adventures of Nobs and Dobs, two lads at large. Offsetting their antics was the parallel epic of the vain and fantastically dressed Miss Popinjay, whose excessively clichéd and fussy femininity led her into endless ludicrous mishaps. Sylvia shared her father's visual imagination: 'As he recounted, he drew amazingly grotesque illustrations which delighted us immensely.'[88]

Yet all three sisters found Father's more serious moods infinitely more enthralling. The crumb trail leading to the origins of Sylvia's intense sensitivity begins here, as she listened to her father with tear-filled eyes while he talked of Percy Shelley, his idealism and his quest

for the perfection of human life and described his poignant grief over
the deaths of his children. She later recalled her elation when her father
read to them from Whitman, 'Pioneers! O Pioneers!'[89]

> O you daughters of the west!
> O you young and elder daughters! O you mothers and
>   you wives!
> Never must you be divided, in our ranks you move united,
> Pioneers! O pioneers![90]

Here are Dr Pankhurst's constant themes of hard work and sacrifice
for the trailblazing pioneer, reinforced by his visionary republicanism
and the idea of the new blood of youths moving west to escape the
older races and their dusty bards. Whitman's emphasis on unity in the
poem speaks to Richard Pankhurst's perspectives on feminism. The
poem stresses the importance of solidarity not for men only, but as
something to be developed between men and women and – vitally –
between women. Sylvia captured in words her father's philosophy for
bringing up feminist daughters:

> He read aloud to us, told us stories, opened to us his beliefs and
> hopes. When we were still but toddlers he was for ever asking
> us: 'What do you want to be when you grow up?' and urging" 'Get
> something to earn your living by that you like and can do.' 'To do,
> to be, and to suffer!' was a favourite phrase of his. 'Drudge and drill!
> drudge and drill!' he would exhort us.
>   Throughout our childhood we heard his beseeching adjur-
> ation: 'If you do not grow up to help other people you will not have
> been worth the upbringing!', his proud joy: 'My children are the
> four pillars of my house!' and his frequent appeal to us: 'Love one
> another!' There was bred in us thus a sense of destiny, and of duty
> to be servants to the commonweal.[91]

Pankhurst continually prompted his daughters and his wife to keep
their eyes open to patriarchal realities and to resist them. He challenged
them with frustrated passion, 'Why are women so patient? Why don't
you force us to give you the vote? Why don't you scratch our eyes out?'[92]
For ever after, Sylvia remembered the violence of the image.

Poetry punctuates Sylvia's recollection of her father's habits. She heard him rising early and reading aloud or reciting poetry to himself during his systematic ablutions. He read as he walked to the bus stop and on the bus to his chambers.

Until the end of her life, Sylvia had his little red-bound Milton, just three inches long, a complete edition in tiny type. Her father bought the smallest editions of all his favourite books so that he could carry them around with him, stowed away in his bulging pockets in between the little black notebooks he always used for his own jottings. Emmeline, brushing his coat before he left for work in the morning, would complain of his curiously disfigured appearance and teased him that surgeons would stop him in the street and ask him to leave his lumpy body for dissection.

Along with the poetry and storytelling were porridge and punishment set against the hot fires of adventure and the imagination. A thunderbolt flashes through Dr Pankhurst's adult personality – the unquiet ghost of the child of lapsed Baptists – combined with the idealist's energy, inexhaustible and always exacting for himself, often exhausting and demanding for others. Sylvia's memories of the discipline of the nursery years are notably precise and unmistakably symbolic in the circumstances of a life where incarceration, food and hunger striking become legendary weapons of her adult struggle with the patriarchal British state.

In the porridge wars with her parents, we hear one of the first examples of Sylvia's insubordinate voice and her testing of her own capacities for resistance. Discipline and porridge in a solidly middle-class family are basic staples of Victorian historical fare, but Sylvia's pugnacity suggests an unexpected twist. There is in her a streak of Jane Eyre (with whom she shares some notable similarities) facing down the horrors of the Red Room. 'In my twenties,' Sylvia later wrote, 'I was surprised to hear my mother telling some friends that before I was three years of age, I had convinced her of the uselessness of beating her children, because when she had employed the means of bringing me to contrition, I had made her feel that she might kill me before I would give way.'[93]

Her father delivered the verbal tellings-off, loftily attributing her bad behaviour to 'a want of conscience', a rebuke she found far more painful coming from him than any of the physical punishments that her parents deputed to Susannah and the servants.[94] Sylvia particularly

resented scoldings for petty reasons: dawdling because of aching feet
in too tightly laced boots, or refusing to eat the always lumpy and cold
daily porridge prepared for the children alone. Her resistance to eating
porridge produced memorably stern censure from her father. For the
rest of her life Sylvia remained obdurate in her distaste for this kind
of food. She detested the Holloway gruel, the staple of the extremely
limited HM Prison Services menu. Even her unchecked enthusiasm
for the Bolshevik Revolution could not extend to eating the traditional
kasha – Russian porridge – offered by her Soviet hosts.

For refusing to take cod liver oil, Sylvia was tied to the bedpost
all day. This was a common punishment for middle-class Victorian
children. Unbearable remorse and a sense of degradation were the
feelings provoked by rebellion against the orders of her mother, but
Sylvia was a repeat offender and just couldn't curb her will to resist.
Interestingly, she attributes her contrition and miseries not to an overly
harsh regime or to the unreasonable expectations of adults, but to her
own disposition towards distressing introspection.

Christabel seemed untroubled by depression at trivial failings and
did not share Sylvia's longing for affection from her parents, since it
became clear that she did not have to work for it as hard as her siblings.
Sylvia sensed that Adela and her little brother Harry shared her own
emotional suffering, though in her own memoirs Adela was adamant
that Christabel and Sylvia were equally favoured by their adoring
parents.[95]

Sylvia later recalled vividly the accidents of childhood that left
permanent marks. Running to fetch a sponge for Susannah, she tripped
and cut her head open by striking it on a trestle table. She remembered
not only the particular design of the table but the patterned plaid
trousers of the doctor who stitched up the wound.

Along with this scar on her head caused by the collision with the
trestle table was the legacy of a very slight limp, caused by a blow to
the hip, which Sylvia described as causing her 'a slight permanent
crookedness'.[96] The Pankhurst children were told not to make a fuss
about injuries: 'Having been exhorted to fortitude, I had schooled
myself to practise it.' Forcing herself to observe self-control, Sylvia
told no one of what she repeatedly refers to as 'the blow'.[97] Susannah
discovered the swelling when she bathed the children as usual that
evening. Her mother couldn't believe it possible she had hurt herself

so badly without complaining. Emmeline took her to the doctor, who assured her the swelling was caused by 'a blow'. Retelling this episode Sylvia repeats 'the blow' so many times that the question of the identity of her assailant starts to scream as loudly as Sylvia evidently didn't when she was struck. The unexplained childhood injury, both physical and emotional, is intriguing. Is Sylvia keeping her counsel out of loyalty or is this a narrative designed to implicate the unnamed sibling perpetrator? 'The accident was one of three, which perhaps accentuated in me a strong reluctance for active sports, inherited from both parents, and a tendency towards nervous despondency, perhaps implanted by their strenuous lives.'[98]

In July 1883, a year after Sylvia's birth, Richard stood in the Manchester by-election. His father-in-law Robert Goulden backed him publicly and bankrolled his campaign. Disaffected by the failure of the Liberal Party to live up to its stated values since it came into office in 1880, Richard resigned from the local Liberal Association and ran as an independent candidate. He adopted a radical programme, demanding universal suffrage for both men and women, the abolition of the House of Lords, disestablishment of the Church, Home Rule for Ireland and the nationalization of land. 'In land,' Pankhurst said in his election address, 'it must be remembered collective ownership is the old institution, individual ownership is the modern innovation.'[99] As his grandson and namesake later remarked, it was scarcely surprising he didn't get elected.[100] Dr Pankhurst forcefully criticized the Liberal government's repressive policies in India and Ireland. He proposed a United States of Europe.

The Liberal press attacked him as a 'wild extremist',[101] and even his old friend and admirer Lydia Becker despaired of him as a 'firebrand'.[102] The *Spectator*, then moderately Liberal in leaning, denounced him for fighting the seat as a fanatic: 'Dr Pankhurst is substantially a French Red of the humane type, and not an English Radical at all.' The magazine was most concerned about Pankhurst's attitude to democratic enfranchisement:

> The most determined Radicals are not unanimous for universal
> suffrage, and are distinctly hostile to the swamping of all male
> votes in that of the large majority of women. They are opposed
> to all those projects, either for confiscation or for the foolish

expenditure of public money, which are concealed under the phrase 'Nationalisation of the land'. They desire to reform rather than to abolish the House of Lords. They are divided – probably about equally – on the disendowment of the Church, thought more than half may be in favour of disestablishment. They are almost to a man against Home Rule for Ireland ...[103]

Although the only other candidate in the election was a Conservative, the Liberal Association told its members not to vote for the 'French Red'. As the *Spectator* put it, 'We admit that Dr Pankhurst is honestly dreaming; and therefore we prefer, if we are forced to make the choice, a sensible Tory to Dr Pankhurst.'[104] He lost the election and after a succession of clients had withdrawn their briefs realized that he was the subject of a professional boycott.

Following his first failed attempt at parliament, Richard founded a Radical Association to challenge the reactionary Liberals and simultaneously took up a case against the powerful Corporation of Manchester on behalf of a fruit and vegetable salesman. Robert Goulden began to despair of his son-in-law and unsurprisingly was alarmed to discover that his own business was now also boycotted. Reliable income and respectability mattered to the Gouldens. Richard's refusal to stand down on his activities and principles became a source of constant argument between Emmeline and her father.

Pregnant again, Emmeline also raised the question of the dowry her father had promised her. Given the financial blow the Gouldens had already absorbed from supporting Richard's family and his political career and that he had four other daughters to take care of, Robert was in no mood to discuss unpaid dowries. Emmeline started packing. She severed all ties, not only with her father but with her mother also and only re-established her relationship with her mother years later after her father had died.

In 1885 Richard and Emmeline left the Goulden household accompanied by their favourite aunt Mary who moved with them to help Emmeline run their new home at 66 Carter Street in Chorlton-on-Medlock in Manchester. Susannah became the housekeeper, to whom Emmeline delegated the day-to-day running of family life. Known to Sylvia always and only as the magical Green Hayes, this house was for her forever remembered garlanded by flower borders of starry pink

London pride, startlingly bright and beautiful amid Manchester's black soot – like fairy flowers, she thought them.[105] Green Hayes was sylvan, like her name.

Emmeline, expecting another baby during the move, suffered her most difficult pregnancy so far, enduring neuralgia, dyspepsia, migraine attacks and bitter arguments with her parents from whom she was now alienated. Adela Constantia Mary, arriving on 19 June, was the third and final Pankhurst daughter.

It's striking to come across Sylvia's recollection that her attempts to challenge her mother's considerable authority gave her early practice in refusing to eat. The children's diet was standard for middle-class children of the age: porridge every morning for breakfast except Sunday when there was bread and butter, and very occasionally an egg between the three of them for a treat. For midday dinner they had potatoes, meat (which was cold on two days and hashed on the third) and sometimes cabbage. Always a rice or sago pudding. For tea they had a cup of milk, bread and butter or sometimes bread and jam, never butter and jam together.

Sundays were the exception. They ate a midday lunch with their parents, with apples or oranges to follow, and were allowed a piece of cake at afternoon tea if Susannah took them in to see visitors. For this they were dressed in pretty little frocks and lace-trimmed pinafores. Sylvia wrote many years later when she had a child of her own:

> Such dietary was generally considered proper for children when
> I was a child, but today it would be held woefully deficient in
> the necessary vitamins. To supply the child with a varied and
> nourishing dietary is more and more tending to become the first
> care in every family, whilst the tendency is for the adults to regard
> strictly simple fare as best for a middle-aged digestion and to seek
> health by resorting to the spartan sparseness which used to be
> imposed on the young.[106]

An early episode with the American feminist Harriot Stanton Blatch concerning food wars with authority lodged itself firmly in Sylvia's consciousness. She remembered the first time Mother called her to be formally introduced. She knew that Mrs Blatch was immensely learned and was in great awe of her. Harriot took one appraising look at Sylvia and declared that she looked pale and delicate. 'She will not eat her porridge,' Emmeline explained. To Sylvia's astonishment, instead of echoing her mother's reproach, Mrs Blatch responded cheerfully, 'Then why give her porridge? There are lots of other good things to eat for breakfast: eggs, fish, bacon, kidneys, fruit!' As an adult, Sylvia would understand and adopt the wisdom of a more varied diet for children, but understandably at the time her loyalty immediately rallied to Emmeline – 'even to hear such words seemed treason to my mother'.[107] Was she not, thought Sylvia, one of the most beautiful women in the world? 'Not one of all the ladies who came to the house, distinguished as I thought them, could compare with her. How clear was her beautiful pallor, how finely arched her delicate black eyebrows, how soft and tender her large violet eyes! She had the loveliness of the moon, and the grace of the slender silver birch. I gazed on her with adoration.'[108]

For those who know something of her story, it is commonplace to assert that from childhood Sylvia identified with her father as a man of action and intellect. That is only half the story. As Sylvia recognized, Emmeline was also a person of action and instinctive intelligence. Her mother was a product of her upbringing: untrained and hampered by her gender, class and culture.

Emmeline's belief in porridge was heart-wrenching. She didn't know any better and simply repeated what her own mother had fed her and her nine hungry siblings. Dr Pankhurst expounded the benefits of green vegetables and fruit, but such food burdened the already overstretched family budget and didn't seem to do his indigestion and stress any good. It did however appear to contribute to Sylvia's evolution into an adult vegetarian.

The Harriot Stanton Blatch episode is an indication of the interconnectedness between the nineteenth-century British and American women's movements. Harriot, daughter of the American feminist leader Elizabeth Cady Stanton, married an Englishman and lived in Basingstoke, Hampshire. She became one of the most active members of the Women's Franchise League, of which the Pankhursts were key founders. Keenly interested in the education of young women, Harriot Blatch protested that even in elementary schools where boys and girls were taught in the same class, arithmetic cards were marked with 'For girls' with easier sums on one side and 'For boys' with more difficult sums on the other.

Harriot told Emmeline that young Christabel was far too sentimental and needed a stiff course in mathematics to counterbalance her perpetual novel reading.[109] This outspokenness greatly impressed Sylvia. It had never so clearly occurred to her that both she and Christabel lacked any systematic education. Several years were to elapse before they were sent (intermittently) to school. In the meantime, there were 'daily' governesses for Christabel and Sylvia, who came on weekdays.

Harriot Blatch provided stalwart support and offered much practical advice to Emmeline. When she stood for the Manchester School Board elections, Blatch recommended cutting the amount of time devoted to sewing for girls in state elementary schools, and advocated drawing, geography and science for both sexes, and raising the school-leaving age. 'Working mothers will rise to the idea if you show how it is a mere case of class legislation.'[110] On campaigning, she advised Emmeline, 'Canvass, canvass … it brings surer success than public meetings.'[111] Blatch had a defining influence on Sylvia, who unlike her mother developed a belief in the value of academic education for young girls and in the efficacy of grass-roots canvassing over public meetings. She became one of Sylvia's key mentors and supporters, playing a significant role in her adult life.

Emmeline engaged a Miss Pearson, who habitually sent her sister, 'Miss Annie', as a substitute. They liked Miss Annie because she made no attempt at formal teaching, instead reading aloud to them the novels of Dickens, Thackeray, Scott and George Eliot. 'The murder of Nancy by Bill Sikes made an indelible impression of horror on me,' Sylvia wrote; 'for years I was haunted by visions of her beautiful face of agony and fear, confronting his brutal strength. The privations of Oliver Twist illuminated for me the public work we knew our father to be doing.'[112] Aunt Mary helped them dramatize the dialogue between Dick Swiveller and the Marchioness, as well as scenes from Thackeray's *The Rose and the Ring*.

Sylvia and her father got along exceptionally well, bonded by her early love of reading, politics and poetry. Christabel, quick, pretty and witty, was easy to love and clearly exceptionally clever. There was something about Sylvia that was less easy to understand immediately. In their intimacy, it was as if her father, of all the family, sensed her difference. In his reedy voice, struggling to hold the tune, he often sang her the song from Shakespeare's *Two Gentlemen of Verona*, 'Who is Sylvia? What is she?' Punning on the Latin meaning of her name, he nicknamed her 'Miss Woody Way'.[113]

When he died so suddenly in her sixteenth summer, her father was still Sylvia's unalloyed hero.

She'd lost her mentor and protector. In those agonizing few days Sylvia learned a mortal lesson that defined her developing character. It was a lesson her father had constantly tried to instil in her and all his daughters. Never, ever, give in to unjustified authority, or bad things will happen.

'I never consulted anyone. From childhood I had always found evasion of anything which appeared to me to be a duty too painful to be persevered in. I knew no peace of mind 'til I had done what appealed to me as the right thing.'[114] Sylvia wrote this in 1937 when she was fifty-five. The claim that she never consulted anyone is nonsense. However, the rest of this statement taps into an emotional truth about the founding trauma of her childhood. Seeking permission from authority may produce bad advice that shelters behind convention and inaction. This might lead in turn to avoidable disaster.

Regarding her attitude to authority, the death of Sylvia's Victorian father raises the question of whether he left her with the solace of belief in God. From childhood Sylvia recalled hearing the servants argue heatedly about whether her father was religious. Ellen, the most intimidating but best loved of their family cooks, was a woman of dark mysterious sayings and strong opinion. She dominated even the robust Susannah. Ellen declared Dr Pankhurst was not at all religious. Susannah and Rose the housemaid disagreed with her, insisting that he could be heard saying his prayers regularly in the bathroom in the morning. Ellen snorted at their ignorance. Those weren't prayers, they were poetry. John Milton's *Paradise Lost* was not the Gospels. Moreover, Ellen added, none of the children had been taught to pray and would all burn in hellfire in consequence. This prospect Sylvia found extremely distressing.

Alongside this, Sylvia was consternated by the idea that Father could be regarded as anything other than a beacon of brightness and inspiration, right in all things. These arguments between the servants prompted her first sense that her family might be unusual. 'Especially when I was alone in the dark the mystery of our apparent difference from other people thrust itself upon me.'[115]

Ellen portentously predicted that evil luck would befall them in this world and the next because of their irreligious state. When the grim prophecy assailed Sylvia in night terrors, she prayed, 'O God, if you are God, I know You will not hurt us. I know it is not wrong that Mother and Father have not told us about You, because I know they are good.'[116] If a God existed, her prayer would be heard. If not, she'd lost nothing by the attempt. This is Pascal's wager, so a telling example of Sylvia's mental aptitude.

Sylvia was only three years old when in 1885 her father's first shot at getting into Parliament was derailed by a smear campaign claiming he was an atheist. These were the external conditions, but Sylvia's route to working it out in the home was much more personal. Her father led her and Christabel gradually to agnosticism through reading and rational argument rather than telling them, in the style of a Victorian patriarch, what to think. They were forbidden to receive religious instruction, but by the time the girls actually went to school it was so late in the day that their views were already fully formed. Sylvia recalled sitting in class pretending to study her extra assignment in history given to her in place of religious instruction, while really listening in awe to other pupils being treated to stories from the Bible. She explored her interest by drawing and painting imagined biblical scenes.

When finally Sylvia and Christabel discussed it with each other, the problem was resolved. They discovered that they were both anxious about overheard conversations between the servants. They went to Father, who listened to their questions and explained that he hadn't discussed it with them before because he wanted them to think about and decide the matter for themselves. He gave them a brief outline of the biblical account of the life of Christ, the Christian dogmas and his own doubts about supernatural interpretation. He presented Sylvia and Christabel with the two rival theories held by agnostics: either Christ was an actual persecuted reformer (his own view), or he was a legendary figure compounded from the stories of many martyrs. He gave them books on the subject to read for themselves alongside an abridged account of Darwin's controversial *Origin of Species by Means of Natural Selection*, published in 1859.

From then on, Sylvia's mind was made up on the subject of Christianity, though not on spirituality generally. Her father's argument removed what previously had been made to appear a question of vice or virtue, good or evil, luck and magic, to the realms of detached, scientific examination. Guilt or moral failure sprang from lack of knowledge or weakness of discernment and concrete will. Notions of virtue were not abstract or detached from material context.[117] Sylvia seemed to be aware that she substituted one religious father figure for another of a different, modern Romantic, scientific and industrial sort:

> I saw my father as a lofty embodiment of the human mind, faring forth amid uncharted heights. The quest of knowledge was now a favourite subject of my drawings. Half-nude figures hewing roads in the rocky mountains, building with rude stone boulders, bearing lamps through the darkness, their unshod feet treading the rude and jagged stones; old scholars poring over great tomes and surrounded by scales and crucibles.[118]

In 1886 Richard Pankhurst gave his views in the witness box, during a libel trial brought against the Tory *Manchester Courier*. During the election, in which he had stood for Rotherhithe, the newspaper reprinted a rival candidate's claim that the Red Doctor was an atheist. From the stand, Dr Pankhurst described himself as 'one of those who are called Agnostics, like Professor Huxley and Mr Balfour'.[119] Though Arthur Balfour's election literature contained the slogan 'Vote for Balfour and Religion!', he was the author of a widely published essay 'Defence of Philosophic Doubt', in which his final position was an expression of the doctrine of agnosticism: 'The world, as represented by science, can no more be perceived or imagined than the Deity, as represented to us by theology; and in the first case, as in the second, we must content ourselves with symbolic images, of which the only thing we can most certainly say is that they are not only inadequate, but incorrect.'[120] Probed about his own opinions, Pankhurst replied,

> I said my position was that I had found for myself that God, the soul and immortality ... were things unknown and unknowable by the human intellect, quite apart from a region which is rarely the region of religion, the region of faith and hope, which region I have never entered in a discussion, because I think it is a sanctuary never to be entered.[121]

God and religion troubled Richard Pankhurst during his adult life only as man-made institutions deployed as political weapons and instruments of power. At the same time his philosophical and scientific temperament and rigorous habits of mind made him logical. Respecting the limits of human knowledge and evidence-based science, he remained open-minded about what could not be understood or disproved. Sylvia was never religious but was always spiritual. Her brother Harry developed a passionate interest in Buddhism and eastern religions, which he discussed with her, but she remained resolutely sceptical of any religions organized around male deities of any incarnation.

Sylvia kept her father's soul and memory alive in the causes that he said were the only things that made life worth living. She learned early on the price to be paid for religious dissent. At Manchester High School, where her father's republicanism and alleged atheism were well known, the Christian girls rushed at Sylvia, demanding to know why she hadn't attended the scripture lesson and taunting her, 'Are you a Jew?' Before she could reply for herself, the Jewish pupils protested, and disowned her. She turned to walk away but all the girls followed with shrieks and laughter, thumping and pushing her, pulling her hair, tearing her hat and coat from their peg and trampling on them.[122]

The question of where Father had gone after his death he had answered already in life, 'playfully, and yet in earnest, "If you ever go back into religion you will not have been worth the upbringing!" '[123] Of all the Pankhurst sisters, Sylvia would be the only one who never returned to religion or the consolations of its Judaeo-Christian philosophies. Christabel and Adela later in their lives both resurrected their relationship to forms of evangelical Christianity. Sylvia remained firmly a child of the secular age of Darwin, Marx and her own secular father.

Her father's funeral was probably one of the first times Sylvia attended a mass gathering held for other than political reasons. His coffin lay on an open bier covered with wreaths. Thousands joined the procession to the Brooklands Cemetery on Saturday 9 July, including an official Independent Labour Party deputation and a diversity of people from the many movements in which he'd worked.

Crowds lined the streets to watch the procession pass through Old Trafford. Gazing at Emmeline sitting opposite her in a carriage, Sylvia thought how beautiful and strangely young her mother looked, 'as though the years since her marriage had fallen from her'.[124] A voice sounded in her ears: 'The widow and the fatherless'. Apt for the moment, that biblical tag, but Emmeline chose agnostic poetic words to be engraved on her beloved husband's headstone, after he had been buried alongside his parents: 'Faithful and true and my loving comrade' – her own adaptation of a line from Walt Whitman.[125]

Decades later in midlife, Sylvia wrote an unpublished short story spirited from the fragment of an adult dream, entitled 'Why the dead do not return'. 'I dreamt that I was dead and was going back to my home … wracked with an unimagined agony, an agony that because it is unlike anything we feel on earth I cannot remember or understand. I only know how it seemed greater than I could bear.' The ghost comes to a room where her sisters sit with their father beside the fire. They recognize her with a start, then from fear forget her instantly. 'Only my father, perhaps because he is dead though in the dream I did not remember it, kept always a sad steady gaze upon me. Yet [he] did not speak, and for the others' fears I could not speak to him. So I hid my face and stole out of the house, knowing that is why the dead do not return.'[126]

3

The Home News & Universal Mirror

The first sixteen years of Sylvia's life prior to the death of her father are a formative tale of growing up in two Victorian cities. London and Manchester are leading characters in Sylvia's story. Through her book-lined homes flowed a constant tide of cosmopolitan visitors from all over Britain and the wider world beyond. The new public galleries, museums and libraries of the self-improving era into which she was born made art, science and cultural history accessible to middle-class children whose parents were minded to encourage their education and civic-mindedness.

Though they never lived there, the spirit of Paris similarly influenced Sylvia's upbringing. France, its philosophy, literature and revolutions, infused Pankhurst political thinking. The French Revolutions, Dr Pankhurst argued, demonstrated the importance of social justice, reform and the primacy of the rule of law. In terms of notions of class hierarchy, the Gouldens were better off and more solidly bourgeois than the Pankhursts. But Emmeline had the disadvantage of belonging to a subordinated class: her sex. As a woman, she was an inadequately educated member of an oppressed majority. Where her husband via the routes of empathy and intellectual grasp understood the power and danger of mob rule, Emmeline shared that majority's instincts directly. Hers was the hard-wired evolutionary fury of the physically threatened and unjustly dispossessed.

Manchester was home for the first five years of Sylvia's life. In 1887, at her mother's instigation, the family moved to London. What Lancashire says today, England says tomorrow, was a popular saying when the industrial north was the political heart of England. London, however, was the home of parliament, and Emmeline believed that living there would further her husband's prospects of becoming an MP. Determined to generate income to support Richard's political ambitions, she landed on the idea of opening a shop, an enterprise for which she possessed absolutely no experience. She found retail premises to rent with living accommodation above at 165 Hampstead Road. The front door of Sylvia's new home opened on to a noisy London street market thronging with potential customers. With its rickety staircases and higgledy-piggledy floors the Hampstead Road property was, Christabel observed, impractical and like something out of a storybook, but their mother was all confidence and enthusiasm, moving in 'a radiant daydream'.[127] The process of buying her stock thrilled her. Daily deliveries arrived, consignments of fancy goods, occasional furniture, plates and jugs. All of these Emmeline enamelled in pale colours and Aunt Mary decorated with flowers. They stitched arabesque cushion covers and drapes from bolts of sumptuous fabrics in the Orientalist themes of what they called 'the East', then so much in vogue.

Emmeline placed the newly painted sign above the shopfront and Emerson & Co. opened for business. It's assumed that the venture took its name from Ralph Waldo Emerson's mantra 'Nothing great was ever achieved without enthusiasm', one of Dr Pankhurst's often repeated tags. Emerson & Co. offered a selection of what Emmeline described as 'art furniture' and interior decor items, peddling contemporary aesthetic ideals and innovative lifestyle choices. The store followed utopian socialist trends: William Morris wallpapers, painted artisanal milking stools, soft furnishings and ornaments inspired by the Arts and Crafts movement. Also displayed for sale were photograph frames for the increasingly popular novelty of family portraits. There were also more conventional late Victorian wares on offer.

Sylvia expressed scepticism about some of her mother's stock. The twee and finicky items of homeware recommended as suitable wedding presents appalled and amused her, particularly a set of table mats made of yellow cloth (Emmeline's favourite colour) stamped with holes for blue silk embroidery supplied for the lucky bride to complete. Sylvia dismissed these sorts of items as 'commercialized kindergarten'.[128] Emerson & Co. supplied toys for the nursery, such as a cardboard Tower of London pierced with holes for cross-stitching. Despite Sylvia's suspicion of the purveying of feminine fussiness, the ethos of Emerson & Co. made a deep impression. It was her mother's fancy-goods shop that first suggested to her the uses of art and design in expressing, branding and selling political ideas. Emmeline's aim of introducing brighter colours and imaginative objects into Victorian homes was creative. Accessible art and crafts spoke a visual, material language. They animated radical, visionary ideals and made tangible the promise of a different lifestyle.

Women of the era had begun to make their bids for professional independence, mostly in teaching and the civil service, but it was still unusually bold for a woman to open and run her own retail business, especially since it was Emmeline's serious intention to try and help subsidize her husband's political ambitions. Loyally supporting his wife's business venture, Richard also thought that her working set a good example for their daughters. That Emmeline was a complete failure as a commercial entrepreneur was beside the point; her purpose in trying to make money and her belief that people benefited from living with beautiful and useful things were in earnest.

Mrs Pankhurst's imaginative enthusiasm and generally good taste in selecting her wares was in inverse proportion to her budgeting abilities and capacity to manage the bottom line. Emerson & Co. lost money and Richard ended up subsidizing the business to keep it afloat. Emmeline bought far more than she ever sold and much of it ended up decorating her own homes or as gifts for friends. Her stylish presence and charm drove sales when she was on the shop floor, but that was all too infrequently. Commuting constantly to and from Manchester with Richard, she neglected the business. Tragedy struck when she was away on one of these trips.

On a bright September morning in 1888 Susannah took the children out for a walk. She pushed three-year-old Adela in a pram. Since her birth, Adela had splints to reinforce weak legs. Frank, now four years old, walked alongside with Sylvia and Christabel. While they were out, Frank started coughing. During the night he fell violently ill. The doctor diagnosed diphtheria and instructed that Emmeline be called back from Manchester immediately. Known as 'the Strangling Angel of Children', diphtheria is a bacterial infection that before the development of treatments and vaccines was a common cause of illness and death among children.

Frank died shortly after his mother returned to London. Richard received the news in the middle of an inquiry. Halfway through the case, he couldn't get free until it ended. Sylvia and Christabel heard their distraught mother shouting that she wished Sylvia or Adela had been taken instead. Frank's death was the first real sorrow to strike the couple in their nine years of marriage. Susannah asked Sylvia if she wanted to see her little brother. 'I went, feeling stricken and stunned, so grieved that I could feel no more. I could not believe it was he, that beautiful little white figure, with dark, still hair and long black lashes.'[129] Sylvia watched the female artist who came to paint two death portraits of Frank. Her mother could not bear to look at them and concealed them in her bedroom cupboard, out of sight.

Defective drains in their rented property were blamed as the cause of Frank's infection. Despite the boasted advances in modern Victorian sanitation, London sewage leaked through faulty pipes and joints, and there was a belief that the disease entered homes through plumbing systems. Frank died before people understood that diphtheria is transmitted person to person via droplets, though by the 1880s there was an imprecise understanding of the idea of infection being carried in the 'miasma' of toxic London air. Emmeline swiftly bundled the girls away to friends in Richmond while she searched for a new home. She persuaded Richard to take a five-year lease on a large house they couldn't afford at 8 Russell Square on the corner of Bernard Street. Emmeline assured Richard that she intended to sublet part of the house to a doctor to make up the shortfall. This plan, of course, never materialized. Besides, Emmeline reasoned with her husband, their working home needed to be large enough to hold political meetings and it was really 'all needed for propaganda activities'.[130]

A respectable middle-class area of locked communal gardens and wide streets, 1880s Russell Square was inhabited by lawyers, newspaper men, medics, academics and well-heeled bohemians. Not far from the Law Courts, London University and Fleet Street, the square was also close to the exciting and risqué areas of Covent Garden and Soho.

The first floor of Number 8 comprised two large intercommunicating rooms used exclusively for Emmeline's 'At Homes' and conferences. The rest of the house they lived in, with two servants – their nanny Susannah and a cook. Emmeline renovated the house from top to bottom. She painted and papered it throughout in her favourite yellow, installing elegant standard oil lamps with yellow shades. She loathed gas and this was the era before the advent of domestic electrification. She installed expensive frosted glass in the library windows and Richard's books almost entirely lined the interior. A frieze of purple irises ran all around the walls of the yellow drawing room. Emmeline put up Japanese blinds made of reeds and coloured beads and covered occasional lamps with scarlet shades. Sylvia remembered how the ruddy light shone through the windows in cheerful welcome when they returned home on dark winter afternoons.

The Russell Square house reflected Emmeline's taste, all supplied by Emerson & Co.: Chinese teapots, old Persian plates, Japanese embroidery, Indian brasses, Turkish rugs. Silks from Wardle's of Leek in Staffordshire and cretonne draperies by William Morris and his imitators set off the white enamelled furniture, ornamented with the fretwork that was so fashionable at the time. 'She revelled in the gorgeous colours of the Orient and all that was brilliant and bizarre in old art and new.'[131]

Sylvia's mother made a huge effort to produce beautiful effects at moderate cost, hanging pictures herself, laying carpets and upholstering furniture. Preoccupied with earning the bread and butter from lawyering and with his political work, Dr Pankhurst paid little attention to his wife's interior decorating and accepted unquestioningly her domestic management, ' "I am a helpless creature!" he often said, handing over even the carving of the joint to his energetic spouse.'[132] On special occasions Emmeline dressed the table elaborately with gauze and flowers. To a large extent she made all her own and the children's clothes. As Sylvia observed, 'Beauty and appropriateness in her dress and household appointments seemed to her at all times an indispensable setting to public work. She was a woman of her class and period, in this as in much else.'[133]

Emmeline thought she had found better premises for Emerson & Co. in Berners Street, legendary for its association with Dickens,[134] but more importantly the premier location for London's best-known cabinet-makers, upholsterers and furnishing companies, including the original Sanderson fabrics and wallpaper. Not long after Emmeline opened the new shop, the building was scheduled for demolition. Even though it was still losing money, she moved the shop once again, this time to 223 Regent Street, opposite Liberty, the luxury department store that opened in 1875, an even more fashionable location with a sky-high rent to match. She repositioned the business, now selling furniture and exotic goods from around the world at more reasonable prices than Liberty. Even at this salubrious location, Emerson & Co. failed to balance its books, despite Emmeline's frequent advertisements for her 'Art Furnishers and Decorators' in popular magazines such as the *Penny Paper*.[135] As Christabel remarked, the family would have been financially far better off without the business, which was now a continuous drain on their father's income.[136]

The recirculation of Emerson & Co. surplus stock sometimes caused consternation among the children. Sylvia awoke on Christmas Day in 1887 to discover, excitingly, an oblong box covered in red plush at the end of her bed, convinced it contained the violin, 'that heart-disturbing, heart-enchanting voice', she longed to learn to play.[137] Expectation turned to tears when she discovered the box to be empty. The other children received similarly empty boxes. There was no extra money for Christmas presents.

Some years later her parents bought Sylvia the violin for which she had yearned, but it remained unused in a locked cupboard. 'Mother, poor busy mother, would find me a good teacher some day.'[138] The teacher never materialized, and Sylvia was profoundly disappointed at not learning to play. Without outwardly protesting, she withdrew to her private world of drawing and painting, a realm that 'was under my own control; I could always return to it'.[139]

As soon as they moved to London, Sylvia's parents threw themselves into the fray of the capital's radical activism. The late 1880s were a time of intensive labour organization in response to the harsh economic times for working people. The predominantly Conservative or Liberal minority administrations met escalating protests, strikes and lockouts with increasingly repressive and violent responses. 'It was a time,' Emmeline recollected, 'when a most stupid reactionary spirit seemed to take possession of the Government and the authorities.'[140] Richard and Emmeline joined protests frequently.

On 8 November 1887 the government banned all further meetings in Trafalgar Square and overnight Londoners mobilized to protest against unemployment and repression in Ireland and to protect their rights of free assembly and free speech. Five days later Richard and Emmeline joined the mass rally of 30,000 demonstrators convening in Trafalgar Square, an event known ever after as Bloody Sunday. Well-known socialists led the speeches, John Burns, William Morris, Eleanor Marx and Annie Besant among them. (All soon became regular visitors to the Pankhurst home.) Armed troops, together with police both on foot and mounted, barricaded the square and fierce fighting broke out, during which hundreds of people were seriously injured and around 300 arrested.

The following Sunday the protest was repeated, and a police horse ran down Alfred Linnell, a legal clerk, who died a fortnight later in hospital. The Pankhursts, riding in a coach with the Linnell family, joined the 100,000 mourners at his funeral, designed to emulate Wellington's thirty-five years before. The Duke's interment had been funded by the public purse. The mass wake of the 'socialist martyr' Alfred Linnell, killed by the police, received no government funding.

In June 1888 Emmeline read aloud to her family Annie Besant's article in *The Link* reporting on the horrendous pay and conditions of the women working at the Bryant & May match factory in the East End's Silvertown. Entitled 'White Slavery in London', Besant's article had been inspired by a speech on female labour given to the Fabian Society by Clementina Black.[141]

The Pankhursts had joined the Fabians when they moved to London, and attended meetings when they could. The Fabian luminaries George Bernard Shaw, Beatrice and Sidney Webb and H. G. Wells all became friends of the Pankhursts and met their daughters, but Sylvia's parents never became central to the Fabian group. As Richard explained to his elder daughters, the Fabians were primarily a group of intellectuals committed to incremental reform. They saw themselves as an elite who thought they knew better than working-class leaders and the international workers' movement what form political change should take and how it should happen. While the Pankhursts fitted in easily with London's trade union leaders and radical socialists, there was a whiff of snobbery about how they were regarded by some of the middle-class intellectuals who dominated the Fabians. As Rebecca West later observed, the Pankhursts were seen as somewhat arriviste. Emmeline's innovative sense of modern fashion and the interior decor in her home were too conspicuous.[142] But the greater social problem was that all the family spoke with Lancashire accents.

Sylvia was five years old when her parents met Keir Hardie for the first time, in November 1888, at the International Workers' Congress in London, organized by the Trades Union Congress (TUC). Socialism, a passionate commitment to the creation of a new British labour party and a love of radical literature brought them together politically. The tragic shared experience of the sudden death of a child bonded them in sympathetic friendship. The Hardies had lost their three-year-old Sarah to diphtheria in 1887; the Pankhursts had lost their four-year-old Frank to the same malady just two months previously.

Keir Hardie was impressed that the Pankhursts attended the conference together, one of the new species of socialist power-couples where the women were as politically engaged as their men. At this congress Hardie also met Eleanor Marx and Edward Aveling, Katharine and Bruce Glasier, who became his friends, and Gabrielle and Robert Cunninghame Graham. Hardie's wife Lillie stayed with the children in Scotland, just as she did the following year when he went to the International Workers' Congress in Paris, where he spent his leisure time with Emmeline and Richard, also attending.

Lillias Wilson and Keir Hardie had married in August 1879. The daughter of a publican, Lillie was tall and handsome, liked to read, knew how to write and was trained as a dressmaker. The two met as youngsters in the temperance movement. Lillie's experience of the family business – her father was an alcoholic – convinced her of the need to take the pledge of abstinence in her teens. Hardie took the pledge at the age of seventeen, supported by his adoring mother, Mary, even though she was an atheist who had firmly brought up her children as unbelievers and was unsympathetic to the religious aspects of the temperance movement.

Lochnorris, a 'substantial three storeys' made of 'sturdy plain stone'[143] overlooks the bank of the River Lugar, one of Robbie Burns' favourite streams, that flows through Cumnock, East Ayrshire.[144] Hardie and Lillie built it with the help of a loan from Adam Birkmyre, a wealthy Jewish businessman dedicated to the socialist cause. Birkmyre offered Hardie the money as an outright gift to build himself and his family a proper house. Hardie refused the gift, but agreed to borrow the money as an interest-free loan, repaid in instalments. Building began in 1891. Lochnorris, as Caroline Benn observes, provided 'a solid stone foundation which gave Lillie domestic standing, if not social respectability, and Hardie an important peace of mind'.[145] He was able to provide his children Jamie and Nan with 'the life of security he never had'.[146] There was a local village school for them, and it was somewhere his siblings and his and Lillie's parents could regularly visit. Lochnorris was Lillie's 'pride and joy'.[147] Its conventional exterior belied a 'surprisingly modern' interior with clean geometric lines and tiles, 'perhaps an Arts and Crafts reaction against Victorian excess',[148] and an expression of Hardie and Lillie's good taste.

The Times had reported on the delegates before the congress opened, with Paris in the middle of a heatwave, capturing both the internationalism of the event and the dominant presence of British trade unions and socialist organizations. This was a very different convention from the Fabian Society meetings the Pankhursts had attended and in this context they were close to the leadership and in step with its radical direction.

> The International Workers' Congress, which is to meet next Monday, will be numerously attended. Credentials have been received from ten different nationalities, but the English are most numerous. Nineteen trade unions or trade councils send representatives, including Mr Burt, M.P., and Mr. Fenwick, M.P., for the Northumberland miners. Six different English societies and 15 branches of the Social Democratic Federation have also appointed delegates. The Belgian Labour party, the trade societies of Verviers and Liège and the miners of La Hestre, the Italian Labour party, some trade societies from Vienna, Hungary, Switzerland, Madrid, and Barcelona, the Labour party of Portugal, and the Knights of Labour of America are all sending delegates. Adhesions from other nationalities are still expected. One hundred and five Parisian trade unions send 253 delegates, and the trade societies of 27 provincial towns have also appointed delegates, among these being eight from Algeria. A large number of workmen's clubs will be represented. Altogether up to the present moment 227 societies, established in 59 different towns or industrial centres, will be represented by 470 delegates.[149]

Hardie and the Pankhursts joined forces for debates and votes on the campaign for the eight-hour working day. In their leisure time, Emmeline introduced Hardie to her favourite city. The men discovered they were as like-minded about literature as they were about politics, and Richard basked in the glow of his emancipated and sophisticated wife. A warm intimacy blossomed between the three. Subsequently Hardie became a regular guest at the Pankhurst homes in both London and Manchester. In Sylvia's words, when Hardie became MP for West Ham South in 1892, her parents 'rejoiced at his election to parliament and ardently admired and supported his independent fight'.[150]

The political and personal alliance between Hardie and the Pankhursts spanned decades until the disastrous rift with Emmeline and Christabel in the final years of his life. Despite the large amount of time they spent together, there is circumstantial evidence of Lillie and Mrs Pankhurst meeting on only one occasion.

While Sylvia's parents became more international and broadened their involvement in London activism, the six-year-old made her entry into politics. During this time, she and Christabel started to attend meetings with their parents and to help in the organization of Emmeline's regular 'At Homes' and conferences. The big yellow double drawing room could accommodate a large number of people. The Pankhursts held meetings on the issues of peace and arbitration, industrial and social questions and, 'of course, on woman suffrage'.[151]

Sylvia vividly recalled being taken to a public meeting at the age of eight in 1890. It was a socialist gathering addressed by Henry Hyndman in a dingy hall. The socialist movement at that time had no money. Meetings were mostly held in ropy premises, often in rooms over rowdy pubs or smelly stables. At another meeting Sylvia attended with her father around the same time, he suggested from the audience that old radicals might find a more congenial home in the Social Democratic Federation (SDF). But he didn't join it, according to Sylvia, because 'he was not attracted by its raucous insistence upon economic interest as the all-embracing motive of sentient man'.[152] This is an unreliable observation. Dr Pankhurst's leanings towards scientific materialism were stronger than the older Sylvia cared to admit when she came to write on the subject. She omits to mention that her father's bookshelves were stuffed with the works of Marx and Engels. According to Adela, 'Karl Marx and the class struggle dominated family life.'[153] Perhaps more decisive were Richard's objections to the infighting within the SDF and the regular expulsions from it, as well as the opposition of its leaders and other prominent committee men to women's enfranchisement. Henry Hyndman and

Belfort Bax implacably opposed votes for women. Feminist leaders like Eleanor Marx, who fought her comrades on this issue relentlessly, were acquainted with the Pankhursts. Memorably, in 1896 when she was thirteen, Sylvia's father took her to a meeting at the Mosley Hotel in Manchester to honour the German socialist leader Wilhelm Liebknecht where Eleanor Marx spoke from the platform, dazzling the feminist teenager.

Sylvia and Christabel were welcome to tag along to political meetings with their parents, but there was no question of them going to school. Their parents encouraged political education but distrusted conventional schooling, suspicious of its reactionary ethos and forced feeding of religious humbug to young minds. Schools for girls were generally second rate, and Sylvia's parents also disliked the unnecessary emphasis on petty institutional discipline. At one point their father became keen for the elder girls to attend a new Marxist-run school for working-class and refugee children. But Emmeline was having none of it. The well-stocked museums, galleries and libraries of London on their doorstep would be education enough. On their frequent trips to the Science Museum, National Gallery and British Museum, Sylvia took along her sketchbook. The Egyptian collection at the British Museum was her particular favourite.

The Pankhurst children launched a manuscript newspaper circulated within the family. They called it *The Home News & Universal Mirror*. Their father contributed letters and editorials on important subjects. Christabel wrote comprehensive reports on political meetings held at Russell Square. Sylvia wrote what she described as 'voluminous screeds', which Christabel helped her copy out.[154] Here is the first sign of her capacity for writing at great length. Sylvia's output included her long-running series 'Walks in London', in which she described anything and everything the children encountered on their trips around town with Aunt Mary and Susannah, and sometimes with their father. She wrote articles recounting visits to the House of Commons, the British Museum, the National Gallery, the Tower of London and the Serpentine recreational lake in Hyde Park. She also drew all the illustrations for the paper. Adela clamoured to be included. Her superior elder sisters allowed her to contribute a couple of stories. Adela wrote first a rhyming rags-to-riches tale about an impoverished widow with many children rescued by a rich benefactor, followed next by a plaintive and troubling tale about a little servant girl whom everyone bullied.

Initially the paper appeared weekly. As it grew larger – mostly due to Sylvia's voluminous contributions – it became monthly. Christabel and Sylvia chronicled the suffrage receptions in their homes: 'Mrs Pankhurst looked elegant in a trained velvet gown,' the 'Misses Pankhurst wore white crepe dresses with worked yokes' and 'the refreshments were delicious, the strawberries and cream being especially so'.[155] The editors of the *Home News* reported enthusiastically on the plentiful quantities of strawberries and cream provided at some of these functions, but at first showed less interest in the subject of the women's suffrage issues discussed.

As well as arranging the chairs and distributing leaflets, Sylvia was tasked with printing the notices, since she had the most artistic hand – 'To the Tea Room' being the most frequently required. Emmeline dressed the rooms with masses of flowers, especially heliotrope, her favourite. It was a modern, novel choice, another example of Emmeline's innovative taste. (This was before the colour purple became a colour of suffrage denoting feminism.) The word heliotrope appeared in the English language in the year Sylvia was born. Shuttling between Manchester and London to keep the whole show on the road, Richard never seemed to complain about Emmeline's extravagance at her salons, though they could ill afford it.

Once the political business of the suffrage meetings was done there were refreshments and usually music and recitations. Sylvia heard the deep, rich contralto of Antoinette Sterling singing Elizabeth Barrett Browning's 1843 poem 'The Cry of the Children' set to music, exposing the plight of children forced into working in the mines and factories of industrial England. The verses combine detailed description of the thoughts and hopes of the children with an outsider's pleas to the public to improve the conditions of their blighted lives. Barrett Browning took many of the details for this work from the report of an 1842–3 parliamentary commission of inquiry investigating the conditions endured by children employed in mines and factories, written by her friend and collaborator Richard Henry Horne.

The American Antoinette Sterling, born in New York State, began performing in England when she arrived in the early 1870s, making her debut in Covent Garden Promenade Concerts and afterwards appearing at key popular venues like Crystal Palace, the Albert Hall and St James's Hall. Controversially, she never wore a corset. This included the occasion when she sang by royal command for Queen Victoria. And she never drank tea. As a child, her patriotism was so stirred by the story of the destruction of tea cargoes in Boston that she resolved to have a lifelong boycott of the beverage. The pro-emancipation Sterling was working as a teacher in Mississippi when the Civil War broke out and her physical safety was violently threatened by local racist thugs. After she had fled by night with a young friend, black activists rescued the pair and escorted them north on the so-called Underground Railroad. In Britain, Sterling met and married the Scottish-American John MacKinlay. The couple lived in Stanhope Place in London, a mile from Russell Square.

Another frequent habitué of these gatherings, especially popular with the children, was Mohammed Abdul Karim, Queen Victoria's favoured Indian attendant. Born in Uttar Pradesh, the son of a hospital assistant, Karim became a servant to the Queen in 1887, her Golden Jubilee Year. His visits to their home intrigued the children and Susannah. Sylvia heard the servants whisper with bated breath that he 'was teaching Hindustani to the Queen', and they marvelled at his ornate turbans and 'flowing robes'.[156]

The domestic intelligence Sylvia overheard was accurate: Karim started teaching the Queen Hindi and Urdu in 1887 and soon afterwards she nicknamed him the 'Munshi', an Urdu word for teacher or clerk. In August, Victoria recorded in her journal: 'I am learning a few words of Hindustani to speak to my servants. It is a great interest to me for both the language and the people I have naturally never come into real contact with before.'[157] On 20 August she noted her enjoyment of the 'excellent curry' Karim had cooked for her, and added that he was teaching her a few lines of Urdu in preparation for an audience in December granted to the Maharani Chimnabai of Baroda.

Victoria appointed Karim her Indian secretary, showered him with honours and obtained a land grant for him in India. Later, she wanted to make him a knight but was blocked by a horrified government who made her settle for the lesser honour of CVO. Karim's intimacy with Victoria and the preferential treatment he received from her during the last fifteen years of her reign made him a controversial and unpopular figure at the xenophobic court. On her death Edward VII immediately revoked all the land, privileges and financial securities bestowed on Karim by his mother.

The racist prejudices of the royal household and its social circles made them utterly incurious about Abdul Karim's life beyond the palace. Little did they guess that Karim frequented Mrs Pankhurst's salons in Russell Square, mingling with republican radicals, including the American anti-racist campaigner William Lloyd Garrison and the feminist leader Elizabeth Cady Stanton. The Indian nationalist leader Dadabhai Naoroji, the first Asian member of the House of Commons, also regularly visited the Pankhursts. Known as the Grand Old Man of India, Naoroji, a Parsi intellectual, educator and cotton trader, was a Liberal Party MP from 1892 to 1895, a member of the socialist Second International and later one of the co-founders of the Indian National Congress. Sylvia read his book *Poverty and Un-British Rule in India* when it was published in 1901, a magisterial political and economic analysis of the draining of India's great wealth into Britain. From the 1850s, Naoroji had been campaigning on this issue from the heart of the empire.

Other visitors to the Pankhurst home included socialists, Fabians, anarchists, suffragists, freethinkers, rebels and humanitarians of all schools. The Ukrainian revolutionary Sergey Stepniak, the Russian revolutionary Nikolai Tchaikovsky and their friend the Italian anarchist leader Errico Malatesta all made a particular impression on Sylvia, as did the Russian refugee anarcho-communist Peter Kropotkin. William Morris greatly enjoyed Emmeline's gatherings but disapproved of her over-elaborate Parisian-style gowns. At the Pankhursts', Morris rubbed shoulders with the Scottish radical John Morrison Davidson, journalist, barrister and trade unionist, and with the communist Tom Mann. Mann, Sylvia noticed, always turned up in a pristine starched white collar, then got so animated and excited when making his speeches that the collar dissolved into a damp rag by the time he had finished.

The Labour leaders John Burns and Ben Tillett were part of the Pankhurst inner circle. The socialist and pacifist Herbert Burrows, Vice President of the Manhood Suffrage League, was another family friend, who worked by day for the Inland Revenue and spent every other waking minute of his life campaigning for radical causes. Annie Besant came often, as did Adolphe Smith Headingley, who thrilled Sylvia and her sisters with the tale of his narrow escape from execution during the suppression of the Paris Commune. Famously, Headingley created the custom of singing Jim Connell's 'The Red Flag' to the tune of 'O Tannenbaum'.

The fabled feminist Paris Communard Louise Michel was a great favourite of Sylvia's – 'the "pétroleuse", as her enemies called her'. Sylvia described Michel as 'a tiny old woman in a brown cloak, intensely lean, with gleaming eyes and swarthy skin, the most wrinkled you ever saw … I regarded her with admiration as a tremendous heroine. She seemed to belong to the magical world of imagination, not the commonplace life of every day.'[158] Sylvia painted Louise Michel in her imagination, sometimes as a fantastic being from fairy tales, at others as a leader at the heart of battle, leaping forward in the darkness, her bare arm uplifted with a flaming torch, a scarlet Phrygian cap pulled over her raven hair, defiant with fierce joy.[159]

The now snowy-haired Victor Henri Rochefort continued to be a regular visitor, although unpopular with Richard. Despite long years of exile in England Henri still did not speak English, so Emmeline chatted to him in her fluent French and her husband in his more punctilious, textbook style. Involved on the wrong side of the Dreyfus scandal Rochefort had shown himself as anti-Semitic. Richard vigorously opposed anti-Semitism, was circumspect with Henri and, unlike Emmeline, far from pleased by his return to their friendship circle in London.

During this period, Rochefort's daughter Noémie, Emmeline's dearest childhood friend, came to stay with her own daughter Lillie and two teenage sons. Sylvia was disparaging about Lillie, declaring her stolid and not very pretty. Her brothers Henri and Armand were of much greater interest. The Bloomsbury neighbourhood found them remarkable, on account of their very short socks and the round navy-blue capes they wore instead of overcoats. The children ran around together in Russell Square gardens and the French boys introduced the Pankhurst girls to games unknown in England.

The Home News & Universal Mirror began to show a growing interest in political issues as well as in strawberries and cream. A sample feature from 1891 gives a flavour of the publication's house style,

Mrs Pankhurst held an At Home at her beautiful house on May 28th. There was a great number of people there. Dr Pankhurst, as

Chairman said in his speech that if the suffrage was not given to
women, the result would be terrible. If a body was half of it bound,
how was it to be expected that it would grow and develop properly.
This body was the human race and the fettered half, women. He
then, with many compliments, called upon Mrs Fenwick Miller
to speak. Mrs Fenwick Miller spoke of the attitude of the political
leaders and the growing power of the Women's Franchise League.
Some opponents tried to prove that women were naturally inferior
to men, but our girls won degrees and honours at the Universities.
Mrs Pankhurst wore a black sort of grenadine with train from
shoulders, and looked very handsome indeed.[160]

Later, Christabel edited out her family's intimate friendships with
revolutionaries and radicals. In her memoir *Unshackled* she focused on
the Pankhursts' non-partisan friends and eminent Liberals, such as the
English pacifist Hodgson Pratt. A great friend of Dr Pankhurst, Pratt
founded the International Arbitration and Peace Association in 1880, of
which Richard was a member.

Christabel also liked Richard Haldane, later 1st Viscount Haldane,
who spoke at their house. Haldane appeared to be the great
parliamentary hope of the Women's Franchise League until Emmeline
and Mrs Jacob Bright, in conversation with him about a Woman
Suffrage Bill, discovered he had absolutely no interest in women's
suffrage being enacted.[161] The Liberal grandee James Bryce, afterwards
Lord Bryce, British Ambassador to the US, was another frequent visitor
to their home whom Christabel enjoyed remembering, alongside their
father's old ally Jacob Bright MP, at the opposite end of the political
spectrum from his conservative anti-suffragist brother, John Bright.
Of the socialists, communists, anarchists, freethinkers, old Chartists
and Communards, abolitionists and radical feminists who flowed
constantly over their doorstep, Christabel seemed to have absolutely
no recollection.

The discussions whirling about the young ears of Sylvia and her
sisters at Russell Square introduced them to all the major radical
issues of the moment. These included the 'New Unionism' which was
broadening and radicalizing the older, more exclusive and less political
craft unions; the socialism of various schools; what Sylvia described as
the 'delightful' prophecies of Kropotkin; the socialist magazine *To-Day*

with its contributions from the much talked-about bright-eyed brilliant young man with sandy hair called George Bernard Shaw; Annie Besant's *Link*; the Fabian tracts; and Robert Blatchford's international blockbuster essay collection *Merrie England*, credited with making the idea of socialism really well known in England for the first time in an accessible, readable form.

Sylvia loved reading Edward Bellamy's Marxist utopian science-fiction novel *Looking Backward: 2000–1887* and listening to the grown-ups discussing the book, which became the third-largest bestseller of its time after Harriet Beecher Stowe's *Uncle Tom's Cabin* and Lew Wallace's *Ben-Hur: A Tale of the Christ*, both of which Sylvia also devoured.

Sylvia listened to discussions on the decision of Edith Lanchester to enter into a free union instead of a legal marriage, a position that her father strongly supported. Given his opposition to Emmeline's suggestion during their courtship that they do exactly the same, this indicates either a notable development in his thinking or a healthy dose of double standards. Eleanor Marx sheltered Lanchester from social opprobrium by moving her into her home, The Den, in Jews Walk, Sydenham, and appointing her as her salaried secretary. Lanchester's love child was born and nursed in Marx's home.

Further matters of marriage, sexual conduct and free love arose over the Dilke divorce controversy, when Sir Charles Dilke was accused in court of adultery. Richard and Emmeline refused to judge the media allegations against Charles, arguing that the man's public work should not be prejudiced by the case. The Pankhursts made a point of being seen by the press calling at the Dilkes' home at the height of the salacious scandal. Charles Dilke, depressed, declared himself ruined. Richard cheerily buzzed him along, assuring him that the storm would pass and that he would live it down. Sylvia marked the example of her parents being loyal to their friends in trouble.

Talk about the new esoteric religion of theosophy, founded by the colourful occult spiritualist, Helena Blavatsky greatly entertained Sylvia. There were witnesses to the certain fact that during a seance Madame Blavatsky had miraculously extended her arm to enormous length in order to light a cigarette from the gas jet in the ceiling. Curious, Emmeline and Aunt Mary impishly attended some seances, but unfortunately nothing remarkable happened in their presence and Emmeline dismissed Blavatsky as an imposter. Recalling this episode,

Sylvia draws an interesting distinction between the empirical and emotional approaches of her father and mother: 'The Doctor was an agnostic; she, lacking his scientific, philosophical temperament and sustained mental training, was emphatically an atheist. Reform, to her, was the main business of life.'[162]

Prominent above all of the other issues discussed in Russell Square was women's enfranchisement and removal of the legal and social disabilities imposed on married women. Dissension over the question of the married women's vote would very shortly come to dominate the Pankhursts' political work.

Other aspects of the Russell Square years went unreported in the *Home News & Universal Mirror*. The enticing lawns and densely flowered banks of Russell Square gardens lay directly opposite their house, containing the statue – rather amusing to the children – of Francis Russell, the 5th Duke of Bedford, dressed preposterously as a Roman senator. The children had permission to play on their own in the gardens, on the strict instruction that they stuck together. Their days alone in their own urban Eden were for a time cut off when 'some big boys asked Adela strange questions'.[163] Christabel and Sylvia confided the questions to Aunt Mary. Prompted by her husband, Emmeline called a family conference with all the girls, first reprimanding them for leaving Adela to play alone and then subjecting them to the excruciating experience of hearing her, very haltingly, trying to introduce them to the mysteries of sex. 'Father says I ought to talk to you,' she began, but did not get very much further and never again referred to the subject, 'leaving us as free from knowledge as before, on the question which disturbed her.'[164]

Following this episode, the children were confined for a time to the patch of ground behind the house. This neglected area offered only some scrubby dried-out grass, a half-dead acacia tree and a lilac that never flowered, all testimony to their parents' lack of interest in gardening. Surrounded by a high wall, the ragged courtyard seemed like a prison yard, but at least they were still outside. 'I used to sit there for hours imagining adventures,' Sylvia remembered.

> The wall would fade away, vistas of trees and flowers would take its place; a lake with swans and water-lilies; a river flowing through meadows, and fringed with yellow irises. Birds sang; lambs bounded upon the grass, a lovely woman in white robes came smiling

towards me, surrounded by dancing children. I flew away on the
back of a great bird, I soared above the clouds, I crossed the seas.
I descended to yellow sands, where groves of palms and flowering
trees came near to the water's edge, and barges lay moored,
laden with bright fruits, gorgeous silks, wrought silver and gold
and precious stones, and all the richest and loveliest things my
childhood mind could conceive.[165]

Years later, the lovely robed woman surrounded by dancing children
in a sylvan grove would be the subject of her last painting. Sylvia
was intensely susceptible to idealistic visions of this sort throughout
her childhood, and used her 'splendid imaginings' as solace for all
the misunderstandings and sorrows. 'Only when the world of dream
refused to open would the carping of a torturing conscience, or the too
vivid realization of the griefs of unhappy people, whether of real life or
of fiction, bring down upon my spirit a cloud of dark despond.'[166]

4

Family Party

Until her twenties, Sylvia's family all supported the same party. When their allegiance diverged, Sylvia mused, 'Families which remain on unruffled terms, though their members are in opposing political parties, take their politics less keenly to heart than we Pankhursts.'[167] Between her birth and the turn of the century, four general elections took place. Richard Pankhurst ran unsuccessfully as a candidate in three of them: in 1883 a year after Sylvia's birth, in 1885 and finally in 1895.

The Liberals and Conservatives vied to hold the balance of party politics in their power and William Ewart Gladstone and the Marquess of Salisbury led as the dominant prime-ministerial figures from the 1880s to the turn of the century. In 1884 Gladstone's administration pushed through the Third Reform Act. This Act further challenged parliamentary resistance to the principle of 'one man, one vote', enfranchised two and a half million new working-class male voters and established a more uniform electorate throughout the country by dividing up most of the old constituencies into single-member seats. In the 1885 general election that followed[168] Sylvia's father stood as an Independent in the Rotherhithe division of Southwark in the south-east London docklands.

Given the disaster of his 1883 campaign in Manchester, Richard was wise to try his chances in a new constituency, this time in a working-class district that shared his radical republican politics.[169] Rotherhithe in the 1880s was grim, its hopeless poverty as terrible as the squalor of the Lancashire factories. Emmeline electioneered alongside her husband, leaving the newborn Adela in the care of her elder sisters and

Susannah. During this period the Pankhursts met the socialist George Lansbury, champion of the East End, women's rights and social justice. Shortly after they married, Lansbury and his wife Bessie Brine moved to Australia, where they encountered unemployment and hardship. Unable to make a life in the Antipodes, they returned to Bow. Lansbury joined the Liberal Party and went canvassing in Bow; he was so appalled by the poverty he encountered that he joined the Independent Labour Party when it was established in 1893. He became an MP, a founder and editor of London's *Daily Herald* and Labour Party leader from 1931 to 1935.

George Lansbury and Sylvia became loyal friends, political allies and confidants. George and Bessie produced twelve children, and all who survived became politically active in their community and beyond. Three of the Lansburys went to prison in the suffragette cause: George, his son Edgar and Edgar's wife Minnie, who died from pneumonia contracted in prison. Annie Barnes, the British-Italian socialist and suffragette, remarked, 'The Lansburys made Poplar. They fought and fought, the whole family.'[170] The dockland borough of Poplar became famous for its political radicalism. The Labour Poplar councillors undertook a range of progressive social reforms including equal pay for women; the building of houses, parks and wash houses; the distribution of free milk; and a minimum wage for council workers significantly above the national average. In 1921 the councillors organized a rebellion against the unfair rates system demanding that London's wealth should be distributed more evenly around the city.

As Richard pounded the streets of Rotherhithe, Helen Taylor, John Stuart Mill's stepdaughter and co-author, stood in a nearby constituency as parliamentary candidate for the Camberwell Radical Association, an unprecedented attempt by a woman to stand for parliament. Richard went to Camberwell to speak for her, but the women's suffrage societies stayed away, considering the move to put forward a woman candidate too daring for their members. Worse still, Helen Taylor had thrown away her skirts and wore only trousers. Emmeline worried that being seen walking around with the unconventional, masculine-looking Helen would cost Richard votes, and she was probably right. Helen Taylor carried on her campaign amid much controversy until the nomination day, when the returning officer refused to receive either the nomination papers or the cash deposit for his expenses. Her electoral contest fulfilled all the requirements for nomination, but under the rules of parliamentary candidature her nomination was rejected because she was a woman.

Richard continued to canvas in Rotherhithe. 'Over the production of wealth preside the laws of nature, but over the distribution of wealth presides the heart of man.'[171] 'What I long and pine for is that our brethren shall have less work to do. I want your life and my life raised to a higher point of power and happiness.'[172] Richard interwove the language of socialism and equality into his speeches. His Tory opponent Colonel Hamilton labelled him a political prostitute: 'I should be ashamed to exhibit myself at street corners like Dr Pankhurst. Look at him in Salisbury Street – a place where I should be ashamed to be seen! The next time you bring out a candidate, bring a gentleman and not a slum politician!'[173]

The slur that Dr Pankhurst was a professed atheist fell like a bombshell in the constituency. The Tories carefully orchestrated a smear campaign reproducing alleged statements by Dr Pankhurst denying the existence of God. These started at a meeting in the presence of Balfour in East Manchester and ended with a well-funded handbill and placard campaign around Rotherhithe. As well as posting up the placards and distributing handbills on the streets, Tory activists placed pamphlets in church pews. Pankhurst denied the libel and reasserted his agnosticism, but the damage was done. As his old ally and friend Jacob Bright MP said in the press in his defence, when it's difficult to find anything in a man's character to attack, label him an atheist.

The spread of free thought and scepticism had been widespread since the Romantics and Darwinism. But attempts to popularize free thought continued to meet with bitter opposition. George Foote was sentenced to jail for blasphemy in 1883 and Charles Bradlaugh continued his battle against the parliamentary oath. Dr Pankhurst had no desire to enter into debate about men's religious beliefs; he just wanted to get on with promoting free and universal education so people could make up their own minds. Nevertheless, candidates who asked for religious freedom, advocated Church disestablishment and argued that affirmation in court and parliament should be made as valid as religious oaths were denounced as atheists.

Sanguine about the furore, Richard absorbed the insults without injury and retained his good humour. Emmeline seethed. Set as she was on victory, the atheism defamation outraged her, and she was troubled by the roughness of the London political crowds. In her experience, Manchester was more civilized. In London she saw her husband's hat knocked off, his nose bloodied from a well-aimed punch, and witnessed helplessly his assault by a mob. She herself was pelted with rotten food.

Emmeline was adamant that Richard needed to fight back and turn around the bad press. His campaign committee had stuck slips over the libellous posters, 'Another Tory lie!' She wanted more of that. Moreover, Richard must go to church with her the following Sunday to prove his respect for religious views even if he did not share them. She wheedled, cajoled, imperiously ordered and, in final desperation, said it would make her ill if he did not, '*I* understand these people, *I* know what to do; you have always got your head in the clouds!'[174]

Such was Emmeline's authority with her husband that she persuaded him to attend the service – not that it made any difference. Hamilton won by 3,327 to Pankhurst's 2,800. In reality, the vote was also affected by the instructions issued by the nationalist leader Charles Stewart Parnell that Irish electors must vote against all Liberal candidates to bring pressure on the government against the coercion of the Irish. Emmeline bitterly protested against Parnell's decision. Once again, her husband tried to persuade her not to take such political tactics too much to heart.

After the election, Sylvia's father became embroiled in disastrous litigation over the religious slur. For nearly two years of her childhood defamation proceedings placed the family under great stress. As a lawyer, Pankhurst knew better. But as a crusader for justice, he did not. He took this action not so much to defend his own name as to test the law as possible protection for radical candidates. Emmeline complained about the conduct of the court proceedings and wrote directly to Mr Justice Grantham. Her letter is a bracing example of her immunity to diplomacy in correspondence,

> My Lord, – Your judgement of Wednesday, and your summing up to the jury to-day, are the concluding acts of a conspiracy to crush the public life of an honourable public man. It is to be regretted that there should be found on the English Bench a judge who will lend his aid to a disreputable section of the Tory Party in doing

their dirty work; but for what other reason were you ever placed
where you are?

> I have, my Lord, the honour to be
> Your obedient servant,
> Emmeline Pankhurst[175]

The controversy rumbled on with the courts initially ruling in favour
of press freedom. Although Richard was eventually vindicated in the
appeal courts, £60 damages and a swiftly retractable apology only added
insult to injury. Yet, ever the idealist, he took some comfort in the law's
attempt to, as Sylvia later put it, 'check the torrent of libel and slander
directed against candidates in those days'.[176]

Ten years later, Richard made his third attempt to enter parliament.
In May 1895 he accepted the invitation of the Independent Labour
Party to be its candidate for Gorton on the outskirts of Manchester.
The Pankhurst children stayed home from school to chalk slogans on
paths and walls, and Sylvia and Christabel went canvassing with their
mother among working-class cottages and tenements. It was a fine
blooding in political campaigning for the thirteen-year-old Sylvia, but
her efforts made no difference. Her father was once again defeated,
this time by a slim majority, as both the Liberals and the Irish again
refused to support his stand. When Sylvia burst into public tears at
the declaration of the poll, her mother rebuked her for disgracing the
family. It was Dr Pankhurst's final attempt for parliament. If he couldn't
win on an ILP ticket in Manchester, he couldn't win anywhere.

Richard and Emmeline's work on women's suffrage continued
throughout their campaigning for a parliamentary seat. The struggle
for labour representation and women's equality were their twin
commitments. The shared fight for women's rights was a personal,
family matter as well as part of a broad political struggle. Richard hoped
above all else to see his wife and daughters vote in his lifetime. Sylvia's
childhood experiences illuminate just how intensely these issues were
entwined in their intimate family life.

An episode involving some young friends demonstrates the
connectedness of the Pankhursts with the feminist and radical
movements. As Sylvia would later observe, families don't change the
world, movements do. For all their serious intention of transforming
the world for the better, there was time for play as well as politics.

'I dreamt that a witch transformed us three sisters into three grey cats and transported us to a desert island,' Sylvia wrote.[177] She turned her dream into a play, and Aunt Mary affably agreed to perform the role of witch. Sylvia scripted parts for their playmates Irene and Helen, daughters of their mother's feminist friend Florence Fenwick Miller, a well-known medic and journalist.

Eager to paint the scenery so she could realize her dream images, Sylvia retrieved some old discarded Japanese screens she'd spotted in the basement, lugged them upstairs with the help of Christabel and Adela and persuaded them to assist her in the laborious job of pasting notepaper over them so that she had a clean white surface for capturing her visions. Discovering the three sisters preoccupied with their messy endeavour, Susannah sensed trouble and informed their mother. Mrs Pankhurst instantly bore down on them, instructing them to desist from 'spoiling' her screens. The word cut into Sylvia, deeply upset by the idea that the beautiful scenes of her dreams were in her mother's eyes merely a child's ruinous graffiti.

Aunt Mary, an accomplished painter who very early on recognized Sylvia's passion for art, quickly intervened before her niece's hurt turned to petulant rebellion. Deftly she suggested that they do away with scenery altogether and simply put up a sign, 'This is a wood', after the theatrical custom of Shakespeare's time. Her aunt's artful compromise was not lost on the word-sensitive Sylvia as she stood, gluepot and brush in hand, thwarted by her mother. Aunt Mary tried to end the stand-off by assuring Sylvia that this way she would still be able to go ahead with her play. Her mother regarded the matter as decided: Sylvia remained dissatisfied.

Soon afterwards, Emmeline's brother Richard – Uncle Bob – a theatrical scene painter by profession, came to spend Christmas with the family. Hearing of the dispute between his sister and niece, he cheerfully resolved the matter by knocking up both scenery and wings from sturdy brown paper and pieces of wood bought for the purpose. Sylvia's magnificent set now looked very professional. Yet despite Uncle Bob's loving efforts to fulfil her heart's desire, her original vision wouldn't leave her: 'I still had hankering thoughts of the beautiful scenes of my dreams, and the unsatisfied longing to cover those large white surfaces I had intended.'[178]

Sylvia's recollection of writing parts in her play for their friends Irene and Helen Fenwick Miller is a reminder of the wider radical milieu in which the Pankhurst children grew older. The camaraderie between the daughters resulting from the friendship between their feminist mothers continued as they grew up. Irene became a WSPU activist, leading direct action, and was several times arrested, tried and imprisoned.

One of the first tiny cohort of women to qualify in medicine in the UK, Florence Fenwick Miller became a campaigner for women's rights during her student days as one of the first women admitted to Edinburgh University. In 1876 she was invited to stand as a candidate for the Hackney division of the London School Board. At twenty-two, this made her the youngest woman ever elected to the largest and most powerful organ of local government then in existence. Educated, political and a member of the women's movement, Florence served on the board because she was interested in the education of working-class people and wished to speak on behalf of elementary schoolgirls and women teachers. She was also motivated by what she described as the 'scandalous shortage' of women with the drive and ambition to pursue interesting careers in the public arena. She forged strong connections with pioneer doctors Elizabeth Garrett Anderson and Sophia Jex-Blake, was well known to the leaders of the major suffrage societies and enjoyed an established reputation among the intellectual elite of the London Dialectical Society.[179]

In 1889 Florence became one of the co-founders, with her friends Emmeline and Richard, of the Women's Franchise League. This pressure group emerged out of a key disagreement over strategy within the suffrage movement over whether or not to campaign for votes for married women. Florence's situation clearly demonstrated the futility and injustice of the argument that married women could be excluded from the vote on the grounds that their husbands could, at least for the meantime, decide their vote for them. Florence was a separated but not divorced working mother, the breadwinner, estranged from a bullying husband from whom she received nothing for the children's upkeep. It was clearly unjust to assume that legal husbands had the right to make decisions for their wives in all circumstances.

Under English common law, married women were immediately excluded from a legal existence separate from their husband by the status of 'coverture' which placed a wife entirely under her husband's legal care and control. The bills for women's suffrage presented to parliament during the 1860s paid no attention to the legal distinction between unmarried and married women and campaigns of the period assumed that dismantling coverture was an integral part of winning votes for all women, whether married or not.

However, when the Liberal Jacob Bright lost his seat in 1874, the women's movement also lost its most radical champion in parliament. Less progressive MPs began to introduce women's suffrage bills explicitly excluding married women, in order to limit the potential size of the women's electorate. The women's suffrage societies, believing that this cautious approach might placate fears and objections to women becoming the majority of people entitled to vote, supported this newly circumscribed approach.

The friendship between Emmeline and Florence and in turn between their daughters shows that arguments between women in the feminist movement over this issue were not merely matters of tactics or realpolitik. For them, it was personal. The Pankhursts opposed the exclusion of married women from the suffrage campaign out of respect for the first-hand experiences of Florence and her daughters, and women like them, whose pressing circumstances the exclusion would ignore.

There were significant advances for the women's movement in the 1880s, and activists began to divide over the best way to keep up the momentum. Long-standing campaigns finally obtained for married women the right to their own property and income and the repeal of the Contagious Diseases Acts, first passed in 1864, and later extended twice. The legislation was an attempt to regulate 'common prostitutes' in order to control the prevalence of sexually transmitted diseases (STDs) within the British army and navy. It required women suspected of prostitution to register with the police and submit to an invasive medical examination. It also granted the police the power to determine who was a prostitute. If a woman was found to be carrying a venereal disease, she would be confined to a 'lock hospital' until pronounced 'clean'. The only alternative to agreeing to the physical examination was three months' imprisonment, later increased to six months, or hard labour. The Contagious Diseases Acts, which did not enforce the examination of men, provoked outrage because they led to the unjust treatment and abuse of the civil liberties of women. The law was eventually repealed in 1886 after successful campaigning by a grass-roots movement led by Josephine Butler, who had founded the Ladies' National Association (LNA) to bring this about.[180]

Women suffragists further advanced their case for the vote by establishing themselves as both voters and elected councillors in local government. The creation of elected county councils in 1888 reinforced these inroads. In the first London County Council elections in January 1889, Jane Cobden and Margaret, Lady Sandhurst, won seats and the council's Liberal majority elected Emma Cons as an alderman. When the right of the women to sit on the London County Council was challenged in the courts, the Pankhursts were among those who joined the pressure groups in support of their inclusion.

The founding of the Conservative Primrose League in 1883 and the Women's Liberal Federation in 1887 provided middle-class women with an opportunity to show their skills in running election campaigns. So successful were women in demonstrating their aptitude for electioneering that later, when they themselves started standing as candidates, all the parties expressed anxiety and consternation at the impact on their own electoral prospects of losing their highly effective women campaigners.

The Women's Liberal Federation (WLF) was formed with an explicit agenda to promote the call for a parliamentary vote more effectively from within the party. Emmeline joined the WLF and became a candidate for its executive committee in 1891. Between 1882 and 1885 she and Richard sat on the committee of the Manchester National Society for Women's Suffrage, frequently siding with the leading moderate suffragist Lydia Baker, despite her refusal to endorse Richard's candidacy for election in 1883.

Thus during Sylvia's formative years in the 1880s, her parents actively participated in the constitutional movement and in organizations that aimed at reform from within. However, Richard and Emmeline became increasingly frustrated by the snail's pace of progress towards winning votes for women. The end of the century was approaching and still they seemed no closer. Further, they had come to the view that the disagreement over what exactly was demanded from parliament was a question not merely of tactics but of values and ethics that could not be put aside for piecemeal gains.

Since the 1870s, from Richard's original draft of the legislation drawn up to enfranchise all women, the proposals had been gradually nudged towards excluding married women and to narrowing the demand for the vote to focus on unmarried women and widows. Husbands could decide for wives. This essentially Liberal position was less calculated to appease public opinion on the sanctity of marriage and the unalterable rights of husbands to rule their wives than it was to allay the fear of the impact on Britain of a newly enfranchised female electorate. Both Liberals and radicals, moreover, feared that middle-class, educated women – by definition from the more elite, reactionary parts of society – would vote Conservative. Attempting to split the women's vote was a classic divide-and-rule political tactic.

In the 1880s the electorate stood at 5.7 million, and four out of every ten men remained disenfranchised. From the gradualist perspective, demanding a vote for all women from the start seemed impractical when so many men also did not have it. Combined with this was the very British belief in the injustice of taxation without representation. Unmarried women and widows who owned their own property and contributed to the state by paying taxes were easier to regard as citizens in the full sense. Conversely, married women were 'covered' by their husbands.

Where she could, Sylvia always dispensed with technical terms in favour of plain expression. Unusually, she was precise about using the legal term 'coverture' in her own language, sensitive to how in this instance the letter of the law expressed the actuality of the human experience. Derived from the verb 'to cover', coverture aptly described the way in which the entitlement of husbands overlay, outweighed, concealed, engulfed, smothered, screened, enveloped and depersoned the women called their wives by means of legal contract.

In 1889 the Liberal MP William Woodall introduced a bill containing a clause that explicitly excluded married women from being allowed to register to vote. Woodall's bill, supported by the leading women's suffrage societies, was wholly out of step with the progressive temperature of the times. Radical Liberals, socialists and campaigners openly critical of marriage as a repressive institution formed an alliance to oppose this clause.

At the AGM of the Central National Society for Women's Suffrage on 21 March 1889, Florence Fenwick Miller, then editor of the long-standing journal the *Woman's Signal*, appeared alongside Richard Pankhurst and Dr Kate Mitchell as insurgents, proposing a resolution condemning the coverture clause that was carried by a resounding majority. Despite several votes against the amendment and a flustered apology by the secretary Florence Balgarnie asserting that the coverture clause seemed to have been 'slipped in, by whom no one seemed to know', the executive committee decided to ignore the membership and continue supporting the clause.[181]

As a result, the suffrage societies split, and those opposed to the exclusion of married women formed the Women's Franchise League (WFL) in July 1889. The committee included Richard, Emmeline, Ursula and Jacob Bright, Harriot Blatch, Jane Cobden, Josephine Butler, Robert Cunningham Graham, Lady Sandhurst and Alice Scatcherd, with Elizabeth Wolstenholme Elmy as secretary. The internationalist perspective of the WFL is illustrated by the inclusion in the committee of Elizabeth Cady Stanton, the American feminist leader, to represent American suffragists. The seventy-four-year-old Cady Stanton was well known in Britain for her role in securing the Married Women's Property Act of 1848, the same year in which she and Lucretia Mott organized the world's first Women's Rights Convention at Seneca Falls, New York.

So by the 1880s the debate over how the demand for the women's vote should be framed focused on the question of whether or not married women should be included in the call. As always, the attempt to divide the movement in the hope of piecemeal reform played directly into the hands of the opposition. How could the married women of England, mothers who formed the mainstay of the imperial nation, possibly be excluded in favour of old washed-up spinsters, obsolete widows, the dubious demi-monde, gold-digging mistresses or outright bohemians? Single women whose primary intent was not to cash in their value on the marriage market and do their reproductive duty were socially irregular figures who aroused fear and suspicion. Much to the alarm of social conservatives, rising numbers of young middle-class women were postponing marriage or, worse, were not inclined to marry at all. Consequently middle-class birth rates were falling.

Male allies of the women's suffrage movement in the Liberal Party felt extremely uncomfortable about proposing bills that excluded wives. For some, this was because it offended their sense of logic and natural justice. For others, it was because it made life at home with their angry feminist spouses intolerable. Women like Lady Dilke and Ursula Bright were not going to remain meek and silent at home while their husbands went off to Westminster to propose legislation that would exclude them.

Outside parliament, Lydia Becker, Millicent Fawcett and their allies largely controlled suffrage organization. They maintained that an initially limited vote offered the only realistic chance of advancing the cause. With good reason, they believed that anti-suffragists supported the more threatening democratic proposal to include married women precisely to ensure its defeat.

Millicent Garrett Fawcett, born in June 1847 in Aldeburgh, Suffolk, was the seventh of ten children. At the age of nineteen, she organized signatures for the first petition of women's rights, though she was too young to sign it herself. She instigated the formation of the National Union of Women's Suffrage Societies (NUWSS) in 1897 and would become its president in 1907, maintaining her leadership until 1919. Millicent Fawcett was also a founder of Newnham College, Cambridge, established in 1871, one of the first English university colleges for women. Her elder sister Dr Elizabeth Garrett Anderson, the pioneer medic, was the first Englishwoman to qualify as a physician and surgeon in Britain, and was co-founder of the first hospital staffed by women.[182] An active socialist and close friend of Karl and Jenny Marx, Dr Garrett Anderson was for a time physician to Eleanor Marx. Another of Millicent's elder sisters, Agnes, established the first interior-design business in Britain run by women.

The question of the married women's vote was the main reason for the formation of the WFL. It was also a response to the decision of the NUWSS to affiliate with other non-suffrage groups, like the Women's Liberal Federation. Because of its failures, the specific circumstances of the formation of the WFL are usually overlooked. But this is at the expense of understanding the lesson provided by its example. Every time the rootedness of political action in everyday women's lives is lost to the record, feminism adds another case of amnesia to its history. Scrutinized more closely, the formation and failures of the WFL are interesting because they were an experimental laboratory for the later development of the Women's Social and Political Union. For Sylvia's childhood political evolution, the WFL was absolutely crucial: it informed and shaped her.[183]

In July 1889 Mrs Pankhurst went into agonizing and protracted labour. Banished from their mother's bedroom, Sylvia and her sisters waited apprehensively. The sounds of her pain alarmed them. At last,

Mrs Pankhurst delivered her second son. A few hours after Harry's birth Susannah noticed Emmeline turn dangerously pale. The nurse told Susannah that Mrs Pankhurst was merely exhausted and there was nothing wrong, but she was not convinced. Ignoring the nurse, Susannah ran out in her cap and apron to summon help. She knocked on the doors of several doctors in the immediate neighbourhoods of Bloomsbury, Fitzrovia and St Pancras, which contained many professional residents. All rebuffed her, saying they no longer took maternity cases. Finally, she found a willing doctor and returned with him to discover Emmeline in life-threatening post-natal haemorrhage. Richard received a telegram demanding his immediate return from Manchester. By the time he got home his wife was out of danger, but it had been a near thing. It was the last time they risked childbirth.

To celebrate Harry's birth and Emmeline's survival, a group of her female friends gathered at Russell Square for a bedside party. They brought gifts and expressed their admiration for Emmeline's new son, understanding how nearly it had been her deathbed. As usual, they discussed sexual politics. The notion that married women, who like all others risked death in childbirth and the threat of domestic violence, should be excluded from the right to vote was unacceptable. Votes for women were a matter of rights and justice, not a tactical exercise. Women's votes could not be sliced like cucumber sandwiches made by female servants, handed out unequally between wives and spinsters at middle-class tea parties. By the time they left Emmeline's bedroom, these women had decided on the formation of the Women's Franchise League.[184]

At their inaugural meeting a fortnight later, the WFL made clear their position that no one should be disqualified from voting by marriage and rejected the proposition that the struggle for voting rights could be separated from the wider struggle for women's emancipation. Wendell Phillips Garrison, son of the prominent American abolitionist William Lloyd Garrison, delivered the keynote speech at the first public meeting of the WLF held at the Westminster Palace Hotel on 7 November. In his speech, he compared the women's suffrage movement with the anti-slavery movement. This was a familiar association to British radicals already well versed in the Romantic tradition in general and the political philosophy of Mary Wollstonecraft and John Stuart Mill in particular. Wollstonecraft and Mill had both drawn attention to the analogy between the dehumanization and disenfranchisement of slaves and the conditions of women under patriarchy.

Lloyd Garrison pointed out that the position of the self-described 'moderates' was more disgraceful than that of the frankly racist and brutal slave-holders, because the 'temporising' and 'wire-pulling' they practised in their bid to achieve partial reform required them to be always mealy-mouthed, 'trying to temper zeal, weaken testimony, decry strong language, and apologise for the wrong-doer'.[185] For the abolitionists the only response was 'immediate and unconditional emancipation'.[186] Speaking from the platform, Richard Pankhurst confirmed this as the position of the WFL on women's suffrage: 'We will not take a piece of justice if thereby we prejudice and injure all the rest.'[187] This insistence on the indivisibility of rights always influenced Sylvia's thinking.

Her understanding would have been developed further the following year the WFL convened an International Conference, held at the Pankhurst home in Russell Square. This meeting declared the 'modern movement' to be one that 'seeks to place society in all its relations upon principles of equal justice, [and] has necessarily attacked the privileges and disabilities grounded on colour, race, religion and class'.[188] Seven-year-old Sylvia and nine-year-old Christabel took great interest in all the proceedings and tried as hard as they could to make themselves useful, writing out notices in big, uncertain letters and distributing leaflets to the guests during the three-day conference that, thrillingly, commandeered every aspect of the life of their home. Significantly, her recollection of this event was the single childhood anecdote that Sylvia included in her 505-page first book, *The Suffragette*, in 1911.

The Women's Franchise League aimed to gather and unify those who rejected the idea that the fight for women's suffrage could be separated from the broader struggle for women's emancipation.[189] Its formative alliance with anti-racist and feminist movements in America, and the inclusion on its committee of key players from both, defined its internationalism and broadly inclusive radical agenda. As well as supporting the call for votes for all women, the WFL declared that no person should be disqualified for election or appointment to any office or position by reason of sex or marriage. The organization worked to secure equality for women in divorce, inheritance and the custody and guardianship of their children.

The WFL was short-lived. It disintegrated in the early 1890s because, as Sylvia saltily observed, many of its adherents became backsliders unable to withstand the vehemence of reproach from the older suffrage societies who believed in the wisdom of tactically splitting the campaign for the vote on the premise that 'Half a loaf is better than no bread!'[190] Young Sylvia learned that the objections of the established women's suffrage societies ran deeper than disagreements over constitutional tactics. The WFL held progressive views on co-education, marriage law reform, trade unionism, internationalism, opposition to racism and colonization, and the abolition of the House of Lords – part of the very parliamentary structure on which the single-issue constitutionalists pinned their hopes. The WFL shared the values of modern British socialism, the worker movement and the emerging Independent Labour Party, making it altogether too strong meat for the cautious constitutionalists aligned with the Liberal and Tory Parties.

Preoccupied by the difficulties of the Women's Franchise League, Richard and Emmeline sent the children off to boarding school in Clacton-on-Sea for a few months with Susannah and Ellen. Sylvia described Clacton as a place that 'opened vistas of squalid life hitherto only imagined from the romances of Dickens'.[191] Street brawls and the carnival-atmosphere inebriation among the day trippers from London scared her. Ellen, on the other hand, took a lively pleasure in the excitement and enjoyed especially the spectacle of two drunken London dockers wrestling in a lurching rowing boat.

In the hope of running into some of her friends, Ellen took them in the evening to the railway station to see the day-trip trains set off on their return journey to London. Overwhelmed by the noisy, ebullient throng and the streaming crowds, Sylvia recalled shivering with fear and clinging to the pram of her young brother. That night, she was 'tortured by hideous visions of the incidents of the day, with Charles Dickens' murdered Nancy and the "Jack the Ripper" victims I had seen pictured in a Sunday paper'.[192] Ellen did Sylvia a great service at the seaside in Clacton. This early childish terror of being a tiny person in a large, potentially uncontrollable gathering, informed by news reports and sensationalist fiction, evolved into an adult confidence, completely at ease within the commotion of mass crowds. More than this, Sylvia actively sought out the bustle and tug of communal street life, a compulsion informed by these early experiences.

Sylvia's alarm at the effects of alcohol, however, never left her, and influenced her later support for the abstinence and temperance movements. She never supported prohibition, but she shared the view of campaigners like Edwin Scrimgeour that cheap alcohol was a vital weapon in the arsenal of the ruling classes to keep the workers down by drowning any potential revolution in drink. During the 1917 Bolshevik Revolution, the Red Guard codes required members of the workers' militia to be 'sober and loyal to the revolution', and stipulated that the 'duty of the Red Guard ... includes the struggle with drunkenness so as not to allow liberty and revolution to drown in wine'.[193]

There were trips to locations more bucolic than Clacton. A town-bred child who'd barely been beyond the suburbs of Manchester or London, Sylvia discovered her love of the countryside when Emmeline sent her two elder daughters to stay at the home of Harriot Stanton Blatch in Basingstoke. The canal, with its water lilies and irises and the fields of scarlet poppies 'seemed like the realization of a dream'.[194] Norah, Harriot's daughter and their playmate, later became a civil engineer specializing in the designing of bridges. Her navy-blue sailor frock, practical short skirt and long, black-stockinged legs impressed Sylvia, as did her boys' short crop and aptitude for daring mischief.

Back home, Sylvia's parents were having a tough time. The commute to and from Manchester was wearing out their father, now often in pain from stomach ulcers. His political career had stalled and Emerson & Co. slid into bottomless cash misère. In the winter of 1892, the end of the Russell Square lease brought a horrendous bill for unforeseen repairs. They had taken on the very end of a ninety-nine-year lease, and the landlords told them they were liable for making good dilapidations over the whole period. If he had ever read it, this detail of the contract Dr Pankhurst's lawyerly eye had overlooked. Once he had dutifully coughed up the stupendous sum, the family discovered that the repairs were never going to be made, as the house was scheduled for demolition to make way for a new hotel.

They could afford London no longer. Sylvia's parents decided it was time to return north. The family took furnished lodgings in the seaside resort of Southport, where for a few weeks Richard took a rest cure at the Smedley Hydro. Without servants, nursery or special food for the children, the girls felt liberated. They saw more of their mother than ever before and ate their meals regularly with their parents. Christabel and Sylvia roamed freely, unaccompanied on the promenade. 'Emancipated from the thraldom of the servants, we felt ourselves to be almost grown-up people.'[195] Temporarily without domestic help, Emmeline's principled objections to the dangers of schooling quickly gave way to the practical force of necessity. Their parents enrolled Sylvia and Christabel at the Southport High School for Girls. Adela managed to persuade her mother that she should go too, despite Emmeline's belief that she was too young.

Sylvia loved school and studied with zest, earning an end-of-term report with glowing grades and endorsement as 'A most promising pupil'.[196] The girls stayed at the school for one term before the family was on the move again. Sylvia recalled, in an anecdote very favourable to herself, that she saved up her pocket money and bought a little leaving present for every girl in her class at the Southport school. 'I was friends with all.'[197] Christabel, however, was neither happy nor popular at the school, she claimed. This seems doubtful. Studious Sylvia was by far the more sensitive, aloof and tricky of the two elder Pankhurst sisters. Christabel was always well liked, though academically lazy. 'It was said of her that she could do better at her lessons if she tried, a reputation she carried with her throughout her school life.'[198]

Sylvia's snide sisterly comment suggests that she probably bought presents for every girl in her class in the hope of making herself more popular. Herself a diligent swot, fiercely brainy and watchful, she was scared by her elder sister's insouciant approach to life and work. Their Southport landlady, however, favoured Sylvia, and gave her a white fox terrier named Vic, whom she was allowed to take to their next temporary home.

From Southport they moved to Disley in Cheshire, to spend the summer in a hilltop farmhouse, where Susannah rejoined them. Sylvia's memories of the Disley summer included blackberrying and haymaking with their mother, now much more relaxed and merry, and ready to ignore their torn stockings and scratched legs. Their father bought them a donkey named Jack, whom they rode astride on a Spanish saddle with a big pommel. Sylvia and Christabel shared a governess with two other little girls who lived in the village. Although she enjoyed studying, Sylvia spent her happiest hours in the fields trying to paint the landscape, accompanied by Vic.

At the end of the summer of 1893 when they left the leafy slopes to return to the smoky city Sylvia was sad. The Pankhursts moved into 4 Buckingham Crescent,[199] in Victoria Park, Rusholme, near Manchester Owens College, and Emmeline was once again able to employ servants. The indomitable Ellen returned to the management of the kitchen. Aunt Mary was no longer with them. When Emerson & Co. and Russell Square were wound up in London, Mary had taken up the teaching of dress-cutting in the technical schools of Lancashire and Yorkshire. Soon afterwards, she married.

Another change that upset Sylvia was the marriage and consequent departure of Susannah, who struck up a romance with the keeper of the Disley golf links and – shortly after Sylvia spotted them kissing over the gate – announced their engagement. Susannah married in the Pankhurst home in Manchester, 'as a member of the family'.[200] Emmeline and Richard supplied champagne, but the bridegroom was so strict a teetotaller he refused even to allow the drawing of a cork for the guests. 'The talk of it,' Sylvia remarked, 'raised in my mind a long train of unsatisfied research into the merits of total abstinence.'[201] A year later Susannah returned unexpectedly to have her first baby in Buckingham Crescent, safer surrounded by women and nearer a doctor than in her cottage on the remote Disley golf course. The servants grumbled uncharitably that Susannah was taking advantage but Emmeline was welcoming and generous. 'She saved my life when Harry was born, and now she has given me the opportunity to save hers.'[202]

From Sylvia's perspective, the years from her eleventh to sixteenth birthday were much taken up with school, the intensification of her passion for art, interesting visitors to their home and the constant drumbeat of her parent's engagement in politics and civil society, revitalized by their return north. Buckingham Crescent consisted of four newbuild houses designed for the professional classes, their back gardens subdivided, but the front lawn undivided. For most of the period when the Pankhursts lived there, two of the four houses remained untenanted, giving the children the run of their gardens. The Pankhursts' only neighbours were the artist Elias Bancroft, his wife Louisa and their young son. The Cheshire-born Bancroft had studied at the Royal College of Art and later taught at Manchester School of Art. Remembered primarily for his landscapes of Wales and Whitby, he was also interested in social subjects, including working hospitals and urban studies. The neighbours became friends and Bancroft quickly noticed Sylvia's talent and love for art.

Rusholme wasn't beyond the range of the smoke from the Coketown factories, but Victoria Park and the relatively substantial suburban gardens made it a verdant and healthy environment. The developers retained as many of the old trees and plants as possible, and Sylvia, ever conscious of the natural environment around her, took detailed note of the profuse white lilac, golden laburnum and – her favourite – the pair of red May (hawthorn) trees.

Richard and Emmeline enrolled their daughters at Manchester High School for Girls. Sylvia, buoyed up by her enjoyment and academic success in Southport, went confidently to school, only to find her optimism dashed. The other girls seemed almost immediately to take against her. She was too independent-minded and too clever, particularly at French. She provoked the irritation of the headmistress and other pupils by asking if she might take modelling and drawing with the students of the upper school, since her art skills were already beyond the level of the juniors. When her schoolfellows discovered that she was not allowed to attend scripture class, the taunting and bullying began.

Sylvia disliked the drudge and drill of the curriculum: the excessive focus on arithmetic; too many French verbs; and the recitation of long lists of historical dates, battles and geographical place names that passed for the study of history. There was too much homework and she had a habit of staying up late to finish the 'perpetual arithmetic' because she had spent the greater part of the evening carried away with her drawing and lost track of time. The disciplinary regime with its writing of lines, detentions and various gradations of punishment for infringements of 'good conduct' seemed to Sylvia 'petty and ignoble'.[203] She particularly hated the large, walled-in gritted playground, bereft of a shrub or blade of grass, comparing it with a prison yard.

For all her grumbling, Sylvia's solid skills in arithmetic and French verbs stood her in good stead later in adulthood. Surprisingly, in all the time she was at the school, she served only one detention – a poor score for a future rebel. 'We were all three regarded as very quiet, well-behaved children, and great astonishment was expressed by the teachers who had known us when we broke forth in the Suffragette Movement.'[204] Sylvia's sunny recollection glosses over the fact that

Adela was so miserable at the school that at the age of eleven she tried to run away and subsequently suffered a nervous breakdown.

In time, Sylvia made herself more popular with her schoolmates, gravitating towards the scholarship kids and the few other children who had radical political parents. Only many years later did she learn of the story that the headmistress, Elizabeth Day, had not wanted the Pankhurst girls at her school. It was said that Headmistress Day appealed to the board to be allowed to reject the daughters of the infamous republican and atheist Dr Pankhurst and his emancipationist wife. Whatever the truth of this rumour, it is clear that Sylvia's teachers and the headmistress turned a wilfully blind eye to the bullying she experienced initially from her classmates. Too clever by half, she also exasperated some of the young teachers who lacked her political awareness. In response to one of her essays for composition class, one of her teachers challenged her, 'If there were no poverty, what would become of all our charities?'[205] In time, it was Sylvia's skill at drawing and painting that finally won her wider admiration and acceptance by the other pupils.

The adversity Sylvia and Adela experienced at school only reinforced Emmeline's belief that the education system as it currently existed destroyed originality and suppressed both independent critical thinking and artistic, creative expression.

Despite Emmeline's scepticism and Sylvia's mixed memories of her time there, Manchester High School for Girls, founded in 1871, was a good choice and offered much opportunity. The school aimed to give girls an education equal to that of boys and tried to make no distinction in religion or social rank (it was not having any religion at all that was a problem). Nevertheless, being of its time, the school placed a strong emphasis on making 'ladies' out of the pupils, including getting rid of their Lancashire accents. According to one of their contemporaries, Teresa Billington-Greig, 'to go to the school was to enter a charmed, snobbish circle'.[206] Manchester High School worked hard on the girls' accents, drilling them in Received Pronunciation (RP), or 'received standard' accent, in the belief that speaking 'properly' might advance their life opportunities. Three decades later in 1922 Lord Reith adopted it as a broadcasting standard, hence the term 'BBC English'. The legacy of the elocution coaching Sylvia received at the school could be heard in her voice ever after. She left Manchester High School for Girls trained in standardized Received Pronunciation, though the school failed to drill out the distinctive Mancunian vowels of her childhood. To our modern ears archaic, RP evolved in the nineteenth century, originally called 'Public School Pronunciation' to mark its association with privilege and elitism. Often believed to be based on the accents of southern England, in fact this style of speaking has most in common with Early Modern English dialects of the East Midlands, the most densely populated and affluent part of England in the fourteenth and fifteenth centuries. By the end of the fifteenth century, 'standard English' had become the established accent of the City of London.

Sylvia's accent evolved into an appealing alchemy of mainstream RP, neutral in many ways, combined with the her Lancashire origins and a speech impediment. When, as a child, Sylvia was learning to talk, it soon became evident that she had a speech impediment so common in Britain it's hard to understand why even called an impediment rather than just a speech characteristic. Known to speech pathologists as 'rhotacism', to the rest of us it is simply recognized as a difficulty in pronouncing your 'r's.

In spoken English this characteristic is manifested as a pronunciation where the spoken 'r' comes out sounding closer to 'w'. The rhotic sounds are the last a child learns and sometimes are never mastered, so she simply substitutes others. This way of uttering the 'r' was also dubbed the 'Winchester r', for its association with speaking posh and adopting the aspirational RP accent.

A Sylvia's adult voice retained her characteristically northern rising intonation. Manchester Girls failed to rid her of these verbal traits. She may have expwessed her love of her pawents and gwandmother and despaired of the misewies of the industwial wookeries of her home city, but when she spoke of the wevolution in FrAnce, the clAss struggle or flowering plAnts, it was with the low-vowel 'short A' feature most common in northern phonology. Radio recordings of her speaking in later life demonstrate that her voice never lost the distinction of her Lancashire dialect, however much the rest of her public-speaking voice conformed to an acquired RP accent.

Sylvia's parents re-embraced Manchester with renewed vigour and threw themselves into activism and community work. In July 1893 Richard rolled up his sleeves and got very involved in the coal-miners' strike of that year, when 400,000 walked out in protest against a 25 per cent reduction in wages imposed as a result of a drop in the price of coal. Dr Pankhurst criticized the employers in the press, and proposed a scheme based on nationalization of the mines, supporting the Mines Nationalisation Bill recently introduced in parliament by Keir Hardie, newly elected MP for West Ham. In 1894 Sylvia's father with justice took some credit for his role in promoting the great Manchester Ship Canal, which opened that year. Richard made the formal application to the Hundred of Salford for certification that the enterprise was complete and fit for the reception of vessels. 'Floreat flumen navigerum Mancuniense,' he concluded. To encourage the use of the new canal that linked Manchester to the Mersey estuary, Dr Pankhurst's speech was widely translated and printed for circulation in foreign ports.

In recognition of his contribution to the project, the entire family was invited to the opening day. On 1 January 1894, the Pankhursts joined the board of directors on the very first boat to pass through the canal. The experience awed Sylvia, who wrote about it elegantly:

> What a sight it was: the gigantic locks working with perfect smoothness. To me the wonder of wonders was the great aqueduct, in which the Bridgewater Canal is carried on high across the Ship Canal. To make way for the funnels of our steamer, the aqueduct swung apart, its waters so wonderfully dammed that there fell from it only a trickle, so small that it appeared as though a teacup had been emptied from the great height.[207]

Emmeline focused her energies at this time on her social work with the aged, jobless and orphans. In the bitter winter of 1894 she worked long hours helping in the soup kitchens for unemployed people. Sylvia went with her mother when she did her rounds of the markets, witnessing her dexterity in cajoling stallholders into contributing vegetables and bones.

Both parents continued to work with the Liberals for the women's suffrage cause. But the intensity and horrors of the poverty they encountered all around them made them rethink their approach, and in 1894 they were among the founder members of the Independent Labour Party, forerunner of the Labour Party. Richard was immediately elected to the ILP National Council, and in December 1894 Emmeline was voted in as the ILP member of the Chorlton

Board of Poor Law Guardians. She was thus one of the first women to be elected to local government in the United Kingdom. She focused her energies on improving conditions for orphaned children in the workhouse. The number of teenage girls with illegitimate babies, often the result of incest, enraged her, as did the sight of eight-year-old girls scrubbing stone floors in the freezing winter, pathetically dressed in sleeveless cotton shifts and without undergarments for either warmth or modesty.

ILP speakers who visited Manchester stayed with the Pankhursts. During this period Sylvia listened to a range of radical ideas canvassed and debated at Buckingham Crescent – Fabianism, socialism, Marxism, positivism, the land tax and the economic philosophy of Henry George. According to Adela, 'Karl Marx and the class struggle dominated family life', producing 'three of the most complete agitators that have troubled the social peace of Britain'.[208] Sylvia claimed no such explicitly Marxist flavour for the family ideology, locating her father rather as a red republican communist:

> A Communist Pankhurst certainly was, in the broad sense which
> would cover William Morris, Peter Kropotkin and Keir Hardie;
> but not in the narrow meaning which has been given to the term
> since the Russian Revolution; he hated violence and believed that
> by appeals to reason and the development of popular education,
> freedom would continue to broaden down from precedent to
> precedent, and the era of equality and fraternity be introduced by
> the votes of enlightened people.[209]

Their Manchester home, Sylvia recalled, 'became a centre of Socialist agitations'.[210] The steady stream of agitators who passed through their home reads like a Who's Who of late nineteenth-century leftism. Keir Hardie, now leader of the ILP, continued to be a regular visitor, as did the Scottish socialist Bruce Glasier, another of the 'Big Four' leading the ILP. Glasier, a close friend of William Morris, was a utopian socialist with a romantic enthusiasm for the medieval style made fashionable by the Victorian Gothic Revival. Glasier's bluestocking labour activist wife, Katherine Conway, one of the first students at Newnham College, Cambridge, passed on to Sylvia her enthusiasm for Greek classicism and smocks. Kate wore sage-green dresses made of serge, cut in the free-flowing Pre-Raphaelite style of Edward Burne-Jones and the Arts and Crafts initiatives like the Guild and School of Handicrafts.

Bluff Robert Blatchford, socialist publisher of the radical *Clarion* newspaper, organ of the ILP, called often at the Pankhursts', along with editors of many other labour publications. The trade unionist Tom Mann, then secretary of the ILP, visited as he had in London. Mann was the outright favourite with Sylvia and all her siblings, who were allowed to romp around with him. The mighty Ben Tillett and James Sexton, who later became known as 'the Dockers' MP', were among the many new trade unionists involved in the ILP who became familiar figures at Sylvia's home.

These were the days when Wilhelm Liebknecht, founder and leader of the German Socialists (SPD), visited Manchester and Sylvia's father took her to meet him at the Mosley Hotel. 'He was then over seventy years of age; a strong, reserved man of powerful mind,' Sylvia recalled.[211] With him was Eleanor Marx, 'daughter of the famous Karl Marx, an attractive personality'.[212] Sylvia's father admired Liebknecht's internationalism and his practical project of conjoining Marxist revolutionary theory with everyday, legal political activity. Between them the Liebknechts, Marxes and Pankhursts produced some notable revolutionary sons and daughters.

By 1896 Eleanor Marx had long since emerged from the shadow of her famous philosopher-economist father, who had died in 1883. British trade unionists and socialists claimed her as 'Our Mother'. Marx was at the high point of her political career, immersed in the emerging Independent Labour Party – and just two years from her shocking death. Wilhelm Liebknecht was father to Karl, who addressed Eleanor Marx as 'Aunt Tussy'. Later, Karl Liebknecht founded the Communist Party of Germany with Sylvia's friend Rosa Luxemburg. Two decades later in 1919, proto-Nazi fascists would murder Wilhelm Liebknecht's revolutionary son, and Sylvia would write about his death in her own internationally distributed newspaper.

Comfortable in the company of what Sylvia described as their 'Bohemian-looking Socialists', her parents had no interest in participating in the conventional social life of professional, middle-class Manchester to which they notionally belonged. This was just as well, because after they left the Liberals and joined the ILP they were no longer welcome. Richard was unsurprised to lose a number of clients. Realizing their need to broaden their social world, he introduced all his children to the working-class Clarion Cycling Club, a spin-off from Blatchford's socialist newspaper. Sylvia recalled pointedly that while her parents bought Christabel a brand-new Rudge-Whitworth that cost a fabulous sum, she got a low-geared, cumbersome machine that a kindly comrade made for her out of gas piping. Nonetheless, cycling became their favourite pastime and Sylvia and Christabel spent most Sundays out in the country away from the grime of Manchester.

On the Sundays when they didn't cycle, Sylvia's parents took them to the talks and the music, arts and science events organized by the Ancoats Brotherhoood. Founded in 1878 by Charles Rowley, the Brotherhood aimed to give working-class people access to art and literature. In the winter of 1894 Sylvia's father delivered on behalf of the Brotherhood a series of lectures on the life and duties of citizenship. He dealt with such topics as society considered as an organism, primitive society, the development of law and ethics, and national and international citizenship. Sylvia attended all of these talks.

Sundays were never a day of complete rest. In the mornings before she set off cycling, Sylvia often went with her father to the narrower, darker streets of Ancoats, Gorton, Hulme and other working-class districts. She recalled her father, standing on a chair or soapbox, 'pleading the Cause of the people with passionate earnestness'.[213] Her experience of her father's oratory, set in the context of the experience of Manchester's slums, made a deep and lasting impression:

> Those endless rows of smoke-begrimed little houses, with never a
> tree or flower in sight, how bitterly their ugliness smote me! Many
> a time in spring, as I gazed upon them, those two red may trees in
> our garden at home would rise up in my mind, almost menacing
> in their beauty; and I would ask myself whether it could be just
> that I should live in Victoria Park, and go well fed and warmly
> clad, whilst the children of these grey slums were lacking the very
> necessities of life. The misery of the poor, as I heard my father plead
> for it, and saw revealed in the pinched faces of his audiences, awoke
> in me a maddening sense of impotence; and there were moments
> when I had an impulse to dash my head against the dreary walls of
> those squalid streets.[214]

Christabel recalled these Manchester years as the best of all in their family life. Sylvia carried more mixed memories. Harry she remembered as being pale and strained, and in fear of both parents, particularly his father. He often played truant to go trainspotting, to watch football or cricket matches, or to chat to and help out builders on development sites. It was at this time that Adela made her attempt to run away from school and was discovered changing out of her uniform by a gardener, who alerted the headmistress.

Following this episode, Adela suffered a nervous breakdown, and refused to speak. She spent a year away from school, partly at home and partly with an aunt in Aberdeen. In Adela's adult view, they tended as children to introspection: 'We lived too much together and within ourselves to be healthy-minded and brooded over troubles that other children in more healthy surroundings would have forgotten in minutes.'[215] This speaks to her own childhood experience, but belies that of her elder sisters. Sylvia certainly could be solitary and introspective, but she was in equal measure outgoing and active.

Perhaps what Adela's alienation points towards is the impact on their lives of their mother and father's radical evangelical humanitarianism, of which Sylvia was less willing to be critical. Richard and Emmeline were fervent also about each other. They liked one another as much as they liked their children, and each was the other's first concern.

Sylvia felt always second to Christabel in her parents' affection. She didn't understand that her elder sister might feel easily displaced. Adela and Harry never seemed to feel that they had loving parents. Either way, the outcome was the same; as Sylvia put it, their father's 'struggle was the background to our lives, and his influence, enduring long after his death, was their strongest determining factor'.[216] In this context, Emmeline's persistent attempts to guide Sylvia towards her art and Christabel towards dancing as real prospective pursuits, rather than towards politics, take on a new light.

In 1895 Richard made his final attempt to enter parliament as candidate for West Gorton. The following year, in June 1896, Emmeline gave her first major public speech at Boggart Hole Clough, in the greenbelt woodlands of Blackley on the outskirts of Manchester, popular for holding larger outdoor ILP meetings. Speaking alongside Keir Hardie and Tom Mann, Mrs Pankhurst defied the council's attempt to ban public assembly at this long-established public speaking ground.

At Boggart Hole Clough, Emmeline was arrested. For the first time an uncomfortable and slightly intimidated British magistrate found himself faced by a statuesque, elegant and wholly unrepentant epitome of bourgeois femininity, dressed demurely in a pink straw bonnet and black gloves. On 5 July a meeting of 40,000 people gathered to celebrate the release of the ILP leaders, the dismissal of the case against them and the success of their protest.

Richard's health worsened. Emmeline rented a farmhouse in Mobberley, Cheshire, and moved her family there temporarily until the end of the summer. She intended to make her husband slow down and take better care of himself in a healthier country environment, at arm's length from his relentless schedule in the city. In the event Richard just ended up commuting daily by train into Manchester. Christabel went with him to keep up her eclectic selection of classes in French, logic and dressmaking. Sylvia was away from school and Manchester for a supremely content six months in Mobberley, spent wandering fields and hedgerows, reading and drawing.

The works of John Ruskin and Richard Jefferies then especially interested her. She was engrossed by Jefferies' apocalyptic visions of environmental catastrophe caused by the degradations of industrial capitalism. His popular post-apocalyptic fiction influenced many later utopian and dystopian writers, including William Morris and H. G. Wells. Sylvia consumed his tales of catastrophes dramatically dislocating the suburban lives of families very much like her own.[217]

Jefferies' *After London; or Wild England*, published in 1885, describes the ecological repercussions of some unspecified disaster, depicting a reversion to barbarism. Little of the old civilization remains and the few books left are only in manuscript, for though the technology of printing is not lost, no one wants to read.

Ruskin greatly influenced Jefferies. Ruskin's argument that the pursuit of material values and worldly success was an invitation to catastrophe found its way into Jefferies' fiction, as did the industrial degradation of the sky and air over Britain. 'Shall the Parthenon be in ruins on its rock – but these mills of yours be the consummation of the buildings of the earth, and their wheels be as the wheels of eternity?' Ruskin asked at the end of 'Traffic', a lecture delivered at Bradford in 1864. 'Catastrophe will come,' he thundered, 'or worse than catastrophe, slow mouldering and withering into Hades.'[218] Sylvia's imagination ranged through these portentous visions, but the approaching storm cloud about to blight her personal landscape blew from a direction entirely unforeseen.

She drew and painted intently and by the time the family returned to Buckingham Crescent she had sufficiently impressed her parents with her endeavours to obtain their agreement to her taking lessons with Elias Bancroft down the road. A new world opened: charcoal, Whatman's drawing paper, art stamps for inking and rubbers of squeezed bread. She loved the experience of three-dimensional drawing: 'I felt a sense of power in seeing the rounded shapes stand forth from my blank paper.'[219] She revelled in still-life groups, arranging jars, bowls and foliage to practise her watercolours at home.

Sylvia turned sixteen in May 1898, secure in the knowledge that she had found her vocation and was supported by her parents in its pursuit.

Two months later, her father was dead.

5

That Scarlet Woman

Few of us understand our childhood until we are older, if we ever do. We experience our early lives twice. Once lived, then remembered. Since infancy goes back into the mists of time before self-awareness and adult consciousness, how we recall our beginnings is a combination of what we think we recollect and what other people tell us about ourselves – the real, the misremembered and the invented. It is the testimony of family, friends and institutions combined with the private archive of our own memories.

Childhood is in this way the least intimate and least private of the phases of our life, a time of dependence that depends so much on the perspective of others. Childhood has in common with biography and history that it is often a story told by others about ourselves.

It would be almost thirty-five years before Sylvia could write the fact simply, 'Father was dead.' The trauma that shattered her sixteenth summer was the primal rupture in her life. Emmeline returned to her home a widowed single mother of four, in the knowledge that the small balance of cash and handful of shares Richard had left behind would not pay the rent or the servants' wages or support the family for more than a few weeks. Overnight, she became sole breadwinner.

We need to travel forward in time and visit, for a while, Sylvia's adult future in order to understand better her childhood past. It's 1928. She is forty-six and starting to write her first memoir *The Suffragette Movement*, 'about me life', as she idiomatically put it.[220] She has already published six books, including a volume of poetry, and is working simultaneously on other large writing projects. *The Suffragette Movement* is destined to become the most popular and controversial of her many books. The memoir begins as a rewriting of her very first work *The Suffragette*, released in 1911 when she was twenty-nine. Sylvia adopts her now habitual process of writing in longhand, later typed up by her secretary. Although this is her usual method, the process is harder than ever before. As she writes, Richard, her first and only child, is beside her in his cradle. Born on 4 December 1927, he is the love child of a free union. His fifty-two-year-old father Silvio Corio, an Italian exile, is also writing, editing political journalism, including Sylvia's, and growing vegetables in their Essex garden. He does most of the cooking and housework.

Sylvia has joined the ranks of the unmarried mothers she so ardently admires – her heroine Mary Wollstonecraft, her socialist comrade Clara Zetkin and the many hard-working single mothers of the East End who have profoundly shaped her political understanding over the past twenty years. Arguably, none of these women had a partner like Silvio Corio. Impenetrable to the prurient but well understood by those who knew her well, their invigoratingly unconventional relationship was the bedrock of Sylvia's and little Richard's lives until Corio's death.

For the first time, Sylvia experiences the challenges familiar to all working mothers. To her friend Nora Walshe, a nurse who worked in the ELFS clinics during the war, she writes, 'I am in despair about my writing. Richard wakes early and keeps me on the go till eleven or so. If I can get him to sleep from then till 1 p.m. it is the best I can hope for frequently – today he woke whenever I put him down and unless I put him to sleep in my arms he won't sleep at all.' On the letter goes, documenting the minutiae of the day in which she searches for shavings of time in which she might write, and ending, 'Actually I find myself so irritable and jaded that when I sit down to write I am often unable to find a sentence … yet in the old days words used to pour out without difficulty.'[221]

Despite this anxiety, Richard's infant years were to be a period of phenomenal literary output for her.

Twinned with this birth, a sorrowful death. Sylvia's mother, Britain's most famous feminist, dies on 14 June 1928. The bill for universal suffrage has passed its second reading in the House of Lords. In a month it will take effect in law, in time for the next general election, the 1929 'flapper election'. Granting the vote to adults aged twenty-one and over, the 1928 Representation of the People Act marks the fulfilment of the cause to which Sylvia, with her mother and her sisters, has dedicated her life. She writes:

> As though Fate had detained her till the completion of the Edifice, Emmeline Pankhurst, who had accomplished so much in making the disenfranchised state of women a burning sore in the body politic, passed away when the final Act became law.[222]

Emmeline had an exquisite sense of the dramatic moment, and dramatically speaking it was a good moment for her to die. For Sylvia, it was disastrous timing.

During her pregnancy, Sylvia attempted several times to visit her mother. Each time she came home weeping. For fourteen years acrimoniously and very publicly politically estranged, mother and daughter had periodically still seen each other privately and corresponded for the main part genially, even affectionately. However, when pregnant Sylvia arrived at the house where Christabel supervised their mother's care, Emmeline flatly refused to see her. Expressing outrage that 'that scarlet woman dared to call',[223] she locked herself in her bedroom and refused to come out until assured that Sylvia had left.

According to hearsay harvested from her friends, when the grandson named after her husband was born, Emmeline was 'horrified and greatly distressed' by the disgrace of her daughter as an unmarried mother.[224] If the gossip Emmeline and Christabel heard was true (it was not), Sylvia barely knew Silvio Corio before becoming pregnant. That Corio was an Italian anarchist refugee doubtless contributed further to the xenophobic Emmeline's sense of injury. But she also had a mother's fear for her seemingly constitutionally rebellious daughter. The intelligence delivered by Emmeline's friends also included rumours that Corio was already father to several abandoned children from previous liaisons, utterly broke and seen often to display a bad temper.

Why did the acknowledged heroine of the British feminist movement who throughout her life had assisted, defended and supported so many unmarried mothers reject her own daughter in the same circumstances? As she turned away the heavily pregnant, supplicant Sylvia, had she forgotten that in her youth she had been a proponent of free union? Perhaps she thought that the seasoned forty-five-year-old Sylvia should be wiser than the naive twenty-one-year-old Emmeline. Sick and depressed and without financial ballast, Emmeline was perhaps frustrated by her incapacity actively to help Sylvia and in no position to tell her middle-aged daughter what to do. Hearsay asserted that Christabel literally debarred Sylvia from seeing their mother, but there's no proof of this and the practical evidence suggests rather that Christabel merely refused to intervene with their mother on her behalf.

A few months after Richard's birth, Sylvia went to the tabloids. This decision may have been an act of revenge against her punishing mother or it might have been that she and Silvio needed the money: perhaps it was a combination of both.

'Sylvia Pankhurst's amazing confession,' yelled the *News of the World*, Britain's most beloved scandal sheet, announcing her first public interview about giving birth 'to a child out of wedlock', as they put it.[225] *The Times* and the Manchester *Sunday Chronicle* ran the story on the same day. Sylvia described her love child as her 'Eugenic baby', prompting further media sensationalism. Not just in Britain, but around the world, the global press ran headlines about Sylvia Pankhurst's 'Eugenic Baby Solution'.

This crude and ostentatious retaliation in the media was well calculated to mortify her mother and sister, all the more for deploying their own tactics against them. For years Emmeline and Christabel had repeatedly renounced Sylvia in the press, most famously in 1916 when her mother disowned her for her pacifist opposition to the war. In April that year, Sylvia helped organize and spoke at a mass adult suffrage and anti-conscription Sunday rally in Trafalgar Square. Word reached her mother across the Atlantic. The WSPU newspaper *Britannia* published the following paragraph, reported and reprinted throughout the local, national and international press:

A Message from Mrs Pankhurst
    Hearing of a demonstration recently held in Trafalgar Square, Mrs Pankhurst, who is at present in America, sent the following Cable: 'Strongly repudiate and condemn Sylvia's foolish and unpatriotic conduct. Regret I cannot prevent use of name. Make this public.'[226]

This was far from the only time Sylvia's elder sister and her mother publicly took issue with her in the press – they had for example announced her expulsion from the WSPU. However, it was the only time that Emmeline stated so brutal a wish as the desire to disinherit Sylvia from the Pankhurst family name.

For twenty years, Sylvia held her peace and never attempted publicly to get upsides with her mother and elder sister. Her kiss-and-tell to the *News of the World* broke the long silence. But she did not refer to Christabel's or Emmeline's disapproval of her unmarried status in any of the publicity.

Emmeline declined rapidly, seemingly from cancer. Some said Christabel kept Sylvia away from their mother during her final illness. Other members of the family and friends from the WSPU claimed that Sylvia's public declarations hastened her mother's end. Ethel Smyth considered it the main cause of her death in 1928: 'Mrs Pankhurst died of chagrin – of pain and horror at the disgrace brought on her name by that disgusting Bolshie daughter of hers.'[227]

Aside from the unkindness of such assertions, they demonstrate poor understanding of Mrs Pankhurst, for whom political difference was demonstrably a far more important factor than conventional sexual shame. Like mother, like daughters. Sylvia understood this point very well. As she remarked on the definitive split between herself, her mother and Christabel over the Great War, the Pankhursts were a family who took their political allegiances keenly to heart.[228]

Sylvia never again saw her mother alive: Emmeline never met her grandchild.

So it is in the context of the life-changing, coincident events of the birth of her baby and the death of her mother that Sylvia sits down to write her memoir of her early life. With both parents dead, she returns to her childhood as an orphan. Sylvia takes her inner child by the hand and sets forth on a literary journey to return to her point of origin. *The Suffragette Movement* interweaves the personal story of the Pankhurst family with the interrelated themes of the struggle for votes for women, the birth of British socialism and the Labour Party, and how to imagine and design a feminist society. The recent historical past is the place where the book is set. The present reality in which Sylvia writes sees the advent of the broadest form of enfranchisement ever experienced. Britain in 1928 is finally an electoral democracy. The people are expecting further change and newly hopeful; the old elites are anxious and fearful. It's a radical moment.

'The book I have in mind to write,' Sylvia explained in a pitch to a potential editor, 'is the inner history of the Suffrage Movement and those who made it and the environment from which they sprang.' As her outline stated, this was the sort of book that could only be written by someone in the inner circle of the drama, who had gained by time and temperament a 'meditative detachment' from the struggle.[229]

What Sylvia produced was an intensely personal memoir of the history of the Pankhurst family and their involvement in the fight for women's suffrage interwoven tightly with external political events. *The Suffragette Movement* is subjective, emotional and partisan. It was criticized, then and now, for never finding the 'meditative detachment' Sylvia originally proposed. But she always regarded the book as an autobiography.

Ray (Rachel) Strachey, women's suffrage campaigner and denizen of the Bloomsbury group, reviewed the book in the *Woman's Leader*, admiring its richness of drama and incident, personalities, prejudices, enthusiasms and quarrels and finding it 'in its way, as complete a revelation of its author's character as the most exacting student of psychology could desire'.[230] Strachey finds 'an evident and undisguised animus against Mrs Pankhurst and Christabel which is almost tragic in its intensity. But after all, bitterness, inaccuracy, misstatement, and animus all lay on the fringes of the militant movement so that they are in a deep sense appropriate to its historian; and though they do not tend to edification, neither did these aspects of the suffragette campaign itself.'[231] Strachey, a Liberal feminist member of the non-militant NUWSS and for five years its parliamentary secretary, resisted the incorporation of the women's suffrage campaign with the Labour Party and was a committed parliamentary gradualist, opposed to socialism, mass movements and militancy. She was also the first biographer of Millicent Garrett Fawcett, her book appearing in the same year as Sylvia's explosive memoir.

If these were not reasons enough for Strachey to put the reviewer's boot into *The Suffragette Movement*, Sylvia gave her further grounds by threatening her with a libel action in 1928 when she published her own account, *The Cause: A Short History of the Women's Movement*, in which she alleged financial mismanagement in the WSPU. Yet while

Strachey strains to curb her evident glee at the feminist faction-fighting revealed in Sylvia's book, it is the animus against her mother and elder sister and Sylvia's account of her childhood that seem most to appal her: 'She gives the picture of her own childhood which is in many ways distressing, and her treatment of the characters of her mother and sister is anything but kind. No doubt that was how she saw it and felt it all, but it can hardly have been how it actually was.'[232]

Strachey's sensibilities are instructive. For her, situating the personal as political was too radical a challenge to the proper order of historical writing. The kind of people who stripped back the pretence of dispassionate objectivity in matters of history and social change were the same kind of people who caused mass turbulence, encouraged militancy and fomented revolution.

Charlotte Drake, an old member of the WSPU, thought Strachey's review 'misleading', and pointed out that she had quoted inaccurately. In her letter to the editor published in the *Woman's Leader*, Drake argued that Sylvia's book was 'very fair and free from bitterness ... and also how true':

> Plenty of books could be written about the suffrage struggle from
> beginning to end, but I doubt if one more comprehensive could be
> written than this book of Sylvia Pankhurst's or one that would give
> such a fair account when you realize it had to be contained in one
> volume. To do the subject justice would need half a dozen volumes,
> and of course we all see things or happenings from our own point
> of view.[233]

Strachey misses the significance of the fact that *The Suffragette Movement* rewrote *The Suffragette*. Published in 1911 when she was twenty-nine, that was Sylvia's first, hastily written history of the militant women's suffrage movement. Emmeline wrote the Preface to her daughter's book from the WSPU offices in Clement's Inn:

> This history of the Women's Suffrage agitation is written at a
> time when the question is in the very forefront of British politics.
> What the immediate future holds for those women who are most
> actively engaged in fighting for their political freedom no one
> can foretell, but one thing is certain: complete victory for their

cause is not far distant ... Perhaps the women born in the happier
days that are to come, while rejoicing in the inheritance that we
of today are preparing for them, may sometimes wish they could
have lived in the heroic days of stress and struggle and have shared
with us the joy of battle, the exaltation that comes of sacrifice of
self for great objects and the prophetic vision that assures us of
the certain triumph of this twentieth-century fight for human
emancipation.[234]

In Sylvia's Introduction, following her mother's endorsement, she refers
to their 'family party', who in 1903 set out determined to make votes
for women the dominant issue of the politics of their time, 'but in
six years drew to their standard the great women's army of today. It
is certain that the militant struggle in which this woman's army has
engaged and which has come as the climax to the long, patient effort
of the earlier pioneers, will rank amongst the great reform movements
of the world.'[235]

In the opening chapter of *The Suffragette*, entitled 'Early Days',
Sylvia offers the briefest passing biographical introduction to her
mother, father and family ancestry. Her and Christabel's childhood
is dealt with by means of a single short anecdote describing how,
aged seven and nine respectively, they helped out writing notices
and distributing leaflets at the founding conference of the Women's
Franchise League held in their home in 1889. Everything to do with
early family life is over in the first few pages, and the 500-page
account that follows is very much in the traditional form of tightly
packed, detailed reportage: all politics, no personal backstory on the
Pankhurst 'family party'.

The Suffragette is crowded with detailed mini-lives and brilliantly
vivid pen portraits of many of the women and men of all ages who
formed the ranks of the movement. In this sense it reads like a group
biography of wildly diverse people interconnected by a common
cause, a quality that carries over two decades later into *The Suffragette
Movement*.

Sylvia's rewriting of her earlier 1911 version is a self-conscious return
to the question of the role of her own family, motherhood, children and
personal experience in understanding broader political struggles. At the
core of this endeavour is the knowledge, now based on experience, that

achieving democratic enfranchisement has not and will not deliver a feminist society. Sylvia wants to explore and demonstrate why and ask what is to be done.

In this context, Ray Strachey's antagonistic but thoughtful review of *The Suffragette Movement* is instructive. On the one hand, she is troubled and made uncomfortable by Sylvia's intense, complex, implicitly critical family portrait. On the other, she is fearful of militancy and what she perceives as extremism and is adamant that neither ever works in Britain. Underlying her anxiety is the fear that these are not two separate elements, but part of the same whole:

> Miss Pankhurst attributes the rise of the women's movement to the same political unrest which led all radical and revolutionary movements of the end of the last century ... Political changes do not come in this country through mass turbulence and ... occasional rioting of small groups. The change of opinion which carried women's suffrage through to victory is a much larger and more important thing than Miss Pankhurst describes.[236]

Here then in 1928 is the beginning of the historical argument in the British women's movement between the suffragists who claimed it was their gradualist constitutional reform that won the day, and the suffragettes who conversely reasoned that without the connection to the earlier socialist, radical movements and – most importantly – militant proto-revolutionary tactics, the political ground would never have shifted.

Sylvia's challenge in *The Suffragette Movement* was intensely serious: to go on a journey into the deeper dimensions of her formative years and see what she discovered there that might throw light on this fight within the feminist family. Disguised as a child, she revisited her past and upbringing in order to try and understand what made her and her family militant extremists and to examine what they had become. How do you make a feminist? Why did she and her sisters emerge as teenage rebel activists poised at the fin de siècle to rock the foundations of the British state? What makes a person militant, a revolutionary or prepared for martyrdom? Simultaneously, she offers answers to the broader political questions. Why did the Pankhurst women change in divergent political directions and fall out as a result?

The memoir is a courageous emotional journey among the shades. Her father, her beloved brother Harry and, most recently, her mother are dead. She and Christabel are painfully alienated. Although she got on relatively better with her, Adela is far away in Australia and so given to running emotionally hot and cold that difficulty also lay in that direction.

So vivid are the Pankhurst family characters that Sylvia reassembles and reanimates in the book and so compelling the story she tells that we are led irresistibly into an alternative, progressive, visionary world – which really existed. This is not a trip to the land of nostalgia. A new, nursing mother buffeted by some of the core judgements of society, and it turns out by her unsupportive and judgemental feminist mother and sister, over marriage, childbirth and homemaking, Sylvia is thinking very much about the uses of the past to understand the needs of the present. 'In all those years of public activity, busy as I was with other matters, I had formed my own conclusions on matrimony, parenthood and the rights of children.'[237]

The Suffragette Movement gives us the opportunity to obtain insight into Sylvia's childhood in a chronology more true to experience – the childhood first lived, then its remembrance, put into the context of its later time of writing. Conjuring her infancy, shadowy images and impressions stand out from the forgetfulness, disconnected but distinctly coloured and lastingly printed in her mind.[238] Of her first year at the Old Trafford house at 1 Drayton Terrace in Manchester where Sylvia was born she summoned up a soft, grey dimness and unrecognizable, flickering figures framed by dazzling light from the windows. She remembered how that outdoor light filtered through the prevailing haze, and the deeper shade of some half-open door. The character of Old Trafford, 'the mysterious shrine of our beginnings, was a centre of earnest and passionate striving'.[239] For Sylvia, the mystery begins with this striving. Toil, struggle, fight – resistance and resilience.

For all its emphasis on the outer world of multifaceted struggles for justice and equality, Sylvia's primal relationship to her childhood was visual, sensual and intensely creative. Her recollections of her early life are forged from an indivisibility of the senses where visions, dreaming, playacting and stories conjured worlds as tangible to her memory as real events. Her recall of indelibly imprinted baby pictures from early life was not uncommon, nor was her sensual experience of the prelinguistic world. But what marks out her memories of her beginnings is her pronounced experience of sensory overload. From the first stirrings of her consciousness Sylvia demonstrates consistently the tendencies of the synaesthete – the neurological phenomenon of the union of the senses that for some children develops when first they encounter abstract concepts.

At the time Sylvia wrote her first memoir, she was midway through life's journey, in a dark wood. Not exactly having lost her way, but trying to find out why she was the way she was. An unusually older mother of a newborn infant, she could not turn to her own recently dead mother for advice and support. Clearly she sought Emmeline's blessing or needed something from her, or she wouldn't have tried to see her during her pregnancy. Whatever it was she wanted from her mother, it wasn't the rejection she received.

In the making of this rebel, violence and visions play a central role. Emmeline remained – in a way that was characteristic of Victorian approaches to child-rearing – somewhat rigid in her approach to discipline, which, Sylvia claimed, involved physical force and 'grew in severity by delegation to others'.[240] Emmeline directed the physical punishments, the servants followed her orders and Sylvia 'frantically resisted' about food:

> For such rebellion against the orders of my mother, though others enforced them, I felt almost unbearable remorse – and sense of degradation; yet from acute physical repulsion I offended in the same manner again and again over a period of years, and shaken by uncontrollable sobbing would end by imploring my mother on my knees, 'Help me to be good!'[241]

This, at least, was how Sylvia represented it in *The Suffragette Movement*, smarting under the grief and rage of maternal rejection twinned with parental death. However, two decades later in a 1953 BBC broadcast about her mother, recorded when she was seventy-one, the mature Sylvia reframes the memory:

> To all of us at home in my childhood, she was the most marvellous and beautiful woman in the world. She was strict with us on one point: we must eat everything. She would have no likes and no

dislikes about food. In all other matters she was lenient ... She
treated her children as reasonable beings – never scolded or struck
... she opposed corporal punishment in schools.[242]

The older Sylvia, herself a mother when she wrote this, bequeathed
a smoothed-out, respectful, idealized version of her mother. By her
later years, she was able to cherish her personal reminiscences and
respect publicly the woman who had become to many a national hero.
Conversely, the memory of Emmeline's strictness around food when
they were children remained an unaltered constant. By the time Sylvia
wrote *The Suffragette Movement*, another set of traumatic experiences
concerning her relationship with her mother and food overlay those
of her early childhood. Sylvia went on hunger strike and was force-fed
more times than any other suffragette. Her mother hunger struck, but
was never force-fed. The government appeared to be nervous of the
public response to abusing so popular an iconic matriarchal, middle-
class figure. Christabel, at the time running the leadership-in-exile from
Paris, was not required to hunger strike and hence was never subjected
to torture.

Sylvia's retrospective midlife journey through her childhood unfolds
less and less as a specific history of one marriage and family and more
and more as a study of archetypes. She is trying to decide between the
father and mother in the role of evolution in the most prototypical
terms – of patriarchy and matriarchy. Understanding that parental
figures are the vehicles through whom the forces of nurturance and
empowerment are transmitted, new mother Sylvia, writing with infant
Richard at her side, is urgently and anxiously trying to work out how to
be a good mother herself and how she and Silvio might not recreate the
stumbling errors of her own well-intentioned parents.

Sylvia's notebooks allow us to fall through a trapdoor in time.
Simultaneously with writing *The Suffragette Movement* and nursing
young Richard, she is drafting 'The Day of the Child', an essay that
the Scandinavian writer Elen Key inspired her to write. Sylvia met Elen
Key in Venice on holiday with some suffragette friends in 1906. Key's
books on family and society had caused a stir, as had her argument
that the twentieth century would be the 'Century of the Child'. Sylvia's
suffragette friends protested hotly that the emancipation of mothers
must come first. Key smiled impassively. 'How true her prediction

proves!' writes Sylvia two decades later. 'This is the day of the child; he has emerged from the bondage of the standards and discipline imposed on him by his elders. For him the era of Authority has passed; the world of knowledge, to be gained by experiment and experience, is open wide.'[243]

In this essay, Sylvia writes about progressive and innovative modern teaching methodologies, particularly those pioneered by the Italian Maria Montessori and the German Friedrich Fröbel whose teaching methods she introduced to east London for the first time. This school of educators declared it the duty of the adult community not to instil knowledge into the child, but to assist her to acquire knowledge for herself. Sylvia demonstrates how education methods based on Darwinian and allied thinking liberated children from the harrowing implications of the concept of original sin. She explores how the flowering of modern children's books and textbooks on science, history, music, drawing, birds and botany opens new vistas of opportunity for freeing the minds of children from the excessive moralizing and misery that Lewis Carroll so forcefully illuminated and criticized in his plea for the liberation of Victorian children's minds and bodies in his Alice stories.

Sylvia incorporates her childhood experience into 'The Day of the Child', describing the Pankhurst household regime of a regular, restricted diet, their clothes – effectively a serge uniform – their lack of fresh air in winter, because it was believed to be bad for them to go outdoors and run around too much. Now that it was an age of open-air babies, 'strange to recall that when I was a child, all we four brothers and sisters spent weeks at a time in winter in our nursery at the top of the house, with a steam kettle going for the youngest who was subject to bronchial colds'.[244]

To be in Sylvia's presence while she writes *The Suffragette Movement* allows us to travel between the different selves that she makes speak to each other across time through the book. She is looking backwards in order to look forward, to the future of her son and other people's children – as she put it in an unpublished interview, 'What I am aiming at: a chance for the children of tomorrow'.[245] The sequence of her memoir-style notebooks provides the substantive evidence trail of how her childhood and midlife selves are in conversation over maternity and motherhood.

While pregnant, Sylvia begins the summary outline of *The Suffragette Movement*. She drafts a note: 'My earliest memories – Old Trafford Seedley and Green Hayes – My father Richard Marsden Pankhurst; his parentage, his work for education. His 13 years Hon. Secretaryship of the Lancashire Union of Institutes. His efforts at the first School Board Selection as a secularist, Gladstone's view'.[246] Abruptly, the note breaks off. Immediately underneath, on the same page, begins her pencil draft of 'The Mother's Month', an essay about maternity and childbirth that ultimately develops into a book, *Save the Mothers*, a factual and analytical study that makes the case for a national system of state-subsidized maternal healthcare.

Richard's birth was difficult and dangerous. She describes the circumstances and how they were saved by the intervention of a maternal health professional who insisted that Sylvia went immediately to a proper nursing home attended by health professionals. She recalls the words of the woman gynaecologist who brought Richard into the world. 'If you had not come into the home when you did I do not think your baby could have been born alive.'[247] As Sylvia observed, the private nursing home was accessible to her only because her rich friends offered to pay.

A few days after Richard had been safely delivered, Sylvia read a series of newspaper articles reporting the appalling facts that in early twentieth-century Britain one mother's life was lost for every 250 babies born, while in every 100 births three infants were sacrificed. Sylvia's own experience of maternity brings her mind more acutely to bear on the problem and to reflect on earlier memories.

Back across the years 'reverberated the shock' of having seen a stillborn infant in her own home and hearing its mother's exhausted lament, 'After all this hard work!' It was the Pankhurst family housekeeper, 'by me much beloved, a dear, devoted woman, whose child had been lost in a long and painful labour'. For hours, the fifteen-year-old Sylvia had hovered about the closed door of her room, waiting for it to be opened in the eager hope that she might 'be allowed to perform some little services for those within, to ease the intense anxiety gnawing at my heart'.[248] With discretion, Sylvia doesn't name the family housekeeper Susannah in this piece of journalism.

Sylvia links this deep, old memory to one more recent, her cousin and namesake lying white and cold next to her wailing motherless newborn.

Sylvia's cousin, one of her father's nieces, was younger, physically more vigorous than her and had, as she puts it, 'lived more normally'. All of which being the case, she should have had better life chances than a forty-five-year-old tortured ex-prison convict with eating disorders and a lifelong indisposition to regular exercise. The difference was that her cousin 'didn't have the care and skill that had been lavished on me'. Marshalling many other examples, Sylvia then lays out her comprehensive plan for minimum medical and legal requirements for maternal and infant care. This essay plants the seed for *Save the Mothers*. The subtitle spells it out: *A Plea for Measures to Prevent the Annual Loss of about 3,000 Child-bearing Mothers and 20,000 Infant Lives in England and Wales and a Similar Grievous Wastage in Other Countries*:

> This book is an urgent plea for a universal, free Maternity Service, and an earnest effort to make plain the great need of Mothers and the grievous hardships, risks and suffering encountered by them in pregnancy and childbirth.

Published in 1930, *Save the Mothers* is written and published in virtual parallel with her personal family memoir, on which so much more controversy is focused. The fact that Sylvia was designing and detailing a 200-page blueprint for a costed, quantified programme for a universally available national maternal health service in the late 1920s, in technical and meticulously evidence-based detail, is less readily recalled than the scandal of her mellifluous memoir.

Save the Mothers is one of several of Sylvia's works used as a guide to forming policy and public health programmes by the architects of the welfare state. George Bernard Shaw, Arthur Henderson, Prime Minister Ramsay MacDonald, Margaret McMillan and Ellen Wilkinson MP were among those who wrote letters of support, published in the book.

Arthur Henderson, then Foreign Secretary and secretary of the Labour Party, wrote to Sylvia to confirm that Labour Party policy was developing along the same lines, which she had suggested. 'Speaking in general terms, I would say what we aim at is a National Maternity Service ... Our object is not only to prevent the present wastage of life, but to secure good health for those many more thousands of mothers and babies who are now left to suffer, perhaps for the rest of their lives, through insufficient care at childbirth.'[249]

Sylvia's literary journey back to the world of her childhood in order to try and understand her relationship with her mother delivered her from the trauma of the intensely personal, individual experience and enabled her to transform it into understanding and action for the greater needs of all women. Simultaneous to giving birth, she delivers the story of her own childhood, parents and family. In her perpetual quest for alternative ways of being and living, she tried to imagine a better future for feminism and its children. This is a repeating pattern throughout her life: the transformation of individual experience into reimagined collective responsibility and creative social change.

PART TWO

Decade of Dilemma 1898–1908

Are we brothers of the brush entitled to the luxury of release from utilitarian production? Is it just that we should be permitted to devote our entire lives to the creation of beauty, whilst others are meshed in monotonous drudgery? ... As a speaker, a pamphlet-seller, a chalker of pavements, a canvasser on doorsteps, you are wanted; as an artist the world has no real use for you; in that capacity you must fight a purely egoistical struggle.

E. Sylvia Pankhurst, *The Suffragette Movement*

6

Not Things Seen, Always the Things Imagined

Sylvia intended to be an artist not an activist. Driven by visions so clear they seemed tangible, she sensed that her contribution was to be as a creative innovator. 'I was continually drawing – not things seen, always the things imagined.'[250] This was Sylvia's mantra for the decade following her father's death. From the age of sixteen to her first imprisonment when she was twenty-five, she believed art to be her vocation. It was her greatest solace in attempting to cope with the loss of her father. Almost providentially, it was the fact of his death that led directly to her going to art school.

As the family tried to balance themselves in the aftershock, Sylvia seemed overly conscientious and serious. In the sadness and madness of grief she shared their determination to keep her father's spirit present and alive. She'd already internalized her parents' insistence on the necessity of public duty and the discipline of 'drudge and drill!' But, as her mother and Christabel were acutely aware, she was burdened by guilt over what she believed to be her inaction and failure during her father's last days. 'It was the collapse of our happy life, of our world as it had been,' Christabel explained. 'Sylvia, poor Sylvia, had met the shock alone … she had been in sole command with no one at hand older than herself, except the servants, when the adored father was taken ill … The responsibility, the shock, were terrible for her. To Mother's grief for her husband was added anxiety for her daughter.'[251]

Adela remembered these as particularly difficult times for herself and Harry, feeling pushed to the sidelines. 'Mother was now involved in public work. We had no friends, we played no games and went nowhere

... we children were not companions for her. She took no interest in our affairs. Christabel seemed at a distance, Sylvia hopelessly depressed, hung about her all the time. Public life was a relief to her.'[252]

In truth, Emmeline, overnight a widow, was fighting hard to support her family. Her husband left little capital and no will. His share portfolio, amounting to £930.69 in the value of the time, was held exclusively in worthy Manchester concerns. Their true patrimony was not material, it was the principled example of his life and the public's memory of him, but they couldn't eat that. Emmeline found a much smaller house at 62 Nelson Street, closer to central Manchester. To share expenses and maintain an adult male presence, her brother Herbert Goulden moved in for a time. Herbert was a staunch supporter of his elder sister and her family, and later during the militant campaign he was beaten up on the London streets when recognized as Mrs Pankhurst's brother. Ellen, their cook and commentator on poetry and religion, remained with them, and Aunt Mary, now Mrs Clarke, came to stay for a while to help them get back on their feet.

Emmeline arranged a house sale for Buckingham Crescent to raise as much ready cash as she could. Most of their furniture was way too large for the new town house. As she'd bought extravagantly, she hoped she could sell well and buy cheaper fittings. Generously, she promised the children they could keep the upright piano, which, at a pinch, would fit in the Nelson Street front parlour. Charles Rowley, of Ancoats Brotherhood fame, came to value Richard's art collection and Emmeline's eclectic prints for modern interiors and advise her on how they might be sold. As kindly as he could, Rowley told her that none of it was of any interest or value. Then he spotted some uniquely promising drawings and paintings and discovered from Emmeline that her middle daughter was the artist.

Declaring her talented, Rowley suggested Sylvia send a selection of her still-life groups to the Manchester School of Art. Originally a design school, the Manchester school opened in 1838, shortly after the Royal College of Art in London, founded earlier the same year. Annie Swynnerton, one of its first women graduates, became also, much later, the first female admitted to the Royal Academy of Art. She was made an Academician in 1922, when she was seventy-eight.

Emmeline thought Rowley's recommendation an excellent idea. Aunt Mary and Cecile Sowerby, one of the children's tutors in London, had frequently pointed up Sylvia's artistic talent to Emmeline. Her father had always encouraged it. An artist whom Aunt Mary met in Paris, Cecile Sowerby, for a while had became their day governess in London. She introduced Sylvia and her siblings to many London museums and galleries. In fact this was her sole teaching method. The Egyptian galleries at the British Museum, a few minutes' walk from where they lived on the other side of Russell Square, were Sylvia's top-ranked favourite. The figurative forms of hieroglyphics fascinated her and the embalmed mummies amazed. Curious about human form, she had told her father that she 'earnestly wished to examine the human skeleton'. He took her to the Royal College of Surgeons Medical Museum in Lincoln's Inn Fields, the largest collection of anatomical specimens in England. Sylvia recalled feeling 'much mortified and wounded' when they were turned away from the doors because children were not permitted.[253] Instead Richard bought her a cardboard anatomical man, designed in multilayered sections. Sylvia's obsession with anatomy can be seen in her perennial curiosity about how to represent movement, mainly in women, both at work and in play. Most predominantly, she was fascinated with depicting dance. Dancing feet repeat throughout her sketchbooks, both shod and bare. The skeletal feet of the Egyptian mummies at the British Museum and her cardboard anatomical man provided her earliest studies for the structure of the foot and its relationship to ground and air.

Sent from Corsier in Geneva, Christabel's last letter to Sylvia before their father died confirms Emmeline's support for Sylvia's artistic ambition. Their mother, Christabel wrote, wanted Sylvia to post a package of gifts from Emerson & Co.'s stock for the Dufaux family and friends. 'Mother says will you make a parcel of "studios" [prints] and put some drawings of your own in – some of your charcoal things etc. Also you must not ride too much on your bicycle.'[254]

Sylvia now felt doubtful about Charles Rowley's advice that she should apply to art school. Shy of showing her work, she had since childhood hidden her sketchbooks, generally under the furniture, where they were found usually by the artistically inclined Aunt Mary. 'I was too heavily conscious of my failure to render adequately my visions', Sylvia explained, 'to endure without pain the inspection of my efforts by the relatively indifferent gaze of other eyes.'[255] Regrettably, there's nothing unusual here about a little girl's lack of self-confidence in her natural talents. What's more striking is Sylvia's visceral anxiety about her ability to render her visions with precision.

Fortunately, Manchester School of Art took a far more optimistic view of her talents. On an uplifting day for the mourning household, a letter arrived informing her that she had an immediate place and a free studentship. Without the scholarship, she wouldn't have been able to go. It's likely that Rowley put in a word about the situation in which Pankhurst had left his family.

Manchester Art School brought Sylvia peace and contentment. 'In spite of our grief and my nervous depression, when absorbed in the work I knew the greatest happiness.'[256] Students and teachers alike welcomed her with kindness, and she settled far more easily into the avant-garde atmosphere of art college than she generally had into the confines of conventional academic school.

Henry Cadness, who ran the design faculty, was an important champion of Sylvia's talent. Lancashire born, Cadness led the Manchester school of textile designing and excelled as an illuminator and painter. His classic work, *Decorative Brushwork and Elementary Design*, published in 1902, has never been out of print. First published as a resource for teachers, it is an inspiring guide to creating patterns and graphic motifs, offering advice on choosing paper, brushes and colours and on developing skills in line, tone and composition. The book contains hundreds of black and white Edwardian designs taken from nature, textiles, pottery and architecture in order to illustrate artistic principles. Leafing through it offers instructive insight into the training that shaped Sylvia's artistic techniques.

Sylvia continued to battle with grief. During her first year at the college she suffered from neuralgia in her face and arms so severe she frequently had to stay at home.[257] These sudden and unpredictable attacks of severe shooting pain were a physical manifestation of her shock and depression at the loss of her father and of coping with the dramatic change in their family circumstances. Although unable to acknowledge it, Emmeline too was needy. Christabel dealt with it by sealing herself in a distant aloofness. Sylvia, more emotionally expressive and demonstrative, comforted Emmeline during her night terrors. She described this as a period of intense intimacy with her mother; they slept together and they wept together.[258]

Emmeline encouraged Sylvia to continue working even when her neuralgia made her too unwell for school, though often she created her own pretexts for keeping Sylvia home for her own emotional support. There was no space for a studio in the cramped new house at Nelson Street, so Emmeline offered Sylvia use of a room of her own above the new Manchester premises of Emerson & Co., at 40–42 King Street, Emmeline sold off stock when left London, but no indication when she restarted the business after their move on the proviso that she kept an occasional eye on the shop, wrote tickets for merchandise and arranged window displays.

Despite Mrs Pankhurst's doughty entrepreneurial spirit, there was still no profit in sight for Emerson & Co. Believing against all rational odds that the venture would provide their future financial security, Emmeline ploughed on. In the meantime, she needed more ready income. The ever-loyal Robert Blatchford and other political friends suggested to her that they would raise a fund to support her and the children. She flatly refused this very practical suggestion as unwelcome charity. But she accepted the far less useful idea of a fund for a public testimonial to her husband, which would have happened anyway. Unfortunately, Dr Pankhurst's memorial would not put food on the table, pay the rent or Ellen's wages, or educate the children.

Respectful of Emmeline's pride, her friends regrouped, and approached her with a new proposition for a paying job, which she accepted. The Board of Manchester Guardians nominated her for the vacant position of Registrar of Births and Deaths, a role providing a steady income and pension. Emmeline resigned regretfully from her position as a Poor Law Guardian, but a few years later took up voluntary work again. In November 1900 she was elected as an Independent Labour Party member to the Manchester School Board.

While Sylvia studied at the Manchester Art School, Britain declared war on the Boer Republics. From October 1899 until May 1902, the South African War (also known as the Second Boer War) was fought between the British and the Boers, descendants of Dutch settlers who had founded two independent South African republics, the Orange Free State and the South African Republic. When gold was discovered in the South African Republic in 1886, the British determined to take the area under their control.

In 1899, the conflict escalated into a fully fledged war, fought in three stages: a Boer offensive against British command posts and railway lines, a British counter-offensive that brought the two republics under British control and a Boer guerrilla resistance movement that provoked an extensive scorched-earth campaign by the British and the internment and deaths of thousands of Boer civilians in British concentration camps.

From infancy, Richard Pankhurst had encouraged his children to support the anti-imperialist Afrikaner struggle. The Liberal Little Englander reaction to the colonial conflict disgusted Emmeline. Even the generally noxious jingo Henry Hyndman called the war 'a struggle between two burglars'. William Morris, who died in October 1896, did not live to see the conflict, but his last speech at the annual New Year's Meeting of the Social Democratic Federation in February 1896 indicated what his opinion would have been.[259] According to Hyndman, Morris 'thought it was a case of a pack of thieves quarrelling about their booty. The Boers had stolen their land from the people it had belonged to; people had come in to help them to develop their stolen property and now wanted to steal it themselves.'[260]

At school, Harry, now ten years old, bravely spoke out for peace. For this he was beaten unconscious by his fellow pupils. His headmaster carried him home in his arms to Emmeline. When Adela likewise vociferously opposed the war during a lesson, a classmate lobbed a book at her head. Although it hit Adela full in the face and injured her, the teacher watched impassively without intervening.

At Manchester Art School, political discord ran equally rampant. Sylvia attended a lecture on ornament given by the socialist artist Walter Crane, former director of design at the college and one of her inspirational mentors. When she was a child her father brought home Routledge's Shilling Toy Books, illustrated by Crane, from which they all sang old English folk songs. Sylvia admired Crane's socialist cartoons, particularly his 'Triumph of Labour', designed to commemorate International Labour Day on 1 May 1891. This piece of political art is widely regarded by critics as a work of real greatness.

Morris's and Crane's work first kindled Sylvia's longing to be a graphic artist and draughtswoman in service to social democratic movements. 'They were artists of the Golden Age. That was the life for me! ... I would portray the world that is to be when poverty is no more. I would decorate halls where people would foregather in the movement to win the new world, and make banners for meetings and processions.'[261] Sylvia had attended Social Democratic Federation meetings with her parents held in nondescript, grubby rooms in backstreets. She'd accompanied them on colourless demonstrations in Hyde Park. She dreamed of making the environment of protest and progressive politics more beautiful.[262]

Walter Crane illustrated his lecture by drawing Britannia's trident, interjecting, 'Let her be as careful to respect the liberties of others as she is in safeguarding her own!' Sylvia quoted this in her report on Crane's lecture for the school magazine, earning the ire of the school's most vocal jingo, Cicely Fox Smith. Later known for her popular books on seafaring and London inns, Cicely sported a military crop and khaki uniform in order to look as much like a soldier as she could. Sylvia's offending report in hand, Cicely charged in on the editor of the magazine, demanding that the whole article be excised and threatening to follow Sylvia home and break the Pankhurst windows.[263] Undeterred by the victimization of her family, in 1900 Emmeline left the Fabian Society in vehement protest at their refusal to oppose the war in South Africa.

Nationwide discord over the South African War escalated beyond community disagreement. The Pankhursts mourned their friend Larna Sugden. At a pacifist rally broken up by drunken pro-imperialist thugs, Sugden was brutally assaulted. She died from her injuries. Sylvia later remarked that although the First World War 'brought its menace to our very homes, the passions it evoked were far less ferocious than those displayed in the Boer War'.[264]

The decline of the Liberal Party and the evolution of the Independent Labour Party NB already used about a dozen times into the Labour Party at the turn of the century were about to play a determining role in the future of Sylvia's artistic career.

On 27 February 1900 the Independent Labour Party, Trades Union Congress and SDF met in Farringdon Hall in London. Keir Hardie carried the motion committing the conference to a 'distinct Labour Group in Parliament', with its own policy and its own whips. Within six years this new formation, the Labour Representation Committee (LRC), was to emerge as the Labour Party. Ramsay MacDonald was its secretary. Its chair and parliamentary leader, Hardie, welcomed its birth clear-sighted about the challenges ahead, and in 1907 referred to the Labour Party as 'my own child'.[265]

The LRC was structured as a federal organization made up of affiliates. Membership was not open to individuals. This would not happen until after the Great War, in 1918. In the early days, LRC leadership was exclusively male, and meetings and conferences male-dominated.

Hardie resigned the chair later in the year to focus on fighting in the autumn general election. Dubbed the 'khaki election', this was the first election of the twentieth century and the last of the Victorian era. Out of a population of 41.15 million, the total electorate in 1900 was 6.7 million. In the total population, women outnumbered men in all age groups. And none of them could vote. The LRC participated for the first time in this election, putting up fourteen candidates. Affiliated organizations received LRC backing, but had to fund their own nominees. Two won their seats: Keir Hardie was returned for Merthyr Tydfil (and Preston) and Richard Bell won Derby. Winston Churchill reached the House of Commons for the first time.

Before 1911, MPs were not paid salaries out of the public purse. Keir Hardie and Richard Bell depended on funding from affiliated trade unions and individual donors to pay their election campaign expenses and the costs of being an MP. Churchill was subsidized by his inherited private fortune. The economics of democratic representation presented a barrier for working-class candidates, male or female. However, there was a fundamentally significant difference when it came to women's suffrage. Candidates and MPs from the labour movement soon began to realize that, in some sectors, they needed the support of women workers in order to get the required union endorsement.

In the textile unions of the industrial north, women made up most of the membership. In the Co-operative Women's Guilds and the Independent Labour Party, women also had their own organizational traditions.[266] This provided opportunities for forging a mutually beneficial link between the interests of labour and women's suffrage, if only the men could overcome their gender prejudice and support women's right to elect them. The classic example arose in the Clitheroe by-election of 1902. David Shackleton, the Labour candidate, a weaver, was forced to declare himself in favour of women's suffrage in order to secure the endorsement of his female-dominated union, the Textile Factory Workers' Association. Radical suffragists woke to the potential for women to use their trade unions to get their right to the vote on the political agenda.[267]

On 22 January 1901, Queen Victoria passed away on the Isle of Wight, aged eighty-one, concluding a reign of nearly sixty-four years.

Her death marked the beginning of the end of absurd fictions about femininity that had crushed the lives of women of all classes in Britain and its empire. The Victorian myth-making factory manufactured stereotypes of gender conformity for men and women rigidly moulded on class and race hierarchies. With the new Edwardian era a radical, feminist incarnation of rebellious womanhood entered the modern age intent on breaking the mould. The impressive family phalanx of republican socialist-feminist Pankhursts emerged among the ranks of its most significant leaders.

In 1901–2, Owens College – precursor to Manchester University – celebrated its golden jubilee by building a grand new venue, the Whitworth Hall, opened in March 1902 by the Prince of Wales, later King George V. Sylvia was among the handful of top students selected to design and illuminate their own dedicated page for the address of welcome prepared as a presentation for the Prince. Dutifully, the young socialist republican applied herself 'for Art's sake', to produce a beautiful contribution to the best of her abilities, and duly received a coveted invitation to join the guests at the royal opening.[268] Come the day, however, Sylvia was to be found leafleting outside the hall in a republican protest organized by the ILP. She and her comrades spent the day selling two publications written by Keir Hardie: a pamphlet on unemployment and an 'Open Letter to the King'. Undeterred by the largely hostile crowds, Sylvia battled on and topped the bill as vendor of the day selling a full two pounds' worth of propaganda.[269]

Sylvia felt guilty about her intermittent absences brought about by depression and illness during her first year at art school. Still lacking confidence, she felt her scholarship undeserved. On top of this she piled another charge of self-induced guilt. Worrying that she was not doing enough to help her mother and Christabel run the shop, she proposed a well-meant but entirely unnecessary scheme to study part-time for her second year so that she could spend more hours working at Emerson & Co. She soon discovered there was really nothing much to do in the shop other than what she already did: write descriptive price tickets, rearrange the displays and sweep pointedly around Christabel's feet as her elegant sister sat attractively draped in display chairs, reading novels. Christabel was under no illusion about her unsuitability for running the shop: 'Business was not good for me and I was not good for business.'[270]

Emmeline encouraged her intellectual eldest daughter to take some classes at Owens College, where her father had been a student and later teacher. Delighted by the opportunity, Christabel took part-time classes in logic, literature and a few other subjects. In October 1900 she went to a meeting of the Women's Debating Society at the college, where the principal gave a talk on 'The Politics of the Poets'. During the discussion that followed, Christabel rose nervously and made a few hesitant remarks. At the end of the meeting, the Society's chair, Esther Roper, came down from the platform and invited Christabel to her home to meet her partner, Eva Gore-Booth. The friendship between the three women developed from there. Both ten years older than Christabel, they became her mentors. She joined their respective organizations, the North of England Society for Woman Suffrage and the Manchester and Salford Women's Trade Council, and fought many battles alongside them, 'with a view to getting woman suffrage recognized as a question of urgent practical importance from the industrial point of view'.[271] Christabel acknowledged their impact on her life in her memoir: 'This was a stage in my political apprenticeship of great and lasting value, and I owed much to the example and sympathy of these two friends.'[272]

Born in Cheshire in 1868, Esther was educated at Church Mission School in London and graduated from Owens College in 1891. Her father was a factory hand who became a lay preacher and missionary. By dramatic class contrast, golden-haired Eva Gore-Booth was born, in 1870, in County Sligo, one of five children of the Irish baronet Sir Henry Gore-Booth, Artic explorer and one of the largest landowners in the west of Ireland. Eva was close to her sister Constance Markievicz.

Aspiring writer Eva and political activist Esther met and fell in love in Italy at the villa of the Scottish writer George MacDonald and his wife in Bordighera. They settled in Manchester and stayed together for the rest of their lives. Both were radical constitutionalists who opposed militant tactics. These were the women under whom Christabel served her political apprenticeship.

Despite a year of working nights and only part-time, Sylvia achieved the accolade of best woman student of the year for 1901, and received a Lady Whitworth Scholarship of £30 and free tuition. She resumed full-time attendance at the school, with no noticeable detriment to the sluggish pace of custom at Emerson & Co.

In 1902, Sylvia scored a hat-trick. She won a National Silver Medal for Mosaic, a Primrose Medal for excellence in design and a travelling studentship – the highest prize available to students at the school. She chose to visit Italy, like so many British artists before her, including her mentor Walter Crane. Never one to miss an opportunity to travel, Emmeline decided to accompany Sylvia on her first trip abroad as far as Geneva, where she could visit her dear friend Noémie, whom she'd not seen since Richard died.

They sailed to Ostend and took the Belgian State Railways to Bruges, a city which enchanted Sylvia. She and Emmeline slept between lavender-scented sheets in a half-timbered attic granary. 'We were so happy together.'[273] Next stop, Brussels, where Sylvia admired the ornate architectural riches of the Hôtel de Ville while her mother launched herself on a vigorous shopping binge and bought hats for all her daughters.

Sylvia's first sight of the amphitheatre of the Alps and Jura mountains encircling Geneva thrilled her. Uninterested in sports, she'd always liked hiking. Here was a glorious new landscape. Every morning before she went out, Emmeline sat for a portrait for Noémie's husband, the Swiss painter and sculptor Frédéric Dufaux. He admired Sylvia's drawings – 'Elle cherche bien les formes' – and suggested that she join him and also paint her mother. Frédéric diplomatically interpreted Emmeline as young, vibrant and beautiful. Sylvia was disappointed with her own results. 'I was by no means pleased with my drawings.'[274] In her portrait her mother appeared older and sad. It was probably a more truthful representation.

In Venice Emmeline and Noémie threw themselves into shopping and sightseeing. Emmeline, as ever, justified her spending spree on the grounds of purchasing stock for Emerson & Co. She bought a large quantity of ornate Murano glass that proved unsaleable to her Manchester clientele. Sylvia 'toiled after' her mother and Noémie's 'speeding steps like a tired dog'.[275] Wearied by their relentless acquisitiveness and their loud bartering in dark shops, she sat down on the steps outside, happy to gaze upon surroundings that seemed to her, as she put it, lovely as the fabric of a dream. Seeing Venice for the first time in the soft, iridescent sunset, she was instantly transported by its stunning contrast with industrial Britain:

a wondrous city of fairest carving, reflected in gleaming waters swirled
to new patterning by every passing gondola. Venice in the brief, violet
twilight; Venice in the mournful loveliness of pale marble palaces,
rising in the velvet darkness of the night; the promised land of my sad
young heart, craving for beauty, fleeing from the sorrowful ugliness of
factory-ridden Lancashire, and the dull, aching poverty of its slums;
Venice, O city of dreaming magic![276]

Sylvia took up lodgings with a middle-aged, unmarried bluestocking
from Manchester, studying on a history research fellowship from the
Victoria Manchester University. 'Lodgings' turned out to be a modest
description for Sylvia's plush new surroundings. The history scholar
was house-sitting for a friend, a Polish countess called Sophie Bertelli
Algarotti, away to avoid the heat of the city summer. Algarotti's elegant
apartment was in one of the old marble palaces in the Calle de l'Arco,
Sant'Antonio.

To Emmeline's delight, the walls of the salon were draped with yellow
brocade and the satin upholstery was a canary yellow. But Sylvia had no
interest in staying indoors, however luxurious. Her mother departed,
streaming with tears and with an enormous amount of luggage. At last,
Sylvia was alone.

She rose every morning at five and went out to paint on the streets,
piazzas and canal bridges. After breakfast, she went to St Mark's
Cathedral to copy the famous mosaics, to the Scuola di San Giorgio
degli Schiavoni to make studies of the Carpaccios, and to churches.
In the afternoons she went to the Rialto to paint crowds, to the Ca'
d'Oro, or to colourful market stalls to sketch portraits of their vendors.
Street children pestered her and passers-by stopped to discuss her work
in bluntly critical terms. Women commented more frequently on the
quality of her looks, rather than the art on her easel. Younger girls
remarked that she was 'brutta' – plain – while older women rebuffed
them: 'Si si, ma simpatica' – 'Yes, but likeable'.[277]

Sylvia stopped reading newspapers, ceased worrying about the world,
read only poetry and, at the end of the day, sat on her balcony trying
to paint by moonlight. Thus immersed, the edges of her grief for her
father began to soften into acceptance.

The arrival of colder weather drove her indoors. Armed with a
letter of recommendation from her Manchester tutors, she joined the

Accademia di Belle Arti. Here she intended to study in the life class under an artist called Tito. The only woman who'd applied to the life class, she struggled to get in. Tito, embarrassed, performed various runarounds and evasions, until she got the better of him by just turning up early in the appointed studio for the class, setting up her easel and refusing to budge.

On this first day, the male students talked among themselves as if the strange-looking English woman was not there and on the incorrect assumption that she did not understand Italian. She'd picked up enough to understand that much of their chatter concerned sex, romance and marriage and very little of it art and aesthetics. However, they left her alone and she settled in quietly. It turned out that there were several other women students in the landscape class, and this was more sociable. Sylvia acquired a circle of friends among the other young female students. Her teacher Ciardi, impressed by her landscape work, asked her to leave her portfolio behind and to her delighted surprise there was a diploma waiting for her when she got back to England.

By this time Sylvia's closest friend in Venice was Sophie Bertelli Algarotti, the Countess who'd kindly thrown open her doors to the visiting Englishwoman. When Sophie returned from her native Poland after the summer, they felt an instant rapport. Sylvia had planned to move on to Florence, but, happy in Venice and in her new friendship, she readily accepted Sophie's entreaties to stay.

The fifty-year-old Sophie Bertelli Algarotti was the widow of an Italian count. She told Sylvia her tragic tale. After many years of lonely widowhood, she'd fallen blissfully in love with a much younger Italian writer, 'the devoted love of her maturity ... a man who became insane on the eve of their marriage, and whom she had visited constantly in the asylum until his recent death'.[278] Sophie's mother had been a lifelong activist in the Polish liberation movement and spent the family's fortune on the national struggle for independence from Russia. When the money ran out, she forged the signature of her infant baby girl in order to make use of her inheritance. Immensely proud of her mother's role in the liberation movement, Sophie seemed to bear no grudge at all about her disinheritance. Her marriage had made her wealthy and, since her second husband's death, independent.

Sophie gathered her friends for intimate salons where she played the piano and Sylvia sang, often the arias of *La Traviata*, first performed in Venice in 1853. In 1855 Alexandre Dumas the younger coined the term 'demi-monde' to describe the world inhabited by Violetta and her sisters, the 'fallen women' of the nineteenth century. Verdi based *La Traviata* – the woman who was led astray – on Dumas the younger's semi-autobiographical novel *La Dame aux camélias*. Telling the story of his affair with the Parisian courtesan Marie Duplessis, the book was published in 1848, the year after her death from consumption at the age of twenty-three. In the 1870s Dumas, an active supporter of women's rights campaigns, described himself as a feminist. His close friends included many European feminist pioneers, such as the Dutchwoman Mina Kruseman. Through her expanding circle of friendship, Sylvia tapped into the networks of modern feminism expanding across Europe.

For all the temptations of the Venetian demi-monde, her obsessional love of her work and growing confidence in her technical knowledge and skills of execution, Sylvia was still the conscientious daughter of her socially evangelical parents. In the glorious Venetian spring of 1903, she received a letter from her elder sister telling her, excitedly, that she had decided to study for a law degree and one day, when the profession admitted women, to become a barrister. It was Esther Roper who said to Mrs Pankhurst of Christabel, 'She ought to be a lawyer.'[279] In order to be coached for her matriculation, required for entrance to the college, she needed to study full time. Sylvia must return to Manchester and help in the shop.

Sophie tried to persuade Sylvia to ignore the letter and stay put. She encouraged her to put her artistic work first, and invited Sylvia to keep her company as her friend and daughter for as long as she wished. Sophie would be her patron and support her – she would have no expenses. Sylvia had stayed on long after the end of her scholarship, living on fifteen shillings a week sent by Christabel and her mother. Despite Sophie's best efforts, duty and guilt won the day. In a series of handwritten notes entitled 'The decisions which have mainly influenced by life', Sylvia reflected on this decisive moment of her youth:

> My decision to return to Manchester was made without any
> hesitation. I was clearly aware that I was leaving a life of security
> where I was happy and beloved and which attracted me above all
> because therein I might study and improve that which was very

precious to me. I grieved also at parting from my dear friend but
I permitted myself no doubts and no regrets.[280]

Her dutiful response, it turned out, was unnecessary. As soon as she
got home, she realized that she wasn't really needed in the shop. This
was a pretext. The real reason for her recall was that Christabel needed
her to look after their mother, who felt displaced from her affections
by her new young activist friends. For Sylvia, the beautiful Venetian
dream, living as an artist with Sophie's enthusiastic patronage, was over.
Gallingly, shortly after she arrived home, Christabel left for a holiday in
Venice with Esther and Eva.

Sylvia landed back in Manchester to a harder life she could so easily
have avoided. For a year she had been free of domestic drudgery and
political activism, living the life of art and the mind first with her
scholarship money, then with her fifteen shillings per week and Sophie's
patronage. Now she was broke, and Emmeline needed her help with
housekeeping, buying food, darning and accounts. On the upside,
she still had use of the studio room above Emerson & Co. It was her
only bolthole. Her irritation at these circumstances proved short-lived.
Almost immediately, she was caught up in the regional revolution that
in her absence had transformed Manchester into the HQ of radical
women's suffrage.

Christabel of the laconic lassitude, easily bored and uncertain of her
direction in life, had disappeared, replaced by a dynamic new elder sister,
both more and less likeable. Under the tutelage of Eva and Esther, she
had discovered her vocation as a brilliant political campaigner. Drawn
increasingly into organized feminist and labour politics, she reconnected
with the Pankhurst family interest in women's suffrage: 'I had been
reared in the suffrage cause and the principle of equality had been lived
out in our home.'[281] Her radical name, she discovered, opened doors.
'My political path was easy. "Dr Pankhurst's daughter" was the passport
to the friendship of one and all, in Lancashire, Cheshire and Yorkshire,
the sphere of my action in my early suffrage days.'[282]

By the time Sylvia was in her teens, in the late nineteenth century,
middle-class women had created a distinct organizing voice. Their
campaigns delivered many successful victories, notably women's right
to access decent secondary and higher education and to enter some of
the professions. Married women had won the right to own property

and to vote in municipal elections. From the 1860s to the late 1890s, the suffrage movement attracted middle-class women constitutional in outlook and gradual in their aims and methods. Temperate incremental change, enfolded into the general movement for equal rights, would they hoped ultimately win the day for women. By 'women', they generally meant themselves. The constitutionalists did not speak to the needs of their working-class sisters. In 1897 the movement regrouped into an umbrella organization called the National Union of Women's Suffrage Societies, led by Millicent Fawcett.

Both members of the NUWSS executive, Roper and Gore-Booth lost patience with the narrow class focus of the NUWSS organization and its message that the work of achieving women's rights was the preserve of the educated middle class and the rich. The pace of change was far too slow. Like Mrs Pankhurst, these women were ILP members, frustrated by the manner in which it continued to shirk political responsibility to make the women's vote a policy priority. The radical Roper recognized the potential for activists to use the trade union movement to advance the cause of women's suffrage in the Labour Representation Committee. She wrote a leaflet, *The Cotton Trade Unions and the Enfranchisement of Women*, urging female members to use their majority position in these unions in the north to make 'Women's Suffrage a Trade Union Question'.[283]

Women trade union activists working within the North of England Women's Suffrage Society led the way in connecting the campaign for the women's vote with established grass-roots trade unionism. Eva Gore-Booth, Esther Roper, Sarah Reddish, Selina Cooper, Sarah Dickenson and others formed a radical group, challenging the class prejudices of the established women's suffrage societies on the one hand and the patriarchal misogyny of the labour movement on the other.

These activists disagreed with the emphasis on the women's vote as a stand-alone right and saw it instead as an integrated part of the wider struggle by which women of all classes needed to transform their lives. To prove their point, they instigated a suffrage petition in 1900 to be signed exclusively by women workers, accompanied by mass action in all factory districts. They formed the breakaway Manchester and Salford Women's Trade Union Council, its objective to campaign through grass-roots women's trade unionism for the women's vote. Initially affiliated to the NUWSS, the Women's Trade Union Council soon seceded from the constitutionalists, who rejected their argument for a principled alliance between feminism and socialism.

In the cotton towns, they launched campaigns urging the female-dominated textile unions to ballot their women members on the issue of women's suffrage. The ballot returns proved overwhelmingly conclusive: women workers wanted the vote. Despite this clear outcome, the LRC and the TUC 'remained obdurately silent or opposed to women's suffrage. A great opportunity was thus sacrificed on the altar of male prejudice.'[284]

Roper and Gore-Booth quickly recognized Christabel's phenomenal oratorical skills, sharp tactical intelligence and fearlessness. She took her place in the leadership of the newly formed Manchester and Salford Women's Trade Union Council and campaigned boldly for its aims of industrial equality and political liberty. Christabel had found her feet, and an exciting new group of friends to invigorate the parlour at Nelson Street.

It was to this vibrant and newly radicalized Manchester milieu that Sylvia returned from her artistic sojourn in Venice.

7

Pankhurst Hall

Sylvia's imperious recall from Venice by her elder sister clearly rankled. 'Soon after my return to Manchester I realized, that so far as my mother's business was concerned, my presence was not required.'[285] Her sense of duty and responsibility was never in question; but nor was her ability never to pass on an opportunity to point up examples of what she regarded as Christabel's narcissistic self-interest and aptitude for putting her own desires and interests ahead of those of everyone around her.

It transpired that Christabel had inadvertently done her a favour. Soon after Sylvia's return, the local Independent Labour Party approached her with a large-scale civic art commission that had dramatic and far-reaching consequences which outplayed any more beautiful renderings of mosaics or Venetian landscapes she might have produced.

The ILP decided to erect an impressive new building called Pankhurst Hall in honour of her father's legacy, located in St James Road, Salford. This was the public testimonial Robert Blatchford had suggested to Emmeline when she refused his offer of raising a cash fund to support the family. The foundation stone had been laid on 26 November 1898, four months after Richard's death, and now, five years later, the building was complete. Though modest by grand Venetian standards, Pankhurst Hall was better than anything the ILP yet possessed. An exciting, brand-new venue for community congregation, designed for meetings, art, culture and social events and to house the ILP branch offices. Appropriately, or so it seemed, the ILP committee asked Sylvia to decorate the lecture theatre and the imposing assembly room. The opening date was already announced, giving Sylvia just a few weeks to complete the commission. It never occurred to her to ask to be paid. To some of her friends, this was imprudent, since she had no income at the time, but no one in the family would have considered it right that this work be anything other than a pure act of love and homage.

Sylvia set to work immediately on the designs and arranged for her friend Richard Wallhead, a fellow pupil from the Manchester Art School, to help her with the heavier construction and installation work. Wallhead worked as a decorator near Manchester and studied part-time as an evening student; a fellow socialist, he was delighted to work on the commission, for which Sylvia ensured he received payment. Wallhead later became chairman of the ILP (1920–2) and the Labour MP for Merthyr Tydfil, a seat he held until his death in 1934. His daughter Muriel was to become Labour MP for Bradford North during Attlee's 1945–50 administration, an indicator of the influence both feminism and Sylvia had on Wallhead's early years.

Working round the clock, they completed the ambitious project on time. Sylvia's capacity for noctural shifts lasting until dawn became legendary among those who knew her. It developed into a persistent habit. As Kate Connelly cogently remarked,[286] Sylvia added an extra day to every week by working through two nights in seven. The Pankhurst Hall commission is the first recorded occurrence of this lifetime pattern.

Sylvia's draft for her design, typically precise, conjures a vision of the finished creation unveiled to the guests at the opening ceremony:

> As this hall bears the name of a pioneer whose life was given for the ideal and for the future, emblems of the future and the ideal have been chosen with which to decorate it.
>
> The Entrance Hall. The symbols are the peacock's feather, lily & rose, emblems of beauty, purity & love; with the motto: 'England arise' and the name of the hall.
>
> The Large Hall. Symbols: Roses, love, apple trees, knowledge, doves, peace, corn, plenty, lilies, purity, honesty, bees, industry, sunflower and butterflies, hope.
>
> The panels illustrate Shelley's line: 'Hope will make thee young, for Hope and Youth are children of one mother, even Love.'[287]

Walter Crane came to speak at the opening ceremony, and praised fulsomely the work of his protégée, the more so since this was public art on a splendid scale, beautiful, useful and expressing dignity and hope. Next, Sylvia braced herself to speak. She'd been asked to give a lecture on the principles of ornamentation and to explain her illustrations to the guests. Poignantly, her public-speaking debut honoured her dead father. He would have approved that she was more focused on explication than sentiment. Extremely nervous, she forgot to take off her gloves when demonstrating on the blackboard, and so punctuated the rest of her talk with a trail of chalky gestures that seemed to suggest an ethereal presence.

Keir Hardie's paper *Labour Leader* praised her tasteful decoration and described it as a true work of love. Sylvia had just turned twenty-one. She came of age with this fitting expression of her artistic vocation and social commitment. It was indeed a labour of love – a tribute to her father of which he would have been proud. Imagine then Sylvia's indignation when she discovered that women were not permitted to join the branch of the ILP housed at Pankhurst Hall. Outraged, Mrs Pankhurst demanded an explanation. The reason given was that the social club attached to the branch was men only. Even more absurdly, the social club rules made it open also to men who were not members of the ILP, though it was closed to all women. Named to honour one of the nation's pioneering champions of women's emancipation, Pankhurst Hall now stood in flagrant, obdurate contradiction to Richard's radical feminist values.

Sylvia's childhood homes, presided over by her feminist father, had been havens of enlightenment. After his death, the realities of being women alone in the world were encompassed in the emblematic hollow façade of Pankhurst Hall. Without women's emancipation and equality between all men, the struggle for democracy proceeded on precarious foundations.

Women played an important role in the ILP, alongside the men. They made up a significant part of the membership and held office in the organization. Yet there remained representatives on the ILP executive actively opposed to votes for women. Here was yet another example of their failure of leadership. Many ILP members, female and male, demanded that the 'Woman Question' should be at the forefront of the national groundswell within socialism.[288] In August 1903, Christabel wrote in the *ILP News*, 'The Labour Representation Committee invites the support of women's unions – what has it to offer in return if it does not intend to press for the representation of women's labour?'[289] Keir Hardie agreed, and was uncompromising in his position that the issue of parliamentary votes for women and women's rights must be founding principles of the newly emerging Labour Party.

For Emmeline the Pankhurst Hall episode proved the last straw. Already, she had been losing her patience with the foot-dragging of the ILP leadership on committing to women's suffrage. For the last two years she had watched and listened to Christabel and her new group of friends, often in her own home, abuzz with far-reaching ideas of mixing socialism with feminist sisterhood in order to radicalize the women's movement. The breakaway Manchester and Salford Women's Trade Union Council made Emmeline acutely conscious of how staid and conformist the Liberal-allied constitutional suffrage movement of her generation still was.

The leaders of the NUWSS, like her, were mothers of the Victorian era. Their daughters and sons were children of the modern age. For some time, she'd felt sidelined by Christabel's transferral of affection to her new friends. Many of these younger women had the opportunity of better education, which was intimidating. Emmeline admired Eva and Esther, particularly the boldness of their free living, but she also resented the way they now commanded Christabel's enraptured attention. According to Sylvia, their mother made no attempt to hide her 'intense jealousy' of Christabel's passionate preoccupation with her new friendships and political circle.[290] She complained constantly to Sylvia that Christabel was never home.

It would be easy but superficial to reduce this to a Freudian catfight between ego-identified mother and eldest daughter. Emmeline's resentment and frustration were understandable in context. Christabel, now on the executive of the most radical women's group in town, had found her vocation. Her new purpose made her more beautiful, a luminous orator, possessed of a superbly quick mind and, as everyone soon realized, the requisite political ruthlessness to crush her opponents without compunction.

Emmeline Pankhurst was no political theorist or intellectual philosopher, but like every great general, she was a good judge of tactical dispositions. Christabel's radical, younger coterie and the

ILP's malingering, exemplified by the Pankhurst Hall patriarchal debacle, jolted Emmeline into renewed action. Now that she had been drawn ineluctably into the progressive good sense of their political strategies, maternal envy was distracted by opportunity and inspiration. Christabel's discovery of her campaigning temperament prompted her mother to rekindle her own firebrand youth.

It was time to go on the offensive.

On 10 October 1903, a Saturday, Mrs Pankhurst invited half a dozen ILP women to convene in her front parlour at 62 Nelson Street. Modest in size, one wall taken up with the upright piano and another with the sewing table, the room was crammed with extra chairs brought in for the meeting. This snug women-only scene was a far cry from Emmeline's grand salons in Russell Square and leafy Buckingham Crescent. At this meeting, the women formed the Women's Social and Political Union. The manifesto they drafted at Nelson Street that day committed the WSPU to securing the female franchise, and justice for women within the labour movement.

> Social reform can never be satisfactory as long as one half of the nation is not represented.
>
> Working men have found that political action is needed to supplement trades unionism and so they have formed the Labour Party. Women Trades Unionists and social reformers now realize that the possession of the vote is the most effective way of securing better social and industrial conditions, better wages, shorter hours, healthier homes and an honourable position in the State which will enable women as well as men to render that citizen service which is so necessary to the development of a truly great nation.[291]

The group of women who founded the WSPU comprised working women, members of the ILP and women who were both working and ILP members. From the outset, they decided that this new union should be women only and an affiliate of the ILP. Over a decade later, Emmeline described the day in her autobiography: 'We resolved to limit our membership exclusively to women, to keep ourselves absolutely free from any party affiliation, and to be satisfied with nothing but action on our question. Deeds, not words, was to be our permanent motto.'[292]

Emmeline had renounced her socialism and trade unionism by the time she wrote this memoir. Her description is accurate on every point except the falsehood that the women launched with the resolve to keep themselves 'absolutely free from any party affiliation'. This is historical nonsense. The WSPU initially formed itself expressly as an affiliate of the ILP. Its founding members were, exclusively, women who were already part of the labour and socialist movements. Throwing open its membership to people from other parties was integral to the movement for the formation of the Labour Party. Like Mrs Pankhurst and her sister ILP members, many women had given up on the Liberals to join the new left.

In 1903, the achievement of universal adult suffrage was considered utterly unattainable – a utopian democratic daydream believed in only by socialist crazies. To understand what followed, it's crucial to remember that, from its inception, the WSPU accepted the principle of a limited franchise, linked to property qualification, on the same terms as men. The Local Government Act of 1894 giving propertied women the right to vote in local elections was the first step towards this capital-based restricted goal.

The Pankhursts were now back on political track. Sylvia, Christabel and Adela became founder members of the WSPU the same weekend. What their younger brother Harry felt about being excluded by his gender is not recorded, but his intention to fight his way into the centre of the feminist action alongside his sisters and mother soon became apparent.

Sylvia supported wholeheartedly the cause of female suffrage. She harboured no doubt that women needed to organize and lobby forcefully within the socialist movement to make it a priority for the men, and reluctant women. However, she was an egalitarian visionary who saw nothing wrong with utopian daydreaming about the aims of democratic socialism. In principle, she supported the goal of universal suffrage. She believed also in the necessary conjoining of the economic and political struggle of women and the working class. Without a class analysis, feminism was a minority campaign group for rich and middle-class women who wanted equality with their brothers and husbands, but had no interest in extending the same rights to their chauffeurs or housemaids.

Sylvia's political upbringing brought her the advantage of pragmatism. Even at the age of twenty-one, she'd learned enough to understand the tension and complexities arising when economic class oppression collided with gendered sexual oppression. The ultimate goal for her, though not for her mother and Christabel, was universal suffrage. To that end, women needed to organize, lobby and persuade in order to demonstrate that they were a subordinated class and an oppressed majority.

Though committed to the practical, strategic need to campaign for women's rights as a single issue, Sylvia was from the outset extremely uncomfortable about the rift growing between the ILP and the WSPU, fuelled by her mother's and Christabel's sexual sectarianism. Art, she was certain, was the force that propelled her. Perhaps some of the gentler young men and the misfits in the worlds of masculinity and femininity that she'd met at art college made her more optimistic about the possibility of making men and women anew.

Emmeline's radical intervention in forming the WSPU grabbed Christabel's attention. Mother and eldest daughter began to work closely together once again. For Sylvia, their renewed alliance created political problems that were deeply and inextricably personal. Emmeline and Christabel stirred up their supporters to launch a broadside at their friend Keir Hardie when next he came to speak in Manchester.

The torrents of WSPU invective unleashed on Hardie dismayed Sylvia, but she learned a valuable lesson from his calm, unruffled response. He understood the women's fury, and found it reasonable. Sylvia described the scene:

> A bevy of angry women prepared to fight him on every point. He raised no objection to the most impatient of zeal. On the contrary he greeted all of this with the keenest sympathy. Votes for women? Of course! The Party must be brought into line, and a big campaign set on foot. A separate women's organization? Excellent! The very thing to provide the necessary spur. A simple one-clause measure to give votes on the same terms as men? Certainly.[293]

Hardie asked Christabel to assemble the evidence and prepare a draft statement. 'The Citizenship of Women: A Plea for Women's Suffrage' was printed and circulated in his name nationally throughout the ILP.

Next, Hardie organized a questionnaire for ILP branches to establish what proportion of women could be regarded as working class among local government voters. The combined research of forty ILP branches found that, of 60,000 women voters, 85 per cent could be defined as working class. He now had the proof he needed to demonstrate to the ILP executive that to call for the women's vote on the same terms as men would hand no advantage to the conservative propertied classes, as was so widely feared in the socialist movement.

Hardie's championing of women's suffrage raises the intriguing question of what it was in his background or make up that made him stick so unshakeably to this policy, even to the point of compromising his otherwise immovable socialist ideals. Asserting that he adored his mother and liked strong women doesn't explain it. Most political men who revered women saw this as no good reason to include them in electoral democracy. Henry Hyndman, Marxist leader of the Social Democratic Federation, recommended that women who wanted the vote should be exiled to a desert island. Philip Snowden, national chairman of the Independent Labour Party, thought Hardie's friendship with the Pankhursts ruined his leadership of the party: 'Hardie never speaks to me. He seems completely absorbed with the Suffragettes.'[294] The party stuck to its policy that votes for women should mean equality for all – universal suffrage. But Hardie supported the WSPU's narrower tactics. The origins of this decision lay not in his loyalty and love for strong-willed women, but in his early experiences as a young trade union organizer in Ayrshire.

Hardie's first employment in the coal pits was to work as a trapper, a job reserved for young boys. Trappers spent their ten-hours-a-day shift opening and closing a door at the head of the shaft to regulate the air supply for miners working below at the coalface. As a young man Hardie was chosen as the spokesman for his fellow miners and this status quickly put him in the front line of conflict with the Lanarkshire coal owners. In 1879, aged twenty-two, he led a delegation of miners to protest against a two-shillings-a-day fall in wages at Newarthill, Lancashire. He and his two brothers David and George were sacked and blacklisted. Hardie was told by the manager, 'We'll hae nae damned Hardies in this pit.'[295] During the all-out strikes of 1880, the Lanarkshire Miners' Association appointed Hardie secretary, and in 1886 the Scottish National Miners' Federation was formed with Hardie as its first secretary. His methods of organization and tactics were controversial, and outside the west of Scotland he was little known.[296] Hardie pushed on, and used his leadership of the Ayrshire miners to get himself to the table at the Trades Union Congress and gradually build a platform for his belief in the need for independent labour representation.

He drew two key conclusions from the bitter defeats he'd experienced in industrial disputes. First, he believed that the employers were too powerful. If the issues of wages and hours were going to be addressed it would have to be through state intervention. Secondly, the miners would have to operate outside the framework of the Liberal Party to achieve this, even though the unions had historically been allied with and supported by the Liberals. Here are early clues to understanding Hardie's support for the suffragettes. Hardie's supreme act of political strategy was his rejection of incorporation into the Liberal Party. Instead, he focused on building an independent new movement. The relationship between the WSPU and the Labour Party, in this sense, was similar to the relationship between the emerging ILP and the Liberal Party.

Hardie understood how the perpetual double shift for women stunted their lives: 'I saw that if the boy went out to work – in effect, he could play or study in the evening, but whatever a woman did, she had another lot of work to do when she got home. This was grossly unfair ...'[297] Isabella Ford, a prominent activist in the NUWSS and no socialist, described Hardie's 'extraordinary sympathy with the women's movement, his complete understanding of what it stands for ... In the days when labour men neglected and slighted the women's cause or ridiculed it, Hardie never once failed us, never faltered in his work for us. We can never forget what we owe him.'[298]

Hardie believed in the power of agitation, what he called the 'divine discontent' of the suffragettes. Melissa Benn reminds us that for Hardie 'the key to politics lay in what he often called "agitation": principled, powerful, often unruly, popular protest'.[299] The principle of limited franchise embraced suffrage equality on the single issue of gender and supported it with a people's movement. Hardie believed this would accelerate the cause and bring greater pressure to bear on Westminster from without than from within. For him, the politically passionate crowd represented his own people – not an external threat by others, but a collective expression of hope and energy. Huge public meetings and demonstrations, and demands for direct representation, were far more familiar to him than the unfriendly, arcane protocols of parliament.

Emmeline was elected to the executive of the ILP at the Easter 1904 conference with the specific task of introducing a Votes for Women Bill into parliament. The WSPU now sat firmly within the big tent of the working-class socialist and trade union movement. By contrast, the NUWSS, with Millicent Fawcett its national secretary, comprised around 500 intellectual, professional, respectable and predominantly Liberal affiliates.

Four years into the twentieth century, the combined forces of socialism and feminism were breaking the fourth wall in the conventional theatre of the battle for the women's vote. The Pankhurst women were the rebel 'family party' at the heart of the new drama, and Sylvia was already its set designer.

Early in 1904 Sylvia's tutors at the art school called her to a meeting. She was amazed, delighted and nervous when they told her they wanted to put her forward to sit the entrance exams for a prestigious national scholarship to London's Royal College of Art, the most influential wholly postgraduate institution of art and design in Britain. Founded as the British Government School of Design in 1837, it became the 'Royal College' almost sixty years later, in 1896. Women were admitted from its founding, but in a segregated 'Female School' with a different curriculum, including life classes in which the live models were, strictly, clothed – men, for example, in medieval suits of armour. Throughout the nineteenth century the school was dominated by a distinctive version of Arts and Crafts philosophy. Socially engaged and progressive, it was a good fit for Sylvia and she for it. During the early 1900s the ethos of the school was changing, particularly in regard to the admission of women. Sylvia might be one of the tiny cohort of women students creating that change.

With Emmeline's enthusiastic support, Sylvia registered and sat the scholarship exams, which were both practical and theoretical. Afterwards, she crept home in utter despair. The rest of the family had gone to the theatre, and she found herself locked out of the house. Having climbed in through an open window, she fell into bed fully clothed, in abject misery. The exams had been a complete disaster. She'd rubbed holes in her paper. Because her hands were sweating and shaking so much, she'd failed to complete the geometry tests. She fell asleep weeping, heartbroken and despondent at her failure.

The results arrived by post. A first-class in every other subject than the incomplete geometry paper wiped out the shortfall and amounted to a grade that put her in first place in the nationwide list of competitors. The Royal College of Art offered a place and a full scholarship. But there were no jubilant scenes at Nelson Street of an ecstatically happy Sylvia dancing with joy, relief and pride with her mother and delighted sisters in the manner of *Little Women*, radical feminism Manchester style. This brilliant achievement lent no support to either Sylvia's ego or to her feminine lack of self-confidence in her own abilities. 'I was surprised, but not elated; the standard is not very high, I concluded.'[300]

It's tempting to wonder if Sylvia's diffidence is highly achieved false modesty veiling a monumental ego, especially when seen from a twenty-first-century perspective where robust female self-confidence is more common. But this doesn't stand the heat of the historical wash. There were very, very few places for young women in the prestigious art academies. In fact, there were hardly any places for women in prestigious institutions of higher learning. Sylvia's doubts about her well-earned success provide a classic example of imposter syndrome – acute feminine anxiety at entering a male-dominated elite institution and fear that she was not good enough.

Sylvia's scholarship paid a handsome £5 per month for the college terms. At face value, this was almost Virginia Woolf's later recommended £50 a year. However, Woolf's £50 was in addition to a room of one's own, after payment of rent and bills. Sylvia's monthly fiver had to cover the ten shillings a week for her rent, food, transport and all her materials for art school. She cut corners by eating cheaply, or not at all, and walking whenever possible. The RCA was based in South Kensington, and Sylvia's one-room lodgings were nearby in Chelsea, on the Cheyne Walk riverside. Even managed frugally, she couldn't stretch her scholarship to cover all her expenses. Many of the other students, especially the young men, were subsidized by independent fortunes, by parental stipends or by living rent-free in family properties in London. None of these applied to Sylvia. To pay for the expensive materials required for her studies, she needed to make up the shortfall. She worried also about helping her overstretched mother by contributing to the family finances.

Not shown on the balance sheet of her weekly expenses was the incalculable additional cost of Sylvia's guilty conscience. Painfully aware of the domestic thrift necessary to keep the household going for the young and increasingly troubled Adela and Harry, Sylvia fretted about the family's financial security. She was no longer costing her mother anything, apart from the rent Emmeline continued to pay for her studio room on King Street above the shop, at her own insistence. However, nor was she actively contributing, either in labour time to Emerson & Co. or in cash by sending money home. Sylvia determined to try and earn the extra money she needed for herself and to enable her to send a contribution back to her mother to help support the family.

To supplement her income, Sylvia embarked on her first entrepreneurial venture. She started selling her own designs for cotton prints to the fashion and home-interiors workshops around Chelsea. Nervously, she stepped out on her first Saturday morning with a basket of sample prints to hand-sell along and around the King's Road. Though the daughter of a shopkeeper who had worked in the storefront of the family business for several years, she felt shy and awkward selling her own work. Despite her hesitancy, from the outset she met with some success. Her Chelsea buyers paid her in guineas. These earnings seemed a fortune: and from her own artistic creations! Sylvia proudly sent the pounds back home to her mother and kept the shillings for bus fares, cups of tea and a newly acquired London habit coffee, which became her favourite beverage.

Gaining in confidence from this, she was puzzled and upset when Emmeline soon told her to put a stop to her extracurricular artistic enterprise. After all, it was her mother's passion and flair for modern interior design and the Emerson & Co. family business that had inspired her to set out in this direction. Up until now, Emmeline had supported the great opportunity offered to Sylvia of studying at the prestigious RCA. Now, suddenly, her mother changed tack. She instructed Sylvia to devote her spare time to collecting as many signatures as she could for a petition in support of the Women's Franchise Bill. Dutifully, Sylvia travelled around London in the evenings after college, and on Sundays went to public meetings where she could drum up support for the petition. She found that the political pitch came much easier to her than the commercial. Campaigning was her comfort zone, the ethos of her childhood home. Learning her craft as an artist, and how to live by it as a young woman without independent means, was a more fragile terrain, requiring nurture and encouragement. Sylvia's mentors were solid in their consistent backing for her career, but her mother's support was her emotional lifeline.

Despite her beginner's anxiety, Sylvia's first steps had been fruitful. She'd discovered she had her mother's entrepreneurial flair, with better business skills. A practical as well as a creative dreamer, she worked extremely hard and systematically to realize her visions. Had this early promise been allowed to develop, she might have been able to live by her artistic talent. But Emmeline didn't have the heart to spare Sylvia entirely for art and Sylvia didn't have the heart to refuse her mother. She wanted to please her. The new demands of WSPU activism divided her concentration, and her fledgling enterprise soon got squeezed out. For the first time, Sylvia sensed a dilemma developing between her artistic vocation and her activist calling.

Sylvia loved the anonymity of the capital's amorphous flow. It enabled her painter's eye to observe and individuate. But without the anchor of her family she felt, at first, lonely in the impersonal vastness of London. Settling into the institutional life of the RCA was also initially challenging. She accurately anticipated the obstacles she would face as a minority female student in a male-dominated academy, but she wholly underestimated the class prejudice that would confront her as a solidly middle-class northerner whose mother was a shopkeeper and whose dead father had been a professional who had left her without the settlement of a private annual income. Manchester Art School had an egalitarian and supportive ethos among both students and tutors. By comparison, Sylvia discovered the RCA to be a hostile, competitive and acutely class-conscious environment, with few – if any – other students with a radical socialist family background and feminist single mother as working head of the household. Then there was her voice. The RP intonation coached into her by Manchester Girls might be considered posh in Lancashire; but in London those hard vowels that she'd never lost sounded like nothing but brass.

It was a relief to discover that nearly all the other young women students were as insecure as she was. They swiftly best-befriended each other in defensive pairs or became cliquey from the necessity of sharing lodgings together in same-sex groups. In living alone, Sylvia was, again, extremely unusual. A bit strange, they thought. At first the female students seemed circumspect towards her. Largely, this was because they were already formed into cohabiting, rent-sharing lodgings; likewise for the men. Every other young woman, it seemed to Sylvia, had a best girlfriend and 'her special man friend'.[301]

Living alone, mixing naturally in a radical activist milieu beyond the college gates, self-composed, intellectual and outspoken, Sylvia appeared a bit lofty and intimidating. In her early days at the college, she felt that she was on terms of distant acquaintance rather than intimacy with most of the other students. Unable to see herself as they did, she didn't realize her effect on them. Worldly and threatening, she habitually questioned all the rules – institutional and social – usually without even realizing or meaning to. After she had left the RCA, she heard that the male students had thought her haughty and imperious, 'but it did not occur to me that others desired to know me unless they made the first advances: the girls did so: the men left the initiative to me, and I, very much absorbed by many interests, made no move'.[302]

This gap in her experience between easy companionability with other young women and the uneasy social barrier distancing her from her male peers in the college was a common experience. Sylvia was not shy in the company of boys and men. She had grown up with brothers, uncles and male cousins, and with a close attachment to a father who taught her she was everyone's equal. In their family home, her parents encouraged the relaxed and free company of many enlightened men, like Keir Hardie, who discussed art, politics and life seriously with her. From childhood, many of the men she knew were people who actively dedicated their working lives to fighting the cause for women's rights. In his 'Sunshine of Socialism' speech in 1914, Hardie said that 'the warming influence of Socialism' could be seen, 'perhaps, most of all in the awakening of women.

> Who that has ever known woman as mother or wife has not felt the dormant powers which, under the emotions of life, or at the stern call of duty are even now momentarily revealed? And who is there who can even dimly forecast the powers that lie latent in the patient drudging woman, which a freer life would bring forth? Woman, even more than the working class, is the great unknown quantity of the race.[303]

The male students at the RCA, and their tutors, certainly found Sylvia a 'great unknown quantity'. She was unlike their sisters and she gave them no familiar point of access through the usual, and more pliantly amenable, conduits of conventional femininity. It did not occur to her that she confused, intimidated or angered most of her male college peers. Her later realization that 'the men left the initiative to me, and I, very much absorbed by many interests, made no move', points to the suggestive social gap into which an older, more mature man might step to satisfy the needs and desires of a bright young feminist woman impatient with the callow youths otherwise on offer.

Sylvia eventually made many good male friends at college, but none of them was of any romantic interest to her. Like her, some were class outsiders, with no family fortunes to float them through London. Others were sexually fluid, outsiders by disposition, who gravitated to Sylvia and she to them, such as Austin Osman Spare. Born in Elephant and Castle, the son of a policeman, Spare, like Sylvia, was a scholarship student. He became one of her close college companions and would be a lifelong friend.

The general air of demoralization and depression among the students greatly surprised her. This was not the affected unhappiness of tortured artistic ennui or general youthful alienation. The cause was institutional. First, the teaching was conducted on a model of constant, hectoring criticism by the tutors in order to make the students reach high and toughen up. Secondly, the student body reacted badly to the introduction of a new college rule requiring them to spend the first six months of their two-year course in architectural school all day, and only their evenings in life classes.

Those not studying architecture protested that this was a waste of their precious time, and Sylvia led the charge. Assuming leadership among her disgruntled peers, she wrote a letter of objection to the policy to the college Principal Augustus Spencer and demanded a meeting to talk with him about it in person. Spencer responded by summoning Sylvia to his office, so that he could reprimand and summarily eject her without allowing her the opportunity to state her case. He thought he'd demonstrated his authority, but he underestimated Miss Pankhurst. 'Thereafter, whenever I met the Principal in the corridor, we glared at each other like two savage dogs.'[304]

Sylvia coolly observed that, had she been received with civility and reasoned with calmly by the Principal, it would not have been difficult to convince her, as a decorative painter, that some study of architecture was essential. It made sense. But the clash between Spencer and the young Pankhurst had nothing to do with cool reasoning and everything to do with the male Principal's intolerance of the young northern woman's mouthy presumption and front.

Now alerted to the institutional sexism, Sylvia began to observe how the RCA treated all the women students. She noticed quickly that while nearly all of them entered the school on scholarships, hardly any achieved further funding awards once they'd got there. The internal selection process overwhelmingly favoured the male students. Augustus Spencer might have wished that he'd been prudent enough to give her a fair hearing in his office over the architectural syllabus-change issue, for this time, Sylvia bypassed the college authorities and went direct to parliament to lodge her complaint.

She solemnly asked Keir Hardie to table a parliamentary question on the point, which he dutifully did, receiving the curt answer that the award of RCA scholarships was in the proportion of one woman to thirteen men. This, it seemed, was deemed more than adequate. No further explanation of the privileging of masculinity over merit was offered. When he heard that the matter had been raised in parliament, Principal Spencer was furious, and glared at Sylvia even more fiercely in the corridors. Yet his open disapproval made no dent in her confidence that hers was a just cause. Her card was now clearly marked as a rebellious troublemaker. Hardie respected Sylvia's challenge to Augustus Spencer's authority as much as the Principal disdained it.

Since childhood, her artistic talent had been established in the Pankhurst family and known to their circle of close friends, among whom Hardie was one of their most intimate and frequent visitors. He had witnessed Aunt Mary gently coaxing Sylvia to stop concealing her secret drawings and paintings under her bed and in other hiding places around the house. He knew that Sylvia's parents had supported her in taking art classes and encouraged her to develop faith and confidence in her gift.

She had now left home and embarked on her independence, a young woman, remarkably, living alone in Europe's largest city, pursuing her creative vocation at the most prestigious arts academy in the country while simultaneously taking her activism to the streets of London. Sylvia was beginning to make friends at college and clearly enjoyed and valued the company of her peers, but this was only one aspect of her life and not socially all-consuming. She prioritized spending time with her brother Harry, at school in Hampstead, and, increasingly, with Keir Hardie. It was while Sylvia studied at the RCA during 1904 and 1905 that her relationship with Hardie evolved, first, into a romance and then into a fully fledged love affair, passionate, ecstatic and tormented. They became lovers, both spiritually and physically.

Since each chose to leave no clear record of it, we cannot know the exact moment when Sylvia and Keir Hardie were prompted by their secret selves to acknowledge that their attraction to each other went beyond platonic friendship. This consciousness may have presented itself to each or both of them long before they acted on it at some point between the winter of 1904 and the spring of 1905, or it, may have developed naturally from her emergence into independent womanhood and have surprised them both. The historian Barbara Winslow has demonstrated how Sylvia's friendship and later love affair with Keir Hardie 'developed Pankhurst's attitudes towards love, marriage and sexuality as well as her political commitment to socialism and feminism'. Lasting for a decade, from about 1904 to 1913 or 1914, this relationship 'strengthened her political convictions and activism. It enabled her to stand up to her mother and Christabel as they not only broke from socialist politics but also turned on her.'[305] Winslow offers insufficient account of the reciprocal ways in which Sylvia influenced and developed Keir Hardie, but her comprehensive portrayal clearly documents his defining role in her political evolution.

Sylvia knew something of Hardie's background because he'd been a family friend and a constant presence in their lives since childhood. As their intimacy grew in London, he told her more about himself. Born in a two-roomed cottage in North Lanarkshire, near Motherwell, in August 1856, James Keir Hardie was nicknamed Jimmy in his childhood. His mother, Mary Keir, worked as a domestic servant and his stepfather, David Hardie, was a ship's carpenter. His biological father, a Lanarkshire miner named William Aitken from Holytown, had seduced Mary and then abandoned her when she told him she was pregnant. Ignoring her appeals, he refused to take responsibility.

Shortly after her baby's birth, Mary brought a paternity action in the Sheriff's Court against William Aitken. Her claim was accepted and a note of the child's paternity added to the birth certificate. Naming the father was 'a sign of Mary's defiance, and it carried over into the boy's upbringing'.[306] William Aitken had disappeared from the area, and Mary brought up her son as a single mother. In 1859, when Hardie was three years old, Mary met and married David Hardie, from Falkirk. His new stepfather claimed James as his own, and from then onwards he was known and registered as James Keir Hardie.

From the age of seven Jimmy worked for his living and to help support his family. His first job was as a messenger boy for the Anchor Line Steamship Company. Over the next three years he earned a pittance in a series of jobs. He worked as an apprentice in a brass-fitter's shop, and as a baker's messenger boy. After that, he got a job smelting rivets in a shipyard and, next, a job working for a lithographer. The printing industry was a revelation, and he enjoyed the work. At ten, like almost all the other boys in his community, he started his job as a trapper in the mines at the Newarthill Colliery. Simultaneously, he began attending industrial night school in Holytown, encouraged by his mother. He walked to his evening classes directly after his ten-hour shifts.

Mary Keir and David Hardie were highly literate, keen readers and atheists, who abandoned religion under the influence of the freethinker Charles Bradlaugh.[307] They taught Jimmy to read and write as a young child. For a short period, he was able to have school lessons with an evangelical minister called Dan Craig. Even though she was a committed and vocal atheist, his mother approved of him doing this, and anything else that brought him education. Among other skills, Hardie taught himself shorthand, which came in useful in his early trade union days and in his later political career. This self-discipline set his habits for the rest of his life. When he entered parliament, Hardie often left the House at eleven or midnight and put in a few hours' volunteering at the Salvation Army with the unemployed and homeless, then returning to his simple lodgings to deal with his correspondence or write. Like Sylvia, he frequently worked through the night, napping only for an hour or so before heading out again in the morning. It was a way of working that in later years led to illness and shortened his life.

When David Hardie was made redundant, he went away in search of work, leaving young Jimmy in charge. Mary was heavily pregnant and the family had no weekly income. Jimmy became the sole breadwinner, working over twelve hours a day for a wage of three shillings and sixpence a week. With this, he tried to support his mother and all his brothers and sisters in their overcrowded cottage. They were always hungry. During this period, one of his brothers fell ill and died, from lack of food and money to pay for a doctor. This experience haunted Hardie for the rest of his life. He had been in his twenty-third year, he assumed his first ever union role as a miners' agent. He was active in the unions since his adolescence.

From these humble working-class beginnings, James Keir Hardie became the first socialist MP in Britain. He stood for election for the first time in 1888 in the Mid Lanarkshire by-election, and came last. In 1892 he stood in West Ham South on the edge of London, a feeder district densely populated by the marginalized women and men who powered and serviced the capital, 'a little isolated republic outside the vast area of the metropolis' where the factory and dockyard owners swept their 'human rubbish'.[308] This time Hardie won. He took his seat in parliament for the first time on 3 August, and was ridiculed by other MPs for what they regarded as the relative informality of his dress. For two years, he sat completely alone as the sole socialist member in the Commons, learning its procedures. Outside the chamber, he had the social conventions of the Palace of Westminster to contend with. He didn't drink alcohol and seemed in every way eccentric. As the historian John Callow writes, 'It was no wonder that he struck establishment commentators as an exotic, unfathomable and extremist figure, who could be mercilessly lampooned in the press as "queer Hardie" on account of his dress, apparent Bohemianism and counter-cultural ideas.'[309]

A decade after he'd first entered parliament, Westminster was still struggling to get used to him. Hardie recalled an incident from 1906, when he had just become the first leader of the new Labour Party. Just before the opening day of the session, he went to the House of Commons to consult some books in the library, but found himself intercepted in a friendly fashion by a policeman.

'Are you working here mate?'
'Yes.'
'On the roof?' (which was undergoing repairs).
'No, on the floor.'[310]

Hardie was far better read than most of the university men in the Commons, who treated him with blistering contempt in the early days. As Robert Cunninghame Graham observed, 'nothing in his address or speech showed his want of education'.[311] He was knowledgeable, adroit at learning parliamentary procedure and prepared to discuss and debate with anyone on equal terms. His hands were always scrupulously clean, but in the condescending eyes of most of the Tory parliamentary elite they were still covered in coal dust. To the less radical and already threatened Liberals, Hardie presaged political doom. He embodied all the revolutionary terrors that threatened their paternalistic free-trade ideology.

During the winter of 1904, when Hardie stayed in London for the weekend, he took to inviting Sylvia and Harry for Sunday dinners and a walk. 'Keir Hardie gathered us both under his benevolent wing,' Sylvia wrote.[312] He cooked them a simple meal himself over the fireplace that served also as stove and oven at his lodgings in Nevill's Court. A gabled Elizabethan building accessed by a narrow passage off Fetter Lane, Nevill's Court was said to be the oldest inhabited house in London. The late-medieval half-timbered five-storey tenement was around the corner from the offices of the *Labour Leader* and a short walk from parliament. Hardie rented No. 14, a single large room divided by partitions and a curtain into a living room with an open coal fire, a bedroom area and 'a tiny box of a kitchen'.[313] The rent was six shillings and sixpence a week. In the little courtyard outside he grew leeks for eating and sun-coloured gowans – marigolds and mountain daisies – which he arranged in Arts and Craft jugs.[314] Hardie's political friends called it a 'slumland' and 'rabbit warren',[315] but he loved the simplicity. In his view, 'My mansion is perfect.'[316] Sylvia wrote that he lived there with 'extreme frugality, cooking his food, doing his housework, blacking his boots, be it said with care, for he was a model of cleanly neatness'.[317]

Two decades later Sylvia recreated Nevill's Court in minute, accurate detail in the stage directions of a play that she wrote secretly in 1921 while imprisoned in Holloway for sedition. The theatre piece, one of two surviving and before now undocumented and unpublished manuscripts written in pencil on HM Government standard-issue toilet paper, is a long, untitled drama that recounts the interconnected story of the Votes for Women campaigns and the emergence of the Labour Party. It charts the relationships – personal and political – between some of the key characters at the heart of these struggles that both united and divided the movement. The manuscript is incomplete; it was smuggled out of the prison in sections by Sylvia's visitors, chiefly her friend and colleague Norah Smyth. In the play, the fictional lead male character, Noah Adamson, represents the real Keir Hardie.

> Noah's room in London. An old fashioned place with walls painted dark green. In the fireplace a hob. On each side engravings of William Morris, Karl Marx, Robert Owen, Ernest Jones and others. Engravings of incidents of the Chartist struggle etc. A few paintings on the wall opposite the fireplace with hobs on either side. A window seat ... a round table in the centre of the room – arm chairs one either side the fire and two very small round tables.[318]

Also on display were a bas-relief of Walt Whitman, a bust of Emerson and a little iron figure of Dr Johnson.

Beside Hardie's big armchair stood a standard lamp draped with the Union Jack. This was a trophy he had captured in South Africa from a mob of British jingoes, right-wing racists and Conservative activists who invaded one of his anti-racist meetings in Johannesburg.[319] Held throughout the key towns and cities of the country, these meetings were part of a campaign against British imperialism and the South African War. The lamp was never used, as Hardie preferred to work by candlelight.

At his home-cooked Sunday dinners, Keir, Sylvia and Harry shared the memory of the drubbing Harry had received from the other boys at school in Manchester when he spoke out against the war and was carried home unconscious by the headmaster. At the time, Hardie had expressed to Emmeline his admiration for the 'wee bairn's courage'. She responded that she would not have expected her children to do anything less than oppose the imperialist conflict so passionately condemned by her husband when he lived. Solicitous and actively supportive of the family after Richard's death in 1898, Keir looked out for Harry's emotional well-being and future prospects. He became a father figure for Harry.

Mrs Pankhurst's resistance to her son's academic education and her perverse notions about what was best for him for a while blocked Hardie's best efforts to champion Harry's opportunities for book learning, which he so greatly prized himself. To his dismay, Emmeline held him up as a role model for the boy. She was heard often repeating the refrain 'Keir Hardie never went to school.'[320] This she used as justification for her argument that Harry did not need too much formal schooling. She believed that her fragile, sensitive son would find his mettle if only he worked as a gardener, farmer, builder or other kind of manual labourer, just as Hardie had done as a child. His poor eyesight made him ill suited to book learning, she argued. She refused to allow him to be prescribed with spectacles, and when the three sisters challenged her on this, they were ignored. Eventually Keir's arguments, supported by Harry's three sisters, prevailed, and Emmeline relented. Hardie, now London-based, offered to act as his guardian while Harry attended the Hampstead school.

On Sylvia and Harry's visits, Keir served them bread and butter and his homemade Scottish scones, baked in the hearth. They drank tea, which he boiled in a saucepan. All keen walkers who enjoyed greatly the green outdoors, the three rambled on Hampstead Heath near Harry's school. If the weather kept them inside, they read aloud together by Keir's hearth in Nevill's Court, where he laid and lit the fire himself.

He showed them his treasured fossil collection, discovered in the workings when he was a child miner, and shared with them his tactile affection for the coal itself. He told Sylvia how he liked 'the grip of it'.[321] She noticed that he always scrupulously washed his hands immediately after touching it. This was a typically Sylvian observation: she understood the meaning of the journey of Hardie's hands, coal-blackened as a child from labouring deep in the pits to spotlessly clean and neat as an adult in parliament, pristine enough to cover endless pages in writing, read books and handle the piles of paper stacked on the large table at which he worked in Nevill's Court. Sylvia loved drawing with charcoal, a preference that became more pronounced when she began to sketch working-class women at their jobs. The emotional connection between Hardie's appreciation of the physicality of coal as tactile object and his feel for 'the grip of it' seems continuous with Sylvia's relationship to the grip of charcoal in her hand when creating her own artwork depicting manual labour.

As will become clear, most of the people who knew at the time, or in the ensuing years, that Sylvia and Hardie had entered into a love affair took their discretion to the grave. However, though it will never be possible to stamp a date on the secrets of their hearts or the moment of the emotional awakening of their romance, we know for certain that this was the period in which their sexual love affair began.

The records of their day-to-day activities and their correspondence – including postcards and telegrams – arranging to meet in London for a walk, dinner or theatre document the development of the relationship. When they had more time, they met at railway stations and went to the country for a day or overnight, for 'rambles in the weald of Kent'.[322]

Later, in 1911, there was an intense period of explicit love letters exchanged between them while Sylvia travelled in America and Canada. Simultaneously, she started writing a series of unpublished short stories, dream pieces and plays, exploring and recording their intensifying love. This process of writing about their relationship continued long after Hardie's death. In the late 1920s Sylvia's fictionalized writing about Hardie developed into a novel, 'Noah Adamson'. She returned frequently to working on it, but it was never finished. In the early 1930s she started writing about their relationship in her political memoirs and life-writing. She embedded an elegant, telling and unabashed narrative arc about their love and life together in *The Suffragette Movement*. In her unpublished memoir 'The Inheritance', Sylvia describes in more detail their countryside hikes and her visits to his apartment.[323]

As will be seen, Frank Smith, Hardie's loyal friend and political secretary, rejoiced in the mutual happiness Sylvia and Hardie discovered with each other, and feelingly empathized with the torments and despair of their difficult circumstances. He fiercely protected their intimate relationship, the truth of which they shared with him. He adored and respected Hardie and Sylvia both individually and as a couple. Frank Smith's sincere and matter-of-fact acknowledgement of their intimate relationship in his correspondence at the time of Hardie's death was deeply compassionate and carried not a trace of censoriousness.

The bond between Sylvia Pankhurst and Keir Hardie was private, not secret. Her mother and Christabel knew about it. Their trusted friends, many of them leading members of the labour and suffragette movements, knew about it. The need to keep the relationship private was imposed upon them by Hardie's public position as leader of the Labour Party. He was a married man with a family and the majority of his Christian socialist supporters cared about the respectability of such things. Hardie's wife Lillie had long known about her husband's liaisons, which predated Sylvia, and were usually less intense and of shorter duration. Hardie had had an affair with an activist and labour organizer, the Welsh-born Annie Hines, daughter of Alfred Hines, well-known autodidact, atheist, Socialist League member and Fabian Society organizer in Oxford, where he worked as a chimney sweep in several colleges.[324] The established rules of their marriage required that Lillie Hardie remained, indisputably, his wife for life and that their family home must be maintained as a separate sphere from his extramarital spiritual and sexual relationships with other women. Rumour may have reached Lillie that Hardie was now having an affair with Mrs Pankhurst, when in fact he was beginning his relationship with one of her daughters.

Among the trusted friends with whom the couple shared their happiness openly, and with whom they socialized, no one cared or would have thought to remark on the age difference between them. This included seasoned feminists, since so many of them had themselves married mature older men. Common and unremarkable at the time, the near twenty-six year age gap between Sylvia and Hardie echoed as it happened the two decades between Emmeline and Richard Pankhurst. Her mother, as would become evident, disapproved of Sylvia's intimate relationship with Hardie largely because she believed their pillow talk might compromise the political tactics of the suffragette campaign, rather than out of moral or sexual judgement. There is no evidence that Emmeline ever tried to tell Sylvia to stop it, or argue her out of it. Nor did she ever try and intervene with Hardie. She knew both of them well enough to see that it wouldn't make any difference. Moreover, Sylvia's mother had her own passionate preoccupations.

During the spring of 1911 an intensely charged relationship sparked between Emmeline and Ethel Smyth, who became each other's constant companions. When Emmeline wasn't working in London or travelling, they lived together in Ethel's cottage in Woking. They were open about their intimacy, and did not ask or expect their friends or anyone in the movement to regard it as a private matter. 'Ethel fell in love with her, attracted by her "authority" as "master",' writes Emmeline's biographer June Purvis. 'But her account of their friendship is not just that of a "soldier's" view of her general' but that of a 'failed love affair'.[325]

Most historians incline to the conclusion that Emmeline and Ethel were lovers,[326] and certainly that was how many of their contemporaries understood their passionate and companionable affair, including the ever-gossipy Virginia Woolf.[327] Purvis sounds a note of caution, finding it 'highly unlikely' that 'they were lovers in any physical sense'.[328] For her part, Sylvia took it for granted that her mother and Ethel were enjoying a lesbian affair, just as Ethel correctly assumed that she was sleeping with the married, older Keir Hardie. Sylvia described Ethel as 'a being only these islands could have produced. Individualized to the last point, she had in middle age little about her that was feminine. Her features were clean cut and well marked, neither manly nor womanly, her thin hair drawn plainly aside, her speech clear in articulation, and incisive rather than melodious, with a racy wit.'[329] Sylvia wrote fondly of Ethel's 'mannish hat' and 'battered and old' plain country clothes, and of the pride with which she adorned these with a new jacket, tie or other accessory in WSPU colours. She liked Ethel's shaggy Old English sheepdog, Pan, and tellingly remarked on Ethel's 'silent, middle-aged housekeeper, a woman with yellow hair and pallid face, who might have been trusted to keep the secrets of a Bluebeard's chamber'.[330] On balance Sylvia liked and admired Ethel as an individual, but was jealous and resentful of the claim she made on her mother's affection and emotional attention.

As becomes evident in the pages of gossipy correspondence among some of Emmeline's women friends and romantic companions, most volubly Ethel Smyth, there was a prurience and inclination to judgement lacking among Sylvia's and Keir's friends. Ethel Smyth had a motivated self-interest in sowing discord between Emmeline and Sylvia, and so is unreliable on points of fact. However, to her voyeurism and vicious intentions history owes an equivocal debt of gratitude for providing, in the form of salacious gossip in correspondence and memoirs, records of conversations with Emmeline about Sylvia and Hardie. The socialists Emmeline and Fred Pethick-Lawrence were kind, empathic and supportive of Sylvia and Keir; the reactionary Conservative Ethel Smyth, conversely, who assumed the right for herself to live an openly sexually unconventional life, prodded Emmeline with the idea of Sylvia Pankhurst being in bed, literally, with the Labour Party and what she deemed to be socialist patriarchy. Sylvia was sleeping with the enemy. As Barbara Winslow observed, Emmeline, Christabel and some other middle-class suffragettes, 'well aware that the leadership of the Labour Party was indifferent, if not hostile, to the women's suffrage movement, came to see men – especially men in the Labour Party and working-class men – as the enemy'.[331] Perhaps Ethel harboured her own jealousy and mistrust of the long and loyal friendship between Hardie and Emmeline. Later, Ethel Smyth betrayed her prejudice against heterosexuality: 'I couldn't help reminding [Christabel] that I always said … that Sylvia would never fall into line and would always be a difficulty … Sylvia will never be an Amazon. If it isn't JKH it will be somebody else.'[332]

Doubtless Ethel would have disapproved of the company that Sylvia was keeping. Away from parliament, Hardie made Nevill's Court a creative egalitarian factory of socialist ideas and campaigning. To his modest lodgings came the constant footfall of diverse people, socialists and social reformers, Russian exiles, Indian independence activists, anti-segregationists from South Africa and other anti-imperialist politicos, writers, painters, musicians and 'dreamers of dreams'.[333] Hardie's door was open to all, except reactionary journalists. For Sylvia, always welcome, it was a home from home, reminiscent of the times before her father died.

Hardie excluded right-wing journalists because the newspapers they wrote for subjected him to relentless defamation, ridicule, vitriol and verbal assault on behalf of their establishment paymasters who bayed for his blood from the day he entered parliament. The radical political press he loved, and everything to do with the arts and culture. Hardie held good journalism in profound esteem and regarded the principle of a free press as inviolable. His love of books, poetry and reading, combined with his experience working for a lithographer in his youth, sparked his deep fascination and love for printing, draughtsmanship and graphic arts. All of these passions were Sylvia's too.

Sharing and discussing their reading was central to Sylvia and Hardie's relationship. The books they gifted one another and exchanged between themselves chart a bibliography of love. The books Hardie gave Sylvia, some of which are preserved in her archive held in Amsterdam, tell their own story, as a few examples show.

On 8 March 1907, Hardie presented Sylvia with a first edition of his newly published book, *From Serfdom to Socialism*, published in London by George Allen in their socialist series, The Labour Ideal. Sylvia's treasured copy is heavily annotated, underlined and filled with her marginalia. Its pages marked up in several different pencil weights as well as black ink, she clearly read the book repeatedly. In 1909 he gave her a gorgeous hand-illuminated edition of Cennino Cennini's 1437 *Treatise on Painting*, with an inscription from his favourite poet,

Robert Burns. The lines, written in black fountain pen in Hardie's elegant cursive, are from Burns' famous 'Ae Fond Kiss': 'Thine be ilka joy and pleasure / Peace, contentment, love and treasure.' Hardie retains the original Middle English 'ilka' used by Burns, rather than Anglicizing it to 'every'. Hardie, not a rich man, lavished this exquisite and expensive gift on Sylvia at exactly the time that her dilemma over whether she should be artist or activist was at its most acute. As their correspondence and Sylvia's autobiography record, he profoundly respected and defended her creative right to be an artist and repeatedly tried to persuade her to stay out of prison and work on her art – advice she ignored.

For her thirty-first birthday in 1913, he gave her a beautiful edition of Maeterlinck's wildly successful play *The Blue Bird*. The book is leather-bound in finest indigo-blue calf. A hand-tooled gold-leaf bird flies towards the title on the front cover of this 'fairy play in six acts', translated by Alexander Teixeira de Mattos and published by Methuen in London. Hardie inscribed the simple words, 'S, with Love, K'. The capitalized L of 'Love' is written with an elaborate flourish. Maeterlinck's *L'Oiseau bleu* is about chasing happiness. It tells the story of a girl called Mytyl and her brother Tyltyl, whose quest for happiness is assisted by a good fairy called Bérylune. A parable of rich and poor, luxury and simplicity, envy and empathy, love and letting go, the play enjoyed phenomenal success when first staged at the Haymarket Theatre in London in 1909. Sylvia and Hardie saw the premiere together. The date of his gift and what Hardie is expressing by it is unbearably poignant. By Sylvia's choice and instigation, 1913 would mark the beginning of the end of their intimate love and romantic relationship.

All this was yet to come. Back in the winter of 1904, Sylvia and Hardie were privately embarking on one of the most sensational political love matches of the early twentieth century. Sylvia's college friends speculated on why she didn't have, like them, 'a special man friend'. 'Suitor' was too old fashioned a term for these bohemian young Edwardian art students, and 'boyfriend' had yet to arrive in the English language from America. However you described your romantic interest, Sylvia didn't seem to have one. Or if she did, it was something that she did not talk about to them.

8

Queer Hardie

Before long, Sylvia was frequently at Hardie's rooms at 14 Nevill's Court on days other than Sunday, and without Harry.

Usually Sylvia and Hardie arranged to get together via short messages on cards sent by the penny post. They met at Nevill's Court, or at one of the new Lyons restaurants. Both enjoyed tête-à-têtes walking together in one their favourite London parks. When a window of opportunity for more time together opened, they could take a train to the country for a long afternoon hike. Hardie played games, like juggling or skimming with stones, insisting she should try. She did, and they found she was 'utterly incapable'.

> 'Did you not play when you were a child?' he asked me. 'All the little girls do it!' I answered: 'You know I never played games!' 'Ah!' he said, with infinite compassion and tenderness, 'that is what is the matter with you! You heard too much serious talk; children ought not to be brought up like that.'[334]

A few years later, an interviewer in Kansas asked her if she 'ever had time for a girl's fun, parties for instance'. Sylvia laughed, 'Oh, I announced to my mother when I was ten years old that I wasn't going to accept any invitations to parties.'[335]

Hardie talked to Sylvia further about his own childhood. Her mother made almost a cult of his autodidacticism, citing him as living proof that there was absolutely no need for conventional education. The school of life, Mrs Pankhurst argued, was the supreme learning

institution. As they walked and talked together, Hardie shared with
Sylvia more tales of his tough upbringing. His mother, whom he
revered, dominated the stories. 'She was no ordinary woman,' Hardie's
sister later confirmed to Sylvia. When as a child he fell ill, she tramped
all the way to Glasgow with him on her back to get him to hospital.
As a little lad, he remembered standing with his mother and siblings in
the road beside their small pile of household items – evicted from their
home. The boss rode by on his horse, and told his mother she might
return to her cottage if her husband would give up the trade union.
'Nay, nay, he'll ne'er do that!' his mother replied.[336]

Hardie told Sylvia about the distant country of his childhood,
unknown to her. But he was an integral character in the landscape of
her early years. Sylvia recalled vividly her girlhood excitement about a
visit when she was – by her own recollection – about twelve or thirteen
years old:

> Keir Hardie was coming! I hastened from school. He was in the big
> armchair, a sturdy figure in a rough, brown, homespun jacket, with
> a majestic head, the brow massive, the gold-brown eyes deep-set.
> Venerable age, vigorous youth seemed blended in him. The strength
> of a rock, the ruggedness of a Scotch moorland, the sheltering
> kindness of an oak, the gentleness of a great St. Bernard dog – these
> similes float through the mind in thought of him.[337]

After her father's death, Hardie was a regular and solicitous visitor to
the Pankhurst home. He and Emmeline worked together on political
campaigns. Sometimes he chaperoned her at social events. Some
people assumed a more intimate relationship between the glamorous
emancipationist widow and the glad-eyed labour leader, particularly
because of the marriage between their political projects. There was a
romance about the idea of Hardie and Mrs Pankhurst being a socialist
love match. The middle-class radical widow and the working-class
political hero, their love child votes for women. However, theirs was
a strong and valued intimate friendship and nothing more. Both had
good rapports with members of the other sex.

Emmeline's view of the influence Hardie came to exercise over her
most difficult daughter was to be another matter entirely. For now, she
regarded him as a family friend *in loco parentis* for Sylvia and Harry in
London. At first no one except those they confided in thought or judged

their relationship to be otherwise. In time, a crisis would develop over the liaison between Sylvia and married father Hardie with far-reaching consequences for her life.

'Like the bit and brace, Keir Hardie and the Pankhursts seemed wrought to work in unison,' Sylvia wrote.[338] As the nature of their bond changed, so too did the varied implications of the simile.

Sylvia introduced Keir Hardie to coffee. In November 1904 they saw Shaw's new comedy *John Bull's Other Ireland* at the Royal Court Theatre and afterwards went for a meal at a nearby restaurant in Sloane Square. When Sylvia asked for a black coffee, Hardie was stunned.[339] Coffee became his favourite beverage. Like Sylvia, an abstaining workaholic, it boosted his long hours toiling through the night. In the unpublished manuscript of her romantic political drama written in prison in 1921, after his death, Sylvia (Freda) and Hardie (Noah) reminisce in a scene set in Nevill's Court:

Noah: Do you remember the first time we had coffee?
Freda: … you were so much astonished not long ago when you found I took coffee without milk that evening in the restaurant in Sloane Square after we'd been to the Court Theatre.
Noah: I was I admit I was as much astonished as if you'd called for a cigar.
Freda: Why?
Noah: Well I was.
Freda: Do you remember that day I fainted.
Noah: I do indeed!
Freda: You looked so terribly upset! Well do you know I should have liked to ask for some brandy but I was afraid you'd be shocked.
Noah: Not at all.
Freda: But you didn't offer me any.
Noah: I never thought of it.
Freda: I believe you would have been shocked. It's only about two or three years since you thought the theatre a wicked place isn't it.
Noah: Oh you'll have to add a nought to that.
Freda: 20 or 30 years ago! Oh it isn't nearly as long as that you know it isn't.[340]

That they went to watch Shaw's political satire on the 'Irish question' together marks the fact that Hardie came to theatre late, led there by the Pankhursts. Brought up in the Calvinistic atmosphere of a Scottish village, he never experienced theatre until his middle age. It was Sylvia's mother who was one of the first to encourage him to enter a playhouse, playfully persuading him to be her chaperone to an entertainment during an ILP conference in a provincial town. New writers like Ibsen and Galsworthy and classics like Shakespeare (whom he'd previously encountered only on the page) subsequently opened up to him brave new worlds. He became a regular and enthusiastic theatregoer.

When the ILP executive held meetings in London, Hardie organized entertainments for the members. They went to see *Romeo and Juliet*, and Hardie's wingman, Frank Smith, a committed socialist, Christian and middle-class man of means, surprised Sylvia by enquiring who was the author of the play. Hardie often cited Ibsen to describe his perspective of himself: 'The strongest man in the world is he who stands most alone.' This telling line he took from *An Enemy of the People*, premiered in London the year of Sylvia's birth, translated by Eleanor Marx. The reference demonstrated Hardie's self-awareness of the essence of his own character.

Trips together to the theatre continued to be an important pleasure for Sylvia and Hardie throughout their shifting relationship. In a letter from America written to Hardie early in 1912, she referred to their friend Israel Zangwill's anti-war drama *The War God*, premiered at His Majesty's Theatre in November 1911. Sylvia knew Hardie would get the shorthand reference, suggesting that they'd seen it together or had discussed it. Between 1904 and 1914, Sylvia and Hardie were much out and about in public. They attended political meetings together, took tea on the terrace of the House of Commons, strolled in St James's Park between his parliamentary sessions and went to the theatre. They walked in Kensington Gardens when she lived for a while near there, or in Richmond Park when she went regularly to visit him convalescing for several months at the Roebuck Hotel on Richmond Hill. Nevill's Court was their sanctuary, a place of shared sociability with trusted friends and political colleagues, and where they could be alone in the delights of their newfound intimacy.

Political activism swiftly dominated Sylvia's extracurricular activities. This was a part of, not separate from, her relationship with Hardie.

It would be impossible to put a hair's breadth between their shared commitment to their ideals and their love for one another.

Sylvia had already many friends in the activist world and it was easier to make new ones in this environment than at the RCA. During her first year at college, Sylvia joined the Fulham branch of the ILP. Soon afterwards she received an invitation to debate with Margaret Bondfield on the subject of votes for women. A trade unionist and women's rights activist, Maggie Bondfield had a background in the shopworkers' unions. (She was destined to become, in 1929, the first female member of a British cabinet as Minister of Labour in Ramsay MacDonald's second administration, and Britain's first woman Privy Councillor.) She was a very brilliant and strikingly beautiful socialist activist.

Little practised in public speaking and awed by Bondfield's impressive reputation, Sylvia begged her older friend Isabella Bird to speak in her stead. The suffragist and socialist Isabella commanded a leading voice in the ILP and held the distinction of having been the first woman ever to speak at the LRC conference.

As the debate got under way, Sylvia – mortified – realized her tactical error and sat in the audience burning with indignation. The fresh, young Maggie Bondfield appeared glowing in an attractive pink outfit. She had worked from an early age in haberdashery and clothing retail, and always looked stylish and well turned out, with dusky eyes and a deep, throaty voice to top the already impressive bill. Charming and vivacious, she took all the shots that her youth and prettiness could win for her against plain, middle-aged Isabella, with her ruddy face and woefully outdated Victorian turban hat crushed down over her straight, undressed hair. Sylvia's heart went out to her, 'whose nature seemed to me so much kindlier and more profound than that of her younger protagonist'.[341] Maggie Bondfield mocked the idea of votes for women as the hobby of disappointed old spinsters whom nobody wanted to marry. What women required, she said, was not votes, but industrial organization.[342] If they were to vote at all, it must be on the basis of adult suffrage – but either way suffrage was of little importance to women.

Pained and enraged, Sylvia wished she had fought Bondfield herself rather than subjecting their old family friend Isabella to this humiliation. 'My heart was in adult suffrage, but this sort of argument was destructive of any sort of enfranchisement.'[343] Youth, vivacity, a pretty face and a well-turned-out appearance would win out over any argument based on logic, justice or reason made by a plain old maid in an outdated hat. The event proved a subtle but significant turning point; Sylvia learned an important political lesson.

Typically, it was an experience she acted on immediately. Just a few weeks later Sylvia accepted an invitation from Dora Montefiore to attend an open-air Sunday rally in Ravenscourt Park in west London. Dora, a friend from Manchester, apologized to Sylvia as soon she turned up. A sudden rain shower had driven the other speakers into the nearest tea shop and Dora was on the verge of picking up her chair and going home. 'We can't give it up!' Sylvia said. Well, in that case you had better take the chair and speak yourself, Dora replied. Sylvia's heart thumped, but her voice was clear and steady and she managed to catch the ear of the Sunday strollers, a few of whom lingered to listen. Her level-headed assessment was that the event seemed tame enough when over, 'ground neither for nervousness nor elation'.[344] But she had stood her ground and spoken. After the Bondfield debacle, Sylvia never again shied away from the responsibility to speak when called upon, however nervous or reluctant she felt.

Margaret and Ramsay MacDonald regularly invited Sylvia to their 'At Homes' at their flat in Lincoln's Inn Fields, busy with their expanding tribe of small children. Sylvia observed that although Margaret's life was eased by 'a substantial unearned income',[345] she had not escaped the double burden experienced by mothers busy outside the home with work, politics and public life. Margaret MacDonald was always in a hurry, and was often to be seen with her blouse on back to front, several buttons undone and its hem riding up over her skirt. One evening, taking off her coat in a bedroom of their flat, Sylvia heard a muffled protest from the bed, and found that the guests had been piling up their coats on top of two sleeping little MacDonalds.

Sylvia met several interesting people for the first time at the MacDonalds'. Emily Hobhouse, just returned from South Africa, told her about her work with the Afrikaners left destitute after the Boer War. During the war she'd reported from inside the British internment centres where Boer women faced squalor, starvation, disease and death, bringing the existence of the concentration camps to the world's attention for the first time. At this first meeting, she also asked Sylvia's advice about where she might find good designs for lace-making.

Hobhouse became an enduring friend and political ally, particularly in their shared involvement in the struggle against imperialism. The Russian literary translator Aylmer Maud interrupted them to talk about Tolstoy.

Not all Sylvia's social life was so enjoyable. Sometimes on Sundays she visited Aunt Mary, now Mrs Clarke, in a depressed south-east London suburb. Though Mary's husband was charming to Sylvia, she sensed that all was not well with her mild and gentle aunt. The husband had adopted a traumatized immigrant street child, whom Mary struggled to manage. A few Saturdays later, Sylvia found her suspicions confirmed. Receiving an urgent note from Aunt Mary telling her that she had left home, she instantly set off to help her and found her huddled in the back room of filthy dilapidated lodgings, clutching the child in a blanket. Mary had no money and no furniture – not even a bed. Sylvia gave her some cash and arranged for a bed to be sent over the next day. Mary went back to her violent alcoholic husband shortly afterwards, but only for a while. She left him again, turned up on Emmeline's doorstep in Manchester, became active in the WSPU and never returned to the abusive marriage.

From Margaret MacDonald to Aunt Mary, Sylvia encountered the difficulties faced by married women, whatever their class.

By the end of 1904, Sylvia had found her feet. She moved to better lodgings at Park Cottage, Park Walk, Chelsea, a street running between the King's Road and Fulham Road. She rented two rooms, 'one unfurnished, and therefore happily free from bric-à-brac'.[346] This was a wonderful development: she now had her own studio. Her Cockney landlords, Mr and Mrs Roe, professional tailors specializing in riding breeches, considered a Tory government always better for business. But Sylvia soon discovered that Mrs Roe responded enthusiastically to the ideas of votes for women, labour and socialism.

Park Walk was not posh. Lodgers and subtenants from different backgrounds rubbed along together, many of them young bohemian artists like Sylvia, whose neighbours were working women and men bringing up large families on limited incomes.[347] Musicians, writers, architects, actors and designers lived alongside soldiers, gas stokers, caretakers and valets. The already infamous Chelsea Arts Club was a stroll of a few minutes from Sylvia's new lodgings. Instigated by the painter James Whistler in March 1891, the Chelsea Arts Club had moved from its original premises on the King's Road to 143 Church Street in 1902. There was a Ladies' Bar for female guests. Membership was opened to women in 1966, six years after Sylvia's death. This might sound late in the day, but relative to other London-based men-only clubs, the Chelsea Arts Club was one of the first to open membership to women.

Sylvia felt at home in Park Walk. She invited her women friends from college to come round to the cottage on Saturday afternoons to paint with her, each taking turns to pose for the rest, since they were not allowed female models in their life-drawings classes at the RCA. She'd found a new friend in the flaxen-haired, flâneurish form of Austin Osman Spare. Spare produced wildly weird work and dressed in an avant-garde get-up of flowing white shirts and red sashes like Lord Byron in his Greek Revolutionary period. He held a deep fascination for the occult, about which he later wrote books in which Sylvia appeared. He also drew a wonderful portrait of her in 1953.[348] Fellow rebels, the two idiosyncratically dressed art students became a familiar sight on the King's Road, often accompanied by another new intimate college friend of Sylvia's, the ethereal Amy Browning. Amy, a passionate feminist, objected to the discrimination against women students, but was no campaigner.

The young women talked long into the night. Sylvia worried about the call of social conscience – was it right that they dedicate themselves to creativity and beauty while the world suffered in abject misery? Amy had no idea why her friend felt this dilemma. Others must solve the problems of the world; they were surely dedicated only to their art? These proved lasting relationships. For the rest of Sylvia's life Austin and Amy continued to be among her closest and most loyal friends.

Just as Sylvia was settled in, enjoying the life of the artist and student activist, Hardie's constant attention and her new circle of friends, her mother descended from Manchester announcing her intention to stay. Emmeline arrived at Park Cottage in February 1905, causing instant disruption. Sylvia apologized to the alarmed Roes for the stream of new visitors, loud discussion and her mother's toing and froing from parliament and political meetings at irregular hours. Often Emmeline returned late at night, swirling with adrenaline, unable to eat properly or settle and sleep, pacing the rooms and pouring out her anxieties, agitation and elation to Sylvia, who made her mother cups of soothing hot chocolate and silently fretted about being able to get enough sleep and be up on time for her 8.30 a.m. classes.

Emmeline had come to London to lobby for the introduction of the Votes for Women Bill, which Hardie agreed to introduce if he could get it on to the Friday-afternoon private members' bill ballot. Sylvia was already busy supporting Hardie in his battle for rights for the unemployed. At last, the King's Speech contained a promise of legislation and the ILP were full steam ahead. At a weekend's notice, Hardie commissioned Sylvia to design a poster campaign for plastering the city with demands for the enactment of the Unemployed Workmen Bill. In the event, there wasn't time for the poster campaign, so her drawing was turned into swiftly distributed propaganda postcards, bearing her new signature monogram E.S.P.

Modernist in line, simple and strong, the drawing depicts a demonstration of female and male workers shoulder to shoulder. They are led by a woman in a white shawl and red apron and a man in his shirtsleeves, jointly holding aloft a black and white placard bearing the slogan 'Workers are Hungry. Vote for the Bill'. Behind it, outlined by a cloud, the edge of another poster is just visible: 'We demand the Right to Work'.[349] Another pen-and-ink sketch entitled 'Feed My Lambs', also used as a postcard for this campaign, depicts a statuesque woman clasping two children to her and feeding them from a pitcher of milk.

Emmeline rebuffed these efforts as a waste of time. She told Hardie that he'd got his priorities wrong. Employment reforms – and all the other reforms – would become a matter of course once women had won the vote. Racked by her conscience for missing college and falling behind on her practice, Sylvia reluctantly accompanied her mother daily to the House of Commons lobby, waiting to leap up and plead their cause to every member who passed. Emmeline was implacable, with good reason. The Liberal Party remained obdurate in its policy of supporting adult suffrage for men only. The very likely arrival of a Liberal government at the next general election meant that the 'Woman Question' would once again be kicked into the long grass. There was no time left: the women's suffrage campaign had dragged on unsuccessfully for more than sixty years. Richard Pankhurst would have been appalled that five years into the twentieth century women still did not have the vote. It had to happen now.

Hardie failed to secure a place in the ballot for the bill in February 1905. Alert to how the marvellous new technology of the telephone accelerated the process of getting things done, Emmeline immediately 'phoned' her feminist friend Alice Bamford Slack, married to the Liberal MP John Bamford Slack. Between them, they persuaded him to take up their bill, which stated that, in all legislation concerning the qualifications for voting, words of the masculine gender should be held to include women. It was the old legal formula used by Richard Pankhurst and the suffragists for decades during the nineteenth century, and a comfortable enough fudge for Bamford Slack to secure sufficient votes to get second place in the order of the day on Friday 12 May. Emmeline returned to Manchester to build the campaign. She didn't seem to have noticed the change in the relationship between Sylvia and Hardie. They had worked together for so long they all felt like family.

Mrs Pankhurst came back to London in May and worked with Hardie to try and manoeuvre their bill into first place. Sylvia spent the intervening time travelling all over London by bus, from meeting to meeting, rally to rally, raising support for the proposed legislation. Alone, she went to a NUWSS gathering and observed in quiet amusement the contrast between the polite discretion of proceedings in the hands of the genteel Millicent Fawcett and the rousing, robust socialist meetings with which she was now more familiar.

Women's organizations from all over the country and abroad excitedly converged on Westminster for the May vote, but their overflowing, pressing presence in Parliament Square, the lobby and every public corridor was ignored by the male members inside the chamber. The bill was 'talked out' (or 'filibustered') with its opponents deliberately speaking for so long that it was impossible to make progress. The House adjourned. Furious with disappointment, Emmeline returned home to regroup.

By the time Sylvia got back to Manchester for the summer holidays, the move towards women's militancy was gaining momentum. She had planned to pass the summer painting, drawing and working on her graphic skills, but it turned out that she spent her entire vacation travelling from one Lancashire town to another attending open-air meetings in train with a group of working women, Christabel and the Manchester and Salford Women's Trade Union Council.

When she arrived home, Christabel and her mother introduced her to a platoon of new WSPU members, whose language, mood and style were markedly different from the old NUWSS leaders. Annie Kenney, a millworker since the age of ten, with a magnificent gift for oratory, a cloud of golden hair and a missing finger torn out by a factory machine, was the new star speaker and mass mobilizer of the group. Annie found her way to the women's movement through the ILP. The schoolteacher Teresa – 'Tess' – Billington, drummed out of elementary teaching by the education authorities because of her refusal to teach religious instruction, matched her large, powerfully built physique with an elemental force of argument and relentless organizational skills, though in Sylvia's opinion she lacked the emotional quality required for great oratory. A self-declared New Woman, Tess refused to make any feminine pretence of subordinating herself to others in thought or deed. She had the fighting impulse and the fists usually ascribed to masculinity, and a deft ability to return blow for blow, as would soon be revealed. When Tess married Frederick Greig in 1907, she refused to give up her surname, so the couple joined their names together and she became forever after Teresa Billington-Greig – known to all as TBG.

Flora Drummond, later dubbed 'the General', was a favourite with Sylvia. Flora possessed a prodigious talent for ingenious interventions and public stunts, a fondness for peaked caps, epaulettes, military outfits and riding a horse at the head of demonstrations flourishing a baton. A native of the island of Arran, she had a standing grudge against the government because, after working hard to qualify as a postmistress, she was disqualified by the sudden raising of the minimum height required for the job. On a holiday trip to Arran, a journeyman upholsterer caused a stir on the sleepy isle by falling off the steamer into the sea and shortly afterwards into stout Flora's arms. They married and she returned with him to Manchester where she trained as a typist and landed a coveted job at the Oliver typewriting office. Flora made a point of telling younger women that it was her husband who had first sent her off to socialist protest meetings, as a result of which she became one of the founding members of the ILP. A rough-and-tumble comedian type, full of self-assurance and audacity, she could always make an audience laugh. Her ebullient fallabout jocularity masked an astute genius for organizing and directing and a sure eye for creating political spectacle.

The WSPU commenced militant agitation in the autumn of 1905. The tipping point came after the infamous Liberal Party meeting on 13 October at Manchester's Free Trade Hall, site of the Peterloo massacre almost a century earlier. Sir Edward Grey, a potential cabinet minister, was the keynote speaker. Grey's wife Dorothy was known to be an ardent feminist. Prior to his arrival, the WSPU asked him to receive a women's deputation while he was in Manchester. Foolishly, he refused. A rising star of the Liberal Party, the young Winston Churchill, prospective candidate for Manchester North West, also attended the meeting, surrounded by a posse of admiring constitutional suffragist women. Sylvia remained unconvinced by Churchill's lip service to women's rights, judging him 'a notorious weathercock in his utterances on votes for women (and much else!)'.[350]

After Grey had finished speaking, making no mention of women's rights, Annie Kenney and Christabel interrupted proceedings, rising and asking the question, 'Will a Liberal Government give women the vote?' There was no answer, except from the stewards who ejected them from the meeting and beat up Annie. In the resulting rumpus, both young women were arrested, shouting 'Votes for Women!'

The next day Christabel was charged with spitting in the face of a police inspector and ordered to pay a fine of ten shillings or go to prison. Annie had the choice of a five-shilling fine or three days in prison.

Naturally both chose jail.

The local press supported them staunchly, but most of the nationals unplugged a sewer of unreserved hostility. The *Daily Mail* sneered, 'If any argument were required against giving to ladies political status and power, it has been furnished in Manchester.' The London *Evening Standard* patronized Christabel, claiming that she had demonstrated her infantile attitude by choosing to go to prison instead of paying the fine like any 'mature and sensible' woman would have done. She deserved the punishment that was 'the lot of children in the nursery'.[351] Owens College later threatened Christabel with expulsion unless she refrained from causing further political disturbance until after she'd completed her law degree.

A month later on 4 December, Arthur Balfour's Conservative government resigned and the general election campaign commenced. The Liberal Party called a mass meeting at the Albert Hall to be attended by all its leaders. Entry was strictly by ticket only. Christabel wrote urgently to Sylvia instructing her to get as many tickets as possible. But there was a tremendous rush on seats and Sylvia could secure tickets only by agreeing that she and a friend would come to rehearsals of

Liberal campaign songs and sing in the choir for the rally. The friend, of course, was Annie Kenney, who was staying with her at Park Walk. Along with a group of Annie's friends in the East End unemployed workers' movement, the women – singing lustily – caused so much commotion at the choir rehearsals that the offer of entry to the big meeting was swiftly withdrawn.

Keir Hardie came to the rescue by managing to wangle a batch of tickets, some of which, the women discovered to their delight, were seats for the private box allocated to John Burns. The position of a box in the Albert Hall presented the perfect opportunity for a suffragette stunt. Sylvia got to work designing the posters, scrolls, calico flags and banners that her friends would hide in their clothes and then unfurl in the hall. This included a giant nine-foot centrepiece to be unfurled directly from the balcony of John Burns' box.

Annie and her accomplices, including Tess Billington, used their tickets to gain entrance. Sylvia, too easily recognized, was barred from entry to the main hall. Once again, Annie Kenney led the women in interrupting the massive meeting to ask the now famous question, 'Will the Liberal government give votes to women?' Once again, there came no reply, in response to which Annie unfurled a white calico flag painted in black letters with the slogan 'Votes for Women'. Simultaneously the group of women at the other end of the hall, led by TBG, let down Sylvia's huge banner from John Burns' box printed with the legend 'Will the Liberal Government give Justice to Working Women?' Pandemonium ensued and the women were ejected from the Albert Hall.

The very next day Sylvia went home for Christmas. As she travelled north, so did Winston Churchill, on his way to speak at Liberal meetings and to canvass in his Manchester North West constituency. The WSPU determined that its members would be present at every meeting. Sylvia spent the festivities engaged day and night in the tedious business of handpainting hundreds of white calico banners with 'Votes for Women' and 'Will the Liberal Government give Women the Vote?' The banners were always snatched away and destroyed as soon as they were displayed, so it was necessary to prepare a great quantity laboriously by hand without any means of mechanical reproduction.

Churchill held his first election campaign meeting of 1906 at a school in Cheetham Hill. Sylvia and Harry attended, flanked by a group of

ILP working men. Sylvia asked Churchill the question leading Liberal MPs now feared most at public meetings. Churchill attempted to ignore her completely. But Harry and the ILP heckled, demanding that Sylvia receive an answer. In the ensuing clamour, Churchill was unable to continue with his speech. Sylvia asked her question for a second time and again he blanked it. The stewards moved to throw her out, but the hall was tightly packed and the ILP working men surrounded her and formed a barrier around her.

Unable to regain control of the meeting, the chairman asked Sylvia to approach and put her question from the platform, which she did, speaking for a few minutes in the continuing uproar. As she turned to leave the stage, Churchill grabbed her roughly by the arm and manhandled her into a chair at the back of the platform, snarling at her to stay put there until she had listened to his reply. Addressing the audience, he berated Sylvia Pankhurst in her hometown for 'bringing disgrace upon an honoured name', and declared dramatically, 'Nothing would induce me to vote for giving women the franchise. I am not going to be henpecked into a question of such importance.'[352]

Sylvia tried again to step down from the platform, but all the men on it stood up and barred her way. Two of the Liberal organizers pushed her into an anteroom with barred windows. One of them screamed at her, jumping about manically, leering at her, calling her a cat and threatening to scratch her face. His incipient violence caused Sylvia to shout out loudly to the passers-by in the street, 'I want you to be a witness of anything that takes place in this room!'[353] A crowd gathered outside, pressing their faces against the barred window, upon which her crazed assailant withdrew from the room, locking her in.

Her supporters noticed another window at the other end of the room with a few bars missing and, with all the excitement of a silent motion-picture caper, Sylvia wriggled and pushed her way out of the window as they pulled her from the outside. A chair was brought, from which she delivered a rousing speech and the gathering turned into a protest, undeterred by the freezing January cold.

Sylvia refused to be intimidated by the rough handling she'd received. Pugnaciously, she responded with levity. 'Of course,' she told the press, 'Mr Churchill found me again at his next meeting. It was the cause of much mirth.'[354] The press loved her story, producing innumerable jokes at Churchill's expense.

Sylvia, Adela and Annie Kenney followed Churchill to every subsequent meeting that he gave in Manchester, relentlessly presenting their question. There was no more kidnapping, and although they were sometimes roughly handled, the Manchester audiences so largely supported them that, if they were ejected by stewards, the people tended to protect them and follow them out of the hall. On several occasions, Churchill found himself left with only his bodyguard to listen to him.

The encounters between Sylvia and Churchill during that winter of 1906 shaped a mutual enmity that followed Churchill for the rest of his political life. Unfortunately for the future Prime Minister, Sylvia would turn out to be his most vocal and active critic in his future London constituency of Woodford. In many ways Churchill intrigued Sylvia, who had a good instinct for understanding worthy opponents. Fools were dismissed, ignored and soon forgotten. Sylvia understood Churchill's intelligence and wit and didn't hold his aristocratic background against him. That sort of class prejudice wasn't her way. From her childhood days attending her parents' Manchester and London meetings and salons at home, she'd met many people from privileged backgrounds who had been able to overcome them and put themselves and their money and social power to good use. Naturally, Sylvia wouldn't much like Churchill's militarism, but that was still to come, and, in his favour, his journalism had been critical of the South African War. In these days of early feminist militancy, it was the combination of Churchill's raw ambition and disdain for women not subordinated in service to him that betrayed the man:

> I felt a contemptuous interest in seeing the desperate eagerness of
> the candidate to win the election, his uncontrolled exasperation
> at our interruptions and arrogant determination not to deal with
> us as he did with other questioners. There was a spice of poignant
> satisfaction in spoiling his meeting as a punishment for his insulting
> attitudes towards women and women's claims. Then the whole
> thing would appear to me as a sordid business, and I would wish
> myself out of it for the rest of my life.[355]

The conflicting reactions Sylvia expressed here are revealing. On the one hand, she was beginning to enjoy the elemental drive of political drama and its call to constant action. She was discovering, perhaps to her surprise, that she had a strong stomach for political combat. Though she abhorred all forms of physical violence, she wasn't deterred by it.

Sylvia was drawn to the frank traffic of political debate and recognized in it the possibility for channelling and regulating the sporting competitiveness and aggression of human nature that otherwise spilled over into war. On the other hand, she would recoil from the extreme passion of her own engagement and the bald offensiveness of the fray. It was not simply that activism diverted her time and energies from practising art for art's sake; it was her awareness that the passion and intensity of those energies were, for her, indivisible.

This was the inviolable legacy of her father: community and service with and for others must come before self-interest. For some, like Churchill, entry into establishment politics and leadership was an inherited birthright paving the way to further self-advancement. That was not the nature of Sylvia's political inheritance. A creative thinker driven by her visions, her quest was to find the best way to realize them. Hers was the pragmatism and practicality of the maker. Her temperament was suited to the life of the socially engaged artist and writer, but the moment in history and family into which she was born made that impossible.

Sylvia combined the life of the apprentice artist with her political activity, working with her mother, sisters and Hardie in the rapidly escalating suffragette struggle. At first, there had been no dilemma. Her talents as a painter, graphic artist and writer dovetailed with her activist world, as she showed creative flair for applying the skills and values of each to the other. She worked hard at developing her artistic technique and in her writing experimented across genres. By now, she had written plays, poetry, essays, short stories and a few draft novels.

In the epoch in which Sylvia grew up, art was a way of looking at the world directly, not looking away. In Sylvia's youth, late Victorian radicals rooted in the Romantic tradition did not think of art and politics as mutually exclusive activities. At any rate, Sylvia did not know how to look away. There was no need. Her mother was supportive and even Christabel understood that Sylvia's art was her means of self-expression. At the beginning unconfident of her talents, she benefited from the active encouragement of her mother and close family friends, especially Hardie, Charles Rowley and her first tutor, their former neighbour

Elias Bancroft. She had the support of some eminent patrons, and the opportunity to study at two of the leading art schools in Britain.

But in 1906 Sylvia's priorities were forced into irreducible tension. In response to the founding of the Labour Party, Sylvia asked, 'What would that Party do for women?'[356] As the militant struggle forced itself to the centre of the British political stage, her sense of dilemma grew. 'Is it just that we should be permitted to devote our entire lives to the creation of beauty, whilst others are meshed in monotonous drudgery?'[357] The external pressures bearing upon her to balance her life between her art and her politics now showed signs of developing into an internalized emotional conflict.

9

The Labour Party – Our Party …
a Reality at Last!

Polling for the momentous 1906 general election took place between 12 January and 6 February. Two days before the polls opened, the *Daily Mail*'s war correspondent Charles Hands coined the word 'suffragette' to describe the militant Pankhurst-led 'ladies' of the Women's Social and Political Union. It was not meant as a compliment. Hands intended to insult, but the WSPU gamely took an instant liking to the term. As Christabel pointed out, it threw emphasis on the direct militant action of 'getting' votes rather than the abstract conceptual 'gist' of meandering hopefully towards enfranchisement by polite gradualist means:

> There was a spirit in it, a spring that we liked. Suffragists, we
> had called ourselves till then, but that name lacked the positive
> note implied by 'Suffragette'. Just 'want the vote' was the notion
> conveyed by the older appellation and, as a famous anecdote had it,
> 'the Suffragettes [hardening the "g"] they mean to get it'.[358]

It is a measure of the prominence of the issue that votes for women and the new militant campaign made popular press headlines in the days running up to the election. Sylvia, back for the new term at the RCA, stood outside the *Daily News* offices in Fleet Street all night watching the results posted in the window. Nearby, Emmeline Pethick-Lawrence, soon to enter Sylvia's life, watched from the roof garden of her flat in Clement's Inn as the results were projected by lantern slide on an elevated white board in the Strand.[359] Sylvia counted with mounting excitement as Hardie's LRC won an unprecedented number of seats. 'The Labour party – our Party ... was a reality at last!'[360] It was a landslide for the Liberals, but the emerging Labour Party had won twenty-nine seats and taken a breathtaking increase of the Liberal vote. Hardie's radical LRC group ran fifty candidates in the election and trebled its share of the vote to 5.9 per cent. Ten per cent of MPs were now working class. Hardie's friend and ILP supporter Emmeline Pethick-Lawrence measured the scale of the political victory: 'A party of only one had increased thirty-fold between 1900 and 1906.'[361]

Born in Bristol in 1867, Emmeline Pethick was the second of thirteen children. Her father, a businessman, was proprietor of the *Western Gazette* newspaper, a socialist and devout Methodist. Emmeline went to boarding school in Devizes at the age of eight, an experience she later described as a welcome escape from the loneliness of the Victorian nursery. In her memoir, she compares nurseries and prisons:

> Nurseries in those days were prisons, as I realized when I found myself for the first time in Holloway Jail and reverted at once to the old sense of helplessness and misery. We were in the hands of those who possessed delegated authority over us, and from that authority there was no appeal. In one sense, it was worse than prison, for there was no public opinion to check abuses. Nursemaids could be tyrants exercising favouritism and venting personal prejudices, unlike the warders in prison, who are themselves under discipline.[362]

After a spell in 'finishing' schools in France and Germany that failed entirely to curb her spirited insubordination, Emmeline rebelled against the wishes of her parents and, aged nineteen, left home and went to London to work as a 'sister of the people' in the West London Mission at Cleveland Hall, Fitzrovia. Here she met Mary Neal, a social worker, philanthropist and passionate folk-dance revivalist who had set up a club for working girls at the Mission. Emmeline helped Mary run the club. Confronted by the poverty of central London cheek by jowl with immense wealth and privilege, she became a socialist.

In 1895 Mary and Emmeline left the Mission and set up their own independent organizations for underprivileged girls. Based in Somers Town, London, the Espérance Club aimed to educate local young women, the majority of whom worked long hours in sewing and dressmaking in poor conditions for low pay. The club focused on creativity and access to culture, encouraging the young women to participate in folk music, dance and drama. The Espérance dance and drama groups performed in and around London for community audiences, giving the girls social confidence and self-assurance. The programmes of evening lectures in politics and worker's rights and of reading groups proved popular.

Mary described the aim of the Espérance Club: 'to bring some of the beautiful things in life within easy reach of the girls who earn their living by the sweat of their brow'.[363] Mary Neal and Emmeline Pethick also launched Maison Espérance, a co-operative dressmaking business to provide employment and empower the young women. Emmeline developed the co-operative, with set working hours and an agreed minimum wage, which was double the pay they were used to receiving. Emmeline also ran a club for Jewish girls and established the Green Lady Hostel in Littlehampton, a holiday home for working girls, on the Sussex coast.

In 1899 Emmeline's dramatic society of young working women was invited to give a performance in the Canning Town Settlement in West Ham. A young lawyer, Frederick Lawrence, hosted and introduced the group to the audience. Recently graduated from Cambridge, a fellow of Trinity College and the son of extremely wealthy Liberal parents, Fred – as Emmeline always called him – was reading for the Bar while living at the Mansfield House settlement in West Ham and studying local social conditions at first hand. He acted as a so-called Poor Man's Lawyer at the settlement, giving legal advice free of charge and using his social network and money to represent the community interests.

After the performance that evening Fred walked Emmeline and Mary Neal back to the station. He told them that he had just completed a book on the economic conditions and wages of men. As he knew nothing about the economic conditions of working women, perhaps, given Emmeline's interest in economics, they might be able to exchange some useful information? As the train left the station and he lifted his hat in parting salute, Mary 'rather shocked' Emmeline by remarking in her characteristically forthright manner, 'I feel that you are going to marry that man.'[364] Soon afterwards, Fred purchased the *Echo*, a left-wing evening newspaper, primarily in order to have a platform to present to the British public the many facts that had been suppressed about the South African War. He commissioned friends from the socialist movement, such as Ramsay MacDonald and Henry Brailsford, to write for the newspaper. He invited Emmeline to join its council, which met weekly to discuss editorial policy. 'Mental sympathy and accord ripened into friendship, and friendship into love,' Emmeline wrote.[365]

At first Emmeline refused to marry Fred because they disagreed over her socialist beliefs. She feared that her practical socialism would arouse discord between them over her working life. By 1901 Fred had become a socialist. When they married in the town hall at Canning Town, their guests included the girls, boys, children, men and women among whom they had lived and worked, old folk from the workhouse and political grandees like David Lloyd George. The newlyweds adopted the joint surname of Pethick-Lawrence and retained separate bank accounts. Their relationship was widely celebrated as a model of modern progressive marriage. Fred was thrilled by Emmeline's pregnancy. When she suffered a miscarriage and they discovered that she could not have children, he wrote to her: 'I am to you a splendid husband and you to me a splendid wife and it is enough!'[366]

In the early years of their marriage Emmeline and Fred helped to develop the Independent Labour Party. Keir Hardie soon became a close friend. It was Hardie who roused Emmeline and Fred to the women's cause, a dead letter as far as she was concerned. 'The days when woman's suffrage was a live issue were over before my time began. The story of the betrayal of the suffrage movement by parliament, and of the death-blow given to it by Gladstone, has been told to weariness.'[367] Emmeline wrote that her early enthusiasms 'were aroused not by ideas of political democracy but by dreams of economic and social deliverance of the toiling masses of the people'.[368] Walt Whitman, William Morris and Edward Carpenter influenced her. She was keen on their concepts of the communitarian 'fellowship' between craftsman and labourer, and on idealistic schemes for new ways of social living, but by her own admission didn't get much further than talking to her friends about the value of living a simple, beautiful and useful life and sharing all they possessed.

Later on, these somewhat dreamy sentiments took more definite form and shape in the new Independent Labour Party founded

by Keir Hardie, but the franchise question did not occupy our
attention. Political interests were subordinate to our fervent desire
to bring about an amelioration of the social conditions of the
workers. Nothing less than this absorbing interest could have
made me indifferent to the question of woman's franchise. I was
convinced that all injustice and wrong would come to an end if a
system of socialism could supplant the old capitalist regime. I had
yet to be awakened to the fact that a system of socialism, planned
by the male half only of humanity, would not touch some of
the worst evils that were engendered by a politically and socially
suppressed womanhood.[369]

Hardie told her that the Pankhursts and the Kenneys had passed through
the same political transition, combining their socialism with a new
demand for women's enfranchisement as a result of their engagement
with working women in the north of England and Scotland, and
the ILP.

Hardie recognized that Emmeline and Fred — now radical
socialists, popular, well connected and immensely wealthy — were
efficient and practical, possessed of already widely reputed financial
and organizational skills that Mrs Pankhurst and Christabel lacked.
In February 1906 Hardie suggested that Mrs Pankhurst call on
Emmeline Pethick-Lawrence to ask her to develop the WSPU in
London. Emmeline Pethick-Lawrence admired Emmeline Pankhurst's
temperament as being 'akin to genius: she could have been a Queen
on a stage or in a Salon', but she was not persuaded. After the meeting
Mrs Pankhurst reported her disappointment to Sylvia: 'She will not
help ... she has so many interests.'[370]

In 1906 it seemed the tide of reaction had turned. Sir Henry
Campbell-Bannerman became Prime Minister, with Asquith, Churchill
and Lloyd George in his cabinet. The election was a victory for those
who had taken the unpopular side in the South African (Boer) War,
opposing what Campbell-Bannerman described as its 'methods of
barbarism': burning Boer farms and herding children and women into
concentration camps where tens of thousands died.

Hardie was returned in Merthyr Tydfil and immediately elected
leader of the LRC committee, which renamed itself the Labour Party.
The national press, which had previously ignored, ridiculed or abused

him, now pursued Hardie night and day. He was in constant demand. Westminster Palace went into shock. Parliament was as uncertain how to react to this unprecedented intake of working-class socialists and trade unionists walking its hallowed corridors as the new Labour MPs themselves were about finding their way around them.

The first rule Hardie laid down was that no Labour MP would be seen drinking in the parliamentary bars: 'Labour and Liquor don't mix.' It was a canny move, simultaneously protecting the inexperienced MPs from the multiple mantraps of the Westminster jungle and sending a reassurance of their seriousness to the voters who had put them there. Gathered for supper at their favourite Lyons restaurant one evening, Hardie, Sylvia and some friends discussed the future optimistically. 'When Socialism comes I shall have a schooner of lager,' Hardie joked. 'No, no, don't break teetotal Hardie!' Philip Snowden pleaded anxiously. 'You don't realize what a great influence it has with men to be able to say that you are a teetotaller.'[371]

For Sylvia, the 1906 election result represented 'a great step towards the Golden Age ... The future seemed full of promise. I went about my work at the RCA (where, so far as I knew, none of the students cared a straw for such matters) with a joyous exhilaration.'[372] Immediately after the election, her mother dispatched Annie Kenney back down south, with the daunting instruction to 'rouse London', equipped with £2 in her purse from the WSPU and a wicker basket containing her shawl and clogs. Annie, like Sylvia, cared passionately about stepping towards the Golden Age.

Sylvia met Annie off the train, took her home to Park Walk and served up some of her vegetarian cooking. This, according to Annie, invariably involved hastily prepared and entirely unseasoned eggs, tomatoes and lentils. Annie arrived with her single instruction and no plan. The two talked long into the night. How should they begin setting about Mrs Pankhurst's command to 'rouse London'?

They considered what they both knew already from their Lancashire activism. The next day, Sylvia consulted Hardie. Go east, he recommended wisely. The following evening Sylvia and Annie were at the opposite end of London in Canning Town, proselytizing for the WSPU among unemployed and barely paid workers struggling below the breadline. To get their attention, they needed to illustrate for working women how their lives would be transformed by the franchise.

'Sylvia and I told them all the wonderful things that would happen to them once women got the vote. Poverty would be practically swept away; washing would be done by municipal machinery! In fact Paradise would be there once the Vote was won! I honestly believed every word I said,' Annie recalled in her memoir. 'I had yet to learn that Nature's works are very slow but very sure ... Poor East End women, we gave them something to dream about, and a hope in the future, however distant that future might be.'[373]

Hardie stressed that attaining that future depended upon how women used their vote once they achieved it. 'The political enfranchisement of women will only mark the beginning, not the end, of their struggle for emancipation. The vote is a weapon which can be used with effect in changing the conditions under which men and women alike suffer under the present system. We want, therefore, to make women Socialists as well as suffragists.'[374]

The two young women quickly developed a strong rapport, notwithstanding Annie's aversion to Sylvia's vegetarian diet. Sylvia benefited greatly from Annie's camaraderie. She handled Annie's correspondence and escorted her around London, introducing her as 'the mill girl who had gone to prison for a vote'.[375] The work expanded Sylvia's self-discovery. 'I had been so horribly nervous when I went to sell my designs, but as soon as it was a question of agitating for a cause, my nervousness was gone.'[376]

In other ways, they were just young women finding their way around Europe's greatest metropolis. London's grandeur, romance and poverty inspired and appalled Annie. In the evenings, when their meetings were over and all their letters done, Sylvia and Annie would read together at Park Cottage 'for a brief half-hour's delight before going to bed'.[377] They selected snatches of verse for Annie to memorize for her speeches, drawing from Tennyson, Shelley, Milton or a Shakespeare sonnet. Both of them loved their special outings to Lockhart's restaurant on the Strand. Annie declared that reading the menu was a feast in itself and enjoyed the prospect of a hearty dinner with gravy. Sylvia just enjoyed not having to cook. Sometimes Hardie joined them. Annie had campaigned for him in Merthyr and they knew each other well.

Following Mrs Pankhurst's failure to recruit Emmeline Pethick-Lawrence to the cause, Hardie set up a meeting between Annie and Emmeline in the hope that Annie might succeed in convincing her and Fred to join the WSPU leadership. This was an astute deployment. Emmeline Pethick-Lawrence vividly describes Annie's persuasive powers. 'She burst in upon me one day in her rather breathless way and threw all my barriers down. I might have been a life-long friend by the complete trust she in me that she showed and by the conviction that she expressed that the only thing needed to bring the movement to complete and speedy success in London was my co-operation.'[378]

Impressed by Annie's courage despite the apparently hopeless scale of the task to 'rouse London', Emmeline asked Annie, 'How do you want me to help you?' 'Mr Keir Hardie told me to ask you to be our national treasurer,' Annie replied. 'Your treasurer!' Emmeline exclaimed. 'What funds have you?' 'That is just the trouble,' said Annie simply. 'I have spent the money already and I have had to go into debt. I do not understand money, it worries me; that is why I have come to you for your help.'[379] Annie persuaded Emmeline to come to a committee meeting at Park Walk the following day, to meet the honorary secretary Sylvia Pankhurst and others for the inaugural meeting of the London WSPU.

After Annie had left, Emmeline felt unhappy about her promise to attend the meeting. 'I had no fancy to be drawn into a small group of brave and reckless and quite helpless people who were prepared to dash themselves against the oldest tradition of human civilization as well as one of the strongest governments of modern times.' She asked her friend and colleague Mary Neal to go with her for support, and the reinforcement of her shrewd judgement and common sense.[380]

The following evening Emmeline and Mary joined Sylvia and the group of women gathered round her table at Park Walk: Annie Kenney, Sylvia's aunt Mary Clarke, her landlady Mrs Roe, Irene Fenwick Miller and the Cornish-born Nellie Martel, who had emigrated to Australia in 1879 and returned to England in 1904. In 1903 Nellie Martel had been one of the four women who contested the federal election of that year, the first at which women were eligible to stand.

This was the occasion of the first encounter between Sylvia and Emmeline Pethick-Lawrence, and the inaugural meeting of the Central London Committee of the WSPU. 'How it happened, I hardly know,' wrote Emmeline, 'but that evening we formed ... and I was formally requested to become honorary treasurer.'[381] She agreed on the condition that her old friend Alfred Sayers, a chartered accountant, would be their honorary auditor and set up the book-keeping system. Emmeline

Pethick-Lawrence, not of a revolutionary temperament, was drawn into a revolutionary movement, and from that day she and Sylvia became intimate and political friends, an alliance that lasted the rest of their lives.

Sylvia's biographer Shirley Harrison observes that the thirty-eight-year-old Emmeline shared the twenty-four-year-old Sylvia's belief in practical socialism. Annie Kenney astutely perceived the vital role Emmeline had to take in the WSPU, making use of her pragmatic, organizational side.

> Mrs Lawrence is not a woman who will play at work or work
> without method or from pure inspiration. She must see where she
> is going, where the road will lead and what obstacles there may
> be to block the path. She was the person we needed. Christabel,
> Mrs Pankhurst and I were too temperamental and purely intuitive.
> So Providence sent the right woman at the right time to help in
> turning the tiny vessel into a great liner.[382]

Providence, that is, in the human and brilliantly strategic form of Keir Hardie.

In her memoir Emmeline recalled her impressions of Sylvia at this first meeting.

> I found Sylvia Pankhurst ... a baffling personality. She was the
> impersonation of what I had imagined those young Russian
> students to be who, in the last decades of the nineteenth century,
> had given up career and status to go amongst the masses of the
> people in order to instruct them, and so to prepare the ground for
> the revolution which they believed would some day take place.
> There was a certain infantile look about her, because her face had
> the roundness and the smoothness of a child. In contrast to her
> childlike face was the outer hardness of her character, the hardness
> of finely tempered steel; she had a strong will, trained to endure.[383]

The new London WSPU agreed that the obvious way to launch their campaign was to organize a march and rally in Trafalgar Square, along with all the other popular movements, on the day of the state opening of parliament on 16 February. Discovering that the square was not available, Sylvia consulted Hardie, who told her to book instead Caxton Hall in Westminster and persuaded a friend to pay for the rental and advertising. The friend was Walter Coats, secretary to the Vacant Lands Cultivation Society. Hardie drafted the Votes for Women handbill, Sylvia laid it out and Annie took it immediately to the women printers' co-operative.

Sylvia bought a large supply of white linen and Indian ink and made banners for the procession to the House of Commons. Simultaneously, she followed Hardie's advice to go to the East End and meet with George Lansbury, the much loved socialist leader. She asked Lansbury for his support in organizing a contingent of women to join the suffrage procession. The future Labour Party leader, a Christian socialist, known as 'the peaceful warrior', was an old friend of Sylvia's father. He soon became a firm friend of hers.

The Suffolk-born Lansbury lived with Bessie, his Whitechapel-born wife, his son Edgar and numerous daughters in a small house in Bow adjoining the family woodyard. Sylvia's friendship with Lansbury and his family became one of the most important allegiances of her life. Lansbury possessed a clear, radical vision for the improvement of the lives of the people of the East End and the development of the area for their benefit. Sylvia shared his vision. No politician of the twentieth century, it was said, walked the high wire between utopianism and pragmatism with greater skill or effectiveness than George Lansbury.[384] His approach influenced Sylvia enormously. His son Edgar became a prominent activist among the male militant suffragettes, and married the brilliant Minnie Glassman, daughter of a Jewish coal merchant, who joined Sylvia and became a leader among the militant East End suffragettes. Later, in 1921, Minnie became one of five women on Poplar Council who, along with their male colleagues and her father-in-law George Lansbury, were jailed for six weeks for supporting the Poplar Rates Rebellion. Minnie developed pneumonia as a result of her imprisonment and died the following year.

From her meeting with George Lansbury, Sylvia went next to the offices of the controversial William Thomas Stead, celebrated journalist, pioneer of investigative journalism, fearless champion of freedom of speech, editor of the *Review of Reviews* and notorious groper of young women. Sylvia asked him to promote their event. Stead obliged with an elegant, enthusiastic eulogy in which he ingeniously likened Annie

Kenney to Josephine Butler. Several Fleet Street editors agreed to give them publicity. W. T. Stead was a staunch and loyal supporter of the suffragettes, but it was a constant struggle to stop him seizing them for a kiss — or, he hoped, for much more — at every opportunity and to make him keep his hands to himself.

With perhaps a touch of hypocrisy, Stead had in 1885 launched an exposé of child prostitution, 'The Maiden Tribute of Modern Babylon', published in instalments in the *Pall Mall Gazette*. A pioneering example of investigative journalism, the 'Maiden Tribute' series revealed in graphic detail the scandalous entrapment, abduction and 'sale' of vulnerable young girls to London brothels. Stead's 'infernal narrative', as he called it, unveiled the criminal underworld of brothels, procuresses, drugs and padded chambers, where upper-class paedophiles revelled in the abuse of underprivileged children. Within days, the 'Maiden Tribute' became an international sensation. The series threw London society into a moral panic and forced the rapid passage of the 1885 Criminal Law Amendment Act, which raised the age of consent for girls from thirteen to sixteen and strengthened existing legislation against prostitution.

Stead and several of his alleged accomplices, including Bramwell Booth of the Salvation Army, were later brought to trial at the Old Bailey as a result of the unlawful methods they had used in the investigation and were convicted of the abduction and indecent assault of thirteen-year-old Eliza Armstrong. From the impoverished Marylebone area of London, Eliza was the real face behind the character of Lily, whose tragic fate in 'A Child of Thirteen Bought for £5' concluded the first instalment of the 'Maiden Tribute' series. Having heard during his investigations that unscrupulous parents were willing to sell their own children into prostitution, Stead sent his agent, a reformed prostitute called Rebecca Jarrett, into Marylebone to purchase a child, to show how easily young girls could be procured. Stead was sentenced to three months in Coldbath-in-the-Fields prison, but was later transferred to Holloway.

Bernard Alfieri, of the Alfieri picture service, was breaking new ground with his cutting-edge photographic illustrations for a new paper called the *Daily Mirror*. The emerging 'photographic newspaper' format was starting to challenge the established tradition of line-drawn illustration. Like Lansbury, Bernard Alfieri proved to be an important and long-lasting friend and ally to Sylvia.

Sylvia and Annie called on Arthur Balfour, to make it clear that, although they were attacking the current Liberal government, this did not imply any friendship towards the Conservatives. Balfour's sister Alice received them, and in tears begged them not to ask her to disturb his meetings, for fear of his anger.

Mrs Pankhurst and Christabel worried about the lack of news from London. Emmeline sent Tess Billington-Greig from Manchester to see what they were really up to. To Sylvia's dismay, TBG dumped her bag on arrival and moved straight into Park Walk, without discussion. The studio that Sylvia had made in her second rented room was now displaced and there could be no more Saturday salons for her college friends. The room became the WSPU London HQ and billet of a militant suffragette encampment.

Caught up in all this activity, Sylvia and Annie continued to forget to update Mrs Pankhurst on their plans. Tess Billington-Greig likewise became absorbed in the campaign launch and proved an inefficient informant. It was hardly surprising that Sylvia's mother soon turned up in no good mood, to find out for herself exactly what they were up to. In her memoirs, Emmeline sedately massages the memory of this episode. She recalls her 'astonishment' at finding out what 'the confident young things' were organizing.[385] At the time, she was furious. Concentrating the full force of her anger on Sylvia, she berated her for her audacity and told her the whole thing would be a sorry fiasco. Caxton Hall was far too big a venue. They wouldn't be able to drum up seventy people to come their meeting and procession to parliament, never mind the clearly unattainable 7,000 for which they were aiming. Sylvia protested that she was acting much on the advice of Hardie, who had suggested Caxton Hall and was financially assisting their plans. This information provoked Emmeline to greater rage.

The timely arrival of the bluff and adept Flora Drummond reduced Emmeline's boil to a simmer. Emphasizing the theatrical spectacle planned for the proceedings, she rallied Emmeline's optimism by declaring that she thought the girls might pull it off. The arrival of an eager press pack hovering around Mrs Roe's house surprised Emmeline. It was too late to cancel. The hall was booked, the event widely advertised. They had to make the best of it.

Come the day, Lansbury's 400-strong East End 'peace army' arrived at Caxton Hall as promised, carried on a tide of red Labour flags. Annie arranged sensibly for each marcher to be received with a fortifying cup of tea and a sugary bun. As the day was bitterly cold and pouring with rain, this was all the more welcome. Caxton Hall filled rapidly to standing room only. Several elite society ladies turned up disguised in their maids' uniforms, curious to see what it was all about but reluctant, as yet, to be identified. One of these was Rosalind Howard, Lady Carlisle, president of the Women's Liberal Federation.

Fired up before the throng, all doubts forgotten, Emmeline delivered an eloquent address. A runner arrived to inform them that the King's Speech, predictably, contained no promise of votes for women. Emmeline moved that the meeting resolve itself immediately into a march on parliament. She walked out into the freezing rain and to a woman the assembly followed her, though many had never set eyes on her before. Sylvia realized that this meeting was a turning point. Gone was the politely muted gloved clapping of the Women's Franchise League. She observed the change in her mother, who having 'shed her old timidity of the nineties' was now confident in her powers, bold in her oratory.[386]

The women's procession, bedecked with red flags and white banners, arrived at the Strangers' Entrance. For the first time that anyone could remember, they found the door of the House of Commons barred to women. Negotiations ensued, with Hardie and several other MPs intervening with the Speaker to urge that the women be allowed to enter. The police remained obdurate. The women, despite the cold and torrential rain, refused to budge. Eventually, permission was granted for twenty women to be admitted at a time. For the rest of the day, the others stood outside waiting their turn.

Shortly afterwards, in his first parliamentary speech as leader, Hardie put votes for women at the top of the Labour Party policy agenda. It was the first time in British history that any party political leader had made such a radical undertaking. The King's Speech had announced the government's intention to abolish plural voting. In the United Kingdom this was the practice that permitted one person to vote multiple times in an election, based on education and professional qualification and property ownership. Those affiliated with a university were allowed to vote in both their university and their home constituencies. Those who owned property in one constituency but lived in another could vote in both. Property owners with holdings in multiple locations had votes in every constituency in which they were landowners. Plural voting also included occupation votes, whereby those who held qualifications or roles in different constituencies – for example, universities, church, local government or business – could vote wherever they held appointments and professional interests. It was not unusual for the small minority to whom this applied to hold anything from five to eighteen votes, and in more extreme cases up to forty or fifty.

The Liberal Party made successive attempts to reform the plural voting system with greater headway in the early twentieth century, but these would be stalled by the outbreak of the Great War in 1914. The Representation of the People Act of 1918 was the first legislation to enshrine the principle that no one could vote more than twice at a general election. Plural voting was finally abolished at general elections in 1948.

Hardie replied to the King's Speech by looking beyond plural voting and urging the need for complete reform of the franchise laws. The Liberal government must put an end to 'the scandal and disgrace of treating women, because they were women, no better than criminals, paupers and peers'.[387]

On 25 April, Hardie attempted to move a women's suffrage resolution. Christabel believed it a foregone conclusion that the motion would be talked out and insisted that the WSPU must protest from the Ladies' Gallery. Sylvia sat with her mother and a dozen or so women in readiness. Their old opponents rose in succession with their jocular schoolboy insults, setting to gleefully with the evident intention of talking the bill out, to the fury of the Ladies' Gallery. Home Secretary Herbert Gladstone fudged and obfuscated, without expressly speaking against. Indignant, the suffragettes looked to Mrs Pankhurst for the signal for their protest to begin. Ignorant of the procedures of the House, they didn't understand that Hardie was waiting until just before the hands of the clock reached eleven to move the closure of the debate and put it to the Speaker to exercise his option to accept or reject the motion.

On many previous occasions, the Women's Suffrage Bill had been talked out because the Speaker refused to accept the closure resolution. However, this was the first time in British parliamentary history that there was a popular Labour leader with a contingent of twenty-eight MPs behind him. Hardie calculated that there was a possibility that this time it just might tip the other way. Unfortunately, the opportunity to put the Speaker to the test was squandered. Unaware of the consequences, Mrs Pankhurst initiated the protest from the Ladies' Gallery. Uproar ensued, the Speaker ordered them from the House and the police rushed into the gallery to remove the women. If there had been any chance of manoeuvring the Liberal government into committing to votes for women in order to buy some support from the new Labour MPs, their disturbance killed it.

In the midst of the rumpus, Sylvia saw Hardie stride from the chamber. 'I knew by his sombre brow and the set of his shoulders we had angered this generous friend.' She set her face and continued with the protest, but felt culpable, 'for I alone understood the difficulty of his stand for us, and realized that his rivals were taking advantage of it to aid them in decrying his whole policy'.[388] She acknowledged ruefully that they ought to have consulted him. As they descended into the lobby, the non-militant suffragists eyed them scornfully and held aloof. But the Labour MPs who had attended specifically to support the Votes for Women Bill gathered around to berate them. Hardie was putting himself on the line for their cause, against the general mood of the party. He had persuaded these Labour MPs to back him; now the suffragettes had ruined the moment with their protest. The following day, the press agreed with them, all except W. T. Stead, who commended the WSPU's 'divine impatience'.[389]

For several heart-wrenching days, Sylvia heard nothing from Hardie – 'they were an age to me'.[390] He broke his silence in the press, robustly defending the suffragette protesters. They were ignorant of parliamentary procedure, he argued, because so long excluded from it. Moreover, they were provoked by the presence of police in the gallery. Sylvia wrote to him immediately, and he agreed to meet. She thanked him for the magnanimous solidarity and apologized for their crass miscalculation. Privately, Hardie expressed his surprise at her mother's ignorance of procedure, given her experience of lobbying. He assured her the matter was closed between them. Sylvia now had a clearer understanding of the pressures exerted on Hardie by his party for his bit-and-brace support for the suffragette cause.

The new London WSPU campaign gained momentum. On 9 March, Sylvia and a group of about thirty women arrived in Downing Street to request an interview with the Prime Minister Campbell-Bannerman.

Ignoring the detectives who tried to send them away, Sylvia, Annie and Irene Miller knocked on the door and rang the bell of Number 10. Irene Miller even managed to push herself inside and make a dash along the corridor to the cabinet room before she was seized. All three were arrested and sent to Cannon Row police station, where they received a message from the Prime Minister, stating the terms on which he would accept a delegation. This seemed a significant victory.

In response, 200 MPs formed immediately a Women's Suffrage Committee, urging the Prime Minister to receive a joint deputation from all organizations interested in votes for women. He agreed, and the date was set for 19 May. A broad alliance of groups, led by the 350-strong deputation, marched from the Boadicea Statue on Westminster Bridge to the Foreign Office where it was received. The procession included the WSPU, non-militant suffragists, Liberals, socialists, Lansbury's East Enders, temperance societies and co-operative workers. Visually the most striking part of the rally was the body of women textile workers from Lancashire and Cheshire who marched under the bright, beautifully made banners of their trade. A huge silage lorry, bedecked with streamers bearing the legend 'We Demand Votes for Women this Session', carried campaigners either too ill or too old to walk. Among them were grandmothers and great-grandmothers who had supported the first petition to John Stuart Mill back in 1866, forty years earlier.

Henry Campbell-Bannerman expressed personal sympathy for votes for women, but regretted that his hands were tied since his cabinet was divided on the issue. He expounded on the virtue of patience, in response to which the elderly Emily Davies snorted loudly. Davies was one of the two women who had handed the first petition to John Stuart Mill in 1866 and who had opened the case for the deputation. Hardie answered the Prime Minister by cautioning that patience can be carried to excess, and urging him to recognize the possibility of the political moment: 'with agreement between the leaders of the two historic parties, and with the support of the other sections of the House, it surely does not pass the wit of statesmen to find ways and means for the enfranchisement of the women of England before this Parliament comes to a close'.[391] The Prime Minister looked at Hardie gravely and shook his head. Clearly, it did surpass his wit. As they left, Annie Kenney shouted out, 'Sir, we are not satisfied, and the agitation will go on.'[392]

Discontented with the outcome, the rally agreed to reconvene at Trafalgar Square. By three o'clock, thousands had assembled. Emmeline, standing on the wide plinth of Nelson's Column, flanked by four crouching lions, addressed the crowd. She was followed by TBG in a startlingly bright blue dress; then the aged, iron-willed Mrs Wolstenholme Elmy. Annie Kenney spoke next, with her shawl over her head and steel-tipped clogs peeping from under her skirt. Then Keir Hardie addressed the mass. Sylvia described 'his rough brown homespun jacket, with his deep-set honest eyes, and his face full of human kindness, framed by the halo of his silver hair'.[393] She was looking at him through a uniquely flattering pair of rose-tinted spectacles. The photographs of the occasion show Hardie with a decidedly more eccentric aspect, looking like a marginally better-dressed, rustic Scottish version of the middle-aged Karl Marx.

Photography surviving from the day also reveals a thronging crowd, packed into the square ear to shoulder, with as many men's flat caps, bowler hats and homburgs as there are women's straw boaters and flower-bedecked bonnets.

The welcome arrival of Emmeline and Frederick Pethick-Lawrence to support the suffragette cause shifted the growing work of the WSPU towards Clement's Inn, the location of Fred's editorial office for the *Labour Record*. In October the WSPU set up offices there, paid for by the Pethick-Lawrences. Fred became business manager of the WSPU. He and his wife set about turning the campaign into a systematically co-ordinated, regulated and accountable organization. Christabel was given the keys to an office of her own and Emmeline worked upstairs in her own flat.

Emmeline Pethick-Lawrence was to remark that at the time Sylvia reminded her of the Russian students who had given up their careers to join the workers and prepare for the revolution,[394] but during the summer of 1906, Sylvia was far more concerned about her future prospects as an artist and earning a living than she was about preparing for revolution. Her two-year scholarship at the RCA had come to its end. She'd successfully completed the foundation course, so the school encouraged her to apply for a place to complete the full five-year diploma. She hesitated, uncertain how she could find work to support herself, study and continue her work in the movement. She suggested to her mother that she give up her role as secretary of the WSPU so that she could find paid employment.

Emmeline refused, insisting that Sylvia stay in the role until Christabel had completed her law degree and was able to come to London as chief organizer of the WSPU. At the same time, she refused to offer Sylvia a stipend for the work to tide her over. Christabel and Adela were already both paid organizers, and adding Sylvia would make for too many Pankhursts on the payroll. For her part, Sylvia had no wish to be a paid employee of the WSPU; but nor could she afford to continue in her voluntary role, especially not for the convenience of her elder sister. Mrs Roe enquired anxiously how Sylvia would continue to pay the rent when she left the RCA. The campaigning was exhausting her and she felt alienated and depressed about not being able to keep up her artistic work. In a sure sign of her nervous state, her neuralgia returned.

Several letters to her mother asking for help to resolve the situation went unanswered. As the last days of the college term approached, Sylvia faced a precarious future just like all the other anxious students. She continued to hope for some response from Emmeline – if only of general encouragement to keep pursuing her artistic vocation. Nothing came. Her mother's silence made it clear that she was expected to do her duty to the movement, regardless of whether or not she could eat or pay her rent. The depth of Sylvia's hurt at Emmeline's intransigence erupts with vehemence in her memoir: 'We were no longer a family; the movement was overshadowing all personal affections.'[395]

Sylvia was alarmed by what she described as the development of her mother's 'incipient Toryism',[396] and with Emmeline's and Christabel's rejection of debate and differences of opinion. She feared their absolutist tendencies, and regarded the Pethick-Lawrences and Hardie as influences crucial to securing a democratic and accountable structure within the WSPU. Christabel and Emmeline were beginning to show signs of breaking ties with the Labour Party, making the checks and balances of the Pethick-Lawrence–Hardie axis all the more crucial.

Burdened by these cares, she was shocked by the news that her younger sister Adela, Annie and several other women had been arrested for agitation in London and Manchester and been shut away in stifling cells in the burning heat of that July. Sylvia resolved on her own course of action. The WSPU London committee was due to meet as usual in her flat at Park Walk that evening. She wrote a neat letter of resignation, left it on the table and with her drawing board and charcoals walked out into the summer night.

Emmeline Pethick-Lawrence, who found the resignation letter, was sympathetic, understanding another side of Sylvia's nature: 'For her own sake she should have done it long before ... many months of work had been interrupted and spoiled by the agitation that was so foreign to her own true nature.'[397] Hardie agreed wholeheartedly that she'd done the right thing. Her mother was furious.

While Mrs Pankhurst tried to reorganize around her daughter's sudden departure, Sylvia decided to move to new, cheaper lodgings. 'And now,' as Emmeline Pethick-Lawrence observed, "she was stranded with her living to earn, and practically no income to fall back on.'[398] Mrs Roe had shown nothing but kindness to Sylvia and the other WSPU organizers had been equally supportive. She did not want any of them to see her 'in what might be a stiff struggle with want'.[399] Pride, and her determination to be financially independent, made her shy away from accepting their help or pity.

Sylvia found two unfurnished rooms in Cheyne Walk on the Thames Embankment, in 'long-haired Chelsea'[400] next door to a house once occupied by the Romantic artist William Turner. Lined with lamps, benches and plane trees, there was, as E. M. Forster wrote, something continental about the Chelsea Embankment.[401] Chelsea was a neighbourhood that placed her at London's artistic bohemian heart. Distracted by her distress at the breach with her mother and her empty purse, it was a while before Sylvia was able to appreciate the consolations of her new riverside neighbourhood.

Besieged by neuralgia and gloom, it took her nearly a week to collect her minimal possessions. To save money, she paid a lad with a handcart to trundle her belongings from Park Street to Cheyne Walk: an easel, camp bed, packing cases of books and paints, and a small bag of clothes. The camp bed and easel, along with a single gas ring, table and chair, were her only furniture. She fed a penny into the slot of the gas meter and sat among her unpacked boxes, feeling sick and depressed. The future was uncertain. She had twenty-five shillings left in the world and her rent was eleven shillings a week. She'd cut her expenses to the lowest ebb, living on Egyptian lentils and loose cocoa sold in the King's Road, which she ate and drank 'with the addition of water alone',[402] another alarming insight into her cooking. These were her sole supplies; fresh dairy and vegetables were too expensive.

All of a sudden, Hardie came knocking at her door. Taking command of the situation, he lifted the heavy items into position, jovially helped her unpack and, when everything was set out and in order, took her for a cheerful dinner at their favourite Italian restaurant.

Next day, it was back to unseasoned lentils, unsweetened cocoa and fairly fruitless job hunting.

Like so many artists before her, Sylvia knew it would be a long time before she might scrape by a living from her vocation, assuming she would ever manage it. As a student of the RCA she was one of a select handful whose qualification from the college opened doors for them, but once inside there were no guarantees. She had no independent wealth to subsidize her artistic pursuits and no interest in purely commercial art. There were two further counts against her: first, that of her sex; secondly, that she yearned to produce mammoth works of art – murals, installations and decorations on a large scale.

In common with the visionary, radical William Blake, whom she admired, Sylvia dreamed of making vast works for public buildings and popular places that would offer beauty and inspiration to be enjoyed by many people, not just by a few art connoisseurs. Where Blake envisaged making an impact through great installations for churches and palaces, Sylvia's aspiration was to create work for secular buildings and public places. Sir William Richmond, who gave her great encouragement when he saw her paintings at the RCA, told her that while large decoration was also his own ideal, few could live by it, since the very limited number of people who could afford to commission on such a scale were not interested in the form.[403]

Sylvia approached magazines and publishers in search of artistic and literary work. Young though she was, her reputation preceded her. Known as a prominent suffragette, vilified in the press, her surname generally provoked a titter in the offices she visited. Most editors assumed she wanted to write about radical feminism, socialism and votes for women and were either unwilling to devote much space to the issues or unwilling to pay her. John Lane at Bodley Head looked kindly on her proposal to produce an illustrated edition of an old classic, *The Open Air*, by Richard Jefferies. Her sketches were excellent, he said, but the book was still in copyright.

When her purse was empty, Hardie came to her rescue, arranging a commission for a couple of illuminated addresses. Off her own bat, she secured a series of paid articles on women's issues under the moniker 'Ignota' for the *Westminster Review*, the Liberal journal once edited by John Stuart Mill, and some other occasional writing helped keep her going.[404] When she earned any surplus beyond her modest needs, she spent it on models for studies, not for selling but to enable her to continue developing her practice. Or she worked for free for the movement, 'till my surplus sped away'.[405] She was self-sufficient. She received no help from her mother. Neither her art nor her activism was subsidized.

The designs and objects she produced for the WSPU during this period, from 1904 to 1914, proved to be some of her most inspired, enduring and – though she could not see it at the time – change-making. Her banner depicting Woman as Mother and Worker was unveiled at the Portman Rooms in 1908. The cartoon for this piece was displayed at the WSPU literature stall at the Hungarian Exhibition at Earl's Court the same year. Setting up a feminist stall at a national trade exhibition was considered an enterprising and highly unusual departure for a suffrage society at the time. This is one of many examples of the innovative campaigning strategies deployed by the WSPU, who publicized their cause by promoting it in unexpected ways and places.

By far the most prized object produced by the WSPU was the now famous portcullis and broad-arrow brooch medal presented to suffragette prisoners on their release. It was Sylvia's conception and design. The exquisite piece is formed of a miniature portcullis, embedded with the emblem of the 'King's broad arrow', or 'pheon' symbol, enamelled in purple, white and green. The broad arrow, signifying government property, was adopted for British prison uniforms in the 1870s. Previously, it had been used on the uniforms of transportees in British penal colonies and, before that, was stamped on military ordnance and other items of state property. The introduction of the symbol is credited to the poet and soldier Sir Philip Sidney, during his tenure in the early 1580s as Joint Master of the Ordnance alongside his uncle the Earl of Warwick, overseeing England's material preparedness for impending war with Spain – a war that, in 1586, took his life. The broad arrow featured in the Sidney family coat of arms.

On Sylvia's brooch, the uncrowned portcullis references the official emblem of the British parliament, an image of the grilled gate associated with both parliament and prisons. The arrow symbolizes the ubiquitous, crude print on every item of prison-issue uniforms, including caps and aprons, which Sylvia reproduced as a key, ironic leitmotif in all the drawings she turned out during her own incarcerations. In creating the design for the suffragette medal, she seized and transformed the arrow into a freedom-loving woman warrior's spear, transposing it into suffragette colours – purple for dignity, white for purity and green for hope. Under the Public Stores Act of 1875, it was a criminal offence to reproduce the broad-arrow hallmark without the government's permission. Sylvia certainly did not ask for this permission.

Later in 1906 she designed the new membership card for the WSPU. A gouache printed in bright colours, it depicts a procession of women in clogs, shawls and pinafores, one carrying a baby, another a pail. The powerful figure at the front, her sleeves rolled up, wearing an aproned skirt and steel-toed clogs, holds a white banner aloft, emblazoned against the blue sky, 'Votes – Votes – Votes'. Beneath the image is printed the mission: 'Women demand the right to vote, the pledge of citizenship and basis of all liberty'. Every member of the WSPU held Sylvia's inspiring design in her hand. As a child Sylvia had taken careful note of the treasured Goulden family heirlooms displayed on her parents' mantelpiece – her great-grandparents' membership cards for the Anti-Corn Law League.

While Emmeline reshuffled the London committee of the WSPU to cope with her departure, Sylvia continued to contribute to the suffragette campaign. Although upset, she jumped at any opportunity to see her mother.

> Mrs Pankhurst, always anxious to secure more workers, would sometimes telegraph me for help at a by-election, or to meet her at Clements Inn, and I would go, throwing all else to the winds. Sometimes I spent my last pence on the 'bus fare to meet her, and walked back, too proud to tell my need. Her frequent complaint that I dressed so poorly I heard with a touch of cynicism, refusing to discuss my financial affairs.[406]

Before their breach over her departure as WSPU secretary, Emmeline had informed Sylvia that Christabel was to take over as leader of the WSPU. Christabel, her mother explained, 'would never be deflected from her purpose in life by her affections, as most women are apt to be. "We are politicians Christabel and I," she often said exultantly. "Christabel is a politician born!" '[407] And what was Sylvia? Was she artist or activist? While at college, she could afford to be both. Now, both came at a cost and neither paid. As she could not bring herself to discuss her financial affairs with her mother, she couldn't ask her advice. Her college friends Austin Spare and Amy Browning were sympathetic, but didn't understand her quandary. An artist put art first. They used their brushes to make their contribution to improving the world.

It was with Hardie that Sylvia was able to explore her predicament most deeply. He supported her resolutely and encouraged her artistic vocation, partly out of a loving veneration for her creative gifts and partly out of pragmatism. He understood Sylvia's heart and character and he knew better than most the sheer magnitude of her energies and her capacity for extraordinary productivity when she set her mind to it. He knew very well that whatever else she did with her life, Sylvia would always be driven to stick with her political cause. He valued deeply the opportunity she had to be properly trained as an artist, and frequently reminded her that this was a rarer chance than political organizing.[408] Knowing her since childhood, he had observed the pressures of duty exerted on her by her parents, particularly by her father before his untimely death. Hardie supported Sylvia by cherishing and encouraging her artistic talent, never making her feel guilty or self-indulgent.

Ultimately, the decision was hers alone to make. Sylvia recalled her dilemma in a significant passage in her memoir:

Always I was torn between the economic necessities of the immediate moment, the desire of further study to equip me for ambitious works and the urging of conscience to assist in the movement. Like many young women of my period, I was distraught by my solidarity with that rage of militancy. There was a solidarity, too, with my family, and with the Union I had helped to form; but more than all these was the poignant compelling appeal to my heart of the victims of social misery, the white faces in mean streets which roused my indignant pity ... I had asked Keir Hardie, Are we brothers of the brush entitled to the luxury of release from utilitarian production? Is it just that we should be permitted to devote our entire lives to the creation of beauty, whilst others are meshed in monotonous drudgery? Now, acting alone the hard struggle of life as an unknown artist, nervous, diffident and in poor health, came the frequent question: Why? As a speaker, a pamphlet-seller, a chalker of pavements, a canvasser on doorsteps, you are wanted; as an artist the world has no real use for you; in that capacity you must fight a purely egoistical struggle.[409]

As anyone who has faced this struggle before or since might have told her, the fact that she was asking the question at all demonstrated that she knew the answer already.

10

Strange Tangle

At this time in her life, Hardie and Emmeline Pethick-Lawrence perceived Sylvia's dilemma with a clarity hidden from others. Few people knew her so intimately, or were as perceptive about the strength of the free spirit that danced irrepressibly within her, guarded as it was by her powerful self-possession. Her mother understood her, but the priorities of the cause for all women must of necessity come before Sylvia's dilemma over how to reconcile her pursuits of art and activism. Viewed in context, this was less unreasonable than it might initially seem, as Mrs Pankhurst was confident of imminent victory. In the next few years, the still youthful Sylvia would be free to return to her artistic vocation for the rest of her liberated life.

To those who knew her less well, Sylvia's diligent and tireless activism after she had left both the RCA and the WSPU London Committee gave no indication of her personal struggle. Her resignation in July had the perhaps unintended consequence of increasing, rather than reducing, the intensity of her participation in the fight for the women's vote. Historically, this was inevitable, since 1906–7 was the period in which the newly launched militant suffragette campaign gained unstoppable momentum.

On 24 October 1906 Sylvia faced the daunting prospect of serving a two-week sentence in Britain's most notorious women's prison. She was twenty-four years old. She had been arrested and held many times before, but this was her first prison sentence. Driven off from Cannon Row police station to Holloway Prison in a springless Black Maria, she heard loud applause as the van passed through the streets of poor neighbourhoods; 'they always cheer the prison van'.[410] Chill autumn darkness closed in by the time the new prisoners were decanted outside Holloway and made to pass in single file through its looming gates.

The previous day, 23 October, a throng of suffragettes led by Mrs Pankhurst had infiltrated parliament and launched a sudden protest attempting to block the lobby of the House of Commons. Policemen drove them out into the street and ten women were arrested in what Sylvia described as the resulting 'scrimmage', including her sister Adela and Emmeline Pethick-Lawrence. The women were scheduled to appear at Cannon Row the following day. Present at their hearing, Sylvia was appalled that the magistrate summarily sentenced all ten of them in less than thirty minutes, without allowing them any defence, and dispatched them to the holding cells.

Sylvia stood up in court and caused a rumpus objecting to the magistrate's conduct. Bundled out of the court by policemen and ordered to clear the area, she refused and drummed up an immediate street protest outside. When the police tried to stop her addressing the crowd, another skirmish broke out and Sylvia was arrested for abusive language and later sentenced to fourteen days 'in the third division' – the worst detention category.

The Prison Act of 1898 ruled that prisoners were to be detained in one of three divisions, according to the nature of their crime. Division 1, which included political prisoners, were allowed unrestricted correspondence and visits, to practise their profession, wear their own clothes, eat their own food and drink some alcohol; were permitted writing and reading matter; and were not forced to work. Divisions 2 and 3 were far tougher, with only the prison uniform to be worn and prison food eaten, and with tightly restricted correspondence. Prisoners were put to compulsory cleaning, stitching of mailbags or hard labour, allowed no reading or writing materials and often put into solitary confinement. These details meant everything in the lives of prisoners in the UK prison system in 1906. The division imposed had a great impact on the coming prison years of Sylvia's life and those of the suffragette women and men imprisoned alongside her.

More than that, these details were components of a system that was the single largest cause of radicalization of middle-class British who had their perspective on the world transformed after being in prison. It bolstered militancy and engendered resistance to the class system. As for many other suffragettes, Sylvia's first imprisonment in 1906 changed her life.

Charmingly, on that first night of her sentence Sylvia asked the wardress who came to lock her in if she could please have a nightdress. The refusal was accompanied by sharp reprimand for not having yet made up her bed. How was this to be done, she wondered, with the scrimp blanket, narrow sheet and stone-hard bolster? Sylvia learned immediately that sleep was one of the hardest things to obtain in Holloway.

In the articles, memoirs and letters she wrote about her first experience of incarceration, she admits her fears freely. Her dread of the clinging damp cold of the uncovered flagstone floors, her horror of the sealed window, the distress aroused by the feeling of tight confinement and by the coffin-like heavy iron doors with their dead fisheye spyhole. The poor ventilation, darkness and vermin intimidated her. She recorded her disgust at the filthy shared bathwater in the tubs in which the prisoners were scrubbed down. The shapeless prison-issue uniform made of mud-coloured serge was uncomfortable, with its rough, gaping bodice and cumbersome skirts like gathered grain sacks. The thick woollen stockings – lumpy and darned – didn't fit and shoes came always in unmatched pairs. The prisoners were ordered to wear at all times cotton caps that fastened under the chin with strings, and blue-and-white-check aprons that Sylvia said looked liked dusters. 'Every article of clothing was conspicuously stamped with the broad arrow, which was painted black on light garments, and white on those which were dark.'[411] Sylvia would take that broad-arrow motif and made it one of the most recognized symbols of the suffragette movement.

As she'd disliked porridge since childhood, the oatmeal gruel was always going to be a problem. Measured amounts of bread, potatoes and suet pudding made up the rest of the prison rations, issued in a pint pot three times a day, between their shifts cleaning their cells and sewing sheets (fifteen per week) and visits to chapel. Later, when she was a more seasoned jailbird, Sylvia quipped that though wholly lacking proper nutrition, the prison rations were rather better than her own meagre diet as a penniless artist. Those who were familiar with her cooking would not necessarily have taken this as a joke.

Three times a week the prisoners were allowed exercise in the prison yard, marching slowly round in single file four yards apart, forbidden to speak to each other or to help the older women who had difficulty walking unaided. Sylvia describes how on this drill she saw and felt the outside world anew – the refraction of light in raindrops, every shade of variation in the glossy plumage of the pigeons. Like most prisoners, after her release she forever afterwards appreciated the sky in a different way.

But like Joan of Arc, to whom she would shortly be likened by the press, it was the sense of loneliness and alienation Sylvia felt when solitary in her single-occupancy cell that was the greatest privation, and Hardie the person she missed most acutely. Without stimulation, human brains go into crisis. From panic to despair; to memory loss and hallucinations; to psychosis, self-mutilation and compulsion to suicide, these are common consequences of solitary confinement. Suffragette prisoners endured extreme physiological and psychological repercussions. Sylvia emerged from her first prison experience as committed to prison reform as she was to the women's vote.

While Sylvia adapted to the harsh and monotonous Holloway regime, Hardie, Lord Robert Cecil and a cohort of other supporters complained in parliament about the punishment of the suffragette prisoners. One of the ten detained at the parliamentary protest and sentenced with Adela and Emmeline Pethick-Lawrence was Annie Cobden-Sanderson, daughter of the Anti-Corn Law League leader Richard Cobden, a founder of British liberalism. Cobden-Sanderson's imprisonment in the third division as a common criminal embarrassed the Liberal government and enabled Hardie and Cecil to get the militant women prisoners accorded the new status of first-class offenders.

Following this intervention, the prison authorities transferred the suffragettes to a different section of the prison. Now able to talk together, they agreed that in solidarity with the women in the other divisions they would refuse the first-division privileges of being allowed to wear their own clothes and have food sent in from the outside at their own expense. They did accept the privileges of a fortnightly letter, newspapers and books. Sylvia wrote immediately to Hardie.

Consulting the prison rules and discovering that she was now also permitted to 'exercise her profession', Sylvia claimed the right to send for a parcel of drawing paper, pen, ink and pencils. When these arrived, she set about sketching prison scenes. Now occupied by her art, the prison 'lost the worst of its terrors', as she had 'congenial work to do'.[412]

After her release on 6 November, Sylvia gave dozens of press interviews, not only to advance the suffragette cause but also to reveal the dreadful conditions of prison life for all inmates. As she told the *Daily News*, to her the worst of it was 'the terrible isolation and loneliness and misplaced work'.[413] To illustrate the interviews, she gave the papers copies of her prison drawings. This defied Christabel's instructions to WSPU women to play down the realities of prison conditions when talking to the press and focus instead on the issues of the women's movement. Christabel did not want votes for women to get lost in campaigning for prison reform. Sylvia disagreed, believing it was good propaganda for the prisoners to reveal their first-hand experiences. She felt a responsibility to raise awareness for the need for prison reforms, 'not for ourselves, but for the ordinary prisoners'.[414] Though sisters of identical upbringing, Sylvia and Christabel were of entirely different mind when it came to class-consciousness.

The sisters were different also in how they looked and spoke. The Scottish suffragette Helen Crawfurd remembered that Sylvia 'was one of those people whom it was impossible to keep tidy; her hair was always tumbling down. One day I met her outside the hotel and noticed that she had her blouse on inside out. I got her behind some packing cases and helped her change it.'[415] Fenner Brockway, a great admirer of Sylvia's unaffected, direct style, noted her careless dress and the manner in which she flung her clothes around herself absent-mindedly like the artist she was. Christabel, he observed by contrast, was exquisitely and expensively dressed, and beautiful, but always cold. She could move an audience, 'not by human emotion as much as calling them to battle'.[416] Conversely, Sylvia, he said, acted and spoke from the heart.

Fenner Brockway was a socialist, pacifist and anti-colonialist who began his career as a journalist and later became a Labour MP. The son of a missionary, he was born in Kolkata in 1888 and educated in Blackheath, London, where he first became interested in politics. A Liberal in his youth, in 1907 he became a socialist after interviewing Keir Hardie, and within a few years was the editor of the weekly *Labour Leader*, organ of the ILP. He was imprisoned for resisting conscription during the First World War, and copies of his 1914 satirical play *The Devil's Business*, about the arms-trade debate, were seized by police under the Defence of the Realm Act. Brockway was first elected to parliament as the member for East Leyton in 1929, and joked that the number of his voters might be providential (11,111: won, won, won, won, won).

On the night of her release the WSPU held a party for Sylvia in their offices. Hardie turned up, as did W. T. Stead, kitted out in the prison uniform he usually wore on the anniversary of his own detention. The next day, Hardie introduced a Women's Suffrage Bill in the Commons. It didn't get anywhere of course, but it gave him the opportunity to tell the Prime Minister that his refusal to offer the April delegation any hope of government action had inflamed militant agitation.

Thoughtfully, Emmeline Pethick-Lawrence suggested a fortnight's holiday in Italy so that they could recuperate from prison. Holidays were a rare treat for Sylvia. She had only once before journeyed outside Britain. Her first trip, also to Italy, in 1902 had been enabled by the travelling studentship awarded to her by Manchester Art School. Sylvia, Annie and Emmeline began their tour in Venice and Torcello, where Sylvia left town to work in the countryside. With her post-prison perspective, she sketched and painted with light in a different way. She decided to go and inspect the women's prison in Milan, to compare it with Holloway. This wasn't quite the sort of sightseeing Emmeline had in mind to soothe them in the wake of their incarceration, but she went along on the tour of the prison and sat patiently while Sylvia sketched and took notes of the conditions which, she concluded, were 'bright and homely' compared with Holloway's 'machine-like grimness'. On the other hand, she found the practice of guarding prisoners with armed soldiers a relic of barbarism.[417] Back in London, she wrote a comparative article, illustrated with her drawings, on British and Italian prisons, published in the *Pall Mall Magazine*.

At the end of the year W. T. Stead commissioned her to produce a cartoon of Boadicea for a new series of children's books he was planning. The picture, of the warrior queen riding into battle on a chariot, was on Sylvia's easel, nearly finished, when she was arrested outside the House of Commons on 13 February 1907 and sentenced to three weeks' imprisonment. The previous day, when parliament reassembled, the King's Speech had once again failed to mention votes for women. In response, Emmeline and Christabel summoned the first 'Women's Parliament' to convene immediately at Caxton Hall. After the meeting, the participants marched to Parliament Square and massed on the green outside Westminster Abbey, where mounted police charged at them.

Sylvia ran, but was chased on foot by constables and thumped. She was among fifty-four women and two men arrested.

Back in Holloway, Sylvia took advantage of the privileges allowed to first-division political prisoners and busied herself drawing scenes of prison life and writing poetry. During the long sleepless nights she fretted that she had left her studio window open and that wind and rain might destroy her picture. But Boadicea proved characteristically resilient and was still intact on her easel when she got home from prison. She wrapped the cartoon and delivered it to Stead's office. The plan for the children's series had been abandoned, but he asked her instead to produce black and white drawings for his bestselling penny booklets. Sylvia's delight at the new commission turned to dismay as Stead lunged at her, seized her in his arms and pinioned her in an unwelcome embrace. Furious, she struggled to get free and ran out of the building without a word. 'His manner of displaying his paternal interest in young women enraged me. Apparently it was a relic of his youth when the woman who appeared asking an editor for work was a rare bird.'[418]

She mentioned the incident to Annie Kenney, who admitted that on several occasions she too had been forced to repel Stead's attempted sexual harassment. When Sylvia ran into Stead at future political meetings, he tried to waylay her, but after the incident in his office she avoided him. He intercepted her at a meeting in Essex Hall, asking, 'Why have you not been to see me?' 'I have been busy,' she answered. 'He stared at me keenly: "That is not the reason!" "No, it is not," I said, and passed on to my seat, wondering why a man who had been so zealous a friend of women's movements should behave like an uncouth bear.'[419]

As 1907 progressed, the break between the Labour Party and the WSPU began to seem unavoidable. Christabel continued to restate WSPU policy that votes for women had to be at the top of the agenda and all other reforms must be stopped until women could participate in their implementation. She would not tolerate a 'divided' allegiance: women must campaign for no other public question except the vote and they must work with no party or organization except the WSPU.

While in October 1906, the Parliamentary Labour Party had committed to putting the issue of women's enfranchisement at the top of its ballot for the forthcoming session, at the Labour Party conference in

Belfast in January 1907, disagreement once again erupted over the issue. The conference voted against sponsoring a Women's Enfranchisement Bill that would give votes to fewer than two million women. Instead, it voted in favour of reaffirming the party's commitment to universal suffrage for all women and men. Keir Hardie startled everyone present by announcing from the speaker's platform that if necessary he would resign from the party over the women's vote:

> I make that announcement with great respect to the Conference
> and with great feeling. The Party is largely my own child, and
> I cannot part from it lightly, or without pain; but at the same time
> I cannot sever myself from the principles I hold. If it is necessary
> for me to separate myself from what has been my life's work, I do so
> in order to remove the stigma resting upon our wives, mothers and
> sisters of being accounted unfit for citizenship.[420]

The Parliamentary Labour Party met at Westminster to find a way to resolve the problem. They agreed to a conscience vote. On the matters of the Women's Enfranchisement Bill and adult suffrage, members were free to vote as they thought fit. For the moment, Hardie's resignation was averted. Sylvia felt 'a blank dreariness' of depression descend.[421] It was absurd to leave the franchise question in a cleft stick like this. The British labour movement must commit wholeheartedly either to the work of achieving universal adult suffrage or to the women's vote on equal terms with the existing male franchise. She admitted that she did not have the heart to flout the opinion of her family, the WSPU and the entire women's suffrage movement. In time, she would change her mind about this. For now, she shared Fred Pethick-Lawrence's opinion expressed in the *Labour Record* that the Labour Party conference decision signalled 'the final severance of the Women's Movement from the Labour Movement'.[422]

In early March 1907 Hardie appeared as guest speaker at a WSPU meeting held at Exeter Hall. In the presence of the Pankhursts and a large number of WSPU members, he surprised the audience by announcing that he was changing his mind about suffrage strategy. If a women's suffrage bill was not granted within the next two years, he would organize a movement himself that would stop at nothing short of adult suffrage. Mrs Pankhurst, chairing the meeting, was deeply shocked. Barely able to treat her old friend with civility, she observed curtly that the speaker had expressed merely his individual view. Silence filled the hall as Hardie stepped down from the platform. No one clapped or offered him a hand. Sylvia, watching him from the front row, could see that he was unaware of the degree of offence his speech had caused.

After the meeting Sylvia and Hardie 'paced the Thames Embankment as I revealed to him the emotions which had seethed about him on the platform, and were surging within me now'.[423] She tried to explain to him her anxiety that he seemed to be about to abandon the cause they had shared for so long. He appeared to be retreating from his Belfast declaration opposing the Labour Party decision on the franchise issue. He above all others surely understood the primary importance of this struggle for justice in her life. 'In my sorrow I said that my friendship with him might even become a competitor with my loyalty to the suffrage cause.'[424]

Here is the flash of the resolute radical in Sylvia, a much younger woman, less experienced, laying it on the line very clearly to her older, politically more powerful male lover-mentor that she might not be able to put her heart before her principles. Hardie listened in silence. They passed a queue of ragged homeless men lining up for tickets for the night shelter. Breaking his long silence, Hardie turned to her and said, 'Do you ask me to desert these?'[425]

They parted with their differences unresolved. Hardie wrote to her immediately, expressing 'sorrowful understanding'.[426] They soon moved on from the argument. Sylvia recalled that the sad farewell that night on the embankment faded like the shadow of a dream. 'Yet the friction which occasioned it continued.'[427]

A little over a month later, Hardie suffered what was later diagnosed as a stroke. Fifty-one, overworked and beset by political and personal dilemmas, the strains and tensions had piled up on him. Assailed by digestive problems, he was in acute pain and could keep nothing down. On a Saturday in April Sylvia called at Nevill's Court and discovered chaos. Frank Smith desperately tried to act as nurse as well as secretary, keeping up with correspondence, spilling medicine and waiting anxiously for the doctor to arrive. To avoid adding to the confusion, Sylvia walked out into the Temple and sat by Oliver Goldsmith's grave, reflecting on the 'strange tangle into which our lives had been wrought'.[428] She returned and then visited for a few hours every day.

Hardie had experienced several breakdowns in his health over the past five years, always attributed by his doctors to overwork and nervous tension. He was always sceptical about his pain and ailments, as his biographer Caroline Benn observed: 'Hardie disliked illness, was not well informed, and believed his best defence was to remain so.'[429] He insisted to Frank Smith that he was recovered, and resumed his punishing schedule.

A week later, shortly after he heard that his proposals to introduce old-age pensions had once again been left out of the budget, Hardie collapsed while trying to dictate an impassioned response to the brutality of the omission. He was admitted to St Thomas' Hospital and his wife Lillie sent for. Before she arrived, Sylvia visited, and Hardie asked for his bed to be moved out into the spring garden and Sylvia sat with him, looking out over the river towards the Houses of Parliament.

Accompanied by Lillie, Hardie spent several weeks recuperating at a hydro in Wemyss Bay. Once back at the family home in Cumnock, he 'relaxed' by finishing a report on Haldane's Army Act, which had made a series of far-ranging reforms of the British army; reading Wilhelm Liebknecht's notes on Marx; and reflecting on internationalism as the only way forward. He decided to embark on a fact-finding and speaking tour of the British empire, without Lillie. All through the summer of his convalescence, a stream of visitors went to Cumnock to see him, including a forgiving Mrs Pankhurst. Frank Smith, Mary Macarthur and other friends passed on reports on his health and activities to Sylvia, but she could not see him. And then she heard he was setting off on a voyage around the world, his future plans unclear.

In July 1907 Hardie departed from Liverpool on the SS *Empress of Britain*, leaving behind for a while his political and personal problems. Local socialists gathered at the dockside to sing the Red Flag and cheer him on his mission 'to experience the world from the perspective of its shared common humanity'.[430]

While Hardie toured Canada, Japan, Malaysia, India, Australia, New Zealand and finally – and most controversially – South Africa, Sylvia set out in the summer of 1907 on an artistic pilgrimage around northern England and Scotland to draw, paint and write about women workers in the north of England. This trailblazing project was launched at the suggestion of the Pethick-Lawrences, and they funded it. Tensions between the sisters had escalated since Sylvia's resignation from the

WSPU committee and Christabel's arrival in London to take over the leadership. With Mrs Pankhurst always firmly taking Christabel's part, a storm threatened to break.

Emmeline Pethick-Lawrence was a great supporter and admirer of Sylvia's artistic career. Observing the work she had produced during her first two Holloway stints and when they were travelling in Italy had made her aware of Sylvia's powerful ability to put her artistic skills to the useful service of her politics. Sylvia possessed a rare talent for illustrating and documenting the undersides of a world in which much contemporary artistic work had very little interest. Thirty years later, Emmeline wrote, 'I know now that under that outer coat of mail there hides a sensitive and tender child ... quiet and shy in those days, she surprised her friends by one brilliant success after another ... The expression of Sylvia's real self was to be found in her creative art and in the depth of her emotional attachment to very few persons.'[431]

Mrs Pethick-Lawrence was also among the few who understood the depth of Sylvia's emotional attachment to Hardie. The clashes between the ILP, the Labour Party and the WSPU over policy on women's suffrage placed stress on the pair's relationship. The level-headed Fred Pethick-Lawrence had made public his belief that the breach between the Labour Party and WSPU policy was now irreconcilable. Sylvia and Hardie were alike in their uncompromising natures and willingness to pursue their political goals regardless of the advice of their friends or the hostility of their enemies. They could debate and agree to disagree over matters of strategy and tactics in their political lives, but the circumstances of their personal difficulties were more intractable. Hardie battled with illness and his fear that the Labour Party in parliament was losing its identity. He also seemed to be struggling with his feelings for Sylvia and his responsibility for Lillie, their marriage and his children. He had a home-loving nature, and a need for the peace and retreat provided by Lochnorris. However, his biographers concur that since around 1901, contrary to the official image projected for the faithful, there had been ' "little" joy for Hardie in the marriage; or for Lillie either'.[432] There had been affairs before, and by 1907 he had compensated by finding joy and sympathy elsewhere, with Sylvia. Their togetherness at Nevill's Court held out the promise of a different way of living and loving. There had never before been any question of him ending his marriage, but his relationship with Sylvia was different. Lillie's arrival in London after his stroke intensified his emotional pressure. The decision to go on political tour offered the opportunity of a respite, time to think and reflect from fresh perspectives beyond his triangulated guilt.

Emmeline and Fred Pethick-Lawrence's suggestion that she go on a painting tour, and their provision of the funding to do it, was not only to create some space between the warring Pankhurst sisters. With subtlety and care for her emotional well-being, they knew Sylvia needed to get away from London, and Hardie's painful absence from it.

Sylvia's immersive tour painting and documenting working-class women's lives was unprecedented. She combined the skills of the artist with the methods of the social scientist to produce an insight into working-women's lives rarely seen before in Britain.

She began her tour in Cradley Heath in the Staffordshire Black Country, producing watercolours and drawings of the women chain- and nailmakers who earned four or five shillings a week. She took lodgings with an elderly woman who ran a sweetshop, and spent her days with the women at the forges in the workshops and the evenings writing up detailed accounts of what she'd seen. The insanitary slum conditions in which the workers had to live and the lack of even basic amenities of town life appalled her. The pub was virtually the only social outlet. There were no libraries, no public baths and only miserable shacks for shops. The women were the drudges of the industry and made only the common 'slap' chain, which required great speed but not technical accuracy, because, Sylvia noted, the trade union prohibited them from doing more skilled work.

Many years later, writing about his mother's artistic pilgrimage, Sylvia's son Richard picked out this poignant detail from her writing: 'It wounded me to see a mother, or sometimes an old grandmother, blowing the bellows at a paltry wage for a lad in his 'teens, already doing skilled work, and occupying an industrial status to which his mother could never attain.'[433]

Sylvia was just about to leave Cradley Heath for Leicester when she received a telegram from her mother instructing her to come to Rutland immediately to help canvass for the WSPU in a by-election. They were short of speakers and needed her. The constituency was tough campaigning. The suffragettes were generally popular among working people but in a few towns tradesmen and Liberal gentry hired gangs of young thugs to roughhouse and intimidate the women's meetings.

After the election Sylvia resumed her research tour, meeting, studying and drawing women in the shoemaking factories. Her next stop was Wigan in Lancashire to observe the 'pit brow lassies' working in the coal mines, as they pushed and dragged and guided the coal-filled tubs to the sorting screens. In an article written later, in 1911, for *Votes for Women*, the WSPU newspaper launched four years before from Clement's Inn, Sylvia described not only the work and conditions, but the muscular strength, endurance and freedom of spirit of the 'splendidly made, lithe and graceful' women who worked at the pits. Watching them working side by side with the men, they appeared almost stronger. Moreover, they enjoyed a 'considerable freedom at the pit'; they 'laugh and call to each other as they pull the tubs about'.[434]

While she was away, Sylvia and her mother corresponded regularly. It was a period of intense internal dispute in the WSPU. Emmeline described the differences that had emerged over tactics and the effects of personality conflicts, all of which had made her decide to tear up the WSPU's elective constitution and make herself 'the autocrat' with the right to appoint and dismiss the committee. Sylvia replied that this was probably not a good idea. 'Do not fear the democratic constitution. You can carry the conference with you. There is no doubt of it.'[435] But encouragement to maintain a democratic approach was of no interest to Emmeline. As Sylvia later observed, she might as well have urged the wind to stop blowing as advise her mother to change her mind. The majority of the committee accepted subjugation to Mrs Pankhurst's dictatorship. Those who did not opted to split from the WSPU and founded the Women's Freedom League, with Charlotte Despard elected as president.

From Wigan Sylvia was summoned again by her mother, this time to help out with the Bury St Edmunds by-election where, to her dismay, there was no Labour candidate. After the election, Christabel demanded they meet at WSPU headquarters in Clement's Inn. One of the organizers working alongside Sylvia had complained that during the campaign she made a speech announcing that she was a socialist. 'Christabel interrogated me ... it had been necessary to convince the people we were not Conservatives. "You should have said we used to be Liberals," said Christabel with her engaging smile. "I do not agree," I answered. We knew each other's tenacity. The subject dropped.'[436]

Not, as it turned out, for very long.

After this showdown Sylvia took to the road again, heading to Staffordshire to visit the potteries. The appalling conditions of the women workers, overexposed to lead and powdered flint dust, seemed even worse than those endured by the chainmakers and coal workers. Here as elsewhere they were subordinated to the men, each employed by the man for whom she toiled – as Sylvia memorably put it, 'the slave of a slave, I thought!'[437]

She was so overcome by the unventilated workshops and choking dust that she fainted twice while trying to sketch. The beauty of the china tableware produced was in inverse proportion to the utter misery of the environment in which it was produced. The exception was Josiah Wedgwood's famous factory, where no lead was used and the working conditions and morale were healthier. The Wedgwoods had originally taken over Sylvia's great-uncle's pottery in Stoke-on-Trent, and the Labour MP Colonel Josiah Wedgwood was later to prove a great help to her, during her years fighting fascism and imperialism. Her son Richard recalled his mother urging friends, where possible, to buy the more ethically produced Wedgwood pottery.

Scarborough was her next stop, painting the Scottish fisherwomen who worked the east coast herring-trail, 'a jolly crowd, amazingly beautiful'.[438] Thence to border country, to the village of Chirnside in Berwickshire, to study women farmworkers, who divided into two distinct groups: the neat, well-spoken country farmhands in quaint, traditional dress and the casually employed potato pickers recruited from the slums of Berwick-on-Tweed, lively with 'oaths and snatches of song'. These latter were a crowd of tattered, hard-pressed women, hungry and sick with privation. The working conditions were appalling. 'So terrible they were that sitting there at my easel I could barely enforce myself to stay.'[439] She did, nevertheless, force herself to stay, and wrote a lengthy article for the *Manchester Guardian* entitled 'How Potatoes Are Gathered', in which she observed how the two groups of women 'eye each other curiously – the poor slum-dwellers from the lanes of Berwick and the rosy-faced Scotch lassies from the leafy lanes of Berwickshire'.[440]

As winter set in, Sylvia moved to Glasgow and got permission to paint in a Bridgeton cotton factory. The little 'half-timers' – child labour – were better able than she to endure the stifling, cacophonous environment in which she passed out several times. She'd chosen Glasgow rather than Lancashire for her cotton study because her brother Harry was living there, labouring for a building contractor constructing new dwellings for workers. Sylvia stayed in a two-room tenement flat with a couple, their daughter and a large basket of Yorkshire terriers. She slept in a traditional cupboard bed in the wall in the parlour, no doubt more comfortable there than she had been on her Holloway pallet. Harry piloted her around the city, introducing her to people in the labour and suffragette movements and chatting to her with great intensity about his developing interest in Buddhism and other eastern philosophies. Sylvia wondered how her gentle, cerebral young brother – six feet tall, unworldly, frail and impractical – coped with swinging around on scaffolding on dark, cold Clydeside winter mornings.

The sketches and paintings that Sylvia produced on her 1907 tour form a remarkable body of work documenting the lives of working women in early twentieth-century Britain. As much of it had to be carried out at speed, in the moment, she worked mainly in gouache. This was a medium she liked and had used in Italy and on the WSPU membership card. She also worked in chalks, charcoal and pastels. Her sitters could spare only short snatches of time. Most often, she was trying to capture likenesses in the fast-moving factory environment, in extremely challenging conditions.

There was little scope for a broad palette of colour and rarely any opportunity of luminosity from natural light. Where she could find natural glow and colour, she captured it – in a shaft of late-afternoon sunlight catching the red hair of a very young girl working in a pottery, or in the pale-blue smocks of the Leicester shoemakers working on benches under daylight filtered through large-paned windows. But mostly the lustre lies in the products rather than the producers – a shining soup tureen, white cotton on bobbins in a spinning mill, the gold of freshly threshed wheat.

Throughout the series, Sylvia renders tools of the trades and machinery with arresting precision. The message is clear: women and instruments of labour are one. Particularly striking, when taken as a group, is the shared attitude of the workers portrayed. These are young girls and women with heads bent perpetually over their work, their eyes focused on labour. The occasional portraits depicting a lifted gaze are of elders, in sedentary tasks reserved for the aged or retired, sitting by the hearth – perhaps the landlady of one of Sylvia's lodgings. Here, as everywhere else in this realist figurative work, Sylvia captures the impact of labour on the women's bodies and faces – prematurely aged by hard lives, their sometimes hopeless expressions. Yet where she encounters it there are also laughter, chatter, smiles and kinship. Commonly this is found among the outdoor workers, because silence was usually strictly enforced in the factories.

Her tour over, in December Sylvia returned to London. Her mother and Christabel called on her a week before Christmas. It was the first time she'd seen them in many months. She took them to a favourite little restaurant in Hampstead she used to go to with Harry during his schooldays and updated them on the time she'd spent with him in Glasgow and on her concerns for his health and well-being. It had been Emmeline's idea to apprentice Harry to the Clydeside builder. She hoped for a positive report, but Sylvia expressed her deep anxiety about his suitability for the work. Her mother and sister invited Sylvia to go with them to Teignmouth in Devon for the upcoming by-election and spend the festive holiday together. She refused.

As Sylvia left home that evening to meet her mother and sister for dinner, she'd picked up a letter left for her on the hall table. During the meal, she read the missive covertly opened on her knee. 'It roused in me a sudden storm of misery, which seemed to be killing my inner life, transforming an inner shrine which had been as a pleasant garden of singing birds, to a waste and barren place. Snakes and writhing creatures, fire and destruction, passed before my eyes; yet neither of the two sitting before me perceived my anguish.'[441]

As she'd refused their invitation, Sylvia surprised Emmeline, Christabel and Mary Gawthorpe on Christmas Eve by turning up unexpectedly at their hotel in Teignmouth during a howling gale. Leeds-born Gawthorpe was a leading WSPU organizer, known for her unrelenting hard work and stamina. She became a pupil-teacher aged thirteen and went on to obtain a first-class teaching certificate. A talented singer and pianist, she put all else aside for the cause. Later, in 1915, she would emigrate to America where she worked for the New York State Women Suffrage Party, for the Labor Party in Illinois and for the Amalgamated Clothing Workers of America trade union in Rochester, New York. Gawthorpe was part of the inner circle of the WSPU committee, and both Emmeline and Sylvia got along well with her.

So strong was the force of the storm when a bedraggled Sylvia arrived at the hotel that the door at the front entrance could not be opened and she had to be let in around the back. She found the festive trio snug together inside, 'merry as crickets', and instantly regretted that she had come. Long-faced Sylvia left on Boxing Day, 'unable to control my restless misery in the face of their cheerful chatter'.[442] Emmeline, who tried to persuade her to stay and relax, was left impatient and angered by her hasty departure. Exasperated by her mood, her mother, sister and Mary wondered at its cause. Only from the point of view of posterity was the trip any sort of success: on Christmas Day Sylvia made an exquisite small sketch of Mary Gawthorpe that captured her best likeness.

Much of Sylvia and Hardie's intimate correspondence during this period is undated. It tends to run in a confluence of continuous conversation, punctuated by the pauses between posting and arrival. Sylvia had returned to London at the end of the year clearly in expectation of being reunited with Hardie after his tour of the empire but had been met instead by the letter on the hall table that so upset her.

An undated letter to Sylvia from Hardie expressing deep emotional distress presents itself as the likely source of the upset. The uncharacteristic spelling errors and crossings out suggest he wrote it while grappling with the effects of his first stroke, which happened during the spring of 1907, while the content makes it clear they are apart and have not seen each other for some time, suggesting he may have written it after his return from his tour. The largely unpunctuated stream-of-consciousness style conveys the urgency of his need to communicate his feelings to Sylvia.

> I feel as though I had passed through fire and water and a long
> valley of bitterness and had come out duller and wiser as though
> I should never feel so acutely any more but that may or not be –
> probably not. At the same time I feel as though I should never feel
> keenly, fervently, other things that I would wish to feel, but only
> calmly and with reserve and with a double sensation of looking all
> round then into the past, the present and the future.[443]

This letter reveals much about the workings of Hardie's heart and his struggle over his love for his wife and for his much younger mistress. But his concerns are also much broader. Certainly he writes plaintively about the quandary he feels himself to be in, torn between the moral conventions of duty and his principled duty to the unconventional.

Yet it is equally important to recall that Hardie is fifty-one years old, has just suffered his first stroke and is cogitating on his confrontation with mortality. Painful and poignant, the letter is a wonderful lyrical affirmation of the desire to hold on to the ability to feel and fight for others in the face of death. Hardie is struggling with his soul.

> I prayed. I longed. I cried in agony to be more stollid [sic] and self-
> contained – I feel I AM now, so I would be in one way, but I would
> not lose the power to pour myself out for others to forget myself
> in enthusiasm for persons and things almost I fear that if I lose the
> ability to be cast down to be all but consumed grief even for slight
> things in any direction so too I shall lose the power to love without
> reserve in that same direction too. I suppose like nature: nature has
> its changing seasons and maybe I have stepped into a new phase
> of life and maybe only into another transient mood who knows
> and the only answer to that is work while you may – so that will
> I do now.

If this emotional outpouring seems to suggest Hardie's struggle with renunciation, his last line also provides proof of his fear of Sylvia's silence: 'I wonder – when will you write to me again.'[444]

Sylvia interpreted Hardie's ambiguous letter as meaning that while he was away he had reconsidered their relationship and intended to end it. If her response to his letter seems over-dramatic, spare a thought for the loneliness and anxiety she had weathered for six months. Returning to London after her miserable Christmas in windswept Devon, she found, to her unexpected happiness, that she had been mistaken. As she discreetly put it, 'I could not foresee that my sorrow would presently be dispelled as suddenly as it came.'[445] Hardie was back in London in the new year, and clearly they saw each other. As political events of 1908 show, Hardie soon 'found a way to fall right back in with Sylvia and WSPU work'.[446]

A fair bit of moralizing has been expended on judging Hardie's effect on Sylvia: far less on her influence on him. The positive aspects of his impact on her are barely acknowledged. It is clear that the actions and values of her adult political life were very much guided by his inspiration and example. Sylvia also had a powerful impact on Hardie and – from a feminist perspective – very much for the better. Deeply revealing are the records of their arguments. Sylvia typically holds her ground. Rather than standing down or bending herself out of shape to keep him sweet – which most of the other women in his extramarital life were prone to do – Sylvia challenged him head-on and walked away until he followed and caught up with her.

Hardie was in so many ways modern, but he was also the product of his upbringing and he was not going to renounce Lillie or the public face of his marriage that so reassured the socially conservative Christian socialists among his constituents and political supporters, however much he longed to. Sylvia's father would have agreed. Public sentiment, Richard Pankhurst explained to his daughter, discriminated against people who challenged the relevance of the marriage institution. That was why he had married her mother, even though they were both committed to the principles of free love. Unmarried, they would have been exposed to slander and it would have been a barrier to their ambitions in public life. Once more, Sylvia heard her father's voice in her head, warning 'that people who have displayed unconventionality in that direction, had usually been prevented from doing effective public work in any other'.[447]

Throughout her life one of Sylvia's most common mantras was 'I always loathed Mother Grundy.'[448] A figurative name for an extremely conventional or priggish person, Mother Grundy was a mythical personification of the tyranny of conformist propriety. The evidence is that Sylvia lived by this mantra. She was private, not secretive about her relationship with Hardie. Throughout her life she maintained that the vitality of life lay in the relationship between personality, what she called the expression and visions of 'the soul', and forces of class, society, politics, world events and the common human cause. At the heart of her affinity with Hardie was her lifelong quest to discover what men could become, and what their relationships with women could be.

It was primarily from her relationship with Hardie that Sylvia learned the exacting price of freedom and the cost of rebellion against the marriage institution against which her father had warned her. The serpentine imagery – 'Snakes and writhing creatures, fire and destruction, passed before my eyes'[449] – that Sylvia used to describe her horror at receiving the letter that so distressed her over the Christmas of 1907 recurs, significantly, in two unpublished short stories she wrote on the theme of her agonizing guilt about their relationship. These surreal pieces, set in allegorical, archetypal dreamscapes, are written under the awkward pen name of S. Prigioniere. During the period Sylvia wrote them, she was imprisoned repeatedly in Holloway. But she was also a captive of another sort, a prisoner of her anguish over what her relationship with Hardie did to Lillie. In 'A dream of the devil's tempting', Lillie is the protagonist and the victim of a Hardie figure led astray and provoked by a cloven-hoofed devil–Sylvia figure.

The story is set in an artist's studio that is also a prison cell. Everything is grey cement. Tall skeletons in Elizabethan dress glide and dance around in a grotesque masque, symbols both of desire and of hunger-striking women in their bulky, bunched prison skirts and bodices. The narrator dreams that she is a devil of a very traditional sort, with forked tail and cloven hoof. The man she is tempting, depicted clearly as a Hardie figure, has a hard-working wife and a cluster of little children. The devil is the villain of the piece throughout. Her lover is her accomplice. She is fully aware of playing on his weaknesses and both of them are certain the wife is their victim.

Violence features throughout.

> I knew that he was almost penniless, that his family were suffering,
> and that though his wife pinched and toiled to make ends meet,
> he was not merely neglectful, but sometimes violently cruel to her
> beside, and I knew that it was I who continued to make him so …
> And whilst I thus was tempting him to do these things my heart
> ached because of them. I was as sad as though I were reviewing the
> failures of my own character, the mistakes of my own life.[450]

Throughout the tale appears the refrain that the life of the wife is one of constant toil. The Sylvia she-devil, seeing her lover's face disfigured, realizes that she has destroyed his equanimity: 'I was suffocating with fear and horror, I knew that I had driven him mad.' It is frequently claimed, disapprovingly, that Sylvia never wrote about Lillie and the effect on their circumstances of her being Hardie's lover. This is untrue. The dream scenes in Sylvia's short story resolve themselves into a tableau: the young wife, slender and fair, puts her arms around her husband's neck to soothe and calm him – his eyes are rolling. A key image of the piece is the light and shadow play of his split face, the distressed side showing his white, mad eye. Instead of returning her embrace, the man spins his wife around, picks up a piece of wood that turns into a gun, puts it against the back of her neck and drives her up on to the roof of a lean-to. She falls backwards on to the gun barrel, and he is about to pull the trigger and shoot her. At that moment the sky pours down molten lead, swirling all three of them into a volcanic whirlpool.

The story ends with the narrator waking. 'What did it mean? Is it that the devil is in our own hearts, and that his tempting is our own giving way to the weaknesses to which we are prone? When I told my dream to one who is wise and good and said, "Heaven would not let him shoot her," he answered, "But Heaven sent lead to make more bullets." '[451]

Decades later, Sylvia produced a detailed outline and chapter breakdown for an unpublished novel entitled 'Noah Adamson', the character in which Hardie would consistently appear in her later fiction and drama. In this mature version, written after Hardie's death, the tortures of conscience are swept aside and replaced by a cogent realist drama. 'Noah Adamson' is described as a novel depicting 'The tragedy of a man of great ability and noble and romantic character who has risen from great poverty to political prominence, condemned to great loneliness of spirit through the inability of the woman he married in early youth to rise with him, and the failure of his political colleagues to reach his own idealism.'[452]

Noah's tough childhood in a northern village is told. Enter 'Lily Burnside, the motherless daughter of a local publican of ill repute'. They take the temperance oath together, marry and quickly become disappointed in each other. Lily resists Noah's work organizing a miners' union, reproaching him for the financial precariousness caused by his idealism. When he's sacked for political agitation, she insists that in future 'material advancement shall take precedence of all else' and tries to force him to take a vacant job as a driver.

Noah resists and persists, is eventually elected to parliament and comes to lead a party, gaining importance and influence. 'Despite the improvement in his position, Lily regards him with unalterable contempt, yet is piqued by the realization that she has slipped out of his emotional life.' Noah's achievements feed her resentment. She complains that she receives 'only a tiny modicum of reflected greatness, and becomes an aggressively complaining *malade imaginaire*, posing as the victim of his neglect'. The plot moves briskly to the entrance of the Sylvia figure. 'In a period of extreme despondency, when he has been tactically out-matched by the grosser elements in his Party, Noah meets Freda Urswick, the daughter of an old friend, a poet, now dead.' Freda lives alone in lodgings and is trying to make her way as a writer. Noah regards her as an earnest young disciple, but soon recognizes that he is in love with her. 'Freda struggles desperately against her growing realisation of his feeling towards her. Herself subconsciously in love, she is unable to maintain her resolve that they must part when he finally declares his love.'

In Sylvia's fictionalization of their story, it is Noah who 'wishes to dare all' and Freda 'who insists that the interests of a movement of which he is the leader must take precedence of their personal happiness'. In consequence, they maintain a secret friendship, 'which entails great isolation for Freda, for they meet only at infrequent intervals. She experiences great sorrow and mental torment, and rare moments of exaltation.'

At this point in the plot, Freda knows nothing of the bitter antagonism and marital breakdown between his wife Lily, whom neither of them mentions. She endures a long period of inner conflict, struggling with qualms of conscience. After her period of heart-searching, she emerges 'convinced that Noah is incapable of cruelty or injustice to anyone' and believing that 'Lily neither gives nor desires from Noah the companionship he needs.'

During Freda's crisis of conscience, 'her mother confides to her her own delusion that Noah is in love with her and that his fatherly interest in Freda springs from that source. When the truth is accidentally revealed to the mother her love for Noah turns to hatred.'[453]

On the unfolding map of their lives, each plot point in Sylvia's novel outline can be charted on real events.

Early in the new year of 1908, nineteen-year-old Harry turned up at Sylvia's lodgings and asked if he could stay with her until he found another job. It hadn't worked out with the developer in Glasgow – he'd been fired. Sylvia put her brother up on her camp bed, fed him and shared with him what cash she had. She had just enough to cover their rent and subsistence for nine days, 'on short commons', an insight into her hand-to-mouth existence.[454] Harry must start looking for another job. Sylvia worried constantly about the frailty of his health and the emotional generosity and gentleness that made him so vulnerable to others. What a great worry to his mother and sisters, this suffragette son.

PART THREE

Rage of Militancy 1908–1914

Like many another young woman of my period, I was distraught
by my solidarity with that rage of militancy.
E. Sylvia Pankhurst, *The Suffragette Movement*

11

The Art of Struggle

The struggle for women's enfranchisement took nearly a century, from the first petition presented to parliament in 1832 to 1928 when women were at last entitled to vote on equal terms with men. The years leading up to the outbreak of the First World War in 1914 were the most intense. For Sylvia, this was a period of self-transformation. The terrain of the suffragette campaign shifted dramatically, the theatre of battle engaged on multiple fronts. As things changed, so too did Sylvia.

Nineteen hundred and eight was a year defined by suffragette spectacle. It began with the WSPU chaining themselves to the railings of 10 Downing Street, secured by large padlocks that the police had to smash before they could drag the women away to Cannon Street police station. Clement's Inn now employed twenty full-time staff and a constant tide of volunteers, working on preparations for the three-day Women's Parliament to be held at Caxton Hall in February. They planned to present a petition to the men's parliament at Westminster on the first day. Knowing they would be blocked, they discussed what form of subterfuge they could devise to get into the palace. Harry, still living with Sylvia, came up with the idea of a Trojan Horse raid to smuggle themselves into Westminster. The WSPU hired two large vans from a London furniture remover and concealed twenty-one activists in the back of each, driven by male supporters disguised in company uniforms.

With Harry's first-rate ruse they made it through the entrance gates into New Palace Yard, into Old Palace Yard and past all the defences to the Strangers' Entrance. There they burst out of the back of the vans and dashed for the doors where startled policemen seized the militants they could catch and threw them back into the road. 'In an instant the expectant calm of Westminster was ended, and the very Speaker in the chair blenched at the sound of the policemen's whistles.'[455] The militant suffragettes had breached the inner sanctum of male political power. 'The bolder members in the House left their places to go lobbyward, grinning. Others pulled hats over their noses, cowered in their seats, and feigned that all was right with the world. In Old Palace Yard everybody ran. They either ran to see or ran for shelter. Even two Cabinet ministers took to their heels, grinning insecurely.'[456]

Harry Pankhurst's operation was a triumph. The stunt caught the media's imagination. The *Daily Chronicle* wrote with admiration, 'the Suffragettes are essentially heroic. First they lash themselves to the Premier's railings; now borrowing the idea from the Trojan horse, they burst forth from a pantechnicon van … A high standard of artifice has been set and it should be maintained.'[457]

Maintained it was. Nineteen hundred and eight was a year of creative protests, stunts, processions, festivals, meetings, mass rallies, arrest, court hearings and widespread imprisonment. Cabinet ministers stopped addressing open gatherings for fear of heckling – or worse – from suffragette militants, and Liberal officials began to bar women from party meetings. On 3 April Campbell-Bannerman resigned on account of failing health. He died three weeks later. Herbert Asquith became unelected Prime Minister on 8 April. Asquith was totally op-posed to women having the vote.

The suffragettes had captured the cultural imagination. Plays, songs, novels, short stories taking the struggle as their theme rapidly started to appear on theatre stages and bookshop tables. In October 1909, H. G. Wells published his feminist novel *Ann Veronica*. His prototype anti-heroine experiences her first direct action in a long fictionalised set piece, recreating Harry and Sylvia's Trojan Horse stunt. ' "It's like Troy!" said a voice of rapture. "It's exactly like Troy!" '[458] Ann Veronica, arrested, tried and sentenced, ends up in Canongate prison, earning her father's implacable fury: directed against her, not the state.

While in the thick of the campaign, the men in Sylvia's life made constant demands on her attention. The Pankhurst women discussed what to do about Harry. Christabel suggested sensibly that he might take a secretarial course and learn shorthand and typing, qualifying him for dry, clean and safe indoor work by which he could earn himself a living. His mother came up with the impractical proposal that he should apply for a ticket to read in the British Library, even though she still flatly refused him permission to wear spectacles. Harry was unable to stand up to his mother on this issue, and anyway was more interested in activism than inclined towards administration or academic research. In this he was like his father. Unlike Richard Pankhurst, he was a very poor reader, because Emmeline continued to regard poor eyesight in youth as a sign of weakness of character rather than genetics. Christabel and Sylvia together decided to take the matter into their own hands. As soon as their mother left London again, they booked Harry an appointment with an optician and had him fitted with spectacles, which they paid for. However, their hope that glasses would help their brother professionally to find better work was not immediately fulfilled. The main benefit of Harry's new range of vision appeared to be that it enabled him to see clearly enough to fall headlong in love with a beautiful young suffragette.

Harry spent Easter working for Christabel's campaign to unseat Churchill in Manchester North West. Here he met the twenty-year-old WSPU activist Helen Craggs, daughter of the politician Sir John Craggs. Helen was educated at Roedean School in the Sussex Downs but her father forbade her studying medicine, despite being a major donor for research into tropical diseases. She joined the WSPU in 1908 at the age of twenty, using the name 'Miss Millar' to spare her parents the embarrassment. 'In Helen's case becoming a suffragette was an extreme act of rebellion and one her parents would neither condone nor forgive.'[459] After the campaign, the lovelorn Harry followed Helen to Brighton where she taught science and physical exercise at her old boarding school, situated on a cliff overlooking Brighton Marina and the English Channel. While spending a rainy night camping out on the cliff in the hope of stealing a glimpse of her, he caught a cold. During the long hours of his chilly vigil Harry, newly kitted out with his spectacles, was able to compose poetry to his first love, returning to his fondness for Trojan War themes:

I saw thee, beloved,
And having seen, shall ever see,
I as Greek, and thou,
O Helen, within the walls of Troy.

Tell me, is there no weak spot
In this great wall by which
I could come to thee, beloved?[460]

Though he could devise a plan to get a suffragette battalion through the
Gothic portals of Westminster Palace in the heart of London, Harry
couldn't seem to come up with a plan to get himself inside the grounds
of a small boarding school.

In April, Hardie returned triumphant from his world tour. Sylvia
had followed his progress. She bought a large scrapbook in which she
had compiled and annotated press cuttings relating to his trip. At the
massive welcome-home rally held for him at the Albert Hall, Hardie
stood up after ten minutes to stop the cheering and singing so that he
could speak. He had discussed with Sylvia his deep concern that her
mother and elder sister had torn up the constitution of the WSPU and
implemented autocracy. He was dismayed by their failure to recognize
the need to prioritize the equality of working-class women within the
movement. In the meantime, they agreed to tolerate Emmeline and
Christabel's methods in support of the principle of the women's vote
overall.

Midsummer 1908 was a highpoint in the temperature of a national
heatwave and in the Votes for Women campaign. In June the NUWSS
called a huge meeting in the Albert Hall, starting with a march from the
Embankment in the dazzling sunshine. An assortment of organizations
participated, including the ILP, Fabians, Women's Co-operative Guild,
National Union of Women Workers and women's Liberal associations.
International suffragists from Australia, America, Hungary, Russia,
South Africa and other countries flew their colours and national flags.
Scientists and professional medical women wore their academic gowns,
writers marched under their scriveners' banner and artists and actresses
paraded alongside nurses, gardeners, typists, factory workers and, to use
Sylvia's modern term, 'home-makers'.[461]

Typically, Sylvia marched with her artist's eye, admiring the 'striking
pageant with its many gorgeous banners, richly embroidered and
fashioned of velvets, silks and every kind of beautiful material'.[462] She
celebrated particularly the seventy large banners made by the Artists'
Suffrage League, emblazoned with images of great historical women –
Boadicea, Joan of Arc, Queen Elizabeth, Elizabeth Fry, Lydia Becker

and Mary Wollstonecraft. 'Altogether the procession,' she wrote in *The Suffragette*, 'was acknowledged to be the most picturesque and effective political pageant that had ever been seen in this country, and every newspaper spoke of its impressive dignity and beauty.'[463]

This line of credit, given so freely and openly in her first account of the movement published in 1911, was withdrawn when she rewrote it two decades later in *The Suffragette Movement*. In the later version, she presents the great NUWSS march negatively as a reaction to the WSPU call for a midsummer demonstration marching on Hyde Park. In 1911 everyone still swam in the struggle's midstream. By 1931 organizations and individuals were jostling with sharp elbows to claim retrospectively their pre-eminent place in history. Factionalism was as fully alive and vigorously kicking in the feminist movement as among the openly fractious socialists or amid the closeted skulduggery of conservativism.

More interesting from a historical perspective than activist infighting is the fact that the women's movement was able to follow the 13,000-strong procession to the Albert Hall on 13 June 1908 with an even larger demonstration on 21 June and swiftly on its heels another mass protest in Parliament Square on 30 June. These rallies and the relentless activism that roused them are representative of many in the months and years of sustained campaigning in that intense period leading up to the summer of 1914.

The WSPU organized the midsummer march and rally to congregate in Hyde Park on 21 June. The event was preceded by an exemplary fortnight of on-the-ground campaigning. Throughout Great Britain, women canvassed door to door, distributed handbills, fly-posted, carried flags in the streets and chalked announcements on pavements. The brainchild of Emmeline Pethick-Lawrence, the new WSPU colours were adopted in May and achieved nationwide recognition before the month was out. A quarter of a million purple, white and green mock railway tickets were printed and given out at stations to workmen and commuter trains. WSPU opened pop-up shops all over London, selling mass-produced, branded suffragette merchandise, all of it printed in the new livery. There were banners and regalia for both body and home; shopping bags printed with images of Christabel, Mrs Pankhurst and other feminist leaders; and printed ties, scarves, sashes, brooches, hatpins and all manner of branded goods. In a limited edition, Sylvia designed an exquisite china tea service elegantly decorated with her trumpeting angel of feminist 'Freedom'.

The General – Flora Drummond – accompanied by a band, pulled up in a steamboat below the terrace of the Houses of Parliament one afternoon when she knew that Lloyd George and his colleagues would be entertaining some ladies for tea. Bellowing through her loudspeaker, she invited them all – especially the Cabinet ministers – to attend the women's procession. Playfully, she promised them police protection and offered the assurance that none of them need fear arrest. As Flora spoke, a flustered Inspector Scantlebury appeared on the terrace accompanied by a cohort of officers and a police boat hove into view, whereupon General Drummond and her brass ensemble steamed away.[464]

Put in charge of the visual choreography of the midsummer 'Suffrage Sunday', Sylvia created a variety of heraldic designs and border decorations. She contracted a firm specializing in the manufacture of banners, bunting and regalia to produce them. She claimed 'no great artistry' for the work, which required 'mass production, in double-quick time'.[465] Many WSPU branches produced their own lovingly hand-stitched or screen-printed standards. Sylvia revelled in this vast production of beautiful and useful public art. The appearance of an individual banner counted for little, she wrote, for 'it was true to say that the creation of a Michael Angelo would have ranked low in the eyes of the W.S.P.U. members beside a term served in Holloway'.[466] Warehouses filled with packing cases of silk banners, flags and ribbons. Decorated buses drove through the streets, cinemas announced the demonstration in their newsreels and London department stores and shops created window displays in the suffragette purple, green and white.

Sunday 21 June was a scorcher for the women's movement. The WSPU arranged for thirty special trains to run from seventy different towns to bring contingents of women to the capital. On the day, each district of London was systematically organized and marchers processed from each of their branches. Mrs H. G. Wells, Mrs Thomas Hardy and Mrs George Bernard Shaw travelled in four-in-hand coaches with Israel Zangwill and other cultural luminaries. H. G. Wells and Thomas Hardy accompanied their wives. Keir Hardie and George Bernard Shaw marched from Trafalgar Square with the ILP and Fabians.

Sylvia's own Chelsea, Fulham and Wandsworth section numbered 7,000. She portrayed the mood as congenial. 'As far as the eye could reach was a sea of human beings. Instead of the sombre darkness of other crowds, the predominating gay hues of the women's clothes and the white straw hats of the men suggested a giant bed of flowers. Under that golden sunshine, that sky of cloudless blue, it was a gala day indeed.'[467] Here was an embodiment of the spirit of celebration and aesthetic pleasure shared en masse, not just a grim column of worthy struggle.

Thirty thousand marchers converged on Hyde Park, joined by a crowd that press and police estimates put at anything between 250,000 and 500,000. Even *The Times* stated that it would be difficult to contradict anyone who claimed the number was a far greater 750,000; 'Like the distance and numbers of the stars, the facts were beyond the threshold of perception.' The *Daily News* agreed that there was 'no combination of words which will convey an adequate idea of the immensity of the crowd around the platforms', while the *Daily Express* praised the suffragettes for providing London with 'one of the most wonderful and astonishing sights that has ever been seen since the days of Boadicea … It is probable that so many people never before stood in one square mass anywhere in England.'[468] Certainly, these were the largest political gatherings since the Chartists.

Christabel dispatched a special messenger to Asquith asking what action the government intended to take in response to the demand expressed at Hyde Park. 'Nothing,' was the Prime Minister's curt reply.[469] The WSPU immediately called a public meeting outside Westminster Palace for the end of the month. When the protesters arrived at Parliament Square they found themselves barred from entry by fifty mounted police and 5,000 more on foot. Sylvia was at the heart of the crowd that rushed forward trying to break the police phalanx and gain access to the House of Commons. Roughs from organized gangs stepped in and confronted them, battering, assaulting and dragging them away. Scotland Yard had hired the gangs from among its informants, it was afterwards revealed. To free her hands and protect herself, Sylvia had to drop her handbag containing her purse and keys. Lloyd George, Winston Churchill, Herbert Gladstone and members of both Houses could be seen watching the tumult from the Westminster Palace windows.

Incensed by the violence and sexual indecency meted out to the women in the square, Mary Leigh and Edith New persuaded a hansom cab to drive them into Downing Street where they hurled two small stones through the windows of Number 10. This was the first act of damage to property committed by the suffragettes. Leigh and New acted unilaterally. Before their resulting trial they sent a message to Mrs Pankhurst making it clear they did not expect her to support their action. She went to visit them in their cells to congratulate them and assure them that their deed had full WSPU endorsement. At their trial they appeared in white dresses, unrepentant and backed by a crowd of suffragette supporters.

In October 1908 Christabel initiated the new tactic of 'rushing' parliament. The WSPU advertised these demonstrations in advance, inviting the public to support the suffragette battle charges against the portals of constitutional power. Sylvia distributed vast quantities of leaflets. Muriel Matters and Helen Fox of the Women's Franchise League chained themselves to the grille of the Ladies' Gallery in the Commons, causing havoc as they shouted 'Votes for Women!' Outside, policemen chased Mary 'La Belle' Maloney around the statue of Richard Coeur de Lion in Old Palace Yard, with four others who had climbed on to the plinth and attempted to address the crowd. Sylvia much admired 'La Belle', nicknamed on account of her one-woman tactic. She followed Churchill around public meetings all over the country and, when he attempted to speak, drowned him out by persistently ringing a muffin bell. Millicent Fawcett condemned both the WFL and WSPU for these 'disturbances of the peace' and appealed to MPs not to change their minds or abstain from voting because of the 'disorder' – 'an exhortation which,' Sylvia remarked, 'seemed to indicate the opinion that they had reason to do so'.[470]

Mrs Pankhurst, Christabel and General Drummond were arrested for incitement. Sylvia, accompanied by her friend Amy Browning, sat through the entire proceedings at Bow Street court. She reported the trial in *Votes for Women*. There is an unmistakable tone of pride and admiration in her description of the defiant panache with which her elder sister turned the trial into daily national media headlines. Christabel conducted her own defence and subpoenaed Lloyd George and Herbert Gladstone to appear. She captivated the press with her cross-questioning of these two big political beasts. Christabel had her period at the time, and Sylvia and Amy made frequent trips to the pharmacy for sachets of painkilling powders to relieve her stomach cramps. The media dubbed her the 'Portia of the Suffragettes', praising her in equal measure for her beauty and her 'brilliant display of persistence in the examination of two Cabinet Ministers'.[471]

Mrs Pankhurst and Flora Drummond were sentenced to three months' imprisonment and Christabel got ten weeks. Emmeline Pethick-Lawrence appointed Sylvia to deputize for her sister while she was inside. Sylvia impressed Hardie and her suffragette colleagues with her energetic and inventive aptitude for leadership during the remaining weeks of the year. In December Lloyd George, at his own suggestion, controversially addressed the Women's Liberal Federation at their annual Albert Hall meeting. The WSPU ignored requests not to disrupt the assembly. Sylvia booked all the seats in the front rows of the arena and packed them with women in buttoned-up overcoats. When stewards and police swooped on them to put a stop to their heckling, the women opened their coats to reveal their prison clothes beneath.

Sylvia had invited the press to Clement's Inn in advance and instructed the protesters who escaped arrest to return directly to the WSPU offices, roughed up, bruised and bloodied with torn corsets and stockings, and not to clean and tidy themselves up first. The stunt produced a sympathetic press. The *Evening Standard* condemned 'the grossly brutal conduct' and 'unnecessary violence' of the stewards, and the *Manchester Guardian* reported that the protesters had been ejected 'with a brutality which was almost nauseating'.[472]

King Edward VII did not share the media's sympathy for the suffragettes. Asquith received a letter from the palace expressing royal 'disgust' at reading in *The Times* about Mr Lloyd George's attendance at the Albert Hall meeting where he appeared to show himself in favour of the women's franchise.[473] Asquith's response summarizes the government's position at the time: 'On the general question, I must point out that in this Cabinet (as would also be the case if the Unionists came to power) female suffrage is an open question. I myself am opposed to it but the great majority of my colleagues including some, such as Grey and Haldane whose opinion I greatly value, are in its favour.'[474]

Women's mock-military infantry assaults, cavalry parades, motor and charabanc demonstrations, and kites and boats covered in posters and flying the suffragette colours kept the spectacle of women's dissent in the public eye. Unlike Millicent Fawcett, the popular press often found wit, ingenuity and heroism in these antics. In February 1909 the Women's

Franchise League took the protest to the air when Muriel Matters, 'that daring Australian girl', sailed her airship over London – 'a cigar-shaped dirigible balloon'. She launched from Hendon, dropping fifty-six pounds of leaflets over Wormwood Scrubs, Kensington, Westminster Palace and Parliament Square, Tooting and finally Croydon, where she came down in the field of a startled farmer.[475] Later, Matters followed Sylvia to the East End and joined the East London Federation of Suffragettes.

While the breakaway WFL proved itself as militant as the maternal body that gave birth to it, Millicent Fawcett's NUWSS was likewise becoming more proactive nationally. The NUWSS affiliated to the growing worldwide feminist movement by joining the International Woman Suffrage Alliance, which held its fifth Congress in London in April 1909. The WSPU kept up the pressure by holding successive Women's Parliaments at Caxton Hall.

Sylvia meanwhile worked flat out on preparations for the Women's Exhibition scheduled for May 1909 in the Prince's Skating Rink in Knightsbridge. Emmeline Pethick-Lawrence had commissioned her early that year, giving her just three months to complete the task of decorating the enormous hall – 250 by 150 feet. It was an exciting, pressurized project. Here was an opportunity to produce inspiring public art on a grand scale, as she had always wanted to do. The venue could be hired only for the period of the exhibition, so all the works had to be prepared outside the building and ready for installation the night before the festival opened.

Sylvia spent three weeks tramping around London by bus and on foot in rain, fog and snow in search of premises large enough to accommodate her twenty-foot-high designs. She found a suitable space in the Avenue Studios on Fulham Road. 'The Avenue' constituted a group of fifteen artists' and sculptors' studios at 76 Fulham Road set up in the late nineteenth century. Here John Singer Sargent spread out to paint his giant murals for the Boston Public Library and Alfred Gilbert created *Eros* for Piccadilly Circus. Sylvia commissioned her friend Amy Browning and two other women who had studied with them at the Royal College of Art to work on the project for thirty shillings a week, the same fee she allocated to herself from the budget provided by Clement's Inn. In addition, she employed four former male students from the RCA to prepare the canvases and to do the heavier lifting at standard decorators' rates of tenpence an hour. For the first time, Sylvia was able to convene a collective of paid artistic workers dedicated to producing the grand-scale murals and decorative installations that powered her imagination.

With characteristic focus, she set about determining the scope and character of the designs and entire decorative scheme according to 'the necessity of doing something which could be executed in two months and one week precisely'.[476] Sylvia drafted and painted the original designs on a quarter scale, after which Amy and her female colleagues enlarged them and painted in the human figures. The men prepared the huge canvases, together measuring 400 by 20 feet. They painted the entirety in a pale-cream base before transferring the full-sized cartoons on to the canvas. Sylvia devised designs for the hall's arches and pilasters, transforming them into four life-sized trees interlaced with vines. She drew inspiration from the work of Walter Crane and William Morris.

Sylvia found this 'large work … an exhilarating experience' and 'felt alive'.[477] She beavered away through the nights and barely slept. Fred Pethick-Lawrence dropped by one evening to ask what sort of stalls she was making for the festival. Until he put the question she'd had no idea that these were her responsibility too. Sylvia shot off to the ice rink, mapped out a plan and handed it over to a bazaar fitter. One of the stalls she invented was a scale recreation of a Holloway prison cell that festivalgoers could get themselves locked into. It proved one of the most popular installations.

The decorations, picked out in the repeated keynote colours of purple, white and green, took for their theme words from Psalm 126: 'They that sow in tears shall reap in joy. He that goeth forth and weepeth, bearing precious seed shall doubtless come again with rejoicing, bringing his sheaves with him.' The colossal, symbolic tableaux and motifs transformed the hall, inspiring and delighting the thousands of visitors who flocked to the exhibition in a holiday spirit.

It was a fortnight's welcome break from militant action, set amid Sylvia's flights of doves, olive branches, groves of spring daisies, daffodils, wild flowers, briar roses, clusters of ripe purple grapes and vividly bright butterflies. There were stalls dedicated to topical political themes, an exhibition of press photographs, a history of the militant movement, satirical sideshows and ju-jitsu lessons, advertised as 'useful for employment in Parliament Square'. Among the issues presented at the polling booth was the bizarre proposal for a so-called Daylight Saving Bill to lengthen winter days, an idea clearly too fantastic ever to become reality.

The thronging crowds entered the exhibition hall underneath the immense figure of Sylvia's sower, who stepped forward purposefully into the future. Overhead, Sylvia depicted a flight of three doves bearing an olive branch. This was included for Asquith's sake – but the Prime Minister never took up the WSPU's invitation to visit the exhibition. In the hall, fourteen-foot-high angels and a brilliant sun ascended over the visitors. The broad arrow, gilded and enclosed in a victory laurel wreath, was repeated among many other symbolic motifs.

It's a mark of her growing confidence in her artistic abilities that Sylvia allowed herself to be convinced by the quality of her work. She felt her installation at the 1909 Women's Exhibition 'assumed an appearance of grace and brilliancy which gave me great pleasure, in spite of my acute consciousness of certain defects of detail'.[478] Many years later, she spoke to her son Richard and to friends about the excitement she felt in producing these decorations.[479] But for a slim folder of black and white photographs, this visionary work is lost to history. It provided an immersive environment for crowds of diverse, intermingled suffragists, suffragettes and their supporters for a fleeting fortnight before it was dismantled. Sylvia's original paintings for the designs were later accidentally destroyed while she was in prison.

Now effectively the official artist of the movement, Sylvia had also been busy creating and producing commercial merchandise for the WSPU shops. Her designs were used on china tea services, banners, badges, greetings cards, badges and tiepins. The most iconic of her patterns were the Angel of Freedom and the portcullis and prison-arrow brooch she designed as the medal awarded to militant suffragettes when they left prison. Some of these items were also for sale in selected London stores, most notably in Gordon Selfridge's innovative emporium, which bought advertising space in *Votes for Women* and other women's suffrage papers. Selfridge flew a WSPU flag over his Oxford Street store. It was a canny move. His business cashed in on women's increased spending power while insuring itself against window smashing.

Exhausted by the months of work on the Prince's Skating Rink project, Sylvia left London before the end of the exhibition. At Hardie's suggestion, she travelled to Ightham in the Weald of Kent to retreat and recover. This was their favourite place for weekend rambles and overnight trips, where they stayed in local inns. Hardie had introduced her to a friend of his who lived there, Benjamin Harrison, a genial village grocer specializing in Eolithic archaeology. Harrison kept a remarkable collection of flint tools in cigar boxes. He showed Sylvia an old cartoon from *Punch* magazine depicting him with a tail, as England's Darwinian advocate for the 'missing link'.

After another tour of militant duty in London, Sylvia returned to the country, renting a small cottage on Cinder Hill near Penshurst on the Kentish Weald, where she settled down to painting by day and writing by night. She occluded the economics of the arrangement, but as they regarded Cinder Hill as a shared home, it seems likely that Hardie contributed to the rent to make it affordable for her. She may have felt an atavistic connection to the area. Recording her father's ancestry, she wrote that 'he was of old Kentish stock, tracing back to remote forebears of Lye and Penshurst before the coming of the Normans', and added that her father's grandfather had altered the family name from 'Penkhurst' to 'Pankhurst'.[480] When Hardie visited at weekends, they enjoyed long walks and picnics along the River Medway and Eden Valley.

Hardie's friend the Jewish American self-made millionaire Joseph Fels, who had amassed his fortune by cornering the market in laundry soap, was a major Labour Party donor and the chief financier of Hardie's recent world tour. Fels had relocated to Britain in 1900, establishing a UK branch of his soap works and settling in a mansion in Kent. Among his many philanthropic enterprises, he pioneered a scheme for establishing collective agricultural colonies aimed at easing working-class urban unemployment. These idealistic new farm communities failed in Britain, but Fels lived to see the success of the kibbutz movement in Palestine, the last farm-colony venture he funded.[481]

Hardie introduced Fels and Emmeline Pankhurst. Fels suggested to her the idea of conscripting Harry to his Mayland farm in Essex. Training as a gardener might be a useful solution to her son's continuing employment problems. Sylvia was sceptical. Harry's sensitive health and impractical nature made him poorly suited to agrarian labour. Harry was badly treated at the farm and suffered frequent illness as a consequence of overwork and living in a permanently damp, unfloored hovel. He said nothing about this to his mother or sisters, who seemed to think his poor health a consequence of his frailty rather than the appalling living and work conditions.

In April 1909 Harry developed a bladder infection. He was brought to the nursing home of the WSPU nursing sisters Gertrude Townend and Catherine Pine in Pembridge Gardens, where Dr Herbert Mills performed an examination under chloroform, much to his mother's alarm. Harry improved sufficiently to be taken to Margate for the weekend by his mother and Christabel, after which Emmeline went back on the campaign trail. She continued to worry about her son's health, and about the cost of his medical bills. Shortly after paying a large account to Dr Mills, she wrote to Harriot Stanton Blatch, her old friend from her Women's Franchise League days, now back living in America. She asked if Blatch could put her in touch with a reliable lecture bureau, and 'spoke of her desire to earn some money so as to be able to secure for Harry the best of medical care'.[482]

They continued to correspond and began to plan for Emmeline an autumn lecture tour of the USA. Blatch was politically and personally sympathetic to her friend's situation. In 1907, she had founded the New York Equality League of Self-Supporting Women, open to 'any woman who earns her own living, from a cook to a mining engineer'.[483] A suffrage society of working women, the organization emphasized the cause shared by industrial and professional women workers.[484] The focus of the Equality League on working women differentiated it from the other suffrage societies in New York City at the time, and was a significant factor in Sylvia's own later lecture tours of America, in which Blatch was highly instrumental. The league was innovative and militant in its style of activism, which appealed to Emmeline. Blatch secured a commitment from the US immigration authorities that Emmeline's prison convictions would be classified as political rather than criminal, and promoted Emmeline as speaking under the auspices of the Equality League.[485]

Back on the suffragette front, the WSPU created a new campaign. They decided to deploy the 1689 Bill of Rights enshrining the right of the subjects to petition the King. On 30 June 1909 the press reported that Marion Wallace Dunlop, a forty-four-year-old artist, writer and WSPU activist, had been charged at Bow Street with wilfully damaging the stonework of St Stephen's Hall in the House of Commons, doing damage to the value of ten shillings. Born at Leys Castle in Inverness, Dunlop studied at the Slade School of Art. Her work had been displayed at the Royal Academy in 1903, 1905 and 1906. On 22 June, using a twelve-inch by ten-inch stamp covered with indelible printers' ink, Dunlop had printed on to the stone wall of St Stephen's Hall:

> 'Women's Deputation. Bill of Rights. It is the Right of the subjects to petition the King, and all commitments and prosecutions for such petitioning are illegal.'

Victor Duval, a twenty-five-year-old clerk from the Men's League for Women's Suffrage, was charged with aiding and abetting her.[486] Two years earlier, in 1907, some forty left-wing male activists, intellectuals and writers, including Henry Brailsford, Henry Nevinson, George Lansbury, Laurence Housman, Harold Laski, Henry Harben and Israel Zangwill, had formed the Men's League for Women's Suffrage 'with the object of bringing to bear upon the movement the electoral power of men. To obtain for women the vote on the same terms as those on which it is now, or may in the future, be granted to men.'

Marion Dunlop was cautioned for her civil rights graffiti, warned that she was now banned from the precincts of parliament and released without charge. Two days later she and Victor Duval returned in disguise. Duval pretended that he had a meeting with an MP. They sat quietly together on the bench in St Stephen's Hall for a while, then Marion whipped out her printers' stamp and blazoned her notice once again on the wall.

For defacing the wall, Dunlop was sentenced to one month's imprisonment in Holloway. She demanded to be treated as a first-division political prisoner. When this was denied, she immediately went on hunger strike on 5 July, acting on her own initiative. When the prison doctor asked her what she was going to eat, she is said to have replied, 'My determination.' After ninety-one hours refusing all food and drink, she was released on 14 July. The militants believed that Dunlop had discovered a powerful new weapon with which to fight the government.

At the same time, fourteen WSPU members were committed to Holloway for smashing the windows of government offices. They refused to be searched, to change their clothes or to obey orders until their demand to be placed in the first division was met. They also broke their cell windows. Violence was used in an attempt to make them comply and various punishments imposed. Two of the women then adopted Dunlop's tactic of going on hunger strike, and others of their cohort soon followed their example.

Alarmed by the grave reports of the medical officers and unwilling to accede to the suffragettes' demand to be recognized as political prisoners, Home Secretary Herbert Gladstone authorized their discharge. On holiday in the fashionable spa town of Marienbad in the hills of Bohemia, Edward VII instructed his Private Secretary to write to Gladstone, 'His Majesty would be glad to know why the existing methods [that is, forcible feeding] which must obviously exist for dealing with prisoners who refuse nourishment, should not be adopted.'[487] The medical ethics of forced feeding had long been a subject of controversy. However, Edward VII clearly demonstrated a strong stomach for enduring the torture of his subjects. In his reply explaining why he had released the hunger-striking women, Gladstone described the option of feeding the prisoners forcibly as 'a very unpleasant operation though frequently resorted to in lunatic asylums and occasionally in prisons'.[488] Within a month Asquith's government had changed its position.

The first forced feeding of hunger-striking suffragettes took place on 24 September 1909 in Winson Green Prison, Birmingham, on the order of the Home Secretary. A group of nine women, including Mary Leigh and Charlotte (Charlie) Marsh, became the first victims of the new policy. Leigh, a working-class militant suffragette, was the first to be force-fed. Enraged by this development, Hardie immediately tabled a parliamentary question demanding a report on the health of Leigh and Marsh and asking whether they had been force-fed and, if so, on what authority this 'horrible ... beastly outrage'[489] was undertaken. Philip Snowden backed him up. The government's defence was that the torture was simply 'ordinary hospital treatment ... frequently applied to men and women – to contumacious or weak-minded persons'.[490] Hardie was horrified at the levity displayed by a large number of MPs at the time, finding it hard to believe that 'a body of gentlemen could have found reason for mirth and applause in a scene which, I venture to say, has no parallel in the recent history of our country'.[491]

Modern science has undertaken thorough research into the physical and psychological effects of hunger striking. People who are in good health at the beginning of a hunger strike are usually at little risk of dying from malnutrition for at least six to eight weeks. Those who are ill can die from malnutrition in as little as three weeks. If a person also refuses all fluids, including water, deterioration is very rapid, with death possible within seven to fourteen days, especially during hotter periods of the year. At the beginning of a hunger strike or fast, hunger pangs usually disappear after two or three days, according to scientific investigations into mass hunger strikes. After the third day, the body starts to use muscle protein to make glucose, a sugar that's needed for cell metabolism. Levels of vital electrolytes, such as potassium, fall to dangerous levels. The body loses fat and muscle mass. After two weeks, people on a hunger strike are likely to have difficulty standing, to suffer from severe dizziness, sluggishness, weakness, loss of co-ordination and low heart rate and to experience a chilled feeling.

After two or three weeks, low levels of thiamine (vitamin B1) become a real risk and can result in severe neurological problems, including cognitive impairment, vision loss and lack of motor skills. After more than a month of fasting, or when more than 18 per cent of body weight is lost, severe and permanent medical complications occur. It can become very difficult to swallow water, hearing and vision loss can occur, breathing can become laboured and organ failure can start to set in. Beyond forty-five days, death is a very real risk, due to cardiovascular collapse or severe infection.

This is the physical damage suffered by hunger strikers. Psychological changes prompting impulsive and aggressive behaviour are common. After a hunger strike has ended, refeeding carries severe risks, since the metabolic changes that occur during fasting can be profound.

During their long walks in the Weald of Kent, Sylvia and Hardie discussed the new policy of forcible feeding of women hunger strikers. 'He told me that the thought of forcible feeding was making him ill.' They debated whether or not she should join the hunger strikers in Holloway. 'I cannot stay here if it continues ... I shall have to go to prison to stand by the others.' Hardie responded that the movement didn't need any more martyrs, it needed her art. 'Finish what you are working on at least!'[492] It was around this time that Hardie gave her the beautiful hand-made copy of Cennino Cennini's 1437 *Treatise on Painting*, which Hardie lovingly inscribed with a phrase from Robbie Burns' 'Ae Fond Kiss'.

In October Sylvia returned from painting in the autumnal woods to find a telegram informing her that Harry was gravely ill and back at the Pembridge Gardens nursing home. She returned immediately and found her little brother in agony and fear, paralysed from the waist down with poliomyelitis. Emmeline had been busy speaking at meetings in London, Edinburgh and Liverpool when she heard the news that Harry had been struck down. She was due to set sail to America in a few days' time for her lucrative lecture tour. Needing money for Harry's care, she stuck to her schedule, though she wrote to a friend, 'I don't like going at all.'[493] Someone had to earn the money to pay for the nursing home and medical bills. Christabel understood the necessity. But Sylvia was harsh in her judgement of their mother's decision to leave her son's bedside. 'So ruthless was the inner call to action, that ... she persevered with her intention ... The movement was paramount. She left us two together, not knowing what might be his fate.'[494] When Sylvia wrote this twenty years later, she was a first-time mother of an infant son. She judged her own mother, entirely unreasonably, as if she had abandoned her son rather than gone out to fight for his survival. Addressing an audience of 2,500 people in Boston, Emmeline spoke about Harry, according to the local *Woman's Journal*: 'As the youngest of her family, he has always been "her baby", and though the doctor assured her it would be all right for her to go, she was in acute anxiety till she got the good news that he was better.'[495]

Sylvia's emotional reaction overwhelmed her pragmatism, as so often happened in her relationship with her mother. Her fear of this abandonment went back further. Harry's illness and Emmeline's departure for America leaving Sylvia feeling responsible for him reawakened the trauma of her father's death on her watch. She clung still to the irrational but understandable belief that, if only her mother had been there, her father might not have died. For Emmeline to leave Harry, with her daughter at his bedside helpless to cure him, revived a fear of abandonment linked to Sylvia's deepest feeling of guilt. Sylvia's condemnation of Emmeline's action shows how invested she was in the belief that her mother, above everyone else, could fix everything. Later, in her biography of her mother, Sylvia retreated from this unforgiving opinion, as she did from many of the other tough judgements she made when she was younger.

Sylvia had gone with Christabel and Emmeline Pethick-Lawrence to see her mother off on the boat train from Victoria. She then returned to Pembridge Gardens and put her life on hold to care for her brother.

Sylvia stayed at Harry's bedside for three months. They talked through the long nights of his pain and fever, Harry veering between acute clarity and delirium. He spoke of his childhood and of their father's death and told her the truth about his hard life at Mayland where the superintendent had bullied him for being a weak, girlish 'muff'. To prove himself, Harry toiled beyond his capacity to the point of collapse. Sylvia saw him as a fallen hero: 'He lay there extended in his nudity, proportioned like the ancient Greeks, lovely as an image of the young Adonis, showing no trace of illness, save only in his clear, smooth pallor.' Dr Mills, attending him daily, described Harry as 'a beautiful boy'.[496] He gently broke the news to Sylvia that her brother would not survive.

In their sickroom intimacy, Harry confessed to Sylvia his passionate love for Helen Craggs, describing their campaign romance in Manchester and her later reciprocation of his love letters when she returned to Brighton. Her family was fabulously wealthy and Harry, living in a mud-floored hut on Mayland and working as a labourer, had despaired of being able to pursue the relationship.

Sylvia took action. She tracked Helen down and pleaded with her to visit him. 'Think of him as your young brother. Tell him you love him; he has only three weeks to live.'[497] Helen showed great tenderness towards Harry, who, Sylvia wrote, was 'transcendent' with happiness to see her. Helen sat with him every day and at night slept on a sofa near the telephone in her rented Bloomsbury lodgings in case Sylvia needed to summon her. They planned his convalescence trip. They would visit Venice and take Sylvia with them. They shared murmured intimacies. 'His illness enclosed those two young creatures within a haven of dream; the hard realities of life were shut away.'[498]

Emmeline returned from America in late December. Mother, daughters and Helen spent a subdued Christmas with Harry at the nursing home. According to Sylvia, her mother resented Helen's presence and rebuked her daughter for not consulting her first before reuniting the young lovers. 'This girl … was taking from her the last of her son.'[499]

Harry died on 5 January 1910, just twenty years old. They buried him in Highgate Cemetery, beside his brother Frank. To Sylvia Emmeline appeared broken and her close friends said that a light went out of her face, never to return. She instructed Sylvia to commission a headstone and choose the words. Richard and Emmeline had never been able to bring themselves to place a stone over their first son Frank, so Sylvia arranged for a memorial to be placed over both brothers, inscribed 'Blessed are the pure in heart'. The resolute atheist Emmeline, who attended church occasionally only for strictly strategic political purposes, had chosen an inscription from Walt Whitman for her adored husband's grave. Here, as elsewhere in her life and writing, the equally unbelieving Sylvia elected for quotation from the popular gospels.

'Sylvia, remember, when my time comes, I want to be put with my two boys.'[500] This turned out to be a wish Sylvia was unable to fulfil.

Feeling grey and cold as the winter, Sylvia dragged herself to the Kent cottage on Cinder Hill abandoned in haste when she'd received that tragic October telegram. While the besieged Liberal government fought the general election campaign of 15 January to 9 February, she packed up the hopeful home in which she had just been getting settled, with its promise of regular shared domestic intimacy with Hardie. It was the only opportunity they had had at making some sort of home together. Gathering her paintings and writings, 'with all their interest gone', she left the brief haven of contentment.[501] Back in London, she gave up the tenancy on the Cheyne Walk rooms and moved to the Cambridge Lodge Studios at 42 Linden Gardens, Kensington, very close to the nursing home where she'd been cloistered with Harry.

Helen, clearly worried by this grief-driven decision to move to that neighbourhood, offered to spend some time with her, but Sylvia refused and honoured Harry's love by urging Helen to try and forget and to move on. For herself, Sylvia just needed time to escape the cast of her own shadow. Helen Craggs impressed Sylvia, who wrote in her memoir, 'Gallantly she played her part, if part it were,'[502] adding that Helen's tenderness towards Harry 'seemed very real'.[503] That 'seemingness' appeared to haunt and discourage Sylvia. Harry and Helen had shared an intimate perfection, a transcendent love endless because it was temporary. By contrast, she and Hardie were forced by circumstance to give up their best opportunity so far to make some kind of secure shared home together.

When Hardie was ill, it was to Lillie that he returned, Lillie who looked after him. Sylvia was shut out, unable to communicate or care for him. The months of Harry's final illness and death and his idealized love for Helen ruptured the promise of Cinder Hill. Dislocated in her grief by the misery of regret and loss, Sylvia experienced profound anxiety and heartache about the circumstances of her own intimate life.

Sylvia wrote Harry's obituary in *Votes for Women*, opening with the Ancient Greek proverb, 'Whom the gods love die young'. She detailed his career working in the movement, campaigning alongside his sisters in Manchester, his experiences of being thrown out of meetings and, on one occasion, being 'brutally kicked for asking a question of a Liberal Minister'. His 'whole heart' was in the women's movement and other just causes for reform:

> There never lived a human spirit on earth who attained earlier to beauty, than the human spirit whose passing all members of the Union during the past week mourned ... Harry Pankhurst was courageous in action and in endurance; he was unselfish, devoted to the public good, and every thought, word, and deed was ruled by the law of love ... He was a fighter in the great cause of justice to women ... Happy even in her grief must be the mother who has borne such a son ... His spirit shines like a star.[504]

Sylvia concluded her obituary with the opening verse from Robert Louis Stevenson's 'In Memoriam':

> Yet, O stricken heart, remember, O remember
> How of human days he lived the better part.
> April came to bloom and never dim December
> Breathed its killing chills upon the head or heart.

Helen Craggs continued to dedicate herself to the militant suffragette cause, working for the leadership of the WSPU at the Clement's Inn offices. Within a few years she would be at the forefront of courageous direct action. The King and Queen visited Cardiff in June 1912. As the royal party proceeded to Llandaff Cathedral, Helen jumped a wall and charged towards the Home Secretary, calling for vengeance for the sufferance of the women in Holloway and shaming him for going about the country when suffragists were starving in jail. Sentenced to a custodial term and forcibly fed as a consequence, Helen herself became one of these prisoners.

Four decades later in February 1957 following Emmeline's death, Fred Pethick-Lawrence married Helen Craggs. He himself died just four years later, leaving her financially secure for life. As it turned out, Sylvia's instincts about the authenticity of Helen's feelings about her brother proved correct. Many years later Helen confided to a friend that Harry had been 'her first and only love'.[505]

12

Insurgence of Women

Sylvia rarely took holidays. She couldn't afford them and leisure unsettled her. When opportunities to travel arose, she immersed herself in the experience. Almost all her trips abroad in her earlier life were at the invitation of Emmeline Pethick-Lawrence, who enjoyed Sylvia's good conversation and intrepid curiosity. In the early summer of 1910 Sylvia accepted Emmeline's invitation to visit Germany for a few weeks to see the Oberammergau passion play, along with Annie Kenney. The women stayed as the guests of Anton Lang, a potter who was playing the leading role. Sylvia produced a watercolour study of his crucifixion. It was an appropriate and unintentionally ironic theme for a political year dominated by the themes of conciliation and betrayal, with Herbert Asquith distinguishing himself in the role of Judas.

In the theatre of war for the women's vote, the years from 1908 to 1912 were a battlefield heaped with successive defeated attempts at constitutional reform. The mounting failures drove the suffrage movement to escalating direct action and civil disobedience. Throughout 1909 the frustration of the women's movement increased. This was the year of the first hunger strikes, followed by forcible feeding. Battles over Lloyd George's proposed budget led to the dissolution of parliament.

In January 1910 Asquith called a general election. The Liberals lost a hundred seats and returned to office with a minority government dependent on eighty-two Irish nationalists and an increased cohort of forty-two Labour Party MPs. During the election campaign, Asquith promised to introduce a Conciliation Bill to allow a measure of women's suffrage in national elections. Henry Brailsford, co-founder of the Men's

League for Women's Suffrage, wrote to Millicent Fawcett, leader of the NUWSS, suggesting that he should attempt to establish a Conciliation Committee for Women's Suffrage, proposing that it could undertake the necessary diplomatic work of promoting an early settlement.

Bertrand Russell stood as the suffragist candidate at a by-election in Wimbledon in 1907. In 1909 the Men's League for Women's Suffrage published a list of prominent men who supported women's suffrage, including eighty-three former government ministers, forty-nine Church leaders, twenty-four high-ranking army and navy officers, eighty-six academics and the writers E. M. Forster, Thomas Hardy, H. G. Wells, John Masefield and Arthur Pinero. By 1910 the Men's League had ten branches in Britain. Cross-party and non-party affiliated, it was non-militant in its tactics, but supported both the WSPU and Women's Freedom League. 'It is impossible to rate too highly the sacrifices that they ... and many others made to keep our movement free from the suggestion of a sex war,' wrote Evelyn Sharp.[506]

On Asquith's return to power a committee was formed, chaired by Lord Lytton and made up of fifty-four pro-women's suffrage MPs from several political parties (twenty-five Liberals, seventeen Conservatives, six Labour and six Irish nationalists). The Conciliation Committee proposed legislation that would have enfranchised female householders and women who occupied business premises, a bill based on existing franchise laws for local government elections under which some women had been able to vote since 1870. The measure would have added a million women to the franchise. The intention was to restrict the number of potential women voters to a relatively small, non-threatening minority to make it as palatable as possible to Conservative MPs. The Conciliation Bill was calculated to appease the suffragist movement by giving a limited number of women the vote based on their property holdings and marital status, in a context where the weakened government might now be more inclined to relent.

The suffrage movement supported the legislation. If it succeeded, the legislation would, it was hoped, rally support from all but the most fanatical anti-suffragists. Millicent Fawcett admitted that many suffragists would prefer a less restricted measure, but argued for the immense advantage to the movement of 'getting the most effective of all the existing franchises thrown open to women'.[507] The WSPU thought the bill too narrow, since it excluded women lodgers, most wives and all working-class women. However, they joined the Conciliation Bill campaign strategically, as a step in the right direction. Emmeline agreed to the idea on behalf of the WSPU and declared a truce suspending the militant campaign subject to the outcome of the Conciliation Bill. Sylvia opposed the draft legislation, regarding it as far too narrow and unjust in its focus on property and marriage qualifications. The Conciliation Bill, passed into law, would merely enfranchise a limited number of middle- and upper-class women. Wealth-based parliamentary representation, in her view, did not meet the minimum requirements of participatory democracy.

Many objected that the legislation would merely ensure votes for the Tories from a minority of elderly propertied widows and spinsters. As Israel Zangwill quipped, 'not Votes for Liberals, or Votes for Labour, but Votes for Women'.[508] Most Liberal and Labour MPs outside the committee opposed the initiative, aware of its divide-and-rule motivation. Following a two-day debate in July 1910, the Conciliation Bill was carried by a majority of 110 and sent away for amendment. At the end of July parliament adjourned until November.

During the peaceful interval of the truce Emmeline Pethick-Lawrence, Sylvia and Annie Kenney set off on their summer adventure to see the Oberammergau passion play. They travelled from Innsbruck through the lush Bavarian mountains, stopping along the way in villages to visit women craftswomen working in cottage workshops, making baskets, toys and furniture.

They arrived in Oberammergau in time for the opening. First performed in 1634 over the graves of Black Death victims, by the time Sylvia saw it the day-long play was presented on a vast open-air stage consisting of six steel arch supports. Sylvia, Emmeline and Annie sat on simple benches, looking up at the 'tremendous spectacle' with sky and mountains as backdrop.[509] Participants in the pageant, which was staged once a decade, had to be residents of the village. Sylvia described the phenomenon of a thousand men, women and children accompanied by a sixty-piece orchestra and magnificent choir performing Rochus Dedler's powerful 1779 score. Visually, she was delighted. 'Some of the most famous Biblical pictures the art of Europe has produced guided the composition of the tableaux.'[510]

She went on, 'Yet it was not the Passion Play, but the life of its people which greatly rejoiced me.'[511] An ancient village of highly skilled craftspeople, wood carvers, potters and fresco painters, working in artisanal co-operatives, Oberammergau revealed to her a collectively organized Arts and Crafts dream come true. The famous carving school fascinated her, as did the circulating library and local art club that distributed reproductions of great paintings for people to borrow and put up in their homes or copy for frescos.

Sylvia filled her new sketchbook with paintings and pencil studies of actors in the play, including the watercolour of their host Anton Lang, the radical potter, performing his lead role in the Crucifixion. Lang, his wife and sister all spoke English, and were eager to learn more about the English suffragettes, especially their friend Lady Constance Lytton, 'whose adventure as "Jane Warton" had sent its thrill thus far'.[512] Constance Lytton, sister of the Conciliation Committee's Lord Lytton, was a highborn and immensely wealthy and well-connected aristocrat. Every time she was arrested and sentenced for militant activity, including stone throwing and window smashing, the police, courts and prison authorities gave her preferential treatment because of her privileged social position. She was put into prison hospital wards or separate apartments, and excused from the compulsory labour enforced on her sister suffragettes. Furious at these class divide-and-rule tactics, Constance Lytton chopped off her hair, put on wire spectacles and ill-fitting rough clothes and adopted the disguise of working-class 'Jane Warton'. Her ruse succeeded. The very next time she was arrested, she was thrown into the same cells as the other suffragettes. She thereby succeeded in exposing the penal system as riddled with class hypocrisy. The media loved the story of this adventurous aristocratic 'Pimpernel' class-warrior, and it travelled far beyond the British and European newspapers to America and far-flung colonies.

Throughout their tour Sylvia painted children and people at work in the mountain villages, and was particularly taken with Partenkirchen where they stayed for a few days. One gouache shows a group of boys in traditional Bavarian costume sitting around the fountain in the village square. In another, a woman in a vibrant blue smock paints figures on ornamental wooden plaques. Sylvia's sketchbook also contains pictures of a potter at work and of a young barefooted lad pulling a cart and, in towns and villages less prosperous than Oberammergau, studies of anxious, hungry-looking children.

While they were in Partenkirchen, the news of King Edward's death reached the travellers. On Christabel's instruction, the WSPU suspended propaganda and protest activities until after the royal funeral. They deferred processions and rallies and published respectfully black-bordered issues of *Votes for Women* displaying portraits of Queen Alexandra and Queen Mary. Sylvia archly observed her elder sister's obsequious editorial tone: 'Christabel, daughter of Republican Dr. Pankhurst, vied with the Conservative organs in her expressions of devotion to the Throne.'[513] There's a nice ironic tickle in the atheist Sylvia making this judgement of her sister while accompanying two faithful believers to the world's most famous Christian passion play.

Along with all the other wings of the women's suffrage movement at this time, the WSPU worked strenuously for the Conciliation Bill. Sylvia argued with her mother about the WSPU's support for the proposals, entirely unsuccessfully. Conveniently, she was able to step back from a row and avoid contributing to what she regarded as the lost cause of the conciliation campaign because she had a pressing book deadline.

Based on the strength of her series of articles about the history of the WSPU published in *Votes for Women*, and of her surname, the New York publishers Sturgis & Walton commissioned Sylvia to deliver a behind-the-scenes and up-to-the-minute account of the British women's militant suffrage movement from 1905 to 1910. It was agreed that she would write a 'just and accurate account of its progress and happenings', packing in as many of its campaigns and incidents as possible. Sturgis & Walton published the feminist economist and novelist Charlotte Perkins Gilman. Perkins Gilman and Elizabeth Wolstenholme Elmy were friends. Elizabeth, who had known Sylvia since childhood, introduced her to Perkins Gilman who in turn recommended Sylvia to her publisher. Elizabeth promised to help Sylvia as much as she could with producing the manuscript. It was thus an American publisher that commissioned and produced the first British 'history of the Militant Women's Suffrage Movement'.[514]

Both Sylvia's mother and Emmeline Pethick-Lawrence thought the book a good idea. They knew the potential publicity and propaganda value of Sylvia's fast, lively, precise and partisan writing. Sylvia possessed an immense capacity for collating facts and figures, understood the law and could be counted on to put the WSPU at the centre of the story. The book would be a convenient fundraising tool. For her part, Christabel calculated that the project might preoccupy Sylvia, diverting the flow of her relentless running critique of WSPU policy and structure. As Sylvia gained confidence as an activist, speaker and organizer who dissented from the family party line, she might be lining up to contend with her elder sister for the leadership.

Christabel proved correct, almost. The responsibility of writing *The Suffragette* to a tight deadline kept Sylvia out of making greater direct political trouble, temporarily. In the thick of the fray during what came to be known as the Black Friday protests in Westminster on 18 November 1910, Sylvia found herself in the unusual position of having to duck confrontation in order to stay out of detention: 'Outside in the square were scenes of unexampled violence. I had promised to report the affair for *Votes for Women*, and I was obliged to avoid arrest as I was writing a history of the militant movement under contract with the publishers.'[515]

The tempering of her activism was relative, of course, to a very high level of engagement, but writing helped Sylvia work out what she thought. In this way, the process of producing her first book set a pattern for the future. Crucially, it provided her with a creative, analytical voice that produced income and professional livelihood in a way that her artistic vocation did not. Sylvia's shift in emphasis from the fine art of painting to the prosaic art of writing was driven by necessity. The urgency of the struggle in the historical moment certainly drove her towards journalism and the art of letters. But it was also a matter of simple economics. Sylvia needed a reliable, flexible profession to survive. Many people wanted to pay her for her writing: the money generated by her art went to the movement.

On the eve of the reopening of parliament in November, ministers announced that there would be no time given to the Conciliation Bill in that session. Asquith delivered a speech making it clear that he intended to shelve it. Keir Hardie attempted to move a resolution for a two-hour debate to advance the bill. On 18 November, following a breakdown in relations between the House of Commons and the House of Lords over the budget, Asquith called another general election for 3–19 December, declaring that parliament would be dissolved on 28 November. It was the last general election in Britain held over a number of days, the last time before the war that those men who could vote went to the polls and – though no one knew it at the time – the last men-only general election in British history.

In response to the demise of the Conciliation Bill into the long grass, the Women's Parliament marched in a deputation of 300 to Westminster on Friday 18 November, Sylvia and her aunt Mary among them. The demonstration was met with a six-hour complete onslaught by the police, which Sylvia described as exhibiting unprecedented levels of state-sanctioned brutality.[516] A policeman struck her in the chest with his truncheon, seized her by the arms and threw her on to the pavement. Women were dragged down side streets, beaten up, sexually assaulted and raped. Black Friday saw the police arrest 115 women and 2 men.

The following day the *Daily Mirror* published a full front-page photograph of Ada Wright lying beaten to the pavement, hands covering her face. The government tried to have the edition withdrawn from sale and ordered that the negative be destroyed.

The Home Secretary Winston Churchill rejected calls for a public inquiry into police conduct. The journalist Henry Brailsford, secretary of the Conciliation Committee, and the psychotherapist Jessie Murray investigated and wrote a report on police conduct, collecting statements from 135 demonstrators, reporting indecency, torn and ripped underwear and obscene language. Some were seized by the hair and forced to their knees, prevented from regaining their footing. Women's faces were punched, their breasts stripped and twisted, nipples pinched and pulled, thumbs broken, throats gripped, faces bashed against railings and ribs broken. Police shoved Rosa May Billinghurst, a disabled suffragette who campaigned from a wheelchair, into a side road, assaulted her and stole the valves from the wheels, leaving her stranded. Numerous women were forced by police to tie their skirts over their heads when taken under arrest. Brailsford's report was detailed and robust in its documenting of disproportionate and unacceptable violence against the protesting women. Moreover, it made explicit the sexualized nature of the brutality.

> The action of which the most frequent complaint is made is variously described as twisting round, pinching, screwing, nipping, or wringing the breast. This was often done in the most public way so as to inflict the utmost humiliation. Not only was it an offence against decency; it caused in many cases intense pain ... The

language used by some of the police while performing this action proves that it was consciously sensual.[517]

There were two fatalities. Henria Williams died from her injuries on New Year's Day. Cecilia Haig, violently and indecently assaulted, suffered illness and breakdown, and died a year later. These were just two casualties of the many resulting from the violence meted out to the women on Black Friday.[518]

Brailsford and his committee obtained 'enough irrefutable testimony not just of brutality by the police but also of indecent assault – now becoming a common practice among police officers – to shock many newspaper editors, and the report was published widely'.[519] The Commissioner of the Metropolitan Police, Edward Henry, denied the charges and claimed that rogue members of the public committed the sexual assaults. On 1 March 1911, in response to a question in parliament, Winston Churchill informed the House of Commons that:

> 'There is no truth in the statement that the police had instructions which led them to terrorise and maltreat the women. On the contrary, the superintendent in charge impressed upon them that as they would have to deal with women, they must act with restraint and moderation, using no more force than might be necessary, and maintaining under any provocation they might receive, control of temper.'[520]

The symbolism of Black Friday made a significant impact on the consciousness of suffrage fighters. Women who had long been abused and bled in private were now battered and bled in public. The epidemic of male sexual violence common in homes, whatever the class of their inhabitants, now exploded on to the streets. And just as in the domestic sphere, it was, according to the arbiters of patriarchy, of course the women's fault. By provoking the sanctity of male authority, the women's movement were asking for it, just like battered wives.

The modern British state became a torturer in 1909 with the advent of forcible feeding. Black Friday of November 1910 made explicit the profoundly sexualized nature of the regime of discipline and punishment inflicted on women who sought to claim their rights as British subjects. Enabled by a rapidly expanding culture of deep surveillance resulting from technological advances in photography, film and recorded sound, resistance to the suffrage campaign was moving into a new phase. History books have long told us that the British government took the country into the Great War in 1914. In fact, Britain's ruling classes declared civil war on half of its own population – women – some years before that.

Black Friday led to a change in tactics. From the introduction of the Conciliation Bill until Asquith's sabotage, the WSPU had maintained a truce on militancy. Black Friday showed that passive resistance was too dangerous. Many members of the WSPU were unwilling to risk being subjected to similar sexual violence, so they resumed their previous forms of direct action against property, such as throwing stones and breaking windows, which allowed time to escape. The police changed their approach too; during future demonstrations they tried not to arrest too soon or too late.

When Sylvia was five years old, her activist parents took part in what became known as the 13 November 1887 Bloody Sunday protest in Trafalgar Square. One of the most notorious attacks on civil liberties in the nation's history, this was the day when a police horse trampled Alfred Linnell to death.[521] Her friend Bernard Shaw freely admitted that he *'skedaddled'* from the police violence that day, unlike her feminist role model Eleanor Marx, who held the front line and stayed in the thick of the fray fighting and wrestling with police alongside the trade unionist Will Thorne.[522] That Bloody Sunday of 1887 proved a watershed in state aggression against the struggle for democracy in modern Britain. Eleanor Marx remarked of the occasion that she was disappointed by the lack of fight in some of the working men.

The suffragettes of Black Friday 1910 strategized new ways to fight. Militant tactics were far from merely an unsophisticated declaration of vandalism against inanimate property; they were a strategy for the articulation of protest while protecting women from extreme physical violence and sexual assault sanctioned by the state, which regarded them as property rather than as citizens.

The weaponization of sexual violence in the war against the freedom-fighting women did not take place only in the theatre of street battle – it was an intimate part of their day-to-day lives, as Sylvia experienced. Several times in her early life she fell prey to unwanted sexual advances, such as from a train guard while travelling alone in Italy and from the radical editor and publisher Stead in his own offices. By today's standards Sylvia's published style of writing about these experiences may seem oblique, but they were explicit for the time.

Sylvia spent Christmas 1910 alone at Linden Gardens, revising the final chapters of *The Suffragette* and working on studies in charcoal for an oil portrait of Hardie. She woke early on Boxing Day morning to the spectral vision of her mother's drained face pressed anxiously against her window. Aunt Mary had been released from prison two days before Christmas, following her conviction for throwing stones at a subsequent action to protest against the police brutality on Black Friday. Emmeline and Mary spent Christmas with their brother Herbert Goulden in Southgate. During Christmas dinner, Mary quietly left the table. Emmeline went looking for her and found her lying unconscious on her bed. Emmeline and Herbert believed the brain haemorrhage that killed their sister was a result of the injuries she had sustained during the protests and the effects of subsequent imprisonment. Mary had escaped an abusive marriage and was working as a suffragette organizer in Brighton. Now a member of the Pankhurst family had become one of the first suffragette martyrs and given her life to the cause. Mary's death would act as a future caution to the authorities when dealing with Mrs Pankhurst, though not when dealing with Sylvia.

The year 1910 began with Harry's death and ended with Mary's. Sylvia had lost brother and favourite aunt, Emmeline her only son and her closest sister. Emmeline accompanied Sylvia on the boat train to see her off from Southampton on 28 December.[523] Sylvia saw in the new year of 1911 in sombre mood aboard the SS *St Paul*, an American express steamship bound for New York (see chapter 13).

On the last night of the voyage Sylvia fended off a 'proposal of marriage' in the form of an attempted sexual assault by the ship's doctor, 'who had occasionally spoken a brief word in passing'.[524] Long accustomed to being alone in the company of men socially, Sylvia had no reason to suspect his interest in her work and invitation of hospitality to discuss it in his professional consulting rooms. Only when things suddenly turned nasty did the significance of the proximity of his bed in the cabin that doubled as his sleeping quarters become apparent.

Reflecting on this episode years later, Sylvia wrote grimly that it was 'mainly motivated, I gathered, by the desire to save me from the militant movement'.[525] The notion that suffragettes required a good dose of corrective rape or at the very least unsolicited sexual attentions to cure them of their independent-minded behaviour was common, particularly when such women had the presumption to travel alone. Two decades later in her late forties, a confident, experienced Sylvia recounted this episode in a self-assured tone clearly laying out that she was not to blame: 'I questioned myself, most searchingly, as to whether I had inadvertently said or done anything to encourage this undue interest ... but was able to exonerate myself from culpability.'[526] At the time it happened, however, her twenty-eight-year-old self wondered if she might have been at fault. She wrote self-critically to Hardie from America about the attempted sexual assault:

> Love I hadn't any more adventures on board ship.
>   I never shall have, I shall take more care. It was silly of me to
> let him take me to see his cabin, even if it was the place where his
> patients went to be doctored and I was quite lucky that the incident
> wasn't more unpleasant than it was. Now I know more about
> ships and how even a silly old buffer of a doctor may be quite a
> dangerous person, I'll never be silly again and altogether am getting
> older and wiser so don't you ever worry again.[527]

To borrow from her phrase about her mother, Hardie was no more likely to stop worrying about Sylvia than the wind was to stop blowing.

By the time she returned to London three months later in April, the newly elected Liberal government had pledged to devote a week of parliamentary debate to the Conciliation Bill. A resubmitted bill passed its second reading with a large majority and Asquith finally pledged to support its passage. This prompted widespread optimism. The truce was back on and Christabel confidently declared in *Votes for Women* that females could now enjoy 'the expectation of taking part as voters in the election of the next and every future Parliament'.[528]

Writing at a furious pace, Sylvia delivered the manuscript for the 500-page book in time for publication in the spring of 1911, completing the final edit while on her first lecture tour of North America and then delivering her corrected galleys to Sturgis & Walton in New York. As soon as the American edition hit the press, London publishers Gay & Hancock imported the printed sheets and released the book in Britain. As well as incorporating and adapting her own journalistic articles published in *Votes for Women*, Sylvia drew on her extensive correspondence with Elizabeth Wolstenholme Elmy for information about the early women's movement. In July 1910 Elizabeth wrote to her, 'You are free to make whatever you please of anything I have sent or may send you, unless I mark them "private" and ask to have them returned.'[529]

The rest Sylvia compiled from an exhaustive array of official parliamentary sources, legal reports, national and local media, union and party records, minutes, memos and correspondence. In the age before the internet, Sylvia's capacity to research, compile, cross-reference and summarize vast quantities of data at great speed and with precision is exemplary. Exceptionally numerate, she had the skills of a human computer. In a different life, she would have made a very good scientist or physicist – empiricism was as strong in her as her futuristic, visionary dreaming. *The Suffragette* was, and still is, criticized for exaggerating the importance of the role of the WSPU at the expense of other organizations and campaigns. What distinguishes the book from others that followed it is the combination of Sylvia's on-the-ground perspective of events as they unfolded and her evidence-based facts and data.

Writing the Preface to the British edition in London in May 1911, Sylvia introduces the work clearly as a validation of the militant movement:

> I believe that women striving for enfranchisement in other lands
> and reformers of future days may learn with renewed hope and
> confidence how the 'family party,' who in 1905 set out determined
> to make votes for women the dominant issue of the politics of their
> time, in but six years drew to their standard the great woman's
> army of to-day. It is certain that the militant struggle in which this
> woman's army has engaged and which has come as the climax to the
> long, patient effort of the earlier pioneers, will rank amongst the
> great reform movements of the world.[530]

She makes it clear that the Pankhurst family takes responsibility for the introduction of militant suffrage tactics, but rightly stresses that 'I believe the effort was greater for those who first came forward to stand by the originators than for the little group by whom the first blows were struck.' Solidarity is all: 'whilst the originators of the militant tactics let fly their bolt, as it were, from the clear sky, their early associates rallied to their aid in the teeth of all the fierce and bitter opposition that had been raised'.[531]

Properly and significantly – given their already well-advanced political differences – Christabel is the only person name-checked in the Preface. There is a moment of reflection on the price of rebellion from twenty-nine-year-old Sylvia that defines the spirit of the book that follows: 'To many of our contemporaries perhaps the most remarkable feature of the militant movement has been the flinging-aside by thousands of women of the conventional standards that hedge us so closely round in these days for a right that large numbers of men who possess it scarcely value.'[532]

The weekend before the coronation of George V in the summer of 1911 the WSPU, NUWSS and other suffrage organizations united together in a great seven-mile celebratory march through London, proclaiming it to be 'The Women's Coronation Procession'. Some 40,000 strong, the 1 June rally was led by 700 ex-prisoners, including Sylvia, who much later described it as 'a triumph of organization, a pageant of science, art, nursing, education, poverty, factorydom, slumdom, youth, age, labour, motherhood, a beautiful and imposing spectacle'.[533] Elizabeth Wolstenholme Elmy, at seventy-eight the oldest suffragette present, stood majestically on a balcony in St James's Street and took a proud salute from the former prisoners as they paraded past.

The UK edition of Sylvia's *The Suffragette* went on sale that same triumphant week. In her memoir, Sylvia chose to quote the *Daily News* leader about the publication of her history book: 'Of one thing there can be no doubt at all: the pioneers of 1905 found woman suffrage an academic question; they have made it a vital issue of national affairs.'[534]

Simultaneously, Sylvia worked hard with Hardie on the amendments to his National Insurance Bill, aimed at increasing the benefits proposed. The WSPU opposed the bill, as they did all legislation in which women were not involved. Sylvia argued that this was illogical. Her amendments proposed benefit increases for the lowest-paid workers, who were by definition mainly women. Hardie passed her recommendations on to the Labour Party committee, along with his own, and moved some of them himself in the House, with her argument. When the bill passed beyond Labour intervention into the House of Lords, Sylvia 'appealed … to the well-known old anti-Suffragist, Lord Balfour of Burleigh [Alexander Hugh Bruce], to take up certain amendments in the interest of the lowest paid workers, mainly women ... He replied with the greatest cordiality, asking me to meet him, and on discussion agreed to a part of what I asked. I felt like a pigmy walking beside his huge figure.'[535]

Sylvia strained to balance this political work with her creative life. She started work on a large, ambitious painting, inspired by her fascination with the revival of English folk dance and song. The suffragette, social reformer and morris-dance revivalist Mary Neal and Emmeline Pethick-Lawrence introduced Sylvia to the dancer, concertina player and choreographer William Kimber and the Fabian, song collector and folk-dance enthusiast Cecil Sharp, who worked together. Neal passionately desired to teach and so pass on traditional English culture.

Born in 1860, the daughter of a Birmingham button manufacturer, Mary Neal escaped her monied upbringing, which she described as 'a pageant of snobbery', went to London and joined the West London Mission to serve the poor. She was one of the founder members of the London WSPU at the inaugural meeting in Sylvia's home in Park Walk. Wholly committed to women's engagement in public service, Neal also became the first female magistrate on a county bench and, with her best friend Emmeline Pethick-Lawrence, pioneered seaside holidays for working-class London girls. She and Emmeline established the Espérance Club in Somers Town in 1895. Folk song, dance, oral poetry and storytelling reached back into pagan times, predating Christianity and community arts passed through generations in which young girls and women of all ages had traditionally participated. Open four nights a week for the next twenty years, the club gained national renown for its displays of English song and dance.

The Espérance troupes were invited to perform in community venues and local town halls around London, and its members received invitations to teach in villages, schools and factories across England. Neal wrote of the changes brought about in the girls' lives: 'It is no small thing for a London dressmaker to stay in the house, as an honoured guest of a country squire, and ride in his motorcar and write letters home at his study table, and feel at the same time that she has something to give.' As the archival work of Mary Neal's great-great-niece Lucy Neal demonstrates, 'It was the energy and interest generated by these slum girls that instigated the first folk revival of English song and dance, a movement that blazed across the countryside.'[536]

Cecil Sharp styled himself the father of the morris-dancing revival, but in fact he was primarily a song collector. Obdurately patriarchal Sharp was no friend to women's suffrage, but he was a very interested student of folk traditions. He claimed that his fascination with folk song and dance dated to Boxing Day 1899, when he was spending Christmas with his family at the home of his mother-in-law in Headington, east of Oxford. The Headington Quarry Morris Dancers, a male troupe, accompanied by their musician William Kimber, performed outside their cottage and attracted his attention. The morris men usually danced at Whitsuntide after Easter, but it was a hard winter and many of them, including Kimber, had been laid off from their jobs in the building trade. They performed out of season to try and earn some extra money. Sharp came out of the house and asked Kimber to return the following day so that he could note down the tunes. The bird-scarer and bricklayer 'Merry' Kimber went on to become the illustrator of Sharp's lectures, where he played the concertina and demonstrated dances. As Kimber's fame grew, so did the prestige of his audiences and the venues in which he played and danced – including the Mansion House, the Albert Hall and Royal Command performances for the King and Queen.

In 1905 Neal read a newspaper interview with Cecil Sharp, and wrote to him to tell him about her Espérance Club girls. They met and decided to join forces and work together in what was initially a happy and fruitful collaboration. Sharp introduced Neal to William Kimber, who coached the Espérance girls. They began to give hugely popular public performances, much reported in the newspapers. So successful was the group that several of the young women were able to leave their jobs as textile workers and become teachers and professional dancers. While watching the performances, Sharp devised notations that he used as the foundation for his first book on morris dancing. It's clear that this work revived and facilitated Sharp's interest in collecting folk songs and dances.

Fêted as the father of the folk revival, he suppressed the influence that Mary Neal and the Espérance girls had had in establishing his reputation, a distortion of the facts in which the male-dominated dance and arts establishment long colluded. As so many times before and since, man took credit for the influence of creative woman's work. The growing tension between Sharp and Neal finally exploded in a public row between them in the *Morning Post*, in which they argued over the interpretation of dance traditions and their roles in the now wildly popular dance revival.[537] Sharp accused Neal's Espérance morris girls of 'hoydenish dancing'. Neal lamented Sharp's flat-footed 'pedantry'. Mary's great-great-niece Lucy Neal observes that Sharp 'has stood over the years for exclusivity and control, and Neal for inclusivity and participation … While Neal "got people dancing" it was Sharp who commandeered the records.'[538] Clearly neither of them could have done it without the genius of William Kimber, the inspiration for the twentieth-century revival of morris dancing.

Well educated in English folk culture traditions thanks to her socialist upbringing and immersion in William Morris' Arts and Craft movement, Sylvia was soon swept up in the early twentieth-century revival of folk music and dance. She worked obsessively on studies of female morris dancers for a large piece depicting a crowd of girls dancing in verdant May woodland. She produced drawings of female nudes in different poses and multiple studies of skirts and legs, feet – shod and bare – and hands, sometimes holding objects. Four studies depicted clothed women standing, walking or moving their hands. Sketches of children, trees and flowers also appear in the portfolio of work Sylvia prepared for this piece. Predominant among her studies are sketches of dancing feet.

Ada Walshe remembered Sylvia's unusual joy and levity when they watched a display of little girls performing traditional folk dance in the East End: 'Some of the dances were religious in style, some pagan, prayers to the sun etc … the floor of the platform had not been washed and the dancers feet became black. The audience roared with laughter and behaved very badly and for once I saw Sylvia almost crying with laughter and trying to hide it.'[539] Sylvia's love of radical dance forms would soon become apparent in her travels in North America.

It seemed that the battle for the vote was really and finally won. But in November Asquith and Lloyd George torpedoed the Conciliation Bill. Although MPs backed the bill at its first and second readings, Asquith refused to grant it further parliamentary time. Instead, the government introduced suddenly a new Manhood Suffrage Reform Bill that tried to prioritize the introduction of universal manhood suffrage. This was clearly a strategy to block the inclusion of a limited franchise of female voters. Asquith refused to abandon the Manhood Suffrage Bill. 'War is declared – declared by the Government upon women!' Christabel wrote in *Votes for Women*. 'The Government's latest attempt to cheat women of the vote is, of course, inspired by Mr. Lloyd George. The whole crooked scheme is characteristic of the man and of the methods he has from the first employed against the Suffrage cause.'[540] The WSPU, outraged at the betrayal, issued a statement announcing the resumption of hostilities. The truce was over.

A cabinet minister Charles Hobhouse inflamed matters further at an anti-suffrage meeting in Bristol where he condemned the Votes for Women campaign for lacking the force of a true popular movement: 'In the case of the Suffrage demand there has not been the kind of popular sentimental uprising which accounted for Nottingham Castle in 1832, or the Hyde Park railings in 1867. There has been no great ebullition of popular feeling.'[541] Hobhouse was referring to the protesters who burned Nottingham Castle to the ground in October 1831 after the incumbent Duke voted against the Reform Bill in the House of Lords. Also to May 1867, when a mass public meeting of the Reform League tore down the perimeter railings to Hyde Park, not for the first time. Karl Marx was among those who took part in the action.

Sylvia described Hobhouse's speech as being 'like a match to a fuse'.[542] The militant campaign was back on. 'Protest imperative,' Emmeline telegraphed from America to Clement's Inn. This time the attacks on private and public property would be on a massive scale and of a more serious, concerted nature. WSPU members carefully organized for their proposed militant operation. Those with cars drove around the country and byways at night-time in groups, collecting supplies of flints, storing them in the homes of those who could be trusted. The covert stockpiling of flint was in preparation for the launch of a mass window-smashing campaign. London hardware shops noticed an unusually brisk trade in hammers. Haberdashers sold thousands of yards of black serge, for making little bags in which to conceal the flint around protesters' bodies.

On 21 November Emmeline Pethick-Lawrence led a large deputation from Caxton Hall to Parliament Square while a smaller cadre of suffragette guerrillas armed with hammers and bags of stones smashed the windows of government offices, the National Liberal Federation, the Guards Club, the *Daily Mail* and *Daily News*, Swan and Edgar's department store, a Lyons tea shop, Dunn's hat shop, two hotels and some smaller businesses, including a tailor's shop and a bakery. A total of 223 were arrested that day, including Emmeline Pethick-Lawrence. Christabel defended the window-smashing campaign. Men had got their vote by riot and rebellion, she told her audience at the Savoy Theatre two days later, and that was how women would get it too.[543]

Lloyd George delivered a speech in Bath, claiming that the Conciliation Bill had been 'torpedoed' by the introduction of the Manhood Suffrage Bill which would pave the way for a 'broad and democratic amendment for women's suffrage and enfranchise, not a limited class of women just to suit the Tory canvasser, but also the working man's wife'.[544] Christabel retaliated in *Votes for Women*, writing that campaigners would never believe that Lloyd George genuinely supported a democratic franchise for women until he undertook to make it a government measure. Emmeline, on her way from the US to Canada on her second North American tour, encouraged British women to engage in a 'civil war'. She would be back soon to rejoin them in the 'glorious struggle'.[545]

Meanwhile, Sylvia organized a huge WSPU suffragette festive fundraiser, held in the Portman Rooms in salubrious Mayfair just before Christmas. She brought out of storage the decorations she had made for the Prince's Skating Rink and repurposed them for the week-long festival. This time, there was budget for a specially designed architectural setting. Sylvia's models, drawings and plans were cast full-sized in plaster and once installed looked, to her delighted eyes, 'as solid and permanent as stone'.[546] *Votes for Women* described the 'exquisite murals from the clever brush' of Sylvia Pankhurst,[547] a treasured accolade for the drawing together of her art and activism.

In the style of the folk-revival movement, she designed stalls and costumes inspired by a picture of an old village fair in a beautiful book of aquatints by the eighteenth-century designer and cartographer John Pine. (The book was another lovingly inscribed gift from Hardie.) The stallholders wore the period costume of 'gentlewomen, fisherwomen, market women, as well as weavers, workers of all kinds, a roast chestnut vendor, and a gypsy fortune-teller with two green birds, as well as a street-crier and a "zany" with his old fool's cap'.[548] Anti-suffrage coconut shies offered the opportunity to take satisfying potshots against anti-suffragists Mrs Humphrey Ward, Lord Curzon and curmudgeonly cabinet ministers. Ethel Smyth and Liza Lehmann organized a programme of concerts and sing-ins. Sylvia designed a magnificent hand-propelled roundabout, which was constructed for her by London carpenters. Hardie rode around on it at the opening to the delight of the thronging visitors, but Sylvia missed the pleasure of seeing him at play. Exhausted by working round the clock, she went home early and fell asleep in her clothes on her studio floor.

The year 1912 marked the continuation of the mass window-smashing campaign. The Labour Party came out in favour of women's suffrage, and later in the year formed an alliance with the NUWSS. By March 1912 Asquith's Liberal government faced major onslaughts on four fronts. The administration was hard pressed by the Irish nationalists, threatened by civil war in Ulster and reeling from the unrelenting industrial unrest of the previous year. On top of all this, it continued to be tormented by the irrepressible WSPU.

Nineteen hundred and eleven had been a year of a thousand strikes, violence in the docks and rioting in the streets. In 1912 came the first national strike by British coal miners. This famous action achieved its main goal: to establish a minimum wage for the first time in the industry. The victory changed for ever the face of industrial and class relations in Britain and its empire. British domestic life went through a process of radical transformation, as captured by D. H. Lawrence in his 1913 play *The Daughter-in-Law*, the first kitchen-sink drama, written decades before the phrase was used to describe working-class theatre. The escalation of the militant suffragette campaign in this period is better understood in the context of the industrial unrest of 1911 and the 1912 miners' strike.

The rise of left-wing thinking fostered a new spirit of rebellion in working-class political culture, challenging the old leadership of the Liberal-leaning trade unions and giving rise to a new 'industrial unionism' reflecting the growing influence of the Socialist Labour Party. Founded in Glasgow in 1905 by the Irish socialist republican, labour leader and supporter of the militant suffragettes, James Connolly, the Scottish SLP extended its influence from the engineering workshops of the Clyde over the borders to Sheffield, Manchester and eventually to the capital.

Sylvia's links with Ireland through Connolly, destined to become the leader of the 1916 Easter Rising, proved decisive in the development of her political thinking during this period, and most critically during the

First World War. Connolly argued for the direct connections between the right of labour to organize and the right of women to vote. Women, like the labour movement, should rely not on any political party but rather on their own efforts.[549] Throughout this pre-war period, Hardie remained steadfast in his support for the suffragette cause. Connolly wrote to him from Ireland, 'When trimmers and compromisers disavow you, a poor slum bred politician, I raise my hat in thanksgiving that I lived to see this insurgence of women.'[550]

For seven years, without interruption and with escalating militancy, the WSPU had criticized and tried to debate with the Liberal government about its risible failure to grant women the vote. Emmeline returned from America in January 1912, bent on intensifying WSPU militant tactics. The words 'Sedition!' and 'The Women's Revolution' were now on Mrs Pankhurst's lips, wrote Sylvia.[551] On 14 February the King's Speech announced a Reform Bill for men only, drafted so that it was impossible to amend it to include women suffrage. Third place in the private members' ballot was secured for the Second Conciliation Bill, but the WSPU knew that the government-backed Reform Bill had sabotaged that already. At a dinner two days later at the Connaught Rooms to welcome home the window-breakers who had served two-month prison sentences, Emmeline wondered at the strangeness of a modern civilization that regarded women's appeal to justice and reason to argue their case for citizenship as 'of less value than the breaking of a pane of glass'.[552] She announced that in the future the suffragettes were going to use was 'that time-honoured official political argument', the stone. 'If the argument of the stone ... is sufficient, then we will never use any stronger argument.'

Exhausted and unwell again, Emmeline then withdrew to Coign Cottage, Ethel Smyth's new home in Hook Heath Road, Woking, which she had built on land chosen for its proximity to the golf course. Ethel took Emmeline to a secluded part of the heath to teach her the art of stone-throwing. Emmeline's training began with the instruction to aim her missile at the largest visible target, a fir tree. 'One has heard of people failing to hit a haystack,' Ethel recalled; 'what followed was rather along those lines.

> I imagine Mrs Pankhurst had not played ball games in her youth, and the first stone flew backwards out of her hand, narrowly

missing my dog. Once more we began at a distance of about three yards, the face of the pupil assuming with each failure – and there were a good many – a more and more ferocious expression. And when at last a thud proclaimed success, a smile of such beatitude … stole across her countenance, that much to her mystification and much to her annoyance, the instructor collapsed on a clump of heather helpless with laughter.[553]

The episode is reminiscent of Hardie trying to teach Sylvia to skim stones and play ball games.

On Friday 1 March, Emmeline, Mabel 'Pansy' Tuke and Kitty Marshall drove in what appeared to be a taxi to 10 Downing Street and smashed two of the Prime Minister's windows. They were arrested immediately. An hour later, at timed intervals of fifteen minutes, units of well-dressed women with hammers hidden in their elegant muffs smashed the plate-glass windows of shops and department stores in London's fashionable West End, followed by another wave two hours later. There were 121 arrests that day for breaking around 400 shop windows and causing an estimated £5,000 of damage. Emmeline received a sentence of two months' imprisonment in the third division and was returned to Holloway.

On Monday 4 March, another unannounced window-smashing action in London led to ninety-six arrests, including that of Ethel Smyth. A WSPU protest was planned for the evening in Parliament Square, announced with handbills that carried Emmeline's signature. The police mustered and quashed the rally.

Having already proved itself unreasonable and repressive by its policy of imprisonment and the horrors of forcible feeding, Asquith's cabinet lost its temper and turned savagely on the WSPU. Enraged by the new escalation of the destruction of public and private property to a mass campaign, the government launched a total onslaught on the organization, attempting to incapacitate it by arresting its leaders.

Scotland Yard received orders to strike. The WSPU leaders were hunted down, with the intention of arresting and trying them for conspiracy. On 5 March police raided the Clement's Inn headquarters with warrants for the arrest of the Pethick-Lawrences and Christabel. Together with Mrs Pankhurst and Mabel Tuke they were to be charged with 'conspiring to incite others to commit malicious damage to property'.[554]

The police found only the Pethick-Lawrences. Christabel was upstairs in her top-floor flat, writing. Fred Pethick-Lawrence managed to whisper to Evelyn Sharp, who ran to Christabel to warn her and with Fred's instruction that she countersign a cheque enabling the transfer of WSPU funds to senior member Hertha Ayrton's bank account before the organisation's accounts were frozen. That done, Christabel escaped by a hair's breadth and made her way to Paris in disguise as 'Miss Amy Richards', to become the mastermind in exile of the militant women's rebellion.

Sylvia was on the other side of the Atlantic in Ann Arbor, Michigan, when she heard the news of the mass window-smashing action on 1 March and the government's retaliation against WSPU leaders.

In Holloway, Mrs Pankhurst was served with the new charge of conspiracy. She was dismayed to learn in prison that during the raid on Clement's Inn the police had taken away with them two cab-loads of her papers and personal family archives.

She had been a most adept and talented homemaker. She left Manchester in 1907 – 'I am giving up housekeeping'[555] – and didn't set about making a new home of her own again until 1916 when she fostered four illegitimate 'war babies'. Their birth certificates were destroyed and they were given new names – Kathleen King, Flora Mary Gordon, Joan Pembridge and Elizabeth Tudor.[556] Emmeline's original intention had been to set up a home for fifty illegitimate female children, but she couldn't get support for the idea, even from her friends.

In the intervening decade, Emmeline was nomadic. At the time of the raid, she lived between an apartment at Clement's Inn provided by the Pethick-Lawrences and the Surrey cottage of her amour Ethel Smyth. 'They went through every desk, file and cabinet, taking away with them … all my private papers, photographs of my children in infancy, and letters sent to me by my husband long ago. Some of these I never saw again.'[557] The dispossession strengthened Emmeline's resolve, tightening her grip on her fight with the British state as it attempted to intimidate her by invading every aspect of her life. Clearly some of the archive was returned to her, or stored elsewhere because a few years after this raid, Emmeline gave Richard's papers to Sylvia, asking her to write his biography. She held back her cherished personal letters from Richard until her death, when they passed to Christabel.

The strategy of orchestrating mass attacks on the new temples of conspicuous consumption was highly effective. Modern retail business depended upon ensnaring the feminine psyche and turning its insecurities to profit. The campaign smashed through conventional stereotypes about women's subordination to sex and shopping. Since childhood a sceptic of consumerism, Sylvia loathed the constraints and waste of time imposed on women by fashion and the distractions of consumption, a theme that came to the fore during the media coverage of her American tours. Her mother and Christabel liked shopping and took a much greater interest in fashion. It was precisely because Mrs Pankhurst understood the role of shopping in women's psyche that she recognized its extraordinary exploitability for political PR. Women of all classes could tap into this rage. The window-smashing campaign was widely condemned in the liberal and right-wing press. *The Times* dedicated an editorial to censuring 'Mrs Pankhurst and her maenads'. Mr Lasenby Liberty, owner of the West End store, said that as a 'victim' of the raid, he would like to ask Mrs Pankhurst 'to state the mental process by which they deem the breaking of the very shrines at which they worship will advance their cause'.[558] Both complaints neatly proved Emmeline's point: the women understood very well the implications of hurling missiles at the false gods of a religion run by men, whom it profited. Women turning against their subordinating roles of shopping and housekeeping meant there was a revolution on the streets and in the home.

Commodity capitalism and its retail theatres provided a fertile public performance space. By the end of the nineteenth century women of all classes enjoyed the use of public areas in cities like Paris and London. Cafés, tea rooms, department stores, promenades, parks, illuminated arcades were places they could go together in groups, unchaperoned. Restaurants, retail consumption and leisure were changed by suffragettes into situationist street theatre. The suffragettes defined a new form of street-level resistance, subversion and civil disobedience, channelling the anger in women to good effect. 'The argument of the broken pane is the most valuable argument in modern politics,' declared Mrs Pankhurst.[559]

For the next two years, from various hotel hideouts and safe houses in her favourite city, Christabel – now in her thirties – 'generalled the last calculatedly reckless stages of militancy',[560] under the alias of 'Amy Richards'. Annie Kenney and other suffragettes, also code-named and heavily disguised, travelled in regular relays to Paris to receive Christabel's updated orders and collect her voluminous flow of copy for her weekly leader in the new official paper of the WSPU, *The Suffragette*.

Christabel made friends with influential aristocratic women in Paris. In her memoir, Annie recalled visiting the palatial apartments of the Princesse de Polignac. The size of the drawing room impressed her, but the 'beautiful books everywhere' even more so. 'I picked up one and found it to be a translation of Sappho's poetry, so pretty, so simple, and yet so profound. The colour of the leather binding was the shade of a ripe pink cherry.'[561] This was the Paris of the salonistes Natalie Barney and Renée Vivien and their Sapphic Amazonian circle of expatriates, artists and writers. The cloak-and-dagger atmosphere of Christabel's courageous, adventurous existence and unwavering emancipationist passion made her an exhilarating figure to the female Parisian demi-monde. There seemed to be some consolations for Christabel's exile.

The socialist leader George Lansbury, who had by now himself been imprisoned and forcibly fed in the suffragette cause, travelled to Boulogne for a secret meeting with Christabel. Lansbury was still recovering his breath from his recent headline-grabbing outburst against the Prime Minister in the House of Commons, when he rushed on to the floor of the House and shook his fist in Asquith's face: 'You ought to be driven out of office … You will go down to history as the man who tortured innocent women!'[562] In November 1912, frustrated by the Labour Party's position on the issue, he decided to resign his seat and seek re-election as a women's suffrage candidate. He sought Christabel's guidance on the tactics he should adopt in his campaign at Bromley by Bow; following her advice, he fought on a single-issue Votes for Women platform, but was unsuccessful.

Henry Harben, heir to the Prudential Insurance fortune, accompanied by a greenhorn Harold Laski, still an undergraduate at Oxford and an active WSPU member, visited Christabel for a conference, representing the Men's Political Union for Women's Enfranchisement, the men's equivalent of the militant WSPU, established in 1910 to assist women suffragettes in every way it could. Lansbury ran the *Daily Herald*, an organ for socialist-supporting suffragettes, and Laski wrote for it. They received a frosty reception from Christabel. Like Lansbury and Sylvia, Harben and Laski argued for closer alliance between the WSPU and militant socialists. The strength of Harben's friendship with her red

sister doubtless contributed to Christabel's froideur towards them. She
wrote to Henry Harben:

> Between the WSPU and the Daily Herald League and movement
> … there can be no connection. Ours is a Women's Movement,
> or at any rate a Mixed Movement. Women must grow their
> own backbone before they are going to be any use to themselves
> or to humanity as a whole. It is helpful and it is good for men
> themselves when they try to promote women's emancipation,
> but they have to do it from the outside, and the really important
> thing is that women are working out their own salvation, and are
> able to do it, even if not a living man takes any part in bringing it
> about.[563]

For several years Sylvia had expressed her discomfort at Christabel's
emerging separatist strategy. Up until now, she'd maintained her public
support in line with WSPU policy, keeping her disagreement a matter
of closed debate within the family and the political leadership of the
movement. That her mother unwaveringly supported Christabel's
position and scolded Sylvia for her 'collaboration' with men added
to the heavy weather brewing between them. A current of increasing
personal tension ran through Sylvia's relationship with her mother
during these years.

In 1911 Ethel Smyth composed her 'March of the Women'. The rousing
beat of imprisoned militants singing this new WSPU anthem during
their exercise in prison yards around Britain became a familiar irritant
to the authorities. In Holloway, Smyth pushed her hand through the
bars of her cell window, conducting the singers with her toothbrush.
Supporters gathered outside the prison walls and joined in the chorus.

Ethel Smyth 'captured the martial spirit' of the militant women
with her anthem,[564] which became the marching song of the suffragette
movement, played by women's bands and sung with great gusto at
rallies and meetings. Smyth captured also the heart of the suffragette
leader with her musical courtship and assiduous attentions. Touchingly,
Emmeline formally introduced Sylvia and Ethel at a smart hotel.
'Recently,' Sylvia observed, Smyth 'had been an anti-Suffragist', but
now she was a 'red-hot militant, entirely subjugated by Mrs Pankhurst,
panting with joy and excitement when she could manage to inveigle her

idol to her cottage near Woking, delighted to be the one member of the Union who addressed the leader familiarly as "Em" '.⁵⁶⁵

Emmeline, Sylvia knew, was slow to respond to affectionate advances, if she responded at all. But since Richard's death she had suffered a great spiritual loneliness. Sylvia watched her mother unbending 'to the wooing of the volatile musician and the power of her music, addressing her as "Dear", a term carrying from her unwonted tenderness'.⁵⁶⁶ An unwonted tenderness that Sylvia craved from her adored but, she felt, withholding mother. This further deflection of Emmeline's attention upset Sylvia and exacerbated the widening ideological breach between them. It added to the disturbance already caused to Emmeline by Sylvia's love for Keir Hardie, which was both sexually and politically inflected.

Though jealous of the affection between them, Sylvia appeared to get along well with Ethel, and maintained an unprejudiced generosity of spirit and admiration for her musical brilliance and unique, captivating eccentricity. Sylvia loved the mixture of strange magic and real popular culture captured in notation by Ethel's eclectic ear:

'Hey Nonny No!' ... was never heard with such great power and weirdness as when she gave it, playing to some casual group of Suffragettes in [her] small cottage. Voices of sailors drinking in a tavern, rude, rough fellows, wild adventurous spirits; voices of merriment; coarse, large laughter; voices of women, foolish, fierce, merry, sad and grieving, voices of horror; voices of Death – all these enwrapt in the rude, wild blast of the storm one heard in that chorus, given by that one magic being.⁵⁶⁷

Ethel treated Sylvia with a mixture of characteristically blunt judgement and human understanding. 'Sylvia is "mis-stitched",' she wrote to Emmeline, and difficult to make 'come to heel', yet Ethel also observed how Sylvia had to struggle with Christabel's primacy. 'When it is a question of obeying one's sister as sole arbiter (for she knows you would do what C. wants & probably doesn't understand it is because your own judgement would go with C's) I suppose its harder.'⁵⁶⁸

In part it was her anxiety about forcing a rift with her mother and Christabel that tempered Sylvia's desire to speak out against the continuation of militant policy: 'it was not in me to criticize or expostulate'.[569] As a committed socialist and at this time still active supporter of the Labour Party, Sylvia maintained the same opinion she had expressed in 1909 when the WSPU launched their earlier, more limited campaign of stone throwing and damage to private property. She continued to argue that the old methods had not yet been exploited to their full potential effect. 'I believed, then and always, that the movement required, not more serious militancy by the few, but a stronger appeal to the great masses to join the struggle.'[570] In this context, her opposition to the WSPU policy of political independence from all men's parties, including the Labour Party, was strategic as well as principled.

Sylvia believed that the WSPU needed steering back towards their socialist roots. She feared the cause would be beaten back for a generation if it divorced itself both from the growing commitment of the Labour Party to women's suffrage and from the adherence of the international socialist women's movement to the principle of universal suffrage. Emmeline's and Christabel's representation of themselves as hard-headed pragmatists steeped in sensible real-world female practicality as opposed to Sylvia's other-worldly, visionary, artistic, writerly intellectual idealism was misleading. Evaluated in the context of the dominant democratic movements of the time at home and abroad, theirs was a far more 'romantic feminism' and hers the clear-sighted realism.[571]

Yet Sylvia's characteristic and deeply ingrained loyalty was not only to her family but to people who put themselves in the front line of battle. 'I would rather have died at the stake than say one word against the actions of those who were in the throes of the fight. I knew but too surely, that the militant women would be made to suffer renewed hardships for each act of more serious damage.'[572]

Sylvia's ambivalence over militant tactics highlighted her views on the nature and responsibility of political leadership. Idolatry bothered her. Patriarchy trained women to follow not lead. She understood that 'in the spate of that impetuous movement, they would rush enthusiastic to their martyrdom, and bless, as their truest saviours, the leaders who summoned them to each new ideal'.[573] She recognized the immense difficulty of holding on to calm thought and a sense of perspective at such a time, 'how readily one daring enthusiast influences another, and in the gathering momentum of numbers all are swept along'.[574]

However, she acknowledged equally that there was never any doubt of the responsibility of the militant leaders for the actions of their followers. 'They accepted that always, without flinching, making themselves an open target for Government attack.'[575] Sylvia's respect for and loyalty to her mother and Christabel on this point were consistent. Most determinedly, it was the questions of class, socialism and men's participation in the women's movement that chipped away at their internal family alliance. Sylvia always supported the long-term goal for universal suffrage. The women's vote was a desirable staging post along the way, but she could not accept the exclusion of working women from this stage of the historical campaign, even as a tactic. Conversely, in Christabel's view,

> Ours is not a class movement at all. We take in everybody – the highest and the lowest, the richest and the poorest. The bond is womanhood! The Socialists are fighting against certain evils, which they believe to be attributable to the spirit of injustice as between man and man. I am not at all sure that women, if they had had their due influence from the beginning, would not have brought about a totally different state of affairs … It comes to this. The men must paddle their canoe, and we must paddle ours.[576]

Sylvia rejected this kind of reasoning. Christabel thought in single-paddle upriver canoes; Sylvia thought in international ocean-going fleets. For Christabel, her younger sister was becoming her socialist bête noire. For Sylvia, her elder sister's utter failure of class consciousness and her separatist tactics threatened to reduce the Votes for Women campaign to a nationwide sex war.

Sylvia challenged Christabel's refusal to acknowledge the hierarchy that existed in the increasingly autocratic WSPU. Everybody might enter the organization, 'the highest and the lowest, the richest and the poorest', and the bond, indeed, was womanhood. But only so long as 'the poorest' knew their place and understood that it was the white middle-class and elite vanguard that took precedence in running the show. Christabel argued that the needs and concerns of working women and issues of economic and social injustice facing the labour movement must be put on hold until the vote was won, since in the face of the arrival of a limited group of women who met the same property qualifications as men at the ballot box, all other social, economic and political iniquities would wither away. A vanguard of educated, middle-class women could be counted on by everyone else to fix the mess of the man-made world and run everything properly and fairly. This was the elixir of good old-fashioned bourgeois revolution in newly branded suffragette bottles.

From Sylvia's perspective, Christabel was now confusing ends and means. For the majority of activists – militant or non-militant – the struggle for the vote provided a focus for the broader struggle for sexual equality and social justice. The non-militant suffragists were beginning to work with the expanding Labour Party. Sylvia held that the WSPU needed to do the same. The policy of non-party alignment had been adopted over a decade earlier primarily as a strategy to win over the Liberal Party to women's suffrage and before the fledgling Labour Party held any seats in parliament. Now all of that had changed and the WSPU, Sylvia argued, needed to adapt themselves to the dramatically altered party political landscape.

13

O you daughters of the West!

Three days after the death of her aunt Mary at Christmas, Sylvia set sail on the SS *St Paul* bound for New York. This was the occasion when her mother saw her off on her first transatlantic voyage. Emmeline had remained with Sylvia after arriving with the terrible news on Boxing Day morning. 'Stunned by our sorrow, we clung together. She shared my narrow mattress, journeyed with me to Southampton, stayed to the last moment on board, smiled at me wistfully from the quay.'[577] As Sylvia steamed westwards her mother mastered her grief to campaign in the elections, in which the WSPU were opposing the government in fifty constituencies. Supporting the international struggle for women's suffrage and promoting the militant cause were the primary political purposes of Sylvia's mission in America. By 1911, women had achieved the right to vote in Colorado, Idaho, Utah, Washington and Wyoming. She would visit two of these states. Aged twenty-eight, already twice imprisoned and a well-known public figure in her homeland, it would be the first time in her life that Sylvia had set foot on soil where enfranchised women citizens walked.

It was a sombre voyage. Oppressed by grief, the blatant and spatially enforced class divisions between passengers depressed her further. Like Eleanor Marx before her making the same crossing in 1886, Sylvia was critical of the behaviour of 'the so-called better classes on board' and felt indignation at how badly the poor third-class emigrants were treated by wealthy tourists.[578] She also felt shame and pity witnessing the ignominious public medical inspections on the gangway of the third-class passengers who had already paid in full for their tickets. Once she'd got over the worst of her seasickness, she kept mostly to her cabin, spending long shifts editing *The Suffragette*. Oppressed by grief for Aunt Mary, she engrossed herself in working on her book and limited social interaction with passengers and officers to mealtimes. Her only relaxation was 'to gaze on the tremendous grandeur of the seas'[579] when the January gale-force trade winds and storms abated long enough to allow her a turn on deck. On the final night of the crossing she fended off the attempted rape by the ship's doctor, desperately seizing his last opportunity.

Sylvia's forthcoming book provided the vehicle for her twelve-week lecture tour. *The Suffragette* was the very first full-length history of the movement. The twofold objective of the trip was to use her moving account of the British suffrage struggle to win popular support in America for the WSPU suffragettes and to win the backing of a number of hugely wealthy individual funders potentially interested in financially assisting the cause.

Her old family friend and feminist mentor, Harriot Stanton Blatch was the driving force behind Sylvia's first transatlantic tour. Blatch had championed Emmeline's first visit to America in 1909. Shortly before she arrived, Blatch had cabled Emmeline on her steamer, 'Welcome to the first political leader among women in the history of the world.'[580] It was Blatch who had amazed Sylvia as a child by defending her dislike of porridge. Instead of trying to make the child eat a breakfast she hated and punishing her if she refused, suggested Harriot to Emmeline, why not give her other good things?[581] According to Sylvia, the outspoken Blatch had also told Emmeline that she thought Christabel 'far too sentimental' and advised that she study mathematics instead of 'her perpetual novel reading'.[582] Whether or not this agreeable criticism of her annoying elder sister was accurate, Blatch preferred and encouraged Sylvia from an early age.

Like Sylvia, Blatch was the daughter of a renowned pioneering mother, both adored and reviled, the veteran American feminist suffragist Elizabeth Cady Stanton. Blatch had returned to the United States in 1902. She discovered that in her absence the feminist movement in her homeland had become quietist, polite and overly genteel. 'The suffrage movement was completely in a rut ... it bored its adherents and repelled its opponents.'[583] Determined to shake up the stultified campaign, she founded the Equality League of Self-Supporting Women in 1907 and two years later brought over her friend Emmeline as a speaker. Inspired by the militant WSPU, Blatch changed the name of her organization in 1910 to the Women's Political Union (WPU) and adopted the purple, green and white of the WSPU in symbolic distinction from the yellow associated with American suffragism. Later, in 1916, the WPU would merge with the Congressional Union led by Alice Paul, who was about to become one of Sylvia's key transatlantic feminist allies.

A publicity photograph shows Blatch and other WPU members flyposting on the streets of New York in the weeks before Sylvia's arrival to publicise her opening lecture at the Carnegie Lyceum on 6 January 1911. The large photograph of Sylvia advertising the event, in which she wears the portcullis and prison-arrow brooch she had designed, is clearly visible on the multiple copies of the poster held by the women activists, powerfully illustrating the political moment of building a transatlantic and transgenerational militant feminist movement. Between the non-militant British and American women's suffrage organizations, channels had already been established. The NUWSS and the National American Woman Suffrage Association (NAWSA) shared publications, reprinted each other's work, jointly attended international conferences and hosted travelling speakers.[584] The WSPU were sidelined from these non-militant networks by their policies and separate organizational structure. Like their British sisters, American suffragists were divided over militancy. Young firebrand Sylvia Pankhurst represented the extreme wing of the movement and, well in advance of her arrival, some argued that associating with English suffragettes would discredit and jeopardize their cause.[585]

As Sylvia was not on the WSPU payroll, her tour had to be self-funding. The Civic Lecture Forum Bureau in New York acted as her speaker agency, organizing bookings, fees, accommodation and payment of expenses. William Feakins, secretary of the bureau, would later become Sylvia's US literary agent.

Sylvia arrived in New York on the morning of 5 January, the first anniversary of Harry's death. It was freezing, great blocks of ice jamming the harbour in the foreground, framed by the jagged silhouette of New York City, 'like a ruined castle on the horizon'.[586] For hours, they were delayed by congestion in the harbour. When they finally docked, 'the Press swooped down on me, all eager for copy, and insisted on my standing to be photographed right in the teeth of a bitter wind such as in England we do not know, whilst all the other passengers stood round to watch'.[587]

Elbowing their way through the reporters, Sylvia's welcoming committee from the WPU greeted her effusively. Lavinia Dock, Eunice Brannan and Beatrice Brow whisked her away to their headquarters in the basement of 46 East 29th Street, where Harriot Stanton Blatch, WPU founder and leader, enveloped her with her characteristic warmth and enthusiasm. Following a round of press interviews, Sylvia's hosts took her to the Martha Washington Hotel, also on 29th Street, where there were more photographers for whom to pose politely before she was treated to a reception dinner. Founded in 1907, the 'Women's Hotel', as the Martha Washington was known colloquially, was the first hotel in New York to provide lodging exclusively for professional women and girls travelling alone. Plush and spacious with over 400 rooms, a public restaurant, private dining salons, a library and a rooftop promenade, the Women's Hotel also housed a number of women's and feminist organizations. In addition, it boasted the conveniences of a drug store, a ladies' tailor shop, a millinery shop, a manicurist and chiropodist, a ladies' shoe-polishing parlour, a stationer's and a newspaper stand.

Soon, Sylvia was walking past photographs of herself displayed on the news-stand. Her arrival in New York and her first appearance at the prestigious Carnegie Lyceum the evening after she docked roused sufficient interest for a three-day round of press interviews. Sylvia as usual presented herself with a scrubbed face, no make-up and simpe tied-back or pinned-up hair. Her long speeches on 'the economic, political and social conditions of Great Britain' startled and impressed, as did the unpretentious, simple aesthetic of her clothing, the 'puritanic simplicity' of her hair and – most surprisingly – unpowdered, unpainted face.[588] Her lack of stays attracted comment from many male journalists. Even those who reported favourably on her political activities couldn't help but regret her refusal to wear a corset.[589] The *Columbus Citizen* found her a 'charmer', admiring her expertise 'on plain and fancy suffragetting', claiming that 'she is heralded here, the militant suffragette. Militant is she? You bet she is – but in the way women have been militant even long before Venus de Milo made such a hit with the men, that they stood for her as a goddess.'[590]

Aroused by her novelty attraction, journalists focused attention on what they saw as her youthful image and English-rose complexion.

According to the *New York Times*, which noted what it described as her 'yellow' satin evening gown, 'The youngest suffragette, as she is called, Miss Pankhurst, is 20, looks younger and might belong with any group of schoolgirls to be seen in New York.'[591] Other papers described her as 'very girlish in appearance', having a 'child face' and 'a soft, pathetic voice that would be quite in keeping with a girl of twelve' and as 'a little rosy-cheeked slip of an English girl'.[592] This infantilizing undermined Sylvia's seriousness, intellect and credentials as a political activist, reducing her unmarried, independent status to a form of arrested development.

Sylvia was also inclined to condescend. The greenhorn reporters 'were exceedingly young, almost like schoolboys, I thought'. Their undisciplined journalistic method appalled her. 'Don't you take notes?' she asked. 'We are not stenographers!' they replied indignantly. Demanding accurate reporting, she sent the bellhop for a supply of notebooks and pencils from the stationer's shop in the hotel lobby and dished them out to the press pack who then, in relays of four to six at a time, 'amiably permitted me to suggest the questions and dictate the answers'.[593] The resulting interviews appeared all over the country, in response to which telegrams with speaking requests poured in. She was now booked up to three times a day, and Feakins was turning down more than he could accept.

North American lecture tours could be lucrative for writers, providing an opportunity to boost insecure finances. In the year of Sylvia's birth, Oscar Wilde made his first hugely successful tour, as had Charles Dickens before him. But they were not women writers, militant suffragettes nor political activists. Sylvia's tour was more akin to that of her socialist-feminist foremother Eleanor Marx, who with her partner Edward Aveling, visited in 1886 as guests of the Socialist Labor Party of North America. Marx returned two years later, this time with Frederick Engels, his first trip across the Atlantic. The German socialist leader Wilhelm Liebknecht, father of Karl, had visited, and the trade unionist Tom Mann worked in the US for a year. Sigmund Freud and his protégé Carl Jung both visited in 1909, the same year that Emmeline Pankhurst made her first circuit. International exchanges between the European socialists and the American labour movement were common and, as Keir Hardie's first trip to the US in 1895 demonstrates, political relations between them were far closer than they are today.[594]

Furthering the feminist agenda, there was a free transatlantic flow of women activists, thinkers, writers and artists. The African-American suffragist and anti-lynching campaigner Ida Wells-Barnett visited Britain in 1893, and gave a lecture at the Pioneer Club at the invitation of Annie Besant. Emma Goldman made several visits to Britain, as – later – did Margaret Sanger and Alice Hamilton.[595]

The people Sylvia met in the United States provided new role models and different perspectives on class. Not on how class functioned, she understood that already, but on how she could escape her own. When the Pankhurst sisters were children, their father had read Whitman's 'Pioneers! O Pioneers!' to them, aimed at encouraging them to break new feminist frontiers. The women-only Pioneer Club in an elegant Mayfair house once home to Lord Byron took its name from Whitman's poem, and many of Sylvia's friends and mentors were members, including Eleanor Marx, Olive Schreiner, Annie Besant, Dora Montefiore and 'new woman' writers like Mona Caird. Of these, Sylvia's political role model Marx had spent the most time in the USA, primarily on her fifteen-week 'agitation tour' in 1886. Making use of her research and her experience of working conditions and the emerging labour movement in the USA, Marx published *The Working-Class Movement in America* in 1888. Not for the first time, Sylvia Pankhurst was very much following in Eleanor Marx's trailblazing socialist feminist footsteps.

Sylvia's three-month itinerary started in New York City before going on to Boston and Philadelphia on the east coast, through the Midwest states as far south as Kansas. Next she went north to Canada, speaking in Ottawa and Toronto, then crossed the border back through New York State – a country in itself – to Washington DC. From there she travelled further along the east coast before tacking due west to Colorado and California. Then she looped back in the direction of NYC, via speaking engagements in Kansas, Michigan and Maryland.

The evening after she arrived in the US, Sylvia gave her first public lecture at the Carnegie Lyceum, the grand performance venue on the lower level of the Carnegie Hall in midtown Manhattan with a capacity to hold 1,000 people. The event was sold out. Seated centre stage, Sylvia was flanked by America's most prominent suffragists and feminist leaders. Her childhood friend Nora Blatch, daughter of Harriot and granddaughter of Elizabeth Cady Stanton, was now a renowned civil engineer and civil rights activist. The writer and economist Charlotte Perkins Gilman, introduced to her by Elizabeth Wolstenholme Elmy, had brokered Sylvia's publishing contract for the US edition of *The Suffragette*. Dr Anna Howard Shaw, physician, suffragist and one of the first ordained Methodist ministers in the USA, sat alongside the socialist sympathizer, Marxist and controversial birth-control advocate Katharine Martha Houghton Hepburn, mother of a then four-year-old future Hollywood superstar.

Sylvia rose to give a barnstorming speech that set the agenda and tone for the rest of her whistle-stop tour. Speaking fluently for an hour and three-quarters, she delivered a justification of feminist militancy, emphasizing the violence inflicted on the suffragettes. Everyone in the audience knew that she had been subjected to physical violence on the streets, arrested, sentenced, imprisoned and forcibly fed. It was less than two months since Black Friday and a fortnight since Aunt Mary's death from the massive brain haemorrhage resulting from police brutality and the conditions of her final incarceration.

Once she had spoken on key suffragette themes, Sylvia turned her attention to the question of women and labour, telling of

'the difference in pay received by the English working women, those at the mines carrying tubs with the men, the identical work, the men getting four shillings ninepence and five shillings, and the women only one shilling sixpence to two shillings fourpence. "The only difference between them was", she said, "that the women tried to make things clean when they were not at work, while the men did nothing." "Shame!" cried a woman's voice.'[596]

From the off, Sylvia worked to integrate her approach to suffrage and feminism with working-class women in the American labour movement. Reporting on the event, the socialist journal *New York Call* reflected on the contrast between Sylvia, who spoke at length 'on the economic, political and social conditions of Great Britain', and her audience of 'parlour suffragettes', wealthy women of Fifth Avenue' and its vicinity 'who automobiled' to the Carnegie Lyceum.

Without exception women in industry are the sweated workers. They are paid lower wages than men, although it has been proved

time and time again that they are doing the same amount of
work. In the shoe trade in England women do the finest and most
skilled work. Yet they get about one-fourth of the price which
men get for the same, and even for cheaper work, which is less
nerve-straining.[597]

The middle-class parlour suffragettes in Sylvia's audience were less
familiar with these discussions of the gender pay gap. Though many of
them longed to be so, few were either gainfully employed or employable.
American socialist women and trade unionists, however, were well versed
in the labour case for women's political representation. Having detailed the
exploitative differences in wages for men's and women's work in the British
mines and shoemaking industries, Sylvia presented the need for women's
direct representation as analogous to that of the political representation of
labour, 'as a means of self-protection and self-presentation'.[598]

    Katherine Connelly astutely observes that, despite Sylvia's concerns
that the British suffrage movement was increasingly being directed by
middle-class women who claimed to speak for, or on behalf of, working
women, on her American tours she tended to present the British
suffragette movement as dominated by working-class women. At the
Carnegie Lyceum she spoke of 'women who work for their living in
factories, in mines and mills, as well as in the home, and who want the
ballot not as a topic for pink tea conversations, but for protection'.[599]
In her close reading of the speech, Connelly identifies that Sylvia was
describing the vision of the women's suffrage movement she wanted to
see created in Britain, rather than the one her mother and sister had
made the dominant force. From the off, she signalled her divergence
from the WSPU feminist family-party line.

    Sylvia's analysis of the socio-economic structure of unequal pay was
lost on the New York Times. Baffled by the disjuncture between, as they
perceived it, the image of the 'Small as a Schoolgirl' Miss Pankhurst and
the words that came out of her mouth, the Times derided her lecture 'as
one would laugh at one's own child talking seriously of the differences
between husbands and wives and the care of children'.[600] Conversely,
some anti-militant-suffrage campaigners took Sylvia's physical presence
among them very seriously as a formidable ideological threat and matter
of economic concern. She was propagating stone throwing, militant
arsonist tactics and the diversion of lecture fees from the American

movement – 'women who did not act like tomboys'[601] – to the British suffragettes: 'people pay hard cash to Miss Pankhurst & want our women to speak for nothing, chiefly because our women have not been in jail'.[602] Sylvia's debut speech in New York, which held her audience in 'rapt attention',[603] prompted these angry complaints from anti-militant suffragists, which continued to follow her throughout the tour. Her hosts around the states found their mailbags bulging with furious letters.

The seniors among these women were old enough to remember Eleanor Marx's tour in 1886, when she encouraged her audiences to 'throw three bombs amongst the masses: agitation, education, organisation'.[604] The inseparability of the socialist project from feminism was one of her key themes all over America, where she found suffragist activists 'ready to engage in the more far-reaching struggle for the emancipation of the workers as well as that for their own sex'.[605] Eleanor Marx spoke and wrote about sweated labour, so named because the sweater 'lives on the woman's earnings, literally on her sweat and blood'.[606] She met and interviewed working women and children about their lives, wages and conditions. Marx's experiences of America expanded and deepened her understanding of the political possibilities of an integrated socialist and feminist programme, and played a determining role in the development of her theory of socialist feminism. Her political essay 'The Woman Question: From a Socialist Point of View' and her study of both working-class feminists and well-to-do suffragists in *The Working-Class Movement in America* were among the very first statements of socialist feminism in western thought, appearing on both sides of the Atlantic. Contemporary reports on Sylvia's 1911 tour through the American states in the local press highlight these resonances: 'she will devote considerable time to the inspection of the condition of the American working classes as compared to those of great Britain'.[607]

The resonances between Sylvia Pankhurst and Eleanor Marx, would have been evident to many in Sylvia's audiences. Those audiences also knew her actual mother. Mrs Pankhurst had carried off her first fundraising lecture tour at the invitation of Harriot Blatch in 1909 with resounding success.

More remarkable than Sylvia attracting controversy for her advocacy of feminist militancy and economic socialism was the fact that she appeared at the Carnegie Lyceum in a satin evening gown. Writing to the always elegantly and appropriately attired Emmeline Pethick-Lawrence later in her journey, Sylvia complained about the pressure she was under to dress up for events: 'The ladies of Des Moines had insisted that I must not wear ordinary clothes, but must go in my cream coloured silk evening frock with its long trailing skirt. It seemed strange to me, but I did as I was bid.'[608] Sylvia felt obliged to respect the preferences of her hosts and paymasters, but it irked her. Hardie, she knew, would understand her irritation at the expectation that she change into evening wear. 'The dress I had to wear at the meeting was creased, as I was a very bad packer.'[609] Later in her trip, one of Sylvia's hostesses set about her tumbled trunk and showed her how to pack neatly and efficiently with tissue paper. The woman, whom Sylvia greatly respected and whose company she much preferred to that of her pompous husband, was a great admirer of Hardie's.

After speaking at a WPU meeting the next day, Sylvia headed to Boston to address 1,000 people at Ford Hall. Sylvia, reported *Votes for Women* back home in Britain, marched in a suffragette procession by torchlight, with music:

> The large number of men in the procession was noticeable. Miss Sylvia Pankhurst walked in the procession among a group of Boston Suffragists. With banners flying and a drum and fife corps playing, the picturesque spectacle attracted large crowds. The Women's Suffrage Bill was being discussed at the State House, and the procession went to Ford Hall, where Miss Sylvia Pankhurst and members of the Massachusetts Women's Suffrage League addressed an overflowing audience. (In fact, three overflow audiences were formed on that memorable evening.)[610]

Harvard students turned out to hear her speak in Cambridge, Massachusetts, and an audience of 800 attended her first Brooklyn event the following evening. While she shook up the parlour suffragettes of Manhattan, the socialists greeted her as one of their own. 'In Brooklyn', reported *Votes for Women*, 'the Socialists demand the vote for women. The Brooklyn Labour Lyceum was the scene of a most enthusiastic meeting on Woman's Day, a day which the Socialist women of America have set aside for the discussion of Woman Suffrage.'[611] In Pittsburgh,

Pennsylvania, she spoke about 'My Life in a London Prison', and in Cleveland, Ohio, on 'Women in Politics'. While in Cleveland she visited the workhouse and spoke with women prisoners. Also in Ohio she got to give her first university sociology lecture to students, at Oberlin College. She swiftly realized that her lectures were booked into the biggest performance venues in many of the towns and cities she visited, and that she was put up in plush modern hotels, to which she was unaccustomed.

By now Sylvia had spent a week travelling on long-distance trains. Her first journey on a sleeper from New York to Pittsburgh had been a culture shock, as she confessed to amused reporters. In America, she discovered, only a curtain separated passenger berths. The *Chicago Sunday Tribune* poked fun at her anxiety about sleeping 'unprotected in an American sleeping car berth, with no door to lock against lurking foes or gentlemen who forget their berth numbers – alas, despair, O agony and grief!'[612] Sylvia was well acquainted with the dangers of unwelcome sexual advances or worse facing the single female traveller. As a student, she'd had to fight off the unwanted attentions of a train guard in Italy and, barely a fortnight since, she'd narrowly escaped attempted sexual assault by the ship's doctor on her voyage to America.

The *Tribune* had an axe to grind with Sylvia, and was reminding her that in a former colony it didn't do to be grand if you came from the old country. Sylvia arrived in Chicago on 18 January at midnight, exhausted. Despite the hour, a press pack awaited her at the Congress Hotel where she was staying. Fretting about her book deadline, she was intent on taking the opportunity of an unscheduled forty-eight-hour window to lock herself up in her hotel room and work on the manuscript. 'I have to do a lot of writing for two days and until I have finished that I will do little talking,'[613] she informed the journalists. Undeterred, the press placed her hotel room under siege.

> Some battered persistently on my door, others invented the most atrocious interviews, which were published with fake photographs in which I appeared an appalling hooligan. A newspaper containing one such caricature was flung over the head of the chambermaid as she entered my room. Seeing it, I capitulated immediately, but the Press men and women did not entirely relent.[614]

The *Tribune* rewarded her capitulation by sending the suffragist Belle Squire to conduct a long interview that ran to a full-page spread, with real photographs and, this time, an accurate cartoon. Squire's own book, *The Woman Movement in America*, was published that year. A sympathetic interviewer, she shared with the readers Sylvia's successes both as an activist and as a talented artist.

Media probing about her romantic life and her appearance irritated Sylvia, who understood all too well its salacious and sexist intent. She dressed up perforce in the evenings, but otherwise wore her usual radically relaxed and simple wardrobe, prompting comments in the press from male journalists about her 'uncorseted figure'.[615] A reporter from the *St. Louis Post-Dispatch* earned a memorable riposte when asking her whether she regarded the harem skirt as emancipatory for allowing women greater freedom of movement. Fashion, she replied, 'seems a trivial matter to me ... certainly the harem skirt is not a vital factor. Let the women emancipate their heads, and their feet will take care of themselves.'[616]

Speculation about her personal life was more intrusive. Unmarried and, as far as anyone knew, not even affianced, her singleness prompted frequent questions about suitors. Sylvia batted them away brusquely, replying that she was 'too busy to get married'.[617] The following year on her return trip she rounded on a journalist who asked her another tiresome question about the leap-year Valentine's Day romantic convention. 'The idea of proposing to a man never entered my head. I have other and more important things to think of. You ask me a silly and personal question.'[618] Sylvia had an inviolable belief in the right to privacy, and objected to the way in which women were belittled and defined by their marriage status and the number of children they produced. Even if her relationship with Hardie had been public, she would have resented it defining her.

In America, a series of introductions leading to new friendships made a substantive impact on her, recalibrating her politics and her intimate life. The six months she spent in America during her two trips in 1911 and 1912 proved critical in her change of heart and head towards WSPU policy, and the development of her own breakaway campaign. Imperceptible to all but herself, they also triggered a parallel tectonic change in her emotional and spiritual life, through a reassessment of the reality of her relationship with Hardie.

Critically, she encountered socialist women trade-union leaders and the principal pioneers of utopian communities running the women's settlement co-operative movement. During her first visit to Chicago in January, she met Jane Addams at Hull House settlement, and later the German-Jewish healthcare pioneer and human rights activist Lillian Wald at her Henry Street settlement in New York.

The first settlement of educated middle-class reformers, Toynbee Hall, built in east London in 1888, was much inspired by the example of earlier American utopian co-operatives. In its turn Toynbee Hall influenced the American settlement movement by prompting Jane Addams to set up Hull House with her lover Ellen Gates Starr in 1889. Starr was a bookbinder and the couple incorporated Arts and Crafts into the ethos of the co-operative, making Ruskin and Morris key influences. Many social settlements sprang up in towns and cities from the 1880s onwards. The women who established them rejected individualistic models of philanthropy based on moral and religious responsibility; rather, they argued the case for the structural causes of poverty and oppression.

By the time Sylvia visited Hull House, it was the most famous settlement in the USA. Addams, who in 1931 would become the first American woman to win the Nobel Peace Prize, influenced a generation of radical women and men on both sides of the Atlantic. As Sylvia noticed immediately, Hull House was organized more democratically than Toynbee Hall, and was a hub for women's campaigns, trade unions, communal kitchens, education, healthcare, arts, crafts and culture. Connections had quickly sprung up between the women's settlement and the university and social science departments, enabling the University of Chicago to lead the way in producing a hugely influential network of women sociologists, economists and thinkers focused on innovative research into working conditions, child labour, immigration and motherhood.[619]

In Britain, equivalent links developed between some progressive universities and working-class communities, as in Liverpool where the radical reformer Eleanor Rathbone fused active work in the suffrage movement, settlement work and political and social reform, later becoming an MP. In the 1930s, Rathbone's highly praised economic treatise *The Disinherited Family*, published in 1924, would become a blueprint for establishing a national maternity service, in tandem with Sylvia's later *Save the Mothers*.

Sylvia's experience of the women's settlement movement in America and its founding leaders informed much of her later work on blueprints and policies for reimagining the social organization of Britain. Her work in east London, establishing the East London Federation of Suffragettes (ELFS), launched immediately after she returned to Britain from her second American tour in 1912, was the first step. 'I wanted to rouse these women of the submerged mass to be, not merely the argument of more fortunate people, but to be fighters on their own account, despising mere platitudes and catch-cries, revolting against the hideous conditions about them, and demanding for themselves and their families a full share of the benefits of civilization and progress.'[620] Sheila Rowbotham describes how British and American women participated and worked together in various types of 'self-help action in communities. Outside the scope of formal politics, the voluntary sector they helped to create enabled many women to gain an understanding of social problems.'[621]

On 21 January, a Saturday, Zelie Emerson and Olive Sullivan from the Chicago Women's Trade Union League took Sylvia on a tour of the Harrison Street jail and police courts. A photograph captured that day shows Sylvia looking pensively into an empty cell, its barred gate ajar. Assembled behind, looking on, are her hosts, including the assistant police matron Elizabeth Belmont, and Sullivan and Emerson, accompanied by the three male members of the group, all spruced up in suits and ties.

Sylvia visited many prisons, reformatories, penitentiaries and prison farms in America and Canada. She described the 'foul, foul stench that reaches out into the street, grows stronger as one enters, and catches the breath as one goes down the stone steps'.[622] Down below was a dim and suffocating subterranean hell. The horror of Harrison Street struck a chord in her that exceeded the horror of them all. 'The worst jail I have visited on this continent was one at Chicago where men and women are kept in darkened cells, serving 30 day terms in a building without any civilized sanitary equipment, the drain being actually an open sewer.'[623]

The prison housed both men and women, those awaiting trial pressed into the overcrowded 'loathsome dens' with convicts serving sentences. Typically, Sylvia quizzed Elizabeth Belmont about the working conditions for the matrons and warders, 'here for long long hours. They suffer much from rheumatism and tuberculosis.'[624]

Sylvia's visit to Chicago was during the final bitter days of the Chicago garment workers' strike that had begun four months earlier in September 1910 and involved 100,100 strikers. The Chicago strike caught the wave of working-class women's militancy that had begun in New York the previous year and spread across the country as women workers, predominantly from immigrant backgrounds, called for a general strike in the garment industry. The Chicago strike broke out when the Hart, Schaffner and Marx clothing factory cut women's piece-worker rates.[625] The women applied for representation from the male-dominated United Garment Workers' Union, who weren't interested in supporting immigrant women they regarded as low skilled. So they turned to the Chicago Federation of Labour and the Chicago Women's Trade Union League (WTUL).

As Eleanor Marx documented in *The Working-Class Movement in America*, Chicago was run by a corrupt system of collusion among employers, police, politicians, organized crime and the social elite who worked together to exploit sweated labour and brutally repressed any attempts at representation or resistance from Chicago workers. During the 1910 action, strikers and pickets, male and female, and protesters who supported them were attacked, beaten, arrested and imprisoned. In two cases, strikers were shot dead by police. Many young girl strikers were dragged to Harrison Street when arrested for picketing. As Sylvia reminded readers in her article for the now friendlier *Chicago Sunday Tribune*,

> I heard of some of the women and girls who had been picketing in the garment workers' strike, as I am told in a perfectly legal way, who had been arrested and thrust either into these police court cells or into the annex, in both of which the risk of contamination at all times is exceedingly great. Happily, their trade union organizations have been able to come to their aid and bail them out within a short time, but it must be remembered that the people being on strike were practically penniless and had no money of their own, and therefore had others not come to their assistance they would have been obliged to continue suffering this terrible form of confinement.[626]

Sylvia had the authority of experience. As she told a journalist later in her American travels, 'Having served two terms in jail I have taken every convenient chance to visit the jails in different cities.'[627]

WTUL activist Zelie Emerson, dubbed by the press the 'scrubwoman heiress',[628] was renowned for her activism in the Chicago garment workers' strike committee, 'engaged in the demanding work of distributing relief to a dispute that lasted nearly four months, involved 45,000 previously unorganized workers and reportedly saw 1,250 "strike babies" born'.[629] Emerson was director of relief work, chair of the Rent Committee and ran the restaurant on Noble Street established to feed strikers and their families.[630] One hundred thousand striking workers and their dependants needed support during the bitter Chicago winter. Seven thousand toddlers wailed for milk in the WTUL headquarters, and linguistic and cultural barriers had to be overcome to co-ordinate workers who between them spoke nine different languages.

The strike became famous for being organized and led by women and for binding together female and male workers across ethnic groups to oppose lousy employers. The university-educated Zelie, who always wrote up her work, described this effort in an article co-written with Katharine Coman in 1911, 'Co-operative Philanthropy: Administration of Relief during the Strike of the Chicago Garment Workers'.[631] Coman, historian, economist, sociologist, educator and social activist also involved in the women's settlement co-operative movement, was the first female statistics professor in the US and the sole woman co-founder of the American Economics Association.

The suggestion of zealousness in the Latin-French-derived name Zelie absolutely suited the firebrand who shared a surname with Mrs Pankhurst's peripatetic interior-decoration shop and an American writer often quoted by both of Sylvia's parents in their stump speeches.[632] Bookish and sporty, Zelie was born in Jackson, Michigan, in 1883. Her mother, Zelie Passavant, from a wealthy philanthropic family, was an intimate of Andrew Carnegie, and rumour held they had wanted to marry. That never transpired, but they long remained friends and she was the unstoppable force who persuaded Carnegie to build the Michigan Carnegie Libraries. Zelie's father Rufus, an industrialist who built a fortune from wood pulp, died when she was thirteen years old, leaving her an income of $10,000 a year and all the cultural capital required to support the society life she was expected to dance her way through. Zelie was having none of such silliness. Instead, she set out to study literature at the University of Michigan. She began her course in 1903–4, but rapidly got involved in student politics. Preoccupied with the need to change the world and with the security of an inherited fortune beneath her feet, she was too impatient to graduate and 'abandoned society for sociological investigation'. She moved to Chicago, living initially at the Northwestern University Settlement and taking a series of jobs: as a hotel kitchen busgirl, as a scrubwoman cleaning floors in a restaurant and as a salesgirl selling toys in a Chicago department store, in order to experience and study working conditions.[633]

At Hull House, Sylvia was introduced to Zelie's Australian friend Stella Miles Franklin. Miles Franklin worked as secretary to her fellow Australian journalist and social reformer Alice Henry at the WTUL and co-edited the league's magazine, *Life and Labor*.[634] Alongside her activism, Franklin achieved literary success on three continents kick-started by her bestselling debut *My Brilliant Career*, the autobiographical novel about a teenage girl growing up in the Australian bush who yearns to break free and become independent. Franklin wrote it while an adolescent living in the outback on her father's cattle farm, and was just twenty-one when it was published in 1901. Her experience working as a domestic servant provided the material for her subsequent book, *Some Everyday Folk and Dawn*, published in 1909.

After meeting her in Chicago, Stella Miles Franklin and Zelie Emerson became Sylvia's friends and useful contacts, but, more than that, they would soon both cross the Atlantic to join her breakaway socialist-suffragette movement and work on her projects in the East End.

Like all great social reformers, Sylvia had particular interest in the way societies managed their systems of rehabilitative justice. She made a point of visiting prisons, some 'like medieval dungeons in their darkness and absence of arrangements for cleanliness of person or clothing'.[635] The horrendous conditions of the Harrison Street Jail in Chicago upset her, as did the barbaric treatment of prisoners in the Tennessee 'tank', a giant pen enclosing numerous smaller cages in which the prisoners were locked like market animals. In her accounts of the American penal system, she details and condemns the lack of privacy, the inadequate provision for exercise and the lidless, unscreened WCs that could be flushed only by external levers controlled by the warders. She expressed compassion for the screaming agony of drug addicts suffering from withdrawal. She enjoyed the artwork of a Welsh miner, convicted for killing a man in a quarrel, who had covered the walls of his cell in paintings of his native valleys, and then he had taken to learning musical instruments. By contrast, she was greatly impressed by the rehabilitative regimes, work and education programmes in the progressive model prisons in New York, Bedford Hills and Framingham, Massachusetts.

On her last day in Chicago the Illinois Equal Suffrage Association hosted a lunch for her in the Chicago Women's Club. In the afternoon she spoke for three hours on 'Life in a London Prison' at the Music Hall in the Chicago Fine Arts Building, and then again in the evening at Northwestern University. A demanding week on the road followed, with multiple events in Kansas, Iowa and Ohio punctuated by night trains on which she got very little sleep.

14

Bridge, Balls, Dinners

By the time Sylvia arrived in Kansas the strain of participating in the elite social events tacked on to every part of the programme by her hosts in every town and city was beginning to tell. On 30 January 1911 she spoke to the Kansas Women's Dining Club, an audience of 300 people. The *Guthrie Daily Leader* reported that Sylvia launched a broadside at the event when she declared, 'Bridge, balls, dinners – I think the women who give their lives to such things as that ought to be swept off the face of the earth.' She paused, eyes sparkling. 'I would love to be one of those to do the sweeping.'[636]

An antidote to bridge, balls and dinners followed two days later, when she was unexpectedly informed at a few hours' notice that she was to address the Iowa state legislature in joint assembly at the Statehouse in Des Moines, followed by another reception. She'd lost her voice by the time she was due to go to Iowa, so an osteopath, Dr Nina Wilson Dewey, was called to her room at the Chamberlain Hotel successfully to restore it by what Sylvia described as a miracle. The two became friends. Sylvia met Nina Dewey again later, and continued to correspond with her once back in England, sending her an account of her forced feeding that Dewey extracted and arranged for publication in the local press. The Iowa Senate and House of Representatives were just about to consider a bill to enfranchise women. As Sylvia entered the chamber, she saw the raised platform holding the President of the Senate and the Speaker of the House from which she was to address the gathering, on the wall behind it an engraved portrait of Abraham Lincoln with the Stars and Stripes draped around it. She noted that many of the legislators occupying the centre of the floor 'sat with their feet upon their desks'.[637] The President and Speaker graciously received her on the platform, and introduced her to the General Assembly. 'It seemed to me a very solemn occasion. I learned that the only woman who had ever before addressed the Iowa Legislature was Susan B. Anthony, who had pleaded for the Married Woman's Property Bill a generation before.'[638]

After another three days of back-to-back speaking events, Sylvia climbed aboard the train from New York to Ottawa, arriving in Canada in the afternoon after a two-hour delay in a snowstorm. An audience of 500 turned out in the evening for her first Canadian event, held at the Russell Theatre. A packed programme of morning, afternoon and evening lectures, receptions and prison visits occupied her next few days in Ottawa and Toronto, before she headed back to New York via Syracuse, to speak to 1,000 people at the Grade Theatre.

In New York her schedule included events in the Labour Lyceum at the Second Baptist Church and the Smith Opera House, and – with delicious irony – a lecture about her prison experiences at the Hotel Astor. In Philadelphia hundreds had to be turned away from the overflowing 600-capacity venue at the New Century Drawing Room. In Washington DC, where women already had the right to vote, similar crowds turned out on 22 February, Washington's birthday, to hear her speak in the Columbia Theatre on 'The New Struggle for Liberty'. In the afternoon she was taken by car to see the Capitol and the Senate Gallery before boarding the train for her second trip to Boston. The following evening she marched at the front of the women's torchlit procession from Boston's Park Square to the State House, addressing the crowds inside and the assembly within.

During the final week of February, Sylvia took part in the 'Suffrage Week' campaign in Albany, New York, where she spoke on the 'Prison Experiences of a Young Suffragette', then on she pressed to Denver, Colorado, via Nebraska, to address the Colorado Legislature in the morning and the Unity Church in the evening. In Denver she stayed with the suffragist leader Sarah Platt Decker.

Warmer weather and bright skies greeted her in California, along with unprecedented comfort, mod cons and a press pack at the Alexandria Hotel. After the now familiar first round of interviews in each state, she spoke in Venice, Pasadena, San Francisco and finally Oakland, where an audience of 2,000 gathered to hear her at the Idora Park Theatre. Her lectures on 'Women in Politics' and 'Women in Industry' went down well in California. Los Angeles loved Sylvia. The California Club hosted a lunch for her, she toured the county prison and juvenile court, which she did not love, and the suffragist Frances Wills hosted a suffragette tea in her home for about seventy guests, including Sylvia's cousin Helen Herendeen and her husband who were wintering at Pasadena's Hotel Mayland. Helen was one of her father's nieces – a Pankhurst – and Sylvia, disappointed, discovered she didn't like her.

On the evening of 12 March Sylvia boarded the Union Pacific from Los Angeles to Lawrence, Kansas, a three-day journey that took her through New Mexico, 'the strangest and most desolate country. What indeed possessed any body of people to settle here?'[639] Her artist's eye picked out the palette of the landscape: 'behind and before us, stretched the dull red sand and withered-looking tufts of grey-green sage bush. On the horizon to right and left, great red stone ridges rose sheer out of the sand.'[640] Passing through a Native American reservation, she saw 'a tiny village of huts built up of sun-dried bricks ... little patches of tilled land ... the tall dried-up stalks of last year's maize ... [T]he whole land is barren and forlorn. It is here that they have driven the poor Indians and now they will say they are lazy and will not work!'[641] She witnessed the colonial dispossession of American First Peoples from their land and culture.

Stretching her legs at a station stop, Sylvia browsed the arts and crafts displayed by the platform vendors. Among them, as she observed in a letter to Hardie, were men 'wearing loose blue cotton suits, with blankets about their shoulders', selling 'bits of turquoise matrix and smokey topaz ... the blue stones that my Darling likes and so I found something for him'.[642] She admired the women 'with short red skirts and white felt leggings' selling 'bead chains and earthenware pottery that they themselves have made'.[643] The best work, she discovered, was to be found inside the store in the middle of the platform, 'an abundance of wrought silver, iron, and copper work, baskets woven with extraordinary fineness, and pottery decorated with simple harmonious pattern'. She watched women and girls 'weaving richly-coloured woollen rugs, but they are merely servants. The whole business is managed by loud-voiced Yankee hustlers, who demand high prices for the goods.'[644]

Back on the train in the dining car, she listened attentively as a local trader boasted about his lucrative commercialization of Indian arts and crafts and described the structure of exploitation involved. 'He is one of those who live by it, and he exports rugs and other things to Europe as well as to New York and other eastern cities.' He employed large numbers of Indians, mostly women, selling their work 'for many pounds; but he tells without hesitation the incredibly small sum he pays the woman for her work'.[645] Quizzed and challenged by Sylvia, he justified his meanness with the age-old excuse wielded against piecework artisans that the women stole or wasted the wool he supplied for them to weave in their own homes.

'Now that the red people well nigh have been exterminated,' Sylvia reflected,

> partly from pure pity and compunction, and partly perhaps because the aborigines are an interesting curiosity like the buffalo or any other rare wild thing, the American Government now wishes to save them from becoming extinct. They are called the 'wards' of the nation, and where the soil of the reservations is too poor, or the conditions are too unkindly to maintain them, rations are dealt out to them. Several Indian Colleges have been set up, where any young man or woman who has even a sixth part of Indian blood may be admitted, and the Government sends out into the reservations to collect free students for these institutions.[646]

Sylvia experienced for herself Haskell College in Lawrence, Kansas, the following day. She discovered that while there was some teaching of regular school subjects – reading, writing, arithmetic, geography, history, drawing – the learning environment was geared to teaching mechanical commercial skills. Her white hosts, its administrators, imagined she would admire the institution and its policies, including the obliteration of indigenous skills and the value of Native American culture in favour of teaching boys building, plumbing and house painting and girls commercial garment making on 'rows and rows of sewing machines'.[647]

Dismayed, she saw they were being taught also to produce 'fancy work', consisting chiefly of 'mats, table centres, and antimacassars', to adorn middle-class homes. Some of these, made of white muslin, were 'dotted over with foolish little pieces of green paper, cut to represent shamrock leaves'.[648] Instead of craft skills and decorative arts, the girls were taught to make 'tawdry artificial flowers', displayed in a depressing showcase. Pushed to the back of it, behind the flowers, Sylvia spotted 'one genuine native Indian rug – a harmonious commingling of brilliant colours grateful to the eye. Seeing it, I said to the teacher: "The girls here still do some of their native weaving, pottery, and rug making then?" "No," was the reply, and then, with evident scorn, "Oh, that rug – that was made years ago. There is no weaving of that kind done here now!" '[649]

In the manuscript for her intended book on America, Sylvia decried the wilful destruction of crafts and decorative arts, 'dying out through poverty and disease in the reservations, and they are being stamped out, even more absolutely, by contact with commerce-made ugliness and false standards in schools and colleges'. Wryly, she observed, 'Soon, those sharp Yankee hustlers will have no more Indian wares to make their money with.'[650] Thirty years later, Sylvia would dedicate herself to the ancient arts and crafts of Ethiopia, ensuring that the teaching of their history and skills was included in the new post-war national school curriculum and, in England, curating exhibitions and presentations of Ethiopian art and culture in early BBC television programmes.

For the remainder of the month Sylvia toured Missouri, Indiana, Michigan, Maryland, New Hampshire, Massachusetts and Pennsylvania. It was not surprising that Hardie became increasingly anxious that his letters didn't seem to be reaching her.

In Indianapolis at a reception breakfast held in her honour she met the novelist Booth 'Tark' Tarkington, already a sensationally famous bestselling Great American novelist seven years before the publication of *The Magnificent Ambersons*. Over hot chocolate, she discovered him to be a reactionary anti-suffragist. She expressed her scepticism about the Great Man with a typically Sylvan prick of the pen, by remarking that Tark's sister had shared with her the confidence that the literary genius never got out of bed before 1 p.m. – in Sylvia's book, behaviour close to criminality. Conversely, the lawyer, journalist and socialist feminist Crystal Eastman impressed her, as did Crystal's little brother Max, editor of the *Masses*, then still 'a very shy young fellow'.[651] Sister and brother co-founded and co-edited the radical arts and politics magazine the *Liberator*. Crystal Eastman later became a co-founder of the Women's International League for Peace and Freedom, and in 1920 of the American Civil Liberties Union.

Sylvia's bookings in St Louis included a turn at the all-male City Club which had temporarily suspended 'its most stringent rule' to allow her to speak there, and directly afterwards a debate with Isaac H. Lionberger, lawyer, capitalist and former Assistant Attorney General of the United States. The venue was the hall of the expensive private school attended by Lionberger's daughter, present in the audience. He attempted to justify an exclusively male franchise on the grounds that women were not able to fight for their country. Sylvia's riposte, 'Do your presidents settle their campaigns for office by prize fights?' received tumultuous applause from the audience. Sylvia won the debate and, according to the press, Lionberger's daughter rushed up to her to congratulate and thank her for 'taking father down'.[652] A Dime Museum in St Louis delivered Sylvia's first exposure to commercial pornography, and saloons where food was free as long as you drank gave her pause to think again about Hardie's arguments for the necessity of temperance in the labour movement.

On 25 March Sylvia was speaking in Detroit, where she was guest of honour at a lunch held by the Men's League for Women's Suffrage. In the evening her hostess Dr Mary Thompson Stevens took her to speak at the Church of Our Father. There, addressing a representative audience composed of all classes, Sylvia pointed out that the conditions of women's labour and wages were much the same in England and the States, that some 24,000 women in Detroit alone were underpaid and that much of the White Slave Traffic was due to this. 'There is an immense field of work open to women in the way of remedying these and other evils, and Miss Pankhurst called upon the women of Detroit to join with their sisters who are already working and fighting. Her earnestness and sincerity made a deep impression upon her hearers,' reported *Votes for Women*.[653]

An article written by Betty Blythe in an Indianapolis newspaper throws light on how Sylvia's image projected her powers to persuade:

Well, it may be true that Miss Sylvia Pankhurst is a 'fighting Suffragette'; but no one would think it to look at her. Dainty, refined, with a mentality rare even in this day of advanced education, Miss Pankhurst is essentially the product of a cultured civilisation. Looking out over that big audience of women who faced the young speaker yesterday, I could not but wonder if any there were in that crowd ready to suffer – and nearly die – for their cause, as had the slender slip of a girl who stood up on the big platform, pleadingly holding out her hands, and looking in her girlish isolation very lonely. But make no mistake: there was neither loneliness nor helplessness. There was a girl who knew what she was talking about; and she was talking about it exceedingly well. She made her hearers sit up and take notice. There was a gasp of surprise as the speaker, a mere girl, told of experiences in English prisons, and out of them, that would try the stoutest heart. And these experiences, tests of courage, strength and endurance, were the means which Miss Pankhurst advised the Indianapolis women who are fighting for suffrage to try.[654]

On 25 March when Sylvia was speaking in Detroit, a fire at the Triangle Shirtwaist Factory on New York's Lower East Side killed 146 workers, predominantly from immigrant backgrounds, because their employers locked them in during their shifts, against regulations. The factory was on the top floors of the building, beyond the reach of firemen's ladders. The fire escape collapsed from the weight of the terrified workers trying to clamber down. Most burned to death inside the building; others died on impact as they hit the pavement, having leapt from the windows in desperation.

One of the survivors, Rose Safran, who had been involved in an earlier strike at Triangle, reflected on the tragedy: 'If the union had won we would have been safe. Two of our demands were for adequate fire escapes and for open doors from the factories onto the street. But the bosses defeated us and we didn't get the open doors or the better fire escapes. So our friends are dead.'[655]

Ten days later Sylvia attended the funeral procession for the victims, organized by the International Ladies' Garment Workers' Union. She described how the 'rain poured from a grey sky' as the 'long procession of saddened workgirls marched in their poor black garments, to show honour and respect to their comrades burnt to death'.[656] One hundred thousand marched in the funeral procession, and some 300,000 lined the streets of the city to pay tribute.

The following week, after completing another round of public events in New York, and visiting state schools and a women's reformatory in Bedford Hills, Sylvia boarded the SS *Majestic* bound for Southampton on 12 April. Shortly before her departure, the *Philadelphia Inquirer* asked her what she thought of the US. 'Delightful,' she replied. 'I would even like to live here. This desire, I must confess, is largely due to the lack of fog, which is so depressing at home in London.'[657]

In a different tone, she wrote critically in *The Suffragette Movement* about the wealthy suffragists who denied or refused to recognize the shared aims and values of the feminist and labour movements.

> I saw great wealth and luxury, the fevered quest of some men to
> spend money, and of some women to get culture, the squalid
> poverty of the new immigrants, the nightmare industrialism ...
> I visited dozens of factories and laundries, and found in some of
> them most horrible conditions. Yet American women constantly
> told me there was no need for them to take an interest in politics,
> because American conditions were so good.[658]

The women of the settlement movement at Hull House and Henry Street, activists of the Women's Trade Union League and all those she met involved in the garment workers' strike had introduced her to the radical American feminists who, whether themselves rich or poor, middle or working class, rolled up their sleeves in the labour movement and organized together to fight the degradations of modern industrialism.

Within nine months, Sylvia was back in America. On 11 January 1912, US immigration officials interviewed passenger number twelve on the shipping list of the SS *Oceanic* that had sailed from Southampton on the 3rd. Twenty-nine years old, female, single. Occupation: artist. Had she been to America before? Yes, last year. Are you a polygamist? An anarchist? No and no. Have you been to prison? Yes, she confirmed, 'twice as a suffragette'.[659]

As she made landfall, New York was deep in a citywide laundry workers' strike, which had begun on New Year's Day, demanding 'More Pay and a Shorter Day'. The workforce, two-thirds women and girls and the remainder men and boys, picketed outside laundries in the freezing snow, intimidated by organized strike-breakers and resisting constant threat of arrest. When they struck on 1 January, they were entirely unorganized. The Women's Trade Union League, led by its New York president Mary Dreir, swiftly helped them form a union.

On 12 January, the day after she arrived, Sylvia joined 'a parade of automobiles through the laundry districts … adorned with pink and black banners', organized by the WTUL, which had set up its strike support HQ at the Harlem Arcade at 211 East 124th Street. In the afternoon Sylvia met a group of thirty women strikers in the 'dingy and dirty' dancehall and asked them to tell her about their work, which she meticulously recorded in her signature large notebook. The stories, characters and lives of these women, ranging in age from adolescents to menopausal widows, she published in her journalism and in future books. Nowhere does she mention her own role in events as the guest speaker at the strike meeting, where she appeared alongside Mary Dreir, the birth-control campaigner, Margaret Sanger and America's leading female industrial activist, Elizabeth Gurley Flynn.

Waiting to speak, Sylvia studied the faces in the crowd, struck by the 'refinement' of the women, admiring their 'dress and general bearing':

> A large proportion of them were certainly American, and it was interesting to notice this, because one is frequently told that over work, under pay, and bad conditions of employment amongst women are confined to the foreign immigrants, and that the American woman does not need to work in a factory, and is always well paid and well cared for.[660]

Of the men, she observed, a larger proportion appeared to be foreign, and their dress and physique poorer, 'though it is very difficult, of course, to generalise in such matters'.[661]

Flynn, an anarcho-syndicalist who insisted that child-rearing and housework were as much part of the productive economy as work for wages, had a global outlook. Unions, she believed, demonstrated 'education in action' and the extension of working people's power required the creation of an international union while resolving divisions and prejudices within the US. Like Eleanor Marx, who was neither anarchic nor syndicalist, Elizabeth Flynn believed that the making of the American working class demanded the overcoming of divisions of skill, gender, race, ethnicity and nationality. She envisaged a unionism based on solidarity without boundaries in which 'the Polack and the Jew and the Turk … forgot their religious and national differences … and felt that an injury to one is an injury to all'.[662]

Getting to know activists like Flynn expanded the knowledge and understanding Sylvia had gained in Britain of women's work as linking the commonality of women's economic and political disadvantages. Flynn was a full-time organizer for the Industrial Workers of the World (IWW), known to all as the Wobblies, and was a lynchpin in the transnational path of global syndicalism. Known across America as a proponent of women's suffrage, rights and birth control, she had much in common with Sylvia, having already been arrested ten times when Sylvia met her, on one occasion chaining herself to a lamp post to delay arrest. She was the inspiration for the song 'The Rebel Girl' by Joe Hill, the Swedish immigrant who was to become, of course, the most famous Wobbly of them all. Theodore Dreiser described Flynn as 'an East Side Joan of Arc', while George Bernard Shaw would soon describe Sylvia as an East End Joan of Arc, but it was an American pastor who first made the comparison.

Sylvia and Elizabeth Flynn also shared a close friend in Jim Connolly, who met Flynn when first invited to America in the spring of 1902. The following year Connolly returned to the US for a seven-year self-imposed exile, and moved to the Bronx, during which time he became very close to Elizabeth Flynn and her father Tom, who also lived in the neighbourhood.[663] The Bronx was a marked change from their suburban middle-class neighbourhood in Newark, but Connolly moved his family there to be back among his Irish-Scottish community of socialists.

Later a founding member of the American Civil Liberties Union (1920), Flynn was a lifelong defender of free speech. She joined the Communist Party USA in 1936, and became its national chair in 1961, by which time she had been convicted of conspiring to overthrow the government and served two years in a federal prison camp, about which she wrote a memoir. She died unexpectedly during a visit to the Soviet Union in 1964, where she was buried in a state funeral with processions in Red Square attended by tens of thousands. When Sylvia spoke with her in Harlem, Flynn was poised to become a leading organizer in the 'Bread and Roses' textile strike of predominantly female immigrant workers in Lawrence, Massachusetts, which ran from January to March 1912. The textile workers walked out en masse, led by Italian women who claimed it was 'better to starve fighting than starve working'.[664] A 'signature chapter' in IWW history, the strike captured national headlines and the sympathies of working-class people across the continent.[665] Founded in Chicago in 1905, the cosmopolitan, multilingual, radical IWW benefited from significant Spanish and Italian leadership from its beginnings. Italians Jo Ettor, Arturo Giovannitti and Carlo Tresca, important figures in the IWW, helped establish the strike and relief committees for the Lawrence action, in which each nationality had a representative and speeches and literature were distributed in multiple languages.[666] Flynn, like Ettor, advocated solidarity, passive resistance, direct action and sabotage as the means to victory, tactics originally imported from Italy.

The Italian influence on the IWW and Sylvia's networking with the Wobblies throws light on a crucially important and overlooked – or perhaps deliberately ignored – development her political consciousness, expressed in the action she took immediately after her return to Britain in April 1912. Sylvia's future thirty-year relationship with an Italian anarcho-syndicalist is the clearest indicator of how the country's politics and culture contributed to her thought.

The IWW was anti-statist, and the impact of her exposure to the Wobblies in America also played a role in her later move to anti-parliamentarianism when she became disillusioned by the British Labour Party's wartime toothlessness.

The trail continues further. Of enormous significance to Sylvia's future was the fact that the IWW organized black and white workers together to overcome the racism pervasive in other American trade unions. They organized, for example, in the 'supposedly impossible American South', in breach of laws and customs that prevented interracial or biracial unionism.[667] It was not by coincidence that Sylvia, on her second trip to America, became more deeply involved in American race politics and broke racist protocols by taking the initiative to speak at Fisk University in Nashville, Tennessee, the prestigious college for black students. National Association for the Advancement of Coloured People (NAACP) founder W. E. B. Du Bois, with whom Sylvia corresponded, had attained his BA at Fisk, before going on to Harvard. The diversity within the American working class that Sylvia experienced as a result of her networking with the Wobblies made a profound impression on her. Observing the complexities of the racial and ethnic divisions in the movement, she was impressed by the degree to which different groups worked together. On one picket line she attended, a young activist spoke in his native Italian, followed immediately by the black strike steward.[668]

Later, Sylvia would come to reappraise her view of the Wobblies as a result of the Bolshevik Revolution, and would agree that the method of the Russian communists who believed in mass education was more effective.

> The British Shop Stewards and the American 'Wobbly's' are obsessed by another idea; they distrust the politician who wears a black coat, however Red may be his Communism. Their distrust of the theorist, the scientist, the administrator is only less than their distrust of the capitalist. They insist on manual control by the worker at the bench; they will tolerate no talk of waiting till he is cultured, and they do not believe anyone is to be trusted even under Communism, who is not strictly controlled by the rank and file.[669]

America was now used to Sylvia, and welcomed her with initial warmth on her return, but the otherwise friendly press swiftly noted and criticized her attitude to equality and US race politics. She was appalled by the treatment of American First Peoples, a subject she raised in her talk to the Fisk students, roundly criticizing the ways in which white people manipulated and exploited those living on the reservations.

The following day Sylvia travelled north to Canada. Having arrived in St John in a snowstorm, she was collected by sleigh and taken to the welcoming home of her hosts Warren Franklin and Ella Hatheway, where real English coal fires and logs burned in every room. She described it as a 'patriarchal family' with three generations all living together under the same roof.[670] Though interested in all the family, Sylvia was most intrigued by Ella Hatheway, who said 'nothing remarkable' yet had an air of distinction about her, 'and one felt at once that she possessed an absolutely fearless and independent judgment'.[671]

A huge lunch was served in the dining room at one o'clock at a table set with silver and china around the centrepiece of 'a gigantic turkey'.[672] Sylvia marvelled at the variety of immense vegetables and the plentifulness of it all, feeling 'spurred to eat twice as much as usual'.[673] It was a stark contrast to the general frugality of her London existence. At lunch they talked politics – imperialism, the probability of war with Germany and Robert Blatchford's recent articles in the *Daily Mail*. Husband and wife argued over the articles, in the process of which Hardie's name came up. Ella instantly came alive with enthusiasm: 'Oh

I like Keir Hardie.'[674] 'He has been a good friend to *our* cause,' Sylvia agreed. 'Yes, I know,' Ella warmly confirmed – but then revealed that she was 'unconverted to the latest militant tactics'.[675]

By the end of Sylvia's stay, she had laid Ella's doubts to rest and converted her to the just cause of militancy. As she was preparing to leave, her new friend came to help her pack her dresses, and told her shyly the story of her chance meeting with Hardie when he had visited St John, an encounter that she felt 'was one of the most important things in her life'.[676]

On the train from St John to Brunswick, Maine, Sylvia reflected on the connection that had bonded them from opposite sides of the Atlantic, and how Ella's life might have been different if it had been less narrow and restricted, less filled with domestic duties: 'if she had been brought into contact with big movements and important crises, she would have been … fearlessly independent and self-reliant in her judgments … and … unswervingly would she have done what she thought right under those circumstances. She would have been what is called great.'[677] So many times in her life Sylvia would make observations like this about the unrealized talents and potential of women she met whose lives were constrained by marriage, maternity and convention.

In Brunswick she stayed at Bowdoin College with a university professor, whose wife introduced her to what she called 'professional circles', keen to impress Sylvia with their abundance of 'culture'.[678] Sylvia argued with a lawyer of the town, who had attended the great WSPU-organized Hyde Park meeting of 21 June 1908 and took it upon himself to explain to her in great detail the central issues of feminism and the women's vote. She found the vaunted Professor of Literature from Bowdoin College 'a most unlearned man', whose manner of thinking illustrated that he would have made 'an excellent plowman'. The president of the university, whom she likened to a walrus, turned out to be a noted anti-suffragist. She had some good meetings with students and the local community, but the people who hosted her – 'oh dear – oh dear! Snobs to say the least of it.'[679]

She returned to New York via Boston, arriving on 20 January for a meeting with William Feakins, now her agent. She stayed with her new friends Alice and Irene Lewisohn in their elegant Fifth Avenue apartment, who had been introduced to them by Lilian Wald. The wealthy philanthropic Lewisohn sisters ran workshops and staged dance, music and theatrical productions with local youngsters in Wald's Henry Street settlement gymnasium.

Daughters of a copper magnate and orphaned in their adolescence, the Lewisohns were to become famous for establishing the experimental Neighborhood Playhouse on the East Side's Grand Street. With their combined social and artistic commitment and their determination to invest their wealth in innovative and radical reform, the sisters were much akin to the Pethick-Lawrences and Lady Constance Lytton. 'I lost my heart to [them], expending their wealth and talents for the creation of a school of dance and drama for the young people of New York's East Side at Henry Street Settlement.'[680]

The following day Alice and Irene took Sylvia to see 'a wonderful child who dances', the child star Virginia Myers. 'The Lewisohns and other people think she is perhaps the greatest dancer alive,' Sylvia wrote to Hardie.[681] Alice and Irene then whisked her to a rehearsal of one of their productions, before she spoke at a suffrage 'At Home' meeting, very much in the spirit of those that she and Christabel had helped their mother organize as children in Russell Square. That evening, she caught the train to St Louis, buoyed up by her enchantment with the 'lovely' Lewisohn sisters. When she returned to New York in April, Alice and Irene took her to a Passover supper, probably with Lillian Wald, who prized the neighbourhood tradition of hospitality. A large proportion of the community around Henry Street were eastern European Jewish immigrants, and the Passover meal – with a multicultural, inclusive local guestlist – was an important festival occasion in the Henry Street dining room, where, as Katherine Connelly recently observed, 'polished menorahs and Russian samovars still proudly sit today'.[682]

After the festive supper, Sylvia watched an enchanting performance of *Sleeping Beauty* in the Henry Street gymnasium, produced by the Lewisohns. Sylvia's dreamlike, lyrical description conjured up the Seven Fairies and Sprites of the Earth and Trees who called 'upon the spirits of woods and seas and air to dance' before singing in chorus refrain, 'Now with elfin pipe and song / Dance yet merrily and long.'[683] Sylvia wrote of the flowery garlands, reedy pipes set to dancing, snowflakes, 'spirits of night and daybreak, sleep and waking, winter and spring'.[684] A few years later, on the other side of the Atlantic, this 'joyous troupe, the piper children and the maiden spirits of the trees', would dance on together in Sylvia's recreation of this performance for a New Year festival at the Women's Arms in east London, with factory worker and activist Rose Pengelly playing the panpipes.

As they danced that evening, Sylvia wrote, 'it seemed to me that we were all whelmed by a flood of love and joy and radiance, and that cleansed of pain and sin, and throwing off social wrongs and false standards of life, we might begin to be brothers and sisters from the hour'. Just a year afterwards, she learned that the little Sleeping Beauty had died from a painful illness that began shortly after the festival, 'the one great joyous event of her short life. For months before she died, she had been unable to go out into the fresh air, for the tenement in which her family lived was up so many flights of steps, and she so weak.'[685]

Sylvia left New York for two days of speaking events in St Louis, Missouri, and a keynote lecture on 'Why More Suffragette Methods Will be Needed to Win the Vote'. From there, she proceeded to Chicago where she was happily reunited with her friends at Hull House and, far less joyously, stayed with her cousin Helen Herendeen and her husband, described in a grumbling letter to Hardie:

> Dear oh Dear how awful is the home of a wife who is absolutely empty headed – poor thing, I probe incessantly to find some interest in anything but food and clothes and a dull blunted passive unintelligence even in them – but find it not – she has no demonstrations of love to spare for her family – nothing nothing. Everything is cheap and hideous in the house and most things in disrepair yet they spend loads of money in stupid comfortless ways and in hotel bills food travel and clothes for all but the little money grub – a kind little man whose mentality has all gone out in making money.[686]

Sylvia took her 'awful' cousin as her guest to a dinner held in her honour at Hull House, hoping it might spark some sisterhood between them as they moved outside Helen's fettered domestic realm. Her good intention fell flat, and she failed to empathize with the fact that her Helen clearly felt out of place and uncomfortable in the alien social environment and was unused to vegetarian food. 'She was a dead weight on my hands all the time and the only comment she made about the place was "they didn't give us a very good dinner there – I couldn't eat that stuff." '[687]

Sylvia continued to complain at length to Hardie about 'my present place of abode with my cousins' for which she blamed Feakins, who 'manoeuvred my staying here against my inclination because he thinks it is the proper thing I suppose', and – more to the point – to save him hotel bills, 'but on Sunday I intend to fly to Milwaukee. I want to see a Socialist city and all that has been done there.'[688]

15

American Letters

Sylvia eagerly anticipated her trip to Milwaukee, fascinated by the fact that the city had elected a Socialist mayor and was attempting to implement municipal socialism. Journalists waited for the arrival of her train at the station, as did Mary Wagner of the American Suffragettes and Martha Heide, assigned to interpret her events with German audiences in the city. After hastily dropping her luggage at the Aberdeen Hotel, she visited the Wisconsin Industrial School for Girls before returning to her hotel to write a letter of introduction to the Mayor of Milwaukee, Emil Seidel. By return, she received a courteous invitation to meet him at City Hall the next day.

In the early twentieth century Britain had a Labour Party that, crucially, entered into an alliance with the trade unions. This alliance did not happen in America, although the Socialist Party made widespread gains in the polls between 1901 and 1912. During 1911, seventy-four US towns elected Socialist mayors or major officers. Supported by the Populist Movement, dynamic coalitions of progressives demanded state regulation of work and living conditions.[689] Women brought their campaigns and influence to bear to reinforce this pressure for moderate change, focusing on both municipal and state policies.

On 5 April 1910, Milwaukee made political history by becoming the first major city in America to elect a Socialist mayor. Emil Seidel, a former pattern-maker who started out as an apprentice woodworker, won a decisive victory in the spring election, beginning a run of Socialist successes at the polls that lasted until Frank Zeidler stepped down in 1960. Seidel went on to become the vice presidential candidate for the

Socialist Party of America in 1912, on a ticket with Eugene Debs, one of the founding members of the Industrial Workers of the World (the Wobblies), destined to be five times Socialist presidential candidate.

Municipal socialism had been germinating in Milwaukee for generations. It was the most German city in America and a significant body of its residents were rebel Forty-Eighters who had found their way to exile in Milwaukee where, passionate about politics and culture, they established a network of schools, music societies, theatre groups and other organizations that made their new home the 'German Athens' of America.

These European intellectual immigrants brought socialist seeds that found fertile soil among the legions of blue-collar Milwaukee immigrants working unregulated hours for a dollar or two a day, without benefits. The alliance between the two groups consolidated after state militia troops unleashed deadly fire against a group of strikers marching for the eight-hour day in 1886. These shootings sparked a populist revolt, delivering a number of factory hands into political office. They were booted out again when Republicans and Democrats joined forces to oust them, but the decade of bootlegging political corruption that held sway between 1898 and 1910 was brought to an end by the leadership of the Socialist tactician Victor Berger who forged a highly effective alliance with organized labour.

Despite brazen red-baiting by the regular parties, a groundswell of popular support finally crested in Seidel's landslide victory and Socialists taking a large majority of seats on both the Common Council and the County Board. Berger went to Washington as the lone Socialist in Congress.[690]

This was the context in which Sylvia arrived for the first time in Milwaukee, immediately disappointing her culture-loving hosts by rejecting their schedule of theatre visits, concerts and official receptions, warning them that 'as little time as possible would I spend at social functions ... I wanted to have time to study as far as possible the institutions and general conditions of Milwaukee.'[691] How very much like Lenin she sounds here. Sylvia's intensity of focus and impatience with flummery is reminiscent of Lenin's similar intolerance of small talk and social time wasting, such as when he stepped off the train at the Finland Station in Petrograd to take control of the revolution. The similarities between their temperament and style are a theme that begins to emerge in this period, and are relevant to the nature of their future relationship.

In preference to entertainment and socializing, Sylvia visited two laundries, which were supposed to be the best from the factory inspector's point of view. She conceded they were fairly well managed but declared that the conditions 'made me sick at heart'. The air was bad and the extent of the mechanization of the work so acutely 'subdivided to the smallest detail' that the women workers seemed merely extensions of the moving parts of the machinery.[692] Sylvia's criticism of the new Taylorism – the supposedly scientific compartmentalization of people's jobs into monotonous and inhuman raw labour – emerges for the first time in her writing about these laundries. This impression was strengthened by the no-talking rule. The wages ranged from four to eight dollars and fifty cents for a forty-five-hour working week, the maximum legal limit for women workers in Wisconsin. Two toilets opened directly on to the factory floor, positioned side by side. Sylvia noticed that the signs on the doors read 'Women' and 'Gentlemen', remarking how the difference in titles reflected their relative positions as employees. The men held all the higher-paid, cleaner-handed jobs.

To Sylvia's dismay, she discovered that City Council meetings were not open to the general public, and that in general the Milwaukee city administration vested too much power in the hands of the mayor and the business interests who supported him. She concluded that the Milwaukee attempt at municipal socialism had so far only managed to produce a middle-class-run technocracy with a top-down approach that excluded working people as participants: 'The Bureau of Economics and Efficiency was too heavily weighted with accountants, businessmen and university professors, who had no practical knowledge of the hardship, toil and struggle of poorer working lives.'[693] It was 'a most powerful force in the Socialist Administration', and yet it 'certainly seemed to consider the methods and machinery before the human beings'.[694] To the alarm of Emil Seidel, with whom she argued ceaselessly, Sylvia recommended that the city adopt a form of soviet-style workers' control of the local government, with, for example, garbage collection and laundry services run by the departmental workers.

For all the strenuous attempts by her Milwaukee hosts to impress her, their efforts were doomed from the start. As soon as Sylvia saw that everything under this socialist experiment was still run by men, she launched into arguments with Emil Seidel and his councillors about women's suffrage, feminism and the point of the struggle for social and economic equalities. 'I was anxious to make him feel that even under socialism it would not be satisfactory to women to leave everything to be managed by men. Also that women need their votes to fight for better conditions just as men do.' Seidel contended that he believed in women's equality, but Sylvia felt he demonstrated little genuine practical enthusiasm. 'We fenced a little on the subject of women's suffrage v socialism. He was anxious to find out where I really stood on the latter question and I [was] not averse to telling him, but not wishing to mix up the two things in order to make a sensational story for the reporter lady.'[695] The arguments became heated – Sylvia literally felt herself flush and heard her voice become fiery.

Class, argued Seidel, preceded questions of gender: 'A woman employer will ground down the women who work for her just as much as a man employer.' 'Yes,' Sylvia replied, 'but look at the position of the woman who … is employed to blow the bellows for the chain maker or the woman who treads the lathe for the turner. What sort of a position is she in?' At this Seidel fell silent and thoughtful, eventually replying in a sad, changed voice, 'She is the slave of a slave.' 'And after that,' Sylvia wrote to Keir, 'we got on better.'[696]

Generally Seidel and his administration were enthusiastic – 'we are just at the beginning!' – but everyone told her that a coalition of disgruntled Democrats, old-guard Republican conservatives and the new Republican insurgents known as the Progressives were forming into an unprecedented bloc to take back power from the socialist experiment at the next election. Sylvia was sympathetic to the obstacles faced by this new administration, but critical of their overly cautious, fearful approach to radical change. For every innovative social reform they made, the right abused them for extravagance. 'I hope they are not going to allow themselves to be crucified in following the behests of economists. I trust that they will not devote much attention to following out the elaborate paper economics of the intellectuals and overlook in the slightest degree the claims of the common people.'[697]

Although Seidel did indeed lose the next election, the Socialists were back two years later, and in the long term Sylvia was proved wrong in her scepticism about the potential impact and longevity of the impact of this Wisconsin Socialist administration. Milwaukee changed perceptibly. The minimum wages for city workers were raised, municipal services expanded and the worst brothels on River Street were closed. A host of other measures improved public works and public schools, and introduced more public parks, larger public libraries and better public health. Other initiatives, including public ownership of utilities and advanced social welfare legislation never came to pass under the Milwaukee Socialists, but they achieved a great shift in the tone and conduct of municipal government towards administrations rooted in transparency, greater efficiency, frugality and prioritizing the needs and rights of working people, reflected in continued success at the polls. Seidel lost his 1912 race for a second term, but voters kept the Socialist Dan Hoan in office from 1916 to 1940 and Frank Zeidler from 1948 to 1960.[698]

On balance, Sylvia's impression of the Milwaukee socialist experiment was favourable. The detail in which she recorded every aspect of the structures of organization in the city and her sympathetic criticisms fed directly into her later blueprints for social soviets and community worker councils, right down to details of garbage collection, water purification and methods of co-operative representation. Sylvia's assessment of Emil Seidel may serve to describe her own approach: 'an idealist, but that rare and priceless treasure, an idealist with a head full of practical details'.[699]

Feakins was responsible for forwarding mail to her, but the difficulties of keeping up with her schedule meant that such letters as were forwarded often arrived after she'd left, exacerbating Hardie's frustrations about keeping track of her. Sylvia had decided that Feakins wasn't maximizing the possibilities for the tour, so she decided to take matters into her own hands and 'manage things a bit myself'. She wrote to Hardie from Chicago, 'I have determined to go South where no one ever goes much, where mother did not go and where, above all things, there is much to do. Awful conditions of labour for women and children especially children and everything generally backward. Moreover it is warm there and the country beautiful I am told.'[700] On the railroad to the South, she penned Hardie a stream-of-consciousness travelogue that stretched to some ninety pages, describing, towards the journey's end, the deep green, the palm trees, the orange groves, the cactus and eucalyptus – with everywhere sunshine.

After pulling into Nashville on the Dixie Flyer, Sylvia's first Tennessee encounter was with the 'negro porter, ever kindly solicitous for the comfort of the passenger, and especially the passenger travelling alone'. The porter helped her ready her bags and then threw open the train door, leaning out with a foot on the step 'even though we had not reached the station'. Through the open door, Sylvia saw a deep pit below, its sides covered with rock, shale and heaps of rubbish. 'Crouching and picking amongst the rubbish were a number of negro women. They were lost to sight in a moment, for our train had entered the station.'[701]

On the afternoon of her arrival, Sylvia was driven out of town to see The Hermitage, the former home of President Andrew Jackson, which was reached through a grand avenue of trees. Sylvia described the colonial pile with its fluted white columns, through which she passed into the 'cold and dreary' interior, the entrance hall covered with a 'hideous hand-painted paper' teeming with six-inch gods and goddesses cavorting through 'meaningless adventures'. 'It seems impossible,' she marvelled, 'that nineteenth century Paris could have produced anything more ugly.'[702] Heavy furniture loaded with tasteless ornaments and stiff, awkward portraits on the walls also failed to impress, and she was much amused that the great four-poster beds were so high that the family were 'obliged to climb up' steps to get into them at night. She felt more at home in the functional, well-worked-in kitchen, with its giant fireplace and spinning wheel, from where she walked outside and down to the family graveyard at the bottom of the garden. 'Just across the field from here, still standing in a row, are the cabins in which the slaves were housed.'[703]

By 1912 Sylvia had lost her patience with the smart society gatherings attached to the lecture tours. In her letters to Hardie over the forthcoming three months she complained about a group of suffragists taking her to 'a stupid play' and told him, through gritted teeth, that on the St Valentine's Day of her arrival in Nashville her hosts 'prevailed' on her 'by the kindest of invitations' to attend the 'Eligibles Ball'.[704] She described the event in horrified detail, from the self-described viewpoint of an 'old fogey', though at twenty-nine she was still an 'Eligible' at the ball. Fancy-dressed Pink Ladies, Quaker Girls, Spring Maids with sun bonnets and very short skirts flirted with eligible young men in uniform black evening dress. Attended by 'negro' servants in livery, other old-fogey chaperones discussed prohibition and ' "Oh! Votes for women." So it went on.'[705] At midnight the dance began,

> and in it joined all the 'eligibles' and many of the chaperones. Mark Twain says that the soul and spirit of a people cannot be understood except by a process of 'absorption', by 'years and years of intercourse with the life concerned.' Therefore I, who am ever an outsider in matters of this kind, whether at home or abroad, could only look on as a foreigner, with curious amaze. I saw young men and women dancing together with slow jerky prancing steps, bodies leaning very much backwards, knees very much bent, arms held out very stiff and wagged jerkily up and down. 'I am sorry' said my hostess, 'that they are dancing the new dances'. I slipped away and left them dancing until the sun shone.[706]

Sylvia's host was apologetic because at the time the new craze for frenetic ragtime-inspired 'animal dances' sweeping the USA was considered scandalous in polite society. The Grizzly Bear, the Camel Walk, the Horse Trot, the Crab Step, the Chicken Flip, the Kangaroo Dip, the Turkey Trot and the Bunny Hug were among the wide repertoire of wildly popular new moves, rooted in African-American slave dancing traditions. The dances varied in style and tempo, but what Sylvia describes fits most closely the Grizzly Bear, in which the knees are bent in a heavy, clumsy manner in imitation of a dancing bear.[707] In some cities the dances were banned and couples fined or arrested for performing them. The press would claim that President Woodrow Wilson announced the cancellation of his inaugural ball in 1913 for fear of ragtime animal dancing.[708]

Sylvia's first speaking event in Tennessee drew 2,000 people to the Ryman Auditorium and was celebrated as a great success by her hosts, the Nashville Equal Suffrage League. She accepted their invitation, in large part because, as she wrote to Hardie, she intended to research working conditions and prisons in the South. Further invitations rolled in, particularly from women's colleges, to the consternation of conservative mothers who furiously protested that these girls should not have been allowed 'to listen to a woman who holds lightly all the virtues our southern girls are taught to cherish'.[709] The suffragist mothers of these daughters welcomed Sylvia to their children's school, but she drew censure from many of them for speaking to black students at Fisk University. The National American Woman Suffrage Association maintained a policy of so-called neutrality towards racism, arguing – like the WSPU in Britain – that the women's suffrage movement was 'separate' from the labour and civil rights movements. When she announced that she was going to speak at the college, 'I was astonished to find every newspaper I opened on my journey thither, protesting against my action.'[710] Some of the press even confidently asserted that Nashville's white feminists would 'prohibit' her from attending the event. *The Crisis*, newspaper of the National Association for the Advancement of Coloured People, covered the controversy, making public the pressure exerted to prevent Sylvia speaking; 'but', it confirmed approvingly, 'Miss Pankhurst kept her engagement'.[711]

She spoke in the chapel of Fisk University, founded, Sylvia noted, a year after the Civil War of emancipation. Her hosts got her there late, and she was rushed immediately to the stage. 'In a moment, I found myself on the platform looking down upon hundreds of dark earnest faces and steady lustrous eyes, that for all their darkness, seemed to glow with inward light.'[712] At times, Sylvia's descriptive language reflects racial stereotypes of the time, veering into the fetish of admiring otherness. Less problematically, her passionate determination to convey the individual beauty and composed intelligence of the students stands in stark contrast to the common language of scientific racism peddling theories of inherent difference and race hierarchy proclaimed by her white hosts.

Throughout, as in her writing about Native American people, Sylvia is categorical in her damnation of the history of slavery and the continuation of systematic, racist exploitation. Talking with the students, she noted the diversity among them, and learned that some 'had come straight from Africa to attend the college'. The choir honoured her with a spiritual rendition of Psalm 55 – 'Oh that I had the wings of the dove!'[713] She describes the melodic arc of the soloist standing up to lead the hymn, and how gradually 'hundreds of other voices joined him, echoing and re-echoing in many-toned chorus'.[714] She bats away the relevance of talking about her own address in response, though speak she did. 'Surely there was never such singing. Who could find words to speak to them of things material after this? I only know that I felt their earnest gaze upon me. They seemed to listen more intently than other audiences.'[715]

She was on the point of catching a train out of Nashville when she received an urgent telephone call from the Socialist Society of Cumberland University, one of oldest and most venerable law schools of the South, begging her to come and speak to them. They put her up in the shabby, down-at-heel West Side Hotel – all the Society could afford – giving her the opportunity to experience 'the most striking contrast to the smart Hermitage Hotel in Nashville, and others of its kind' that she had stayed in, 'where all the furniture looks as though just sent in from the maker's and every visitor has his, or her, own private bathroom, with porcelain bath and gleaming taps'.[716] At the West Side, the smoke-filled saloon bar doubled as the check-in reception, and the shared bathroom was at the opposite end of the building to her threadbare bedroom. She ate her typical Southern lunch – fried mutton, dried beans, corn cake – at the shared dining tables with the delegates of a Methodist Conference, before a troop of law students and two local women activists picked her up and took her in the rain to visit the two factories of Lebanon – named after a grove of cedar trees which provided the wood for the pencil factory. After that, she visited a blanket factory. She interviewed the employees and recorded in detail the production process and working conditions in each. In particular, she analysed the division of labour: 'Negroes and white men were working side by side together,' but their wages were not equal. Below the sawmill, 'girls and women' sorted, paid by the piece. All worked in air clogged with dust amid the 'nerve wracking noise of machinery' – she found it almost impossible to breathe or hear above the din.

> The virtual impossibility of manufacturing under the fierce
> competitive system in which we live, except at a financial loss, or
> at an infinitely more serious loss of health and happiness to the
> workers, is everywhere apparent. How long will it be, one wonders,
> before some community of free men and women sets itself steadily
> to build up a true Republican brother and sisterhood in which this
> odious system shall find no place?[717]

Back in Nashville, Sylvia visited the penitentiaries, making a close study of the inmates and their conditions which she recorded in her notebooks. She wrote long letters to Hardie recounting her observations and experience in minute detail. This process she repeated in all the states she toured, where the conditions in some of these penal institutions appalled her, most of all the Tennessee prison known as 'the tank'. 'Having served two terms in jail,' she told a reporter, 'I have taken every convenient chance to visit the jails in different cities.'[718] In the opening speech of her tour, at the Carnegie Lyceum, she had told the audience about the reform that suffragette prisoners in Britain had brought about. Drawing material from her letters to Hardie, notebooks and lengthy journalistic articles, her American manuscript, published for the first time over a century later in 2019, includes a defining emphasis on the US penal system, and what she learned from it.

Throughout February, blizzards, delays and mistakes in her bookings constantly derailed her schedule. Feakins was not on the ball, it was a tough winter and she had probably returned too soon after the 1911 tour. More decisive factors were her turning away from the socialite aspects of the programme that had dominated the previous year, and on 1 March the launch of the mass window-smashing campaign in London's West End, organized by the WSPU. Sylvia was in Ann Arbor, Michigan, when she was taken by surprise by the news. She discovered that the renewed militancy instantly affected attitudes towards her in America. 'At the first shock of it many American supporters were estranged. People about me drew away, becoming reserved and distant, or uttering a grieved rebuke.'[719] Students at Ann Arbor and Socialists were supportive, helping her to get information from the press and joining her in sending messages of support to Clement's Inn. The audiences of 'the great meetings' Sylvia addressed as she travelled dispatched many telegrams of sympathy and solidarity, but 'individuals were cautious of committing themselves'.[720] As she continued on her expedition, she learned how much the new wave of WSPU direct action launched in November 1911 exercised a deterrent effect on support in constitutional suffragist circles with long historical mutual links with Britain.

More immediately, it affected her programme. The Mount Morris Church in Harlem cancelled their booking for Sylvia to lecture there on 1 April: 'We are in favour of women's suffrage as such and we want to hear Miss Pankhurst, but after the English outbreak she endorsed the methods of the militant suffragettes. Just at present we have no desire to endorse militant methods.'[721] The Chicago WTUL and the editorial

office of *Life and Labour*, the monthly bulletin of the National WTUL
edited by Alice Henry and Stella Miles Franklin, tried to organize a 'fair
play' meeting for Sylvia, but as Miles Franklin recalled, 'as with Sodom
and Gomorrah, there were not enough of us to save the situation'.[722]

Sylvia maintained her defence of militance. Her choice of 'Life in
a London Prison' as one of her three lecture subjects for the 1912 tour
provided an effective catch-all hook to contextualize British militancy,
explaining to American audiences the repressive measures of the Liberal
government and its refusal to grant women's citizenship. The weather
abated and crowds picked up. Six hundred people turned out at the
Garrick Theatre in Detroit – Sylvia always did well in the industrial
cities.

She revisited Canada before returning to New York and the warm
hospitality of the welcoming Lewisohn sisters. In the final weeks of her
trip, traversing New York State, Sylvia spoke three times alongside the
Socialist trade union organizer and garment worker Rose Schneiderman,
an avid reader known for borrowing books from other workers before
she and her lifelong partner Maud Swartz, an Irish-born printer, could
afford their own. She read the serialization of Émile Zola's *J'Accuse* in
the Yiddish evening paper *Abend Blatt*, admitting later, 'I devoured
everything I could get my hands on.'[723]

Sylvia ended her tour where she had begun in 1911, at the Carnegie
Lyceum, giving a lecture to which all her new New York friends received
an invitation. Her subject, 'Militant Methods – Why?', was a clear
statement of intent to her audience: it was also a question she would
continue to ponder deeply on her voyage home, as the mighty clash
with her sister and mother would demonstrate. A year on, the venue
was the same, but Sylvia was not. Many transformations had taken
place for her during the six months she spent in America in 1911 and
1912. She had learned to shake hands 'in the American way',[724] with a
much firmer grip than was generally preferred in Britain. Handshaking,
in greeting and congratulation, she discovered, was ubiquitous among
American feminists and women professionals of all social and economic
classes, whereas in Britain it was less common practice among middle-
and upper-class women. Sylvia enjoyed the direct approach, plain-
speaking openness and energetic curiosity she discovered among the
transatlantic sisterhood. A transformation had also taken place in how
she felt about Hardie. She had met Zelie Emerson, who had committed

to following her across the Atlantic to help organize in Britain. Crucially, she understood better the conjunctures between international socialism and the global struggle for women's emancipation.

On 3 April Sylvia held a midnight reception in the stateroom of the SS *Mauretania* for friends and colleagues who had gathered in force to see her off. She set sail at one o'clock in the morning. 'Life in the States,' she mused, 'seemed a whirl, with harsh, rude extremes, rough and unfinished, yet with scope and opportunity for young people and with more receptivity to new ideas than is found in the old countries: I thought that some day I might become an American citizen.'[725] She never returned.

Drafting the Preface for her intended book about her six months touring North America, Sylvia begins, 'I have called this book American Letters because' – then she breaks off the sentence and draws a vertical line down the remainder of the page. Her final version of the Preface completes the explanation: 'The following pages were in the first place written in the form of letters to a friend in England.'[726]

The letters exchanged between Sylvia and Hardie during her travels in America prove their intimate relationship. They are filled with endearments, sexually explicit longing, separation anxieties and profound reflection on the nature and quality of their bond. Hardie, who wrote extensive reportage in the form of correspondence about his own world travels for publication in the socialist press, supported Sylvia's plan to adapt her letters for publication. In May 1915, knowing that he was nearing the end of his life, he wrote to her to tell her what items of his he would like her to have. Most importantly,

> I have a great many letters of yours, especially those from America,
> & a good many others. They are well worth preserving, and
> I should like to return those to you. I could let you have the whole
> of those now at Nevill's Court; & you could use your discretion as
> to which are most worthy of being kept & published and which
> should be destroyed.[727]

When Sylvia reproduced this letter in her second memoir *The Home Front*, published in 1932, she edited out the phrase 'and which should be destroyed'.[728] The vertical line that Sylvia drew down the page of her draft Preface was a mark of discretion. To write a book based on her letters, she needed to excise the secret within her private life laid bare throughout their pages – literally cut the heart out of the correspondence.

The episodic, thematic and lyrical manuscript that she produced was never published in her lifetime,[729] and 'American Letters' was her only working title. Katherine Connelly, the saviour of this important work that adds so much to what we know about her in this period, points out that 'there were in fact two friends in England to whom letters from Sylvia formed the basis for her American book'.[730] Sylvia corresponded also with Emmeline Pethick-Lawrence, her good friend and co-editor with her husband Fred of the WSPU newspaper of *Votes for Women*, where in April 1911 Sylvia's article 'Some American Impressions' appeared.[731] Significantly, Sylvia chose to write to the two people in her life who most closely shared her developing disaffection from her mother and sister's policy and manner of running the WSPU.[732]

Transatlantic ideological differences were formative in Sylvia's American education. These travels focused and developed her understanding of how to frame politically the impact of differences in human experience. Jane Addams, whom Sylvia met at Hull House in Chicago, knew her Marx, but, as Sheila Rowbotham points out, Sylvia's sensitivity to how subjective factors determined relationships between people of different classes and races was beyond Karl Marx and Frederick Engel's theorizing: 'In Marxist groupings, primacy was always given to the proletariat as the catalytic anti-capitalist force – a view which contrasted sharply with the emphasis on women's significance in American reform circles.'[733] Sensitivity to the subjective intersections between class, race and gender differences was not, however, beyond the understanding of Marx's daughters. First-wave British Marxist-feminists Eleanor Marx, Annie Besant and Dora Montefiore struggled to find a framework within which effectively to express dissatisfaction and antagonism about the asymmetry of male and female experience, especially on matters traditionally regarded as the sphere of the domestic – sex, motherhood and child-rearing.[734] But they had a good go, and were early supporters of the need for the unionization of women workers and the vote.

Sylvia had read the same books as the American feminist activists and social theorists she met – Olive Schreiner on women and labour, Beatrice Webb on the co-operative movement, the German socialist August Bebel on the vital importance of women's conscious agency – and, so equipped, her reading converged with new forms of thinking. In 1891 Blatch published her essay 'Voluntary Motherhood', in which she argued that women should have control over conception and child rearing. Georgia Kotsch, writing in 1911 in the *International Socialist Review* – which Sylvia read – took up the theme, contending that 'the mother function' and 'the mother instinct' were the 'last citadel' of masculine psychology's strategy for managing women.[735]

One of the pleasures of following Sylvia's American letters is the sense of the cinematic evoked in these chapters of her life. This filmic effect is due largely to her visually expressionistic correspondence with Hardie that forms a stream-of-consciousness travelogue. Condensations of emotion, vivid scenes, character study and significant observation are the structuring elements of this on-the-road real-time commentary, rather than itinerary and episodic chronology. Interwoven with long drafts for political and journalistic articles, sketches of dreams and landscapes viewed from train windows, Sylvia's American journals appear at first disordered because their narrative time is not sequential; it is the atemporal life of the mind. Symbolic, condensed, these 'impressionist paintings in words and emotions', as her biographer Shirley Harrison aptly describes them,[736] fuse Sylvia's artistic imagination with the visual language of film rapidly emerging as the dominant popular form of the early twentieth century, dramatizing the psychological interiority of her journey. Set in the contrasting landscapes of great train journeys across deserts, past tumbleweed, verdant orange groves and sprawling industrial jungles, Sylvia's sense of loneliness and her condensation of dream life and real life shift to a proto-modernist stream of consciousness.

She wrote to Hardie more than any other. Her travelogues are essentially made up of a succession of often very long letters to him. The descriptive letters – whether her word-picture landscapes from the trains or her accounts of political meetings – are intermingled with some of the most intense and explicit love letters of their sexual liaison. Yet it is clear on Sylvia's return in 1912 that something has shifted, on her part. She loves him still, and seemingly with more intensity, but there is a new intelligence to the manner in which she approaches the relationship – a sense of self-protection, and a greater awareness of the unalterable constraints beyond which their possible future together cannot realistically be imagined.

Emmeline Pankhurst

Richard Pankhurst

[Left to right] Adela, Sylvia and Christabel
Pankhurst

Harry Pankhurst

Self-portrait of Sylvia,
in pastel, c. 1907-1910.

Untitled. A small boy on an Italian
Street; painted by Sylvia in Venice,
c. 1902.

Dancing Feet,
watercolour
by Sylvia.

Sylvia in her studio, while at art school.

Keir Hardie sitting in front of his fireplace at Nevill's Court.

Poster of Keir Hardie on the cover of *Labour Leader* newspaper, which he edited between 1888–1905.

Sylvia's Labour Party membership card.

Keir Hardie speaking on women's suffrage in Trafalgar Square in 1908. Emmeline Pankhurst stands in the background, facing the crowd.

The Portcullis and Arrow brooch, given to suffragettes who served prison sentences. Designed by Sylvia, it depicts the prison gates of Holloway Prison and Prison Arrow that marked all the prison uniforms, c. 1909.

Portrait of Sylvia wearing her Portcullis Brooch and Hunger Strike Medal, c. 1910.

Prison sketch by Sylvia of an inmate of Holloway prison. Reproduced in *Votes For Women*, January 7, 1909.

Suffragette rally in Hyde Park, 23 July 1910. [Left to right] Emmeline Pethick-Lawrence, Christabel Pankhurst, Sylvia Pankhurst and Emily Wilding Davison.

Sylvia being taken into custody on 1 January, 1912, after a women's suffrage rally in Trafalgar Square.

Sylvia recovering from a hunger strike at the Paynes' home after her release from Holloway Prison, July 1913.

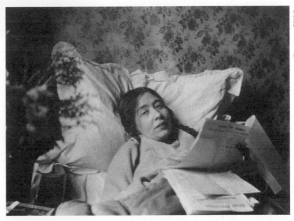

Sylvia being carried by the crowd in a bath chair, weakened by hunger, thirst and sleep strikes during her stay in Holloway Prison, June 1914.

Self-portrait of Sylvia in her Holloway Prison uniform, pastel and charcoal, c. 1907.

Poster promoting Sylvia's 1909 exhibition at the Prince's Ice Skating Rink.

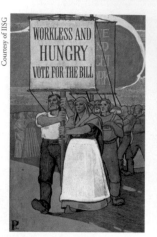

Picture postcard designed by Sylvia for Keir Hardie's *Unemployed Workmen's Bill* of 1905. Sylvia's monogram signature appears in the bottom left-hand corner.

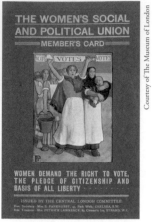

The WSPU Membership Card, with Sylvia's design on the front.

One of Sylvia's mural installations that decorated the walls of the Prince's Ice Skating Rink, during her exhibition in 1909.

[Left to right] Emmeline,
Christabel and Sylvia
at Waterloo Station,
4 October 1911.

Changing the Bobbin,
painted by Sylvia during
her tour of the industrial
workplaces of the north
of England in 1907.

Sylvia during her first USA
and Canada Lecture Tour,
Toronto, 1911.

[Left to right] Norah Smyth, Sylvia Pankhurst and Zelie Emerson, outside the East London Federation of Suffragettes, 1912.

Sylvia on a scaffold painting 'Votes For Women' on the shop front of the East London Federation of Suffragettes at 198 Bow Road.

Close up of the above.

Hardie was anxious about not hearing from her with more frequency, and frustrated by not being able to keep up with her schedule. On 11 March 1911, two months into her first trip, he wrote, 'In one letter you say you hope to be back in New York first week in March and that seems clearly impossible. I am not grumbling, sweet, but only telling you of the difficulties of keeping up with your movements.'[737] When embarked on his own globetrotting, Hardie had often gone silent for weeks at a time, sending brief postcards that punctuated his immersive schedule, telling her not to expect letters and that she mustn't worry. Hitherto, however, he had been accustomed to the reassurance of being always able to locate her. Now for the first time in their relationship he was not always sure where she was. He kept the tone of his anxiety initially light, but it became more marked, particularly when the subject of their surviving correspondence turns to the subject of sex, as it so often does. Separated by the Atlantic, inspired by the new telegraphic technologies, Sylvia contemplated the possibilities of forms of spiritual, transcendent contact – congress on a higher plane. Hardie replied very hastily by return of post to insist on the necessity of material, physical contact to nurture and maintain their bond.

The pain of being separated from him in America reinforced the perennial sense of loss she experienced even when they were together in Britain. The presence of his absence that she experienced, which tormented her in her dreams, nightmares and daytime reveries, was qualitatively little different for her from living with only part of him in London – always accepting that he had another, autonomous life, to which he would imminently once again disappear. Perhaps also the rekindling of the Whitmanesque themes of self-discovery and the greater autonomy of the American women she met enabled Sylvia to reflect on and place greater value on her relative youth. It was in the nature of America to prompt contemplation of the future. Hardie was never going to separate from Lillie and the family, and no one could know what time they had left.

In their correspondence, Hardie and Sylvia often reflected on their anxieties about each other. When Hardie told her that he had had a dream in which he was worrying about her,[738] Sylvia replied on 22 January 1911:

My dearest Love, You mustn't dream those dreams about me. My darling, when I read about it I felt ashamed that I so often worry

you by telling you of things that worry me and of things that I think
may go wrong and of the periods of depression that come to me, and
I half felt as though you were my own dear baby, as though I could
take you up in my arms and send you to sleep, a real peaceful,
dreamless sleep. I longed so much to have my arms around you.
I wanted to wake you with kisses and tell you I was there.[739]

She goes on to apologize once again for her 'silliness' in going to the
ship's doctor's cabin. She describes the depression she experienced at
being separated from him – doubtless exacerbated by a good dose of
transatlantic seasickness – 'That day I stayed in bed all day and felt ill
and got the blues very badly and wasn't good but cried for you many
times in the day and night too.'

Another night, she burned her arm on a hot-water bottle put in her
cabin bed – 'I had forgotten my indiarubber one and they put a nasty
tin one in the bed, which seemed nearly red hot.'[740]

To elicit his sympathy, she describes the scar from the burn. What's
striking about the hot-water-bottle incident emerged later. Sylvia
complained to him more about the discomfort of this minor burn than
ever she would about her subsequent torture in prison, the forcible
feeding or her own consequent infirmities. It's indicative of how much
she lives in her mind – her capacity for visionary transcendence over the
prosaic embodiment of physical pain.

Sylvia and Keir commonly describe their dream life to each other in
this correspondence, unravelling the surreal narratives as best they can.
In the same 22 January 1911 letter:

During the night I dreamt vividly that I was climbing in the dark
up a stone dilapidated staircase without a handrail. It was in a
narrow well and went up to a great height. As I was nearing the top,
a man in dirty white overalls and a red and white striped knitted
cap caught my ankle from behind with a wire which seemed to
sting ... I was a man too I think, I am not sure. I got to the top, a
sort of stone ledge, he was below me coming up the steps. He got
me by the wrists. He had to lean across like this [here she inserts a
sketch] ... Oh I haven't the patience to draw it properly but it was a
struggle.[741]

No psychoanalytic services are required here to unpack the significance of Sylvia's dream in relation to the attempted sexual assault, here conflated into a dream image, part butcher, part leery sailor.

From Boston in February 1911 she wrote to Hardie again.

> Oh Dearie, I do wish I were with you. How is my Darling? Oh Dear, I don't want anyone but you but I want you so ... I think fate ought to have given me a bigger share of what I do want ... I am afraid I shan't get a letter from you before I go West but what use is a letter anyway ... if I can't have my darling always he is dearer and better than anyone in the world ... only I want you now and I can't bridge over the distance. Why can't we Dear?... Just think if we could only have half an hour, even ten minutes to talk to each other every day ...[742]

How much Sylvia would have appreciated the enhanced opportunities for communication provided by new technologies, whose potential impact she fully appreciated:

> ... I'm not sure when one looks into it that all this isn't going to work a more tremendous social change than at first one supposes. Don't you sometimes feel as though a door was going to open in your mind and teach you something quite outside your knowledge and imagination? Oh I am so sure just outside the circle of the things we know, there it is waiting for us to find.
>
> If such a clumsy thing as wireless telegraphy can exist, surely there isn't anything unreasonable in being able to communicate our human thoughts ... Something has come into my head now. It is that when people have discovered the full power of thought transference, the joy and satisfaction of being able to intermingle our ideas with all their finest shades instead of having to rely on clumsy words which were invented for buying and selling and superficial intercourse will be greater than anything we can understand ... we shall be able to play with our minds producing sparkling shafts of new thought ... of course there will no longer be misunderstandings and mistakes. They spring from poor, foolish, inadequate words ... and much as I love my Darling's arms around

me, sweet as kisses are, I rather think it will tend to make us less
dependent on those things. If you carry that idea through it leads
you a long way ...[743]

Her speculative musing on what the emergence of telegraphy might
suggest for new forms of human 'thought transference' makes for
interesting reading in the age of digital communication. She knew
Hardie might not welcome these mystical ideas, but, in reflective mood,
continued:

> Now you will say perhaps all this is nonsense. Socialism is the cure
> for all ills. Ah well may be but Socialism couldn't bridge over for
> me that ocean wide. Moreover, I don't think I go the right way to
> work. When we are parted I pine and long and eat my heart out ...
> but when I am with you I chatter away and use silly words feebly
> to express my mind and thoughts and I prattle about nothing
> whatsoever ... When I come home I shall sit and look deep down
> into your eyes and try to know what you are thinking and to make
> you know what I would say ... then we must have just one time
> each day to send a message, you see one begins like that ... and the
> power gradually grows and some day the door suddenly opens and
> it is clearer than day. Well, writing has made me feel better. Love
> and kisses. Goodnight my love. S.[744]

As always, Sylvia is interested in making the future a place we want to
visit. This is a suggestive reflection of her belief that materialism alone
is not enough, combined with her profound grasp of how technologies
change bodies and human capacities.

Once again Hardie responded swiftly with a restatement of the
importance of keeping things very much grounded in the materially
embodied:

> Don't you think the satisfaction which comes from the pressure
> of my arms around you must be the transference of something
> from the one to the other? And so too with kissing. And if this be
> so surely the transference of something from the one to the other
> could be effected without actual physical contact. To that extent
> I agree with you but without the touch of the actual pressure there

could not be the same satisfaction and the wordless talk would only make distance more terrible. That at least is how I feel about it. But tonight I am sleepy. We sat [in the Commons] from three yesterday afternoon till ten this morning and had to be back at the house by noon. Beyond feeling sleepy I am no whit the worse. I am in good fettle ... I understand just how you feel dearie and the time will come. I like to think of you going over the same ground, speaking in the same halls and meeting the same people as I have. I can think of myself as a pioneer smoothing the pathway for the coming of my little sweetheart ... May it be ever so ... K[745]

And there's the little nudge of anxiety: the need to remind her that he is the mentor, she the protégée. Without the option of ensnaring each other with marriage and reproduction, they are continually set on a course of readjusting a relationship based purely on love and work – and, within that, the exploration of what this kind of loving comprises. Unlike her role model Eleanor Marx, Sylvia was not fatally hobbled by the desire for, or false promises of, future marriage and children, nor by the disappointing realities of their actual arrival. Other deluded young women has tried to and press these aspirations more forcibly on Hardie – with no success. Sylvia clearly yearned for an authentic relationship with him, but this never took the conventional form.

Hardie's anxiety about keeping track of Sylvia was exacerbated by the fact that the mail system couldn't easily keep pace with her schedule. Forwarded mail so often arrived after she'd left that Feakins quite reasonably deemed it more sensible to hold on to her correspondence until she could collect it in New York. The lovers of course did not see it this way.

Travelling west, the barrenness of the landscape and dereliction of the economic inequality had increasingly depressed her. 'My Darling', she wrote in January 1912 in maudlin mood to Hardie,

I am longing to be in your arms away from it all ... Oh these long journeys for a single meeting!

How desolate the country is that we are passing through ... great open wastes where the snow has fallen ... there are none of those dainty silver birches that abound in Massachusetts ... the trees here have stems and boughs all blackened and seem mostly to have writhing and distorted shapes. We pass by frozen swamps and rivers, the very shrubs that stick up from them are black ... Sometimes there is an isolated factory with great chimney pouring forth black smoke, as we go further west, the ice is often melted and there are great pools in the badly paved streets ... Even in the towns one rarely sees a human creature for hours ... only a negro standing by the line, a man waiting with his lean horse and rickety old carriage till we pass by, a woman and child in grey faded garments dejectedly crossing a muddy road.[746]

In this mood, she found no consolation in hope:

Well might one think that this country, instead of being one where huge fortunes are being made, were a land of bankruptcy and decay, but the men who grow rich here are for the most part too much in a hurry about it either to live decently or to let others do it. New machinery is put in, the old is thrown out and left to rot by the roadside ... The very houses built of wood are run up anyhow, there is no time even to level the ground on which to build them ... Oh what a tragedy mankind has made of this poor land ... I wish I'd never seen the ugly place ...[747]

The intensity of her longing and loneliness did not abate, despite Hardie's evident anxiety that she was moving too fast, beyond his reach in March 1911.

Love and kisses my sweetheart. Don't notice my grumbles. It will all come right and I will try hard to save money in expenses ... I haven't had a letter yet, Dearie but perhaps tomorrow. Love I'm longing for a sight of you but it won't be so very long will it? Dearie take care of yourself and now I must stop. This place makes thinking too hard to bear and I'm longing too much to be sitting with you in the firelight. I trust all is well with you my Angel Dear. If only wishing could bring me to you. Heaven bless you my angel. S[748]

Her mood lightened and expanded as the sun came out and the environment softened, 'How wonderful it is! ... It is beautiful, glorious in its immensity and yet awful in its lonely space.' She longed even more for Hardie – 'if you were there … I should hear the buzz of the myriad insect life that no doubt is there, a bird would start up at our feet – we should find lizards and strange cactus plants. But now I can see bones whitening on the sand. We pass the dead body of a horse lying beside a dried up stream. NO dear it is too sad Heaven take care of my dearest till I come home.'[749]

Sylvia's American experiences returned her to her underlying spirit of revolt against the class-bound constraints obstructing the progress of the British women's movement. The trips also bolstered her finances. She succeeded in being frugal with her expenses and saving the money she earned in lecture fees. Her six months in the United States thus freed her economically for a period and gave her renewed confidence in ploughing her own furrow in 1912:

> I determined that on my return home I would give all my time as
> a voluntary worker in the active movement, doing whatever I saw
> required to be done which would not be attempted without my
> intervention. What I had earned in America would maintain me for
> some time. I would add to it by writing occasional articles.[750]

On her return, Sylvia began immediately the work that led to the establishment of her East London Federation of Suffragettes (ELFS). Simultaneously, she would be writing her book about America intended for swift publication, while it was still topical. Every moment over the next few years that she wasn't sitting down to reflect on the theory, she was striving to answer in practice the question the book posed: how to build a mass movement of working women shoulder to shoulder with the socialist labour movement. The contemplation of class and race in the women's movement that she explores in the American manuscripts mirrors the political class struggle she was grappling with in her own 'family party', about to enter its final decisive battle.

16

Sex War

In 1912 the constitutionalists of the NUWSS, still led by Millicent Garrett Fawcett, along with some other non-militant societies forged a successful working alliance with the Labour Party that prevailed until the successful inclusion of women in the 1918 Franchise Act.[751] Sylvia's continuing support for working with the Labour Party meant that her campaign tent appeared to be pitched alongside the non-militant, constitutionalist camp. This, combined with the fact that she shared pillow talk with the socialist leader of the Labour Party, made her troublesome and suspect in the eyes of her elder sister and mother.

Such was the topography of her personal and political landscape when Sylvia returned from America at the beginning of April 1912. Pausing in London only long enough to wash and change into the disguise of a nurse's uniform borrowed from Kate Pine at Pembridge Gardens, Sylvia crossed the Channel, took a train to Paris and changed her clothes again at the railway station. To ensure that she was not followed to Christabel's flat in the Hôtel Cité Bergère, she took three different taxis, walking between them.

Where others reported the atmosphere of pressure and anxiety Christabel experienced in Paris, Sylvia represented her sister's exile as if it were an extended holiday. She found her 'entirely serene', enjoying the 'exciting crises' of the WSPU from the distance enabled by her new life where she indulged her love of the shops and the Bois de Boulogne. After the strenuous office routine of Clement's Inn, 'Paris meant relaxation.'[752] With lofty disapproval, Sylvia observed how her elder sister dashed off her articles at great speed so that she was ready for sightseeing, 'for which I had no heart, keyed as I was for the struggle, and awed by the suffering for so many in imprisonment and loss of health, friends, employment, which I knew the heightened militancy would produce'.[753]

She barely concealed her anger at her elder sister's apparent insouciance. As she poured the coffee, Christabel asked her what art she would like to see during her visit, a kindly suggestion respecting her sister's passion and a deft deflection from political discussion. Irritated by Christabel's light-hearted approach, Sylvia reminded her that the four most prominent leaders of the movement, including their mother, were in detention and she in exile. Mother, moreover, was facing a conspiracy trial. The purpose of her visit was to find out what she should take responsibility for in light of these practical constraints on their joint leadership of the WSPU. Everyone was needed, and what did Christabel think she might best do to help? '"Behave as though you were not in the country!"' Christabel replied cheerfully. '"When those who are doing the work are arrested, you may be needed, and be called upon."'[754]

To Sylvia this answer was 'ludicrous'. Did her sister expect her to hide as if she were afraid? 'Well, just speak at a few meetings,' Christabel conceded. Sylvia was not fooled by her sister's cool amiability. She was clearly so absolutely convinced that her own policy was the only correct one, 'so intensely jealous for it', that she thrust aside the slightest hint of deviation from her tactics. Christabel miscalculated by not tasking Sylvia and keeping her busy. For the sake of unity in the movement, Sylvia later wrote, she was prepared to continue to subordinate her views in many matters to Christabel, 'but her refusal to ask any service of me would leave me the more free to do what I thought necessary in my own way'.[755] A crucial error on Christabel's part.

Refusing to allow Sylvia to express her own views on WSPU policy, Christabel diverted the argument with the suggestion that they set off to the Panthéon to look at the paintings by the great symbolist and muralist Puvis de Chavannes. Sylvia, still exasperated but defeated, conceded that she would like to see the collection. From there Christabel took her to her favourite boutique where she bought a dress and insisted that her reluctant sister did the same. Sylvia was never an enthusiastic shopper. It was all too much for her: she left by the night boat, 'unable to endure another day'.[756]

This was the first episode in the breakdown of the relationship between the two feminist sisters, signposted by a series of meetings in Paris, each progressively worse than the last, until the final breach. Sylvia judged Christabel harshly, as only a sister can. Christabel was under no illusions about the criticisms levelled at her continuing exile. Back in October 1905, she and Annie Kenney had been the first suffragettes to be jailed:

> Any laurels that might belong to the pioneer prisoner would
> certainly wither from my brow. But I could not depend on any of
> the others to stay abroad through thick and thin. Least of all could
> I depend on Mother to do it! I knew her ardent spirit too well ...
> Whatever my limitations, I knew that in two respects I was well
> equipped – in the capacity to control affairs from a distance, and in
> the capacity to read the mind of particular cabinet ministers and of
> the government in general.[757]

The tension brewing between Christabel and Sylvia represented in microcosm what was happening in the WSPU and the organization's impending factional split over the conduct of the campaign. While Christabel was careful to emphasize the primacy of women's organizations transcending all man-made political parties and ideologies, Annie Kenney was more matter of fact about representing the realities. 'An autocracy suits my conservative, liberty-loving nature ... The true and inner secret of the Militant Movement was that we were an autocracy. No committee has, or ever will, run a revolution.'[758]

In July 'Amy Richards' (Christabel's alias) again travelled to Boulogne for a meeting with the Pethick-Lawrences. Emmeline and Fred had been jailed, forcibly fed (and, in Fred's case, expelled from the Reform Club) and were about to be bankrupted by the government. They went to France to plead with Christabel for a slackening of the militant campaign. Christabel rejected their request.

To Sylvia the evolution of the WSPU into a dictatorship unilaterally determining the scale of militant policy without consultation with the membership was unacceptable. It was another example of the organization's move away from the needs and interests of working women. Emmeline and Fred shared Sylvia's ambivalence about the wisdom of policies of property destruction and more violent direct action. Up until now, they had been less concerned about their own participation in undemocratic leadership practices. The consequences of continuing to support the 1907 shift of WSPU organization to autocracy now caught up with them.

Following her argument with Christabel in April, Sylvia returned to an England in uproar to which she further contributed by intervening on the question of torture of suffragette hunger strikers. She wrote a covering letter and circulated a report to MPs and the press containing the statements of prisoners who had been forcibly fed.[759] In the ensuing furore, she challenged the Home Secretary Reginald McKenna to prosecute her for criminal libel. In this she was supported and encouraged by many of her political opponents who wanted to see her put on trial, but Hardie defended her, anxious as he always was to keep her out of prison.

In May her mother's conspiracy trial alongside the other leaders who had been charged began at the Old Bailey. Sylvia sat through the proceedings, 'weighed down by a deep sadness that all this struggle should still be necessary for the winning of so simple and obvious a reform'.[760] Throughout the months of the trial the forcible feeding continued. Meetings, memorials, petitions, protests on behalf of the hunger strikers consumed her energy, but she could do nothing to allay her anxiety about her mother. She had spent the past couple of months speaking at a relentless succession of public mass meetings and rallies around London and its environs.

The WSPU planned a spectacular Bastille Day rally in Hyde Park. Sylvia enjoyed the break from constant public speaking to supervise the creation of hundreds of scarlet caps, banners and flags in her Kensington studio. When her busy volunteers ran out of white fringe, she found a supply at Barker's on Kensington High Street, left over from Queen Victoria's funeral – a nice irony. The day before the demonstration the studio garden became crammed full with red caps and banners. 'Two lovely girls sat out there through the blue twilight and black night, with the lamplight on their faces, till the fresh, clear, dawn, with the rosy glow in the sky, sewing away at the red dragons of Wales, which I, in the studio, was drawing on scarlet flannel, with lighted candles stuck in bottles around me to reinforce the gas.'[761]

Clement's Inn issued a resolution repeating its demand for a limited vote based on marriage, property and education qualifications.

Opposition to this class-based policy grew among those committed to votes for all women, including the working-class female majority who would be excluded. Sylvia drafted her own resolution for Hyde Park, repudiating 'the introduction of any measure to extend the Parliamentary Franchise which does not sweep away both the sex and marriage disqualifications at present erected against women' and demanding that the government 'introduce into the Reform Bill provisions for securing political equality for men and women'.[762] She urged provincial unions to join the call. Mass demonstrations gathered in Aberdeen, Edinburgh, Dundee, Newcastle, Sunderland, North and South Shields, Hull, Jarrow, Manchester, Bradford, Halifax, Sheffield and many other large municipalities. Sylvia rushed between cities and towns, helping to organize the demonstrations and speaking at many of them.

In the midst of this she received a telegram from her elder sister containing a request to burn down Nottingham Castle, as an echo of its destruction in 1831. It didn't seem to matter to Christabel that the Castle had been owned by Nottingham City Council for the last thirty-four years.[763] 'The request came as a shock to me,' Sylvia wrote. 'The idea of doing a stealthy deed of destruction was repugnant to me ... I had the unhappy sense of having been asked to do something morally wrong.'[764] She replied to Christabel with the suggestion that she lead a torchlit procession to the castle, 'to fling my torch at it, and to call the others to do the same, as a symbolic act'.[765] In July Christabel implemented her secret arson campaign. Sylvia opposed this furtive militancy and the price it exacted from socially vulnerable rank-and-file suffragettes.

She and Adela helped with the Manchester by-election. During all this activity, Sylvia was laying plans for launching an East End WSPU campaign.

In Dublin, a group of suffrage prisoners went on hunger strike. As the English were denied the status of political prisoners, the Irish struck with them in solidarity. All were released without forcible feeding except Mary Leigh, one of the first stone-throwing suffragettes, and Gladys Evans, a young shop assistant employed at Selfridges whose father was an owner of *Vanity Fair* magazine. The government let it be known that it intended either to let the women die or to send them to a criminal lunatic asylum. Political and public tension grew. Sylvia accepted an invitation to speak at a demonstration in Phoenix Park in

Dublin demanding the release of Leigh and Evans. She ended the day locked in a cell in Mountjoy Prison. After obliging her to cool her heels, the police escorted her to the docks and deposited her on a boat back to England.

On her return, two events caused seismic shifts in the direction of the movement and of Sylvia's life.

In October 1912 the internal debates within the WSPU came to their definitive conclusion. The Pethick-Lawrences returned to England from Paris and, shortly after another secret summit with Emmeline and Christabel, announced their departure from the WSPU. The final breach happened for two reasons. First, because the Pethick-Lawrences refused to support Christabel's policy of introducing new and more extreme tactics focused on property destruction on an extensive scale. Secondly, because they opposed her resolution to attack the Labour Party on the same terms as the government. At a barnstorming meeting at the Albert Hall, Mrs Pankhurst had announced that, in the future, property would be as gravely endangered by the suffragettes as by the Chartists of old. The unity between the leadership quartet of Pankhursts and Pethick-Lawrences that had been maintained, however uneasily, was then irreparably broken. In order to choke the WSPU of their funding, the government was poised to bankrupt Emmeline and Fred of the Pethick-Lawrence fortune they had selflessly put into service to bankroll the suffragette campaign for so many years. This made the breach at this point all the more brutal on Christabel and Emmeline Pankhurst's part. As their last collective act, they put out a joint statement:

> At the first re-union of the leaders after the enforced holiday Mrs Pankhurst and Miss Christabel Pankhurst outlined a new militant policy, which Mr and Mrs Lawrence found themselves altogether unable to approve. Mrs Pankhurst and Miss Christabel Pankhurst indicated that they were not prepared to modify their intentions, and recommended that Mr and Mrs Pethick Lawrence should resume control of the paper *Votes for Women* and should leave the Women's Social and Political Union.
>
> Rather than make schism in the ranks of the Union, Mr and Mrs Pethick-Lawrence consented to this course.[766]

The Pethick-Lawrences continued to publish *Votes for Women*, with Sylvia's permission to continue using her cover design. The WSPU announced the launch of their new newspaper, *The Suffragette*. In 1914, the Pethick-Lawrences would hand over *Votes to Women* to the United Suffragists.

Sylvia found herself in a position where she no longer shared a large enough raft of principles to stay afloat with either faction. While she agreed with Emmeline and Fred on opposing Christabel's new covert militancy and the onslaught on the Labour Party, she disagreed with all of them over their rejection of the vital importance of democratic procedure: 'The Union was an autocracy: none of the four most concerned thought it necessary to consult its membership.' As Sylvia observed, the root of the problem went back to the abandonment of the democratic constitution in 1907. 'They differed less with each other, I thought, than I had often differed in view with them.'[767]

Sylvia was not opposed to militancy as long as it was public and in plain view. She objected to covert operations, deploring the practices of furtive destruction, evasion of arrest and the surveillance it imposed upon the participants who had little social or economic power to protect themselves. Their punishment would be harsh: 'for these unknown girls there would be no international telegrams; the mead of public sympathy would be attenuated'.[768]

WSPU officials now recruited and advised eager young suffragettes, sent them on night missions lugging heavy cases of petrol, paraffin, touchpapers and housebreaking tools. These perilous expeditions succeeded in setting ablaze empty stately homes, churches and national heritage sites. The operations were well planned so the perpetrators mostly escaped, but sometimes they were caught. The priority was to avoid endangering human life, but, Sylvia wrote sorrowfully, 'works of art, the spiritual offspring of the race, were attacked without ruth'.[769] The extent to which her opposition to the more extreme militancy campaign was motivated by the genuine pain she felt at the damaging and destruction of art cannot be underestimated.

The old, defiant, symbolic militancy performed in the sight of all, punished with a severity out of all proportion to its damage, if damage there were, had roused an enormous volume of support;

had brought the Cause to the fore, would keep it there. What the
movement required, that it might reap what had been sown, was,
in my opinion, a broader and more confident appeal to the people,
and the effort, which assuredly would be crowned with success, to
make the movement a genuine mass movement.[770]

Coupled with the implementation of the new militant campaign, the
public tone of Christabel's misandry, supported by her mother, moved
from a debate within the movement to a statement of policy, if not
principle, in 1912.

Christabel had written a series of articles on sexually transmitted
diseases. She now pulled these together in a pamphlet, *The Great
Scourge*, laying out her sex manifesto. The pamphlet shocked Sylvia
deeply, as did the morally puritanical register of Christabel's new and
unworkable 'Votes for Women and Chastity for Men!' slogan. In her
pamphlet, Christabel claimed that 80 per cent of all Englishmen of
all classes carried venereal disease and were hell-bent on the deliberate
infection of Englishwomen. She took the feminist argument away from
the justice of natural rights and towards moral hysteria. Christabel had
started her political career among the women-textile-workers' labour
representation committees, working almost entirely on the industrial
status of women. Now she was playing to the easily charmed gallery of
the hidebound middle-class moral-purity movement.

Sylvia carefully picked apart the unreliability of her sister's statistics
and perhaps wilful lack of understanding of epidemiology. But her
thorough, evidence-based critique was far too heavy on fact, science and
numbers and could not compete with Christabel's rousing, simplistic
and factually incorrect declaration about the inborn depravity of men.
As Sylvia observed, the advantage of the 'great scourge' propaganda was
that it cut across party lines. Crucially, it appealed to the sensitivities
of 'those frail hot-house blooms', Conservative supporters of women's
suffrage, whom the WSPU were eager to cultivate. 'Christabel,' Sylvia
concluded, 'was now, in effect, preaching the sex war deprecated and
denied by the older Suffragists.'[771]

Fred Pethick-Lawrence, Keir Hardie and George Lansbury all
represented different political perspectives, but they had made common
cause in supporting the militant suffragette movement to prevent the
outbreak of sex war. Christabel's outright declaration of hostilities in

1912 broke the honestly brokered alliance with good men who had put their lives and careers on the line for the women's suffrage cause. It was also the second deciding factor in Sylvia's break for freedom from the move of the WSPU to conservative moral purity and the politics of the right. The assertion that 'women were purer, nobler and more courageous, men … an inferior body, greatly in need of purification; the WSPU being the chosen instrument capable of administering the purge',[772] smacked of the British imperialist language of class and racial purity that revolted Sylvia. Women were not morally superior to men, they were just equally flawed humans. 'Sex,' Sylvia wrote some years later, 'was one of the great mysteries: there is nothing in it and there is all in it,' an epigrammatic reflection of her assessment of its simultaneously complex and utterly simple nature.[773]

Sylvia couldn't stomach her mother and sister's separatism. They constantly criticized her for speaking at socialist meetings and for inviting men to speak on suffragette platforms. Some of their friends and followers nudged them to regard her intimate relationship with Hardie as proof of her collaboration with patriarchy, as if the politics of class had no place in the matter. The extent to which this prurient commentary about Sylvia's sex life was part of the conversation is demonstrated in Ethel Smyth's correspondence. Ethel Smyth understood that Christabel, marooned in Paris, was anxious that Sylvia might get their mother on her side and weaken Emmeline's resolve to reject any form of alliance with the Labour Party or other socialist groups. Ethel wrote a meddlesome letter to 'My darling Em' from the Tewfik Palace Hotel in Helouan, Egypt:

> I think C's one preoccupation – only half a one! – was lest Sylvia
> should get round your maternal heart re their differences of
> opinion!! While I was in Paris … I couldn't help reminding C that
> I had always said that, given S's brain formation or something she
> would never fall into line & would always be in difficulty, given the
> fact that C is not on the spot. Sylvia will never be an Amazon. If it
> isn't J.K.H. [Hardie] it will be someone else.

UnAmazonian Sylvia couldn't be trusted, Smyth proposed, because of her sexual relationship with the male 'enemy'.[774]

The WSPU abandonment of working with the newly emerging Labour Party and the socialist movement to whom they owed both their existence and historical moment finally put Sylvia, Christabel and their mother on opposing sides of the barricades. Sylvia understood the broader question of divide and rule in class terms. 'In the East End, with its miserable housing, its ill-paid casual employment and harsh privations bravely borne by masses of toilers, life wore another aspect. The yoke of poverty oppressing all, was a factor no one-sided propaganda could disregard. The women speakers who rose up from the slums were struggling, day in and day out, with the ills which to others were merely hearsay.'[775] True, the WSPU had their established middle-class speakers who evolved from the earlier suffrage movement, 'but it was from our own East End speakers that our movement took its life'.[776]

To try and raise the consciousness of affluent women to whom manual labour and privation of basic necessities were unknown, Sylvia organized groups of East End speakers in the plush drawing rooms of Kensington and Mayfair. Her next step was to persuade the Kensington, Chelsea and Paddington WSPU branches to assist her in setting up and supporting WSPU shops in Bethnal Green, Limehouse and Poplar respectively. Sylvia's ingenious twinning strategy was a logical and practical extension of the successful drawing-room meetings.

Sylvia did not rouse the East End or take ideas of women's collective action there; it was the other way round. She brought the long-established tradition of women's organization in the East End and participation in the suffrage and suffragette causes up to the West End, in an effort to try and educate middle-class women, to remind them of their relationship to working women and to cement their network and activist relationships. To co-ordinate activities, Sylvia proposed setting up an East End branch in Bow that she would run and persuaded the WSPU HQ to pay the rent. With her new friends Norah Smyth and Zelie Emerson, she went in search of premises. They found, appropriately, an old baker's shop near George Lansbury's house available for immediate lease.

They aimed to make 198 Bow Road a political home of hope for the women and children of the district. Sylvia describes how they scrubbed and polished the interior until it was spotless. She climbed a wooden tower scaffold and painted the legend VOTES FOR WOMEN on the shopfront in beautifully gilded characters. As she worked, an intrigued throng gathered around her. The real, expensive gold leaf she had used gleamed in striking contrast to the soot, dirt and dilapidation around the old bakery, reflecting the brightness and energy of the crowd. The lustrous classic Roman lettering, freshly painted shopfront and sparkling windows sent a clear, inviting message – nothing here is too good for the women workers.

Norah, the photographer among them, captured the moment in two memorable images: in one, Sylvia kneels at the top of the scaffolding applying the lettering above the shopfront, intent on her work, as if in an artist's studio. In the next, a diverse crowd of east Londoners have gathered around to watch her. Aloft, robed in her flowing artist's smock, Sylvia presents the image of a twentieth-century female Michelangela painting the roof of her beautiful and useful Sistine chapel. Below, in the foreground of the photograph, looking out from the crowd directly at the lens, is a young East End girl in a cap. We do not know her name, but she is at the epicentre of this visual story, whose meaning Norah so eloquently captures.

Sylvia began the year on a transatlantic steamship to North America and ended it in her new east London home adjusting to the fumes from the nearby tanneries and soap works. She never again moved back up west. Two dominant factors were decisive in prompting this break with the geography of her middle-class past: her experiences in prison and her six months travelling through America.

'Streets are the dwelling place of the collective,' wrote Walter Benjamin.[777] Sylvia's was a middle-class though financially precarious British upbringing, but in her childhood she had some experience of observing life from a more egalitarian street level, accompanying her father when he made speeches outside factories on those rainy Sundays. Her widowed mother's working life for the council engaged the family with the reality of the lives of others around them. The ethical and philosophical life of the Pankhurst children encouraged by their parents focused always more on populace and polis than on the front parlour. Many aspects of Sylvia's home life and political education predisposed her to this move.

Christabel faced tough political and personal challenges in conducting her leadership from London and Paris. Her emotional resilience and composure were won at high cost, and she was in many ways courageous. Nevertheless, she lived in great personal comfort far above street level, and hovered iconically above the hoi polloi. Her adoring followers loved her for her air of inaccessible celebrity. Her brilliant mind, charismatic oratory and ethereal beauty made her seem an aloof, desirable goddess. Sylvia in her artisanal smock with her undeviating socialist idealism was more of a Cockney's mate. Emblematically, in her final act of extreme suffragette militancy, Sylvia would lie down on the London pavement outside parliament and refuse to get up again unless the government agreed her terms, to the point of death. She got from the West to the East End of London by travelling via America. It was her epic journeys in 1911 and 1912 to the western frontier of capitalism and her socialist resistance to it that charted her new political topography. Those odysseys were the agent of change that shifted her definitively to east London and, irrevocably, further to the political left.

17

Not as Suffragettes, But as Sisters

A photograph from 1912 shows a smiling Sylvia wearing the 'extravagant' full-length and spectacularly badly fitting fur coat she had bought in December 1910 for her first American winter tour. She fondles a cat of evidently finer-quality fur held in the arms of a statuesque, grinning Norah Smyth. 'Smyth', as Sylvia always referred to her, looks distinguished in a well-cut double-breasted naval-style trouser suit, topped with crisp shirt collar and tie. To Sylvia's other side is a compact Zelie Emerson, arms akimbo, hands shoved firmly into the pockets of a wilfully misshapen cardigan, also worn over a shirt collar and tie. Zelie and Sylvia are looking at the cat. Norah looks out at the camera.

Sylvia, Smyth and Zelie moved to east London as a team. The triumvirate worked and sometimes lived together for the next few years, functioning as a tight and highly effective cadre.

Zelie and Norah encouraged and defended Sylvia, who had lost the emotional protection of her mother and Christabel. Norah's practicality, loyalty, wealth and business skills provided the bedrock for Sylvia's East End operations. Zelie's political and organizational abilities, strength and fighting spirit combined with her fierce love and adoration inspired and motivated Sylvia. Zelie and Smyth possessed great physical dexterity and courage, both were passionate about Sylvia and shared her belief in mass social democracy as the necessary condition for guaranteeing women's rights. Both were wealthy heiresses, determined to smash their way out of the class and gender constraints and disadvantages of their privileged backgrounds.

Zelie first engaged with feminist ideas in university women's groups. After meeting Sylvia in 1911, she increased her direct active campaigning for women's suffrage, speaking at suffrage meetings and getting involved in local Chicago protests and press stunts. Shortly before she sailed to Britain, Zelie addressed a meeting in Michigan state, speaking 'of conditions in England and why women were moved to act as they did in the cause of the vote'.[778]

'Zelie Emerson,' wrote Sylvia, 'had scurried back to us from the United States, eager to be in the thick of it.' When she arrived in Britain, Zelie appraised the political situation on the ground. She swiftly outlined to Sylvia the work that needed doing. 'She was stirring me up to do something for our old Bow Road district. Presently she was ladling out soup in Tryphena Place, Bow Common Lane, an unsavoury neighbourhood, her black eyes frowning intent, and her red lips pursed – her little plump figure hurrying, scurrying.'[779] Since Sylvia was already so self-stirred, stirring her up was no mean achievement, and a telling indication of Zelie's personality. For the next two years, Sylvia and Zelie lived, worked, travelled and went to prison together.

In May 1911, shortly after Sylvia returned from her first American adventure, Norah Smyth's father died, leaving her a personal fortune of around £20,000.[780] In the coming years, Norah was to invest almost all of it in Sylvia's East End movement and in alleviation of Sylvia's personal financial crises, which amounted to much the same thing.

Born in 1874, Norah Smyth grew up in Cheshire in a turreted mansion set in famed 220-acre gardens. Her father, Hugh Lyle Smyth, was chairman of the family business, Ross T. Smyth & Co., the world's third-largest grain-trading multinational, which operated out of Liverpool and dominated the Anglo-American sector. He refused university education to all of his daughters, and forbade them from marrying except to his choice of groom. In 1906, Norah and one of her sisters went to a WSPU rally in Trafalgar Square and became active in the local suffragette movement. Norah was thirty-eight when her father died. Relieved of the patriarchal constraints on her life and liberated by her financial independence, she left directly for London where she cropped her hair short, ditched her dresses and invested in a new wardrobe of masculine suits, shirts and ties, men's brogues, and a double-breasted coat and peaked driver's hat. Newly kitted out in this smart livery, she became Mrs Pankhurst's most trusted chauffeur. Her father had refused her academic education, but she had learned how to drive, a skill that equipped her for freedom.

Smyth, it was said, was much loved by all. She had one blue eye and one brown. She acquired a pet monkey that she named Gnome. As well as monkeys, she loved cats and gave them mythological names: Tristan and Isolde, Thisbe and Pyramus, Oedipuss and Midas. Smyth made all of her fortune available to the East London Federation of Suffragettes and its related east London projects. She was a key financier of the ELFS' newspaper, Zelie's brainchild the *Woman's Dreadnought*. Nellie Cressall was very fond of Norah, 'more level-headed than Sylvia' and 'always ready with the money. I used to say to her, "You know, it's all your money we're using," and she'd say, "I don't mind, it's in a good cause." She was a tower of strength.'[781] Norah could afford this giving, since she managed her investments well.

Cressall, a founder member of the ELFS, was an East End-born labour activist and suffragette. Renowned as a fine speaker, she would be elected to the Poplar Council in 1919, alongside her husband George, who was George Lansbury's political agent for thirty-two years. In 1921 she became one of the Poplar councillors imprisoned for refusing to obey a court order requiring the imposition of unfair taxation. When she was sent to Holloway, she was six months pregnant with her son Samuel. In 1943 she became the first female Mayor of Poplar. She was credited with having discovered Aneurin Bevan in 1907 when he knocked on her door and volunteered to help the labour movement. She had eight children, one inevitably called Keir. 'I only had one girl [Bessie]: if I'd had another, she'd have been called Sylvia.'[782] Nellie kept a large photograph hanging on her wall of Sylvia and Zelie walking together along the Embankment.

On 13 July 1912 Norah narrowly escaped arrest when attempting an arson attack on an eighteenth-century mansion lived in by Lewis Harcourt MP. The mansion stood in gardens designed by Capability Brown that ran down to the Thames near Oxford. Norah and Helen Craggs – Harry Pankhurst's erstwhile sweetheart – hired a canoe, packed it with hammers, matches and fire accelerants and paddled up the Thames at dusk. They were poised to commence their assault on the mansion when a PC Godden caught them red-handed. While he seized and arrested Helen, Norah legged it. Pursued by police dogs, she sprinted over the fields, retrieved the hidden canoe and paddled it to Abingdon from where she took a train to Reading. 'In Reading I changed my clothes in a public toilet before crossing the Channel to Europe where I hid 'til the dust settled.'[783] Norah Smyth was more than compensating for her fettered youth.

On her return to London, she moved into Linden Gardens with Sylvia, where Zelie also stayed when she arrived from the US. From here, the three launched the East End WSPU branch at 198 Bow Road, initially paid for by WSPU HQ. For a while, they maintained the tenancy on Linden Gardens, until first Sylvia and then Norah moved to live as well as work full time in the East End.

Photographs of these three friends at leisure together are rare. The fur coat and pussycat photograph of the triumvirate together is unusual because Smyth is in the picture rather than taking it. Best remembered as the person who bankrolled the ELFS and for her indefatigable work as managing editor of *Woman's Dreadnought*, Norah Smyth was also a phenomenally talented and brilliant pioneer of British documentary photography. Her inheritance made Sylvia's East End project possible, and her cameras captured the history, bequeathing a rich visual storyboard of this period of Sylvia's life. The shift to visual culture tracks the great social and cultural developments of the epoch they lived through, so subtly captured by Virginia Woolf's pen in *The Years* (1937).

In east London – the real heart of the city – cinemas were pushing out the music halls and dramatically changing the character of popular entertainment. Widened access to commercially produced photographic equipment for those who could afford it enabled more people to record and document their own lives and communities. Parallel with this, the new technology radically transformed state surveillance techniques. The suffragettes now became the first militant extremists in Britain subjected to constant, usually covert, photographic observation. The boundaries of public and private life were going through a highly contentious process of reframing.

As soon as Sylvia docked at Southampton, she headed directly to Paris for that catalysing sisterly summit with Christabel that proved so decisive to the future of the British feminist movement.

Shortly after Sylvia's return from Paris in April, George Lansbury told Sylvia that he had settled on Monday 15 April 1912 for the launch of his new newspaper, the *Daily Herald*. Little did he know he'd have the disaster headline of the century. Nor that W. T. Stead, the man Roy

Jenkins describes as the most sensational figure in nineteenth-century journalism, would be one of the drowned. During the night of 14 April, the SS *Titanic* went down, taking more than fifteen hundred souls. After the ship had hit the iceberg, Stead was seen helping women and children into boats and several witnesses claimed they saw him give away his own life jacket. He died honourably in extremity. His reported actions were consistent with his support for women and his oft-demonstrated physical courage. This goes some way towards explaining why his old friends, including Sylvia, in later memoirs went gently on his well-known reputation for sexual harassment and unwelcome predatory behaviour. Stead genuinely championed the women's vote, suffragettes and social reform for the East End.

Exactly a month later on 15 May, the conspiracy trial opened at the Old Bailey, with Sylvia's mother and the Pethick-Lawrences in the dock. In *The Suffragette Movement* Sylvia wrote about it with all the gusto of classic courtroom drama, drawing on her articles covering the case published at the time in *Votes for Women* and Lansbury's new *Daily Herald*. Later the same month, Sylvia was at the ILP Conference in Merthyr, where Hardie observed that she spoke with a new gravitas and increased self-confidence. He made a speech looking to a future in which not just the bonds of poverty would be broken, but equally the shackles of moral convention, which would be shattered only when women stood free and equal side by side with their husbands, brothers, lovers and friends.

Sylvia's intimates remarked that she appeared embarrassed by his public frankness and were puzzled that she didn't seem to appreciate the rare acknowledgement. However, Sylvia knew – as most did not – that Hardie's allusion was not solely to her and that when he referred to lovers in the plural he meant it literally. During her transatlantic travels Sylvia had time to reflect on Hardie's inability to meet her emotional needs. Her newfound state of independence in America brought her to an awareness that this could never change. 'Sylvia,' Caroline Benn suggests, 'was taking her life forward, instinctively protecting herself from the fate of a life's work dedicated to supporting the great man – the fate of most of the rest of the women in his life.'[784] Rose Davies, another of Hardie's amours, with whom he appears to have started an intimate flirtation in 1910 that developed into a relationship,[785] had come to a similar conclusion and was also beginning to create distance from him and re-engage in her own marriage. Hardie now had the more pliable and less problematic young Agnes Hughes to sit at his feet and admire him. Aggie came without the complications of obliging him to worry constantly about having to save her from state torture or militant martyrdom and, unlike the married Rose Davies, without the encumbrance of a husband. Angelic Aggie was also a calculating and self-interested operator, who unlike Sylvia had no compunction about insinuating herself into the heart of the Hardie household by befriending Lillie and their only surviving daughter Nan (Agnes) in the guise of presenting herself as the family's loyal amanuensis. Hardie and Lillie's sons Jamie and Duncan had long since been apprenticed to engineering firms in Glasgow, while Nan, Hardie's favoured child, stayed to run the household with her mother and never left home.[786]

Lillie marked Aggie out for favour in January 1913 by sending her a box of the New Year shortbread that the Hardies gifted only to family friends. But she was not fooled. Perhaps she felt pity for the unwitting and unskilled ingénue who was as yet unaware of her place in the queue, and of Hardie's failing health.

That summer, Sylvia went hoarse from her schedule of public speaking all over London, including the 14 July Bastille Day spectacular held in Hyde Park on her mother's 'official' birthday. During these months, she was busy arranging the move to the East End. In August Hardie was off again to the USA where he spent two months campaigning for the Socialist presidential candidate Eugene Debs. While there, he addressed meetings over the border in Canada.[787] Accompanying Hardie on the voyage to New York was the thirty-three-year-old May Stoddart, on her way to marry his son Jamie. To the great relief of his parents, Jamie had finally made good. He had succeeded in recovering from the gambling addiction that had troubled him for many years and threatened to ruin his life, and set up a viable carpet-cleaning business on Third Avenue, Brooklyn. He worked hard to develop the business and save money, and was now in a position to marry and support the ever loyal and long-suffering May, who was the inspiration for his recovery and survival. On 29 August Hardie witnessed their Brooklyn wedding, dressed in their Sunday best. Lillie, as ever, was absent. She had no appetite for a transatlantic crossing nor for her son's wedding in a distant, alien city.

By the time Hardie returned to Britain in the autumn he found that George Lansbury had taken his pre-eminent position as the champion of the women's vote,[788] and Emmeline and Christabel had declared war on the Labour Party. Sylvia was busy bedding into east London. The state of their relationship at this time was very delicate. In their private lives, Sylvia was questioning their future together and Hardie was sadly coming to realize her growing obduracy on this point. Meanwhile, their political co-working continued undisturbed and as steadfast as ever, spurred by the escalation in the militant campaign.

Sylvia now discovered the true heart of London. No longer was it Dickens' East End of rookeries and Artful Dodgers sticking their thumbs into grubby breeches. Electrification enticingly illuminated the new cinemas and revivified pubs. Parks boasted newly dug and landscaped boating lakes. Trams, paddle steamers and expanded rail links created greater access to the nearby Kent coast for day trips to the beach or hop-picking holidays in the summer. The mighty London docks towered over everything, the source of trade and the city's livelihood, filling every inhabitant's belly. Berthed ships eclipsed church steeples, casting their shadows over the streets. 'Here the riches of the world passed through the hands of England's poorest and most degraded people.'[789] Everyone in the community worked, one way or another, for the shipyards, or lived with a dockworker. The world still depended on sturdy ships, and the Deptford and Rotherhithe shipbuilders were known to be the best in the world. On the streets of east London, shipwrights were sovereign, a loyal, communitarian tribe with Wesleyan tendencies, who from the 1780s had been passionate and effective unionizers – no one prospered without his brothers. The master woodcarvers who created captains' cabins were unsung artists. Their carving appeared on the lintels of fine houses and in churches, and when there was no work shipbuilding they made skilful housebuilders. Now the London docks had been joined by modern industries. Sylvia explored the Silvertown gasworks and heavy engineering and chemical factories where wages were low, job insecurity high.

Women had to work: unskilled workers' families could not survive without female labour. Once again, she was following in the footsteps of Eleanor Marx, who had unionized women gas workers and had worked tirelessly during the Silvertown strike, rarely going home. Marx had also helped organize workers in the Thames Estuary chemical factories.

Over a third of the East End female workforce were employed in domestic service. In the decade from 1911 to 1921 this proportion declined by 20 per cent as a result of the war. Four per cent of women worked in the rag trade; 12 per cent were clerical workers; 8 per cent worked in commerce and finance; and 6.5 per cent in teaching and nursing.[790] The sweated trades employed thousands of women and some men – subcontractors producing artificial flowers, beadwork, sacks, nails, clothing. Sylvia focused on these, as women outnumbered men two to one in the sweated industries. She pursued her now customary research into factory conditions, studying closely the dire environment where for a pittance women made artificial flowers with dangerous chemicals, sewed sacks and clothes or prepared wooden pips for strawberry jam. Many were married to dockers. The minimum wage (laid down by the 1909 Trade Boards Act) was often ignored. Sylvia wrote about this in the *Daily Herald* on 29 October 1912. A woman at a meeting had interrupted her as she referred to the legislation to tell her that the 'outworkers' were not paid the regulation minimum wage. Unemployment and alcoholism were more prevalent among women than among men – accompanied by illegitimate birth, infant mortality and a brisk trade in prostitution.

Poverty laid down firm political foundations for men and women workers – dockers, laundresses, gas workers, sweated workers and ladies' maids. Back in 1905 Sylvia had designed the posters for a joint demonstration of the WSPU alongside George Lansbury and East End socialists – 1,000 working women marching to support the Unemployed Workmen's Bill. There were other processions from the East End between 1905 and 1906 and in that year the Canning Town branch of the WSPU was founded, followed shortly afterwards by the Poplar Branch. Both branches met regularly between 1907 and 1912 and frequently asked for speakers and strike support. From the outset they were at odds with WSPU central command who were increasingly unwilling to work on the interconnection between labour issues and women's suffrage. The Canning Town WSPU was made up predominantly of ILP members or sympathizers and naturally demanded votes for all working women.

As early as 1907, Adelaide Knight resigned in protest against the WSPU leadership failing to keep their promises to working women.[791] Born in Bethnal Green in 1871, Adelaide Knight came from a tough background. Disabled, she overcame lifelong battles with ill health and challenges to her physical mobility to become one of the first leader of the working women in the WSPU. She joined the ILP with her sailor husband, Donald Adolphus Brown, son of a Guyanan Royal Navy officer. Both were socialists. Their mixed-race marriage in 1894 caused some local controversy. Donald supported Adelaide's feminist activism, and took her surname. Adelaide became secretary of the first London branch of the WSPU. In June 1906 she was arrested alongside Annie Kenney and WSPU activist Mrs Sparborough when they tried to gain an audience with Herbert Asquith. Sentenced to six weeks in prison, Adelaide relied on Donald to take care of their small children, the youngest just eighteen months old. She maintained her resolve during her imprisonment, singing the Red Flag every morning and evening and using hairpins to scratch the lyrics on to the windowsill of her cell. Increasingly dismayed with the lack of democracy in the WSPU, Adelaide resigned as branch secretary in March 1907. The following year she was elected to the West Ham Board of Guardians, where she served until 1910. Now, she rejoined Sylvia's breakaway initiative.[792]

In May 1913, Sylvia, Zelie and Norah formally constituted the East End WSPU. Other founder members included Adelaide Knight, Melvina Walker, a former ladies' maid married to a dockworker, and Elsa Dalglish, a landscape painter. These women met in an amusing way. Sylvia and Zelie were speechifying in Bow, using a cart as a platform. A group of mischievous boys tried to overturn it. Elsa and Melvina intervened and sent the boys packing. Sylvia and Zelie invited them to 198 Bow Road for tea.

For the first year until the definitive split, the WSPU central office paid the rent for Sylvia's East End branch and provided other supplementary support. When Christabel and Emmeline denounced Sylvia and cut off the WSPU funds, the Prudential Insurance heir Henry Harben stepped into the breach, pledging £50 per year for three years to start up the new breakaway East End Federation of Suffragettes (ELFS), and topped it up generously thereafter. Norah Smyth, elected treasurer, was the other key funder, and helped launch their newspaper in 1914. She ceaselessly met requests for emergency loans, but no one could remember her ever calling in a single one. Norah could afford this giving, since she managed her investments well.

One of the first local initiatives of the East End WSPU was to organize a rent strike, based on Zelie Emerson's knowledge of rent-strike organization in Chicago. A 'No Vote! No Rent!' leaflet aimed to assure women that they would be protected if they took action. Sylvia wrote: 'A couple of years ago the garment workers of Chicago, in America, were obliged to strike against rent, as well as against sweated employment, because they could not pay ... There was only one eviction in Chicago; there will be no evictions in London when women begin the "No Rent" strike for the vote.'[793] From the outset it was clear that Sylvia was making use of organizational skills learned from the radical American women's unions as well as from the northern British women textile workers who had inspired the founding of the WSPU.

The broader impetus of Sylvia's immediate East End WSPU campaign focused on the women's vote, following the WSPU policy of forcing the Liberal government to draft a bill enfranchising women and to campaign against the government until this was done. Alongside the rest of their WSPU sisters, they heckled, held public debates, demos and mass marches, hunger struck when imprisoned and were force-fed. Where they differed was on their insistence that this vote must include working women. But there were fundamental divergences with the WSPU. Their structure was democratic, with all officers elected. Men were warmly welcomed and actively encouraged to join. Officer roles and leadership were reserved for women, but men could participate at every other level of organization and support.

Contrary to WSPU policy, the East London suffragettes would not attack the Labour Party but worked with it. This included supporting Labour candidates unsympathetic to women's suffrage or who would consider it only in the context of universal suffrage. On 19 November 1913 Sylvia wrote to a Mr Lapworth, 'It's so hard to induce working women to come out and make speeches and really take a prominent part in political movements that we must, even apart from the vote, be constantly laying emphasis on the woman's side of things; but nothing is further from my wish than to be bitter and disagreeable towards the men and especially the men down here who have stood by us so splendidly.'[794]

Sylvia and Zelie had set the momentum for the ELFS's East End activism on Monday 17 February, when they attracted a crowd who listened to them speaking from a cart stationed outside a local council school. Zelie, a star speaker and with the novelty of an American accent and idiom fascinating to East End Cockneys, attracted a large audience. Sylvia spoke next, urging the women in the crowd to make the sacrifice of imprisonment, even though it would cause them hardship and suffering. Feeling the ending of the meeting a little muted after so rousing a call to martyrdom, she lobbed a stone at a nearby undertaker's window. The undertaker, Bromley Public Hall and the local Liberal Club ended up with smashed windows. Once again, Sylvia and Zelie were arrested, and with them a local dressmaker, Mrs Watkins, the very young East End suffragette activist Alice Moore and Annie and Willie Lansbury, daughter and son of George. Willie, Sylvia recalled, shouted wildly 'Votes for Women!' as the police dragged him off to Bow police station.

Sylvia, Zelie and Willie received sentences of two months' hard labour for causing malicious damage to a £3 plate-glass window, with no offer of fines as alternative to imprisonment. The others were given one month. The women served their sentences in Holloway and Brixton prisons. Processions and demonstrations were organized to support them. The sentences were tougher on the lives of the East End women, who lost their jobs and worried about their children. The ELFS raised money and arranged childcare facilities to help alleviate the problems, following the working principles of women's strike committees. Zelie's expertise was crucial to these initiatives. As an organizer of the Chicago Women's Trade Union League, she had been in charge of a restaurant devoted to feeding strikers and their families, chair of the Rent Committee and a director of the relief work during the Chicago garment workers' strike of 1910.[795]

Annie Barnes from Stepney, among the earliest recruits to the ELFS, recalled that from the outset Sylvia prepared them for militancy. She warned them that they would need to be prepared to 'face anything' and should expect to be in danger.[796] Annie Barnes' first risky mission was to accompany Sylvia and a group of ELFS to the top of Tower Bridge,[797] carrying bags stuffed with Votes for Women leaflets which they released into the air over the heads of the people below. Sylvia urged them to be as quickly as possible so as to get down before the police caught them.

In between prison terms, Sylvia took part in mass rallies that built the profile of the East End movement. Christabel became increasingly secretive and hidden from view; Sylvia became more visible and consistently in the public eye. The groundswell of enthusiasm for the East London WSPU approach to mobilizing demonstrated itself in the Victoria Park rally in May 1913, joined by trade unions, suffrage societies and the Labour Party. Sylvia, barely able to walk thanks to a recent hunger strike, was carried on the crest of a wave by this united democratic front wearing bright-red Liberty caps in their thousands.

On 25 March 1913 Home Secretary Reginald McKenna had introduced the Prisoners (Temporary Discharge for Ill-Health) Bill. This legislation enabled the government to release seriously weakened hunger strikers on a special licence that required their rearrest when their health was deemed to have sufficiently recovered to continue serving their sentence. When it passed into law the suffragettes instantly dubbed it the 'Cat and Mouse Act'.

Then came the watershed moment of the 1913 Epsom Derby. According to the King's diary, 4 June was 'A most disappointing day', because a woman called Emily Wilding Davison spoiled his trip to the races. Home early from the aborted event, he and Queen Mary sat brooding in the garden with a cup of tea. Five days later Emily Davison died, never having regained consciousness after leaping in front of the King's horse Anmer. Sylvia, dressed in white like all the other suffragettes, planned to attend the 14 June funeral in London with her mother. As soon as Mrs Pankhurst emerged on to the street, however, detectives rearrested her under her Cat and Mouse order and drove her back to prison. This was a spiteful and petty piece of policing to prevent her honouring Davison's sacrifice, but it did nothing to dent the impact of this mass procession of women in white which brought central London to a standstill. Davison's funeral took over the capital and occupied the national media's hysterical, unfavourable front pages. The militant suffragettes now had a martyr. This iconic funeral became a turning point in the militant campaign, imprinting itself on the nation's consciousness.

In an interview reported nationwide on her arrival in New York in January 1911, Sylvia, referring to the police brutality she had witnessed in suffragette demonstrations in London, had stated that thousands of Englishwomen were ready to 'rush beneath the hoofs of the mounted police and die as the Christian martyrs of old died in the arena for their faith'.[798] Martyrdom formed a substantive tactic of militancy and presented a powerful indictment of state violence, as was acknowledged by the government's prevailing fear of hunger strikers dying.

Sylvia drafted an emotional retort in heroic verse form to honour Davison, entitled 'O Deed Majestic! O Triumphant Death!' She sent it to the *Daily Mail*, which wanted to publish it, but Sylvia changed her mind and withdrew it, judging the sixteen-line poem 'an eccentric manifesto':

The crowded, trivial race-course and the glaring sun,
The swift rush out into that horror of the horses' hoofs, a frantic
clinging impact.
Then, unseen, the column of flame that rises up to Heaven as the
great heart bursts – the ascending spirit is set free.
O deed of infinite majesty! Great heart that no one could
ever know!
Mean, sordid things they write of her in printed sheets whose
objects fill our mind with petty things ...[799]

Between 1912 and 1914 Sylvia was mostly speaking and protesting on the streets, organizing, or in Holloway, with a few interludes travelling in Scandinavia and Hungary. During this high point of the militant campaign, suffragettes set stately homes ablaze, ripped-up railway upholstery, destroyed golf courses to make them unplayable, slashed great masterpieces in art galleries, smashed the orchid house at Kew Gardens and trampled its plants. Great-grandmothers applied for gun licences and cut telephone wires. Women chained themselves to railings; police and gangs attacked them in public. The media showed photographs of protesting women dragged by the hair through the streets of British cities. Women were arrested and force-fed in their tens of thousands.

Sylvia's health progressively deteriorated as a result of repeated hunger and sleep strikes. Refusing sleep as an act of protest was one of her specialities. In Holloway, single-occupancy cells were about nine feet high and either about thirteen feet by seven feet or ten feet by six feet.[800] Sylvia's method of sleep striking was to walk back and forth between door and wall of her cell without pause or resting until she literally fell down with exhaustion. Each time she was released from prison, she was beset by injuries, illness and malnutrition. During the summer of 1913, she went on hunger and thirst strike to ensure she was released on temporary licence in time for a rally at the Bromley Public Hall on 21 July. Alarmed by her fainting fits, the prison doctor signed her temporary discharge and two wardresses took her to stay with her friends the shoemakers Mr and Mrs Payne in their small house at 28 Ford Road, off the Roman Road in Bow.

The Paynes moved their marital bed downstairs into the front parlour and gave Sylvia sole use of their small upstairs bedroom. For several months this became her convalescent retreat. They tied up the doorknocker and closed the business in order to give Sylvia rest. Norah captured her lying in bed supported by comforting pillows and an eiderdown and surrounded by newspapers. Sylvia is so emaciated the papers seem disproportionately enormous. As she slowly recovered, she caught up on writing a number of articles and essays and keeping up her correspondence. Detectives hung around outside. Locals, now protective of Sylvia as one of their own, objected to the harassment. The resulting furore caused regular noise and altercation on the street between the police and Sylvia's supporters.

Dr Flora Murray, who had attended her mother and many other 'mice' hunted down by the Cat and Mouse legislation, nursed Sylvia back to health. Her mother came to visit, and they swapped war stories about their prison experiences. Thereafter, Sylvia wrote in her biography of her mother, 'we were chasing each other in and out of prison, as though it had been a race between us, until she had served forty-two days in ten imprisonments, and I, in nine imprisonments, had served sixty-five days'.[801] On several occasions they were both in Holloway at the same time but prohibited from seeing each other. Emmeline recalled, 'I was put into solitary confinement because in the exercise yard I spoke to my daughter … My daughter was also penalized because she waited for me to catch up with her as we marched round the yard. This seems a bit harsh.'[802]

The Paynes' home was a far cry from Nurse Pine's suffragette convalescent hospital in its gracious Kensington villa. Sylvia was always welcome there, but there was no question of her returning there now. She belonged to the East End. She described the house and neighbourhood in an article she wrote at the time, 'A Prisoner of Bow', particularly Jessie Payne's constant battle with the bugs. The cry of the bug exterminator advertising his services was a familiar sound on East End streets, offering to rid people's homes of the infestations associated with poverty – bed bugs, beetles, fleas, cockroaches, ants and other insects. On sleepless nights Sylvia's candle illuminated them in battalions crawling over the walls and Jessie's wedding curtains, despite constant disinfection. In these modest surroundings Sylvia received many visitors, including the Bishop of London. Hardie arrived with gifts and letters of support, Smyth with a constant stream of letters requesting help and advice.

A photograph of Emmeline also taken in 1913 makes an interesting pair with Norah's photograph of Sylvia in bed. Emmeline rests in bed at Kate Pine's nursing home in plush west London, her gaunt and pinched face clearly the parental mirror of Sylvia's. On her nightstand is a photograph in an ornate frame of Sylvia in her fur coat and a large hat. The nightstand is otherwise crowded with bouquets of flowers. Emmeline's head leans towards the photograph, drawing the eye towards Sylvia. Her proud maternal smile is unmistakable. Given the political trouble between them at the time, this is a deliberate and telling image of solidarity.

The ELFS grew throughout 1913. As more police were sent to their meetings, the women responded by returning to the tactics of the early suffragette days. They dressed up, disguising themselves with wigs, veils and misleading costumes. They planned feints and diversions and made use of doubles. Sylvia declared herself impatient with these techniques but deployed them with a flamboyance and an aptitude for dramatic and risky escapades that rather contradicted her objections. These militant suffragette years were Sylvia's training for her later career in the international political underground.

At the 21 July Bromley Public Hall meeting that she was so anxious to get out of prison to attend, Sylvia turned up concealed within a long dark coat with upturned collar and with a hat pulled down over her eyes. She jumped on to the platform and threw off the disguise. Greeted by thunderous cheers she gave a rousing speech about breaking the chains of poverty. The police tried to arrest her as she left the stage. The crowd turned a hose on them and flushed them out on to the street, allowing Sylvia to duck into an alley where she hid all night in an empty stable. Just before dawn the following morning, Willie and Edgar Lansbury turned up in a cart piled with wood, some of which they nonchalantly offloaded into the stable. The Lansbury boys then tied Sylvia in a large sack and put her in the back of the cart, surrounded by sackloads of logs. Satisfied that she was concealed, they drove her to Epping Forest where Bessie Brine, George Lansbury's sister-in-law, gave her shelter until the police gave up the search.

At the end of July Sylvia was in disguise again when driven into Trafalgar Square for a rally. 'There was a strange, deep, growling sound in the crowd about me I had never heard before: the sound of angry men.'[803] She wore a motley ensemble of curly red wig, shepherd's plaid coat and voluminous skirt. Her front was stuffed with newspapers to bulk out her emaciated body, and over the top of all this she wore a transparent veil. Captured, arrested and back in Holloway after she revealed herself, Sylvia felt rising frustration. 'I was at first so horrified by the return there I felt I could have knocked my head against the wall.'[804]

The escalation of state violence against the suffragettes called for new strategies in response. Supporters started showing up at meetings with sticks and batons to defend themselves. The East End favourite, the 'Saturday Night', became the weapon of choice among the women – a length of tarred rope, twisted, knotted and usually weighted with lead. This sidearm originated in the docks, an old sailor special. The press covered the street violence lustily: 'Wild Scenes in the East End', 'Threat of Gunpowder and Violence', 'Socialist-Suffragette Riots'.[805]

Urged to take a holiday to convalesce, Sylvia decided to tour Scandinavia with Smyth to see for herself the new feminist policies that, it was said, had put the region so far ahead in dismantling patriarchy and establishing women's equal rights. She accepted invitations to give lectures on her experience of forcible feeding. Hardie gave her letters of introduction and a list of his political contacts to visit, though reviewing the list he admitted, 'I cannot say if it is suffrage or socialist.'[806]

Sylvia and Smyth set off for Scandinavia in August, first stop Helsinki. Finland was still an autonomous Grand Duchy of the Russian empire. (It would not become independent until 1917.) Here they were intrigued to meet some of the first women in the world elected to a modern parliament, in particular Ida Aalle-Teljo. In 1906, the Finnish national assembly – Eduskunta – under pressure from socialist-led general strikes, became the first parliament in the world to adopt full gender equality, making Finland the first country in Europe to allow universal and equal suffrage, irrespective of class, gender, wealth or inherited position. The 1907 general election returned nineteen women to the Eduskunta, nine socialists and ten from middle-class parties. To distinguish between them, the socialists wore white and women from liberal and right-wing parties wore black. These women worked within their own parties to improve women's status and promote social welfare legislation, but they also participated in all other legislative work. The Finnish feminist movement saw no need to have a separate party for women.

From Finland they moved to Denmark, where the social services dazzled Sylvia: 'Admirable Denmark seemed to me the happiest, most fraternal and, therefore, noblest country in the world!'[807] The Danish public and press loved her, the national and local media reporting her tour in detail. 'Miss Pankhurst,' they noted, 'is very impressed by what has been achieved for women … in our country, without the use of violence'.[808] The German socialist Clara Zetkin had initially called for an International Women's Day at the socialist conference in Copenhagen in 1910, early evidence of Denmark's progressive attitude to women's status. At Elleborg in Hellebæk Sylvia and Norah were the guests of veteran feminist campaigner Johanne Münter of the Danish Woman Suffrage Association.

In Lillehammer, Norway, Sylvia gave a lecture arguing that the British suffragette movement was moving in the right direction, but slowly. She stressed the importance of getting the support of the masses, and that when the women's suffrage campaign worked more closely with the workers' movement 'everything would develop faster'.[809] She deplored the social conditions endured by working women in Britain, and their appallingly low wages.

Sylvia was the guest speaker at an event organized by Norsk Kvind-estemmeretsforeningen – the Norwegian Association for Women's Voting Rights – when she once again described the bad living conditions for women of the English lower classes: 'It is true, what I learnt from my father in my childhood … that behind every poor man there will always be an even poorer woman … Our goal is the same as for all reformers … We want the right to vote so that we can have influence on the laws.'[810]

During their first visit to Kristiania (Oslo) the pair stayed at the Hotel Regina, from where Sylvia gave a string of interviews and posed for photographs, 'together with Miss Smyth, the movement's clever chauffeur'.[811] Sylvia's speech to the students' union at the prestigious University of Oslo, then known as the Royal Frederick University, caused controversy. The writer and prominent literary critic Hjalmar Christensen denounced the students' union for inviting 'hysterical women' like Pankhurst to give speeches at their university meetings. It was a full house. Most people applauded, some whistled, as Sylvia delivered her ninety-minute address on 'The English Woman's Struggle for the Vote'. At the end of her address, the chair, Dr Wallem, thanked her for her historical discourse, adding that he could not think of anything so perfectly complete as the English gentleman, 'but I don't think we have the English suffragette in mind when we try to evoke the ideal woman'.[812] Suitably disgusted, Sylvia cut short the event and left the hall shortly afterwards.

In Sweden, Sylvia and Smyth were hosted by Anna Fredrika Carlberg, known to all as Frigga. The writer, social worker and feminist Frigga Carlberg was a member of the central committee of the National Association for Women's Suffrage (LKPR) and chairperson of the Gothenburg branch of the Swedish Society for Woman Suffrage from 1902 to 1921. Focusing on women's issues and the living conditions of poor people, her novels and plays directly influenced campaigning and public policy. Sylvia and Smyth also spent time with the formidable feminist activist Augusta Tonning, who later became a politician and gave much support to the British women's movement.

John Chaplin, chair of the Anglo-Swedish Society in Gothenburg, notes that 'it had to be made very clear by Frigga and Sylvia that this visit was a private invitation and not sanctioned by the National Association for Women's Suffrage (LKPR). Sylvia was considered too militant for Swedish tastes although there was clearly a good deal of interest in her speech as the hall was booked only a couple of days in advance and yet, according to accounts, the hall was full.'[813] Numbers are not given, but Chaplin estimates an audience between two and three hundred. The police transcript of Sylvia's long lecture, in English, was recently discovered by an archivist after 106 years. Dated 13 October 1913, the cover note to the fifteen-page typed report is on headed notepaper from the Remington Typewriter Company. The police informant explains that, while most of the transcript is verbatim, for the 'latter part of the lecture ... I have made a sort of précis of her remarks from memory which I hope will be enough for your purpose'.[814] As Helen Pankhurst wryly observed, the police spy clearly gave up from exhaustion, lacking the stamina to keep up with Sylvia.[815]

While in Gothenburg Sylvia and Norah also visited one of the orphanages run by Carlberg, and an art gallery, which Chaplin suggests was probably the private Fürstenberg Gallery. Carlberg commented afterwards in a letter to her daughter, 'Thank God that we invited Sylvia Pankhurst here – we are not yet living in Russian-like conditions but we have freedom of speech in this country.'[816] At the time the Tsar was closing newspapers and locking up journalists.

Hardie's list of introductions included the leader of the Swedish socialists, Karl Hjalmar Branting, whom Sylvia and Norah met in Stockholm. In 1920 Branting would become the first Social Democratic (SDP) President of Sweden, and he went on to serve three terms, but would already disappoint Sylvia greatly by supporting the Mensheviks and condemning the Bolshevik seizure of power in Russia.

On their return journey, Sylvia and Smyth again spent some time in Denmark, where the periodical *Kvinden og Samfundet* – 'Woman and Society' – ran an article describing how Miss Pankhurst spent her 'holidays'. In six days, from 2 to 8 October, she visited a workhouse, a women's prison, a pioneering tuberculosis clinic, several municipal schools, a teacher training college, a home for the elderly, the headquarters of a trade union for female domestic workers, a dairy and the Royal Danish porcelain factory. She delivered two speeches at open meetings and spent three hours at the Danish parliament, listening to a debate about voting rights for women. The press made daily demands for interviews, and noted that 'wherever she was she wrote notes in a big note book'.[817]

On 13 October the ELFS and other local organizations held a homecoming reception at Bow Baths Hall. Sylvia and Norah, buoyed up with idealism by their Scandinavian tour, landed back in Britain with a bump. Detectives raided the hall and tried to arrest Sylvia as she spoke. 'Jump, Sylvia, jump!' shouted the audience, crowding round the platform to protect her. A fight broke out with the police, during which supporters passed Sylvia along over their heads, delivering her to Kosher Hunt, an East End ex-prize fighter, now her personal bodyguard. Kosher disguised her in his jacket and scarf and they disappeared into the sheeting rain and dark.

As the police rushed the hall, Zelie had set about them with her Saturday Night special to cover Sylvia's escape. They retaliated by knocking her unconscious and fracturing her skull. This injury had severe long-term effects on Zelie's physical and mental health and, as a consequence, on her relationships with those closest to her, including Sylvia.

Undeterred by the fracas, the following evening Sylvia tried to turn up to speak at Poplar town hall. Disguised as a washerwoman, cradling a mock baby bundle on the top deck of an omnibus, she almost made it to the town hall entrance, but was recognized and sent straight back to Holloway, this time protesting with nine days of hunger and thirst strike. When released, she could no longer walk, so for the rest of the year was carried to meetings on stretchers and chairs.

Christabel and Emmeline looked on with growing unease at the impact of Sylvia's work in the East End. Ultimately, however, it was the question of Ireland and not the working women's vote that proved the final straw for her sister and mother.

James Larkin was gaining ground, advancing the cause of the Irish Transport and General Workers' Union which had been formed by Sylvia's friend James Connolly. On 26 August the Dublin bosses tried to demolish the ITGWU by declaring a lockout. The management denied employment to the employees by closing down workplaces – 'locking out' the workers. In the resulting riot, police killed protesters and Larkin was arrested. The lockout lasted until 18 January 1914. The British government ignored direct pleas for assistance from the employees, who were starved into going back to work. Lansbury's *Daily Herald* ran a campaign that brought children over from Dublin to English homes. The Pethick-Lawrences looked after several of these temporary refugees in their Surrey home. Sylvia's latest Cat and Mouse licence had expired, but she agreed to speak at the Albert Hall on 1 November at George Lansbury's mass rally in support of Larkin and the Dublin victims.

Christabel was furious. She issued a statement from Paris stating that Sylvia had spoken at the Albert Hall meeting as an independent and not as a representative of the WSPU. Sylvia gamely sent a rejoinder to all WSPU branches, defending her stance, and calling the argument 'this little storm in a tea cup … There was a time when the WSPU held far more meetings than any other society. That is not the case today. People are asking whether I or the East London Federation of the WSPU have formed any kind of alliance with The Daily Herald League. The answer is quite simply: "no we have not".'[818]

As they very certainly had, this statement naturally upset their male East End supporters and required some deft revision. While Sylvia worked to repair the damage her denial of the East End alliance had caused, Christabel wrote to her from the western front: 'It is essential for the public to understand that you are working independently of us. As you have complete confidence in your policy and way of doing things, this should suit you perfectly. There is room for everybody in the world, but conflicting counsels inside the WSPU there cannot be.'[819]

Around the same time Adela received a letter from Annie Kenney asking her to promise never to speak again in England. Adela had recently completed her training at the agricultural college Rode Manor in Somerset and been appointed their head gardener. Emmeline and Christabel, alarmed by Sylvia's accelerating independence, worried that she would persuade Adela over to her socialist side.

Like numerous suffragettes, Norah Smyth wore conventional women's clothing only when absolutely necessary for disguise. January 1914 was one of these occasions, when she had to borrow a nursing uniform from the ever obliging Kate Pine to accompany Sylvia, summoned by her sister to Paris. 'I realized', wrote Sylvia, 'that, like so many others, I was to be given the *congé*.'[820] Although uninvited, Norah accompanied Sylvia in order to represent their members properly and for support. For the journey, she treated them to the luxury of a private cabin from Harwich. Unusually, Sylvia's uncle Herbert Goulden insisted on accompanying them to the boat to see them off, making her even more certain that the axe was about to fall. Sylvia, 'miserably ill in body and distressed by the reason of my journey', crossed to the Hook of Holland oppressed by seasickness, nightmares and fear of the police detectives that her uncle had seen boarding the boat.[821] These turned out to be in pursuit of diamond thieves, not her, so the pair made it safely to Paris, where they found Emmeline alarmingly unwell and in poor spirits.

Their audience was held at the Princesse de Polignac's luxurious mansion, where Christabel was staying. With Fey, her Pomeranian, on her lap, Christabel got straight to the point as soon as they arrived. The East London Federation of the WSPU must become a separate organization. *The Suffragette* would announce this and, unless they immediately chose to adopt a new one for themselves, 'a new name would be given to us'.[822]

With Emmeline and Norah as witnesses, Christabel listed in detail Sylvia's misdemeanours. Her delinquency in having spoken at Lansbury's pro-Larkin meeting at the Albert Hall was particularly emphasized. She had persisted in working with Lansbury and the Labour Party, contrary to WSPU policy. Further, the East London WSPU had a democratic constitution, deviating from the centrally run command-and-control autocracy dictated by Clement's Inn. Sylvia's East End campaign was unnecessary, 'a working women's movement was of no value: working women were the weakest portion of the sex: how could it be otherwise? Their lives were too hard, their education too meagre to equip them for the contest. "Surely it is a mistake to use the weakest for the struggle! We want picked women, the very strongest and most intelligent!"'[823]

Like her friendship with Lansbury, her sister crisply informed her, Sylvia's friendship with Henry Harben was wrong. Also, her East London suffragettes were diverting funds that might otherwise have gone to the central WSPU. This accusation infuriated Norah, who knew better than anyone how the funding and accounts of their operation worked. She held her tongue, but not for long.

In view of all of this, Christabel concluded, Sylvia's East London suffragettes had to become an entirely separate organization, having proven their inability to operate in compliance with WSPU policy.

They paused for lunch and drove in the Bois de Boulogne, Christabel with Fey on her arm. Sylvia was in no mood for the superficial social niceties of lunch and drives in the park, and was profoundly alarmed by her mother's frail state for which, in her view, Christabel appeared to make little allowance. By the afternoon the conversation had turned outwardly hostile. Norah burst the diplomatic bubble by exploding finally on the point of funding. She challenged Christabel on her assertion that East London funds had been 'diverted' from Clement's Inn. Christabel retorted that she couldn't understand why such a 'simple' organization as theirs needed any money at all to function. Up until now depressed and mostly silent, their mother tried to interject with an offer of some supporting funds to Sylvia. Christabel cut across her, 'Oh no, we can't have that! We must have a clean cut.'[824]

Christabel had made her decision clear about the class bias of the movement, as she later explained in her memoir:

Surveying the London work as I found it, I considered that in
one sense it was too exclusively dependent for its demonstrations
upon the women of the East End. The East End women were
more used to turning out in numbers, for many of them have
done so in connection with Labour demonstrations, and at the
very beginning of our London campaign it was natural for our
organizers to rely mainly upon them. It was, however, the right
and duty of women more fortunately placed to do their share, and
the larger share, in the fight for the vote which might be, whatever
our hopes to the contrary, long and hard. Besides critical murmurs
of 'stage army' were being, quite unjustly, made by Members of
Parliament about the East End contingents, and it was evident
that the House of Commons, and even its Labour members,
were more impressed by the demonstrations of the feminine
bourgeoisie than of the feminine proletariat. My democratic
principles and instincts made me want a movement based on no
class distinctions, and including not mainly the working class but
women of all classes.[825]

Her characteristic chop logic on the question of class and equality
continues:

No! We must show no respect of persons. An individual gift for
command and organization, united with freedom from domestic
and other circumstances, gave the title to manage departments of
the work. Consequently it was sometimes found in our WSPU
that directions would be given by a junior in age to seniors, or by
one of less to those of more social consequence. But true equality
reigned with us between women of every class. All belonged to the
aristocracy of the Suffragettes.[826]

So Christabel moves from democracy to aristocracy in the space of just
one paragraph.

The clean break was publicized with surgical precision through a brief
WSPU press release and an announcement in *The Suffragette* published
on 13 February 1914. Several national newspapers excitedly took up the
press release and printed the statement to whip up the story of the
internecine suffragette split – it was too good an opportunity to miss.

For Sylvia, all of this was just so much external noise. She was coping with something much more profound than tomorrow's chip-paper media sensationalism. After the dreadful meeting, just before she left Paris, Christabel took Sylvia aside so that they were at last alone together. She said that she hoped they might sometimes meet, 'not as Suffragettes, but as sisters'. Sylvia wrote, 'To me the words seemed meaningless; we had no life apart from the movement. I felt bruised, as one does, when fighting the foe without, one is struck by the friend within.' Memories of their childhood flooded her mind, 'the little heads clustering at the window in Green Hayes'; Christabel's 'pink cheeks and the young green shoots in the spring in Russell Square; my father's voice: "You are the four pillars of my house!"' [827]

And so her elder sister expelled Sylvia from the family party, while her mother stood by silent, without objecting.

Not long afterwards Adela also stepped into the Paris dock to be read the rap sheet of her failings, this time led by Emmeline. Christabel added her criticisms, starting with the fact of her younger sister's professed socialism. According to Adela, Sylvia had tried to recruit her for the East End campaign. It was this that prompted Annie Kenney's letter instructing Adela to desist from public speaking in Britain. Emmeline suggested that Adela travel to Australia on a one-way ticket, offering to write her letters of introduction. On 2 February 1914 Adela sailed alone for Canberra. Her mother gave her £20. 'It was very little and I often wondered what she thought I would do in Australia when it was spent.' [828]

Adela saw the Pankhurst daughters as casualties of the movement. She said of her mother, 'I was young and she was old. Our points of view could not be the same. Tolerance was certainly not to be learned in the school in which she had been trained. If she had been tolerant and broadminded she could not have been leader of the Suffragettes. She had nearly forgotten me as a daughter ... and I must confess I had largely forgotten her as a mother ... It was part of the price paid by us for votes for British women.' [829]

Emmeline Pethick-Lawrence, Helen Moyes and Sylvia all thought Emmeline Pankhurst and Christabel ruthless in getting rid of Adela. Sylvia and Adela were too socialistic and too charismatic for Christabel. Publicly, Adela defended her mother. She buried the pain of her rejection in the criticisms written into her long 1917 play, *Betrayed*. The mythical country of Orrin in which the drama is set struggles for Home Rule. Autocratic matron Mrs Morley, the Emmeline Pankhurst figure, delivers her ultimatum to her socialist son, Edward (Adela), in which we get the flavour of that last meeting in Paris:

> We have been forbearing with you for a long time. I have excused you because you were young and because you were given a responsible position too early. But I tell you, neither Spencer [elder son, the Christabel figure] nor I will tolerate open insubordination. As to money, I will give you none until you leave your present associates, and consent to take up a position in ... the colonies ... If you persist in your present attitude, I will publicly disown you.[830]

What is so bracing about the political Pankhurst daughters and their great militant matriarch of a mother is how they collectively defy the conventional trope of motherhood as an unrealizable ideal and ultimate scapegoat for everything. Their family story demonstrates the impossibility for women of conforming to social expectations of being a perfect mother or a perfect daughter and of being fully human as a civic and political subject in the world. For all the differences between them, their uncompromising refusal to perform these conventional roles of mothers and daughters remains at the core of their radicalism and change-making.

Sylvia returned in January 1914 to anxiety and irritation among the East London members about their expulsion from the WSPU. Swift on the heels of this row came the unedifying wrangle over the organizational name between the now officially factional Pankhursts. Emmeline and Christabel objected to Sylvia's preferred East London Federation of Suffragettes because of the 'S'. They argued that the concept of suffragette was synonymous with the WSPU. Sylvia claimed that she proposed a variety of alternatives to the East London members but none of them appealed – the Bow quarter wanted to be the ELFS. So they plumped for the name most objectionable to Clement's Inn and added the equally offensive bright red for liberty and socialism to the purple, white and green.

Nicely timed for the day after the WSPU's national announcement of Sylvia's severance, she held the first public meeting marking the formal transition of the East End WSPU to the ELFS at Bromley Public

Hall on Bow Road. It was a Valentine message for her mother and sister. In her speech Sylvia made it clear that the ELFS opposed WSPU tactics of individual acts of arson and destruction of property. Mass communal action, she argued, would be more effective than individual and dramatic acts of terror – however successfully these stunts grabbed the headlines. By contrast, the ELFS policy was for collective militancy in plain and public view.

To underline the point, Sylvia invited the Bromley Hall meeting to march to the local bank and police station and join in some communal window smashing. Police arrested and imprisoned Sylvia and Zelie, making an excellent start to the ELFS campaign. Emmeline paid their fines immediately, to Christabel's annoyance.

As Christabel had decreed that *The Suffragette* would no longer report any of their activities, the ELFS started their own newspaper, the *Woman's Dreadnought*, a weekly 'reporting from the working-women's point of view', launched on International Women's Day, 8 March 1914, with an initial circulation of 20,000 and produced by an East End printer. To mark its introduction the ELFS held a suffragette demonstration in Trafalgar Square, decked out in purple, green, white and red, signalling its internationalist, socialist politics. Mounted police met the demonstrators with violence and the following day a magistrate grumbled that half of Scotland Yard had to be deployed in central London to keep this load of desperadoes in order.[831]

Zelie pounded the streets trying to sell advertising space to shops and manufacturers. Lipton's Cocoa and Neave's Food took out three-month trial contracts. This was a PR coup; purveyors to the Russian royal family and most of the crowned heads of Europe, both were significant brands that continue to this day as global multinationals. Working-class East End suffragettes and socialists were seen as an interesting potential market. Ideally Sylvia wanted the paper to be free, but they couldn't afford that, so each edition was a halfpenny for the first four days after publication and thereafter the remaining copies were distributed free door to door around east London.

The *Woman's Dreadnought* ran until July 1924, changing its name along the way to *Workers' Dreadnought*. It was the first newspaper Sylvia edited. After *Dreadnought*, she created and ran a series of successful international newspapers and continued doing so until her death. In another life, being a newspaper editor could have been her full-time professional calling. It was one of her great talents.

Meanwhile, other media outlets eager for Sylvia to write about the battle with her mother and elder sister contacted her with commissions. The *New York Times* wanted 1,000 unexpurgated words from Sylvia attacking the WSPU. The paper told Norah Smyth, who handled the correspondence, to brief Sylvia to say that the WSPU were smashed, insolvent, disorganized, and that the Cat and Mouse Act had crushed the militant movement. When Sylvia's copy naturally arrived without any of this material, the editor Ernest Marshall returned it unpublished.

Between February and June 1914 Sylvia was imprisoned nine times. Emmeline was frequently in and out of Holloway during the same period, though the authorities prohibited them from meeting while in the prison.

From her cell, Sylvia made plans to lead a procession from the East End to Westminster Abbey for the service on Mothering Sunday, 22 March. Released on 14 March, she wrote to the Dean of Westminster asking him to include a remark on votes for women in the Mother's Day Sunday service. From Bow to Westminster is a six-mile walk. Extremely weak and unwell on her release, Sylvia couldn't do it on foot. The ELFS borrowed a wheelchair, but it buckled instantly in the crush of people around her, so they hoisted it up and carried her shoulder high above the crowd all the way to Westminster.

They arrived at the Abbey to find the gates shut and locked against them. Guards told them there was no room for them inside, so their rebel priest C. A. Wills conducted an outdoor service. Sylvia addressed the rally, transcendent – 'All pain had left me. The air seemed intensely restful and still. When my turn came I spoke without effort, feeling that the people and I were united in a great triumph of love'.[832] The ELFS hired an ambulance to take her home and she vomited in spasms in the back of it for the entire journey.

Sylvia received an invitation to go to Budapest over Easter on an all-expenses-paid speaking trip with a share of the ticket prices going to the ELFS. Norah encouraged her to go and to take Zelie with her.

Shortly before she left, Sylvia went on a morning walk in a dense pea-souper and literally bumped into the frontage of 400 Old Ford Road next door to the Lord Morpeth Arms, looming out of the fog. Variously a school and a factory, the premises had a public hall that held up to 300, connected to the main house by a wide, flat-roofed lobby and living accommodation. With some make-do and mend it looked like a promising prospect for a new, expanded headquarters of the ELFS, 'to organize a lending library, a choir, lectures, concerts, a "Junior Suffragettes Club", and so on'.[833] From here she could set about realizing the blueprint for her next projects, devised during her prison thinking time, where she drew up plans for the long-term future of the ELFS and programmes for social reconstruction.

With financial support from Henry Harben the community got to work. Men from the Rebels' Social and Political Union helped paint, decorate and restore the house as the ELFS HQ and a communal home for Norah, Sylvia and the Paynes, who now had more space than they had had at 28 Ford Road.

While the renovations were under way, Sylvia left for Budapest with Zelie. On their way, they dropped in unannounced on Christabel in Paris. The maidservant, who had seen footage of the famed hunger striker Sylvia in cinema newsreels, shrieked when she opened the door. Christabel wasn't home, but when she did appear it was all very cool and she evinced absolutely no interest in their Hungarian trip or in what was happening in east London. Zelie was horrified and Sylvia could see she was on the verge of blowing up, so they left without eating their lunch.

The duo spent Easter Sunday in the gorgeous bronze and gold St Stephen's Basilica in the heart of Pest, listening to the priest declaiming eloquently against socialism, as their translator explained. They went on a sightseeing tour of the city, absorbing its colour and vibrancy. In a newly built showcase suburb for 30,000 people Sylvia encountered a concrete example of how her vision for the East End could be made reality. The fact of state provision for orphans and destitute children amazed her. That said, she thought the women's prison was worse than Holloway. Of course they visited the prisons – this was a Sylvia Pankhurst holiday.

Addressing a large crowd at the Vigadó Concert Hall on the Pest embankment, Sylvia described the struggle for the vote by British women and received a standing ovation in support of the hunger strikers, 'in their heroic fight for human freedom'.[834] The invitation to speak at Vigadó was an honour about which Sylvia was modest in her memoirs. Designed by Frigyes Feszl in 1859 and inaugurated in 1865,

Vigadó was already a legendary concert hall, the second largest venue in the city. A grand mixture of Oriental and Hungarian art nouveau, it had played a prominent role in Hungarian history and culture. Here in 1873 the city of Budapest was born by merging the towns of Pest, Buda and Óbuda (Old Buda). Concerts by world-renowned musicians – including Franz Liszt, Richard Wagner, Johannes Brahms, Claude Debussy, Béla Bartók, Johann Strauss, Antonín Dvořák, Arthur Rubinstein and Sergei Prokofiev to name a few – took place in Vigadó.

From Budapest Sylvia and Zelie went on to visit Vienna, where they were fêted and filmed for newsreel. Their hosts presented them with tickets for a box at the Vienna State Opera House where they saw *Die Walküre* and the next day walked in the peaceful Vienna Woods, gathering violets from amid the roots of the beech trees. In her memoirs, Sylvia likens herself to 'a caged wild thing … liberated among the trees. Poor town-bred children, what joys you miss!'[835]

While she was away the ILP celebrated its twenty-first birthday. Lillie attended and Hardie gave her a warm public accolade: 'Never, even in those days, did she offer one word of reproof. Many a bitter tear she shed. One of the proud boasts of my life is to be able to say that if she has suffered much in health and spirit, never has she reproached me for what I have done for the cause I loved.'[836]

This public acknowledgement gave voice to private home truths. Hardie's health was failing. Sylvia wrote about him wistfully at the time, unaware of the severity of the change in his health. She noted that he'd given up his flamboyant ties and taken to dressing in grey and dark clothes. She took this as a sign of inner change and sombre mood reflecting the deepening of his struggle with his party over the issue of war and peace. It seems never to have occurred to her that she might be a significant cause of the loss of colour in his life.

18

Cat and Mouse

In her twenties, Sylvia was surprised to hear her mother telling some friends that, before she was three years of age, her middle daughter had convinced her of the uselessness of beating her children, 'because when she had employed the means of bringing me to contrition, I had made her feel that she might kill me before I would give way'.[837] Emmeline Pankhurst understood the extent of Sylvia's powers of resistance a long time before the British state.

On 17 February 1913 when Sylvia and Zelie smashed that undertaker's window after an East End meeting organized by the newly formed ELFS, they ended up in prison for two months. They were sentenced on Tuesday 18 February and entered Holloway the same day, immediately announcing that they would hunger strike. The government was growing more fearful of such resolution undeterred by repeated twice-daily forced feeding. Some sectors of the press and parliament might happily leave them to starve themselves to death, but there was a palpable swing of public opinion in favour of the justness of the brave and now widespread suffragette cause. Asquith had the measure of their determination and didn't want an army of martyrs on his hands.

When McKenna introduced his Prisoners (Temporary Discharge for Ill-Health) Bill on 25 March 1913 while Sylvia was serving her sentence in Holloway. The legislation would turn her into the nation's most 'moused' militant. She'd experienced her first forced feeding in February 1913, and by the end of the year she would hold the unenviable record for being the prisoner most frequently subjected to this form of torture.

The Home Office issued Holloway with Cat and Mouse temporary discharge licences for Sylvia Pankhurst during every calendar month after the Act came into force in April – and sometimes several.

Asquith dreaded a battle with an army of prison martyrs. Instead his government created a confrontation with a mighty militant Pankhurst 'mouse' with her own organized street army and a terrifying capacity for martyrdom. Sylvia's response to systematic state torture, total surveillance and the attempt to constrain and degrade every aspect of her life and beliefs was twofold: to organize collective resistance among the similarly oppressed and, as an individual, to fight to the death. She named her fighting force the People's Army, but everyone else called it Sylvia's Army. As to Asquith's nightmares about an army of martyrs, Sylvia alone became a figure of political self-sacrifice of leviathan proportions: 'I was always convinced that the element of martyrdom provided the highest and keenest incentive to our movement. I knew that the hallowing influence of sacrifice cemented the comradeship of the great mass movement which had grown up.'[838]

In 1909 the press had said that the suffragettes were no longer a movement but a 'whirlwind', likening them to 'hornets' and 'hooligans'. However, by 1913 their sustained campaign was achieving a shift in public opinion. Even the *Daily Mail* now asked Sylvia to write articles about her prison experience for it, and protested in its own op eds about forcible feeding:

> It will not do. No one who has read the reports of their sufferings
> … such as … Miss Sylvia Pankhurst's story in yesterday's *Daily Mail*
> can have any other feeling than this – that however necessary it may
> be to use such methods in the case of the insane, their application
> to women, who, in the full possession of their senses, choose to
> offer violent resistance, is barbarous and uncivilized. It converts a
> sentence of a month's or two months' imprisonment into a sentence
> of unbearable torment degrading the community which inflicts it.
> What we suggest is that Mr McKenna should cut forcible feeding
> completely out of his scheme.[839]

Sylvia was the only Pankhurst subjected to this form of torture. Emmeline was a physically and mentally courageous hunger, thirst and sleep striker. Fearing the consequences of abusing so popular a public icon, the government refrained from force-feeding her, though she was subjected to many other forms of life-threatening harassment and mistreatment. Exile in Paris placed Christabel beyond prison and beyond the reach of the mouth vices and clamps, rubber tubing, funnels and stomach pumps used by medical officers for the process. So it fell to Sylvia – of the three, the most reluctant – militant, to endure repeated forced feeding during her successive prison sentences of 1913 and 1914.

The forcible-feeding policy continued from 1909 to 1914, ending only when the WSPU surrendered their militant activity on the declaration of the First World War. When Lord Robert Cecil protested against the practice, urging instead his old proposal that militants should be deported to the most inhospitable British colonies, McKenna defended his approach on the grounds that he had to cope with 'a phenomenon absolutely without precedent in our history'.[840] Those who advised him not to release the hunger strikers believed that the women would surrender if there were no chance of their release. In his speech to parliament on 11 June 1913, McKenna astutely warned against underestimating the determination of the militants:

> We have to face the fact, however, that they would die … in many
> cases they have got in their refusals of food and water beyond the
> point where they could help themselves … There are those who …
> think that after one or two deaths in prison, militancy would cease
> … So far from putting an end to militancy, I believe it would be
> the greatest incentive to militancy which could ever happen. For
> every woman who died there would be scores who would come
> forward for the honour as they would deem it, of the crown of
> martyrdom … They have a courage, part of their fanaticism, which
> undoubtedly stands at nothing … They would seek death; and I am
> sure that however strong public opinion outside might be today in
> favour of letting them die, when there were twenty, thirty, forty or
> more deaths in prison, you would have a violent reaction of public
> opinion … We should have woman after woman, whose only
> offence may have been obstructing the police, breaking a window,
> or even burning down an empty house, dying because she was
> obstinate. I do not believe that is a policy which, on consideration,
> will ever recommend itself to the British people, and I am bound

to say for myself that I could never take a hand in carrying the policy out.[841]

McKenna added ruefully, 'I have on many occasions ... had the prisoners examined by doctors, but in no case have they been willing to certify them as lunatics.'[842]

By intellect and temperament Sylvia was an unwilling extremist. Yet the double standards by which women's behaviour was judged differently to that of their fellow men violated her sense of fair play. McKenna's signalling adjective in his speech is 'obstinate'. Disobedient women will die because they are difficult, self-willed and non-conforming, not because they are courageous freedom fighters willing to give their lives to fight for their human rights and a cause regarded as a civil right for men to strive for since the birth of Greek democratic ideals. He acknowledged the women's bravery, but not the justice of their cause.

From McKenna's perspective, a hunger-striking Sylvia was simply an older, insubordinate version of the girl child who resisted eating the porridge she loathed, even at the risk of incurring her beloved father's wrath. And perhaps there was something in that, after all. Women's eating habits differed from men's. Millions of working mothers and grandmothers were accustomed to going hungry in order to feed their families. In a different context, many elite and middle-class women managed – or rather mismanaged – and distorted their eating behaviour in order to squeeze themselves into corsets and stays. Or they deployed refusal of food as a form of externalized passive resistance to the boredom or hysteria produced by the mind-numbing constraint of their respectable lives over which, like children, they had no control.

Suffragette women's disobedience and insubordination were provocations prompting the sanction of more rational beings in order to maintain good sense and public order. The government policy of forcible feeding was an obscene violation of women's – and suffragette men's – bodies. However, the government's line was that these protesters were victims of wilful self-harm.

Read the voluminous pages of Hansard, scan the stuffed vaults of Home Office files, Scotland Yard reports and cuttings from reactionary media, and you will find that the British state represented itself not as the active agent propagating this torture policy, but merely as an apparently passive object subjected to intolerable incitement and forced by ungovernable women to react. The state didn't do it. Draconian legislation didn't do it. Patriarchy didn't do it. It was suffragettes who inflicted this torture on themselves by refusing to eat. No one more so than the socialist firebrand Sylvia Pankhurst. Her name became synonymous with the most extreme forms of personal resistance and eagerness for martyrdom. Both her mother and George Bernard Shaw depicted her as the modern Jean d'Arc. And like Joan, Sylvia raised an army.[843]

Sylvia wrote a letter to her mother that was published in *The Suffragette* on 12 March 1913:

> I am fighting, fighting, fighting. I have four, five, and six wardresses every day, as well as the two doctors. I am fed by stomach-tube twice a day. They prise open my mouth with a steel gag, pressing it in where there is a gap in my teeth. I resist all the time. My gums are always bleeding. The night before last I vomited the last meal, and was ill all night, and was sick after both meals yesterday ... By the way, I was told that Dr. Ede says Mrs. Branson [a suffragette hunger striker also in Holloway] has a defect in her heart. Can something be done? ... I am afraid they may be saying we don't resist. Yet my shoulders are bruised with struggling whilst they hold the tube into my throat. I used to feel I should go mad at first, and be pretty near to it, as I think they feared, but I have got over that, and my digestion is the thing that is most likely to suffer now.   SYLVIA

Sylvia was correct to assume that the prison authorities were repressing the truth about the regime to which she was subjected. They assured the media that she was well looked after, in good health and – most gallingly – a well-behaved, model prisoner. Sylvia had been on thirst and hunger strike for three days before she was threatened with forced feeding. She allowed herself only a daily mouthwash, careful not to swallow the water, refusing all other liquids and food.

When the warning of forced feeding came, she panicked initially. She describes the extremity of her visceral fear as she tried to escape from her locked and barred cell. She desperately gathered her few possessions including prison mug, plate and shoes, to use as missiles against her assailants. Realizing the futility of her situation, she calmed herself and spent the night stiffening her resolve to face the twice-daily torture that began the next day. This breathtaking feat of mental and physical self-control indicates the depths of her belief in the justness of her cause and her extraordinary courage.

In her detailed press reports of the torture she endured, Sylvia was unusual in explicitly describing the experience of forced feeding as a form of rape. Many other victims of the treatment, concerned to preserve their dignity, confined these aspects to personal diaries, private correspondence or later published memoirs. But Sylvia bravely published the facts of the sexualization of this widespread torture. One key account in *The Suffragette Movement* stands for many others. Knowing that it describes not a horrific, singular experience but a twice-daily ritual that lasted for weeks at a time over a period of twenty months of her life makes it an even tougher read.

When her cell door opened, it was filled by a menacing group of at least six wardresses, all much bigger and stronger than her:

> They flung me on my back on the bed, and held me down firmly
> by shoulders and wrists, hips, knees and ankles. Then the doctors
> came stealing in. Someone seized me by the head and thrust a sheet
> under my chin. My eyes were shut. I set my teeth and tightened
> my lips over them with all my strength. A man's hands were trying
> to force open my mouth; my breath was coming so fast that I felt
> as though I should suffocate. His fingers were striving to pull my
> lips apart – getting inside. I felt them and a cold steel instrument
> pressing hard around my gums, feeling for gaps in my teeth. I was
> trying to jerk my head away, trying to wrench it free. Two of them
> were holding it, two of them dragging at my mouth. I was panting
> and heaving, my breath quicker and quicker, coming now with a
> low scream which was growing louder ... A steel instrument pressed
> my gums, cutting into the flesh ... 'No, that won't do' – that voice
> again. 'Give me the pointed one!' A stab of sharp, intolerable agony.
> I wrenched my head free.[844]

Until then, she wrote, she hadn't had a clue what it meant, really, to clamp your mouth shut. The force required to try and resist the invasion. 'I fought against it with all my strength, but, cutting its way into the flesh, it worked its way in, and then they turned a screw which gradually forced my jaws apart.'[845] She described feeling faint and nauseated – her head swimming. Then she heard suddenly a new voice in the cell, high-pitched, distressed and strange. Only afterwards did she identify it as her own screaming.

> Again they grasped me. Again the struggle. Again the steel cutting its way in, though I strained my force against it. Then something gradually forced my jaws apart as a screw was turned; the pain was like having the teeth drawn. They were trying to get the tube down my throat, I was struggling madly to stiffen my muscles and close my throat …[846]

They got the tube down her throat. She felt the pain as it scraped its way right down into her stomach. It felt, she recalled, 'like a rope of fire'. A sickening, rushing, burning sensation in her head; her eardrums seemed to be bursting. 'I was unconscious of anything then save a mad revolt of struggling, for they said at last: "That's all!" and I vomited as the tube came up. They left me on the bed exhausted, gasping for breath and sobbing convulsively.'[847]

As soon as she was able to, Sylvia made herself retch until she brought up what had been forced into her. Lying on the bed, head down, choking and straining, she feared that her eye cords would snap. She used the phrase 'pulling myself together'. During her Holloway torture, idioms became literal acts.

'The same thing happened in the evening,' Sylvia wrote, 'but I was too tired to fight so long.'[848] The following morning and evening, again. And the day after that. Day after day, morning and evening, the same struggle. Sylvia decided to use no violence, but each time resisted. Each time she was outnumbered and overcome. Sometimes, the doctors rammed the tube violently up one of her nostrils. Once they hurt her so badly that the matron and two of the wardresses burst into tears, begging the impervious doctors to desist.

The forced-feeding 'medicine' poured through the oesophageal tube was a combination of branded supplements and sustenance usually prescribed for invalids and children. Allenburys vitamin powder, malted Horlick's and Sanatogen supplements were mixed with milk, raw egg and cocoa. Variations included oxtail soup and chicken broth instead of the milk and cocoa. Virol malt extract was added often, and sometimes lemon juice for vitamin C.

Between these brutal episodes, Sylvia was locked in solitary confinement. Warders placed tempting dishes of luxurious foods in her cell: roast chicken, fresh fruit, vegetables, jellies, cheeses and soothing Brand's Essence. She remarked that the varied colours of the food diverted her painfully blood-flooded eyes from the drabness of the cell. But she had 'no more inclination to eat the still life groups on my table than if they had been a painting or a vase of flowers'.[849]

The first time such an appetizing feast was laid out on the table in her cell, she placed it all under her bed and covered it at nightfall, fearful that it might undermine her will or that, ravenous, she might eat it in her sleep during the night. But she hid the tray out of sight under her bed only once. The next day, she realized that to leave the delicious, tempting food on the table in view of the fisheye as the wardresses passed by during the night would be a material sign of her defiance. From that day forward, the warders had to remove the food, finding it exactly where they had placed it the previous day, untouched except by insects, mice or rats.

'At first I kept a regular diary, but as the toll of days lengthened into weeks I lost heart in it; the events it chronicled were too hateful to be dwelt upon.'[850] She gave it up and 'used my paper for more inspiring things, with fear that it might be filled up too quickly'.[851] Instead, she turned her hand to writing a play telling the biblical story of David and Bathsheba, and to writing verse. As well as the paper and pencil with which to write her diary and stories, Sylvia was also permitted a small slate and chalk. She sketched on her slate to try and divert her mind from the torture and avert despair. She drew an illustration to the opening lines of *The Rubáiyát of Omar Khayyám*: 'Awake! For morning in the bowl of night / Has flung the stone that puts the stars to flight.' Another depicted Ezekiel chapter 34, which she read in her prison Bible. Sylvia gave the fat, parasitical shepherds of the story the faces of cabinet ministers, 'but a slate is a dismal thing to draw on; one cannot long retain one's zest in making drawings to rub out'.[852] She gave up, and surrendered herself to night visions prompted by passages read from the Bible during the day.

'Infinitely worse than the pain was the sense of degradation,' for herself and her torturers, who she believed came to the task with 'loathing and pity and would have refrained from it if they could'.[853]

Sylvia gives an especially thoughtful place in her testimony to the agents of her torturers. Throughout her accounts, she takes care to record any sympathetic action, look or sign by a wardress. She notes that some wardresses resigned from their jobs rather than continue with forced feeding. This despite the fact they were working women with families to feed, and were paid substantial additional wages to recompense them for the strain imposed by assisting with the twice-daily torture regime.

To cope with her own sense of degradation, Sylvia dissociated. She felt she was being 'broken up into many selves, of which one, aloof and calm, surveyed all this misery, and one, ruthless and unswerving, forced the weak, shrinking body to its ordeal'.[854] She writes how, deep within, she felt her split selves struggling with each other, imagining each possessed of a voice that combined with the others in a collective protest. She creates a memorable image of multiplying her sense of self into a collective in order to envision resistance that she transformed into embodied physical opposition to her captors.

Sylvia usually wrote formally structured verse in prison, striving to condense the struggle to maintain hope under incarceration and to convey the smart of absence from lovers long endured. Metaphors of walls, inaccessible blue skies, the importance of birds and their song evoke the daily privations and cruelties of unjust confinement and the mental anguish of being forcibly locked in. The prosody of these poems stand in notable contrast to the movement of poetic consciousness and psychological realism in her always vivid, innovative prose, whose internal rhythms, flows, caesuras and startling, compressed word imagery range freely. Sylvia's memoirs are an enactment of the revolutionary 'life writing' for which Virginia Woolf called. Women writers, Woolf argued, needed different experiments in style in order to express unscripted and repressed female experience. Sylvia found scope to explore these modernist forms and inventions in her life writing. Yet the restrained conventions through which she expresses herself in her Romantic lyric prison poetry are profoundly affecting. She inscribes the personal trauma of incarceration, torture and solitary confinement and their political meaning with powerful, metred constraint.

On Saturday 15 March, a month into her sentence, Sylvia decided to start a campaign of sleep striking. 'Then, nerved by deliberate purpose, I began to pace up and down the cell: five steps to the window end, abruptly turning, five steps back to the door; pacing on and on ... I felt very sick, and faint, terribly faint, but I would not stop.'[855] Despite interventions by the principal medical officer, wardresses and other doctors, she refused to stop this walking sleep strike. She discovered that one unexpected side effect of this new form of resistance was that the pacing relieved her extreme constipation, which was suffered by everyone subjected to forcible feeding. Typically, Sylvia focused on this positive aspect rather than on the horrendous effects of sleep deprivation on the human body and mind.

There was no mirror in the cell, but she could see herself in the polished tin reflector behind the cell's single gas light. 'I paused an instant to look: my face was white, my eyes horrible, like cups of blood.'[856] Her legs became swollen and she fell against the walls. 'At times all went black, and I fell, but did not lose consciousness, and after an instant I rose again and continued on the march.'[857] The head warder asked the doctor if they should tie Sylvia on to the bed. He replied, 'No; she'll soon get tired of that [pacing her cell].'[858] Sylvia kept going for twenty-eight hours before she collapsed. 'A thought came to me, "Home Office doctors." I knew that they had been sent for in some cases. I believed if they saw me now they would report it dangerous to force food on me any more.'[859] She asked the next warder who checked her cell to bring the doctor and governor together, and, when they came, asked for permission to petition the Home Secretary for an independent medical examination. They agreed, on the condition that she would at least consent to drink two cups of milk that Sunday evening and also the next morning, so that she had at least some sustenance before the Home Office doctor arrived for the consultation. She accepted the terms. On the evening of Monday 17 March, Dr Maurice Craig was sent to Holloway by the Home Office and confirmed that continuing to force-feed her would endanger her life. The following day Dr Craig reported:

> I am of the opinion that she is now in such a highly nervous state
> that, if forcible feeding has again to be resorted to, she might have
> a severe mental and nervous breakdown; therefore, on this ground,
> I consider it will be impossible to continue feeding her in this
> way. But I wish it to be understood that it is not the actual feeding
> which is injuring her, but the mental excitement which she works
> herself into before, during and after each feed, together with the
> strenuous resistance she always offers.[860]

It would take until Wednesday to process her release papers; until then, she had to continue drinking the twice-daily milk.

Keir Hardie told her later that Reginald McKenna had spoken to him of her twenty-eight-hour non-stop cell march: 'Sylvia *is* a plucky girl!'[861] The Home Secretary seemed as pleased, Hardie remarked, as if he was celebrating a high-performing young employee. Sylvia never forgot the remark. During the war when he was at the Board of Trade and Sylvia was a member of a deputation to discuss rations and allowances, McKenna approached her, stretching out his arm: 'I must shake hands with you. You are the pluckiest girl I ever knew!' She refused his hand. Churlish, perhaps; but at the time his government had still not granted women the vote nor even the dignity of being addressed as adults.

Some of these 'plucky girls' were also anally and vaginally 'force-fed'. Sylvia describes elsewhere in her memoir how a hunger striker in Perth prison in Scotland was assaulted three times a day with attempted 'force-feeding' through her rectum. Another had hot wires applied to her ears to burn them during feeding to try and lessen her resistance. Oral forcible feeding was the most common form of the torture, but establishing the prevalence of other methods is difficult. On the one hand, the prison medical authorities removed these practices from the official records. On the other, most suffragette women understandably avoided the pain and humiliation of revealing the violence of vaginal and anal forced feeding. They simply didn't want to talk about it. Suppressing these abuses in their memoirs and published accounts helped them to maintain their dignity, though it did nothing to heal the trauma.

Wednesday 19 March came and went, with no further news about her release. Sylvia made a request to the prison governor to let her communicate with her uncle Walter Goulden, to ask him to go to the Home Office and request her release papers. The governor refused. She 'became horribly depressed' and 'lay on the bed, unable to stay my tears'.[862] That evening, a prison officer unexpectedly unlocked her door and said they were taking her to Zelie's cell. Sentenced and imprisoned together, Sylvia and Zelie had been separated in solitary cells and kept apart deliberately to undermine their morale.

Zelie was laid out on her narrow prison bed. Her wrist and arm were bandaged and she could barely move. 'Shocked at her condition, I took her in my arms, uttering foolish words: "Oh, my little sweetheart! Oh, my little sweetheart!"'[863] Sylvia discovered that Zelie had tried to kill herself. Using a small blunt penknife smuggled into her cell, she'd dug into her flesh until she found the artery. But when she tried to sever it, she found it too tough, 'like an indiarubber band' she explained to Sylvia.[864] The wardresses had discovered her through the cell-door fisheye as she sawed away at her blood-drenched arm. They bandaged and tried to sedate her, but she became feverish, crying out desperately for Sylvia. Without permission and in breach of the prison regulations forbidding contact between them, the wardresses helped Sylvia along the corridor to Zelie's cell and hovered outside, watching from the door.

Ashamed at having relented, Sylvia determined to recommence her hunger strike immediately. She refused to touch the milk. She was refused permission to say goodbye to Zelie before she left Holloway. It was several days before Zelie, hoping every hour for another visit, discovered cruelly that Sylvia was no longer in the prison.

Sylvia entered Holloway weighing 132 pounds. When she was released on Good Friday, 21 March, she had dropped to 97. After calling in on her studio in Linden Gardens, she went to the Pembridge Gardens nursing home.

The Act allowed the Home Secretary to free the suffragettes when they had starved themselves almost to the point of permanent harm and required them to report back to prison. Once the Cat and Mouse legislation came into force, most of the London 'mice' went to recover under the supervision of Kate Pine, whose hospital was soon nicknamed Mouse Castle. At first Kate Pine did not recognize Sylvia. Within a few hours Hardie was there, weepy and haggard, looking uncharacteristically dishevelled. She apologized for causing him grief. Her mother arrived a little later and was visibly shocked by her condition, despite her familiarity with the British penitentiary regime.

Emmeline herself was temporarily out of prison on Cat and Mouse licence. On 3 April she had been sentenced to three years' penal servitude for conspiracy. She went on hunger strike as soon as she entered Holloway in April, for nine days consuming nothing but water. Released on special licence on 12 April, she avoided rearrest a fortnight later and went to convalesce with Ethel Smyth in Hook Heath, Woking. On the morning of 19 April, the WSPU attempted to blow up a house which Lloyd George was having built for himself near Walton Heath Golf Club, some twenty miles away from Ethel's home. The construction was funded by his friend George Riddell, proprietor of the *News of the*

World, and later to be raised to the peerage. The WSPU activists who carried out the operation claimed that Mrs Pankhurst had no prior knowledge of their plan. As their leader, she accepted responsibility for their actions.

In and out of prison on Cat and Mouse licence over the next five months, hunger striking, refusing medical examination, contracting jaundice from which she never recovered, Emmeline suffered a deterioration in her health almost to the point of death. Hardie, outraged at her barbaric treatment, asked questions and protested relentlessly in parliament and the press. During a spell of detention in July, Emmeline decided to force her release by following Sylvia's example of walking up and down her cell until she collapsed, gasping and barely conscious. The medical officer reported that Emmeline was 'evidently in an emotional state and seemed distressed at her own position and also because she thought her daughter [Sylvia] might be in the same plight as herself'.[865]

Sylvia's constitution changed for ever as a consequence of continuous hunger striking and forced feeding over a period of nearly twenty months. Their shared physical resistance became a bond between mother and daughter. Later in the year, Emmeline addressed 3,000 people at a rally in Madison Square, Manhattan. Her eyes filled with tears when she spoke about the imprisonment and forcible feeding of her daughter Sylvia.[866]

While recovering from her Holloway ordeal, Sylvia now experienced a new torture in the form of extreme anxiety about those she had left behind in Holloway – particularly Zelie. In her memoir, she makes an odd remark about Zelie's suicide attempt: 'What was the matter with her?'[867] Placed in context, it can be seen that Sylvia experienced Zelie's response as an act of attempted abandonment. They were in the same wing of the same prison, fighting the same form of torture with merely the length of a corridor between them. Outside prison, they fought together, shoulder to shoulder, mutually reliant and co-dependent for survival. How could Zelie even think of leaving her? It placed a qualification on their love and on Sylvia's belief in Zelie's resilience not previously present in their relationship.

Deeply troubling to Sylvia was the thought that the attempted suicide made her responsible for Zelie's life. She had encouraged Zelie to leave America and become involved in the British suffragette struggle. To save her life, she would now have to get her out. The suffragette supporter and socialist Dr Charles Mansell-Moullin persistently raised his concerns about the effect of Zelie's skull fracture and other head injuries on her physical and mental health, and suggested to Sylvia that she needed a long period of medical treatment and convalescence back home in America. Charles Mansell-Moullin was the husband of the WSPU activist Edith Mansell-Moullin, who also had served time in Holloway. One of the founders of the Men's League for Women's Suffrage, he protested tirelessly to press and parliament against the violent and abusive treatment of the suffragette women. On 22 November 1910, the *Daily Mirror* had published his letter complaining about the way the police were treating members of the WSPU during demonstrations.

> The women were treated with the greatest brutality. They were pushed about in all directions and thrown down by the police. Their arms were twisted until they were almost broken. Their thumbs were forcibly bent back, and they were tortured in other nameless ways that made one feel sick at the sight … These things were done by the police. There were in addition organised bands of well-dressed roughs who charged backwards and forwards through the deputation like a football team without any attempt being made to stop them by the police; but they contented themselves with throwing the women down and trampling upon them.

Mansell-Moullin had performed emergency surgery on Emily Wilding Davison after she had thrown herself in front of the King's horse, but was unable to save her.

Until this juncture, Zelie represented a fulfilment of what Hardie could not – an undivided loyalty. The fear of suddenly losing those dearest to her that had haunted Sylvia since her father's sudden death cast its shadow over this relationship. For Sylvia, who clung so tenaciously to the principle of life and now felt responsible for Zelie's life, the suicide attempt was a turning point.

Sylvia's articles about her torture were published widely, appearing in the *Daily Mail*, the *Standard*, the *Morning Post*, the *Daily Herald* and *The Suffragette*,[868] among many other national and regional newspapers. Her detailed and frank accounts caused a public furore, and contributed to a revolt of public opinion against forced feeding. The articles struck a blow against the government's attempts to repress popular awareness of what was really happening to the women in Holloway and other prisons. Hardie backed up her reports by stating in the Commons, 'The endurance and heroism these women are showing in prison equals, if it does not excel, anything we have witnessed in the field of battle. When they have fought for their freedom, give them a chance. Do not torture them in prison, and feed them as you would a half-worried rat in a cock-pit, and then let them out, and then take them back once more to prison to undergo all these horrors and tortures.'[869] The *Medical Times* condemned the torture: 'Rather than be party to such an outrage we would resign the most lucrative appointment ever held by a member of the "noble profession".'[870]

Sylvia wrote extensively about the physical effects produced by hunger and thirst strike. She documented her experiences for the period 1913–14 in a typescript entitled 'A Suffragette Year', in which she included professional medical opinion: 'A doctor who has tended the hunger strikers gives the following list of effects produced by hunger and thirst strike: nervous shock, emaciation, weakness, heart trouble, anaemia, dyspepsia, jaundice, constipation, cystitis. The effects which the doctor says are to be feared include heart failure, appendicitis, uraemic coma, convulsions, displacement of organs (through loss of internal fat), mental derangement.'[871]

Alongside Hardie and Lansbury, George Bernard Shaw was one of the most vocal and persistent critics of the government's forcible-feeding policy. Sylvia constantly emphasized the psychological as well as physical effects of the torture in her publicity, and Shaw followed her lead. In a speech at Kingsway Hall delivered on 18 March 1913, he said:

> If you take a woman and you torture her you torture me. These
> denials of fundamental rights are really a violation of the soul. They
> are an attack on that sacred part of life that is common to all of us,
> that part which has no individuality, that which is real, the thing of
> which you speak when you talk of 'the life everlasting' … the denial
> of these fundamental rights to ourselves, in the persons of women,
> is practically a denial of the life everlasting.[872]

In later years, Sylvia grew impatient with Shaw's trimming and temporizing on crucial political issues. In particular, his stupidity over fascism bemused and dismayed her, but she never once hesitated to give him credit for his consistent and uncompromising public support for the suffragette campaign and his condemnation of the state torture of women and refusal of their human rights.

King George was anxious about the impact of the hunger strikers and forcible feeding on public opinion and morale. He'd had a bad time at the state opening of parliament on 10 March. Suffragettes bearing a petition rushed his coach on the Mall. When he got to Westminster, his peers were distinctly thin on the benches for the usually well-attended state occasion. The palace wrote to the Home Secretary expressing the King's welcome for the Prisoners (Temporary Discharge for Ill-Health) Bill:

> His Majesty quite recognizes that the accounts written by women of their sufferings in prison are probably much exaggerated, if not actually untrue, but unfortunately the public see and believe these stories.
>
> The King is glad that your Bill will, to a great extent, do away with the need for 'forcible feeding' and His Majesty trusts that, without publishing the fact, this unpleasant duty will only be resorted to in extreme cases, such as that quoted by you of women convicted of taking or attempting to take Human life and when there is every reason to believe the offence would be repeated on their release.
>
> Are there many cases in which by means of 'Forcible Feeding' the prisoners are able to complete the full term of their sentence?
>
> The King's point is that ... if the women's health breaks down through their starving themselves they will fail to arouse that sympathy which is evinced towards them when they claim 'Forcible Feeding' as the cause.[873]

McKenna's reply informed the King that since the beginning of the year six prisoners had been released after forcible feeding of whom only three had completed their sentence. Those who had not completed their sentence were May Billingshurst, who was paraplegic, Lilian Lenton, who had pneumonia-related pleurisy, and Sylvia Pankhurst, who had served five weeks of an eight-week sentence.[874]

Since the beginning of the militant campaigns, the treatment of working-class prisoners had typically been much harsher than that dispensed to the wealthy and influential. Over the years, this changed.

Aristocratic, elite and middle-class women now regularly went on hunger strike and were subjected to forcible feeding. The exposure of class hypocrisy over the treatment of suffragette prisoners had a comparable impact on women, much as life in the trenches would help knock down class barriers between men. Although on a smaller scale, prison experience radicalized a significant cohort of privileged women into class consciousness. Working women engaged with their notional class superiors as equals or as their leaders in the political hierarchy. Middle-class and elite women previously shielded from the realities of life learned about the real world and their place in it for the first time when they went to prison. Working women engaged with them for the first time in a context other than servitude and impersonality.

Lady Constance Lytton became the symbolic example of the possibility and danger of radical feminist politics to the British establishment and the class system on which it was based. Her brilliant prison memoir, *Prisons & Prisoners*, published by William Heinemann in 1914, is remembered for demonstrating the power and extraordinary self-contained forbearance of women's religious faith when converted to belief in a just secular cause. The suffragette forms of resistance, including Sylvia's, drew heavily on the iconography of Christian martyrdom common in the British radical tradition.

Because she was titled and an extremely wealthy aristocrat, Constance Lytton was persistently placed in prison hospitals when she arrived to serve her sentences. She was separated from other prisoners and not required to do the manual labour and constant cleaning demanded of all ordinary women convicts. To draw attention to this preferential class system, Lady Lytton famously reinvented herself in the guise of plain 'Jane Warton' and joined the ranks of the untitled women prisoners.

Lytton, who had a heart condition, died young as a consequence of imprisonment and the effects of forcible feeding. She suffered a heart attack in August 1910, and subsequently a series of strokes which paralysed the right side of her body. As a consequence, she learned, 'in the most painstaking manner', to write with her left hand.[875] Because she was unable to sit in a chair, she kneeled at her desk to work. 'In my ignorance and impudence,' she states in her Preface, 'I went into prison hoping to help prisoners. So far as I know, I was unable to do anything for them. But the prisoners helped me. They seemed at times the direct channels between me and God Himself, imbued with the most friendly and powerful goodness that I have ever met.'[876]

The radicalization of class-privileged women in Britain ran along parallel historical lines with the Russian women born into noble families who in the same period became revolutionaries. Russia had a long tradition of hunger strikers, including women. One of these, Vera Figner, sentenced to death for her role in the assassination of Alexander II, wrote, 'The idea of martyrdom was instilled in girls by the Christian tradition and was reinforced by the struggle for the rights of the oppressed.'[877] Other aristocratic women turned terrorist revolutionaries were executed for their role in the assassination, but Figner's sentence was commuted and she served twenty years in prison before later becoming an icon of the 1917 February Revolution.

The ethical foundation of Russian radicals in the Christian traditions of dedication and self-sacrifice was mirrored in the suffragette movement. Unlike Constance Lytton, Sylvia was a lifelong atheist, but nonetheless used the symbolic values of religious martyrdom to fashion her own methods of survival. Lytton's Preface describing how a woman could not only endure but transcend imprisonment and torture provides an insight into the self-containment practised by these militants. It eloquently expresses the depth of the desire for freedom from a whole system of oppression. As Lytton shows, even their privileged lives were already a form of imprisonment. Her mantra of feminist self-avowal casts an illuminating light on the extremes of self-command these women, including Sylvia, had to build within themselves to survive:

> Lay hold of your inward self and keep tight hold. Reverence
> yourself. Be just, kind and forgiving to yourself. For the inner you
> of yourself is surely the only means of communication for you with
> any good influence you may once have enjoyed or hope some day to
> find, the only window through which you can look upon a happier
> and more lovable life, the only door through which some day you
> will be able to escape, unbarring it to your own release from all that
> is helpless, selfish and unkind in your present self.
>
> Public opinion, which sent you to prison, and your gaolers, who
> have to keep you there, are mostly concerned with your failings.
> Every hour of prison existence will remind you of these afresh.

Unless you are able to keep alight within yourself the remembrance of acts and thoughts which were good, a belief in your own power to exist freely when you are once more out of prison, how can any other human being help you? If not the inward power, how can any external power avail?

But if you have this comforter within you, hourly keeping up communication with all that you have known and loved of good in your life, with all the possibilities or good that you know of – in your hands, your mind, your heart – then when you are released from prison, however lonely you may be, or poor, or despised by your neighbours, you will have a friend who can really help you.[878]

Sylvia had many friends and supporters. The prison authorities, under the instruction of the Home Office, worked hard to engineer acts of spite designed to undermine her self-confidence and increase her sense of isolation. Hardie, for example, applied formally to the Home Secretary for permission to visit her during one of her spells in prison. McKenna refused him. This was an unworthy snub to a long-serving parliamentarian and the former leader of a political party. The Holloway authorities delayed delivering her parcels and 'mislaid' items brought in person to the prison by friends and supporters. Norah Smyth wrote letters of complaint, demanding that Sylvia be given the parcels and items to which she was entitled.

At one point Sylvia wrote to Hardie, but her letter was returned with 'Insufficiently addressed' scored across the front of the envelope. This was an act of petty cruelty. Most people in Britain knew how to get a letter to Keir Hardie. Scotland Yard knew his residential addresses better than his own family did, as well as the nature of the relationship between Hardie and this Pankhurst. The British state silenced communication between Sylvia and Hardie, drove Zelie to try and kill herself and kept Sylvia apart from Emmeline in the same prison.

Only the prison censor read the sorrowful letter to Hardie that never reached its destination. In it, Sylvia confesses her torture-induced hallucinations, her isolation and paranoia. 'I felt once that a dear friend was beside me in the cell and afterwards there smote upon me sometimes that this dear friend was dead.'[879]

Sylvia's subsequent career demonstrates that it was through her experience of prison that she finally learned to perform that most radical of feminist acts defined by Constance Lytton. She became a reliable friend to herself.

The bulging Home Office files on Sylvia's imprisonments during 1913 and 1914 run to thousands of pages. Some were released in 2005. Most were sealed until 2014. These remarkable records contain not only the letter to Hardie, but also printed forms and reports completed by hand, typed transcripts, marginal notes and commentary from various state institutions and government departments. Between the buff covers are reams of daily correspondence between the Home Office, Downing Street, Windsor Castle, Buckingham Palace, Holloway Prison, Scotland Yard, the Metropolitan Police, newspaper editors, MPs, clergy, doctors and medical specialists – official and private. The files contain carefully annotated newspaper clippings from the national and regional press, with commentary attached written by civil servants on the accuracy of the media reporting. Mixed in with these records is unsolicited correspondence from supportive members of the public protesting against Sylvia's treatment or from self-appointed citizen informers reporting on and condemning her every activity.

Alongside these files we have Sylvia's own correspondence, manuscripts and published writings produced over a period of three decades. Combined, these archival resources provide the most detailed and vivid first-hand account of this ignominious episode of suffragette torture in British history.

When Sylvia went on hunger strike and was forcibly fed, the government's Chief Medical Officer was required to submit reports twice a day, sent to Downing Street by courier or transmitted by telephone. Combined with the other records and official correspondence on her case, these provide an almost hourly account of her life inside Holloway. The Home Office files give us the perspective of the authorities, and offer intriguing insights into the attitudes of the government, senior ministers, mandarins, King George V and a variegated host of Britain's male ruling elite towards suffragette women in general and Sylvia Pankhurst in particular.

The daily medical reports required summary assessments of Sylvia's 'Health' and 'Attitude'. Her 'Attitude' is repeatedly described as 'violently restive' or 'rather spare', a disapproving assessment of her refusal to co-operate or make any effort to be amenable to the regime. Sylvia's 'spareness' evokes an image of her developing emaciation over the course of her multiple imprisonments. It is also an apt description of her Spartan tendencies, illustrated in her reputation for stirring up rebellion.

In the first report from Holloway on 18 February 1913 at the beginning of her two-month sentence for causing malicious damage to that £3 plate-glass window, the prison officer explained his reason for putting her in a solitary cell: 'as she is rather spare I thought it would be better to separate her from the others, as she might have a bad influence over them ... She is being kept strictly isolated from the others.' Sylvia refused food, the report informs, both morning and evening. 'She will be reported tomorrow for misconduct if she continues her present attitude.'[880]

Sylvia's sister detainees, Zelie Emerson (aged twenty-six), Alice Moor (twenty-two), Eva Watson (thirty-eight) and Annie Lansbury (thirty), were all reported as having 'General Conduct' that is 'good'. Alice and Eva had dangerous pre-existing conditions that threatened their health. All of these women were convicted and sentenced together for smashing the same window, and all were on hunger strike but kept in isolation in separate cells. By contrast, Sylvia's 'General Conduct' is most frequently recorded as 'INDIFFERENT'. At other times, she is noted as being, again, 'violently restive'.

Meanwhile, the male suffragette of the group, twenty-seven-year-old Willie Lansbury – Annie's brother – was in the Pentonville Prison hospital, where the doctor expressed his anxiety about whether 'he would be fit for forcible feeding ... if the question arose'. Here, as elsewhere, the medical officers experienced ambivalence and confusion over the prospect of having to force-feed men or aristocratic women. For all other women, the question never arose. Willie, the doctor reported, was 'Emotional and depressed: frequently gives way to tears'. Willie did not have the camaraderie shared by the women in Holloway. Even in solitary, they knew they were in it together, and could sing, shout or occasionally spot each other in the exercise yard.

Between February 1913 and August 1914 Sylvia was subjected to a regime of intense surveillance that breached all notions of individual privacy. She consistently resisted and 'refused all examination', so the doctors built their reports on superficial checks. They assessed the quality of her complexion, the strength or weakness of her voice, her breath odour, her pulse, whether or not she had slept and, if so, for how long, and whether she had defecated and, if so, the quality of her stools. Day after day the doctors disdainfully recorded her 'breath offensive' and her attitude 'sullen', her mucus blood-stained, or noted that she 'looks pinched'. We learn about the variations in her daily pulse rate, her bowel movements and the temperature of her fingers and toes.

This regime of all-encompassing surveillance was intended to render her helpless, and yet we know from Sylvia's own writing how much eluded the sight and understanding of her torturers. Her natural talent for resistance flashes through these degrading reports. When they asked her about her sleep, she responded by telling them that she escaped during the night into visions: 'she states she only slept towards the morning, and was then disturbed by vivid dreams'.[881] An infantilizing tone runs through these statements, representing Sylvia as a wilful child. She acquired 'the art of being sick at will', and indulged in 'voluntary starvation'.[882]

There are hundreds of daily reports in these hefty files, stretching over a period of eighteen months. Yet they are produced with so little variation that they read like endless duplicates of almost the same document. To question 1, 'What is the physical and mental condition of the prisoner?', the answer is most commonly 'Refuses examination'. To question 2, 'Is the prisoner taking food voluntarily?', the form reports 'No'. To question 3, 'If refusing food and water what sorts of food have been offered to the prisoner with a view to inducing a different attitude?', the doctor replies 'various appetizing foods'. It is question 4 that asks for a statement of 'General Conduct' and usually gets the answer 'INDIFFERENT'.[883]

The Home Office played roulette with the lives of these women. After the introduction of the Cat and Mouse Act the reports frequently recommended that Sylvia is 'To be released when she has starved herself to the point of endangering life'. The unfortunately named Dr Forward, one of her prison medical officers, wrote that he used to think Sylvia would go mad at first, and she often seemed to be pretty near to it, as the prison authorities feared. But she 'got over that'. Forward found her 'Intolerably persistent'. Nervous symptoms, extreme insomnia and wild derangement of her digestive functions meant, she claimed, that if they continued to force-feed her, she would die. However, the Home Office physician sent for a second opinion concluded that the process of forced feeding did not endanger her life. Rather, it was the mental excitement which she worked herself into before, during and after each encounter that produced the danger to her health, together with her strenuous, unrelenting 'intolerably persistent' resistance.

While Keir Hardie was asking the Home Secretary in the Commons whether Sylvia was still confined in Holloway and, if so, whether she was being forcibly fed, the Home Secretary was receiving reports of her sullen attitude, 'languid' behaviour and unrelenting insubordination. 'Lies on bed night and day' and 'refuses to undress'. In August 1913 Dr Maurice Craig wrote, 'I have always regarded her as one who might develop mental symptoms if forcibly fed for a lengthened period.' A memorable piece of British understatement: at the time Craig wrote this Sylvia had been forcibly fed twice a day for extended periods over a total of seven months.

The repetitive nature of the files and the understatement belie the true horrors. The torturers became bored and impatient with the endless paperwork. After a few months, the number of reports delivered as hastily transcribed telephone messages increased and the twice-daily written forms became less detailed. The transcripts of telephone messages from Holloway to the Home Office convey succinctly Sylvia's plight: 'her pulse 100 ... looks rather thin ... walking about all night ... symptoms of starvation more pronounced today ... tongue coated ... breath bad. Starvation after tomorrow inadvisable.'[884]

The files swell into a labyrinthine compendium of dates, statistics and subjective opinion as they attempted to control Sylvia's movements. The pattern is always the same. She is discharged from prison on Cat and Mouse licence. Her licence expires. Yet another report is sent from Holloway to the Home Office, stating 'Sylvia Pankhurst did not return to prison yesterday as ordered.' The Home Office direct Scotland Yard to track her down. They do so, and ambush her. She resists arrest and her personal bodyguard of men and women – the People's Army – fight with the police to protect her. Sylvia is rearrested and taken back to Holloway, where she immediately goes back on hunger strike, is forcibly fed, and the whole process begins again.

The long, repetitive lists of dates of her detentions, temporary discharges and rearrest are accompanied by dramatic police reports, newspaper articles and Special Branch memos that provide detailed evidence of her adventures. Here are the accounts of her subterfuge, disguise, wigs, veils, hats, once a faked pregnancy, another time a fake baby who gets thrown across a London bus. There are street fights, violence and capers across London. The files contain screeds of verbatim police transcripts of Sylvia's political speeches, for which she usually received an additional sentence for public incitement, 'stirring up revolt' and using 'inflammatory language'.

There is also a hefty Home Office file dedicated to George Lansbury's June 1914 campaign to draw attention to government double standards and cruelty in their treatment of suffragette women. Determined to bring widespread public attention to the hypocrisy and sex and class prejudice of the vile Cat and Mouse policy, Lansbury wrote an open letter to both the King and the Queen – 'as the leading woman in the land' – in which he compares his case with that of Sylvia Pankhurst.[885]

In 1913 Lansbury was arrested alongside Sylvia and sentenced for the same offence of 'inciting men and women to commit outrages of Suffragette agitation'. He received a sentence of one month: Sylvia received three. Lansbury went on hunger strike in Pentonville, and was released under a Cat and Mouse licence. He was not force-fed, the prison authorities said, because this procedure was not administered except in the case of serious offences. When his licence expired, Lansbury was not rearrested, despite the fact that he had spoken all over the country making exactly the same kind of speeches for which he had been sentenced originally. Therefore, by the time of writing his letter on 11 June 1914, he had still not served his sentence.

Moreover, Lansbury reminded George V and Queen Mary, he had been extremely busy in the meantime encouraging open defiance of the law and organizing resistance to Their Majesties' state. This is confirmed by contemporary Metropolitan Police reports closely documenting Lansbury's activities and verbatim transcripts of his public speeches. In 1913 Lansbury became president of the Rebels' Social and Political Union – the male suffragettes – and from then on was prominently associated with Sylvia Pankhurst's ELFS. On their behalf he took over 400 Old Ford Road, Bow, in his own name. 'Previously', the police files noted, 'Miss S. Pankhurst residing at that address'. Despite all of this, and the expiry of his Cat and Mouse licence, Lansbury had never been rearrested.

By contrast, Sylvia, convicted at the same time for the same offence of incitement, hunger struck and was force-fed. Like him, she was released under Cat and Mouse, 'but in her case she has been taken back to prison at least eight times. Last night she was re-arrested and is now lying in Holloway on hunger strike, and slowly but surely is being starved to death.' The inconsistency in their treatment showed that 'the administration of law in this country has become a farce and a sham'. He went on, 'She is re-arrested in the name of the King and in the same name I am released, and what I wish to ask is why should a man in my position be allowed to go free and a young woman be forced back into prison time after time?'[886] Given this gross instance of 'partiality so alien to the spirit of justice', Lansbury wrote that he was impelled to ask the King to exercise his prerogative to order the unconditional release of Miss Pankhurst or to order his own rearrest immediately.

The King's reply revealed that he was more concerned about national monuments than about the spirit of British justice. His secretary, Lord Stamfordham, wrote from Buckingham Palace to Home Secretary McKenna to ask why Mr Lansbury had not been rearrested under the Cat and Mouse Act and why he was not force-fed when he refused food in prison. More pressingly, however, 'His Majesty is horrified to hear of the Suffragettes' last attempt at Westminster Abbey: the wretched women have no respect for our most ancient and cherished monument.'[887]

McKenna replied to the palace that Lansbury was neither force-fed nor rearrested because his offences were not serious enough. 'The case of Miss Pankhurst is quite different as she persists in open defiance of the law.' Lansbury, the Home Office asserted, had been careful to avoid any language of incitement to crime that would cause his rearrest. This was consistent with the behaviour of other women who had been discharged and not rearrested because 'they intended to refrain from further militant action'.[888]

As any ELF or member of the male suffragettes knew, none of this was remotely accurate. The Metropolitan Police reports on Lansbury's activities erroneously claimed that the Rebels' Social and Political Union was 'otherwise known as "Sylvia's Army"'. This conflated the men's union with the people's militia founded and led by women and properly named, by Sylvia, the People's Army. The police report was accurate in one respect only – this force was by now commonly known to all as 'Sylvia's Army'.

19

Sylvia's Army

Sylvia announced the launch of her People's Army at the end of October 1913:

> I say to you that not until there is a popular uprising will you secure
> for us the vote. That is necessary. There is going to be drilling in
> the East End. We are going to fight and we will do far more than
> the Ulster people. Get on with this drilling. Arm yourselves. Let us
> fight and we shall win.[889]

When Sylvia wrote this call to arms, she was a pacifist. Her father's repeated invocation to 'drudge and drill!' stayed with her from her Victorian childhood. She viewed her proposal for an army of women and men to take to the streets in disciplined formation and show their preparedness to fight largely as a campaigning strategy and publicity stunt: 'The government is so cowardly that even the appearance of force will make it give way.'[890]

The term 'Army', Sylvia wrote, 'was in our case rhetorical rather than militarist'.[891] She did not envisage a civil uprising to overthrow the government by force, like the struggle developing in Ireland, but 'always a popular movement of the character which has preceded the Reform Acts'. The militancy springing up on so many fronts needed channelling to useful effect. 'I saw that our movement was awakening masses of women, and men also, to a desire for better conditions. I saw that the police now shrank from attacking us in the East End; I wanted that shrinking accentuated.'[892] At a practical level, the People's Army aimed at being an organization that men and women could join 'in order to fight for freedom, and in order that they may fit themselves to cope with the brutality of government servants'.[893]

Sylvia's thoughts on the need for a trained workers' army evolved from her experience of the violence used against the suffragettes during that intense pre-war period of militancy. By the end of 1913, the Home Office and Scotland Yard had pushed the suffragettes beyond the point of passive resistance. Speaking alongside Sylvia at a public meeting in front of the East India Dock gates in July that year, Mary Leigh, the first suffragette sentenced to prison for stone throwing, told the cheering audience, 'Get your stones ready. Get your matches ready; get your paraphernalia of which we are such past masters in the use and tonight, let us light a bonfire in London which is bound to be seen by the whole world.'[894] Sylvia encouraged men to join her army: 'I hope that large numbers of men will at once respond too and form themselves into a citizens' corps for this purpose. It is but just that they should do so, for women have always been found to support men in their struggle for political and economic liberty.'[895]

In the course of Sylvia's many arrests, she was roughly handled. Her captures resulted in community street fighting with the police. In January 1914 police raided an ELFS meeting in Shoreditch. An Inspector Riley grabbed Sylvia by the arms and dragged her across a passageway while she yelled, 'Votes for Women!' Riley's detective sidekick threatened her, 'If you call out again, I'll give you a smack across the head.' When she retorted, 'How dare you,' he gagged her with his handkerchief and verbally abused her: 'You're always talking about morals, but your morals are down in the depths of hell.'[896]

This was just one of numerous episodes of violence meted out to militant suffragettes. Sylvia urged women to learn the art of self-defence: 'We have not yet made ourselves a match for the police and we have got to do it. The police know jiu-jitsu. I advise you to learn jiu-jitsu. Women should practise it as well as men.'[897] The west began to learn about the Japanese martial arts of unarmed fighting at close quarters in the nineteenth century. The 'New Art of Self Defence' was introduced into fin-de-siècle London by the English engineer Edward William Barton-Wright, returned from living in Japan. Barton-Wright established a blended martial arts form drawing primarily on Japanese jiu-jitsu, but including other traditions. Influential figures from the British armed services and police attended his lectures and demonstrations and joined his elite training academy, known as the Bartitsu Club. In the early twentieth century, martial-arts training was introduced into the London Metropolitan Police. In 1903 Sir Arthur Conan Doyle famously used 'baritsu' as a plot device in *The Return of Sherlock Holmes* in order to explain how Holmes had escaped falling to his death at the Reichenbach Falls with Professor Moriarty.

The first encounter between the suffragettes and jiu-jitsu took place at a WSPU meeting. Edith Garrud and her husband William, who together ran a martial-arts school in London's Golden Square, were booked to attend, but William was ill, so Edith went alone. He was London's leading jiu-jitsu trainer, having popularized Barton's innovation. 'Edith normally did the demonstrating, while William did the speaking,' explains Tony Wolf. 'But the story goes that ... Emmeline Pankhurst encouraged Edith to do the talking for once, which she did.'[898] Standing 4 foot 11 inches, Garrud began teaching the suffragettes. By 1910 she was regularly running suffragette-only classes and writing for the WSPU's newspaper, *Votes for Women*, which stressed the suitability of jiu-jitsu for women who had to deal with physically larger, more powerful forces in the shape of the hostile police and government. *Health and Strength* magazine printed a satirical article entitled 'Jiu-jitsuffragettes'. *Punch* ran a cartoon of Garrud holding her own against several policemen, captioned 'The suffragette that knew jiu-jitsu'. The term 'suffrajitsu' soon came into common use. The Pankhursts encouraged all suffragettes to learn martial arts, which became a powerful aid to their safety and survival.

Since the implementation of Cat and Mouse policy and the escalation in state-sanctioned brutality that came with it, the ELFS had been developing into an informal militia. Suffragettes turned fire hoses on police who attempted to break up meetings, dropped wooden benches from galleries on to their heads, threw tables and set about thumping them with chairs. They had adopted the Saturday Night as their weapon of choice – that long club of knotted rope dipped in tar and weighted with lead.

The police were particularly brutal to the East End suffragettes. They attacked a free-speech meeting in January 1914 while Sylvia was speaking, beating Mary Leigh unconscious, thrashing Zelie Emerson with a club and breaking the arms of two other women. According to Sylvia, being taunted as 'puss' by the mice in the crowd riled the uniformed constables.

At her trial in February 1914, Zelie Emerson told the court that she had carried a Saturday Night ever since her skull was fractured by a police truncheon at a rally in Victoria Park. The prosecuting lawyer asked her, 'Did you see a notice it was the duty of all friends to go armed?' 'Yes,' she replied, 'I always go to meetings armed ... for over two years I have been closely associated with the People's Army and the WSPU in the East End. I have been called a dirty dog on hundreds of occasions.'[899]

The suffragettes paid close attention to the fact that the Liberal government took no action to prosecute Sir Edward Carson and the Protestant Ulster rebels opposing Home Rule for Ireland for acts of treasonous militancy. Carson had formed a well-trained, disciplined army organized 'to fight to the death against Home Rule'.[900] Sylvia had no truck with Carson's politics, but the tactic of his citizens' army inspired her as a practical tool. As she explained to George Lansbury, 'there would be no fear of suffragettes going back to prison if they had an army like Sir Edward Carson's'.[901]

The historian Barbara Winslow has told the story of drilling in Edwardian Britain, showing how and why it impacted on the period.[902] Drilling was common practice at the time, promoted by organizations such as Sir Robert Baden-Powell's recently established Boy Scouts and – at the other end of the political spectrum – by Robert Blatchford and Clarion Club socialists. The poor state of health of working men revealed by the South African (Boer) Wars in the 1890s shocked the nation, prompting the introduction of drilling across the country, not least by churches and socialist Sunday schools. Christabel and Emmeline, as Sylvia knew, based some of their organizational ideas for the WSPU on the model of William Booth's Salvation Army. The sons of the elite had training corps at public schools, such as Eton and Gordonstoun, and above all there was Sandhurst. Women and working-class people had to organize for themselves.

Most importantly, Sylvia's friend and champion of the militant suffragettes James Connolly provided the key source of inspiration. Connolly first announced the formation of his Irish Citizen Army at a suffragette meeting in Dublin during the Dublin General Strike in November 1913. He highlighted the connections between the right of labour to organize and the right of women to vote. Like the labour movement, women should rely not on any political party but on their own organizational efforts. Sir Francis Fletcher Vane, a former captain in the British army, was also interested in the creation of a working-class 'Labour Army'. 'The Labour Training Corps,' he had written in the *Daily Herald*, 'has been instituted to provide the rank and file of the Labour Party with the means by which they can perfect themselves in that simple form of drill which will enable them … to protect their own comrades when unjustly attacked.'[903]

A hereditary baronet, Sir Francis Fletcher Vane was a democrat with socialist and republican sympathies. A career officer, he spoke on anti-war platforms; a loyal imperialist, he challenged jingoism and was highly critical of the conduct of the British army in the Second Boer War. His ancestor, Sir Henry Vane the younger, was the civilian leader of the Commonwealth bloc in parliament during the English Civil War who retired from politics rather than acknowledge Cromwell as Lord Protector. After the Restoration of the Stuart monarchy he was tried for treason and executed in 1662.

Born in Dublin in 1861 to an Irish mother and an English father, Francis Vane grew up in Sidmouth, Devon, before attending Oxford Military College. He served in the Worcester Militia and Scots Guards, and did a stint in a submarine mining unit of the Royal Engineers. During a residency at Toynbee Hall, east London, in 1886 he founded a Working Boys Cadet Corps. He served in South Africa through most of the Second Boer War and became a magistrate, but was sacked for being 'pro-Boer'. From 1902 to 1904 he was a correspondent in South Africa for the *Manchester Guardian*, *Daily News*, *Westminster Gazette* and *Truth*. He wrote a pamphlet attacking British war methods published by the South African Newspaper Company, followed up later by an expanded version entitled *Pax Britannica*. Vane stood unsuccessfully as the Liberal candidate for Burton on Trent in the 1906 general election, following which he became active in suffragette and, later, anti-war campaigns. In 1909 he became London Commissioner of Scouts in Baden-Powell's organization, from which he was sacked for not following policy, having objected vociferously to the growing militarism. He became President of the (separate) British Boy Scouts in 1909 and merged them with the Boys' Life Brigade to form the National Peace Scouts. A year later he founded the Italian Scout movement, called Little Scouts of Peace.

From 1918 to 1927 he lived and worked in Italy, but left in 1927 when the Fascists suppressed the Italian Scout movement.[904]

The Times published Sylvia's East End speech calling for her volunteer force: 'If there is any man here who has been in the Army or knows anything about drilling, will he please communicate with me and we will start drilling!'[905] Francis Vane responded to her appeal, offering a cohort of army officers to train her people, with him in command. Vane drafted a pledge for new recruits: 'I promise to serve the common cause of Justice and my Comrades under our duly elected Officers. I will be a friend to all and ... to every member of the People's Army. I am a sincere believer in a Vote for every Woman and every Man.'[906]

The inaugural meeting of the new militia took place at Bow Baths on 5 November 1913. Norah Smyth was appointed captain of the army. Sylvia, 'disguised as a very sporting lady', arrived at the meeting in an open-topped racing car with Francis Vane and some of his ex-military friends. The government was furious that Sylvia had once again eluded arrest despite the expiration of her Cat and Mouse licence. The Home Office ordered 300 mounted police to descend on the meeting, giving the new army immediate opportunity to try out their manoeuvres. The People's Army unseated some of the mounted police and drove the rest out of the neighbourhood. Dressed as Sylvia's decoy, George Lansbury's daughter Daisy was seized and arrested, enabling the real Sylvia to lead the victory parade through Bow the next day.

The same month at a rally in Bow Baths, Sylvia announced that the army was nearly strong enough to march on parliament, in response to which, reported the *East London News*, the crowd lifted her enthusiastically on to their shoulders and carried her home singing the Red Flag.[907]

The army drilled weekly on Tuesday nights. Training usually consisted of around 100 people marching in formation, carrying clubs. By the following winter of 1914 around 700 women had joined. The *Daily Herald* boasted that the police were wary of the new militia, and claimed that it had 'already put the fear of God into the hearts of the special Scotland Yard variety quartered in the East End'.[908] The East End women appeared also to have scared their usually stout-hearted drillmaster. After a few training sessions, Francis Vane took fright at their intense seriousness. He was committed to drilling and scouting as non-military community- and solidarity-building exercises developed over time. He believed in mediation for all conflict where possible. He had not previously encountered activist women like this. They were too fighty. Understandably, he was alarmed by their urgent need to battle with police and, potentially, soldiers deployed at demonstrations. The violence done to the suffragettes shocked him. Vane had also agreed with local trade unionists to form them into a corps for deployment in trade disputes, but underestimated how quickly they needed to get to work and on to the front line of industrial battles.

To resolve his caution, Vane presented Sylvia and Norah with a list of names of army officers who would drill the corps and promptly disappeared to Italy, whence he sent nervous dispatches with apologies and general advice on how to proceed: 'You see I did not know your rapid methods, and my interview with the Trade Unionists led me to suppose that they would move slowly but surely ... I had a card from Mr Lansbury asking me to come back as soon as possible. But I cannot until after Christmas.'[909] Smyth responded brusquely, regarding him as feeble, ignoring his congratulations, advice and instructions and merely informing him that 'Major Roskell (whom we call Mr Rendall, as he did not wish his name mentioned) is drilling us at present ... Mr Nevinson hopes to help us after Christmas.'[910] Sylvia dismissed Vane as a 'broken reed who offered much and did nothing'.[911] This judgement would change when Vane staked his army career on attempting bravely to prevent a cover-up of military murders in Dublin during the Easter Rebellion in 1916. He was in command at Portobello Barracks in Dublin during the Uprising. He tried to have a Captain Bowen-Colthurst arrested for the murder of Francis Sheehy Skeffington and others. Bowen-Colthurst's arrest occurred only after Vane had travelled to London to report the murder directly to the War Office. As a result, Vane was dismissed from the army. He dedicated himself to writing a book on the 1916 rebellion, *The Easter Rising*, but publication was prevented by the Army Censor in 1917 and the manuscript destroyed. His book *War Stories*, documenting incidents from South Africa, the First World War and the Easter Uprising, was also suppressed. At the 1918 general election Vane chaired meetings for Labour and Liberal candidates. He died in 1934.

Poplar Borough Council also became worried about the strength of Sylvia's women, especially after police started setting up roadblocks in the East End in an attempt to prevent the People's Army from drilling.

In the winter of 1914 the council passed resolutions banning local halls from renting their venues to individuals or organizations associated with militancy. The new regulations also forbade any organization that sympathized with the militant suffragette movement from holding a public meeting in the borough. The ELFS retaliated by systematically disrupting any meeting held in a public hall unless a suffragette speech was given.

Local allies of the suffragettes deluged the council with letters and depositions of complaint. The Poplar Trades Council, the Labour Representation Committee, the Cubitt Town branch of the Gas Workers' Union, the Poplar Labour League and the East End branch of the Electrical Trades Union all objected in solidarity with the East End suffragettes. The Men's League for Women's Suffrage, the Rebels' Social and Political Union and the British Socialist Party followed these up with a request that Poplar Borough Council meet a deputation. The councillors agreed, but at the meeting refused to change their decision. When next they convened, George Lansbury tried unsuccessfully to persuade them to rescind their restrictive policy.

In response, the People's Army launched an offensive inside the council chamber. Seven years before the birth of legendary 'Poplarism', Old Poplar town hall, with its high Victorian Gothic architecture, Venetian details and copper-domed octagonal tower, became the site of a suffragette battle launched from the gallery of the council chamber. The troops shot off popguns, bags of flour, red ochre, blue paint powder and a variety of other ingenious, harmless substances. Rushing the councillors, they overturned ink pots, tore up agendas and threw official papers and chairs into the air. Councillors who attempted to lash out at them physically were set about with Saturday Night clubs. At the heart of the fracas, three well-known male anti-woman's-suffrage councillors came off worst after engaging in hand-to-hand combat with female members of the People's Army. As a consequence, the council banned the public from attending all council meetings. Disgusted by the decision, Lansbury strode to the town clerk's desk, ripped up all his papers and stalked out of the chaotic chamber. Famously, he would be back when he became the first Labour Mayor of Poplar in 1919.

Inevitably, the right-wing press attacked the People's Army. *The Times* ran an editorial denouncing and ridiculing the notion of women being in an army. It described them contemptuously as Amazonian lesbians wielding broomsticks. The ELFS swiftly responded:

> In reply to your extraordinary editorial comments ... the People's Army is not composed of Athletic Amazons as you say but of working women and men who have been toiling all their lives for their daily bread and have hitherto found neither time, energy, nor superfluous cash to cultivate athletics ... So far as the weapons employed by our recruits have not been broomsticks but life preservers made of India rubber or rope – in some cases weighted with lead pokers and good stout sticks. You refer to the formation of our army as 'flat-footed tomfoolery' and 'the negation of everything that makes for popular advancement of advantage'. You would do better to abuse the Liberal government for its refusal to grant freedom for women, its introduction of the crude and disgusting practice of forcible feeding and for its brutal treatment of the Dublin strikers.[912]

In 1914 the ELFS launched another brigade to which the national press paid absolutely no attention. Sylvia named it the Junior Suffragettes Club. A photograph shows a smiling group of the Bow Junior Suffragettes in Victoria Park. Some of the girls proudly hold copies of their broadsheet magazine. Sylvia had encouraged them to launch their own junior newspaper, providing funding from the ELFS and assisting them with editing and printing.

Among members of the Junior Suffragettes Club, green-eyed, russet-haired factory worker Rose Pengelly became a favourite of Sylvia's. Rose, who lived with her extended family on Ranwell Street in Bow, joined the Junior Suffragettes as a founder member, at the age of twelve. She had worked at the Backs Asbestos Pipe Factory on Old Ford Road. In an issue of *Woman's Dreadnought* she described how she had to pack the heavy 'saggers of ware' and carry them to the furnace.[913] She was made to run errands for the factory housekeeper, peeled potatoes and washed the factory owner's shirts and bed sheets. She referred to him as 'the governor'.

At the age of fourteen in 1914, Rose led her colleagues out on a strike, marching them in procession down the road to the ELFS Women's Hall, her red hair blazing the trail. The women took the action in support of male co-workers striking for higher and equal pay. For this action Rose was sacked and gained the nickname 'Little Sylvia', by which she was known ever after.

Sylvia describes meeting Rose shortly after she was sacked. ' "What are you doing in Ranwell Street?" I asked her, knowing the chronic poverty of that little alley. "All out of work, all helping each other," she chirruped gaily, flashing a merry smile to me from her clear green eyes, her red plaits tossing. Yet I saw she was pale, and her gait not as buoyant as usual.'[914] Sylvia encouraged her to lead the Junior Suffragettes. A brave activist, Rose loved dancing and was a talented musician, often playing the pan flute at fundraising picnics.

In the spring of 1914 Old Ford Road was advertised as the site of the new ELFS headquarters and community hall. There was a library, and an auditorium for lectures and concerts. The Junior Suffragettes Club and Women's Hall were there for the use of everyone in the community. The official opening and house-warming was held on Sylvia's birthday, 5 May 1914. The next day Zelie sadly set off back to America. She'd agreed to leave with extreme reluctance. Her health was broken. She was strained and her figure shrunken. She'd sustained serious injuries from fighting with the police and from prison torture by forcible feeding. 'I had the greatest difficulty to induce her to go,' Sylvia wrote, 'and suffered many a painful hour of distressful heart-searching on her account. I was grieved to lose her.'[915]

Zelie would come back to England to help the ELFS during the First World War. After her return to America following the war, she sent a letter that Sylvia preserved among her papers:

> Dear Sylvia,
>   I have not heard from you so I conclude that you do not wish to see me. However I would like to know what was the cause for your not wanting me to speak for us any more … I know I am a 'self righteous little prig' but would like to know what else I am to you … Of course you know that nothing that has happened or may happen between us can ever alter my feeling toward you and perhaps some day … I may be of service to you and the cause for that is after all the only thing that really matters …

The letter ends with a painful poem:

To Sylvia Pankhurst

I

You did not understand, and in your eyes
I saw a vague surprise,
As if my voice came from some distant sphere,
Too far for you to hear;
Alas! In other days it was not so
Those days of long ago

II

Time was when all my being was thrown wide
All veils were drawn aside
That you might enter anywhere at will
Now all is hushed and still
Save for a sound recurring more and more
The shutting of a door

As ever. Yours Zelie Emerson.
PS. Thanks for the hair.[916]

Sylvia maintained her silence and left no explanation about Zelie. In one so loyal and consistent in her deep attachments, there is about the private mystery something suggestive of a case where 'a woman may do that for love's sake that shall kill love'.[917] Sylvia never mentioned having sent Zelie a lock of her hair. But she did not destroy Zelie's letter and by keeping it in her archive preserved the mystery for posterity.

Immediately after her release from Holloway on licence on 30 May 1914, Sylvia launched a campaign to organize a deputation of working people to the Prime Minister. Delegates were elected by direct ballot at a series of great open rally meetings held in the East End. Sylvia took this action in response to Asquith's objection that the popular women's suffrage movement 'was not democratic, and the movement not of the masses, but of the classes'.[918]

The mass meetings selected the candidates for the deputation and unanimously endorsed the demand for a vote for every woman over twenty-one. Sylvia wrote to Asquith requesting him to receive the deputation on the evening of 10 June 1914, or any earlier date convenient for him. He refused.

In her reply, Sylvia detailed the scale of the movement and the will of the women and men who attended so many meetings in halls and outdoor rallies. 'A large proportion of the women of East London are living under terrible conditions … The women are impatient to take a constitutional part in moulding the conditions under which they have to live … I cannot think that that if you realized the strength and earnestness of the movement here … it would fail to make an impression on you.'[919] She issued an ultimatum, so far unprecedented in her political career:

> I regard this deputation as of such importance that I have
> determined should you refuse to receive the deputation and I be
> snatched away from the people … and taken back to Holloway, my
> 'Cat and Mouse' licence having expired, I will not merely hunger
> strike in Holloway, as I have done eight times under this present
> sentence, but when I am released, I shall continue my hunger strike
> at the door of the Strangers' Entrance to the House of Commons,
> and shall not take either food or water until you agree to meet this
> deputation. I know very well from what has happened in the past
> that I am risking my life in coming to this conclusion because, so
> far, you have almost invariably refused the appeals which Suffragists
> have made to you. At the same time I feel it my duty to take this
> course, and I shall not give way, although it may end in my death.[920]

Once again, Asquith refused. Sylvia wrote to Hardie, Will Thorne, the Bishop of London and the Bishop of Kensington asking them to join her procession to parliament. Hardie was away so unable to attend. The others, most of whom who had previously supported her, failed altogether to reply. Perhaps Sylvia's public threat that this was a cause for which she was now prepared to die seemed too extreme. Perhaps it frightened them. Christabel, on the other hand, supported the logic of militancy, even if she didn't support her sister. She wrote to Emmeline Pethick-Lawrence from her Parisian exile, 'You know, anti-militancy does affect the reasoning faculty adversely.'[921]

On all fronts, temperatures ran high. When Asquith's second refusal was announced at the next open rally, the women present nearly turned on a nurse whom they suspected of being a police spy. Sylvia had to call in stewards to prevent them from beating her up.

On the evening of 10 June, Sylvia was brought out on to the street on a stretcher carried on the shoulders of four men, among them Henry Nevinson. The Reverend C. A. Wills jeopardized his livelihood by saying a prayer to the crowd from an upstairs window. The procession got no further than Grove Road before the waiting police swept down on them, knocked Sylvia from her stretcher and bundled her into a taxi where detectives waited to return her directly to Holloway.

The procession reformed, and continued to Westminster, accompanied by throngs of protesters gathered along the route, lining the streets of east London and the City, Fleet Street, the Strand and on to parliament. Ranks of police lined the route. Only George Lansbury, as an ex-MP, was allowed through. The women made speeches in Parliament Square, thus breaking the law. When Asquith received the politely written request to meet the deputation, he once again refused.

Sylvia was released at dusk on 18 June, dangerously weak and in excruciating pain. Reluctantly, Norah followed her instruction to drive her directly to Westminster, where a group of women awaited her, accompanied by Josiah Wedgwood and Keir Hardie. Her condition horrified them. Hardie went back into the palace and approached the Prime Minister to try and persuade him to speak with Sylvia and her representatives. Asquith retorted that Sylvia was blacklisted for having thrown a lump of cement at the Speaker's painting, and moreover she still owed the Speaker a written apology for having broken the rules of the House.

Hardie brought this message back to Sylvia, who agreed to write the apology note on the spot. She then instructed them to lay her stretcher down by the plinth of the statue of Oliver Cromwell near the Strangers' Entrance where she would remain, without eating or drinking, until either Asquith agreed to meet the East End deputation, the police forcibly removed her or she died. 'My mind was concentrated on the object, emotionless and unfearing, like one who is running a race.'[922]

George Lansbury joined Hardie and Wedgwood and all three went once more to the Prime Minister, conveying Sylvia's apology and the terms of her lie-in. They returned with the news that Asquith had finally relented: he would see six of the elected delegates the following Saturday, 20 June. Amid cheering and laughter, Sylvia was lifted into

Norah's car. On the way back to the East End she asked, 'Do you not think we could stop for a drink of water now?'[923]

The suffragette activist and Poor Law Guardian Julia Scurr led the elected deputation to Downing Street on 20 June. Her husband John later became a Labour MP. Mrs Jane Savoy, a brush maker, described by her neighbour George Lansbury as 'the best woman in Old Ford', was undeterred by her dropsy and painful heart condition. Mrs Byrd was a mother of six, living on her husband's weekly wage of £1 10 shillings. Mrs Daisy Parsons, born Marguerite Millo, was later elected as a socialist borough councillor on the West Ham Council and in 1935 would become West Ham's first woman mayor. Elsie Watkins and Jessie Payne completed the six. George Lansbury was also at Downing Street for this historic meeting.

Julia Scurr made and received the introductions, and was first to speak. Sylvia helped prepared her statement:

> Parliament is constantly dealing with questions affecting the education and care of our children, with the houses in which we live, and more and more with every item of our daily lives. Our husbands die on average at a much earlier age than do men of other classes. Modern industrialism kills them off rapidly, both by accident and overwork. We can here speak with much feeling on these matters for we know by bitter experience the terrible struggle with absolute want that our widowed sisters have to face through no fault of their own. We feel most earnestly that it is gravely unjust to pass legislation in matters of this kind without consulting the women of this country. We would further point out that whilst women are taxed on exactly the same basis as men, and like men are obliged to obey the laws, they are allowed no voice in these questions.

Jessie Payne told of her terrible life as a sweated labourer working as a cigarette packer in a factory where she had earned less than a shilling a day. Men were allowed time for lunch but women were not. Because they had nowhere to eat, they had to consume their food in the lavatory. Jessie Payne emphasized that trade unions would not tolerate such conditions. She went on to describe her life with her daughter, who suffered debilitating mental illness. Medical doctors recognized only the authority of fathers, causing enormous problems for mothers who had no voice in trying to look after their sick children. 'I think we ought to have a voice in the different laws for women, because when you make laws, such as this Mental Deficiency Bill, it is all very well to make them; but unless you have had dealings with the mentally deficient people you do not know what they really need.'

Jane Savoy stepped forward, and from her handbag produced a brush:

I am a brush maker, and I work from eight in the morning till six at night making brushes ten hours a day, and while I work I have to cut my hands with wire, as the bristles are very soft to get in. I have brought brushes to show to you. This is a brush I have to make for 2d, and it is worth 10s 6d. As I have to work so hard to support myself I think it is very wrong that I cannot have a voice in the making of the laws that I have to uphold. I do not like having to work ... without having a voice on it, and I think when a woman works ... she has a right to a vote, as her husband has. We want votes for women.

One by one they told their stories to Asquith. His hostility softened. It was the first time in his sheltered, privileged life that he had listened to articulate working women talking about their lives. 'I think it is a very moderate and well-reasoned presentation of your case and I will give it, you may be quite sure, very careful and mature consideration.'[924] Then came the equivocation: 'If you are going to give the franchise to women, you must give it to them on the same terms that you do to men ... That is, make it a democratic measure ... If the change has to come, we must face it boldly, and make it thoroughgoing and democratic in its basis.'[925]

A general election was expected before the end of the year, so Sylvia knew they had to keep up the pressure. For the moment, it looked for as though the ELFS had the government on side. This was astute political manoeuvring: Sylvia had given Asquith an alternative to appearing to cave in to WSPU militancy.

George Lansbury followed up immediately by organizing a breakfast meeting at the House of Commons attended by himself, the Chancellor Lloyd George and Sylvia. The outcome was that Lloyd George agreed to put his full support behind a Reform Bill including women's enfranchisement and a pledge to resign if he failed. Lansbury interpreted the meeting more positively than Sylvia. Lloyd George's offer was conditional on the end of militancy, and he wanted Christabel to deliver to him in person the commitment to a truce.

Sylvia felt she had fluffed it, and she was right. On the morning of the breakfast meeting, Norah wasn't around to drive her to the House of Commons. Worried about money, Sylvia took a long bus trip from Bow to Parliament and arrived hungry and tired. Lloyd George sat in front of a window, the light from which burned her damaged eyes. She failed to ask him for a written guarantee and she was too unguarded with him, stating frankly that she doubted Christabel would concede unless the government made the first move and showed goodwill through implementing a legislative measure. Lloyd George briskly deflected this by stating he would only discuss the matter personally with Christabel himself, fully aware that such a meeting was unlikely to take place. Sylvia realized as she left that she was empty-handed. Lansbury wrote immediately and enthusiastically to Christabel who, predictably, answered as Sylvia had anticipated, 'No truce'. This time Sylvia offered to visit Paris to talk with Christabel in person, but she responded with a telegram sent to Norah, not to Sylvia: 'Tell your friend not to come.'[926]

In mid-July, Emmeline Pankhurst, exhausted, escaped across the Channel to join Christabel in Brittany. Sylvia gatecrashed a garden party given by the Bishop of London, who may have regretted ignoring her letter asking him to support her petition to Asquith. On 26 July, disregarding the expiration of her Cat and Mouse licence, Sylvia, together with Norah and the ELFS, including the Junior Suffragettes, went for a picnic in Epping Forest, a place Sylvia loved. Among her drawings and sketches there are many studies of its hornbeams and beeches. In the evening she spoke at Helions Bumpstead to striking Essex agricultural labourers. The 1914 north-west Essex farmworkers' strike was by now national news. There had been near rioting and police patrolled the country lanes in force. Many speakers had been to address the strikers, including George Lansbury and John Scurr, but the largest meeting of the strike gathered to hear Sylvia speak on the green outside the Pig & Whistle pub. Afterwards, she led a procession of

2,000 through the village. The strike organizer asked her to send down some of her suffragettes to set fire to hayricks and scare the farmers, who would think it had been done by the labourers. 'I answered that our organization did not commit arson.'[927]

On the same day, British soldiers from the King's Own Scottish Borderers shot dead four civilians and injured more than thirty other unarmed protesters on Bachelor's Walk in Dublin. This massacre would shortly come to dominate Sylvia's activities.

At the end of July, Sylvia and Norah went on a trip to Penshurst in Kent, near her favourite Cinder Hill. They booked into the Leicester Arms under assumed names. Hardie planned to join them. He tripped up by sending a telegram to 'Pankhurst'. The innkeeper panicked; his landlord Philip Sidney, Baron De L'Isle would be furious if he had them as guests. Suffragettes had recently attempted to set fire to Penshurst Place, ancestral home of the Sidney family since 1552. The innkeeper begged them to keep their aliases, not to wear any ELFS badges or anything that would give them away and to keep quiet about Hardie's identity. When Hardie arrived, the three discussed the next election and agreed that the call for universal suffrage for both men and women should be the Labour Party's main manifesto call. Universal suffrage for men over twenty-one did not come until 1918, and was only extended to women in 1928.

As Hardie left for an emergency meeting of the International Socialist Bureau in Brussels to discuss the Balkan crisis, he warned them of the worsening international situation. He returned early from Brussels to London, to keep his commitment to spend the weekend with Aggie Hughes at Nevill's Court. They went to the Fleet Street Picture Palace and he took her for a smart supper at the Savoy Hotel. They returned to Nevill's Court to find the press waiting at the door. The French socialist leader Jean Jaurès had been assassinated in Paris. One of Hardie's oldest political friends, Jaurès had been due to preside at the 9 August meeting of the International, convened to oppose impending war. In June, the British press had missed the significance of the assassination of Archduke Ferdinand and his wife in Sarajevo by the Serbian secret society the Black Hand, concentrating instead on events in Ireland. Austria declared war on Serbia in June and Russia was the next to be drawn in.

On her return from their trip to Penshurst, Sylvia departed immediately for Dublin to investigate the Bachelor's Walk massacre and participate in organized protest against the government's response.

Hardie was now under steadily intensifying attack for his pacifism. He still believed the worldwide working class was strong enough to impose 'international peace by the threat of social war'.[928] The press battered him in print and he was abused in public as never before. Tories, Liberals and – worse – his own fellow Labour Party members bashed him in the Commons. The bulk of the trade union leadership turned against him. Ramsay MacDonald began to receive some of the same treatment. Hardie was hooted at and hustled constantly, right up to his front door at Nevill's Court. He and MacDonald were attacked on the street when recognized, and, following physical assault and death threats, had to take precautions. They appealed for protection. Sympathetic Labour and Liberal MPs waited for them to finish their business in the House at night and walked them home from parliament. Old friends like the ILP stalwart Bruce Glasier travelled with Hardie on trains as bodyguard. MacDonald suffered deeply from the ostracism. In future he sheltered himself by moving to the centre.[929]

On Sunday 2 August, the ILP held anti-war demonstrations and meetings throughout Britain, while the cabinet met three times in one day. The veteran anti-war activist Emily Hobhouse sent desperate letters to everyone who might be persuaded to avert the catastrophe, including her old ally Lloyd George, who had so vehemently opposed the Second Boer War. 'Few English people have seen war in its nakedness,' she wrote to the *Manchester Guardian*, supporting its call for British neutrality and reminding readers of her experience of the Second Boer War. 'They know nothing of the poverty, destruction, disease, pain, misery and mortality which follow in its train … I have seen all of this and more.'[930] Crowds gathered outside newspaper offices for the latest information.

That same Sunday a huge rally convened in Trafalgar Square, presenting a united democratic front of speakers from every shade and faction of Labour Party, trade union and socialist opinion – all their usual differences buried as they teamed up to oppose a capitalist war. On Monday 3 August Germany declared war on France. The same day, Hardie spoke passionately against war once again in the Commons and the terrible suffering it would bring to the poor. As he spoke, 'a cold, cold wind began blowing at his back. It was the sound of the National

Anthem being sung – softly.' Will Crooks and Labour MPs from his own side led the singing.[931]

Early on the morning of 4 August, German troops crossed the Belgian frontier. Opinion in the British cabinet now swung overwhelmingly towards intervention. The following day, Britain declared war on Germany. Sylvia heard the news in Dublin. On 7 August the Home Secretary Reginald McKenna offered an amnesty to suffragette prisoners only on condition that that they would undertake not to commit further crimes or outrages. The WSPU leadership asked Mrs Mansel, cousin of the Liberal Chief Whip, to contact the Archbishop of Canterbury and invite him to act as an intermediary with the government. They reached a deal: release and reprieve for all who agreed to shelve their militant suffrage campaigning with immediate effect and to work for the war effort. On 10 August McKenna announced that within a few days all suffrage prisoners would be released unconditionally. Two days later, Emmeline Pankhurst sent a letter to all WSPU members calling for a suspension to militancy until further notice.[932]

On 8 September Christabel reappeared at the London Opera House, for the first time after her long exile, 'to utter,' Sylvia wrote, 'a declaration, not on women's enfranchisement, but on "The German Peril".'[933] Mrs Pankhurst toured the country, making recruiting speeches.

PART FOUR

In the Red Twilight 1914–1924

European war will almost certainly lead to European revolution, the end of which no man can foresee.

Keir Hardie

20

Peacework

As for so many other millions of people, Sylvia's wartime experience ushered in a period of enormous transition in her life.

In March 1916 the East London Federation of Suffragettes became the Workers' Suffrage Federation. In July 1917 their newspaper, the *Woman's Dreadnought*, became the *Workers' Dreadnought*. A year later, the organization was once again renamed, becoming the Workers' Socialist Federation, operational until 1921. The change from suffrage to socialism was more significant than that from women to workers. Sylvia credited ELFS activist Mary Phillips with coming up with the newspaper's name when they launched it in 1914.[934] 'It would not have been my choice, but the members generally acclaimed it, and I fell in with their view.' She 'wished it had been "The Workers' Mate" … "Mate" was a favourite term of address with our people in the East End, and to my mind a most genial and sympathetic one.'[935]

These name changes signpost clearly Sylvia's wartime political evolution and the development of the ELFS from an East End socialist suffragette campaign group to a national federation for revolutionary socialist transformation led by a woman who was now recognized as Britain's leading left-wing feminist anti-war agitator.

Sylvia entered the First World War a socialist and reluctantly militant reformist and Labour Party-supporting suffragist and emerged from it a left-wing revolutionary communist.[936] Her feminism remained constant. Since 1906 she'd argued feminism that did not put grass-roots organization by working women front and centre and challenge existing hierarchies based on race and class was no sort of feminism at all. Sylvia's war was fought in the home-front trenches of a conflict that forever shattered the battle lines of class in Britain.

On the declaration of war, Sylvia was in Dublin immersed in investigative journalism focused on the recent Bachelor's Walk massacre. On 26 July 1914 British troops returning to barracks suddenly opened fire on a jeering civilian crowd of, mainly, children. Sylvia's series of articles in the *Woman's Dreadnought* dug deeply into the facts and reconstructed carefully what had happened. Through her painstaking and extensive interviews, including with the mothers and relatives of the dead and injured children, she produced a detailed exposé that blew the lid off the heavily censored official versions of events.

Since childhood a supporter of Home Rule and Irish republicanism, Sylvia maintained close links with Irish activists – nationalists, suffragists and feminists. Scotland Yard surveillance recorded that Miss Sylvia Pankhurst had been the house guest of her friend Maude Gonne when she went to Dublin to address a meeting on votes for women. Her movements in Ireland were always closely followed, but not always successfully, as later events would demonstrate.

On the declaration of war, Sylvia admitted that she'd failed to heed Hardie's 'heart-wrung warnings of the great catastrophe' approaching.[937] Her horizon had narrowed 'to the fierce, immediate struggle' for the women's vote.[938] Stunned by the 5 August announcement of hostilities, she took passage back to England that night on a crammed boat amid a riot of wildly drunk young recruits, some in brand-new khaki, others still in civvies.

In a scene reprising her childhood fears of drunken revellers, Sylvia expressed her anxiety at 'grossly intoxicated' mobs, 'incognisant as oxen'.[939] Women at the dockside clinging miserably to departing sons, lovers and husbands, the sad keening of the men on the ship off to likely death or permanent maiming, their purpose 'untouched by the cleansing fires of enthusiasm'.[940] A multitude of masculinity, 'each one leaving behind him the desolate grief of women'.[941]

For the next four years women and children left behind on the home front became Sylvia's political priority. She expressed her horror at the consequences of war:

> The lads would be pressed as slaves to the hideous work of carnage;
> the maidens, their fair eyes red with the scalding tears of new

bereavement, left to the sad loneliness and loss of their unfruited love. Throughout Europe would be a vast widowhood, the cries of fatherless children, the groans of injured men; a gigantic arrest of human progress; a huge vanquishing of the higher life of culture, and the finer processes of thought; a triumph, sadly immense, of the annihilating power of violence, maintained by great stores of wealth, drawn up from any and every source, and ultimately from the hard toil and harsh privations of the people; beneath all a great hunger, till famine prove the victor.[942]

During the sleepless overnight voyage, Sylvia travelled in her imagination once again through the countries she and Norah Smyth had visited in the spring. They had made a grand tour of European radicals and movements, visiting Hungary, Austria, Germany, Belgium and France: 'bitterly would they suffer under the guns of contending armies! Women struggling for emancipation, Socialists, educationists, libertarians and reformers of every school, each and all had spoken of universal peace.'[943]

Back at the ELFS HQ, Sylvia found that her women friends who had been united over the struggle for the vote were now divided over the question of supporting or opposing the war. She, sat on the sofa between Norah Smyth and Jessie Payne, argued, 'This war, like the Boer War and all the others we have known, is fought for material gains. It is not glorious and noble, but a hideous blot on the escutcheon of the European governments, a huge and shameful loss to humanity.'[944]

Norah challenged Sylvia's teatime lecture: 'If Mrs Payne and I were France and Germany, and you were Belgium, would you think it right for us to fight out our quarrel on top of you?'[945]

'You must look deeper and further into it than that, Smyth, if you want to understand it,' Sylvia retorted.

Attempting to make the peace, Jessie put her deft shoemaker's hand soothingly on Sylvia's knee, patiently and affectionately explaining the situation to her in a perfect parroting of press rhetoric depicting the miseries of poor little 'Plucky Belgium'. Jessie was caught up in the atmosphere of excitement whipped up on the streets by the catastrophe: 'What would you do if you saw a great strong man killing a baby?' she asked. Norah chipped in with an arresting image. 'Suppose I pointed a pistol at you?' Then the two women chimed together, with variations on the theme of 'They started it first: are we to let them carry on until they've killed everyone?'[946] This was not just a debate among friends. Norah and Jessie were Sylvia's co-founders, officers and leading spokeswomen of the ELFS. They represented the pro-war views of many of their members and supporters, both working and middle class.

Having long before disowned their former allegiance to the labour and socialist movements, Mrs Pankhurst and Christabel were natural supporters of a capitalist, nationalist war. In their view, women's patriotic war service would earn them the right to the vote after it ended. The whole nation now was militant, and it was far more important to fight the Greater Prussian Patriarchy than to battle Englishmen at home, vulnerable in their hour of need and requiring more than ever the support of a sanguine, bellicose matriarchy to stiffen its resolve. '[S]uffragettes,' Christabel explained, 'believe that it is our duty to do all we can to rouse the individual citizen to fight for the freedom and the independence of this country and this Empire ... as militant women, we may perhaps be able to do something to rouse the spirit of militancy in men.'[947]

However, before 1914 most socialists, progressive trade unionists and radical feminists supported the pacifist argument that the ruling classes and those with capitalist interests used war as a mechanism to resolve domestic problems at home and challenges to imperial interests abroad. The policy of the Second International was that workers of all countries should unite and strike against war. Socialists opposed the capitalist warmongering of governments and the nationalism stirred up to get people on side and fighting. But now, as Sylvia wrote, 'Internationalism seemed vanquished; its most prominent sponsors turned war mongers.'[948]

Not only her family but old friends and people she admired, including H. G. Wells and Peter Kropotkin, turned fiercely jingo. 'They flinched from the huge conception that a perpetual reaching out for new fields of exploitation was inherent to the Capitalist system.'[949] To Sylvia it seemed evident that free-market rivalry and imperialism, bolstered by rabble-rousing patriotic nationalism, was the 'vast master-cause of the war'. It was a brutal and ruthless exploitation, the unmasking of a world of disillusion peopled by 'harsh' and 'revolting' truths. 'In the great chaos and tortuous convolutions of this unbodied thing we call

Capitalism, wherein too often we are as corks, tossed on the ocean, all this was vague, amorphous. How could one make it plain to those whose untutored minds craved only for curt, neat slogans?'[950]

Sylvia refused to be stripped of her conviction that economies could be differently organized, but struggled with how to represent her vision.

> How convey to them, as a living certainty, my own unfaltering belief in a society, consciously and concertedly providing for the needs of the world's population, estimating it, catering for it, eliminating scarcity, and avoiding glut? How convince them that today's haphazard production of commodities, turned out without measure to compete for buyers in the world market, is destined to be outlived by advancing humanity; to become the horrified amazement of the historian, when a co-operative social system has made possible a general spirit of fraternity unknown today?[951]

Discovered by Sylvia on that foggy early-morning walk, 400 Old Ford Road was now home for her, Norah and the Paynes, as well as being HQ of the East London Federation of Suffragettes. As made clear by the sofa debate on her return from Dublin, the challenge she faced now was how to convince the ELFS that they must oppose the war.

The executive committee met the same day to determine the organization's response to the war and to vote on the future direction of policy. There were three options on the table: to continue suffragette activities regardless and ignore the impact of the war; to respond directly to the war by trying to alleviate suffering and hardship in the East End; or to capitalize on the situation by working on PR campaigns exploiting the war in order to gain members. The executive committee voted for the second option.

Aware that her pacifism for the moment put her in a minority position, Sylvia decided to bide her time until public anti-war sentiment developed. This was a wise strategy. Too many people had relatives signed up to fight and many were enjoying the novelty of disruption to life's normal routines. It was yet early days. She knew she wouldn't have to wait long before the realities hit. In the meantime, the WSPU deal with the government to suspend militant action and support the war effort in exchange for release and clemency for suffragette prisoners deepened the great political rift between Sylvia and her mother and

Christabel. Emmeline Pankhurst's unalloyed enthusiasm for the war and the new WSPU policy, supported by her eldest daughter, drew from a wellspring beyond the question of achieving women's suffrage, as Christabel explained. 'The truce she declared for the duration of the war had undoubtedly a decisive influence in securing peace at home during war abroad. If the Suffragettes had continued their pre-war campaign during the war, others with a grievance might have followed suit!'[952] And none more so than her younger socialist sisters Sylvia and Adela.

Christabel ended her self-imposed exile in Paris, begun in March 1912. Protected by the amnesty, she returned to London, appearing for the first time at the London Opera House on Kingsway on 8 September 1914. The London Opera House, its rooftop adorned with figures representing Melody and Harmony, opened in November 1911. It occupied an entire block on Kingsway, between Portugal Street and Sardinia Street, and was built for Oscar Hammerstein, whose idea was that it should rival the Covent Garden Opera House. The building was opulent and enormous, capable of seating over 2,600 people.[953] Sylvia described the scene of her sister's widely advertised return: 'The empty stage was hung with dark green velvet. She appeared there alone, lit by a shaft of lime-light, clad in her favourite pale green, graceful and slender.'[954] A 'dainty, smiling, blushing figure', crooned the *Daily Mail*, as Christabel stood amid the flags of the Allied forces decorating the auditorium and a women's band thumped out national anthems.[955] Her WSPU 'adorers' filed up to present her with wreaths that she laid out in a semicircle at her feet.

The charming tableau sparked Sylvia's scepticism. Christabel made no reference to militant suffrage. At all. Not a word. The audience remained uncomfortably silent, when Victor Duval of the Men's Political Union for Women's Enfranchisement shouted out, 'Votes for Women!' Christabel rebuked him impatiently, 'We cannot discuss that now.' Sylvia listened with dismay to her sister's speech, 'wholly for the War; light, dialectic, as though of some academic political contest; no hint appeared of the appalling tragedy. I listened to her with grief, resolved to speak more urgently for peace.'[956]

Christabel did, however, speak of women's citizenship and put forward her theme of how militant women could rouse the militant spirit of men. To Christabel and Emmeline, war was an opportunity. They would jump on the war horse and spur it to ride to the woman's vote. 'War was the only course for our country to take. This was national militancy. As Suffragettes we could not be pacifists at any price.'[957]

There had been no communication between Sylvia and her elder sister since the Lloyd George initiative in the summer. Backstage, Sylvia found Christabel alone in the speaker's green room, apparently busy with some papers. 'Is Mother here?' Sylvia enquired. Without raising her eyes, Christabel responded that she would be coming soon. That was all. They sat in silence until Emmeline arrived, surrounded as usual by an entourage of women. 'We exchanged a brief greeting, distant as though through a veil.'[958] Sad and irritated 'beyond measure' by the awful meeting, Sylvia left the Opera House alone, ignoring the solidarity cheer that went up for her from a group of women gathered outside the doors.

Emmeline and Christabel went back to Paris, from where they announced that they would shortly return to England, 'to partake in rallies for recruiting men into the army'.[959] They did not try and see Sylvia again, and she first heard the news in the press of their return to England for their patriotic speaking tour. She wept when she read the announcement, overwhelmed by 'a surge of old memories and affections, which broke over me – I thought of my father's peace crusade of the 'seventies in which [her mother] had met him, the girl, Emmeline Goulden, in the ardour of her youth; his unswerving life-long advocacy of Peace and Internationalism, in which, for nineteen years, she had supported him; her stand with us, her children, against the Boer War – all this negated, a vast rift lay between our past and her present intention!'[960]

She wrote a letter appealing to her mother. It met with a rebuff: 'I am ashamed to know where you and Adela stand.'[961] The pain of losing her brother haunted Sylvia's argument with her mother. She was shocked to read a speech in which Emmeline said that she wished her boy had been marching with the armies. Sylvia was sure that Harry would have loathed the war and – especially given his sincere search among ancient eastern philosophies and ethics – would most likely have been pacifist. She writes in *The Home Front*, her memoir of the war years: 'A doubt sprang to my mind; would he have been coerced into enlistment by his love for her?[962] Anguished that her mother could contemplate sending Harry to destruction, she struggled with Emmeline's misapprehension of her own son. 'How could she know so little of him that she had failed to sense how alien, how hideous in its bestial hate and gross materialism, this butchery must have been to him?'[963] Poor Harry, in death as much as he had been in life still pulled apart in the family tug of war between the women who all thought they knew what was best for him.

Keir Hardie stood upon his integrity in a different way. In reply to the taunt 'Where are your two sons?', Hardie answered, 'I would rather see my two boys put up against a wall and shot than see them go to the war.'[964] Though disagreeing vehemently on the war, Emmeline Pankhurst and Keir Hardie presented the lives of their sons as subordinate to their political principles and the greater cause of the movement. Sylvia and Adela knew what that felt like.

Both Sylvia and Emmeline were guilty of projecting on to dead Harry, unable to speak for himself. For Sylvia's part, the symbolism of Harry's vulnerability to the sacrifice of war was uppermost in her mind because she wrote *The Home Front* with her own infant son Richard beside her in his cradle. As she did in her work *The Suffragette Movement*, she reflects on motherhood from a perspective of doubling and disjuncture. She speaks as the alienated daughter of her mother at the same time as becoming herself the mother of a young son whose death in a pointless war is unconscionable.

' "Let us go over to France," I said to Smyth. "One ought to know what one can." '[965] At Christmas 1914, Sylvia and Norah took the boat train to Paris via Boulogne. Sylvia noted that their passage was eased by their British passports and accents. From the train window she saw Boulogne transformed into a British military base. In Paris she was struck immediately by the 'less ostentatious' way the war was run compared to Britain; it was 'too near a reality for Paris to make a show of it as they did over here'.[966]

She saw famous department stores refitted as relief workrooms for unemployed women and the finest hotels converted to military hospitals. At the luxe Hôtel Claridge in the Champs-Élysées, she found her suffragette colleague Dr Flora Murray and a staff of women running a hospital with the support of the French government, because the British War Office had refused their application for assistance. Defying convention, Flora Murray gave equal treatment to all ranks in her hospital, placing officers and privates side by side on the same wards. After they'd had tea – 'the thin bread and butter and toasted bun of a modest English household'[967] – with Dr Murray and her orderlies,

Sylvia and Norah were left alone to speak with the injured French and British patients. Most of the soldiers expressed their extreme anxieties about their girlfriends, wives and children, preoccupied by how little food and money they had to survive on. They talked to their visitors about the horror of the war and its ugliness, detailing their experiences in the trenches that had brought them to the hospital as casualties.

The duo were invited to join the audience of a Christmas play staged by some convalescents called *The Deserter*, 'a grim satire on army life', and derisive of its class hierarchy. The privates in the audience hooted their approval. ' "Is it like that in the Army?" I asked a young convalescent beside me. He answered seriously, "Oh yes; just like that." ' Quizzed further, the lad confirmed it was true that they were sentenced to death for running away. Yes, the courts martial he had seen were just like that, and, yes, the sentenced had to dig their own graves before facing the firing squad.[968]

Sylvia and Norah next went to visit their friend and ELFS financier Henry Harben, 'Fabian-Suffragist – *Daily Heraldite*', running a war hospital at the Hôtel Majestic, and at several other converted hotels, out of his own pocket. Here there was no English tea and buns. Harben stuffed them with strong coffee and French pastries 'as restoratives', before leaving Sylvia to walk the wards and meet as many patients as she could, 'figures heavily swathed in bandages, racked in their torment … Algerians, Moors, Tunisians unable to speak to nurse or doctor, ghastly in pallor; an English boy of nineteen, incurably injured, bandaged from head to foot.' She spoke to a Yorkshire footballer who'd lost for ever the use of foot and hand. One of the doctors asked him what he would do to survive when he went home. 'I don't know,' the young man answered, 'unless the government have some idea of setting me up in a little business.'[969] She moved on, appalled by witnessing wards full of soldiers mutilated by grenades.

For all their differences, she longed to see her mother, who was staying with Nurse Pine in Christabel's flat in Paris while she was away on a lecture tour of the USA. The meeting was arranged. According to Sylvia, it was another disaster. They met at the flat, where sitting 'at her fireside' Emmeline would speak of nothing but the war, articulating 'the bellicose thesis which Christabel, now her unchallenged mentor, was propounding at the time: "The blockade! A war of attrition! Intern them all! She seemed a very Maenad of the War with her flashing eyes." ' Sylvia represents herself as the peacemaker at this encounter, resolved to avoid a quarrel. When her mother demanded suddenly, ' "What are *you* doing?" with a strain of contemptuous irony in her voice, which I well knew from childhood, I answered only, "In the East End." '970 Whatever her tone, Sylvia's mother had given her a cue that she stubbornly refused to take.

In an attempt to fill Sylvia's truculent silence, Norah intervened to bang on randomly about their recent trip to Scarborough. But Sylvia couldn't gather herself to bridge the gulf. As usual in these encounters, there is the sense that she is expecting – hoping – that her mother will do the emotional labour. 'We were distant from each other as though a thousand leagues had intervened; an aching void, in truth; for we were near, so poignantly near in the memory of old efforts and old loves.'971

Sylvia describes how her senses were bruised by the disjuncture between her mother's familiar, trusted physical mannerisms and the shockingly unfamiliar themes she used them to express. There is a weary finality in her departure, 'a sad anti-climax to a life's struggle – the thought knelled like a death bell in my brain. I was glad to get away, exhausted by sorrow.'972

That tolling bell is followed by a strikingly modernist break in Sylvia's memoir where she recalls these events. A line of dots – a graphic caesura – and a half-empty page are followed on the next by a pen portrait amplifying the sense of emotional abandonment by her mother:

> At Senlis, we were told, we should most readily see the damage done by the German advance in the first weeks of the War. The destruction was more hideously complete than I had imagined possible. The buildings had been systematically demolished and reduced to mere heaps of debris. It was difficult to realise that these deserted ruins had so lately been inhabited. A solitary woman stood sorrowing beside the charred remains of her home.973

As soon as the war began, pacifist women across Europe, America and beyond launched peace efforts to end it. But with the realities growing daily more terrible, censorship tightened. The Christmas Day truce of 1914 and the football game in no-man's-land between the trenches of the Western Front is now famous, a popular story, supported by correspondence and photographs suppressed for many years. Sylvia recalls (among others) how this 'brief manifestation of human solidarity, banned from official reports, was never permitted to recur'.[974] Peacework was subject to even more draconian censorship and propaganda. Worse than being pilloried as traitors to their nations and sons, women radicals and neutralists had the greater problems of contending with division over the war on two fronts: the feminist and the socialist movements.

At the outbreak of the war, there were attempts to resurrect the Socialist International. The Dutch offered their neutral soil as a place to parley and try 'to perform the difficult task of resuscitation'.[975] The socialist parties of the northern neutral countries led the way by meeting in January 1915 and issuing a manifesto denouncing the war as a product of capitalist imperialism and its secret diplomacy and calling on socialists of the warring nations to be active for peace and to work with renewed energy to overturn the status quo.

The leaders of the socialist parties of the belligerent nations rejected this manifesto. Led by the British, a conference supposedly representing the socialist movements of France, Belgium, Russia and Britain issued a counter-declaration strongly supporting the Allied cause and confirming the commitment of socialists of their countries to fight until victory was achieved. They would not meet the socialist parties of the countries 'with which the capitalist governments of their countries were in conflict' until the war was won.[976]

In Britain, the ILP condemned this belligerent policy, but Ramsay MacDonald, party to the initiative, urged that it be treated in a spirit of compromise and characteristically encouraged his critics to take the longer view. MacDonald surprised many when he resigned the Labour Party leadership within a week of the declaration of hostilities, to be replaced by Arthur Henderson. But, as Caroline Benn points out, 'MacDonald had a future to win'[977] and short-term social dishonour was a worthwhile risk. After the war, people would want a new start. While the Labour Party was divided within itself and compromised by its co-operation with the government, MacDonald and the Union of Democratic Control (UDC) attempted 'to take up a distinctive position which will in due course be the rallying centre for those who will wish that this war should not have been fought in vain'.[978] Founded in August 1914 by MacDonald, Sir Charles Trevelyan, Edmund Morel, Arthur Ponsonby and Ralph Norman Angel, the UDC became a powerful British pressure group calling for greater public scrutiny and control of diplomacy. Critical of the conduct of British foreign policy and its reliance on 'secret diplomacy', the UDC advocated transparency, was an early champion of the League of Nations and was largely supported by Labour and Liberal MPs.

Meanwhile, European countries with more established parliamentary socialist parties also had better working relationships with prominent socialist-feminist women leaders. On 2 December 1914 Karl Liebknecht was the only member of the Reichstag to vote against Germany's participation in the war. Liebknecht, Clara Zetkin, Rosa Luxemburg and other socialists drew up a manifesto calling for immediate peace, without annexations (that is, without seizure of foreign lands, without forcible incorporation of foreign nations) and without indemnities. They called for the securing of political and economic independence for every nation, disarmament and compulsory arbitration of international disputes. At Christmas, Liebknecht sent a message to the ILP in London urging the formation of the new Socialist International. On 10 March 1915 Liebknecht repeated his refusal to back the war. On 18 March thousands of women rallied outside the Reichstag, calling for peace. They had organized secretly with Liebknecht, who addressed them from a Reichstag window. As punishment, he was sent to the front, despite his immunity as a member of parliament.

The same month a conference of socialist women met secretly in Berne. Clara Zetkin, appointed leader of the Women's Office of the SPD when it was founded in 1907, was now deeply disillusioned by its nationalistic support for the war. She joined forces with Rosa Luxemburg to convene the women's international conference, attended by delegates from all factions of warring nations, 'who met in their old fraternity, to utter a call for the speedy ending of the war and a peace which should impose no humiliating condition on any nation'.[979] This women's event went largely unreported, and was derided by pro-war women commentators offered unlimited column inches in which to undermine their sisters. Reflecting on these actions in 1935, Sylvia wrote admiringly, 'Women Socialists of all countries had overcome the nationalist hysteria of war time, which held the male leaders of the International in its grip.'[980]

Clara Zetkin and Rosa Luxemburg's plan to travel together over frontiers to meet with socialists of all the warring nations was forestalled by Rosa's arrest in Germany. Clara visited her in prison and then went on to Holland, but was turned back from the Belgian frontier, and was soon herself arrested in Germany and indicted for treason; because of her poor health she was released from prison after four months. She persevered with the conference, but by then SPD leaders had declared it an offence against party discipline to distribute the conference manifestos or attend the event.

Dutch suffragists led by Dr Aletta Jacobs demanded that belligerent governments call a truce to allow them to define their peace terms and called for a women's international peace congress at The Hague. They appealed for the submission of all international disputes to arbitration; democratic control of foreign policy; full political enfranchisement of women; inclusion of women in the peace negotiations; and democratic self-determination of territories.

Simultaneously, a group of women organized on the British front for peace. At Christmas 1914 one hundred British women addressed the 'Open Christmas Letter' to the women of Germany and Austria urging them to join together in calling for a truce. Leading signatories alongside Sylvia Pankhurst included the instigator of the letter, Emily Hobhouse, Helen Bright Clark, Margaret Gillett, Isabella Ford, the Liberal politician and Quaker pacifist Anna, Lady Barlow, and the social worker and internationalist Catherine Courtney, Lady Courtney of Penwith.

Mary Sheepshanks, editor of *Jus Suffragii* – the official newspaper of the International Women's Suffrage Alliance – bravely published the controversial letter. The majority of British suffrage societies strongly opposed her pacifist and internationalist feminist editorial policy. When German and Austrian women responded positively to the letter with an invitation to the international peace conference at The Hague, this opposition became more entrenched. After the war, Mary Sheepshanks' courage and the principled stand of her newspaper earned her praise from around the world.

Dutch and German suffragists agreed to pay two-thirds of the costs of the women's peace conference, and awaited the response from Britain. The NUWSS represented British women in the International Suffrage Alliance. Their leader Millicent Fawcett rejected the invitation and denounced the conference. A group of dissatisfied secessionists from the NUWSS joined forces with the ELFS and other organizations to answer the invitation, and at a meeting at Caxton Hall, 200 women volunteered to go to The Hague.

Millicent Fawcett and Christabel and Emmeline Pankhurst now found themselves in the novel position of being on the same side. They condemned the women's peace conference and declared it akin to treason to talk of reconciliation. Their organizations gained widespread publicity for their patriotic nationalist opposition. Nina Boyle, in a leader in *The Vote*, the organ of the Women's Freedom League, scorned the presumption of women 'who imagine it possible for them ... to be an international power, and set in motion reforms vaster and more quixotic than any body of men with franchise, representatives, and Cabinet Ministers in their pocket, would venture to attack at the present moment'.[981] French suffragists were, overall, equally emphatic in their denunciations. Conversely, the initiative met with positive support in the USA, where women tried to lobby their leaders, including former President Theodore Roosevelt. The USA was not in the war at this point; it was to enter in April 1917.

Pacifism was for the moment proving unpopular in the East End. Funders steadily withdrew financial support from the ELFS. Norah Smyth upped her contributions to operational costs and directly underwrote the local emergency war-relief fund. She gave support in the form of donations and interest-free loans, all of which she wrote off.

Sylvia lost sleep over the rising costs of her uncompromising stance. Was it imprudent? She could keep quiet and support the popular position, protecting the ELFS' hard-fought-for projects and stopping the fall in their membership and reputation. She repeatedly weighed up the options of whether to stay silent or to speak. 'I was guided by the opinion that freedom of thought and speech is more important than any good which can ever come of concealing one's views, and by the knowledge that in the hour of its greatest unpopularity the pioneering cause needs one most.'[982]

The governments of Germany, Russia, Austria, France and Belgium permitted women to attend The Hague peace conference. In Britain, 200 women delegates requested permission to attend. The Foreign Office trimmed the British delegation to twenty-four, and handpicked the list of women to whom they agreed to issue permits to travel; but most had their passports withdrawn and were refused permission to travel. Sylvia observed, 'It is impossible to describe the atmosphere of repression which overhung the movement.'[983] In the end, three British women made it to The Hague, Emmeline Pethick-Lawrence being one of them.

Well aware that she would never make the final selection, Sylvia had already sent her resolutions ahead to the congress. She shared her proposals with an enthusiastic and approving Hardie, and they redrafted them together at Nevill's Court. Sylvia's resolutions covered the abolition of secret and sectional treaties and alliances; the creation of a permanent peace treaty uniting all nations; abolition of national armies and navies; a democratic international court of arbitration and extension of its powers. Her father would have approved. These proposals drew inspiration from his own detailed schemes for an international court of justice and a league of co-operating nations. It was an opportunity, now increasingly rare, for Hardie and Sylvia to spend time working intimately together. These days their mutual solidarity was most usually directed through political and press channels.

Sylvia's friend Jane Addams, described by John Burns as 'America's finest citizen',[984] presided over the peace conference which opened on 28 April 1915 and closed on 1 May. In January that year Addams and Carrie Chapman Catt had formed the Women's Peace Party in Washington DC. Three thousand women attending the meeting voted for a political platform calling for the extension of suffrage to women and creating a conference of neutral countries to offer continuous mediation as a method of ending war.

More than 1,200 delegates from twelve countries attended The Hague women's peace congress – including Germany, Austria-Hungary, Italy, Poland, Belgium, Britain and the United States – but not France.

The demand for a truce made in the original appeal from Dutch women did not make it to the final resolution of The Hague peace congress. However, the gathering resolved to request belligerent governments to end the bloodshed and begin peace negotiations, mediated by a council of the neutral governments. This initiative foundered ultimately on the refusal of the US government to participate, because it rejected the principle of mediation led by neutral nations, declaring it 'utterly impracticable'.[985] If there was going to be mediation, it had to be led by President Woodrow Wilson and America, 'to their everlasting glory' – and to secure American interests in exploiting developing markets in other parts of the world.[986]

Jane Addams, convinced that the war was reactionary and benefited only the arms industries, continued unsuccessfully to try and persuade President Wilson to mediate a negotiated end to hostilities and dissuade him from agreeing to American military involvement. On her return home after the conference, she spoke around the US calling for increased food production to aid European starvation caused by the war. At the time vilified for these activities, a decade after the armistice she would become a national hero and Chicago's leading citizen. In 1931 she was awarded the Nobel Peace Prize, the second woman to receive the honour. Bertha von Suttner, the first woman to win the Nobel for peace, had died in June 1914, a month before the outbreak of the war she had struggled so long to avert.

The Hague peace conference resulted in the formation of the Women's International League for Peace and Freedom (WIL). Jane Addams was a co-founder, serving as president from 1919 until her death in 1935. All women's organizations working for peace were invited to participate in the founding meeting of the British section of the WIL – suffragists, socialists, Quakers and ELFS. Sylvia was elected to the executive. She immediately moved resolutions that the name should be changed to the Women's International Peace League and that women who were not British citizens should be allowed to join. Both motions were defeated.

As the majority of the London members were secessionists from the NUWSS, the WIL adopted a moderate and cautious tone. Sylvia objected that 'even the British wives of aliens were excluded from participating',[987] but she worked hard in a spirit of compromise within the organization for as long as possible. She genuinely respected the WIL and many of its leaders and members, despite their nervousness at being associated with radicalism. The WIL was also too timid to support demonstrations objecting to the harsh sentences against women like Nellie Best who violated the controversial Defence of the Realm Act (DORA). Nevertheless Sylvia robustly defended the principles of its work: 'It carried no fiery cross; but tried in a quiet way, sincerely, if at times haltingly, to understand the causes of war, and to advance the cause of peace by negotiation, and the enfranchisement of women.'[988]

The Women's International League came under fire from all directions: the government, Millicent Fawcett and the other WSPU leaders, her mother and elder sister. Sylvia remained an active member, supporter and critical voice within the organization for two years. Affiliation required a registered membership of 5,000, so the ELFS didn't qualify to join. But Sylvia still slogged to the all-day meetings and despite her criticisms of its approach proposed the establishment of an East End branch. Working with the WIL provided a way of ensuring that the ELFS functioned within a broad network of other initiatives and did not become 'insular' – the word she used at the October 1915 executive committee meeting.[989]

Despite the squeamishness of the WIL, she continued to argue that it was necessary to work with middle-class women and former political opponents to bring the unnecessary war to an end. She was finally forced to draw the line in 1917 when the WIL refused to condemn a gross violation of the rights of one of its own founding and most prominent members. Emily Hobhouse, who had travelled to Belgium to investigate the truth of British stories about German atrocities. On her re-entry to Britain, she was seized by border police. She was ignominiously strip-searched and branded a traitor by the government. To Sylvia it was a disgrace that the WIL remained silent about this abuse of one of Britain's leading human rights activists. Sylvia and Emily had been friends and allies since they met at the home of the MacDonalds shortly after Emily's return from South Africa. Sylvia had been one of the initial signatories to Hobhouse's 1914 'Open Christmas Letter', and they had worked together on the women's peace congress, with the South African Olive Schreiner. Hobhouse died in 1926. In an unfinished manuscript drafted towards the end of her life, Sylvia set down her intention to write a chapter about 'my friendship with Emily Hobhouse' and the subsequent chapter was to be about her friendship with Olive Schreiner.[990] Sadly, she appears to have never fulfilled these intentions.

The ELFS' anti-war policy remained at odds with popular support for the war. Membership and funding continued to fall away as a result of Sylvia's stance. Daily she considered compromising, as urged by many on her executive. Yet she found that she could not stand down from her pacifist principle. As always in her most desolate inner struggles, it was the sacrifice of her artistic vocation that returned to haunt her in these lonely moments of leadership:

Yet it was often hard to choose thus sternly, flying in the face of what seemed prudent, casting to the winds the result of laborious effort; hard, not on my account; for I had shed all personal aims when I gave up painting in the years of the Suffragette struggle before the War; hard only on account of the work I was striving to do, and the people who looked to me for aid.[991]

21

The Dogs of War

As Sylvia had anticipated, public opinion shifted as the hardship and realities of war dug in. At the end of October 1914, the *Glasgow Herald* reported that Sylvia Pankhurst had spoken out against the war at a huge ILP meeting held in the city, arguing that peace must be made by the people and not by diplomats and politicians. This speech made her one of the first suffragettes to speak out publicly against the war. Initially her outspokenness and her emergence as an anti-war agitator caused great discomfort to her East End colleagues and suffragette allies, but just a year later the ELFS were able to adopt a clear anti-war position.

The ELFS started to think about how they could implement practical measures at local, community, municipal and factory level to alleviate the effects of the war, and which organizations to ally with for this purpose. They worked hard, largely unsuccessfully, to oppose draconian anti-civil-liberties legislation and government repression during the war years.

The war started out with a volunteer national army, in line with liberal beliefs in individual freedom. But by 1915 trench warfare required a guaranteed supply of replacement recruits abroad and an urgent need to crack down on the increasingly voluble and unsettled civilian population at home. Strikes began among engineering workers on the Clyde and dockers in Liverpool as early as the beginning of 1915 as hungry workers demanded their rightful share of the increased profits generated by their extra war work.

Parliament had passed the Defence of the Realm Act (DORA) in August 1914, making it illegal to spread information 'likely to cause disaffection or alarm' among either the military or civilian population. The aims of DORA, a gross infringement of civil liberties, was to ensure the flow of more recruits into the forces and to discipline and regulate the workers in defence-related industries. DORA permitted the arrest of suspects without warrant, unlimited search powers and the right to seize documents or anything else deemed suspicious. People arrested under DORA could be tried and imprisoned by military court martial, even if they were civilians, and treated as if they were soldiers on active duty. Constantly amended, DORA was supplemented in May 1915 by the Munitions Act, attempting to regulate all aspects of the lives of workers employed in the munitions industry. This prepared the way for the introduction of conscription for single men from January 1916 and universal manhood conscription four months later.

The impact of this legislation on women was one of Sylvia's chief preoccupations. Regulation 40D issued under DORA making it compulsory for women suspected of being prostitutes to be inspected and registered for venereal diseases outraged her. Further, it made it an offence for women to have sex with a member of His Majesty's Forces if they had an STD. This attempt to reintroduce the state regulation of 'vice' – policing women's sexuality – revived feminist debates about morality and hypocrisy. This backdoor revival of the Contagious Diseases Acts, successfully repealed in the previous century thanks to the indefatigable campaigning of Josephine Butler, appalled Sylvia. She was dismayed that feminists who had previously campaigned against the state regulation of vice remained silent.

Living at street level, Sylvia experienced first-hand how this pernicious legislation demonized unmarried mothers, widows and women managing their families while their men were away at war. Using a popular term for an excessively nosy person, she wrote, 'Paul Pry was still at large,'[992] imperilling women unemployed or widowed by the war. This introduction of police surveillance of soldiers' wives she found particularly distasteful and profoundly hypocritical. In non-judgemental terms she produced detailed case studies of her neighbours and local women whose sexual lives and alcohol consumption were monitored in an Orwellian manner. She kept the issue in view with constant reporting in the *Woman's Dreadnought*, monitoring and exposing the activities of the police and special 'sex' constables. Where possible, she got George Lansbury and poor law and town hall officials to intervene. Throughout the winter of 1914–15, the *Woman's Dreadnought* ran a series of articles exposing and protesting against the Metropolitan Police's efforts to snoop on the wives of sailors and soldiers on active duty, which was intended to enable the government to revoke the separation allowances paid if the wives were found to be 'badly behaved'. The separation allowance was paid by the government to a soldier's dependants to ensure they were not left destitute. Surveilled women faced the threat of being stripped of their only access to their husbands' wages, or blackmailed by the officers in charge of inquiries into their behaviour. Sylvia's *Dreadnought* articles drew on her personal experience of the apparatuses of surveillance during the militant suffragette campaigning. She aimed to amplify the voices of working women, drawing attention to the ways in which surveillance made these women particularly vulnerable.[993]

Norah Smyth's photographs of the period include a series of images of women bundled up in eiderdowns and blankets at Old Ford Road, sleeping on shelves, chairs and makeshift camp beds in order to evade the hastily rushed-through National Registration Act of 1915 which provided for a register of all men and women between the ages of fifteen and sixty-five, later used to aid conscription. Women were required to give their age, marital status, the number of children they had and their occupation. The registration form also asked if they were able or willing to undertake any skilled work. ELFS did not want to be drafted into war work that they did not support. National Registration raised concerns about civil liberties – it was the gathering of personal information by the state on an unprecedented scale. In July and August the ELFS staged meetings and demonstrations opposing the Act.

Sylvia wrote to Lloyd George, now Munitions Minister, inviting him to meet a deputation of women who wanted to talk to him about the registration of workers and the soaring costs of food and coal with which their low wages could not keep pace. The war intensified hunger, poverty and desperation. The delegation wanted to demand equal pay for equal work. Lloyd George, a strong supporter of general conscription, declined to meet this proposed delegation. Sylvia published his refusal, gaining the ELFS substantial support for their next demonstration against the Registration Act from a range of bodies including trade unions and the British Socialist Party, but only some Liberals, since they were divided on the subject of conscription. At this rally, Sylvia denounced war profiteering and women's sweated labour, arguing that the register was constructed solely for the purpose of exploiting the workers.[994] The *East London Observer* reported that she ended her speech by announcing her own refusal to sign the register, 'for she, like millions of Englishwomen, still did not have the vote'.[995]

In July 1915 miners in South Wales struck in defiance of the Munitions Act. Sylvia took up their cause. In September she spoke at an anti-war, anti-conscription rally in Bristol, as she did at similar meetings in South Wales and Belfast, when crossing the Irish Sea was perilous, patrolled as it was by German U-boats.[996]

As Sylvia travelled up and down the country speaking against the war, conscription and government outlawing of wartime strike action, her mother and sister also toured Britain speaking passionately in favour of the war, conscription and industrial profiteering. In 1916 Sylvia spoke at a number of meetings in Glasgow alongside George Lansbury and the leading 'Red Clyde' revolutionary John Maclean. Some newspapers used the term 'Red Clydeside' to refer to the rising tide of socialism in Glasgow and along the banks of the River Clyde, including Clydebank, Greenock, Dumbarton and Paisley. The area had a long history of political radicalism going back to the 1820s. This groundswell of support for a socialist labour movement in Scotland was rooted in working-class opposition to the war. Sylvia supported women who successfully organized a rent strike and urged shop stewards to hold their ground on opposing conscription, as well as backing or encouraging a succession of illegal strikes throughout the war.

In May 1917 a group of schoolchildren in Burston, Norfolk, who had set up their own strike school, invited Sylvia to come and speak to them during the official opening programme of the new school.[997] On 14 April 1914 radical teachers Tom and Annie Higdon had been dismissed from their jobs in Burston. That day, the school's pupils, children of poor farm workers, marched around the village under a banner inscribed with 'Justice' and placards demanding 'We want our teachers back'. Supported by their parents, these children started what became the longest strike in British history. The boycott of the local authority school lasted twenty-five years. The children and their parents, supported by trade unions, set up an alternative strike school that ran until the end of the dispute in 1939. Initially classes were held on the village green and in the winter moved into old workshops. A national appeal to build a new school, supported by the ILP, trade unions and co-operative societies, enabled the strike school to open its new premises officially in May 1917. The Russian novelist Leo Tolstoy was among the many contributors to the fund for the new building. On 13 May, a week after her thirty-first birthday, a charter train from London brought Sylvia and John Scurr to speak at the opening, accompanied by supporters from the National Union of Railwaymen.

The ELFS anti-war activity in London adopted the same methods used during the pre-war suffragette campaigns. Huge meetings gathered at the gates of the East India Docks and processed to Victoria Park. Soldiers and sailors participated in the demonstrations that, although large, were smaller than the pre-war suffragette marches.

The symbolic high point of the anti-war agitation was the Trafalgar Square march and rally of 8 April 1916. In mid-March the ELFS had renamed themselves the Workers' Suffrage Federation (WSF), with a revised political ambition 'To secure Human Suffrage, namely, a Vote, for every Woman and Man of full age, and to win Social and Economic Freedom for the People', a mission reflecting the evolution of their social work. They set about organizing the Trafalgar Square demonstration with friendly unions, the ILP, the British Socialist Party and trades councils. Charlotte Drake, along with twenty other WSF women, was arrested in East London's Isle of Dogs for pasting up posters advertising the march, bearing slogans such as 'War is Murder' and 'The Soldiers in the Trenches are Longing for Peace'.

On the day, the Workers' Suffrage Federation led the march on the usual six-mile route from Bow via Poplar to Trafalgar Square. Reports estimated that the protesters congregated in the square numbered around 20,000, apparently the largest anti-war rally to date. Norah Smyth's photographs, supplemented by those of press reporters and undercover Scotland Yard detectives, show the platform at the base of Nelson's plinth occupied by Sylvia, Charlotte Drake, Melvina Walker, Dr Barbara Tchaykovsky and Eva Gore-Booth. A Glasgow city councillor told the crowd about the engineers' strike on Clydeside and updated them on the circumstances of workers arrested under DORA.

A sign of her skill with early, slower technology, Norah's camera captured the moment just after jeering soldiers and sailors hostile to their anti-war campaigning threw ochre dye at the speakers and leapt on to the platform to assault them.

Shirley Williams wrote in her Foreword to the 1987 edition of Sylvia's war memoir *The Home Front*: 'There were two home fronts in First World War Britain, and they were very different – the home front of middle-class England and the other which ran through the dingy terraces of the working class.' It was a 'society of such brutal class division, so callous in the administration of its partial and biased laws, that one is amazed not only that we today share with it the same country, but that we also share with it the same century'.[998] The work of the ELFS and subsequently WSF enabled some East End communities to reorganize to challenge and change these stark inequalities.

The separation allowances announced by the government at the outbreak of hostilities were issued by the War Office to the wives of privates, corporals and sergeants, plus weekly allowances for London living and child allowances until the age of fourteen for boys and sixteen for girls. Most were either paid woefully late or never arrived, and all were at minimal rates. To pay the weekly rent women all over the country were forced to sell their furniture and clothes. Prices rose. Mothers with families of up to ten children had no immediate means of feeding them and faced threats of eviction. Sylvia saw a calico banner hung across a neighbouring street: 'Please, Landlord don't be offended / Don't come for the rent till the War is ended.'[999] The slogan came from a poem originally published in *Reynolds News* during the great dock strike in 1889:

> Our husbands are on strike, to the wives it is not honey,
> And we think it right, not to pay the landlords' money.
> Everyone is on strike, so landlords do not be offended,
> The rent that's due, we'll pay you, when the strike is ended.[1000]

'Starvation,' Sylvia wrote, 'that strange, dull gaze, daily stared in my face from the eyes of mothers and children.'[1001] Women fed their children on boiled bread and went hungry themselves. Sylvia met the wife of a greaser who had disappeared when his ship was commandeered. For four days she'd been without food for her six children. Appointed to the Poplar Committee, whose purpose was to help local people, Sylvia turned up with a comprehensive list of ideas, including subsidized low-cost restaurants. Comprised predominantly of well-fed, middle-aged, middle-class men and some women, the committee also included Violet Millar (future wife of Clement Attlee), Julia Scurr of the ELFS and Susan Lawrence, later to become one of the first female Labour MPs.

Convened by the Mayor on 17 August 1915, the meeting decided nothing, then adjourned for eight days. Exasperated, Sylvia wondered at their failure to understand the urgency of the hardships facing the community. Driven by the dream she had grown up with, 'to wipe out poverty, to transform the dreary wastes of the slums to a pleasance of happy well-being',[1002] she determined that the ELFS would take matters into their own hands.

On 31 August Sylvia and Zelie opened the ELFS' first Cost Price Restaurant at Old Ford Road, based on Zelie's successful relief restaurant during the 1911 Chicago strike. From idea to opening, the conversion and construction was achieved in just one week. Willie Lansbury, now running his father's timber yard, provided wood and fittings for the furniture, made by local men from the Rebels' Social and Political Union who worked through the nights to get it done. Gas stoves and boilers were hired locally and willing supporters donated crockery and glass. All around the district and beyond, people with allotments donated produce, chicken carcasses and ingredients for bread. Those who could donated money.

During the last four months of 1915, the Cost Price Restaurant served around 400 meals a day. 'I'll never forget those dinners,' Nellie Cressall recalled. 'They were made of meat pudding, greens and potatoes. They had it with a slice of spotted dog all for 1 penny. It did not pay of course. But I think many a life was saved by the sacrifice and service of the people who carried on all through the war and after.'[1003] Norah's photographs show very clearly the dignity of that penny, picked up by the press, who dubbed the restaurants 'Sylvia's Penny Carltons'. The women are seen eating lunch with their children at the restaurant, their hair smoothed and clothes made tidy for the communal meal. Sometimes, a woman wears a Sunday-best hat. Often, a folded *Dreadnought* lies on the table by their plates, spectacles placed atop.

On the downside, Sylvia's appointments of Mrs Ennis Richmond and her sister Miss Morgan Brown, as head cook and restaurant manager respectively, turned out to be controversial. The two women described themselves as 'food reformers' and 'experts' in modern food and nutritional values, which involved cooking with a lot of dried lentils and beans. This caused Sylvia painful indigestion and relentless wind, exacerbating the problems she still experienced in consequence of hunger and thirst striking in prison.

More problematically, the women customers expressed outrage at Ennis Richmond's whacky ideas about food preparation and nutrition. She insisted, for example, on putting potatoes *unpeeled* into the soup, explaining that the skins contained valuable vitamins. Hungry as they were, the women surreptitiously examined the skin in their soup and declared it a shame 'to give such "muck" to poor people!'[1004] Sylvia tackled Ennis Richmond on their behalf, trying to explain to her that their customers interpreted the potato skins as a sign of contempt. Decent people peeled their potatoes before putting them in the soup. Ennis, however, was resolute: either the skins stayed on the potatoes, or she would leave.

Sylvia appealed to Hardie for advice. 'What shall I do? … Shall I permit the Expert to improve the people against their will?' To her great surprise, Hardie answered her decisively, 'I think so.' The levity of the exchange gave way to a more fractious undertone. When Sylvia persisted, Hardie sighed, 'Have we fallen so low that we must discuss potato skins?' Sylvia smarted at the rebuke, but recognized its truth. 'In the struggle to provide for our people my mind was withdrawing itself from the thought of the great tragedy over there.' Hardie thought of nothing else. Perpetually conscious of the carnage, 'in his deep eyes, was the restless agony of a man in torment'.[1005] He predicted, 'European war will almost certainly lead to European revolution, the end of which no man can foresee.'[1006]

Ennis Richmond's approach to cooking was in line with the government campaigns encouraging people to make domestic economies, abstain from luxuries and 'Eat Less Meat'. As awareness of state-run war racketeering, stockpiling, wastage and inefficiency distributing provisions to troops became more widespread, strikes broke out. In the course of the war, food became a staple issue of discontent.[1007] 'Sylvia's

Penny Carltons' symbolized an act of resistance against the unnecessary hunger caused by war.

In the conclusion to *The Home Front*, Sylvia reflects on the strenuous work of the East End peace campaign. Street after street was visited, pavements chalked, leaflets distributed from door to door. Speakers stood on chairs in the street, in markets and outside factory gates. Sylvia kept at it, she said, 'spurred by anxiety, which could find respite only in effort'.[1008] To quiet her restless mind, she required action. ELFS/WSF activist Emma Boyce, their roving organizer, accompanied her on much of this campaigning, following 'slowly after with her sore feet … She was old and battered by life, the hard life of a working-class widow toiling to bring up her children. She presently had one of them sent back to her from the War, an incurable cripple.'[1009]

In her neighbourhood, Sylvia saw children gathering on doorsteps in the dusk, reaching up to knock at the front doors of their homes, in vain. The men gone, mothers not yet returned from the gun factory, the hungry children waited outside in the cold.

> I was seething with energy. Racked with pain, prostrate with
> headache, at times I might be, yet within me was a rage at this
> merciless War, this squalor of poverty! Oh! that all the wealth and
> effort the nation was squandering might be to rebuild these slums,
> to restore these faded women, these starved and stunted children.[1010]

The energy of pure rage motivated Sylvia during the war: a rage for peace. Her anger that the leaders of the militant suffragette campaign had betrayed all women was boundless. She possessed no hatred of foreign enemies. For her, the enemy was the capitalist war on the home front.

Sylvia's Workers' Suffrage Federation converged with the British Socialist Party and the ILP in its demonstrations against the collapse of Labour Party opposition to the war, and picketed the 1917 Labour Party conference, held in Manchester, where delegates targeted the WSF women with particularly venomous abuse. Sylvia found it especially galling to receive this treatment in her home town. It was reminiscent of the pillorying the Pankhurst family had received for their pacifist views against the South African Wars when they were children. Led by her father, their anti-war position at that time was supported by no one more vigorously than her now bellicose mother and elder sister.

The behaviour of the Labour Party towards the WSF during the war, combined with its generally supine policy positions, convinced Sylvia that it no longer represented working people. Under her father's tutelage, her belief in participatory democracy was based on the premise of the future viability of a rock-solid British parliamentary democracy that was representative, subject only to reform of the second chamber. She had continued to agree that the representative British parliamentary system needed to be restructured and diversified, not dismantled. The failure of the Labour Party to contest the war combined with the folding of internationalist socialist parties on their hitherto pacifist policy moved her towards examining seriously, for the first time, alternative forms of democracy and anti-parliamentary political positions.

In May 1915 Asquith had formed a wartime coalition government. The new cabinet included nine Conservatives and one Labour minister (George Henry Roberts), with the Liberals continuing to hold most of the key positions. Labour MPs and trade union leaders served in more junior positions in the ministries. In December 1916 a new coalition was formed by David Lloyd George, who became Prime Minister, and which included Labour's Arthur Henderson, who continued to serve in it until its dissolution in January 1919.

At the 1918 Labour Party Conference, Sylvia, inspired by the Russian Revolution, moved the resolution on behalf of the British Socialist Party (BSP) that the Labour Party withdraw its participation entirely from the coalition government. The motion was lost and she was ridiculed. She left the conference resigned to the futility of working during wartime with the Labour Party, now fully persuaded of its inability to rise to the current political moment. These experiences significantly informed her later argument with Lenin, with important consequences for the political fortunes of the left in Britain.

The treatment of Keir Hardie by Labour proved another decisive factor in Sylvia's departure from the party ranks. Hardie's illness, depression and heartbreak over the war and the failure of socialist internationalism in opposing it caused him to become withdrawn and despondent. They never lost touch and he was always solicitous and kindly, but Sylvia feared the change in him. As with her reaction to Zelie Emerson's struggle for survival in Holloway, she seemed to be emotionally threatened by loss of spirit or hope in those closest to her.

To state that Sylvia Pankhurst was unusually resilient and possessed of almost magical reserves of optimism, hope and the physical and emotional energy required to support them would be an understatement. A powerful personality, she needed her loved ones and intimates to be equal to her in strength, if not to be even stronger. Since the death of her father, Hardie had been her bedrock, an essential underpinning to all she had done. The deep personal and political friendship between her father and mother and Hardie and his presence and support when her father died framed her early life. It provided a form of unbroken psychological continuity. Since she was sixteen, Hardie had carried her father's torch lighting the way for her.

After one of their final meetings alone together, Sylvia described how she had 'left him heavy with anxiety'. Waiting in Bishopsgate for the bus east to Old Ford Road, a thought, 'tragic and luminant, seized me – not my thought it seemed, but one from without'.[1011] This is Sylvia's second great epiphany. The first was the idealistic Russell Square vision of her childhood, where she conceived the hope of a commonwealth where 'all should be "better than well."'.[1012] This second vision has adult foresight. Significantly, it comes 'from without' and occurs at the breaking point of the wartime Labour Party's relationship with Hardie:

> In a flash I realised the long struggle sustained in the advanced
> countries, through many generations, to waken the masses that they
> might gain control of their national parliaments: I saw them at last
> make entry into the citadel, only to find it empty, the power gone –
> removed to an international government wherein the dead weight
> of backward peoples would strangle all progress for generations
> to come. Was this the truthful augur of Internationalism? Was
> it thus that privilege and poverty would be buttressed in their
> ancient reign? Profound melancholy closed down on me. How
> static was this poverty, cruel and stultifying, with which we warred!
> All schemes for international arbitration and agreement seemed
> empirical. The belief flared up insistent that only from a society
> recreated from the root, replacing the universal conflict of today
> by universal cooperation, could permanent peace arise. Yearning

for the golden age of the coming equalitarian society, I passed, in thought, to the extremist pole, whereat all save a world-embracing social rebirth and reconstruction seemed mere trumpery.[1013]

Her mother and sister's active role in dismantling Hardie's character devastated Sylvia. They colluded in the public assault on his reputation. When Emmeline's pacifist husband had died, Hardie had been Emmeline's mainstay, stalwart in his personal support for the family. Politically he had maintained his solidarity with them throughout nearly twenty years of the suffragette struggle, to the considerable detriment of his authority in leadership and of his own standing within the party. Now, Emmeline and Christabel betrayed him.

The sequential breakdown in the relationship between Sylvia and her elder sister and mother that took place during the pre-war years through the series of arguments in Paris always included Christabel's little Pomeranian, Fey, who presided over each of these momentous family summits. Christabel's remoteness from the realities of the streets on which Sylvia worked and lived was symbolized by the dainty, petite Fey, tucked under her elegant arm or seated on her lap during imperious audiences.

Shortly after visiting the ailing Hardie at Nevill's Court, Sylvia 'woke early one Sunday morning with a dream of him fondling some little puppy, as he often did ... There was always a strong attraction between the dogs and him; not one of them approached him but he must have to do with it.'[1014] Hardie mourned his dogs who had died 'as old friends', and wished that he could have one at Nevill's Court – but he travelled too much. Remembering how her childhood home had been full of pets, all the years Sylvia lived alone Hardie had urged her to get a dog. Following the impulse of this vivid dream Sylvia took herself off to the dog market on Bethnal Green Road in search of an Old English Sheepdog, 'the most human of dogs, as far as I know them'.[1015] There were no sheepdogs to be had, but she found a litter of what the vendor assured her were retrievers and chose the fattest, round as a barrel, with long black silky fur. Sitting on the bus with him on her lap, she fantasized about how happy Hardie's face would be when she arrived with this unexpected gift: 'I could see his amused surprise at this new arrival – imagined his way with it.'[1016]

Hardie's right-hand Frank Smith gently intervened. Hardie had returned home to Cumnock, and there was no way of sending the puppy north to Scotland, even if the transport could be arranged, Hardie was now too ill to receive such a gift. What Frank couldn't bear to tell Sylvia was that Hardie, deeply attached to all his pets, had recently surprised and upset his family and friends by suddenly ordering all of his beloved dogs to be sent away immediately from Cumnock.

Sylvia called the puppy Donald, named after the best-loved of the pit ponies Hardie had befriended in childhood. She decided to keep him – she hoped just for a while – until Hardie's health improved. In the East End, people took to calling the puppy Jimmie, which was Hardie's childhood nickname. After a week Sylvia accepted the majority decision that the puppy's name was Jim, not Donald.

Jim soon became devoted to Sylvia. He turned out not to be a retriever after all, but a crossbred Old English Sheepdog who grew an iron-grey coat. His golden-brown eyes Sylvia imagined to be 'like the eyes of him I bought him for'.[1017] She rarely had enough time for Jim, but she kept him with her when she could. Where possible, Jim trotted beside her around the East End and on demonstrations and rallies. She enjoyed his pranks and his demolition of shoes and hats, and was indifferent to his muddy paws indoors. All the ELFS adored him. He was fed in Sylvia's Penny Carltons and petted by all. 'Yet he was my dog, though I never fed him and on the whole had little time to notice him.' He responded generously to the little attention she gave him, 'as a good dog will, repaying our poor care of them, in affection, a thousand-fold'.[1018]

When Sylvia was away, Jim lay in the passage outside her bedroom door at night, or, if he could slip past the beady eye of Jessie Payne, slept on the bed, messing up the sheets with his wet, muddy paws and fur. Knowing Sylvia's step, he sprang to the door to greet her before anyone else. 'Dear Jim, dear dogs, so faithful in your ungrudging love which satisfies us not.'[1019]

Meanwhile, Christabel's refined lapdog travelled in carriages in the Bois de Boulogne, curled up on luxurious sofas in the sumptuous apartments of the Princesse de Polignac and waited for Christabel in her basket in the green room of the London Opera House. Just before Christmas 1913, Fey made a dash for freedom from her life of chocolates, silk and gentility. The *Pall Mall Gazette* passed on the intelligence that

Miss Christabel Pankhurst had lost her 'small brown Pomeranian' in Paris and was offering a handsome £4 reward for the dog's return. The *Express* correspondent suggested that 'the money may be earned with comparative ease by anyone who cares to walk about the streets of Paris shouting "McKenna!" and seeking a responsive bark'.[1020]

Sylvia's Jim lived in a different, parallel world. He appears in Norah Smyth's photographs, sometimes spotted in the midst of a great street protest, elsewhere tumbled amid jostling groups of smiling children playing with him outside their East End homes. Wherever he is in the picture, Jim is always at street level.

22

Mothers' Arms

In March 1915 Sylvia and her friend Lady Sybil Smith took the train to Maidenhead where they were greeted by a flamboyant Nancy Astor and piled into her luxurious limousine with other guests invited for the weekend to the Astors' renowned political salon. Lady Astor drove them herself to Cliveden House at the breakneck speed for which she was renowned. Along the way she entertained them with her singing, with interludes of vigorous political opinion and, at one point in the journey, with abuse of a horse rider in civvies. As they sped past she yelled out to him, 'Why aren't you in khaki?' and then launched into a diatribe against slackers who didn't join up and fight.

As they raced through the Kent countryside to its most magnificent estate, Lady Astor shared the ideas set out in the book she was currently reading which argued that indulging in luxury increased the poor man's burden – ' "I am going to be austere!" she shouted, eyeing us all with a glance of challenge.'[1021] Soon, they arrived at magnificent Cliveden, a wedding gift from Lady Astor's father-in-law, William Waldorf Astor, the richest man in America.

Feeling from the outset 'like a fish out of water', Sylvia was uncomfortable around Nancy Astor, who, she thought unkindly, 'looked like a bit of Dresden china with her flaxen hair and pink and white skin'. She wished herself 'a thousand miles away from her hospitality'.[1022] The only moment of genuine empathy Sylvia achieved the entire weekend was when a telegram arrived one evening during pre-dinner cocktails bearing the news to one of Lady Astor's sisters that her beloved fiancé had been killed.

Sylvia's discomfort stemmed from the fact that she and Sybil had arrived as supplicants at the Astors' house party. They needed investment from wealthy supporters, many of whom Sylvia knew from her WSPU days. To provide alternatives to the below-rate sweated labour justified in the name of 'war relief' work, the ELFS had set up two model factories in the East End. First, they opened a boot and shoe factory. Next followed a toy factory, which employed fifty-nine people and ran on a not-for-profit co-operative basis. Everyone received pay of fivepence an hour or eleven shillings a week.

Sylvia had set up the co-operative factories as an alternative to the Queen Mary Workshops. In August 1914 Sylvia had written to Queen Mary outlining her criticisms of the conditions in the workshops set up in Her Majesty's name to give work to unemployed women at appalling wages. Sylvia dubbed them 'Queen Mary's Sweatshops'. She tried to persuade local and national government to raise the rates of pay in factories. Having failed, she changed tack and set up her own. They couldn't make the boot and shoe factory break even, and now the toy concern was struggling too. Sybil suggested and arranged the drawing-room fundraising meeting at Cliveden.

Lady Sybil Smith, daughter of Lord Antrim, had joined the ELFS to help Sylvia run their first nursery. Driven mad by the boredom of a cloistered life as a Mayfair socialite, Sybil seized the opportunity provided by the war and decamped to the East End four days a week looking after babies while their mothers were at work. She brought the crèche an exquisite new doll's house taken from her own children's nursery. It was this gift that sparked the idea of setting up the toy factory. German toy imports, the women realized, had ceased thanks to the war. There was a gap in the market.

Sylvia invited her old friend Amy Browning from her student days at the RCA to come and help with design and fabrication, rekindling her own interest in arts, crafts and textiles. She roped in Herr Niederhofer, an expert German woodworker employed at the Lansbury woodyard who made beautiful carved wooden toys as a hobby, very much like the ones Sylvia had seen on her holiday in Austria. They instituted a policy in the factory for the women workers: if one of them designed a suitable toy, the factory purchased the template and paid the designer a royalty on sales.

The toy co-operative started with wooden toys, then diversified into the manufacture of dolls – black, yellow and white – all of which sold well. Rag baby dolls were particularly successful. Monkeys, lambs, terriers and other stuffed animals followed. Soon, other local factories made poor-quality, cheap copies of their new popular artisanal designs and undercut their prices. Trying to reassert their business position, Sylvia filled a taxi with toys and took them for appraisal by Gordon Selfridge and his radically feminist daughter Rosalie, who had supported the suffragettes robustly before the war. The quality of the toys is illustrated by the retailers that stocked them: Marshall and Snelgrove's flagship store on Oxford Street, Liberty on Regent Street and Gamages in Holborn, known for its toy department and Christmas catalogue coveted by children across the nation.

In response to Sybil Smith's request, Lady Astor had suggested the teatime fundraiser. Seeking new investors from among the Cliveden guests, Sylvia and Sybil set out their toys on display in an ornate grand salon. Well-dressed women swept in to hear the presentation and inspect the toys. A factory established and run by women was an unusual and intriguing proposition. Sylvia appealed to their sympathy.

> I spoke to them quietly of the hard, grey life in the East End; of
> the women and girls making toys in our little factory; drudges,
> errand girls, charwomen learning to paint, the sausage-filler turned
> designer. I strove to reveal to them within our poor ones the eternal
> psyche, striving for release from its dull prison.[1023]

Her pitch was well received: 'many people enjoy having their hearts touched – then pass to the next sensation, quite unchanged'.[1024] Unchanged or otherwise, the women contributed to a generous cash collection and made future pledges before they swarmed to a buffet 'laden with glittering delicacies, consuming, or discarding with a nibble, over the teacups, heedless of that austerity our hostess preached'.[1025]

As the house party gathered for pre-dinner drinks, Sylvia watched Arthur Balfour, in the centre of an admiring throng, talking with 'flippant, senile elegance' as he condemned the mendacity of the government. Nancy Astor was genuine in her intention to assist the toy factory, since she sat Sylvia next to her husband at dinner. Sylvia's affable host got off entirely on the wrong foot when he opened their conversation by telling her about 'two remarkable letters' he'd received from her marvellous sister. Unawares, he ploughed on, telling her that he'd been so impressed by Christabel's letters that he shared them with the War Office and ministers in charge of foreign trade.[1026] Sylvia changed the subject. She'd rather talk with him, she said, about his work to secure pure, clean milk for children, which she admired. Milk distribution for children, she told him, had been the ELFS' first war-relief effort.

Dinner over, Sylvia found it strange 'in the midst of the Great War to be filing out with the women, while the men sat on chatting with their wine, as they did in the time of our grandfathers. In the rush of an agitator's life, I had forgotten that such foolish customs still obtained.'[1027] For a while, she sat on an ottoman, awkwardly alone. In time, a troupe of 'lovely beings' bore down on her.

'What are you doing for the war work?'
'Nothing! ... I am not connected with War!'
'Of course we are all connected with the War!'
The lovely women turned their backs on me, I felt the icy atmosphere of their disdain.[1028]

Sylvia's is an unforgiving depiction of Nancy Astor: her hostess 'shouts', sings in 'strident tones', 'shrieks', 'struts', 'shrills' and 'jars'. In one instance, she is even 'notorious for her sauciness', which is rich coming from Sylvia.[1029] The source of Sylvia's animus was the same as that wellspring of pain and disagreement with her own mother and sister – the war itself and its price in the blood of young men. 'I think that every German should commit hari-kari by falling on his own sword!' Lady Astor patriotically declared. The 'babel of high-pitched merriment' that so assaulted Sylvia's senses was the clamour of well-fed jingoism.[1030] Coupled with her nationalistic bigotry, Nancy Astor's loudly proclaimed anti-Semitism appalled Sylvia. This tension was implicit between the women when they discussed the work of the ELFS, underpinning Astor's judgement that the morality of the East End women should be improved.

An exchange between hostess and guest as they walked the gorgeous landscaped grounds of Cliveden captures the antagonism between this Pankhurst and the woman who became Britain's first female MP. In what

Sylvia heard as 'tones of high patronage', Nancy questioned her about her work in the East End. 'I hope you teach the women to be good?' 'I do not consider that my province,' Sylvia answered; 'they know as much of goodness as I do. I try to spur them to revolt against the hideous conditions under which they live.' In response, Nancy Astor 'uttered a deprecating snort, and spoke of their need of "higher things"'.[1031]

Astor later wrote to Sylvia to tell her that she would never have funded her toy concern, let alone invited her as a guest into her own home, had she known at the time the extremity of her pacifism and socialist politics. Astor also upbraids Sylvia for increasing the wages of the toy-factory employees an outrageous £1 per week instead of the ten shillings set by the government, which funded the Queen Mary Workshops.

Nancy Astor may have regretted aiding the toy initiative, but might have approved of the fact that it prospered for a while due to the ruthless capitalist business practices of its sometime manager, Regina Hercbergova. To add to the difficulties caused by the undercutting of wages and prices by rival factories ripping off their designs, Regina was a problem, as Keir Hardie had recommended and introduced her, which made it awkward to get rid of her.

The factory was supposed to be run collectively, guided by a definite constitution and a workers' committee. Unbeknown to Sylvia and the leadership of the ELFS, Hercbergova set up her own business management system. A furious row erupted when her activities came to light.

According to Sylvia's version of events, she realized soon after Hercbergova arrived that, despite her claims to management expertise, she was in fact clueless about how to run a factory and keep the books. Although Regina was obsequious and flattered her, Sylvia wasn't fooled. But Hardie had sent Regina to Sylvia, asking her to give her a job. To try and deal with her inexperience and lack of the qualifications she claimed to possess, Sylvia brought in her businessman uncle Herbert Goulden. Uncle Herbert trained Regina for her job, far too well. The outcome of his instruction was that Regina swiftly grasped the most effective capitalist methods – cost cutting, increasing her own wages and decreasing those of the staff – while running roughshod over the co-operative, socialist ethos on which the factory was supposed to run. Regina sued Sylvia for libel after the publication of *The Home Front* in 1933, in which she revealed Regina's malpractice. The outcome of the legal action exposed the depth of Regina's venality. More interestingly, the evidence revealed the full extent of Norah Smyth's unstinting generosity towards this and all the other ELFS projects.

To help the defence case, Norah was required to submit to the court her relevant diary excerpts, correspondence and accounts. These provide an interesting peek into the unconventional toy factory. One employee recalled that Norah arrived punctually at 9 a.m. and gave helpful hints about how the toys should be shaped. Regina never appeared before 10 a.m. and was usually not seen until lunchtime or later. The younger women in the factory took advantage of being unsupervised to sing and play. Regina's tantrums added to the general cheerful indiscipline. In 1921, while Sylvia was in prison once again, Regina would seize the opportunity to take over the factory and push Sylvia off the organizing committee, a detail omitted by Sylvia in her own version of events. Whatever the shenanigans, Nancy Astor's sometime support and that uncomfortable importuning weekend at Cliveden proved worthwhile. Impressively, the factory was still a going concern in 1921.

Norah photographed the women at work in the toy factory making their beautiful and useful William Morris-inspired creations. In her youth, Sylvia had toured the north to sketch and paint women factory workers in order to document their lives. Now Norah's camera replaced her brush. The toy factory provided truly creative labour, and greatly enhanced the lives of the women involved in the co-operative project.

Norah's photographs tell the story of a kind of success. Published originally in the *Workers' Dreadnought*, one captures three women surrounded by plenty of glue, paint pots and brushes, creating a glorious wooden circus, complete with elephant, clowns and ballerinas. An older woman sits between two much younger. All are smiling, concentrating on their painting and wearing clean smocks. A patch of sunlight illuminates the dust-free environment of their cottage industry.

Although the ELFS had been inspired by the suffrage issue, the war had pushed them into emergency relief projects, setting up welfare provision which the government should have organized but which was non-existent. The removal of working men and boys to war left women – traditionally the most impoverished workforce – to support their communities in an environment where wages were already suppressed and unemployment rife.

The factories remained on too small a scale to make any real impact on unemployment and the increased wartime poverty of the East End, so Sylvia's wartime projects have been described as a form of 'feminist social work'.[1032] The ELFS provided an established community base from which to organize urgent social welfare on the ground and simultaneously sustain steady anti-war work.[1033] Their war work was an expression of active citizenship, but disagreement arose about this new direction. In 1917 Emma Boyce complained at a meeting that the ELFS appeared now to be more like 'a charity organization with suffrage tacked on'.[1034]

The day-care centres, nurseries, milk and food programmes, baby clinics and libraries set up by the ELFS might look like humanitarian relief initiatives, but charities did not publish radical policy manifestos demanding, for example, the immediate nationalization of all food supplies. On 15 August 1914, the *Dreadnought* published the ELFS' resolution proposing that 'During the war, the food shall be controlled by the government in the interests of all the people in order that we may feed or starve together without regard to wealth or social position. To make sure that the food supply is properly controlled, we demand that working women shall be called into consultation in fixing the prices to be charged for food and the way in which the food is to be distributed.' Sylvia's approach to these projects was imaginative and creative. Run by women, community-based, they drew on the most innovative thinking from around the world on health, nutrition, education, maternity, childcare and model work practices.

Post-war governments adopted Sylvia's methods and programmes for new national policies. Her work was studied by the Attlee administration when it was developing the National Health Service for its launch in 1948.

In 1931 Sylvia was instrumental in the establishment of the Socialist Workers' National Health Council, which held its first annual general meeting a year later on 12 March at Friends House, Euston Road. The Council emerged alongside the Socialist Medical Association established in November 1930 to organize the campaign for a state medical service. Modelling itself on the earlier democratic socialist schemes developed in Germany and Austria for basic medical treatment services, trade unions, the labour movement and the Labour Party funded, supported and campaigned for the state service. Medical and political activists agreed that if any success was to be attained a Socialist Medical Association must be affiliated to and exercise its influence through the Labour Party. The constitution of the new organization conformed to that of the Labour Party. Its three principal aims were:

1. To work for a Socialized Medical Service both preventive and curative, free and open to all.
2. To secure for the people the highest possible standard of health.
3. To disseminate the principles of socialism within the medical and allied services.[1035]

Years later, the founders of the World Health Organization declared that 'the enjoyment of the highest attainable standard of health is one of the fundamental rights of every human being'.

Socialist members of the British Medical Association (BMA) organized debates and meetings, and up and down Britain BMA branches endorsed the establishment of a state medical service. Opponents at the debates argued that a state service would lead to the disappearance of the family doctor, that its cost would be prohibitive and that the personal factor in the practice of medicine would vanish. All these arguments applied only to the middle class and the well-off already blessed with 'family doctors'. Countrywide, it was the younger members of the BMA who most fully supported the initiative, but there was a large number of older members of the medical profession who, while not initially prepared to accept all the principles of the SMA, were in favour of any proposals for the establishment of a state service.

The Socialist Workers' National Health Council committed itself to the 'socialisation of the National Health, in its constructive, preventive and curative aspects', and set up a nationwide organization with district committees, 'to co-ordinate socialist forces against the vast vested professional, trade and political interests which exploit workers' lives, health and sickness, for profit or for power'.

The ultimate goal of the National Council was a socialist policy and scheme for the establishment of a National Medical and Allied Service, 'which will afford the best and fullest benefit of medical and allied sciences, free and open and utilised by all'.

In preparation for the first AGM of the Socialist Workers' National Health Council Sylvia wrote 'Outline of Socialist Scheme for the National Health and Medical Allied Medical Services' in 1932.[1036] Her scheme 'provides a free medical service to all with all that Medical Science can give, and its cost is born by the National Exchequer, as is education and other public services'. It prioritized 'social responsibilities and humanity to one and all', and should have a hospital infrastructure provisioned with the best equipment, adequate to scale and 'up to date'.[1037] Sylvia's blueprint covered legislation, structure, management and administration, public finance, architecture, medical services – hospitals, clinics, outpatients, home visiting – and medical training for nurses, doctors, surgeons, specialists, administrators and managers and the provision and regulation of medicines and equipment. The detailed and thoroughgoing plan, structured in functional sections, is objective and practical throughout.[1038]

The scheme she proposed would be under worker control through central and local government authorities and departments, requiring reorganization of the Ministry of Health, disability and mental health departments, maternity and child welfare, school medical support and National Health insurance. Sylvia set out the process and structure for this reorganization, detailing duties and responsibilities of departments and individual personnel, qualifications and conditions of service. Hospitals and health centres are considered in detail. Her creative programme for public health education for the lay public and specialists is a delight to read. Numerical and financial data sets, disability, invalidity and mental-health benefit payments are documented in the annexes to the proposal.

In her appendix, she argued the case for a rapid implementation against the longer-term 'transitional stage' towards a state medical service usually proposed by political parties: 'The doctrine of the inevitability of gradualism (which must be the motive for an evolutionary transitional scheme) means, to most that hold it, that gradualism in preferred to socialism "for [their] life".'

In the introductory overview she included an analysis of current party political policies regarding the question of a publicly funded healthcare system accessible to all. No such scheme existed within the sphere of the present party 'practical politics', she pointed out, for reasons of 'economy'. 'It is "put off" and not worth fighting for.'[1039] In the appendix, she sets out existing procedures and health policies of the Labour Party and the TUC. The proposal ended with a political appeal: 'Let the government come to the aid of the workers as it did to the aid of the bankers!'[1040]

From 1915, women started joining the industrial workforce in huge numbers. No longer firefighting the consequences of chronic unemployment, the ELFS were able to shift their attention to issues affecting the protection of women workers: the abolition of sweating, training, education and development for women and securing equal pay. The *Dreadnought* published detailed exposés of hellish working conditions, such as in the dark, unsanitary basement in Limehouse where women made the turtle soup served in porcelain tureens to the royal family.

The Labour Party, socialist organizations, trade unions and both Liberal and Conservative governments claimed themselves committed to ensuring the best conditions possible for women engaged in making anything that would help win the war – uniforms, tinned bully beef, boots, munitions. In this area, the ELFS propaganda and agitation work achieved widespread traction.

Sylvia's involvement in infant healthcare and education evolved out of the milk-distribution scheme she set up, initially run from the Women's Hall at Old Ford Road. This was the programme she brought up with Waldorf Astor at that Cliveden dinner. Most of the babies brought to the clinic were too sick to digest their feed. Sylvia had discussed the problem with her old friend Dr Barbara Tchaykovsky from the WSPU. They started four mother-and-baby clinics and milk stations in London, making doctors available to advise mothers and treat children, without charge. Alice Johnson joined Tchaykovsky as the clinic's second doctor. They established one of the first clinics in the old disused stable in Bow where Sylvia had once hidden all night in a haystack evading recapture by the police.

The ELFS opened several more relief offices, at 319 East India Dock Road and in Crowder Hall on Bow Road. The Poplar Woman's Hall was opened at 20 Railway Street and another at 53 Leonard's Street, Bromley. The Canning Town ELFS Women's Centre opened under the direction of the brilliant, formidable Daisy Parsons, who later became the first woman mayor of West Ham. A member of the six-strong working women's deputation to Asquith in June 1914, Parsons continued to work with Sylvia throughout the war. The centres provided free milk to mothers with babies, as well as Virol malt extract, eggs and barley. Sybil Smith ran the nursery. The doughty airship activist Muriel Matters had studied recently with Maria Montessori. She joined the ELFS to set up and run a Montessori school for the older children.

Barbara Tchaykovsky had run the White Cross League for child victims of the dock strike in May 1912, and joined the ELFS in opposition to Emmeline and Christabel's support for the war. She pointed out that during the first year of the war 75,000 British soldiers (2.2 per cent of the combatants) had been killed. During the same period over 100,000 babies in Britain (12.2 per cent of those born) had died. In 1915 nearly 1,000 mothers and their babies attended the ELFS clinics and many more benefited from the clean-milk programme. George Lansbury helped fundraise for the scheme and many suffragists made generous donations. In 1915 the ELFS' milk bill alone ran to over £1,000. Glaxo and Nestlé donated baby food and milk in exchange for advertising space in the *Dreadnought*.

Norah Smyth's photographs document the expansion of the clinics programme. On the corner of Old Ford Road and St Stephen's Road stood an empty pub called the Gunmaker's Arms, opposite the munitions factory on Gunmaker's Lane. It was available for rent.

Just before the outbreak of the war, in the spring of 1914, Lavinia Dock, who ran medical and nursing projects at the Henry Street settlement in New York, visited Sylvia and Zelie at Old Ford Road. She wrote to a friend about her visit to the ELFS to observe their 'work among the toilers on the East Side':

> Sylvia has the settlement idea in her mind. She was deeply
> impressed with our settlement, especially, and she is planning a
> settlement life down there for herself ... Then, after the vote is won,
> she looks forward to settlement life, a return to her art, but always
> keeping a political centre as a main purpose. She is a wonderful and
> inspiring girl.[1041]

In April 1915, the ELFS reopened the Gunmaker's Arms as a day nursery and mother-and-baby health clinic called the Mothers' Arms. It was the new ELFS headquarters, and the hall at the back became the venue for the biggest of Cost Price restaurants. Bessie Lansbury, wife of George

Lansbury, was appointed director and Maude Florence Hebbes ran the nursery. In a speech at the Caxton Hall in 1916 Israel Zangwill said, 'The hope of the world lies in changing the Gunmaker's Arms into the Mothers' Arms!'[1042]

After the war, Stella Miles Franklin came to visit Sylvia and wrote about her work in what she described as 'the dark pit of East London',[1043] blasted and more deeply impoverished by the conflict. They had met in Chicago at Hull House and Franklin had kept track of the progress of the east London campaign through her close friend Zelie. Sylvia's home and ELFS headquarters at Old Ford Road is described by Franklin as a 'tumbledown house', with an 'impoverished meeting hall' tacked on the back providing premises for the Cost Price Restaurant. Sylvia introduced Franklin to the nursery and Montessori school, showed her round the clinic and free medical advice centre, then walked her to the toy factory, where she was impressed to learn that the beautifully made toys were 'in great demand' and stocked by leading London department stores.[1044]

Maude Hebbes ran the Mothers' Arms nursery until it closed in 1921. Her next job was as the first nurse employed by Marie Stopes, who put her in charge of her pioneering birth-control clinic in Marlborough Road, Holloway. Hebbes had qualified as a midwife in 1908 and was active in the WSPU, treating women injured in violent demonstrations and dangerously ill from the effects of forcible feeding. On several occasions she had loaned Sylvia her uniform as a disguise so she could evade the police. She left the WSPU with Sylvia to become a founder member of the ELFS.

The Mothers' Arms was the flagship of the four ELFS mother-and-baby clinics. Maude Hebbes appears in many of Norah's photographs, holding underweight babies with great tenderness, or playing with children and encouraging them to laugh and romp around. When Marie Stopes interviewed her for the position at the Society of Constructive Birth Control's pioneering new clinic, Maude told her that she had read both of her books, *Married Love* and *Wise Parenthood*. Sylvia read these books too, and they were discussed at the lectures and meetings held in the old tap room of Mothers' Arms.[1045]

Sylvia brought the mothers-and-infants clinic and the day nursery together under one roof with the Montessori school for older children run by Muriel Matters. 'The public houses are with few exceptions the best built and most efficiently preserved premises in the East End,' Sylvia wrote.[1046] The Mothers' Arms scrubbed up into a utopia of progressive childcare. The ELFS painted it throughout in sunshine and white paint, put up bright chintzes in the windows, with handmade quilts and proper sheets on the cots, and decorated the walls with illustrations from Walter Crane toy books. Sylvia painted the ELFS initials in gold on the outside walls, wreathed in bright red liberty caps. Women going to the small-arms munitions factory across the road dropped off their infants on their way into work.

Sylvia turned the pub's bar into the reception and lecture room of the clinic, installed giant cupboards with sliding doors to store medicines and baby foods, and large drawers for baby carry cots and maternity outfits. Sylvia's old schoolfriend Lucy Burgis from Manchester High School for Girls managed and maintained the maternity and nursery clothes. The children shed their shabby clothes, stockings and boots when they arrived in the morning and were bathed and dressed in the fresh, bright nursery garments. Their clothes and shoes were then cleaned and mended ready for the end of the day. Nurses and teachers took the children out into nearby Victoria Park. Those old enough to walk held on to a long rope. The Mothers' Arms day nursery could accommodate forty children – but there were applications for ten times that number of places.

Lady Sybil Smith went hunting among her elite friends with time on their hands to do some voluntary work. Lady Lutyens sent one of her daughters to 'develop a social consciousness',[1047] and Sylvia packaged the story of the Mothers' Arms for the press with great canniness. As a result of her publicity, the Corporation of London and the Ministries of both Health and Education provided direct financial grants. West End theatre managers organized Sunday benefit fundraisers and all sorts of people interested in progressive healthcare, social work and child education came to look round.

The Mothers' Arms embodied a fully functional pilot model of Sylvia's 200-page case study and manifesto published in 1930, her 'urgent plea for a universal free Maternity Service, and an earnest effort to make plain the great need of mothers'.[1048] Sylvia's effectiveness at radical maternity, child and healthcare reform was based on assiduous reading and research. She drew her knowledge from diverse sources: traditional feminist arguments about the need to educate women as doctors and surgeons as well as nurses, such as those put forward by Mary Wollstonecraft;

modern Montessori methods; and innovative social reform programmes for maternity, childcare and education in Scandinavian countries. As its architects attested, Sylvia's East End work on maternity and childcare services provided functional blueprints for developing policy during the post-war creation of the NHS.

George Bernard Shaw amiably agreed to Sylvia's invitation to speak in her fundraising lecture series at the Mothers' Arms. The event made a hefty £75 profit for the ELFS' projects. But Shaw's equivocal speech had disappointed Sylvia, who chaired the event. In some of its passages, he was decidedly jingo and cheerfully contradicted the opinions he expressed in his essay 'Common Sense About the War'. Embarrassed, Sylvia nevertheless maintained sufficient courtesy for Shaw to compliment her on having 'the family charm'.[1049] Afterwards, they exchanged frank letters. Sylvia regretted his inconsistency. He was a household name. What he said mattered. She tried to persuade him to take a clear stand. Shaw replied that in helping to save babies she was doing a terrific job, but to oppose the war was utterly hopeless. 'How can you hope to convert the public,' he asked, 'when you cannot even convert your mother and Christabel?'[1050] A direct Shavian hit.

Sylvia was never cross with Shaw for very long. The bracing intellectual jousting between them was too much fun. While Sylvia despaired at his prevarications, she sensed his heart was in the right place and admired his frankness, even when she disagreed with his position. In January 1916, the ELFS opened the New Year by organizing children's parties in Bow, Poplar and Canning Town. George Lansbury joined in with local labour organizers to support the effort. 'Children are only children once,' Sylvia wrote, 'we wanted to compensate them as far as we could for the dark days of war.'[1051] They gave the children a late Christmas, interwoven with a spring pageant to bring promise for the new year. Norah Smyth's 'whimsical' cousin Georgie Mackey donated a huge seasonal fir tree and Father Christmas – in the disguised form of Norah – presented the children with gifts. George Lansbury gave a puppet show. Sylvia invited GBS to judge an essay-writing competition. Fully entering into the spirit of the occasion, Shaw awarded first prize to Miss Molly Beer of 9 Brabazon Street, Poplar:

> *In account with* G. Bernard Shaw
>   Correcting two mistakes in grammar 1d

Striking out two apostrophes put before 's' when there was nothing belonging ½d

Completing the word 'affectionately' as it was written 'affec' 1d

Counting 22 kisses for Miss Pankhurst 1.½d

I award Miss Beer a special prize of 3d. for laziness. She was in such a hurry to get into bed that she wrote the shortest essay … so she has only 1d to pay.[1052]

Norah Smyth's photographs show women smiling with infants sitting in their laps at the WSF Mother and Infant Clinic at Poplar. In another, Mrs Schlette distributes fresh milk at 20 Railway Street to a hall packed with girls and boys presenting their own bottles. Some turn towards Norah's camera to give a wink or smile. The nursery is full of well-clothed infants and blanket-lined prams. Sybil Smith sits comfortably amid them, dangling an infant.

Norah's photograph of children taught by the Montessori method at the Mothers' Arms reveals in close detail their varied, creative teaching materials and absorbed expressions. Another of the same class at lunch shows the children carefully serving each other at table from trays, dressed in smartly striped aprons. Among the images are photographs of severely emaciated, malnourished babies. However, Norah is consistent generally in ensuring that her subjects maintain their dignity, resilience, humour and individuality. There is no prurient indulgence of shocking filth, nor clichés of working-class inertia. All her subjects are active, engaged, alert and owners of the space of their urban environment. There are no Dickensian urchins, jaunty cockneys or slum dens. Those who had grown up Victorian knew their Mayhew and their Malthus – Smyth and Pankhurst were determined to offer a version of East End life demystified and undramatized.[1053]

With all the energy he had left, Hardie had fought the war and the government tooth and nail since August 2014. The government bashed workers and trade unionism, denouncing them for limiting output and undermining the war effort. One of Hardie's final exchanges with Lloyd George in the Commons was a defence of munitions workers. A twelve-hour day and seven-day week now was the norm, but the government blamed any shortfalls and problems on the putative drunkenness, poor timekeeping and slothfulness of the workers. Lloyd George, Minister of Munitions, denounced workers' laziness and drinking habits 'in the same breath' as urging forward manufacturing output.[1054] Hardie protested:

> In time of war one would have thought the rich classes would grovel on their knees before the working classes who are doing so much to pile up their wealth. Instead, the men who are working eighty-four hours a week are being libelled, maligned and insulted; and on the authority of their employers, the lying word, accepted without inquiry by Lloyd George, went round the world that the working class were a set of drunken hooligans. That is the reward they got. The truth is that the shifts could be arranged to overtake all the work.[1055]

Lloyd George protested that Hardie had misrepresented him. Hardie continued relentlessly: 'I pointed out that the employers, when before you, had put the whole blame on the drinking habits of the workers, and you, by accepting their statement without challenge, had given world currency to the fiction that the workers were drunken wasters.'[1056]

Despite his failing health, Hardie had insisted on attending the opening session of parliament in February 1915. He persisted in trying to continue with his usual routine of public speaking and meetings and angrily scotched rumours in the party and press about his illness. Sometime between February and May, Sylvia received a telegram from him while speaking at Poplar Town Hall, instructing her to take no notice of press reports that he had collapsed. 'My anxiety aroused, I rushed off to Nevill's Court as soon as the meeting was over. He disclosed that he had a seizure in the House of Commons. Dr Addison had gone to his aid. It was the first sign of a grave condition.'[1057]

On 19 May 1915 the Labour Party had met to decide whether or not it should join in the wartime coalition government, 'the ultimate incorporation'.[1058] After bitter argument, Arthur Henderson agreed to serve in the cabinet. MacDonald described it as a 'heartbreaking' decision. His friend Charles Trevelyan predicted correctly that this was the end of the Liberals. Four of the six ILP MPs opposed identifying with the government, but all the other Labour MPs supported its war policy and its so-called non-political recruiting campaign. Hardie heard the news in a hydro in Caterham, Kent where he'd spent some time convalescing the year before with Lillie. It was the final blow.

Reassurances from political colleagues that they'd just have to move forward and keep the party intact when the war ended made no impact. For Hardie, it was over. Towards the end of May, he decided he would no longer attend parliament and determined to return to Scotland.

The press hounded Hardie, making no allowance for his illness. Zelie put into Sylvia's hands the copy of *The Suffragette* that reproduced a cartoon from *Punch*, portraying the Kaiser giving a vulgarized Keir Hardie a large bag of money: 'Also the Nobel prize (though tardy) / I now confer on Keir von Hardie.'[1059] Sylvia wrote to her mother in sadness to tell her that she had seen the cartoon and informing her plainly, ' "He is dying." I believed that her old love for him must flame out against further insults, did she know his state. She did not answer me.'[1060] Sylvia's thoughts returned to her childhood home in Manchester, where she'd first met Hardie. She recalled her father's great love for him, and 'how staunch a friend Keir Hardie was to us in the after years!'[1061]

She heard that the WSPU had sent Flora Drummond to Hardie's Merthyr constituency to campaign for the new Labour candidate lined up to replace him, a violent jingo called Charles Butt Stanton who specialized in smashing up peace meetings – which explains why the WSPU were supporting a Labour contender. Flora, who had named her son Keir, had in the past spent many evenings sitting on the hearthrug at Nevill's Court and had frequently sought Hardie's assistance for WSPU problems.

Frank Smith made the arrangements for packing up Hardie's London life. He sent Sylvia a letter dictated by Hardie, requesting her to meet him the following week at Nevill's Court. Hardie intended to sell most of the stuff that was there. He wanted to return the portrait she had made of him, and – significantly – her letters. He asked that he might keep the picture of the child she had painted at Penshurst as a gift for him: 'The one over the fireplace I have so closely associated with you that I should not like to part with it.'[1062] He maintained always that the child looked like her.

Of the letters, he particularly wanted to return those she had written to him from America. 'They are well worth preserving.' Many of them were also emotionally and sexually explicit and thus compromising: 'you could use your discretion as to which are most worthy of being kept and published and which should be destroyed ... I must leave the matter entirely in your hands. I have not now the capacity for dealing with such a matter.'[1063]

Reading the letter, Sylvia saw that the word 'now' had been inserted in ink in Hardie's own hand. 'So that was his thought: to give permanency to those letters I had written to him in the unconscious communion of friendship.'[1064] This is what, finally, he could offer: not to deny their relationship by destroying their intimate correspondence. The decision was to be hers.

Their final meeting at Nevill's Court in the first week of June was unlike any before. For the first time since they'd met when she was twelve, they were tongue-tied in each other's company. Struggling to maintain her self-control, Sylvia painfully rejected Hardie's offers of keepsakes as he urged her to choose what she wanted. 'I don't want to be given anything!' she exclaimed. She'd wanted him. And now it had come to this. Frank Smith came in, but his presence did nothing to ease the situation. 'Keir in his agony, mysterious, unkenned, seemed to loom over us like some great, tragic ruin.'[1065] Already Sylvia had transposed him back into the rock for which he was named. When Frank Smith left the room on an errand, she summoned the courage she knew she had to find to take her leave. 'I felt him near me, heard for the last time his voice: "You have been very brave!"'[1066]

Throughout their relationship, they had maintained a conversation in postcards, short text and image messages, from just around the corner in London or across far-flung continents. The final postcard Sylvia received from Hardie at the end of July was written from Caterham hydro, shortly before his return to Scotland. 'Dear Sylphia, In about a week I expect to be gone from here with no more mind control than when I came.' The sign-off, simply, 'Love'. The misspelling of her name and the trembling hand confirmed what she'd been told of his deterioration. Yet truth was embedded in the slip. She had been his very sylph-like Sylvia, a spiritual, visionary, potentially transformative force in his life. For Hardie, Sylvia had embodied, among other things, a medium delivering news from a better future.

This was the last direct word she received from him. Hardie spent his final summer in Cumnock with his family, approaching his fifty-ninth birthday. In September, he was taken to hospital in Glasgow, where he died at noon on Sunday the 26th, with Lillie and his daughter Nan at his side.

That afternoon, unawares, Sylvia was speaking at an anti-conscription rally in Trafalgar Square, alongside Henry Hyndman, Charlotte Despard, Emmeline Pethick-Lawrence, the MP Will Anderson and trade union leaders, including John Hill and Fred Bramley. She saw newsboys with posters of a special edition come running into the square, shouting out their headline, drowned by the noise of the rally. She couldn't hear what they were saying. One of the press placards brandished by the news runners came into focus – 'DEATH OF KEIR HARDIE'.[1067] Barbara Tchaykovsky saw that Sylvia was looking faint and made her sit down on Nelson's plinth with her head between her knees. 'I felt as they who had lost their dearest in the war, for the war had killed him, as surely as it had killed the men who went to the trenches and were shot.'

The night brought torment: 'the mind sought to transform what might have been to what was'. Never would this palpable sense of the possible life unlived with Hardie leave her. 'The regrets surged over me – for words unsaid and things undone, for hours unlived … ah, to have seen the last of him! Within me rose the great rebellion against the cruelties of our life, and its denials … its foolish, vain denials …'[1068] She blamed everyone for letting him down, and none more than herself. Her anguish conjured 'scenes of make-believe', the image of the entirely self-sacrificing helpmeet she never could have been, even if Lillie had got out of the way:

> To have stood beside him; travelled with him; laid aside all else to
> support and cherish him. Not one had borne that part towards him
> fully. All their work, their families, their health, their incapacities –
> not one had said: 'I will give my all to serve with him, and to
> serve him'. Lesser men and women have known such serviceable
> companionship. Not you, O you tower of strength! In the lonely
> heights of your isolation, this was denied to you![1069]

The first storm of grief passed to more dispassionate public duty. In the dawn, she imagined him 'mantled in his great reserve, impregnable'. Her silent rock. 'I felt the charge laid on me to make a more pointed and urgent struggle against the war and the influences which gave it birth.'[1070] Calmer, practical, she spent the day drafting his obituary for the *Dreadnought*.

While Sylvia wrote her memorial, the nationals diminished Hardie with faint praise or scorn, all unable to rise above the politics of the moment. *The Times* mention was curt and dismissive: Hardie, it asserted, stupidly created a 'cleavage' between himself and 'patriotic fellow labourites'. He was 'the most extreme of British politicians ... one of those who spent their lives expressing the views of a minority' and 'advocating unpopular causes'.[1071] On top of which, he was Scots and 'dour'. This latter was one of the most laughable misrepresentations of Hardie.[1072] To the *Mirror*, Hardie 'was one of the best hated men of his time'.[1073]

In parliament, to its eternal disgrace, nothing was said to acknowledge or honour Keir Hardie's death.

Sylvia's obituary steamrollered over all the trimmers – clear, compassionate and entirely free of the maudlin regrets that characterized her later depressed reminiscences: 'Keir Hardie has been the greatest human being of our time: when the dust raised by opposition to the pioneer has settled, this will be known by all.' She captured his essence, showing his uncompetitive nature. Astutely, she observed that he had 'loved humanity as others love their immediate families'. This was a forgiving take on the nature of his emotional generosity and its consequences for his intimates, to whom it often felt indiscriminate and indicative of personal insecurity. Some suggested then and now that Sylvia ought to have stated in her obituary that Hardie's wife Lillie and their three children survived him. Was Sylvia's silence on this born of discretion or righteous anger? It would have been proper and good mannered to follow the convention – and entirely hypocritical. Lillie certainly would have held Sylvia in contempt for doing it. Sylvia knew far too much of the truth to sentimentalize the 'little mother' public narrative legitimizing Hardie's guilt and inability to live a free life.

Sylvia was always a successive drafter when writing, but there are more iterations of this obituary in her manuscripts than for any other article she ever wrote. She romanticized Hardie, returning him to the Scottish granite from which he was hewn in mist-wreathed prose that Walter Scott would have admired:

Fate fitly named this man, who was braver and more steadfast
than the general human kind; Keir (Rock) was his mother's name,

Hardie, his father's. This hardy rock was a child of nature, an outcrop of the Scottish moors. His father was a fisherman and he too, a fisher of souls for socialism, had the weather-fashioned look of those who follow the calling of the sea. He was built for great strength, his head more grandly carved than any other; his deep-set eyes like sunshine distilled, as we see it through the waters of a pool in the brown earth ...[1074]

Sylvia and Hardie spent years in conversation about spirituality, faith and religion. Both had been brought up in radically atheist households by parents who rigorously discouraged belief in religious mysticism. Unlike Sylvia, Hardie developed into a believer in radical Christian socialism.

The first joyous revelation of his life was religious. He wished that all might live according to the Sermon on the Mount. When he first heard of Socialism he shrank from it as material, but as he grasped the fullness of its ideal he realized that it could make Christ's teaching practical ... he came to look upon State Socialism as the necessary prelude to a free Communism ... Had Keir Hardie lived in a communistic world, he would have been a great writer, painter or musician.[1075]

Rightly, she focused on the years of isolation, ridicule and abuse that characterized his political journey: 'The first Labour Member of Parliament, he was for years absolutely alone.'[1076] At the end of his political life, he was isolated once again, as a pacifist in wartime who so angered people that he had to have a personal bodyguard wherever he went in public. 'He had hoped that the strength of the growing socialist movement would make this war impossible. Undoubtedly his grief hastened the ending of his life.'[1077]

Her summary assessment was accurate and fit testimony: the keynote of Hardie's contribution, she concluded, was that 'he made the Labour movement a coherent political force'.[1078]

The ILP paid for Hardie's funeral in Glasgow, where crowds lined the streets and processions brought the city to a standstill. Women marched in phalanxes to honour his lifelong stand for them. Lillie, their three children and all Hardie's siblings were present. Tactfully, Sylvia stayed away. She sent a wreath of laurel tied with the purple, green and white colours of the suffragettes, with the added red of her own ELFS.

May O'Callaghan, Sylvia's sub-editor at the *Dreadnought*, commissioned George Bernard Shaw to write a piece about Hardie. He delivered his copy with a covering letter saying that his article was 'not nearly so good as Sylvia's'. As an expression of his admiration, he asked for a lifetime subscription to the *Dreadnought* in exchange for paying a full ten years upfront, cheque enclosed.

Recognizing its candid truth, Sylvia found Shaw's quintessentially Shavian piece almost too bitter to stomach. He put it bluntly:

> There is, I feel sure, a very general feeling of relief in the House of Commons and in the Labour Party now that Keir Hardie's body lies mouldering in the grave ... I really do not see what Hardie could do but die. Could we expect him to hang on and sit there among the poor slaves who imagined themselves Socialists until the touchstone of war found them out and exposed them for what they are? ... [T]hat the workers themselves – the Labour Party he had so painfully dragged into existence – should snatch still more eagerly at the war to surrender those liberties and escape back into servility, crying: 'You may trust your masters: they will treat you well' ... this was what broke the will to live in Keir Hardie.[1079]

Memorial services raised hymns, prayers, speeches and vigils up and down the country. Sylvia buried herself in work. Heartbroken, Frank Smith wrote to Sylvia, 'What a loss is ours. I don't think anyone, among the many thousands who mourn for him, knew, understood or loved him better than you and I.'[1080]

Not that they knew him as well as they thought, as it turned out.

At a Labour conference Kate Glasier told Sylvia the secret of Hardie's illegitimacy, revealed in the first – and only – chapter of his unfinished autobiography discovered at Cumnock after his death. Kate and Sylvia were having tea alone together at the International Women's Suffrage Club in Grafton Terrace, Kentish Town. 'Hardie wasn't his name, you know. Hardie was only his stepfather ... that's why he was so absolutely different from the rest of them.'[1081] Sylvia asked to see the manuscript and it was sent to her on loan, 'two brief, pregnant galleys of print'. It confirmed Kate Glasier's story. Hardie wrote that his birth was branded with 'the bar sinister'. 'He spoke of his mother Mary Keir; but of his father not.'[1082]

Sylvia wondered at the 'beautiful silence' with which Hardie had guarded his revered mother's secret, the secret that prevented him from ever getting beyond the first chapter of his autobiography. Hardie's attempts at writing this personal memoir are a fable of self-sabotage. He'd had a go at starting to write it in London during the early days of their relationship and then told Sylvia that he'd lost the finished first chapter somewhere in the *Labour Leader* office and 'could not bring himself to begin it again'.[1083] He tried again several times, but each time the pages were by some mishap mislaid.

Hardie's miscarried autobiography is an unborn literary orphan holding hands with the terminated biography of Karl Marx attempted by his youngest daughter. Eleanor discovered that her father was father also to Freddy Demuth, whose secret paternity the Marx daughters had attributed to Friedrich Engels. Unable to be the bearer of this revelation, Eleanor Marx ceased the project.

Later in 1915 Sylvia met Hardie's sister Agnes Aiton in Glasgow for the first time. They became friends and corresponded. When she was speaking or at meetings in the city Sylvia stayed with Agnes, who told her things about her brother that brought 'sorrow and wonder to my heart'.[1084] Hardie had enjoyed the embrace of many women. In the end, it was to his mother's arms that he remained most loyal.

Sylvia endured her bereavement with her own 'beautiful silence' and much dignity. Those true friends who knew about the depth and longevity of their relationship were discreet, tender and solicitous. It required grim fortitude and resolute self-composure to grieve alone. Those who could, tried to comfort her. Sylvia now had to endure yet another occlusion of the significance of her love in his life – this time in his death.

Sylvia wondered at all she hadn't known about Hardie, particularly his lifelong concealment of his illegitimacy to protect the story of his mother's life. She felt ambivalent about the circumstances that prevented them ever living together as they'd longed to, except for their brief time in their rented Kent cottage on Cinder Hill near Penshurst. 'Waves of thought were rending me, grief at the sadness of life, amaze at its poignant drama. Novels, romances, what is the need of them? Not one is so strange, so poignant as the true romance of Life.'[1085]

23

Welcome to the Soviets

Sylvia's widespread reputation as an anti-war militant grew from December 1914. Already an established voice against the war by the time of Hardie's death, Sylvia's grief for him infused her peacework with a new transcendental fervour.

In December 1915 Sylvia, Norah Smyth and Jim visited Merthyr Tydfil, where Sylvia longed 'to renew myself in the communion of memory with him who had made the name of that place a household word'.[1086] Sylvia and Norah met up with old political friends, 'gathered together as a little company of believers, working and hoping for the dawn of Peace to break, in a world distraught by war'.[1087] They took Jim for walks in Gethin Woods, and Sylvia showed Norah the far-reaching views of the South Wales valleys and the Brecon Beacons that Hardie had shown her on their hikes. They helped the local ILP women dress the Christmas tree for a children's party. A choir of children treated them to a recital of the verses Hardie wrote for the melody of the Welsh anthem. Wherever Sylvia went in Merthyr, she remembered the times they had spent there together.

Sylvia had lost Aunt Mary, many close friends and Keir Hardie to death by principle. Emily Davison's martyrdom she saw as symbolic of the price exacted by fighting for radical social change. The rift with her mother and Christabel wounded her deeply. While Hardie was alive, he provided an emotional bridge between their shared political past and a possible future in which they might reconcile. With his death, this psychic bridge collapsed. But Sylvia did not.

To pull herself out of the miseries of 1915 and her grief for Hardie, Sylvia threw herself into organizing a festival to start the year. With the arrival of 1916 the ELFS organized New Year parties in Bow, Poplar and Canning Town. 'Children are only children once; we wanted to compensate them as far as we could for the dark days of war.'[1088] The centrepiece of the Bow Baths parties, photographed by Norah, was a spring pageant performed by the Junior Suffragettes, diverse both ethnically and in class terms. 'Its flowers,' Sylvia recalled, 'were our East End blooms: dark Mary Carr from poor little Ranwell Street, where people all helped each other, the two pretty Cohens, one as slender as the lily she represented and the other, Nellie, my secretary, glowing as a ripe peach.'[1089] Violet Lansbury played the Spirit of Spring and pale Lily Gatward, decked in the ELFS purple, white and green flag, embodied the Spirit of Liberty. The Spirit of Peace was played by 'a stern, stiff' young Joan Beauchamp, who later became the editor of *Tribunal*, the newspaper of conscientious objectors, and went to prison for it. A quartet of 'merry' three-year-olds led the parade, the middle two girls in red liberty caps. They held banners emblazoned with 'PEACE' and 'PLENTY'.

To Sylvia, 'the central loveliness of it all' was the now sixteen-year-old Rose Pengelly, arising as the sylvan Spirit of the Woods – the figure closest to Sylvia's heart. Elf-like, her red-gold hair and rosy skin dancing in the limelight, Rose played 'upon Pan's reeds' and 'danced with unimagined grace, artless, untaught – a vision of youth's loveliness, the denizen of a slum!'[1090] 'I had loved her,' Sylvia wrote, 'since that day ... when she led the strikers from Back's asbestos factory into our Women's Hall, telling us they had nicknamed her "Sylvia".'[1091]

Rose danced in the first Bow Baths party pageant on Thursday, 'a glimpse of moving ecstasy, which made my heart tremble with its beauty'.[1092] On Saturday she should have danced again at the second Bow Baths occasion, but tragedy struck. A blade for box making sliced her flute-playing fingers. Sylvia, horrified, described the accident: 'the knife of the machine she was working descended on her pretty right hand, rending and mangling the thumb and a couple of fingers'.[1093] As Rose lay unconscious in a spreading pool of blood, her co-workers ran to ask permission from a policeman to purchase a tot of brandy to revive her. Licensing hours were now restricted and a wartime regulation called the 'No Treating Order' required that alcohol had to be paid for by the person supplied. Rose's employer made no offer of help and refused to pay a cab fare to get her to hospital. Her co-workers were threatened with the sack if they took time off to take her there, so Rose had to go alone. Roughly bandaged, she walked to the station, paid for her own ticket for the train to the London Hospital in Whitechapel and sat in the crowded outpatients department until late at night. When finally she was seen to, her crushed thumb and two fingers were amputated.

On her 1912 tour of America, Sylvia had visited several women's laundries, including one named The Ideal in Milwaukee. Though presented to her as a model laundry, it made her 'feel sick at heart'.[1094] She had written then of watching workers tackling machinery that was old, stiff and hard to work. 'To prevent their fingers being caught in some of the machines the women had to practise constant vigilance.'[1095] Rose Pengelly was ever vigilant, but had fallen prey nevertheless to a terrible industrial accident. Unable to dance in the second performance of the spring pageant, Rose was honoured as the heroine of the evening. (In 1921, she would marry and settle in Devizes, Wiltshire, where she had a son.)

For the following three years, until the armistice in November 1918, Sylvia worked for peace with a renewed and formidable courage in what was at first a wildly unpopular cause. The significance of her contribution to the national anti-conscription and peace movement in Britain was all too clear when in 1917 the *Workers' Dreadnought* became the first London publication, and the second in the country, to publish the letter from Lieutenant Siegfried Sassoon, MC, 3rd Battalion, Royal Welsh Fusiliers, to his commanding officer, declining to return to duty.

The statement, written by Sassoon, Bertrand Russell and John Middleton Murry and distributed widely to opinion makers and the press, first appeared in the *Bradford Pioneer* on 27 July and in the *Workers' Dreadnought* the following day. The Liberal-turned-Labour MP Hastings Lees-Smith read Sassoon's letter in the House of Commons two days later. The next day, it was printed in *The Times*.

I am making this statement as an act of wilful defiance of military
authority, because I believe that the war is being deliberately
prolonged by those who have the power to end it.

I am a soldier, convinced that I am acting on behalf of the
soldiers. I believe that this war, upon which I entered as a war
of defence, has now become a war of aggression and conquest.
I believe that the purposes for which I and my fellow soldiers
entered upon this war should have been so clearly stated as to have
made it impossible to change them and that had this been done the
objects which actuated us would now be attainable by negotiation.

I have seen and endured the sufferings of the troops and I can
no longer be a party to prolonging these sufferings for ends which
I believe to be evil and unjust. I am not protesting against the
conduct of the war, but against the political errors and insincerities
for which the fighting men are being sacrificed.

On behalf of those who are suffering now, I make this protest
against the deception which is being practised upon them; also
I believe it may help to destroy the callous complacency with
which the majority of those at home regard the continuance of
agonies which they do not share and which they have not enough
imagination to realise.[1096]

For three years the *Dreadnought* had campaigned consistently against the
war. As early as December 1914, Sylvia had published Karl Liebknecht's
'Why I Reject Voting for the War Budget', in which he explained his
courageous anti-war stand as the first deputy to vote in the Reichstag
against allocating funds for war spending. Liebknecht's protest had
resonated across Europe and gave new hope and energy to socialist
anti-war initiatives. His reasoning was disseminated around Germany
as the first of the underground circulars later entitled *Spartacus*. Sylvia
continued to publish Liebknecht regularly in the *Dreadnought*. In his
1914 speech, he had declared:

None of the peoples involved in this war wanted it, and it did not
break out to promote their welfare – not in Germany or anywhere
else. It is an imperialist war, a war to dominate the capitalist
world market and secure for industrial and financial capital the
possession of important territories for settlement ... We must
demand a speedy peace, a peace that humiliates no country and
involves no annexations. All efforts to that goal should be welcomed
... The only secure peace will be one based on international

working-class solidarity and the freedom of all peoples. Therefore, it is now the task of the proletariat in every country to carry out common socialist work in every country for peace ... I approve the emergency spending for relief [and] all measures to alleviate the hardships of our brothers at the front and of the sick and the wounded, who have my fullest sympathy ... I protest, however, against the war and those who launched it and direct it; against the capitalist policies that gave birth to it; against the capitalist goals that it pursues ... against the military dictatorship; and against the continuing neglect of social and political responsibilities on the part of the government and the ruling classes.[1097]

Sylvia saw the impact of the war in the chaos of the lives of working people dependent on daily and weekly wages. Recruits were ill supplied. Their mothers and wives petitioned the War Office about the reports they received in letters from their sons and husbands who were fighting for food and short of clothes. Asquith recorded in his memoirs that Kitchener had admitted that the recruits were inadequately supplied with clothing, boots and other essentials. Soldiers were forced to purchase at inflated prices from the regimental stores, profiting suppliers.

Meanwhile, war contracts and privation forced soldiers' wives and daughters into sweated labour that generated big profits that somehow would never seem to find their way back to paying off the war loan. The avarice of the shipowners in turning war contracts into profit for themselves and hunger for workers propelled Sylvia into forming, in February 1915, a League of Rights for Soldiers' and Sailors' Wives and Relatives, 'to spur the women on to stand up for themselves and each other' in order to resist the increasingly draconian regulations issued under the Defence of the Realm Act.[1098] At the heart of this broader campaigning work, she positioned her grass-roots organizing to get women's voices heard.

Sylvia infuriated Kitchener's deputy, Harold Baker, by turning up at the War Office with a deputation of ELFS activists and soldiers' wives and mothers. Baker, 'immaculately tailored, arrogant with class prejudice',[1099] physically baulked at the evident poverty of the women and objected to Miss Pankhurst that the spacious chamber in which he'd received them was in fact far too small a room to contain them. He addressed Sylvia as if the small group of women were a teeming crowd.

SYLVIA PANKHURST

There were only nine of them. Turning to Sylvia sharply, he tried to silence the women:

'I only want to hear the officials; I do not want to listen to the actual cases!'
    'But surely you want to understand their point of view and to know what their actual experience is!'
    'This is not a Court of Inquiry … it is no use listening to them.'
    'This deputation is to represent the opinions and experiences of the women concerned.'[1100]

The episode is typical Sylvia. Enable individuals, groups and communities. This is what she understood as one of the key elements of participatory democracy. Facilitate agency. Work for opportunities for people, especially women, to advocate for themselves. She deployed her own class confidence and experience to get other people through the door, into meetings, and then obdurately flexed her muscle to try and ensure they got a fair hearing. This emphasis on facilitating other people's agency was key to Sylvia's strategies of empowerment for democratic socialism.

Barbara Winslow has documented in detail how during the war the ELFS expanded increasingly beyond the East End. Before 1914 there had been an ELFS branch in north Hackney. By 1916 London branches were established in Holborn, Hoxton, St Pancras, Holloway and Islington. By 1917 the ELFS/WSF had thirty branches across England, South Wales and Scotland, focused in heavily industrial regions where they allied with socialist and industrialist organizations. The expansion diversified the membership. Men were admitted as members, undergoing a tighter process for their nomination and approval than women. Men had to be nominated and seconded by the local branch executive and then approved by the national executive committee. Before 1918 men were not allowed to serve on the executive committee.[1101]

Sylvia's East End war relief projects expanded locally. Her anti-war campaigning extended nationally. Simultaneously, events in Ireland in the spring of 1916 heralded another profound political evolution in Sylvia's life and thought.

She was at the ILP conference in Newcastle when she heard the news of the Easter Rising. It was many years since she had last attended an

ILP conference, but this year all the organizations and societies that campaigned for peace converged around the party, as it was still directly in touch with a mass base. Many delegates were conscientious objectors on parole pending decision on their exemption appeals. Hardie's absence loomed over them. Katharine Glasier denounced the 'hideous blasphemy of war' with great fervour, quoting Hardie, Walt Whitman, William Morris and Edward Carpenter.

A rift emerged between the conscientious objectors and the ILP executive, who backtracked on their original pledge to resist conscription. They had urged members of the party to do likewise and suggested that they would provide financial and legal support for objectors and their families. In January 1916 the Military Service Act had been passed. This imposed conscription on all single men aged between eighteen and forty-one, but exempted the medically unfit, clergymen, teachers and certain classes of industrial worker. In response to this legislation, the ILP executive changed tack and warned members and branches that any behaviour on their part that could be interpreted as an incitement to disobey could render individuals and the party open to prosecution under DORA.[1102]

By the end of the conference, divisions on strategy and tactics remained, but there was consensus on the broad principles. Closing the proceedings, Bruce Glasier urged unity: 'One half of the manhood of the ILP will be in prison before we meet again. We shall require to stand very near one another.'[1103]

There were rumblings from Westminster and Whitehall that conscription should be applied to Ireland. It was in the context of this, coupled with the insecurity of Home Rule, that Sylvia opened the newspapers to read about the Irish rebellion.

On Easter Monday 24 April 1916, a stream of urgent telegrams about a surprise insurrection in Dublin landed on the desk of Viscount French, recently appointed commander of the Home Forces. Around 1,750 nationalists took up arms in an attempt to gain Irish independence from the United Kingdom. James Connolly's Irish Citizen Army marched up O'Connell Street. Standing out among the rebel leaders was the fleet figure of Constance Markievicz – described by Yeats as a 'gazelle', wearing the uniform that she had designed for the army.

As they approached the General Post Office, Connolly gave the order to turn and charge. Within minutes they took possession of the building and garlanded it with a huge green flag decorated with a golden harp and the words 'IRISH REPUBLIC', also designed and made by erstwhile art student Constance Markievicz. On the front steps of the GPO, the poet and activist Pádraic Pearse read out the Irish Declaration of Independence, announcing the establishment of a provisional government for Irishmen and Irishwomen. 'Ireland, through us, summons her children to her flag and strikes for her freedom.' The father of Máire Nic Shiubhlaigh printed the proclamation. As a member of Cumann na mBan – the Irishwomen's Council - Máire Nic Shiubhlaigh commanded the women at Jacob's Biscuit Factory during the Rising.[1104] This republican women's paramilitary organization had been formed in Dublin on 2 April 1914.

During the Dublin General Strike in 1913, police had violently broken up a strike action organized by the Irish Transport and General Workers' Union (ITGWU). In response, James Larkin and James Connolly had founded the Irish Citizen Army as a citizens' guard to the ITGWU, led by former British army officer Jack White. Connolly had announced the formation of this military force at a suffragette meeting. The same month, Sylvia had announced the launch of her People's Army.

Connolly and Michael Mallin led the 1916 Easter rebellion. The Irish Citizen Army was intended to be a highly disciplined force but was hampered by its small numbers, of around 250 men. Supplementing the rebel forces, the Fianna boys and girls acted as messengers and runners during the uprising, and those who were sufficiently trained joined the combat. Na Fianna Éireann, known as the Fianna, an Irish nationalist youth organization, had been founded by Bulmer Hobson and Constance Markievicz in 1909. In Irish mythology, Fianna were small, semi-independent warrior bands.

In response to news of the revolt, Viscount French immediately dispatched two infantry brigades to Ireland and put all other home front units on alert. The Prime Minister and Kitchener authorized him to order further troops to Ireland, under General William Henry Muir Lowe. Born in colonial India to a father in the Indian Civil Service, the Sandhurst-educated Lowe had seen action in Egypt, Burma and the South African Wars.

Lowe's British soldiers surrounded rebel-held central Dublin and the authorities declared martial law. Meanwhile, the rebels cut telephone lines, occupied railway stations and other strategic buildings. They built barricades, blockading major streets with cars and digging trenches on St Stephen's Green. The outside of the rebels' temporary HQ displayed the legend 'We serve neither King nor Kaiser, but Ireland'. Insurgents, blockaded in shops, factories and private homes, fought on, evacuating their wounded through back doors and smashed walls. The heavily shelled General Post Office went up in flames that illuminated the sky above the street battlefield by night. Famously, the final HQ of the short-lived rebel army convened in Hanlon's fish shop on Moore Street.

'Day by day,' Sylvia wrote, 'came news of amazing doings: the little Republic of a week, established by a tiny majority, with promises of "equal rights and opportunities" for all citizens; the suppression of the rebels, with their "job lot" of old arms, by machine-guns, bombs, bayonets, and poison gas, massacres, imprisonments, executions.'[1105] Markievicz referred to three great movements – labour, nationalism and the women's movement – converging to bring about the revolutionary upheaval that was manifested in the Rising and its aftermath.

The Easter Rising struck a blow against England's imperial hubris and remains a landmark in Irish nationalist history, but it failed to spark a nationwide uprising and remained limited mainly to Dublin. British troops outnumbered the poorly armed rebels by twenty to one. The British intercepted weapons promised by the Germans. People who tried to run ammunition to the freedom fighters were seized on the streets and brutally treated. 'When the soldiers came,' Sylvia wrote, 'there began, indeed, heartrending slaughter – slaughter perpetrated by both sides, but the Rebels, untrained men, women and boys, had for arms only "a job lot of rifles", whilst the authorities opposed them with machine guns, bombs, bayonets, and cannon.'[1106]

By the end of the week, official counts put deaths at 400 and wounded at 2,500. The British military authorities court-martialled the leaders of the revolt and sentenced fifteen to execution. The last of the condemned to be brought before the firing squad in Kilmainham Jail courtyard was a badly injured James Connolly, carried in on a stretcher and then tied to a chair to be shot. Outrage at the executions reverberated throughout the world. Connolly was a close personal friend to both Sylvia and Keir Hardie. He had proved himself a stalwart supporter of the militant suffragettes and of Hardie's controversial stand in his advocacy of their cause, despite his own primary commitment to the struggle for universal suffrage. Sylvia wrote later of the Rising, 'The hopeless bravery of it, the coercion and the executions which followed, to me were a grief cutting deep as a personal sorrow.'[1107]

In the days of the 1913 Dublin lockout, Sylvia had spoken alongside Connolly on the Albert Hall platform, the action for which her mother and sister publicly disowned her. 'I mourned him as one who had lived laborious days in the service of human welfare; a man of pity and tenderness, driven to violent means, from belief that they alone would serve to win through to a better life for the people.'[1108] Unable to condone armed resistance, Sylvia understood its wellspring.

She admired the 'pure fire of idealism' blazing amid the destruction and carnage of this rebellion led by women, socialists and poets. Fifteen of the company of young poets 'glorious and radiant in their fervour for the renaissance of their national literature, of the old lovers of Ireland and the lads who burned to die for her were executed'.[1109] On the morning of his execution, the art student Grace Gifford married her lover Joseph Plunkett in prison, an event that touched Sylvia deeply.

Sylvia had still been a youngster when Constance's pacifist sister Eva Gore-Booth introduced them in the earliest days of the WSPU. Sylvia recalled Markievicz 'driving a four-in-hand at Winston Churchill's by-election in defence of the barmaids' right to serve behind the bar; ladling out soup to the starving poor in the Dublin lock-out, drilling her company of Boy Scouts'.[1110] Which soon included girls.

In the context of the government's news blackout on the Easter Rising, the *Woman's Dreadnought* swiftly became an important source of reliable and up-to-date information. Sylvia tasked her keen eighteen-year-old Irish correspondent Patricia Lynch with reporting on the events. Lynch ducked the government blockade on entrance to the city and spirited herself into Dublin with the help of a politically sympathetic army officer who got her through the roadblocks by pretending she was his sister. Risking prosecution, Sylvia published Pat Lynch's report 'Scenes from the Irish Rebellion' in the Saturday 13 May edition of the *Woman's Dreadnought*. The issue sold out immediately and it was reprinted multiple times.

Sylvia gave Pat Lynch her first job at the *Woman's Dreadnought* as a cub reporter and encouraged her. Born in Cork City in 1898, Lynch later became a professional journalist and well-known author of novels, short

stories and children's books. Her article written as Sylvia's war reporter
on the ground in Dublin described the air heavy 'with burning, and
dense clouds of smoke' that obscured the war zone in O'Connell Street
and along Eden Quay, which even when the rain came, 'and after three
days of it', were 'still smouldering'. 'Could the Germans do worse to us?'
she heard one person say to another. 'They tell us to pity the Belgians;
it's ourselves needs pity, I'm thinking.' Lynch interviewed an elderly
woman, shrouded in black and weeping, mourning the death of her
only son, a Sinn Feiner killed in the fighting, ' "As much ammunition
was being used for one sniper as would wipe out a German regiment,"
she said, adding bitterly, "But then the English don't hate the Germans
the way they hate us." '[1111]

Sylvia's thunderer 'The Irish Rebellion' had appeared a week earlier
on Saturday 6 May:

> Justice can make but one reply to the Irish rebellion, and that is to
> demand that Ireland shall be allowed to govern herself. Differences
> of opinion in England, Scotland, or Wales as to what measure of
> self-government Ireland is to have ought not to affect the matter –
> by the 'freedom of small nations' which the British Government has
> so bombastically sworn to defend, this is essentially a question for
> Ireland herself to decide. Let a popular vote be taken in Ireland as
> to whether she shall be an independent self-governing republic, or
> an autonomous part of the British Empire, like Australia and New
> Zealand. That is the only method by which the Irish difficulty can
> be solved and Ireland learn content.[1112]

Sylvia condemned the 'firm and vigorous administration' demanded
by *The Times* for Ireland as just another term for coercion. She
criticized suggestions from a 'professing-Liberal' Professor Longford
that conscription should be applied to Ireland and the Irish rebels set
free on condition that they join the army. This, she predicted, would
only lead to graver trouble in the near future. 'Ireland has been held
in subjection by force too long not to retaliate with what force she can
when provoked beyond a certain point.'[1113]

Analysing the Home Rule Act, designed to provide self-government
within the United Kingdom for Ireland, and the backstory of the
myriad forces and factions arrayed against it in Ireland, Sylvia weighed

up the rights and causes of the international industrial working classes against the nationalist desire for self-determination:

> To many of us, who believe that neither race nor creed should
> separate the workers of the world, it is a matter of regret that
> the old position of Larkin and Connolly should now seem to be
> somewhat obscured. We believe that the co-operative millennium
> cannot be reached till Capitalism is overthrown by the workers.
> Yet we know the impatience which many an earnest reformer feels
> with the slow growth of the proletarian movement. We understand
> the revolt of the impetuous Celtic temperament against being tied
> to slow-moving England, more conservative than either Wales
> or Scotland, England, who, with her strong vested interests and
> larger population, is always the predominant partner in the British
> Isles. We sympathise with the dream of so many ardent lovers of
> Ireland to make of her an independent paradise of free people,
> a little republic, famous, not for its brute strength, but for its
> happiness and culture, something unique in all the world, holding a
> position amongst the nations like that of Finland, who, until Russia
> trampled on the constitution which she won, not by bloodshed,
> but by a universal strike, was thought here to be, and probably was
> politically, the most free of all lands.[1114]

Sylvia evaluated where this rebellion stands in the long struggle for Irish independence. Still a self-proclaimed anti-materialist, she nevertheless ended this powerful piece with a socio-economic analysis of Ireland that reads like a well-written page of Marx. Here as elsewhere she argued with the style and precision of a historical materialist. Yet she claimed elsewhere that she regarded it as a reductive way of approaching the world. Her father had been a great reader of Marx and Engels. Her own heavily annotated edition of *Capital*, published in 1912 by William Glaisher and bound in handsome red cloth, tracks her systematic reading of Marx's theory of capitalist economics.[1115]

Sylvia made a cooler assessment of the rebellion in *The Home Front*, written a decade later. Reflecting on the significance to her of Easter 1916, she declared, 'To me the death of James Connolly was more grievous than any, because his rebellion struck deeper than mere nationalism.'[1116] In temperate analytical prose very different from the in-the-moment newspaper editorializing, Sylvia took the measure of Celtic Twilight romantic mythologizing. 'It is a truism that countries held under an alien dominance remain politically stagnant and, to a large extent are culturally repressed. Recognition of this made me a supporter of Irish nationalism.'[1117]

She entertained no illusions about the long-term struggles of decolonization: 'Yet after national self-government had been attained, the social problems with which we in England were wrestling, would still be present in Ireland.'[1118] The 'pure fire of idealism' burned in the poetic romanticism of cultural rebellion, but it was politics that drove it. 'Some of the Irish deceived themselves with dreams ... Were English rule but removed ... happy fraternity without social strife would establish itself. I was under no such illusions. I saw Ireland as she was; backward, politically, industrially, culturally.'[1119]

Sylvia regarded Connolly as the decisive actor in the rebellion, and by far the ablest personality in the Irish labour movement.

> Connolly was of another order than these dreamers ... He had
> buttressed experience by economic study. Though he had thrown in
> his lot with the Sinn Fein patriots, he remained an internationalist
> ... I knew that the Easter Monday rebellion was the first blow in
> an intensified struggle which would end in Irish self-government,
> a necessary step in Irish evolution ... Yet Connolly was needed so
> seriously for the after-building; him, at least, it seemed Fate should
> have spared.[1120]

Sylvia's intimacy with the leaders of the rebellion was well known. Only much later did it become public that she had been in Ireland during the Easter Rising. In her unpublished draft manuscript 'The Inheritance', Sylvia tantalizingly outlines her preparatory notes for writing about being in the thick of it.

> What I knew of the Irish Rebels. Larkin, Connolly, Countess
> Markievicz, Arthur Griffith, De Valera and others. Sheehy-
> Skeffington as I knew him. I debate at the Abbey Theatre under the
> chairmanship of W. B. Yeats. I attend Dial Eireanne during the civil
> war. The Mayor's Mansion House reception stopped by the military.
> I am close to the bayonets. A shot is fired over our heads. The

Limerick Soviets. *Dreadnought* is raided for expressing sympathy
with the Irish rebels. Maude Gonne McBride and her son. Ireland
as whole: the poverty of the West. Dublin – the beautiful city
in decay. A. E. George Russell – the poet painter and would-be
financial expert of cooperators. A general view of Irish politics. The
Labour Party. Tom Johnson and W. O'Brien. Liberty Hall. A land
of grief and reaction.[1121]

Sylvia took a lot of trouble to try and understand what was happening
in Ireland. Over the years, the coverage in the *Dreadnought* produced
commentary considerably more nuanced than appeared in any other
left-wing paper. Positions shifted, or were contradictory, as Sylvia and
her contributing journalists worked out how the politics developed.
As early as 1919, the *Dreadnought* objected that 'The Irish middle
classes … are the mainstay of Sinn Féin.'[1122] Shortly after that Sylvia
wrote an article warning about the dangers of sectarianism: 'Ireland
should learn from East London to settle her religious differences
by walking over them to unity against foreign imperialism.'[1123] On
another occasion the newspaper charged 'Downing Street, Dublin
Castle and Carsonism' with attempting to 'invoke religious hatred, as
a last resort, to maintain Imperial Capitalism in Ireland'.[1124] In another
issue, the *Dreadnought* complained that 'Carson and his lieutenants
are making use of the religious weapon to smash trade unionism in
Belfast.'[1125]

Within a year of the Easter Rising, the Russian Revolution dawned
for Sylvia 'as a great hope in the midst of disaster'.[1126] In 1903 the Russian
socialist movement had split between two groups, the Bolsheviks
('majority'), led by Lenin and Trotsky, and the Mensheviks ('minority'),
under the leadership of Martov. The Bolsheviks believed the Tsar had
to be overthrown and a workers' state established. The Mensheviks
favoured alliance with the middle class and existing establishment.
In 1912 the two groups formally separated. The early months of 1917
brought news of mass protests against food rationing in Petrograd, the
Russian capital. Erupting on 23 February, eight days of revolutionary
activity and fighting with the police ensued, at the end of which the
mutinous Russian army sided with the revolutionary forces.

On 2 March the Tsar Nicholas II abdicated the Russian throne.
Members of the Duma, the Russian parliament, formed a Provisional

Government and assumed control of the country, sharing power with the soviets, grass-roots community assemblies dominated by the urban industrial working class and soldiers. Throughout 1917 the Mensheviks led the Soviets, particularly the powerful Petrograd Soviet, whose vice chairman was Alexander Kerensky. Lenin, who had led the Bolsheviks from exile, returned to Russia on a sealed train in April 1917 and campaigned for an immediate end to Russia's participation in the war. The February Revolution (which took place in March by the western New Style calendar) was welcomed by all progressives in Britain, but Sylvia was among the very first to recognize that another more radical revolution must follow and to anticipate the rise of the Bolsheviks.[1127] Before many others, she saw Lenin coming.

The Workers' Suffrage Federation was among the first British socialist groups to establish contact with Moscow. In her manuscript for 'In the Red Twilight', which she began working on from 1924, Sylvia describes her early, enthusiastic response, greeting events in Russia as 'the Social Revolution I at once recognized it and affirmed it to be', the starting point of 'the World War I revolution, the rising of the masses against war which would usher in the Socialist order of universal fraternity – that bright hope of the multitude which from childhood I had shared'.[1128] She started writing this contemporary account of the death of communism and the rise of fascism at a crucial moment of change in her political life.

Immediately after the February Revolution, on 19 March 1917, the WSF held a meeting discussing and passing a series of resolutions responding to the events in Russia. They sent a message to Kerensky and Nikolai Chkheidze, congratulating the Duma for overthrowing Tsarist autocracy and eagerly anticipating the early election of a constituent assembly by secret ballot and adult suffrage. Notably, at this point adult suffrage remained for Sylvia a central concern. The WSF sent a further message to socialists, the press and Russians living in Britain and France, congratulating Russian workers on taking their first successful steps towards establishing 'a genuine democracy' and bringing about 'a speedy end to the war'.[1129]

The final resolution at this historic WSF meeting fired a broadside directly at the British government. As the Russians attempted to democratize their Constituent Assembly and Germany initiated adult suffrage, the WSF demanded that the British parliament introduce a new measure providing for adult suffrage. A mass meeting was called at the Albert Hall to congratulate the Russian people on their Charter of Freedom which, the *Woman's Dreadnought* announced in its headline, 'includes ADULT SUFFRAGE'.[1130]

In June 1917, the United Socialist Council, which included the ILP, the British Socialist Party (BSP) and the Fabian Society, organized the Leeds Convention which established a Council of Workers' and Soldiers' Delegates for Great Britain. Sylvia observed with wry amusement how George Lansbury, Ramsay MacDonald, the socialist politician William Anderson, husband of the trade unionist and women's rights campaigner Mary Macarthur, and others 'staked out their claim to office in the expected British Revolution'.[1131]

For Sylvia, the potential for a soviet-run society created unprecedented opportunities to eradicate and transform existing models of social and political organization. Her practical philosophy of socializing the basic necessities of life and consumption remained central to her interpretation of democratic socialism. Her feminism drove her insistence on participatory democracy and the need to extend the framework of what counted as class-consciousness and active citizenship. As the leading historian of this subject Sheila Rowbotham demonstrates, the international socialist women's movement of this period fought not merely for political equality with men. The demand for gender equality was a limited claim to individual rights. Rather, it included a broader demand for access to resources and power for working-class women.[1132] Sylvia's community action in the East End and the rent strikes in Glasgow and in other British towns formed part of a global pattern, evident also in the US, Canada and Mexico in the same period where poor women rebelled over the price of food and housing.[1133]

Sylvia introduced the term 'social soviets', although she had been promoting the concept since 1917, for the first time at the National Administrative Council (NAC) of the shop stewards' movement held in January 1920. The purpose of the meeting was to discuss theories and models of soviet power. Sylvia was much inspired and informed by Rosa Luxemburg in her thinking on this. Luxemburg tried to theorize an alternative to Lenin's view of the party, encouraged by the mass strikes in Europe before, during and after the war.[1134] Sylvia contributed to the agenda for the January NAC rank-and-file convention. Russian soviets were largely factory-based. Sylvia's social soviets proposed involving the entire working class in a new form of organization, not just through the industrial worker base. She thought that soviets – committees of recallable delegates elected by and answerable to mass meetings of working-class people – would be much better able to bring about this objective than parliaments. Social soviets would be organized around where people lived – the advantage being that home and local community were areas over which women workers potentially exercised greater transformative powers. This arrangement would enable the increased participation of women, older people, the unemployed, the disabled, elders and the socially marginalized – anyone not 'formally' employed in the industrial workforce.

Mass layoffs in the engineering and munitions factories following demobilization in 1918 weakened the organizing power of the shop stewards, naturally making the soviet model a more viable alternative. Social soviets could revitalize the participation and representation of unemployed workers. Leading socialist organizations, including the British Socialist Party and the Socialist Labour Party, discussed and theorized a new society based on soviets. William Gallacher of the BSP, chair of the Clyde Workers' Committee, led the way by publishing his thoughts in his pamphlet *Direct Action*. Other organizations followed suit, publishing articles, studies and think pieces assessing principles and structures of socialist tactics, organization and workers' committees. None of this work raised discussion of the role of working women, mothers or housewives. Gender difference was deemed of secondary importance, or overlooked entirely.

In 1918 Sylvia published her first attempt at describing a political structure for her feminist-inspired social soviets. In the *Workers' Dreadnought* of 26 January, she described their proposed structure organized through workers' committees much like branches of the main party:

> As a representative body, an organization such as the All-Russian
> Workers', Soldiers', Sailors' and Peasants' Council is more closely
> in touch with and more directly represents its constituents than the
> Constituent Assembly or any existing Parliament. The delegates ...
> are constantly reporting back and getting instructions from their

constituents; whilst Members of Parliament are elected for a term of years and only receive anything approaching instructions at election times. Even then it is the candidate who, in the main, sets forth the programme, the electors merely assenting to or dissenting from the programme as a whole.

Two years later in June 1920 she was ready to publish 'A Constitution for British Soviets' in the *Workers' Dreadnought*. She emphasized the potential role of what she called 'household Soviets': 'In order that mothers and those who are organisers of the family life of the community may be adequately represented, and may take their due part in the management of society, a system of household Soviets shall be built up.'[1135]

Famously, Marx and Engels chose not to codify in their work the forms of organization necessary for a working-class revolution. The Paris Commune of 1871, the first glimmer of hope for a future socialist society, contained elements closer to Sylvia's vision of social and community soviets than to worker councils. The latter appeared for the first time in the 1905 Russian revolutionary factory councils, emerging from that point as the basis of the Russian revolutionary movement, built on democratically elected and recallable leadership.

Sylvia filled the pages of the *Dreadnought* with case studies of soviets and how they worked, or didn't. She published blueprints for feminist-designed soviets. This analysis took place in the context of the establishment of soviet-style workers' councils, in Fife, Glasgow and Methil in Scotland, Cork in Ireland, Manchester in England, Bologna in Italy, and in parts of Bulgaria and Germany.

Sylvia's fascination with the possibilities of a society organized on socialist principles was grounded in a strong belief in local community control and the democratic mechanisms by which this could be integrated with national and international representation on behalf of the broadest, most diverse base possible. During her 1911 trip to America she'd studied the Milwaukee experiment in municipal democratic socialism very closely. There it appeared to her that primarily white, male, middle-class professors and businessmen made decisions on behalf of ordinary working women and men who were rarely materially enabled or encouraged to participate in the day-to-day running of the city. Conversely, her experience of Bologna's municipal socialism, based on the Russian soviet model, impressed and encouraged her.

Sylvia studied deeply and systematically the nature of political organizations that revolutionaries should build. All her life she'd thought about this. From her childhood devouring of science-fiction fantasies of utopian socialism to her father's radical reformist programmes for every political, legal and economic institution in Britain and beyond, this was a lodestar guiding her life.

How to apply the principles of the Bolshevik Revolution to British conditions? Marx and Engels had recognized that the venerable edifice of the British parliamentary system posed the question: reform from within or revolutionize without? Sylvia's current thinking had moved to the latter. Mary Davis argues that 'despite her enormous achievements as an agitator and organiser, her grasp of Marxist theory (what Lenin regarded as the basis for revolutionary action) was weak and that whilst she undoubtedly had both sympathy and contact with workers, her politics in this regard displayed an impatience and lack of understanding of the historical forms of workers' organisations'.[1136] Sylvia's design for her social soviets supports Davis' analysis. She struggled with determining how to integrate effectively existing industrial workers' organizations with her conceptualization of social soviets that required the distribution of participatory and representational power outside the traditional and modern industrial workplace. Davis emphasizes Sylvia's resolute persistence in trying to reconcile the realities of the majority of women's lives (materialist feminism) with the still male-dominated politics of the only progressive game in town: socialism. This is her driving political passion and at the heart of what makes her a trailblazer for twenty-first-century feminism.

Sylvia's designs for social soviets represented a strenuous attempt to find a way to involve all working-class people in the revolution, not just working men. Unemployed men and women, children, elders, those excluded unfairly from the workplace by disability and – crucially – mothers and housewives who kept the whole show going through unpaid domestic and reproductive labour. The visionary searchlight of her political imagination strove to illuminate how these groups might become agents of a British revolution and not just its beneficiaries.

The concept of soviets was understood in the British labour movement. However, from its rank and file to intellectuals and activists, the relationship between worker committees and a revolutionary party was harder to grasp. Britain possessed an established history of alliance between political parties, trade unions and labour organizations and an albeit deeply flawed parliamentary system. Russian soviets operated independently of the revolutionary party, whereas in Britain there was a tendency to envision them as effectively the same as the local revolutionary party organization. Lenin understood clearly, as Sylvia did not, that in Britain these structures were far less clear-cut than they were in Russia.[1137]

On 3 June 1917 the convention of socialists met in Leeds to discuss the implications of the Russian Revolution, to decide how to bring an immediate end to the war and to consider whether Britain should, in the words of one of its advertising leaflets, 'Follow Russia'. Over 3,000 anti-war socialists and pacifists gathered together of whom 1,150 were delegates from democratic organizations. Socialist figures including Ramsay MacDonald, Philip Snowden and Bertrand Russell played a leading role in the proceedings. Known colloquially as the Leeds Conference, this historic gathering was formally titled the 'Great Labour, Socialist and Democratic Convention'. It convened to discuss the possibility of Britain following Russia by overthrowing autocracy, enfranchising everyone and setting up local councils of workers and soldiers.

Even as the delegates gathered, the French army was confronted by massive mutinies and Britain itself experienced the aftershock of engineering strikes involving over 200,000 workers. Representation was drawn from trades councils, local Labour Parties, trade unions, the ILP, British Socialist Party, other socialist societies and women's organizations, including the WSF and Women's Labour League. The National Council for Civil Liberties, co-operative societies, peace societies and May Day committees also sent delegates.

At the time Lloyd George headed a coalition that included Labour. An alarmed Lord Milner sent the Prime Minister clippings from left-wing newspapers and urged him to 'instruct the Press ... not to "boom" the Leeds proceedings too much'.[1138] A surveillance report sent to the War Office confirmed that there could be no doubt that the conference 'is intended to lead, if possible, to a revolution in this country'.[1139]

The conference was held in a cinema with electric organ and mock-Gothic façade. The delegates kicked off proceedings with a rousing rendition of the Red Flag and a minute's silence in memory of Keir Hardie. Charlotte Despard, in her signature black mantilla and sandals, delivered a militant speech and committed to establishing a workers' and soldiers' soviet in Newcastle. Despard was elected to the thirteen-member provisional committee; as was Sylvia. Bertrand Russell spoke on behalf of imprisoned conscientious objectors before receiving a standing ovation for announcing his intention to establish a London soviet.

The conference opened with salutations and fraternal greetings sent from the executive of the Russian Soldiers' and Workers' Deputies, which suggested meeting its representatives between 15 and 30 July in Stockholm (*Cheers*), being the most convenient place for the conference. The meeting then moved to set up local Councils of Workmen's and Soldiers' Delegates on the Russian model. Speaking in support of the resolution to establish the Provisional Committee, Sylvia made a radically feminist call for the inclusion of working women and mothers as representatives:

> I trust you will all support this resolution, because it is an attempt
> to make a straight cut for the Socialist Commonwealth that we all
> want to see. I believe that this Provisional Committee will be the
> Provisional Government, like the Russian Socialist Government,
> some day; and I am very glad to feel that at last we shall come out
> of this slough of despond, and that the workers will be united in
> common action. We have had resolutions which have talked about
> 'encroachments upon liberty,' but we have never had real liberty in
> this country. What we want to do is to extend the bounds of liberty
> further and further. The revolution in Russia is not only political
> but also industrial. I hope you are going to see to it that some of
> the women you choose are those sweated workers and the mothers
> who live in the hovels and slums. I hope you are not going to leave
> them out when you form your Committees and your Central
> Government. (*Cheers*.)[1140]

So saying, she proposed the amendment of the name from Councils of *Workmen's* and Soldiers' Delegates to non-gender specific *Workers*, in keeping with the Russian original and recognizing the inclusion of women. She further demanded that these structures be called the Workers', Soldiers' and Housewives' Councils, reminding colleagues that unemployed women and housewives were active members of the working class and thus must be included in all organizations purporting to demonstrate socialist equality.[1141]

She won on the gender-inclusive workers but lost on the housewives. The conference established a Council of Workers' and Soldiers' Delegates, and appointed as members of the central committee the thirteen conveners of the conference, including Charlotte Despard, George Lansbury, Ramsay MacDonald, Tom Quelch, Robert Smillie and Philip Snowden. It was agreed that the thirteen would be added to by the votes of district conferences covering the whole country. The Leeds Conference also voted to support the war aims of the Russian Provisional Government, notwithstanding the fact that Ramsay MacDonald had told his constituents a month earlier that the Bolsheviks were a party of thoughtless anarchists whose minds were filled with violence and hatred. Sylvia wrote of MacDonald in *The Home Front* that she was 'anxious to think well of him', because, despite his 'political gyrations and very obvious weakness' she appreciated his stand against the war, and wanted to promote solidarity and unity in the ranks,

> ...yet I could never overcome my distrust of him; he woke it within me perpetually by his tortuous strategy. To go by the straight road to a clear-cut objective seemed impossible to him. He must always be travelling roundabout, with so much concession to the opposite pole, that unless rudely thrust on by a strong force behind hm, he was apt to end to the rear of the point from where he started.[1142]

The government immediately banned the Workers' and Soldiers' Council. Soldiers and right-wing mobs violently attacked attempts at congregating for the regional conferences, so district representation had to be selected and balloted by post. Unwillingly, Sylvia was elected to represent London and the Southern Region. As she put it archly, they 'cast their eyes round for a woman'. On the grounds that they needed an appropriate candidate, not just the token female most conveniently to hand, she refused the nomination. The men totally ignored her and went ahead and balloted her name anyway. 'One woman was enough to put on a committee these days but a woman they must have to

placate the suffragists.'¹¹⁴³ As she wrote later in her wryly titled article
'When I sat with the present Prime Minister on the Workers' and
Soldiers' Councils', Sylvia and Ramsay MacDonald on this occasion
sparred in a ridiculous but telling way. Looking pointedly at Sylvia,
MacDonald complained that there was only one working sailor elected
to the executive committee, with the overt implication that she – and
not any of the other majority block of white men – had stolen the place
of a trade unionist or soldier. On the one hand, Sylvia abhorred the
tokenism of shoehorning on to the executive the nearest vocal, middle-
class white woman whom the men knew. On the other, once she was
there, they turned on her with resentment for being a female intellectual
activist who'd 'taken the place' of a by-definition male working soldier
or sailor. Damned if she did: damned if she didn't.

The right-wing press blustered that the establishment of the Workers'
and Soldiers' Council was a violation of the rule of law, blithely ignoring
William Anderson's motion at the Leeds Conference which stressed
that the Council was not intended to be subversive or unconstitutional.
George V expressed grave fears on behalf of the unelected monarchy. Will
Thorne, former leader of the militant gas workers who had been tutored
by Eleanor Marx and was now MP for West Ham, calmed the royal nerves
by assuring His Majesty that 'I've seen these things happen many times
before in days gone by, and in my humble judgment there will never be
a physical violent revolution in this country.'¹¹⁴⁴ Under vehement external
pressure from the coalition government and due to the internal weakness
of its own organization, the Council soon ceased to exist.

Sylvia forged ahead. The WSF made genuine practical attempts to
set up social soviets. WSF member Joe Thurgood, a bootmaker from
Ashford in Kent and keen Bolshevik, organized the WSF workers'
committees. Sylvia was tasked with seeing to the organization of social
committees. The WSF held a meeting at Bow Baths in March 1920,
festooning the venue with banners announcing 'WELCOME TO THE
SOVIETS'. Sylvia's keynote speech praised the Italian and German
soviets and reported on their progress. At home, she argued, the rise
in food prices would cause rebellion. She urged the establishment of
'soviets in our streets, in our workshops and in our factories'. Harry
Pollitt encouraged East End women to raid the docks to challenge food
prices, and Melvina Walker urged young WSF men and women to
'push the Labour leaders along and out of the way'.¹¹⁴⁵

The same month Sylvia published her 'Constitution for British Soviets', citing East End women's track record of political organizing as case studies for success. The coalition government of which the Labour Party was a small part was failing to control food prices; social 'household' soviets were urgently required to deal with the direct problems women faced with food supplies, milk, transport and housing. She detailed structures, with precise constitutive numbers, for her proposed Poplar, Bromley and Bow District Household Soviets.

Sylvia published further articles in the *Dreadnought*, attempting to integrate her philosophy of feminism with both Lenin's and Trotsky's analyses of soviets. 'These are the workshop committees of the mothers for the streets and the houses they live and work in are *their* workshops. The women must organise themselves and their families and help in the general struggle of the working class to conquer the power of government.'[1146] The problem, as always, was how to counteract women's lack of social power consequent on their lack of industrial and business power.

Inevitably, the WSF attempts to establish soviets utterly failed for the very good reason that there was no working-class revolutionary upheaval in process in Britain to create the necessary conditions for their formation. Social soviets couldn't simply be superimposed on existing structures. However, Sylvia's intentions and efforts enabled her to confront in practical ways the problem of women's double role at home and in the workplace. She claimed to have read and been influenced by Engels. Certainly she tackled head-on the question of the sexual division of labour and the essential value of women's unpaid domestic labour to capitalist economics. Yet how to resolve the problem of the gendered division of power between factory, family and home? Women workers, she argued, would be covered by their factory soviets, but this failed to answer the question of how men could share equal responsibility for domestic labour, reproduction and child-rearing.

24

Anti-Parliamentarianism

In May 1908 Lenin had been in London again, this time to complete the research for his book *Materialism and Empirio-Criticism*. Living at 21 Tavistock Place in Bloomsbury, he worked daily in the British Museum. This was the month of the massive suffragette Suffrage Sunday rally in Hyde Park. The year 1908 was a high-water mark in the national campaign for votes for women. So widescale was the suffragette direct action in 1908, you didn't need to be an avid reader of the papers – or a Russian revolutionary journalist – to be aware of the ubiquity and dominance of the issue. Lenin and his wife Nadezhda Krupskaya had heard of the Pankhursts long before Sylvia knew of them.

The geography of Lenin's and Sylvia's London coalesced: Bloomsbury, Gray's Inn Road, Tavistock Place, the British Museum. At different times they frequented the same political groups and the same places. Both worked with the Social Democratic Federation and attended radical meetings in the East End, where they met, admired and were informed by Jewish immigrants from the Russian empire, who were open to ideas of international socialism.[1147] Sylvia possessed a fundamental faith in the people: Lenin started with very little, and ended with none. Aside from this entirely different view of humanity, they shared some significant characteristics.

Both were brilliant expositors, able to encapsulate and get their ideas across clearly. Both were superb journalists and indefatigable propagandists, class warriors, political schemers and natural-born faction fighters, though he was more talented at the latter than she. They enjoyed debating each other robustly in print and, when finally they met, would get along very well. Sylvia held on to her hopes for Lenin's leadership and the Bolsheviks from 1917 until finally denouncing him for introducing the New Economic Policy in 1921. The depth of her disappointment showed the measure of her hopes for the communist revolution. It was also a reflection of her disillusionment with a person in some regards rather like herself in personality if not politics – though she wouldn't have recognized that in the mirror. For his part, as will be seen, Lenin created an entire political theory in Sylvia's honour and wrote a famous pamphlet in April 1920, 'Left-wing Communism': An Infantile Disorder, published in May, globally distributed in an effort to silence Comrade Pankhurst's persistent refusal to accept Lenin's party line for Britain. Lenin respected Sylvia's mind and recognized her potential importance to the British revolutionary left, consistently singling her out for attention. Comrade Pankhurst was to be taken seriously.

Though still much overlooked, the political relationship between Sylvia Pankhurst and V. I. Lenin made a significant impact on the shape and future of the British Communist Party in particular and the British left in general.

The first explicit references to Lenin and Bolshevism in the Dreadnought appeared on 30 June 1917. Prior to that, a handful of pieces in Sylvia's paper mentioned the labour and socialist movement in Russia. A Boxing Day report in December 1914 on the anti-war protests in Germany and Russia referred to Lenin's essay on the war and social democracy as 'the manifesto of the Russian Socialist Party'.[1148] Before 1917, there were a few further articles on Russian socialism; Sylvia's long analytical review of the autobiography of Marie Sukloff, one on the people in the assassination attempt on General Dubasov; and a book review about socialism and the war by the American political activist and analyst William English Walling, founder of the National Women's Trade Union League in 1903 and among the co-founders of the National Association for the Advancement of Colored People in 1909.

Sylvia understood the dual power struggle in Russia from the outset and, as early as March 1917, grasped that the Soviets could become the next government. As she repeatedly reminded her audiences, it was women textile workers celebrating International Women's Day who sparked the February 1917 revolution. She kept a close eye on developments. In the 24 March issue, a mere two weeks after the overthrow of the Tsar, Sylvia explained to *Dreadnought* readers, 'there are virtually two governments in Russia: the Provisional Government appointed by the Duma and the Council of Labour Deputies ... responsible to the elected representatives of the workers and soldiers'. No one else in Britain was writing or publishing anything like this.

At the beginning of June, while others on the British left were still singing his praises and predicting a Menshevik government, Sylvia predicted the overthrow of Alexander Kerensky, who, she wrote, had utterly failed to 'realise the greatness of the moment he would lead'.[149] By the end of the month, she came out fully for the Bolsheviks. When Lenin and the Bolsheviks made their first appearance in the *Dreadnought* on 30 June 1917, Sylvia cut straight to the chase with notable clarity of foresight, supporting the Maximalists and Leninists who wanted to cut loose from the capitalist parties altogether and establish a socialist system of organization and industry in Russia.

The key question was whether it was possible to establish a socialist republic within a capitalist Europe mid-war. Sylvia believed that British socialist leaders would hang back until there was a socialist foundation in western Europe, rather than throw themselves behind an eastern European Russian socialist government leading the way. Established socialist organizations looked to strengthen their presence in parliament and persuade the frightened Liberals to adopt their programmes. For Sylvia, this limited vision risked missing the opportunity of the moment.

The Bolsheviks, Sylvia argued, showed a radically alternative approach. In August, the *Dreadnought* informed its readers that the Petrograd soviet was moving towards Lenin's position that Free Russia must refuse to continue fighting in a capitalist war. When finally the Bolsheviks came to power in in October 1917 (November by the western New Style calendar), *Dreadnought* welcomed the revolution and supported immediately the Bolshevik dissolution of the Constituent Assembly.

On 17 November 1917, she published 'The Lenin Revolution: What it means to democracy', in which she compared the TUC and Labour Party with the Russian Revolution in order to answer the question: 'Why is the UK so far behind the Russian?' She compiled a list of the shortcomings of the British left and labour movement, including the constant nervous looking out of the corner of their eyes at the capitalist press. 'The Russian problem is our problem: it is simply whether the people understand socialism and whether they desire it. Meanwhile, our eager hopes are for the Bolsheviks of Russia: may they open the door which leads to freedom for the people of all lands.'[1150]

By this clear rejection of any form of pre-existing parliamentary democracy, Sylvia propelled herself further to the revolutionary left, a position in keeping with her support for soviets or workers' councils as the best new form of participatory democratic government. Sylvia declared that 'the old bourgeois parliamentarianism has seen its day'.[1151] To explain the Bolsheviks to Britain and counter the opposition of the right-wing and social democratic press, she ran articles by leading Bolsheviks – including Alexandra Kollontai, Lev Kamenev, Maxim Litvinov and Lenin, and their international supporters such as Louise Bryant.

While all others either prevaricated or condemned outright the October Revolution, smaller organizations and left-wing publications *The Socialist*, *The Call* (later *The Communist*, official organ of the BSP) and Sylvia's *Workers' Dreadnought* came out clearly for the Bolsheviks. They carried material from Russia including reports and translated articles and appeals. In retaliation, the government used the Defence of the Realm Act against all three newspapers to raid their offices and intimidate their editors and journalists. In 1918, for the first time since its inception in 1890, the British May Day rally was banned, under Regulation 9A of DORA.

The drawing up and implementation of the 1918 Representation of the People Act coincided with the Russian Revolution. For Sylvia, these combined historical events represented what mattered to her most: equality, justice, women's rights and socialism as the best available means of achieving them. Her political turn to left-wing communism and support for anti-parliamentarianism in this period cannot be understood without an awareness that for her the legislation of 1918, for which she'd fought since almost a child, was a great disappointment. The Act provided the vote for women over thirty who met a property qualification and for all men over twenty-one. This fell far short of what she had envisaged.

When the Representation of the People Act came into effect on 6 February 1918, Sylvia's response was thoughtful, analytical and critical – but certainly not celebratory. From before her birth, her family had worked for this cause. Now aged thirty-six and already a political veteran, she could see that the class divisions, not only protected but further entrenched by the qualified vote, would ensure that its impact was at best limited, at worst counter-productive.

Working-class women, particularly the young, grafted during the First World War. From the 1880s, working women had formed the activist base for women's suffrage. Despite this, it was primarily middle-class and aristocratic women who benefited, and those with some education or property. The legislation did not remove sex discrimination or establish equal suffrage. It entrenched class prejudices designed to quiet that spectre so feared by British elites – voter registration giving voice and power to the popular majority: working men and women, poor housewives, the unemployed.

Enfranchisement was extended to women ungraciously, in grudging spirit, in a fearful atmosphere. Middle-class women, it was hoped, would provide a bulwark against advancing threats of social unrest, Bolshevism and socialism escalated by the horrendous death and deprivation caused by the war. Voting patterns demonstrated this to be the case. Between 1918 and 1928, newly enfranchised women overwhelmingly voted Conservative.

In March 1916 the ELFS had evolved into the Workers' Suffrage Federation. The following year its annual conference declared itself for state redistribution of resources, particularly food and mothers' pensions, against conscription and the National Service Act and in favour of 'the socialist commonwealth'.[1152] In July 1917, when the WSF changed the name of its newspaper from the *Woman's Dreadnought* to *Workers' Dreadnought*, it reframed its statement of aims a little in order to clarify that 'Social and Economic Freedom for the People' would be established 'on the basis of a Socialist Commonwealth'. Contrast this with the policies of Christabel and Emmeline's new separatist Women's Party launched the same year, replacing the WSPU. 'While the Women's Party is in no way based on sex antagonism,' Emmeline Pankhurst explained, 'it is felt that women can best serve the nation by keeping clear of men's party political machinery and traditions, which, by universal consent, leave so much to be desired.'[1153] That immediately begged the question, if your object is to 'keep clear of men's party political machinery and traditions', why form a political party with parliamentary ambitions that mimics them? As the socialist Susan Lawrence sensibly wrote in *The Labour Woman* magazine in response, 'there was an objection to a Party [that was] really political calling itself a non-party organization'.[1154]

The Women's Party supported the war effort and called for armed intervention by the Allies to restore order and save Russia from the Bolsheviks who, Emmeline claimed, were German agents.[1155] Far from presenting an alternative. these policies made members of the Women's Party instant handmaidens of a warmongering imperialist patriarchy, neatly summed up in its jaunty jingo slogan, 'Victory, National Security and Progress'.

Welcoming the advent of the patriotic Women's Party, the right-wing press warmly wished Mrs Pankhurst 'God-speed' in saving the country from left-wing socialist MacDonaldism and the Labour Party's angling for the women's vote.[1156] Sylvia saw the Women's Party as a 'phalanx of the Tories' and an attack on the entire socialist movement, not least herself.[1157] The *Common Cause*, official organ of the NUWSS, warned entirely accurately that the party 'will of course be an autocracy like the old WSPU'.[1158] Christabel stood in the 1918 general election as a Women's Party candidate in alliance with the Liberal–Conservative coalition in the Smethwick constituency. Once again, no evidence here of 'keeping clear of men's party political machinery and traditions', and no evidence of any interest in the question of solidarity with the women who supported the Labour Party candidate, who narrowly defeated Christabel by 775 votes. In the inter war years, Sylvia reviewed her position on the viability of a women's party. During the 'full hurly burly' of the 1935 general election campaign, she reflected in her essay 'Women's Rule in Britain', 'the amazing thing is that we women hold the electoral majority here. If we combined in a Party of our own, our Party would be in power. Women would form the Government and fill all the offices from the Prime Minister downward.'[1159] In 1936, a reader of her newspaper would write to ask why there was still such a scarcity of women in parliament. Sylvia replied that men continued to control the main political parties, to the exclusion of women and, because women had come so late into politics, they had little chance of success standing as independent candidates.[1160]

Sylvia was consistent in her opposition to limiting the vote to women over thirty who were householders or married to householders, excluding younger, propertyless women. In 1916 she had written to the

British Socialist Party newspaper *The Call*, laying out her views on why she could not support such legislation:

1. A woman is not to vote until 30 years of age, though the adult age is 21.
2. A woman is on a property basis when enfranchised.
3. A woman loses both her Parliamentary and local government vote if she or her husband accept Poor Law Relief; her husband retaining his Parliamentary and losing his local government vote if he accepts Poor Law Relief.
4. A woman loses her local government vote if she ceases to live with her husband, ie. if he deserts her, she loses her vote, he retains his.
5. Conscientious Objectors to military service are to be disenfranchised.[1161]

Given that women's participation in the war economy made it unfeasible to deny them the vote any longer, Sylvia believed this bill was selling out their political advantage far too cheaply. It was also caving in to a form of intentional class-based divide-and-rule between women that the war had already deeply undermined between men. With class differences between men decreasing as a result of the war and radically more fluid than ever before, class divisions had to be reconsolidated somewhere else – between women.

Until 1917 the WSF maintained the position that the vote would enable women workers to exert influence over the fundamental decisions affecting their lives. Universal suffrage would 'make Parliament obedient to the people's will'. If it was the people's will that a socialist society should be established, they could make this happen by electing socialists to parliament. A precondition of this reformist parliamentary strategy was that suffrage should be extended to every woman and man. The overthrow of the Tsarist autocracy and the commitment to establishing 'a constituent assembly … elected by the men and women of Russia by secret ballot and on the basis of Universal Suffrage' explain Sylvia's enthusiastic reaction to these events, based on a pro-parliamentary model for bringing about social democracy.[1162]

Until 1917 the WSF viewed the February Revolution from the perspective of the suffrage issue. After 1917 it viewed the issue of suffrage through the lens of the October Revolution and the establishment of worker councils.

In March 1917 the WSF had looked forward to the establishment of the Constituent Assembly with keen anticipation. The October Revolution, however, prompted Sylvia to change this position, catalysing the WSF's ideas into an anti-parliamentary stance. Until 19 January 1918, the statement of universal suffrage based on parliamentary representation appeared as the newspaper's mission on the cover of *Workers' Dreadnought*. From 19 January, the slogan ceased to appear. The following week's issue carried Sylvia's article praising the Bolsheviks' dissolution of the Constituent Assembly in Petrograd eight days previously. In January 1918 the Bolsheviks dispersed the Constituent Assembly before its first meeting, and Sylvia endorsed their action.

The emergence of the soviets in Russia, regarded as the means by which the revolution had been achieved and as the administrative machinery of the post-revolutionary society, persuaded the WSF to reject the parliamentary route to socialism. Dedicated to the struggle for socialism, galvanized by the Russian Revolution, Sylvia revised her former perspective that the struggle for suffrage was an adequate mechanism for political participation, for unseating the vested interests of the elites and for social transformation.

The view of the WSF executive committee was that soviets were 'the most democratic form of government yet established'. The organization's commitment to 'Popular Control of the Management of the World' was not abandoned, but transferred to the mechanism of worker councils. Sylvia thought that soviets would be much better able to bring about this objective than parliaments. In her article on the dissolution of the Constituent Assembly, she argued: 'As a representative body, an organization such as the All-Russian Workers', Soldiers', Sailors' and Peasants' Council is more closely in touch with and more directly represents its constituents than the Constituent Assembly, or any existing Parliament.'[1163] In February 1918 Sylvia asked: 'Is it possible to establish Socialism with the Parliament at Westminster as its foundation? ... we must consider very seriously whether our efforts should not be bent on the setting aside of this present Parliamentary system under which the peoples suffer, and the substitution for it of a local, national and international system, built upon an occupational basis, of which the members shall be but the delegates of those who are carrying on the world's work.' She specified what she meant by occupational, suggesting that these delegates 'shall be themselves workers, drawn, but for a space, from the bench, the mine, the desk, the kitchen, or the nursery; and sent to voice the needs and desires of others like themselves'.[1164]

At the annual conference in May 1918, the Workers' Suffrage Federation changed its name to the Workers' Socialist Federation, replacing its former slogan, 'Socialism, Internationalism, Votes for All' with the new call 'For Revolutionary International Socialism, the ending of Capitalism and Parliaments, and substitution of a World Federation of Workers' Industrial Republics'. Mercifully, this was shortened to 'For international socialism'. Membership was open to all men and women, and subscription to the *Workers' Dreadnought* fourpence per month, four shillings per annum. The WSF pledged its opposition to the continuation of the war and declared its commitment to the abolition of all armed forces. All conscientious objectors should be released immediately, and the policy of militarization in schools cease. No more drilling and no more sacking teachers for their political or religious objections to the war.

Calling on the British government to recognize the Soviet government, the WSF urged British workers to oppose all political candidates who supported the war and to endorse instead only internationalist socialist candidates. It declared the parliamentary system defunct and proposed instead the establishment of local worker-controlled councils on the soviet model elected through a local, national and international system, which shall render Parliament unnecessary by usurping its functions. Land, production, distribution and exchange should be placed under industry-based community control. These industry- and market-specific workers' committees would replace parliament. The conference called for self-determination for India and Ireland, and defined the WSF as explicitly anti-colonialist.

In June 1918 Sylvia spoke at the Labour Party Conference against intervention in Russia. The chairman tried to stop her and shut her up. She appealed to George Lansbury for support. Kerensky attended the conference as its special guest to appeal for the intervention. The hall attempted to shout him down, but Arthur Henderson embraced him and hushed the delegates, and Kerensky got a fair hearing.

The attitude of the official Labour Party at this time to the Bolsheviks was antagonistic – they did not understand their language and they did not like their manners. Henry Brailsford denounced the Bolsheviks in the *Daily Herald* as 'fanatics who have carried the Socialist view of the class war to its logical but exaggerated conclusion'. Nevertheless, Sylvia urged people to vote Labour in the 1918 general election called immediately after the Armistice, while continuing to be engaged in successive disputes with the local Poplar Labour Party. Throughout 1918 the WSF's views on parliamentarianism were in the process of transformation. When a group of Sylvia's admirers in Sheffield asked her to stand as a candidate in the Hallam constituency in the general election that year, she declined: 'in accordance with the policy of the Workers' Socialist Federation, she regards Parliament as an out-of-date machine and joins the Federation in working to establish the soviets in Britain'.

The WSF announced that it would not run candidates and would only support socialists, but that it would not prevent members from working for Labour candidates. Sylvia at this point also still supported involvement in parliamentary elections as a means of giving voice to revolutionary ideas: 'The expected General Election interests us only so far as it can be made a sounding-board for the policy of replacing capitalism by Socialism, and Parliament by the Workers' Councils. We shall be at the elections, but only to remind the workers that capitalism must go.'[1165]

Despite its growing anti-parliamentarianism, the WSF supported three Socialist Labour Party candidates: Jack Murphy, best known as J. T. Murphy, Arthur MacManus and William Paul, as well as David Kirkwood of the ILP and the BSP's John Maclean, known as 'the Scottish Lenin'. Sylvia travelled to Glasgow in mid-November 1918 to open a large fundraiser in aid of Maclean's election campaign.

The *Workers' Dreadnought* celebrated May 1918 by leading with an in-depth two-part feature entitled 'Karl Marx and Fleet Street (1865–67)', written by a new contributor called Silvio Corio.[1166] An Italian anarchist socialist, journalist, editor and printer, Corio was a recent addition to the newspaper's staff.

Sylvia wrote to Adela in Australia inviting her to write for *Workers' Dreadnought*. Recently married, Adela and her husband Tom Walsh now lived in Sydney. Walsh was a communist and leader of the seamen's trade union. Adela had only just been released from prison in Sydney, having served her sentence for anti-conscription campaigning. She emerged from incarceration to learn that the workers had won in Russia and the war was nearing its end. As the Armistice was under negotiation in November 1918 Adela took a taxi to St Margaret's Hospital, returning home by train with her new baby boy named for her father.[1167] Both of the boy's parents were prominent communist activists, leaders in the Australian labour movement and supporters of the Russian Revolution.

While the correspondence between Sylvia and Adela shows renewed warmth between the sisters, now again working together, baby Richard's maternal feminist grandmother showed no interest in the arrival of her first grandchild. Her 'sparkling young middle-class English journalist' daughter, who might have done so much better for herself, infuriated Emmeline by marrying an Irish, left-wing, working-class ex-Catholic sailor.[1168] Richard Pankhurst had deemed trade unionism outdated, and Emmeline had it in for all Irish after their failure to support her pro-Home Rule husband in his election campaign. (It was only shortly before she died that Emmeline acknowledged Tom Walsh as her son-in-law.[1169])

Sylvia would reprint in the *Dreadnought* Adela's articles on domestic feminism, written for the *Australian Communist*. 'Communism and Social Purity' and its companion piece 'Capitalist Home Life' combined engaging homespun political philosophy with analysis of the situation of the working wife and mother: 'Marriage today involves such a terrible sacrifice, the family is such a source of carking care.'[1170] The homely, relatable style of these articles evokes the child Adela who so successfully entertained her audience by describing the anatomy of the family cat.

The daughter of a middle-class family, Adela now laboured as a trade union wife, who had to juggle her work with bringing up a large family of five children on a low income. The Walsh family lived in rented homes mostly without running water or electricity, and all their furniture was second-hand or bought on hire-purchase. The revolutionary Marxist myth of liberation for working-class housewives appealed directly to Adela's experience.[1171] She was now responsible for three stepchildren and two infants of her own. She named her second baby, born in October 1920, for Sylvia. Perpetually penny-pinched, Adela despaired at the everlasting 'No' said to children who asked for tiny pleasures – and received instead 'smackings and scoldings' from frustrated parents unable to provide 'frugal comfort in a world where everything abounds'.[1172]

Back in Britain, Sylvia, disaffected by the Labour Party's disastrous wartime compromises and antagonistic response to the Bolshevik Revolution, left the party, gave up on the electoral parliamentary system altogether and adopted a hard stance against conservative trade-union leadership.

Sylvia's distrust of the Labour Party had built up over time. Initially, the party aroused her misgivings through its lack of support for women's suffrage. Then it supported the war and abandoned Keir Hardie. The party refused to help Jim Connolly and the martyrs of the Easter Rising. Even so, the WSF continued to work seriously within the Labour Party until 1919, when there was an almighty row over pro-soviet WSF banners displayed on a truck during a Labour Party rally held in Victoria Park in east London. In consequence, Norah Smyth and Melvina Walker were expelled from the party.

The 1919 WSF annual conference took place shortly after the establishment of the Third International – commonly known as the Communist International (CI). It resolved immediately to affiliate to the International, and simultaneously disaffiliate from the Labour Party. Voting on its policy commitments to working women, the conference backed the establishment of maternity centres based on the model set up by the Bolshevik feminist Alexandra Kollontai, at the time Russian Commissar for Social Welfare. Critically, at this 1919 conference, Sylvia's WSF resolved to rename itself the Communist Party, pending upcoming unity negotiations with the British Socialist Party, the Socialist Labour Party and the South Wales Socialist Society.[1173] This resolution was to cost Sylvia dearly.

While the Labour Party made itself unpopular by participating in the wartime coalition and the Russian Revolution changed the boundaries of the possible, the shop stewards' movement, founded in Glasgow shipyards in 1915, had spread to munitions factories. From the Taff Vale dispute of 1901 to the Great Unrest of 1910–14, early twentieth-century Britain had been dominated by the impact of changing industrial relations, quelled only by the declaration of war. The 1911 Liverpool General Transport Strike brought the country closer to mass civil unrest and potential uprising than ever before. In a show of force by the authorities, two gunboats sailed up the Mersey and the army turned out on the streets, excepting the Liverpool regiments, which were confined to barracks because the government felt unable to rely on their loyalty. Throughout the summer the strikers and their supporters fought running battles with the police. These rank-and-file-led struggles frightened even the national union leaders into complying with the government's request to negotiate an end to the strike. The 'Red Clydeside' period that began in 1915 as a consequence of the war and ended only in 1920 is chiefly remembered for the 1919 strike of over 100,000 workers calling for a forty-hour week, which was savagely attacked by the police and led to the battle in George Square in Glasgow on what became known as Red Friday.

Elsewhere the police themselves became strikers for the first time. The successful police strikes of 1918 and 1919, which included prison officers, prompted the government to crush their union and ban them from union affiliation, terrified that they were losing control of the force. The Metropolitan Police struck in August 1918 for the first time in their history, demanding union recognition, a wages increase and the reinstatement of the dismissed Police Constable Thommy Thiel, provincial organizer of the National Union of Policemen and Prison Officers and delegate to the London Trades Council. The next police strikes in May 1919 spread to Liverpool and other cities. The support of prison officers for the strikes deepened the government's alarm.

Anxiety about the economic consequences of the war and about the increasing British industrial militancy it had unleashed, reveals itself in the titles of official publications, especially from 1917 and in the immediate aftermath of the war: 'The Coming Crash of Peace', 'The Socialist Illusion', 'How to Pay for the War' and 'Incentives in the New Industrial Order'. That the end of the war presaged a new class and industrial order was undisputed. The question was how to tackle the challenge.

Young men who had enlisted or been conscripted before they'd ever had a job or been educated, trained or apprenticed, returned from war to find wages suppressed by the sudden surge in the available labour force, and women efficiently doing work previously reserved for men. With the German Ruhr supplying Britain with coal as part of the draconian reparations imposed by the peace, there was less work for miners. The young John Maynard Keynes had urged that the Versailles peace conference should set the conditions for economic recovery. Instead, the conference focused on borders and national security and set excessive reparations at a level that Keynes perceived would ruin Europe.

During the war, shop-floor leaders elected by the workers, not formally part of the trade union structure, had organized themselves into workers' committees, defying both government and the official trade unions and popularizing the idea of direct action. Unemployment caused by demobilization and the cessation of war work created a ready-made civilian army primed for agitation and class conflict. Disappointment with the conduct of the Labour Party and older-established socialist organizations during the war enhanced the standing and credibility of socialist militants, grass-roots participatory democracy and forms of direct action – particularly in support of countrywide demands for shorter hours and increased wages. Reducing working hours was necessary, the trade unions argued, in order to create sufficient employment for the suddenly expanded workforce. It was also a reaction to the non-stop excessive shift hours demanded during the war.[1174]

Rank-and-file demands for the direct action of a general strike put pressure on the trade union leaderships to call for reduced hours and stabilized wages. At the end of 1918 unions began negotiations with the shipbuilding and engineering bosses for a forty-seven-hour week. In January, a general strike began in Belfast. Clydeside engineers followed, demanding a forty-hour week. It was these actions that led to Red Friday.

The strike spread to miners, municipal workers, bakers, builders, carpenters, gas workers, joiners, paper workers and railway workers. From Edinburgh to Greenock, Leith, Perth and Rosyth, Scotland joined the strike. Shipbuilders and repairers in London walked out, demanding fifteen shillings a day. Strike committees virtually controlled many towns, organizing food distribution and issuing permits for gas and electricity.

From the perspective of business owners and government, the most worrying aspect of this agitation was that, although these strikes were all happening simultaneously, none of it was nationally co-ordinated. When the Electrical Trades Union voted to come out in support of all strikers nationally, Britain was faced with the threat of total blackout.

The government responded by invoking the wartime Defence of the Realm Act and declaring the ETU strike illegal. At the same time, the miners were negotiating a charter demanding a 30 per cent increase in wages, overhaul of hours and conditions and nationalization of the mines with joint control between the state and mineworkers.

Cowed by government threats and failing adequately to co-ordinate the scope of their newfound power delivered by their rank and file, the trade union leaders retreated from what could have been a revolutionary general strike. Frustrated and impatient with their timorousness, Sylvia boomed in the *Dreadnought* that trade union officialdom was becoming 'a mere parasite on the workers' movement'.[1175] Whatever the failings of the union leaders, it was the complementary failure of the armed forces, police and industrial workers to join together that more decisively averted open class war. At the end of 1918 and on into early 1919, soldiers and sailors mutinied at Calais, Dover, Folkestone, Osterley Park and Rhyl. The police strikes were simultaneous to this.

Missing the opportunity to combine their forces, the unions were picked off by the old divide-and-rule tactics of piecemeal negotiations with individual industries. Workers won some small victories, lost others. Throughout the summer of 1919 and into 1920, the tidal ebb and flow of advances and retreats showed that the working classes remained in fighting mood. The cotton workers struck and won a forty-eight-hour week in the summer of 1919. Both skilled and unskilled railway workers went out on strike in support of wage cuts to unskilled workers. London compositors supported them by refusing to set or print newspapers containing propaganda against the railway employees. The municipal elections of November 1919 delivered dramatic Labour successes in London, Durham and South Wales. The dockers forced the government to mediate in disputes with their stonewalling employees, and gained ground in improving work conditions.

Simultaneous to the industrial action of 1919–20, campaigning against Allied intervention in Russia gained momentum. By 1918 Sylvia was active in the London engineers' movement and playing a growing national role in encouraging workers to defend the Russian Revolution. She became a member of the vigilance committee of the Amalgamated Society of Engineers (ASE), and pledged to strike for workers' control over food distribution and production. The miners of South Wales invited her to speak to them. On the Clyde, she addressed to both the overwhelmingly male shop steward movement and the women leading the no-rent strikes. Wherever she went, she urged rank-and-file male workers to look for solidarity and make common cause with women's campaigns, just as Eleanor Marx had done before her.

In January 1916 Sylvia had written in the *Dreadnought*, 'The new Trade Unionism, which is so active on the Clyde, wished to emancipate the workers from the position of incoherent dependent tools, whether of employers, Governments or officials sprung from their own ranks. It wishes every worker in the trade to take his or her own part in moulding the policy of the union, and each trade union to take its part in making the nation a co-operative commonwealth.'[1176]

Here Sylvia entered the weathered debate between craft unions and industrial unions. As old as the British labour movement itself, it marked a political dividing line between radicals and reformists. Craft unions organized workers along occupational lines. Industrial unionism proposed the organization of all workers in a specific industry regardless of craft, gender, age, race or ethnicity. The WSF supported the position of the revolutionary socialists that industrial unionism was the only way to overcome differences between skilled and unskilled, men and women, black and white, young and old. By stressing the common interests of workers, industrial organization could work to overcome the racial and gender divisions reinforced by job classifications and hiring discrimination. In addition, the larger size of industrial unions and their density in some communities made mass political action more effective, compared with the lobbying and special-interest politics that fitted with narrow craft interests. Socialist supporters of industrial unionism, including the WSF, argued that it represented a qualitative step forward for workers, shoving aside the hidebound conservatism and self-protectionism typical of many craft unions and organizing within mass production industries that were central to the economy and thus to the power of the workers.

The task for Sylvia and like-minded revolutionary socialists, many of whom had been active in the shop steward movement, was to organize a rank-and-file campaign committed to resistance to the employer and the state. Workers' committees needed to function on a local, national and international scale in order to galvanize political solidarity with those outside the waged labour market – women, unemployed, young and old – and with colonized nations fighting British capitalist imperialism. Given its majority female membership and its East End headquarters, the WSF was poorly positioned for systematic workplace organizing, so the decision to focus on co-ordinating and promoting campaigns made practical and strategic sense. The *Dreadnought* was the machine that powered the WSF campaigns, organization, information, propaganda, analysis and critique.

As editor, Sylvia never missed an opportunity to support and promote working women's campaigns. In August 1918 the paper reported on the strike by the London transport women workers for equal pay. Following a meeting at Willesden garage, the women there came out on strike immediately, refusing to wait for sanction from male trade-union officials. Inspired by their action, women transport workers of Acton and Hackney followed suit, refusing to return to work pending negotiations as their union leadership requested. They won. In September women workers on the London Underground came out on strike, supported by the National Federation of Women Workers, which charged the government with discriminating against women in jobs that had been done by men before the war.

For a year from March 1918, the engineer and west London ASE member William (Billy) Watson wrote a regular column in the *Dreadnought* on industrial unionism and workshop committees entitled 'Workshop Notes'. In these, he provided publicity and co-ordinating information for the shop steward movement. Workers' committees from around the country submitted reports on their activities. Watson's articles both shaped and reflected WSF activity. Like Sylvia, he understood and explained the complex arguments being debated between government, the Labour Party, the TUC and other unofficial organizations.[1177] Watson followed the WSF commitment to women's equality, showing the ways in which it continued to be an issue that the labour and socialist movement had still not adequately taken up.[1178]

The ASE still excluded women, and Watson wrote columns protesting against this discriminatory policy and arguing that, since women were now employed in all grades of engineering jobs, they must be represented on the until now exclusively male Woolwich Arsenal Shop Steward Committee. The Woolwich Arsenal was a large employer in the East End. Laid-off ex-servicemen and discharged munitions workers became key to unemployment discontent in the region.

London workers were never as extensively organized into committees as elsewhere in industrial England and Scotland, especially Glasgow. But workers' committees did exist in Acton, Hammersmith, Chiswick, Croydon and elsewhere, particularly in aircraft factories. Metalworkers, railway workers, tram workers, tube workers and woodworkers were also active, leading Watson to declare optimistically that London should become the Petrograd of Britain.

Not surprisingly, by now the WSF had its own designated police informant, Basil Thompson, assigned by Scotland Yard to infiltrate and spy on its activities. As his prolific intelligence demonstrated, Thompson's reports were crucial to achieving Billy Watson's arrest and imprisonment for sedition in March 1919. Soon afterwards, it emerged that Watson himself was a police informant. On his release from prison he admitted accepting money from Scotland Yard, claiming in his defence that it was a double bluff to ensure that he supplied them with misleading information. The case was a complex one, and the London shop stewards were undecided on the question of Watson's guilt or innocence. Either way, his credibility was blown. He stopped writing for the *Dreadnought* and stepped down from the ASE. The cabinet files confirm that Watson was indeed a police informant, but an utterly useless one, because he was 'so drunken and untrustworthy that his communications were discredited'.[1179]

25

Sylvia's Communist Odyssey

In March 1918 Sylvia established the People's Russian Information Bureau (PRIB), to co-ordinate British support for the revolution. The Estonian violinist and revolutionary Eduard Sõrmus, who had trained and lived in Russia, was now living in Merthyr Tydfil. He appealed to Sylvia to convene a conference and set up an organization to disseminate the truth about the Russian Revolution.[1180] Sylvia took his proposal to a WSF committee meeting, which voted unanimously to establish PRIB.

Sõrmus studied at the St Petersburg Conservatoire and later in Paris and Berlin. Exiled from Russia after his participation in the 1905 revolution, he was warmly welcomed in Britain both for his brilliant talent and for his outspoken opposition to Tsarist tyranny. Sõrmus became a key artistic figure in the socialist labour movement and in British Jewish cultural life. His recitals at venues including the Jewish Trades Hall in Leeds, Welsh working men's institutes and community halls, often accompanied on the piano by his British wife Virginia, garnered rave reviews. Their performance of a Bach chaconne and 'Ar Hyd y Nos' was described in a local paper as one of the finest musical programmes ever given in Ammanford, high praise from a Welsh critic.

The first conference of the People's Russian Information Bureau was held on 24 July 1918 in Chandos Hall, London, electing a committee to run the campaign, with Sylvia representing the WSF. The Socialist Labour Party, the British Socialist Party, the National Union of Railwaymen, the Independent Labour Party and the Labour Representation Committee formed the initial core of the committee. By February 1919 they had been joined by over 100 more affiliates, including the local Labour Party, the Herald League, trade unions, co-operative guilds and the Communist League. Sylvia's secretary Nellie Cohen and her best friend May O'Callaghan, who managed the offices of the *Dreadnought*, took responsibility for running the PRIB office, located a floor above in the Fleet Street HQ. May O'Callaghan was now sub-editor of the *Dreadnought*. The East End-born Nellie Cohen (later Rathbone), daughter of Polish Lodzer Jews who settled in Mile End, possessed formidable clerical and organizational skills. She was a political 'secretary' in the most traditionally masculine sense of the word. Nellie and May shared a flat with a fellow communist, Daisy Lansbury, daughter of George Lansbury.

Sylvia spoke frequently at Sórmus' concerts, and he became an active member of PRIB. Some thought he should confine himself to classical music recitals and shut up about the revolution, dubbing him the 'insolent Russian Bolshevist violinist from Merthyr'.[1181] On 14 February 1919, the *Abergavenny Chronicle* would report that he had been arrested under the Aliens Restriction Act for preaching revolution in South Wales while camouflaged as a Russian violinist. His violin was confiscated until he hunger struck. After it had been returned to him, he played for other prisoners and composed his 'Song of Sorrows'. Deported from Britain, Sórmus returned to Germany, where he had once studied music and where his fundraisers became enormously popular. In Germany he became known as 'der rote Geiger' – the Red Violinist. Targeted by the Nazi Party, he was dragged from the stage and arrested at a performance where he was raising money for a children's orphanage. Nazis smashed his violin at another concert in Magdeburg, and his Jewish landlord was murdered in Dresden. Sórmus fled to France where, in 1947, Marc Chagall would paint the Red Violinist as *Le Violoniste Bleue*, with Sórmus playing floating under a full moon, over the landscape of a Russian-Jewish village, evoking their shared cultural heritage.

Scotland Yard launched a surveillance operation on the People's Russian Information Bureau as soon as it was set up in July 1918. The Home Office collected PRIB leaflets that quoted letters 'alleged to have been received from Russia without passing through censorship'.[1182] Detectives raided the home of the PRIB's treasurer, and from this and other manoeuvres concluded that its main objective was to work up an agitation against the Allied intervention in Russia.

Basil Thompson tracked funds received from Russia in 1919 and 1920 to pay for the work. PRIB produced vast numbers of pamphlets and leaflets, translating the work of communists abroad and circulating it around Britain. Proving herself coolly adept at espionage and covert ops, Sylvia received letters and documents from Russia via the shipping lines and sent them back the same way. A ship's doctor called Nosovitsky who worked on the Cunard Line brought her a copy of the new constitution of the Soviet Republic, so Sylvia was the first to have the constitution translated into English and published, in *Dreadnought*. Nosovitsky was one of several shadowy figures Sylvia was introduced to and worked with who might have been double agents. In her manuscript of 'The Inheritance' where she writes about these men, each one is tagged with the same question, 'Was he genuine?'[1183] This included a Finn called Anderson who during his mission to London fell in love with 'my secretary'. Scrupulous about not identifying Nellie Cohen, Sylvia did write about the 'mysterious intrigues' resulting from the romance and 'the trouble I foresaw from it'. Anderson's arrest, shortly before her own, led to what Sylvia described as 'spymania amongst the comrades'.[1184]

Nellie and her younger sister Rose Cohen had brilliant minds and were hauntingly beautiful, with brown eyes, long dark hair, magical smiles and resolute communist politics. Their father Morris, a Polish Lodzer Jew, was a 'Ladies Costumier' in Globe Road, Mile End, where they grew up, and both were always exquisitely dressed.'[1185]

Maxim Litvinov, the Soviet government's representative in Britain, was also deeply involved in the PRIB. Sylvia records in 'The Inheritance' that she organized clandestine printing for him and notes that it was Litvinov who introduced her to the colourful Theodore Rothstein, whom she worked with extensively, never in an uncomplicated way. The Lithuanian-born Rothstein escaped the Tsarist pogroms and emigrated to London in 1891, joining the SDF four years later. By profession a journalist and translator, he wrote for numerous newspapers, including the *Daily News*, the *Manchester Guardian*, *Justice* and the *New York Call*, and was active in the National Union of Journalists. He became a friend and close confidant of Lenin, who visited him on his trips to London. Rothstein supported the formation of the British Socialist Party in 1911, became a senior member of its executive and, by 1917, was a Bolshevik. He strongly opposed the First World War while, perhaps surprisingly, working for the Foreign Office and War Office as a Russian translator and interpreter. Litvinov appeared illogically jealous of Sylvia's position in the British movement and anxious for the soothing attention of others. Sylvia thought that 'his vanity [made] him a poor conspirator'.[1186] In her draft manuscript notes, she writes intriguingly, 'What I did for him: printing and diamonds.'[1187] Around this time she made a covert trip to Berlin, noting later that she might write 'about my adventures there'. If she did, the account is lost or destroyed.

After ten months in office, Litvinov was arrested by the British and used in a prisoner-exchange negotiation with the Soviet government. The British authorities wanted Robert Bruce Lockhart, the former British Consul General in Moscow in 1918, who had used his diplomatic position to co-ordinate the activities of British spies and had plotted to overthrow the Soviet government. For this, he and his coterie had been arrested by the Soviets.

At the beginning of 1919, the British government sent troops to Archangel to assist the counter-revolutionary White Armies. PRIB publicized this and raised national awareness about the steadily increasing Allied intervention in Russia, arousing widespread dismay, particularly among organized labour. Sylvia wrote many leaflets calling on workers to fight against Allied intervention.

In January 1919 a broad group of radical organizations, including the WSF, convened a 'Hands Off Russia' conference and elected a steering committee of fifteen, including Sylvia, to co-ordinate anti-intervention activity. Sylvia later wrote that Theodore Rothstein had 'started' the Hands Off Russia committee.[1188] On May Day Sylvia, Melvina Walker, Amelia O'Mahoney and others led a deputation from Hyde Park to the St Stephen's Entrance of the House of Commons to demand 'Hands Off Russia'. Sylvia and Amelia O'Mahoney were arrested on charges of obstructing the police, and appeared before the magistrate Sir John Dickinson the following day. Attending as a witness, Melvina Walker explained the anti-intervention campaign to the court and their support for the establishment of a Soviet Republic. Sylvia had her say before Dickinson discharged them. She felt that she had not received the treatment she had a right to expect from the parliament of her purportedly democratic homeland. 'We had come to the close of one war, and the Empire was being dragged into another with Russia and Hungary, and probably with other countries in order to prevent the establishment of Soviets and Socialism in Europe.'[1189] On 21 March 1919, the Hungarian Soviet Republic had been proclaimed, but it only lasted until 1 August, when it was overthrown by the entry of the White Romanian army into Budapest, led by the Hungarian counter-revolutionary Admiral Miklós Horthy.

All of these events had taken place in the context of post-war 'revolution' in Germany. By September 1918 Germany had known it could not win the war. On 23 October the Allies told Chancellor Max von Baden that no armistice would be possible without an unconditional German surrender. While Baden attempted to negotiate a ceasefire, the German Admiralty gave orders for one last major North Sea battle, against unwinnable odds. The German navy was outnumbered and outgunned by the Allied fleet. Although officers drank toasts to this final 'honourable' suicide mission, their men rebelled. On 29 October sailors aboard two ships at Kiel mutinied, and within forty-eight hours the revolt had spread to other ports and naval stations. On 3 November the Kiel sailors, joined by workers from the city, seized their officers and took control of their ships. Next they formed elected councils, modelled on the workers' soviets of the Russian Revolution the previous year.

The naval mutiny quickly developed into a fully fledged political revolution. Workers' councils were established in many of Germany's major cities and demanded the abdication of the Kaiser and local princes, the scrapping of aristocratic privilege, the political empowerment of the Reichstag and the adoption of socialist policies. On 9 November the Kaiser abdicated and Germany began its transition to republican government. The Social Democratic Party (SPD), which had backed the war, led by Friedrich Ebert and Philipp Scheidemann, took control of the government. The SPD had backed the war. They were challenged from the left by Karl Liebknecht and Rosa Luxemburg, who, with Clara Zetkin, Leo Jogiches and others, had broken away from the SPD and in 1916 officially founded the Spartacist League, a socialist revolutionary movement, and had been imprisoned for organizing opposition to the war.

Shortly after his release, at a mass meeting on 9 November, Liebknecht publicly declared a 'free socialist republic of Germany' and raised a red flag. Rosa Luxemburg was released from prison that evening. A lifelong supporter of democracy within the Marxist tradition, who developed and adapted Karl Marx's insistence on the connection between capitalism and imperialism, Luxemburg was ambivalent about the German revolution. She had greeted both the February and October Revolutions with enthusiasm, because they had been galvanized by general strikes, a key revolutionary mechanism about which she had theorized throughout her life. From her perspective, the German uprising was clearly not a grass-roots socialist revolution, but was key for widespread political education among workers and citizens of the new republic, to prepare them for revolutionary activity. She wrote extensively about the German revolution despite never being at its front line.

At the end of December 1918, the Spartacists convened a congress and founded the Communist Party of Germany (KPD), challenging the SPD leadership. In early January 1919 they launched a failed communist uprising, known as the Spartacus Revolt, in Berlin. On 15 January Luxemburg and Liebknecht were captured and brutally murdered in the Eden Hotel, where they were in hiding following the suppression of the uprising, by members of the conservative paramilitary Freikorps. The day before, Luxemburg had written: 'The leadership failed. But a new leadership can and must be created by the masses and out of the masses. The masses are the crucial factor. They are the rock on which the ultimate victory of the revolution will be built … "Order reigns in Berlin!" You stupid lackeys! Your "order" is built on sand. Tomorrow the revolution will "rise up again, clashing its weapons", and to your horror it will proclaim to the sound of trumpets: I was, I am, I shall be!'[1190]

Sylvia was devastated when she heard of their assassination. She immediately composed an elegy entitled 'Rosa and Karl', celebrating equally their heroism and their humanity:

Rosa, whose verderous [sic] thoughts bloomed 'mid the dusk
Of prison cells, and whose up-soaring mind
Broke forth beyond the bars and winged its flight
Past all conventions of the sordid throng;
Thy lustrous eyes turned skyward on the clouds,
With dreaming looks, writing of birds and flowers,
To lull the sharpness of another's pain.

Rosa, that doctoral in the school would teach,
And wrote grave tomes of deep and wide import,
And entered zestful into argument,
Swaying vast crowds, beloved of simple folk;
O, prophetess sublime and undeterred …
Great Karl, that knew no pause, heroic friend
That vaulted onward to that vasty goal
Where freedom waits, O glorious Freedom's self …
You saw that vision of future days,
And followed it, unheeding of the wrath
Of jealous power that compassed thee about
With murderous menace of wild men at arms.[1191]

In March 1919 the Third (Communist) International (CI) was founded in Moscow by the Bolsheviks, and a courier from the International attended the WSF's 1919 conference the same month with the recommendation that a Communist Party should be formed in Britain. The WSF voted to change its name once more, this time to the Communist Party, the executive committee following the suggestion from Moscow to 'take steps towards linking up with the Third International and other communist groups in Britain'.[1192] Shortly afterwards, the executive decided to drop the new name, 'in case it prejudiced negotiations with other groups'. This explains why, in some historical accounts, the WSF is described interchangeably as the British Communist Party during the period between March 1919 and June 1920. Many British revolutionaries had long studied and argued about the nature of the organization they should establish.[1193] Negotiations for a united Communist Party had begun in May 1918 when the British Socialist Party (BSP) suggested that its newspaper *The Call* and the *Workers' Dreadnought* be amalgamated.[1194] Sylvia later claimed that she had initiated the move, though the records show this was clearly not the case. The merger did not take place because Edwin Fairchild of the BSP, who would have become joint editor of the new paper, would not endorse soviets and commit to the dictatorship of the proletariat. Relations between the two organizations remained cordial, and they continued to work together.

For the next sixteen months Sylvia focused her political work on clarifying the WSF's anti-parliamentary political programme, establishing affiliation to the CI and engaging in negotiations with other socialist groups in Britain, which were working together to establish the British Communist Party – referred to on the left as 'the unity negotiations'. After two decades of working for women's suffrage within the parliamentary system, Sylvia now believed in the policy 'abstentionism': 'that *on principle* revolutionaries should never participate in bourgeois parliamentary activities such as voting or running for Parliament'.[1195] Combined with her opposition to affiliation with the Labour Party and the official trade union organizations, this positioned her as forming a left-wing opposition within the CI.

Simultaneously, up and down the country, Labour Party and trade union meetings passed resolutions condemning intervention in Russia. In June 1919 the Labour Party annual conference, held that year in Southport, voted by a large majority to demand an immediate end to intervention and called for a twenty-four-hour general strike in support of Russia and Hungary to enforce its demand. The TUC parliamentary committee blocked this by refusing to back the resolution for a general strike. The WSF held a fundraiser in Old Ford Road to raise money for agitation in London dockyards, and the veteran socialist labour leader Tom Mann got to work among the dockers persuading them to refuse to load munitions destined for delivery to the enemies of Russia. The WSF held countless open-air and town-hall meetings all over London in a great push against intervention.

In the midst of all this communist-inspired activism, Sylvia had fallen in love with an anarchist: Silvio Corio, the Italian who had joined *Dreadnought* as a staff journalist and rapidly moved into editing, producing and managing it. Born in Saluzzo, in the Piedmont region, on 26 or 28 October 1875, Silvio Celestino Corio was the son of Eugenio Corio and Domenica Chiara. His father keenly supported the Risorgimento, the struggle for Italian independence and unity. As a youngster Silvio joined the Turin Socialist Club. By his early twenties he'd become involved with the anarchist movement and was associating with its leading lights, such as Alessandro Clama and Enrico Ricchiero. Like many left-wing socialist Italians of his generation, he adhered to anarchist rather than communist thinking, following the Russian Prince Peter Kropotkin and the Italian Errico Malatesta in preference to Marx.[1196] The young Corio trained as a printer and typographer. When conscripted, he turned his hand immediately to producing propaganda and as a result served most of his military service (July 1897–December 1898) in a disciplinary 'prison' battalion. His political beliefs and his support for the emerging Italian trade union movement saw him pushed into exile.

He fled to France to escape the repression of anarchists and socialists by the government of Luigi Pelloux, and there after lived as a stateless refugee. In Paris Corio fell in with the anarchists around Felice Vezzani, who published the news-sheet *Vita Nuova* (New Life) aimed at Italian exiles in France. In 1900, the French authorities issued him with an expulsion order prompted by an article about Italy that he wrote for the French anarchist paper *Le Libertaire*. He went into hiding, helped by, among others, Emma Goldman who was living in Paris. Caught and briefly imprisoned, on his release he headed to exile in London, arriving in 1901, and lived for a while with fellow anarchist Arturo Campagnoli. Silvio worked first as a street trader, then as a barman and waiter in Italian restaurants and cafés, while editing and printing the fortnightly *L'Internazionale* (January to May 1901) and simultaneously working with Carlo Frigerio on his book *Lo Sciopero Generale* (The General Strike). Corio also helped the Irish war correspondent Francis McCullagh with his book *Italy's War for a Desert*, which covered McCullagh's experiences reporting on the ground in Tripoli and is a brilliantly well-documented study of Italy's ruthless invasion of Libya in 1912.[1197] Corio interpreted or served as a guide for Italian socialists visiting England, including Errico Malatesta, Giuseppe Modigliani, Giacinto Serrati and the Treves brothers, all of whom, like Sylvia, later resolutely challenged Lenin's international policies.[1198]

After meeting in London, Malatesta and Corio became friends. Corio helped with the founding of Malatesta's Popular University on the Euston Road, conceived as a way of spreading anarchist ideas. Passionate about the Popular University, Corio taught design there and was deeply disappointed when it had to close in 1905 for lack of funds.

In late 1902, with twenty others, Corio signed a press statement announcing the launch of a new fortnightly paper, *La Rivoluzione Sociale*. As well as editing this with Frigerio, he contributed, under the name of Crastinus, to the magazine *Germinal*, run by anti-organizational anarchists. By 1904 the Italian anarchists in London had rallied to Malatesta's pro-organizational ideas. They lived mostly in the West End, and established relations with German, French and English anarchists and with the Jewish movement in the East End. All frequented the international anarchist clubs in London.

Corio attended the International Anarchist Congress in Amsterdam in 1907 as a delegate and there met British anarchist Guy Aldred, with whom he shared a critical view of the current organization of trade unions. In the same year, he assisted with *The Voice of Labour*, set up by some members of the *Freedom* journal collective and aimed at agitation among British workers. *Freedom* had been launched in 1886 by volunteers, including Kropotkin and Charlotte Wilson. Originally its subtitle was 'A Journal of Anarchist Socialism', but it was changed to 'Anarchist Communism' in June 1889. Corio wrote an article criticizing Henry Hyndman, leader of the Social Democratic Federation, who supported the building up of the British navy, and this was translated and published in Aldred's monthly journal *The Herald of Revolt*. Corio also took part in the activities of the Studi Sociali group, formed in London in 1911 to strengthen international anarchist propaganda. He wrote extensively on the war in Libya for several newspapers and many journals and came to specialize in that conflict and in Libyan history. In 1913 he participated in the founding of the new anarchist paper *Volontà* in Ancona, another Malatesta initiative, becoming its London correspondent. The same year he participated in the famed International Syndicalist Congress held in London.

For ten years, Silvio eked out a precarious existence with his partner, the socialist Clelia Alignani, also from Turin. They had a son Percy and a daughter Beatrice Roxane, nicknamed Rockie. (Silvio had an older son by a previous relationship, who worked in Genoa and periodically visited his father for a few days when he was in London on business trips with his employer.[1199]) Following the breakdown of the relationship, the children remained with their mother.

Corio's associates Errico Malatesta and Emidio Recchioni were critical of Italy's participation in the European war. Recchioni was to become a conspirator in the 1931 plot to assassinate Mussolini. From 1916 Corio was vocal in his anti-war stance. He started working with *Freedom* as a printer and around the same time joined the editorial board of the *Workers' Dreadnought*. Most of his contributions to these papers were anonymous or pseudonymous; even so, he was soon threatened by the Aliens' Act of 1918, which could have resulted in deportation to his homeland where a firing squad awaited him.

Corio attended the peace conference in Paris in 1918 and the international socialist conference in Berne the following year. He made covert trips to Italy, where he appears to have been carrying out clandestine work for Malatesta.

An unsubstantiated tale held that at one stage in his life 'Corio converted to Islam and joined the Ahmadiyya, an Islamic brotherhood with headquarters in India.'[1200] Given that he was a lifelong anarchist-atheist sceptic, this is nonsense. The rumour stems from the fact that Silvio got involved with nationalist friends in the Ahmadiyya global Islamic revival movement, which had been founded in the Punjab in the late nineteenth century. Corio lived for a time in lodgings at the Ahmadiyya Muslim Mission House, close to the mosque in Melrose Road in Southfields and stored some possessions there, as recorded in his correspondence.[1201]

In the early stages of their relationship, the new lovers, Sylvia and Silvio, squabbled about the management of the *Workers' Dreadnought*. Silvio's use of a pseudonym for his journalism annoyed Sylvia. She seemed at this stage ignorant of or insensitive to the extent of his vulnerability as a stateless refugee. The tiff provided Silvio with a welcome opportunity to write her a playful love letter in which he makes delicious sport of the felicity of their sharing the same proper name, in its masculine and feminine forms. Their son Richard Pankhurst, a subtle man, many decades later chose this as the only love letter between his parents to submit to the public domain from his mother's correspondence. It speaks, in Corio's third language, to two great loves of his life: linguistics and Sylvia,

> 'Apologia Pro "S" being a Fragmentary Essay on Politics':
>   Technicalities; Editorial rights and despotism; the alphabet, its value and importance; names and anonymity; to which is appended a moral: a contrition: a disclaimer: and in addition to: a few grammatical and ungrammatical errors together with: some useful and candid remarks on various happenings of daily life: by 'An Illustrious Author'.[1202]

The rolling epistle bristles with literary allusion, such as to Thomas
Carlyle and the Scriblerus Club and to Alexander Pope's *The Rape of the
Lock*. There is semantic frolic: Amper Sand appears personified. Turning
to the similarity of their names, he dwells on the form of the ' "S" in
front of me at the time of writing, visible to the inner eyes of the mind
… "S" leant over me, in its – or is it hers – graceful forms – willowy, her
graces pleasant to behold, piteously supplicant: Have mercy upon me!
… begone, temptress! display not upon my weak intellect the flexious
lines of thy body.'

Silvio plays with the 'E' and 'P' of her initials, entwined in her
distinctive ESP graphic signature. Parrying the question of his
pseudonym, Silvio Corio writes that his name indeed is a good one,
and he gives his father credit for making it harmonious. However, it
'is un-English', an 'alien' name difficult for a journalist in these times;
whereas 'you are of these islands' and moreover a well-known public
figure. Silvio concludes this twelve-page flight with:

> Dearest, Now two lines to you … It seems it is a long time since
> I have seen you … Yes I am afraid we shall have to wait for the spring
> before we go once more to Richmond Park. Richmond Park, now
> that I know you seems to me Paradise itself. How strange that but
> a few hours should cut so deep in one's mind. Tonight, every night
> I am sad. I miss you. You do not know how much. As ever, S.[1203]

In the summer of 1919, Sylvia and Silvio Corio decided to go together to
the conference of the Italian Socialist Party (PSI) in Bologna. The British
and Italian governments had placed both of them under surveillance
and restricted their free movement, so the only way to pass through the
borders was by clandestine means. They planned a radical grand tour
of Europe. As well as attending the PSI conference in Bologna with
Corio, Sylvia planned to attend the Western European Secretariat of
the International in Frankfurt, at the invitation of Clara Zetkin. Their
journey to Frankfurt would take place amid the recent tumultuous
events in Germany, where many socialists – Zetkin included – were in
hiding or under house arrest.

This trip was the first journey the lovers made together. His
homeland was an extremely dangerous place for Silvio to be. The

PSI at the time comprised a broad spectrum of left-wingers, from reformist parliamentary socialists to revolutionary socialists and other revolutionaries like Antonio Gramsci, Angelo Tasca and Palmiro Togliatti. Some, like Gramsci, envisioning workshop committees and a people's militia, looked to Soviet Russia for inspiration. Others, like Amadeo Bordiga and his ultra-left anti-parliamentary faction, equally admired the Russian example, but argued strongly for independence from Moscow and against taking their lead directly from Lenin and the Bolsheviks. Sylvia worked with and admired both: Bordiga for his tactic of abstentionism from corrupt parliamentary processes and Gramsci for his factory council movement. The Italian co-operative movement and the Turin metalworkers also inspired her and she regarded the factory council movement, which led the Turin factory uprisings, as being far ahead of workers'-committee organization in Britain.

Bordiga condemned the workers'-council movement as just another reformist modification of classic trade union structure, and a distraction from the job of creating a properly homogeneous proletarian party, built on individual commitment to the party and led, if necessary, by an 'audacious minority'.

The Bologna conference pledged the allegiance of the Italian Socialist Party to the Communist International. Sylvia addressed the delegates, bringing solidarity greetings from British workers, welcoming the development in revolutionary activity and arguing for the abstentionist faction as the 'most logical': 'It is difficult for me to understand how you can possibly make propaganda to win seats in parliament – a body which you mean to abolish in a few months – when you ought to be absorbed in the work of revolutionary preparation and when the most urgent need is to convince workers that the time for Parliaments is passed.'[1204] She learned a great deal in Italy, about the labour and socialist movements in Turin and Milan, and about the successes of the Italian co-operative movement. Meeting the leaders of the Italian socialist movement in Bologna, she discovered its successful programme of municipal socialism – particularly work by socialist councillors in schools and in establishing food centres. She visited gardens, schools, mountain care homes for the elderly, communal restaurants and land-reclamation projects.

In Bologna, Sylvia experienced her first bitter taste of emerging fascism. Rumour was that Mussolini was hiding in the city, for now 'a discredited chauvinist'.[1205] The Mayor Francesco Zanardi invited the British conference delegates to a reception. As they entered the town hall, they were attacked by fascist Blackshirts.[1206] In the same year a small group of men met in a businessmen's club to launch the Milan Fighters' Fascio. It wasn't all so grim and earnest. Sylvia wrote of the 'beautiful city of Bologna', of how they talked of politics and Dante beside its leaning tower, which features in the poet's *Divine Comedy*, and of how street musicians serenaded them under the stars.

Following the Bologna conference Sylvia set off alone without visa or passport towards Germany, climbing the Alps from Italy into Switzerland. Resistant to all forms of healthy organized exercise, Sylvia was an Olympian-standard walker when a political mission marked the destination. A young Swiss comrade guided her along goat paths over the mountains into Germany, crossing the frontier by night, and on into Stuttgart rendezvous with Norah. This was a demanding journey of three days and two nights, dossing down for the night in shepherds' huts. Police raids on people's homes forced many into hiding. The underground network introduced Sylvia to activists, including Paul Levi, Mieczysław Broński and other refugees. Levi had been head of the German Communist Party since the assassination of Liebknecht and Luxemburg. The Polish communist Broński, known as Braun, had accompanied Lenin on the sealed train back to Moscow in 1917.

Sylvia's hike was not yet over, as she and Norah had to walk to Clara Zetkin's country home, the only safe way for them to get there undetected. Sylvia and Clara had met several times before, but over the following days they got to know each other much better. Sylvia declared Clara a 'remarkable woman' and admired her 'enormous power'.[1207] Clara suffered from chronic ill health, but Sylvia observed that she never allowed this to deflect from her 'devotion to the cause'.[1208] During their stay, Clara dictated to Sylvia 'The Life and Times of Rosa Luxemburg', which Sylvia printed in English in the *Dreadnought*. Zetkin, at the time probably the world's leading feminist, argued that bourgeois feminism was a tool too easily used to divide the unity of both the working classes and women. Small wonder she and Sylvia got along famously.

The three women proceeded together to Frankfurt for a secret meeting of the Third International. This was occupied territory to attend the conference, but Sylvia discovered that, rather than getting on with the work, 'Comrades take the waters, eat cake in the cafés, amuse themselves.' They returned to Frankfurt for another conference organized by a 'supposedly learned society', which also turned out to be held in a succession of restaurants and involved male comrades talking revolution while waiters brought in platters laden with beef and beer.[1209] This was not at all the ascetic Sylvia's idea of how it should be. In Berlin she was introduced to members of the Spartacist group, whom she was immensely relieved to discover were less given to beer-and-beef restaurant philosophizing. This was more like it.

Sylvia rendezvoused with an agent described as 'the eye of Moscow' who passed on to her £500 funding for PRIB and the Hands Off Russia campaign. After receiving the money and instructions from Russia, Sylvia and Norah went on to Amsterdam, no doubt to the great relief of her 'idling' comrades. Sylvia's conclusion from her experience in Germany and Italy was that the Russians were 'grossly misinformed on the strength of the movement in these countries', which was far weaker than they believed.[1210]

Theodore Rothstein, who – operating under various aliases, including Veltheim, Anderson and Rubinstein – managed the channelling of funds provided by Lenin to pro-Bolshevik groups, already directed subsidies to the *Dreadnought*. All of this Sylvia later wrote up in her unpublished works 'In the Red Twilight' and 'The Inheritance', but at the time these activities were secret, known only to the participants and to British spooks and their European contacts.

By now the *Workers' Dreadnought* was the most visible communist publication in Britain. Sylvia's ideas travelled internationally through the many socialist journals and newspapers to which she regularly contributed. In 1918 she wrote a series of articles for *Avanti*, organ of the Italian Socialist Party, circumventing the censors by clandestine means to get her copy to Italy. These pieces dug into the secret wartime treaties between Tsarist Russia and the Allies, detailing proposals for carving up Europe and the Middle East following the conclusion of the war.

During the same period Sylvia enjoyed the unique position of being Antonio Gramsci's only regular foreign correspondent for his journal

L'Ordine Nuovo (The New Order), established in May 1919 in radical Turin, for which she wrote almost monthly. She contributed also to a range of theoretical and other journals. The activities of the WSF and Comrade Pankhurst received reciprocal international coverage, including in Amadeo Bordiga's *Il Soviet*. This demonstrates the reach of Sylvia's international network, as does the range of articles by communists that she published in the *Dreadnought*, including leading lights such as Clara Zetkin, Alexandra Kollontai, Rosa Luxemburg, Karl Liebknecht, Lenin and Herman Gorter.

In 1919 Sylvia was the British correspondent for the *Communist International*, official newspaper of the Comintern executive. Between June and September, it published several articles by her. The first argued against the war of intervention, appealing to British workers and soldiers to oppose counter-revolutionary aggression and urging them to accept that Labour MPs would not take a firm stand against intervention. In parliament, she wrote, courage evaporates 'like a child's soap bubble'.[1211] All nations involved in the war had imperialist designs, and the working classes of all countries should turn their attention to waging an international civil war against capital. Her next two pieces discussed 'The Workers and the League of Nations' and 'The Workers and the Social Traitors in England'.

By 1919 the WSF had arrived at a committed anti-parliamentary position. In March Sylvia wrote, 'Circumstances are forcing the Socialists of every country to choose whether they will work to perpetuate the Parliamentary system of government or to build up an industrial republic on Soviet lines. It is impossible to work effectively for both ends.'[1212] The WSF passed a resolution calling for all parliamentary and municipal elections to be ignored and for efforts to be made to expose the futility of workers wasting their time and energy.

The WSF stood fast on the position of 'No Parliamentary Action' in their discussions with other organizations. This anti-parliamentarianism aligned it with revolutionary British Marxist-anarchists, predominantly Guy Aldred. In May 1919 Aldred had observed that 'the *Workers' Dreadnought*, under the editorship of our comrade, Sylvia Pankhurst, has been making great strides intellectually speaking, and seems now to have become a definite Revolutionary Marxian Anarchist weekly with a clear outlook on the question of Soviet Republicanism as opposed to Parliamentarism'.[1213]

Two key points were proving 'stumbling blocks' to communist unity in Britain: refusal to engage in the parliamentary process and opposition to affiliation with the Labour Party, both insisted on by Lenin.[1214] Of the three other groups leading the communist unity talks, the South Wales Socialist Society agreed with the WSF, the Socialist Labour Party opposed Labour Party affiliation but supported parliamentary participation, while the British Socialist Party, by far the largest of the organizations involved, 'favoured both participation and parliamentarianism'.[1215] On 16 July 1919, Sylvia wrote to Lenin asking for his support for the WSF's anti-parliamentary stance in the British communist unity negotiations: 'if you were here, I believe you would say: Concentrate your forces upon revolutionary action; have nothing to do with the Parliamentary machine. Such is my own view.' Parliamentarianism, she believed, was holding back the advance of communism in Britain.

> The Labour movement in England is being ruined under my
> eyes by parliamentary and municipal politics. Both leaders and
> masses are only waiting for elections, and, while preparing for
> the election campaign, quite forgetting the socialist work ... they
> totally suppress all socialist propaganda in order not to frighten
> the electors. The British Socialist Party takes pride in the election
> of members to the municipal councils; but their election is
> not a signal for revolutionary agitation therein. They accepted
> the departmental office and became part of the machinery of
> capitalism.[1216]

Sylvia's letter to Lenin also explained inaccuracies in the reporting by the BSP newspaper *The Call*, which claimed that in June 1919 the WSF had set itself up unilaterally as the official Communist Party of Great Britain. She clarified that though her WSF had voted in favour of changing its name to the Communist Party, this was still pending.

Lenin admired Sylvia. Though critical of her anti-parliamentary stance in the British context, he took seriously her potential role in the creation of a British communist party, not the least because of her credentials as an experienced and tireless campaigner for parliamentary representation. On 28 August he sent her letter and his reply for publication in the *Communist International*. His response opens with some mollifying noises about anti-parliamentarians being among 'the best, most honest and sincerely revolutionary representatives of the proletariat'. But what, he asks, if communists sincerely committed to the soviet system cannot unite owing to disagreement over parliamentary participation?

> I should consider such a disagreement immaterial at present … the question of parliamentarianism is now a partial, secondary question. I am personally convinced that to renounce participation in parliamentary elections is a mistake on the part of the revolutionary workers of Britain, but better to make that mistake than to delay the formation of a big workers' Communist Party in Britain, out of all the trends and elements listed by you. We Russians, who have lived through two great revolutions, are well aware what importance parliamentarianism can have, and actually does have during a revolutionary period in general and in the very midst of a revolution in particular … Soviet propaganda can, and must, be carried on in and from within bourgeois parliaments.
> With Communist greetings,
> Lenin[1217]

This was not the response from the leader of the revolution that Sylvia had hoped to receive.

26

Comrade Pankhurst

In the 21 February 1920 issue of *Workers' Dreadnought*, Sylvia published an article she had written entitled 'Towards a Communist Party', outlining the progress of the unity negotiations for the formation of a united British Communist Party, on the basis of affiliation to the Third International, the recognition of the Soviet system instead of parliamentarianism and the recognition of the dictatorship of the proletariat.

> The Communist Party must keep its doctrine pure, and its independence from reformism inviolate. Its mission is to lead the way without stopping or turning by the direct road to Communist Revolution. Do not worry about a big Communist Party yet; it is better to build a sound one. Never let us hesitate, lest we should make it too extreme.[1218]

Purity and inviolability clearly would get nowhere in the necessarily messy business of changing the world. Too long accustomed to assuming a position of leadership, Sylvia had developed a vanguardist weakness. These lofty, entirely unrealistic words stand in contradiction to her usually solid good sense and to her understanding that all viable change must be built through a genuine and broad participatory movement.

That February Sylvia, alongside representatives of British socialist and Marxist parties, attended the founding conference of the short-lived 'ultra-left' Amsterdam Bureau of the International. Here she met two fellow anti-parliamentarians, the Dutch communist theoreticians

Anton Pannekoek (an astronomer) and Herman Gorter, who, a year later in September 1921, had formed the Communist Workers' Party of the Netherlands (KAPN), modelled on the German Communist Workers' Party (KAPD). Together they drew up an 'appeal to our English friends to unite on the basis of no affiliation with the Labour Party'. This conflicted with Lenin's view and hastened the dissolution of the Bureau.[1219]

At the Amsterdam conference, Sylvia proposed an international general workers' strike in support of Russia and against intervention. Herman Gorter seconded her motion, adding an amendment that the German revolution must also be defended. Both motions were accepted. In the event, the attempt at an international general strike failed because solidarity did not hold – key French and Italian unions backed out at the last minute, rendering the strike only partial. However, in Britain, the London dockers turned out in force, as did South Wales miners and workers in boot and shoe factories in Norwich. Sylvia and George Lansbury spoke themselves hoarse at rallies in Trafalgar Square, Victoria Park and Bethnal Green, but at this preliminary stage the attendance at the demonstrations was small.

In June 1920 Lenin made the Scotland Yard raids on the offices of the *Workers' Dreadnought* the previous month international news when he wrote about them in his 'Letter to the British Workers', published in *Pravda* and by the BSP in *The Call*, both on the 17th. The *Dreadnought*, the *Daily Herald* and *Russia Outlook* reprinted it two days later, following which it was taken up by the global press.

On 14 May Scotland Yard had swooped on the offices of the *Workers' Dreadnought* and arrested Sylvia's business manager, Harold Burgess. During the fortnight following his detention police returned to search the *Dreadnought* offices a further six times in Sylvia's presence. While her premises were raided she was de facto detained for the period of the search. Lenin wrote:

Sylvia Pankhurst has been arrested in England. This is the best possible answer the British government could give to this question which the non-communist British labour 'leaders' who are captive to bourgeois prejudices, are even afraid to put, namely against which class is the terror directed – against the oppressed and the exploited or against the exploiters and oppressors? When they speak

of 'freedom' do they speak of freedom for the capitalists to rob,
to deceive, to befool the toilers from the yoke of the capitalists,
the speculators and the property owners? Comrade Pankhurst
represents the interests of hundreds upon millions of people who
are oppressed by the British and other capitalists. That is why she is
subject to White terror, deprived of liberty etc.[1220]

In the ensuing months Sylvia and Lenin entered into an escalating
argument about the character and policy of what would become the
British Communist Party. The debate began in amity, with Sylvia one
of the key players, and ended with her expulsion from what became
the official British Communist Party and a battle for the soul of the
Dreadnought. According to Lenin, all of this happened because Sylvia
had unfortunately contracted an acute case of what he described as the
'infantile disorder' of 'ultra-leftism'. Having diagnosed her condition,
consulted directly with her on her self-treatment and published his
findings on the cure internationally, Lenin continued to hope for
Sylvia's speedy recovery. The patient, however, did not agree that she was
suffering from any sort of political disorder.

Lenin entitled his tract '*Left-Wing Communism': An Infantile Disorder*.
Sylvia retorted robustly with a pithy, witty edit to Lenin's sexist title,
referring to it as 'Left Childishness',[1221] neatly skewering its infantilizing
of a woman comrade's intellect and its all too familiar implication of
the general derangement of the minds of women who presumed to
occupy the public sphere.

The seeds of Sylvia's final exclusion from the British Communist Party
that she had worked so hard to bring about were sown in her argument
with Lenin over anti-parliamentarianism and Labour Party affiliation.
Albert Inkpin's British Socialist Party adopted orthodox Leninism, pro-
parliamentarianism and the strategy of Labour Party affiliation. The
Scottish Socialist Labour Party (SLP) and Sylvia's Workers' Socialist
Federation (WSF) were now committed to anti-parliamentarianism,
independence from trade unions and advocating a general strike. The
SLP had around a thousand members, and by now the WSF a few
hundred. Being so much smaller, the two organizations feared correctly
that unity would mean losing their left-wing platform.

Sylvia attacked Inkpin in the *Dreadnought* and he returned the favour
in *The Call*. The unity talks were scheduled to reconvene in August, but

Sylvia and the WSF decided to go it alone. With seven other affiliated groups, the WSF dissolved itself on 19 June and reconstituted itself as the Communist Party, British Section of the Third International (CP-BSTI), based on non-affiliation to the Labour Party and refusal to participate in elections, with the *Dreadnought* as its official newspaper. This inaugural meeting was small enough to take place in the flat shared by Nellie Cohen, May O'Callaghan and Daisy Lansbury. *The Call* derided Sylvia's 'fatuous fooling' and dismissed the CP-BSTI as a 'tiny and uninfluential gathering', but in reality the BSP and SLP were infuriated by Sylvia's presumption.[1222] They wrote to Lenin complaining about her and asking him to endorse their move to exclude her from the August unity convention.

In her unpublished account of these years 'In the Red Twilight', Sylvia summarized the chapter of her life that followed. 'Lenin sends a wireless message he will debate with me and [she] writes "Left Childishness".'[1223] Lenin sent his memorandum on 8 July in the run-up to the congress:

> I consider erroneous the tactics pursued by Comrade Sylvia Pankhurst and the Workers' Socialist Federation, who refuse to collaborate in the amalgamation of the British Socialist Party, the Socialist Labour Party and others to form a single Communist party. Personally I am in favour of participation in Parliament and of affiliation to the Labour Party, given wholly free and independent communist activities. I shall defend these tactics at the Second Congress of the Third International on July 15, 1920 in Moscow. I consider it most desirable that a single Communist party be speedily organised on the basis of the decisions of the Third International, and that such a party should establish the closest contact with the Industrial Workers of the World and the Shop Stewards' Committees, in order to bring about a complete merger with them in the near future.[1224]

Sylvia launched her response to Lenin's condemnation in the *Dreadnought* with a gloriously sardonic salvo against the revolutionary leader: 'My reply to you is that I would like to defend my tactics in the Moscow Congress, but I have been refused two visas by two intervening countries. If you, through your influence in the Labour Party and your parliamentary friends can obtain for me a passport, I shall gladly meet you in debate.'[1225]

Then, without waiting for a response and with neither passport nor visas, Sylvia set out on a clandestine journey to Moscow, with the security services of three nations attempting to follow her. The official British delegation included William Gallacher, Dave Ramsay, Jack Tanner, William MacLaine and Tom Quelch. Sylvia received her credentials as a Consultative Delegate for the WSF – with a voice, but no vote. The Home Office had confiscated her passport and it was the embassies of Norway and Sweden which had refused her visas.

Conversely, in 1917 Lloyd George had instantly granted her mother's request for passports for herself and WSPU colleagues to visit Russia as 'patriotic British women, loyal to the national and Allied cause'.[1226] Opposed to international Marxists, particularly to pro-Bolsheviks like her daughter, Mrs Pankhurst had seen it as her patriotic mission to encourage Russia to stay in the war and speak against 'minority representatives [who] are going to preach class war and the universal strike. While talking in favour of peace with the German aggressors, they advocate class war. I want to say to the Russian people that those who first taught democratic ideals did not preach the class war.'[1227] Emmeline Pankhurst left Britain accompanied by a media fanfare and sailed into Petrograd docks to a public welcome, flags flying.

Three years later the government prohibited her socialist daughter from leaving Britain. Trailed by the security services and on the watchlist at every port, Sylvia was obliged to leave Britain by subterfuge. Driven by her determination to debate directly with Lenin and the Comintern, she embarked on her risky mission from Harwich, in disguise. Assisted by comrades, she stowed away on a freighter bound for Norway and Sweden, where she expected to pick up a 'Soviet steamer'.

The solid-sounding 'steamer' turned out to be an old fishing smack, 'unpainted for many years ... scarcely eight feet across and her gear rusted and weatherworn', in which she spent 'hours of misery' in the icy seas making the voyage to Murmansk. In her memoir *Soviet Russia as I Saw It*, Sylvia writes airily that they 'bounded over the waves, away from Capitalism'.[1228] As the unpublished manuscripts for 'The Inheritance' and 'In the Red Twilight' show, this was a cheerfully roseate retrospective gloss on her seasickness, on the choking fumes coughed out by the temperamental engine and on the fact that she managed only with great difficulty to prevent herself from slipping overboard in a squall that turned into a storm. The tempest forced the captain to seek shelter in the nearest port, and after a rough night they proceeded to Murmansk and on to Petrograd. The following day Sylvia took the train to Moscow, where she booked into a hotel, adorned with red banners and packed with delegates from all over the world.

The cultural preferences of her comrades amused her. The British delegation was, she noted, deeply unhappy about the ample quantities of what they regarded as unpalatable caviar and fresh rye bread supplied by their hosts. But they cheered up instantly on discovering the generous daily supply of free cigarettes, cheroots and matches. For her own part, Sylvia once again found herself challenged by her dislike of porridge that had followed her from nursery to prison. This time it was in the form of the staple *kasha* served at most mealtimes. Her alarmed description of this ubiquitous Russian gruel is the subject of one of the longest footnotes in her travel memoir.

Each international delegate received a traditional peasant blouse in their conference gift pack. Sylvia observed that while the Russians and southern Europeans looked terrific in this revolutionary garb, the British delegates didn't carry them off quite so well. This might have been a metaphor for the difficulty of making Bolshevik methods suit the small island of highly industrialized modern Britain rather than a sprawling peasant-dominated continent crawling away from the yoke of the Tsars.

Between conference sessions Sylvia explored Moscow, fascinated by its combination of strangeness and familiarity. St Basil's Cathedral was 'like a schoolboy's Christmas nightmare and yet it possesses a strange barbaric beauty'.[1229] She deplored a new statue of Karl Marx as the worst she'd ever seen, remarking that many talented British art students might find good regular work improving public art in Bolshevik Russia. In Petrograd, the style of the eerie tinted negatives in the propaganda shops on the Nevsky Prospekt had stirred her perennial interest in design and printing techniques, as did the wider experience of art and culture in the process of rapid radical transformation.

There were sound political reasons why Comrade Pankhurst and Comrade Gallacher arrived in Moscow as the only two dissenters in the British delegation. Both had significant influence in the British unity movement, whatever the disclaimers of the British Socialist Party. Lenin argued that British revolutionaries had to differentiate themselves from reformists and demonstrate to the working class the ultimate uselessness of gradualism and parliamentarianism. Tactically, in order to do this, the Communist Party of Great Britain should properly engage in political discussion with the working class, and that required affiliation with their existing structures of political representation. 'Millions of backward members are enrolled in the Labour Party, therefore Communists should be present to do propaganda amongst them provided Communist freedom of action and propaganda is not thereby limited.'[1230]

Theoretically logical, this position, Sylvia argued, overestimated the size and influence of the British Labour Party. It was not a mass party in the way Lenin envisaged it. In her view, Lenin equally underestimated the Labour Party's commitment to open political debate when he wrote:

> Comrades Gallacher and Sylvia Pankhurst cannot deny that …
> while remaining in the ranks of the Labour Party, the British
> Socialist Party enjoys sufficient liberty to write that such and such
> leaders of the Labour Party are traitors, champions of the interests
> of the bourgeoisie and their agents in the Labour movement; this is
> absolutely true. When Communists enjoy such liberty, then taking
> into the account the experience in all countries, and not only in
> Russia … it is their duty to affiliate with the Labour Party.[1231]

Lenin argued that it was necessary for the Labour Party to have a trial period in office in order to expose the futility of reformism and the unreliability of Labour officials. When, inevitably, they failed, workers would look to the communists. Sylvia countered: 'We assert that the Labour Party will in any case come to power, that the BSP cannot disassociate itself too clearly from the Labour Party's reformist policy and must by no means enter into alliances or arrangements with it. We believe that Communists can best wean the masses from faith in bourgeois parliamentarianism by refusing to participate in it.'[1232]

She laid out her position more explicitly in her manuscript of 'In the Red Twilight': 'When the workers have passed through trade unionism and Labour Parliamentarianism, through industrial unionism and developed a Marxian appreciation of the class war, and are striving to build up amongst the workers within their own industries, the organization and consciousness from which the soviets will spring, they are unlikely to turn their attention back to parliamentarianism in any form.'[1233]

The other British delegates debated against Pankhurst and Gallacher's position. Each speaker was allotted five minutes, but Sylvia somehow persuaded congress officials into allowing her thirty. The extra time was just another twenty-five minutes in which to lose the argument. Her fiery agitator's speech misjudged the need of the moment for measured advocacy. Even allowing for ample misogynist bias in the reporting of her address, she'd spoken for too long and buried her arguments in rhetoric.

In the final days of the conference, Lenin launched his attack on anti-parliamentarians, targeting Willie Gallacher and Sylvia Pankhurst in particular. He sent Sylvia a message summoning her to a meeting with him at the Kremlin to discuss the 'British question' with red-bearded Nikolai Bukharin and the US journalist turned Bolshevik revolutionary, John Reed, among others. John Reed was now romantically partnered with the journalist Louise Bryant, who wrote for Sylvia's *Dreadnought*. Congress hummed and whirred with the news that Comrades Pankhurst and Gallacher were in for a mighty dressing-down from the leader. Sylvia described her journey to the meeting, starting with the issue of her pass by the security chief: 'The Commandant wrote out a little pink *probusk*. The motor car took me over the cobbles to the walls of the Kremlin. The Red Guards, five or six of them, checked the car to examine my *probusk*, and three times afterwards I was obliged to display it before I reached my destination.'[1234]

Sylvia strode undaunted into the Kremlin with her bulging file and signature large notebook tucked under her arm, deportment upright and imposing. She passed 'the Czar's big bell, which lay on the ground with a piece chipped out of it'. She paused to look at the 'great entrance', with its 'mighty staircase ... all hung with long red flags blazoned with the sickle and corn-sheaf, and ... a painting of "Labour", huge and naked, breaking the chains that bind the earth, hideous and ill-proportioned, but having a certain effective vigour'. The walls of the corridors and antechambers were plastered with 'photographs, posters and literature. The Russian Communists are indeed great propagandists!'[1235] The Committee Room, formerly the Tsar's palatial bedroom suite, was the venue for the meeting. The stage was finally set for the Pankhurst–Lenin showdown.

As she entered the room, Lenin detached himself from a meeting in progress and 'with smiling face came quickly forward from a group of men waiting to get a word with him'. She thought him more 'vividly vital and energetic, more wholly alive than other people'. He seated Sylvia in prime position beside him at the table. David Wijnkoop, co-founder of the Dutch Communist Party, sat on her other side and interpreted. 'Lenin', she noted, 'has a complete knowledge of English: he more than once humorously pulled up Wijnkoop for misinterpreting the speakers.'[1236]

Bukharin, editor of *Pravda*, Karl Radek, Grigory Zinoviev and 'Big Jack' Reed also sat around the table. 'Young and vigorous' Bukharin had, she thought, 'the expression of one to whom life is full of enjoyment … During Committee meetings he is continually drawing caricatures of the delegates, but no important point in the discussion escapes him. Today he drew Wijnkoop as a solemn, pompous owl.' The Pole Karl Radek, a Spartacist comrade and one of the founders of the German Communist Party, now a member of the Bolshevik Central Committee and in charge of western propaganda, Sylvia found Radek 'smiling and cheerful, with a detached dreamy air'. In contrast to Radek's 'calm and humour', Zinoviev was impatient and a little contemptuous and 'the controversy seemed to bore him'. Sylvia added, 'One of the American delegates said of Zinoviev that he always talks to one as though he were taking a bath.'[1237]

Under no illusion about who was going to win the argument, everyone played along. 'We, who were in opposition on certain matters, nevertheless argued our case in spite of the hopelessness of the task, and Lenin argued against us, as though our defeat had not been a foregone conclusion,' Sylvia wrote.[1238]

Sylvia didn't pull her punches. 'Though I am a socialist,' she told Lenin, 'I have fought a long, long time in the suffrage movement and I have seen how important it is to be extreme.'[1239] Lenin argued that socialists differed from communists, and emphasized the need for affiliation and co-operation, citing the repeated mistakes made in Germany, France and Russia. Turning one of his full charm offensives on Comrades Pankhurst and Gallacher, he advised them to return to Britain and join the CPGB. When the conference assembled that evening in the Old Throne Room, Lenin announced that the British delegation and 'even Sylvia Pankhurst' were now in full accord. It appeared she had conceded that Lenin was right after all: the need for unity was paramount.

Lenin's contradictory positions irritated Sylvia. Parties belonging to the Comintern, he declared, should break with 'opportunistic' kinds of socialism that rejected the need for the 'dictatorship of the proletariat'. Yet simultaneously he demanded that British communists should affiliate themselves to the British Labour Party. Lenin's argument was that communism in the United Kingdom was as yet too frail to set up an independent party. 'Pankhurst might have raised a fuss if all eyes had not been on the map of the war front,' observes Lenin's biographer Robert Service. 'Everyone at the Congress concentrated upon the question of how to aid the process of Revolution presently being advanced on the bayonet tips of the Red Army.'[1240]

Sylvia certainly learned a different perspective from the experience of being in Soviet Russia and the reality of the vast international congress with its diversity of delegates discussing the imminent possibility of multinational revolution. Lenin in person exposed her susceptibility to the truly clever and intellectual political man:

> At first sight one feels as though one has always known him … the photographs are not like him: they represent an altogether heavier, darker and more ponderous man in place of this majestic and mobile being … rather short, broadly built, he is quick and nimble in every action just as he is in thought and speech … his rather bright complexion looks sandy because it is tanned and freckled by hot sun … His bearing is frank and modest, his brown eyes twinkle with friendly amusement …[1241]

Yet twinkling eyes and glittering radical brains only went so far with Sylvia. For all his fully turned-on charm, Lenin was contemptuous of most women, and Sylvia knew it. Unlike Eleanor Marx, Sylvia never interpreted loyalty to individual love as a just reason for self-immolation or for giving up her own assertive rights. This Pankhurst had had a far more explicit and intentional feminist upbringing than her socialist sister role model Marx. But it wasn't just the lessons in sexual equality learned in the nursery of the Pankhurst household that better equipped her. It was precisely the example of what had happened to women she admired who had gone before: Marx commited suicide due to crushing disillusion with her father (primarily) and an unworthy 'repellent' partner (secondarily).[1242]

Lenin had secured his arguments with Sylvia (and Gallacher) in 'Left-Wing Communism', which was distributed to all delegates. Lenin criticized Comrade Pankhurst's ideology and derided it as 'intellectual childishness, not the serious tactics of a revolutionary class'.[1243]

Ideologically at variance, Comrades Pankhurst and Lenin were perhaps more alike in their pragmatism. Just as Lenin needed to keep the British parliamentary labour movement onside, Sylvia needed to return to Britain with the funds urgently required to keep the WSF and the *Dreadnought* afloat and, by extension, to sustain opposition to the Leninist party line. Later events suggest that Sylvia may have been strategically pretending to comply in order to secure her campaign finances. Lenin was the international man of the moment, for now better as ally than as opponent. She might even really have been persuaded by his argument for unity at that moment in the Kremlin, surrounded by the evidence of Bolshevik power and its potential to turn the ship of global capitalism in midstream.

When Lenin addressed the congress immediately after their meeting, delegates from all points of the globe met his confirmation of British unity with roars of approval and lusty singing of the Internationale as they picked him up and carried him above the heads of the throng. Even a soul made of such stern stuff as Sylvia might be impressed and swept along on this hopeful new tide.

Herman Gorter rounded on Lenin for leading Sylvia astray on the question of resisting political opportunism:

> In England, more even than anywhere else, there is always a
> great danger of opportunism. Thus also our Comrade Sylvia
> Pankhurst, who from temperament, instinct and experience,
> not so much perhaps from deep study, but by mere chance, was
> such an excellent champion of Left Wing Communism, seems to
> have changed her views. She gives up anti-parliamentarism, and
> consequently the cornerstone of her fight against opportunism,
> for the sake of the immediate advantage of unity! By so doing
> she follows the road thousands of English Labour leaders have
> taken before her: the road towards submission to opportunism
> and all it leads to, and finally to the bourgeoisie. This is not to be

wondered at. But that you, Comrade Lenin, should have induced
her to do so, should have persuaded her, the only fearless leader
of consequence in England, this is a blow for the Russian, for the
world revolution.'[1244]

Lenin was right about education from within and Sylvia was wrong.
On the other hand, she was correct that Lenin overestimated the size
and nature of the Labour Party. Nowhere in these debates does it occur
to Lenin to address the question of why a former militant suffragette
might by 1920 be justifiably sceptical of placing confidence in British
parliamentary representation. It hardly needs to be mentioned that
feminism of any sort, socialist or otherwise, was not part of Lenin's
agenda. For her part, Sylvia characteristically respected the Bolshevik
achievement of deeds, not just words: 'Moreover, I was loathe [sic] to
break with those who had placed the Soviets in power without great
consideration. I felt they had been through the fire of battle, they had
the courage to rise and had at least achieved something, whereas we [in
Britain] were only talking still.'[1245]

   At other moments, Sylvia's doubts surfaced, even while she was still
in Russia. She recalls one night 'escaping from the perpetual stream
of humorous anecdote' among the delegates at the hotel, enabling
her to escape 'down to the banks of the Moscow river with Mikhail
(Gruzenberg) Borodin', the translator of 'Left Childishness'. As they
watched 'big comets with long tails of light, and frequent shooting
stars', Borodin talked to her about his long exile in London, and
compared the 'dull visionless life of a British worker, mentally starved,
though perhaps comparatively well fed, with the desperate, hungry
struggle, lit by tremendous hopes and dreams that has brought Soviet
Russia where it is. In the great, panelled dining-hall of a millionaire's
mansion, now occupied by Communist workers, Borodin's meagre
supper, a little piece of cold meat and a spoonful of rice, had been left
waiting.'[1246]

   For as long as Sylvia remained in Russia maintaining her outward
show of unity, she was rewarded with star treatment. Driven to the
Bolshoi Opera in the former Tsar's limousine, she was seated in the
Royal Box to watch the performance. Following an exhausting tour of
the usual Moscow sights, she headed off with a group including Jack
Reed to explore real life outside Moscow. They visited a metal factory,

a 'House for the Mother and Child' and model schools and hospitals. Sylvia made copious notes about her visits to soviets and co-operatives, and like many others at the time inhaled the fumes of progressive social transformation while ignoring evidence of the oppressive behaviour of the Bolsheviks to those who opposed them.

She approved of Red Russian prohibition. 'Today it is believed that the Russian people have mostly forgotten the very existence of alcohol,'[1247] she wrote, without so much as a snifter of irony and directly after a long night spent in the company of Jack Reed and soldiers drinking bootleg vodka. Though equally intoxicated by events, Sylvia's Russian memoir is no match for Reed's bestselling *Ten Days That Shook the World*. Her style is as earnest as Reed's is racy. The unpublished complete manuscripts of her later works 'The Inheritance' and 'In the Red Twilight' reveal that it was her studied intention to buck the sensationalizing trend in witness memoirs. *Soviet Russia as I Saw It* in its entirety is barely the length of one of her many chapters about Russia in the longer manuscripts. She also leaves out all the interesting stories about herself, just as she did when she wrote about her travels in America. Jack Reed made himself the centre of the action, Sylvia removed herself from the narrative to the position of observer. Nowhere in the published book are there accounts of her many speeches in Soviet Russia – such as the occasion of her addresses to the Red Army and the Red Navy. Nor, regrettably, does it include her night of 'dancing with the Red Navy'.[1248] Other elisions were practical. To protect others, her account of how the Norwegian government tried to catch her and hand her over to the British on her way back home naturally had to be suppressed for a later date, alongside much else too revealing of the still live operations of international networks.

Sylvia sent a detailed book proposal and working manuscript for 'In the Red Twilight' to Victor Gollancz over a decade after the events. Gollancz admired Sylvia, but he didn't need to read further than the detailed chapter breakdown to realize that the book was dynamite his publishing house couldn't afford in legal bills and scrutiny from the security services. It was a book that could be published safely only abroad, or in Britain in the future, when it had become history.

The value of Sylvia's slim contemporary memoir *Soviet Russia as I Saw It*, published in 1921 by her own publishing house, the Dreadnought Publishers, lies in its power as an observation written before Lenin instituted the New Economic Policy of reversion to capitalism. Sylvia's focus on women and children in her account is unusual for the time. Her revolutionary travelogue is rich with insightful portraits of personalities, particularly women, such as the statuesque Red Guard soldier who speared their conference passes on the tip of her bayonet before using it to point them into the hall.

Sylvia also took the opportunity to deliver a good thumping to Labour Party trimmers:

> Bourgeois democrats of capitalist countries complain that the
> Russian dictatorship of the proletariat is the dictatorship of the
> Communist Party ... Ramsay MacDonald, who has talked glibly
> against Bolshevik dictatorship in Russia, has actually opposed
> proportional representation in Britain, on the ground that it might
> militate against large government majorities. He argued that strong
> governments with large majorities are best.[1249]

Her description of the Commissariat of Public Health reads like a blueprint for the NHS.[1250] She compared the education values in Britain, especially indoctrination into the ideology of empire, with the new communist education system for the youth of Russia.[1251] She was fascinated by the introduction into the education system of Jacques-Dalcroze's experimental method of 'eurythmics' – teaching concepts of rhythm, structure and musical expression using movement. As always, she was deeply interested in creative innovations that enabled students to gain physical awareness and experience of music, dance and art through training that takes place through all of the senses, particularly kinaesthetic. The new linguistic possibilities forged by social transformation also intrigued her – 'proletcult' (people's culture) being a clear favourite, judging by the frequency with which she repeated it. Among other gems in this travelogue is Sylvia's approval of post-revolutionary women's dress and sensible shoes, in preference to the silly stilettoes that hobbled women still footbound by capitalism.[1252]

For all this, Sylvia was alert to the challenges and telltale signs of troubles ahead. Mostly, she picked these up from the women she met, such as Helen Gorielova, garment textile worker and organizer of the Petrograd women. 'She has her prototype amongst the revolutionary proletarian women of Russian origin in many European cities; you may see her like any day on the East Side of New York. She works hard and lives almost as poorly now that the Workers' Soviets are in power, as she did under Capitalism.'[1253] An ardent communist, Gorielova lived only to serve the cause. Like many women, she learned to shoot in the revolution and could handle a revolver or a carbine (a rifle proved too heavy for her).

Sylvia also enjoyed the company of many other women she met who do not appear in her 1921 memoir, but do feature in her later 'In the Red Twilight' manuscripts. One of these was Tamara Ketlinsky, once living in a fashionable district near Hyde Park, 'who became a proletarian'. Ketlinsky's father joined the Bolsheviks and was shot by White Russians; she returned home to continue his work.

Back to Britain travelled Comrade Pankhurst with her fellow delegates, Willie Gallacher, Jack Tanner and Dave Ramsay. To avoid the blockade maintained by the Allied intervention on the side of the anti-communist 'White' forces in the southern Baltic states of Latvia, Lithuania and Estonia, they had to take a circuitous, clandestine route home around the northern Baltic. The return journey was so perilous it made her bumpy ride outward seem like a smooth passage. The first stage of the journey was by rail from Moscow to Murmansk, via Petrograd. At about two in the morning, a fire broke out on the night train. The woman in the top berth above her leapt down and raised the alarm. As the door of their compartment was opened, smoke came pouring in. Sylvia and her fellow passengers 'gasped for breath, our eyes streamed with tears and smarted horribly'.[1254] It was impossible to find their coats and shoes, 'the smoke was too suffocating and painful'.[1255] The train rushed on for a few seconds, then jolted to a stop. Sylvia jumped on to the track and ran to the railway bank with the other passengers, where she stood while the train was sprayed with a hosepipe, and a carriage was removed. Shivering in her nightdress and without shoes, she observed, 'It was unpleasant. It might have meant getting one's death of cold in mid-winter. As it was, I got a chill from it.'[1256]

Willie Gallacher recalled the episode rather differently. He had shared a compartment with Ramsay and Tanner. According to him, when the engineman stopped the train, 'We were out of that carriage in record time. But Sylvia …? I went back in and found her nearly suffocated. I raised her over my shoulder and got her outside.'[1257] Gallacher described how he manfully carried Sylvia through the smoke-filled, smouldering corridor to safety.[1258] In case it was missed, he emphasized his gallantry in his memoirs: 'That was the beginning of a responsibility that rested on me until we parted ... She was a pretty helpless subject on a journey, and required quite a lot of looking after.'[1259]

From Murmansk, they boarded a Norwegian fishing boat bound for Vardo, the easternmost port town in Norway. A group of comrades came to wave goodbye to them from the quay. The four British delegates stood on the deck and sang the Internationale as they sailed out under sunny skies, their friends on the shore joined in, and the Red Guard who had checked their passes raised a salute. Within hours a fierce storm blew up and Sylvia became violently seasick. 'The boat was throwing somersaults,' Gallacher recalled. 'Sylvia was very sick. We laid her on the top of the little hatchway, covered her with a waterproof. I wedged myself between the hatchway and the gunwale of the boat, and held her there all through the night. What a night!' The seas lashed over the craft, threatening 'to wash Sylvia and myself into the great unknown. But we stuck it out.' Sylvia got a 'bit maudlin' and started 'reciting a childhood poem about rains and storms and how she crept beneath an oak and how the "oak it sheltered me". Then she moaned, "Gallacher, you're my oak!" I have been called a lot of things in my time, but I think Sylvia beat them all.'[1260] As with the railway-fire episode, Sylvia makes no mention of Gallacher's chivalry in her own memoir, which is particularly odd, given her habit of taking every opportunity to cite a tag of poetry. She simply and crisply recorded that 'great waves tossed us, drenching our deck and us with it. Most of us were sick, and all of us were cold.'[1261]

When the storm subsided, a rowing boat came out to take them to shore, where they clambered over a slippery outcrop of rock and seaweed to get to relatively drier marshy land. Both Sylvia and Gallacher identified this cove as Zipnavalok, a Soviet wireless station, where a detachment of the Red Navy was quartered. There the British delegates from the CI received a cordial welcome, and in the evening were treated to a special dinner in their honour, including prized supplies of English tea, sugar, flour cakes and bully beef, rations left behind by the British army after the Allied intervention in 1919. The Red Army had defeated them in the region, and they beat a hasty retreat, abandoning equipment and supplies. As Gallacher remarked: 'It was the commonest sight imaginable to see northern peasants with a nice suit made of finest English khaki.'[1262] Members of the local community and Communist Party came to the supper, after which the tables were cleared away for dancing. 'Sylvia had come through it very well', said Gallagher, 'and though, like the rest of us she had got badly shaken, she wasn't long in getting back to her old lively self with the staff at the station.'[1263] In her account, Sylvia offered her assessment of who were the best dancers at the supper party.

The following morning they resumed their voyage, once more, according to Gallagher, encountering heavy seas. 'I must honestly say,' he wrote, 'that it seemed worse than the night before, and the old oak tree had to function once again.'[1264] Again, Sylvia makes no mention of needing to cling to her 'oak', nor even that they encountered any particularly rough weather. She does note, however, that they annoyed their Norwegian captain, who sensibly wanted to leave at dawn to catch the best weather. 'We ignored his instructions and ate our breakfast, which was fortunate, as we did not arrive till late afternoon.'[1265]

The skipper delivered them safely into the harbour of Vayda-Guba, a coastal village situated beyond the Arctic Circle in Murmansk Oblast on the Kola Peninsula, the northernmost point of Russia. It was 'a barren spot, greatly inferior to Zipnavalok', according to Sylvia; 'it lay on a cruel grey coast of jagged slate, with two wrecked hulks lying on either side of the bay'.[1266] She was hosted by a prosperous trader, Comrade Petersen, and his Norwegian wife, while Gallacher, Tanner and Ramsay stayed in a cottage on the other side of the harbour.[1267] 'Comrade Petersen,' she explained, had been sent to Vayda-Guba, 'by the Communist Party to lead the organisation of the fishing industry.' Bored by the 'long dark winters and the harsh climate [he] was said to have enriched himself by trading with foreign vessels'.[1268]

In the morning, after his cup of coffee and piece of black bread, Gallacher went to let Sylvia know that their boat was ready to leave. Mrs Petersen came to the the door, and looked at him in surprise when he asked for Sylvia. 'She waved her arm towards the mouth of the harbour and, I gathered, indicated that Sylvia had gone. I couldn't understand it.' He went and spoke to the skipper, who knew some English, asking him what had happened. 'You could have knocked me down with a twelve-pound hammer when he told me that she had gone with a Soviet trader that had been lying over on her side of the harbour.

The names we called her, when I reported to the others! To slip off like that, without a word – that's gratitude!'[1269]

Sylvia's account of her unannounced pre-dawn departure is opaque, to say the least. Candles and fuel for lamps were in short supply in the village, and 'there was not a match to be had in the place. The household had gone to bed at dusk. It slept, and I with it, when suddenly came a knocking at the window and a voice crying: "You must be dressed in four minutes, and across the bay in a motor boat in half an hour." '[1270] She describes how she 'crept over the slippery rocks in the darkness' with Petersen, who led her to a group of 'comrades' who rowed her out to the motor boat. 'This was a tiny craft to cross' the Barents Sea, 'with one mast and without a cabin, quite open, with only a shelter over the motor at the rear, and a single man to steer her. I leaned my back to the mast, and the curl of the waves that broke on our prow splashed over my face. The skipper made a shield for me with the end of the sail, but the waters defied his efforts to keep them out.'[1271] As both Sylvia and Gallacher recorded, it was here, on this stage of the Arctic route, that two French delegates, and their crew of three fishermen, were drowned a few days later. One of them was the soldier, writer and activist Comrade Raymond-Louis Lefebvre. Like the British, the French delegates had to take the circuitous route home due to the Allied blockade. When Gallacher, Ramsay and Tanner finally reached Vardo, they cabled Moscow 'recommending that no more delegates should be sent by the Arctic route'.[1272]

Sylvia offers only one clue in her 1921 memoir to why she was the only passenger in the motor boat, a partial explanation for why she had so abruptly parted company from the others. She 'landed before the dawn, but the place shall not be written, for I learnt that the British authorities had wired the Norwegians to stop me as I returned through from Soviet Russia. So I returned to the British Empire.'[1273] According to Gallacher, Comrade Petersen had secured her passage on a Soviet trader. Whether or not this was the case, all that we know for certain is that her return to the British empire involved, as she mentioned briefly in 'In the Red Twilight', being smuggled on to a ship to Christiania (Oslo) and then on to a third, where she was instructed to pretend that she was an English stewardess who had abandoned her job on another ship. On this vessel, some sailors tried to assault her sexually and a struggle ensued, from which she escaped to her final, unidentified passage home.

Sylvia wrote up her travel diary and published *Soviet Russia as I Saw It*, one of the bumper crop of first-hand accounts of the Bolshevik Revolution which became an internationally popular publishing trend in 1921. Sylvia's has none of the kick of Jack Reed's, but, unlike him, she wasn't there for the actual fighting. Her observations focus on the immediate aftermath, the reconstruction and the possibilities for social transformation and political justice for which she yearned.

While it may have seemed that Comrade Pankhurst had returned from Moscow committed to unity, in compliance with the terms agreed at the International, it didn't take long for the shine to wear off her encounter with Lenin.

27

Discontent on the Lower Deck

In the autumn of 1918 German sailors had refused to take orders any more and control of the fleet was seized by a council of workers, soldiers and sailors. 'It is the beginning of the Revolution,' Sylvia declared in the *Dreadnought*. 'As it is in Russia, so it is in Germany!'[1274] Germany proclaimed itself a republic in November, and in January 1919 came the Spartacist Rising in Berlin. In April Bavaria declared itself a soviet republic with Munich its capital; it lasted a month.

Simultaneously, military disturbances exploded in Britain. On the one hand, events in Russia spurred the labour movement into revolutionary optimism; on the other, disillusioned troops were becoming increasingly militant. Established on 3 June 1917 at the Leeds Convention, the Council of Workers' and Soldiers' Delegates was in position to provide an effective national, and international, co-ordinating structure.

The slow process of demobilization after Armistice on 11 November 1918 meant that there were still large numbers of British troops in France after the war. Demonstrations by Royal Artillery units at Le Havre in December rattled the British military command and the government, which tried to pass them off as drunken seasonal high spirits rather than politically motivated riots. Ten thousand men mutinied in Folkestone in January 1919 and refused to return to France. Fifteen hundred men from the Royal Air Corps in Osterley Park commandeered trucks and drove them all the way to Whitehall in a protest convoy. Rioting in Rhyl caused five deaths and twenty-three serious injuries. In Dover, 4,000 men demonstrated in solidarity. Twenty thousand British soldiers mutinied in army camps surrounding Calais, and British soldiers posted in Egypt organized workers' councils.

'In the Red Twilight' Sylvia describes how during these widespread disturbances sailors flew the Red Flag from the mast of HMS *Kilbride* at Milford Haven in protest against their low wages and against government intervention in Russia. The Workers' Suffrage Federation distributed a leaflet addressed 'To British Sailors: urging them not to sail to Russia', and growing numbers of sailors refused to do so, and ships with troops who refused to fight had to be turned around and sent home. The police harassed the WSF. Members were arrested and jailed for incitement and sowing disaffection among His Majesty's Forces.

Throughout the lower decks of the British Royal Navy, there was considerable discussion of mutiny. In the summer of 1918, the situation at Portsmouth had been serious enough to scare the Admiralty into immediate improvements in pay and conditions to avert trouble, with an able seaman's pay more than doubled to four shillings a day.[1275] Demands for 'lower deck' organization were taken seriously and agitation for trade union representation spread through the service. In the post-war period, they movement of the Royal Navy achieved unprecedented victories. Far from comprising 'a mass of dumb Jack Tars waiting to be led by the nose', they were organizing as never before.[1276] From the turn of the century, the lower decks developed a very effective movement for reform. Their death-benefit societies functioned effectively as quasi-trade unions. Their vibrant independent press, particularly the monthlies *The Bluejacket* and *The Fleet*, published nationally, successfully promoted campaigns for reform. In the first two decades of the century, this had led to significant improvements in lower-deck conditions that dragged the navy into modernity. Along the way were a number of mutinies and many collective acts of insubordination. This campaigning reached a high point in 1919.

Sensing the moment and dissatisfied with the speed of progress, Sylvia ramped up the work of the *Workers' Dreadnought* in appealing for international working-class solidarity. In May 1920 she boldly printed Lenin's 'Appeal to the Toiling Masses', a tract blacklisted by the Home Office. Harry Pollitt stored copies of the popular leaflet under his bulging mattress and worked hard with other WSF members to distribute them. 'Many of the comrades could be seen outside the

London Docks and shipyards selling "Hands Off Russia" literature and our members were also selling inside. Day after day we posted up placards, sticky backs and posters on docksides, and in various places in the ships and lavatories.'[1277] Pollitt particularly admired the ingenuity of the militant suffragette Melvina Walker: 'Walker was unbelievable – she was always talking to groups of women shopping in Crisp Street ... telling them about Russia, asking them to tell their husbands to keep their eyes skinned for munitions.'[1278]

In the spring of 1920, a number of these husbands reported to Sylvia that barges in London and in Belgian ports were being loaded with munitions destined for the White Russian campaign against the Bolsheviks. Harry Pollitt went on to the docks and tried to persuade the stevedores to refuse to load the barges. They appeared to ignore him completely, turning their backs and carrying on working as if they could not hear him. Pollitt stood alone, puzzled and dejected. Quietly, an old docker took him aside and told him in a low voice not to worry. Shortly afterwards, when the cargo was loaded from the barges on to the ships, every single tow rope mysteriously snapped and the entire consignment sank irretrievably into the North Sea.

Melvina Walker, Harry Pollitt and a dedicated band of comrades kept the work in the East End docks going tirelessly for two years. As Sylvia put it in the *Dreadnought*, these activists 'kept the communist flag flying at East India Dock gates week in and week out during the Russian war'.[1279] In May 1920 their work finally paid off. On the 10th dockers began to load HMS *Jolly George* at East India Dock. After about twenty minutes, the stevedores realized the cargo was labelled 'OHMS Munitions for Poland'. The coalmen then refused to fuel the ship unless the munitions were unloaded. A group of dockers went to see their union officials, who confirmed that if the munitions weren't taken off the ship, the union would back a strike. By the following day, the action had spread and on 15 May the stevedores unloaded the munitions on to the quayside, backed by a resolution that strikers would prevent HMS *Jolly George* from loading munitions for Poland in any British port. By the end of May, the example set by the London dockers had led to a national refusal by dockers' and railway unions across Britain to load munitions.

The *Jolly George* victory created a turning point. The government now became intensely concerned about escalating discontent in the armed services and industries and the effectiveness of anti-intervention campaigning. War demobilization immediately produced a new set of problems. Civil unrest in Ireland and other colonies strained the resources available for meeting Britain's increasingly unpopular imperial commitments, as did counter-revolutionary intervention in Russia and the Rhineland occupation. An Allied force – including the British Army of the Rhine – occupied territory on either side of the Rhine from December 1918 to June 1930 both to protect France from further German incursions and to help enforce the reparations soon to be imposed by the Versailles peace treaty. The allegiance of young working-class soldiers and sailors throughout the British armed forces became questionable, an insecurity that dovetailed with the revolutionary discontent among the European fighting forces by whom they had been inspired.

Police and informants spying on Sylvia and other WSF members identified them as dangerous agitators in Britain's first 'Red Scare'. It was in May 1920 that Scotland Yard raided the offices of the *Workers' Dreadnought* and arrested Harold Burgess, sentencing him to six months for subverting the Irish Guards. Later in the month, police arrested the prominent WSF activists Lillian Thring and Bertram Colonna at a PRIB demonstration protesting against intervention in Russia outside the Polish diplomatic mission in London.

Sylvia's political relationship with Russia was already a matter of debate in parliament. She makes regular appearances as the subject of exchanges recorded in Hansard. For example, in the Commons on 1 July 1920, regarding the Soviet Trade Delegation, the Liberal MP for Jarrow Godfrey Palmer rose to ask the Prime Minister Lloyd George 'whether he is satisfied that M. Krassin, the agent of the Soviet Government of Russia, is fulfilling his pledge not to engage in any political action in this country; and whether he is aware that M. Krassin has had interviews with Miss Sylvia Pankhurst, who has been actively employed in propaganda work for the Soviet Government, and that in other ways he has broken the pledge under which His Majesty's Government agreed to enter into commercial negotiations with him?'[1280]

On behalf of Lloyd George, Bonar Law replied that there was no reason to believe Krassin had broken his commitment not to engage in any political action in Britain. Palmer continued, 'Is the Rt Hon.

Gentleman aware that the woman referred to in the question is in the pay of Lenin, and that she is endeavouring to disaffect British soldiers, and propagate Bolshevik doctrines?' 'That may be true,' said Bonar Law, but refused to be drawn into discussion about Sylvia and stuck to the matter of Krassin's political activities.[1281]

In October 1920, shortly after her return from her first trip to Russia, Scotland Yard detectives arrested Sylvia under Regulation 42 of the Defence of the Realm Act. Special Branch had set traps to catch her as she re-entered Britain the previous month, but she managed to elude them. The *Sunday Express* revelled in its reports that Sylvia had 'completely outwitted the Special Branch of New Scotland Yard'.[1282] The *Daily Express* had even more fun with the story when she visited Manchester:

> 'Sylvia's World Revolution – Postponed by a Dogfight' Hush! The revolution has started. Sylvia Pankhurst has returned from Russia. She has re-appeared in the city of her parents and flung the gauntlet full in the face of capitalism.
>
> Whilst she was doing that this afternoon, there was the most interesting dogfight I have ever seen … It was a beautiful fight. Even the Communists admitted it. The meeting inside was suspended and … windows … were framed with intense faces watching the progress … One of the dogs, a black and white terrier, took liberties with one of the most anti-Bolshevist dogs in the district. The two dogs were evidently discussing the Zinovieff theory of the Third International. Oh it was grand! At the climax a woman – anti-Bolshevist and believing in home, family and country – threw a bucket of cold water over the pair and they separated.
>
> What a Sylvia![1283]

Sylvia's own newspaper explained that its editor had been arrested under DORA and printed her warrant for violating Regulation 42, which proscribed any 'act calculated or likely to cause sedition or disaffection among any of His Majesty's forces, or among the civilian population'.[1284] This contentious *Dreadnought* issue, dated 20 October, contained four offending articles: 'The Datum Line' by Sylvia, 'Discontent on the Lower Deck' by Dave (Douglas) Springhall (under the alias S.000,

Gunner), 'How to Get a Labour Government' by Theodore Rothstein (under the alias Rubinstein) and 'The Yellow Peril and the Dockers' by Claude McKay (alias Leon Lopez).[1285]

The subject of the 'The Datum Line' was the agreement between the coal miners and the government regarding pay and conditions. In this Swiftian article Sylvia restated her position that parliament was part of the oppressive machinery of the bourgeois state and argued that it was the duty of revolutionaries to destroy it and follow William Morris' recommendation in *News from Nowhere* that the buildings be turned into storehouses for manure.

As editor of the *Dreadnought*, Sylvia was held responsible for the three other articles.

The Jamaican revolutionary and communist poet Claude McKay was a full-time *Dreadnought* journalist. When he arrived in London McKay had been appalled by the racism in the *Daily Herald* and tried unsuccessfully to get the paper to publish his articles. *Herald* headlines like 'Black Scourge in Europe', 'Black Peril on the Rhine', 'Brutes in French Uniform', 'Black Menace of 40,000 Troops' and 'Appeal to the Women of Europe' horrified him. He wrote a letter to *Herald* editor George Lansbury and pointed out that his 'black scourge' articles were stirring up racial prejudice: 'I thought it was the duty of this paper as a radical organ to enlighten its readers about the real reasons why the English considered coloured troops undesirable in Europe instead of appealing indirectly to illogical emotional prejudices.' Lansbury only penned McKay a note saying he was not personally prejudiced against 'Negroes',[1286] and left it at that.

McKay wrote next to the editor of the *Workers' Dreadnought*, which published his letter immediately and in full. He also received an invitation to visit Sylvia's office at his earliest convenience.

> I found a plain little Queen-Victoria sized woman with plenty of long unruly bronze-like hair. There was no distinction about her clothes, and on the whole she was very undistinguished. But her eyes were fiery, even a little fanatic, with a glint of shrewdness … Pankhurst had a personality as picturesque and passionate as any radical in London … and in the labour movement she was always jabbing her hat pin into the hides of the smug and slack labour leaders. Her weekly newspaper might have been called 'The Dread

Wasp'. And whenever imperialism got drunk and went wild among the native peoples, the Pankhurst people would be on the job.[1287]

Sylvia hired the surprised McKay as a staff journalist on the spot and gave him an assistant called 'Comrade Vie', whom McKay suspected of being an undercover international revolutionary. Sylvia tasked McKay with writing a series of articles about London dock life from an anti-racist perspective, describing and comparing the experiences of black and white sailors. She assigned him, as correspondent focusing on the Australian, American and Indian press, to cover and comment on stories of interest to *Dreadnought* readers. Claude McKay wrote numerous articles on a wide range of issues, including the Garvey movement and black nationalism in the USA, revolutionary coal miners in the Rhondda Valley and TUC conferences.

The *Dreadnought* was the only British socialist newspaper at the time to employ black journalists and Claude McKay was said to be the first black political journalist to be employed full time on the staff of a modern national British newspaper. Sylvia also engaged Reuben Samuels, a sailor, to become a regular correspondent for the paper. McKay and Samuels led on stories about racism and imperialism, and how to oppose them.

Claude McKay and Sylvia bonded over anti-racism and communism, but his attitude to her leadership ambitions in the fledgling Communist Party (BSTI) betrayed less progressive views on gender. This is illustrated in a letter discovered recently by the historian John Callow written by McKay to Willie Gallacher just a week before Sylvia's arrest. In the letter, McKay prods Gallacher's leadership ambitions by criticizing Sylvia's:

> You seem so high above petty actions and deceit that you ought to be the man to weld the little warring forces together who are not wasting their energy fighting amongst themselves. I am really quite close to Sylvia & the more I see of her, study her manner & gauge her intellect, the more I recognise how hopeless & what madness it is for her to aspire to be a leader.
>
> She is no doubt a sharp, clever woman quite well at grasping and sizing up current events. But I don't think she has any vision into the future nor has she the head & depth necessary in a great leader

that gather followers around him & make him obey, trust and respect him.

If Sylvia tries to be imperious, she is funny, if she tries to be greatly sympathetic she is a failure. Her worth is to be an agitator & no more. The comprehensive mind necessary for high constructive work is lacking in her. But there is no doubt that she is splendid at 'gingering' up people. I don't think she has an equal in that.[1288]

Earlier in 1920 McKay had met a radical young Royal Navy sailor named Douglas Springhall, known to all as Dave. Born in Kensal Green, Springhall joined the navy during the war at the age of fifteen. Ferociously intelligent and a keen reader of the *Dreadnought*, Springhall visited the newspaper's offices requesting revolutionary literature for his eager shipmates. Shortly afterwards, he wrote to McKay detailing the level of discontent among navy sailors. McKay and Sylvia edited his letter, which described growing unrest on an unnamed battleship, listing pay grievances and highlighting the abolition of marriage allowances and free railway passes for men under twenty-five:

> Men of the Lower Deck: Are you going to see your class go under
> in the fight with the capitalist brutes who make millions out of
> our sacrifices during the war? Comrades, here is fertile ground for
> propaganda to win the Army and Navy to the cause of the workers
> … You are the sons of the Working Class, therefore it is your duty
> to stand by that class and not the class of the Government which
> is responsible for the starving of your ex-service brothers. Hail the
> formation of the Red Navy, which protects the interests of the
> working class, and repudiate the dirty financial interests which you
> are protecting now![1289]

This was read as incitement to mutiny, alongside the other allegedly seditious articles. Sylvia had published much material like this before in *Dreadnought*. However, this time the government determined to act.

On Monday 18 October 1920, Inspector Lionel Kirchnez of the Scotland Yard Special Branch entered the premises of an organization now calling itself the Communist Party-British Section of the Third International at 152 Fleet Street. Seizing several party documents,

including the latest edition of the group's paper, the *Workers'*
Dreadnought, Kirchnez proceeded down the block to the *Dreadnought*'s
publishing office at 10 Wine Office Court.

Hearing the police arrive, McKay sprang into action. Stuffing the
original Springhall article down his sock and concealing it under his
wide trouser leg, he sauntered out into the corridor. Arranging his face
into what he described as 'a big black grin', he walked into the WC
where he shredded and flushed the evidence down the toilet. Then he
escaped the building by pretending nonchalantly to the unsuspecting
police that he was just a Fleet Street messenger and in no way associated
with the newspaper.

Meanwhile, Inspector Kirchnez walked in on Sylvia Pankhurst,
writing in the composing room. Instructing her to stop, he held up the
confiscated *Dreadnought* issue and asked if she held herself responsible
for it. To which she replied, 'Yes, I certainly do.' As the inspector
searched among the manuscripts, she told him, 'If you are looking for
[the] letter, you won't find it, because I anticipated a visit from the
police.'[1290]

The following day, City Police Detective Hugo Smith accompanied
by two other officers dressed in plain clothes arrested Sylvia at the
printing office.[1291] As they read aloud her warrant, she interrupted
them: 'Are there any more to come?' The next day, she was charged
before Sir Alfred Newton at the Mansion House Police Court with
violating Regulation 42.[1292]

Sylvia's arrest coincided with extreme unrest across Britain. That
same week the coal miners started a nationwide strike and railworkers
threatened to come out and join them. Also on 18 October, a rally
against unemployment turned into a riot as processions led by workers
carrying red flags pushed their way through police lines to get to
Downing Street. Military leaders expressed their concern to the Home
Office that there were insufficient troops in England to manage the
unrest. The timing of Sylvia's arrest was not a coincidence.

This was the second time Sylvia had been arrested under DORA's
wartime emergency powers. In October 1918 she spoke near a military
camp in Creswell, Derbyshire, calling on the working class to demand
peace from the government. She encouraged her audience with the idea
that a soldiers' strike might not be far off, warning the government
'to be a little wiser, or the soldiers will take it on themselves'.[1293]

Arrested on the spot for inciting sedition and brought before the local magistrates, she defended her actions on the grounds that they were less seditious than the publication of secret treaties by other British mainstream newspapers. She was found guilty and fined £50.[1294] That week in Westminster, the Liberal MP Joseph King has asked 'whether the Government has taken any decision to suppress the advocacy of Socialist opinions'.[1295]

Now Sylvia entered the court on Thursday 28 October 1920, looking very pale and tired. As she spoke, she gained colour and energy.[1296] According to some reports, she carried a bouquet of red carnations, but in fact she wore a single red carnation pinned to her lapel. Appearing for the Director of Public Prosecutions, Travers Humphreys told Alderman Newton, 'I shall ask you to look over the paper, but I should be sorry to nauseate you by reading the whole of it to you.'[1297] Delivering her own defence, Sylvia introduced as exhibits letters she had written to Lenin that week. This cannot have helped her case.

It is rarely to be recommended that someone facing criminal charges, let alone those jeopardizing their liberty, should conduct their own defence. This is the case even when the accused is a qualified lawyer, hence the adage that counsel who embarks on such an exercise has a fool for a client. Nonetheless, there can be a rational explanation for such a dramatic choice other than a defendant having taken leave of their senses. Sylvia's DORA trial was many years before the post-Second World War introduction of legal aid and it came at a time when she was short of both finances and supportive friends who might have helped to fund or conduct a professional defence. Further, the charges were brought under sweeping wartime provisions. These would be extremely difficult for the publisher of the four offending articles to resist without the assistance of today's Human Rights Act, incorporating into United Kingdom law incorporated the right to freedom of expression.

So Sylvia would understandably have seen these proceedings very much as a political trial over political charges. The tactic of speaking for herself was both one familiar to the veteran suffragette and helpful in reminding her audience of her already established place in a wider struggle for civil liberties going back to the Chartists. In 1908 Christabel had ably conducted her own defence at Bow Street Magistrates' Court, cross-examining witnesses in a court at a time when female law graduates were not allowed to practise law, but prisoners could defend themselves.

Conducting her own defence gave Sylvia licence to paint a compelling canvas broader than the rules and system stacked against her, citing liberally from political literature to highlight the absurdity and arbitrariness of the law and pleading her poor health arising from past incarceration and torture. And if, as was to be the result, these efforts proved in vain, the court room would be her platform and her imprisonment her righteous sacrifice once more.

Alderman Newton offered the opinion that 'the punishment of six months' imprisonment which I pass on you is quite inadequate'. The *Daily Herald* reported the next day that Newton referred to 'treason felony' and 'hard labour'. However, after a whispered consultation with the clerk, he added: 'Having regard to your sex, I order it to be in the second division.'[1298]

Granted leave to appeal, the court released Sylvia on bail put up by Norah Smyth, who raised the cash by mortgaging their company the Agenda Press, for which she, Sylvia and Silvio Corio were trustees. Sylvia's bail was conditional on her agreement not to participate, in any capacity, in the running of the *Dreadnought* or to attend any political meetings or other forms of public assembly. In the absence of its editor, the *Dreadnought* proclaimed, 'Let us be of good cheer. Other comrades must try to carry on Sylvia Pankhurst's work ... The arm of the capitalist is heavy and strong. It is put forth to crush the revolutionary workers and their leaders. Let us brace ourselves for the battle.'[1299]

Sylvia was anxious that a return to prison would further damage her already compromised health. She continued to suffer from the consequences of repeated hunger striking and forced feeding during the pre-war years. Along with the physical effects, she had to assess the measure of her own mental resilience. Her militant suffragette days amply proved her capacity to endure imprisonment in a just cause. As a militant suffragette, she by necessity broke unjust, irrational laws. This sentence was a gross infringement of press freedom and pretty much all of her civil liberties.

Sylvia's appeal was set for 5 January 1921 in London's grandiose Guildhall. She appeared with her hair apparently unbrushed, once again wearing a neat red carnation in her buttonhole. So arrayed, she treated the court to an impassioned ninety-minute peroration that held everyone rapt. Except the judge.

Sylvia's speech included the story of her life, the sacrifices of her beloved art and her family to pursue her father's mission of liberating the oppressed from their oppressors. She reminded the court that she had faced death many times for her beliefs – 'I have gone to war, too' – and had shortened her life in consequence. Her current state of health would not withstand another prison term.

Sylvia described her East End life and the privation of the people of her community. As she stood in the dock, the shabbiness of her wardrobe spoke for itself. The clothes she wore were second-hand and her lifestyle frugal, she explained to the court. She rounded on her accusers: 'it is wrong that people like you should be comfortable and well fed, while all around you people are starving'. In support of her argument, she quoted her 'heroes', Karl Marx and Friedrich Engels, and read passages from William Blake, William Morris and Edward Carpenter. She turned to the specifics. Defending her publication of McKay's piece 'The Yellow Peril', she explained that the article was written as a plea to workers not to turn on their black brethren. She set her defence in the context of her own experience:

> I was returning home one evening down the West India Dock Road
> and I found the place thronged. I asked, 'What is the matter?' And
> I was told, 'They are stabbing coloured men.' Some were killed
> that night and for three nights that went on in Poplar. Out of work
> soldiers and other unemployed were stabbing the coloured men.
> This is some time ago now, though it was since the war; we have
> had it in other towns and docks as well as East London. The fact
> was that the trade union was objecting to the employment of these
> coloured men. They were left here in this country, and the men out
> of work, seeing, they thought, they were going to get their jobs,
> took to stabbing them … Leon Lopez, being himself a coloured
> man – who is not a British subject perhaps – felt this keenly, and he
> put his letter in this paper; and I, as editor, felt he had a right to put
> it there and point out to the workers that unemployment is caused
> by deeper things than this.[1300]

And here it is, crystal clear: marking the next significant evolution in Sylvia's political focus, the transition to putting the fight against racism at the front and centre of all her work. From now until her death, she will not deviate from this priority. Strategies of divide-and rule-propping up colonial imperialism abroad and discord among working people at home depended upon peddling ideologies of racial bigotry. The fight against racism, Sylvia argues, is at the heart of the labour, socialist and feminist movements.

Despite the eye-watering length of her monologue, Sylvia mesmerized her listeners, both fascinated and appalled by her outrageous, sensational soulfulness. The judge, Sir John Bell, however, remained impervious, and upheld the sentence. Moreover, he added, six months' solitary confinement was a wholly inadequate punishment given the seriousness of her offence.

Sylvia never named Claude McKay or Dave Springhall. Neither of them forgot her loyalty. McKay continued to write for the *Dreadnought* while Sylvia served her sentence.

The communist agitator Springhall was dismissed from the Royal Navy for associating with extremists. He wanted to visit Sylvia in prison, but McKay advised him against doing so since they were all now under continuous surveillance. Springhall went on to join the Communist Party of Great Britain (CPGB) and its affiliated Young Communist League. He stood unsuccessfully as a Labour Party candidate for Richmond Town Council, then later as a communist candidate. In 1924 he was a delegate to the Fifth Congress of the Communist International. Two years later he became acting secretary of the Young Communist League, serving during the British general strike, for which he was twice jailed. During the Spanish Civil War, he served as political commissar of the British Battalion, then later as assistant commissar of the XV International Brigade. He became editor of the *Daily Worker* in 1938, then briefly served as the CPGB's representative in Moscow.

By 1940 Springhall was a national organizer for the CPGB. He cultivated a contact at the Air Ministry, Olive Sheehan, who was one of a small ring of communist supporters in the Ministry and provided Springhall with, among other things, classified information about the radar countermeasure device WINDOW (known better by its later name, Chaff). Their arrangement was uncovered when Sheehan's flatmate overheard a conversation about classified information, and

Springhall was arrested and convicted in 1943 on a charge of passing classified information to the Soviet Union. The trial was held in camera because of the still secret nature of WINDOW. Springhall's MI5 file was released in May 2004.

He was sentenced to seven years' penal servitude and served four and a half years. He was also expelled from the Communist Party of Great Britain, which strongly disapproved of his espionage activity as it had not been sanctioned by the party leadership and was contrary to its policy at the time. Later, he travelled through eastern Europe to China, where he worked as an adviser to the China Information Bureau of the Press Administration. He died in Moscow in 1953. His grave is located at the Babaoshan Revolutionary Cemetery in Beijing.

Springhall's file also shows that he acted as a distribution agent in the armed forces for material regarded as seditious during and after the First World War, for which he had been discharged from the navy in 1920. As a result of this activity he was kept under surveillance and his correspondence was closely watched. McKay's caution was well founded.

Sylvia stuck to the principle of press freedom and speaking truth to power, but was unsparing in her assessment of the greenhorn journalists she encouraged and protected. In her unpublished manuscripts she entitles this incident, 'How I went to prison to shield three young men and how little they deserved it'.[1301]

Soviet newspapers publicized Sylvia's trial and conviction. She received many letters of support from Russia, but most of the British press avoided reporting the case and only a few hundred people turned out for the protest against her imprisonment held in Trafalgar Square. George Bernard Shaw sent her an open letter, published in the *Dreadnought*, under the title, 'The Lion and the Hairpins'. Shaw was sympathetic, but couldn't resist wagging his finger at her once again:

> My dear Sylvia Pankhurst
>   I am very sorry your appeal has not succeeded; though, like all the sensible people in the movement, I am furious with you for getting into prison quite unnecessarily. Why didn't you make up your mind to keep out of prison instead of persistently breaking into it? The lion will let you put your head into his mouth, because

the law says he must; but if you shake your hairpins in his throat, he is only too glad to have an excuse for snapping. However, there is no use scolding you now; so keep up your spirits, and look forward to the day of your deliverance.[1302]

Had Sylvia been allowed pen and paper in Holloway, she might have replied to the now fabulously successful Shaw that she looked forward equally to the bright day of his deliverance from smug pomposity. Aptly, Shaw's *Heartbreak House* – 'A Fantasia in the Russian Manner on English Themes' – had just opened at the Garrick Theatre. The critic Louis Crompton remarked of the play that it was peopled by characters who though they 'often talk grandly and eloquently about the future of humanity' are obviously 'not going to act on their convictions'.[1303] Shavian characters who were, therefore, very unlike Sylvia.

Noticeably, Shaw entirely missed the point of Sylvia's protest against racism, but among the commentariat he was hardly alone in that.

Sylvia appealed against both her prison sentence and her assignment to the second division. From Holloway she petitioned for first-division privileges, asking that Rule 243A be applied to her. In 1910, Home Secretary Winston Churchill had granted this to address the reputational crisis facing the government during the women's militant suffrage movement. Public pressure exerted on the Home Office forced it reluctantly to allow to 'highly strung' and 'neurotic' suffragettes privileges based on medical grounds.[1304] If permitted by prison commissioners, prisoners (suffragettes, conscientious objectors and DORA offenders) could access better food, wear their own clothes and receive reading and writing materials.

At the end of Sylvia's petition, she reminded the Home Office that the government had granted privileges to those 'charged with offences committed from political and conscientious motives', including herself, for suffragette militancy in 1913–14.[1305] 'I am one of those who took part in the struggle to obtain Rule 243a and I do not feel justified in relinquishing that just amelioration which was won after much hardship and many hunger strikes had been endured. I therefore again ask for its application in my case.' Her need for particular foods, she explained, was necessitated by her colitis and inflammatory conditions. The medical examiner confirmed her health problems during her trial.

The cold and damp conditions of her second-division cell would make her ill. '[S]ince in my opinion I have not committed a crime but have done as my principles and conscience dictated, I object to wearing prison clothes and to submitting to the number of other indignities from which Rule 243a exempts those to whom it is applied.'

Distinguishing between criminal and political offences, Sylvia positioned herself within the tradition of dissenters, including Chartists, Irish Fenians, suffragettes, conscientious objectors and defenders of freedoms of conscience and expression. 'For a person of active mental life,' she argued, 'it is no small thing to be deprived for six months of writing materials ... I would point out that it is unusual throughout the world to deprive political prisoners of material for writing and study and that many of the finest books have been written in prison by political prisoners of various nationalities.'[1306] This seeded an idea in her. She would spend her sentence writing, somehow, even without paper and pencil. The question was: how?

The last occasion Sylvia served time, six years previously, she'd been carried on a constant tide of support. It was hard to be back in Holloway in a dank, solitary cell without the same scale of solidarity. She was put to cleaning duties and carrying coal buckets. The prison authorities still denied her access to reading and writing materials, except for one small, child's-size slate and a stick of chalk. The WSF held 'enthusiastic and well attended' meetings outside Holloway every Sunday at four o'clock, chaired by Norah – who literally stood on a chair to run proceedings. 'Communist songs were sung and cheers given for Comrade Pankhurst, which we are sure, must have penetrated the thick and dismal walls of the prison.'[1307] Sylvia's supporters sang the Red Flag and tramped around outside the gates parading banners protesting 'Six Months for Telling the Truth'.[1308]

Sylvia briefly considered hunger striking, but her health was already too fragile and the prison doctor had diagnosed her with endometriosis. Norah reminded her that the government had recently allowed Terence MacSwiney, the Lord Mayor of Cork, to die while on hunger strike in October 1920. As the weeks wore on, Sylvia's health collapsed. The prison doctors put her on a diet of bread, eggs and milk, and had her moved to the infirmary wing where she remained for the rest of her sentence.

Her only writing materials were that small slate and piece of chalk; this prohibition was far the worst punishment. Despite these restrictions and the indignity of regular intimate physical searches, Sylvia managed to write a great deal. The series of poems she created became the anthology *Writ on Cold Slate*, published in 1922 shortly after her release. The collection is lyrical and philosophical, expressing her sense of alienation and the depression experienced in Holloway. Some poems capture the quickness of her interest in the lives of other women prisoners; others create an uncanny effect, haunting the reader with Sylvia's bleak weariness and dejection at being back in prison.

In the title sonnet, she deploys the ephemeral image of the slate and chalk. All that she thinks and writes is now temporary, under erasure.

Whilst many a poet to his love hath writ,
boasting that thus he gave immortal life,
my faithful lines upon inconstant slate,
destined to swift extinction reach not thee.

In other ages dungeons might be strange,
with ancient mouldiness their airs infect,
but kindly warders would the tablets bring,
so captives might their precious thoughts inscribing,
the treasures of the fruitful mind preserve,
and culling thus its flowers, postpone decay.

Only this age that loudly boasts Reform,
hath set its seal of vengeance 'gainst the mind,
decreeing naught in prison shall be writ,
save on a cold slate, and swiftly washed away.[1309]

Sylvia created these works by an ingenious covert process. As the poems tell us, she initially drafted them in chalk on her slate. Then, as I have discovered, before the lines were 'swiftly washed away' she transcribed them with a soft pencil onto sheets of standard issue HM Prison toilet paper. Using this medium, she expanded, revised and successively redrafted the poems and other writings throughout her prison sentence.[1310] Sylvia concealed these in the underclothes of her prison uniform and slipped them to Norah when she came to visit, or passed them to other patients in the infirmary to spirit out of Holloway via their visitors or on their own release. Running as it does to hundreds of sheets of rough beige, perforated toilet paper, the survival is miraculous. Sylvia complained to Norah that 'the stuff I write all rubs off because it flops around in my pocket,' but this very line has survived for nearly a century on its little square of rough toilet roll, along with the hundreds of others.

These compressed bundles contained poems, correspondence for Norah to transcribe and post, and the draft of a near-complete five-act play. While Sylvia redrafted and printed the prison poems, the ambitious dramatic piece remains unpublished and never performed. Later, she transformed the subject of the play into a novel (unfinished). As with the poems and letters, the toilet-paper manuscripts are fragmented. Sections are overwritten, discontinuous, duplicated or missing. However, the process of transcribing them all together reveals the structure and coherence of the play. An almost completed redraft was smuggled successfully out of Holloway.

George Bernard Shaw upbraided Sylvia for breaking into prison. Little did he know that while there she would use her time usefully, writing a groundbreaking political drama. Sylvia's play tells the intertwined story of the parallel emergence of the Labour Party and the Votes for Women campaign. At the centre of the piece stands the story of how the Pankhurst suffragettes emerged from the socialist ILP and then diverged from it. 'Miss Christabel' and her mother feature as reported figures of political discussion in the play, rather than appearing as onstage characters.

The arguments and shared interests between the labour movement and the suffragettes dominate the multi-layered themes of the piece, which include the relationship between young suffragettes and their fathers, brothers and lovers; temperance and its importance to the labour movement; trade union formation; how to organize an election and the constant truth 'that socialism won't come from wishing'.

The hero, Noah Adamson, is based on Keir Hardie. The Lillie/wife figure is distributed between a number of different characters, in order to reflect the different stages of her relationship with Noah. (In the later novel plan, 'Lily' would appear with her own name.) Sylvia is Freda McLaird. Years later when she began to turn the material of the play into her novel entitled 'Noah Adamson', she cast herself again as Freda, this time with the surname Urswick.

The full cast is large, the lead characters predominantly working class and recognizably based on figures from the suffragette, labour and trade union movements and from Keir Hardie's personal life. In the opening act, set in Noah Adamson's 'committee rooms in a London constituency', Noah debates with Thomas Fenton of the ILP, challenging him on settling the problem of the Labour Party position on the women's vote:

Noah: Ah, there I agree with you! The Suffragette question being set aside by the Labour Party in favour of a direct fight to secure Socialism. My feeling would be very different, but we are only too aware that the Party has not got so far as that, and that the majority of the Parliamentary Party and the Executive are actually afraid of socialism or even opposed to it. No Fenton, this is not a question of Votes for Women or Socialism. The question of Socialism has to got to be fought inside the Labour Party unfortunately. And even you, Tom, are keen on pressing for Reforms – old age Pensions, unemployment, and education Bills, palliative measures only indirectly consistent with the fight for Socialism.

Thomas: Oh, don't misunderstand me Adamson, I'm *not* against you helping the women in the least. I only wish the Party would take up their question and get it settled. What I mean is, I do not think it worth splitting the Party on such an issue. Moreover I don't think you could split the Party on it if you were to you would isolate yourself and lose your influence, which is so necessary just now. You would cut yourself off from office in the Party, lose the Chairmanship and your seat on the Executive and leave the field clear to the reactionaries … It would be a thousand pities to throw away your position in the movement for something that, after all, is not Socialism. Already your influence has been weakened by your support of the WSPU …And the WSPU ostentatiously declares it does not support the Labour Party 'any more than any other Party.' Miss Christabel with her airy insistence on the neutrality of her precious Union, takes the wind out of your sails, in my opinion. In fact, she puts you in a devil of a hole to my mind. Neither you nor anyone can expect the Labour Party, or the Liberals for that matter, to take kindly to such a method! And isn't she impudent, upon my word!

Miss Christabel comes under political scrutiny by her sister in this play. Fenton admits that Mrs Pankhurst has done 'splendid work' for the ILP in her time, and 'I know that the WSPU was entirely formed of Socialist women in the first place, but they are getting some very odd recruits these days.' He warns of the dangers of the neutral policy. However well intended as a weapon to fight the Liberal government, it runs the risk of appealing 'to a most reactionary set of women who only want the vote as a barrier to progress and to stop any social legislation'. Noah Adamson listens to him attentively as he continues, 'Socialism has quite a back seat in the WSPU now; indeed there's no blinking the fact that it's out of it altogether. Miss Christabel is a dark horse. I shouldn't be the least surprised at her turning Tory and dragging her mother along with her.'

A beautiful setpiece discussion evocatively describes 500 gas workers coming out on strike and congregating for a meeting outside the Red Lion pub in a fictitious Perk Street. There's a fair amount of didactic but useful voter education. 'Remember', says Noah Adamson,

> that meetings are not all what really counts is the steady persistent
> spadework, arguments and systematic distribution of literature. We
> want more helpers (voters) and every one who is cheering ought
> to take up actual work in the movement. And not for the election
> only the election is merely an incident. The employing class has far
> greater resources and means of spreading its propaganda we can
> only out do our opponents in enthusiasm we appeal to every one
> of you to come forward this is your fight as much as ours.

In a mirror of Sylvia's life and mind, the play moves from pragmatic political scenes like this to lyrical conversations between women laced with cultural allusions. It's easy to picture her conjuring scenes of the art and literature she loved for imaginative comfort. 'Hogarthian' faces appear; Luther nails his Ninety-five Theses to Wittenberg's Schlosskirche; Pallisy the gifted potter throws his furniture into the fire to stoke his kiln; Michelangelo's *David* is invoked, and the suffragette characters 'wonder if the Greek lassies had such times as ours!'

The third act moves forward in time, shifting the scene of the drama to the evocative true-to-life recreation of Keir Hardie's London lodgings at Nevill's Court, meticulously detailed in the stage notes.

Freda McLaird, about twenty-five years old, appears for the first time in a series of intimate scenes with Noah Adamson. The play shows how their relationship develops from working together. Freda has been editing Noah's latest article. He asks for her opinion. 'I wasn't satisfied with it. I told you I went through it twice dictating. Of course I've been too busy – no spare time to write it.' Freda agrees that because he was tired when he first dictated it, the arrangement of the argument wasn't very good.

I went through it and rearranged the sections, leaving the old numbers on the pages so you could go back to them if you preferred. By my arrangement you can discard several pages that are repetition and you would have to rewrite a few. I've put slips of paper with notes to show you what I mean. I can't see anything else wrong with the article I think it is excellent I hope you won't mind my suggestions – you told me to do it you know. Here it is.

Nowhere else do we have a detailed record of the editing process shared by these two prolific political writers. Hardie was open and generous in acknowledging Sylvia's work with him on his articles, speeches, drafting of policy and legislation, all skills she learned from her father who before her had shared the same process with Hardie.

Their work complete, the scene shifts to a new atmosphere of intimacy:

Noah: I never could speak of what I felt most deeply. I have always had to suffer without words.

Freda: Oh I don't believe it. You only imagine it's so because you're so lonely here by yourself ... I never thought – I couldn't imagine – you thought of me as anything else than the daughter of two old friends. Your little girl who had not her own father. How could I think of – [Freda pauses. Resumes.] Do you remember the little pussy you told me about ... the one the man on the bus was carrying?

Adamson joins in the reminiscence. They discuss how the man examined the kitten 'then shoved it back in his bag without seeing that it wanted a little affection'. 'But I am not a little pussy,' says Freda. 'No, you are not a little pussy,' Noah murmurs, as he leaves his chair and crosses the stage to sit on the arm of Freda's. He touches her on the cheek with his hand. She starts slightly, and leans forward to avoid touching him.

Noah: Have you never wanted to feel a man's arms around you in love?

Freda: [Slowly with a sigh puts her closed hand against his cheek to hold him back and looks sadly at him. Then with a low voice] Oh you have other people.

Noah: I'll give up the other people.

Freda: [proudly] I shouldn't like you to do that I shouldn't like to be the cause of making anyone else unhappy.

Noah: You know I am too fond of you Freda.

Freda: What does it mean?

Noah: Just what it says.

Freda: [drops her head] Oh let me be still your little girl always and not spoil the little flower.
   [He withdraws his hand and sits quite still. Freda gradually leans so that she just touches him. He waits. After some moments he slips onto his knees and puts his arms round her gently.]

Noah: Are you longing sometimes?
   [Freda bolts upright and looks at him.]

Noah: You had better go then. You'll be quite safe. Better take care of yourself.
   [Freda looks at him miserably. He helps her to put on her coat then opens the door and motions her to precede him]

Noah: I'll come down with you.

Freda leaves. Later in the act, she returns, her intention wordlessly clear.

Although struggling with depression in Holloway, Sylvia did not loosen her grip on her politicking. Batches of the Holloway toilet-paper manuscripts are taken up with draft correspondence for Norah, most of it concerned with trying to resolve the financial problems caused by the interruption of funds from Bolshevik Russia after the raid for the WSF, the *Workers' Dreadnought* and the People's Russian Information Bureau. These funds were couriered by 'a Swedish Comrade', via clandestine routes, delivered directly to Sylvia. Norah, as treasurer, was 'always most punctilious about keeping various funds separate'.

Due to the interruption of their funds from Russia after the raid on the *Dreadnought* offices, Norah had to cross-subsidize all the projects from her own and Sylvia's money. This included their support for the Young Socialist League, which they'd helped through a difficult period by inviting it to share the *Dreadnought* offices and printers in order to produce their youth magazine, *Red Flag*, a publication that caused Scotland Yard considerable alarm.

Sylvia tasked Norah Smyth with transcribing a complicated letter written in laborious pencil draft on many layers of toilet paper about the channelling of funds from Russia through Sylvia herself and the WSF to various socialist and communist projects in Britain. The intended destination of the monies, usually delivered by the Swedish communist courier, became a matter of dispute between Comrade Rothstein and Comrade Pankhurst. Sylvia urgently tried to resolve the disagreement from prison in order to ease the financial difficulties she knew the WSF faced in her absence. That Sylvia's role in taking delivery of these underground monies and distributing them around Britain was one of the factors that prompted the government to arrest her, undisclosed at her trial. The raid of the *Dreadnought* and the sedition charge were as convenient an excuse as any other to get her off the streets and intercept the revolutionary funding stream.

28

Left Childishness?

The prospect of completing her sentence revived Sylvia's spirits. She wrote Norah a bossy letter on her now customary perforated toilet paper with instructions to organize a schedule of meetings for the day of her release, starting with an immediate campaign breakfast at Eustace Miles' vegetarian restaurant in Covent Garden. Her invitation list included Labour MPs and party officials, and key press figures, 'including press agencies English, American, colonial, etc with offices in London'.[311] ILP, Communist Party branches, the Hands Off Russia Committee, worker groups, university socialist groups, Fabian researchers, friendly borough councillors, League of Rights and penal reform activists also received invitations. Her personal guestlist included Charlotte Despard, Emmeline and Fred Pethick-Lawrence, Henry Brailsford, Henry Nevinson, Israel Zangwill, Daisy Greville, Countess of Warwick, Dora Montefiore and George Bernard Shaw, who she hoped would speak. His critical letter upbraiding her roundly for 'getting into prison quite unnecessarily' had clearly glanced off her.

Sylvia instructed Norah to set up a fundraiser meeting for the evening, for 'a well mixed crowd', whom she would address on the subject 'From Russia to Holloway – What I Saw In Russia'. She was happy to speak about the communist programme or anything else. 'I know there is trouble and I am doing what I can – any efforts at corruption have failed.'

Sylvia then proposed a schedule for meetings up and down England, Scotland and Wales before shifting into money and personal matters. 'If the trouble can't be overcome then don't despair just say its fate but don't give in till all is gone. No letter no visit it is a living death in here. As ever, ESP. (PS. The meetings must be crammed into the month of June).'[1312]

Sylvia emerged through the Holloway prison gates on 10 May 1921, frail and emaciated. Norah Smyth and Jesse Payne helped her to their car, and Norah drove them, as Sylvia instructed, straight to Eustace Miles' restaurant, a popular haunt from their suffragette days.

Miles, a Cambridge-educated health guru, Olympic-class tennis player, prolific author and radical vegetarian, and his wife Hallie had opened their 'Food Reform' restaurant in May 1906. In March 1907 the WSPU chose it as the venue for a breakfast celebrating the release from Holloway of the prisoners who had been arrested when taking part in the deputation from the first Women's Parliament. Many similar breakfasts were subsequently held there, including a celebratory event for the women who had taken part in the Harry Pankhurst-inspired pantechnicon Trojan Horse raid on Parliament. In 1910, the restaurant was the venue for the inaugural meeting of the Men's Political Union for Women's Enfranchisement. The suffragette Edith Craig, daughter of the actor Ellen Terry, sold *Votes for Women* from a pitch specially reserved for the purpose in front of the eatery and Bernard Shaw was among the restaurant shareholders.

Eustace and Hallie offered the use of meeting rooms above the bright, plant-filled ground-floor dining room for free as long as people bought their food and drink. The 'Simple Life' movement held lectures there, and Miles offered the audience 'ozonized air' to breathe as they listened to edifying talks on such subjects as 'The Religion of the Great Mother', to the accompaniment of a lantern show produced by Vera Holme. The restaurant was popular with carnivores who enjoyed the bohemian atmosphere, and it did very well during the First World War, when meat-free cooking was a necessity. The Miles' popular radical vegetarian destination stayed in business for over thirty years.[1313]

Sylvia returned from Holloway in bloody mood. At her appeal, she'd argued that the serious state of her health militated against her being sent to prison, especially for merely publishing articles containing the ideas of Karl Marx and William Morris which easily could be found in libraries and bookshops all over Britain. She protested that she'd received better treatment in prison as a suffragette and claimed provocatively, 'I've been to Russia and prisoners are better off there than here.'[1314]

But the intensity of her anger and bitterness about this arrest and imprisonment are startlingly out of character: this was because Scotland Yard had tried to set her up. Using a police plant, they stung her with the mortifying suspicion of acting as a police provocateur, stirring up civil disobedience among unemployed workers. Theodore Rothstein, who wrote one of the *Dreadnought* articles for which Sylvia was convicted, 'How to Get a Labour Government', tried to flee London after her arrest. Detectives caught and detained him, claiming to have found a letter from Sylvia on his person. Allegedly this incriminating missive proved that she and Comrade 'Veltheim' (Rothstein) had been involved in what Sylvia later described as 'fantastic and absurd adventures' including gun running, currency laundering and inciting violence among the East End unemployed.[1315]

Most people believed the letter to be the imaginative work of Scotland Yard, but Sylvia was infuriated by the attempt to undermine her reputation. Her friend and admirer John Maclean, Scottish Marxist, member of the BSP and Bolshevik Consul in Scotland, had been the first person to be arrested under the Defence of the Realm Act for his support of Russia in 1918. He too had been tried and convicted for sedition and was also a former prison hunger striker. Maclean wrote in his newspaper *Vanguard* in November 1920:

> The report of the trial of a Finn who is alleged to be a courier
> between Lenin and the revolutionaries in this country has brought
> to light a letter supposed to be written by Sylvia Pankhurst. She
> is supposed to tell Lenin that she got lads to create disturbances
> amongst the unemployed whilst Lansbury and other London
> mayors were discussing matters at 10 Downing Street. If she
> wrote it, then Sylvia acted as a police provocateur, consciously
> or unconsciously. At any rate whether guilty or not, the work
> was that of the police to head back the dangerous outburst when
> unemployment grows worse as the year proceeds.[1316]

From a friend, this was rather qualified support. Maclean knew as well as anyone else on the left that Sylvia was targeted as a suspected enemy of the state, and would say with good reason, since she was a former militant extremist, current self-professed anti-parliamentarian, unwavering supporter of Irish liberation, Bolshevik sympathizer, founder of the first British Communist Party (BSTI) and so recently returned from her meeting with Comrade Lenin in Moscow.

At the end of May, *Dreadnought*'s front page extended 'A Woman's Welcome to Comrade Sylvia Pankhurst on Release from Holloway, celebrating her 'spirit of great self-sacrifice', and her display of the 'enthusiasm and zeal of the real revolutionary who sees the goal'.[1317] The next issue, on 4 June, featured Sylvia's front-page article describing her prison life and laying out her programme for penal reform. A large, eye-catching modernist cartoon captioned 'TO FIGHT AGAIN! Comrade Sylvia Pankhurst' depicts Sylvia's unmistakable form emerging through the Holloway prison gate, underneath the 'OUT' door, her head held defiantly high. In the opposite direction, a long, line of 'Communist' members file past her through the 'IN' door.

Sylvia's imprisonment for sedition coincided with the formation of a united British Communist Party just two weeks after she started serving her prison sentence. The second Unity Convention was held in Leeds on 19 January to agree the formation of the British Communist Party. Nora and other representatives of the WSF attended. They now had to choose between sticking to their founding principles or 'continued participation in the mainstream of the international communist movement'.[1318] One-third of the WSF membership had already resigned over the issue. The remaining 200 members decided to follow the policy of the CI and entered the CPGB at the Leeds Unity Convention, where the united party was finally founded. Sylvia's final contribution to the unity negotiations 'consisted only of a recommendation that the CP (BSTI) enter the CPGB as an opposition group determined to win the party over to left-wing policies'.[1319]

In opposition to Sylvia's arguments, those of the WSF and of other significant left-wing communist leaders and smaller groups, the Unity Convention fully embraced the policies of the Third International. This, crucially, included the BCP accepting the principles of parliamentary participation and Labour Party affiliation, though by this time the party had made it clear that it would reject applications for affiliation from the communists.

In Sylvia's absence, the *Dreadnought* tried to keep up the left-wing opposition campaign, publishing articles discussing anti-parliamentarianism, trade unions and other unity issues. However, since the Home Office had succeeded in cutting off the inflow of Russian funding to the paper. Struggling with mounting debt, *Dreadnought* slid rapidly towards bankruptcy. Despite Norah's generosity in trying to keep it afloat, there were limits to her own ability to fund the newspaper, and with the agreement of the board, she wrote to the Russian government minister and feminist Alexandra Kollontai requesting interim funding. Sylvia's East End supporters also raised a special *Dreadnought* Fund by personal subscription 'as a mark of appreciation of her work and devotion to the cause',[1320] which Norah presented to Sylvia as a New Year's gift on behalf of the donors; from Holloway she asked Norah to convey her gratitude.[1321]

By the summer of 1921, Albert Inkpin's 10,000-strong British Socialist Party, and Lenin himself, conclusively outmanoeuvred the WSF. Sylvia's public argument with Lenin during the unity negotiations and her imprisonment are examples of intransigence based on idealism rather than pragmatism. She hankered after a more radical, fresher start than Britain was ready for, as Lenin well understood. As Karl Marx wrote in the 'Critique of the Gotha Programme', the new society will be stamped with the birthmarks of the old order from whose womb it emerges. There is no 'pure' point from which to begin. To believe in this form of tabula rasa – in the possibility of starting again with a blank page – was the illusion of so-called ultra-leftism. This was the position Lenin described as Sylvia's 'infantile disorder'. In its revolutionary zeal, this idealism refused absolutely to work with the compromised tools of the present: social reform, trade unions, political parties, parliamentary democracy, and so on.[1322]

For her part, Sylvia understood very well the misogyny and patriarchal attitudes built into the strategies deployed to sideline her. The campaign for women's suffrage and the arguments of feminism had also been diagnosed as an 'infantile disorder' for 300 years. Sylvia's entire life so far had been shaped by this disorder. Being accused of another form of juvenile delinquency did not seem very different.

Either way, the argument turned out to be academic as regards parliamentary representation. In 1921 the Communist Party of Great Britain made formal application for membership of the Labour Party and was rejected immediately by an overwhelming majority. Communists, Labour leaders argued, would not be able to follow the party's democratic constitution.

Sylvia had returned home from Soviet Russia only to face arrest, a sedition trial and six months' imprisonment that took her off the political scene at a crucial time. On her release, she had to confront the grim realities of Lenin's strategy. The CP-BSTI, Sylvia's party, merged with the Communist Party of Great Britain (CPGB), from which point the *Workers' Dreadnought* ceased to be its official organ. From then on she would report openly on controversies within the party, determined to ensure ongoing debate. She met with a sub-committee of the CPGB executive which presented her with a set of conditions to which they knew she would never agree. Her request to meet the full executive committee received no answer. Instead the sub-committee issued her with a directive instructing her to cease publication within a fortnight, which inevitably she ignored. In September she finally received her summons to appear before the full executive, to whom she made her uncompromising case for a left-wing group within the CPGB and a policy of allowing open debate. Liberally deploying the repeated watchwords of 'party discipline', the CPGB responded by expelling Comrade Pankhurst 'following her repeated forthright condemnations of CPGB and Comintern policies'.[1323] They demanded that she hand over the *Dreadnought* to the Communist Party. Sylvia responded by accusing the executive of playing at the dictatorship of the proletariat while in reality fearing to be really revolutionary. She was, she wrote in the *Dreadnought*, extremely saddened to see that even in Russia there was as yet no sign of the withering of dictatorship, which was supposed to be only a temporary transitional state. 'The Communist Party of Great Britain is at present passing through a sort of political measles called discipline which makes it fear the free expression and circulation of opinions within the Party.'[1324]

Throughout it all, Sylvia kept her eye on the best in culture. On 19 June she wrote a letter in longhand on *Workers' Dreadnought* notepaper to the American 'Red Dancer' Isadora Duncan, whose *Liszt – Harmonies poétiques et religieuses S. 173, No. 7 Funérailles ('Funeral')* had just premiered at Queen's Hall.[1325]

Dear Madam,
    I watched your wonderful performance last night with admiration, and since you are going to Russia, an act which is

deeply significant and symbolic in these days, I should greatly
like to interview you for the above paper. Could you give me
an appointment for this purpose either one day this week from
Wednesday onwards? Perhaps some time in the evening next
Saturday or at Queen's Hall might be most convenient to you –
but that is as you wish if you will oblige me by granting me the
interview. I should also be grateful if you would send a press ticket
for the *Workers' Dreadnought* representative.[1326]

Neither interview nor press ticket materialized. Duncan opened her first
school in Moscow in 1921, on the invitation of Anatoly Lunacharsky,
the Commissar of Enlightenment in the first Soviet government.[1327] Like
Sylvia initially a Bolshevik enthusiast, Duncan became disillusioned
with the failures of the revolution.

Meanwhile the row over the *Dreadnought* continued to rage, driven
also by unresolved internal disputes between the members of Sylvia's
CP-BSTI and her partner Silvio Corio over his dominant role in the
running of the paper. Corio acted as its editor even though officially this
was Sylvia's title and role. Moreover, as an anarchist, Corio was not a
member of the Communist Party. The deputy editor May O'Callaghan
alleged that it was Corio's behaviour – 'drunken' rows and high-
handedness with other members of the press – that led to Sylvia losing
her grip on the *Dreadnought*.[1328] In addition, Joe Thurgood accused
Corio of financial mismanagement. Whether these claims were fact or
fabrication, it was incontrovertible that Corio's anarchism placed him
in opposition to the formation of communist parties. Sylvia offered
to resign the editorship, but as no one volunteered to replace her she
was re- elected. She continued to publish the *Dreadnought* under the
strapline 'Organ of the Communist Party', still criticizing the CPGB
for being a Moscow puppet with no mind of its own.

By the summer of 1921 Sylvia's public clash with Lenin at the height
of the unity negotiations and her imprisonment for sedition allowed
Lenin and Albert Inkpin, backed by the greater membership strength
of the BSP, to outmanoeuvre her.

She published Herman Gorter's 'Open Letter to Comrade Lenin'
replying to the now internationally debated pamphlet *'Left-Wing
Communism'*. Gorter declared, 'without a doubt ... I also am a victim'
of this infantile disease. 'Your observations about the confusion that

revolution has caused in many brains, is quite right ... I know that. The revolution came so suddenly, and in a way so utterly different from what we expected.' Gorter confirmed to Lenin that 'Your words will be an incentive to me, once again, and to an even greater extent than before, to base my judgement in all matters of tactics, also in the revolution, exclusively on reality, on the actual class-relations, as they manifest themselves politically and economically.'

Gorter praiseed Lenin for the success of his 'brilliant' tactics in Russia, but argued that this proved nothing for western Europe. The Soviets, the dictatorship of the proletariat, the methods for the revolution and for reconstruction, all these he accepted. 'Also your international tactics have been – so far at least – exemplary. But for your tactics for the countries of Western Europe it is different. And this is only natural. How could the tactics in the East and West of Europe possibly be the same?' He proceeded to take apart Lenin's pamphlet, on the premise that the starting point in the argument is erroneous. Lenin is mistaken in his judgement that the conditions of the western European revolution are analogous with the Russian one, 'that is to say the class-relations', which led Lenin to mistake the cause from which left-wing opposition originates. 'Therefore the brochure SEEMS to be right, as long as your starting-point is assumed. If, however (as it should be), your starting point is rejected, the entire brochure is wrong. As all your mistaken, and partly mistaken, judgements converge in your condemnation of the Left movement, especially in Germany and England ... I imagine I had best answer your brochure by a defence of the Left Wing.'[1329]

Gorter commended the Communist Party of Sylvia Pankhurst, for striving, 'above all, to raise the masses as a whole, and the individuals to a higher level, to educate them one by one to be revolutionary fighters, by making them realise (not through theory only, but especially by practice), that all depends on them, that they are to expect nothing from foreign help, very little from leaders, and all from themselves'.

While the *Dreadnought* continued to argue with Lenin, Alexandra Kollontai, People's Commissar for Social Welfare in the Soviet government, still appeared regularly there. Kollontai was the most prominent woman in the Soviet administration and now known internationally for founding the 'Zhenotdel' – Women's Ministry – in 1919. The Women's Ministry worked to improve the conditions of every aspect of women's lives in the new Soviet Union, combating illiteracy, educating women about the new marriage, educational and work laws established by the revolution, and ran effectively until it was closed, under Stalin, in 1930. Kollontai was from the outset a robust internal critic of the Communist Party. At the end of 1920 she sided with the Workers' Opposition, the left-wing faction of the party rooted in the trade unions. Kollontai wrote articles on a range of feminist subjects and also thoughtful, informative pieces on the development of the workers' opposition in Russia, a left-wing faction that wanted to operate within the Communist Party. Investment from the savings of Norah Smyth and the Pethick- Lawrences kept Dreadnought alive until 1924, as an 'independent communist voice'.

All of this increasingly riled the CPGB. In September 1921 Sylvia published a long article in *Workers' Dreadnought* laying out in detail her arguments with the Communist Party, concluding, 'And so I leave the Party but not the movement. I am tired, comrades. I have had a long struggle.'[1330] Investment from the savings of Norah Smyth and the Pethick-Lawrences kept *Dreadnought* alive until 1924, as an 'independent communist voice'.[1331] Just after Sylvia's expulsion from the Communist Party by the CP executive committee and the disbanding of WSF, she endorsed the manifesto of a newly formed Fourth International, a collective of left-wing organizations convened by Herman Gorter (not to be confused with Trotsky's later Fourth International of 1939). This initiative, known as the International of Opposition Parties, included Belgian, Bulgarian, Czech and Dutch left-wing communists who condemned the lack of democracy and the development of bureaucracy within the Russian-led Third International and the intolerance of its leaders in relation to communist parties of other countries. Although still a revolutionary socialist, Sylvia was becoming increasingly opposed to the direction of travel in the Soviet Union. In October 1921 she called on communists to leave the Third International and join the democratic opposition represented by the Fourth. In terms she had demonstrated already in her pacifist opposition to Labour Party policy during the First World War, she robustly defended the right of criticism within the movement and spelled out her position on party allegiance.

I shall never adopt the motto 'The Party Right or Wrong' – I shall always go for what I believe to be best. I think that is the only way to avoid becoming a hindrance to progress. A Communist Party, a Party of Revolution, must, I think be very stern, very unyielding, very exclusive towards the Right elements, but ever tolerant toward the Left elements.[1332]

Her unwavering defence of democratic socialism continued as she published articles by and defended the rights of left-wing Russian dissidents, and spoke at concerts with exiled Russian left-wing musicians, Eduard Sôrmus and Bohumir Ulman. In January 1921, on the anniversary of the deaths of Rosa Luxemburg and Karl Liebknecht, Sylvia dedicated the front page of the *Dreadnought* to her eloquent tributes to them both.

Rosa Luxemburg was one of Marx's most perspicuous and intelligent followers. Gifted with shrewdness and complete independence of thought, she refused to accept any traditional formula on trust; she probed every idea, every fact … Rosa Luxemburg was never satisfied with the insipid and dry theoretical disquisitions so dear to the heart of our erudite Socialists. Her speech was brilliantly simple; it sparkled with wit and was full of mordant humour … She was a splendid theoretician of scientific Socialism, but had nothing in common with the paltry pedants who cull their wisdom from a few scientific works … Socialism was for Rosa Luxemburg a dominating passion which absorbed her whole life, a passion at once intellectual and ethical … Rosa Luxemburg will remain one of the greatest figures in the history of international Socialism.[1333]

Dreadnought serialized Rosa Luxemburg's *The Russian Revolution*, and in February 1921 Sylvia printed both Luxemburg's and Karl Liebknecht's letters from prison.

When Lenin introduced his New Economic Policy in March 1921, a programme that included the encouragement of private trade, Sylvia immediately wrote a leader setting out her diagnosis that a manageable contagion had now passed to something chronic and fatal. Lenin had caught the terminal disease of becoming a clay-footed politician like all others, readmitting capitalism by the back door and buying himself the protection of big money and its free-market companies:

> Lenin. We address you as representative of the Russian Soviet Government and the Russian Communist Party. With deep regret we have observed you hauling down the flag of Communism and abandoning the cause of the emancipation of the workers. With profound sorrow we have watched the development of your policy of making peace with Capitalism and reaction. Why have you done this?[1334]

Arguably, Sylvia possessed experience and understanding of British politics that exceeded Lenin's. She'd been much closer to seeing the corrupting influence and unctuous seductions of power and privilege, having grown up in one of the oldest traditions of parliamentary government, whereas Lenin came from a country with no tradition of bourgeois government. Sylvia thought him uninformed and inflexible in his misunderstanding of the specific history and context in Britain. He thought her rigid and caught in the trap of asserting pure principles and therefore relegated to the sidelines. Writing to Teresa Billington-Greig decades later in 1956, Sylvia reflected:

> I did not join the official party being convinced the policy was unworkable. I believed that Russia, almost a world in itself, could establish socialism within its own borders. For this I was dismissed as a sentimental dreamer, but afterwards that became (ostensibly at least) the official policy. I believed that the correct policy for Russia was to make life happy and prosperous for the mass of people and to avoid atrocities and brutalities both in the interests of the home population and to render socialism attractive to the rest of the world. Such a task was hard, perhaps too hard, but that, I am convinced should have been the aim ... On the whole Russians do not seem to have bothered about world public opinion ... their propaganda ... converted some but their ruthlessness estranged others. I lost sympathy with their methods but I was, and am, a socialist.[1335]

Though immersed in the internal battle over communism, Sylvia's political radar did not fail her, even while rapidly losing ground on many fronts in her campaign organizations. The *Dreadnought* was among the first and few publications in Britain where the name of a young leader of the newly formed Nazi Party began consistently to appear in news and editorials warning of the dangers of fascism emerging in Germany. Closely tracking the threat arising in the confrontation between communism and fascism, Sylvia and Silvio Corio kept their sights constantly trained on the activities of Benito Mussolini in Italy and Hitler's new party in Germany.

The December 1923 general election returned a minority Labour government, with Ramsay MacDonald as Britain's first Labour Prime Minister. An unprecedented thirty-four women candidates stood for parliament – thirteen Labour, one Labour/Co-op, twelve Liberal, seven Conservative and one Independent. Among the eight women who won their seats, Lady Astor, Sylvia's nemesis, was returned for a second time. Lady Astor, Sylvia wrote, was among those women who 'entered Parliament merely as the deputies of their husbands'. Astor's case, 'from a democratic standpoint', was 'particularly objectionable ... since [Lord Astor] was thus given a voice in ruling the people through both Houses of Parliament'.[1336]

Sylvia felt she was guarding against the chauvinism of delusions of female superiority. From her perspective, this was more than bear-baiting old adversaries. 'The woman professional politician is neither more nor less desirable than the man professional politician: the less the world has of either the better it is for it.'[1337] She harboured no illusion about the crucial moment that brought these women entry into parliament:

> It is interesting to observe that the legal barriers to women's
> participation in Parliament and its elections were not removed until
> the movement to abolish parliament altogether had received the
> strong encouragement of witnessing the overthrow of parliamentary
> government in Russia and the setting up of Soviets ... The
> upholders of reaction ... were by no means oblivious to the growth
> of Sovietism when they decided to popularise the old parliamentary
> machine by giving to some women both votes and the right to be
> elected.[1338]

Workers' Dreadnought welcomed 1924 with the cheerful New Year message that 'Parliamentary Government is a failure; it does not grip the interest of the masses.'[1339]

Having declared his likely successor Joseph Stalin 'unbearable' Lenin died on 21 January 1924 in the hills outside Moscow. Arthur Ransome, creator of *Swallows and Amazons*, wrote in the *Manchester Guardian*, 'Even the irreconcilable enemies of the Revolution are unable to disguise their respect for one of the greatest figures in Russian history.'

On 30 May the secretary general of the Italian Socialist Party Giacomo Matteotti made an unvarnished denunciation of the Fascist Party and Mussolini to the Chamber of Deputies. He challenged the results of the recent elections and, once again, denounced the violence and abuses that had brought the party to power. He ended, 'I've said my piece ... now get ready for my death.' Less than two weeks later, on 10 June, six fascist *squadristi* kidnapped him as he walked along the banks of the Tiber in Rome. In August his mutilated body was discovered hastily buried just outside the city, near Riano Flaminio. The Matteotti Crisis shocked world opinion and initially threatened to cause the downfall of the fascists.

Born in the same month and year as Sylvia, Giacomo Matteotti had entered politics after graduating from the University of Bologna law school and practising as a lawyer. He was elected to the Italian Chamber of Deputies in 1919 and re-elected in 1921 and 1924, by which time he had become secretary general of his party. Simultaneously, Mussolini was conducting terrorist attacks on leftists. Matteotti's disappearance created a sensation, as did the discovery of his body. The opposition deputies withdrew from the Chamber to protest against the murder and to work for Mussolini's overthrow. But the parliamentary forces proved ineffective in keeping public opinion aroused and failed to take decisive action against him. After a prolonged judicial inquiry, the six suspects arrested for the murder were allowed to walk free.

Mussolini, at first taken aback by his loss of public favour, went opportunistically on the offensive. On 3 January 1925 he took full responsibility for the murder of Matteotti as head of the Fascist Party and dared his critics to prosecute him for the crime. The Matteotti Crisis marked a turning point in the history of Italian fascism. Mussolini abandoned any notion of working with parliament and established a police state, including suppression of the opposition press, exclusion of non-fascist ministers and formation of a secret police.

In 1924 that Sylvia started making notes for her new book 'In the Red Twilight'. She began working on this masterwork on the death of communism and the ominous rise of the fascist lust for power at the time when many people in Britain appeared willing to accept Mussolini and subsequently even Hitler as modernizing reformers, and when Churchill was cheerfully declaring himself 'charmed' by Mussolini. Sylvia wrote articles analysing the use of violence by the fascist movement. She investigated why women joined it and their role and position within it. She criticized the Labour Party for not taking sufficient heed of the fascist menace.

Norah wrote Sylvia a long missive beseeching her to rethink her ultra-left-wing politics. After Sylvia's release from prison in 1921, Corio had written to Shaw requesting financial support for their operations. Shaw replied:

> I have known for some time past that Sylvia is in difficulties …
> though I am quite as much disposed to make a spoiled child of her
> as the rest of her friends I am not really sorry that she should lose a
> toy so expensive and dangerous as a printing press, and have a spell
> of total abstinence from *Weltverbesserungswahn* [the illusion that the
> world could be better].[1340]

A decade later in 1931 Shaw would defend Joan of Arc's greatness in a BBC broadcast and recommended that if listeners wanted 'to find what women can feel when they have the whole power of society marshalled against them, and they have to fight it', they should consider Sylvia Pankhurst and the suffrage movement. 'Miss Sylvia Pankhurst, like so many other women in that movement, was tortured: in fact, except for the burning, she suffered many actual physical tortures that Joan was spared.' Shaw advised that reading Pankhurst's work provided a much better depiction of Joan's trial than the 'very dry historical accounts'.[1341]

But in the early 1920s some of Sylvia's friends and even her political colleagues found her Joan of Arc style of unyielding battle for her causes tiresome. On 25 March 1923 Sylvia spoke at an anti-fascist rally in London, the first of many. Still they thought her extreme and alarmist. A decade later, the very same people saw her urgent, tireless early warnings of the fascist menace in an entirely different light.

PART FIVE

Modern Times 1924–1945

I'm sorry, but I don't want to be an emperor. That's not my business. I don't want to rule or conquer anyone. I should like to help everyone – if possible – Jew, Gentile – black man – white. We all want to help one another. Human beings are like that. We want to live by each other's happiness – not by each other's misery. We don't want to hate and despise one another. In this world there is room for everyone. And the good earth is rich and can provide for everyone. The way of life can be free and beautiful, but we have lost the way.

Charlie Chaplin, final speech, *The Great Dictator* (1940)

29

The Red Cottage Tea Room

During the last year of its publication, the *Dreadnought*'s front page advertised 'Red Cottage Tea Room – Weekend Outings and Teas', illustrated with a woodcut of a bucolic scene. Two women and a man sit – Sylvia, Norah and Silvio – in the garden of a country cottage, sun-hatted, sipping tea amid verdant flowers and foliage.

In July 1924 Sylvia shut down the *Workers' Dreadnought*. By then Old Ford Road had been closed up and Sylvia had moved into a small, dilapidated, vermin-infested, weather-boarded cottage at 126 High Road, Woodford Green, a suburb on the border of north-east London and Essex next to Epping Forest.[1342] George Lansbury had introduced Sylvia to Epping Forest during their Bow days. They would go for long rambles, discussing their lives and politics, trying to solve the problems of the world. Sylvia and Norah had discovered Vyne Cottage, set back from the main road connecting London and Epping. 'Cottage' dignified what was little more than a ramshackle makeshift structure – more of a habitable shed than a house. A toddler at the time, Leslie Powter recalled, 'It was an absolute slum.'[1343] There was one indoor cold-water tap, no electricity and an outdoor privy, no foundations and abounded with damp and rats. The upside of Vyne Cottage, as its name more truthfully suggested, was the garden, where Leslie's mum grew the flowers that she sold locally. Sylvia set up home in one half of the dwelling and the Powter family of five lived in the other half, which had two small partitioned bedrooms. According to her son, Sylvia had 'earlier purchased' the piece of land on which the single-storey cottage stood, so it seems that the Powters, already resident, became her tenants.[1344] Sylvia changed the name to

Red Cottage and decided to open a tea room and bookshop for study groups and talks.

Silvio built the Red Cottage Tea Rooms as an extension to the cottage. Mrs Ashman, a Woodford neighbour, recalled that 'the tea rooms were put up in sections by him and my husband about 1924–5. Mr Corio laid the floor while my husband put on the roof. He wasn't able to climb. The tea rooms were run by Sylvia Pankhurst with help by Mr Corio.'[1345] She added that her husband greatly enjoyed Corio's genial company and the work, punctuated as it was by regular cups of tea and chat.[1346] Mrs Powter supplied the tea room with dahlias and other flowers and produce from her garden. Sylvia and Norah had cohabited for over a decade, but it seems that Sylvia lived there alone initially, and that Silvio moved in some months later. There's evidence that the devoted Norah was hurt by this displacement from the centre of Sylvia's life.[1347]

Tea and cake, like bread and beer, have always been vital ingredients of rebellion and revolution. Tea rooms featured in the suffragette era of the Pankhurst women. The Teacupp Inn just off Kingsway near the Clement's Inn offices had been a great favourite with the WSPU. Its proprietor, Mary Hansell, ran regular advertisements in the WSPU paper *Votes for Women* – 'Dainty luncheons and Afternoon teas at moderate charges. Home cookery. Vegetarian dishes and sandwiches. Entirely staffed and managed by women.'[1348].

Tea drinking contributed to brewing the October 1917 revolution. At the time, more Russians drank tea than vodka, contrary to the current cultural stereotype. Tolstoy couldn't write without it. Lenin needed it to think. Stalin also was a great tea drinker. Along with their passionate love of angling, it was one of the few things the two leaders had in common. Traditionally vodka drinking remained the preserve and habit of aristocrats, the elite and depressive poets and writers, whose mores came to define a class-based notion of Russianness for the British.

In January 1924 the Labour Party formed its first government and Lenin died in Moscow, having failed to remove Stalin from the General Secretaryship. Following Sylvia's expulsion from the Communist Party, the WSF disbanded. The *Dreadnought* outlived Lenin by six months, ceasing publication in July. Sylvia never excused Lenin's amoralism nor forgave him for traducing the promise of the Bolshevik

Revolution. His successor never fooled Sylvia for a moment. From the outset she regarded Stalin as damaged goods. She criticized his foreign policy in scrupulous detail. She repeatedly published articles damning his human rights abuses. She rejected 'corporate socialism' in long analytical articles and disapproved of everything that came out of the new Moscow government. On her visit to Russia in 1920 she had met many of the early Bolsheviks. Knowing them personally, she never believed their alleged forced 'confessions'. Later, she published writings by Soviet defectors who attacked Stalin's role in the Spanish Civil War.[1349]

The defeat of Ramsay MacDonald's Labour minority government and the Conservative landslide victory in the October 1924 general election – the third election in less than three years – was attributed to the forged Zinoviev letter published by the *Daily Mail* four days before the election. The forgers have never been identified. Christopher Andrew in his authorized history of MI5 is confident that it was confected by unidentified White Russians and then accepted as genuine by SIS (MI6).[1350] Andrew concedes that several MI5 officers may have helped publicize the letter, so both MI5 and MI6 were murkily involved. The Zinoviev letter conspiracy had little impact on support for the Labour Party, which increased by about one million votes compared to the 1923 general election. However, it scared anti-socialist Liberals, who switched their support to the Conservative Party out of fear of the 'Red Peril'.

Winston Churchill took up his new seat as a 'Constitutional and Anti-Socialist MP' for Epping, which included Woodford. As the British Bulldog entered Woodford, his old nemesis Miss Pankhurst also moved into the neighbourhood and established herself as his best-known and most troublesome constituent. Churchill was to represent the constituency during his second term as Prime Minister, right through until he retired aged eighty-nine at the 1964 general election.

Sylvia had travelled with great purpose through life. Now, as a consequence of her expulsion from the Communist Party, she was without a newspaper and without her own grass-roots organization. She was in her forties. Her love affair with Corio had developed into a serious committed relationship, and couple decided to move further east, from urban Bow to leafy Woodford Green.[1351]

In the summer of 1923, the *Workers' Dreadnought* ran its first advertisements for 'Red Cottage Teas', 'For Outings and Weekends ... Buses 34, 40a, 10a pass the door. Opposite "Horse and Well"'. Opened in 1730, the Horse and Well pub remains a going concern.[1352] At the bus terminus next door to the pub, drivers and ticket inspectors changed shift before the return journey. Sylvia hoped to tempt them with tea, bacon sandwiches, cakes and biscuits as an alternative to beer and gin at the Horse and Well. She hoped they might also be interested in the books, pamphlets and informative talks offered alongside Red Cottage tea and sandwiches.

She also aimed to cater for local passing trade and day trippers to Epping Forest. Her Bow pals, activist comrades and international friends passing through Britain were all welcome, as well as anyone else who might be interested in tea and buns accompanied by a stirring of socialist education. Crucially, Red Cottage served also as a stable community centre. It provided a crèche to feed and look after the children of strikers, and an information bureau and social club for refugees.

The Red Cottage bookshop offered a wide selection of titles, including Jack London's books on class war and revolution; Charles Bradlaugh on religious doubt; Edward Carpenter on civilization and its cure; evolutionary scientific thought from T. H. Huxley and the works of Olive Schreiner. Arthur Ransome – *Guardian* journalist, children's author and Russian spy – published a hugely popular book, *The Truth About Russia*, always available at the Red Cottage bookshop, as were the writings of William Cobbett, Mary Wollstonecraft, Clara Cole, Henry George, Keir Hardie, Maxim Gorky, Peter Kropotkin, William Morris, Karl Marx, Friedrich Engels, Antonio Gramsci and Alexandra Kollontai. Sylvia and Silvio, who helped her run the bookshop, made sure that it covered a broad range of historical and economic subjects, from the Protestant revolution to studies of the wage system, the industrial revolution and communism. For those in search of something lighter to digest with their scones, faint hope might be offered by guidebooks on British rural rides, modern English grammars and James Leakey's basic introduction to Esperanto.

Corio was an ardent bibliophile. Book loving and a fascination with language and print were among the shared passions that drew Sylvia and Silvio together. He spent much time in the British

Museum Reading Room. His son remembered vast piles of Readers' Book Application Forms stacked on the mantelpiece at their later home in Woodford. Like Friedrich Engels, Corio found comparative linguistics and etymology fascinating. He went fossicking in the second-hand bookshops on Charing Cross Road and spent money he couldn't afford on a compendious collection of dictionaries in every language under the sun, a key symbol among his son's later memories of his father. Richard also described his father as 'a great devotee of Italian poetry', who 'delighted in reciting Dante and other Italian poets to me'.[1353]

Two years after Sylvia launched her cheerful clapboard community tea room on the road to Essex, her mother and elder sister established a genteel tea shop in a Mediterranean resort on the French Riviera. In mid-August 1925 Mrs Pankhurst, Christabel and Mabel Tuke selected Juan-les-Pins near Antibes (between Nice and Cannes) as the location for Emmeline's new business venture. The English Tea-Shop of Good Hope boasted a sea view. Emmeline and Christabel hoped to attract a clientele including tourists, French Anglophiles and dowager expats. Their refined venue offered exquisite interior design and most definitely no socialist books or other improving literature in sight.

The English Tea-Shop of Good Hope, like all of Emmeline's commercial ventures, was an enterprise more of good hope than of good management. With her usual flair, the premises excelled in their decor – tangerine tablecloths and vibrant flower-filled window boxes aimed to tempt tourists and expats through the door to try Mabel's cakes and scones. Unlike her mother, Emmeline was no baker or jam maker. The business lasted barely a season. Homesick British dowagers nursed pots of tea but lacked sufficient appetite to support Mabel's daily baking. The women found the winter surprisingly cold. They packed it in and returned to London by the end of the year. Emmeline's chintz-and-scones Antibes tea shop advertised her maternalistic, imperial feminism. Her response to the 'exceedingly and increasingly serious and alarming' international situation was to stress women's vital role in protecting the moral tone and stability of nation and empire.[1354] Meanwhile, back in suburban Woodford Green, her middle daughter, proprietor of the Red Cottage Tea Room, continued to promote left-wing causes, espouse free love and decolonization and sell bacon sandwiches, cupcakes and socialism to bus drivers and students from the London School of Economics.

In the 1920s, elite London tea rooms became popular places of rendezvous for exiled White Russians and Nazi sympathizers among the British upper classes. In 1923 Admiral Nikolai Wolkoff and his family opened the Russian Tea Room in Harrington Road, South Kensington, near the Natural History Museum. In the late 1930s the Tory MP Archibald Ramsay, representative for Peebles and Southern Midlothian, established his secret Right Club in the Russian Tea Rooms in London, intended to 'co-ordinate the work of all the patriotic societies'.[1355] Anna Wolkoff, couturier to Wallis Simpson and later a German spy, became secretary of the anti-Semitic, pro-Nazi organization. Archibald Ramsay explained in his autobiography that 'The main object of the Right Club was to oppose and expose the activities of Organized Jewry in the light of evidence which came into my possession in 1938. Our first objective was to clear the Conservative Party of Jewish influence, and the character of our membership was strictly in keeping with this objective.'[1356] The culture of the tea shop drew new battle lines in British politics between rising right-wing extremism in support of fascism and the forces assembling to oppose it.

Sylvia roped in a Welsh woman, Annie Barnes, as baker for the Red Cottage Tea Room. Sylvia's cooking skills remain a matter of historical dispute, but certainly did not stretch to baking. The general view that she was a poor cook owes something to the novelty of her intermittent vegetarianism and equally to the fact that she never had much money to spend on food. It may owe as much to implicit criticism or envy of her lack of enslavement to the conventions of housewifery; but certainly she was no domestic goddess. Based on her experience of living with Sylvia while she was an art student, Annie Kenney declared herself thoroughly alarmed by her friend's dependence on unseasoned lentils and any possible combination of muddled eggs and tomatoes. This way of cooking was a matter of pinched economy and efficiency for Sylvia. Conversely, Annie loved restaurants and all opportunities for fine dining, and possessed a connoisseur's appreciation of food and leisured conviviality.

In a BBC interview Annie Barnes claimed once to have discovered Sylvia in the kitchen at Red Cottage boiling rashers of bacon for butties.[1357] Her son Richard reported that she was a good cook and that he liked her food.[1358] Silvio saw to the grocery shopping, cooking and washing up. Sylvia loved Italian food. Now she had a partner with an expert flair for his native cuisine. British visitors invited to supper at Red Cottage expressed surprise at unusual dishes like macaroni cheese or rustic pepperonata and pasta and at the preponderance of 'salad'. Mrs Ashman remarked on the health aspects of the family's diet: 'The vegetables were mostly salads that were grown.'[1359] Silvio prepared, served and cleared these meals in between chess moves with Richard.

Sylvia favoured simple fare. As an art student in London, economy governed her preferences. She enjoyed Hardie's Scottish scones which he baked himself on the hearth at Nevill's Court. It was Hardie who first took her to an Italian restaurant. Later, the digestive problems caused by torture in prison determined what she ate. As her life progressed, Sylvia possessed neither the money nor interest in keeping an elaborate larder and table. Like many socialist radicals of her age, and even more militant suffragettes, the politics of food and its production concerned her, particularly the critique of violence against animals implicit in vegetarianism. The long-established link between radical feminism and refraining from violence against animals combined with her education from Keir Hardie in the Christian socialist arguments in favour of ethical eating.[1360]

During war rationing and general scarcity, Sylvia pragmatically relaxed her vegetarian precepts and took her nutrition where she could get it. Her vegetarianism prevailed during her early and middle years. Later in life, a combination of illnesses, menopause and moving to an African country returned Sylvia to moderate consumption of animal protein. She liked offal – particularly brains and tongue – but disliked bacon, ham and other pork products.[1361]

Norah O'Connell (Walshe) wrote of Red Cottage in a letter to the historian David Mitchell, 'It was a curious household, so untidy and casual.'[1362] 'Untidy' and 'casual' were Norah's polite euphemisms for Sylvia and 'Mr Corio's' openly free-love union and their unconventional lifestyle. Red Cottage is where Sylvia and Corio set up home together for the first time. The garden, Silvio's domain, was indeed the best part of it. Red Cottage had no foundations and abounded with damp and rats. The woodcut conjures a rare and welcome moment of rest in this enjoyment of Silvio's garden. For the most, it was hard work, lots of it, and struggling always to get by.

Annie Barnes, who'd never seen Silvio before, thought Mr Corio the gardener when she met him for the first time digging outside. He was an unflashy dresser, anarcho-radical-rustic Italian peasant style. According to Mrs Ashman, 'Mr Corio was a small man, a bit on the plump side, about five foot three inches, grey haired, gentle in manner, and spoke good English.'[1363] Two or three times a week Corio set off to visit London in his best suit and trilby, 'but', said Mrs Ashman, 'my husband couldn't say what for'.[1364] Of Sylvia and Silvio, 'They kept themselves to themselves, and got on very well together by what my husband saw.'[1365] This perspective of Sylvia and Silvio as a rather mysterious couple illustrates the sliding doors of their lives. To London's network of Italian political refugees, Africans, Russians, Indians, socialists and radicals of all sorts, they were well-known, gregarious friends and community leaders. In the eyes of some of Sylvia's former middle-class suffragette circle and her mother and sister's friends, Corio appeared to be a scruffy, apparently penniless Italian immigrant refugee about whom little was known except that he shared Sylvia's subversive political world and had spent a fair amount of time working in restaurants and bars.

For a decade, Sylvia and Norah had lived their daily lives as each other's primary companion and friend, prison walls notwithstanding. Norah was her conduit to the outside – organizing parcels, letters, singing and vigils outside the prison gates, and dealing with sensitive, confidential personal and political information. According to Norah Walshe, 'It was said that Miss Smyth saw that Sylvia went out to her meetings looking reasonably tidy.' Norah worked with Sylvia in Bow for three years during the war: 'Norah Smyth was Sylvia's great friend in those days. They lived together in a wretched place in Bow and Miss Smyth tried to look after her health and protect her ... she was a very reserved woman. When Sylvia became attached to Richard's father the friendship snapped (so I was told). I don't know if they were ever friends again.'[1366]

The relationship between Sylvia and Norah was already under strain prior to Corio's arrival. As their correspondence shows, Norah took issue with Sylvia's swerve to communism and the ultra-left, concerned about its impact on the WSF. As Sylvia readjusted her political course in response to Lenin's betrayal and regrouped her energies to fight fascism, she and Norah reconciled. There was a temporary falling out over a financial misunderstanding, but by 1928 they were once again firm personal friends and political allies, working shoulder to shoulder.

Following her bust-up with the right-wing communists during her period of ultra-ultra-leftism, Sylvia continued to explore her own political thinking and ideals. At the core was her belief in democratic socialism. These combined with her habit of re-examining her point of view in the face of facts and events on the ground. From their first emergence into public view, Sylvia was alert to the dangers of Mussolini's and, subsequently, of Hitler's rise to power. She recognized the origins of fascism in Italy and their imitation in Germany. 'There is no doubt in my mind ... that Mussolini and Hitler are definitely working together, and that though there is some rivalry over Austria and the German speaking territories in Italy, they are quite prepared to let these difficulties rest at any time if they can strike a blow against France and Britain thereby ... It is simply gangster rule, and there will be no peace in the world until these dictators come down.'[1367] If democracies dealt swiftly and decisively with Mussolini, she argued, Hitler might be averted. Back in 1919, she and Silvio had witnessed *squadristi* beating up fellow members of their socialist delegation on the steps of the Bologna city hall. In 1922, the couple followed and reported events attentively as Mussolini hijacked Gabriel D'Annunzio's 'March on Rome'.[1368]

During this decade Sylvia became founder and co-founder of three significant anti-fascist organizations: Friends of Italian Freedom, Italian Information Bureau and Women's International Matteotti Committee. She participated in the Women's World Committee Against War and Fascism. The League for the Boycott of Aggressor Nations elected her as their vice president, as did the British Non-Sectarian Anti-Nazi Council.

Silvio Corio was decisive in rousing Sylvia to sound the alarm about the incipient rise of Italian fascism. Her significant adult relationships centred on profoundly socially engaged people, with distinctly inspirational names: Keir, Zelie and Silvio. Though in ideological sympathy with all of them, with none of them did she agree entirely. Their challenges to her thinking were key to the quality and endurance of the relationships. Their commonality was the desire to try and make the world a better place. Fortunately for the anarchist socialist revolutionary Silvio, he entered Sylvia's life at the high point of her turn to anti-parliamentary communism. She understood his anarcho-syndicalism in the context of Italian politics. Following their politically timely convergence, the couple evolved together in the urgent cause of the fight against fascism and racist imperialist colonialism during the 1920s. Their son Richard, born into this milieu, became a child of modern times. Some of her comrades wondered or worried about Sylvia finding unexpected new love with an anarchist. At the time they met, there was common ground between her left-wing communism and his libertarian socialism, but far more importantly their common fight against fascism united them. Sylvia wrote in her manuscript for *New Italy* of 'Anarchists, who remain apart from all others'.[1369] Perhaps this apartness was a key to their compatibility.

After the *Workers' Dreadnought*, Sylvia and Silvio launched several short-run journals together. In 1923 they set up an illustrated political-cultural magazine, another *Germinal*, which included new fiction, drama and poetry, but it ran for only a few issues. When first they met, Silvio helped Sylvia with the printing of *Soviet Russia as I Saw It*. Silvio continued his journalism and printing activities during this time, producing a growing compendium of informative anti-fascist publications, but gradually moved away from anarchist activity in favour of supporting Sylvia's campaign for Ethiopia against Mussolini's fascist regime.

The Ethiopian empire was commonly known in Europe as Abyssinia, an ancient name derived from the Amharic and Arabic words for 'mixed' or 'mixture', referring to the diversity of peoples who lived in the region. Mussolini promised the Italian people 'a place in the sun', intent on building up Italian colonial possessions at a time when, as Neelam Srivastava puts it, 'colonialism was beginning its decline and anti-imperialist movements were developing in various parts of the European empires'.[1370] Ethiopia, above all others, was the prize, the essential jewel in the crown of what Mussolini saw as the new Roman empire: Africa Orientale Italiana.

The ancient civilization of Ethiopia was the only place in Africa that had so far escaped any form of European colonization. Invading Ethiopia would serve to unify Italian-held Eritrea and Italian Somaliland. Mussolini also wanted vengeance. In 1896 Ethiopia had won, resoundingly, the First Italo-Ethiopian War which began in 1895 and culminated in the Battle of Adwa, where Emperor Menelik II's Ethiopian army inflicted what was seen as a humiliating defeat on the Italian force. The Ethiopian victory curbed Italy's empire-building efforts in Africa, and became the first overwhelming defeat of a European power by an African nation during the colonial era. The treaty of Addis Ababa, signed in October 1896, ended Italy's claim to a protectorate over of all of Ethiopia. Four years later, another agreement defined the borders of the Italian colony of Eritrea and significantly reduced its territory. Further treaties fixed the borders of Ethiopia with its European-ruled colonial neighbours.

The decisive outcome of the First Italo-Ethiopian War inspired modern African nationalist consciousness and the struggle for independence from white colonization on the continent and throughout the global African diaspora. Lemn Sissay encompasses the significance of this historic victory in his poem about the battle:

> Remember this, the Europeans
> Carved up our homes with blood thirst,
> Not because we were the Third World
> But because we were the First.
> Because we held gold in our hearts,
> Because we had diamonds in our eyes,
> Because oil ran through our veins,
> And a blessing hung in our skies.
> ...
> Remember this; how the story washed
> Across the continent enslaved
> Flooded with the story of Adwa
> In a whispered tidal wave
> From Kenya to Senegal
> From Morocco to the Gambia.
> The liberation began in Adwa, 1896,
> And ended in South Africa.[1371]

In November 1934 Mussolini's policy of aggression against Ethiopia would escalate. A border incursion at the Walwal oasis in eastern Ogaden precipitated an international diplomatic crisis. The League of

Nations had been founded in 1920 to provide a forum for resolving international disputes, intended to ensure the prevention of future wars through the principle of collective security, and Ethiopia had joined it in 1923. Attempts to avert Mussolini's imperialist expansionism would fail, and in October 1935 the Second Italo-Ethiopian War would begin when the fascist dictator illegally invaded and the League was powerless to stop him.

Comparisons have been made between Sylvia and Virginia Woolf,[1372] who share the same birth date and many common social, political and literary interests, to which however they took very different approaches. A more striking similarity in skills and temperament – and their roles in the lives of brilliant women – exists between Silvio Corio and her husband Leonard Woolf. Both were writers, journalists, typesetters and printers running their own publishing houses. Both were practical gardeners, and skilled in keeping Sylvia and Virginia on track. They also shared critical views of European colonialism and a keen interest in Ethiopia. In his 1928 book *Imperialism and Civilization*, Leonard Woolf had attacked the notion that the British empire was a civilizing force. Rather, expansionism 'was a belligerent, crusading, conquering, exploiting, proselytizing civilization'. Indeed, the imposition of imperialism 'on subject peoples at the point of the bayonet and the muzzle of the howitzer [had] heavily overweighted the blessings with a load of war, barbarities, cruelties, tyrannies and exploitations'.[1373]

Greatly concerned about the Ethiopian situation, Leonard Woolf wrote a pamphlet entitled *The League and Abyssinia*, published in 1936 by the Hogarth Press. This explored the problems the 'Ethiopian question' presented to international law and collective security under the League of Nations covenant. In Woolf's view, 'The old methods of imperialism and the 1906 agreements, which authorize Great Powers to conquer, control, and exploit the weaker Powers, are inconsistent and incompatible with the League system, which excludes conquest and guarantees independence and territorial integrity to weaker states.'[1374]

Sylvia and Silvio lived within the local and international network of Italian radical politicos. They had met Antonio Gramsci in Turin in October 1919. *L'Ordine Nuovo* published Sylvia's series 'Lettere dall'Inghilterra', translated by Palmiro Togliatti. In November 1926 Togliatti became general secretary of the Italian Communist Party (PCI), succeeding Gramsci and holding office until 1934; he held it again from 1938 until he died in 1964. His supporters nicknamed him *il Migliore* (the Best). In 1930 Togliatti became a citizen of the Soviet Union and Tolyatti, a city in the province of Samara, was named in his honour.

At Red Cottage, Sylvia wrote the manuscripts for 'In the Red Twilight' and 'The Inheritance'. Simultaneously, she researched and drafted another monumental book that became *India and the Earthly Paradise*, published in 1926 by the Bombay Chronicle Press, Sunshine Publishing House.

Owing to the political situation, India was topical in British publishing in the 1920s. Lord Curzon released his memoirs in 1926, the same year as Annie Besant published *India: Bond or Free?*, which followed her 1915 book, *How India Wrought for Freedom*. William Wedgwood Benn assisted Sylvia with research for her book on India in the British Museum Reading Room. Three years after its publication, Benn was appointed Secretary of State for India. Sylvia's old friend Fred Pethick-Lawrence, always hugely supportive of her writing projects, also helped her with her India project; and later he too became Secretary of State for India. Sylvia laid out her stall in the Preface:

> The mutuality and communism of Ancient India still, in a measure, persist unto this day. There yet remain traces of her old voluntary institutions for mutual aid, her producers' associations co-operating for the common welfare.
>
> Side by side with these, contending against them, often superseding them, have arisen, in continual succession, the dominations and exploitations of native priests and rulers, of foreign invaders from the East, of Western imperialists, and finally of modern capitalism with its growing tendency to discard nationality.
>
> Abysmal poverty has resulted from these exploitations. The long burden of military and bureaucratic rule has checked and thwarted development in every field.
>
> Superstition and enlightenment, those constant rivals for dominion of the evolving mind, have borne their part in the long struggle.
>
> Vast stores of natural wealth; immense untapped potentialities of human energy are locked in India.

The ruling economics and philosophy of a dying epoch would keep them in bondage for exploitation by the powerful few. But the ideals of a new time call for admittance.

The wealth of both East and West must be developed in freedom by the great fraternity of mutual aid, for the common enjoyment of all our peoples and for the building of the Earthly Paradise towards which India and all nations of the earth are surely wending.[1375]

Beginning with a historical survey of Ancient India and the Buddhist Renaissance, Sylvia moved through analyses of Indian law, property, caste as a social institution, marriage, family, the Mogul emperors and British land tenures. As she proceeded to the Akali movement and the Jaito massacres, Sylvia included a study of the Indian Peasants' Union and an interpretation of village *panchayats* as executive committees that, as Keir Hardie had suggested, could be reformed to become the basic organ of democratic local government.

In the chapters on self-sufficiency and the Homespun Movement, Sylvia introduced Gandhi and his work. Drawing comparison between Irish republicanism and the Indian non-cooperation movement she pointed out, 'The great difference between the Sinn Fein of Easter-week and the Swaraj of Gandhi, is that the former was a professedly warlike movement, and the latter is pledged to passive resistance.'[1376]

The impact of British rule on India runs throughout the 638-page book. The other dominant theme is every aspect of the lives and struggles of women. Sylvia devoted long sections to making detailed arguments against arranged marriage, child labour, domestic abuse and female genital mutilation (FGM). In her conclusion, she posed the question, 'how shall we build the Earthly Paradise, the fraternal life of the future?'[1377] For answer, she turned first to William Morris, rather than to Karl Marx.

Sylvia's childhood home at Russell Square thrummed with conversation about British imperial rule in India. The Indian nationalist politician and thinker Dadabhai Naoroji, MP for Finsbury Central, had been a frequent habitué of her mother's salons. In 1886, when Sylvia was four years old, Naoroji, a Parsi intellectual, educator and cotton trader, was elected president of the Indian National Congress, a political party founded the year before. He became the first British

Indian MP for the Liberal Party between 1892 and 1895, and a member of the socialist Second International. Aged nineteen, Sylvia read his book *Poverty and Un-British Rule in India* when it was published in 1901. This is a magisterial political and economic analysis of the draining of India's wealth into Britain, an issue Naoroji introduced into British politics in the 1850s. In 1904, Naoroji became the first delegate of the Indian National Congress sent to the Sixth Congress of the Second International. His brief was 'to alert world socialism to the evils of the Raj'.[1378]

Sylvia's art-school mentor Walter Crane had visited India with his wife in 1907 and produced a beautifully illustrated travel book of his drawings, *India Impressions*. The authoritarianism of the British Raj appalled the Cranes; Indian people and culture charmed them. In the same year Keir Hardie first toured India, where British intelligence reports recorded anxiously that he was consorting with nationalist revolutionaries, among them some who became India's founding fathers, including Gandhi's colleague Gopal Krishna Gokhale.[1379] Sylvia met many of the Indian activists who visited Hardie at Nevill's Court and followed Gandhi's work from the beginning. She consistently criticized the Labour Party for not standing up strongly enough for Indian independence, just as Keir Hardie had done before her.

Rajani Palme Dutt, a founding member of the Communist Party of Great Britain, wrote for the *Workers' Dreadnought* from 1917 to 1921. She knew also his brother Clemens, equally involved in the Communist Party. She met Dhanvanthi Rama Rau when she moved to England in 1929, and through her encountered others in the London-based Women's Indian Association, including the Bengal-born independence activist, poet and women's rights campaigner Sarojini Naidu, who studied at Girton College, Cambridge.

Hardie's criticism of British policy in India had earned him as many enemies as his radical socialism. Long before his first visit to the subcontinent, he regularly denounced Indian poverty and low wages and the refusal of the British to give Indian people any say in their own government.[1380] 'The sooner the people of India controlled their own affairs the better.'[1381] He lambasted the educated English classes for wanting to keep India as a gravy-train employer for their own sons. On his political tour of India in 1907 he declared that the country should be as free as Canada to determine its own national life, pointing to racism as the cause of the difference between the governance of the two colonies. He supported 'agitation though not violence', and promised to relay Indian demands to MPs in Britain.[1382] On his return to the UK in 1907, Hardie intensified his attack on conditions under British imperial rule, and never let up from applying pressure in parliament on the issue for the rest of his life. His shilling pamphlet *India: Impressions and Suggestions*, published in 1909, 'outlined what was to be the Left's position on India for the next fifty years'.[1383] He vehemently denounced the brutal British repression of Indian nationalists. Famously, he sent a telegram from Bengal stating that India was 'at the mercy of the corruptest police in the world'.[1384]

While Sylvia busied herself writing about communism and anti-imperialism, Christabel sold highly successful religious books in America, launching her second career as a Second Adventist preacher and writer. In the 1918 general election, Christabel had attempted to enter parliament as the Women's Party 'Patriotic Candidate for Smethwick and Supporter of the Coalition'. The Women's Party candidates were supported by the alliance of the Conservative Party and the David Lloyd George-led coalition faction of the Liberal Party. Christabel labelled her Labour opponent, the experienced trade unionist John Emanuel Davison, and his supporters Bolsheviks, and told voters, as did many other Conservative candidates in the election, that they had to choose between the Red Flag and the Union Jack.[1385] Christabel failed to win the seat, and it was at this point that she turned away definitively from politics to religion and became a Second Adventist.

Emmeline had accepted a lecturing job from the Canadian National Council for Combating Venereal Diseases, and moved to Vancouver Island to take up the position. In 1923 she became a Canadian citizen, though she remained a largely itinerant lecturer, touring mainly in North America. In the spring of 1924 she moved to the British colony of Bermuda, with the children and their nurse-governess Mrs Jean Cookson, where she stayed for about a year. Emmeline hoped the warm and balmy climate would restore her failing health. Christabel moved with her, but, now chief breadwinner for the family, was often away from their shared home, preaching on the mainland.[1386]

By the spring of 1925, financial problems were pressing again. Christabel once more tried her hand at writing popular journalism for the British press. Emmeline came up with the idea that they could open a new family business on the Mediterranean coast, to be nearer England. In June 1925 they docked in Avonmouth, near Bristol, and then travelled to Paris. By August they were in Nice, where the children were delighted to be swimming in the sea, and by September they had settled on Juan-les-Pins in Antibes.[1387] At Christmas, Emmeline, Christabel and the children returned to England after the failed tea-shop enterprise. A year later Emmeline published an article in the *Evening News*, 'Women Can Defeat the Reds!',[1388] while her recalcitrant middle daughter sat up all night drafting her new book 'In the Red Twilight' in her Red Cottage in Essex.

On 2 October 1926, the Toronto *Daily Star* published 'Trio of Pankhursts Far Apart in Ideals', with the sub title 'Mrs Pankhurst Against Communism, Sylvia Teaches It, Christabel Very Religious':

> Mrs Emmeline Pankhurst and her two daughters have been given the title of England's most remarkable family trio. Mother and daughters all sit down at the same tea table, now and then, but their interests in life, and their aims, politically and religiously, and their methods of bringing about their respective reforms designed to regenerate society, are as far apart as the poles ... they never discuss politics or religion over the teacups. Mrs Pankhurst ... has taken up cudgels against Communism, while her daughter, Sylvia, goes on more energetically than ever, advocating the teachings of Lenin. Miss Christabel ... is tremendously interested in religion. She loathes politics. Mrs Pankhurst herself has joined the Conservative Party and for weeks has been addressing meetings in her endeavor to rouse the British women voters against Communism and all its works.[1389]

Life had been easier for Sylvia when they had the Atlantic between them. In the autumn of 1926 Emmeline accepted the invitation from the Conservative Party to stand as their candidate for Whitechapel – of all unlikely constituencies.

Reputedly Sylvia wept when she heard the news. Her sister was a born-again Christian and her mother a born-again Conservative.

She wrote to *Forward*, the socialist journal, a letter that subsequently appeared summarized in most of the national dailies.

> Permit me, through your columns, to express my profound grief
> that my mother should have deserted the cause of progress ...
> For my part I rejoice in having enlisted for life in the socialist
> movement, in which the work of Owen, Marx, Kropotkin, William
> Morris and Keir Hardie, and such pioneering efforts as those of my
> father, Richard Marsden Pankhurst, both before and during the
> rise of the movement in this country, are an enduring memory. It is
> naturally most painful for me to write this, but I feel it incumbent
> upon me, in view of this defection, to reaffirm my faith in the cause
> of social and international fraternity, and to utter a word of sorrow
> that one who in the past has rendered such service should now, with
> that sad pessimism which sometimes comes with advancing years,
> and may result from too strenuous effort, join the reaction ...[1390]

In 1933 Adela wrote of her sister, 'Readers should understand that in Sylvia's eyes to cease to be a socialist, if one had ever been one, is a moral crime.'[1391] This assertion excises the fact that their mother and Christabel had politically excommunicated Sylvia not just once, but twice, and taken the trouble to publish her banishment in the national press. They had also publicly disowned her as a 'Pankhurst', and later Christabel had even demanded that Sylvia desist from allowing her son Richard the right of using his family name.

By the autumn of 1927, Emmeline was living in London with her sister Ada Goulden Bach at Gloucester Street in SW1, 'close to Eccleston and Warwick Square and what is called Pimlico or if one is snobbish South Belgravia. I get down to Whitechapel in half the time and Westminster in a few minutes.'[1392] Emmeline deserves empathy. She campaigned hard for the Whitechapel seat. At best, the Tories merely tolerated her for her potential public image and conservative women's vote-catching value, but kept her always firmly at social arm's length from the party. The carless, propertyless Mancunian Mrs Pankhurst was patronized from the lofty heights of their propertied, car-owning, privately educated elite lives and their landed family connections. As her secretary Nellie Hall-Humpherson put it, she was 'badly treated' by the Conservative Party, 'like a poor and unwanted step-relation'.[1393]

Christabel brought a Pomeranian dog round to Pimlico as a seasonal gift for her mother. On Christmas Eve, it fell ill and died. A grim augur. Nellie missed her Christmas dinner with her husband as a result of wandering around with the dog's corpse looking for somewhere to bury it on Christmas Day.[1394] Emmeline's health that winter was poor. The London pea-souper fogs got to her, and her eating was irregular.

Emmeline's frailty made her friends unwilling to break the news to her that Sylvia had delivered an appropriate seasonal blessing. On 3 December Sylvia gave birth in a nursing home to her first and only child. She named him for her father, Keir Hardie and Emmeline Pethick-Lawrence: Richard Keir Pethick Pankhurst. Aged forty-five, Sylvia's own solution to resisting 'that sad pessimism which sometimes comes with advancing years' was to become a mother.

30

Free Love

Charlotte Drake offered to assist Sylvia with a home birth, but Emmeline Pethick-Lawrence and Lady Sybil Smith, thinking this unsafe, intervened and booked her into the Fitzjohn's Avenue nursing home in Hampstead and insisted on paying the bill. Sylvia wrote instantly to Norah after Richard was born, 'Yes, dear friend, he is a fine, healthy, beautiful child, perfect in every way and yet I am told that if I had not come here when I did I should not have brought him out alive.'[1395] In the new year, Emmeline Pethick-Lawrence invited Sylvia to bring her baby and convalesce with her and Fred at their home. Sylvia told them that her experience had brought home to her more urgently than ever before the need for a state-funded national public maternity service in Britain.

Shortly after Richard's birth a misunderstanding over money occurred between Sylvia and Emmeline. Before she went into the nursing home, Sylvia had taken a loan from her ever generous friend to pay for the costs of Silvio building for her an office and writing shed in the garden of Red Cottage. As chief breadwinner, Sylvia's best option was to support her family by means of her pen.

Inevitably, Silvio overspent on the building work and alarmed Emmeline with anxious requests for more cash that were unaccounted for. Sylvia, 'in the dark' about this until she returned home with Richard, and aghast at the miscalculation and the demands made on Emmeline, wrote to apologize to her old friend in the most plaintive and abject terms.[1396] Her papers contain many successive redrafts of the letter. 'Dearest Emmeline, I keep trying to write to you. I feel so miserable that it should be so and above all that you should think I have deceived you.' 'I keep trying to write to you and beginning again. I am so miserable that you should feel you do not love and trust me any more. It is only Richard beside me gives me the heart to try to make you see it a little less hardly.'[1397] Emmeline seemed satisfied by her explanation and what she recognized as the most heartfelt terms of regret Sylvia had ever expressed. Always the pragmatist, Emmeline empathized with Sylvia's situation. In due course, the two once again worked together closely. Regular gifts for Richard and consistent interest in his development continued throughout his childhood. When not exchanging frequent missives about his health, teething and schooling, the women could frequently be spotted together protesting outside parliament against Mussolini's fascism and settler colonialism.

Sylvia wrote to her mother immediately to tell her the news of baby Richard's arrival. However, when the letter arrived at Gloucester Street Ada Pankhurst made sure her sister never saw it. She sifted the post, removed the envelope addressed in her niece's handwriting and told the mystified Nellie, who usually took Emmeline's correspondence to her, to keep quiet about it.[1398] Emmeline knew the baby was due around Christmas. During her pregnancy, Sylvia tried several times to visit her mother, but when the pregnant Sylvia arrived at the house, Emmeline refused to see her. According to Mrs Pankhurst's foster-child Mary Gordon, her mother locked herself in her bedroom 'like a sulky girl and refused to see Auntie Sylvia when that scarlet woman dared to call'.[1399] Gossip maintained that Christabel barred the front door and refused Sylvia entry to the house, although several family members and friends corroborated Mary Gordon's version.[1400]

Ethel Smyth wrote in her memoirs about the amity between Emmeline and Christabel who 'worked perfectly together, being, as Mrs Pankhurst often said, different sides of the same medal'.[1401] While they were, according to Smyth, the ideal combination as members of the same family, the relationship between Emmeline and Sylvia was all discordance and disharmony.[1402] Presenting her version of the events at the end of Mrs Pankhurst's life, Ethel Smyth wrote:

> It may as well be stated … that … Mrs Pankhurst, once a member
> of the ILP, came to feel something like horror of the Labour Party,

whereas Sylvia was one of their warmest adherents. The perhaps inevitable alienation between mother and daughter was fated to culminate in a tragic and sinister episode during the tragic last weeks of the former's life.[1403]

Emmeline made no attempt herself to contact Sylvia or to meet her new grandson. As long as the public remained unaware of the story, Mrs Pankhurst could also ignore it.

On 29 March 1928 she sat in the Ladies' Gallery as parliament passed the second reading of the Representation of the People (Equal Franchise) Bill. By allowing all women to vote from the age of twenty-one, the bill added another five and a half million female voters to the existing nine million. In the upcoming election, women would be the majority of the electorate for the first time. Emmeline had made the decision to go and live in Whitechapel. The commute from the West End tired her out, particularly as she refused to use the London Underground, even where the trains ran overground. And and to win the Whitechapel seat, she knew it was really necessary to be a resident of the constituency.[1404] As Emmeline packed up and moved into her new rooms at 9 High Street, Wapping, the news of what she regarded as a shameful family secret hit the national headlines.

That evening, Mrs Pankhurst was scheduled to chair a meeting for her fellow Conservative candidate Commander Lindsay Venn. He received an advanced briefing that he would be asked questions about whether it was true that one of Mrs Pankhurst's unmarried daughters had recently given birth to an illegitimate baby of dubious paternity. Venn warned Emmeline what to expect, and when the question was put to her in the meeting, she replied curtly that she did not discuss private matters in public.

A few days later on Easter Sunday 8 April, Emmeline attended church with her old friends Kitty and Alfred Marshall. The same morning the *News of the World* ran a sensational front-page Sunday special feature, 'EUGENIC BABY SENSATION. SYLVIA PANKHURST'S AMAZING CONFESSION', accompanied by a large portrait photograph of a beaming Sylvia cheek to cheek with adorable baby Richard cuddled in her arms.

Like her mother and elder sister, Sylvia did not discuss private matters in public. However, unlike her mother, she did not regard the birth of her love child as a private matter. 'I opened my eyes, and I saw that my youth was fled. Then I said: it is time that I should have a child of my own, in whom I shall live again,' she wrote of her unconventional, risky decision to have her first child at the age of forty-five.[1405] Sylvia's joyous public celebration of her new maternal mission, a form of midlife resurrection, was for her own mother a mortifying public social crucifixion. It was said that Emmeline never again spoke in public.

The *News of the World* had bought 'Sylvia's amazing confession' from the American press who published the interview the previous day. 'Miss Pankhurst' espoused 'marriage without a legal union', and had given her son her own surname, not that of his father, a fifty-three-year-old 'foreigner'. (Silvio was fifty-two.) She regarded her son as a 'eugenic' baby since both his parents were intelligent, healthy people. She could not understand why her mother and family ignored her. If Emmeline read the article, she might have been surprised by Sylvia's statement that she had written a letter to her mother about the birth of her child but had received no reply. This was the letter Ada Pankhurst had stolen from Emmeline's letter tray and bullied Nellie to keep quiet about.

During the 1920s and 1930s, eugenic ideas enjoyed common currency and wide debate in Britain. 'This was,' writes Clare Hanson, 'a period of optimism and intense speculation in relation to the transformative possibilities of science'.[1406] Popular texts written for the 'intelligent layman' were published in relatively cheap format in the 'Today and Tomorrow' and the 'Thinker's Library' series. J. B. S. Haldane, Ronald Mache and Garet Garrett featured among those writing for a general readership about advances in biological science, and about the extension of knowledge and control over the human body. These writers examined what they called the 'eugenic problematic', offering perspectives ranging from keen support to qualified and considerate criticism.[1407]

Before the First World War, eugenic thought had already made its way into medico-social texts increasingly preoccupied with public health issues, and gained greater traction after the war, which dramatically highlighted the great chasm in health and education between working-, middle- and upper-class Britons.

Sylvia's 'confession', circulated widely in the world media, used popular eugenic terminology to bolster her choice in favour of 'voluntary motherhood', the concept of the individual woman's rights over her body, birth control and fertility: 'I wanted a baby, as every complete human being desires parenthood, to love him and cherish him, to see him grow and develop and to leave behind me a being who will, I hope, carry on the best that is in me and my stock.'

Many radical feminists and free lovers of her generation used the concept of voluntary motherhood to distinguish from 'enforced motherhood', patriarchy's vital weapon and 'the chief cause of the degradation that gives birth to human woe'.[1408] Sylvia's mentor Harriot Stanton Blatch wrote a renowned paper on 'Voluntary Motherhood' in 1891, supporting the individual human rights of women to choose and placing women's control over reproduction in a wider social and economic context. She argued that women should have the right of control over conception and child-rearing, access to good education and the means of working for financial independence.

Sylvia's closest friends and feminist network were some of the leading birth-control and safe-abortion campaigners on both sides of the Atlantic, such as Margaret Sanger, Marie Stopes, Dora Russell, Emma Goldman, Crystal Eastman and Alexandra Kollontai. Arguments about birth control and eugenics rumbled through the socialist and feminist movements during Sylvia's youth in the 1890s and onwards. The neo-Malthusian social case for limiting population as a means of reducing world poverty and misery always and inevitably bumped up against the case for individual human rights and objections to statist social engineering.

The British scientist and geographer Francis Galton coined the term 'eugenics' in 1883 to describe the study of selective breeding. Galton's first cousin Charles Darwin had produced a scientific evolutionary theory of the competitive struggle for survival in the natural world. Galton's aim was to produce a social theory that complemented natural selection, designed to show that a better future could be secured for all and social problems solved by engineering reproduction to produce 'better' people. Cultural eugenics pitched itself against the fear of increasing democratization in a period when working-class people – the so-called masses – were pressing for change in the organization of production. From the off, eugenics was always a positive–negative: to encourage the 'best' traits in people to reproduce a better human race while constraining those deemed to be 'unfit' from reproducing: 'The loaded question was, of course, who decided who was "fit" and who was "unfit".'[1409]

Birth-control activists of the late nineteenth and early twentieth centuries grappled not only with resistance within the labour and progressive movements but with censorship, harassment, arrest and prison sentences. Anti-socialist feminists harangued and undermined their socialist feminist sisters for dragging sex into politics, accusing them of factionalism that would split progressive parties and the labour movement.[1410] In Britain, Labour Party women voted over and over again at the annual Women's Conference for birth-control advice to be made legal in welfare centres, and were repeatedly defeated at main conference. Ramsay MacDonald insisted that birth control was a private, not a political, issue and successive Labour leaders, aware of their dependence on a strong Catholic vote.[1411]

Sylvia's matriarchal fetishizing of motherhood is as distasteful to the modern ear as the language of eugenics, but in the context of the times, defending the right to be an unmarried mother at forty-five and celebrate maternity as a positive choice would have been heard and understood differently. Marie Stopes both saved and changed the lives of millions of women, children and men. Her 1918 bestseller *Married Love*, its sales outstripping mass popular fiction of the era, was a mere fraction of her work – activist graft, relentless campaigning, from organized teatime talks on married love to her 'Mothers' Clinics' that provided free contraceptive advice and help for all women, especially working-class women. (Stopes would later be condemned for backing neo-Malthusian eugenics.) Lynn Segal offers a cogent historical analysis of what the work of these birth-control campaigners meant in a historical context, as the originators of the radical idea that the female body was political: 'it was the maternalist, utopian thinking of these radical women from the 1920s that led to the eventually successful campaigns for public provision of birth control and state endowment for motherhood – though these have been contested ever since'.[1412]

Invited to 'discuss eugenics', Sylvia responded,

'You ask if my baby boy is eugenic,' she said. 'It is good eugenics,
I believe if one desires parenthood, to consider if one is of sufficient
general intelligence, bodily health and strength, and freedom
from hereditary diseases to produce AN INTELLIGENT AND

HEALTHY CHILD. I believe that of myself, I believe that, also, of my baby's father. Indeed, I consider my "husband" has many gifts with which to endow our child.'[1413]

Her use of the language of popular eugenics put Sylvia in company with a diversity of leading lights of the time, when the appeal of eugenics reached across all parts of the political spectrum – Winston Churchill, Teddy Roosevelt, Shaw, H. G. Wells, Beatrice and Sidney Webb, Helen Keller, Francis Crick, to name but a few. Social reformers and progressives adopted it in the US, and the Fabians in Britain, 'who believed in the need for evolutionary change, but feared class conflict'.[1414] It found simultaneous favour with imperialists concerned to strengthen the white British race, and with those anxious about racial 'dilution' and 'swamping' caused by the migration of workers. Eugenics could equally be embraced as a positive force by feminists and socialists fighting for the rights of mothers, and birth controllers and advocates of free love.[1415] What differentiated Sylvia and other feminists was that they considered eugenics a potential weapon to help women exercise choice, rejecting involuntary motherhood and, even more radically, organizing 'birth strikes' in order to release women from the burden of physical reproduction and enable them to flood the ranks of competitive labour in all industries and professions.

Sylvia's complete and unpublished three-act play 'The Rectegenetic Child' has the subtitle 'A Study in Matrimonial Futurism'.[1416] It is dramatically one of the most successfully achieved of her plays, and explores the impact of the pioneering futuristic science of artificial insemination on the relationship of a Manchester couple, Mary and Edward, desperate for a child. Mary's sister has given her a book in which, 'only in a footnote … it said in America … they … some people have … that a doctor could … by injecting'.

Edward understands and shares Mary's intense desire for a child and the pain of her disappointment at their inability to produce one. He offers to do anything and everything possible, but is utterly appalled by the eugenic idea of experimenting with artificial insemination, the 'abominable proposal to experiment with injecting the semen taken from another man – or some chemical preparation? in the one case odious; in the other utterly fantastic. No good can come of it … I don't like the idea of experimenting in such matters.'

The play sets up Mary's baby hunger against Edward's immovable resistance to non-traditional biogenetic interference, despite his shared desire for a child. He vehemently opposes eugenics and thinks if conception is going to happen at all, it must be 'naturally'.

Housekeeper Mrs Jackson and Nurse Smith discuss how Mary's 'craving for motherhood' is 'a disease with her'. 'She does take on about it, poor dear!' exclaims Mrs Jackson. 'My word, she doesn't know the troubles she's been spared!' Nurse Smith reflects in detail on the phantom pregnancy of one of her patients. Here Sylvia was writing from experience – she had endured a phantom pregnancy in the year before she conceived Richard. Nurse Smith picks up a printed circular left in a bowl by Mary:

> It's about having babies! [Reading] Rectegenesis. I wonder if that means through the rectum?
> *Mrs Jackson:* What, up the back?

Their comic ribaldry turns to serious investigation of the article,

> *Nurse Smith:* Oh, I see; it's a vaginal chemical process ...
> 'Rectegenesis, from <u>Recte</u> = rightly and Genesis = Creation. That is to say rectification of the failures of nature in the sphere of reproduction. Professor Solon I. Kindermacher has triumphantly succeeded in bringing Science to the assistance of Nature, in order that children shall be well born, and that the natural and praiseworthy desire of childless couples for parenthood shall be satisfied.' Science coming to the aid of nature, you see, Mrs Jackson.

And this is the subject of Sylvia's play – science coming to the aid of nature, probing the ethics of birth control, artificial insemination and the feminist question of the rights of women over their bodies. There are no easy answers. Mrs Jackson is convinced no right-thinking woman would go for such crazy eugenic solutions. Nurse Smith strongly disagrees: 'I believe that crowds of people will go for it.'

With reluctance, Edward consents to their trying the experimental treatment, though struggling with the idea that the process constitutes bringing 'rank adultery' into their marriage, since the semen comes from another man. This he discusses with his cousin Siegfried, fifteen years his junior, visiting from London, and so breaks his promise to Mary to keep the matter their secret. Meanwhile, Mary, elated, heads to London to visit the specialist for the treatment. Siegfried comes to visit her at her hotel and argues with her about the dangers of submitting herself to 'this quackery', saying he is sure Dr Kindermacher is a fraud and bullying her into anxiety and uncertainty about her decision. He accuses Edward of being a dog in a manger for taking her youth hostage. Siegfried suggests an alternative method to the now distraught Mary: 'You only need a decent normal man to father it, some one you could be fond of ...' Rising and turning off the electric light, he declares, 'Woman! Let there be love! Let there be ardour!'

The third act opens five years later, with Siegfried visiting Manchester for the first time since his return from India. In the now happy home he is introduced to Mary and Edward's 'strong, intelligent, sweet-natured' little boy Harry, 'all that a mother's heart could desire!' But while Siegfried is staying with them, Edward is devastated to discover that the up-until-now apparently angelic Harry has been begging money from servants and neighbours. This, he confides despairingly to Siegfried, proves his belief that the sperm donor was a 'degenerate', probably a convict. 'The low traits have appeared all too soon, Sig. It is the first downward step. The boy will become a wastrel and a criminal in the end.' Siegfried has to set him right. As he is about to do so, Edward is distracted by the headlines of his newly delivered newspaper lying on the table:

Edward: Good God Sig! 'The blow has fallen! The imposture is revealed!'

 Sig: What?

 Edward: You can read the thing for yourself. [Taps the paper, which he holds at arm's length, reading the headlines] 'THE ARTIFICIAL PRODUCTION OF CHILDREN FRAUD. RECTEGENETIC PROFESSOR EXPOSED! ARREST OF SOLON I. KINDERMACHER! DECEIVED HUSBANDS' CHARGES! WIVES COMPLAIN OF RAPE!'

 My wife has done this!

Professor Kindermacher has been inseminating his 'patients' by the most conventional sexual method and blackmailing the desperate women to keep their silence. The revelation leads Edward to believe that Kindermacher forced himself on Mary, until she tells him that she never attended the scheduled appointment with Kindermacher in London, and that Siegfried is in fact Harry's father. Mary argues with Edward and Siegfried, defending her choice to have a child and asserting Harry's right to have two fathers, thus demonstrating that Sylvia took a far from simple and straightforward view of the science of eugenics and reproductive rights. Through Monica, Mary's sister, the whole is interlocked with an exploration of 'the logical development of the striving towards sexual freedom expressed by Bernard Shaw, Meredith, Thomas Hardy and all the great novelists of the last generation. William Morris was the only one who dared to be logical, in my opinion ...' The play closes with little Harry rushing to Mary and leaping into her embrace. She hoists him on to her shoulders, exclaiming, 'They are both your fathers! Tell them that we are love, and life and joy!'

Sylvia's neatly typed and signed manuscript of 'The Rectegenetic Child' is undated, but sits in the archive amid a body of unpublished plays, draft novels and short stories produced after Richard's birth, and the manuscript for her published programme for maternal health.

In maternal health, particular interest focused on the class differentials in the birth rates between working women and constrained or idle middle-class women. Statistics consistently suggested more successful birth rates and lower maternal mortality rates for hospital and clinic births. Home births, for women of all classes, demonstrated a much lower success rate and far higher risks of complicated labour, birth injuries and risk of mortality. Two years after her sensational interview in the *News of the World* Sylvia published a pioneering book on childbirth and maternity written from a thoroughly anti-eugenicist position. Informed and – as ever – driven by her own experience, Sylvia published her polemic on maternity, *Save the Mothers*, in 1930. Her argument is that all women, regardless of class, are vulnerable. Rich, elite, middle-class women forced into unsupported, unhygienic home births suffer unnecessary mortality in equality of suffering with crushingly poor women giving birth in unimaginable conditions. There is no trace of the 'degeneracy' of the poor or genetically undeserving in this superb tract on the urgent need for state-provided modern maternity services for all women, rich and poor. In all her writing on maternity and feminism, Sylvia stressed that ability and character are not a matter of class and that difference comes from the unjust economic and social inequalities resulting from wealth for a minority and poverty for the majority.

In *Save the Mothers* Sylvia contested the then popular view that the so-called hospital classes received better maternity provision than wealthy elites. She argued that only those who had access to private healthcare could be assured of receiving appropriate, safe maternity treatment based on the latest modern science. Her treatise on maternity and mortality rates makes the case for national state provision for the very best maternity services to be made available to all women in public hospitals. Based on wide evidential statistical surveys, empirical medical data and the latest medical science research from around the world, *Save the Mothers* presents the very antithesis of a platform for eugenic theories. Sylvia's very uneugenicist argument is that neither class nor reproductive 'stock' will have any bearing on successful childbirth or the life chances of the child. Every mother-to-be, she proposes, should have access to first-class treatment and maternal healthcare at the point of childbirth.

At forty-five, it was inevitable that Sylvia experienced a challenging pregnancy in the 1920s. Her age and medical history combined to make it hard. The experience of being physically slowed down shocked and horrified her. The term 'elderly primagravida' applied to women of thirty-five and over pregnant for the first time. Given her health challenges, including long-term endometriosis, her successful midlife pregnancy quite rightly made Richard's advent all the more wonderful to her.

Aside from her sensational tabloid article, there's no evidence elsewhere of Sylvia pursuing any systematic enquiry into eugenics beyond its topicality as a popular form of social-scientific improvement with the potential to tackle economic and educational inequalities. Her ideas of upliftment, common at the time among idealists including socialists, focused on policies of intervention and social engineering: everyone – by which Sylvia meant the working masses – should have access to the better healthcare, nutrition, education, housing and culture that the elites had by accident of birth enjoyed from time immemorial.

The upper and middle classes were, in Sylvia's eyes, 'socially en-gineered' by the manipulation of resources and power to favour a minority, not a 'naturally' superior breed, or 'stock'. It was a reactionary truism of the time that the ancestrally highborn and moneyed ran the world by the birthright of natural superiority rather than the accident of birth that bestowed upon them privileges of education, security and ready-made position in the world.

In her *News of the World* interview. Sylvia launched a defensive attack on the notion that moral and social soundness are provided only by the institution of marriage. In place of convention, she offers the example of people choosing to reproduce without the sanction of matrimony as a reasonable choice. In the glare of the international media, she is shadow-boxing with her mother. Emmeline shunned Sylvia and her new grandson, sorrowfully acting out the role of being the victim of a great public disgrace. Yet as a young mother herself Emmeline had both privately and very publicly supported women friends whose circumstances were regarded as beyond the pale: single mothers, divorcees, lovers caught in adultery scandals.

Mrs Pankhurst's first proper campaign had been to look after the interests of illegitimate, orphaned and discarded children. All of this Sylvia remembered from her childhood. And yet here was her own mother treating her in the most conventional way as if she were a social degenerate and an embarrassment to the Pankhurst family.

All the elements of Sylvia's story contradict the fundamental precepts of 'positive' eugenic propaganda. She is much too old to be responsibly reproducing. She is unmarried. The refugee immigrant foreigner father of her bastard child, old, short and broke, is in eugenicist terms a catastrophic choice. The mischief of Sylvia's tabloid confession lies in her opportunistic use of eugenic tropes as a way to fight with her mother. The fact that she is deeply hurt and over-sensitive about Emmeline's reaction to her love child is no excuse: it is an explanation.

It's curious and interesting that Sylvia's first public act in her maternal voice is notably also the first inauthentic media intervention of her career. There was a professional motivation: motherhood was expensive. Corio was loving and supportive, but earned little money. Sylvia needed to drum up some publicity for the Sylvia Pankhurst brand – or rebrand. The American interview about Richard's birth paid a handsome fee in much-needed money and put her back in international public view. This supported a platform of new writing projects on feminist subjects.

In the 1920s, Richard's illegitimacy and mixed ancestry meant something. By the prejudices of the day, his father was a foreigner. So it's testimony to Sylvia's powers of propaganda that the media attention and fan mail and the equal measure of social opprobrium and hate mail focused on her actions and choices as a woman, and rarely on the nationality or economic penury of her partner.

In an interview with *Reynolds's Illustrated News* after Richard's birth, Sylvia responded to questions about her unmarried status and the controversy surrounding it:

> My son is the child of a happy union of affection and long
> friendship of two people who care for each other. His father is not
> a wealthy man but he is a man of fine character. I do not believe it
> is eugenic or fair to children that they should be brought into the
> world except as a natural result of affection between their parents.
> I do not seek publicity but want to share the joys of motherhood
> with my darling.[1417]

Sylvia's public announcement attracted widespread publicity at home and abroad. When Annie Barnes' father read the feature in the *News of the World*, he travelled immediately all night to fetch his daughter home to Wales, 'as we wasn't having her work for that kind of woman'.[1418] The bulging mailbags of letters Sylvia received took a very different view to that of the outraged Mr Barnes. This fan mail must have buoyed Sylvia and Corio up, compensating for her mother's excommunication.

The torrent of letters, many of them running to great length, offers the testimony of many lives, poignant love stories and personal tragedies. Mostly from women, the correspondence focuses on marriage, the difficulty of divorce, domestic abuse, the struggle for free love and notions of free union. Putting aside a few from oddball male 'medics' of questionable qualification, interested priests and pseudo-social theorists, the letters notably demonstrate no interest at all in the eugenics aspect of her story.[1419]

Helen Craggs, now Mrs McCombie, and 'completely buried' with her two small children, 'being without a maid', wrote to congratulate Sylvia warmly and 'with very much love' on Richard's birth and hoping they might reconnect, though she expects 'the small lad is an occupation in himself'.

Elsy Jackson wrote from Chalfont St Peter in Buckinghamshire after reading Sylvia's Sunday 'confession':

> your romance is beautiful in my opinion and I wish to congratulate you – my ideas on marriage are the same as yours. Why should a few words out of a book read by a parson (who is only a man) make a difference to a union between two people – and yet convention steps in and prevents them living together unless they are 'joined together' by God in a church or registry office. To my way of thinking – if there is a mutual love and understanding that is the bond of Him. I have always had free ideas of thinking on this subject, and am now the age of 32, but still very young in my looks and ways ...

Elsy confessed, 'at present I live rather a lonely life – too much so', alone with her mother, as her father deserted them twenty years previously. Elsy tells Sylvia that her mother is 'just the same as myself' having missed many an offer for the sake of living 'a clean respectable life' and 'kept up appearances etc'. But why, she asks, continue? They are both fed up and ready to ignore scandal: 'one gets hopelessly bored to death with ordinary things – and longs'. Elsy doesn't envy her married friends their routine, or husbands who 'seek single girls company' – 'and why?!' Elsy apologizes for expressing herself poorly, 'but I am very pleased and interested with your story, perhaps you will understand a little what type of girl I am – not', she heavily underlines for emphasis, '*stodgy* – and how I feel – I simply love men's company. Elsy M. Jackson.'

From Cheadle Hulme, Stockport, Mrs Campbell wrote 'in all admiration' to 'congratulate your son on having chosen you his mother a woman of such grand courage. A few more women like you and there will be some hopes of a more reasonable and cleaner minded attitude towards the whole business of sex, marriage and parenthood generally.'

'A Woman (Who lives on the Earth, but not in the Clouds)', wrote to congratulate Sylvia on her bravery in facing the world alone: 'We each of us have our own views and ideas of life as it is and as it should be, but we are not ready enough to give them voice. God made Nature with all its wonderful secrets. Man made *wars* with all its Horrors, and after effects. And I believe it is the women that will eventually straighten out the tangle by standing by their ideas of right and wrong.' This letter was in response to a piece attacking Sylvia in the press on 'moral, legal, and religious' grounds. A Woman lambasts the hypocrisy of Church and law that marry and divorce people yet draw distinctions between the children of divorced couples and unmarrieds who, like her, live together with their children. And why, she asks, should divorced and remarried couples regard themselves as superior to never-marrieds?

> Dear Miss Pankhurst,
>   Do please give the smug dear a dressing down, and so, starting a little bit of soul searching all around. We talk of the Heathen with their customs but really are we any better. There are millions spent destroying life, with nothing left to preserve life. Silly vain existence … its nearly time some of the smug conceited people were knocked off their perch with their ideas they found in the ark. So I do hope you will be able to help lots of the 'Other Woman' which in my opinion are often far better women than the legal wife.

Confidential letters from married women in abusive relationships appear all too frequently. Testimony from cowering, terrified wives writing of 'unprincipled, unfaithful, brutal husbands', including 'men who would be known to you in public life', expressing the impossibility of escape or of being able to talk about the 'unspeakable torture' of 'suffering physically', and speculating on whether they might reveal their identities to her. Other women write to Sylvia about their alcoholic husbands, or men from whom they'd divorced and refused to take any financial support for themselves or their children, as they did not think anything was due to them or thought it wrong to take without giving anything in return. Sylvia and her secretary Nellie Rathbone acknowledged as many of these letters as they could, and where necessary offered advice or recommended confidential contacts who might be able to help.

On Easter Tuesday, from Harley Street an admirer wrote as a 'representative of all the other mediocrities' who long for 'organisation, co-operation and guidance for the thousands of women who will not dare to follow without this help', who long for leadership in organizing 'a new institution that will supplant legalised marriage'. There are not

enough role models, this correspondent wrote, to show young women –
including feminist women – alternatives to the conventions of marriage
and childbirth within it, 'we must grow a new Type!' It's unlikely, she
mused, that a 'man's mind is going to think out the new conditions
for us, they must come out of ourselves. And who is going to do it? Is,
perhaps, the greatest of all needs that of raising the general standard of
ideals until, instead of talking of the "woman" question, the world will
include us in the HUMAN question?'

Editor Will Cullen sent a request to Sylvia asking her to write an
article for the *East London Advertiser* explaining herself 'more fully, why
you of all women, should advocate marriage, without a legal bond'.
Her 'remarkable policy' is 'one I consider most impracticable, from the
working class point of view'.

Cullen's objection is that the working-class majority has no recourse
to the divorce court or means to access it, and marriage is essential for
protecting 'the upkeep of the child'. He tried to engage Sylvia in an
important discussion on how men can be compelled to accept responsibility
for women and children. Sylvia agreed with some of his substantive points,
but disliked his hectoring tone, and annotated the letter, 'Am not prepared
to write for his rag. NO time – please ignore this request.'

There were the usual letters from cranks and hobby-horsers, including
W. H. Baxter from Knapping Mount in Harrogate who sent her some
of his sex manuals on how to conceive 'following the law of animals'
and hoping that 'your child has been born in perfect purity as every
child has a perfect right to be born'. As a result of Mr Baxter's field
research, 'it has been my contention for over twenty years that when a
woman desired a child and did her duty at conception, that such child
would be a male ... no doubt your case confirms this opinion'.

Fred McGowan wrote cheerfully from his oil and hardware store
in Clapham, congratulating Sylvia on her 'courageous protest against
bourgeois marriage laws' and fully endorsing her actions. Though her
views 'do not quite tally with mine' the essence for Fred 'is that you
have rebelled – and rebels against the present marriage laws are badly
needed'. He optimistically concludes, 'I suspect that it will be found that
the ideal "sexual system" of the future ie. the one yielding the greatest
possible happiness to the greatest number of people (including posterity)
in sexual matters – will be no system at all,' and adds admiringly, 'Your
latest act has increased the debt which the people owe to you.'

Henry Neil sent salutations from Long Island, New York: 'Congratulations, You are a brave woman. Ten million people have just read the … announcement of your love child, most of them think that it is barbarous to compel a woman to sign away the ownership of her own children in a wedding contract in order to be a respectable mother.' Neil encloses a copy of his new novel, *All Things are Possible*, on this very subject. 'The winning character is a love baby who grows into a perfect woman. You will enjoy and agree with its every word.' He asks her to send 'a photo of yourself holding your baby'. Sylvia, eternally vigilant, notes that this is Judge Neil, 'who has done so much for Mothers' Pensions', and instructed Nellie Rathbone to send the requested photograph of her and Richard for him to use in his book. Others send her their poems about free love, or simple straightforwardly comradely congratulations.

As the letters of support poured in, Sylvia heard nothing from her mother. How painful this silence must have been for her. David Mitchell suggests that Emmeline felt 'as if a moral as well as a physical slum had opened to engulf her … It seemed as though Sylvia's conduct had been, not a matter of perverse principle, but a blow deliberately aimed at her: just as, to Sylvia, it seemed that Mrs Pankhurst's Whitechapel foray was a calculated personal affront.'[1420]

Christabel also interpreted Sylvia's actions as a personal attack. She repeatedly complained to friends that the newspaper headlines referring to 'Miss Pankhurst' caused her no end of embarrassment as she feared being mistaken for the subject of the scandal. 'That was the biggest blow I ever received and the repercussions have not really ceased,' she told Grace Roe over two decades later. 'The whole publicity was skilfully engineered to harm me.'[1421] [1422]

In Sylvia's biography of her mother, published in 1936, Sylvia wrote with sympathy and admiration about the difficult last year of Emmeline's life. There is not a whisper of her own hurt in this dispassionate account. 'Early in 1928,' she wrote, Mrs Pankhurst 'resolved to settle in her own constituency, an heroic step, for she was in need of the most solicitous care.'[1423] Sylvia wrote with compassion about the depth of Emmeline's sadness at having to part with her foster-child Mary, who could not come with her to Whitechapel. Her schooling was better served by allowing her to be looked after by her wealthier and better-placed ex-suffragette friends. 'The child's prospects and need of education had given her many an anxious hour' and though Mary was to be very well looked after in a good home, 'the wrench cut deeply'.[1424]

Sylvia describes Emmeline establishing herself that spring 'in her little lodging' in Whitechapel, 'Proudly and graciously, with that hard-held composure she knew so well to preserve'.[1425] Her mother felt 'suddenly homeless – a mere lodger. The sense of being needed and necessary fell away from her. The war was won, the vote was won. The Royal Assent to the last Act in securing complete political equality had been set. There was a loosening of her grasp on life, but she spurred herself to another effort.'[1426] 'If I could only get my strength back,' Emmeline kept saying, 'I know I've got five years of good work in me yet.'[1427]

Emmeline had been greatly cheered by a letter from Adela expressing tenderness and regret for the long rift between them. Adela's letter announced that she and her husband Tom had come round to her mother's point of view about the destructiveness of class conflict and were now promoting the message of industrial peace between employers and workers, encouraging them to forget the struggle of labour against capital and to act together for the common good. Emmeline replied immediately, with a letter of 'whole-hearted reconciliation'.[1428]

On 31 May 1928 Christabel and Emmeline's sister Ada arranged for her to leave the small airless room in Whitechapel and moved her to a nursing home in Hampstead. Several physicians tried to improve her condition, without success. Her relapse into her old conditions of jaundice, painful nausea and inability to digest food progressed to pneumonia and an undiagnosed stomach condition.

Emmeline asked if Christabel could fetch her old physician Dr Chetham Strode, who treated her after her hunger strikes (by pumping her stomach) and restored her to health after her prison sentences. She was then moved to a nursing home at 43 Wimpole Street, so that she could be within calling distance of where Dr Strode lived. By now Emmeline was so weak that only Christabel and a couple of old trusted friends were allowed to see her. She slipped into unconsciousness and, with Christabel at her side, died on Thursday 14 June, just one month before her seventieth birthday.

The final cause of death was registered as septicaemia due to influenza. Christabel wrote that Mrs Pankhurst died peacefully: 'My greatest comfort is the look of joy on her face that I saw when I went back into the room where we had watched beside her to the end ...

It seemed to fade afterwards and just peace and contentment and beauty were left – as I have never seen them on any other. But that first look of great joy I shall always have before me.'[1429] Christabel was now a conservative evangelical Adventist who had publicly proclaimed 'Christ as her Saviour ... her unquestioning faith in the accuracy of the Scriptures ... and her certain conviction of the coming again of Christ as the hope and solution to the world's problems'.[1430] Christabel was in no doubt that Mrs Pankhurst had departed for a better place.

No one reported or recorded Emmeline expressing the wish to see Sylvia in the final weeks of her life before she lost consciousness. Christabel refused Sylvia's repeated and increasingly desperate requests to be permitted to visit her.[1431] Cruelly, Ethel Smyth laid the blame for Emmeline's terminal decline and death at Sylvia's door. 'Mrs Pankhurst died of chagrin – of pain and horror at the disgrace brought on her name by that disgusting Bolshie daughter of hers.'[1432]

On Sunday Emmeline's body lay in state on a purple catafalque in Cambridge Place chapel in London's West End. Thousands of women came to pay their respects. A photograph taken outside the church shows dense crowds thronging to gain access, marshalled by police. In the foreground, a Goulden–Pankhurst family group stand for an awkward, unsettled portrait. At the centre, only Emmeline's sister Ada attempts to look at the camera. To her right, Christabel glances away distractedly. Standing between and behind them, Sylvia, puffy-faced, also looks away. Christabel stayed at Cambridge Place all that Sunday, returning several times to see her mother's body, as if, people said, she could not believe that she was really dead.

At the end of the day Mrs Pankhurst's coffin was taken to St John's Church, Smith Square, in Westminster, where four former suffragettes kept vigil throughout the night. The following day, 18 June, mourners lined the streets of west London to watch Mrs Pankhurst's funeral cortège pass on its way to Brompton Cemetery, a spectacle likened by the *Daily Mail* to 'a dead general in the midst of a mourning army'.[1433] The WSPU flag and Union Jack draped Mrs Pankhurst's coffin on its flower-covered bier. More than a thousand women wearing purple, green and white processed to the graveyard behind the chief mourners, led by Christabel and Sylvia.

At the open grave the sisters stood a little apart, Christabel supported by a group of her friends. Near Sylvia stood a cluster of her intimates, looking after baby Richard. The following year Christabel would visit Sylvia to ask that Richard should not carry the family surname, since people mistakenly believed the boy to be her own son. The ensuing row ended with Sylvia telling Christabel to stay out of her personal life, as she had out of hers.[1434]

Two years later, on 6 March 1930, the former Prime Minister Stanley Baldwin unveiled Mrs Pankhurst's statue in Victoria Tower Gardens, adjacent to the Houses of Parliament.[1435] There was no question of the statue of a woman being permitted in Parliament Square alongside the male national icons. Sylvia sat with her three-year-old toddler in the general audience. Snubbed, she had not been invited to join the official guest party, nor to speak, though she was the only one of the three Pankhurst sisters in Britain. Christabel, on a lecture tour of America, was unable to attend and Adela too far away in Australia to be able to afford the trip. The former suffragette Kitty Marshall deliberately excluded Sylvia from the planning and from the day's programme.

The Reverend Canon Woodward said prayers and led the hymn singing, Stanley Baldwin made a patronizing speech about Mrs Pankhurst having unquestionably won 'a niche in the Temple of Fame', and Fred Pethick-Lawrence, now a Labour MP, spoke more robustly about Emmeline's statue typifying 'for all time the revolt of womanhood' against outmoded, false patriarchal conceptions that women should be relegated to secondary status, and waste their lives merely as 'ministers to the happiness, the comforts, or the vices of man'. Emmeline's friends and suffragette veterans bedecked the statue with WSPU pennants, Sylvia's 'Suffragette prison medal', the portcullis and prison-arrow brooch, and wreaths. Listened to by millions on their home radios, the occasion was an early example of mass radio broadcasting of a public event.

Kitty Marshall's exclusion of Sylvia from the ceremonial of the day had the unintended effect of freeing up Sylvia's time to write extensively about her mother in the national and international press.

The day before the unveiling of Mrs Pankhurst's statue, Sylvia published an article in *The Star* entitled 'My Mother. Rebel to Reactionary'. A full-blooded portrait, the thickly descriptive essay ranges widely, reminding readers of her radical father, Mrs Pankhurst's husband, and of the extraordinary contribution of Emmeline and Fred

Pethick-Lawrence. Her mother's breach with them, she wrote, remains a 'matter of deep regret'. In summary, Sylvia wrote that her mother 'could do the outrageous thing without appearing outrageous, or losing her charm. A detective confided in after years to an ex-militant: "Mrs Pankhurst was my idea of a queen."' Sylvia reflected that her mother's interest in fashion and shopping, and her limited reading habits, 'mainly confined to novels', were 'surprising in one whose life was so largely given to public causes'. 'Her greatness', Sylvia concluded, 'was in her courage and devotion, indomitable and unflinching, deaf to all criticism, prepared to meet all hardships.' She considered the direction of her mother's later life: 'That she lost the reformer's quality in her declining years and grew as intolerant in her reaction as she had been stubborn in her pioneering, will not be recorded against her. That failing has been a common one amongst reformers.'[1436]

Sylvia produced a number of similar articles throughout the year, prompting Emmeline Pethick-Lawrence to write to her at Christmas, 'I wish *you* could have written your Mother's Life, because I feel that you would have made of it – a work of art. Her life and character present rare materials for a deep human story.'[1437] Christabel had announced several years previously that she was going to write a memoir about their mother. At the time Sylvia was busy with both *The Suffragette Movement* and *Save the Mothers*. 'There are great heights and depths, marvellous light, and sombre darkness,' in her character, Emmeline continued. 'If Christabel ever writes her life, it will be unutterably dull, "Me & Mother" stuff ... outside the ever diminishing numbers of devoted followers – nobody is interested in the paragon of wisdom and conduct.'[1438] Rather, says Emmeline, 'Her arc of flight, through Liberalism, Socialism, extreme revolution, to Conservatism is of full interest.'[1439] She continued, 'Even in her villainies she is intensely dramatic ... as when she repudiated you and Adela and again when she expressed extreme horror and reprobation of you in following the example of Mary Wollstonecraft, Elizabeth Elmy and many other pioneers of the Woman's Movement.'[1440]

As it transpired, five years later Sylvia did publish a biographical monograph about her mother. That same year, Christabel completed her manuscript, but decided it would not be published during her lifetime.

In 1933 Sylvia and Silvio moved upmarket to a proper brick-built Victorian house. Woodford council condemned Red Cottage for demolition, though Sylvia owned the land. The council rehoused the Powters in a snug new-build with indoor plumbing and modern amenities. The Pankhurst-Corios crossed the railway line. The three-storeyed West Dene, at 3 Charteris Road, boasted a large tree-filled garden and was a five-minute walk from Woodford Station, just an hour by steam train to London's city centre. Sylvia and Silvio lived at West Dene for almost thirty years. It was to be Sylvia's final home in England.

Richard recalled the character of the house as defined by print and communality. In several rooms books (both history and literature) lined the walls. A top-floor room was stuffed full of back issues of his parents' new newspaper, *New Times and Ethiopia News*, where he played hide and seek with his friends amid the tottering stacks. Another room housed 'a mountain of pamphlets and newspapers in many languages and of every political and religious persuasion', often sent in exchange for *New Times* or 'in an attempt to influence its editor'.[1441]

Appropriately, the extensive 'largely unkempt' garden contained the qualities of a Sylvan wood – apple trees, pear trees and an abundance of raspberry, blackberry, black- and redcurrant and gooseberry bushes.[1442] An ancient oak presided at the back of the garden just beyond their fence. Silvio continued to take charge of the cooking and washing up. When working, his son remembered, his father often put on a long grey overall coat. Occasionally, a woman came in to catch up on the backlog of washing and cleaning.

For a while Richard enjoyed the companionship of a Danish au pair named Gurli Jensen, in Britain to study English. Otherwise, 'sundry European refugees from time to time helped out in the house'.[1443] There was much carrying up and down of coal and coke, lighting or cleaning fires, and regular chimney sweeping, 'an art or craft in itself'.[1444]

Sylvia and Silvio paid the bills by letting a third of the house to tenants. The aged and mysterious Mrs Green occupied 'a gloomy, generally locked' room on the top floor, and 'made a solitary appearance every few months'.[1445] By contrast, the West Indian couple occupying the first floor welcomed Richard as an extension of their own family. Glamorously, this duo ran the local Broadway Music Saloon, and it music fascinated and delighted the boy. A family who listened constantly to pirate wireless stations came next, providing a further source of novel entertainments from Radio Normandie and Radio Luxembourg.

The Pankhursts, their tenants and the constant tide of visitors – most of them political refugees from all points of the globe – shared the teeming space with various domestic animals. Dogs were generally Airedales, accompanied by the occasional tortoise, Sylvia's cats and Silvio's Goatie, kept (mostly) in the garden. Silvio milked Goatie, so Richard became far more used to goat's milk. His father 'was heartbroken when she died of pneumonia'.[1446] Richard proved imaginative and endearingly geekish in naming successive pets as he got older. A statuesque cat became Todtleben, after a Russian hero of the Crimean War, and a Khaki Campbell duck was given the Euclidean geometrical nickname of Cyclic Quad. During the rationing of the war years, Richard became responsible for a dozen chickens and sometimes ducks, whose eggs were shared among friends. He recalled his pleasure in presenting Emmeline and Fred Pethick-Lawrence with a monthly box of eggs.

Sylvia and Silvio didn't own a radio until around 1935, and although they read the *Manchester Guardian* and *The Times* every day, these appeared boring to Richard as a child, with their front pages devoted to dull advertising while the news, 'with only small headings', was relegated to the inner pages.[1447] The continual flow of visitors provided a much more colourful and interesting source of information about international events – from Italy, Germany, Austria, Hungary, Poland, France, Belgium, Sweden and Spain. After the Italian invasion, these were joined by an increasing number of visitors from Ethiopia and its supporters, including the West Indies and countries all over Africa.

'My parents were old-style libertarian socialists. They were also committed anti-fascists, anti-racists and anti-colonialists. So, by and large, were many if not most of their friends, not a few of whom I met – or heard talking – as a child.'[1448] Sylvia replicated the best of her own upbringing for her son: Richard's descriptions evoke Sylvia's own memories of her open-doored, political childhood homes in Manchester and London.

Of his parents' once scandalous partnership, Richard wrote crisply, 'Following the practice of many who shared their political and philosophical point of view, and anticipating later more widespread practice, they on principle never married.'[1449] Nor did it seem out of the ordinary to him that he bore his mother's surname – that was also part of their worldview. There were, however, serious dangers that parents would naturally hide from a child. At the time of Richard's birth and infancy, Silvio was a vulnerable stateless refugee. Marriage could expose Sylvia and her son to the risk of deportation to a country whose 'great dictator' had identified both of his parents as enemies of the state. Even after his mother's death, the *Daily Mail* persisted in salaciously harassing Richard about the identity of his father and confecting speculative stories about his nationality, as if it had ever been a secret.[1450]

Silvio and his children Percy and Roxane stayed in touch other, and he provided some financial support during Roxane's school years, and the two youngsters occasionally visited Woodford Green.[1451] Rockie wrote letters to her father updating him on her academic progress and assuring him that she was keeping cashbook accounts of her spending, but their meetings appear to have been irregular.

Rockie worked hard to put herself through school. After their mother died, she and Percy continued to live together in north-west London. Awarded a full Night School Scholarship to the School of Economics, Rockie went in search of Sylvia to ask her for financial help with her subsistence so that she could afford to take up the scholarship. In this undated letter Rockie wrote to Sylvia:

> I very seldom see my father now, and the money he gives us is less than negligible. It is not surprising therefore that I have been rather hard pressed lately and I need many things – winter clothes etc.
> … I am wondering if you can give me a little financial assistance.
> If you could, it would come at a time when it could not be more appreciated. I shall be glad when the school year is ended and I shall have the chances of a better job.[1452]

This was a well-judged letter, and exactly the right way to approach Sylvia for help. Sylvia's reply is not recorded, but it seems that she assisted Rockie, and maintained the family bond. As evoked in family photographs and memories, Helen Pankhurst recalls that 'the relationship was good'.[1453]

Richard's arrival brought a shock of change to Sylvia's life that challenged even her infinite adaptability and inexhaustible work ethic. Between 1926 and the mid-1930s, Sylvia published a steady stream of books. Written at

STAND UP FOR THE SOLDIER'S WIFE!

A PUBLIC MEETING

WILL BE HELD BY

THE EAST LONDON FEDERATION OF SUFFRAGETTES
and THE UNITED SUFFRAGISTS,

AT

THE CAXTON HALL,

WESTMINSTER,

ON

Monday, November 16th, 1914

at 8 p.m. (doors open 7.30)

TO PROTEST AGAINST

The Government's attempts to insult the
Soldier's Wife by threatening her with Police
Supervision, the stoppage of her allowance,
exclusion from the public house (while men
are admitted), and other restrictions on the
liberty of women.

Chair: Miss EVELYN SHARP

Speakers:

A SOLDIER'S WIFE

Mr. H. BAILLIE-WEAVER

Mrs. DRAKE

Mr. H. W. NEVINSON

Miss SYLVIA PANKHURST

ADMISSION FREE.

A few Reserved Seats at 1s. to be obtained from the Ticket
Secretary, United Suffragists, 3 Adam Street, Strand, W.C.

Printed by Geo. Barber, Furnival Press, Furnival Street, E.C.

Suffragettes selling copies of the *Women's Dreadnought* on Roman Road in the East End of London.

Printed handbill advertising a protest meeting against government proposals to restrict women's liberties during the First World War.

The Junior Suffragettes' pageant at the ELFS' New Year party, Bow Baths, East London, 1916. Middle row, left, sixteen-year-old Rose Pengelly plays the panpipes. A few days later she lost the thumb and two fingers of her right hand in a factory machine accident at work.

A postcard of Sylvia with one of the East End children from the Mothers' Arms' creche, run by the East London Federation of Suffragettes (ELFS).

The ELFS' Toy Factory.

The Mothers' Arms' toddlers taught via the Montessori method.

The Cost Price Restaurant in the Women's Hall, Bow, East London.

Harry Pankhurst during his last illness, paralysed by poliomyelitis. He died on 5 January 1910, aged 20.

Remembering Keir Hardie, who died on 26 September 1915.

The fallen martyrs in *The Workers' Dreadnought*. Rosa Luxemburg and Karl Liebknecht were murdered on 15 January 1919.

Emmeline Pankhurst's funeral, St John's Church, Smith Square, Westminster, 18 June 1928. [Right to left] Christabel, Sylvia and their maternal aunt, Ada Goulden Bach.

WOMEN'S WILL
BEAT ASQUITHS WONT

Emmeline Pethick-Lawrence, left, and Israel Zangwill at the Women's Sunday suffragette rally, 21 June 1908. Protestors dressed in white, green and purple held a thousand banners aloft.

Anti-war march from Bow to the Houses of Parliament, organized by Sylvia in June 1914.

Sylvia addressing Trafalgar Square anti-conscription rally, April 1916. The little girl next to her has been hit with red ochre paint, aimed at Sylvia by agents provocateurs.

A breakfast celebrating Sylvia's release from Holloway Prison, May 1921. She had been imprisoned since October 1920 for sedition. Nellie Cressall [to Sylvia's left] and Jessie Payne [to Sylvia's right].

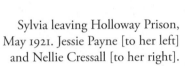

Sylvia leaving Holloway Prison, May 1921. Jessie Payne [to her left] and Nellie Cressall [to her right].

Sylvia with Japanese delegates at the London Naval Conference, April 1930.

Sylvia at the Second Congress of the Third International in Moscow, summer 1920. The group includes Marjory Newbold (standing second from left), Dave Ramsay (standing fifth from left), John Reed (standing sixth from left), Tom Quelch (standing seventh from left). Seated second and third from the left are Willie Gallacher and Jack Tanner.

RED COTTAGE

TEAS

LR

Red Cottage, Woodford, Essex, where Sylvia and Silvio lived and ran tea rooms and a bookshop, advertised in *Worker's Dreadnought*, 22 March 1924.

Sylvia and her son, Richard Keir Pethick Pankhurst, 1928.

The family in Romania, 1934. In the front, Arcadiu Petrescu and Richard. Standing behind them left to right, Silvio Corio, Judge Petrescu, Sylvia and Mrs Petrescu.

Sylvia speaks against Fascism and Nazism, London 1935.

Sylvia's newspaper, the *New Times & Ethiopia News*.

A photograph of the Anti-Air War Memorial, Sylvia's 'Stone Bomb', designed by Eric Benfield, in Woodford.

Courtesy of Helen Pankhurst

Courtesy of Redbridge Museum

Richard and Rita's wedding in Addis Ababa, 17 September 1957. Pictured outside the Pankhurst home with a family friend [left] and their best men, Afewerk Tekle [in front] and Mengistu Lemma [standing to the right].

Sylvia and Haile Selassie.

Courtesy of IISG

Anti-Mussolini poster parade outside the House of Commons, 1946. [Left to right] Mrs M. A. Cotton, Sylvia, Mrs. Tedros and Mrs. Kerrie.

Art copyright Jerome Davenport, image courtesy of Blank Walls

2018 homage to Sylvia, painted by Australian street artist Jerome Davenport, otherwise known as Ketones6000, on the Lord Morpeth pub, Old Ford Road, Bow. The pub is next door to the site of the ELFS' Women's Hall.

the Red Cottage, *India: The Earthly Paradise* was the last great tome Sylvia
published before Richard's birth. In the years immediately following
Richard's arrival Sylvia managed to produce a succession of significant
works, despite the challenge of motherhood. She wrote concurrently
several longer books and shorter monographs while turning out lectures,
letters and articles for journals, magazines and newspapers.

Throughout the 1920s, Sylvia pursued her interest in modern
language reform, first expressing her enthusiasm for the idea of an
international language in her journal *Germinal*, founded in 1923: 'The
Germinal Circle is intended to assist in the artistic expression of current
thought, in order to bring art into contact with daily life and to use
it as a means of expressing modern ideas and aspirations.'[1454] Sylvia
wrote in the second issue, 'I sing of the peoples. I sing of the peoples
united; I sing of the peoples creative; the peoples alert without master;
of themselves they are master.' Her vision of 'the people' as creative,
autonomous and unified drove her cultural and political work in this
period 'and also informed her commitment to the development of an
international language'.[1455]

Delphos: or the Future of International Language came out
in London and New York, a forward-looking tract reflecting
Sylvia's futuristic mood brought about by the imminent advent
of her child. Beginning her argument for the logical necessity of
'interlanguage' – or Interlingua, as she called it – Sylvia reflected
on mankind's failure to achieve a general means of international
communication in the realm of language, 'with a smile and shrug
of inept apology, powerful industrialists, famous statesmen, and
learned savants confess their inability to exchange with each other
the simplest of ideas'. Yet, she observed, with superb prevision of
future technologies,

> in other provinces mankind is knitting the globe to a remarkable
> unity. The interchange of materials between distant countries
> has led to an interdependence of peoples undreamt of in
> earlier times. World activities and needs are, and will be, ever
> more and more coordinated ... The aeroplane, the telegraph,
> the telephone; of late wireless telegraphy and photographic
> telegraphy; and now television, allow us to maintain a rich and
> constant communication with every part of the globe. It is not

too much to prophesy that sensations other than those of hearing
and sight will soon be transmitted by similar methods: we shall
not only see, but smell, the flowers in the old home-garden; the
ozone of the seaside and the latest electric and sunbath-treatment
will reach us as readily as the broadcasted concert. By some allied
means we may even feel the touch of distant hands.[1456]

This last line touchingly evokes the love letters she exchanged with Keir
Hardie when she was in America, as they speculated on the possibilities
of synchronicity. These technological developments are popular, Sylvia
argueed, because accessible to all economic classes: 'The youth of the
poorest homes are able to install the wireless. Radio-broadcasting thus
becomes a great force, making towards the adoption of an international
auxiliary language.'

Sylvia pointed out that while the BBC attempted to standardize
the pronunciation of English, it needed to consider the power of the
wireless set to 'carry the people far beyond the confines of their native
tongue':

The spoken word to-day encircles the globe and can be stored up
for future generations. Our children's children will hear the singing
of Nellie Melba, and, if they should think worth while, the speeches
of this year's statesmen. Yet language-barriers deprive the far-sent
word of the universal comprehension given to music.

The work of the League of Nations and all international congresses,
Sylvia asserted, is constantly hampered by the 'mechanical business
of interpretation and translation', which exacerbated political and
trade rivalries and blocked 'the desire for world-friendship long latent
amongst the kindlier and wiser people of all nations ... now quickened
to an ardent flame by the agonies of the World War. With all its faults,
the so-called League of Nations is the response of governments to this
deep and ever-growing sentiment.'

Sylvia surveyed the history of the search for an international language,
from the fall of Latin as a lingua franca to Descartes' 1629 theory of a
universal language so easy that 'It will not be a marvel that uneducated
people should learn in less than six hours to compose with the aid of
a dictionary ... I believe that this language is possible, and that one

could discover the science on which it depends, by means of which the peasants could better judge the truth of things than do the philosophers at the present time.' She introduced and analysed Esperanto, 'a claimant star which appeared in the interlanguage firmament in 1887', tracing the history of its emergence and showing how it is the foundation on which Interlingua will be built.[1457] Sylvia had long championed Esperanto. In November 1921 *Dreadnought* had launched a serialized primer: 'Are you Learning Esperanto? See our Esperanto Primer. Beginning this week. Specially written for Communists.'[1458]

She examines the emergence of other forms of international communication, from Morse Code, invented in 1832 (foreshadowed in method by Bacon's cipher as early as the sixteenth century); the maritime signal code adopted by England and France in 1862 and soon after by all nations; the Gregorian calendar; maps, mathematics, chemistry, botany and other sciences, the measurement of time and the notation of music. She throws in Dewey's 1873 decimal classification of books, the adoption of the Roman alphabet, becoming more widely used in printing German, Turkish and Far Eastern languages. She explores the composite languages grown up along the frontiers of conquest, commerce and immigration, including 'Benguela, Lingua Geral, Hindustani, and Chinook'.

Sylvia's advocacy of Interlingua continued with her 1928 lecture 'Is an International Language Possible?', published on behalf of the Academia Pro Interlingua. Here she argued that a new international language could attain widespread recognition if the education system and media got behind it, reminding her audience that Descartes, Pascal and Leibniz were passionate proponents, and more recently Friedrich Nietzsche, who 'declared the coming of universal language to be as certain as aviation'.[1459]

Sylvia's deadline loomed for *The Suffragette Movement*. She wrote to Norah Walshe asking for help. They had lost touch after the war until Norah read about Richard's birth in the papers. Early in January 1929 Sylvia wrote to Norah in terms most working mothers with a young child would recognize, with or without a book deadline:

I told you, I think, I had a contract to write a book. I am in despair about my writing. Richard wakes early and keeps me on the go until eleven or so. If I can get him to sleep from then till 1pm it is

the best I can hope for frequently – today he woke whenever I put
him down and unless I put him to sleep in my arms he won't sleep
at all … If I do make him sleep I have more trouble at bed time
… If I get him to sleep at 6pm I am lucky; it is more likely to be
7.30pm and I have to sing to him and rock him to accomplish
it … Some days I have managed to work between 11.30–12.30,
when I have my meal and again from 8-11pm and once or twice
from 12pm–1am but I can't keep that up … The solution is to get
someone to take care of Richard part of the time regularly, so that
I can count on it …[1460]

Norah helped, taking Richard out sometimes to enable Sylvia to get
on with the book. 'Richard's father,' Sylvia explained, 'has been ill with
sciatica so I can't count on him to help me with the boy; indeed when
he is at home I get less done than when he is out! I don't want to hand
my little boy over to anyone – I know how important it is that he
should be rightly handled … I find myself so irritable and jaded that
when I sit down to write I am often unable to find a sentence … yet in
the old days words used to pour out without difficulty.'[1461]

Sylvia ploughed on throughout 1929. By 1930 Richard was unwell
and the exhausted Sylvia was at the point of collapse. An old suffragette
friend Joan Hodgson came to the rescue with an invitation for mother
and child to stay for a while in Bedfordshire, where Richard was
operated on for tonsillitis. By mid-year, things had improved. Other
friends helped out, and Sylvia's writing projects progressed. Nineteen-
thirty saw the publication of *Save the Mothers*, endorsed by heavyweight
leaders and specialists from all relevant areas of public life and extremely
well received.

Unrelated to these maternal themes, Sylvia decided to translate
the work of the nineteenth-century Romanian Romantic poet
Mihail Eminescu, perhaps a surprising choice given his conservative
nationalistic views. Proclaimed then and now Romania's national poet
and godfather of the modern Romanian language, Eminescu spoke to
Sylvia's long-standing interest in folk art, music and dance – especially
Romanian. Assisted by Dr I. O. Stefanovici and a pile of dictionaries
assembled by Silvio, she produced an anthology of heroic verse carrying
the torch for social justice that impressed even Shaw: 'The translation
is astonishing and outrageous: it carried me away. Sylvia: you are

the queerest idiot-genius of this age – the most ungovernable, self-intoxicated, blindly and deafly, wilful little rapscallion-condottiera that ever imposed itself on the infra-red end of the revolutionary spectrum as a leader; but that you had this specific literary talent for rhyming and riding over words at a gallop has hitherto been a secret.'[1462] Without his permission, Sylvia published Shaw's letter as the book's Preface.

Richard's health improved and Sylvia got the hang of motherhood. In July 1930 she wrote to update Norah Walshe: 'Most days I make a point of being free from 4pm to 6pm when Richard goes to bed … I seem to be terribly rushed and in arrears and I find it difficult to keep even that time free but I try … We are trying to start a Montessori nursery school.'[1463] By October the Montessori nursery at West Dene had opened, with nurse, socialist, feminist and pacifist Vera Brittain as honorary treasurer and attended by four pupils, including one of Fenner Brockway's daughters. 'Richard knows all his letters (capitals) and begins to have some ideas of the others and has also the idea of word building. He is very quick and has good command of his limbs.'[1464]

With *The Suffragette Movement* in the pipeline for publication in 1931, Sylvia turned her pen to *The Home Front*, which she delivered in February 1932, dedicated 'to Emmeline Pethick Lawrence, whose generous appreciation encouraged the penning of this record'. Vera Brittain wrote a letter to Sylvia congratulating and praising her for the book before she reviewed it favourably in *The Clarion*.

Regina Hercbergova's decision to sue Sylvia for libel over her representation of her in *The Home Front* had the happy result of bringing Sylvia and Norah Smyth closer. Punctilious Norah, now living in Florence, had kept all the records and accounts relating to the business. In correspondence with her, Sylvia bemoaned her teeth troubles and Silvio's skin eruptions. Norah sent advice. Sylvia replied that she is booked in to have all her teeth removed and thanked Norah for the recommendations for Silvio's skin complaints. (In the event, Sylvia did not have all her teeth removed.)[1465]

The British Library is in possession of a highly entertaining and typically fat file entitled 'Sylvia Pankhurst and the Society of Authors', containing all her correspondence with this union for British writers between 1930 and 1935. Engaged in constant wrangles with her agents and publishers, Sylvia applied constantly to her union for advice and support on how to stand up to both and how to resolve contractual disputes.

The publication of her surprisingly even-toned biography of her mother in 1935 became the occasion of one of these contractual wrangles. Commissioned to write a short monograph of 40,000 words, Sylvia delivered two versions to her publishers, one the commissioned length and another version of 80,000. Following hearty argument, the shorter went to print. Though in this case the longer proved the better version, the publishers understandably didn't want to pay extra for uncontracted work.

For a while, Sylvia shifted operations to the Welsh border, while Richard undertook a trial period enrolled as a day boy at Dora and Bertrand Russell's experimental school. Away from his father, pets and London home, Richard never settled. Being allowed to board with the other children might have given him a better chance of fitting in, but Sylvia seemed unprepared to consider this option, despite the gentle suggestions of the progressive Russells that she might return to London and leave the boy to find his own feet.

Richard was too young to be aware that in 1930 Oswald Mosley formed the New Party, by 1932 known as the British Union of Fascists, organizing on Sylvia's old home ground, the East End of London. In Ethiopia, on 2 November 1930, Ras Tafari was crowned Conquering Lion of the Tribe of Judah, His Imperial Majesty Haile Selassie I, King of Kings of Ethiopia, Elect of God. These two events were to have far-reaching and definitive impact on Sylvia's life and so in turn on her son's.

31

Fascism as It Is

Sylvia understood from the beginning the threat posed by the emergence in Italy of the original Strongman of Europe.

Her youthful passion for Italian art combined with her fascination for the role the region had played in the history of democratic ideals predisposed her to Silvio Corio. Italy, the land of her early artistic enchantment, cradle of radical visions, now choked under a violent police state with censored press and despotic penal islands. The crushing of the socialist and workers' movements and free speech in Europe's oldest attempt at democracy dismayed and horrified her. In the 1930s she became immersed in the cause of Ethiopia's struggle against Mussolini's war of imperialism. The significance of his unprovoked invasion of Ethiopia in 1935 was clear to the world at the time: the test case in the fight against fascist dictators threatening the entire world order. Nelson Mandela recalled, 'I was seventeen when Mussolini attacked Ethiopia, an invasion that spurred not only my hatred of that despot but of fascism in general.'[1466]

By experience and intellect Sylvia was well positioned to perceive, early on, that fascism was emerging as a doctrine that threatened the prospect of creating a stable peace in Europe.[1467] Chauvinism, authoritarianism, racism, misogyny, the celebration of militarism, pandering to the ideological aggression of capitalist economics, to the self-interest of social and economic elites – all these Sylvia recognized as new, disfigured forms of old unresolved problems. Decades of front-line experience in the suffragette movement and later among unreconstructed hardmen of the left honed her instinct for identifying bullies and sociopaths. The state torture she had suffered at the hands of her homeland when a young woman gave her the clear measure of the real limits of liberalism.

Fascism, Sylvia recognized, could not be argued, negotiated or coaxed out of existence. Deterring its aggression necessitated force of arms, boycott and organized collective resistance. She relinquished her long-held and hard-fought-for pacifism. Her son described her as remaining 'in spirit largely a pacifist', who hoped the League of Nations might locate its missing backbone and rally the good sense and courage to fight back.[1468]

Always critical of the punitive terms of the Paris peace settlement, Sylvia agreed with Sir Alfred Milner's assessment that the Versailles Treaty created 'a Peace to end Peace'. Hitler wrote in *Mein Kampf* just a few years later, 'What a use could be made of the Treaty of Versailles … How each one of the points of the Treaty could be branded in the minds and hearts of the German people until sixty million men and women find their souls aflame with a feeling of rage and shame … with the common cry, "We will have arms again!"'[1469]

From the outset of the 1920s and throughout the 1930s, Sylvia wrote an uninterrupted torrent of letters to Whitehall officials and MPs. Most of them either ridiculed or impatiently ignored her warnings. 'It never occurred to them,' Caroline Benn observes, 'that she might be right about Jews under Hitler, the oil, the aerial bombings, Palestine, and Fascism in Europe and Japan.'[1470]

The 19 August 1922 issue of *Dreadnought* offered an early warning: 'Now Mussolini dominates the situation with his fascisti … they have broken the back of the working class movement.'[1471] In a steady stream of articles in the *Dreadnought* and elsewhere, Sylvia argued that fascism in Italy fed on the chaos following the collapse of the Italian left in 1919. From her perspective, the defeated Italian soviets and disunited democratic socialist movement failed to mount adequate organized resistance, leaving the path opened for the scared middle classes to look to Mussolini for what they imagined would be stability and order.[1472]

In her exacting analysis, Sylvia placed responsibility squarely on the failure of the left. However, the historical evidence demonstrates that equal culpability lay in the abnegation of responsibility by the inert, self-interested middle classes who in the vacuum of social instability created by the Great War feared the impact of democratic socialism on their privilege and found the power-sharing proposed by communism distasteful.

The March on Rome in October 1922 symbolized dissatisfaction with the socialist and moderate coalitions attempting to achieve democratic governance of the nation and revive the severely damaged economy. That there was anger at being badly treated, despite promises from their allies on the winning side during the Versailles peace settlement, Sylvia would agree. In the face of the Blackshirts preparing to enter and take over Rome, the King, parliament and press lacked the fortitude to stand up to the threat. Fearing civil war, they offered Mussolini leadership of a coalition government.

In 1924 Giacomo Matteotti's tract *The Fascisti Exposed: A Year of Fascist Domination* rolled off socialist presses in London. The leader of the United Italian Socialist Party, Matteotti distinguished himself as Mussolini's most courageous and fiercest opponent. Sylvia, Silvio and their Italian exile community were among the first in Britain to read Matteotti's new work. It contains a detailed 'Chronicle of Deeds' for the month of May 1923.

> Genoa: at Marassi-Guezzi fascists strike workmen found in public bars, fire revolver and rifle shots, and set fire to the Friendly Society's premises.
> Rome: workers distributing leaflets for May Day arrested. The fascist militia tear the red carnations from passers-by.
> Milan: Chamber of Labour entered during the night, and an attempt made to set it on fire.
> Parma: the worker Tosini Guido killed by fascists.
> Milan: fascists attack a restaurant in the Strada Paullese, where dancing is going on.
> Pompeii: several fascists ill-treat some young ladies who were carrying red flowers to the Madonna.[1473]

The list continues in similar vein for another fifteen densely packed pages.

It was on 30 May 1924, that Matteotti stood up in parliament and made his brave speech challenging the results of the recent elections. Matteotti's slaughter by fascist thugs led to a crisis that should have led to Mussolini's overthrow (see pp. 601–2). Instead Il Duce turned the setback into an opportunity to transform Italy into a full-fledged dictatorship. Matteotti's murder sparked the formation of the anti-fascist movement guided by his motto, 'You can kill me but my ideas will never die.'

Sylvia persistently challenged the active approval and the more passive policies of appeasement that encouraged Mussolini and his pupil Hitler. Throughout the 1920s and 1930s she urged British politicians and opinion formers to reconsider their support for Mussolini and to question their mistaken belief in the potential effectiveness of appeasement. She constantly urged her local MP Winston Churchill to direct his attention to the danger of what was happening in Italy rather than focusing only on Germany. Those elements within British social elites who offered enthusiastic support for Mussolini included politicians, like Churchill, the centre 'moderate' and right-wing press, such as the *Observer* – whose stated editorial policy was to support Mussolini's continuation in power – and avowedly socialist pundits like her old sparring partner Shaw. Sylvia was relentless. 'Miss Pankhurst only wants to be tiresome,' wrote a harassed Foreign Office official obliged to deal with yet another of her unstoppable flow of letters. 'Does it matter what Miss P. thinks? She's a crashing bore who will deserve to be snubbed if in fact it were possible to snub her.'[1474] While busy being a consistently 'tiresome', repetitive, 'crashing bore' about the threat posed by fascism from the moment of its inception, during the 1930s Sylvia was also juggling with the challenges of bringing up her young son in partnership with Silvio and producing a battalion of books, tracts, and journalism. She maintained the continuity in her campaigning without much noticeable interruption.

On 30 March 1933, George Lansbury received a letter from Sylvia, cautioning him about the 'reactionary class dictatorship against the socialists' embodied by Hitler's new regime and about the Nazis' 'terror against the Jews'. She warned that 'we are not awake to it as the Jews are'.[1475] Elsewhere, she wrote about the problems on the North West Frontier and British massacres in India. She dissected the problem of Palestine and Jewish settlers in the Middle East and their quarrel over territory; 'the two ... must learn to live together,'[1476] she argued.

In her remarkable tract *The Truth about the Oil War* (1922), Sylvia predicted that oil would one day cause global wars beginning in the Middle East if international action were not taken to control and regulate trade in this valuable resource in the world's collective interest:

> Oil concessions are those for which the great capitalists scramble most eagerly to-day. Oil shares are amongst the most profitable of all shares ... Whoever owns the oil in peace-time; in wartime the oil will be seized by those armies and navies which control the road to it and the territory where it lies. They will seize it for their own use, and prevent its use by others.[1477]

In 1932 Corio received a letter from Carlo Rosselli, leader of the Italian émigré democratic resistance movement Giustizia e Libertà (Justice and Liberty). Rosselli reported that Matteotti's widow Velia and her two sons were being kept under house arrest and subjected to round-the-clock police surveillance, with a searchlight directed into their home all night to deter visitors. The boys were forbidden from using their father's name and one was forced to give the fascist salute to a photograph of the dictator. Matteotti's grave was repeatedly vandalized, and his widow prohibited from visiting it.

Rosselli told Corio that an Italian doctor, Mario Germani, had braved police harassment and the searchlight to visit Velia. For this act of friendship, he was arrested and exiled to the crowded penal colony of Ponza. Richard later drew together the historical dots that connected these events and helped form the context of his own political childhood: 'It was on this island that the Ethiopian Emperor Haile Selassie's cousin Ras Imru was imprisoned only a few years later, and where Mussolini, by a nice irony, was himself detained after his fall from power.'[1478]

Sylvia responded to Rosselli's report by founding a Women's International Matteotti Committee (WIMC) to raise awareness of Velia's persecution and to campaign for her release from house arrest, drawing attention to the totalitarian character of the fascist regime. Bertrand Russell, Professor Harold Laski – the renowned political scientist, Labour Party activist and Richard's future university professor at the London School of Economics – George Lansbury, by then leader of the Labour Party, and Emmeline Pethick-Lawrence lent their influential names to the committee. Shaw GBS, however, declined, a decision that led to a slanging match by correspondence with Sylvia.

In a June 1931 BBC broadcast, Shaw had compared Sylvia with Joan of Arc, 'who wasn't listened to either'.[1479] Two years later, refusing to serve on the committee and to sign its petition, he explained why he now wasn't listening to her either:

> What the memorialists, including your incorrigible pugnacious self, are doing, is making an attack on the fascist regime in Italy, under cover of sympathy with the distressed widow and her orphans. Obviously the effect will be to irritate the Fascists ... If you want to soften the Fascist Government, you must accept at least that it is a government and approach it as a friend ... assuming its desire to be just and humane ... But if you do not care a rap ... go ahead by all means and pile on the agony ... only you must not expect me to sign it ... you cannot cure nations – least of all the English Nation of the vice of lecturing other nations on their moral inferiority. Nor shall I cure you.[1480]

In response, Sylvia accused Shaw of being oblivious to 'the corporate state ... soviet and fascist' that threatened them all.[1481] Naturally she took exception to his argument about the vice of the English lecturing other nations, 'for the simple reason that I do not recognize nationality at all in this matter. It is a question of ideas and ideals – you know ... and everyone else knows – that I should be just as eager to do this for Mrs Matteotti if she happened to be English or ... a native of Ireland, India, Egypt or any other nation under British rule.'[1482]

By now coming to the conclusion that Shaw genuinely didn't understand fascism, as opposed to just pretending that he didn't for his own self-interested professional convenience, Sylvia proceeded to explain its ideology to him at some length, and continued. 'Italian fascism is simply a capitalist dictatorship,' she wrote, 'a manifestation of capitalism which it creates when it finds itself in difficulties, to protect itself from the rising power of the workers ... 'I see the Italian situation as one of the phenomena which have developed in this transition period which, in a book I am writing now, I have called *In the Red Twilight*.'

Sylvia prodded Shaw with the reminder that had he been born Italian rather than Irish he would be one of Mussolini's victims. His terse reply came by postcard: 'No: you can't bully me; and you can't even bully Mussolini ... I know perfectly (human error excepted) what I am about.'[1483] He did not know, however, that in order to fundraise for the campaign Sylvia had by then cannily auctioned all his previous correspondence with her, for an excellent return.

One of Richard's earliest childhood memories is rooted in his early awareness of his parents' involvement in international political struggles. Nearly seven years old, he came down from his bedroom one morning to find the large round mahogany sitting-room table 'covered with innumerable shining objects, like knives, of different shapes and sizes'.[1484] Sylvia was collecting surgical equipment for the treatment of some 3,000 Italian detainees interned on the island of Ponza.

One of the prisoners on Ponza was a young Max Salvadori, a Giustizia e Libertà activist. Through the Matteotti Committee his mother Giacinthia discovered her son's whereabouts and succeeded in visiting him on Ponza, where she learned that the doctor on the island was his fellow detainee Dr Germani. The fascist authorities refused his request for surgical equipment to treat the prisoners. They turned to Sylvia for help.

Publicizing the launch of the WIMC appeal, Sylvia wrote to the *Manchester Guardian* on 2 August 1933, 'Some months ago, in the columns of your paper, I drew attention to the appalling sentence of ten years' imprisonment passed by the Special Fascist Tribunal of Italy upon Dr Germani for having desired to assist the widow of the murdered Italian Deputy Giacomo Matteotti to leave her native land on account of the terrible persecutions she has suffered since her husband's death.'[1485] She described Dr Germani's desperate need for 'a case of surgical instruments and disinfectants', to alleviate suffering and stem the 'many unfortunate' deaths on the island. Sylvia attached a carefully documented list of the internees on Ponza known to be gravely ill, thus drawing public attention to their plight. Appealing to British medics and surgeons to assist, she listed the names of women and men, details of their illness and condition, and the cause. Most frequently the cause is beating and violence from the fascist militia.

The WIMC's appeal raised sufficient funds to purchase the equipment, packed up and dispatched from their Woodford home to Italy by Richard's parents. However, contravening written assurances from the Italian Embassy in London, the equipment was confiscated on arrival and never reached Ponza.

In March 1933 the Non-Sectarian Anti-Nazi League to Champion Human Rights had launched an anti-Nazi boycott of German products in opposition to Hitler's anti-Semitic policies. An alliance of international critics co-ordinated a worldwide, efficiently organized economic boycott against German goods that lasted until the outbreak of war in 1939. On 24 March the *Daily Express* approvingly announced the boycott, providing readers with information about how to support it, under the headline 'Judea declares War on Germany'. Sylvia sat on the UK anti-Nazi boycott committee.

Simultaneously, in the summer of 1933, she and Silvio organized an International Day of Protest in support of victims of Italian fascism as part of their continuing attempt to raise awareness of its dangers to the British public. The *Manchester Guardian* ran a feature, citing Sylvia extensively,[1486] and her appeal on behalf of the victims of Italian Fascism suffering in the prisons and islands of deportation was also published in newspapers in Switzerland, the USA, Spain and Sweden:

> Fascism denies and destroys all freedom of thought, party, press, association; exploits and enslaves the workers; tramples on every popular liberty won during the last two centuries; re-establishes the juridical concepts of the Middle-Ages; is guilty of the maltreatment and murder of its political opponents. The Italian political victims, upheld by a high faith in human destiny, have for eleven years resisted unprecedented torture and persecution. Over them lies the agonising sorrow that their families, isolated from friends, surrounded by Fascist hatred, the object of continual menace, daily face the risk of death or violent assault and suffer a miserable poverty every day intensified. Their heroic endurance should be made known to all the world.[1487]

The WIMC succeeded in improving Velia Matteotti's situation and that of her children. In September 1933 the authorities released them from house arrest into the supervision and care of the Church. But Velia's heart and health were broken. She died the following year.

Richard recalled his excitement at meeting the Italian-Jewish Carlo Rosselli when he visited Woodford on a summer's day. They spent the afternoon out in the garden, where Rosselli thrilled the child with tales of his daring jailbreak (in 1929) from captivity on the heavily guarded penal colony on Lipari, off the Sicilian coast, reputed to be impossible to escape from. Rosselli had been sentenced to five years' internment there for presenting to Velia Matteotti a wreath to be placed on her husband's grave. Years later Richard learned the political truths behind these Boy's Own adventure tales. Rosselli and two fellow detainees escaped to Paris, where Rosselli set up the militant anti-fascist Italian resistance HQ. Later, Rosselli was seriously wounded fighting in the Spanish Civil War. Unwavering in his mission to defeat Mussolini, he coined the famous slogan, 'Oggi in Spagni; domani in Italia' (Today in Spain; tomorrow in Italy). In June 1937 he and his brother visited the French resort town of Bagnoles-de-l'Orne where they were murdered by a group of French fascist *cagoulards*. *New Times* ran the tragic headline: 'Carlo Rosselli and his Brother Nello Assassinated ... by Order of Fascist Rome ... on the Anniversary of the Murder of Deputy Giacomo Matteotti'.[1488] Recalling Rosselli's famous message when he went to fight in the Spanish Civil War, Sylvia paid tribute to their friend: 'The Rossellis live ... They live, and will live, as long as memory lasts, in the heart of all lovers of Liberty.'[1489]

The emblem of Rosselli's newspaper was a fiery sword of justice. As a tribute, *New Times* now adopted this as part of its own logo, and often reproduced his work in its pages. For the remainder of her life, Sylvia kept a portrait of Rosselli in her study.

Sylvia's admiration of Rosselli, known for his non-Marxist 'liberal socialism', is indicative of the direction of her thinking at this time. The British Labour Party and radical movements had greatly influenced Rosselli's theory of reformist liberal socialism. Sylvia read his book *Socialisme Libéral*, published in 1930, which contained a passionate critique of classical Marxism in favour of democratic socialist revisionism synthesizing Italian and British political thinking and practice.

The assassination of the Rossellis was part of a brutal campaign of reprisals unleashed during 1937. On 19 February there was an attempt to assassinate Marshal Graziani, Viceroy of Italian East Africa, during a public ceremony in the capital.[1490] In retaliation, the Italian occupiers launched a horrific three-day massacre in Addis Ababa, followed by widespread summary executions. Without the work of the Indian journalist Wazir Ali Baig, news of this atrocity would have taken much longer to filter through fascist censorship and the self-censorship of pro-Italian European journalists into international news.

Then the Djibouti correspondent for the *New Times*, Baig had previously worked as a news gatherer for the *Daily Mail*'s war correspondent in Ethiopia, Evelyn Waugh. The *Mail* dispatched Waugh to cover the conflict in August 1935. He expressed himself happy to be writing for 'the only London newspaper which seemed to be taking a realistic view [pro-Italian, pro-fascist and pro-Nazi] of the situation'.[1491] The readers of the *Evening Standard* on 13 February 1936 were informed by Waugh that Ethiopia was 'still a barbarous country ... In the matter of abstract justice, the Italians have as much right to govern; in the matter of practical politics, it is certain that their government would be for the benefit of the Ethiopian Empire and for the rest of Africa.'[1492] Baig did all the legwork while Waugh drank cocktails in the Itegue Taitu Hotel in Addis and mused on the idea of writing a satire about sensation-seeking foreign correspondents. Unlike his boss, Baig strongly opposed the Italian invasion.

Baig sent detailed eyewitness reports to Sylvia: 'Thousands Murdered in Addis Ababa: Corpses Burnt, Soaked in Petrol ... Fascism Stamped with Eternal Infamy'. Sylvia wrote in her leader:

> The awful holocaust of Addis Ababa has stirred the world. Even the diplomats in their chanceries betrayed their horror. They protested to the Italian aggressors, ignoring all fear of diplomatic incidents, and sent through to Europe the news of the slaughter, which the Fascist press censorship would have hidden from the world, as it has hidden so much else of cruelty and wrong.[1493]

Sylvia's experience of the 'eternal infamy' of fascism, and what its censorship hid from the world, had been deepened and informed by a family trip through Nazi Germany in the summer of 1934. Her well-received translation of Mihail Eminescu's classic works, acclaimed even by GBS, had occasioned the first and only pre-war Pankhurst-Corio family holiday. An unexpected invitation had arrived in Woodford, for Sylvia to attend the unveiling of a statue in honour of the poet, erected in Constanța.

The most obvious route was through northern Italy, but Silvio would have been arrested, so the little family travelled through Germany, changing trains in Berlin. To help Richard sleep on the journey to the Nazi capital, his parents tore pages from *The Times* to shade the ceiling lamp. The border guards inspecting their compartment at the German frontier ripped down and impounded the 'seditious' foreign pages.

Sylvia, Silvio and Richard passed through Berlin shortly after President von Hindenburg's funeral in August 1934. Richard recalled long Nazi flags with black borders hanging from key government buildings. They went into a grocery shop to buy provisions for the long journey ahead. Silvio paid, but the shopkeeper pushed the heavy bag of supplies on to Sylvia to carry, which she took to be symbolic of the status of women in the new Reich.[1494] The Nazi ascent to power immediately excluded women from the Reichstag, provincial parliaments and local government to which they had been elected in considerable numbers after 1918. 'Women,' Sylvia wrote,

> according to the dictum of Hitler, must return to the three K's, *Kirche, Kinder and Kueche*, to which the last century opponents of women's enfranchisement desired to confine them. According to Goebbels 'whilst man masters life, woman masters the pots and pans'. The German *Financial Times*, January 1934, observed, 'The self-supporting woman injures man, not only by being his competitor, but also by depriving him of his pride of being the family's breadwinner.'[1495]

These first-hand experiences confirmed what Sylvia already knew. On 11 June 1934, the *Manchester Guardian* had reported her speech in Hyde Park the previous day at an international women's peace rally, beneath the headline: 'WOMEN AND FASCISM: Miss Pankhurst's Warning':

> Miss Sylvia Pankhurst sees in Fascism a menace to feminine freedom. She gave grave warning as to the possible results for women of the war for which she believes Fascism is heading. 'Britain', she declared, 'was the last bulwark among the great nations so far as democracy for women was concerned. In Germany, the vote for women had been taken away. They had a war Government

put into power. It was only a great revolt amongst the German
people, or force too great for Hitler from outside, that would
prevent 'that bruiser' from throwing his forces against the people
of the world. 'Women,' she continued, 'we stand here as the last
bulwark for women in Europe. If war comes, I cannot say what will
happen to such freedom as we have won. To stop this imminent war
is the first and most important thing for all of us today.'[1496]

Sylvia spoke tirelessly around the country on this theme. Her schedule
demonstrates that she was effectively now reintegrating with the
Labour Party, from which she accepted a constant flow of invitations.
She spoke to a large audience in the Silksworth Miners' Hall at a
meeting organized by the Houghton-le-Spring Women's Federation of
Labour Sections. Here she gave an address on 'War and Fascism', and
was afterwards presented with a vote of thanks and a bouquet by the
federation's president, Mrs Wake of Ryhope.[1497]

Sylvia devoted a section of her 'Fascism as It Is' series in *New Times*
to 'Women under the Nazis'. Documenting in detail the exclusion
of women from all employment by public bodies, government
departments, local councils, hospitals, charities and – as far as possible –
even schools, Sylvia pointed out that among the women eliminated
'are the very people who, since the Revolution in 1918, have actually
created government departments dealing with infants' welfare and
the education of girls and women'.[1498] She warned against the reaction
now turning back the clock in Germany on hard-fought-for feminist
advances:

> There is no question here, either of race or political view. Women
> are excluded on the clear basis of womanhood and that alone.
> Many famous actresses like Elisabeth Bergner, Fritzi M. Massary,
> Elisabeth Lennartz, and Greta Mosheim, can no longer appear in
> Germany either because of Jewish race or political opinion, but
> many hundreds of medical women have been obliged to renounce
> the practice of their profession simply because of their sex.[1499]

For twenty-five years German women had possessed the right of
admission to universities and the right to practise in the professions.
Now only 10 per cent of qualified applicants were permitted to enter

university and women had been rigorously weeded out of the scientific, legal and medical professions. In the same article, Sylvia wrote about concentration camps and forced-labour colonies. She also focused on anti-Semitism, discussing particularly the forced sterilization of Jewish women.

The Pankhursts' summer vacation by the bright-blue Black Sea proved a brief enchantment. Her son recalls that Sylvia 'fell in love with Romania, its beautiful countryside and fine peasant costumes, and spent many happy days admiring the Byzantine-style paintings in its medieval churches. (As a child I found these inspections in the summer heat almost unending …)'[1500] They garnered a large collection of postcards that Sylvia stored in her Romanian scrapbooks.

More fun for Richard than the tiresome traipsing round endless Byzantine-style churches were the then unspoilt Mamaya Beach and the swimming pool at the Hotel Lido boasting the marvel of an artificial-wave machine. There were sightseeing trips in horse-drawn buses, and Richard's father took him boating in the exquisitely landscaped park and to see the exotically uniformed palace guards.

The colour photographs illustrating the national newspapers impressed Sylvia, as did the novelty of railway stations made beautiful by carefully tended flower beds and hanging baskets, features which prompted her to write an article describing the practice in the local Woodford press.

Eminescu's statue, carved by the sculptor Oscar Han, was unveiled on 15 August, Navy Day, in the presence of King Carol II, who recited the first stanza of Eminescu's poem 'Unto the Star', included in Sylvia's collection.

Unto the star that now appears,
So far indeed the transit;
Its light would take a thousand years
To reach our vision's orbit.[1501]

Richard became pen friends with Arcadiu Petrescu (Dudu), the son of one of their hosts, Judge Petrescu, who was in charge of organizing the Eminescu celebrations. The two boys continued their correspondence and friendship into the communist era and adulthood, when Dudu, by then a prominent neurologist, was obliged to arrange for his letters to be posted from neighbouring countries in order to avoid police attention. In the next century, Dudu wrote from Bucharest to one of Sylvia's biographers, 'The friendship between Richard and me is one of the best feelings that I have. Sixty-eight years of correspondence interrupted only by the war.'[1502] Her son clearly inherited her capacity for consistent letter writing and long-term friendship.

Dudu's mother wrote an article about Sylvia's visit for a Romanian women's magazine. She fondly detailed the usual traveller's mishaps of confused schedules, missing luggage and the unexpected dietary requirements of her guests. Sylvia had requested goat's milk for Richard and Mrs Petrescu panicked when Sylvia informed them that she and Richard were strictly vegetarian. Mrs Petrescu wrote as romantically about the great British feminist legend as the legend herself wrote about Romanian folklore and Byzantine churches: 'her eyes', Mrs Petrescu enthused, 'seemed to have borrowed from the grey of the far away ocean, from the shores of which she had come to Romania'.[1503]

The family also spent time with Nicolae Jorga (spelt Iorga in her book), who wrote the introduction to Sylvia and Stefanovici's Eminescu translations. Sylvia, Silvio and Richard enjoyed getting to know Jorga and his family. Later, the Romanian fascist Iron Guard would brutally murder him. But even at the time clear intimations of the future blighted the trip. Sylvia was shocked to discover that the Iron Guard was gaining power in the country and to learn that fascist ideas had already penetrated the Romanian women's movement.

Princess Alexandrina Cantacuzino, a leading force in Romanian women's liberation, invited Sylvia to meet in 'her big palace' in the Calea Victoriei in Bucharest, 'an opulent museum teeming with the precious, the curious and the rare'.[1504] She showed Sylvia her superb collection housed in the palace she called home, including Byzantine art, and 'a graceful Botticelli, a deep Rembrandt, a slick Velasquez'. Alexandrina described her impressive pioneering role in the Romanian women's movement and articulated her positions on the current European political situation. She believed there was still time to save Europe from the disasters of the armistice and Versailles, but not by a revision of treaties.

Sylvia was impressed, until she asked her hostess for policy specifics. Came the reply, 'I believe in corporations; they would send the best representatives to transact the nations' affairs, not their worst as we get everywhere at present ... Parliamentarianism must go! You, above all, must approve it, you who are always to the Left!'

'You mean corporations as in Italy?... I am absolutely opposed to Fascism and its dictatorship!' Sylvia protested. 'Democracy, whatever its shortcomings, is the only constitutional bulwark of popular right against vested interests under this system. We have seen in Italy and Germany the appalling results of its overthrow!'

'Oh we do not want a dictatorship in Romania; we want democratic corporations. No one in Romania desires dictatorship.'

'The Iron Guard?' Sylvia shot back at her. Princess Alexandrina dismissed the argument, and invited Sylvia to a reception at the Woman's House two days later. The Princess's hospitality, as described by Sylvia, included 'exquisite preserved fruit served on dainty filtered dishes', and goblets of 'clear, cold water', filtered from the famed sweet waters of the Dâmbovița. The Princess introduced Sylvia to the group of lively emancipated women, and their talk 'led almost immediately back to the corporations', desired by all present. Sylvia 'urged the danger of a dictatorship'.

'But why not a dictatorship?' two of the women chimed.

'Dictatorship is the absolute negation of the women's movement, the death of progress,' Sylvia answered hotly.

'But why?' one of them persisted.

'Because it rests on force,' she replied.

At which the Princess Alexandrina intervened, took Sylvia's arm and swept her away to tour the Woman's House.

In conversation at the lunch reception given in the magnificent banqueting hall, her hostess, then president of the National Council of Romanian Women and recently prominent in the European feminist international, revealed that she and her colleagues 'welcomed the attempt to fashion a corporate state which would "get things done" and rouse the country to new heights of self-sacrifice and communal effort'.[1505] Alexandrina concluded by explaining why corporativism did not mean a curtailment of liberty, since Romania was 'essentially democratic'. 'Whether you realize it or not,' Sylvia replied, '– and I think you do – you are working to bring in a Fascist dictatorship which will destroy all that the women's movement has gained!'[1506] It was a bitter end to what had been the family's first and last Mediterranean holiday. Richard enjoyed the fascinating trip. Twenty years into his as yet unimagined adult future, a chance encounter at the Toynbee Hall in London's East End would forever entwine his heart and family life with all things Romanian.

On their return home, Sylvia continued her speaker tour and lecture series on 'The Menace of War and Fascism', delivered in London, Cardiff and Manchester, and in smaller towns and villages all over England, Wales and Scotland. Her talks were now illustrated with her first-hand accounts of her family's journey through Nazi Germany.

32

The National Anti-Fascist Weekly

By 1934 Germany, under the leadership of its new Chancellor, was flagrantly defying the terms of the Versailles peace settlement by escalating rearmament and introducing conscription. The following year Sylvia would find herself in the unusual position of being joined in agreement by King George V, when he told the British Ambassador to Berlin, 'We must not be blinded by the apparent sweet reasonableness of the Germans but be wary and not taken unawares.'[1507]

At the end of 1934 the Italians and Ethiopians clashed over the wells at the Wal Wal oasis in the Ethiopian Ogaden Desert on the border with Italian Somaliland, which sparked an international diplomatic crisis that led, ten months later, to war. Mussolini was seeking a pretext for invading Ethiopia, and the The Wal Wal 'incident' was orchestrated from Rome. The Ogaden provided essential trading access to the Red Sea and Indian Ocean. Addis Ababa and Rome had long wrangled over the exact line of the Ethiopian–Somali border, but the fact that the Wal Wal oasis belonged to Ethiopia was undisputed. The three colonized Somalias – Italian, British and French – surrounded Ethiopia.

On 5 December Italian soldiers from the garrison fort at Wal Wal attacked Ethiopian forces guarding the wells and a bloody two-day battle ensued. The next day Emperor Haile Selassie protested about the aggression. The Italian forces were supported by two tanks and three aircraft armed with machine-guns and bombs. The battle ended on the 7th, with an estimated 110 Ethiopians dead and forty to fifty

Italians and Somalis. The following day, Italy demanded an apology and compensation for what it claimed was Ethiopian aggression. On 3 January 1935 Ethiopia appealed to the League of Nations for arbitration. Unchecked, Mussolini pressed on with his strategy of building up his forces for imperialist invasion.

On 22 December 1935, the Italian Air Force began using poison gas. The indiscriminate use of this weapon of warfare on Ethiopian civilians as well as combatants, caused horrific torture and suffering on a mass scale, and violated the Geneva Convention of 1926. In April 1935 Sylvia composed a battalion of letters to her MP Winston Churchill advocating the imposition of sanctions on Mussolini's Italy. In one of these, published in the *Woodford Times*, she deplored the fact that 'Horror has been piled on horror in the atrocious campaign, without any effective step being taken by this government or the league.'[1508] She urged Churchill to protest in the House of Commons. His secretary sent a brusque rebuff in reply. Sylvia persisted, challenging the cowardice of the government and the League of Nations in their dealings with Mussolini and Hitler. In 1936 Sylvia and Churchill corresponded again over the case for sanctions on Italy, loans to Ethiopia and the League of Nations, debating the broader issues of international justice, the aggression of the Italian and German dictators and danger to world peace.[1509] On 7 April 1936, Sylvia wrote a long response to Churchill's most recent letter:

> The danger to world Peace and to the freer nations arising from the
> Fascist dictator states, of which you write, has been present in my
> mind from the first. In the days when I read, with regret, speeches
> favourable to the Mussolini regime from yourself and others,
> I was already working strenuously to bring this danger before the
> British public. The ideals and practices of Fascism are obviously
> directed towards war and conquest. It is for this reason that it was
> and is especially important to prevent a victory for Italian Fascism
> in Africa. To permit Fascism to reap a victory there would be
> absolutely disastrous, and yet at the moment there appears to be
> the greatest possible danger that such a victory is to be allowed
> by Britain and France ... You rightly declare that the German
> and Italian dictators are arming more every day. It is, therefore,
> criminal folly to allow a success to Fascism in Africa ... Had fascist

aggression in Africa been firmly checked at the start, the world
would present a very different picture today.'[1510]

She also took him to task once again on the consequences of the British
government's failure to check Mussolini's fascist aggression, 'Malice,
weakness and folly have produced the greatest betrayal of history.'[1511]
Churchill replied thanking her for her 'long letter which I have read
and on which I have reflected. You may be sure that all the matters
about which you write absorb my mind.'[1512]

The temper of this correspondence reflects the events of the previous
year, when all attempts at international diplomacy failed. Mussolini was
allowed by the League of Nations to reject all arbitration offers, and
on 3 October 1935 the Italians invaded Ethiopia. Mussolini believed
his planes, lethal poison gas, tanks and larger army would knock out
the Ethiopian army in one decisive blow. He was mistaken. The Italian
advance on Addis Ababa slowed to a congested crawl as it tried to pass
through the mountains. The Italian supreme commander General Bono
was stood down and replaced with the mercilessly brutal Marshal Pietro
Badoglio. As well as misjudging the terrain on the ground, Mussolini
underestimated Ethiopian resistance. He overlooked the fact that he was
taking on a nation of warriors legendary for their utter fearlessness. The
established conventions of Ethiopian warfare gave his forces advantage
in the early stages. Ethiopian warriors were trained to engage in head-
on, hand-to-hand combat to the death. Battles were fought by day.
Night was for water, food and rest until re-engagement in the morning.
Only criminal bandits fought by night.

Against overwhelming odds and despite antiquated weapons and
shortage of everything needed to fight a modern war, the courageous
Ethiopians held their own against the Italian invasion longer than
anyone imagined possible. They came very close to invading the
Italian-blockaded territory of Eritrea. In response, Mussolini's generals
ruthlessly exterminated a generation poised to lead their country into
the twentieth century. From the outset Haile Selassie understood that
guerrilla warfare would be the only feasible strategy if the Italian invaders
were ultimately to be vanquished. He found it hard to persuade his
commanders and feudal warlords, to whom the principles of guerrilla
warfare seemed ignominious. It was only after Mussolini's troops had
entered Addis Ababa in May 1936 that the Ethiopian fighting forces fell

in behind Selassie's strategy – a plan the Emperor often found difficult to stick to himself.

At the end of November 1935 Haile Selassie donned khaki field uniform and travelled to the front. As commander-in-chief of the army, the Emperor carried full responsibility for the strategic conduct of the war. He oversaw every aspect of military operations, managing dispatches, briefing heads of the armed forces, constructing roads, handling diplomatic negotiations with recalcitrant chiefs, codifying regulations and deciding tactics for engagement against western arms. He was trained in handling anti-aircraft machine guns. On 19 January 1936 the American historian John Spencer, one of Selassie's foreign policy advisers, witnessed the Emperor put on a steel helmet and swing himself into position on a 20mm Oerlikon anti-aircraft gun in anticipation of an attack by Italian aircraft. 'His Majesty frantically motioned for me to run for cover. Reluctantly, I moved aside a few feet under a eucalyptus tree so that I could continue to see what the Emperor might do. When the planes came overhead the Emperor started firing.'[1513] At the Battle of Maychew in March 1936 Haile Selassie manned an Oerlikon for the duration of the bitter day-long battle, refusing to leave his post for safety as his nobles and army officers died around him. Mussolini, who thought of himself as the new Caesar, never risked anything more dangerous than the short ride on a liveried white horse from his office to the Piazza Venezia to make one of his rallying speeches.

Ethiopia had joined the League of Nations in 1923, the first African country to do so. The Italian attack breached League of Nations principles, but despite public outrage in Britain and France, both countries' governments prevaricated and America refused to be drawn in. Having tested their resolve and got the measure of it, Mussolini consolidated his invasion. Solidarity with Ethiopia was galvanized around the world. In London, Sylvia joined the London-based Abyssinia Association, formed to support Ethiopia.

These events coincided with political changes in the leadership of Britain. In 1929 Ramsay MacDonald had become Prime Minister for the second time, leading a Labour government which lasted until 1931, when a national coalition government was formed with Conservative and Liberal support. MacDonald, to the consternation of many Labour MPs, remained in office as Prime Minister, but the Lord President

Stanley Baldwin, the former Conservative Prime Minister, was the effective head of the coalition government. On 7 June 1935, the ailing MacDonald exchanged offices with Baldwin. On 20 January 1936, King George V died, and the Prince of Wales ascended the throne as King Edward VIII, Nazi advocate and friend to Hitler. Baldwin found his hands immediately full with the constitutional crisis presented by Edward's intention to marry the no less fascistically well-connected American socialite Wallis Simpson.

Mussolini had invaded Ethiopia in October 1935 with an army of 476,000 men, including 87,000 askaris – African soldiers co-opted to fight for their colonial overlords, mostly from Eritrea with a smaller number from Somalia. The Italians had 500 tanks and – most significantly – 350 fighter planes loaded with poison gas. In addition, they had 19,000 lorries and other forms of motorized vehicles, 100,000 horses, mules and donkeys, 1,500 artillery pieces, over half a million rifles and muskets and 15,000 machine guns.[1514] The Ethiopians mustered an army of 250,000 troops, two dozen tanks and eight airworthy aircraft, mostly transports, not fighter planes. Despite its modern military superiority the Italian army found it extremely difficult to make advances between October 1935 and March 1936, an effective resistance that enraged Mussolini.

Around the world, Haile Selassie, the Lion of Judah, came to symbolize the end of the age of white colonialism and people rallied to Ethiopia's support. In London, outraged socialists clashed with Mosley's Blackshirts, who supported the invasion. There were demonstrations in Toulouse, Mexico City and parts of South America and Asia. In Accra, 500 black citizens wanted to sign up and fight for Ethiopia; in Cape Town, 6,000 black South Africans petitioned the government for the right to volunteer for Haile Selassie. Muslim Arabs in Spanish and French Morocco assembled a small mercenary army, intending to travel overland through the Sahara and along the Upper Nile to join the fight.[1515]

As Jeff Pearce's masterly history of the war ably demonstrates, support for Ethiopia was at its highest in America. In August 1936 some 20,000 people poured on to the streets of Harlem in solidarity with the cause, many 'calling themselves "African" in a remarkable show of black power before the term had even been coined'. Waving the Ethiopian tricolour of green, yellow and red the crowd shouted 'Death to Fascism!' and

'Down with Mussolini!'[1516] In September, around 7,000 people crowded into Madison Square Garden for a pro-Ethiopia protest. Three-quarters of those taking part in this rally were white New Yorkers sympathetic to the cause. Tens of thousands of African Americans wanted to sign up and fight for the black nation, a hope shared by many in west Africa, and by expatriates in London and Paris. In the American capitals of black consciousness – New York, Chicago, Pittsburgh and Detroit – Ethiopia became the symbolic centre of the fight against white racism and colonialism. The American government moved swiftly to prevent any black Americans acquiring passports or visas to travel out of the USA, while Italian volunteers who signed up to fight for Mussolini were permitted to travel. Riots broke out between black and Italian neighbourhoods of New York, a tension that spread across America as the war progressed.

During 1934 and 1935 the so-called Peace Ballot (officially entitled 'A National Declaration on the League of Nations and Armaments') was held in Britain – a nationwide questionnaire to establish the public's attitude to the League of Nations and collective security. Those organizing it had hoped that it would demonstrate national support for the principles of the League. The results and the Trades Union Congress vote of September 1936 showed that millions of white people were on the side of an African nation at a time when the British persisted in presiding over the world's most extensive empire. The TUC motion demanded 'all the necessary measures provided by the Government to resist Italy's unjust and rapacious act'. Nearly three million members voted in favour, against 170,000 opposed. The Foreign Office monitored the constant stream of volunteers presenting themselves at British embassies.[1517]

On 10 October 1935 the League of Nations had condemned the invasion by fifty votes against Italy's one. But no action was taken to close the Suez Canal, essential for the easy passage of Italian troops to East Africa. The trifling economic sanctions imposed excluded trade in all oil-based products. Without petrol, Italy could not have flown planes or fuelled tanks and armoured vehicles. As Sylvia had written in *The Truth about the Oil War* in 1922, the British oil kings were in a plot with the government to secure domination of the world oil markets. In her view, western capitalist interests in the oil industry drove all foreign policy in the Middle East and Africa.[1518]

Sylvia considered her job was to try and 'save the world from another war', as she wrote to Cosmo Lang, the Archbishop of Canterbury.[1519] Her letter to the *Manchester Guardian* read: 'As to the story that Sanctions will lead to war, I do not take that seriously. As I view it, both Fascist Italy and Nazi Germany are going to make war wherever they find a sufficiently good chance of success, and I am perfectly convinced that if the [Italian] armies come back from Africa with a victory, a new enterprise will be entered upon before long.'[1520]

In the same year Sylvia wrote to Norman Angell, Labour MP and Nobel Peace Prize winner, voicing her concern about Oswald Mosley and his British Union of Fascists (BUF): 'as I see it, all Fascisms are one in their menace to society, that of Italy, of Germany, of Austria, of Japan, and in this country ... Mosley'. Angell agreed, and was also alarmed by the 'British government's encouragement ... to fascist policy in Spain and elsewhere'. Angell demonstrated in his critical journalism the ways in which the government was brokering diplomatic and economic deals with fascist dictators in order to protect and advance the interests of the British empire. He argued that the issue of capitalism versus communism was now irrelevant. The real issue was 'how a modern state fulfils its economic functions without sacrificing the individual ... how can we have peace without sacrificing freedom?'[1521]

Sylvia joined the call for more robust League of Nations action to constrain Mussolini. Ethiopian forces continued to resist the invasion, hampering the advance of Italian forces towards the capital despite their overwhelming ascendancy in modern armaments. Frustrated by the slowness of progress, Mussolini ordered his Commander-in-Chief Marshal Badoglio to deploy poison gas. Dropped from the air, and accompanied by conventional bombs, this aerial assault succeeded in killing and mutilating Ethiopian soldiers, livestock and civilians. In breach of all the international protocols of war, the Italian Air Force bombarded Red Cross hospitals.

Appealing to the League of Nations to uphold its Covenant, Sylvia argued that the honour of Britain was at stake. If Britain failed to support Ethiopia against this chemical-warfare-wielding fascist army, it would actively collude in 'leaving humanity defenceless against the menace of an international conflict, yet more hideous and devastating than that which afflicted us in 1914–1918'.[1522]

In August 1936 she wrote, 'We are in the world war of Fascism against Democracy.' She continued:

> This war began in Ethiopia; now it has spread to Spain, where the government democratically elected by the Spanish people, in constitutional form, is being attacked by the Fascists, who were defeated at the ballot box. The Spanish Fascists would already have been defeated in the test of force which they have chosen, were it not that they are being assisted by the Fascist powers outside. Italy and Germany are assisting them …[1523]

In 1935 Sylvia wrote a series of letters published in the *Manchester Guardian*, in which she took the government to task for failing to support the League of Nations and stand up for Ethiopia. Her letter, published on 22 February, argued that secret commitments to Italy made by Britain prevented it from supporting Ethiopia and explain why the Foreign Office refused Ethiopia's attempts to purchase aircraft in order to bomb Italian military supply depots.[1524] 'The Italo-Abyssinian war is upon us. Unless the peoples of Europe will rise to the menace overhanging them, another greater catastrophe will shortly follow.'[1525] Urging British public opinion to 'make itself heard', she warned that the dictatorships of Germany and Italy were 'poisonous snakes' which, 'warmed in the bosom of the democratic states', would 'wound them to the death'.[1526]

In the following months further letters by Sylvia appeared in *The Times*, *Daily Telegraph*, *Daily Herald*, *Daily Express*, *News Chronicle* and numerous local, provincial and international papers. Laying bare the economic and diplomatic facts, Sylvia pointed out that though Ethiopia was prevented from importing defensive weapons, Italy could easily obtain anything it wanted to support its military requirements, the 'greater part' of which came from Britain; South Wales coalfields supplied Italy with coal, while the British-based Suez Canal Company raked in profits from the tariffs paid for soldiers passing through its channel.

Daily, systematically, Sylvia forensically unpicked and challenged Italian fascist propaganda. She disputed the assertion that Ethiopia was the last stronghold of slavery in the world, documenting Selassie's recent reforms and abolitionist policy. Answering the fascist argument that Italy needed an empire in the sun to house its expanding surplus population, Sylvia pointed out that Italian emigrants had always completely ignored government attempts to persuade them to settle in Eritrea. As everybody knew, the majority of Italian emigrants headed west to the USA.

Despite the evidence of Selassie's reforms and abolitionist policy about slavery, many other colonial countries accepted the Italian propaganda about slavery. Sylvia highlighted the astounding hypocrisy of European nations suddenly developing a conscience about supposed slavery in Ethiopia as an excuse to stand by and do nothing about Italian aggression. Mussolini had announced clearly his intention to extend the age of white colonialism. He broadcast loudly and clearly to the world his sociopathic promise to recapture the glories of ancient imperialism and create the new Roman empire in East Africa. Why then, Sylvia asked, was the world not hearing him? 'The talk of slavery in Abyssinia should make all honest people blush, for no one cared about it until Italy desired to put the slavery of a nation equipped with modern arms upon the Abyssinian neck.'[1527]

Through 'criminal ... sloth' the League had failed to prevent the threatened invasion, and now was at risk of allowing war. 'Is the conscience of Europe dead? Is there no honest thinking left in Britain? Cannot an appealing voice which the Government dare not disregard, insist on the Italo-Abyssinian question being taken up by the League of Nations with real determination?'[1528]

Deriding the hypocrisy of the League members who required the Ethiopians to 'keep the peace', she heaped shame on 'the great League of civilized powers, which was set up to prevent questions in dispute ever again being decided by the arbitrament of war, turning a deaf ear to the plea of one of her own members'.[1529] That Ethiopia, the only African member of the League of Nations, was a small country pleading for intervention from stronger powers made the spectacle all the more invidious.

Those like myself, who from its first inception, uttered warning against the theories and practice of Fascism, which has since spread with so disastrous results to Germany, and who pointed

out from the start the policy of Fascism was first civil war and
then foreign war, must now sadly say: 'We told you so'. In doing
so another warning must be issued. If the Fascist Government
is allowed by the rest of the world to succeed in its aggression
against Abyssinia, this will be but the prelude to yet more terrible
aggression.[1530]

Sylvia's position was underwritten by her anti-imperialism. She
reminded readers of the *News Chronicle* of Kipling's poetic line 'Take
up the White Man's Burden', which was supposed 'to indicate that it
was the mission of the peoples of modern civilization to civilize the less
advanced peoples'. The white man then, in the shape of Mussolini, was
taking it upon himself 'to be engaged in civilizing the Abyssinians by
the atrocities of the gas bomb and the shell'.[1531] She continued that the
fascist government condemned the 'youth of the gifted Italian race':

> all we who in 1918, cried 'Never Again', know that today the
> mothers of Italy weep for their departing sons. For my part,
> whatever the colour of the skin, I make no distinction between
> mother love, whether it be in Africa or Europe.[1532]

This is one of the most precise statements of Sylvia's integrated
understanding of the intersection of oppressions. She thoroughly
understood the depth and force of the threat of fascism. Her way of
thinking was rooted in those ideals expressed in 'isms' and 'ists' that
George Bernard Shaw had cautioned should be camouflaged in the
interests of reasonable persuasion: humanitarianism, democratic
socialism, pacifism, egalitarianism, internationalism and that particularly
English form, conscientious libertarianism. This eloquence came from
the heart. When she wrote, 'I make no distinction between mother love,
whether it be in Africa or Europe,' she was writing as the mother of a
son of Italian heritage.

Sylvia's press campaign focused on women's responsibility for
the cause of collective security. 'There never was a time when it was
more urgent than this for women to make use of the great influence
they gained when they became enfranchised citizens.'[1533] Rallying as a
former suffragette, she reported receiving bags of letters every day from
'women thanking me for my repeated protests against the inaction of

the League ... and of the British Government in face of Italy's breach of the Covenant and diabolical attack on a Member State of the League'.[1534]

> All these women appeal to me to know what they can do and
> urge me to give a lead which will enable them to come together to
> struggle for international justice as women struggled for national
> justice in their fight for the vote.[1535]

As the League loitered and the British government continued to prevaricate, refusing Ethiopia's applications for secured loans to fund its protection and resistance against occupation, Sylvia urged the immediate imposition of sanctions, at that time still a novel policy idea. She argued for sanctions in moral terms: 'Failure or hesitancy now would be the deepest possible dishonour.'[1536] Sylvia's son – of an Italian father – points out that his mother wrote 'at this early stage as a friend of Italian freedom, rather than of Ethiopia as such'. Sylvia concluded that immediate action was not only a duty towards Ethiopia but the greatest good that could be done for the people of Italy, whose best interests would be served by stopping this 'wanton war'.[1537]

Stopping wanton war was also the chief concern of Sylvia's favourite filmmaker and actor, Charlie Chaplin. His films had been banned in Germany by the Nazis – who believed he was Jewish – ever since they took power in 1933. Asked years later on his seventieth birthday in 1959 for his views on the future of mankind, Chaplin said, 'I hope we shall abolish war and settle all our differences at the conference table.'

Back in 1913, South Woodford Cinema had opened with a seating capacity of 601. In 1934 it was enlarged and refurbished in Art Deco style and reopened in November as the 1,600-seat Plaza Cinema at a gala launched by Winston Churchill and featuring a screening of Claudette Colbert in Cecil B. DeMille's *Cleopatra*. Sylvia loved the Plaza. Richard recalled her first taking him there in 1935 when he was eight years old, and she made sure they saw every new Charlie Chaplin film. In 1936 they went to see *Modern Times*, premiered in London on 11 February. On 5 May – Sylvia's fifty-fourth birthday and the day the Italian army entered Addis Ababa – the first issue of her newspaper *New Times and Ethiopia News* went to print, published by Walthamstow Press, 'the most modern of London suburban printing works'. It was dated 9 May, the day Mussolini proclaimed victory, the 'end' of the war and the beginning of a fascist empire in Africa.

Chaplin's *Modern Times* and his exercises in devising a philosophy of utopian idealism based on a more equitable distribution not just of wealth but of work decided Sylvia's choice of the title for the weekly newspaper that was to occupy her for a third of her working life, and, as Richard put it, 'take her along many then unimagined paths'.[1538]

The banner headlines of the launch edition spelled out the paper's position: 'REMEMBER: Everywhere, Always, Fascism means War', and 'WE STAND FOR INTERNATIONAL LAW AND JUSTICE'.

> The cause of Ethiopia cannot be separated from the cause of international justice … We shall set ourselves resolutely to combat fascist propaganda [and], to secure the continuance and strengthening of sanctions … We shall strive to induce measures by the League to resist the Fascist usurpation, and to aid and defend Ethiopia, and will persistently urge that Britain take the responsibility of initiating an active League policy …
>
> We shall urge that Britain shall herself individually give aid to Ethiopia …

The paper committed to urging 'in season and out' that the facts of the Italo-Ethiopian War be broadcast 'in all languages to inform all peoples' – especially in Italy where the free press was denied.

New Times published a series of articles by Ethiopia's minister in London, Wärqenäh Eshäté, known to most Britons as Charles Martin. These moving accounts demonstrated the trust Ethiopia had placed in the League and international law, and the grotesque realities of the war. Sylvia commissioned a diverse range of contributors of differing points of view, backgrounds and interests, including activists, writers, academics, teachers and anti-fascist Italian refugees now based in London, Paris and across the USA. Anti-Nazi refugees from central Europe were prominent among contributors, notably the Austrian Ruth Schulze-Gaevernitz and the Hungarian Béla Menczer. Two Swedes, the humanitarian aviator Count Carl von Rosen and the flamboyant air force General Eric Virgin, kept company on the pages of the newspaper with countless anarchists and American radicals.

Rome watched Sylvia's activities closely. When she organized another fête and bazaar celebrating Ethiopia and continuing to focus attention on its plight, the Italian journal *Azione Coloniale* objected that Sylvia's newspaper was stuffed with 'nonsense' and 'poisonous recriminations'. The petitions received from Ethiopian fighters testified, conversely, that poison was, in fact, part of the arsenal of Mussolini's forces.

On Sunday 4 October 1936, Oswald Mosley attempted to march a contingent of some 3,000 Blackshirts, funded directly by Mussolini, from Tower Hill through Aldgate and Shadwell, a predominantly Jewish neighbourhood. Sylvia was among the tens of thousands of outraged local residents of London's East End, Zionists, socialists, Irish dockworkers, communists, anarchists and left-wing Labour groups who gathered to prevent Mosley and his BUF from marching through their neighbourhoods.

This mass opposition blocked their path and roared, 'They shall not pass.' Estimates of the numbers varied from 20,000 to 200,000. A police force of 6,000 officers tried to clear the area, but failed. The march was diverted via Cable Street. Three sets of barricades, incorporating an overturned lorry and other vehicles, had already been set up there, with broken glass and marbles strewn across the street. Thousands of local people massed behind each barricade, and the protesters exploded homemade bombs and threw marbles at the feet of charging police horses. They rained down a fusillade of projectiles on the marchers and the police attempting to protect them. East London and its supporters forced Mosley and his Blackshirts into retreat, a humiliating defeat. Throngs of anti-fascist protesters congregated in Victoria Park to mark the victory, with great relief but also anger at the role of the police.

Along with many others, Sylvia criticized the timorous and appeasing Labour and Jewish newspapers and community leadership organizations which had urged their members to stay away and 'ignore' the march. The victory at Cable Street carried enormous symbolic value. It demonstrated the effectiveness of a united democratic front. It also prompted Mussolini and Hitler to cut off their funding and political support from Italy and Germany. Deeply unimpressed by Mosley's failure, Mussolini refused him further money and dismissed the BUF's claims to credibility. He concluded that Hitler and he would have to do the job themselves to ensure it was done right. Shortly afterwards,

Sylvia spoke at a rally in Victoria Park co-ordinated by a coalition of radical Jewish organizations to orchestrate opposition to Mosley and the Blackshirts. Fascist thugs threw missiles. Sylvia was injured by a rock thrown at her head.

The Battle of Cable Street demonstrated clearly that opposition to Mussolini and support for Ethiopia were not restricted to political activists and intellectuals. The British public expressed strong support for Ethiopia, motivated by a sense of patriotic shame at Britain's failure to protect a legitimate member of the League of Nations family. There was also respect for Ethiopia as an independent nation that had never been colonized. Large numbers of letters to *The Times*, the *Daily Telegraph* and other leading national newspapers denounced alien aggression, demanded the imposition of sanctions and called on the government to do the right thing. 'One feels ashamed', wrote one reader of *The Times*, 'to belong to a civilized nation which allows an innocent victim to be savagely attacked by a ruthless aggressor.'[1539]

Britain was divided between society and state. Overwhelmingly, British public opinion was strongly pro-Ethiopian. Among the many Conservative MPs and other members of the minority elite there were those, like Evelyn Waugh, Bernard Shaw and Lord Rothermere, owner of the *Daily Mail*, who staunchly supported Mussolini and fascist Italy.

The general population, along with Sylvia, George Lowther Steer and the highly influential Abyssinia Association, were sympathetic to the plight of the Ethiopian people. The South African-born Steer, son of a newspaper manager, played an influential role in shaping Sylvia's consciousness and her understanding of the Ethiopian situation. From deep inside the action, he wrote eyewitness accounts of the Italian–Ethiopian struggle and the Spanish Civil War that alerted Europeans to the atrocities committed by Italians in Ethiopia and by Germans in Spain.

When the fifty-five-year-old Pablo Picasso, supporter of the Spanish Republic and sworn enemy of Franco and his followers, read George Steer's report from Guernica, it inspired him to record the atrocity in a huge mural painting.[1540] 'Painting is not just done to decorate apartments,' he said. 'It is an instrument of war … against brutality and darkness.'[1541] On a Monday night, 26 April 1937, five foreign correspondents covering the civil war drove out to the fire-bombed town of Guernica, interviewed survivors and witnessed the carnage, gagging on the smell of charred meat – human and animal.[1542] Four of the reporters filed their copy immediately, but Steer held back and investigated further and identified the aeroplanes as German. 'He revealed to the world the dirty secret that Nazi Germany was deeply embroiled in the Spanish Civil War, hugger-mugger with General Franco's "insurgents".'[1543] His story caused a global outcry.

In the years before the Second World War, when he gave up journalism and became a British soldier, Steer was the only journalist to report from Ethiopia, the Basque country and Finland, 'where small nations fought for their lives against great powers, and lost'.[1544]

Like Sylvia, Steer actively campaigned for Selassie. As a soldier, he would help liberate Ethiopia in the first Allied victory of the war, driving at the front of the column with Haile Selassie on his victorious return into Addis Ababa.[1545] Evelyn Waugh seethed with jealousy and resentment of Steer for the success of his influential journalism and hard-hitting, bestselling books, all the more so because he regarded Steer as a colonial runt of inferior breeding and rough manners, 'a South African dwarf ... never without a black eye', an outsider to the British establishment.[1546] Steer, who grew up in a liberal household in the Eastern Cape, described himself as 'a South African Englishman', but his tutors at Winchester College in the 1920s thought that the brilliant, sunburned boy with his natural allegiance to the underdog 'showed a colonial disregard for the conventions of this country'.[1547] Steer's bestselling account of the war from the Ethiopian side, *Caesar in Abyssinia* (1936), stood in direct contrast to the English Waugh's pro-Italian version of events, *Waugh in Abyssinia* (1936).

From 1936 to the outbreak of the war, in addition to her weekly 2,000- or 3,000-word editorial for her new newspaper, Sylvia produced weekly instalments for her two serials, 'Fascism As It Is' and 'How Hitler Rose to Power', totalling 200,000 words. The first ran to 120,000 words over nearly fifty issues. The second, when complete, amounted to 80,000 words. She extended the hours of her working week by staying up always at least once and sometimes twice throughout the night before sending the paper to press. She did not type, but drafted in clear longhand. Richard would come down to breakfast to find her at her desk, 'engulfed in a sea of paper'. After she'd sent her handwritten copy to the printer, she turned to answering and writing letters, a daily activity.[1548]

In October 1936, on her return from a trip to Geneva to attend the League of Nations assembly on Ethiopia's continued membership of the League, Sylvia wrote an article explaining her philosophical beliefs and the reasons for her focus on the Ethiopian and anti-fascist struggle. In this piece she explains, 'We have chosen advisedly the prefix *New Times*; for we desire to be no mere chronicle, uncritical and without purpose, but to take an earnest part in building the hopeful edifice of the future.'[1549]

Haile Selassie had led his Ethiopian warriors in battle since the beginning of the war, living in military encampments and manning anti-aircraft guns. When Mussolini's armies entered Addis Ababa, the Emperor wanted to return immediately to fighting, to the death, the hallmark of the Ethiopian warrior. Only with great difficulty was he persuaded to board a train into exile with his family and entourage. At the very last moment, he once again nearly turned back, but his diplomats persuaded him that, as a statesman, he must live another day to launch an appeal to the International Court in Switzerland. The Emperor appointed his cousin Ras Imru Haile Selassie as Regent in his absence, and sought asylum in Britain. As his train pulled into Waterloo Station on 3 June 1936, Sylvia was among the welcoming committee. A Pathé newsreel captures a striking image of her, standing expectant on the platform waiting for his train to arrive, gloved and hatted, a newspaper under her arm. As he stepped off the train with his entourage, Sylvia presented Selassie with a copy of *New Times and Ethiopia News*, then in its fourth issue, and a 'beautifully printed Memorial of Welcome' signed by contributors to the paper and the nine-year-old schoolboy Richard Pankhurst:

> Welcome to our land, millions of whose people honour the valiant suffering of Ethiopia under the cruel and unprovoked aggression of the Fascist dictatorship.
>
> We testify our gratitude for the great and heroic service You have rendered the cause of International Peace and Justice, and our sympathy, fraught with sad and passionate indignation, for the grievous sorrow, and the cruel atrocities inflicted upon Your people.
>
> We pledge our sincere devotion to the cause for which You stand, and our determination to strive that might shall not triumph over right, and that the outcome of this appalling, yet profoundly memorable struggle, shall be Peace with Honour, Freedom and

Prosperity for Ethiopia, and the vindication of Public Law and
Human Right throughout the world.[1550]

This is an effective summary of the work Sylvia undertook to support
Ethiopia for the rest of her life.

While the huge London crowds waiting outside Waterloo Station
waved banners proclaiming 'Welcome to the Emperor' and shouting 'Well
done, Abyssinia' and 'Down with Fascism and war', Sir Oswald Mosley's
Blackshirts were organizing a fascist rally in Hyde Park for Saturday 6
June, to protest against the presence of Selassie and his family in Britain.

The Jewish philanthropist Sir Elly Kadoorie hosted the Emperor and
his family at his home in Prince's Gate, Kensington, near the Ethiopian
Legation, where Sylvia had her first private audience with him a few
days after his arrival, and she informed him briskly, 'I am a republican.
I support you not because you are an emperor, but because I believe
your cause, the cause of Ethiopia, is a just one.' Haile Selassie replied
quietly, 'I know.'[1551] During his years in exile, Sylvia would become, in
the assessment of one of his most reliable biographers, Asfa-Wossen
Asserate, one of Selassie's 'most important supporters in the sphere of
politics and public relations'.[1552] *New Times and Ethiopia News* provided
the key platform for that support.

In this initial interview published in the next issue, Selassie stressed
that the invasion of Ethiopia had been unanimously condemned and
that the 'violation of international conventions regulating warfare'
should be recognized as 'important not to Ethiopia alone but to all the
countries of the world'. World opinion 'cannot remain indifferent before
the use of poison gas, the bombardment of Red Cross Ambulances
and of open towns, and the destruction of civilian populations'. Sylvia
asked him what he was going to request of the League of Nations.
'We shall demand the application of the Covenant by all the means
which are at the disposal of the Member States,' was his reply. From the
outset, Sylvia focused attention on the future: what did the Emperor
consider the most important achievements of his reign, and what were
his intentions on returning to Ethiopia after the defeat of the Italian
occupation? Selassie told her, 'The construction of schools, hospitals,
roads; financial reforms; the purchase of the Bank of Abyssinia and
its transformation into a State bank; the fight against slavery and
establishment of schools for freed slaves.'[1553]

When Sylvia had seen Haile Selassie for the first time, on 3 June, his 'gentle graciousness which impresses all' impressed her too, as did his eyes, in which burned 'the quenchless fire of the hero who never fails his cause'. The 'mental anguish, the physical pain and weakness under which he laboured were more sadly evident when I met him for a personal interview than in a crowd'. Sylvia had earned his trust.

On 25 July, she met him for another interview, pleased to see that his 'bodily health had greatly improved during his stay at Worthing', though his profound grief and anxiety for his people shone through as before. Despite his diminutive frame, he had not been broken by the terrible campaign that might have destroyed many of the strongest. His 'great qualities of mind and heart' reassured her of his capacity to 'solve the appalling difficulties of his nation and his people'. In private correspondence with friends written four years later in 1940, she expressed her concern about his vulnerability. 'He was very friendly … more so than I had ever seen him, and I felt sorry for him because he seemed so utterly helpless. He is, as you know, a very small man of frail physique and I wondered how he was going to enforce the right of his country, and wished more energy could be displayed.' This remark tells more about Sylvia's resources of energy and resilience than it does about Selassie's lack of them.

Contrary to nonsense assertions that she idolized him, Sylvia's correspondence shows her measure of Selassie and her continuous reassessment of his capacities, particularly when it came to the depth of his Christian belief in divine providence.

> I am not necessarily for the Emperor against any other ruler of
> Ethiopia, but though he may not be as strong as many people,
> I think he is humane and he has shown that he is not willing to
> compromise with the Italians. He has the qualities and defects of a
> man who relies on providence. He is not a soldier by temperament.
> But he did expose his life in the trenches for five months, which is
> more than most of the rulers of today would consider doing on any
> account. He is genuinely keen on social reform and his reign would
> be beneficial for his country, I feel sure.

She never disguised her concern about what she regarded as Selassie's naivety about the cunning and duplicity of European statesmen.

'With all his ability and dignity, I often felt, when I went to see the Emperor after Italy declared war [against Britain and France in June 1940], as though I was talking to a sick child who did not know how to deal with the politicians about him.'[1554] This aspect of his personality deeply touched her. He had genuinely placed faith in the justice of the League of Nations. As he put it in his interview with her in August 1936, 'Is the League now prepared to permit Ethiopia to perish for her faith?' When he went to Geneva to protest to the League against the unjust invasion, he had to witness the lifting of sanctions previously imposed. When he asked what the League would do to help fifteen million Ethiopians waiting for him to return with a reply, 'no state member proposed a single measure to assist them in any way, or made any attempt to stop the war in a peaceable fashion'. The League denied his request for a loan of £10 million, while its member countries profited from supplying Italy with resources to produce armaments and fight the war against Ethiopia. 'Must our brave people still struggle and suffer until death? The blood that is being shed is not the blood of a dog. It is the blood of our common humanity, and God will find his way of defending this cause. Since we are of the same descent, being all sons of Adam, and all human, I do not know why the peoples of the world cannot feel the suffering of Ethiopia in her deep trouble.'[1555]

Criticisms for her support of an undemocratic hereditary emperor glanced off Sylvia. From the outset, she made it clear that she supported the principle, not the office, of the person. Where were these vaunted western European democrats when Ethiopia needed the enforcement of the principles of the League of Nations, to which it was entitled as a member? Sylvia stuck to the principle of self-determination for African countries, which she argued should be left alone to decide their own preferred future. After the successful campaign when the Emperor was back in Ethiopia, there was no justification for their war allies to maintain military and administrative presence in their country. The British forces of liberation in Ethiopia should give up their temporary occupation to prove that they had no plans to achieve outright colonial annexation. As she wrote, bluntly, the British should 'clear out of the country and leave her to manage her own affairs and to surmount her own difficulties in her own way'.[1556] In 1941 Foreign Secretary Eden declared that the British government had no 'territorial ambitions in Abyssinia', while its officials were in fact secretly pressing Selassie to cede the Ogaden to British-occupied Somalia, and Borana to the British colony of Kenya.[1557]

As Sylvia argued, those noticeably white western Europeans who criticized her support for a paternalistic hereditary king when they couldn't locate their own backbones to resist Mussolini's fascist advance on Ethiopia appeared to lack equal self-awareness of the paternalism of their own belief that they could best determine the political organization of the countries they had colonized. Sylvia was in line with thinkers and activists of the global black-consciousness movement, including young black African leaders like her personal friends Jomo Kenyatta and Tom Mboya from Kenya, who understood and supported the significance of Selassie's cause from the outset.

Sylvia's *New Times* rapidly became an internationally published British newspaper. Translated across the world into multiple languages, it reached every continent of the globe. Corio worked quietly and largely anonymously as co-editor. He wrote articles under the alias of Crastinus, shared thinking with Sylvia on commissioning and editing, and spent one day a week in Walthamstow at the printing press directing the layout. Once the paper hit a circulation of 10,000 and received sufficient donations from regular subscribers, Sylvia arranged for weekly complimentary copies to be sent to a long list of members of both Houses of Parliament and other influencers. Volunteers sold the paper at meetings and rallies and Sylvia used her well-seasoned tactics for targeted campaigning. During the Peckham and Balham by-election in the summer of 1936, *New Times* opened a pop-up shop selling pro-Ethiopian and anti-fascist publications, the proceeds of which went to the London-based Ethiopian emergency relief fund run by the Legation.

She made extensive use of visual narrative to get her story across, including the sharp satire of political cartoons. In the 1930s there were many opportunities for visual documentary provided by the rapidly proliferating technology of photography. Obtaining pictures through its network of contacts on the ground, *New Times* published images of atrocities suppressed or ignored by other news agencies. Italian troops supplied a steady source of photographic evidence, from mixed motives: some boasting macho-fascistic swagger, keen to show off their crimes, others supplying the images as a form of resistance to express their appalled dissidence.

The biased pro-Italian, anti-African coverage of the Ethiopian crisis by the BBC became increasingly a matter of concern for anti-fascists in Britain generally and a particular target of Sylvia's relentless criticism. The Foreign Office fulminated against Miss Pankhurst's publication of photographs documenting war crimes in the *New Times* and her steady output of pamphlets and leaflets. Italian diplomats complained constantly, particularly about the *New Times* propaganda distributed in Italy and among the invading forces. The Foreign Office made regular sorties to the Home Office and protested directly to the government to try and shut down Sylvia's unremitting publication of atrocities committed against Ethiopia. She reproduced photographs of the Italian Air Force deploying poison gas and bombing the British Red Cross; of dismembered Ethiopian fighters and civilians; of the severed heads of resistance fighters held aloft as trophies by Italian troops; and of a portable gallows on which six Ethiopian patriots had been hanged.

Sylvia packed the pages of *New Times* with statements by the Ethiopian government in exile that received little if any attention in the rest of the British press. When Haile Selassie made his famous address to the League of Nations, speaking of the atrocities committed in Ethiopia and asking 'What reply will I have to take back to my people?', her *New Times* was the first to publish his complete unedited speech.

From the outset, Sylvia's position was typically clear and unequivocal. The Ethiopian crisis was symptom not cause. If governments sat on the fence between Italy and Ethiopia, fascist tanks would soon roll over and crush all of Europe. Neutrality was too shallow a soil in which to build effective resistance to another global war, intent on destroying the messy struggle for democratic forms of civilization against self-interested barbarism:

> *New Times* is opposed to the conception of dictatorship. It understands that fascism destroys all personal liberty and is in fundamental opposition to all forms of intellectual and moral progress. We draw a profound distinction between the Italian Fascist Government and the Italian people, who are enslaved today, but whose freedom is slowly but surely being prepared by the martyrdom of thousands of heroic men and women, guardians of an inextinguishable faith: murdered, tortured, imprisoned, exiled

in poverty and sorrow, they keep high and untarnished the ideal of justice.[1558]

Outside Britain, the paper's most rapid expansion of circulation occurred initially in West Africa and the West Indies. Soon, African nationalist presses across the continent were reproducing news, articles and photographs from *New Times*, with or without attribution. Regarding it as an open source, Sylvia and everyone else involved in the paper had neither the time nor the interest to insist on citation, permissions or copyright that would impede the urgent need to disseminate its information as fast as possible.

Amid the many files of letters received by the paper both from continental Africa and from Africans working and studying across the world was a missive from a West African student in Britain: 'if it were not for your paper the young Africans would not know what is happening in Africa today, as the whole of the press in Europe has no room to publish the Ethiopian case'.[1559] A later series of articles launched by the paper, 'Africa to Africans', became immensely popular all over the home continent, and penetrated further south of the Sahara into heavily censored colonial states, including Kenya and South Africa.

In response to the horrors of imperial air warfare in Ethiopia, Burma and India in the 1930s, Sylvia joined artistic forces with the sculptor Eric Benfield to create an unusual, inspired Anti-Air War Memorial – a public monument for peace that became known as Sylvia's 'Stone Bomb'. Benfield described his work as 'protesting in stone'.[1560] Sylvia conceived the idea of putting up Britain's first public peace monument on the now derelict piece of land she still owned on the site of Red Cottage. Benfield's brilliant design is an enduring piece of modernist statuary, which he explained in a cogent humanitarian statement. 'Those who had preserved bombing were politically and morally dead, and this was their gravestone.'[1561] Its plinth rises up into a pyramid on which the stone torpedo is mounted on its nose as if perpetually falling from the sky. The small bomb is eighteen inches long, with fine serrated fins that seem to whistle through the air. On a plaque at the foot of the plinth is inscribed:

to those who in 1932
upheld the right

to use bombing planes
this monument is raised
as a protest against war in the air

Sylvia dedicated the memorial ironically to the British delegation to the League of Nations, which had 'upheld the right to use bombing aeroplanes' at the World Disarmament Conference in Geneva in February 1932 on the grounds that it was necessary, as her son laconically put it, 'to bomb the tribesmen of northern India to keep them in order'.[1562] Sylvia had witnessed the first Zeppelin raids over London during the First World War. In 1932, she had protested against British bombing of rebels in Burma and north-west India.

The monument, unveiled on 20 October 1935, was vandalized immediately. As Patrick Wright has recorded, 'It was smeared with creosote on its very first night ("the traditional way to object to any stone sculpture", as Benfield observed, happily counting himself into "the select band who have had their public work tarred").'[1563] Shortly afterwards the stone bomb itself was stolen. Benfield immediately set about making a new one, and plans for the new unveiling were announced in the launch edition of *New Times* printed on 5 May 1936, Sylvia's fifty-fourth birthday. 'In these days of ever threatening war, the necessity of effective and ceaseless opposition cannot be over-emphasised,' wrote Daisy Greville, Countess of Warwick. 'The powers of Science have given aerial war a capacity of devastation and destruction without parallel in the history of mankind.' It was vital that people became 'more fully alive to this danger' and, with this aim in mind, it was intended to:

> erect a model in stone of an aerial torpedo bomb ... There are
> thousands of memorials in every town and village to the dead,
> but not one as a reminder of the danger of future wars. The
> People who care for Peace in all countries must unite to force
> their Governments to outlaw the air bomb. We must not tolerate
> this cruelty, the horror of mangled bodies, entrails protruding,
> heads, arms, legs blown off, faces half gone, blood and human
> remains desecrating the soil. We must not assent to this merciless
> destruction of men, women, children and animals.[1564]

Sylvia had tried to organize a big event for the initial unveiling to draw attention to the impending danger. Local media loyally covered the event, but national press and broadcasters showed little interest. Fenner Brockway recalled that very few people believed Sylvia's madcap notion that civilians would be bombed from the air. Only her Ethiopian comrades took the invitation seriously, turning out in force and sending their most senior diplomat to the occasion. The publicity caused by the vandalizing of the first monument 'ensured that the second unveiling', in June 1936, 'achieved much greater interest than the first. Ethiopia was represented once again, but this time there were also representatives from Germany, France, Hungary, Austria and British Guyana.'[1565] Ethiopians, who had by then experienced repeated aerial massacres, publicized and supported the peace monument – and the opportunity to highlight its ironic charge against the failures of the League of Nations – more than any other nation, most particularly Sylvia's own.

Ten weeks after Sylvia had launched her anti-fascist newspaper, right-wing military officers in Spanish-occupied Morocco launched a coup. Within days, civil war in mainland Spain broke out between socialists and fascists. By prior arrangement, Germany, Italy, Japan and other sympathetic European regimes immediately supported Franco's insurgent generals and declared their support for his nationalist war. 'Two Victims of Fascism – Spain and Abyssinia', declared the *New Times* headline, printing photographs of Spanish children killed by German and Italian bombing alongside satirical cartoons ridiculing the official pretence that support for Franco by fascist Italy and Germany was limited merely to the loan of willing volunteers.[1566] To support the resistance, Sylvia began to issue Amharic editions of *New Times*, spirited into occupied Ethiopia along concealed networks.

The newspaper's twinned focus on keeping the Italian invasion of Ethiopia and the Civil War in Spain in its headlines was an early sign of Sylvia's understanding that her anti-fascism was inseparable from her anti-colonialism.[1567] Some readers wrote to her and said, 'Focus on Spain!' Others complained that they wanted to read only about Ethiopia. Ethiopia-sympathizer Lord Auckland, up until then a regular subscriber, sent her a ringing complaint:

> Lord Auckland will be glad if the Editor of the Ethiopian News
> will discontinue to send him that paper, as it has now evidently

degenerated into a pro-Communist sheet and is full of inaccuracies regarding the situation in Spain and the Balearic Islands. If the Editor sees fit to consolidate the Ethiopian cause with that of the Communists of Spain, she will go a long way towards losing the sympathy of those, Lord Auckland included, who in the past have been sympathetic towards Ethiopia and her cause.[1568]

A while later, Sylvia received a letter from Barcelona thanking her for her paper's continuing support for the Spanish anti-fascist struggle, but suggesting she should devote most of her activity to Spain, 'at present the most important thing in the world and of the greatest consequence'.[1569]

Ignoring both positions, Sylvia kept the paper firmly committed to covering both conflicts. When armed resistance to Franco in Spain collapsed in 1939, she joined a women's delegation hoping to persuade the Foreign Office to allow refugees asylum in Britain. Anti-fascist volunteers from free countries were able to return home from Spain, but those from Italy, Germany and Falangist Spain were forced into French detention camps without any facilities. Commissioned by Sylvia to investigate the conditions in the French refugee camps, Nancy Cunard turned in a series of on-the-ground reports revealing in detail the hardship experienced in the camps, where former volunteers died of starvation and cold.

Simultaneously, Sylvia and Silvio worked hard with Carlo Rosselli to produce anti-fascist pamphlets printed in Italian. The couple also got to work assisting Rosselli with smuggling these into Italy, frequently under the noses of British customs officials.

In December 1936 Italian forces captured the Regent Ras Imru, Haile Selassie's cousin and his representative in the west of the country and flew them in chains to Italy, ending Ethiopian resistance in the west. Charles Martin, Ethiopian Ambassador in London, wrote to Sylvia laying out the implications. As Ethiopia could no longer claim to have a government, the abduction was likely to lead to the League of Nations recognizing the Italian 'conquest'. Sylvia organized a petition addressed to the Secretary General of the League of Nations demanding the release of Ras Imru, held in detention in Italy and now one of the few surviving Ethiopian leaders who had not been shot. As part of this campaign and to consolidate the voice of a united democratic front, she threw herself and the paper into organizing an intense schedule of public events – from political meetings and conferences in support of justice for Ethiopia at Central Hall in Westminster to garden-fête fundraisers, bazaars and film screenings.

Through this programme Sylvia corralled a broad coalition of individuals and institutions: the Federation of Peace Councils, the Church of England and the Free Church, trades unions, women's organizations and co-operative guilds. The India League, the League of Coloured Peoples, the African Service Bureau, the Negro Welfare Association and the Kenya Association joined forces as consistent supporters. Despite the seeming staidness of their titles, these were radical organizations. Jawaharlal Nehru sent messages of support from the Indian National Congress. Jomo Kenyatta and the Sierra Leonean union organizer and journalist Isaac Wallace-Johnson, founder of the West African Youth League, supported Sylvia's campaign for a united democratic front, as did the Dean of Winchester and the Quaker Isabel Fry.

In between these events, Sylvia travelled to Geneva to report on and lobby at the League. As Ethiopians continued 'fighting tooth and nail for independence', she expanded the focus of the paper beyond the consistent reporting of fighting and political issues to deepening understanding through articles and full supplements on Ethiopian history and culture. 'What Modern Ethiopia Achieved for Herself', for example, recounts the millennial reach of Ethiopian civilization preceding Mussolini's barbarian 'civilizing mission'.

In May 1937 Neville Chamberlain succeeded Baldwin as Prime Minister, and the next year saw the policy of appeasing Mussolini and Hitler reach its peak: Hitler annexed Austria to Germany; Chamberlain's Conservative government signed the Anglo-Italian agreement, recognizing Mussolini's 'conquest' of Ethiopia; and Hitler, Mussolini, the French Premier Édouard Daladier and Chamberlain signed the Munich Pact, surrendering the Sudeten area of Czechoslovakia to Hitler.

In March 1938 anti-fascist organizations in Britain arranged a demonstration in Trafalgar Square to 'Save Abyssinia and the League'. Sylvia spoke alongside radical lawyers, politicians, publishers, trade unionists and peace councils. Throughout this period *New Times* reported the continued Ethiopian patriotic resistance, informing readers that the provinces of Wollo, Tigre and Gojjam were almost entirely 'free of the Italians', and in another issue revealing that the invaders were again using poison gas.'[1570] The paper gave prominence to a leaked report by the Duke of Aosta, the fascist Viceroy, which informed Rome that 'Italian influence extended only as far as machine-gun bullets could reach, and that "in the event of a European war, the invasion could not last a month".'[1571] On 6 May, the eve of the next meeting of the League of Nations, Sylvia organized a rally in Central Hall, Westminster, under the slogan 'No Recognition of Italy's Conquest of Ethiopia'. Haile Selassie's daughter, Princess Tsehai, and the American singer Paul Robeson joined the speakers, alongside national and international organizations.

The New Times headline on 1 October, the day after the signing of the Munich Pact, condemned Chamberlain's appeasement. 'STAND BY CZECHOSLOVAKIA. Peace Can Only Rest on Justice and Respect to Treaties. Further Concessions to Dictators Will Destroy Us All'. The front page declared, 'In the Event of War it is the Bounded Duty of All Freedom-loving Persons to work with determination for the Defeat of the Fascist States', and carried a lead article denouncing the signing of the Pact as 'The BASEST DAY in BRITISH HISTORY'. Sylvia's editorial observed that the 'outstanding feature of Mr Chamberlain's shameful pact with Mussolini was his cynical and callous thrusting aside of the principle of justice and the rights of the Ethiopian people who are now fighting bravely with extraordinary success ...' Deriding Chamberlain's eulogy of 'new Italy' as the 'crowning insult', she declared, 'The mask is off! Mr Chamberlain has revealed himself as a supporter of Fascist theory and practice.'[1572] She concluded: 'The pact will not stand.' Sylvia once again organized a petition, this time addressed to Chamberlain, its delivery accompanied by another protest meeting in Trafalgar Square.

In April 1939 Sylvia expanded her campaigning by opening a New Times Bookshop on Farringdon Street in London, stocking pro-Ethiopian and anti-fascist publications, and providing a central London venue for meetings, events and book launches.

When they were little girls living in Russell Square, their mother tasked Sylvia and Christabel with arranging the chairs and putting out leaflets for her political and literary salons. Subsequently, Sylvia helped Emmeline in her Emerson & Co. businesses. Mrs Pankhurst's retail enterprises were all beautifully fitted, exquisitely stocked commercial failures, but they were successes in terms of her inventive, forward-thinking imagination. One day, she said, everyone would want easily accessible shops selling beautiful and useful ready-made interior furnishings for their homes. Sylvia's foray into providing books and buns at a destination venue – the Red Cottage Tea Room – paved the way to her innovative Farringdon bookshop, whose combination of politics, culture and community developed from the days of talks, lectures and events at the Mothers' Arms in Bow.

Sylvia programmed a series of 'Meet the Author' Thursdays at her bookshop, inviting writers to speak about and sign their works. The veteran campaigning journalists Henry Nevinson and Henry Noel Brailsford featured in the series alongside Vera Brittain, the acclaimed New Zealand novelist Robin Hyde and the political interviewer Betty Ross. Peter and Irma Petroff had been friends since Sylvia met them in Soviet Russia. She invited them to speak about their political autobiographies and their experience as Jewish communist refugees. Another popular speaker, Cobina Kessie – law student and activist from the Gold Coast – was one of several controversial 'children of empire' studying in Britain whose dissident activities and opinions were prompting an anxious Foreign Office to monitor their activities closely.

The New Times Bookshop operated successfully as a hub of progressive thinking and emerging new writing from around the globe until German bombs destroyed it during the summer of 1940.

Sylvia understood the propaganda value of cinema. In 1937 she saw two Italian fascist films, *The Birth of an Empire* and *The Path of Heroes*.[1573] Their brutality substantiated everything she had been writing about and she immediately understood their value in Britain as anti-fascist, pro-Ethiopian propaganda. She persuaded Gilbert Murray, a leading voice in the League of Nations Union, to watch *The Birth of an Empire* with a view to arranging a public screening in London. Murray was appalled that 'We are asked to look at scenes which make an impression of beautiful display and skill in flying, but which really represent acts of abominable cruelty inflicted on people who for the purpose of the entertainment are treated as if they did not matter ... The action represented is not war but mere massacre.'[1574] There could be no more 'dastardly cowardice', Murray wrote, than 'showering bombs and poison gas day after day upon a people who have no aeroplanes and no effective arms with which to hit back'.[1575] He added, 'The culminating horror of this exhibition is not physical but psychological,' that Mussolini, 'instead of sinking with shame at the knowledge of the deeds done in his name and by his own family, is actually proud of them and boasts of them to the world'.[1576]

Sylvia arranged a screening of the film at the Regal Cinema in Marble Arch on 19 December 1937, together with two Ethiopian films. She scheduled a second screening of *The Birth of an Empire* at the Phoenix Theatre, Charing Cross Road, for 15 February 1938, in the presence of the Emperor and Dr Martin. The Italian Embassy got wind of the plan, and quickly arranged for the film to be withdrawn from circulation. Undeterred, Sylvia managed to obtain a copy, and screened the film at the Kingsway Hall on 31 March at a Memorial Concert for the Ethiopian Dead. She organized a further showing of the film in her native Manchester on 13 May at the Houldsworth Hall, Deansgate.

Addressing the meeting after the Kingsway Hall viewing, Sylvia reminded the audience that the merciless terror they had just witnessed on screen still continued: 'planes are still bombing little homes, setting their fragile walls aflame, and blowing to mangled fragments their defenceless occupants. Agonised people … are still convulsed by terror and grief. The war goes on.'[1577] Sylvia's son Richard identified this speech as significant: it marked the moment that she publicly announced her change of position from committed pacifist to supporter of necessary Ethiopian armed resistance:

> The awful thing is that we who hate war are compelled to rejoice
> because Ethiopia's valiant soldiers are still in arms. They refuse
> to submit to the aggressor. They are a daily standing proof that
> the cruel and unjust aggression does not pay. They are a shield to
> other nations against the aggressive designs of the dictator who
> is compelled to employ finance and forces in Ethiopia which
> otherwise would be used in other parts of the world. They will yet
> be the force which shall participate in the fall of Mussolini in the
> revolt which his vast and costly failure in Abyssinia will precipitate
> against his cruel and costly rule in Italy itself.[1578]

In 1940 Sylvia saw another Charlie Chaplin film at the Plaza Cinema. *The Great Dictator*, the first he made with dialogue, ended with a speech that Chaplin is said to have rewritten and rehearsed more than any other in his career:

I don't want to rule or conquer anyone. I should like to help
everyone – if possible Jew, Gentile – black man – white. We all
want to help one another. Human beings are like that. We want
to live by each other's happiness – not by each other's misery. We
don't want to hate and despise one another. In this world there is
room for everyone. And the good earth is rich and can provide for
everyone. The way of life can be free and beautiful, but we have lost
the way. Greed has poisoned men's souls, has barricaded the world
with hate, has goose-stepped us into misery and bloodshed. We
have developed speed, but we have shut ourselves in. Machinery
that gives abundance has left us in want. Our knowledge has made
us cynical. Our cleverness, hard and unkind. We think too much
and feel too little. More than machinery we need humanity. More
than cleverness we need kindness and gentleness. Without these
qualities, life will be violent and all will be lost …

Many argued that this speech was superfluous, and roundly criticized
Chaplin for including it in the film. 'Remember – everywhere, always,
fascism means war,' Sylvia had written back in May 1936. Perhaps those
who thought Chaplin too overtly politicized in his film also found Miss
Pankhurst's warnings about fascism 'tiresome'. Even three years after
the war had broken out, her refusal to be silenced on the subject of
international justice had, in the opinion of the Foreign Office, turned
her into 'a crashing bore'.[1579]

Sylvia marked the twenty-fifth anniversary of the outbreak of the
First World War in 1939 with a grim leader, facing a world once more
'under the shadow of the guns'. On the day war was declared in 1914,
she was stunned, but, now eternally vigilant, she had this time seen the
enemy approach from afar: 'The Enemy is Fascism. There can be no
respite from it till it is overthrown.'[1580] Angered by her constant barrage
of articles about Ethiopian resistance and the repressive policies of
fascist colonialism, Rome once again launched an attack against Sylvia
and her paper – this time on the radio.

33

War in Woodford

At West Dene in Woodford, Essex, there was no sharp intake of breath as the family gathered around the wireless to listen to Neville Chamberlain's address to the nation. By Sylvia's reckoning Chamberlain's policy of appeasement had taken Britain to war years before: the Second World War had begun on 3 October 1935 when Mussolini invaded Ethiopia. By September 1939, she was already fully immersed in fighting the colonial wars that had raged ever since the Italian leader launched his imperialist mission of conquest in Africa.

When Hitler invaded Poland on 1 September 1939, Sylvia was fifty-seven, her son eleven and Silvio about to celebrate his sixty-fourth birthday. Japan and China had been at war in the Pacific for two years. Sylvia would say there most certainly had never been peace in her time. The Russian Revolution had attempted to make direct war against capitalism. The redrawing of the map at Versailles rearmed nationalism for a century and beyond. Sylvia and Silvio had opposed the Munich Pact and the Molotov–Ribbentrop pact of August 1939, allowing Hitler to run amok in the east. Sylvia fully supported the declaration of war on Germany by Britain and France, regarding it as long overdue.

At the actual outbreak of the war, Sylvia immediately added a new tagline to the masthead of *New Times and Ethiopia News*: 'THE NATIONAL ANTI-FASCIST WEEKLY'. In contrast with her stance on the First World War, she now advocated complete military victory against the Axis powers. She condemned Chamberlain for preferring his individual policy of appeasement to collective international action through the now useless League of Nations. Her criticism of the Prime Minister, however, was mild by comparison with her condemnation of the Soviet Union for entering into the Molotov–Ribbentrop pact, over which neither Russian people nor the German had any say.

> The Communist Parties of Britain and France will doubtless find some method of justifying this Pact to their own satisfaction, but their non-communist allies, who had great faith, are dismayed … It is a stunning blow. Yet for ourselves we are not stunned by it, nor wholly surprised. We knew that there was always a risk that the Soviet Union would even now hold aloof from the struggle – the desperate struggle – between all that is best in European democracy and the brutal forces of fascism.[1581]

She detailed Stalin's totalitarian terror and complicity with fascism, and rededicated the *New Times* to working for its overthrow. Sylvia published relentless criticism of Stalin's Russia, condemning the invasion of Finland and publishing exposés of the Soviet Union's cynical and manipulative 'support' for the Spanish Republic. Among many articles about Stalin's purges was an article by the defector General Krivitsky about 'The Execution of the Old Bolsheviks', some of whom Sylvia had met years earlier in revolutionary Russia and had stayed in touch with until they were brutally executed. *New Times* was one of the first British journals to publish Krivitsky's revelations.

War on a new front meant making a list of practical tasks and getting on with them immediately. The only significant change was that Silvio and most of their community of Italian friends and colleagues were now potentially 'enemy aliens'. This didn't make much practical difference personally as Sylvia's and Silvio's passports had been withdrawn and visas permitting them to leave Britain refused on numerous occasions since 1918. But the restrictions impacted enormously on many of their friends.

Until Mussolini's entry into the war, Britain and Italy remained allies and Sylvia's opposition to the fascist state angered the Foreign Office. The Foreign Office was struggling to placate Il Duce, who had objected to the anti-fascist content of Sylvia's newspaper. Mussolini's diplomats had declared *New Times* a violation of the 1938 Anglo-Italian treaty, which restricted negative propaganda between the nations. To mollify its Roman ally without outraging Britons' love of their freer press, the Ministry of Information, operating from Senate House in Russell Square, deployed wartime censorship powers to prohibit Sylvia from dispatching *New Times* to neutral countries, which officially included Italy. She was permitted to continue to write and publish what she liked in Britain.[1582]

On the evening of the announcement of Mussolini's declaration of war on Britain and France on 10 June 1940, Sylvia and Silvio were enjoying one of their frequent casual supper parties. As usual, Silvio cooked, and Italian refugees predominated among their guests, several of whom were Jewish-Italian anti-fascist activists. Richard, aged twelve at the time, remembered that his parents and their friends 'cheered when they heard the BBC news announcement that "Signor Mussolini" had declared war. They knew that this action, which they had long been awaiting, meant their days of exile were numbered.'[1583] Britain's policy of appeasing Mussolini with promises of territorial concessions in Africa in exchange for neutrality was over. Haile Selassie had already offered Ethiopia's allegiance before the dictator's declaration of war. On 16 May the Emperor had sent dispatches to the British and French governments, assuring them of the 'complete and loyal cooperation of the Ethiopian people', and offering 'the immediate assistance of several thousand experienced riflemen'.[1584] The British government finally had to decide to support Ethiopian liberation from Italian colonialism. The timing of Selassie's confidential notes is significant. On 10 May Winston Churchill had replaced Chamberlain as Prime Minister, and shortly afterwards had appointed Anthony Eden as Secretary of State for War.

The morning after the supper party, a knock at the front door announced the unexpected arrival of their most hostile and difficult neighbour, a retired pro-fascist British army officer who had met both Il Duce and the Pope in Italy. Until now he had pointedly ignored and shunned them, expressing horror to their other neighbours at Sylvia's wrong-headed politics. Hat in hand, he apologized to Mr Corio for his rudeness to his wife. He'd thought she had been 'barking up the wrong tree'. Now he understood that she had been right after all. Collarless, in

706   SYLVIA PANKHURST

the overall he wore for working at home, Silvio extended a handshake and his usual hospitality of an invitation into the house for a cup of tea. Not long afterwards, Sylvia received a letter from barrister Francis Beaufort-Palmer, 'a friend of all oppressed peoples'[1585] and contributor to *New Times* in support of Ethiopia: 'I suggest that you open a fund for a contribution to buy Mr Chamberlain a hat to eat.'[1586]

The Foreign Office changed tack in its attitude not only to Sylvia but to Corio, who found himself immediately invited to give an Italian broadcast on the BBC. His son recalled that the BBC introduced the broadcast with the rousing music of the 'Inno di Garibaldi', which half a century earlier had so inspired Italians fighting for independence and unity. Mussolini's entry into the war effectively nullified the Anglo-Italian agreement. This was a turning point in Sylvia's long campaign against the dictator she regarded as the founder of fascism. She reminded readers that Mussolini had declared war on the anniversaries of the murders of both Giacomo Matteotti and Carlo Rosselli.

On Thursday 13 June, the Italian Ambassador Signor Bastianini, his staff and around 300 other Italians who had taken refuge at the London Embassy were preparing to catch a train for Glasgow to join a ship ready to take them to Lisbon. Sylvia went to deliver a personal send-off: 'Miss Sylvia Pankhurst, the ex-suffragette, walked up to the Embassy this morning, threw a copy of the *New Times and Ethiopia News* on the Embassy steps and went away. One of the policemen on duty picked up the paper and put it in his pocket.'[1587]

That *New Times* reaffirmed the paper's commitment to ensuring recognition of the full independence of Ethiopia and other territories occupied by fascist Italy, Albania and the Greek Dodecanese islands. 'Ethiopia is our ally in the struggle against the Axis Powers':

Help to Speed the Victory!
  Mussolini's Declaration of War assures:
  ABYSSINIA'S FREEDOM;
  THE FALL OF FASCISM;
  AXIS POWERS WILL PERISH TOGETHER
  Our Policy Vindicated

Sylvia called for Haile Selassie's immediate recognition by the Allied governments. Some members of the House of Lords, she noted, commiserated with the King of Italy, on the grounds that could hardly be held responsible for Mussolini's war. She retorted that Victor Emmanuel certainly cut a 'pitiable figure lacking the moral courage to withstand the crimes of the dictator', from whom he had accepted the title 'Emperor of Ethiopia'.[1588]

The British government was initially unwilling to withdraw its recognition of Italy's occupation of Ethiopia and Albania, even after Rome's declaration of war. Britain had been party to treaties recognizing Italian supremacy in the partitioning of East Africa throughout the scramble for the continent, and had consistently refused to treat Ethiopia, an independent country, as being on an equal footing with European sovereign states. Sylvia observed that War statesmen of 'civilised countries' used African territories as bargaining chips in the settlement of inter-European disputes.

From the platform of her newspaper and other national media channels, and in letters with which she bombarded ministers, Sylvia urged the government to withdraw recognition of Mussolini's occupation of Ethiopia, recognize the country's full right to independence and accept it as an ally, according Haile Selassie's government in exile equal status with the European refugee governments from Nazi-occupied countries. Further, it should commit to the total dismantling of the Italian colonial empire and recognize the full independence of Albania. She also drafted a series of parliamentary questions for MPs to put to the Commons. These pressed the Foreign Office to acknowledge that Italy's unprovoked entry into the war entitled Britain 'to reserve full liberty of action' in respect of previous agreements. The government duly committed to recognizing Haile Selassie's administration as the lawful authority in Ethiopia, with the status of an ally, but having confirmed this pledge, proceeded to do absolutely nothing to implement it.

By the autumn of 1940 it was clear that the government was dragging its heels on derecognizing the Italian 'conquest' of Ethiopia, annulling the Anglo-Italian agreement or committing itself to Ethiopia's independence and full status as an ally. The Emperor was in Khartoum, in Sudan, 'a half-resented, semi-prisoner of the British administration',[1589] and isolated from his parliamentary and civil society supporters in Britain. The Governor-General Sir Stuart Symes and General William Platt, in charge of the East Africa command, were opposed to allowing the Emperor to return to Ethiopia and lead his forces. At the end of October, Anthony Eden and General Wavell, British Commander-in-Chief in the Middle East, arrived in Khartoum and, according to Selassie's American adviser John Spencer, 'forced Platt to renounce his opposition to the use of the Emperor as a means of combating the Italians. To that end, Wavell, with Eden's approval, arranged the appointment of Colonel Orde Wingate, as the Emperor's staff officer.'[1590] There was no formal treaty, but an agreement was reached to recognize Haile Selassie as leader of a war of liberation, entitled to full freedom of action. Orde Wingate was confirmed as overall commander of the guerrilla operations. His brief was to contribute to the British East African Campaign by assisting Ethiopian patriots and hold down Italian forces in the north-west of the country. Wingate interpreted his mandate as including the liberation of Ethiopia and the reinstatement of Emperor Haile Selassie.

Born in India where his father was a colonel of the British Raj, Wingate was brought up an evangelical, fundamentalist Christian in the Plymouth Brethren sect. He declared frequently that he felt a kinship with Oliver Cromwell and before going into battle always quoted to his troops liberally from the Old Testament. He attended Charterhouse and the Royal Military Academy at Woolwich, after that mastering fluent Arabic at the London School of Oriental and African Studies. In the 1920s he commanded a company of the Sudan Defence Force. Transferred to Palestine in 1936, he led a paramilitary commando unit made up of British soldiers and members of the Jewish Settlement Police (JSP), also known as the Notrim.

Since the nineteenth century, Ethiopia had held an image in the west of being an African kingdom that was both ancient and Christian. The Ethiopians continued to claim the truth of the legend that their dynasty and the people themselves were descended from the Tribes of Israel and that they possessed the Ark of the Covenant – or the Holy Grail – in the Cathedral of St Mary of Zion in Aksum. In Palestine, Wingate got involved in the kibbutz movement and Zionism. His dream was to ride triumphantly into a liberated Jerusalem on a white horse. His plan to found a Jewish army never materialized on the scale he planned it, but it eventually took the form of the Jewish Brigade. His close friends Chaim Weizmann and David Ben-Gurion declared him an extraordinary friend of the Jewish people and the Zionist cause. Wilfred Thesiger, British military officer, writer and explorer, who served with Wingate in Ethiopia, described him as 'an idealist and a fanatic ... He should have lived in the time of the Crusades.'[1591] Frustrated by British inaction up to this point, Wingate surprised Haile Selassie with his fervent determination to restore the Emperor to his throne and ensure that Ethiopians played a full part in their own liberation.

Wingate flew to Gojjam to consult with Colonel Daniel Sandford on the plan for taking back Ethiopia. Sandford, who knew the country better than anyone else in the British armed forces, was to be the military liaison to the bands of resistance in Ethiopia. In due course, he and his wife would become close friends of Sylvia's. Wingate put together a tiny army of about seventy British commandos, 800 men from the Sudan Frontier Battalion and about 800 Ethiopian Patriots – the resistance fighters known in Amharic as *Arbegnoch*. Wingate called it Gideon Force, after the Old Testament judge chosen by an angel to deliver the Israelites from oppression by the Midianites. On 20 January 1941, the Emperor and his entourage, including his two sons and the diplomat Lorenzo Taezaz, flew to the Sudan–Ethiopia border in two Hurricane fighters, courtesy of – ironically – the South African air force which had been deployed to the Allied East African campaign. Wingate, who was there to meet him, had organized an appropriate ceremony, including bugle call and raising the imperial standard up a pole. 'For the first time in five years, Haile Selassie stood on Ethiopian soil as the colors of his nation flew proudly overhead.'[1592]

Sylvia learned, through the press, that Selassie and Eden had met in Khartoum, but realized that no statement of official British policy had resulted from the meetings, and she kept up pressure on this point in her editorials, repeatedly demanding that British government confirm the independence of Ethiopia as a British war aim and the annulment of the Anglo-Italian agreement. The Foreign Office continued to issue assurances that Britain had no territorial ambitions in Ethiopia, but Sylvia didn't believe them. The Foreign Office files, released long after her death, show that she was right to mistrust the claims. Colonial Office documents, from November and December 1940, confirm the intention to establish a protectorate over Ethiopia, and its partial dismemberment, described as 'frontier rectifications', in favour of the three neighbouring British territories, Anglo-Egyptian Sudan, the British colony of Kenya and British Somaliland.

Sylvia had devised a campaign, launched in June, that drove the BBC, the Foreign Office and several government ministers to apoplectic fury. The Sunday evening after Mussolini's declaration of war, Sylvia 'listened to the radio with great interest' to an evening recital of the 'National Anthems of the Allies'. Surprised that the Ethiopian national anthem was not played, she wrote immediately to the BBC, the government and various newspapers, highlighting the omission. The variety of explanations offered by the BBC over the ensuing months for leaving out the anthem makes for highly amusing reading. Sylvia wondered aloud, in *New Times* and in parliamentary questions put by MPs on her behalf, whether the exclusion of the Ethiopian anthem was from fear of offending the racist apartheid state of South Africa, whose own white-supremacist nationalist anthem was included. On 29 October fascist Italy invaded Greece, thus making that country an ally. The following Sunday the BBC played the Greek national anthem, while still omitting to broadcast that of Ethiopia. In December Luxemburg was added to the list, and in April 1941 Yugoslavia.

The non-playing of the Ethiopian anthem became a cause célèbre. By the end of April 1941, the success of the Liberation Campaign, combined with political lobbying, the relentless pressure of Ethiopia's supporters and the groundswell of British popular support for its cause had broken down the Foreign Office opposition to recognizing the nation as an ally. Haile Selassie and the victorious liberation forces entered Addis Ababa on Monday 5 May, Sylvia's birthday. The following Sunday, Sylvia sat down to listen once again to the broadcast and was 'pleasurably satisfied' to hear, finally, the long-awaited anthem.[1593] In the *New Times* she praised the Ministry of Information, which 'rose brilliantly to the occasion by including the National Anthem of Ethiopia among those of all Allies, and by sounding it first of all, for in fact Ethiopia was the first of the Allies against the Axis to suffer invasion and to take up the dauntless fight against the enemy'.[1594] Long before, Sylvia had learned the political art of uncompromising persistence and the need within democracy to hammer fearlessly away at the same point through representative channels of persuasion and argument. With age, this capacity matured into a sublime indefatigability whose wellspring seemed limitless. Her lifelong rebellion against authority was now honed to a fine art.

A measure of Sylvia's effectiveness in her anti-fascist work came in the form of two death threats in 1940. A Nazi supporter from Rochester warned her that Hitler would be in Britain very soon, and that if she did not desist from publishing her paper 'it would find itself without an Editor'. The next, signed on behalf of 'Italian London Fascists', also advised that 'the invasion of England will take place in a few days', at which time 'You will pay with your life.' Sylvia published both letters in *New Times*, August and September that year. She and Silvio continued to leave the back door at Charteris Road unlocked. At the end of the war, Nazi records revealed that Sylvia's name was on the Gestapo Special Wanted List of 2,820 people to be arrested when the Germans invaded Britain in 1940. George Steer, along with many others she numbered as friends and colleagues, was also among those to be rounded up by the Gestapo. After the war, Rebecca West found herself on the list alongside her friend Noël Coward, to whom she quipped, 'My dear – the people we should have been seen dead with.'[1595] Sylvia so infuriated Mussolini that he soon took up both pen and microphone against her directly.

While Silvio arranged for the construction of two Anderson air-raid shelters in the garden, Sylvia got to work organizing her Women's War Emergency Council. Based on her East End experience of the First World War, the Council advocated measures for introducing price controls and rationing and securing allowances for soldier's families. These included separation allowances, soldiers' pensions and control of food prices and of other essential provisions. Beginning as a local initiative, the model of the programme soon spread all over London. This time her initiatives met no obstruction, but were warmly welcomed and encouraged by local councils and swiftly taken up by central government. To her surprise, she received a respectful invitation to attend consultative talks at the War Office to advise on the implementation of these measures as national policy.

Her son noticed the disappearance of pots, pans and utensils from their kitchen as the former pacifist Sylvia packed up domestic hardware for delivery to the local metal-collection point for the government's manufacture of Spitfires and Hurricanes. There were further changes in the kitchen, as Richard explained: 'We had until then been vegetarians – I firmly so ... However, in view of wartime difficulties, and the need for simplicity, my parents decided when necessary to eat meat. Not for the first, or last, time were considerations of animal welfare avowedly subordinated to those of humans.'[1596] Fortunately, rationing didn't much affect his supply of sweets, since his parents gave him their allowance.

Silvio covered the Anderson shelters in the garden of West Dene with thick turf and soil. The government issued one shelter per family, and they were free to those with an annual income of less than £250. For those who didn't fall into this category, the price was £7. The second shelter at West Dene was allocated to the Pankhurst tenants, who subsequently moved out. It soon became apparent that Woodford lay directly beneath the Luftwaffe's flight path to central London. When air raids became regular, Sylvia put Richard to bed in one shelter while she and Silvio continued to work in the house. If the bombing became heavy, they would rush out to the other shelter.

Richard recalled vividly a night spent with his parents in Bethnal Green Underground station when an air raid interrupted their journey home from Liverpool Street. He was put to bed on an 'immense and dusty pile' of railway records, more than four feet high and dating back decades. 'Later as a student of economic history at the London School of Economics I wished that I had had the time to study them for they would have constituted the basis of fascinating research in transport history.'[1597] Before leaving central London for Woodford, the family had enjoyed a spaghetti supper in Charing Cross at an Italian eating house run by an anti-fascist restaurateur friend of theirs. The next day they heard that he had been killed during the night when the restaurant had been hit in the bombing.

Sylvia wrote a poem about the Blitz, 'Blackout in London Town Tonight'. The verses express fear of aerial bombing – 'Spare these still homes where millions sleep' from the 'maddening glare of incendiary bombs' – and her love for London and its 'sheer, stark majesty'.[1598]

Unlike so many other youngsters, Richard was not evacuated. To circumvent the unpredictable and potentially dangerous steam-train commute, Sylvia moved him to Bancroft's, an independent school founded in 1737, situated nearby on Woodford High Road.[1599] Aside from being able now to walk to school, Richard was relieved to escape from one of his former teachers who had visited Germany for the 1936 Olympics and had ever since enthusiastically propounded to the children the wonders of Hitler and Nazism. Sylvia volunteered West Dene as a collection and distribution point for clothes and essential supplies for evacuated children, dispatching innumerable parcels around the country.

Voicing her regret for the violent backlash in Britain against Italian shopkeepers, Sylvia's first editorial on Mussolini's entry into the war emphasized that the Italian military autocracy 'does not represent the Italian people over whose "corpse" of democratic liberties Mussolini boasts he "marched"'. Italian shopkeepers and restaurateurs were in no way responsible for the activities of Mussolini and his 'gangsters'. Sylvia listed and honoured the 'heroes and heroines' of the resistance, including the many interned in Mussolini's penal islands: 'Ardent anti-fascist exiles are ready to fight to liberate Italy from the shameful yoke of Fascism, as they fought, ill-equipped, against its extension in Spain.'[1600]

Corio picked up this theme in an article published simultaneously in English and Italian, urging the need to reject 'false patriotism' and underlining that there 'is not a single thread of solidarity between us Anti-Fascists and those who have fettered into abject slavery the Italian people. Mussolini is the traitor, not we!' Responding to the dictator's call to arms, Corio answered, 'Yes, we shall fight, proud to do so, at last – against you!… You have stolen the freedom of our native land; we shall reconquer it arms in hand … We shall free the Italian name from the shame you have cast upon it.'[1601]

The British Home Office and a number of Conservative apologists for fascism had no intention of missing a new opportunity for divide and rule, particularly where it related to a group containing such markedly radical activists. Swiftly, it became evident that the government agencies dealing with 'enemy aliens' in Britain were failing to differentiate sufficiently between Italian fascists and anti-fascists. Ani Anzani, secretary of the Italian section of the League of the Rights of Man and a regular contributor to *New Times*, was interned, alongside former members of the International Brigade who had fought in Spain and Jewish refugees from Mussolini's ethnic-cleansing laws. Too many prominent fascists, meanwhile, were left at large in Britain, among them the founder of the London *fascio*, Mussolini's UK support group.

In tragic consequence of this miscarriage of justice – as Sylvia described it – Anzani and a group of other anti-fascists drowned at sea when the *Arandora Star* – on which they were being shipped to detention on the Isle of Man – was torpedoed by a German submarine. Immediately, Sylvia launched a campaign on behalf of the survivors interned on the island. In a series of articles telling the personal, human stories of the Italian residents, she sought to create empathy and understanding for their plight.

One typical example from this series, entitled 'Fascists at Large, Anti-Fascists Interned', recounted the case of Aldo Cosomati, married to an Englishwoman. Right-wing inmates saw one of his anti-fascist cartoons in a newspaper and beat him up, without any intervention from the guards. Successive articles exposing this and similar cases, as well as letters to ministers and other activist methods from her repertoire, led to success in that most of these injustices were redressed. The government, however, never conceded culpability for prejudicial treatment of 'enemy aliens', or the unnecessary loss of life on the *Arandora Star*.

Home Office files show that MI5 kept its eye on Sylvia's correspondence and her movements from 1936. In 1940, she wrote to Viscount Swinton as the chairman of a security committee investigating fifth columnists, sending him a list of active fascists still at large and of anti-fascists who had been interned. A copy of this letter on MI5's file carries a note in Swinton's hand reading, 'I should think a most doubtful source of information.'[1602]

Released in May 2004, this reconstituted MI5 file chiefly concerns Sylvia's post-suffragette years, though there are summaries of her earlier activities, including notes on the *Workers' Dreadnought* and the Workers' Suffrage Federation from 1914. The main body of the file follows her from the launch of the *New Times and Ethiopia News* in 1936, and contains reports of meetings she addressed, transcripts of her speeches, notes of interviews with her and the product of a 'watch' maintained on her correspondence.

The file concludes that Sylvia's chief source of information was her long-term Italian partner, Silvio Corio. After the liberation of Ethiopia, it details her activities there, documenting her strong support for a union of Ethiopia with ex-Italian Somaliland, later to become part of the independent state of Somalia. The file would consider in 1948 various strategies for 'muzzling the tiresome Miss Sylvia Pankhurst'.[1603]

During the war – initially undetected by her MI5 watch – Sylvia went round to the London flat of Orde Wingate, just back from fighting in the Ethiopian liberation campaign. He had been summarily recalled from Addis Ababa and gagged, as he was regarded as too embedded as a commander of Haile Selassie's resistance forces. He knew, as did everyone in Addis at the time, that Sylvia was a trusted ally.

Sylvia discovered Wingate's return by accident, thanks to her friend and former suffragette Millie Gliksten, who chanced to see him in the corridor of the apartment block off Park Lane where they both lived. Thirty years earlier, Millie had hidden Sylvia in her home for several days to help her evade rearrest under the Cat and Mouse Act. By the time Sylvia met him at the age of thirty-seven, the enthusiastic young Zionist Wingate had already gained extensive experience and some international notoriety. Sylvia took Richard with her to meet Wingate at his apartment, where he gave a detailed, vivid account of the Ethiopian campaign. He also outlined his strategy for capturing Libya. His pent-up energy fascinated Richard, as did his ambitious idea for launching a 'Lawrence of Arabia type attack' on the Italians in Libya from the South'.[1604] The object of their discreet meeting was for Wingate to lend Sylvia a copy of his classified official campaign strategy. The following day, his wife Lorna arrived in Woodford by train to retrieve the copy.[1605] Wingate intended to stand for parliament as a Labour candidate, but died in what many claim to be a mysterious plane crash in Burma in March 1944.

The Allied campaign for the liberation of Italian East Africa began in January 1941 and ended less than three months later. As soon as Allied troops reached Addis Ababa, Sylvia got to work calling on Italian anti-fascists to make clear that they would renounce any post-war claim to Ethiopia once Mussolini was defeated.

The question of the future of the Italian colonies in Africa now came to the fore, most specifically that of Eritrea, founded half a century earlier and the launchpad for two Italian invasions of Ethiopia, in 1895 and 1935. Ethiopia's successful resistance to the nineteenth-century 'scramble for Africa' was the cause of its being singled out for revenge during the age of totalitarian conquest in the 1930s. Mussolini's invasion in part sought to avenge Emperor Menelik II's defeat of the Italian army at the Battle of Adwa in 1896. Ranking with the later defeat of Russia by Japan in the Russo-Japanese War as one of the great setbacks of European imperialism, the Battle of Adwa was misrepresented as having been an encounter with an army of disorganized Africans with spears somehow accidentally beating the Italians. Independent Ethiopia was slowly but steadily modernizing, an affront to the fascist ideology of black barbarism. By invading Ethiopia, Mussolini could avenge and colonize simultaneously. Prior to partition during the European colonial conquest of Africa, Eritrea formed an integral part of Ethiopia. In the years of Italian colonization, many Eritreans went to work in

Addis Ababa or, denied education by the fascists, went to Ethiopian schools. The most promising were sent abroad to study, like many other Ethiopians.

In August 1935 the Emperor established a government press bureau under the directorship of the thirty-five-year-old Eritrean-born Dr Lorenzo Taezaz, who had been secretary to the Governor of Asmara before he was driven from his homeland by Italian racism. As a result of a chance meeting in Aden, Selassie had sponsored Taezaz by means of a scholarship enabling him to study abroad so that he could return to become an agent of modernization and reform in Ethiopia. He was one of the new cohort of gifted Young Ethiopians – *jeunesse éthiopienne* – in whom the Emperor was investing to build the nation's future.[1606] Taezaz went to Montpellier to study law, served on the Boundary Commission before Wal Wal and ran the Emperor's counter-espionage service working with Ethiopian Patriots against Italian spies in Ethiopia. During these years he became the country's most senior diplomat. He drafted Haile Selassie's speech to the League of Nations, following which he was appointed Ethiopia's Permanent Delegate to the League. At the end of the war with Italy, he became Minister of Foreign Affairs. He was among Sylvia's close friends including several from the Eritrean region, the diplomat Ephrem Tewelde Medhen and Mr Tedros, a waiter, who with his West Indian wife and children were among the newspaper's staunchest supporters. From these Eritreans came Sylvia's belief that the colony should be reunited with the rest of Ethiopia from which it had been hacked within her lifetime. She laid down this position in March 1941, a few days before the Allied occupation of the Eritrean capital, Asmara, and before Haile Selassie raised the question of the colony's future. 'With Italy removed,' Sylvia wrote, 'Eritrea with its seaboard should return to Ethiopia.' Ethiopia needed access to the sea, 'by the recovery of at least some part of her ancient coast'.[1607]

In a series of articles entitled 'The Post-War World I Want', African contributors argued that Eritrea and Italian Somaliland should be reunited with Ethiopia, as did Rastafarian commentators from the West Indies. Meanwhile, Britain administered Eritrea as occupied enemy territory. Fascist legislation, and racial laws, remained in place, the press was censored and political organization prohibited. Selassie would grant 500 acres of fertile land to the 'Black People of the West' in

1948, as a gesture of appreciation for their massive support to Ethiopia during the Italian occupation of 1935–41.[1608] The first immigrants to arrive were African-American Jews, who soon moved on to Liberia or Israel. Following them, in 1963, came a dozen Rastafarians, whose numbers expanded further following Selassie's visit to Jamaica three years later.[1609]

By the autumn of 1941 it became clear that Sylvia's concerns that Britain was attempting to replace the Italians as de facto ruler of Ethiopia were entirely justified. A series of delegations and talks at the Foreign Office, along with consultation with Orde Wingate and Sir Philip Mitchell, an administrator of the former Italian territories, brought her to this conclusion. Most people in Britain believed that the struggle for Ethiopian independence had been completed by the Allied liberation. Conversely, Sylvia realized that it was now necessary to fight for the country against its supposed liberators. Under the cloak of the war, Britain was trying to turn Ethiopia into a protectorate. Readers comfortable in the assumption that Ethiopia had been liberated woke to the announcement, in September 1941, that 'INDEPENDENCE OF ETHIOPIA IN DANGER: All Her Friends Must Be On The Alert: REASSERT YOUR FAITH IN FREEDOM'S CAUSE.'[1610] Sylvia explained in detail that no Ethiopian government was yet permitted. The British government was substituting military and police forces under British officers, placing British judges in the Ethiopian courts and dragging its feet on de jure recognition of Ethiopian independence. The days of imperialism, Sylvia warned, were far from dead. This and many other articles, supported by representation to the government and MPs of all stripes, led to a succession of probing questions put to Anthony Eden, by then Foreign Secretary, to smoke him out. What was really going on in Ethiopia? Eden responded with evasion. Shortly after this it emerged that British officials were conspiring not only to establish quasi-protectorate control over the country, but in addition to annex several provinces, particularly Boran and Ogaden. Sylvia followed up her political demands for Ethiopian independence and the withdrawal of British administration with a series of articles headed 'Ethiopian Mystery', digging into British attempts to annex parts of Ethiopia and reporting on 'the Emperor's Fight with his Liberators'.

On 31 January 1942, Haile Selassie was forced by the British occupation authorities to sign an Anglo-Ethiopian agreement, which recognized Ethiopia's independence but simultaneously imposed a system of British advisers and administration at every level of Ethiopian governance, while leaving Britain in occupation of vast territories. Under the treaty, the Ogaden became a protectorate under British military administration and the so-called Reserved Area adjoining the frontier of British Somaliland was placed temporarily under British control. Controversially, this reversed the agreement made under the Anglo-Ethiopian treaty of 1897, by which Britain had recognized the Reserved Area as Ethiopian territory. The 'failure to guarantee Ethiopia's territorial integrity', Sylvia argued, highlighted Britain's continued pursuit of a 'colonial solution' and its intention 'to dismember her'.[1611]

Sylvia organized a piece of mischief to demonstrate that Ethiopia, widely vaunted as the first country to be freed from Axis domination, was still predominantly under foreign control. She laid on a commemoration conference at the Institute of Archaeology in London, ostensibly to celebrate Britain's tardy recognition of Ethiopia, and packed it with long-standing supporters, foreign diplomats and press offered the opportunity to find out what was really going on. MPs and ambassadors of countries which had never recognized the occupation of Ethiopia told the story the Foreign Office was trying to suppress. The Archbishop of Canterbury, Dame Elizabeth Cadbury, Eleanor Rathbone MP, Viscount Cecil and many of Sylvia's other consistent supporters in this cause sent messages of support.

A few months later Sylvia held another conference at Cowdray Hall in West Sussex that caused the government further embarrassment. Harold Moody of the League of Coloured Peoples was among the keynote speakers, who also included representatives of the Women's Co-operative Guilds. The conference passed resolutions demanding recognition of Ethiopia's right to the Ogaden, and its right of access to the sea.

To meet growing interest in the future of the region, Sylvia launched a series of articles entitled 'Ethiopia and Europe on the Horn of Africa', and penned a leader in which she confidently declared that the colonial era would shortly meet its end. Another regular feature series, 'Oppression and Revolt', tracked resistance throughout Axis-occupied Europe.

In August 1942 Haile Selassie's twenty-three-year-old daughter, Princess Tsehai, died in childbirth. Sylvia had first met her when she accompanied her father into exile at the age of seventeen. Princess Tsehai, as Richard Pankhurst described, had 'spoken to the world by radio from Addis Ababa at the time of her country's invasion in 1935–6, and later served as interpreter for her mother, and mine, and was well known in Britain as she had served as a nurse in London during the Blitz'.[1612] Tsehai trained as a nurse at Great Ormond Street Hospital and graduated as a state-registered paediatrics nurse in 1939. Then she enrolled, as Sylvia said in a tribute to her, 'at the bottom of the ladder to get further training at Guy's Hospital'. On her return to Ethiopia after her father's restoration to the throne, Tsehai worked at Dessie Hospital. Her ambition was to introduce the best in modern healthcare for women and children in a modernized Ethiopian hospital service. To honour Princess Tsehai's life, Sylvia launched a project for the founding of a commemorative hospital in Addis Ababa, its first modern hospital. Sylvia convened a Princess Tsehai Memorial Hospital Council chaired by the Welsh businessman, former Liberal MP and philanthropist Lord Davies.

The successful Allied landings in Sicily in July 1943 and the fall of Mussolini a few weeks later pushed the question of the future of Italy into the headlines. Sylvia led with 'NO! TO FASCISM, WITH OR WITHOUT THE "DUCE"'. She was dismayed that the Allies had established a collaborationist government under Marshal Badoglio, who was responsible for the use of poison gas and the bombing of the Red Cross in Ethiopia. Sylvia ran an editorial declaring that 'Badoglio, "Duke of Addis Ababa", Must Go, Too'. *New Times* published comprehensive indictments of the Marshal, and called for the overthrow of the Italian monarchy in favour of the establishment of a republic.

In Ethiopia, Badoglio was a named war criminal. In order to avoid charges being brought against him, Ethiopia would be excluded from the United Nations War Crimes Commission. The UN, with fifty-one founding member states including Ethiopia, was established in October 1945 to promote international co-operation, world peace, human rights and international justice. It thus replaced the League of Nations. Though the Allies later conducted highly publicized trials of German and Japanese war criminals, there was no Nuremberg for Italian criminals. According to modern historians, Britain and the

United States succeeded in frustrating the UN war crimes investigation into Italian atrocities.[1613] Neither Badoglio or Graziani, 'The Butcher of Ethiopia', was ever tried for Italian war crimes committed in Ethiopia.

Sylvia continued to run extensive articles on Ethiopian history and culture, including a serialization of the seventeenth-century German scholar Ludolf's *New History of Ethiopia*. Each week, Richard copied out the next instalment longhand for the printer.

British officials in Ethiopia accelerated their efforts to annex parts of the country as the end of the European war approached, in preparation for shoehorning the inclusion of the territory into the peace treaty. Sylvia denounced these moves in March 1944: 'Gross Breach of Faith! Intrigues to Dismember Ethiopia! Plan for Faked Plebiscite by British Military Authorities in the Reserved Area'. Another article revealed that colonials in Sudan were demanding Tigray province, 'Historic Centre of Ethiopian Culture …'[1614]

These claims enraged a number of Conservative MPs, two of whom put parliamentary questions asking the government to take steps to stop Sylvia's 'propaganda' and prevent her paper's publication in March 1944. Brendan Bracken, Minister of Information, responded that he had read the articles, but felt that Britain's record could speak for itself. Eleanor Rathbone leapt to her feet to declare that *New Times* had been 'a very useful watchdog in the interests of Ethiopia', and that if its allegations were inaccurate the best way of proving it would be 'to give a definite assurance that no such plebiscite has been arranged or is contemplated'. Ducking this challenge, the Minister retaliated: 'This paper contains attacks on England which are worthy of Goebbels. It has insulted the British troops who have rescued Ethiopia, and in my opinion is a poisonous rag.'[1615]

The following month Sylvia published her first report on the emergence of the Eritrean nationalist and anti-colonial movement demanding reunion with Ethiopia, and included the text of British wartime leaflets dropped in 1941 that promised the Italian colony exactly this. Italian anti-fascists wrote about their opposition to an Italian return to the colonies, pointing out that although Mussolini's fascism had been defeated, the 'amoral self-centred and aggressive nationalism of a politically ignorant and arrogant ruling class' was still very much alive.[1616]

In parliament, the Labour MP Percy Barstow, one of Sylvia's parliamentary friends, asked Eden whether Britain opposed the return of the colonies to Italy, and whether the Italian empire was 'irrevocably lost', to which Eden replied, 'Yes, Sir.'[1617] Attempts were immediately made to renege on the commitment.

At the end of 1944, Sylvia visited Ethiopia to view the site for the Tsehai Memorial Hospital. She sailed from Britain through the Mediterranean to Alexandria in Egypt. Shipping was scarce due to the war and she had to apply for special government permission to obtain passage and berth. 'It was wonderful to be sailing to Ethiopia, of which I have been thinking for eleven years – ever since the attack at Wal Wal had revealed Mussolini's intention to break the peace of the world.'[1618] She flew from Cairo to British-occupied Asmara, capital of Eritrea, where she met unionist leaders and the Asmara Native Council, which presented her with a gorgeous bouquet of flowers in the Ethiopian national colours of green, yellow and red. In particular, she met and befriended the Eritrean unionist leader Tedla Bairu, who had graduated in Italy. She also met and argued with numerous British colonial officials and expressed public sympathy for the unionist cause, especially at lectures and events attended by British officials. Sylvia recalled that the British Military Administration still retained fascist racial legislation. Over the entrances to cafés, restaurants, cinemas and hotels were the signs 'Vietato per Nativi' or 'Vietato per Indigeni' – Prohibited for Natives. Italian taxi drivers were forbidden from carrying Eritrean customers.

Disgruntled by encounters with British and Italian colonials in Asmara that ranged from the politely fractious to outright hostility, Sylvia was relieved to meet Muslim and Christian Eritrean unionists who warmly welcomed her support.

British intelligence followed Sylvia throughout her journey. Reports quoted her as declaring that the entire Horn of Africa should 'one day be united under native government and that Ethiopia might have an outlet to the sea'. Remarking that her views were 'undoubtedly … embarrassing to the British Military Administration', MI6 also recorded that Sylvia publicly expressed the incendiary view that 'the methods used by the suffragists to realize their ideals should be used by other idealists'.[1619]

Arriving in Addis Ababa Sylvia was greeted by many Ethiopian friends who had been exiled in Britain. As she toured extensively, she wrote continuously every day, drafting a series of articles on the schools, hospitals and other institutions she visited. Invited to broadcast over Addis radio, she described her experience of the country's reconstruction.

During her trip, on 19 December, the second Anglo-Ethiopian Agreement was signed. Britain was still to occupy a third of Ethiopia – the Ogaden and the Reserved Area. She wrote: 'After nine years of struggle to secure Justice for Ethiopia and to induce the government of my own country to act with justice, to fulfil its pledges and honour the principles it has professed on our national behalf, I must declare my intention to oppose this policy which removes from Ethiopian jurisdiction a third of the country ...'[1620]

Four months later, Sylvia called a conference in London to challenge the continued occupation of Ethiopia. She reported at length on her recent visit and explained her anxieties at the curbing of its independence. The conference passed a series of resolutions, one of which demanded the fixing of an early date for the withdrawal of British military administration and for Britain's compliance with principles of international justice. Another, moved by Jomo Kenyatta, declared, 'This Conference demands that the ex-Italian colonies, Eritrea and Somalia, be returned to Ethiopia.'[1621]

Sylvia continued to raise funds for the Princess Tsehai Memorial Hospital. Postal appeals, bazaars, fêtes and concerts brought in a steady flow of donations for the project, now under construction. At a fundraising concert in Central Hall, an uncensored version of Verdi's 'Hymn to the Nations' was played, with nice irony. In December 1943, Arturo Toscanini had conducted this work in a performance for inclusion in a War Office information documentary about the role of Italian-Americans in aiding the Allies. Toscanini added a bridge passage to include arrangements of the Star-Spangled Banner for the US and the Internationale for the Soviet Union and Italian partisans.

The tenth-anniversary issues of *New Times* in May 1945 gave no cause for celebration. Articles on fascism, Ethiopian history and the Italian colonies showed that eternal vigilance remained the keynote. The Eritrean author Alazar Tesfa Michael reported in 'Eritrea Today' that the British military authorities still kept fascist legislation in force with the racist colour bar. More optimistic was an article about the work of the German-Ethiopian David Hall establishing Ethiopia's first co-operatives. The paper published a series of pamphlets, three written by Sylvia, which surveyed British policy in Ethiopia and Eritrea, and also contained a thorough critique of British colonialist ambitions.

Sylvia's friend the West Indian Pan-Africanist T. R. Makonnen had financed *New Times* to produce a grisly serialization of articles documenting 'Italy's War Crimes in Ethiopia', also published as a separate pamphlet, *Italy's War Crimes in Ethiopia*. Containing photographs of fascist atrocities taken by the perpetrators, it aroused widespread alarm in the Foreign Office, evident in their extensive files of reports and correspondence discussing it.

The plan adopted by the new Labour Foreign Secretary Ernest Bevin to create a 'Greater Somalia', chiefly at Ethiopia's expense, confirmed the Attlee government's intention to annex the Ogaden as part of the post-war settlement. Sylvia addressed 'An Open Letter to Mr Bevin', with the headline 'HANDS OFF ETHIOPIA!', and got to work organizing public meetings and petitions rallying Ethiopia's supporters.

In July 1946 Sylvia travelled to the Paris peace conference to lobby for Ethiopia and report on the proceedings. She distributed copies of Makonnen's *Italy's War Crimes in Ethiopia* widely, in opposition to Italy's attempt to canvass at the conference for a return to Africa. She discovered that Enrico Cerulli was a member of the Italian delegation and that its members were giving out copies of their own booklet in praise of Mussolini's occupation of Ethiopia. Cerulli was a former fascist colonial official who had previously advised the fascist delegates at Geneva. By the conclusion of the conference, Italy had agreed to renounce its colonies and return all loot stolen from Ethiopia, but simultaneously made it clear that it intended to launch diplomatic initiatives to reassert its presence in Africa.

Sylvia kept her attention trained on the future. After the war, a cohort of Ethiopian students arrived to study in Britain. Six of them became Sylvia's wards and among Richard's closest friends. Many of them wrote articles for *New Times*, ensuring that it continued to live up to its name, including two future Ethiopian prime ministers, Endalkachew Makonnen and Mikael Imru. The dramatist Menghestu Lemma became one of Sylvia's most cherished friends, as did her beloved Afewerk Tekle, whom she came to regard as a second son. She published many of Tekle's paintings and cartoons in *New Times*. Later he became Ethiopia's leading national artist and cultural icon defining Ethiopia's African Renaissance style. They remained close.

Three years after renouncing all claims to its former colonies as part of the Paris Peace Treaty of 1946, the Italian government would launch a campaign to regain them. The Italian Foreign Minister Count Sforza won support for the plan from many Catholic member states of the UN, particularly in South America. *The Times* of London recognized this initiative, and gave its support to a proposal for Eritrea to be placed under joint British, French and Italian control. 'ITALY MUST NOT BE ALLOWED TO RETURN TO AFRICA', responded Sylvia.

Angered by the possibility of the return of Italian colonialism, young Eritreans in increasing numbers took up arms to fight for reunion with Ethiopia – reported by *New Times* as 'LIFE AND DEATH STRUGGLE IN ERITREA'.

In November 1949 the UN General Assembly came to the ludicrous compromise that Libya should become independent after three years, Somalia placed under Italian trusteeship for ten years and Eritrea's future subjected to yet another commission of inquiry, composed of Norway, Pakistan, Burma, Guatemala and South Africa, all of whom, except Norway, had reason to oppose the unionist cause.

Italy seemed set to grab back control of Eritrea, leaving Ethiopia once again without access to the sea. Sylvia organized another of her signature poster parades from Fleet Street to Westminster: '1940 Britain urged Somali people to fight for freedom; 1949 Britain voted at UNO for Italian forces to return to Somaliland'; and 'Power Politics at UNO instead of Justice. UNO Commission packed four to one against Ethiopia going to Eritrea'. She dispatched a sequence of letters to the press, signatories including nine MPs, the socialist academic G. D. H. Cole, the Dean of Gloucester, Canon Douglas, and Gordon Selfridge's daughter Princess Rosalie Wiasemsky.

The Foreign Office became increasingly angry with what they considered to be Sylvia's 'undue scrutiny and publicity', her continued attacks and her habit of publishing their correspondence. It was 'well to remember,' warned an internal FO memo by Derek Riches in August 1945, 'that anything sent to her is liable to be published in full in her paper,' and that replies to letters from other correspondents were likely to be sent directly to Miss Pankhurst. Sylvia's agitation pushed the Foreign Office to exasperation: 'Miss Pankhurst is bombarding the Secretary of State and PM with paper ...' Diplomats protested that one of her pamphlets had been favourably reviewed in the Russian media: 'After reading this outrageous pamphlet it had struck us that it was a pity that this "widely known suffragette leader of former days" was allowed to malign and slander us with impunity.'[1622] The British Legation in Moscow – knowing full well that she was a vociferous critic of Stalin and that *New Times* constantly opposed him and criticized Soviet policy – attempted to spread the rumour that Sylvia was a Soviet agent, as so clearly 'unpatriotic' in her criticism of Britain's sins in the world. A Foreign Office official considering whether there was 'any legal means of hauling Miss P. over the coals' sensibly concluded, 'even if there were I should deprecate action as Miss P. would use the Court as a public platform and would get in some shrewd blows against H.M.G., while no judge could stop her talking'.[1623] Others were less measured in their response. Daniel Lascelles, later British Minister to Ethiopia, wrote to the British Legation that all his colleagues agreed 'wholeheartedly with you in your evident wish that this horrid old harridan should be choked to death with her own pamphlets', but, he warned, 'Even if we can get her in court ... we would be ill advised to try, since the proceedings would be a wonderful propaganda opportunity to herself and her friends both here and in the Soviet Union. Infamous as her slanders are, it is a fact ... that public probing into our record since 1941 in the Ogaden would produce quite a lot that would embarrass us.'[1624]

The struggle over the future of the former Italian East African colonies continued throughout 1950. In January, *New Times* published a letter on the 'Eritrean Crisis' signed by a lengthy list of Eritrean patriots. An article by Bereketab Habte Selassie recalled the tons of leaflets dropped over Eritrea by the RAF during the war promising that Eritrea 'should be united with their brothers and their Motherland'. Hearing that the British administration in Eritrea was offering generous rewards for the capture of Eritrean freedom fighters, Sylvia and Emmeline Pethick-Lawrence published a joint protest under the rider 'BLOOD MONEY'.

Sylvia and Peter Freeman (a Labour MP) convened a conference in the House of Commons, attended by a number of agencies, including the United Nations Association and Labour Party, and by African delegates. They passed a resolution urging the government to 'honour the pledge made to Ethiopia during World War II to return Eritrea to Ethiopia', and another regretting the decision to allow the Italians to

return to the former Somaliland colony. Sylvia followed up by drafting
a letter to Foreign Secretary Ernest Bevin, signed by seventeen Labour
MPs. When the second commission of inquiry went to Eritrea in the
spring of 1950, *New Times* organized its last conference on the ex-
colonies, also held in a Commons committee room.

The struggle came to an end a few months later when the UN General
Assembly, following the unexpected recommendations of Norway,
Burma and South Africa, decided on 2 December that Eritrea should be
federated with Ethiopia, under the Ethiopian crown. Many of Sylvia's
supporters, and a fair number of her detractors, gave her public credit
for her role in the outcome. From Selassie, she received 'gratitude' for
the 'courageous and unaided effort' with which she had defended 'a
cause which at that time seemed to be well-nigh hopeless':[1625]

> Since that time the publication with which your name is
> indelibly associated has rendered the greatest services to the cause
> of Our Empire. As that publication which, without interruption,
> alone, through all these years, has communicated to the world
> facts and information of importance concerning Our Empire,
> it constitutes today a vast and indispensable storehouse of
> information and reference. It has become an influential and
> effective spokesman for causes which Ethiopia must defend
> and for which the support of world public opinion must be
> obtained ... We would wish particularly to bear testimony to
> the admirable and sustained qualities of devotion to all that is
> represented by Ethiopia, which We have always found in yourself.
> Gratitude and appreciation are yours without the necessity of our
> stating so. You are a tried and sure friend who will always enjoy
> Our deepest esteem.[1626]

Meanwhile, by the summer of 1950, the Princess Tsehai Memorial
Hospital Council in London had raised £48,000 and continued to
hold successful fundraisers. Isabel Fry, the actor Donald Wolfit and
the exiled Chief Seretse Khama of Bechuanaland (later Botswana) were
among speakers at a series of garden parties. At the end of 1951, Sylvia
visited Ethiopia for the second time, to attend the opening of the
hospital. Her articles from this trip included an immersive description
of the Asmara slums, and an account of the 'wanton destruction' of

the docks at the Ethiopian port of Massawa, implemented by the British administration. 'Why are We Destroying the Eritrean Ports?' became the subject of a longer series of historical pieces that were later incorporated into her groundbreaking 747-page volume *Ethiopia: A Cultural History*. Other articles focused on the history of Kenya and Uganda. Later, Richard used his mother's work on Kenya as the basis of his own book on the country's history. During the 1950s, mother and son became increasingly involved in the Kenyan struggle for liberation from British rule.

By the early 1950s, the Reserved Area was the only part of Ethiopia remaining under foreign control. Sylvia and Emmeline Pethick-Lawrence kept up the campaign opposing British occupation, supported by Peter Freeman, Arthur Henderson, church leaders and academics, including the loyal G. D. H. Cole. The British colonial administration complained constantly to the Foreign Office about the paper's destabilizing effect, resulting in it being censored as a 'Prohibited Publication' in British Somaliland. In 1954 the occupation of the Reserved Area would finally come to an end, and national sovereignty was restored throughout Ethiopia.

After eighteen years, *New Times and Ethiopia News* had completed its mission in 1954. Two years later, on Sylvia's seventy-fourth birthday, the last issue appeared. With it came the announcement of the launch of a new publication called the *Ethiopian Review*, subsequently changed to *Ethiopia Observer*. In the final edition of *New Times*, Sylvia published a poem, 'O Addis Ababa, O Fair New Flower' – a eulogy to the city shortly to become her home. For the next four years she edited her new monthly publication with Richard, with copy sent back to England and printed in Manchester. She wrote a large proportion of the *Ethiopian Review* herself, which involved extensive travelling over vast distances in the little Fiat gifted to her by the Ethiopian government. Each issue was dedicated to a separate aspect of Ethiopian life. After her death, the publication appeared quarterly and was edited for the following sixteen years by her daughter-in-law and son, who modestly observed, 'Like Sylvia's more famous weekly out of which it had been born, it thus spanned a generation.'[1627]

Bancroft's School is situated near where Sylvia's Stone Bomb still stands on the site of the old Red Cottage Tea Room. During the war Richard regularly walked past his mother's memorial presaging the advent of aerial warfare against civilians. He joined the Air Training Corps (ATC), for which he was kitted out with a badly fitting air-force-blue uniform and taught how to recognize Spitfires, Hurricanes and other British and German fighters and bombers of great interest to a young boy. He proved particularly proficient in tapping out the Morse code.[1628] Richard enjoyed several exciting weekends at RAF bases, learning how to rotate an anti-aircraft gun, 'a skill which, as things turned out,' he remarked laconically, 'I was never required to use.'[1629]

The small-engine-operated V1s – doodlebugs – frightened and fascinated Richard. Dubbed Hitler's Secret Weapon, the doodlebugs flew overhead, leaving smoke trails on their way to London. At night they burned through the sky like meteors. More impressive still were the V2 rockets, crashing down without any prior warning. Attacks by V1s and V2s continued to near the end of the European war. 'It was with an intense feeling of relief, almost of liberation, when we realized that they had come to an end: that one could live one's life without the constant threat of death, and at last sleep undisturbed at night.'[1630]

But Victory in Japan Day in August 1945 had not been the end of the war for them. With former Italian colonies still occupied by Britain, Sylvia's war was not over until Britain vacated them and gave up its own colonial possessions. Finally, while Stalin remained dictator of the Soviet Union, there could be no peace. The so-called Cold War, for Sylvia, was merely intensification by a few degrees of the deep freeze that began, for her, in 1921, when Lenin sold out the revolution.

PART SIX

African Consciousness 1945–1960

The great work of Sylvia Pankhurst was to introduce black Ethiopia to white England ... and to make the British people realise that black folks had more and more to be recognised as human beings with the rights of women and men.

W. E. B. Du Bois, *Ethiopia Observer* (1961)

34

Suffragette & Son

For Sylvia, the end of the European war coincided with her son finishing school. She asked Frida Laski for advice about the possibility of university and potential scholarship opportunities. Mandatory maintenance grants for students to cover tuition fees and living costs would not be introduced in Britain until 1962. A supporter from Sylvia's East End days, Frida arranged an interview with her husband, Professor Harold Laski at the London School of Economics, who tasked Richard with writing a historical essay on a subject of his choice. He wrote about the Chartist movement of the 1840s, in which his great-grandparents had participated.

Harold Laski approved the subject matter and content, but warned Richard about his purple prose with the marginal annotation: 'No flowers by request!'[1631] Judging by the objectivity, understatement, clarity and often roguishly droll understatement of his adult writing style, it was advice Richard took to heart. His mother was the chief inspiration for Richard's approach to research and writing, but selectively. Sylvia had two very distinct styles: one of absolute rapier-like, shorn-back, evidence-based factual precision and succinct argument; the other one of picaresque narrative, liberally adorned with garlands and bouquets. Which style she chose to use depended always on context and intention. Richard followed her precision and forensic research methods but not the outward expression of her unstopped passion when she was in flowery mode.

According to Frida Laski's fruitier version of Richard's application to the LSE, Sylvia accompanied her son to his interview. 'Sylvia was a demon mother. Richard was completely subjugated. When my husband asked him a question, she would answer. My husband got quite annoyed, sent them both away and told Richard to come back by himself.'[1632]

Offered a place and passing the scholarship exams, Richard opted to study politics and economic history and joined the institution with its reputation for being 'a hot-bed of "Reds"', which he soon discovered to be largely untrue. The LSE was the most culturally and racially diverse university in Britain, and its comfortable internationalism made it feel to Richard like a home from home.

At the beginning of his first term at the LSE, Richard ran into his schoolfriend Basil Taylor, also a fresher. Basil became a frequent visitor to Charteris Road, and was much impressed by Richard's mother, whom he was later to liken at this stage of her life to Margaret Thatcher: 'She could be amiable one minute and then suddenly she was there, eyes flashing, tense and tight. She had tremendous presence and invited great respect – the sort of woman who made you feel you should stand up when she sat down.'[1633] Basil's comparison couldn't have been more ideologically off-beam, but what's telling is that he likened Sylvia to the most powerful woman in British public life at the time.

Basil Taylor kept a diary during his student days, which chronicles how Richard quickly roped him in to helping out with the family campaigns. At one of Sylvia's garden-party hospital fundraisers, he recalled, 'I sold several copies of her recent book *Ex-Italian Somaliland* and many baskets of strawberries.'[1634]

Richard and Basil formed a group with Sylvia's Ethiopian protégé Afewerk Tekle and fellow LSE students from Africa, who turned West Dene into their second home and, in time, into an informal cultural centre. Tekle, then aged seventeen, had finished at public school and was just about to start at the Slade School of Fine Art following an intervention by Sylvia who had recognised his abilities and became mentor to his artistic endeavours. Silvio fed the young people Italian suppers. These were usually accompanied by the delicious luxury of bread rolls and fresh butter – so scarce during the war years – accompanied by the offer of strong Russian tea, for which Sylvia had acquired a taste during her Moscow travels. Mr Corio, Basil noted, would also serve 'Red pepper sauce and boiled rice with grated cheese', which might have been a young Englishman's way of describing the novelty of eating his first risotto.

The boys also enjoyed going to the pictures together – or, as Basil described it in his diary, to a 'new American technicolour film'. They rushed out to see the popular bodice-ripper period drama *Lorna Doone* when it opened. Richard, neat and tidy in his 'buff gabardine suit' and generally quietly spoken – except when 'worked up' about politics and the injustices of the world – intrigued his friends with unexpected interjections revealing unwittingly how exciting it was to have Sylvia Pankhurst for a mother. When Richard and Basil discussed Hollywood's popularization of political and social themes, for example, Richard said that he'd met the Boulting brothers, who had produced and directed the 1947 political drama *Fame Is the Spur*, and that 'he and his mother were impressed by their cultural vulgarity'.[1635] This film dramatized Howard Spring's novel based on the career of Ramsay MacDonald. Spring recognized his debt to Sylvia's *The Suffragette Movement*. As a result, the director Ray Boulting invited her to visit the film set at the Denham Studios in Buckinghamshire. 'She assumed that she had been asked for advice, and, although very busy, agreed to go.' Richard went with her. Sylvia 'expressed dissatisfaction' with the set. The women's prison dress was totally wrong. Boulting informed her that 'her advice was not required as the costume had already been decided upon'. Sylvia replied that 'if her advice was not wanted she saw no need for her to remain'.[1636] Boulting later conceded that she had been invited purely for an on-set photo shoot to provide advance publicity for the film.

Easy talking about their public and political interests, Richard was reticent about discussing his family. His friends clearly discussed the unconventional domestic arrangements of his welcoming home, with its always open door and free flow of people, interesting food, discussion and views. Since she had announced it in the international media, Sylvia did not regard Richard's free-love birth or the identity of his Italian father as a secret. In the early 1950s Richard was unusual in having unmarried parents and a father who lived and worked at home, did most of the cooking, shared the domestic responsibilities of the household and did a larger amount of housework than his female partner.

These aspects, however, did not seem to be as curious to Richard's British LSE friends as his father's exotic Italianness and elusive class background. Returning from an evening at West Dene, Basil Taylor reported to his diary that they had been served a vegetarian dinner and that 'Also with us were Mr Corrio [sic] … who is/may be Richard's father if a hint of Tekle's is right.' Continuing with snobbish condescension, Taylor muses, 'He does not speak English as well as he ought … and is rather "an old dear" and very pleased to see us. He was dressed more as an odd job man … Indeed Richard is the only tidy part of the household!'[1637] Small wonder Richard kept the details of his family background to himself. Basil Taylor remained blithely unaware of Corio's professional and political hinterland.

Richard's parents worked together closely on all their projects – the newspaper they launched and ran together, articles they wrote and edited together, the Freedom Press, and their anti-fascist campaigning. They included Richard in their endeavours – just as Sylvia's parents had done with their daughters – and in time he grew into the role of working as his mother's researcher and co-author. Silvio took Richard to meetings and introduced him to his political network. In a letter of 8 October 1953, Corio wrote to say that he would like to attend the forthcoming conference of the Syndicalist Workers' Federation (SWF),

> if permitted – merely as an observer. And – if you have no
> objection – I will take with me Richard. He is very interested in
> the Labour Movement of today. Before long his book on Wm.
> Thompson will be published by Messrs. Watts & Co. It should have
> appeared already but these people are so slow. He is now teaching
> Economics for the W.E.A. [Workers' Educational Association] at
> Woolwich, thanks to his Ph.D. degree. He wants to know, at first
> hand, the opinions of English workers of today.[1638]

Richard's first book, titled *William Thompson: Britain's Pioneer Socialist, Feminist, and Co-operator*, was an adaptation of his PhD thesis. After leaving LSE, Richard would specialize in African history and economics, enrolling at the School of Oriental and African Studies as a part-time student, and studying Amharic.

Richard postponed his military service until he had completed his doctorate. Conscientious objection to conscription was allowed, but only for outright pacifists opposed to all and any kind of war. Persuaded by his mother's example, Richard had no objection to the principle of a 'just war', but was 'totally opposed to Britain's seemingly endless colonial wars, and the use of British troops in repressing indigenous nationalist movements in Africa and Asia'.[1639] Determined to demonstrate his opposition to colonial oppression, Richard rejected his call-up papers.

His lawyer advised him to plead conscientious objection to war as a pacifist, but at his tribunal Richard took a different tack. Fascism and Nazism he would have fought willingly, he said, but he objected to the use of force against native Kenyans as an unjust war. Citing the state of emergency in Kenya as a current example, he pointed out that the number of Africans arrested and detained as suspected Mau Mau rebels exceeded the total number of white settlers on whose behalf the Kenya Emergency had been proclaimed. Richard declared his refusal to be party to the repression implemented by the Colonial Secretary Oliver Lyttelton, but, he added, would be prepared to participate in detaining the Minister. The tribunal rejected his contentions, and, after fining him twice, left him alone to get on with his work. Richard's conscription tribunal unleashed the launch of yet another Pankhurst public campaign, which both the Home and Foreign Offices were keen to shut down, since Miss Pankhurst and Son persistently ignored the press censorship imposed on the British and colonial media on all matters relating to the Mau Mau.

In his first skirmish with the state on a point of principle, Sylvia's son proved himself a worthy chip off the old block. Richard's tribunal hearing was supposed only to allow him to offer his defence; instead he turned it into a public platform to condemn colonial oppression and support the Kenyan cause of decolonization. Sylvia testified on Richard's behalf at his tribunal. 'SUFFRAGETTE AND SON: AT 70 SYLVIA PANKHURST SPEAKS FOR THE MAN WHO MADE HEADLINES AS A BABY', reported the *Evening Standard* in January 1953, in a lively interview syndicated to the *Liverpool Echo*.

Sylvia allowed journalist Louisa Reid to come and interview her at home in Charteris Road. They sat facing each other across a round mahogany table, drinking coffee. Reid observed the faded photograph of Keir Hardie looking down on them from the chimney piece. Near it hung Sylvia's self-portrait wearing prison dress while serving one of her many sentences as a militant suffragette.

Sylvia still has a vaguely 1910 look: grey hair scooped back, an ancient black corded silk coat over a drab cardigan, no nonsense, no jewellery, not so much as a ring. And of course no make-up. Lipstick in particular she abhors. Not only does it spoil the shape of the mouth, she asserts, it reveals the 'slave mentality'. I passed my tongue over my pinked lip before asking her about PhD son Richard who has twice refused registration as a conscientious objector. 'Richard is going to resist,' she announced calmly. 'His case is rather like that of John Bright in the Crimean War and that of Lloyd George in the Boer War. He would not have minded fighting the Nazis but he would not want to fight in Kenya.'[1640]

It was logical to object to particular wars, Sylvia continued, and particular weapons. She could not imagine Richard killing anyone. He had always been a gentle boy, and even disliked toy soldiers. There was no time for playing at imaginary war games in the Pankhurst household. She described her fourteen-hour working day to Louisa Reid, which began with her reading a mixed bag of correspondence from women concerning the hard realities of their lives: letters from women abandoned by their husbands, unmarried mothers seeking legal affiliation orders, widows asking how to access their pensions.

Reid turned her questioning to the domestic life of the SUFFRAGETTE AND SON household. There was usually daily help, Sylvia said, and, when the housekeeper couldn't turn up, 'we all go into the kitchen and cook something when we feel like it. But food is not important to us.' As to money, 'I manage. I've had two useful legacies from friends who were with me in the suffragette movement ... There are royalties from my books and money from articles.'[1641]

The apathy of Englishwomen appalled her, she admitted. Married women still had precious few rights. In Ethiopia, if a marriage broke up, the wife was entitled to half of the communal property. Women should be fighting for peace, picketing the United Nations, lobbying parliament, 'as we fought for the vote'. There were many other issues women should be organizing around. 'Films are deplorable. Many crimes are directly influenced by American gangster violence. When Richard was smaller, I used to take him to the pictures sometimes, but we were always having to come out – all those insipid blondes and people being murdered.'

As well as the impact of cinema and TV, Sylvia was concerned about developments in the modern toy industry. Having set up and run a toy factory herself, and with a keen interest in child development and education, this was a subject in which she had perennial interest: 'I was reading the other day about little children being sold real daggers. Why don't women *do* something about it?'

Sylvia and Richard visited Kenya for the first time a few years later in 1958, but the country was already part of their lives. Jomo Kenyatta had long been a regular visitor to Woodford. Subsequently, Richard became friends with the Kenyan leader Mbiyu Koinange, through the Movement for Colonial Freedom, founded by his mother's friend and veteran British Labour leader Fenner Brockway. Sylvia and Brockway had met when he was a very young conscientious objector, refusing to join the British army during the First World War. Richard's first book after his PhD was a political history of Kenya. The country was not an abstract or academic subject for the white Richard Pankhurst living in Essex and studying in his hometown of London – it was part of his family upbringing, through his mother's friendship circle and people who lived in his home. Nothing would induce him to fight his friends in whose call for independence he had played an active part.

After Sylvia's return from her second African trip, she and Richard worked flat out on the book that they had started working on together, *Ethiopia and Eritrea: The Last Phase of the Reunion Struggle, 1941–1952*, which would be published in 1953 by their own new family publisher, Lalibela House, based at 3 Charteris Road. Once he'd submitted his doctorate, Richard devoted as much time as possible to researching the book, while Silvio edited, copyedited and proofed their co-written sections of the manuscript. Silvio was bedevilled by intensifying asthma and recurrent infections, but showed no sign of slowing down – if anything, he was busier. To fund the publication, Sylvia finally sold the old Red Cottage land. Haile Selassie knew where the money had come from to publish this campaigning tool and platform for the unionist case.

Exhausted by the marathon of completing the bulky manuscript in record time by April 1953, Sylvia rushed up Snakes Lane in Woodford with overdue proofs for the printer in Manchester to catch the last post. The bulging package contained the manuscript, which was loaded with facts, figures, reports, transcriptions of documents and illustrations

compacted together into a phenomenally coherent narrative covering
Ethiopian and Eritrean history and contemporary politics. Sylvia had
plumped out during the past two decades, rounding into a pleasing and
commanding full-figured maturity that matched her formidable status
as Britain's guardian of justice and immovable force of eternal vigilance
keeping the establishment in check and speaking truth to power.

The combination of overweight body, heavy manuscript and stress
on the long hill to the Woodford Green post office did for her. She
caught the post, but on her return collapsed just outside the gate of
West Dene. Basil Mackenzie diagnosed severe coronary thrombosis. For
many hours, her heart attack was thought fatal. She pulled through and
began a period of convalescence under Basil's supervision and lovingly
tended by Silvio, Richard and her friends.

Lying in bed recuperating, fed by an anxious Silvio and incapacitated
in a way she had not been since the forced-feeding episodes over forty
years earlier, Sylvia was surprised and to receive a letter from Christabel,
written to her from Santa Monica on the day of her seventy-first birthday.

Sylvia dear,
  This is your birthday and I am writing to wish you, with my
love, many happy returns of the day. I hear you are not as well as
usual and I hope that you are improving and feeling stronger in
this spring and your birthday month. Your mind often goes back,
I know, as mine does to those good years of our childhood, when
we still had Father & Mother & the home they made for us. When
I went through mother's papers in 1928, I found among them a
letter that I wrote to you from Geneva, where I was when father
died, in which I said to you how happy we had been … We had
wonderful parents for whom we can always be thankful, whose
memory is as vivid with us now as it has ever been. Your son must
be a great joy & comfort to you & I am sure there is a beautiful
bond between you & him … The years are passing by & what
strange … unexpected events & conditions they have brought us
and are bringing in the world. I view the things that are happening
all over the globe with concern, but with strong, with invincible
hope in the final triumph of goodness & justice & of glory
surpassing all human dreams.
  God's in His heaven: all must & will be right with the world.[1642]

She signed off with 'Again my birthday love, Your sister, Christabel'. In finally acknowledging Richard for the first time, Christabel sent her sister the most welcome and beautiful of birthday gifts. Sylvia, delighted, wrote back immediately. Christabel confirmed that shortly after the arrival of Sylvia's letter the photo of Richard arrived: 'Thank you and thank him for this portrait of such a well-grown & clever looking young man.'[1643] In touch again after so long a silence, the sisters corresponded further. Christabel wanted to discuss family papers, which she believed Sylvia had, but she also reverted to childhood memories. They did not discuss contentious events, nor it seems from Christabel's letters, did they discuss Adela. There was an intense exchange of missives again in the spring of 1954, prompted by the publication of two books about the suffragette movement, Vera Brittain's *Lady into Woman: A History of Women from Victoria to Elizabeth II* and Ray Strachey's *The Cause: A Short History of the Women's Movement in Great Britain*, both of which, they agreed, required interventions with authors and publishers to make factual corrections.[1644] The correspondence between the sisters was to continue until Christabel's death.

Richard never met either of his aunts. Like Sylvia, Adela had a heart condition that worsened as she aged. They shared highly charged, stress-driven personalities, but in Adela's case this was exacerbated by chain-smoking roll-ups. Shortly before she died in May 1961, Adela wrote, 'I never meant to take up politics as a career. I wanted to write books and go in for music.'[1645]

Sylvia was 'totally incapacitated' for a few weeks. Basil Mackenzie ordered her to take a longer period of convalescence, reminding her constantly that her coronary had been near fatal. Sylvia carried on her correspondence and writing from her bed, and then bounced back. She alarmed Basil and her personal assistant Ivy Tims by giving everyone the slip one day, catching the train to town and turning up to address a rally in Trafalgar Square. Here she clambered on to the speaker's platform beneath Nelson's Column and joined in the demands for the reinstatement of Seretse Khama, exiled from Bechuanaland. The first anyone knew of her escapade was when they heard her speech reported on the BBC news.

No sooner had she finished the last book than Sylvia launched into another, *Ethiopia: A Cultural History*. This tour de force of 735 pages she dedicated to Haile Selassie, 'Guardian of Education, Pioneer of Progress, Leader and Defender of his People in Peace and War'. On its publication in 1955, the book received enthusiastic, appreciative and positive reviews, most notably from the *Times Educational Supplement*. Richard laboured once again as his mother's chief researcher, further building the deep knowledge that would make him later one of the world's leading Africanist experts and the founder of the discipline of Ethiopian historical studies in Addis Ababa.

Just eight months after Sylvia's severe coronary, she lost her soulmate of over thirty years. Silvio died on 11 January 1954, aged seventy-eight, in Woodford Green, attended by Basil Mackenzie. In 1953 during the months preceding his death, Silvio was still trying to re-establish a Popular University in London. In November he had attended the International Working Men's Association congress, an anarcho-syndicalist organization. Sylvia arranged for his cremation to take place in Manor Park, Walthamstow, two days after his death. Come the day, she could not attend the funeral. Richard recalled that his mother wept unceasingly for days when his father died. The intensity of her grief must have terrified him. Never before had he experienced his mother unable to cope. Basil Mackenzie feared that her grief might trigger another coronary, and asked Richard to persuade her not to attend Silvio's funeral.

Exactly two months later on 11 March, Emmeline Pethick-Lawrence died and, again, Sylvia did not go to the funeral. She wrote to Emmeline's husband:

Dear Fred,
    I feel you might perhaps think it churlish of me not to have been at the crematorium. But I cannot help crying so much and getting upset when I care so poignantly that I felt I should only be a bother to other people ... When Richard's father died, Richard asked me not to go to the crematorium with him because he knows I am like that and he told me he would be upset if I came and begged me not to go. I can't control my tears and all that. You know I am not very well now – sometimes I feel almost the same as before but anything upsets me. I never go out now unless someone will drive me in a car and very seldom at all.
    I should have been ashamed to go and be a trouble ... though I would desire to manifest my love and admiration for beloved

> Emmeline ... I have lost one of the pillars of my world, the dearest
> of long loved friends ...[1646]

All her life, Sylvia showed up. She took principles of accountability, responsibility and public duty not only to exacting but to exhausting levels. For her friends and loved ones she was all heart and compassion. Silvio's and Emmeline's deaths, following so closely together, stunned her. Her father, in her childhood, spoke of his wife and their three daughters as the four pillars of his life. Sylvia's echo of his words on the loss of the twin pillars of her life partner and dear friend speaks for itself. Richard spoke only of his mother's reaction to his father's death. He kept to himself how he felt about it.

Sylvia's letter to Fred Pethick-Lawrence, in the context of her other correspondence, is startling. Nowhere else has she ever written about the inability to control passionate emotion as a negative – 'I can't control my tears and all that.' Her refusal of emotional constraint on occasions where it was conventionally expected – from the dock, in formal political meetings – had been one of the hallmarks of her political career. Some regarded it as wilful; others loved and admired her for her unfettered passion and commitment. It astonished, embarrassed, appalled or delighted and inspired. Here, in the fear expressed to Fred about the intensity of her emotion, was a sign of self-awareness of the physical impact her extreme sensitivity exacted on her older self.

Gifted with the constitution of a working dray horse, the years of flogging her body caught up with Sylvia when she suffered her first coronary. It was primarily stress of overwork and her compromised medical history from hunger striking and forced feeding that contributed to her ill health. Sylvia had no other addictions. She rarely drank alcohol, and then in moderation. On the other hand, she was averse to any form of organized exercise unless it involved marching for miles on a demonstration, running away from police or crossing the Alps undetected by state security services. She had walked a great deal in her younger years, for economy and campaigning as an art student and activist. At leisure, she had spent some of her happiest times strolling in London parks and hiking in the Kentish Weald and in Wales with Keir Hardie.

After Silvio died, Sylvia locked herself away and wrote his obituary. The January 1954 issue of *New Times* devoted the entire issue to Corio, 'a great comrade', honoured in his own right. The measure of her private grief emerged shortly afterwards, when she put up a 'For Sale' sign at Charteris Road. Bereft of her closest intimates and adrift in 1950s England, Sylvia packed up and left. The prompt for this decision came directly from Haile Selassie.

In October 1954 the Emperor returned to Britain for an official state visit, the scale of which stood in marked contrast to the unenthusiastic welcome he had received from the British government in 1936. The royal welcome extended by the recently enthroned Queen Elizabeth II 'put to shame' what he had he received thirty years before, when no royal salutations from Edward VIII were extended to welcome his arrival. The Foreign Secretary Anthony Eden had suggested to the King that it would be 'a popular gesture if the British monarch received the Emperor at Buckingham Palace. "Popular with whom?" snapped the king. "Certainly not with the Italians." '[1647] This time, the Guards' band played the Ethiopian national anthem as the royal carriages passed out of the Victoria Station forecourt in procession to Buckingham Palace a martial echo of the dark days when Sylvia had campaigned for the reluctant BBC to play the anthem on national radio.

After laying wreaths at the tomb of the Unknown Warrior in Westminster Abbey and a visit to Clarence House to call on Queen Elizabeth the Queen Mother, the next event in the programme was the welcome to the City of London at the Guildhall, still under repair from wartime bombing. Sylvia stood with the delegation of VIP guests alongside Lord Amulree, the Archbishop of Canterbury, the Edens, the Attlees, cabinet ministers and Dominion high commissioners. Right-wing newspapers that had previously supported Mussolini's invasion of a 'barbarian' nation in need of 'civilizing' performed elegant reversals, waxed lyrical about renewed Anglo-Ethiopian relations, falling over themselves to praise the dignified Emperor Selassie who had stood up to the fascist bullies before they recognized the need:

> He is in fact a hard-working and very practical ruler in the
> most modern fashion, in labouring to equip his people with the
> amenities of twentieth-century civilization with the least possible
> disturbance to their inherited social order. In his belief that the way
> of true progress is to graft the new stock on the ancient roots he has
> perhaps his closest affinity with the mind of his British hosts.[1648]

When Sylvia and Haile Selassie met privately during this state visit, he reminded her of his standing invitation to her and her son to move to Ethiopia where a warm welcome and much useful work awaited them. Knowing of her recent loss, Selassie's graciousness and timing was impeccable.

For Richard it was a year of endings and beginnings.[1649] He had met, by fateful chance, Rita Eldon at Toynbee Hall, where he was teaching. Rita was tutoring in the extramural department of London University alongside her job in the Press Library at Chatham House. They met because of Lawrence Fabunmi, a Nigerian PhD student enrolled at the LSE to research the modern history of Sudan, and Frank de Halpert, the Toynbee Hall registrar. Alongside teaching, Richard was busy writing, researching at the National Institute of Economic and Social Research, and, with his father gone, helping his mother produce *New Times* – having taken over Silvio's roles on the paper and at Lalibela House. He described his night-school teaching British economic and social history in the University of London's extramural department as 'exciting because it entailed travelling northwards as far as Watford and southwards to Woolwich, on several occasions at night by ferry across the River Thames'.[1650] The evening of Richard and Rita's fateful meeting, they were both teaching at Toynbee Hall. Lawrence Fabunmi visited the Chatham House Press Library many times to study files on Sudan. Here he met Rita and they became friends. One day Fabunmi unexpectedly proposed to Rita, as he had done to several of her friends. He met her 'inevitable refusal' by thrusting a chapter of his thesis into her hands and asking her to read and correct it. Rita took the thesis chapter with her to Toynbee Hall that evening, where she was teaching French conversation. As she was signing the register, Richard, also just arriving, caught sight first of lovely Rita and then of the envelope she was carrying with Fabunmi's name on it. Richard had met Fabunmi at the LSE. Seizing his opportunity, he asked Rita how she came to know him. Frank de Halpert, taking registration, then introduced them, 'and that', said Rita, 'was the beginning, but by no means the end of my acquaintance with Richard'.[1651]

Rita's memory of her first visit for dinner with his mother at Richard's home was marked by the 'pretty awful' food. Rita was shocked and mystified by the strange table Sylvia kept, which had become disorganized since Silvio died.

At the beginning of their relationship, Rita's parents, particularly her mother, were anxious about her choice of Richard. They were set on her marrying the 'immensely learned, and absolutely reliable' Basil Robinson, 'courteous in the old school style', Keeper of Metalwork at the Victoria and Albert Museum, 'a typical product of English public schools, confessing to me that he had been beaten three times, and, when he reached that stage himself, beat a junior boy three times'. As well as 'excellent manners', her mother pointed out to Rita, Basil offered a solid income and lived in London.[1652]

When Rita announced that she was going to move to Africa, a place she'd never visited before, to 'live in sin'[1653] with Richard and Sylvia, the Eldons had been initially very unhappy and challenged her on Richard's poor prospects and the fact that he came firmly attached to a notorious mother. Uncomfortably aware that Sylvia had never married Richard's father and that their prospective bookish son-in-law was an internationally announced love child, Rita's parents worried about her intention to live with Richard without a fixed wedding date in view.

Rita recalled the first time her prospective mother-in-law visited her family home in Swiss Cottage for dinner. Rita's mother Charlotte – known as Lottie – immaculately turned out and always stylish, was blithely unconcerned with feminism, and appeared on the face of it utterly unlike Richard's. 'My parents,' Rita said, 'thought I was an adventuress and couldn't understand how I could think of living in the same house as "that strident woman". They were very much against our marrying because they didn't think I could keep her in check.'[1654]

> 'What has Richard done in life?' my parents asked me. Would he
> be able to keep me? Was I proposing to live in the same house with
> a mother-in-law, that virago of a woman, well known for fighting
> with everybody? Did I know what was involved in living in Africa?
> Did I want to live so far away from them?[1655]

But Rita knew her own mind and was undeterred. As it would turn out, Richard's and Rita's parents had more in common than their doted-on children initially anticipated. Sylvia delighted Richard and Rita by being on her best behaviour. Following her son's instructions, she assured the Eldons that she was strongly in favour of the youngsters getting married. She had little if no regard for the institution, but her son's happiness was of paramount importance to her. Following this dinner, Rita's parents 'became resigned to the inevitable',[1656] an experience shared by many over the decades whom Sylvia had lobbied on a campaign point. In this instance, however, she was merely the cavalry. Rita Eldon knew her own heart and determined to follow it. Her show of grit boded well for her relationship with her future mother-in-law. The 'adventuress' Rita developed a fine relationship with Sylvia, in time became an unequivocal feminist and – mercifully – improved Richard and Sylvia's eating habits when, alongside full-time employment, study and social work, she took over the supervision of the Pankhurst household in Ethiopia. When Rita's parents came to visit, they fell in love with Sylvia, Ethiopia and their daughter and son-in-law's friends, and themselves became happy adventurers in a new and exciting milieu.

35

The Village

In 1936 George, husband of Annie Barnes, a keen gardener, went round to Sylvia's house in Woodford to take her some plants. He ordered his supply of flowers and shrubs from the country, and any left over he would give Sylvia for her garden. George was also 'a bit of a comic ... He was a caution, my husband,' Annie said fondly.[1657] She recalled how on this occasion George came home 'very puzzled'. 'There's a lot of black people in Sylvia's house.' He hadn't seen Sylvia, only the housekeeper who opened the door.

'Who are all these black people?' George asked her, indicating the party congregated in the garden.

'Shh! Mr Barnes!' chided the help. 'It's the Emperor!'

'The Emperor!?' he said. '*I'm* the Emperor.'[1658]

Among the guests at West Dene that day was a young Kwame Nkrumah. In June 1958 on a state visit to Ethiopia by Nkrumah, new President of Ghana and hero of the moment, would become the cause of jubilant celebration in Addis Ababa. The *Ethiopian Herald* would print a special edition in sepia ink in his honour, and commission Richard Pankhurst to write his biography. Sylvia received an invitation to attend an official cocktail party for Nkrumah at the Ghion Hotel, and the President approached her and asked fondly how things were at 'the Village'.[1659]

Nkrumah had nicknamed Sylvia's Woodford home 'the Village' during his student days in London. At West Dene he congregated with the Kenyans, Ethiopians, Egyptians, Nigerians, Somalis, Eritreans,

South Africans, Afro-Caribbeans and African Americans invited by Sylvia to make it their home from home. Sylvia's always open house became a hub of radical African consciousness, new free jazz and political intelligence and gossip in Essex. Silvio was popular among this pan-Africanist diaspora, for both his political knowledge and his macaroni cheese. Only-child Richard enjoyed the extended family attentions of the group of lively exiles who missed their younger siblings, nephews and nieces. They welcomed the inquisitive little boy into the gatherings – where he listened to their debates about art and politics and the African music they brought with them.

Mussolini's invasion of Ethiopia and Eritrea swiftly forged alliances between anti-fascists and anti-colonialists. The activists and thinkers who congregated in Woodford on the eve of the Second World War already understood the ideological connections between them. African Americans who went to fight for republican Spain had previously wanted to go and fight for Selassie against Mussolini. As one African-American partisan put it, 'This ain't Ethiopia, but it'll do.'[1660]

After his first visit to Woodford for tea, Jomo Kenyatta became a regular visitor. In Sylvia's global village he met the Senegalese historian and politician Cheikh Anta Diop; the American thinker W. E. B. (William Edward Burghardt) Du Bois; the Jamaican Pan-Africanist Amy Ashwood Garvey, co-founder, with her ex-husband Marcus Garvey, of the *Negro World* newspaper; the Guyanese-born financier and activist George Thomas Griffith – better known as T. Ras Makonnen; the physician Harold Moody, founder of the League of Coloured Peoples; Julius Nyerere, future President of Tanzania; and the Trinidadian writer and journalist George Padmore, among significant others. Jomo Kenyatta rallied to Ethiopia's support immediately when Mussolini invaded in 1935. Then living in London, he founded the Society of African Friends of Abyssinia and spoke at nearly all of Sylvia's pro-Ethiopia and anti-fascist meetings. Sylvia read his book *Facing Mount Kenya*, published in 1938, and passed it on to her bookworm son who gained from it an early appreciation of Kikuyu life and culture. Of the many visitors to West Dene, Richard was particularly impressed by T. Ras Makonnen (George Thomas Griffith), who had adopted this name as an act of solidarity with the Ethiopian struggle, to which he devoted his considerable wealth and energies.

Around 1938 Makonnen moved to Manchester, where he opened restaurants and a nightclub. These all proved exceptionally successful ventures, especially following the wartime arrival of African-American troops. Jomo Kenyatta was one of Makonnen's employees. In a further campaigning venture, Makonnen opened a bookshop serving the nearby Manchester University. This groundbreaking African-studies bookshop was a vital source of influence on the teachers and students of modern history and politics. Makonnen gradually bought a number of houses in Manchester for the express purpose of letting them to black tenants struggling with exclusion by racist landlords.

Makonnen used the proceeds to finance his *Pan-Africa* journal and to support political campaigns to build a British-based Pan-Africanist movement. At his own instigation, he paid for the production of Sylvia's pamphlet *Italy's War Crimes in Ethiopia*. Richard recalled that the bibliophile Makonnen gifted him a copy of Prosper Hippolite Lissagaray's *History of the Paris Commune of 1871*, edited and translated into English in 1886 by his young lover, the multilingual Eleanor Marx.

Another frequent visitor to the Village, the Trinidadian writer and journalist George Padmore, also befriended Sylvia. He was part of Nkrumah's delegation on the state visit to Addis in 1958, and after the official cocktail party at the Ghion Hotel, they all met up informally.

Amy Ashmore Garvey and Sylvia discovered a particular rapport and became close friends. Garvey gave Sylvia an exquisite small Benin bronze statue, which can be seen in photographs of Sylvia's study always in pride of place. Marcus Garvey was a fierce critic of Selassie, arguing the need for a democratic Ethiopian republic and unconvinced by the cloak of reform the Emperor wrapped around his restricted constitutional monarchy.

Peter Abrahams, another friend of Sylvia's who was a regular caller at the Village, became the first black South African novelist published in Europe and the US. Born in Vrededorp, Johannesburg to an Ethiopian father and a mixed-race South African mother, Abrahams was forced to flee his homeland as a result of his opposition to the white supremacist regime. His reputation, as one of South Africa's most distinguished twentieth-century writers, spanned five continents. His novel *The Path of Thunder* (1948) was made into a ballet by Gara Garayev, the eminent leading composer of Soviet Azerbaijan. His next book *Wild Conquest*

(1949), about the Great Trek and interracial love, forged a new literary movement. The novelist and pundit C. P. Snow wrote presciently of Abraham's work, 'It may be the forerunner of an entire school of African literary art,' thus accurately identifying Abrahams as the father of modern South African writing. During his time in London before he moved to Kingston, Jamaica, Sylvia commissioned Abrahams to write several popular articles for *New Times*. He educated Sylvia about South African apartheid, the mining industry, politics and identity, all subjects of his novels and journalism.

Another South African friend who informed Sylvia about the country's current situation was the writer and journalist Colin Legum, born in the Orange Free State to Lithuanian immigrant hoteliers. He wrote for the London *Observer* and accomplished the considerable achievement of steering the newspaper away from its default pro-imperialist, pro-Italian position to an anti-colonial editorial line. Later, Colin and Margaret Legum co-authored *South Africa: Crisis for the West* (1964), making the case for economic sanctions against the South African regime in order to bring an end to apartheid, which was a highly controversial and unnecessarily extreme position at the time. Also much preoccupied with Ethiopian politics, Legum later visited Addis for the Second Conference of Independent African States, and predicted the coup that followed six months later in December 1960.

Before 1945 many of the leading figures in the emerging Pan-Africanist liberation movement of necessity lived and worked in the diaspora. During the war years, most based themselves in London and Manchester. The October 1945 Fifth Pan-African Congress in Manchester marked the end of this phase of the movement. After 1945 the focus of activity switched to mainland Africa. George Padmore, the young Nkrumah, W. E. B. Du Bois and Peter Abrahams played leading roles in organizing the October 1945 Fifth Pan-Africanist Congress, regarded as the unifying event in the multifaceted, disparate, anti-colonial struggles of the time. Peter Abrahams was among the representatives of the African National Congress (ANC). Seen as the most significant of the seven congresses held by the Africanist movement, the Manchester convention passed resolutions supporting the criminalization of racial discrimination and decrying imperialism and capitalism. *New Times* reported in detail every aspect of the event and its policy resolutions. The mainstream

British press barely noticed it. The Manchester Congress marked the end of this phase of the movement. After 1945 the focus of activity switched to mainland Africa.

In the post-war period this generation of new leaders educated Sylvia, and her son in turn, in the radical flourishing of African consciousness: the political philosophy supporting the urgent need for decolonization. In 1957 Sylvia left her Woodford village and followed her friends to live in Africa.

Though this change took place in the final chapter of her life, Sylvia's journey to Ethiopia began in her earliest childhood.

When she moved to Addis Ababa, it was to put herself at the heart of the transnational action. Ethiopia was the intersectional point for freedom struggles all over the world. Sylvia's relocation was the culmination of an odyssey winding back to the origins of human history and forwards to the future of the world. The date of Ethiopia's founding is set at 6280 BC, over 8,000 years. The first King of Abyssinian Ethiopia in 4470 BC was Emperor Ori; Haile Selassie was its 334th ruler. On the map of Sylvia's life, her journey to Africa began in Manchester – Britain's most radical city – before transferring to London, where she made the significant symbolic and actual move from West End to the East End, then on into the Essex borders, where she established her internationalist Woodford village. From there, having lived in England all her life, she relocated from London to Addis Ababa, and never returned.

Sylvia was brought up in Manchester and London without racial prejudice in a home actively engaged in the movement to abolish slavery and racism. Emmeline Pankhurst read to her daughters *Uncle Tom's Cabin*, her own abolitionist mother's favourite novel. For all its failings by modern standards, Harriet Beecher Stowe's bestseller contributed hugely to changing popular perceptions of black Americans and slavery on both sides of the Atlantic.

Racism had never been acceptable in the Pankhurst home. Family friends and political visitors gave Sylvia early integration into a diverse, egalitarian, polyphonous community. By the time she was adolescent, she had met and talked with black American abolitionists, Indian nationalists, activists, poets and revolutionaries in her own home.

Because Keir Hardie socialized with black and Asian people for the first time in the Pankhurst home, the Pankhursts enlarged his opportunities to engage with racially diverse people and his exposure to anti-racist thought. He had grown up with the racial prejudices common in his community, expressing racist and anti-Semitic sentiments about 'filthy foreigners ... some fleeing pogroms'.[1661] Within a decade of making this racist statement, he was reviled in the mainstream press for his championing of Indian independence and his fierce opposition to all forms of racism, including anti-Semitism. Radical socialist Jewish philanthropists became his most loyal and generous lifelong political funders. Hardie became the first Westminster politician to declare that South Africa had made a state policy of racism.

Eleanor Marx, Olive Schreiner and Israel Zangwill were among the Jewish activists and intellectuals who inspired Sylvia from a young age, and – the last two became friends and supporters. Sylvia thought and wrote about socialist Zionism, and through Zangwill came to understand the rejection of biblical-homeland Zionism in favour of territorialism, according to which thinking a Jewish homeland could be anywhere appropriate, including – or especially – within old empires. The homeland didn't have to be in or near the old Holy Land. Zangwill understood very early on that biblical-homeland Zionism would inevitably run the risk of becoming theocratic rather than democratic.

When Zangwill's drama *The Melting Pot* opened in Washington DC in 1909, former President Theodore Roosevelt shouted from his box that it was a great play, and in 1912 Zangwill received a letter from Roosevelt in which he said *The Melting Pot* was one of the very strong and real influences upon his thought and life. Sylvia followed all of this closely: Zangwill was a staunch supporter of the radical suffragettes and a constant friend.

Sylvia began writing in earnest about anti-Jewish racism, for example, in the 26 May 1917 issue of the *Woman's Dreadnought* she had reported in detail on what she described as 'the first British anti-semitic pogrom', the anti-Jewish riot in Bethnal Green. She concluded by honouring the conscientious objection of young British Jews and refugees, adding, 'There is much talk today of creating a Jewish state in Palestine and granting self-government to them there under British rule. Will the Jews be made conscripts also in Palestine?'[1662] Two decades later, the *New Times* covered the fighting between Palestinians and Zionist settlers. Sylvia saw this as an existential threat to world peace: 'The conflict between the Arabs and the Jews is tragically sad and unnecessary. These two races must agree to live together.'[1663]

In November 1938 Frank Van Gildemeester, president of the International Committee for Jewish Refugees, sent an appeal to President Franklin Roosevelt asking for help in creating the world's largest Jewish city on the banks of Lake Tana in 'Abyssinia', in the highlands of Italian-occupied Ethiopia. Gildemeester's organization was an entirely separate operation to the Netherlands-based Committee for Jewish Refugees, and functioned in a manner at variance with its policies. Later Jewish historians investigated Gildemeester's highly questionable motives, arguing that he aimed to profit from assisting wealthy people whom he made pay into funds for 'poor Aryans'. But Roosevelt gave his support to the scheme and reportedly wrote to Mussolini, asking the dictator to allow Jews to settle in his empire.[1664] Sylvia, who condemned Hitler's persecution of the Jews, and was busy finding homes in Britain for Jewish refugees, strongly objected to the project. On 17 January 1939, she wrote to Roosevelt warning him that the proposed plan to settle Jewish people in Ethiopia was 'impossible' because 'they would be massacred by the inhabitants of the country who are fighting for their liberty and independence'.[1665]

Racism was endemic in the British socialist and labour movements. Black, Indian, mixed-race, Chinese and Jewish workers were denigrated in some sectors of the trade unions and anti-Jewish racism was widespread. Socialist politicians, like Henry Hyndman, and trade union leaders, like Will Thorne, reproduced anti-Semitic tropes and stereotypes: this was all the more inexcusable given their close association with the Marx family in general and Eleanor Marx in particular, who had so inspired and supported them.

Since Sylvia's first meeting with Hardie when she was twelve years old, all his political journeys – both physical and intellectual – became hers. By the time he was a young adult he was freed from the prejudice that bedevilled most of his contemporaries. His early racial bias, based on blinkered ignorance, helped make him compassionate and empathetic towards others who suffered the same witlessness. He had been brought to his senses by education and experience, and so too could others be. Hardie's travels in India and South Africa consolidated his experience. After this his understanding of the need for political equality for all races and religions became a positive belief.[1666]

Hardie first visited South Africa in 1907, on his 'trip round the Empire' funded by his industrialist friend, Jewish visionary and philanthropist Joseph Fels.[1667] Fels picked up a large bill for radical political international travel that year. That same year he also paid for Lenin to attend the social democratic congress in Britain.

Hardie's voyage took him initially to Canada, then to India, New Zealand and Australia, where he met up with his old friends the former coal-miner Andrew Fisher and the indefatigable Coventry-born trade unionist Tom Mann. Fisher had become Australia's first Labour Prime Minister, while Mann busied himself revolutionizing Australian labour organization.

Hardie's 1907 tour ended in South Africa, where he met up with Olive Schreiner. Now back living in South Africa, Schreiner was reviled by racist white society, most virulently by British expats and colonial South Africans, but she was a crucial influence on British radical awareness and thought on racism in the nineteenth and twentieth centuries, and educated her contemporaries – Eleanor Marx, Henry Havelock Ellis, Israel Zangwill – on the problem of racism and empire, and in turn enlightened Sylvia and Keir Hardie. Her contribution was long remembered in South Africa. In December 2003, President Thabo Mbeki would posthumously award the Order of Ikhamanga (Gold) to Olive Schreiner 'for her exceptional contribution to literature and her commitment to the struggle for human rights and democracy'.

On Keir Hardie's speaker tour of South Africa and on his return to Britain, he put racism and economic inequality within the same frame. The problems of poverty and low wages experienced by Indian workers and black South African miners, he said in his speeches, were the same as those of the miners of Lanarkshire and South Wales. All suffered appalling living conditions while the bosses and landowners exploited them and lived well. But Hardie went further. There was no reason why 'South Africa should be made a white man's country'.[1668] Trade unions should open themselves to black membership and whites must share farmland with black people.

Conservative activists, colonial jingoists and right-wing racists hounded Hardie in a braying pack, breaking up meetings and smashing windows at the hotels where he stayed.[1669] When he came home, he showed Sylvia the Union Jack that he'd grabbed from one of his assailants while fighting his way out of a meeting in Johannesburg attacked by far-right pro-war British-expat jingos. He displayed the trophy on the wall at Nevill's Court as a memento of his part in the war against imperialism, and, as he told the multitude of visitors who passed through his modest lodgings, a marker of his political evolution from prejudiced youthful ignorance to adult understanding of racism.

Sylvia was brought up anti-imperialist. The South African wars were the first she remembered. Her parents firmly supported the Boer struggle against British colonial repression. All of the Pankhurst children suffered physical and verbal abuse at school for their anti-war stance. It was the memory of these years that made it so painful and inexplicable to Sylvia that her mother and Christabel turned their coats towards imperialism and racist xenophobia.

Just as her friendships with Peter Abrahams and Colin Legum further developed Sylvia's understanding of modern sub-Saharan Africa, her work on Ethiopia and friendship with Haile Selassie and other leaders informed her of the role Ethiopia and Selassie played in supporting liberation movements in Africa. Nelson Mandela wrote of Ethiopia as 'the birthplace of African nationalism' and of Selassie's influence as 'the shaping force of contemporary Ethiopian history'.[1670] With typical wit, he dubbed the diminutive Emperor the 'African Giant'. In his autobiography, *Long Walk to Freedom*, Mandela explained how the Ethiopian example had inspired and contributed to the formation of the ANC in South Africa in 1912, to bring all Africans together as one people, to defend their rights and freedoms.

Prior to the establishment of the Organization of African Unity in 1962, Nelson Mandela met with Haile Selassie and explained the plight of South Africans living under apartheid. Mandela wrote:

> Ethiopia has always held a special place in my own imagination and
> the prospect of visiting Ethiopia attracted me more strongly than
> a trip to France, England and America combined. I felt I would be
> visiting my own genesis, unearthing the roots of what made me an
> African. Meeting the Emperor himself would be like shaking hands
> with history.[1671]

Under the alias of David Motsamayi (meaning 'the walker') Mandela travelled to Addis Ababa to the first congress of the Pan-African Freedom Movement for East, Central and Southern Africa, convened under Ethiopian auspices. He was shocked when he stepped on board the Ethiopian Airways flight from Khartoum to Addis:

> I had never seen a black pilot before, and the instant I did I had to quell my panic. How could a black man fly an airplane? But a moment later I caught myself: I had fallen into the apartheid mindset, thinking Africans were inferior and flying was a white man's job. I sat back in my seat and chided myself for such thoughts. Once we were in the air, I lost my nervousness and studied the geography of Ethiopia, thinking how guerrilla forces had hidden in these very forests to fight the Italian imperialists.[1672]

Mandela received military training in Ethiopia, and learned how to handle a rifle and handgun, fire a mortar and make a bomb. He also learned the 'art and science of soldiering'. On Selassie's authorization, he was issued with an Ethiopian passport, enabling him to re-enter South Africa under an alias. He wrote of the impact Selassie made on him: 'It was the first time I had witnessed a head of state go through the formalities of his office, and I was fascinated. He stood perfectly straight, and inclined his head only slightly to indicate that he was listening. Dignity was the hallmark of all his actions.'[1673]

By the time Sylvia first visited Ethiopia during the war in 1944, she had made several trips during her life to America and France, travelling always over land and sea. Her first visit to the African continent at the age of sixty-two was also her first thrilling experience of flying. Haile Selassie had invited her to come and inspect the proposed site for the Princess Tsehai Hospital, presenting the invitation as a private visit. The timing also happened to coincide with the anniversary celebrations of his coronation. Sylvia tried to take Richard with her, arguing that her son could assist her by holding the tape measure and recording data for her hospital survey, but the War Office refused permission for him.

Sylvia left Liverpool early in October 1944 in a sea convoy, arriving in Alexandria five weeks later. From Cairo she flew, in a plane full of naval and army officers, to Asmara in Eritrea. Colonial Asmara appalled her. The guests and conversation at the Ministry of Information lunch gave her a rude and immediate introduction to the lie of the land. She met 'an Ethiopian gentleman who I afterwards learned is locally known as the Eritrean Quisling'.[1674] She also met Professor Edward Ullendorff, then editor of the *Eritrean Weekly News*. He told her why he opposed the return of Eritrea to Ethiopia and supported a British mandate in both countries. He censured Sylvia and her newspaper for being insufficiently critical of Ethiopia, to a chorus of supporting approval from the other guests.

Sylvia heard the same opinions expressed in the mess of the British military administration and by other colonials. Ullendorff bothered her. In a rapid dispatch back to the *New Times*, she wrote, 'I could not help feeling it a mistake to confide so important a propaganda medium as the sole weekly newspaper in the language of the people (Tigrinya) to an editorship sharply opposed to Eritrean reunion with Ethiopia and even to Ethiopia's independence.'[1675]

Other shocks followed. Why were her passport and vaccination certificate checked by Italian officials? Due to a shortage of British personnel was the answer given.

Back at her hotel, things looked up. A deputation of Muslim and Christian Eritrean reunionists presented her with a welcoming address, accompanied by a bouquet of roses tied in the green, yellow and red colours of Ethiopia: 'Sword of the Press! We have read your paper with which you fight for our country ... our Motherland, Ethiopia.' Each member of the delegation shook her hand. 'I knew they were appealing through me to all in Britain and throughout the world who have aided the Ethiopian people so far, to keep true to the end, to heed and understand their heartfelt desire for reunion.'[1676] Professor Ullendorff chuntered: her intervention in Eritrea was 'disastrous'. Other specialists disagreed. 'What she wrote was true. The Brits *were* robbing Eritreans. Of course they did not like what she was saying.'[1677] Regardless of their differences, Edward Ullendorff and his wife would send prompt letters of condolence and warm admiration when Sylvia died.

At her request, Sylvia visited Asmara proper, referred to by colonial overlords as 'the native quarter'. Writing in the *New Times*, she contrasted conditions in these townships, without water, sanitation or infrastructure, with colonial Asmara, 'the bright and gay city of trees and gardens devoted entirely to strangers from overseas'.[1678]

The flight from Asmara to Addis dazzled her, despite altitude sickness: 'The Red Sea a lovely peacock blue, the Arabian shore to the left of us; the African shore to the right where the glorious blue sky faded to pale, misty green on the horizon ... everywhere sea and sand peppered by the dried up water courses, with tiny tufts of brownish green. The blue, blue sea turns green at the edge with a fringe of white beaches.'[1679]

The sharp reascent after refuelling en route hit her with another wave of altitude sickness, but excitement at overflying Ethiopia got the better of her faintness and nausea: 'A lake, rivers, then a wide stretch of vivid green broken by water came into view ... A flock of white birds far beneath us ... the plateau. I cannot describe the feeling it gave me.'[1680] High on oxygen deprivation, she painted idealized images of peasant tulkuls with their grass roofs (in reality smoke-filled, dark and poorly ventilated) and wrote just as if she had indeed discovered the lost golden kingdom of the Queen of Sheba and Prester John: 'Except for extensive woods capping the heights, every yard seemed cultivated ... a marvellous country, greatly favoured by nature, peopled by industrious cultivators.'[1681] This was a rose-tinted idealization of hard peasant existence. But rather this romanticism than the racist stereotypes that presented Ethiopians as indigent barbarians still scratching in the dust, despite being the world's oldest Christian civilization.

Addis Ababa, one of the highest capital cities in the world, rose from a dusty plain – an irregular urban sprawl out of which grew jewels: the churches, the imperial palace, the great Mausoleum of Menelik and Italian colonial buildings. A delegation comprising some of Ethiopia's most senior government officials honoured Sylvia with an official welcome as she stepped off the plane on to the tarmac. Photographs show her, dressed in an unusually well-tailored jacket and neat straw hat, shaking hands with Chancellor and Minister of the Pen (the Emperor's principal secretary) Wolde-Georgis Wolde-Yohannes; Selassie's private secretary Teffera-Work Kidane-Wold, and *Ato* (Mr) Makonnen Habtewold, influential adviser to the Emperor. The British Minister to Abyssinia Sir Robert George Howe, displeased by the status granted to Sylvia's visit, wrote disapprovingly in his report to the Foreign Office that she had been met at the airport by 'nearly all the leading political figures, as well as by her former Ethiopian acquaintances in England', and from the airport had been 'escorted by a convoy of official cars to the house in the former Italian Legation prepared for her use'.[1682] Access to the grounds of the property, known as Villa Sahle Selassie and set amid flowerbeds of arum lilies and vivid red cannas, with clusters of red currant bushes, was along an avenue of graceful eucalyptus.

Sylvia experienced for the first time the smell of the eucalyptus trees that permeated the 'forest capital'. Non-indigenous Australian eucalyptus dated from Menelik's day, sucking the moisture out of the water table and playing havoc with local flora, but Sylvia loved their golden-green canopy and perhaps felt compassion for that doughty air of resilience rustling through eucalyptus everywhere outside of its native Antipodean habitat. The colloquial Amharic term for the trees, Bihar Zaf, literally 'sea tree', perfectly captures the distinctive sound made by wind currents through their branches.[1683] Ever pragmatic, Sylvia admired Menelik's decision to plant the alien trees. Not only did eucalyptus provide a ready, fast-replenishing source of building material enabling Ethiopians to create permanent settlements, but it also created a public-health benefit by reducing endemic malaria. Plantations of eucalyptus dried the land, diminishing the mosquito population in malaria-infested areas and dramatically lowering the incidence and impact of the disease, as the trees did elsewhere in Africa. With their thirsty roots and their leaves dripping acid on the earth, the 'sea trees' had a deleterious effect on the long-term health of the soil, but conversely provided abundant building material and proved hugely beneficial for human health.

Sylvia was shown to her living room with a log fire burning in the hearth and a large bouquet of flowers to welcome her – red and white carnations, scarlet and pink geraniums. A study was laid out for her, equipped with a large desk and plentiful writing materials. An Ethiopian army major introduced himself as her designated escort, and two menservants appeared to wait on her. Briskly, she asked Tafara Worq, 'What is the programme?' 'Complete rest for today – tomorrow you will see Their Majesties,' he offered. Dissatisfied with this reply, Sylvia asked to be taken for a drive right away. On her return she went straight to the plush study to start the first dispatch to *New Times*: 'I seem to be living in a dream. I was in Addis Ababa, strange yet familiar. The many photographs I had seen were now put together.'[1684]

She describes seeing the Ethiopian people in traditional dress, as well as donkeys, mules and their picturesque burdens, including enormous black jars, baskets, tables, straw umbrellas and bundles of eucalyptus to fuel ovens. 'A woman in a black cape riding a mule with an umbrella to shade her; a man, all in white, on a mule with a gaily embroidered scarlet saddle. I was enchanted and bewildered.'[1685]

Over the next few weeks, Sylvia undertook a strenuous tour of the country, visiting schools, war orphanages, handicraft co-operatives, a Greek-managed tobacco factory and a cotton factory under the management of a Manchester textile expert. She saw abandoned Italian tractors and cars in the process of being reconditioned. She took delivery of a large collection of 'Fascist atrocity photographs taken from dead or captured Italian soldiers'.[1686] These she later put to repeated use in *New Times* and in pro-Ethiopian propaganda leaflets, provoking the Foreign Office to near apoplexy.

Asked to make a national broadcast from the Addis radio station, Sylvia praised what she had seen and committed herself to continue working for Ethiopia and reunion with Eritrea. She spoke of how impressed she had been by a Somali chieftain who petitioned the 'Sword of the Press' to represent the cause of British withdrawal from the Ogaden; she also informed listeners that she had been told that Somalis who refused to surrender their arms were refused water from wells guarded by the British military occupation, and chiefs were pressurized to say that they wished to remain under British rule.

Signed on 19 December 1944 while Sylvia was in Addis, the new Anglo-Ethiopian Agreement was a flimsy stopgap, setting no time limit to British occupation of the Ogaden and making a pathetic reconstruction grant of £3 million spread over three years. Compared with the £87.5 million granted to Italy by the UN, it was deeply insulting.

Speaking to the Ethiopian–Eritrean Association on her return to England, Sylvia reminded her homeland of its obligations. She jogged the memories of her British audience about the UK government leaflets, produced in consultation with Haile Selassie and dropped by RAF planes, promising reunion with Eritrea after the defeat of Mussolini. Yet Italian judges and Italian fascist laws remained in place in Eritrea with the support of the British authorities. She had received a report of the execution by the Italian occupiers of five Eritreans for murdering one Italian, and a whole village gunned down for the murder of another. The fascist colour bar was kept in force, and public meetings forbidden in Eritrea.

The Conservative MP Maurice Petherick wrote to Anthony Eden on 6 February 1945, fulminating against Sylvia's attacks on the new accord and on British intentions in Ethiopia:

Subject to further consideration, the agreement with the Ethiopians
seems a very reasonable one in the circumstances, but this
confounded Pankhurst woman who has always been 'plus fuzzy
wuzzy que les fuzzies-wuzzies' is making all kinds of disgusting
allegations against British administration and about supposed
British intervention.[1687]

Contradicting her lifelong republican conviction, Sylvia offered no
robust criticism of the extremities of luxury at the imperial palace when
she visited it. As one historian remarks, 'Unlike other correspondents,
she found nothing absurd in the rich ceremonial, the tremendous
flunkeydom, which surrounded the tiny figure of Haile Selassie.'[1688]
Perhaps the altitude had got to her, but she clearly succumbed to the
aesthetic overload of pomp and circumstance.

The servants who waited on us wore the velvet uniform,
photographs of which I had seen in the American magazine Life.
Terribly hot they must be in a tropical climate I thought, not
realizing that all the year round Addis Ababa is neither hot nor
cold. Nor did I realize how beautiful this uniform looks in the grey-
walled palace – the coat of rich bottle green, the vest and trousers
deep ruby crimson. They are straight, handsome men who wear it,
and they served us with friendliness and grace. One thing to learn
in Ethiopia is this: the people are kind, from the highest to the most
humble, they love to help you, but there is nothing servile about
them.[1689]

Especially when you are the personal guest of the Emperor. Sylvia's
reputation as Sword of the Press and valiant champion of the Ethiopian
cause justly preceded her, but that did not excuse her failure to address
the extreme disparities between the wealth of the elites and the struggling
peasantry out of sight in the Highlands. The intrepid Dervla Murphy,
who travelled through Ethiopia on foot and mule in the early 1960s,
would agree with Sylvia's assessment of the kindness and lack of servility
among even the most impoverished Ethiopians in the remotest part of
the Highlands. But it is hard to imagine Murphy not taking Sylvia to
task over her silence, at least initially, on the excesses of the anachronistic
royal court and the endemic poverty among the general population.[1690]

In turn, Sylvia might reply with a reminder of what they were up against in the context of the times. Murphy, at an individual level unquestionably the most intrepid explorer and greatest travel writer of her generation, steered clear of the fearful difficulties and complications of realpolitik required of those actively engaging in struggles for political change. During Sylvia's visit, the newly established British Embassy in Addis sent an intemperate dispatch to Anthony Eden:

> Miss Pankhurst clearly set out on her journey with her mind already made up; she was going to a citadel of freedom populated by brave, virtuous and wholly admirable defenders, beset by the machinations of European imperialists ... Miss Pankhurst's sense of her own importance, which shelters inadequately behind an affectation of modesty, received great encouragement here when she was met by all the leading political figures.[1691]

Reports of Sylvia's activities caused controversy at the Foreign Office. The retired senior diplomat Lord Vansittart, furious at her public criticisms of British foreign policy, wrote to Sir Orme Sargent, Deputy Under Secretary for Foreign Affairs, demanding to know why she been granted a visa: 'Miss Sylvia Pankhurst seems to have done a great deal of mischief there ... Who is responsible?' Sir Orme replied that the Foreign Office 'had no desire whatsoever to promote the lady's journey ... she is in fact one of our most persistent and unscrupulous persecutors'; however, 'we really had very little choice in the matter once the ban on foreign travel had been lifted'.[1692] Whitehall anxieties proved entirely justified. The moment Sylvia hit African soil she started advocating the cause of Pan-Ethiopian Eritrean nationalism and insisting that Britain must end its military occupation of the Ogaden.

So there was Sylvia's choice, between backing the statesmen of her homeland who deemed it acceptable in official correspondence to refer to black people as 'les fuzzies-wuzzies' on the one hand and, on the other, lending her elbow and pen to a monarchy committed to the African struggle for independence, the expanding global political movement against racism and the central symbolic figure in Rastafari ideology.

Other official engagements of Sylvia's visit included laying wreaths at the tomb of Princess Tsehai, at the Ethiopian Liberation monument and at the monument to the victims of the Graziani massacre of 1937. The latter action once again irritated the British Embassy. On the morning of the Orthodox Christmas on 7 January 1945, Sylvia joined the royal party, amid 3,000 schoolchildren assembled to sing to Haile Selassie and receive gifts from him. Confronted by an entire school class of wounded and disabled boys and girls, Sylvia wept. She followed up with an article about the effects of war on Ethiopian children, 'victims of Italian ferocity whose scars attest the wickedness of Fascism'.[1693] That same morning, Sylvia joined a service in the Church of the Saviour of the World, and allowed the sumptuously robed Coptic priest to anoint her cheek and lips with holy water. This appears to be the only recorded instance of Sylvia attending a church service.

In the new year, the Emperor awarded Sylvia two decorations at a public ceremony, the Ethiopian Patriot's medal and the Queen of Sheba medal, created to honour women. For the Patriot's medal, a unique decoration was designed just for her, embodying five palms, 'the most palms anybody can have,' Sylvia boasted, one for each of the years of her struggle against the fascist occupation.[1694] She wrote to the Foreign Secretary Anthony Eden:

> I was surprised to hear my name called during the ceremony and to be presented with the Order of the Queen of Sheba and a special decoration which has been introduced for service to the cause of Ethiopian liberation during the five years of the Italian occupation. Of course I was most grateful for the unexpected honour … but Mr Howe, the British Minister, afterwards pointed out to me that a British subject may not accept such decorations without obtaining the permission of His Majesty the King.[1695]

Sylvia wrote this letter to Eden on the instruction of Sir Robert George Howe. The most senior British diplomat in the region, Howe had spent a decade fighting with Sylvia and trying to obstruct her activities, unsuccessfully, and he was mightily 'peeved at the award'.[1696] He told Sylvia that she had better write immediately to the Foreign Secretary to obtain the Crown's permission for the award she had already received. Simultaneously, Howe also wrote to Eden to complain: 'When I reproached the Emperor's Private Secretary for his failure to obtain His Majesty the King's prior permission for the award (a regulation of which *Ato* Tafara Work [Teffera-Work Kidane-Wold] is perfectly aware) he apologized on the ground that there had been no time to obtain such permission.'

Sir Ronald Campbell, Assistant Under-Secretary of State at the Foreign Office, expressed the Foreign Office's umbrage, writing on 7 March that 'the lady is a blister and deserves a rap'. His colleague Robert Dunbar agreed; he took 'a rather poor view', he wrote, of the application for permission to wear the decoration, 'since Miss Pankhurst's support for the Ethiopian cause has usually taken the form of abuse of His Majesty's Government, whom moreover she has lately criticised rather disloyally in connection with the new Ethiopian agreement', whose terms were still under discussion. Dunbar knew, however, that refusal 'would be likely to lead to a row if Miss Pankhurst was denied the permission which she seeks' because 'she would exploit the popular sentiment in favour of Ethiopia to get the refusal reversed'.[1697]

The Ethiopian diplomats had outmanoeuvred them. 'Very reluctantly, therefore', Dunbar recommended the Foreign Office's grudging capitulation, suggesting 'that she might be given restricted permission as an exceptional measure dictated by considerations of expediency, and if you [the Foreign Office] think that the King would approve this solution will you send a formal request'. Dunbar added, 'It is to be hoped that the Emperor will not wish to decorate all the people who helped him when he was in exile here, and we are considering the possibility of conveying a hint that it would be embarrassing if he were proposing anything of the kind.'[1698]

Once she had sent off her letter to Eden, Sylvia continued blithely unconcerned by the diplomatic row. She was enjoying the airy six-room villa put at her disposal – 'two bathrooms', Sylvia marvelled, with 'arum lilies and red currants in the garden'. The 'excellent' servants and 'beautiful' table decorations impressed her, but not the battalions of ants. She wrote to her secretary Mrs Westrope, 'I am busy all the time and one can't work so hard here. In the mornings one feels the height ... It is neither too hot nor too cold, lovely sunshine, flowers and trees.'[1699] This is a rare admission from Sylvia that the altitude affected her. In time, she adjusted. After decades living at sea-level in the mizzled lowlands of the Thames Valley, the temperate climes of Addis' sunny plateau, at 7,500 feet, were a revelation.

36

Patriot

From the time of her return from Addis Ababa in 1945, Sylvia worked tirelessly to present Ethiopia's claims to repossess the former Italian colonies of Eritrea and Somalia. She put the case in her booklet *The Ethiopian People: Their Rights and Progress*, published in 1946. Robert Gale Woolbert described the it in his capsule review in *Foreign Affairs*: 'An historical résumé of Ethiopian progress in recent decades and of her rights to such border areas as Eritrea'.[1700]

Sylvia argued that British and French Somaliland, along with Eritrea and Somalia, should have been joined with Ethiopia to form a natural geographic and economic unit. During sixty years of Italian colonial rule large numbers of people had emigrated from Eritrea and Somalia to Ethiopia, where they were given full citizenship, education and, frequently, government posts. 'Racial discrimination, economic stagnancy, and slavery (both open and in the form of forced labour) were the hallmarks of Italian "civilization".'[1701]

The evidence of European travellers and explorers proved that in the early nineteenth century, Eritrea was regarded as part of Ethiopia. Sylvia contested the claims that the Somalis were natural enemies of Ethiopia and that the outbreak of bloody civil war between pro- and anti-Ethiopian factions in Eritrea and Somalia was inevitable; or that both regions would suffer economically under Haile Selassie, who was hard pressed to finance Ethiopia's own development. Further, she disagreed with experts who maintained that the British military administration of the Ogaden and Reserved Area was necessary to prevent serious incidents on the border with Somalia.[1702]

She hoped mistakenly that the Labour Party victory of 1945 would bring greater credence to the cause of reunification. In fact, Cold War conditions meant that Britain was ready, like the US and Soviet Russia, to try and gain influence in Italy, including by negotiating for a return of Eritrea or Somalia – or parts of both. Ethiopia was excluded from the conference that worked out the peace terms with Italy.

Sylvia threw her weight against what was either a hostile or an indifferent British press, encouraging reunionists in Eritrea and ex-Italian Somaliland to demonstrate and bring pressure on the UN. By 1947 Italian newspapers were accusing her of active complicity in provoking riots in Somalia's capital Mogadishu, which broke out again in 1948 and 1949 in defiance of a ban on demonstrations imposed by the British military regime. In 1949 the *Giornale d'Italia* charged her with the 'principal moral responsibility' for bloodshed in clashes between police and the Somali Youth League. At the end of the year, the issue was settled when the UN voted in favour of Italian Somaliland becoming a UN trusteeship called the Trust Territory of Somaliland, placed under Italian administration for ten years. In January 1950 the war criminal General Guglielmo Nasi, Graziani's deputy in Ethiopia, was appointed administrator of the Italian colony of Somaliland, but so great was the international public outcry, Nasi was withdrawn.

Infuriated by her persistent unionist tirades, the Italian government banned the *New Times* and all Sylvia's books and pamphlets from Italy and Somaliland, along with the *Daily Worker*, various other communist and Pan-African publications – and *Camera Studies in the Nude*. Sylvia led poster parades from Fleet Street to the Houses of Parliament. She lambasted *The Times* for claiming that Ethiopia lacked any indigenous culture, art or notated music. She stated that there was a growing stream of refugees to Ethiopia from the 'Italian terror' in Somalia.

In September 1951, shortly before Attlee's Labour government called a snap general election for 25 October, Sylvia received an invitation from Haile Selassie to attend the grand opening of the Princess Tsehai Hospital on 1 November. In the event the Conservative Party won the election and Sylvia's MP Winston Churchill was returned as Prime Minister. This marked the beginning of Labour's thirteen-year period in opposition.

Accompanied by Richard and her friend Basil Mackenzie, Lord Amulree, chair of the trustees of Sylvia's fundraising committee and their family doctor, Sylvia set off on her second visit to Ethiopia. She stayed there until the new year, working with the Selassie administration on the campaign for unification, researching and touring. They were put up in the government villa that Sylvia had stayed in before. Richard was delighted to be reunited with some of his university friends from the LSE, just returned from Britain and taking up jobs, mainly in government service. They took him to their favourite restaurants and cafés in thrumming Addis, and also 'tried to introduce me to the intricacies and mysteries of Ethiopian government and politics'.[1703]

Sylvia, Richard and Basil attended a concert at the Hager Fikir theatre as the Emperor's guests, and toured new schools, medical facilities and factories. A visit to Gondar, the old seventeenth- and eighteenth-century capital, dazzled Sylvia and Richard. Years later Richard chronicled Gondar's history in his two-volume compendium of Ethiopian towns and cities. Together, mother and son watched the sun set over the vast Lake Tana, much of which flowed into the Nile.

Sylvia made speeches and spoke on national radio. Addressing a reunion of resistance fighters held at the Addis Ababa National Theatre, she condemned the post-war treatment of Ethiopia. The failure to reunite Ethiopia, Eritrea and Somaliland was 'one of the great injustices of history … My own country was largely responsible for the failure. We were only in part exonerated by what we did to assist the liberation of Ethiopia from the enemy yoke in 1941. In the former Italian Somaliland liberation will come also, and we must work for it.'[1704]

The official opening ceremony of the completed teaching hospital took place on 2 November, with Sylvia accorded the tribute of being guest of honour. Lieutenant-Colonel William Byam, who had qualified at St George's Hospital in London and after his military career in the RAMC subsequently lectured there for twenty-five years in tropical diseases, was appointed director of Ethiopia's first teaching hospital. 'The Princess Tsahai [sic] Memorial Hospital,' Sylvia wrote, 'is destined to be of immense importance to Ethiopia in the training of nurses and, subsequently, of physicians and surgeons.'[1705] She wrote at length about the hospital in *New Times*, describing the new hospital, its staff and equipment, and continued to fundraise, describing the plans for its future development.[1706]

While Sylvia continued on her official schedule, Richard went to visit a Sudanese college friend in Omdurman, Sudan, Mohamed Osman Yassein, who introduced him to other friends, many of them western educated.[1707] They in turn brought him into their networks, including several communist activists opposed to the British occupation. Richard's new acquaintances educated him in Sudanese politics, and discussed their attempts to fuse together the interests of north and south. Mohamed drove Richard through the desert to visit the Gezira cotton-cultivation scheme, believed to be a prototype for economic development throughout Africa. Walking around the site, Richard recalled his old LSE teacher, the historian Jack Fisher, advising him that, 'in evaluating prosperity, one should investigate the contents of peasants' houses'. As Richard reported grimly to his mother, 'Throughout my stay I was not introduced to a single Sudanese woman.' Before returning home alone to finish his doctoral thesis on William Thompson, Richard threw a party for his friends. His guests were a mixed group who had studied in the UK and in North America: 'There were lengthy, good-natured discussions on the burning issue: whether Britain or the US provided the best, and most relevant, education for Ethiopian students.'[1708]

During her long stay in Ethiopia Sylvia gathered research for their 350-page co-authored book *Ethiopia and Eritrea*, making the case for unification:

> Dedicated to the gallant people of Ethiopia who throughout the
> ages have never surrendered their freedom; to their brothers and
> sisters across the Mareb who at length have been liberated from
> three generations of colonial bondage; and to those generous British
> men and women who have always remembered that justice and the
> friendship of peoples are greater than imperial interests and will
> remain fruitful when the old colonial empires are no more.[1709]

The 15 September 1951 issue of *New Times*, published shortly before Sylvia's second journey to Africa, provides a representative snapshot of her key preoccupations at the time. This issue contains articles on finance in Ethiopia, South African apartheid and new UN postage stamps. The emphasis in the paper on South African matters illustrates Sylvia's engagement in the struggles of the whole continent – her interest and obsessions were not focused singularly on Ethiopia and she never lost sight of the broader context.

As within Britain and elsewhere, Sylvia monitored right-wing nationalism in the post-war world. In South Africa, the Netherlands-educated pulpit preacher Daniel François Malan won forty-three seats for his Reunited National Party in the House of Assembly in the 1943 election. In the 1948 election this party, allied with the smaller Afrikaner Party, appealed to both Afrikaner and Anglo-British racial prejudice and won a narrow majority in the House of Assembly. This enabled D. F. Malan to form the first exclusively Afrikaner government of South Africa.

This September 1951 edition of *New Times* also contains a long article by Walter Sisulu, general secretary of the African National Congress, extracted from a pamphlet issued by the ANC for distribution to the UN. Entitled 'South Africa behind Bars', the feature provides a detailed summary of the current situation in South Africa, analysing D. F. Malan's white-supremacist government and its policy of implementing absolute apartheid via the Group Areas Act, the Suppression of Communism Act, the Mixed Marriages Act and the Immorality Amendment Act. Sisulu's article clearly explains each piece of legislation. The report proceeds to describe the everyday so-called 'petty' apartheid of public segregation, then provides detailed information on the restructuring of parliament, the withdrawal of the franchise from multi-ethnic Cape Coloured people (of mixed European white and African black or Asian ancestry), the persecution of Indian politicians and banning orders on international travel. It describes the tightening of the pass laws, the controversial compulsory ID system used to control the movement of black, Indian and Coloured people in South Africa, and concludes with a description of the degradation caused by the Bantustan system, the policy of ethnic cleansing by which means the white supremacist National Party created ten 'Bantu homelands' as supposed 'autonomous' territories for designated ethnic groups, stripping the people forced into them of their South African citizenship and making those who worked in South Africa 'immigrants' in their own country.

In 1955 *New Times* welcomed the newly revised Ethiopian constitution, which enshrined election of members of parliament by full adult suffrage. Article Four of the constitution clearly retained the theocratic basis of Ethiopian government: 'By virtue of His Imperial Blood, as well as by the authority He has received, the person of the Emperor is sacred, His dignity is inviolable, and His power indisputable.' The *Economist* characterized Haile Selassie as 'comparable in modern history only with the Tsar of Russia or the Sultan of Turkey', pointing out the alleged reluctance of educated Ethiopians to 'do jobs which entail putting on overalls' – as if, snorted Sylvia in her *New Times* rebuttal, this reluctance were not still unduly common in class-ridden Britain.

Also in 1955, alongside the new constitutional revisions, Ethiopia issued an Imperial Charter for an Animals' Protection Society: 'it is Our desire to promote the mitigation of animal suffering and the advancement of the practice of humanity towards the inferior classes of animated beings'. Despite Britain's vaunted self-image as an animal-loving nation, neither The *Economist* nor the BBC had anything to say about the protection of animal rights. Challenging this, and the errors in a BBC programme on the Ethiopian government which criticized the Emperor's 'benevolent despotism', Sylvia's *New Times* editorial continued, 'It often happens that when some rare creative humanitarian genius is devoting all the force of unusually abounding energies to the welfare of his creatures, the very magnitude of the resultant achievements attracts a multitude of destructive and bitter critics. Yet these critics usually offer no adverse comment on rulers whose lives are entirely devoted to personal pleasure.'[1710]

Indicative of Sylvia's attitude is her response to an article published in the *Manchester Guardian* by a disillusioned American schoolteacher who had worked in Addis for nine years. He deplored the insanitary, rudimentary school premises and the disgraceful extremes of wealth and poverty and claimed that the families of Ethiopian students supported in their study overseas were 'held as hostages for their return'.[1711] Yes, wrote Sylvia in her letter of reply, of course there was poverty in Ethiopia, that was why it received assistance from the Point Four Program, the first global US foreign aid programme for so-called developing countries, introduced by President Harry S Truman in January 1949. The talk about hostages was untrue, and wilfully ignored the fact that many of the Ethiopians studying abroad were orphans whose parents had been killed by the Italians. As 'the one percent of Ethiopians whom your correspondent considers live in luxury know nothing of such riches as are found in America,' she would like to 'inquire whether he recommends equalitarian communism for the USA as well as for Ethiopia'.[1712]

In 1955 John Gunther published his brash, lively, hugely popular exposé of Ethiopia, *Inside Africa*, offering the reader an easy-to-read survey of contemporary African politics to arm them for dinner-party and senior common room conversation in the increasingly alarming context of anti-colonialism, rising African nationalism and black consciousness. Praised by white western critics for providing a precious mine of detailed information about contemporary Africa, the book was in fact more of a minefield of misinformation and unthinking prejudice. Gunther's chapters on Ethiopia and Haile Selassie demonstrated the good sense of allowing a temporary continuation of autocracy and paid tribute to the Emperor's abilities and integrity as a leader. Then they dissected Ethiopia to try and see how it worked, and found it wanting on every count.

Press censorship, Gunther found, was rigid, self-censorship and bribery of government officials endemic, educational attainment mostly pathetic and sanitation so basic that it was only the altitude that prevented widespread epidemics. The capital city, 'New Flower', Gunther observed, 'looked as if it had been dropped piecemeal from an aeroplane carrying rubbish', and the Christian clergy he deplored for being the most numerous and illiterate in the world in a county where half the population was either Muslim or pagan. The new constitution hardly passed for democracy, since it allowed no political opposition and the Emperor selected the members of the upper house of parliament himself. Dissenting politicians were carted off to a version of Ethiopian 'Siberia'.

As for the Emperor himself, Gunther energetically continued, in his large pith helmet and long flowing khaki cape he resembled nothing so much as a 'mushroom' – a very small mushroom, since a cushion had to be placed under his feet so that his feet didn't dangle when he sat on the throne.

Sylvia matched Gunther with equal vigour in her rebuttal of his book, to which she dedicated an entire issue of *New Times* in April 1956. Gunther's account was heavily dependent on Margery Perham's *The Government of Ethiopia* (1948), an armchair academic book by an ill-informed but vocal Oxbridge advocate of British trusteeship of Ethiopia. The colonialism-friendly Perham, like Gunther who followed her, held the view that although the Italian invasion was cruel, the fascist occupation had given Ethiopia 'a badly needed jolt', and it could not be denied that the money Italy had invested in public services and infrastructure formed 'the bedrock of the country's physical progress'.[1713] Sylvia was aghast at Perham's defence of fascism and British imperialism, and no less dismayed by her representation of Ethiopia as a barbarian backward nation.

The problem of Ethiopia was not a simplistic choice between defending white racist colonial fascism and supporting an ancient autocratic indigenous monarchy trundling towards reluctant reform. Perham's account ignored, or pretended to ignore, the adroit patience with which Haile Selassie managed his return to power, using political connections and the military might of his allies to defeat the fascist Italian forces. As with so many other western European academics, Perham suffered from an amnesiac state when it came to considering the slow evolution into democracy, over many centuries, of her own British homeland.

This was when Sylvia got to work on writing her monumental book about the cultural history of Ethiopia, published at the end of 1955, *Ethiopia: A Cultural History.* An epic survey from ancient stirrings to modern times, the book recounted the history of indigenous Ethiopian art and culture spanning a thousand years, from illuminated manuscripts and notated music to the educational achievements of the Coptic Church, and was admired by critics. It chronicled in detail the successive invasions by Portuguese and Protestant missionaries and by Egyptian and Turkish forces, and the Italian usurpation. Inevitably, favourable reviews and scrupulous research did nothing to make Sylvia's a popular book in Britain. Gunther's was shorter, easier to read, more entertaining and bathed the reader in the warm balm of reconfirming their existing racial and cultural prejudices. And Sylvia's was by no means an unpartisan history, which jarred on readers who wanted to get there by themselves.

Shortly before leaving England in 1956, Sylvia arranged a meeting with the Foreign Office to ask if the rumours were true that Britain intended to try and resume control of the Ogaden and run it from the British Somaliland protectorate. Officials confirmed that this was, regrettably, necessary, since Ethiopian police were unable to 'control border banditry'.[1714] Further, the Foreign Office considered it to have been a mistake to promise self-government by 1960 to the Somalis under Italian trusteeship. This meeting confirmed Sylvia's suspicions that

Ethiopia was beset by scheming Britons, General Nasi and his Italian 'Peace Corps' and trigger-happy Kikuyu-murdering British settlers in Kenya. Just as with Russia in 1919, here was a 'gigantic underdog … encircled by yelping capitalist curs'.[1715]

The early 1950s had brought not only the return of the Tories to government but a change of monarch. George VI died in February 1952, and was succeeded by his twenty-five-year-old daughter Elizabeth II. The Princess was at Treetops luxury game lodge in Kenya on the night her father died. The following afternoon, beside a trout stream in the foothills of Mount Kenya, Prince Philip broke the news to her. Called Sagana, the fishing lodge where she learned that her life was forever changed had been gifted to her as a wedding present.

Sylvia's first direct introduction to Kenyan politics came through her friend the Ethiopian diplomat Birhanu Tesemma and his German wife Edith. Tesemma served in the London Embassy, where first he met Sylvia. Exiled in Kenya during the Italian occupation, he later became Ethiopian Consul in Kenya, where he and Edith befriended rising African nationalists working for independence. Birhanu and Sylvia corresponded for years, and later he and his wife introduced her and Richard to Kenyan freedom fighters and future leaders.

On the personal front, these were tough years for Sylvia. She had suffered her first heart attack in April 1953. The following January Silvio died. Emmeline Pethick-Lawrence followed him only weeks later. Haile Selassie's state visit to the UK in October 1954 brightened the horizon of a doleful year. During this official state visit, Selassie reminded the recently widowed Sylvia of his open invitation to her to come and live in Ethiopia. Richard, who had recently completed his PhD, received the offer of a job at the new national university in Addis Ababa.

As other African countries began to move towards democratic republican independence in the 1950s, Ethiopia's position became a focus of attention among its Pan-Africanist allies. Sylvia had corresponded with W. E. B. Du Bois, the leading Pan-Africanist intellectual and stalwart supporter of women's suffrage since the Fifth Pan-African Congress held in Manchester in 1945, where they had met. In March 1946 she had lobbied Du Bois to leverage his influence among African Americans to raise support in the US for Ethiopia's claim to Eritrea. She claimed to be operating independently of the Ethiopian government.

'We never ask for any official approval for what we do for Ethiopia. The Legation is perfectly able to tell the Foreign Office if it chooses, that we are acting independently and cannot be controlled.'[1716]

In the ensuing correspondence, Du Bois discussed with Sylvia the challenges in the geopolitics of black consciousness. 'Whenever we try ... to help our fellow Africans in other parts of the world, our work is looked upon as interference and with that attitude goes usually the assumption that we are busybodies who must be ignored.' He honoured her work: 'No one has appreciated more than I the long and courageous effort you have made for the freedom of Ethiopia; but I strongly believe that you would be helped in your alliance with American Negroes if your understanding of their efforts were more complete.' Du Bois tried to steer Sylvia to a subtler understanding of the divide-and-rule tactics deployed by competing colonialisms – whether British imperialism or American capitalism. 'The Ethiopians themselves for a long time have been misled by the idea that any appearance of sympathy between them and American Negroes would be unwise.'[1717]

They kept in touch. One of Sylvia's seasonal greetings survives from 1948, when she sent him 'a merry Christmas and happy New Year' message on a photographic card of a smiling boy saluting, above the caption 'Young Ethiopia'.[1718] In 1954 they corresponded over Haile Selassie's state visits to the UK and US. Knowing her influence with the Emperor, Du Bois wrote to Sylvia in February asking her to intercede on behalf of black Americans to ensure that they would be able to meet him during his visit.[1719] It was a matter of vital importance. Sylvia responded by return assuring Du Bois that she would write immediately to the Emperor exactly as he had requested, 'but perhaps I might mention to you that Ethiopia does not recognise the term "negro" as applied to the whole of the African people ... I promise that I will put the matter to His Imperial Majesty, and I am sure he will do what he can to meet the desire of the Afro-Americans, or Negroes, if you prefer to call them so.'[1720]

The reflection on terminology is an indicative piece of diplomacy on Sylvia's part, revealing her growing understanding of the political tensions within global Pan-Africanism. In their earlier correspondence in 1946 discussing how to encourage African-American support for the Ethiopian cause, Sylvia had told Du Bois about her experiences in Tennessee over thirty years before: 'I have always had sympathy for the

American Negro and had some lively experiences when I was in the United States on that account.'[1721] When Du Bois came to compose an admiring public eulogy for Sylvia after her death, he wrote of the shared, collective struggle of 'black folks' and 'black Ethiopia'.[1722]

Continuing their discussion about the Emperor's state visit in 1954, Du Bois wrote to Sylvia again on 10 March, concerned that she so far had not succeeded in getting a firm commitment that Selassie would meet with African-American delegations on his state visit to the US. Sylvia replied immediately, sharing his anxiety and assuring him that she would decide what to do to progress the matter. 'I would add, however, that in view of the present situation in Kenya [referring to the Mau Mau Uprising] I feel that we British are not really in a very good position at the moment for criticizing other people's governments, as we have such a mess-up in a territory for which we are responsible.'[1723]

Ethiopian democratization was proceeding slowly. The first post-war direct election in 1957 produced voter registration of a quarter of the population. Five million people registered out of the estimated population of twenty million entitled to vote. On polling day, just over three million turned out. Among the candidates for the 210-seat elected Chamber of Deputies, the lower house of parliament, were six women and several of Richard's LSE- or Oxford-educated friends. Members of the upper house, the Senate, were appointed by the Emperor. It was a start, but there was still a very long way to go.

On the other hand, it is hard to find any British homeland or colonial media covering the election that did not apply far more stringent standards to Ethiopia than ever it did to the centuries-long, laborious process of democratization in Britain. This lack of self-reflection would be laughable had it not shown so starkly the prevailing cultural racism of Britain in the 1950s.

Writing, many years later, one of the most astute appraisals of her mother-in-law's career, Rita crisply set the context for this period of her life: 'Sylvia, as an anti-colonialist, and anti-racist, was keenly interested in the African struggle for independence then being waged in many parts of the Continent.'[1724]

In February 1956 the National Portrait Gallery received a letter from Sylvia asking if they would like to have her portraits of Keir Hardie. The trustees accepted. Sylvia and Richard packaged them up and her son took these unique pictures on the train to Charing Cross to deliver them to the gallery on Trafalgar Square. Here for five decades his mother had delivered political speeches in support of every just cause from the women's vote to pacifism, to fighting fascism and supporting the liberation of South Africa from apartheid. In the early years, Sylvia and Keir Hardie stood shoulder to shoulder on Nelson's plinth addressing mass rallies. It was here in 1915 that she had learned of his death.

On 5 May 1956, her seventy-fourth birthday, Sylvia closed the *New Times and Ethiopia News* after two decades of publication and began the arduous work of sorting and packing half a century of archive – newspapers, books, pamphlets and correspondence. She was tidying up. Anyone under the impression that Sylvia was preparing to slow down into a quiet, graceful dotage for the final chapter of her life would soon discover otherwise.

37

Look for Me in a Whirlwind

Sylvia's fifty-ninth birthday on 5 May 1941 had been a day of jubilant celebration, for on the same day Haile Selassie re-entered Addis Ababa, exactly five years after its occupation by Mussolini's Italian forces. Ever since 5 May has been celebrated in Ethiopia as Arbegnoch Qen – Patriots' Day. Twelve days after this triumphant re-entry, Sylvia received a telegram from Selassie: 'You will share my joy at re-entering my capital. Your unceasing efforts and support in the just cause of Ethiopia will never be forgotten by myself or my people.'[1725] The Ethiopian press announced that a major thoroughfare in the centre of Addis Ababa was to be named in her honour; connecting Ethiopia's first university to the heart of the city, Sylvia Pankhurst Street remains to this day a bustling thoroughfare.

In her British homeland, there were no state honours or streets named for Sylvia. Mrs Pankhurst's statue, unveiled by Stanley Baldwin in 1930, stood beside Westminster Palace in Victoria Tower Gardens and in 1936 the government had appointed Christabel a Dame Commander of the Order of the British Empire. In the middle of her eighth decade Sylvia remained in the swim of an uninterrupted political life spanning two centuries and two world wars. Her struggles were in the present. Keeping a firm grip on her pen and in now superbly accomplished oratorical voice, the Sword of the Press fought on.

On May Day 1956, Fred Pethick-Lawrence received one of Sylvia's last letters from London:

Dear Fred,
    I am going away to Ethiopia for a long time and shall have to say goodbye to you and everyone. Probably I shall never return ... In many ways I am sad to go – to part with dear friends – and packing and disposing of house and goods is a terrible toil.[1726]

West Dene sold easily. While Sylvia believed she had sold the property to a private buyer, within a few months it was bulldozed to make way for profitable semi-detached new-builds kitted out with the all the mod cons. Locals curious about the neighbourhood celebrity turned up for Sylvia's auction of household contents. The tea chests stacked in every room were stuffed predominantly with books and papers – an archive of half a century's activism. These went by cargo ship, addressed to Sylvia Pankhurst, c/o H.I.M. the Emperor's Private Secretary, Addis Ababa, Ethiopia.

Shortly before her departure, a reporter from the *Woodford Times* came to Sylvia's home do an interview about her emigration to Ethiopia, and found the house full of tea chests stuffed with documents, papers and books, and the furniture labelled ready for auction.[1727] In the photograph taken to accompany the piece, Sylvia sits with smiling eyes, poised for departure.

Ivy Tims, Sylvia's friend and personal assistant, drove her, Richard and their half-Persian cat Pitti to experience the new Central Terminal Area at Heathrow, designed by the British architect Frederick Gibberd and opened the year before by Her Majesty the Queen.

Gloved and hatted in a style out of fashion even before the war, the now stout Sylvia emigrating to Ethiopia was every inch the battle-seasoned feminist matriarch. Haile Selassie, ten years younger than her, treated her generally as a sometimes adviser, problem fixer and trusted friend. They were comrades in the same cause. They debated and, when they disagreed, worked each other round with diplomacy or manipulation.

Sylvia did not entertain the notion that Selassie was the Second Coming of Christ. For Sylvia's detractors, now as then, it was much easier to patronize and write her off as enthralled by a father-figure king presiding over the mystical ancient white fantasy land of Prester John rather than to grapple with the contemporary realities of Pan-Africanism, the philosophy of black consciousness and the fight for decolonization.

Pitti the cat, reluctantly secured in her travelling basket, accompanied Sylvia and Richard on their BOAC flight from London to Athens, from where they transferred to an Ethiopian Airlines plane via Cairo, Khartoum and Asmara to their final destination. As they overflew Egypt, the Suez War began, heralding the death knell of British imperialism. Sylvia blew into Africa on the winds of change.

The party landed in Addis on 4 July. Richard recalled the brilliant Ethiopian sunshine, 'much more luminous than a British summer's day', and the 'intoxicating smell of the eucalyptus trees'.[1728] A welcoming committee of Ethiopian dignitaries and friends drove them to their temporary accommodation in the annexe of the modest government-run Genet Hotel, functional quarters formerly part of an Italian workers' housing scheme. Pitti survived the plane journeys – an unusual experience at that time for humans, never mind cats. Rita Pankhurst later remarked that Pitti was most likely the first British cat to emigrate to Ethiopia.[1729] The intrepid feline settled in easily given the warmer Addis climate, though she could never again be persuaded to get back into her travelling basket.

Next day, Sylvia and Richard drove to the office of Teffera-Work Kidane-Wold, promoted in 1955 to the Emperor's principal private secretary, to announce their arrival formally, and to pick up their mail and hear the news. All discussion focused on what Richard described as 'Mr Eden's Egyptian Fiasco'.[1730] Two days later they were able to access a radio reporting on the Suez crisis. Reading the political weather accurately was one of Sylvia's great aptitudes. Her friends loved her for it: it exasperated her enemies. When she arrived, Ethiopia was one of only three independent African states, alongside Egypt and Liberia; the following year, they would be joined by Kwame Nkrumah's Ghana, liberating the British slaving colony of the Gold Coast. Hindsight makes clear that the winds of change were blowing harder, but it was not so easy to judge at the time.

Elsewhere, the post-war European colonial situation was appalling. South West Africa had been under South African control since 1915, increasingly oppressed by white Afrikaner nationalism. In the

British colony of Rhodesia – named in the nineteenth century after an ambitious diamond-mining prospector – a young farmer and fighter pilot turned politician called Ian Smith, son of a Scottish cattle breeder and butcher, appeared to be gaining ground for his white settler movement. The Central African Federation further consolidated Anglophone white minority rule over vast territories. The French showed no sign of being dislodged from Algeria, while the Belgians continued to control the Congo and the Portuguese Angola and Mozambique.

Richard took up a post at the University College of Addis Ababa, then the country's only institution of higher education, teaching economics, general economic history and ancient Egyptian history. His general course on African history proved too controversial for the more conservative elder professors, because it was anti-colonialist. Richard, however, kept his job: because of his backing by Haile Selassie and his government.

Boldly, Rita Eldon set out alone to join Richard and Sylvia in November: 'I had little awareness of Ethiopia other than having caught a fleeting glimpse of the Emperor as he passed through a City of London street.'[1731] The night before she flew into the unknown, Rita dreamed she was in a valley with mountains rising steeply on either side. 'I climbed up one of these and got to the top, only to discover that beyond the top there was a sheer drop, and nothing beyond that, like a mountain on a stage set. However, this did not deter me.'[1732] Her dream served her well: this is a concise imagining of the topography of the Ethiopian Highland plateaus.

Rita's friends also tried to deter her from what they considered her madcap and alarmingly bohemian scheme of following the impecunious Richard and his extraordinary mother to Addis Ababa, of all places. The heartsore Basil, who had been complacently convinced of his ultimately stronger suit, tried to dissuade her right up to her departure. He wrote a poignant, prejudiced little poem of discouragement for Rita about 'the land of Prester John', warning that it offered only hotel rooms that 'smell', meagre food, venomous snakes and scorpions, and 'fierce Somali bandits'. Moreover, she should prepare herself for sexual predators coveting her 'curvilinear' attractions and gird her loins for vile colonial expat snobbery.[1733] Passionately in love and with a sense of adventure incomprehensible to poor Basil, Rita, undeterred, put on her smart, fashionable hat and gloves and boarded the BOAC flight alone. The Suez Crisis having interrupted the usual route across Egypt, she travelled instead via Tripoli.

By the time Rita arrived in the temperate, dry Ethiopian autumn season, Sylvia and Richard had moved to an Italian-built villa fringed by a eucalyptus grove. The property, situated next door to the Tsehai Hospital that Sylvia had helped build, was made available to them by the government, and was not, as sometimes asserted, a gift from the Emperor. Sylvia described their new home to Fred Pethick-Lawrence:

> Dear Fred,
>   We at last have a charming house surrounded by eucalyptus trees. We reach it up an avenue of eucalyptus … we have some geraniums some of which grow to 8 feet high and mean to have some more as well as other flowers. There is a room in front … which has windows the entire length. This is where I work. There is a little veranda where we have lunch and a round summer house with a thatched roof with a window on two sides. I believe that will be a good place for writing on chilly days (of which there are many at present) … The earth is very light here. Much of it is red. It is volcanic.[1734]

The eucalyptus grove stood in the residential compound for Trans World Airlines pilots that bordered their property, situated near what was then Addis airport. The house was accessed by the luxury of a narrow asphalt lane, shared with the nearby Netherlands Embassy. Sylvia rattled along this eucalyptus-lined lane in her Fiat Millecento, loaned to her by the government along with her driver Yami, who also helped with maintenance around the house.

Sylvia loved the eucalyptus trees. Emperor Menelik II had imported the silver-leaved Australian eucalyptus when he built the new city for his Empress Taitu. The story goes that Taitu preferred the fertile plateau with its hot springs and flowering trees to the location of the military camp atop the Entoto Hills. Over the ages, the verdant, well-positioned site had been the location of several capitals. In the 1880s, Menelik started building a new one. Taitu, it is said, named it Addis Ababa – New Flower – for the sun-yellow mimosa blossom that grew there in abundance.

The first eucalyptus trees in Ethiopia were planted around St George's Cathedral. People quickly realized that the fast-growing, hardy trees were practical as well as gracious. Their lithe, strong trunks provided a ready supply of firewood, could be used for scaffolding and offered a source of income. Within a few years the sea-trees were everywhere, defining the character of the city. 'Long eucalyptus branches, wrapped into heavy bundles, were strapped to women's backs and bent them double in the dawn, men fashioned walking canes and used them to drive oxen or to sling across their shoulders as they swaggered down the roads. Eucalyptus smoke flavoured the food, the beer, the very air; a copse of mature eucalyptus meant a child's books, a coat for school, a dowry or funeral dues; it was insurance, and it was wealth.'[1735]

Knowing it would be of great interest to him, Sylvia in her letter to Fred goes on to paint an elegant picture in words of the countryside, before signing off with a typically Sylvian conclusion:

What awful news about Suez!… The stopping of the Suez Canal is ruinous to this country. Coffee is their greatest export, after that hides, skins, oilseeds, honey, beeswax and various agricultural products. Coffee is far and away the greatest source of revenue. It goes in largest quantity to the USA and after that Britain and Europe … the East does not take it. The Emperor's visit to India is opportune and some trade will result but not to compare, I fear, with coffee. Transport problems in this mountainous land make cereals a costly export and cereals can be obtained more cheaply from the great farms, highly mechanized elsewhere …[1736]

As would be expected, Sylvia familiarized herself thoroughly with the economic and political landscape before inspecting the prospects of the geraniums in her new Anglo-African garden.

Sylvia rejoiced that Rita was willing to take over the running of the house, for when she arrived, their new home 'resembled a storehouse'.[1737] Tea chests were stacked from floor to ceiling, thirteen containing a full set of *New Times and Ethiopia News* on its way to the National Library archives, and the remainder mostly stuffed with Sylvia's and Richard's books and papers, artworks and precious mementos or objects, such as her Benin statuette from Amy Ashwood Garvey. Items practically useful in the way of setting up home – linen, tableware, cosy ornaments – were in notably short supply came with Rita.

They needed basic furniture – tables, chairs, sofas and storage cupboards. The tiled floors they covered with Ethiopian carpets and fur rugs, obtained from the carpet seller outside the old Post Office. Richard loved bargaining, and struck up an excellent rapport haggling with the carpet seller. They enjoyed battling away for several days or even weeks over each rug. A furry acquisition arrived in the form of a large dog named Poodlepie, who became famed in the neighbourhood for the unrestrained attention he paid to the neighbourhood bitches. Later, a Great Dane called Maxie and a minuscule dachshund called Minnie expanded the Pankhurst pack.

Their multilingual chef Askale was as delighted by Rita's arrival as Richard. An accomplished cook, Askale could prepare the cuisines of most of the languages she spoke – Amharic, French, Arabic, Greek, Italian and Aderé, spoken by the Harari. Despite this proficiency, she had struggled to plan menus that worked for Sylvia whose digestion had suffered permanent damage from the hunger strikes.

Delighted by Rita's appreciation of food, Askale learned to cook Romanian and Jewish dishes, and was ever anxious to show off her culinary skills, and remained with the family for twenty years. There was also a great deal of eating out at official functions, at which were served an abundance of overly rich foods that did nothing to help Sylvia's digestion or waistline. Initially reluctant to accept the constant flow of invitations and the alarming codes of formal dress they required, Sylvia came to understand that these events were an essential opportunity to network and nobble people for the things she wanted to get done.

Rita got a job at the new National Library, still at the very early stages of its development. Her work building the library over the forthcoming years made a major and decisive contribution to the development of the institution and its collections. Rita was also asked to prepare lists of books for parliament and the palace, and Richard threw himself wholeheartedly into helping her prepare these. Rita made a huge impact on educational life, devoted to expanding access to the library for children and students.

Their post came simply to Addis Ababa Post Office Box number 1896, chosen for the date of the Battle of Adwa. The same month Rita arrived, Sylvia and Richard launched the *Ethiopian Review*, successor to the *New Times*, and all copy and correspondence for the new paper was also sent to PO Box 1896.

Rita and Richard married on 17 September 1957. To the great disappointment of their Ethiopian friends, they completed the marriage and reception celebrations in just one day, avoiding ostentation. A week before their marriage, Sylvia wrote a reassuring letter to Rita's parents, who could not come for the wedding. 'I hope they will be happy and care for each other. My son has been since his birth more than anything in the world to me and I have therefore naturally observed matters carefully.'[1738] She noted that the young couple were good companions, helping each other with their work, the specifics of which she recounted for Rita's parents, knowing how assiduously they had invested in her education. 'They have spent many hours working together very pleasantly. This sort of collaboration gives a mutual interest in the daily round and they agree well together in such occupations ... I have therefore hope that their union will be founded upon a firm and enduring basis of mutual interests and that they will feel that they belong to each other.'[1739] With compassion and tact, Sylvia expressed her understanding of how sad they must feel to have their daughter choosing to live so far away, and praised Rita for having 'work of her own which she considers useful and in which she has considerable scope and is appreciated for her ability and diligence'.[1740]

On the day of the wedding, Afewerk Tekle invited them for a champagne lunch in his exquisitely decorated apartment, raising a toast to absent parents, 'whereupon', wrote Rita, 'both Sylvia and I burst into tears'.[1741] Haile Selassie sent a large silver cigarette box lined with red velvet and adorned with his monogram. The Crown Prince sent a sumptuous red carpet, despite Sylvia's gaffe of forgetting to invite his wife to the wedding reception. All three Pankhursts returned to their desks the next day. Three weeks later Rita lost her wedding ring, probably, she thought, while planting raspberry canes and climbing roses in the garden.

The honeymoon was in the walled city of Harar, famed international commercial centre of the sixteenth century, the fourth holy city of Islam and one-time home to the poet and merchant Arthur Rimbaud. Sylvia accompanied them, to research a special issue of the new *Ethiopia Observer* dedicated to the city. Recaptured from the Italians for the Allies by the 1st Battalion of the Nigerian Regiment in March

1941, old Harar retained Italian features, including the Grand Hotel, where the Pankhursts stayed in an interconnecting suite. Richard and Rita's friends were highly amused that his mother went with them on honeymoon, but the newlyweds saw little of Sylvia as they took to intensive sightseeing and she busied herself researching her special issue on Harar.

This became volume 2, number 2 of the *Ethiopia Observer*, illustrated with a beautiful painting of the city by Afewerk Tekle. Later, in an exchange of their works, Sylvia acquired Tekle's painting of Rimbaud's house in Harar. The Pankhursts noted that the farmers in the area – once famed for its coffee, bookbinding, poets and mosques – had turned to more profitable *khat* (*Catha edulis*), also known as the Flower of Paradise, whose leaves are chewed for their stimulating effects, alleviating fatigue, promoting excitation, increasing confidence and suppressing sleep and hunger. Richard and Rita met the Sandhurst-trained Sikh officers and their wives preparing for the opening of the new military academy.[1742]

Once they had returned to Addis, it was time to settle in and learn, as Rita put it, 'life à trois'. She wrote regularly to her parents, 'in the business of reassuring them'.[1743] Returning to these letters fifty years later, Rita looked for what her younger self had really felt about her new life and mother-in-law. Shortly after her arrival in Ethiopia, Sylvia took her on a visit to the Shashemene Leprosarium, the subject of an newspaper article. They shared a bedroom.

> In the morning, as we dressed, I was given the history of Ethiopia
> up to Emperor Menelik. I found Sylvia charming. I am quite falling
> in love with her. We have an occasional evening alone together,
> and get along splendidly, even on the subject of Richard. She is
> remarkably objective about him. Somehow it seems quite normal
> that we three should form a unit.[1744]

In one letter, Rita challenges the assertion made that Sylvia was reputed to be overly 'talkative'. Yes, Rita said, it was true that when they had certain visitors Sylvia talked a lot, but this public persona did not translate into her private, intimate sphere. 'I am never aware of it when we are alone, the three of us. In all honesty I can say we hit it off very well. At first Richard acted as a kind of mediator, but now we are apt to gang up against him, rather than quarrel about him.'[1745]

Elsewhere, Rita wrote frankly about her insecurity in relation to her mother-in-law, recalling that Sylvia 'was not demonstrative in personal relations but I think she was pleased that Richard had found a partner. I can't help feeling, however, that she might have preferred someone more familiar with public political affairs. If this was so, she never gave any sign of it.'[1746]

When Rita's parents Charlotte and Alexander Eldon visited, it was a great success and overturned all their anxious assumptions about 'living in Africa'. Richard, Rita and Sylvia took them on memorable trips to Yeka Mikaél rock church and on a picnic on Mount Ziquala, marked on the 1460 map of Venetian cartographer Fra Mauro and a place of pilgrimage since time immemorial. An extinct volcano, the mountain is a landmark visible from great distances, and on a clear day can be seen from Addis Ababa.

Rita's mother admired her daughter's developing garden, amazed by its variety of vegetation, and equally enjoyed Askale's excellent cooking. Rita's father immediately made friends with their friends, 'a characteristic of his which gave me [Rita] much pleasure'.[1747] Back in London, the Eldon home in Wadham Gardens, Primrose Hill, became open house to many Ethiopian friends and dignitaries passing through, studying or working in London. All were warmly welcomed, were offered accommodation and enjoyed Charlotte Eldon's generous traditional Jewish-Romanian cooking.

Now in her mid-seventies, Sylvia maintained her customary dynamic routine, showing that she had fully adapted to the altitude. She was sometimes in poor health, and admitted to stomach pains, but these rarely slowed her down. 'I found that her energy was incredible,' wrote Rita. 'She never complained about the altitude.'[1748] Richard, conversely, continued to experience some respiratory difficulties. Sylvia was usually in bed by midnight, had breakfast at 8 a.m. and then, if she had no appointments, was at her desk working solidly until lunchtime. The woman who had walked up and down her cell uninterrupted for twenty-eight hours on thirst and hunger strike, and had worn through more shoe leather marching for just causes than any other surviving British twentieth-century activist, could still rarely be induced to exercise for its own sake. Richard noted that she suffered from swollen ankles, 'but her spirit remained indomitable. She was seldom discouraged and never complained.'[1749] By her own admission, as she'd written in *The Suffragette*

Movement, she had 'a strong reluctance for active sports, inherited from both parents',[1750] finding any excuse to bunk off and read instead. Rita tried to coax her out for a regular stroll at lunchtime, or at weekends, in the afternoon, 'but work is really her life'.[1751]

Like mother, like son. Rita discovered in her husband a similar disposition. Richard put on weight, and had no interest in dieting until one day he read in the newspaper that Colonel Nasser was a trim 11 stone 11, and decided to achieve the same weight as the handsome Nasser and put himself on a strict diet. 'He has, I was surprised to find, a remarkable fund of will-power, perhaps influenced by his mother's ability, while in prison, to endure hunger strikes. In later years, when we were scouring the hills in search of man-made caves, he would go without food or drink, other than a grapefruit, all day long, whereas he proved resistant to going for a walk in the neighbourhood without an approved motive.'[1752]

Rita found that her mother-in-law enjoyed walking around the garden, to discuss where and how to plant, for example, some newly arrived roses. She continued to discover Sylvia less thorny than anticipated: 'she is far more human, generous and sweet than you or I expected', she told her parents. 'We really do pull it off remarkably well. She is a most understanding, sincere, and kind-hearted person.'[1753] The Eldons educated themselves in Sylvia's career. They sent Rita a newspaper cutting about suffragettes that she and Sylvia discussed together. Soon afterwards they were all taken aback and hugely impressed to discover, belatedly, Sylvia's work in translating Eminescu, and to find that her translations had been so publicly praised by George Bernard Shaw. 'In truth I had left Romania too young to read Eminescu and had very little knowledge of Sylvia's activities before she left England,' Rita wrote.[1754]

Afewerk Tekle was their first house guest. He moved in with them, bringing his maid and a selection of favourite opera recordings, while his traditional Gondar-style house was under construction. In the evenings, as they listened to opera on their gramophone, Afewerk worked on the drawings and plans for his house – an artistic and architectural masterwork – while Sylvia beavered away at her desk, with the door open so that she could hear the music. Afewerk proved to be a 'charming, helpful and generous guest' and, as soon as his grand design house had been completed, invited them for dinner and a tour.[1755]

Sylvia and Afewerk had 'a special relationship', founded on his early years living in London when she had taken special care to encourage his artistic career.[1756] She greatly admired his talent, understanding his aesthetic mission, and was equally a critical friend. Occasionally, he got the sulks when Sylvia tried to check some of his excesses, such as charging inflated prices for government-commissioned work. But he would always reappear breezily full of love and enthusiasm after the appropriate period of pique had passed.

Percy Arnold arrived as their second house guest to assist the Ethiopian Royal Chronicles Department in the completion of the Emperor's autobiography. The first part, covering his life up to his arrival in Britain in 1936, Haile Selassie had already written, making using of his time in exile to compile notes and write the manuscript, in Amharic. This section required editing and, for international distribution, translating into English. The second part, covering the subsequent period from Selassie's exile to his triumphant return, required a very ghostly ghostwriter – the Emperor no longer had the time.

In July 1957 Haile Selassie invited Sylvia for a meeting and asked for her help. The book was falling behind schedule. Her productivity and speed were legendary. Would she please take on the task? Deftly, Sylvia ducked the bullet, urging that the project required nothing less than a full-time professional to work on it. Shortly afterwards, Richard received a request to meet with Ato Kebbede Mikaél, head of the Chronicles Department, who asked him to undertake responsibility for the entire autobiography. 'This I was unwilling to do, as I felt incapable of entering into the Emperor's mind and writing about events in the first person, as would have been needed in an autobiography. I did not believe, moreover, that such a work could effectively be supervised by a committee.'[1757]

Richard handled the matter with tact equal to his mother's. Diplomatically, he recused himself on the grounds that he was currently involved in writing an economic history of Ethiopia, which required all the time he could put into it outside his teaching responsibilities and sub-editing the *Ethiopia Observer*, a role many others would have considered a full-time job on its own. Kebbede gracefully accepted Richard's refusal, but with a condition: it was his sole responsibility to find an alternative ghost. As if briefed for espionage, Richard was dispatched to England with strictly confidential instructions to find another suitable author. On no account must the matter reach the press.

Grateful for the bonus of a few days consulting references in the British Museum's Reading Room, Richard accordingly left for England and – with some difficulty – came up with two candidates, one of whom was the retired journalist Percy Arnold, secretary of the Commonwealth Writers' Association in London, who'd written a popular modern history of Cyprus. Thus Percy Arnold arrived in Addis Ababa on his secret mission, apparently a friend of the family visiting Ethiopia for some sightseeing. The Pankhursts drove Percy in the Fiat Millecento to a famous Rift Valley ravine some thirty miles outside Addis, hiked along the edge of a sheer rift dropping down into a deep gorge and picnicked with a splendid view, heckled by baboons trying to steal their sandwiches.

Despite all the inducements, Percy proved an unsuccessful appointment. He expected the committee to do the research work for him and present him with a working draft, whereas they expected him to do his own homework and write up the final text. Richard's other proposed candidate might have proved more adept for the commission. John Rosselli, a journalist on the *Manchester Guardian*, was the son of Silvio's dear friend and comrade Carlo Rosselli, founder of the anti-fascist Justice and Liberty movement, who had been tragically assassinated alongside his brother by fascists in France. Haile Selassie's two-volume autobiography, *My Life and Ethiopia's Progress*, covering the period 1892 to 1942, would not be published until the 1970s, worked on by many assistant writers, and translated into English by Professors Edward Ullendorff and Harold Marcus.

Percy Arnold might have taken some tips from Christine Sandford, who together with her husband Daniel Sandford ran Mulu Farm, two and a half hours' drive north of Addis. Christine was the author of *Ethiopia and Haile Selassie* (1946) and a biography of the Emperor *The Lion of Judah Hath Prevailed* (1955). These she produced at the same time as bringing up children, running the farm clinic and managing education projects, including a school in Addis, while baking her own bread and making cheese, butter, jam and cakes. Mulu Farm produced the only strawberries available in the Addis Ababa market. Mrs Sandford would preside over traditional tea and sandwiches on the lawn, watered by the Blue Nile, in her wide-brimmed straw hat decorated with a riot of dried flowers.

Richard described the ruddily robust Sandfords as 'the northernmost of the Kenya settlers'.[1758] Settlers they were, but in the parlance of the day the Sandfords had 'gone native' and thrown in their energies with the liberation movement. Daniel Sandford worked alongside Orde Wingate and shared his views. Sylvia took Richard and Rita to meet the Sandfords in February 1957, the first of many visits. Sylvia approved of the Sandfords' 'socially conscious' children, their community development and their social work.

Daniel Sandford, an ex-gunner (DSO and bar), had played a significant role in the British effort to mount a rebellion against the Italians, working with Orde Wingate. He had come to Ethiopia in the early 1920s as a farmer. He wrote for *The Times* and *Daily Telegraph* as their 'Abyssinia' correspondent, and became a friend and confidant of Haile Selassie. In September 1939 Sandford had been brought out to Cairo by General Wavell, who had to work on a covert plan known as Mission 101 to assist the Ethiopian rebellion in the western province of Gojjam, which the Italians had never been able to suppress. Wavell made Sandford a colonel, put him in charge of the Ethiopian section of Middle East Intelligence and sent him to Khartoum to co-ordinate the revolt. In Khartoum Sandford put together a hand-picked crew of old Ethiopia hands, many connected to Wingate's Gideon Force campaign.

One vital element of Mission 101 was to get the Emperor out of exile in England to Khartoum in the last week of June 1940. Sandford picked George Steer, who described him as 'Myopic, optimistic, hairy and hale', to help in the clandestine mission to spirit Haile Selassie out of England to the Sudan by Daimler to Plymouth, by flying boat to the Egyptian–Sudanese border and finally by train from the Egyptian border to Khartoum, on which the Emperor travelled on a ticket under the alias of 'Mr Smith'.[1759]

Another history book caused Sylvia some trouble in 1957. Roger Fulford's *Votes for Women: The Story of a Struggle*, published by Faber & Faber, cheerfully assured readers that forcible feeding 'was not dangerous', while heaping all manner of distortion and stereotype on the suffragettes, most particularly those named Pankhurst. Sylvia wrote to Christabel, and she replied immediately, heartily agreeing and sharing Sylvia's annoyance, though with a different emphasis on its causes. Christabel was incensed that Fulford's book gave her very little credit for her leadership role in the WSPU campaign, while Sylvia was more irritated by his historical inaccuracies and what she felt were slurs on their parents.

> I am horrified ... by the manner in which [Fulford] expresses his 'deep obligation' to me while distorting everything I have ever written. This is of course odious ... I am most wounded and horrified by the belittling of dear father ... I consider it your duty to act. I have done my best to defend the WSPU on previous occasions which means defending mother and you. It is your turn to come forward in the interests of historic truth ... This letter may appear peremptory to you but it is not intended in that way ...
>   For my part all that sort of atmosphere – I mean the old rivalries of the WSPU and the Women's Freedom League is utterly distasteful. I never cared to have a position in the WSPU or anything like that. In the East End I felt I was helping people just as I have done ... in Ethiopia. I would rather shut ears and eyes and have nothing to do with Fulford and all the rest.[1760]

Now reunited by a common enemy, the correspondence provided the opportunity for a refreshing clearing of the air all these years later. Christabel's lengthy, robust rebuttal of Fulford, propelled by the hot winds of her indignation, showed that she'd lost none of her marvellously righteous indignation on behalf of herself and her mother, and of WSPU policy. In her own way, Christabel now even tried to express support for Sylvia. Sending festive greetings to Jessie Kenney and Fred Pethick-Lawrence, she celebrated the deStalinization of the Soviet Union and 'the gallant and incredibly heroic fight for freedom by the women of Hungary': '... I like to think that they have in mind the record of the British Suffragettes.' She asked Fred if he had seen the entry on Emmeline Pankhurst in the *Encylopaedia Britannica*. Noting its many worrying omissions, she observed that on the one hand the entry made no mention of her mother's statue in Victoria Tower Gardens and on the other introduced extraneous errors, such as reference to 'Sylvia's *communism* etc'. Taking her younger sister's part, Christabel wrote, 'Sylvia does not, I suppose, call herself a communist now.'[1761]

In a letter to Christabel, Sylvia had noted:

[Richard] asks me to send you his love: he is family conscious.
Having been an only child he likes the idea of having relations
and was amused by Zuleika Dobson [heroine of Max Beerbohm's
satirical novel of the same name, supposedly modelled on
Christabel] and is interested in the lady concerned. He is a Professor
and is considered a great man by the students. I suppose you know
Richard's father is dead.[1762]

Touchingly, Sylvia seems at pains to impress her sister with a show of social conventionality, and reflects, 'I have tried in my life to follow and learn what I imbibed from Father and not to desert the cause to which he dedicated his life and energy – human welfare and progress in its many aspects. Often I have been mistaken ... I was probably mistaken in giving up my art but what I conceived to be duty impelled me to courses which made the achievement of good and successful work in art impossible.'[1763] Sylvia's lost life as an artist was much on her mind during these years. She brought with her from London a brand-new set of brushes and paints, intending to take them up again. But the brushes and paints remained unused.[1764]

Richard felt that the renewed contact between his mother and aunt 'did not lead to any real meeting of minds'.[1765] As far as politics went, this was an accurate assessment. The sisters sensibly skirted around contentious issues, but shared their concern with 'hurrying to catch up time', acknowledging their shared childhood and its enduring values. Six months later, on 12 February 1958, aged seventy-seven, Christabel died alone from a heart attack, sitting bolt upright in a chair, watching TV and sewing by her picture window overlooking the Pacific in her Santa Monica home. Her friend Grace pleaded with a mutual contact, 'I have not Sylvia or Adela's address, so, dear Enid, please cable both of them if you have not already done so.'[1766]

Sylvia did not make any public statement about Christabel's death (nor did Adela), but Sylvia spoke and wrote about it a great deal in her correspondence at the time. 'I much regret to learn,' she wrote to Rita's parents, 'that she was alone with no friend present when the end came – one can never know what that meant to her.'[1767] Christabel's death brought back memories of the early days of the WSPU, and more so, as she wrote to Fred Pethick-Lawrence, 'of our childhood together, when we did everything together and went everywhere together'. To Pearl Murcheson, she gave fulsome credit to Christabel's 'leading part' in the advances women had made in the twentieth century, and to her role in ensuring they 'had wide publicity throughout the world'. In other correspondence, Sylvia wrote about Betty – Christabel's adopted daughter. Aurea Elizabeth Tudor had joined the Pankhurst family initially as one of Emmeline's four fostered 'war babies'. Christabel later adopted Betty and after the war focused on organizing her single-parent family and providing Betty with a good education. Tragically, Betty died from alcoholism in 1952 following the failure of her marriage. 'My sister never mentioned the girl in later years,' wrote Sylvia, 'but she had been very fond of her when she was a little child.'[1768]

The closure of the Suez Canal presented Sylvia with challenges for the launch of the *Ethiopia Observer*, published each month simultaneously in Addis Ababa and London. Sylvia arranged to have it produced in Manchester by the Percy Brothers printing works, which had printed the *New Times and Ethiopia News* for many years, and their team was familiar with setting Sylvia's mainly handwritten articles. As she knew that the *Observer* would circulate widely outside Ethiopia, production in Manchester would speed up international distribution and keep down postal costs.

Researching, writing and editing this new monthly journal became Sylvia's constant occupation during the last years of her life. She researched and wrote most of the articles in her distinct cursive that right up until her death remained remarkably firm and clear. The Sword of the Press held her pen in a firm grip until the very end.

Post-war expansion of international airmail services made possible both the production of the journal in Manchester and its swift international distribution. Sylvia and Richard airmailed the longhand copy to Manchester where it was set in linotype. When the proofs came back from Manchester, they pored over the layout together. This process regularly produced considerable tension between them, as Rita related to her parents: 'She and Richard sometimes shout at each other, and are so rude that it appals me, but it is all superficial, usually about the layout of the *Observer*, but I never come into it at all, and it is usually sharp and short. Today they are at it again because it is proof day.'[1769] Richard concurred: 'This entire operation, which required much measurement, was often frustrating, and made both of us tense and irritable.'[1770]

The first issue had hit the racks in December 1956, declaring its twofold mission. First, 'to mirror each and every facet of Ethiopia's present renaissance'.[1771] 'It will be the first periodical ever published simultaneously in England and Ethiopia, and will contain definitive articles on economics, politics, history, culture, education and the arts.'[1772] Its second, broader mission was to cover continent-wide current affairs in order to realize fully the role Africa played in the future of the world.

Each issue usually focused on a specific theme or locale. The first presented Ogaden, the second Addis Ababa. Subsequent issues took the subjects of Ethiopian women, public health, industrial progress, Ethiopia's first general election, Pushkin's Ethiopian ancestry, the Battle of Adwa and the Queen of Sheba. Afewerk Tekle provided gorgeous cover illustrations. Sylvia promised that the *Ethiopia Observer* would publish articles on wide-ranging topics 'concerned with Ethiopia past, present and future. It is hoped that each issue will be of immediate and permanent interest.'[1773]

For the paper, Sylvia travelled all over the country on constant journalism safaris, visiting schools, hospitals, economic and agricultural development projects and ancient historical sites and cities. Armed always with pencils and her signature outsized notebook, Sylvia traversed thousands of miles of the country, often by Land Rover over rough tracks, 'not only to get copy, but to keep Ethiopia on its toes'.[1774] Government officials either welcomed or dreaded her visits to their projects, knowing they would be written up in her widely distributed paper. If officials overestimated the extent to which she had the direct ear of the Emperor, Sylvia did nothing to correct the misapprehension. Collecting hard facts and practical details, she acted to solve problems where she could. Informed that odourless mats were required on which to dry coffee beans, she arranged for the inmates of a rehabilitation centre to get to work immediately making bamboo mats in quantity in time for the next harvest.

Sylvia was either fact finding on her frequent journalism safaris, at her desk in Addis or working on other projects in the capital. With unusual tact, she avoided complaining about some of the complexities of life in Addis Ababa. Since her son was half-Italian and the country and its people one of her adopted nations, she had no good reason to object to the continuing presence of Italian hoteliers, restaurateurs and shopkeepers. Nor did she seem to carp about the influx of Nazis fleeing to the city after 1945 to escape war trials. Instead, she focused on raising concern about the dwindling of British influence – perhaps as a stratagem to highlight the benefits of one over the other. She was concerned that British teachers, numerous before the war, were now reduced in numbers. The British Council closed its office in Addis, feeling it was operating in a hostile environment. Certainly the Ethiopian government remained determined to extricate itself from the danger of becoming a British 'protectorate'.

38

Ethiopia Observer

Most of her life Sylvia lived in highly urbanized environments amid smoking chimneys, soot-streaked factories, London fogs and the industrial emissions of the Docklands' coal, gas and manufacturing plants. The years in Woodford greened her life within the restrained pastel palette of suburban London spring. She'd brought colour to all the places she lived and worked: now, in Ethiopia, the colour came to her.

Running a newspaper was a habit of Sylvia's life launched with the *Home News and Universal Mirror* in her childhood. In that, her first publication, she reported on the collection in the British Museum. Now she was able to explore the places from where the great African art she adored had originated. Between 1956 and 1960 the research required for the *Observer* articles provided abundant excuses for exploration and adventure. She met cattle-herding cowboys attending night school, feminist nuns in progressive convents and monks who shared their bean mash and home-brewed beer with her in their tulkul dormitories.

Sylvia's Africa copybooks, running to thousands of pages, filled with sketches, maps, diagrams, poems marked up in scansion, unfold into a cultural and historical map of Ethiopia, vast in scale, minute in detail, multilayered in vision. Sweeping descriptions of landscape run into histories of ancient cities reaching back into biblical times, juxtaposed with intimate, vivid pen portraits of individual people and their present lives.

Sylvia's enchantment with her new environment was prompted in part by the new perspective brought to her artist's eye by the experience

of flight – the marvel of the world seen from the aerial view of an aircraft window. She loved the variation in the breathless heights of mountains and depths of plummeting gorges, the deep tracks of winding rivers, the weightless feeling of being in the clouds, at such great height flying through the mountains that she felt she was walking on the roof of the sky. 'It seems not a real world but a toy world or a beautiful map.'[1775]
On the ground, individuals emerged:

In the dull early dawn some people are wearing brown homespun blankets wrapped around themselves in a cloak … A horseman well clad in shamma [traditional shawl], straw hat and khaki riding breeches his horse wearing a red saddle cloth is accompanied by a couple of humble plodding donkeys carrying heavy firewood. A handsome coal-black crow with a white breast hovers lazily around us or stalks slowly on. A brilliant white shamma with a red border approaches on a mule which shies unexpectedly at the sight of the stationary car and foams slightly at the mouth as the rider draws tight the reins. A pigeon perches on the top of a bundle of tall sticks propped against a tulkul.[1776]

She was fascinated by the Arab horses, descendants of the world's most famous pedigree bloodlines, painting word pictures of their brown and scarlet livery and brightly coloured saddlecloths. Visiting the ancient city of Harar with Afewerk Tekle, she described 'a treasury for the tourist and the antiquarian who are able to find curiously wrought old silver and other enticing handicraft ware' in merchants' shops. 'It is a never ending source of picturesque subjects for the painter and photographer.'[1777] From the old city, she moved her pen to rendering the modern new town outside the wall, laid out with gardens and civic spaces.

The history of seventeenth-century court life and plumbing in Gondar deeply absorbed her. She wrote at length about the famous sunken bath filled from heated underground water pipes, about the swimming pools and gardens built by Emperor Fasiledes (1632–67) and about the fine architecture of the numerous castles she visited.

Over half a century later, it's easy to miss the significance of Sylvia's endeavour. Back in time behind the distortions of the mirror of colonization, her detailed and systematic work aimed to establish in the present the ancient art and authority of Ethiopian civilization. Deliberately, she pitched a different vision and history against racist imperial propaganda about supposed African 'barbarism'.

Sylvia hugely enjoyed the hotel at the spa town of Ambo, famed for its hot mineral springs and producer of Ethiopia's favourite mineral water. The small, elegant hotel perched on high ground, popular for those nearby hot springs, was much frequented by Somalis with whom she struck up political conversation. She liked the modish pleated skirts and low-heeled pumps worn by the Ethiopian waitresses. After her meal she inspected the baths in detail, from tiles to plumbing system, and the sanitation. She remained for a while in 'this pleasant little haven' to write up her notes, protected by mosquito nets.[1778]

Always, colour and texture caught her eye, making her a soft target for seduction by Ethiopia's 'velvet' landscape, 'brilliant green', sunrise-yellow flowering acacias, blue mists, purple valleys, burnt umber to dark-red savannahs. Between Dire Dawa and Lake Alamaya, Sylvia daydreamed out of the car window observing the wild ducks, goats, cattle and camels. But her travels in Ethiopia were far from being all African picturesque.

Juxtaposed with this, there is much industrial sublime and agricultural science and mechanization. She wrote detailed descriptions of the operational headquarters of high-tech geophysicist exploration sites, or of a cement factory employing '200 Ethiopians, 20 Europeans, 2 Greeks, accountant and chemists, Belgian chiefs of sales. The rest Italian technicians.' She documented the level of education and salaries of employees, the workshop output, exports, worker conditions, structures of organization. She repeated exactly the same process for documenting a crushing mill, a cotton factory, a grain-washing factory and coffee plantations.

She applied a similar level of detail to studying every school she visited. In the eastern Highlands, she visited Catholic and Swedish missions and government schools, analysing the pupils, reading the curricula, looking at the books and assessment systems. In Gondar, schoolgirls presented her with a magnificent bouquet of pink gladioli tied with ribbons in the Ethiopian national colours while greeting her with a speech: 'Welcome to Gondar, we know you are a friend of Ethiopia.'[1779]

Sylvia is not yet thought of as a travel writer, yet once pieced together and compiled into a whole this substantial body of work, a lifetime's pursuit, stands among the best of her generation. It is one of her many parallel careers, hidden in plain view. As a young art student, she took her immersive pioneering tours of the north of England to study working conditions for women. Then followed her two tours of the United States of America, writing and drawing all the way. From her travels in Bolshevik Russia came a further stream of journalism and a book, *Soviet Russia as I Saw It*, along with her writing on Romania and other European journeys. Then, later in life, the personal discovery of a continent new to her: Africa.

Reading Sylvia's early travel journalism about Clydeside or California produced in her twenties alongside her writing about Ethiopia and Kenya in her seventies, it is striking how the tempo remains utterly unchanged. Relentless pace, energy, sharpness of vision, curiosity, attention to minute detail; all these and more are consistent across the epochs of her life. There is something grand and outrageous about the velocity of her energy. Even while enduring increasingly poor health, Sylvia ploughed on, fascinated by it all.

Her travel journalism, journals and broadcasts covering a decade in Ethiopia are in some ways reminiscent of her American travels in 1911 and 1912. There were some significant similarities. The USA and Ethiopia were both developing industrial economies and emerging experiments in liberal democracy. Both presented to the itinerant traveller vast, far-flung territories of breathtaking grandeur and variation, which miniaturized the scale of their own place in the landscape. The USA and Ethiopia both struggled to transition from agriculture to industry. In both countries, Sylvia traversed great distances, in both she met cowboys and social entrepreneurs trying to establish co-operatives, and in both she focused acutely on women's lives and work.

The differences between her youthful experiences in America and her mature encounter with Ethiopia appear in Sylvia's internal landscape. Half a century later she is more confident. Gone is the youthful preoccupation with anxieties of the self. The American notebooks struggle with personal relationships when she projected on to the outer landscape a reflection of her inner alienation. Now in later life, the painful feelings of inadequacy and anxiety have receded. She is still questing, but she has come into her own.

She admires and presents both beauty and ugliness as facts to be lived with. She is in love with the object and its truth. Or she is objectively clear in her disagreement with untruth. This conviction discomfits others, but it no longer discomfits her. By contrast with her American private journals and published journalism, these Ethiopian copybooks are shorn of the youthful anxiety and anomie, the constant niggle that some essential truth, or need for decision, eludes her.

Sylvia's travel writing, published journalism and intense, prolific, energetic notebooks of this period convey the sense of a liberation of mind and a centred certainty of soul. Unburdened of the baggage of self, she seemed to enjoy being an older unconventional woman, occupying her mature personhood as a terrain she might map for herself.

The notebooks are not chronological, so we see Sylvia's writing mind continuing to operate in an imaginative space–time continuum. Interspersed with an account of a journey through the vast gorge of the Blue Nile are successive drafts of poems. Nestled between a flight to Jimma in the west and arriving in Sinclair in the Ogaden appears a draft manuscript of 'Dogland', her shaggy-dog children's adventure written for a canine-besotted Richard from their Woodford days. Then, between inspections of hospitals where she notes the exact number of beds, the voltage of the radiology and details of the training and qualification of the nurses and doctors, appears a thundering poetic satire of current events, 'Sam Hoare, No more!'[1780]

So while Sylvia stands in a long tradition of British explorers in Ethiopia, she is distinctively unlike them.

Mostly, Richard and Rita accompanied her on the expeditions. They travelled in Sylvia's little old Fiat or in their Volkswagen Beetle, along the network of narrow Italian-built roads or beating along dirt tracks, riverbeds and grassy escarpments. Driving to the geophysicists' camp at Jimma, 'the road winds up corkscrew fashion in magnificent mountains well wooded with green bushes and trees'.[1781] They frequently drove for hours without encountering any other motorized vehicles, but mules and camels were numerous along the way. Andreas Esheté, a student at Menelik II High School, established in 1898 as Ethiopia's first modern school, and volunteer intern in the National Library, often accompanied them on these missions, his skills as an interpreter creating many opportunities, including invitations from peasant farmers to join delicious meals of traditional spiced stew and sourdough flatbread, the ubiquitous *injera*.

Andreas 'gradually became a part-time member' of the Pankhurst household, helping Rita in the garden with pruning and weeding and joining Richard on expeditions to the sheep market to bargain for the best purchase to bring home in the back of the VW as a gift for the house staff for Ethiopian Christmas.[1782] Andreas Esheté was a natural intellectual and he and Richard struck up a working relationship. In 1958 they published a joint article in *Ethiopia Observer* on the history of indigenous self-help associations, Andreas' first publication. Later Andreas studied philosophy at Williams College and Yale University in the US, held professorial chairs at a number of American universities, published work in moral and political philosophy and produced a lifetime of writing on Ethiopia.

On other occasions, Afewerk Tekle would take the three of them on eventful excursions, usually including memorable picnics in inspiring locations.

Ethiopia was in a phase of post-war modernization, and Sylvia wanted to visit as many schools, hospitals and clinics as possible as well as agricultural and industrial developments. One of her early trips was to the Wenji Sugar Estate, 170 miles south-east of Addis, where a Dutch company had established a sugar plantation of Indonesian cane with the aim of producing enough sugar to supply Ethiopian needs.

In May 1957, around the time of her birthday, they set off again to Jimma, heartland of Ethiopia's coffee-growing region, to visit an agricultural secondary school about which Sylvia wrote an article. They flew by transport plane, along with chickens and produce, looking out of the windows over spectacular scenery. An American director ran the school, staffed by ten families from Oklahoma who trained boys in improved agricultural methods, particularly for coffee growing. In the evening, the boys arranged to interview Sylvia, complete with microphone and PA.

This was the first time Rita heard Sylvia address a public audience. 'She was a born speaker, clear, to the point.'[1783] The boys plied Sylvia with questions about African politics and Ethiopia's place among other independent African countries, and asked her also about London and the role of women. The students presented her with a pale-blue plaster-cast plaque, on which appeared in relief the single word – 'Others'. On this trip Sylvia saw one of her London-educated wards, now returned home, training others and working to improve conditions in the Jimma Hospital. From a wealthy family, the woman had chosen not to live a life of ease in Addis Ababa. This confirmed the legend of the plaque. Sylvia passed on her father's values and the primacy of living life for others.

Sylvia's writing about her trip to the thirteenth-century monastery of Debre Libanos remains one of the most vivid penned about this famous holy site, a particular favourite of Haile Selassie who as a youth followed the excavations with great interest when he was titular governor of the borderland Selale district.

Tragically, the Debre Libanos monastery became better known in the modern world for the massacre that took place there during the war with the Italian fascists. After the attempt on his life in February 1937, the colonial Governor Rodolfo Graziani claimed that the monastery's monks and novices had been involved in the conspiracy and, without further investigation, ordered colonial troops to massacre the inhabitants. They murdered 297 monks and 23 laymen. The remains of these victims lay unburied until the 1940s when a tomb was built to honour and contain them.

By the time of Sylvia's visit in the 1950s, there were only a handful of disciples and students left at the monastery. After the massacre, the survivors dispersed in fear, unable to return until the end of the war. Sylvia recounted her arrival at the imposing entrance. Alongside an elegant sketch of the church, she described the 'rich gold embroidered robes' of the *debteras*, holding brilliant gold-fringed umbrellas. The *debteras*, unordained members of the clergy well versed in Ethiopian Orthodox Church rituals, liturgy and scriptures, traditionally assist with services, performing the holy singing, music and dance. Only men were allowed to approach the monastery, but the *debteras* invited her to their quarters and entertained her in their dormitory, sharing their dinner of milk, *injeras*, boiled beans and home-brewed beer. Bananas and lemons grown in the monastery's orchard brought colour to the meal.

In 1958 Sylvia made a trip to the Qoqa Dam and Reservoir, driven by Major Assefa Lemma, chief of the Electric Power Authority, and his wife, Siniddu Gebru, newly elected to the Ethiopian parliament as one of its first women representatives, to see how the works, scheduled for completion by 1959, were progressing. The workforce included Ethiopian labourers, Ethiopian and Italian technicians and Norwegian supervisors.

On several occasions in the last years of her life, Sylvia was game for camping out overnight. Richard and Rita would curl up in sleeping bags, while Sylvia hunkered down in the car, bolstered by the pillow and eiderdown she always took with her, and wrapped in the Siberian rug brought by Rita's parents from Romania. There were picnics in the midday sunshine, making tea with their rudimentary gas stove, and numerous hours spent sitting at the side of the road while Richard tinkered with a broken-down engine. Her husband, Rita reported, 'specialized in starting defective cars and driving by night'.[1784]

In December 1958 Sylvia went on an extended fact-finding trip to Eritrea. At seventy-six, and given her medical history, her stamina was impressive. She flew to Asmara, then to Massawa, back to Asmara, then on to Assab and back home to Addis. The material she garnered provided content for five issues of *Ethiopia Observer*, and consolidated her belief in the cause of reunification of Eritrea and Ethiopia. Back in Addis, she attended the opening ceremony of the Economic Commission for Africa, and at the reception reported to Haile Selassie on her visit to Eritrea and her confidence in the campaign for reunification. As he left the event the Emperor called out to her, 'C'est grâce à vous.'[1785]

In April 1958 the First Conference of Independent States was held in Accra. Haile Selassie announced fifty four-year scholarships for secondary school students from other parts of Africa to study at Ethiopian institutions of higher learning. As Richard observed, 'these students, though few in number, made a notable impact on young Ethiopians, and helped to break down the country's traditional isolation'.[1786] Things were changing. Sylvia suggested that they charter buses and take the scholarship students on picnics so they could discover more about Ethiopia.

As another strategy for supporting the new generation, Sylvia produced a special student issue of the *Ethiopia Observer*, packed with political, historical and cultural articles written by these youngsters, many of whom later became leaders. The Pankhursts threw open the doors of their home to visiting African leaders and students, who were invited to give informal talks with Sylvia acting as moderator. A family friend, the Eritrean unionist leader Tedla Bayru, became a frequent visitor to these meetings. Cheikh Anta Diop of Senegal spoke at one of these popular 'At Homes', as did Kenneth Kaunda and Simon Kapwepwe from Zambia and the chair of the Kenya African Union, James Gichuru. Other Kenyan speakers included Jaramoji Oginga Odinga, Mwai Kibaki, Peter Mbiyu Koinange and a young Tom Mboya.

Another sign of a shift towards radicalization in Ethiopia was the launch of the Africa Society, founded by Ras Imru's daughters in January 1959. Chaired by Yodit (Judith) Imru – the only woman Director General in the Ethiopian government – and her sister Hirut, an expert in social work, the Society aimed to raise awareness among the Ethiopian public about African issues, to publicize and rally support for African independence struggles and to popularize Pan-Africanist philosophy and ideals. The group had significant impact, developing a more international and broadly cosmopolitan outlook in Ethiopia.

Rita Pankhurst established a hugely popular lecture series at the National Library, programming events at which diverse leaders from colonial or newly liberated territories were invited to speak. Julius Nyerere, Mbiyu Koinange and Oliver Tambo delivered lectures that created national headlines. Other speakers came from South West Africa, Rwanda-Burundi, Liberia, Libya and the emerging West Indies. Audiences of over 500 people regularly attended these.

Secretly, Mau Mau refugees were granted asylum in Ethiopia. Richard knew and socialized with many of them. He recalled a dinner hosted by General Aman Mikael Andom discussing guerrilla tactics in the conduct of the Kenyan resistance. Two decades later, Andom became the first post-imperial acting head of state following the coup d'état that ousted Haile Selassie in September 1974.

In August 1958 Sylvia, Richard and Rita visited Kenya. They were taken on a trip to the Masai Mara before it was established as a wildlife sanctuary. In Nairobi they were mostly entertained by members of the local Indian community, many of them deeply committed to African independence, like the Punjabi Hari Chhabra, from Delhi University, who was completing a thesis on Indian–African relations. On their way back, Richard and Rita accepted Chhabra's invitation to make a quick trip to Uganda. Richard went to buy the train tickets. 'You will be travelling First Class, of course,' said the ticket master. 'Why of course?' 'Because you are European. Europeans travel First Class, Asians Second Class, and Africans, Third Class.'[1787]

Following their visit, Rita wrote about the social changes brought about by the Mau Mau rebellion and Richard penned a polemical article for an Ethiopian magazine about the Mau Mau, the ongoing struggle and Kenyatta's imprisonment.

Sylvia and Mbiyu Koinange had been friends since Fenner Brockway introduced them in London at a meeting of the Movement for Colonial Freedom (later known more handily as Liberation). Brockway instigated its founding in 1954 to challenge the Labour Party's official policy not to support independence leaders. Seventy MPs, including Tony Benn, Harold Wilson and Barbara Castle, supported the campaign. Brockway chaired and Tony Benn acted as treasurer. The movement gained instant support from rank-and-file Labour Party members and trade unions, launching a formidable public campaign and tabling over 1,500 parliamentary questions.

A brilliant public speaker, Mbiyu Koinange was greatly admired among African students in Britain, who looked to him as a leader. While studying in America, he debated with an Italian colonial official about Mussolini's invasion of Ethiopia. When he visited Woodford, Sylvia asked him to speak at several of her meetings, and to chair a fundraiser for the Princess Tsehai Hospital. Mbiyu and Richard's Romanian father-in-law Alexander Eldon forged an enduring friendship. As his sons were at school in Ethiopia, Mbiyu Koinange visited Addis frequently. His lecture on the political situation in Kenya was so popular that people who couldn't get into the hall smashed windows and clambered in that way in order to to hear him.

In October 1958 Tom Mboya visited Sylvia and Richard in Addis. They'd met him two months before on their trip to Nairobi and had invited him to give a lecture on the Kenyan political situation in Rita's National Library programme. The event was standing room only. Richard borrowed a loudspeaker from the US Information Bureau so that Mboya could be projected beyond the hall. From him Sylvia learned about developments in the African trade union and co-operative movements. The purpose of his trip to Addis was to test the Ethiopian government's attitude to trade unions and to suggest that a cohort of

Ethiopians should be sent to the Labour College in Kampala, Uganda, to study trade union leadership. Warmly received by Haile Selassie, Mboya attended official functions and had discussions with Selassie's nieces, who wanted his advice on starting a co-operative settlement in Ethiopia.

Sylvia, Richard and Rita held a tea party for Mboya at their house, cramming over sixty guests into their living room. Mboya spoke, and Sylvia chaired. Rita's letter home to her parents ruminated on 'his outstanding intelligence, his dynamism and his objectivity in assessing a given situation'.[1788] Many agreed on Mboya's leadership potential, but, as a Luo, Richard remarked, he was not popular with the Kikuyu.

At the end of February 1959, Sylvia visited Debre Birhan, north-east of Addis Ababa, to observe an American teacher-training facility about which she would write for the *Ethiopia Observer*. Debre Birhan had been the Ethiopian capital in the fifteenth century, named Mount of Light by Emperor Zera-Yaqob when he saw it illuminated by Haley's comet in 1466. The town is at an altitude of around 11,500 feet and the party were there in the chilly rainy season. Neither altitude nor inclement weather seemed to bother Sylvia, who got on with her interviews and note-taking in the residential school.

From the moment Sylvia arrived to live permanently in Ethiopia, she continued her dedicated work for the Princess Tschai Hospital. A decade earlier she'd curated a fundraising exhibition for the hospital of Ethiopian arts and crafts at Foyle's bookshop on London's Charing Cross Road. She appeared on BBC television to talk about it. Her focus on raising awareness of the history of Ethiopian art and culture was significant. Propagated by imperial superiority and fascist propaganda, the myth of so-called African barbarism prevailed still in many British representations of Africans. Evelyn Waugh sneeringly dismissed the ambitious new programme of civic development in Ethiopia as 'abortive modernism' and missed no opportunity to harp on the theme of the primitive backwardness of 'Abyssinians'. Waugh demonstrated historical ignorance and racist xenophobia typical of the time: 'they had no crafts. It was extraordinary to find a people with an ancient and continuous habit of life who had produced so little.'[1789]

In the 1947 BBC broadcast Sylvia shows presenter Freddie Grisewood examples of Ethiopian arts and crafts – antique and modern – from her

Foyle's exhibition: fine antique glassware, jewellery, leatherwork and exquisite metalwork.

Sylvia made radio appeals, organized garden parties and induced Dame Sybil Thorndike, Sir Donald Wolfit – one of her favourite actors – and Wendy Hiller among other well-known celebrities to give charity recitals or matinees. She'd made her friend the physician and Liberal peer Basil Mackenzie president of the Council of the Princess Tsehai Memorial Hospital. Mackenzie fondly recalled Sylvia and her approach to the project:

> She was dumpy and untidy, rather the shape of a cottage loaf. But she had immense personal charm, and was quite ruthless in a naïve way. She would overspend on equipment by thousands of pounds after the committee had agreed on a go slow. She always said the money would come in, and it always did. But we had our anxious moments. It was a sign that she had done something drastic when she arrived particularly untidy, wisps of hair floating, papers awry, flustered – and then confessed.[1790]

At a fundraising bazaar in 1949 Wendy Hiller beseeched the attendees to help achieve the last £15,000 of the £100,000 target, 'not only for the sake of improving health services in Ethiopia, but to keep Miss Pankhurst from going to prison again'.[1791] In a radio broadcast Sylvia listed Haile Selassie, Her Majesty Queen Elizabeth II, General de Gaulle, trade unions, co-operative societies, women's groups, miners, nurses, doctors, writers, artists and pensioners from various professions among donors to the project. Trinidad and Tobago had sent £1,000.

Now Sylvia found that much needed to be done to develop the hospital further. Before she left England, she'd wisely arranged for Gordon Selfridge's daughter, now Princess Rosalie Wiasemsky, to replace her as the hospital's London representative. Ethiopia still needed to produce its own doctors, and it remained a challenge to recruit suitable personnel from abroad. The hospital's British directors expected the Ethiopian Ministry of Public Health to familiarize itself with and follow their organizational procedures, never questioning whether that might not meet local requirements. This produced obstructive tensions and struggles over who would compromise.

Sylvia continued to do fundraising, driving the purchase of essential equipment and – a direct echo from the old days at the Mothers' Arms – organizing clothes collections for hospitalized babies in need. She began the campaign for a separate maternity ward, a blood bank and an orthopaedic centre for the manufacture of artificial limbs. The latter was proposed by a brilliant British orthopaedic surgeon, Oscar Barry, who in a separate initiative realized that many young polio victims begging in the streets could regain the use of their limbs through surgery to break and reset them. On several occasions, Sylvia stopped her Fiat abruptly on the streets of Addis and persuaded young beggars to go to the hospital and receive successful treatment, at her expense.

The number of homeless people begging on the streets deeply troubled Sylvia, so she pitched in with a group of Ethiopian friends to establish a voluntary organization called the Social Service Society aimed at rehabilitating street people. The dynamic new Mayor of Addis Ababa, Dejazmatch Zewde Gebre Selassie, whom Sylvia had known when he was a student at Oxford immediately after the war, put his muscle into the project, creating a designated, fenced area in which large corrugated-iron sheds were erected to house and feed the destitute and provide craft training, especially in making knotted Ethiopian wool carpets. However, the hastily constructed municipal barracks, with inadequate living facilities, quickly proved an unattractive alternative to life on the streets, and the Mayor's successor used this resistance as an excuse to drop support for the initiative before it had opportunity to develop further.

The Social Service Society achieved more success with other initiatives. Rita got involved, and she and Sylvia worked together very effectively, including setting up a Singer sewing-machine project to train women in dressmaking and tailoring, still chiefly a male preserve. The establishment of the first youth sports ground in the city proved another fruitful venture. On this, Rita and Sylvia worked together with Lieutenant Girma Wolde-Giorgis, who later became the President of Ethiopia, from 2001 to 2013.

Many of the projects followed in the tracks of Sylvia's perennial concerns: public health activism, education, political participation. The health of babies and new mothers remained a priority. As ever, Sylvia took a practical approach. A UNICEF scheme operated in Ethiopia distributing dried milk for malnourished children, but it was failing badly, as mothers mostly took the powder to market to sell. Sylvia investigated and discovered that there were no guidelines, demonstrations on how to use it or instruction or provision of appropriate beakers or boiling facilities. Sylvia and her friend Geoffrey Last, an English headmaster, persuaded UNICEF to fund the necessary equipment and then set up regular demonstrations showing how to prepare and use it. As a result, Sylvia modestly recorded, 'Health was demonstrably improved.'

Sylvia also considered how to address the appalling maternal mortality rates suffered by Ethiopian women, at the time among the highest in the world. She established education programmes, focusing on infant and maternal health. Sylvia also made direct interventions to create clinics and facilities for people with stigmatized diseases. Her first initiative in this sphere was to support the setting up of a leprosy centre in Addis Ababa.

During the East End days of the First World War when Sylvia's Workers' Suffrage Federation turned its energies to community projects and public relief, Emma Boyce had commented that the federation seemed more like 'a charity organisation with suffrage tacked on'.[1792] This tension between social work within existing society and working for more enduring long-term structural change is a key feature of Sylvia's long career. In Ethiopia, the dilemma appeared as a tension between participating in the emerging culture and policies of post-war 'international development' and working for state-level, widescale radical social and political change.

Sylvia thought always about how to integrate the apparatus of community and government: this was one of the tenets that drove her life. She was unable to walk past a person or community in need if the problem could be addressed with a practical intervention in the immediate present. This emotional humanity, one of her great strengths, produced simultaneously a vulnerability to compromise with the status quo in order to get things done. This inner contradiction, so personal to her worldview, was reflected outwardly in the modern post-war world as the contradiction and dilemma between the continuing colonial co-dependence of economic development aid and political independence for post-colonial African nations.

Richard and Rita shared Sylvia's values and embodied the perspective of the next generation. Richard was exposed directly to the anti-colonial struggle in Africa as a student at the LSE and became friends with a number of its future thinkers and leaders. His historical studies inspired him to write for the *New Times* a lengthy serialized article on the abolition of slavery in the USA and the subsequent period of reconstruction. Later he penned a number of theoretical critiques of colonialism, disputing the 'then prevalent colonialist argument that the nationalist movements in contemporary Africa had been created by a tiny proportion of the population, the so-called intelligentsia, who were "unrepresentative" of their countries'. Contesting this, Richard argued that the masses supported the precepts of nationalist independence and rejected 'the pretensions of their colonial rulers'.[1793]

Among Richard's other early journalism were two long historical articles on Kenya and Uganda. He chronicled the power grab by a minority group of white colonizers and argued that the Mau Mau rebellion then taking place 'was a just response to selfish and repressive policies of the settlers'.[1794] Peaceful means had failed. Kenyans were left with no choice but armed resistance. Richard's articles on Uganda focused on the role of missionaries in European colonization. Dr Krishna Dutta Kumria, founder of the Swaraj (Freedom) House on Percy Street in London's Fitzrovia in 1942, was greatly impressed by these pieces. Editor of the London magazine *Africa and the Colonial World*, Kumria published Richard's work in 1954 as a book entitled *Kenya: The History of Two Nations*, with an introduction by Frida Laski. Richard also reproduced this work as a series for the British railway workers' newspaper in London. Years later, in 1961, his mother's friend Jomo Kenyatta visited Addis, shortly after his seven years of imprisonment and internal exile had come to an end. Kenyatta was now leader of the re-established Kenya African National Union party. Rita pressed into his hand this book by his friend's son, whom he'd known as a child in Woodford.

39

Iron Lion Zion

The busy pace of life in the early days in Ethiopia, Rita remarked, 'was nothing to the state of affairs that followed'.[1795]

In addition to their regular employment, all three handled several other jobs. Alongside her role at the National Library, Rita worked with Sylvia on her city community projects. Then came an official request from the Emperor's office asking Rita to curate an ambitious exhibition at the palace, which she accomplished with ingenuity and aplomb despite the short notice.

Between teaching, marking, steering a passage through academic institutional politics and producing the newspaper with Sylvia, Richard pressed on through the last stages of copy-editing the English version of the new Ethiopian government's first Five Year Plan.

Forty-five years older than both of them, Sylvia sustained an equivalent workload. 'If she was not on her travels,' Rita wrote,

> Sylvia would go to her desk when we left for work – Richard at
> the University College of Addis Ababa, where he taught, and I at
> the National Library of Ethiopia. She was usually still at her desk
> when we returned at lunchtime, and again in the afternoon. After
> supper she often went back to her desk. When the historian, Brian
> Harrison, once asked me what we did for our holidays it came to
> my notice that we did not indulge in them.[1796]

The government commissioned Sylvia to produce a compendium of pictures illustrating Ethiopian buildings and architecture, historical and contemporary. Some of this material she repurposed into a special issue of *Ethiopia Observer*, focusing on architecture. She steeped herself in learning about Ethiopian history of art, religion and folk culture with the same intense concentration and passionate interest she had demonstrated at the Royal College of Art in her youth. At the centre of her active engagement in the contemporary stood her mentoring and friendship with Afewerk Tekle and his circle of emerging talent. Characteristically, Sylvia focused on caucusing for the inclusion of the study of art in the Ethiopian school curriculum and education.

In October 1958 Sefton Delmer, chief foreign affairs correspondent of the *Daily Express*, announced, 'SURPRISE! LOOK WHO'S HERE! MISS PANKHURST!' In an article reporting on Sylvia's work in Ethiopia, Delmer covered her attendance at the opening of an exhibition of children's art curated by the Soviet Information Centre.

> Solemn Ethiopians trot around admiring water colours and crayon
> sketches by six to sixteen year olds from Ocholsk to Omsk. And
> who is this genial blue eyed English gentlewoman with the silvery
> hair hobnobbing with the comrades over vodka and zakusi? Why,
> it's that grand old suffragette Sylvia Pankhurst. Here in Addis
> Ababa, with energy undimmed, she is carrying on a campaign to
> liberate Africans from their European oppressors.[1797]

Sylvia, Richard and Rita were frequently expected to attend at the palace on state occasions. Mostly these were gala evening receptions. The state opening of parliament and some other events took place, inconveniently, in the morning. At first, because they were neither on the diplomatic list nor on that of government officials, printed invitations often arrived late or not at all, causing chaotic last-minute scrambles to dress appropriately and arrive on time. Strict etiquette required Sylvia and Rita to wear long dresses and gloves. It took the trio some time and a few conspicuous sartorial clangers to work out correct dress for Richard. Because they arrived at the palace crammed into their small Fiat, the imperial bodyguards usually relegated Yemi their driver to a distant corner of the car park, requiring them to walk to the venue and making them late. All three found state occasions stressful in the early days and they soon wearied of the time consumed by such events, which reduced the hours in their working days while significantly expanding their waistlines.

Addis boasted a wide selection of record stores and treating themselves to new recordings became a favourite indulgence. The *New Statesman* arrived reliably from London on postal subscription and dutifully they listened to the 9 p.m. BBC World Service broadcast for news of the increasingly distant-feeling Europe. 'We were soon bound up with Ethiopia,' Rita recalled, 'developing interests of quite a different nature from those pursued in England.'[1798]

Richard and Rita bought a second-hand Toyota, which opened up the city to them. They drove across town to their favourite Chinese restaurant, or to one of the city's four cinemas. There were visits to the theatre, including the National Theatre, elegantly decorated in powder-blue and dark-strawberry hues. Sylvia joined them sometimes if pressed, but usually she preferred to work in the evening. She agreed to accompany them the second time they saw the Russian director Grigori Kozintsev's *Don Quixote*, the first film version in widescreen and colour. Rita recalled vividly the impact of the 'exquisite photography, each picture like a Spanish painting, splendid acting and real poetic truth'.[1799] Submitted to the 1957 Cannes Film Festival, this Soviet drama played to great acclaim in Britain and America, starring Nikolai Cherkasov in the title role and Yuri Tolubeyev as Sancho Panza.

Though they all enjoyed staying in of a night, in the land of extreme hospitality there was no escape from going out. Weddings, garden parties, official receptions, art openings, government events and all manner of occasions called them on parade with the grim regularity of marching drill. Sylvia doughtily trundled to perform her duty, rigged out in her limited assortment of wildly outdated hats and her only smart gloves, which struggled to stay in a pair. Her idiosyncratic ensemble took its place modestly amid the grand fashionable clothes and accessories glittering at the extravagant receptions. Increasingly, this excess and expenditure in a land so poor became the subject of vocal critique within Ethiopia and, later, in TV exposés abroad.

Rita admitted to having soon 'had my fill of lavish parties', but she 'felt obliged to attend, as Sylvia felt a need to be present at such gatherings in order to be in contact with important people'.[1800] Sylvia discovered quickly the sameness in this regard between the elites of England and Ethiopia: promoting her projects required her to hobnob at 'see and be seen' social functions. One of Rita's typically detailed letters to her parents paints a clear picture of the over-indulgences of the onerous and tiresome wedding season. Sitting down to write having just returned from a marquee lunch reception, she jests that it was a rather small and homely affair of merely 200 guests. In a few hours, they are off to another, 'one of those mammoth parties for the wedding of one of the Emperor's two grandsons' for about 2,000 people. More parties loomed ominously the following week, and they'd still had no time to recover from the wedding for the stepdaughter of the Minister of Information held at the weekend:

> huge tent, small tables, Ethiopian Orchestra, buffet, cutting of wedding cake, champagne etc. There must have been about a thousand people. One shudders to think of the cost, merely of food and drink, let alone bridesmaids' outfits, hiring of tables and chairs, orchestra, invitation with gold lettering etc.[1801]

Three months after Sylvia's death there would be an attempted coup against Selassie staged by his trusted bodyguard, followed fourteen years later by a major famine, an attempted revolution, an invasion from Somalia and civil war. Eritrea, which Sylvia was keen to see federated to Ethiopia, would once again break off from it. Even Selassie's most hard-line critics argue that his leadership divided into two distinct periods of good before and bad after. Some of the seeds of his destruction lay in these excesses.

Sylvia had taken issue with her own mother, her elder sister and V. I. Lenin long before she first met Haile Selassie in 1936, and she was a critical friend to him from the outset. Yet there are some telling clues that she had a shrewd sense of what might be coming and what was needed to avert disaster. Among these, her resolute focus on putting her energies and expertise into the next generation was probably the most telling.

During the final decade of his reign, Selassie and his government's leadership fell apart. The ageing and weary Emperor refused to abdicate and allow his son to take the helm. Increasingly brought to account by a progressive civil society movement demanding a faster pace of change, and riven by infighting and scheming between rival factions vying for power, the power structure collapsed. It was followed by an opaque Soviet backed military junta that ruled Ethiopia from 1974 to 1987, the bloody Derg regime that in a few months of 'Red Terror' in 1977–8 killed some 20,000 Ethiopians, most of them left-wing students. A similar number escaped and fled the country. The corruption, narcissistic self-importance and government inaction that overcame the last ten years of Selassie's leadership followed a career up until then distinguished by remarkable achievements.

Sylvia was no fan of any system of monarchy. As far as the Ethiopian King of Kings was concerned, she had told him at the outset that, as a republican, she supported him not because he was an emperor, but because she believed in his cause, the cause of Ethiopia. Despite this, she eulogized him as 'a special man of destiny, elect of God, Conquering lion of the tribe of Judah, King of Zion, King of Kings, Emperor of Ethiopia, chevalier sans peur et sans reproche (i.e. a knight without fear and reproach) and epitome of true nobility'. She described him as 'the soul of resistance to Mussolini'.[1802] Elsewhere, she deployed the language of nobility to make a comparison between Selassie and a toiling proletarian, in whose 'irresistible, eyes burned the quenchless fire of the hero that never failed his cause. One sees in his build and bearing those features full of meaning, those fine and eager hands, the worker who toils unceasingly for the public weal, untouched by personal ambition or material desire for wealth or safety.' "[1803]

Above all else, to her Haile Selassie was a living symbol of international justice.[1804] Selassie managed to see off Mussolini's fascist occupation and hold together a vast feudal empire for nearly fifty years. As one commentator remarked, he succeeded in heaving feudal Ethiopia if not into the twentieth century, then at least into the late nineteenth. Many of Selassie's reforms – the abolition of slavery being the key example – were bold acts of defiance against ancient feudal landlords and provincial princes whose support he needed. His decision to set up a new university based on international models was a courageous modernization project, designed to create a new generation of progressive young Ethiopians inevitably hostile to the old autocracy and hence to his own existence.

According to Rita and contrary to popular belief, Sylvia saw relatively little of the Emperor once she lived in Addis. He made time for her on the few occasions when there was a specific issue she wished to raise with him. 'In several letters to him, aware of the need for further reforms, she proposed the establishment of producers' cooperatives, and advocated free trade unions and democracy – with little success.'[1805]

He introduced the franchise for all women and men over twenty-one and implemented a programme of gradual reform of the old system. Two years after Sylvia moved to Ethiopia, the first women were elected to parliament. While Selassie senior maintained a policy of incremental progressive change at home and integration within the international family of democracies abroad, the next generation within his own family already took the view that Ethiopia required more radical and immediate change.

Consistent with her perennial interest and investment in young people, Sylvia maintained an indirect active channel to Haile Selassie through his youngest son, Prince Sahle Selassie. Sahle Selassie had been educated in England, as had several of Haile Selassie's granddaughters. 'The Emperor was well aware of her positive influence on the young Royals,' observed Geoffrey Last. Last had lived in Woodford before he moved to Addis to become headmaster of the Medhane Alem School, but they had never met in London. In Addis, they became friends. 'She came to see me often and we worked together on her many projects. She shared the Emperor's concern that since Ethiopia was a strongly Christian country, too many people were leaving their money to the church; she wanted to encourage them to remember the hospitals and the schools instead when they died.'[1806]

Many of Geoffrey Last's pupils at the school were the sons of Ethiopian and Somalian chieftains. Haile Selassie steered them into the school and away from their fathers' feudal seats to provide them with a modern education and 'lessons in practical politics'.[1807] There was no doubt of his commitment to building a new cohort of modern leaders and administrators. Many of these young men, though children of relative privilege, were amputees, victims of hand-grenade attacks, survivors of brutal, dislocated childhoods.

Questioned on the wisdom of Sylvia's loyalty to Selassie, Last, a first-hand witness, took the temperature of the times: 'It is arguable that, being the Emperor's unofficial mouthpiece, she closed her mind to the fact that some of her idealism was misplaced. There were, for instance, many Somalis who did not want to be united with Ethiopia. They had too much fun with the Italians and wanted their freedom.'[1808]

Geoffrey Last reported that Sylvia 'was incensed that only the educated and the wealthy were getting benefits from government reforms and felt that they should be giving something back to the community'.[1809] Last's observation provides a sharp insight into Sylvia's mind: she identified personally with these children as having a common heritage. Like her, they came from the equivalent of middle-class security, comfortable families with a history of community leadership and social service. Where others saw difference of race Sylvia identified through class. Far from a developmental attitude of maternalistic upliftment to the disadvantaged she saw in these young girls and boys children very much like her younger self, Christabel, Adela and Harry – except that these youngsters already had the advantage of a far better school education. Her father's exhortation, 'If you do not work for other people you will not have been worth the upbringing,'[1810] she applied equally to her own child as to other people's children, and most particularly to children born into privilege – British or Ethiopian.

In her eighth decade, the terrain had changed for Sylvia but the clearly drawn battle lines remained the same: the inequalities and injustice framing social relations between rich and poor, capitalism and socialism, haves and have-nots. The scenery had dramatically altered, but the core elements remained consistent with the key concerns that drove her life. Already at seventeen, suffragette Sylvia had had to think very carefully about the choice between revolution and reform. A reluctant militant, she was in this regard more cautious than her radical father. Now a seasoned and experienced elder, the same proposition presented: are you going to work for the radical breach of revolution or find the best reforming methods to fix gradually from within? Between Sylvia at seventeen and Sylvia in her seventies stood Lenin and the failure of his revolutionary government to deliver on the potential of the Bolshevik Revolution. Standing beside him were her mother and her elder sister, whose Napoleonic aspirations for a new civil code radicalizing the lives of women resulted only in handing back their ballot cards to the age-old reactionary patriarchy which they'd once aimed to dislodge.

From Rita's up-close perspective, Sylvia had 'great admiration for the Emperor': respecting him as the country's pre-war modernizer; as a symbol of Ethiopian resistance to the fascist invasion and as a leader who had outmanoeuvred British attempts to dominate the country. She understood his power as a unifying force and saw him, 'in a sense, as a benevolent ruler in the context of Ethiopian monarchy'. Sylvia, Rita said, felt that Haile Selassie 'could carry the country forward. Though not blind to the deficiencies of his government, she was reluctant to join in the criticism by other foreigners, having, as she said, experienced so much inefficiency in the East End, under a longer established bureaucracy.'[1811] Unlike many of her left-wing counterparts at the time, she did not put aside or wilfully ignore the questions of European imperialism and racism when evaluating the position from Africa.

In her admiration for Haile Selassie, Sylvia was in good company. African nationalists who had spent their lives struggling against white imperialism accepted honours from the Lion of Judah, helping to build Addis Ababa as the executive capital of the New Africa. Seasoned revolutionaries such as Jomo Kenyatta, Kwame Nkrumah, Ben Bella and Sekou Touré acknowledged Selassie as the elder statesman of African self-determination. By 1960 Ethiopia was accepting aid from Khrushchev's deStalinizing Soviet Union and Marshal Tito's People's Republic of Yugoslavia. Haile Selassie was one of the most vocal international leaders urging people to observe the duty of boycotting South Africa.

In 1978 the Polish journalist and literary charlatan Ryszard Kapuściński published his now discredited fantastical account of – ostensibly – the life and fall of Haile Selassie, reducing the state of the Ethiopian court to fatuous comic opera. *The Emperor: Downfall of an Autocrat*, heralded as a masterpiece, overnight became a runaway bestseller, translated into dozens of languages, heaped with literary prizes and later adapted as a popular London stage play. Kapuściński worked for the Polish Press Agency. He claimed that he had travelled to Ethiopia to get an insider's view on the coup of 1974, interviewing former servants and people close to the Emperor. Readers lapped up his grotesque portrait of a paranoid African megalomaniac, which became the accepted view of Haile Selassie. When Kapuściński died, tributes flooded in from his well-known literary admirers. In fact, he was a highly imaginative and talented liar whose greatest ability was to produce colourful and lyrical fictions. If it had any substance at all, *The Emperor* was a clever surrealist tapestry purporting to tell the story of Ethiopia but in fact offering a thinly veiled tragicomic satire of Kapuściński's own Soviet-style communist homeland, then bent under the tyrannical weight of Edward Gierek, First Secretary of the Polish United Workers' Party (the communists) from 1970 till his removal in disgrace in 1980. Kapuściński's 'magic journalism' may be an intriguing parable of Polish politics,[1812] but its conflation of an African emperor's court with an eastern European Communist Party was a toxic concoction of fantasy and prejudice.

Other writers, such as Evelyn Waugh and Thomas Packenham, enjoyed huge literary success in the Atlantic and Anglophone colonial world for their bestselling books based on journalistic assignments (Waugh) and exploration (Packenham) in Ethiopia. Waugh supported Mussolini and the cause of fascism. Packenham did not. He understood, long before many other writers, the role of Ethiopia and Haile Selassie at the centre of the jigsaw of African and twentieth-century history. Written from very different perspectives, Waugh's and Packenham's works popularized renewed interest in Ethiopia, so long the subject of white colonial mythology. Haile Selassie advised the white western powers:

> Do not seek to perpetuate, in some different guise, the old forms
> of economic and political exploitation and oppression. Africa needs
> and desires and welcomes the help of others, but must nevertheless
> be left to develop herself, her people, her resources, as Africans
> determine. Leave to us, freely and without qualms, the choice
> between good and evil, between justice and injustice, between
> oppression and liberty. Our choice will be the right one, and history
> will judge us, and you, the better for it.[1813]

Selassie chose to end Ethiopia's self-imposed isolation from the rest of Africa. As Thomas Packenham astutely observed, this made him an enlightened leader who could see the future through the lens of anti-imperialism, black consciousness and African nationalism. Haile Selassie was an emperor who knew that the Ethiopian throne would not survive the modern impetus towards republican democracy and a just rule of law built into the ideals of post-colonial liberation movements. The last Emperor was a bold modernizer. From 1941, he ruled the country unchallenged for nineteen years, playing opponents off against each other, depriving aristocrats of their private armies and for two terms chairing the Organization of African Unity in a manner that earned him admiration from fellow leaders. But the pace of change in Ethiopia seemed excruciatingly slow, particularly to the increasing numbers of Ethiopians educated abroad.

Aged seventy-six and at the time unwell, Sylvia determined to visit a UNESCO Community Development Training Centre at Majete, a town in north-eastern Ethiopia that was an eight-hour drive away over rough terrain. The final leg of the journey was along steep escarpments, through winding valleys and tunnels and across dry sandy riverbeds. Richard and Rita suggested that it might be too strenuous a trip, earning the biteback, 'Do you think I have come to the end of my active life?' After a challenging, adventurous journey, Sylvia enthusiastically inspected the school and spoke to staff and trainees, in blistering heat. Come evening, there was entertainment and dancing, to the strumming of a banjo. 'Sylvia, as fresh as a cucumber and fresher than the rest of the party, was of course busy gathering information.'[1814] Only after they got back home did she admit that she'd had a headache throughout the tour.

One of her last 'journalistic safaris' was a long trip to a prison farm at Robi. She slept in the prison hospital, ate the same food as the inmates and noted approvingly that prisoners were not confined in cells, but instead usefully employed learning skills that would set them up in trade.

Rarely could Sylvia be persuaded to go out unless with an objective in view. Occasionally she accepted suggestions for a little sightseeing and relaxation with no other purpose. She loved the wooded hills above Addis Ababa, the deep meandering streams and the lofty eucalyptus, flourishing 'in the season of great rains … a blending of blues, greens and greys, haunting in its wistful loveliness'.[1815]

Driven out to the countryside, Sylvia would sit alone, silently, meditating on the great vistas of mountains, valleys and lakes. She observed the dusky purple rainclouds in the highlands, which, by the time she arrived back in Addis Ababa, had 'vanished in the calm of a mellifluent golden sky'.[1816] 'I often feel I should like to paint again in this beautiful country,' she wrote to the sculptor Elsa Fraenkel, 'but I am always busy and I feel that if I were to make a start I should be terribly disappointed with what I could produce after this interval of fifty years.'[1817]

Just before her seventy-eighth birthday, in 1960, an X-ray revealed a duodenal ulcer. The doctor prescribed a milky diet. The difficulty was that she ate too little. By mid-August she seemed quite well, but Richard took the precaution of connecting an emergency alarm bell from her bed to their cook Askale's rooms.

Having left Britain, Sylvia found that she was honoured in her absence. Elsa Fraenkel asked Sylvia for permission to organize another exhibition of her artwork. Held in 1959 at the French Institute in London, the exhibition was opened by the Indian High Commissioner, Mrs Vijaya Lakshmi Pandit, and supported by the Royal India, Pakistan and Ceylon Society along with the Suffragette Fellowship and the old Woman's Freedom Leaguers. Sylvia sent Elsa a set of old photographs of the giant designs she had created for the WSPU fête of 1909, to be displayed at the exhibition.

The Townswomen's Guild in Woodford also contacted Sylvia in Addis to request her permission to include her in their pageant of 'Women through the Ages'. 'I am delighted at your enterprise,' wrote Sylvia in her gracious reply.[1818] Around the same time the BBC asked her to participate in a programme about George Lansbury, the British Labour leader who had so staunchly supported the suffragettes. The BBC recorded her on tape, and sent it by airmail to London, from where it was broadcast in July 1960.

The last great public event Sylvia witnessed was on 15 September, when the Ethiopian runner Abebe Bikila returned from the Olympic Games in Rome with a gold medal for the marathon event, the first Ethiopian Olympian.

Richard and Rita left for a three-day camping trip with friends in the Rift Valley lakes on the early morning of Sunday 25 September. They asked Sylvia to join them: 'she looked and felt well and had often said she would like to go camping',[1819] but she stayed behind because she had two meetings scheduled for the Monday. One of these was to discuss the establishment of a blood bank at the Princess Tsehai Hospital with the anaesthetist Dr Ghose, the other to discuss the position of Ethiopian women in the new Civil Code with her friend the parliamentarian Siniddu Gebru.

On Monday evening, besieged by sudden pain in her chest and arms, Sylvia used the emergency bell to call Askale, asking her to telephone the doctor, who came to the house immediately and advised her to go to the hospital. Sylvia said she'd rather not. The doctor stayed with her for a couple of hours and she assured him that she would go to the hospital in the morning for an examination.

Warning against the tendency to overburden the contingent moment of death with symbolism and conclusive meanings, Samuel Beckett remarked, 'Death has not required us to keep a day free.'[1820] If death had the temerity to ask Sylvia Pankhurst to keep a day free, it is likely she would have replied briskly that she did not have the time.

On the morning of Tuesday 27 September the duty matron at the Princess Tsehai received a telephone call from Sylvia saying she felt much better and felt no need to come to the hospital. At lunchtime Dr Catherine Hamlin, co-founder of the Fistula Hospital in Addis, took an urgent call from Askale informing her that Sylvia was again unwell. Catherine and Reg Hamlin, both surgeons, were friends of Sylvia's. Catherine, an internationally renowned obstetrician and later Nobel Peace Prize nominee, had met Sylvia through their shared concern for the suffering of Ethiopian women during and after labour. To address high female mortality rates, Hamlin established the first Fistula Hospital in the world, based in Addis Ababa. Catherine and Reg went directly over to Sylvia's bungalow and found her 'in great pain', quickly realizing she was suffering a coronary thrombosis. They sent for morphine and oxygen from the hospital nearby, and the doctors thought that a clot had moved to the brain because half of her face was slightly paralysed. 'Knowing what a great friend of the Emperor she was, we rang the palace straightaway.'[1821] Her old friend Princess Tenagne, the Emperor's eldest daughter, arrived soon afterwards, but Sylvia did not recognize her. They sat with her, Catherine Hamlin holding her hand: 'she thought it was Richard and said she was glad he had come'.[1822]

Sylvia died at 4 p.m. On the wall above her bed hung the election manifesto written by her father as an Independent Labour Party parliamentary candidate for Gorton, Manchester in 1895. Returning home at 6 p.m. from their camping trip, Richard and Rita were surprised by Askale, distraught, rushing out into the garden to meet them. Sylvia lay in the bedroom, 'looking just like the photographs of her own mother'.[1823]

The news spread quickly and Teffera-Work Kidane-Wold arrived swiftly with condolences from the Emperor, who asked where Sylvia should be buried. Richard thought the best place was with the other Ethiopian patriots, 'with whom she identified herself and who considered her one of themselves'.[1824] Teffera-Work Kidane-Wold asked for a list of their friends and assured them that everything else would be organized by the government. By this time, Afewerk Tekle and many other friends were there, and others were soon arriving.

With quiet fortitude, Richard took a photograph of his mother when she was laid out, performing a service to her friends and history at this time of profound distress. 'R. is of course in a bad state,' wrote Rita, 'but controls himself well.'[1825]

Shocked, Rita sat down to compose a brief air letter to her parents the next day: 'It was all over when we returned. Doctors had been called, Princess Tenagne, British Embassy ... It was a complete surprise as we had left her looking and feeling so much better than usual.' Rita notified Fred Pethick-Lawrence and Henry Harben so they could share the news in England, 'also printers and blockmaker. I should inform you that the *Ethiopia Observer* will continue for 2 or 3 issues which are already prepared, to be followed by some sort of memorial issue to the Editor. That will doubtless be the end.'[1826] People had been bringing wreaths since the morning, including one from the National Library staff who came en masse to support Richard and Rita. More people were beginning to arrive for the funeral. The house and garden filled with friends, whom Rita needed to greet, 'so shall just say that we feel very lonely without her'.[1827]

By coincidence 27 September was the date of the annual religious festival of Mesquel – the Feast of the Exaltation of the Holy Cross. On this day the Roman Empress Helena, later canonized, was supposed to have discovered Christ's true cross in Jerusalem in the fourth century.

On Selassie's instruction Sylvia was to be buried at Holy Trinity Cathedral – known also as Selassie Cathedral – with a full state funeral. He flew back immediately from Dire Dawa to attend.

The procession set off from the house at 3.15 p.m. on Wednesday 28 September, passing through the Princess Tsehai Hospital compound where nurses, doctors and other hospital staff lined the way. 'It was hard to believe that one day she was out admiring the flowers in the garden and the next the wreaths were on top [of her coffin].'[1828] Rita described how the gate in the garden fence separating their property from the grounds of the hospital was always kept locked. On this day, it was opened for Sylvia's casket to pass through.[1829] 'It was a terrible moment,' wrote Richard, 'the sun shining on the white uniforms of the staff, the coffin on its last journey through the Hospital and the town.'[1830]

Haile Selassie and a phalanx of members of the imperial family, the cabinet and the diplomatic corps joined old friends from the time of their exile in London, new friends made since moving to Addis and many people who knew her by reputation only who came to pay their respects, bringing their children with them. Among diplomats present at the funeral were the British Ambassador and the Consul. Reporting on the event to the Foreign Office they wrote that 'a very large crowd, mostly Ethiopian, but also members of the European community, was present at the Cathedral ... as far as we know, no other foreigner has been similarly honoured'.[1831]

Sylvia was given a grave in the Kiddist Selassie Menbere Tsebaot Church cemetery in front of Trinity Cathedral, the first European to be accorded such an honour. She remained the only non-Ethiopian buried among the Ethiopian patriots who had fought the fascist invasion, until her son Richard was buried alongside her in 2017. Richard too was given the distinction of a state funeral. When he died, aged eighty-nine, in February 2017, Foreign Minister Workneh Gebeyehu described him as 'one of Ethiopia's greatest friends'.[1832] Rita Pankhurst died two years later, in May 2019 and was laid to rest in another part of the cathedral compound.

As a further honour, Sylvia's funeral service was conducted in Ge'ez, a ceremonial language used solely for religious occasions, intelligible to the most observant Coptic Christians present. Rita described the service in a letter to her parents, noting 'the various abunas [bishops] intoning church chants, Coptic fashion'.[1833] The funeral oration was delivered by Ras Andargachew Massai, husband of Princess Tenagne, and one of Ethiopia's most powerful political figures. He and Sylvia had met when he was Ethiopian Consul at Djibouti, during the Italian occupation. His eulogy addressed mourners in language accessible to those who could not understand the Ge'ez; 'when a person or country is in trouble, friends become scarce', he began, but 'she came forward as a friend of the suffering and friendless people of Ethiopia during the dark period of the Ethiopian occupation. We consider her as Ethiopian.'[1834] He continued:

Sylvia Pankhurst is the great lady who, following in the steps of her mother, was throughout the advocate of all human beings who were refused their rights ... We must remember that she served Ethiopia in the country's darkest hour not only with all her moral support but also by selling her property to obtain money with which to assist Ethiopian exiles, so that she became poor.

Therefore Ethiopia's friend, the great Englishwoman Sylvia Pankhurst, should be called a true Ethiopian Patriot ... Sylvia Pankhurst, the Emperor and the Ethiopian people, whom you sincerely and honestly served, now stand weeping around you. Your history will live forever written in blood, with the history of the Ethiopian patriots. Since by His Imperial Majesty's wish you rest in peace in the soil of Ethiopia, we consider you an Ethiopian. May God, who has surely witnessed your noble deeds, keep you in a place of honour.[1835]

Haile Selassie stood to attention for the two-hour duration of the service. The Emperor then led the mourners as Sylvia's coffin, draped in golden cloth, was borne outside to her grave immediately in front of the cathedral for burial, surrounded by the Imperial Guard in full regalia, ceremonially robed Coptic priests and acolytes holding aloft gorgeously embroidered and fringed traditional parasols.

Sylvia being a name unknown to the Ethiopian Orthodox Church, she was given the designation Welette-Christos, Daughter of Christ. Over her coffin, Coptic priests performed ancient rites entirely discordant with Sylvia's lifelong iconoclastic atheism but in keeping with her aesthetic appreciation of customary arts and Ethiopia's ancient culture. The *Manchester Guardian*, produced in the city of her birth, published their report the next day, 29 September: 'Observers said it was the most outstanding tribute ever paid at a non-royal or non-official funeral in Ethiopia.' At the time of Sylvia's death, Catherine Hamlin, recording the state honours accorded to her by Ethiopia, noted that 'Miss Pankhurst had never been decorated by her own country, which I thought was disgraceful.'[1836]

Tributes poured in, from her homeland, from India, Israel, America, Mexico, Japan, Germany, Sri Lanka, and from all over Africa – from Accra to Cairo, Nairobi to Johannesburg. The global tributes were a roll call of the illustrious, the venerable, the radical, revolutionaries, visionaries, rascals and thousands upon thousands of what Sylvia would never think of as ordinary people. The great and recognizably good wrote their tributes alongside the most humble and unknown. Roxanne and Percy wrote to Richard from their home in Westerham, Kent, 'Wherever we are is your home.'[1837] Fenner Brockway spoke in the problematic language of the time but nonetheless with genuine passion for many in the British labour movement when he acknowledged her contribution to combating racism in her homeland: 'She was one of the first to stand for racial equality and against discrimination of the blacks, not only black Africans but brown Indians. She deserves deep recognition as one of the pioneers of that struggle.'[1838] One of Sylvia's Ethiopian drivers sent warm tribute, as did Addis schoolteachers. 'Kind Miss Pankhurst,' wrote Beine Selassie, 'helper of the poor and mother of the orphans, worked night and day without rest, used all her energy and her brilliant mind to help the people. What makes me sad is that there were so many things she wished to complete.' The American poet Lynn Martin stated incisively, 'She was a very grand person in both the casual and exact sense of that word.' A Polish refugee wrote remembering her as 'one of the few people in England who was kind to me'.

From Australia, Adela's telegram offered, succinctly, 'Deepest sympathy'.

Geoffrey Last expressed the opinion that Haile Selassie's decision to stage such a high-profile funeral might have been strategic: 'Sylvia was in cahoots with all the early African rebels. The Emperor needed a spectacular unifying event and her death offered such an opportunity.'[1839] If that was the case, it is unlikely Sylvia would have objected to providing Selassie with such an occasion for effective statecraft. Certainly she would have approved of the pageantry. So far away in time and geography, in such a different context, the sea of white robes of the Coptic priests and their umbrellas held aloft visually echoed the flowing white dresses and banners of the mass suffragette rallies Sylvia had choreographed in the streets of early twentieth-century London.

Geoffrey Last's narrow view that Haile Selassie had political motives for her state funeral underestimated the popularity and respect Sylvia had earned in her adopted homeland. The scale of the occasion reflected the genuine feeling and outpouring of grief from Ethiopians and Africans from all over the continent. Tributes came from all parts of

Ethiopian society and from across the political network of the African world. W. E. B. Du Bois made a typically thoughtful assessment.

> I realised ... that the great work of Sylvia Pankhurst was to introduce black Ethiopia to white England, to give the martyred Emperor of Ethiopia a place of refuge during his exile and to make the British people realise that black folks had more and more to be recognised as human beings with the rights of women and men.[1840]

Other radical leaders also spoke. Semakula Mulumba in Uganda declared, 'We have lost the general of the most sincere and selfless fighters for freedom, justice and democracy.' Joseph Murumbi of the Kenya African Union said, 'We Africans will always regard her as being a great friend of our people.' Lij Endalkatchew Makonnen, Ethiopian Ambassador in London, stated, with exquisite diplomacy, that 'Her whole life exemplified the liberal and humanitarian spirit which gives Britain her undisputed position of moral and spiritual leadership.'

London marked Sylvia's death with a memorial service at Caxton Hall, with accolades from Frederick Pethick-Lawrence, Basil Mackenzie and numerous peers from both sides of the House. In what was still then British Guiana, the churches held a series of memorial services to honour Sylvia as a champion of all colonial peoples.

Richard wrote to his mother's old friend Elsa Fraenkel, 'Even now I can scarcely believe I have lost her. Of course I saw her getting old but she was so active to the end, so full of ideas.'[1841] Rita had marvelled to her parents, 'To the end she was full of plans for the beggars, artificial limbs for cripples, etc etc.'[1842] It is safe to imagine that Sylvia would have been glad that Richard sat down the day after her magnificent state funeral to write a formal letter thanking the Emperor for his 'great generosity to my Mother'.[1843] He knows, her son continues, that she would have felt greatly honoured by the Emperor's presence at the service, and the sympathy of the entire family, as well as by the place assigned to her in the graveyard of Selassie Church. 'She was proud to be considered one of Ethiopia's patriots when she was alive and would have been pleased to know that she would rest among them after her death.' Richard described to the Emperor how Sylvia continued her activities to the very end. On her desk was her work in progress reviewing the new Civil Code for the *Ethiopia Observer* and letters raising support for a new wing of the Tsehai Hospital to expand the maternity school and provide training of district midwives. Richard told Haile Selassie about the meetings Sylvia had scheduled for the day she died.

One scheme Richard was anxious to ensure was kept on track was Sylvia's project to establish an orthopaedic centre for the manufacture of artificial limbs, which she hoped could be set up very near the Princess Tsehai Hospital 'so that patients could be individually fitted'. Sylvia had secured a partnership with the Rotary Club for the scheme, which was well under way, including a programme to train disabled people at the Kolfe Rehabilitation Centre as carpenters employed to produce the limbs. On 1 October, he and Rita attended one of the Centre's committees which she usually took part in, 'to push her various plans there'.[1844] Sylvia had been concerned also to keep children off the streets by establishing a chain of well-equipped, greened playgrounds in different parts of the city. 'I know she wanted to ask Your Imperial Majesty whether part of HH Ras Hailu's estates with the swimming pool could be opened as a public garden or whether this land was already allocated for other purposes.'

Just before she died, Sylvia had become anxious about the circumstances of African refugees and students in Ethiopia, 'for whom Your Majesty is providing'.

Richard and Rita immediately took on the responsibility of attending Sylvia's scheduled meetings, committees and projects, even as they dealt with the steady flow of condolence messages. 'Letters are beginning to follow the crop of telegrams which included one from Tom Mboya as well as ... members of our family,'[1845] Rita told her parents.

Richard and Rita made an inventory of the wreaths, telegrams and letters of condolence that poured in. Many of these reflections on her life they reprinted in the memorial issue of the *Ethiopia Observer*. 'Unfortunately there are few photos – she never could be bothered with that,' Rita told her parents.[1846] The following Sunday, she started clearing Sylvia's bedroom. 'R. is beginning to feel the loss at the deeper level and needs a lot of looking after.'[1847] The next day, Richard went back to work for the new college term and Rita returned to the library. Both hoped that work would make things easier.

In his supercilious letter to the Foreign Office reporting on the funeral, the British Consul in Addis inveighed at length against Sylvia's misguided opposition to British government policy over Eritrea and

Somaliland. He also noted that her son Richard taught 'history of a strong anti-colonialist variety' which had proved embarrassing to the Canadian Jesuits who ran the University College. Their attempts to remove Pankhurst Junior from his position, the Consul confided, 'have invariably been frustrated'. The letter ended, 'It will be interesting to see whether Dr Pankhurst will survive now that his mother's protection has gone.'[1848] Richard did, and in 1962 he became the founding director of the Institute of Ethiopian Studies at the University College of Addis Ababa and in 2004 accepted the honour of an OBE bestowed by the British government for his services to Ethiopian studies. The historian Jeff Pearce wrote, 'Richard's books brought a new calibre of insight and depth to examining the country's history and culture. He formalized Ethiopian History as an academic field and then became its greatest contributor.'[1849]

Richard and Rita continued to live and work in Ethiopia, with the intermission of a few years in exile back in England during the revolution. Sylvia's first grandchild Alula, born two years after her death, by fitting coincidence on 27 September, was named in honour of Ras Alula, the nineteenth-century Ethiopian leader. Richard was writing a history of Ethiopia when Helen was born in 1964, hence her name: Helen Sylvia Tarik (the Amharic word for history).

Ten weeks after Sylvia died, two commanders of Emperor Haile Selassie's Imperial Guard led a failed coup, taking advantage of his absence on an extended tour of Brazil. The putschists were correct in claiming that there was political stagnation in Ethiopia, but the general populace was not in sympathy with them – the Ethiopian people did not rise up or offer support through strikes or a mass protest movement.

In 1972 the Emperor celebrated his eightieth birthday, still refusing to announce his successor. The opportunity to accelerate moderate reform had been squandered. Loyalists begged Haile Selassie to abdicate and pave the way for constitutional democracy.[1850] Two years later came the inevitable uprising. Haile Selassie was quietly smothered with a pillow in his palace bedchamber.

'It was all so predictable – and avoidable. That was at the heart of the tragedy,' wrote Thomas Packenham, who concurs with the cool assessment of Haile Selassie's masterly biographer Asfa-Wossen Asserate: 'His many services to the country will carry more weight than the great mistakes he undoubtedly made.'[1851] Packenham goes further, making clear the significance of Haile Selassie's services to the world at large: 'To Europeans he represented the pioneer in the struggle against fascism. To millions of Africans he came to symbolise their own struggle for independence. He gave them back their dignity robbed by centuries of European exploitation. This was the ultimate irony: a despot at home (even if a benevolent one), he was regarded abroad as the champion of liberty.'[1852]

In her last letter to Rita's parents, written in January 1960, Sylvia told them, 'You would see great changes here as all the eucalyptus trees ... have been cut down, but we are compensated by seeing the mountains and woods at some distance ... They are now growing again very fast. Some of them are already three or four feet high.'[1853]

Like Sylvia, the eucalyptus were irrepressible.

The Australian eucalyptus was admired for the practical benefits it had brought to Ethiopia, and the way its striking groves 'defined the landscape'.[1854] Fast-growing eucalyptus made permanent settlement and the construction of towns and great cities possible in Ethiopia for the first time, providing a ready supply of both building material and fuel alongside its extensive medicinal properties. In time, as people became more knowledgeable about the 'dire effects' of the roots of these thirsty trees on the water table and other native vegetation,[1855] and new sources of building materials and fuel became more readily available, the old eucalyptus groves were cut down to make way for indigenous trees and bushes and a wider variety of succulents, tropical plants and European varieties.

'At first', wrote Rita, 'we considered it a great misfortune when the eucalyptus in the pilots' compound bordering our garden were all mercilessly hewn down. [The pilots were at this time from Trans World Airlines. TWA was nurturing Ethiopian Airlines, which soon became independent.] The old eucalyptus trees lining our access road were cut down at the same time.'[1856] As they came to understand the deleterious effects of the trees on the habitat, the Pankhursts followed suit and decided, reluctantly, to cut and uproot the ones remaining on their land. 'All gardeners in Addis Ababa were agreed they spelled death to any garden, having numerous water-consuming roots as well as leaves dripping acid on the soil.'[1857]

These the Pankhursts replaced with 'graceful' indigenous zigba – *Afrocarpus gracilior* – East African yellowwood and aloes, whose flowers are a delicacy much appreciated by Addis' monkeys. On the advice of the prominent local horticulturalist Professor Stash Chojnacki and Afewerk Tekle, who showed them round the already famed gardens of the former government official Sibhatu Gebre-Iyesus, they also planted an indigenous olive tree and a South American pepper tree, sowed all manner of seeds and planted cuttings. Sibhatu Gebre-Iyesus, who turned to business and landscape gardening after becoming disillusioned with government service, created original and distinctive gardens that combined Ethiopian, tropical and European botanicals, including ever-resilient English rose varieties. Rita and Richard expanded their rock garden, planted a cactus grove, planned a greenhouse in which to grow tomatoes and tropical plants and invested for the first time in a lawnmower, 'to which instrument Richard had objected on the ground that it encouraged unemployment'.[1858]

Sylvia regretted the loss of the eucalyptus trees. At the time of her death, she was composing several poems to them:

O lofty, lofty Eucalyptus tree
Bowing your dusky crests to every breeze
How upright in your serried ranks you stand
As did your forbears in th'Australian land.[1859]

Sylvia mourned the uprooting of the trees that had made such an impact on Ethiopia's development. Like her, they were welcome immigrants, transplanted from their native soil and able to make a defining contribution to the country that invited them in. The eucalyptus also infused Ethiopia with its characteristic fragrance – a refreshing scent of minty pine, sweetened with a touch of honey.

The lives of many people who otherwise would probably be starving or dead depended on eucalyptus, in Ethiopia, Argentina and numerous other countries. These trees have more uses, especially in the medicinal field, than any other species. Menelik II approved eucalyptus plantation in 1895, when Sylvia was thirteen years old, the year she met Eleanor Marx. By 1960 the enabling work of the eucalyptus was done and it could be phased out for the next stage of development.

According to legend, in the beginning of time there were a group of aboriginal Australians gathering wood to make a fire. They collected different kinds of branches. As they prepared the fire, they heard a new sound that scared them. At first they thought it was the call of an evil spirit. As the sound was pleasant, they investigated further and realized the music was the spirit of the wind blowing through a branch of eucalyptus hollowed by termites. This was the origin of the didgeridoo, the instrument used in rituals to connect with the spirit of the ancestors. Sylvia's fondness for the trees, with their 'lofty' bearing, yet bowing their 'dusky crests to every breeze', expressed in the poem written in the final year of her life, whispered eloquently the spirit of her own connection to all the world, and her place in it, standing 'upright' alongside the 'serried ranks' of all peoples who are, essentially, migrants. Unbowed, a fighter to the end, Sylvia was not an old colonial lady wistfully contemplating the changed boundary of her own garden. In her final poetic elegy to the sea trees, as in all her work, Sylvia found a natural figure that expressed her spiritual place in the boundless interconnectedness of the local and intimate with all the confluences of the wider world.

In a visionary essay, Sylvia once wrote, 'What I am aiming at. A chance for the children of tomorrow.'[1860] In 1951 Vera Klein moved into Charteris Road with her husband and little daughter Ann. The Kleins ran a shop in Woodford Green. Sylvia used to go in from time to time, and the neighbours became acquainted. Vera remembered seeing Richard and Silvio pottering around the garden, which, she remarked, 'was always in a shocking state'.[1861] She continued:

You would never have imagined that she had done all those things. She was just a little old-fashioned lady in black, dumpy and mild-spoken. To look at she reminded me so much of Queen Victoria in her later years. Of course we all knew about the baby [Richard] and the suffragettes, and we used to say with pride that Sylvia Pankhurst lived in Woodford. I took my daughter to tea there ... and Miss Pankhurst showed us round the house, which was in a terrible mess, just as though it had been a palace. She handed us a teacup without a saucer and with a spoon in it, but with such an air as though a full tea set had been laid. She had real dignity. My daughter ... who was very young then (about 10), told her what to do to get the garden in order, and Miss Pankhurst listened very carefully and patiently.[1862]

Afterword

When I am Gone

Sylvia was such an accessible and clear-eyed writer. I hope that those who have read this far will support my wish that her collected works will be published in full at last. They offer so much encouragement and wisdom in this new difficult age. Characteristically, most of her writing is not about herself. An exception is a piece she was asked to contribute late in life, to a collection by notable women on how they would like to be remembered after they were gone. Parts of the Sylvia Pankhurst entry almost read like a matter-of-fact alternative to the famous bereavement poem 'Do not stand at my grave and weep'. While Mary Elizabeth Frye gave us, 'I am not there, I did not die!' Sylvia wrote of herself:

> Personal ambitions were to her both puny and ephemeral, because she realised that, when in a thousand years, all we who strive and labour in our passing days are dust, mankind will still be working out its destiny. She desired it might always be true of her that she never deserted a cause in its days of adversity. To give her energy to its early struggles was her habit, never waiting until advocacy had become popular. When victory for any cause came, she had little leisure to rejoice, none to rest; she had always some other objective in view.[1863]

Yet the many objectives of her nearly eight decades of brave struggle all sprang from a single, simple and principled vision of what she describes as a 'an equalitarian society, in which by mutual aid and service, there should be abundance for all to satisfy material and spiritual needs'.[1864]

Elsewhere in her latter years, Sylvia also wrote of her lifelong loathing of 'Mrs Grundy', a cypher for every prurient gossip who sits in cruel judgement over the lives of others. Gerald Martin described biographical subjects as having lived public, private and secret lives. The first is the business of the biographer; the second, in Sylvia's case, she decided for herself; and the third is nobody's business. It is a sadness, perhaps, when the three categories become so blurred that history cannot fully protect the secret garden of the soul. This is my view of the intimate relationship between Sylvia Pankhurst and Keir Hardie, witnessed by close and trusted friends but only reliably documented in correspondence between the pair when she travelled America. Her letters to him he returned out of respect for her privacy and agency before his death, entrusting her to 'use your discretion as to which are worthy of being kept and published and which should be destroyed'.[1865] Sylvia chose to save their love letters for posterity. These her son subsequently included in her public archive. The same applies to the very few and more cryptic intimate letters surviving from Zelie Emerson.

Musing on the political differences amongst the Pankhurst women, Adela had remarked, 'Readers should understand that in Sylvia's eyes to cease to be a socialist, if one had ever been one, is a moral crime.'[1866] A century later, it is Sylvia's appealing morality that make her attractive to many, as the historian Lyndall Gordon put it, 'because she was a socialist who always stuck to her principles. She is easy to admire.'[1867] Sylvia's friend Elsie Bowerman, WSPU activist, lawyer and *Titanic* survivor, remarked that 'Sylvia was of course attached to the left wing of everything.'[1868] In fact she was not so simple. Her allegiances were complex, wide-ranging and often surprising. In 1965 Nellie Cressall, the ELF activist who became Sylvia's friend, remembered, 'Mrs Pankhurst came to this meeting in Bow, and afterwards, I was standing quite near, she tackled Sylvia. "What have you decided, Sylvia?" she said. "Are you coming with me, or are you going to stay with these women?" Sylvia said she was staying with us. She was happy with us and felt her work lay in the East End.'[1869]

There are few memorials to Sylvia Pankhurst in the country of her birth to which she committed so much of her life's work. Perhaps this would not have mattered to a self-styled 'citizen of the world' with her eyes on the far future. However, Britain might reflect on why it was necessary for the Dutch government to ensure the preservation of the legacy of such an important woman of the twentieth century. An earthquake and coup in Ethiopia fast followed in the wake of her death in 1960. This prompted her son Richard to seek immediate safe-keeping of her papers. It was the Dutch who offered refuge. Imagine the fury in parts of the press in which this Pankhurst and her struggles so often featured if such international solidarity had been required to save the writings of her sometime nemesis and occasional ally Winston Churchill.

Sylvia is best recognized in continuing campaigns for the values and causes closest to her heart. The plight of refugees is a critical example, as we live through the world's greatest forced displacement of people since World War Two, now exacerbated by the Covid-19 pandemic. Vanessa Redgrave's 2017 documentary *Sea Sorrow* features one of Sylvia's many pre-war letters urging the Home Office to expedite and extend refuge for European Jews seeking to escape Hitler's death camps. It is easy to imagine what she would have made of the so-called hostile environment, bulldozers in Calais, or caged children separated from their parents on the US-Mexican border. As she wrote in November 1938 after Kristallnacht, 'May we not plead for somewhat more humanity in dealing with these cases?'[1870]

Speaking of how perspectives of her grandmother have shifted during her own life, Helen Pankhurst described how attitudes to the different Pankhursts have changed: 'When I have been approached about my surname and the Pankhurst legacy, outside Ethiopia and in the UK in particular, most often it is Emmeline who people knew about and admired. However, some would come up to me and say something like you know it was your grandmother Sylvia who was my favourite!' Helen describes how interest in Sylvia has 'increased over time as in many ways the world has moved in the direction of her thinking.' She points out that Sylvia 'kept her focus on poorer women and those discriminated against for many other reasons' and was 'what we would now call an intersectional feminist'. But the 'growing interest' in Sylvia, she observes, 'remains segmented. People tend to know just one part of the story and are interested in her work as a suffragette or a socialist, or they might know about her work combatting fascism and colonialism or her work in Ethiopia, they might know she was an editor or a painter. Yet it is the whole that is so astonishing.'[1871] While we await the successful completion

of the fundraising campaign for Sylvia's long-overdue statue on east
London's Clerkenwell Green, we can enjoy alternative appropriate
monuments. The Tate has acquired four of her 1907 paintings of
women working in Glasgow mills and Staffordshire potteries from the
Pankhursts' private collection. Their display will be a fitting tribute to
Sylvia's career as an artist. Nellie's words stand as a living memorial to
her achievements:

> We all loved her. She was a warm, human person. Of course she'd
> had a better education than me. But she used to say: 'Nellie, I may
> have had a better education, but you've had the experience.' She was
> tireless, she had real vision, ideals. So different from the politicians
> of today. When I tell people all the things she did, they don't believe
> me. And after the way she suffered in prison.[1872]

Researching this book, I followed Sylvia's journeys as far as possible.
Fully to appreciate the esteem in which Sylvia Pankhurst, the socialist,
feminist, anti-fascist, pro-liberation internationalist, is held by so many
in the world, I made my last trip to her final home in March 2019.
My time in conversation with Rita Pankhurst in Sylvia's study, and
reading at her desk, with its view of the garden, was unforgettable and
invaluable.

Sylvia's grandson Alula took me to the Sylvia Pankhurst Café on
Sylvia Pankhurst Street in central Addis – itself a poignant moment
given her personal and political relationship to food, hunger and street
protest. Alula explained the reason for my visit, and an interested crowd
soon gathered. People shared stories about Sylvia, told to them by their
parents, several of whom had known her. As the sun dipped over the
brow of the hill and we got up to leave, I was stopped by an Ethiopian
man who had just arrived outside the café. He'd heard my reason for
being there and broke into a heartfelt tribute to this woman and her
contribution to his nation. His final words on what she meant to him
will never leave me: 'After God, Sylvia Pankhurst.'

Rachel Holmes
1 May 2020

Abbreviations

CP	Christabel Pankhurst
ESP	E. Sylvia Pankhurst
IISH/SPP	International Institute of Social History/Sylvia Pankhurst Papers
RKPP	Richard Pankhurst
RP	Rita Pankhurst
THF	ESP, *The Home Front: A Mirror to Life in England during the World War* (London: Hutchinson, 1932)
TSM	ESP, *The Suffragette Movement: An Intimate Account of Persons and Ideals* (London: Virago, 1977)

Notes

PREFACE

1 ESP, 'On parents, children and matrimony', n.d., IISH/SPP/ARCH01029/
   141
2 Stella Miles Franklin, *A Gregarious Culture: Topical Writings of Miles
   Franklin* (Brisbane: University of Queensland Press, 2001), p. 71
3 Ibid., p. 70
4 Shirley Harrison, *Sylvia Pankhurst: A Crusading Life, 1882–1960*
   (London: Aurum Press, 2003), p. 15
5 Nellie Cressall to David Mitchell, 5 April 1965, David Mitchell Collection,
   Museum of London Library, GB 389 73.83
6 Sheila Rowbotham, *Hidden from History: 300 Years of Women's Oppression
   and the Fight against It* (London: Pluto Press, 1973), p. 168
7 ESP to Teresa Billington-Greig, editorial remarks on 'How I Would
   Like to be Remembered' (c. 1955–7), cited in Patricia Romero, *E. Sylvia
   Pankhurst: Portrait of a Radical* (New Haven & London: Yale University
   Press, 1990), p. 282
8 Melissa Benn, 'An Agitator: The Enduring Principle of Agitation', in
   Pauline Bryan (ed.), *What Would Keir Hardie Say? Exploring Keir Hardie's
   Vision and Relevance to 21st Century Politics* (Edinburgh: Luath Press,
   2015), p. 149
9 Cited in Emrys Hughes, *Keir Hardie* (London: George Allen & Unwin,
   1956), p. 138
10 George Bernard Shaw, Preface, *Saint Joan* (London: Penguin, 2001), p. 4
11 *Pravda*, 17 June 1920; V. I. Lenin, *Collected Works*, 4th English edn
    (Moscow: Progress Publishers, 1965), vol. 31, pp. 139–43

12 George Orwell, 'Fascism and Democracy' (first published in the *Left News*, February 1941), in his *Fascism and Democracy* (London: Penguin, 2020), p. 2

13 Elizabeth Robins, *The Convert* (New York: Macmillan, 1913), pp. 174–5

14 *Britannia*, 28 April 1916; and see June Purvis, *Emmeline Pankhurst: A Biography* (London & New York: Routledge, 2003), p. 285

15 Barbara Castle, *Sylvia and Christabel Pankhurst* (London: Penguin, 1987), p. 18

16 *News of the World*, 8 April 1928

17 RKPP and RP, *Ethiopian Reminiscences: Early Days* (Los Angeles: Tsehai Publishers, 2013), p. 4

18 ESP, 'Italian Fascism', IISH/SPP/ARCH01029/152

19 ESP, 'The Inheritance', unpublished MS, IISH/SPP/ARCH01029/55

20 ESP, 'Fascism today', n.d, IISH/SPP/ARCH01029/152

I AUTHORITY

21 E. Sylvia Pankhurst, *The Suffragette Movement: An Intimate Account of Persons and Ideals* (London: Virago, 1977), p. 150

22 Ibid., p. 148

23 ESP, *TSM*, p. 124

24 Ibid.

25 Ethel Smyth, *Female Pipings in Eden* (London: Peter Davies, 1933), p. 248

26 ESP, *TSM*, p. 147

27 Ibid., p. 147

28 ESP, *TSM*, p. 148

29 Ibid.

30 Ibid.

31 Ibid., p. 149

32 Ibid, p. 149

33 Ibid., p. 150

34 Ibid.

35 Ibid.

36 Ibid.

37 Ibid., p. 151

38 Ibid.

39 ESP, *The Life of Emmeline Pankhurst: The Suffragette Struggle for Women's Citizenship* (Boston & New York: Houghton Mifflin, 1936), p. 41

40 ESP, *TSM*, p. 151

41 Purvis, *Emmeline Pankhurst*, p. 10; ESP, *The Life of Emmeline Pankhurst*, p. 9

42 Emmeline Pankhurst, *My Own Story* (London: Vintage Books, 2015), p. 4

43 CP, *Unshackled: The Story of How We Won the Vote*, ed. Lord Pethick-Lawrence of Peaslake (London: Hutchinson, 1959), p. 35
44 Ibid., p. 34
45 Ibid.
46 ESP, *TSM*, p. 56
47 CP, *Unshackled*, p. 21
48 ESP, *TSM*, p. 56
49 Purvis, *Emmeline Pankhurst*, p. 16
50 CP, *Unshackled*, p. 25.
51 Richard Pankhurst, cited in ibid., p. 2
52 Rebecca West, 'Mrs Pankhurst', in William Ralph Inge (ed.), *The Post-Victorians* (London: Ivor Nicholson & Watson, 1933), pp. 479–500 at p. 479
53 Cited in Verna Coleman, *Adela Pankhurst: The Wayward Suffragette, 1885–1961* (Melbourne: Melbourne University Press, 1996), p. 4
54 Purvis, *Emmeline Pankhurst*, p. 9
55 ESP, *The Life of Emmeline Pankhurst*, p. 7
56 Cited in Purvis, *Emmeline Pankhurst*, p. 11
57 ESP, *The Life of Emmeline Pankhurst*, p. 11
58 ESP, *TSM*, p. 47
59 Cited in Purvis, *Emmeline Pankhurst*, p. 12
60 ESP, *TSM*, p. 64
61 ESP, *The Life of Emmeline Pankhurst*, p. 12
62 West, 'Mrs Pankhurst', p. 497
63 ESP, *The Life of Emmeline Pankhurst*, p. 15
64 Ibid., p. 13

2 RED DOCTOR

65 ESP, *The Life of Emmeline Pankhurst*, p. 16
66 Ibid.
67 ESP, *TSM*, p. 55
68 Cited in CP, *Unshackled*, pp. 20–1
69 Cited in ibid., p. 21
70 Cited in ibid., p. 22
71 ESP, *Richard Marsden Pankhurst: A Eulogy by his Daughter* (Redditch: Maurois Press/Read Books, 2011), p. 1
72 ESP, *TSM*, p. 7
73 Martin Pugh, *The Pankhursts: The History of One Radical Family* (London: Vintage, 2008), p. 16
74 Emmeline Pankhurst, cited in Midge Mackenzie, *Shoulder to Shoulder* (London: Penguin, 1975), p. 4

75 ESP, *Richard Marsden Pankhurst*, p. 5
76 Thus a worthy antecedent to Manchester's thriving cultural scene and festivals in later centuries. See Alexandra Mitchell, 'Middle-Class Masculinity in Clubs and Associations: Manchester and Liverpool, 1800–1914', PhD thesis, University of Manchester, 2011
77 ESP, *Richard Marsden Pankhurst*, p. 6
78 Cited in ibid.
79 Ibid., p. 15
80 Ibid., p. 4
81 The same day that Josephine Butler, feminist, suffragist and social reformer, gave evidence to the House of Commons Select Committee on the Operation of the Contagious Diseases Acts
82 ESP, *TSM*, p. 58
83 ESP, 'Sylvia Pankhurst', in Countess of Oxford and Asquith (ed.), *Myself When Young by Famous Women of Today* (London: Frederick Muller, 1938), pp. 259–312 at p. 262
84 CP, *Unshackled*, p. 17
85 ESP, *TSM*, p. 106
86 Ibid.
87 Ibid.
88 Ibid., p. 67
89 Ibid.
90 Walt Whitman, 'Pioneers! O Pioneers!', in *Leaves of Grass* (Philadelphia: David McKay, 1891–2), p. 185
91 ESP, *TSM*, p. 67
92 Ibid., p. 97
93 Ibid., p. 101
94 Ibid., p. 102
95 Ibid., p. 101
96 Ibid., p. 59
97 Ibid.
98 Ibid.
99 Ibid., p. 21
100 RKPP, *Sylvia Pankhurst: Artist and Crusader* (New York & London: Paddington Press, 1979), p. 10
101 *Manchester Guardian*, 28 September 1883
102 ESP, *TSM*, p. 64
103 Ibid., pp. 62–3
104 Ibid., p. 63
105 Ibid., p. 66

106 'The Day of the Child', n.d., IISH/SPP/ARCH01029/141

107 ESP, *TSM*, p. 105

108 Ibid.

109 Ibid., p. 104

110 Cited in Purvis, *Emmeline Pankhurst*, p. 41

111 Cited in ibid.

112 ESP, *TSM*, pp. 84–5

113 RKPP, *Sylvia Pankhurst: Artist and Crusader*, p. 11

114 ESP, 'Some Autobiographical Notes', in *Jaarboek/Yearbook International Archives for the Women's Movement*, vol. 1 (Leiden: E. J. Brill, 1937), pp. 88–98 at pp. 94–5

115 ESP, *TSM*, p. 109

116 Ibid.

117 ESP, *TSM*, p. 110

118 Ibid.

119 Ibid., p. 77

120 Ibid., p. 76

121 Ibid.

122 Ibid., p. 121

123 Ibid., p. 110

124 Ibid., p. 152

125 'Bold, cautious, true, and my loving comrade', from Whitman, 'As Toilsome I Wander'd Virginia's Woods', in *Leaves of Grass*, p. 240

126 IISH/SPP/ARCH01029/171

3 THE HOME NEWS & UNIVERSAL MIRROR

127 CP, *Unshackled*, p. 6

128 ESP, *TSM*, p. 85

129 Ibid., p. 88

130 Ibid., p. 89

131 Ibid., p. 90

132 Ibid.

133 Ibid.

134 Dickens' maternal great-aunt ran a lodging house in Berners Street and here the fifteen-year-old Charles stayed when he got his job as a solicitor's clerk in Gray's Inn that saved him from the sickening blacking-factory job. Later, Dickens installed his nineteen-year-old mistress Nelly Ternan, her mother and two sisters in a house on Berners Street

135 Purvis, *Emmeline Pankhurst*, p. 38

136 CP, *Unshackled*, p. 28

137 ESP, *TSM*, p. 84
138 ESP, 'Sylvia Pankhurst', p. 263
139 Ibid.
140 Emmeline Pankhurst, *My Own Story*, p. 19
141 The definitive work on the Bryant and May matchwomen and their place in history is Louise Raw, *Striking a Light* (London: Bloomsbury, 2009). Raw restores the matchwomen to their proper place in labour history, correcting Annie Besant's self-perpetuated distortions about the significance of her role in the strike
142 Rebecca West, 'Mrs Pankhurst', *The Post-Victorians* (London: Ivor Nicholson & Watson, 1933), pp.479–500
143 Caroline Benn, *Keir Hardie* (London: Hutchinson, 1992), p. 80
144 Ibid.
145 Ibid., pp. 79–81
146 Ibid., p. 80
147 Ibid.
148 Ibid.
149 *The Times*, 13 July 1889, p. 7
150 ESP, *TSM*, p. 119
151 CP, *Unshackled*, p. 28
152 ESP, *TSM*, p. 111
153 Coleman, *Adela Pankhurst*, p. 19
154 ESP, *TSM*, p. 107
155 CP, *Unshackled*, p. 29
156 ESP, *TSM*, p. 98
157 Shrabani Basu, *Victoria and Abdul: The True Story of the Queen's Closest Confidant* (Stroud: The History Press, 2010), p. 43
158 ESP, *TSM*, p. 91
159 Ibid.
160 CP, *Unshackled*, p. 29
161 Ibid.
162 ESP, *TSM*, p. 92
163 Ibid., p. 103
164 Ibid.
165 Ibid., pp. 103–4
166 Ibid., p. 105

4 FAMILY PARTY

167 ESP, *TSM*, p. 595
168 The campaign took place during 1885; the date of the election was 12 January 1886

169   See Pugh, *The Pankhursts*, p. 39

170   Annie Barnes, *Tough Annie: From Suffragette to Stepney Councillor: Annie Barnes in Conversation with Kate Harding and Caroline Gibbs* (London: Stepney Books, 1980), p. 27

171   ESP, *TSM*, p. 71

172   Ibid., p. 72

173   Ibid.

174   Ibid., p. 75

175   Ibid., p. 77

176   Ibid., p. 79

177   Ibid., p. 107

178   Ibid.

179   Jane Martin, 'To "blaise the trail for women to follow along": sex, gender and the politics of education on the London School Board, 1870–1904', University College Northampton, 1999, http://eprints.ioe.ac.uk/2136/1/G%26E_Martin_1999Blaise_the_trail.pdf

180   See https://webarchive.nationalarchives.gov.uk/+/http://yourarchives. nationalarchives.gov.uk/index.php?title=The_Contagious_Diseases_Acts

181   ESP, *TSM*, p. 95

182   Elizabeth Garrett Anderson was also the first dean of a British medical school, the first female doctor of medicine in France, the first woman in Britain to be elected to a school board and, as mayor of Aldeburgh, the first female mayor and magistrate in Britain

183   Where others pass over it, Katherine Connelly astutely identifies the significance of the WFL to Sylvia's political formation in her childhood. See *Sylvia Pankhurst: Suffragette, Socialist and Scourge of Empire* (London: Pluto Press, 2013), pp. 9–10

184   ESP, *TSM*, p. 95

185   'Women's Franchise League Report of Proceedings at the Inaugural Meeting', cited in Connelly, *Sylvia Pankhurst*, pp. 9–10

186   Ibid., p. 10

187   Ibid.

188   'Programme of the Women's Franchise League International Conference', cited in ibid.

189   Ibid., p. 9

190   ESP, *TSM*, p. 96

191   Ibid., p. 110

192   Ibid., p. 111

193   Helena Stone, 'The Soviet Government and Moonshine, 1917–1929', *Cahiers du Monde Russe et Soviétique*, vol. 27, no. 3/4 (July–December 1986), pp. 359–79 at p. 359. As Stone dryly observes, 'However, as the

workers' militia could not resist the temptation to drink, a special commission put an end to the drunken riots through the generous use of machine guns.' For alcohol and revolution, see also Jonathan Davis, 'A New Socialist Influence: British Labour and Revolutionary Russia, 1917–1918', *Scottish Labour History*, vol. 8 (2013), pp. 158–79

194 ESP, *TSM*, p. 111
195 Ibid., p. 113
196 Ibid., p. 114
197 Ibid.
198 Ibid.
199 Later renamed Daisy Bank Road
200 ESP, *TSM*, p. 114
201 Ibid., p. 115
202 Ibid.
203 ESP, *TSM*, p.122
204 Ibid., p. 122
205 Ibid., p. 123
206 See David Mitchell, *Queen Christabel: A Biography of Christabel Pankhurst* (London: Macdonald & Jane's, 1977), p. 329
207 ESP, *TSM*, p. 142
208 Adela Pankhurst, cited in Coleman, *Adela Pankhurst*, p. 20
209 ESP, *TSM*, p. 21
210 Ibid., p. 126
211 Ibid., p. 128
212 Ibid.
213 Ibid., p. 124
214 Ibid., p. 126
215 Adela Pankhurst, cited in Pugh, *The Pankhursts*, p. 34
216 ESP, *TSM*, p. 4
217 See https://www.saylor.org/site/wp-content/uploads/2011/01/VictorianWeb-Richard-Jeffries.pdf. For a comprehensive bibliography of works by and articles and lectures about Jefferies, see http://www.richardjefferiessociety.org/p/the-life-of-richard-jefferies-with.html
218 John Ruskin, *Traffic* (London: Penguin Classics, 2015)
219 ESP, *TSM*, p. 146

5 THAT SCARLET WOMAN

220 Cited in Romero, *E. Sylvia Pankhurst*, p. 6
221 ESP to Norah Walshe, undated, David Mitchell Collection, Museum of London Library, GB 389 73.83. The letter is addressed from Red Cottage,

so can be dated to the period 1928–9, before the family moved to West Dene, Charteris Road

222 ESP, *TSM*, p. 608

223 David Mitchell, *The Times*, 25 July 1975

224 See Romero, *E. Sylvia Pankhurst*, p. 168

225 *News of the World*, 8 March 1928

226 *Britannia*, 28 April 1916

227 Ethel Smyth cited in Louise Collis, *Impetuous Heart: The Story of Ethel Smyth* (London: William Kimber, 1984), p. 65

228 ESP, *TSM*, p. 595

229 Sylvia's book outline submitted to Sir James Marchant, 25 June 1928, Northwestern University Library, Special Collections, IISH/SPP/ARCH01029/301

230 Ray Strachey, 'The Suffragette Movement', *The Woman's Leader and the Common Cause*, vol. 23, no. 3 (20 February 1931), p. 19

231 Ibid.

232 Ibid.

233 Charlotte Drake, 'Letters to the Editor', *The Woman's Leader and the Common Cause*, vol. 23, no. 6 (13 March 1931), p. 47

234 Emmeline Pankhurst, Preface, in ESP, *The Suffragette* (New York: Sturgis & Walton, 1911), p. i

235 Introduction, in ESP, *The Suffragette*, p. ii

236 Strachey, 'The Suffragette Movement', p. 19

237 *Daily Mirror*, 4 November 1935

238 A borrowing from Sylvia's colleague Olive Schreiner's *Story of an African Farm* (1883) (Oxford: Oxford University Press, 2008), p. 101. 'The year of infancy, where from the shadowy background of forgetfulness start out pictures of startling clearness, disconnected, but brightly coloured, and indelibly printed in the mind. Much that follows fades, but the colours of those baby pictures are permanent.'

239 ESP, *TSM*, p. 3

240 Ibid., p. 101

241 Ibid.

242 Sylvia Pankhurst on Emmeline, BBC Archive, https://www.bbc.co.uk/archive/sylvia-pankhurst-on-emmeline/zjfghbk

243 'The Day of the Child', IISH/SPP/ARCH01029/144

244 Ibid.

245 ESP, 'What I am aiming at: a chance for the children of tomorrow', IISH/SPP/ARCH01029/141

246 Untitled MS planning chapter outline of *TSM*, IISH/SPP/ARCH01029/51

247 ESP, 'The Mother's Month,' IISH/SPP/ARCH01029/51 and 59

248 'The Mother's Month', IISH/SPP/ARCH01029/51 and 59

249 Arthur Henderson, letter to ESP, cited in ESP, *Save the Mothers: A Plea for Measures to Prevent the Annual Loss of about 3,000 Child-Bearing Mothers and 20,000 Infant Lives in England and Wales and a Similar Grievous Wastage in Other Countries* (London: Alfred A. Knopf, 1930), p. 185

6 NOT THINGS SEEN, ALWAYS THE THINGS IMAGINED

250 ESP, *TSM*, p. 105

251 CP, *Unshackled*, pp. 33–4

252 Adela Pankhurst, cited in Harrison, *Sylvia Pankhurst*, p. 30

253 ESP, *TSM*, p. 108

254 General Correspondence, 1898–1959, IISH/SPP/ARCH01029/7–15

255 ESP, *TSM*, p. 105

256 Ibid., p. 155

257 RKPP, *Sylvia Pankhurst: Artist and Crusader*, p. 27

258 ESP, *TSM*, p. 152

259 See https://www.marxists.org/archive/morris/works/1896/second.htm

260 See Anna Vaninskaya, ' "My Mother, Drunk or Sober": G. K. Chesterton and Patriotic Anti-Imperialism', *History of European Ideas*, vol. 34, no. 4 (2008), pp. 535–47

261 RKPP, *Sylvia Pankhurst: Artist and Crusader*, p. 21; and see ESP, 'Sylvia Pankhurst', p. 267

262 Ibid.

263 ESP, *TSM*, p. 156

264 Ibid.

265 Cited in Benn, *Keir Hardie*, p. 481 n. 35

266 See Mary Davis, *Sylvia Pankhurst: A Life in Radical Politics* (London: Pluto Press, 1999), pp. 16–19. This analysis is drawn from and indebted to Davis' work

267 See ibid.

268 ESP, *TSM*, p. 155

269 RKPP, *Sylvia Pankhurst: Artist and Crusader*, p. 28

270 CP, *Unshackled*, p. 40

271 Ibid., p. 41

272 Ibid.

273 ESP, *TSM*, p. 159

274 Ibid.

275 Ibid., p. 161
276 Ibid., p. 160
277 Ibid., p. 162
278 Ibid., p. 163
279 CP, *Unshackled*, p. 42
280 ESP, 'The decisions which have mainly influenced my life were as follows' IISH/SPP/ARCH01029/10 and 365
281 Ibid., p. 41
282 Ibid., p. 42
283 Cited in Davis, *Sylvia Pankhurst*, p. 17
284 Ibid., p. 18

7 PANKHURST HALL

285 'The decisions which have mainly influenced my life were as follows', 10 December 1930, IISH/SPP/ARCH01029/365
286 Kate Connelly, conversation with the author, 'Thinkers for our Time: Sylvia Pankhurst', British Academy, 5 December 2017
287 RKPP, *Sylvia Pankhurst: Artist and Crusader*, p. 40 Shelley's lines are from *The Revolt of Islam* (1818), Canto 8, verse 27, lines 3434–5
288 See Harrison, *Sylvia Pankhurst*, p. 40
289 Connelly, *Sylvia Pankhurst*, p. 18
290 ESP, *TSM*, p. 164
291 See Harrison, *Sylvia Pankhurst*, p. 41
292 Emmeline Pankhurst, *My Own Story*, p. 36
293 ESP, *TSM*, p. 169
294 Cited in Fran Abrams, 'Women's Suffrage: Unfailing Support', in Bryan (ed.), *What Would Keir Hardie Say?*, pp. 87–96 at p. 92
295 William Knox, 'Trade Unionism: Independent Labour Representation', in Bryan (ed.), *What Would Keir Hardie Say?*, pp. 61–72 at p. 64
296 See ibid., p. 65
297 Cited in Melissa Benn, 'An Agitator: The Enduring Principle of Agitation', in Bryan (ed.), *What Would Keir Hardie Say?*, pp. 149–56 at p. 152
298 Cited in ibid., p. 154
299 Ibid., pp. 149–50
300 ESP, *TSM*, p. 170
301 Ibid., p. 172
302 Ibid.
303 Keir Hardie, 'Sunshine of Socialism' speech, 11 April 1914, Bradford. See full speech at https://labourlist.org/2014/04/keir-hardies-sunshine-of-socialism-speech-full-text/

304 ESP, *TSM*, p. 171
305 Barbara Winslow, *Sylvia Pankhurst: Sexual Politics & Political Activism* (London: Routledge, 1996), p. 4
306 Benn, *Keir Hardie*, p. 4
307 Bob Holman, 'Christianity: Christian & Socialist', in Bryan (ed.), *What Would Keir Hardie Say?*, pp. 37–47 at p. 37
308 John Callow, 'West Ham: A Splotch of Red', in Bryan (ed.), *What Would Keir Hardie Say?*, pp. 111–22 at p. 112
309 Ibid.
310 Alan Haworth and Diane Hayter (eds), *Men Who Made Labour: The PLP of 1906 – the Personalities and the Politics* (London: Routledge, 2006), p. 229
311 Cited in Benn, *Keir Hardie*, p. 55
312 ESP, *TSM*, p. 173
313 See Benn, *Keir Hardie*, pp. 176–7, and ESP, *TSM*, pp. 173–4
314 Benn, *Keir Hardie*, p. 185
315 Ibid., p. 177
316 Ibid., p. 185
317 ESP, *TSM*, p. 174
318 ESP, 'Noah', autograph draft of a play written on prison toilet paper, British Library, Archives and Manuscripts, Add MS 88925/1/2: 1920–1
319 Benn, *Keir Hardie*, p. 232
320 ESP, *TSM*, p.306
321 ESP, *TSM*, p. 174
322 ESP, 'The Inheritance'
323 Ibid., passim
324 Benn, *Keir Hardie*, p. 109
325 Purvis, *Emmeline Pankhurst*, p. 160
326 Purvis provides a comprehensive bibliographic survey of writing about Emmeline Pankhurst and Ethel Smyth's relationship at ibid., p. 394 n. 34
327 Ibid.
328 Ibid., p. 160
329 ESP, *TSM*, p. 377
330 Ibid.
331 Winslow, *Sylvia Pankhurst*, p. 7
332 Ethel Smyth, cited in ibid., p. 8
333 ESP, *TSM*, p. 174

8 QUEER HARDIE

334 ESP, *TSM*, p. 177

335 ESP, *A Suffragette in America: Reflections on Prisoners, Pickets and Political Change*, ed. and with an introduction by Katherine Connelly (London: Pluto Press, 2019), p. 14

336 ESP, *TSM*, p. 175

337 ESP, 'Sylvia Pankhurst', p. 270

338 ESP, *TSM*, p. 131

339 Ibid., p. 174

340 ESP, 'Noah', autograph draft of a play written on prison toilet paper, British Library, Archives and Manuscripts, Add MS 88925/ 1/ 2: 1920– 1

341 ESP, *TSM*, p. 178

342 Ibid.

343 Ibid.

344 Ibid.

345 Ibid.

346 Ibid., p. 180

347 See Cathy Hunt, 'Ellen and Sylvia: Chelsea, 1906', 12 February 2018, https://cathyhunthistorian.com/2018/02/12/ellen-and-sylvia-chelsea-1906/

348 See Richard Pankhurst, *Sylvia Pankhurst: Artist and Crusader*, p. 187

349 RKPP, *Sylvia Pankhurst: Artist and Crusader*, p. 54

350 ESP, 'Sylvia Pankhurst', p. 280

351 ESP, *TSM*, p. 190

352 Ibid., p. 193

353 ESP, *The Suffragette*, p. 47

354 ESP, 'Sylvia Pankhurst', p. 280

355 ESP, *TSM*, p. 194

356 Ibid., p. 166

357 Ibid., p. 218

9 THE LABOUR PARTY – OUR PARTY ... A REALITY AT LAST!

358 CP, *Unshackled*, pp. 62–3

359 Emmeline Pethick-Lawrence, *My Part in a Changing World* (London: Gollancz, 1938), pp. 142–3

360 ESP, *TSM*, p. 197

361 Pethick-Lawrence, *My Part in a Changing World*, p. 143

362 Ibid., p. 24

363 Roy Judge, 'Mary Neal and the Espérance Morris', *Folk Music Journal*, vol. 5, no. 5 (1989), pp. 545–91 at p. 547, http://www.maryneal.org/file-uploads/files/file/1989s1a.pdf

364 Pethick-Lawrence, *My Part in a Changing World*, p. 123

365 Ibid., p. 124
366 Correspondence between Frederick and Emmeline Pethick-Lawrence, Frederick Pethick-Lawrence MSS, Trinity College Library, Cambridge University
367 Pethick-Lawrence, *My Part in a Changing World*, p. 145
368 Ibid.
369 Ibid., pp. 145–6
370 Ibid., p. 146
371 ESP, *TSM*, p. 177
372 Ibid.
373 Annie Kenney, *Memories of a Militant* (London: Edward Arnold, 1924), p. 59
374 Hughes, *Keir Hardie*, p. 134
375 ESP, *TSM*, p. 197
376 Ibid.
377 Ibid.
378 Pethick-Lawrence, *My Part in a Changing World*, p. 147
379 Ibid.
380 Ibid., p. 148
381 Ibid.
382 Annie Kenney, cited in Harrison, *Sylvia Pankhurst*, p. 66
383 Pethick-Lawrence, *My Part in a Changing World*, p. 149
384 See Harrison, *Sylvia Pankhurst*, p. 62
385 Emmeline Pankhurst, *My Own Story*, p. 49
386 ESP, *TSM*, p. 199
387 Ibid., p. 200
388 ESP, *TSM*, p.210
389 See Harrison, *Sylvia Pankhurst*, p. 3
390 ESP, *TSM*, p. 211
391 ESP, *The Suffragette*, pp. 77–8
392 Ibid., p. 79
393 Ibid., p. 80
394 Pethick-Lawrence, *My Part in a Changing World*, p. 148
395 ESP, *TSM*, pp. 215–16
396 Ibid., p. 221
397 Pethick-Lawrence, *My Part in a Changing World*, p. 165
     Ibid.
398 Ibid.
399 ESP, *TSM*, p. 216
400 E. M. Forster, *Howards End* (London: Penguin Classics, 2012), p. 141

401 Ibid., p. 134
402 ESP, *TSM*, p. 217
403 RKPP, *Sylvia Pankhurst: Artist and Crusader*, p. 61
404 Ibid.
405 ESP, *TSM*, p. 218
406 Ibid., p. 219
407 Ibid., p. 192
408 Ibid., p. 320
409 Ibid., p. 218

                         IO STRANGE TANGLE

410 ESP, *The Suffragette*, p. 109
411 Ibid., p. 112
412 Cited in RKPP, *Sylvia Pankhurst: Artist and Crusader*, p. 69
413 Ibid.
414 ESP, *TSM*, p. 140
415 Cited in Winslow, *Sylvia Pankhurst*, p. 13
416 Cited in Romero, *E. Sylvia Pankhurst*, p. 49
417 ESP, *TSM*, p. 140
418 Ibid., p. 255
419 Ibid.
420 Ibid., p. 246
421 Ibid., p. 248
422 Ibid.
423 Ibid., p. 249
424 Ibid.
425 Ibid., p. 248
426 Ibid., p. 249
427 Ibid.
428 Ibid., p. 257
429 Benn, *Keir Hardie*, p. 166
430 Ibid., p. 230
431 Pethick-Lawrence, *My Part in a Changing World*, p. 149
432 Kenneth Morgan, cited in Benn, *Keir Hardie*, p. 179
433 ESP, *TSM*, p. 62; and RKPP, *Sylvia Pankhurst: Artist and Crusader*, p. 76
434 ESP, 'Pit brow women', *Votes for Women*, 11 August 1911. See Kathryn
     Dodd (ed.), *A Sylvia Pankhurst Reader* (Manchester: Manchester
     University Press, 1993), pp. 37, 40
435 ESP, *TSM*, p. 262

436 Ibid., p. 270
437 ESP, 'Sylvia Pankhurst', p. 290
438 Ibid.
439 Ibid., p. 291
440 ESP, 'How Potatoes Are Gathered', *Manchester Guardian*, republished in *Berwickshire News & General Advertiser*, 14 January 1908
441 ESP, *TSM*, p. 272
442 Ibid.
443 Keir Hardie to ESP, General Correspondence 1898–1959, IISH/SPP/ARCH01029/7–15
444 Ibid.
445 ESP, *TSM*, p. 272
446 Benn, *Keir Hardie*, p. 237
447 Ibid., p. 56
448 ESP, 'I always loathed Mrs Grundy', n.d., IISH/SPP/ARCH01029/158
449 Ibid., p. 272
450 ESP, 'A dream of the devil's tempting', unpublished MS, IISH/SPP/ARCH01029/171
451 Ibid.
452 ESP, 'Noah Adamson', unpublished MS, IISH/SPP/ARCH01029/170
453 Ibid.
454 ESP, *TSM*, p.273

11 THE ART OF STRUGGLE

455 H. G. Wells, *Ann Veronica* (London: Virago, 1980), p. 194
456 Ibid.
457 Cited in Diane Atkinson, *Rise Up Women! The Remarkable Lives of the Suffragettes* (London: Bloomsbury, 2018), p. 88
458 Wells, *Ann Veronica*, p. 192
459 Atkinson, *Rise Up Women!*, p. 93
460 Cited in ESP, *TSM*, p. 325
461 ESP, *The Suffragette*, p. 242
462 Ibid., pp. 242–3
463 Ibid., p. 244
464 Ibid., p. 245
465 ESP, *TSM*, p. 284
466 Ibid.
467 Ibid., p. 285
468 Ibid.
469 ESP, *TSM*, p.286

470 Ibid., p. 294

471 Joyce Marlow (ed.), *Suffragettes: The Fight for Votes for Women* (London: Virago, 2000), pp. 74–5

472 ESP, *TSM*, p. 297

473 King's Private Secretary to Asquith, 3 December 1908, Royal Archives, Windsor Castle, cited in Harrison, *Sylvia Pankhurst*, p. 101

474 Asquith to King's Private Secretary, 7 December 1908, cited in ibid.

475 See Robert Wainwright, *Miss Muriel Matters: The Fearless Suffragist Who Fought for Equality* (London: Allen & Unwin, 2017), ch. 18

476 RKPP, *Sylvia Pankhurst: Artist and Crusader*, p. 115

477 ESP, *TSM*, p. 305

478 Ibid.

479 RKPP, *Sylvia Pankhurst: Artist and Crusader*, p. 123

480 ESP, *TSM*, p. 4

481 Benn, *Keir Hardie*, p. 194

482 See Purvis, *Emmeline Pankhurst*, p. 126

483 Cited in ibid., p. 136

484 Ibid.

485 Ibid.

486 'Charge of Wilful Damage', *Morning Post*, 30 June 1909, cited in Marlow (ed.), *Suffragettes*, p. 92

487 King's Private Secretary to Herbert Gladstone, July 1909, Royal Archives, Windsor Castle, cited in Harrison, *Sylvia Pankhurst*, p. 104

488 Ibid., p. 106

489 Hansard, House of Commons, 27 September 1909, vol. 11, col. 924, https://hansard.parliament.uk/commons/1909-09-27/debates/189fb749-320f-4229-908b-54f1a583619f/CommonsChamber

490 Charles Masterman replying for the Home Secretary, ibid.

491 Cited in Harrison, *Sylvia Pankhurst*, p. 108

492 ESP, *TSM*, p. 320

493 See Purvis, *Emmeline Pankhurst*, p. 137

494 ESP, *TSM*, p. 321

495 *Woman's Journal* (Boston), 30 October 1909, cited in Purvis, *Emmeline Pankhurst*, p. 138

496 ESP, *TSM*, p. 321

497 Ibid., p. 323

498 Ibid.

499 Ibid.

500 Ibid., p. 324

501 Ibid.

502 Ibid., p. 323
503 Ibid.
504 ESP, 'Harry Pankhurst', *Votes for Women*, 14 January 1910
505 See Purvis, *Emmeline Pankhurst*, p. 142

12 INSURGENCE OF WOMEN

506 Cited by John Simkin in https://spartacus-educational.com/Jbrailsford. htm
507 Millicent Garrett Fawcett, *Women's Suffrage: A Short History of a Great Movement* (London: T. C. and E. C. Jack, 1912), p. 88
508 ESP, *TSM*, p. 337
509 Ibid., p. 335
510 Ibid.
511 Ibid.
512 Ibid., p. 336
513 Ibid., p. 337
514 ESP, *The Suffragette*, Preface
515 ESP, *TSM*, p. 342
516 Ibid.
517 Conciliation Committee for Woman Suffrage, *The Treatment of the Women's Deputations of November 18th, 22nd and 23rd, 1910 by the Police* (London: Women's Press, 1911)
518 Ibid.
519 Paul Foot, *The Vote: How It was Won and How It was Undermined* (London: Viking, 2005), p. 211
520 Hansard, House of Commons, 1 March 1911, vol. 22, cols 367–8, retrieved from https://api.parliament.uk/historic-hansard/commons/1911/mar/01/ metropolitan-police-and-suffragettes
521 Purvis, *Emmeline Pankhurst*, p. 26
522 See Rachel Holmes, *Eleanor Marx: A Life* (London: Bloomsbury, 2014), pp. 298–300
523 ESP, *Emmeline Pankhurst*, p. 98
524 ESP to Keir Hardie, n.d., 1911, General Correspondence, 1898–1959, IISH/SPP/ARCH01029/7–15
525 ESP, *TSM*, p. 346
526 Ibid.
527 ESP to Keir Hardie, n.d., 1911, General Correspondence, 1898–1959, IISH/SPP/ARCH01029/7–15
528 ESP, *TSM*, p. 352

529 Elizabeth Wolstenholme Elmy to ESP, 13 July 1910, General Correspondence, 1898–1959, IISH/SPP/ARCH01029/7–15
530 ESP, *The Suffragette*, Preface
531 Ibid.
532 Ibid.
533 ESP, *TSM*, p. 353
534 Ibid.
535 Ibid., p. 354
536 This section is drawn from the groundbreaking work by Lucy Neal, who recovered her great-great-aunt's archive and restored this hidden history. See Neal, 'Poverty knock', on the secret history of morris dancing, https://www.theguardian.com/stage/2009/feb/07/morris-dancing-lucy-neal-victorian
537 Ibid.; Records of the English Folk and Dance Society, Cecil Sharp House, Vaughan Williams Memorial Library. This EFDS collection and the hidden feminist history it recovers exist thanks to the dedicated tenacity of Lucy Neal.
538 Neal, 'Poverty knock'
539 Ada Walshe, cited in Harrison, *Sylvia Pankhurst*, p. 124. This is from the Walshe letters in the Mitchell Papers, Museum of London
540 Christabel Pankhurst, *Votes for Women*, 10 November 1911, cited in Purvis, *Christabel*, p. 256
541 ESP, *TSM*, p. 373
542 Ibid.
543 Purvis, *Emmeline Pankhurst*, p. 174
544 Ibid.
545 Ibid.
546 ESP, *TSM*, p. 354
547 RKPP, *Sylvia Pankhurst: Artist and Crusader*, p. 140
548 Ibid.
549 See Winslow, *Sylvia Pankhurst*, pp. 56–7
550 ESP, *TSM*, p. 376
551 ESP, *Emmeline Pankhurst*, p. 103
552 Cited in Purvis, *Emmeline Pankhurst*, p. 178
553 Smyth, *Female Pipings in Eden*, pp. 208–9
554 *Votes for Women*, 8 March 1912
555 Cited in Purvis, *Emmeline Pankhurst*, p. 94
556 Ibid., p. 279
557 See ibid., p. 180
558 Ibid.

559 Emmeline Pankhurst, 'The argument of the broken pane', *Votes for Women*, 23 February 1912

560 David Mitchell, 'The Pankhursts in Paris', typed MS in the Mitchell Papers

561 Kenney, *Memories of a Militant*, p. 176

562 George Dangerfield, *The Strange Death of Liberal England* (Stanford: Stanford University Press, 1997), p. 151

563 Cited in Mitchell, 'The Pankhursts in Paris'

564 Romero, *E. Sylvia Pankhurst*, p. 59

565 ESP, *Emmeline Pankhurst*, p. 106

566 Ibid.

567 ESP, *TSM*, p. 376

568 Ethel Smyth to Emmeline Pankhurst, 15 January 1914, cited in Purvis, *Emmeline Pankhurst*, p. 247

569 ESP, *TSM*, p. 316

570 Ibid.

571 For the concept of romantic feminism, see S. S. Holton, ' "In Sorrowful Wrath": Suffrage Militancy and the Romantic Feminism of Emmeline Pankhurst', in H. L. Smith (ed.), *British Feminism in the Twentieth Century* (Aldershot: Edward Elgar, 1990), pp. 7–24

572 ESP, *TSM*, p. 316

573 Ibid.

574 Ibid.

575 Ibid.

576 Christabel Pankhurst letter to Henry Harben, 1912, cited in David Mitchell, *The Fighting Pankhursts* (London: Jonathan Cape, 1967), p. 35

13 O YOU DAUGHTERS OF THE WEST!

577 ESP, *Emmeline Pankhurst*, p. 98

578 Holmes, *Eleanor Marx*, p. 271

579 ESP, *TSM*, p. 346

580 See Purvis, *Emmeline Pankhurst*, p. 137

581 ESP, *TSM*, p. 105

582 Ibid., pp. 105–6

583 Harriot Stanton Blatch with Alma Lutz, *Challenging Years: The Memoirs of Harriot Stanton Blatch* (New York: G. P. Putman's Sons, 1940), p. 92

584 See ESP, *A Suffragette in America*, p. 12

585 Ibid., p. 29

586 ESP, *TSM*, p. 347

587 ESP, *A Suffragette in America*, p. 65

588 Cited in Katherine Connelly, ' "Miss Pankhurst Has Some Jolts in Store": Sylvia Pankhurst's Tours of North America and their Place in

Suffrage History', paper at Women's Suffrage and Political Activism conference, Murray Edwards College, Cambridge, 3 February 2018, p. 4. I'm grateful to Dr Connelly for generously permitting me to reference work unpublished at the time of writing

589 Cited in Winslow, *Sylvia Pankhurst*, p. 21

590 Cited in ibid., pp. 20–1

591 *New York Times*, 7 January 1911

592 See ESP, *A Suffragette in America*, pp. 18–19

593 ESP, *TSM*, p. 347

594 Benn, *Keir Hardie*, p. 130

595 Sheila Rowbotham, *Dreamers of a New Day: Women Who Invented the Twentieth Century* (London: Verso, 2010), p. 31

596 Connelly, ' "Miss Pankhurst Has Some Jolts in Store" ', p. 4

597 See ESP, *A Suffragette in America*, pp. 38–9

598 Connelly, ' "Miss Pankhurst Has Some Jolts in Store" ', p. 4

599 Ibid.

600 See ESP, *A Suffragette in America*, pp. 18–19; ESP, *TSM*, p. 347

601 See ESP, *A Suffragette in America*, p. 29

602 See ibid.

603 See ibid., p. 18

604 See Holmes, *Eleanor Marx*, p. 285

605 See ibid., p. 279

606 See ibid., p. 281

607 Cited in Katherine Connelly, 'Sylvia Pankhurst, the Suffragettes of East London and the Garment Workers of Chicago', in *Chicago History: The Journal of the Chicago History Museum* (forthcoming)

608 Cited in ESP, *A Suffragette in America*, p. 14

609 Cited in ibid.

610 *Votes for Women*, 21 April 1911, p. 472

611 Ibid.

612 Cited in ESP, *A Suffragette in America*, pp. 22–3

613 Cited in ibid., p. 19

614 ESP, *TSM*, p. 347

615 Cited in ESP, *A Suffragette in America*, p. 24

616 Cited in ibid.

617 Cited in ibid., p. 23

618 Cited in ibid.

619 Rowbotham, *Dreamers of a New Day*, p. 8

620 ESP, *TSM*, p. 417

621 Rowbotham, *Dreamers of a New Day*, p. 7

622 Cited in ESP, *A Suffragette in America*, p. 23

623 Cited in ibid., p. 95

624 Ibid., p. 23

625 For a fuller account of the strike and its context, see Connelly's Introduction in ibid., p. 41

626 Ibid., p. 43

627 Ibid.

628 *Chicago Tribune*, 4 April 1912

629 Connelly, ' "Miss Pankhurst Has Some Jolts in Store" ', p. 6

630 ESP, *A Suffragette in America*, p. 43

631 *Survey*, vol. 25 (4 March 1911), pp. 942–8

632 See, for example, ESP, *TSM*, p. 489

633 Patricia Greenwood Harrison, *Connecting Links: The British & American Women's Suffrage Movements, 1900–1914* (Westport, Conn.: Praeger, 2000), p. 178

634 See Jill Roe, *Her Brilliant Career: The Life of Stella Miles Franklin* (Cambridge, Mass.: Belknap Press, 2009), p. 14)

635 ESP, *TSM*, p. 349

14 BRIDGE, BALLS, DINNERS

636 ESP, *A Suffragette in America*, p. 14

637 Ibid., p. 148

638 Ibid., p. 149

639 ESP to Keir Hardie, undated, [March 1911], IISH/SPP/ARCH01029/9

640 ESP, *A Suffragette in America*, p. 138

641 ESP to Keir Hardie, undated, [March 1911], IISH/SPP/ARCH01029/9

642 Ibid.

643 ESP, *Suffragette in America*, p. 139

644 Ibid., pp. 139–40

645 Ibid., p. 140

646 Ibid.

647 Ibid., p. 141

648 Ibid.

649 Ibid., p. 142

650 Ibid.

651 ESP, *TSM*, p. 349

652 ESP, *A Suffragette in America*, p. 43

653 *Votes for Women*, 21 April 1911

654 Ibid.

655 Rowbotham, *Dreamers of a New Day*, p. 182

656 ESP, *A Suffragette in America*, p. 66
657 Ibid., p. 4
658 ESP, *TSM*, p. 349
659 ESP, *A Suffragette in America*, p. 1
660 Ibid., p. 75
661 Ibid.
662 Rowbotham, *Dreamers of a New Day*, p. 185
663 Marjorie Murphy, 'Jim Larkin, James Connolly, and the Dublin Lockout of 1913: The Transnational Path of Global Syndicalism', in Peter Cole, David Struthers and Kenyon Zimmer (eds), *Wobblies of the World: A Global History of the IWW* (London: Pluto Press, 2017), pp. 239–53 at p. 243
664 Cole, Struthers and Zimmer (eds), *Wobblies of the World*, Introduction, p. 6
665 Saku Pinta, 'The Wobblies of the North Woods: Finnish Labor Radicalism and the IWW in Northern Ontario', in ibid., pp. 140–55 at p. 146
666 Cole, Struthers and Zimmer (eds), *Wobblies of the World*, Introduction, p. 6
667 Ibid.
668 See Winslow, *Sylvia Pankhurst*, p. 20
669 ESP, *Soviet Russia As I Saw It* (London: Workers' Dreadnought, 1921), pp. 51–2
670 ESP to Keir Hardie, undated, [January 1912], General Correspondence, 1898–1959, IISH/SPP/ARCH01029/7–15(9)
671 Ibid.
672 Ibid.
673 Ibid.
674 Ibid.
675 Ibid.
676 Ibid.
677 Ibid.
678 Ibid.
679 Ibid.
680 ESP, *TSM*, p. 349
681 ESP to Keir Hardie, 22 January 1912, IISH/SPP/ARCH01029/7-15(9)
682 ESP, *A Suffragette in America*, p. 87
683 Ibid., p. 85
684 Ibid., p. 91
685 Ibid., p. 92
686 ESP to Keir Hardie, undated, [January 1912], IISH/SPP/ARCH01029/7–15(9)
687 Ibid.

688 ESP to Keir Hardie, undated [late January 1912], IISH/SPP/ARCH01029/
7–15(9)

15 AMERICAN LETTERS

689 Rowbotham, *Dreamers of a New Day*, p. 6
690 For this material on socialist Milwaukee, see John Gurda, 'Socialism before it was a four-letter word', *Journal Sentinel*, 3 April 2010, http://archive.jsonline.com/news/opinion/89804422.html
691 ESP to Keir Hardie, 5 February 1912, IISH/SPP/ARCH01029/7–15(9)
692 ESP, *A Suffragette in America*, p.78
693 ESP, *A Suffragette in America*, p. 117
694 Ibid., pp. 113, 117
695 ESP to Keir Hardie, 5 February 1912, IISH/SPP/ARCH01029/7–15(9)
696 Ibid.
697 Ibid.
698 See Gurda, 'Socialism before it was a four-letter word'
699 ESP, 'A Socialist Administration – The Milwaukee City Council', in ESP, *A Suffragette in America*, p. 109
700 ESP to Keir Hardie, undated [late January 1912], IISH/SPP/ARCH01029/
7–15(9)
701 ESP, *A Suffragette in America*, p. 155
702 Ibid., p. 157
703 Ibid., p. 158
704 Ibid.
705 Ibid., p. 159
706 Ibid., pp. 159–60
707 See Nadine George Graves, ' "Just Like Being in a Zoo": Primitivity and Ragtime Dance', in Julie Malnig (ed.), *Ballroom, Boogie, Shimmy Sham, Shake: A Social and Popular Dance Reader* (Champaign–Urbana: University of Illinois Press, 2009), pp. 59–61, for a discussion of the Grizzly Bear. I am grateful to Dr Katherine Connelly and Dr Dana Mills for their assistance in identifying the Grizzly Bear as the dance that Sylvia witnessed
708 See https://www.history.com/news/banned-animal-dance-turkey-trot-woodrow-wilson
709 ESP, *A Suffragette in America*, p. 153
710 ESP, *TSM*, p. 348
711 Cited in ESP, *A Suffragette in America*, p. 154
712 ESP, in ibid., p. 161

713 Ibid. The wording is Sylvia's. The more usual biblical translations are 'the wings of a dove' and 'wings like a dove'.
714 Ibid.
715 Ibid., p. 162
716 ESP, *A Suffragette in America*, p. 165
717 Ibid.
718 Cited in ibid., p. 94
719 ESP, *TSM*, p. 382
720 Ibid.
721 ESP, *A Suffragette in America*, p. 32
722 Cited in Connelly, 'Sylvia Pankhurst, the Suffragettes of East London and the Garment Workers of Chicago'
723 Rowbotham, *Dreamers of a New Day*, p. 182
724 ESP, *TSM*, p. 348
725 Ibid., p. 350
726 ESP, *A Suffragette in America*, p. 8
727 Hardie to Pankhurst, 27 May 1915, IISH/SPP/ARCH01029/7–15(9)
728 ESP, *THF*, p. 226
729 Dr Kate Connelly's groundbreaking work *A Suffragette in America*, published by Pluto Press in 2019, achieved the first publication of Sylvia's American manuscripts and is a landmark in feminist scholarship. Connelly faithfully organized and annotated the labyrinthine papers, the bulk of which are written longhand in pencil, into the shape of the book that Sylvia had planned. Connelly also meticulously reconstructs the first accurate timelines of both Sylvia's 1911 and 1912 tours
730 ESP, *A Suffragette in America*, p. 11
731 Ibid., p. 10
732 Ibid.
733 Rowbotham, *Dreamers of a New Day*, p. 30
734 Ibid.
735 Ibid., p. 118
736 Harrison, *Sylvia Pankhurst*, p. 115
737 Keir Hardie to ESP, 11 March 1911, IISH/SPP/ARCH01029/7–15(9)
738 See Benn, *Keir Hardie*, p. 289
739 ESP to Keir Hardie, 22 January 1911, IISH/SPP/ARCH01029/7–15(9)
740 Ibid.
741 Ibid.
742 ESP to Keir Hardie, 26 February [1911], IISH/SPP/ARCH01029/7–15(9)
743 Ibid.
744 Ibid.

745 Keir Hardie to ESP, 10 March 1911, IISH/SPP/ARCH01029/7–15(9)
746 ESP to Keir Hardie, 22 January 1912, IISH/SPP/ARCH01029/7–15(9)
747 Ibid.
748 ESP to Keir Hardie, undated, [March 1911], IISH/SPP/ARCH01029/
     7–15(9)
749 Ibid.
750 ESP, *TSM*, p. 383

16 SEX WAR

751 Marlow (ed.), *Suffragettes*, pp. x–xi
752 ESP, *TSM*, p. 383
753 Ibid., p. 384
754 Ibid.
755 Ibid.
756 Ibid.
757 Mitchell, *The Fighting Pankhursts*, p. 33
758 Kenney, *Memories of a Militant*, pp. 73–9
759 ESP, *TSM*, p. 385
760 Ibid., p. 388
761 Ibid., p. 395
762 ESP, *TSM*, p. 396
763 A fact pointed out to me by Peter James
764 ESP, *TSM*, p. 396
765 Ibid.
766 Cited in Purvis, *Emmeline Pankhurst*, p. 197
767 ESP, *TSM*, p. 413
768 Ibid., p. 402
769 Ibid., p. 400
770 Ibid., p. 402
771 Ibid., p. 522
772 Ibid., p. 523
773 ESP, 'Now That I am Nearly Fifty', *The Times*, 14 September 1930
774 Ethel Smyth to EP, 9 December 1913, Smyth Letters, cited in Purvis,
     Emmeline Pankhurst, p. 239
775 ESP, *TSM*, p. 523
776 Ibid.
777 Walter Benjamin, *The Arcades Project*, ed. Rolf Tiedemann, trans. Howard
     Eiland and Kevin McLaughlin (New York: Belknap Press, 2002), p. 243

17 NOT AS SUFFRAGETTES, BUT AS SISTERS

778 Cited in Connelly, 'Sylvia Pankhurst, the Suffragettes of East London and the Garment Workers of Chicago'

779 ESP, *THF*, p. 44

780 The contemporary value of this figure can only ever be very approximate as there are so many variables. The latest Bank of England calculation (2019) for £20,000 in 1911 is £2.3 million (https://www.bankofengland.co.uk/monetary-policy/inflation/inflation-calculator)

781 Nellie Cressall to David Mitchell, 5 April 1965, David Mitchell Collection, Museum of London Library, GB 389 73.83

782 Ibid.

783 Harrison, *Sylvia Pankhurst*, p. 131

784 Benn, *Keir Hardie*, p. 300

785 See ibid., p. 268

786 Ibid., p. 166

787 Ibid. p. 268

788 Ibid., p. 304

789 Winslow, *Sylvia Pankhurst*, p. 28

790 Ibid., p. 29

791 Ibid., p. 32

792 Later Adelaide Knight became one of the founder members of the Communist Party of Great Britain, with her friend Dora Montefiore

793 IISH/SPP/ARCH01029/231

794 ESP to Mr Lapworth, 19 November 1913, IISH/SPP/ARCH01029/191

795 See ESP, *A Suffragette in America*, pp. 41–2

796 Annie Barnes, *Tough Annie: From Suffragette to Stepney Councillor: Annie Barnes in Conversation with Kate Harding and Caroline Gibbs* (London: Stepney Books, 1980), p.14

797 Annie Barnes recalled this as leafleting London Bridge, but the spiral staircases and galleries suggest the structure of Tower Bridge

798 Cited in ESP, *A Suffragette in America*, p. 31.

799 ESP, *TSM*, p. 469

800 June Purvis, 'The Prison Experiences of the Suffragettes in Edwardian Britain', *Women's History Review*, vol. 4, no. 1 (1995), pp. 103–33 at p. 108

801 ESP, *The Life of Emmeline Pankhurst*, p. 134

802 *Toronto Star Weekly*, 16 October 1926

803 ESP, *TSM*, p. 486

804 Ibid., p. 487

805 Cited in Harrison, *Sylvia Pankhurst*, p. 150

806 Benn, *Keir Hardie*, p. 310

807 ESP, *TSM*, p. 494

808 *Fyens Stiftstidende*, 3 September 1913

809 *Aftenposten*, 8 September 1913

810 *Social-Demokraten*, 27 September 1913

811 *Social-Demokraten*, 4 September 1913

812 Trondhjems Adresseavis, 29 September 1913

813 John Chaplin, correspondence with Helen Pankhurst and the author, 2 February 2020. See https://angloswedish.wordpress.com

814 Ibid.

815 Helen Pankhurst, conversation with the author, 31 January 2020

816 Ibid.

817 *Kvinden og Samfundet*, no. 17 (1913)

818 Cited in Harrison, *Sylvia Pankhurst*, pp.151–2

819 Cited in Purvis, *Christabel Pankhurst*, p. 345

820 ESP, *TSM*, p. 516

821 Ibid.

822 Ibid., p. 517

823 Ibid.

824 Ibid., p. 518

825 CP, *Unshackled*, pp. 66–7

826 Ibid., p. 67

827 ESP, *TSM*, p. 518

828 Cited in Harrison, *Sylvia Pankhurst*, p. 156

829 Ibid.

830 Cited in Coleman, *Adela Pankhurst*, p. 55

831 ESP, *TSM*, p. 530

832 Ibid., pp. 532–3

833 ESP, *TSM*, p.542

834 ESP, *TSM*, pp.539–40

835 ESP, *TSM*, p. 540

836 Benn, *Keir Hardie*, p. 320

18 CAT AND MOUSE

837 ESP, *TSM*, p. 101

838 Ibid., p. 505

839 Ibid., p. 453

840 Ibid., p. 568

841 Ibid.
842 Ibid.
843 The assertion that Sylvia's zealotry was a form of self-aggrandizement found its way into much later conservative feminist histories. As history turned right in the 1980s and 1990s, even feminist biographers claimed that her excessive and sustained protest was driven by a hysterical determination to outdo all others in extremism in order to get her mother's attention and approval rather than by a resolute ethical and well-organized struggle for women's rights and the implementation of laws to support them
844 ESP, *TSM*, p. 442
845 ESP, *Daily Herald*, Wednesday 26 March 1913
846 ESP, *TSM*, p. 443
847 Ibid., pp. 443–4
848 Ibid., p. 444
849 Ibid., p. 442
850 Ibid., p. 445
851 Ibid.
852 Ibid.
853 Ibid., p. 444
854 Ibid.
855 Ibid., p. 447
856 Ibid., p. 448
857 Ibid.
858 Ibid.
859 Ibid., p. 449
860 Dr Maurice Craig, 'Report re Miss Sylvia Pankhurst', 18 March 1913, TNA HO/144/1558/234191
861 ESP, *TSM*, p. 451
862 Ibid., p. 449
863 Ibid.
864 Ibid., p. 450
865 Purvis, *Emmeline Pankhurst*, p. 228
866 Ibid., p. 235
867 ESP, *TSM*, p. 451
868 *Daily Mail, Standard, Morning Post, Daily Herald*, all 26 March 1913; *The Suffragette*, 28 March 1913
869 ESP, *TSM*, p. 454
870 Ibid., p. 452
871 ESP, 'A Suffragette Year', IISH/SPP/ARCH01029/133

872 ESP, *TSM*, p. 451

873 Cited in Harrison, *Sylvia Pankhurst*, p. 145

874 Ibid.

875 Midge Mackenzie, 'Introduction', in Lady Constance Lytton/Jane Warton, *Prisons and Prisoners: Some Personal Experiences* (London: Virago, 1988), p. xi

876 Lytton, *Prisons and Prisoners*, p. xiv

877 Judy Cox, *The Women's Revolution: Russia 1905–1917* (London: Counterfire, 2017), p. 24

878 Lytton, *Prisons and Prisoners*, pp. xiii–iv

879 ESP, *TSM*, p. 445

880 TNA HO/144/1558/234191/Part 1: 18.02.1913

881 Ibid.

882 TNA HO/144/1558/234191/28.2.1913

883 For just three of many examples, see TNA HO/144/1558/234191/ 20.02.1913, TNA HO/144/1558/10.03.1913 and TNA HO/144/1558/ 14.03.1913

884 TNA HO/144/1558/234191/21.10.1913

885 George Lansbury to His Majesty King George, 11 June 1914, TNA HO/ 144/1264/237165

886 Ibid.

887 Stamfordham to McKenna, 11 June 1914, TNA HO/144/1264/237169

888 McKenna to Stamfordham, 12 June 1914, TNA HO/144/1264/237169

19 SYLVIA'S ARMY

889 *The Suffragette*, 31 October 1913

890 *The Suffragette*, 11 November 1913

891 ESP, *TSM*, p. 505

892 Ibid.

893 Ibid.

894 Cited in Winslow, *Sylvia Pankhurst*, p. 55

895 Cited in ibid., p. 57

896 See ibid., p. 55

897 *The Times*, London, 20 August 1913

898 Camila Ruz and Justin Parkinson, ' "Suffragitsu" – How the suffragettes fought back using martial arts', *BBC News Magazine*, https://www.bbc. co.uk/news/magazine-34425615

899 Cited in Winslow, *Sylvia Pankhurst*, p. 54

900 Ibid., p. 56

901 Cited in ibid.

902 This account is based on ibid., pp. 56–9
903 Cited in ibid., p. 57
904 See https://www.wcml.org.uk/our-collections/activists/francis-fletcher-vane/
905 *The Times*, 10 August 1913
906 ESP, *The Suffragette*, p. 505
907 *East London News*, 25 November 1913
908 *Daily Herald*, 29 October 1913
909 ESP, *TSM*, p. 507
910 Ibid.
911 Ibid.
912 *East End News*, 25 November 1913, cited in Winslow, Sylvia Pankhurst, pp. 58–9
913 Sarah Jackson and Rosemary Taylor, *East London Suffragettes* (Stroud: The History Press, 2014), p.159
914 ESP, *THF*, p. 20
915 ESP, *TSM*, p. 543
916 Zelie Emerson to ESP, nd. IISH/SPP/ARCH01029/183
917 Robins, *The Convert*, p. 214
918 ESP, *TSM*, p. 564
919 Ibid., p. 566
920 Ibid.
921 Cited in Harrison, *Sylvia Pankhurst*, p. 163
922 ESP, *TSM*, p. 570
923 Ibid., p. 571
924 Ibid., p. 575
925 Ibid.
926 Ibid., p. 583
927 Ibid., p. 589
928 Cited in Benn, *Keir Hardie*, p. 322
929 Ibid., p. 328
930 Cited in Adam Hochschild, *To End All Wars: A Story of Protest and Patriotism in the First World War* (London: Macmillan, 2011), p. 90
931 Benn, *Keir Hardie*, p. 325
932 June Purvis, 'Did Militancy Help or Hinder the Granting of Women's Suffrage in Britain?', *Women's History Review*, vol. 28, no. 7 (2019), pp. 1200–34 at p. 1210
933 ESP, *TSM*, p. 593. The London Opera House is not to be confused with the Royal Opera House; see https://womanandhersphere.com/2013/11/13/walkssuffrage-stories-the-london-opera-house-kingsway/

934 ESP, *TSM*, p. 525, and see Elizabeth Crawfurd, *The Women's Suffrage Movement: A Reference Guide, 1866–1928* (London: UCL Press, 1999)
935 ESP, *TSM*, p. 525
936 Barbara Winslow documents this transition: 'In 1914, she [Sylvia] was a socialist suffragette, pacifist, and sympathizer with the Independent Labour Party. By the time of the signing of the Armistice in 1918, Pankhurst was an International Socialist and revolutionary feminist.' Barbara Winslow, 'Sylvia Pankhurst and the Great War', in Ian Bullock and Richard Pankhurst (eds), *Sylvia Pankhurst: From Artist to Anti-Fascist* (New York: St Martin's Press, 1992), pp. 86–120 at pp. 87–8
937 ESP, *THF*, p. 11
938 Ibid.
939 Ibid., p. 14
940 Ibid., p. 15
941 Ibid.
942 Ibid.
943 Ibid.
944 Ibid., p. 16
945 Ibid.
946 Ibid.
947 Cited in Purvis, *Christabel Pankhurst*, p. 370
948 ESP, *THF*, p. 31
949 Ibid., p. 16
950 Ibid.
951 Ibid., p. 17
952 CP, *Unshackled*, p. 288
953 See https://womanandhersphere.com/2013/11/13/walkssuffrage-stories-the-london-opera-house-kingsway/
954 ESP, *THF*, p. 66
955 See Purvis, *Christabel Pankhurst*, p. 372
956 ESP, *THF*, p. 66
957 CP, *Unshackled*, p. 288
958 ESP, *THF*, p. 66
959 Purvis, *Christabel Pankhurst*, p. 374
960 ESP, *THF*, pp. 66–7
961 Ibid., p. 67
962 Ibid.
963 Ibid.
964 Ibid., p. 34

965 Ibid., p. 119
966 Ibid.
967 Ibid., p. 120
968 Ibid., p. 121
969 Ibid., p. 123
970 Ibid., p. 124
971 Ibid.
972 Ibid.
973 Ibid., p. 125
974 Ibid., p. 146
975 Ibid.
976 Ibid., p. 147
977 Benn, *Keir Hardie*, p. 328
978 Ibid.
979 ESP, *THF*, p. 148
980 Ibid.
981 Ibid., p. 149
982 Ibid., p. 150
983 Ibid.
984 Ibid., p. 152
985 Ibid., p. 153
986 Ibid.
987 Ibid.
988 Ibid., pp. 153–4
989 Winslow, 'Sylvia Pankhurst and the Great War', in Bullock and Pankhurst (eds), *Sylvia Pankhurst: From Artist to Anti-Fascist*, p. 99
990 IISH/SPP/ARCH01029/55
991 ESP, *THF*, p. 150

21 THE DOGS OF WAR

992 ESP, *THF*, p. 108
993 Stephanie J. Brown, 'An "Insult to Soldiers' Wives and Mothers": The *Woman's Dreadnought*'s Campaign against Surveillance on the Home Front, 1914–1915', *Journal of Modern Periodical Studies*, vol. 7, no. 1–2 (2016), pp. 121–62
994 Winslow, 'Sylvia Pankhurst and the Great War', in Bullock and Pankhurst (eds), *Sylvia Pankhurst: From Artist to Anti-Fascist*, p. 95
995 Cited in ibid., p. 94
996 Ibid., p. 99
997 Ibid., p. 100

998 Cited in Harrison, *Sylvia Pankhurst*, p. 170
999 ESP, *THF*, p. 19
1000 Cited in Winslow, *Sylvia Pankhurst*, p. 62
1001 ESP, *THF*, p. 43
1002 Ibid., p. 42
1003 Cited in Harrison, *Sylvia Pankhurst*, p. 173
1004 ESP, *THF*, p. 45
1005 Ibid.
1006 Cited in William Stewart, *J. Keir Hardie: A Biography* (London: Independent Labour Party, 1925), p. 341
1007 ESP, *THF*, pp. 209–13
1008 Ibid., p. 436
1009 Ibid.
1010 Ibid., p. 36
1011 Ibid., p. 152
1012 ESP, *TSM*, p.104
1013 Ibid.
1014 Ibid., p. 229
1015 Ibid.
1016 Ibid.
1017 Ibid., p. 236
1018 Ibid.
1019 Ibid.
1020 *Pall Mall Gazette*, 23 December 1913, p. 9

22 MOTHERS' ARMS

1021 ESP, *THF*, p. 142
1022 Ibid.
1023 Ibid., p. 143
1024 Ibid.
1025 Ibid.
1026 Ibid.
1027 Ibid., p. 144
1028 Ibid.
1029 Ibid.
1030 Ibid., p. 145
1031 Ibid., pp. 145–6
1032 See Winslow, 'Sylvia Pankhurst and the Great War', p. 100
1033 See ibid.

1034 Minutes of the General Meeting of the WSF, 15 January 1917, cited in ibid., p. 101

1035 See https://www.sochealth.co.uk/national-health-service/the-sma-and-the-foundation-of-the-national-health-service-dr-leslie-hilliard-1980/why-a-national-health-service/why-a-national-health-service-chapter-2-the-socialist-medical-association/

1036 ESP, IISH/SPP/ARCH01029/132

1037 Ibid.

1038 Cited in ESP, *THF*, p.235

1039 Ibid.

1040 Ibid.

1041 Cited in ESP, *A Suffragette in America*, p. 51

1042 Cited in ESP, *THF*, p. 429

1043 Cited in Connelly, 'Sylvia Pankhurst, the Suffragettes of East London and the Garment Workers of Chicago'

1044 Cited in ibid.

1045 Clare Debenham, *Marie Stopes' Sexual Revolution and the Birth Control Movement* (London: Palgrave Macmillan, 2018), p. 145

1046 ESP, *THF*, p. 173

1047 Ibid., p. 174

1048 ESP, *Save the Mothers*, p. ix

1049 ESP, *THF*, p. 239

1050 Ibid.

1051 Ibid., p. 274

1052 Ibid., pp. 275–6

1053 Val Williams, *Women Photographers: The Other Observers, 1900 to the Present* (London: Virago, 1986), pp. 40–6

1054 Benn, *Keir Hardie*, p. 341

1055 Cited in Stewart, *J. Keir Hardie*, p. 388

1056 ESP, *THF*, p. 156

1057 Ibid., p. 34, and see Benn, *Keir Hardie*, pp. 336–7

1058 Benn, *Keir Hardie*, p. 343

1059 ESP, *THF*, p. 228

1060 Ibid.

1061 Ibid.

1062 Ibid., p. 226

1063 Ibid.

1064 Ibid., p. 227

1065 Ibid.

1066 Ibid.

1067 Ibid., p. 230
1068 Ibid., p. 231
1069 Ibid.
1070 Ibid.
1071 See Benn, *Keir Hardie*, p. 351
1072 *The Times*, 27 September 1915
1073 *Daily Mirror*, 27 September 1915
1074 ESP, IISH/SPP/ARCH01029/9
1075 Ibid.
1076 Ibid.
1077 Ibid.
1078 Ibid.
1079 *Woman's Dreadnought*, 16 October 1915
1080 Frank Smith to Sylvia, 26 September 1915, cited in ESP, *THF*, p. 231
1081 ESP, *THF*, p. 237
1082 Ibid., p. 238
1083 Ibid.
1084 Ibid.
1085 Ibid.

23 WELCOME TO THE SOVIETS

1086 ESP, *THF*, p. 274
1087 Ibid.
1088 Ibid.
1089 Ibid., p. 275
1090 Ibid.
1091 Ibid.
1092 Ibid.
1093 Ibid.
1094 ESP, *A Suffragette in America*, p. 78
1095 Ibid., p. 82
1096 *Workers' Dreadnought*, 28 July 1917
1097 *Woman's Dreadnought*, 26 December 1914
1098 ESP, *THF*, p. 131
1099 Ibid., p. 78
1100 Ibid.
1101 See Winslow, *Sylvia Pankhurst*, p. 78
1102 A second Act passed in May 1916 extended conscription to married men.
1103 ESP, *THF*, p. 320

1104 Ruth Taillon, 'Socialism, Feminism and the Women of 1916', Sylvia Pankhurst Memorial Lecture, 13 August 2016

1105 ESP, *TSM*, p. 321

1106 *Woman's Dreadnought*, 13 May 1916

1107 ESP, *THF*, p. 321

1108 Ibid.

1109 Ibid.

1110 Ibid.

1111 Patricia Lynch, 'Scenes from the Rebellion', *Woman's Dreadnought*, 13 May 1916, and *Rebel Ireland: 'Thoughts on Easter Week, 1916' by E. Sylvia Pankhurst; 'Scenes from the Rebellion' by Patricia Lynch; 'The First Sinn Fein Member of Parliament' by May O'Callaghan* (London: The Workers' Socialist Federation, 1919), p. 7

1112 ESP, 'The Irish Rebellion: Our View', *Woman's Dreadnought*, 6 May 1916

1113 Ibid.

1114 ESP, 'Thoughts on Easter Week', in *Rebel Ireland*, p. 3

1115 Karl Marx, *Capital*, from the library of Sylvia Pankhurst, IISH call number 2008/4757

1116 ESP, *THF*, p. 322

1117 Ibid.

1118 Ibid.

1119 Ibid.

1120 Ibid.

1121 ESP, 'The Inheritance'

1122 Cited in https://www.historyireland.com/decadeofcentenaries/sylvia-pankhurst-irish-revolution/

1123 Ibid.

1124 Ibid.

1125 Ibid.

1126 ESP, 'The Inheritance'

1127 Ibid.

1128 ESP, 'In the Red Twilight', unpublished MS, IISH/SPP/ARCH01029/146–50

1129 *Woman's Dreadnought*, 31 March 1917

1130 Ibid.

1131 ESP, 'The Inheritance'

1132 Sheila Rowbotham, Introduction to Winslow, *Sylvia Pankhurst*, pp. xiv–xv. This section borrows directly from Rowbotham's pioneering work documenting this history

1133 Ibid.

1134 Ibid.
1135 *Workers' Dreadnought*, 19 June 1920
1136 Davis, *Sylvia Pankhurst*, p. 82
1137 I follow Davis wholly here: see ibid., pp. 82–3
1138 Cited in Hochschild, *To End All Wars*, p. 273
1139 Cited in ibid., p. 274
1140 *Workers' Dreadnought*, 21 July 1917
1141 *Workers' Dreadnought*, 21 July 1917
1142 ESP, *THF*, pp. 319–20
1143 Cited in Winslow, *Sylvia Pankhurst*, p. 147
1144 Cited in Raymond Challinor, *The Origins of British Bolshevism* (London: Croom Helm, 1977), p. 182. Open source full text also available at https://www.marxists.org/history/etol/writers/challinor/1977/british-bolshevism/index.htm
1145 *East London Advertiser*, 20 March 1920
1146 *Workers' Dreadnought*, 27 March 1920

24 ANTI-PARLIAMENTARIANISM

1147 Robert Service, *Lenin: A Biography* (London: Macmillan, 2000), p. 149
1148 *Woman's Dreadnought*, 24 March 1917
1149 *Woman's Dreadnought*, 2 June 1917
1150 *Workers' Dreadnought*, 17 November 1917
1151 *Workers' Dreadnought*, 26 January 1918
1152 *Woman's Dreadnought*, 2 June 1917
1153 Cited in Purvis, *Emmeline Pankhurst*, pp. 301–2
1154 Ibid., p. 304
1155 See ibid., p. 301
1156 See ibid., p. 304
1157 Ibid., p. 303. For an alternative view of the Women's Party challenging Sylvia's position, see June Purvis, 'The Women's Party of Great Britain (1917–19): A Forgotten Episode in British Women's Political History', *Women's History Review*, vol. 25, no. 4 (2016), pp. 638–51
1158 Purvis, *Emmeline Pankhurst*, p. 304
1159 ESP, 'Women's Rule in Britain', IISH/SPP/ARCH01029/129
1160 ESP to Mrs Ross-Clyne, 3 July 1936, Women's Library Archives, GB106 9/20/053
1161 Cited in Winslow, *Sylvia Pankhurst*, p. 100
1162 Cited in Mark Shipway, Anti-Parliamentary Communism: The Movement for Workers' Councils in Britain, 1917–45 (London: Palgrave Macmillan, 1988), p. 4

1163 *Workers' Dreadnought*, 26 January 1918
1164 *Workers' Dreadnought*, 16 February 1918
1165 *Workers' Dreadnought*, 2 November 1918
1166 *Workers' Dreadnought*, 4 May 1918
1167 Coleman, *Adela Pankhurst*, p. 86
1168 Ibid., p. 80
1169 Ibid., p. 81
1170 Adela Pankhurst, 'Communism and Social Purity', *Workers' Dreadnought*, 26 February 1921
1171 Coleman, *Adela Pankhurst*, pp. 89–90
1172 Ibid., p. 89
1173 See Winslow, *Sylvia Pankhurst*, p.107, and minutes of Bow Members meeting, 5 May 1919, IISH PP 8211c
1174 Winslow, *Sylvia Pankhurst*, p. 108
1175 *Workers' Dreadnought*, 1 February 1919
1176 *Woman's Dreadnought*, 8 January 1916
1177 See Winslow, *Sylvia Pankhurst*, p. 114
1178 Ibid.
1179 Cited in ibid., p. 23

25 SYLVIA'S COMMUNIST ODYSSEY

1180 ESP, 'In the Red Twilight', cited in full n. 1094
1181 *Llais Llafur*, 5 May 1917, and see https://fournationshistory.wordpress.com/2017/05/22/wales-and-the-russian-revolution/
1182 Cited in Winslow, *Sylvia Pankhurst*, p. 119
1183 ESP, 'The Inheritance'
1184 Ibid.
1185 See Francis Beckett, *Stalin's British Victims* (Stroud: Sutton Publishing, 2004)
1186 ESP, 'The Inheritance'
1187 Ibid.
1188 Ibid.
1189 *The Globe* (London), 2 May 1919, p. 8
1190 Cited in Dana Mills, *Rosa Luxemburg* (London: Reaktion, 2020), p. 156
1191 ESP, 'Rosa and Karl', *Workers' Dreadnought*, 19 January 1924, and manuscript drafts of poem [January 1919], IISH/SPP/ARCH01029/62
1192 ESP, *Communism and its Tactics (1921–22)*, ed. and introduced by Mark A. S. Shipway (Edinburgh: self-published by Mark Shipway, 1982), Introduction, p. iv. ESP's *Communism and its Tactics* was first published as a series of articles in the *Workers' Dreadnought*, 26 November

1921–11 March 1922 and republished with some revisions in the issues of 27 January–10 March 1923

1193 ESP, *Communism and its Tactics*, p. 150

1194 Winslow, *Sylvia Pankhurst*, p. 162

1195 Ibid, p. 135

1196 RKPP and RP, *Ethiopian Reminiscences*, p. 7

1197 Ibid., p. 8

1198 Ibid.

1199 See Silvio Corio to Hazrat Mirza Basheer-ud-Din Mahmud Ahmad, 20 April 1922, IISH/SPP/ARCH01029/316. I asked Rita and Alula Pankhurst, but they can't recall the son's name; because he was so much older he never became part of the extended family in the way Rockie and Percy did. Silvio writes about him, but does not name him in his correspondence.

1200 Romero, *Sylvia Pankhurst*, p. 161

1201 Silvio Corio to Ahmad, 20 April 1922

1202 Silvio Corio to ESP, [no date], IISH/SPP/ARCH01029/315

1203 Ibid.

1204 Cited in Winslow, *Sylvia Pankhurst*, p. 142

1205 ESP, 'The Inheritance'

1206 ESP, 'In The Red Twilight'

1207 ESP, 'In the Red Twilight'

1208 Ibid.

1209 ESP, 'The Inheritance'

1210 ESP, 'The Inheritance'

1211 Cited in Winslow, *Sylvia Pankhurst*, p. 136

1212 Cited in Mark Shipway, *Anti-Parliamentary Communism: The Movement for Workers' Councils in Britain, 1917–45* (London: Palgrave Macmillan, 1988), p. 7

1213 Ibid., p. 8

1214 ESP, *Communism and its Tactics*, Introduction, p. v

1215 Ibid.

1216 Cited in Vadim Valentinovich Zagladin et al. (eds), *The International Working-Class Movement*, vol. 4: *The Socialist Revolution in Russia and the International Working Class (1917–23)* (Moscow: Progress Publishers, 1984), p. 379. ESP's letter and Lenin's reply were published in *Communist International* two months later in September 1919

1217 See https://www.marxists.org/archive/lenin/works/1919/aug/28.htm

26 COMRADE PANKHURST

1218 *Workers' Dreadnought*, 21 February 1920
1219 See https://www.leftcom.org/en/articles/2000-01-01/sylvia-pankhurst-the-real-meaning-of-the-revolutionary-years
1220 *Pravda*, 17 June 1920; Lenin, *Collected Works*, pp. 139–43
1221 ESP, IISH/SPP/ARCH01029/147
1222 Ibid.
1223 Cited in Mary Davis, *Sylvia* Pankhurst, p.81
1224 Lenin's message was published in *The Call* on 22 July 1920. See https://www.marxists.org/archive/lenin/works/1920/jul/08.htm
1225 *Workers' Dreadnought*, 24 July 1920
1226 Purvis, *Emmeline Pankhurst*, p. 293
1227 Ibid.
1228 ESP, *Soviet Russia as I Saw It*, p. 8
1229 Ibid., p. 34
1230 Lenin, *On Britain*, cited in Winslow, *Sylvia Pankhurst*, p. 156
1231 Ibid., cited in Winslow, *Sylvia Pankhurst*, p. 157
1232 ESP, *Soviet Russia as I Saw It*, p. 48
1233 ESP, 'In the Red Twilight', IISH/SPP/ARCH01029/147
1234 ESP, *Soviet Russia as I Saw It*, p. 40
1235 Ibid., pp. 40–1
1236 Ibid., pp. 41–2
1237 Ibid., pp. 42–3
1238 Ibid., p. 52
1239 Cited in Harrison, *Sylvia Pankhurst*, p. 208
1240 Service, *Lenin*, p. 411
1241 ESP, *Soviet Russia as I Saw It*, pp. 41–2
1242 ESP, *TSM*, p. 128
1243 Stephen Graubard, *British Labour and the Russian Revolution* (Cambridge, Mass.: Harvard University Press, 1956), pp. 133–4; V. I. Lenin, *'Left-Wing Communism': An Infantile Disorder*, 8th edn (Moscow: Progress Publishers, 1981), p. 69
1244 Herman Gorter, 'Open Letter to Comrade Lenin: A reply to "'Left-wing communism": an infantile disorder', *Workers' Dreadnought*, 12 March–11 June 1921
1245 ESP to an unnamed anarchist, 1921, cited in Harrison, *Sylvia Pankhurst*, p. 158
1246 ESP, *Soviet Russia as I Saw It*, p. 39

1247 Ibid., p. 182
1248 See ESP, 'In the Red Twilight'
1249 ESP, *Soviet Russia as I Saw It*, pp. 68–9
1250 Ibid., pp. 136–8
1251 Ibid., p. 81
1252 Ibid., p. 171
1253 Ibid., p. 19
1254 ESP, *Soviet Russia as I Saw It*, p. 167
1255 Ibid.
1256 Ibid., p. 168–9
1257 William Gallacher, *The Last Memoirs of William Gallacher* (London: Lawrence & Wishart, 1966), p. 156
1258 Ibid.
1259 William Gallacher, *The Rolling of the Thunder* (London: Lawrence & Wishart, 1947), p. 18
1260 Ibid.
1261 ESP, *Soviet Russia as I Saw It*, p. 187
1262 Ibid., p. 19
1263 Gallacher, *The Last Memoirs of William Gallacher*, p. 157
1264 Ibid., p. 158
1265 ESP, *Soviet Russia as I Saw It*, p. 191
1266 Ibid.
1267 Ibid. p. 192
1268 Ibid.
1269 Gallacher, *The Last Memoirs of William Gallacher*, p. 158
1270 ESP, *Soviet Russia as I Saw It*, p. 194
1271 Ibid.
1272 Gallacher, *The Last Memoirs of William Gallacher*, p. 158
1273 ESP, *Soviet Russia as I Saw It*, p. 195

27 DISCONTENT ON THE LOWER DECK

1274 *Workers' Dreadnought*, 9 November 1918
1275 See   https://www.marxists.org/history/etol/revhist/backiss/vol8/no3/carew.html
1276 Ibid., and see Anthony Carew, *The Lower Deck of the Royal Navy, 1900–39: The Invergordon Mutiny in Perspective* (Manchester: Manchester University Press, 1981)
1277 Harry Pollitt, *Serving my Time: An Apprenticeship to Politics* (London: Lawrence & Wishart, 1940) p. 111
1278 Ibid.

1279 *Workers' Dreadnought*, 15 May 1920

1280 Hansard, Soviet Trade Delegation, HC Deb 01 July 1920, vol. 131, cols 624–7

1281 Ibid.

1282 Cited in Harrison, *Sylvia Pankhurst*, p. 209

1283 *Daily Express*, 27 September 1920

1284 TNA, HO/144/1697/414256, *Daily Telegraph*, 21 October 1920

1285 Winslow, *Sylvia Pankhurst*, pp. 127–8

1286 Claude McKay, *A Long Way from Home* (New York: Harvest Books, 1970), p. 74

1287 Ibid., pp. 63–4

1288 Claude McKay to William Gallacher, 10 October 1920, CP/IND/GALL/ 02/04, Gallacher Papers, People's History Museum, Manchester. I am grateful to Dr John Callow for sharing this letter with me immediately after he discovered it during his own work on Willie Gallacher

1289 *Workers' Dreadnought*, 20 October 1920

1290 'Appeal of Miss Sylvia Pankhurst against sentence of six months imprisonment […] for articles in the *Workers' Dreadnought*, October 1920' (trial transcript), p. 10, IISH/SPP/ARCH01029/254

1291 TNA, HO/144/1697/414256, *The Dispatch*, 20 October 1920

1292 TNA, HO/144/1697/414256, *Daily Telegraph*, 21 October 1920

1293 TNA, HO/144/1558/234191, *Sheffield Daily Telegraph*, 29 October 1918

1294 Ibid.

1295 TNA, HO/144/1558/234191, 'Miss Sylvia Pankhurst', 30 October 1918

1296 TNA, HO/144/1697/414256, *Daily Herald*, 29 October 1920

1297 TNA, HO/144/1697/414256, *Daily Telegraph*, 21 October 1920

1298 TNA, HO/144/1697/414256, *Daily Herald*, 29 October 1920

1299 'Sylvia Pankhurst Arrested', *Workers' Dreadnought*, 23 October 1920

1300 'Sylvia Pankhurst's Appeal', IISH/SPP/ARCH01029/254. The 'Verbatim Report of Sylvia Pankhurst's Appeal' was published in *Workers' Dreadnought*, 15 January 1921

1301 ESP, 'In the Red Twilight'

1302 GBS to ESP, *Workers' Dreadnought*, 15 January 1921

1303 Louis Crompton, *Shaw the Dramatist* (Lincoln, Nebr.: University of Nebraska Press, 1969), p. 155

1304 TNA, HO/144/1697/414256, 'Petition', 13 January 1921, Sylvia Pankhurst to Home Secretary

1305 Ibid.

1306 Ibid.

1307 *Workers' Dreadnought*, 15 January 1921

1308 Cited in Shirley Harrison, *Sylvia Pankhurst*, p.580
1309 ESP, *Writ on Cold Slate* (London: The Dreadnought Publishers, 1922),
       p. 5
1310 The British Library Archives and Manuscripts hold an archival acquisition
       Add MS 88925/1/2: 1920-1 given to the library by Richard Pankhurst.
       This is a separate archive from the main body of Sylvia Pankhurst Papers
       bequeathed by the Pankhurst family to the International Institute of
       Social History (IISG) in Amsterdam. This British Library MS holding
       includes a previously disordered cache of MS writings in pencil on HM
       Prison toilet paper, that I have sorted, ordered, and transcribed and are
       made available to readers here for the first time. The most significant
       elements of this fascinating archive comprise poetry, a play, and political
       correspondence channelled through Norah Smyth.

28 LEFT CHILDISHNESS?

1311 ESP to Norah Smyth, British Library, Archives and Manuscripts, Add
       MS 88925/1/2:1920-1921
1312 British Library, Archives and Manuscripts, Sylvia Pankhurst, Add MS
       88925/1/2: 1920–1
1313 Elizabeth   Crawford,   https://womanandhersphere.com/2012/09/
       07/suffrage-stories-suffragettes-and-tea-rooms-the-eustace-miles-
       restaurant-and-the-tea-cup-inn/
1314 *Glasgow Herald*, 31 May 1921
1315 ESP, 'In the Red Twilight'
1316 John Maclean, 'The Unemployed', *Vanguard*, no. 12, November
       1920, p. 7
1317 'A Woman's Welcome to Comrade Sylvia Pankhurst on Release from
       Holloway, May 30th', *Workers' Dreadnought*, 28 May 1921
1318 ESP, *Communism and its Tactics*, Introduction, p. v
1319 Ibid.
1320 The list of donors was published in *Workers' Dreadnought*, 15 January 1921
1321 Ibid.
1322 Terry Eagleton, *Why Marx Was Right* (New Haven & London: Yale
       University Press, 2011), p. 71
1323 ESP, *Communism and its Tactics*, Introduction, p. vi
1324 *Workers' Dreadnought*, 17 September 1921
1325 For an introduction to Isadora Duncan's revolutionary dance and
       politics, see Dana Mills, *Dance & Politics: Moving beyond Boundaries*
       (Manchester: Manchester University Press, 2017)

1326 Irma Duncan Collection of Isadora Duncan materials, Folder 107, New York Public Library, Letter, 19 June 1921, London, to Isadora Duncan, [London] [1] p. on 1 l. I am enormously grateful to Dr Dana Mills for drawing this letter to my attention

1327 See Mills, *Dance & Politics*, pp. 28–47

1328 Cited in Winslow, *Sylvia Pankhurst*, p. 167

1329 Herman Gorter, 'Open Letter to Comrade Lenin: A reply to "'Left-wing communism': an infantile disorder"', *Workers' Dreadnought*, London, 12 March–11 June 1921

1330 *Workers' Dreadnought*, 17 September 1921

1331 *Workers' Dreadnought*, 24 September 1921

1332 Cited in Winslow, *Sylvia Pankhurst*, p. 174

1333 *Workers' Dreadnought*, 15 January 1921

1334 *Workers' Dreadnought*, 4 November 1922

1335 ESP to TBG, Papers of Teresa Billington-Greig, Correspondence from Sylvia Pankhurst, 1956, Women's Library Archives, GB 106 7TBG/2/B/05

1336 *Workers' Dreadnought*, 15 December 1923

1337 Ibid.

1338 Ibid.

1339 *Workers' Dreadnought*, 5 January 1924

1340 George Bernard Shaw to Corio, in Romero, *E. Sylvia Pankhurst*, p. 154 n. 68

1341 'Inquisition Persists, Says Shaw in Radio Address on Joan of Arc', *New York Herald Tribune*, 31 May 1931

29 THE RED COTTAGE TEA ROOM

1342 126 High Rd, South Woodford, London E18 2QS, is now the site of a supermarket

1343 RKP, *Sylvia Pankhurst: Artist and Crusader*, p. 185

1344 Mrs C. Ashman to David Mitchell, 15 September 1965, David Mitchell Collection, Museum of London Library, GB 389 73.83

1345 Ibid.

1346 See Harrison, *Sylvia Pankhurst*, p. 217

1347 See Elizabeth Crawford, https://womanandhersphere.com/2012/09/07/suffrage-stories-suffragettes-and-tea-rooms-the-eustace-miles-restaurant-and-the-tea-cup-inn/

1348 RKPP, *Sylvia Pankhurst: Counsel for Ethiopia: A Biographical Essay on Ethiopian, Anti-Fascist and Anti-Colonial History, 1934–1960* (Hollywood, Calif.: Tsehai Publishers, 2003), p. 2

1349 Christopher Andrew, *The Defence of the Realm: The Authorized History of MI5* (London: Allen Lane, 2009), pp. 148–50. With thanks to Peter James for educating me on this point

1350 Harrison, *Sylvia Pankhurst*, p. 217

1351 Cited in ibid.

1352 The Horse and Wells, going strong since 1730, is still selling beer and gin, and has recently seen off property developers trying to turn it into flats.

1353 RKPP, *Ethiopian Reminiscences*, p. 20

1354 See Purvis, *Emmeline Pankhurst*, p. 338

1355 Cited in https://spartacus-educational.com/2WWrightclub.htm

1356 Ibid.

1357 See Harrison, *Sylvia Pankhurst*, p. 218

1358 Mary Davis, conversation with the author, 2017: Mary Davis reporting discussion with Richard Pankhurst on subject of his mother's cooking

1359 Mrs C. Ashman to David Mitchell, 9 September 1965, David Mitchell Collection

1360 See Tristram Stuart, *The Bloodless Revolution: Radical Vegetarians and the Discovery of India* (London: HarperCollins, 2006)

1361 RKPP and RP, *Ethiopian Reminiscences*, p. 140

1362 Norah Walshe to David Mitchell, 2 November 1964, Mitchell Papers, Museum of London

1363 Mrs C. Ashman to David Mitchell, 9 September 1965

1364 Ibid.

1365 Ibid.

1366 Norah Walshe to David Mitchell, 2 November 1964, David Mitchell Collection

1367 RKPP, *Sylvia Pankhurst: Counsel for Ethiopia*, p. 26

1368 See Lucy Hughes-Hallett, *The Pike: Gabriele D'Annunzio – Poet, Seducer and Preacher of War* (London: Fourth Estate, 2013), pp. 498–500

1369 IISH/SPP/ARCH01029/152

1370 Neelam Srivastava, *Italian Colonialism and Resistances to Empire, 1930–1970* (Cambridge: Cambridge University Press, 2018), p. 15

1371 Lemn Sissay, 'The Battle of Adwa, 1896', in his *Listener* (London: Canongate Books, 2008), pp. 53, 57

1372 See, for example, Wendy S. Dunst, 'Virginia Woolf and Sylvia Pankhurst: Radicals, Pacifists, Visionaries', 25th Annual Conference on Virginia Woolf, June 2015

1373 Leonard Woolf, *Imperialism and Civilization* (London: Hogarth Press, 1928), pp. 9, 16

1374 Cited in Srivastava, *Italian Colonialism and Resistances to Empire*, p. 184
1375 ESP, *India and the Earthly Paradise* (Delhi: B. R. Publishing Corporation, 1985), Preface
1376 Ibid., p. 549
1377 Ibid., p. 617
1378 Benn, *Keir Hardie*, p. 189
1379 Ibid., p. 231
1380 Ibid., p. 230
1381 Cited in ibid.
1382 Cited in ibid.
1383 Ibid., p. 232
1384 Kenneth O. Morgan, *Keir Hardie: Radical and Socialist* (London: Weidenfeld & Nicolson, 1975), p. 192
1385 Purvis, *Emmeline Pankhurst*, p. 314
1386 Ibid., pp. 335, 336
1387 See Purvis, *Christabel Pankhurst*, pp.449-452
1388 Purvis, *Emmeline Pankhurst*, p. 344
1389 Mitchell Papers, newspaper clippings folders
1390 David Mitchell, *The Fighting Pankhursts*, p. 177; Purvis, *Emmeline Pankhurst*, p. 345
1391 Adela Pankhurst, 'My Mother, an Explanation and Vindication', 1933, Adela Pankhurst Walsh Papers, National Library of Australia, Canberra, and see June Purvis, 'Emmeline Pankhurst (1858–1928), Suffragette Leader and Single Parent in Edwardian Britain', *Women's History Review*, vol. 20, no. 1 (2011), pp. 87–108
1392 Cited in Purvis, *Emmeline Pankhurst*, p. 347
1393 Cited in ibid.
1394 Ibid., p. 348

30 FREE LOVE

1395 ESP to Norah Smith, [post 3 December 1927), IISH/SPP/ARCH01029/ II
1396 ESP to Emmeline Pethick-Lawrence, [XXXXX -date], Ibid.
1397 Ibid.
1398 Purvis, *Emmeline Pankhurst*, p. 348
1399 David Mitchell, *The Times*, 25 July 1975
1400 See Romero, *E. Sylvia Pankhurst*, p. 306 n. 27
1401 Ethel Smyth, *Female Pipings in Eden*, p. 202
1402 Ibid., p. 220
1403 Ibid., p. 221

1404 Purvis, *Emmeline Pankhurst*, p. 349

1405 ESP, 'In the Days of my Youth', undated typed manuscript [c. 1930–1], IISH/SPP/ARCH01029/10

1406 Clare Hanson, 'Mass Production', in her *A Cultural History of Pregnancy: Pregnancy, Medicine and Culture, 1750–2000* (London: Palgrave Macmillan, 2004), p. 114

1407 Ibid.

1408 Rosa Graul cited in Rowbotham, *Dreamers of a New Day*, p. 84

1409 Ibid., p. 88

1410 Ibid., p. 97

1411 Ibid.

1412 Lynn Segal, *Radical Happiness* (London: Verso, 2017), p. 114

1413 *News of the World*, 8 April 1928

1414 Rowbotham, *Dreamers of a New Day*, p. 88

1415 Ibid.

1416 ESP, 'The Rectegenetic Child', undated, IISH/SPP/ARCH01029/174

1417 Cited in Harrison, *Sylvia Pankhurst*, p. 220

1418 Mrs C. Ashman to David Mitchell, 15 September 1965, Mitchell Papers

1419 All correspondence cited in this section is at IISH/SPP/ARCH01029/17

1420 Mitchell, *The Fighting Pankhursts*, p. 197

1421 Purvis, *Emmeline Pankhurst*, p. 350

1422 Ibid., p. 351

1423 ESP, *Emmeline Pankhurst*, pp. 173–4

1424 Ibid., p. 174

1425 Ibid.

1426 Ibid.

1427 Mitchell, *The Fighting Pankhursts*, p. 197

1428 Purvis, *Emmeline Pankhurst*, p. 351; Mitchell, *The Fighting Pankhursts*, pp. 197–8

1429 Cited in Purvis, *Emmeline Pankhurst*, p. 352

1430 Ibid., pp. 440–1

1431 Ibid., p. 351

1432 Ethel Smyth cited in Collis, *Impetuous Heart*, p. 65

1433 Cited in Purvis, *Emmeline Pankhurst*, p. 353

1434 Ibid., p. 356

1435 Ibid., p. 355

1436 ESP, 'My Mother: Rebel to Reactionary', *The Star*, 5 March 1930

1437 Emmeline Pethick-Lawrence to ESP, 26 December 1930, IISH/SPP/ARCH01029/11

1438 Ibid.

1439 Ibid.
1440 Ibid.
1441 RKPP and RP, *Ethiopian Reminiscences*, p. 2
1442 Ibid.
1443 Ibid., p. 3
1444 Ibid.
1445 Ibid.
1446 Ibid.
1447 Ibid., p. 4
1448 Ibid., p. 5
1449 Ibid., p. 4
1450 *Daily Mail*, 29 September 1960
1451 See Roxane Corio to Silvio Corio, 19 October 1921, IISH/SPP/ARCH01029/315
1452 Roxane Corio to ESP, undated, IISH/SPP/ARCH01029/315
1453 Helen Pankhurst, note to the author.
1454 Morag Shiach, ' "To Purify the Dialect of the Tribe": Modernism and Language Reform', *Modernism/modernity*, vol. 14, no. 1 (2007), pp. 21–34, https://www.researchgate.net/publication/249907253_To_Purify_the_dialect_of_the_tribe_Modernism_and_Language_Reform. As Morag Shiach points out, 'The cultural project in which Pankhurst was involved here is explicitly understood as a form of popular politics.'
1455 Ibid.
1456 ESP, *Delphos: The Future of International Language* (London: Kegan Paul, Trench, Trubner, 1928), p. 5
1457 Ibid., p. 30
1458 *Workers' Dreadnought*, 26 November 1921
1459 Shiach, ' "To Purify the Dialect of the Tribe": Modernism and Language Reform'
1460 ESP to Norah Walshe, undated, 1929, David Mitchell Collection, Museum of London Library, GB 389 73.83
1461 Mrs C. Ashman to David Mitchell, 9 September 1965
1462 GBS, Preface (reproduced in facsimile), in ESP and I. O. Stefanovici (eds and trans.), *Poems of Mihail Eminescu* (London: Kegan Paul, Trench, Trubner, 1930), p. x
1463 ESP to Norah Walshe, 9 July 1930, David Mitchell Collection, Museum of London Library, GB 389 73.83
1464 ESP to Norah Walshe, July 1930, David Mitchell Papers, Museum of London, and cited in Harrrison, *Sylvia Pankhurst*, p.225

1465 Rita Pankhurst and Alula Pankhurst, conversation with the author, March 2019

31 FASCISM AS IT IS

1466 Nelson Mandela, *Long Walk to Freedom* (London: Abacus, 1995), p. 349
1467 See Benito Mussolini, co-written with Giovanni Gentile, *The Political and Social Doctrine of Fascism (1932)*, trans. Jane Soames (London: Hogarth Press, 1933)
1468 RKPP, 'Sylvia and *New Times and Ethiopia News*', in Bullock and RKPP (eds), *Sylvia Pankhurst: From Artist to Anti-Fascist*, pp. 149–91 at p. 150
1469 Cited in Hochschild, *To End All Wars*, p. 358
1470 Benn, *Keir Hardie*, pp. 409–10
1471 *Workers' Dreadnought*, 19 August 1922
1472 See Winslow, *Sylvia Pankhurst*, pp. 184–5
1473 Giacomo Matteoti, *The Fascisti Exposed: A Year of Fascist Domination* (London: ILP Publications, 1924), p. 84
1474 Cited in RKPP, *Sylvia Pankhurst: Counsel for Ethiopia*, p. 191
1475 Cited in Benn, *Keir Hardie*, p. 409
1476 *New Times and Ethiopia News*, 11 March 1939
1477 ESP, *The Truth about the Oil War* (London: Workers' Dreadnought Publications, 1922), p. 1. See https://www.marxists.org/archive/pankhurst-sylvia/1922/oil-war.htm
1478 RKPP and RP, *Ethiopian Reminiscences*, p. 9
1479 Benn, *Keir Hardie*, p. 409
1480 IISH/SPP/ARCH01029/163
1481 Benn, *Keir Hardie*, p. 409
1482 IISH/SPP/ARCH01029/163
1483 Ibid.
1484 RKPP and RP, *Ethiopian Reminiscences*, p. 9
1485 IISH/SPP/ARCH01029/152
1486 *Manchester Guardian*, Friday 22 September 1933
1487 Ibid.
1488 Cited in RKPP, 'Sylvia and *New Times and Ethiopia News*', p. 160
1489 Cited in ibid.
1490 See Ian Campbell, *The Plot to Kill Graziani: The Attempted Assassination of Mussolini's Viceroy* (Addis Ababa: Addis Ababa University Press, 2015)
1491 Evelyn Waugh, *Waugh in Abyssinia* (Baton Rouge: Louisiana State University Press, 2007), p. 49
1492 Jeff Pearce, *Prevail: The Inspiring Story of Ethiopia's Victory over Mussolini's Invasion, 1935–1941* (New York: Skyhorse Publishing, 2014), pp. 49–50

1493 Cited in RKPP, 'Sylvia and *New Times and Ethiopia News*', p. 160

1494 RKPP and RP, *Ethiopian Reminiscences*, p. 11

1495 Dodd (ed.), *A Sylvia Pankhurst Reader*, p. 222

1496 *Manchester Guardian*, 24 June 1934, p. 12

1497 *Sunderland Echo & Shipping Gazette*, 3 July 1934

1498 ESP, 'Women Under the Nazis', undated, IISH/SPP/ARCH01029/150

1499 Ibid.

1500 RKPP, *Sylvia Pankhurst: Artist and Crusader*, p. 190

1501 ESP and Stefanovici (eds), *Poems of Mihail Eminescu*, p. 112

1502 Harrison, *Sylvia Pankhurst*, p. 230

1503 Ibid.

1504 This and all following in this section from ESP, IISH/SPP/ARCH01029/45

1505 ESP, IISH/SPP/ARCH01029/45 and see Mitchell, *The Fighting Pankhursts*, pp. 248–9

1506 Ibid., p. 249

32 THE NATIONAL ANTI-FASCIST WEEKLY

1507 Cited in Professor Vernon Bogdanor, 'King George V', Lecture, Museum of London, 17 January 2017, p. 10

1508 *Woodford Times*, 17 April 1935

1509 For this correspondence, see RKP, *Counsel for Ethiopia*, pp. 39–43

1510 ESP to Winston Churchill, 15 April 1936, ibid., p. 40

1511 Ibid., p. 42

1512 Ibid.

1513 Cited in Asfa-Wossen Asserate, *King of Kings: The Triumph and Tragedy of Emperor Haile Selassie I of Ethiopia* (London: Haus Publishing, 2015), p. 120

1514 Ibid., p. 114

1515 Pearce, *Prevail*, p. 4.

1516 Ibid.

1517 This summary is based on Jeff Pearce's extensive and detailed work on international solidarity in ibid., passim

1518 ESP, *The Truth about the Oil War*, pp. 1–27

1519 Cited in RKPP, *Sylvia Pankhurst: Counsel for Ethiopia*, p. 37

1520 Ibid., p. 38

1521 Benn, *Keir Hardie*, p. 409

1522 *Cornish Guardian*, 9 April 1936

1523 *New Times and Ethiopia News*, 1 August 1936

1524 Letter of 22 February 1935 to *Manchester Guardian*, cited in RKPP, 'Sylvia and *New Times and Ethiopia News*', in Bullock and RKPP (eds), *Sylvia Pankhurst: From Artist to Anti-Fascist*, p. 150

1525 Letter of 20 June 1935 to *Manchester Guardian*, cited in ibid.

1526 Ibid.

1527 *News Chronicle*, 12 July 1935, cited in RKPP, 'Sylvia and *New Times and Ethiopia News*', p. 152

1528 Ibid.

1529 Cited in RKPP, 'Sylvia and *New Times and Ethiopia News*', p. 152

1530 *The Times*, 30 September 1935.

1531 Cited in RKPP, 'Sylvia and *New Times and Ethiopia News*', p. 151

1532 Cited in ibid.

1533 *Daily Herald*, 17 April 1936

1534 Ibid.

1535 Ibid.

1536 *Manchester Guardian*, 3 October 1935

1537 RKPP, 'Sylvia and *New Times and Ethiopia News*', p. 153

1538 RKPP, *Sylvia Pankhurst: Counsel for Ethiopia*, p. 21

1539 Cited in Srivastava, *Italian Colonialism and Resistances to Empire*, p. 150

1540 Steer's influence on pro-Ethiopian support in Britain is covered in detail by Neelam Srivastava in ibid. – see pp. 154–65. Srivastava shows also why and how there was widespread support from the British public for the Ethiopian cause, if not from the government; she pulls together the best scholarship to date – see ibid., p. 161

1541 Cited in ibid., p. 3

1542 Nicholas Rankin, *Telegram from Guernica: The Extraordinary Life of George Steer, War Correspondent* (London: Faber & Faber, 2003), p. 1

1543 Ibid.

1544 Ibid., p. 5

1545 Ibid.

1546 Ibid., p. 35

1547 Cited in ibid., p. 7

1548 RKPP, *Sylvia Pankhurst: Counsel for Ethiopia*, p. 23

1549 *New Times and Ethiopia News*, 17 October 1936

1550 RKPP, *Sylvia Pankhurst: Counsel for Ethiopia*, pp. 47–8

1551 Ibid., p. 48

1552 Asserate, *King of Kings*, p. 131

1553 RKPP, *Sylvia Pankhurst: Counsel for Ethiopia*, p. 48

1554 Ibid., p. 113

1555 Quotations not from RKPP, *Sylvia Pankhurst: Counsel for Ethiopia* in this section are from Tekeste Negash, *Woven into the Tapestry: How Five Women Shaped Ethiopian History* (Los Angeles: Tsehai Publishers and Loyola Marymount University, 2016)

1556 RKPP, *Sylvia Pankhurst: Counsel for Ethiopia*, p. 176

1557 Ibid., p. 167

1558 *New Times and Ethiopia News*, 9 May 1936

1559 Cited in RKPP, 'Sylvia and *New Times and Ethiopia News*', p. 158

1560 Cited in Patrick Wright, 'Dropping their Eggs: The History of Bombing', *London Review of Books*, vol. 23, no. 16 (23 August 2001), https://www.lrb.co.uk/the-paper/v23/n16/patrick-wright/dropping-their-eggs

1561 Cited at https://www.londonremembers.com/memorials/stone-bomb-anti-war-monument

1562 RKPP, *Ethiopian Reminiscences*, p. 13

1563 Wright, 'Dropping their Eggs'

1564 *New Times and Ethiopia News*, 5 May 1936

1565 Wright, 'Dropping their Eggs'

1566 Cited in RKPP, 'Sylvia and *New Times and Ethiopia News*', p. 158

1567 The best analysis of this crucial aspect of Sylvia's thinking can be found in Neelam Srivastava's work on Sylvia and her contemporaries in *Italian Colonialism and Resistances to Empire*, pp. 147–93

1568 Cited in ibid., p. 168

1569 Cited in ibid., p. 169

1570 RKPP, 'Sylvia and *New Times and Ethiopia News*', p. 162

1571 Ibid.

1572 Cited in ibid., p. 163

1573 RKPP, *Sylvia Pankhurst: Counsel for Ethiopia*, p. 62

1574 Ibid.

1575 Ibid., pp. 62–3

1576 Ibid., p. 63

1577 Ibid.

1578 Ibid.

1579 FO annotations to ESP letter to Anthony Eden, 13 January 1942, cited in RKPP, *Sylvia Pankhurst: Counsel for Ethiopia*, p. 191

1580 Cited in RKPP, 'Sylvia and *New Times and Ethiopia News*', p. 165

33 WAR IN WOODFORD

1581 Cited in RKPP, 'Sylvia and *New Times and Ethiopia News*', in Bullock and Pankhurst (eds), *Sylvia Pankhurst: From Artist to Anti-Fascist*, p. 166

1582 See RKPP, 'Sylvia and *New Times and Ethiopia News*', p. 167

1583 RKPP, *Sylvia Pankhurst: Counsel for Ethiopia*, p. 96
1584 Ibid., p. 95
1585 Cited in RKPP, 'Sylvia and *New Times and Ethiopia News*', p. 156
1586 Ibid., p. 96
1587 *Shields Daily News*, 13 June 1940, p. 6
1588 Cited in RKPP, 'Sylvia and *New Times and Ethiopia News*', p. 169
1589 Leonard Mosley, *Haile Selassie: The Conquering Lion* (Englewood Cliffs, NJ: Prentice-Hall, 1965), p. 237
1590 Cited in RKPP, *Sylvia Pankhurst: Counsel for Ethiopia*, p. 114
1591 Cited in Asserate, *King of Kings*, p. 148
1592 Pearce, *Prevail*, p. 485
1593 RKPP, *Sylvia Pankhurst: Counsel for Ethiopia*, p. 133
1594 Ibid., pp. 133–4
1595 Rankin, *Telegram from Guernica*, p. 4
1596 RKPP and RP, *Ethiopian Reminiscences*, p. 23
1597 Ibid.
1598 IISH/SPP/ARCH01029/92
1599 At the time of writing Bancroft's School does not list on its website Richard Pankhurst among its Old Bancroftian alumni, an oversight that perhaps might be corrected. See https://www.bancrofts.org.
1600 Cited in RKPP, 'Sylvia and *New Times and Ethiopia News*', p. 167
1601 Cited in ibid.
1602 MI5, Releases of 21 May 2004, Communists and Suspected Communists: Sylvia Pankhurst, TNA KV 2/1570
1603 Ibid.
1604 RKPP and RP, *Ethiopian Reminiscences*, p. 26
1605 Ibid.
1606 Rankin, *Telegram from Guernica*, p. 23
1607 Cited in RKPP, *Sylvia Pankhurst: Counsel for Ethiopia*, p. 139
1608 Over the past forty years, the global Rastafari movement has established a community at Shashemene with several individuals and families settling on the land, some raising children and grandchildren.
1609 See BBC Magazine, 12 September 2014, https://www.bbc.co.uk/news/magazine-28059303 and Jeff Pearce, *Prevail* (2014)
1610 Cited in RKPP, 'Sylvia and *New Times and Ethiopia News*', p. 175
1611 Cited in ibid., p. 178
1612 Richard Pankhurst, *Sylvia Pankhurst: Counsel for Ethiopia*, p.4
1613 See for example the work of Filippo Focardi and Lutz Klinkhammer, 'The Question of Fascist Italy's War Crimes: The Construction of a Self-Acquitting Myth (1943–1948)', *Journal of Modern Italian Studies*, vol. 9, no. 3 (2004), pp. 330–48
1614 *New Times and Ethiopia News*, 4 March, 18 March 1944

1615 Cited in ibid., p. 181
1616 Cited in ibid.
1617 Richard Pankhurst, *Sylvia Pankhurst: Counsel for Ethiopia*, p.209
1618 RKPP, *Sylvia Pankhurst: Counsel for Ethiopia*, p. 209
1619 Ibid., p. 210
1620 Cited in RKPP, 'Sylvia and *New Times and Ethiopia News*', p. 182
1621 Cited in ibid., p. 183
1622 RKPP, *Sylvia Pankhurst: Counsel for Ethiopia*, pp. 234–5
1623 Ibid., p. 235
1624 Ibid., pp. 235–6
1625 Ibid., p. 236
1626 Cited in ibid.
1627 Cited in RKPP, 'Sylvia and *New Times and Ethiopia News*', p. 190
1628 RKPP and RP, *Ethiopian Reminiscences*, p. 25
1629 Ibid.
1630 Ibid., p. 24

34 SUFFRAGETTE & SON

1631 RKPP and RP, *Ethiopian Reminiscences*, p. 56
1632 Frida Laski to David Mitchell, cited in Harrison, *Sylvia Pankhurst*, p. 258.
1633 Cited in Harrison, *Sylvia Pankhurst*, p. 258
1634 Basil Taylor, cited in ibid., p. 259
1635 Ibid.
1636 Rita Pankhurst, 'Sylvia Pankhurst in Perspective: Some Comments on Patricia Romero's Book *E. Sylvia Pankhurst, Portrait of a Radical*', *Women's Studies International Forum*, vol. 11, no 3 (1988), pp. 245–62 at p. 248
1637 Basil Taylor, cited in Harrison, *Sylvia Pankhurst*, p. 259
1638 See Silvio Corio's letter at http://radicalhistorynetwork.blogspot.com/2013/05/silvio-corio-and-son.html
1639 RKPP and RP, *Ethiopian Reminiscences*, p. 81
1640 *Liverpool Echo*, 8 January 1953
1641 Ibid.
1642 CP to ESP, 5 May 1953, in Richard Pankhurst, 'Suffragette Sisters in Old Age: Unpublished Correspondence between Christabel and Sylvia Pankhurst, 1953–57', *Women's History Review*, vol. 10, no. 3 (2001), pp. 483–537
1643 Ibid.
1644 Ibid.
1645 Cited in Coleman, *Adela Pankhurst*, p. 174

1646 ESP to Frederick Pethick-Lawrence, March 1954, Frederick Pethick-Lawrence MSS, Cambridge University, Trinity College Library
1647 Pearce, *Prevail*, p. 341
1648 *The Times* cited in ibid., p. 195
1649 Ibid.
1650 RKPP and RP, *Ethiopian Reminiscences*, p. 81
1651 Ibid., p. 92
1652 Ibid., p. 95
1653 Ibid., p. 114
1654 Rita Pankhurst, conversations with the author, 23–26 February 2019, Addis Ababa
1655 RKPP and RP, *Ethiopian Reminiscences*, p. 96
1656 Ibid.

35 THE VILLAGE

1657 Barnes, *Tough Annie*, pp. 56, 57
1658 Ibid., p. 57
1659 RKPP and RP, *Ethiopian Reminiscences*, p. 201
1660 Cited in Srivastava, *Italian Colonialism and Resistances to Empire*, p. 151
1661 Cited in Benn, *Keir Hardie*, p. 232
1662 *Woman's Dreadnought*, 26 May 1917
1663 *New Times and Ethiopia News*, 11 March 1939
1664 See RKPP, 'Plans for Mass Jewish Settlement in Ethiopia (1935–1941)', *Ethiopia Observer*, vol. 15, no. 4 (1973), pp. 235–45
1665 Cited in RKPP, *Sylvia Pankhurst*, p. 76
1666 Benn, *Keir Hardie*, p. 412
1667 Ibid., p. 232
1668 Cited in ibid.
1669 Ibid.
1670 Mandela, *Long Walk to Freedom*, p. 349
1671 Ibid.
1672 Ibid., p. 348
1673 Ibid., pp. 350–1
1674 Cited in Mitchell, *The Fighting Pankhursts*, p. 291
1675 Cited in ibid.
1676 Cited in ibid.
1677 Geoffrey Last, head of the Medhane Alem School in Addis, cited in Harrison, *Sylvia Pankhurst*, p. 261
1678 Cited in Mitchell, *The Fighting Pankhursts*, p. 291
1679 Cited in ibid.

1680 Cited in ibid.
1681 Cited in ibid.
1682 Howe to FO, 12 January 1945, cited in RKPP, *Sylvia Pankhurst: Counsel for Ethiopia*, p. 213
1683 I am grateful to Helen Pankhurst for informing me of the Amharic colloquial name.
1684 *New Times and Ethiopia News*, cited in Mitchell, *The Fighting Pankhursts*, p. 292
1685 Ibid.
1686 Ibid., p. 293
1687 Maurice Petherick to Anthony Eden, 8 February 1945, TNA FO 371/46950, J.563
1688 Mitchell, *The Fighting Pankhursts*, p. 293
1689 ESP cited in ibid.
1690 See Dervla Murphy, *In Ethiopia with a Mule* (London: John Murray, 1968)
1691 Cited in Harrison, *Sylvia Pankhurst*, p. 256
1692 Cited in RKPP, *Sylvia Pankhurst: Counsel for Ethiopia*, p. 215
1693 Cited in Mitchell, *The Fighting Pankhursts*, p. 294
1694 Louisa Reid, *Liverpool Echo*, 8 January 1953
1695 Cited in RKPP, *Sylvia Pankhurst: Counsel for Ethiopia*, p. 216
1696 Cited in ibid.
1697 Cited in ibid.
1698 Cited in ibid.
1699 Cited in ibid., p. 213

36 PATRIOT

1700 Robert Gale Woolbert, 'The Ethiopian People: Their Rights and Progress', *Foreign Affairs*, January 1947, https://www.foreignaffairs.com/reviews/capsule-review/1947-01-01/ethiopian-people-their-rights-and-progress
1701 Mitchell, *The Fighting Pankhursts*, p. 308
1702 Ibid. David Mitchell is paraphrasing this from Woolbert, 'The Ethiopian People: Their Rights and Progress'
1703 RKPP and RP, *Ethiopian Reminiscences*, p. 79
1704 Cited in ibid., p. 311
1705 ESP, Letter to the Editor, *Canadian Medical Association Journal*, vol. 66, no. 1 (January 1952), pp. 77–8 at p. 78
1706 *New Times and Ethiopia News*, 3 May 1952
1707 RKPP and RP, *Ethiopian Reminiscences*, p. 80
1708 Ibid., pp. 80–1

1709 ESP and RKPP, *Ethiopia and Eritrea: The Last Phase of the Reunion Struggle, 1941–1952* (Woodford Green: Lalibela House, 1953), dedication
1710 Cited in ibid., p. 314
1711 Cited in ibid.
1712 Cited in ibid., p. 315
1713 Cited in Mitchell, *The Fighting Pankhursts*, p. 316
1714 Cited in ibid., p. 317
1715 Ibid., p. 318
1716 Ibid., ESP to W. E. B. Du Bois, 27 March 1946, mums312-b111-i455
1717 Ibid., W. E. B. Du Bois to ESP, 31 July 1946, mums312-b111-i456
1718 Greeting card from ESP to W. E. B. Du Bois, December 1948, W. E. B. Du Bois Papers (MS 312), mums312-b121-i233, Special Collections and University Archives, University of Massachusetts Amherst Libraries
1719 Ibid., W. E. B. Du Bois to ESP, 16 February 1954, mums312-b142-i353
1720 Ibid., ESP to W. E. B. Du Bois, 26 February 1954, mums312-b142-i354
1721 Ibid., ESP to W. E. B. Du Bois, 11 October 1946, mums312-b111-i470
1722 W. E. B. Du Bois, *Ethiopia Observer*, vol. 5, no. 1 (1961)
1723 Ibid., ESP to W. E. B. Du Bois, 15 March 1954, mums312-b142-i356
1724 Rita Pankhurst, 'Sylvia Pankhurst and Ethiopia', undated essay, p. 12, www.sylviapankhurst/com/her_campaigns/sylvia_ethiopia. At the time of writing, www.sylviapankhurst.com is offline while under reconstruction. Citations here are from a PDF of the article in the author's possession. The website is scheduled for relaunch in 2020 in a joint project by the Redbridge Museum & Heritage Centre, Woodford County High School and New City College, Ilford, Essex, supported by the Heritage Lottery Fund.

37 LOOK FOR ME IN A WHIRLWIND

1725 Haile Selassie telegram to ESP, 17 May 1941, cited in Harrison, *Sylvia Pankhurst*, p. 249
1726 ESP to FPL, 1 May 1956, cited in Harrison, *Sylvia Pankhurst*, p. 268
1727 *Woodford Times*, 10 July 1956
1728 RKPP and RP, *Ethiopian Reminiscences*, p. 97
1729 Rita Pankhurst, conversations with the author, 23–26 February 2019, Addis Ababa
1730 RKPP and RP, *Ethiopian Reminiscences*, p. 99
1731 Ibid., p. 95
1732 Ibid., p. 96
1733 Ibid.
1734 Cited in Harrison, *Sylvia Pankhurst*, pp. 269–70

1735 Aida Edemariam, *The Wife's Tale: A Personal History* (London: Fourth Estate, 2018), p. 245

1736 Cited in Harrison, *Sylvia Pankhurst*, p. 270

1737 RKPP and RP, *Ethiopian Reminiscences*, p. 133

1738 Ibid., p. 118

1739 Ibid.

1740 Ibid.

1741 Ibid., p. 120

1742 Ibid., pp. 124–5

1743 Ibid., p. 127

1744 Ibid.

1745 Ibid., p. 128

1746 Rita Pankhurst, 'Sylvia Pankhurst and Ethiopia', pp. 13–14

1747 RKPP and RP, *Ethiopian Reminiscences*, p. 125

1748 Ibid., p. 127

1749 Ibid., p. 128

1750 ESP, *TSM*, p. 59

1751 RKPP and RP, *Ethiopian Reminiscences*, p. 126

1752 Ibid., p. 140

1753 Ibid., p. 127

1754 Ibid.

1755 Ibid., p. 135

1756 Rita Pankhurst, cited in ibid.

1757 Ibid., p. 136

1758 Ibid., p. 232

1759 Rankin, *Telegram from Guernica*, p. 174

1760 Cited in Harrison, *Sylvia Pankhurst*, p. 272

1761 Purvis, *Christabel Pankhurst*, p. 507

1762 Cited in ibid., p. 513

1763 Cited in Harrison, *Sylvia Pankhurst*, p. 272

1764 Rita Pankhurst, conversations with the author, 23–26 February 2019, Addis Ababa

1765 RKPP, 'Suffragette Sisters in Old Age', p. 483

1766 All this cited in Purvis, *Christabel Pankhurst*, p. 522

1767 All this cited in ibid.

1768 All this cited in ibid.

1769 RKPP and RP, *Ethiopian Reminiscences*, p. 127

1770 Ibid., p. 100

1771 RKPP and RP, *Ethiopian Reminiscences*, p. 100

1772 See Mitchell, *The Fighting Pankhursts*, p. 318

1773 RKPP and RP, *Ethiopian Reminiscences*, p. 100
1774 Mitchell, *The Fighting Pankhursts*, p. 318

38 *ETHIOPIA OBSERVER*

1775 IISH/SPP/ARCH01029/92
1776 Ibid.
1777 Ibid.
1778 Ibid.
1779 Ibid.
1780 Ibid.
1781 Ibid.
1782 RKPP and RP, *Ethiopian Reminiscences*, p. 138
1783 Ibid., p. 240
1784 Ibid., p. 239
1785 Ibid., p. 129
1786 Ibid., p. 220
1787 Ibid., p. 225
1788 Ibid., p. 203
1789 Cited in Srivastava, *Italian Colonialism and Resistances to Empire*, p. 162
1790 Cited in Mitchell, *The Fighting Pankhursts*, p. 311
1791 Cited in ibid.
1792 Minutes of the General Meeting of the WSF, 15 January 1917, cited in Winslow, 'Sylvia Pankhurst and the Great War', p. 101
1793 RKPP and RP, *Ethiopian Reminiscences*, p. 67
1794 Ibid.

39 IRON LION ZION

1795 RKPP and RP, *Ethiopian Reminiscences*, p. 141
1796 Rita Pankhurst, 'Sylvia Pankhurst and Ethiopia', p. 15
1797 Sefton Delmer, *Daily Express*, 20 October 1958
1798 RKPP and RP, *Ethiopian Reminiscences*, p. 138
1799 Ibid.
1800 Ibid., p. 152
1801 Ibid., p. 153
1802 Keith Bowers, *Imperial Exile: Emperor Haile Selassie in Britain, 1936–40* (Bath: Brown Dog Books, 2016), Kindle location 2260–72
1803 Ibid., location 2272
1804 Ibid.
1805 Rita Pankhurst, 'Sylvia Pankhurst and Ethiopia', undated essay, p. 17

1806 Cited in Harrison, *Sylvia Pankhurst*, p. 273

1807 Ibid.

1808 Cited in ibid.

1809 Cited in ibid., p. 275

1810 ESP, *TSM*, p. 67

1811 Rita Pankhurst, 'Sylvia Pankhurst and Ethiopia', undated essay, p. 18

1812 See Adam Hochschild, 'Magic Journalism', *New York Review of Books*, 3 November 1994

1813 Cited in Mitchell, *The Fighting Pankhursts*, p. 321

1814 RKPP and RP, *Ethiopian Reminiscences*, p. 242

1815 Cited in Mitchell, *The Fighting Pankhursts*, p. 320

1816 Cited in ibid.

1817 ESP to Elsa Fraenkel, Papers of Elsa Fraenkel, Women's Library Archives, LSE, GB106 7EFR/1

1818 Cited in Shirley Harrison, *Sylvia Pankhurst*, p. 274

1819 Rita Pankhurst to her parents, 1 October 1960, correspondence in private collection of Rita and Richard Pankhurst, Addis Ababa

1820 Samuel Beckett, *Proust and Three Dialogues with Georges Duthuit* (London: John Calder, 1987), p. 17

1821 Catherine Hamlin with John Little, *The Hospital by the River: A Story of Hope* (Oxford, UK & Grand Rapids, Mich.: Monarch Books, 2004), p. 95

1822 Rita Pankhurst to her parents, 1 October 1960, correspondence in private collection of Rita and Richard Pankhurst, Addis Ababa

1823 Rita Pankhurst to her parents, 28 September 1960, correspondence in private collection of Rita and Richard Pankhurst, Addis Ababa

1824 RKPP and RP, *Ethiopian Reminiscences*, p. 258

1825 Rita Pankhurst to her parents, 28 September 1960, correspondence in private collection of Rita and Richard Pankhurst, Addis Ababa

1826 Ibid.

1827 Ibid.

1828 Rita Pankhurst to her parents, 1 October 1960, correspondence in private collection of Rita and Richard Pankhurst, Addis Ababa

1829 Rita Pankhurst, conversations with the author, 23–26 February 2019, Addis Ababa

1830 RKPP and RP, *Ethiopian Reminiscences*, p. 259

1831 Ibid., p. 260

1832 https://www.telegraph.co.uk/news/2017/02/17/ethiopians-call-state-funeral-richard-pankhurst-champion-ethiopian/

1833 Rita Pankhurst to her parents, 1 October 1960, correspondence in private collection of Rita and Richard Pankhurst, Addis Ababa

1834 RKPP and RP, *Ethiopian Reminiscences*, p. 259

1835 Memorial Issue, *Ethiopia Observer*, vol. 5, no. 1 (1961)

1836 Hamlin with Little, *The Hospital by the River*, p. 95

1837 See Harrison, *Sylvia Pankhurst*, p. 276

1838 Fenner Brockway, interview with Caroline Benn, in Benn, *Keir Hardie*, p. 98

1839 Cited in Harrison, *Sylvia Pankhurst*, p. 276

1840 *Ethiopia Observer*, vol. 5, no. 1 (1961)

1841 RKPP to Elsa Frankael, 9 October 1960, Papers of Elsa Fraenkel, Women's Library Archives, LSE, GB106 7EFR/1

1842 Rita Pankhurst to her parents, 28 September 1960, correspondence in private collection of Rita and Richard Pankhurst, Addis Ababa

1843 Richard Pankhurst to H.I.M. The Emperor Haile Selassie I, 29 September 1960, correspondence in private collection of Rita and Richard Pankhurst, Addis Ababa

1844 Rita Pankhurst to her parents, 1 October 1960, correspondence in private collection of Rita and Richard Pankhurst, Addis Ababa

1845 Ibid.

1846 Ibid.

1847 Ibid.

1848 RKPP and RP, *Ethiopian Reminiscences*, p. 262

1849 Jeff Pearce, https://medium.com/@jeffpearce/remembering-richard-pankhurst-6cb40a4c483c

1850 Cited in Asserate, *King of Kings*, p. xii

1851 Ibid., p. 318

1852 Thomas Packenham, Preface, in ibid., p. xiii

1853 RKPP and RP, *Ethiopian Reminiscences*, p. 156

1854 Ibid., p. 155

1855 Ibid.

1856 Ibid.

1857 Ibid., p. 157

1858 Ibid.

1859 RKPP, *Sylvia Pankhurst: Counsel for Ethiopia*, p. 249

1860 ESP, 'The Day of the Child', IISH/SPP/ARCH01029/141

1861 Vera Klein telephone conversation with David Mitchell, 23 August 1965, transcript, David Mitchell Papers, Museum of London

1862 Ibid.

AFTERWORD: WHEN I AM GONE

1863 ESP, 'When I am Gone', undated, IISH/SPP/ARCH01029/158
1864 Ibid.
1865 Hardie to ESP, 27 May 1915, IISH/SPP/ARCH01029/7–15(9)
1866 Adela Pankhurst, 'My Mother, an Explanation and Vindication', 1933,
      Adela Pankhurst Walsh Papers, National Library of Australia, Canberra,
      p. 2, cited in Purvis, 'Emmeline Pankhurst (1858–1928), Suffragette
      Leader and Single Parent in Edwardian Britain', p. 90
1867 Lyndall Gordon, conversation with the author, 2017
1868 Elsie Bowerman, letter to David Mitchell, 6 January 1965, David
      Mitchell Collection, Museum of London, GB 389 73.83
1869 Nellie Cressall, conversation with David Mitchell, 5 April 1965,
      transcript, David Mitchell Collection, Museum of London Library
1870 ESP, *Manchester Guardian*, 22 November 1938
1871 Helen Pankhurst, conversation with the author, January 2020
1872 Ibid.

Select Bibliography

Andrew, Christopher, *The Defence of the Realm: The Authorized History of MI5* (London: Allen Lane, 2009)

Aptheker, Herbert (ed.), *The Correspondence of W. E. B. Du Bois* (Amherst, Mass.: University of Massachusetts Press, 1978), vol. III

Asserate, Asfa-Wossen, *King of Kings: The Triumph and Tragedy of Emperor Haile Selassie I of Ethiopia* (London: Haus Publishing, 2015)

Atkinson, Diane, *Rise Up Women! The Remarkable Lives of the Suffragettes* (London: Bloomsbury, 2018)

Barnes, Annie, *Tough Annie: From Suffragette to Stepney Councillor: Annie Barnes in Conversation with Kate Harding and Caroline Gibbs* (London: Stepney Books, 1980)

Basu, Shrabani, *Victoria and Abdul: The True Story of the Queen's Closest Confidant* (Stroud: The History Press, 2010)

Beckett, Francis, *Stalin's British Victims* (Stroud: Sutton Publishing, 2004)

Beckett, Samuel, *Proust and Three Dialogues with Georges Duthuit* (London: John Calder, 1987)

Ben-Ghiat, Ruth and Fuller, Mia (eds), *Italian Colonialism* (London: Palgrave Macmillan, 2008)

Benjamin, Walter, *The Arcades Project*, ed. Rolf Tiedemann, trans. Howard Eiland and Kevin McLaughlin (New York: Belknap Press, 2002)

Benn, Caroline, *Keir Hardie* (London: Hutchinson, 1992)

Berger, John, *Ways of Seeing* (London: BBC and Penguin, 1972)

Blatch, Harriot Stanton, with Alma Lutz, *Challenging Years: The Memoirs of Harriot Stanton Blatch* (New York: G. P. Putnam's Sons, 1940)

Bowers, Keith, *Imperial Exile: Emperor Haile Selassie in Britain, 1936–40* (Bath: Brown Dog Books, 2016)

Brown, Stephanie J., 'An "Insult to Soldiers' Wives and Mothers": The *Woman's Dreadnought's* Campaign against Surveillance on the Home Front, 1914–1915', *Journal of Modern Periodical Studies*, vol. 7, no. 1–2 (2016), pp. 121–62

Bryan, Pauline (ed.), *What Would Keir Hardie Say? Exploring Keir Hardie's Vision and Relevance to 21st Century Politics* (Edinburgh: Luath Press, 2015)

Bullock, Ian and Pankhurst, Richard (eds), *Sylvia Pankhurst: From Artist to Anti-Fascist* (New York: St Martin's Press, 1992)

Carew, Anthony, *The Lower Deck of the Royal Navy, 1900–39: The Invergordon Mutiny in Perspective* (Manchester: Manchester University Press, 1981)

Castle, Barbara, *Sylvia and Christabel Pankhurst* (London: Penguin, 1987)

Challinor, Raymond, *The Origins of British Bolshevism* (London: Croom Helm, 1977)

Cole, Peter, Struthers, David and Zimmer, Kenyon (eds), *Wobblies of the World: A Global History of the IWW* (London: Pluto Press, 2017)

Coleman, Verna, *Adela Pankhurst: The Wayward Suffragette, 1885–1961* (Melbourne: Melbourne University Press, 1996)

Collis, Louise, *Impetuous Heart: The Story of Ethel Smyth* (London: William Kimber, 1984)

Conciliation Committee for Woman Suffrage, *The Treatment of the Women's Deputations of November 18th, 22nd and 23rd, 1910 by the Police* (London: Women's Press, 1911)

Connelly, Katherine, ' "Miss Pankhurst Has Some Jolts in Store": Sylvia Pankhurst's Tours of North America and their Place in Suffrage History', paper at Women's Suffrage and Political Activism conference, Murray Edwards College, Cambridge, 3 February 2018

Connelly, Katherine, *Sylvia Pankhurst: Suffragette, Socialist and Scourge of Empire* (London: Pluto Press, 2013)

Connelly, Katherine, 'Sylvia Pankhurst, the Suffragettes of East London and the Garment Workers of Chicago', in *Chicago History: The Journal of the Chicago History Museum* (forthcoming)

Cox, Judy, *The Women's Revolution: Russia, 1905–1917* (London: Counterfire, 2017)

Crawfurd, Elizabeth, *The Women's Suffrage Movement: A Reference Guide, 1866–1928* (London: UCL Press, 1999)

Crompton, Louis, *Shaw the Dramatist* (Lincoln, Nebr.: University of Nebraska Press, 1969)

George Dangerfield, *The Strange Death of Liberal England* (Stanford: Stanford University Press, 1997)

Davis, Jonathan, 'A New Socialist Influence: British Labour and Revolutionary Russia, 1917–1918', *Scottish Labour History*, vol. 8 (2013), pp. 158–79

Davis, Mary, *Comrade or Brother? A History of the British Labour Movement* (London: Pluto Press, 1993)

Davis, Mary, *Sylvia Pankhurst: A Life in Radical Politics* (London: Pluto Press, 1999)

Day, Sarah, *Mussolini's Island* (London: Tinder Press, 2017)

Debenham, Clare, *Marie Stopes' Sexual Revolution and the Birth Control Movement* (London: Palgrave Macmillan, 2018)

Dodd, Kathryn (ed.), *A Sylvia Pankhurst Reader* (Manchester: Manchester University Press, 1993)

Eagleton, Terry, *Why Marx Was Right* (New Haven & London: Yale University Press, 2011)

Edemariam, Aida, *The Wife's Tale: A Personal History* (London: Fourth Estate, 2018)

Faulkner, Neil, *A Radical History of the World* (London: Pluto Press, 2013)

Fawcett, Millicent Garrett, *Women's Suffrage: A Short History of a Great Movement* (London: T. C. and E. C. Jack, 1912)

Focardi, Filippo and Klinkhammer, Lutz, 'The Question of Fascist Italy's War Crimes: The Construction of a Self-Acquitting Myth (1943–1948)', *Journal of Modern Italian Studies*, vol. 9, no. 3 (2004), pp. 330–48

Foot, Paul, *The Vote: How It was Won and How It was Undermined* (London: Viking, 2005)

Forster, E. M., *Howards End* (London: Penguin Classics, 2012)

Franklin, Stella Miles, *A Gregarious Culture: Topical Writings of Miles Franklin* (Brisbane: University of Queensland Press, 2001)

Gallacher, William, *The Last Memoirs of William Gallacher* (London: Lawrence & Wishart, 1966)

Gallacher, William, *Revolt on the Clyde: An Autobiography*, ed. John Callow (London: Lawrence & Wishart, 2017)

Gallacher, William, *The Rolling of the Thunder* (London: Lawrence & Wishart, 1947)

Graubard, Stephen, *British Labour and the Russian Revolution* (Cambridge, Mass.: Harvard University Press, 1956)

Hamlin, Catherine, with John Little, *The Hospital by the River: A Story of Hope* (Oxford, UK & Grand Rapids, Mich.: Monarch Books, 2004)

Hanson, Clare, *A Cultural History of Pregnancy: Pregnancy, Medicine and Culture, 1750–2000* (London: Palgrave Macmillan, 2004)

Hardie, J. Keir, *From Serfdom to Socialism* (London: George Allen, 1907)

Harrison, Patricia Greenwood, *Connecting Links: The British & American Women's Suffrage Movements, 1900–1914* (Westport, Conn.: Praeger, 2000)

Harrison, Shirley, *Sylvia Pankhurst: A Crusading Life, 1882–1960* (London: Aurum Press, 2003)

Haworth, Alan and Hayter, Diane (eds), *Men Who Made Labour: The PLP of 1906 – the Personalities and the Politics* (London: Routledge, 2006)

Hochschild, Adam, *To End All Wars: A Story of Protest and Patriotism in the First World War* (London: Macmillan, 2011)

Holmes, Rachel, *Eleanor Marx: A Life* (London: Bloomsbury, 2014)

Hughes, Emrys, *Keir Hardie* (London: George Allen & Unwin, 1956)

Hughes-Hallett, Lucy, *The Pike: Gabriele d'Annunzio – Poet, Seducer and Preacher of War* (London: Fourth Estate, 2013)

Hunt, Cathy, 'Ellen and Sylvia: Chelsea, 1906', 12 February 2018, https://cathyhunthistorian.com/2018/02/12/ellen-and-sylvia-chelsea-1906/

Inge, William Ralph (ed.), *The Post-Victorians* (London: Ivor Nicholson & Watson, 1933)

Jackson, Sarah and Taylor, Rosemary, *East London Suffragettes* (Stroud: The History Press, 2014)

Judge, Roy, 'Mary Neal and the Espérance Morris', *Folk Music Journal*, vol. 5, no. 5 (1989), pp. 545–9, http://www.maryneal.org/file-uploads/files/file/1989s1a.pdf

Kenney, Annie, *Memories of a Militant* (London: Edward Arnold, 1924)

Lee, Hermione, *Virginia Woolf* (London: Chatto & Windus, 1997)

Lenin, V. I., *Collected Works*, 4th English edn (Moscow: Progress Publishers, 1965), vol. 31

Lenin, V. I., *'Left-Wing Communism': An Infantile Disorder*, 8th edn (Moscow: Progress Publishers, 1981)

Lytton, Lady Constance (under pseudonym Jane Warton), *Prisons and Prisoners* (London: Virago, 1988)

McKay, Claude, *A Long Way from Home* (New York: Harvest Books, 1970)

Mackenzie, Midge, *Shoulder to Shoulder* (London: Penguin, 1975)

Makonnen, Ras, *Pan-Africanism from Within*, ed. Kenneth King (Oxford: Oxford University Press, 1973)

Malnig, Julie (ed.), *Ballroom, Boogie, Shimmy Sham, Shake: A Social and Popular Dance Reader* (Champaign–Urbana: University of Illinois Press, 2009)

Mandela, Nelson, *Long Walk to Freedom* (London: Abacus, 1995)

Marlow, Joyce (ed.), *Suffragettes: The Fight for Votes for Women* (London: Virago, 2000)

Martin, Jane, 'To "blaise the trail for women to follow along": sex, gender and the politics of education on the London School Board, 1870–1904', University College Northampton, 1999, http://eprints.ioe.ac.uk/2136/1/G%26E_Martin_1999Blaise_the_trail.pdf

Matteoti, Giacomo, *The Fascisti Exposed: A Year of Fascist Domination* (London: ILP Publications, 1924)

Merridale, Catherine, *Lenin on the Train* (London: Allen Lane, 2016)

Mills, Dana, *Dance & Politics: Moving beyond Boundaries* (Manchester: Manchester University Press, 2017)

Mills, Dana, *Rosa Luxemburg* (London: Reaktion, 2020)

Mitchell, Alexandra, 'Middle-Class Masculinity in Clubs and Associations: Manchester and Liverpool, 1800–1914', PhD thesis, University of Manchester, 2011

Mitchell, David, *The Fighting Pankhursts* (London: Jonathan Cape, 1967)

Mitchell, David, *Queen Christabel: A Biography of Christabel Pankhurst* (London: Macdonald & Jane's, 1977)

Morgan, Kenneth O., *Keir Hardie: Radical and Socialist* (London: Weidenfeld & Nicolson, 1975)

Mosley, Leonard, *Haile Selassie: The Conquering Lion* (Englewood Cliffs, NJ: Prentice-Hall, 1965)

Murphy, Dervla, *In Ethiopia with a Mule* (London: Eland Publishing, 2012)

Mussolini, Benito, co-written with Giovanni Gentile, *The Political and Social Doctrine of Fascism (1932)*, trans. Jane Soames (London: Hogarth Press, 1933)

Negash, Tekeste, *Woven into the Tapestry: How Five Women Shaped Ethiopian History* (Los Angeles: Tsehai Publishers and Loyola Marymount University, 2016)

Orwell, George, *Fascism and Democracy* (London: Penguin, 2020)

Pankhurst, Christabel, *Unshackled: The Story of How We Won the Vote*, ed. Lord Pethick-Lawrence of Peaslake (London: Hutchinson, 1959)

Pankhurst, Emmeline, *My Own Story* (London: Vintage, 2015)

Pankhurst, E. Sylvia, *Communism and its Tactics (1921–22)*, ed. and introduced by Mark A. S. Shipway (Edinburgh: self-published by Mark Shipway, 1982)

Pankhurst, E. Sylvia, *Delphos: The Future of International Language* (London: Kegan Paul, Trench, Trubner, 1928)

Pankhurst, E. Sylvia, *Ex-Italian Somaliland* (London: Watts, 1951)

Pankhurst, E. Sylvia, *The Home Front: A Mirror to Life in England during the World War* (London: Hutchinson, 1932)

Pankhurst, E. Sylvia, *Housing and the Workers' Revolution* (London: Workers' Socialist Federation, 1918)

Pankhurst, E. Sylvia, *India and the Earthly Paradise* (Delhi: B. R. Publishing Corporation, 1985)

Pankhurst, E. Sylvia, *The Life of Emmeline Pankhurst: The Suffragette Struggle for Women's Citizenship* (Boston & New York: Houghton Mifflin, 1936)

Pankhurst, E. Sylvia, *Rebel Ireland* (London: Workers' Socialist Federation, 1919)

Pankhurst, E. Sylvia, *Richard Marsden Pankhurst: A Eulogy by his Daughter* (Redditch: Maurois Press/Read Books, 2011)

Pankhurst, E. Sylvia, *Save the Mothers: A Plea for Measures to Prevent the Annual Loss of about 3,000 Child-Bearing Mothers and 20,000 Infant Lives in England and Wales and a Similar Grievous Wastage in Other Countries* (London: Alfred A. Knopf, 1930)

Pankhurst, E. Sylvia, 'Some Autobiographical Notes', in *Jaarboek/Yearbook International Archives for the Women's Movement*, vol. 1 (Leiden: E. J. Brill, 1937), pp. 88–98

Pankhurst, E. Sylvia, *Soviet Russia as I Saw It* (London: Workers' Dreadnought, 1921)

Pankhurst, E. Sylvia, *A Suffragette in America: Reflections on Prisoners, Pickets and Political Change*, ed. and with an introduction by Katherine Connelly (London: Pluto Press, 2019)

Pankhurst, E. Sylvia, *The Suffragette* (New York: Sturgis & Walton, 1911)

Pankhurst, E. Sylvia, *The Suffragette Movement: An Intimate Account of Persons and Ideals* (London: Virago, 1977)

Pankhurst, E. Sylvia, 'Sylvia Pankhurst', in Countess of Oxford and Asquith (ed.), *Myself When Young by Famous Women of Today* (London: Frederick Muller, 1938), pp. 259–312

Pankhurst, E. Sylvia, *The Truth about the Oil War* (London: Workers' Dreadnought Publications, 1922)

Pankhurst, E. Sylvia, *Writ on Cold Slate* (London: The Dreadnought Publishers, 1922)

Pankhurst, E. Sylvia and Pankhurst, Richard K. P., *Ethiopia and Eritrea: The Last Phase of the Reunion Struggle, 1941–1952* (Woodford Green: Lalibela House, 1953)

Pankhurst, E. Sylvia and Stefanovici, I. O. (eds and trans.), *Poems of Mihail Eminescu* (London: Kegan Paul, Trench, Trubner, 1930)

Pankhurst, Helen, *Deeds Not Words: The Story of Women's Rights, Then and Now* (London: Hodder & Stoughton, 2018)

Pankhurst, Richard, 'Suffragette Sisters in Old Age: Unpublished Correspondence between Christabel and Sylvia Pankhurst, 1953–57', *Women's History Review*, vol. 10, no. 3 (2001), pp. 483–537

Pankhurst, Richard, *Sylvia Pankhurst: Artist and Crusader* (New York & London: Paddington Press, 1979)

Pankhurst, Richard, *Sylvia Pankhurst: Counsel for Ethiopia: A Biographical Essay on Ethiopian, Anti-Fascist and Anti-Colonial History, 1934–1960* (Hollywood, Calif.: Tsehai Publishers, 2003)

Pankhurst, Richard, 'Sylvia and *New Times and Ethiopia News*', in Ian Bullock and Richard Pankhurst (eds), *Sylvia Pankhurst: From Artist to Anti-Fascist* (New York: St Martin's Press, 1992), pp. 149–91

Pankhurst, Richard and Rita, *Ethiopian Reminiscences: Early Days* (Los Angeles: Tsehai Publishers, 2013)

Pankhurst, Rita, 'Sylvia Pankhurst and Ethiopia', undated essay, www. sylviapankhurst/com/her_campaigns/sylvia_ethiopia

Pankhurst, Rita, 'Sylvia Pankhurst in Perspective: Some Comments on Patricia Romero's Book *E. Sylvia Pankhurst, Portrait of a Radical*', *Women's Studies International Forum*, vol. 11, no 3 (1988), pp. 245–62

Pearce, Jeff, *Prevail: The Inspiring Story of Ethiopia's Victory over Mussolini's Invasion, 1935–1941* (New York: Skyhorse Publishing, 2014)

Pelling, Henry, *A History of British Trade Unionism* (London: Penguin, 1992)

Pelling, Henry, *A Short History of the Labour Party* (London & Basingstoke: Macmillan Press, 1982)

Pethick-Lawrence, Emmeline, *My Part in a Changing World* (London: Gollancz, 1938)

Pethick-Lawrence, Frederick, *Fate Has Been Kind* (London: Hutchinson, 1943)

Pollitt, Harry, *Serving my Time: An Apprenticeship to Politics* (London: Lawrence & Wishart, 1940)

Pugh, Martin, *The Pankhursts: The History of One Radical Family* (London: Vintage, 2008)

Purvis, June, *Christabel Pankhurst: A Biography* (London & New York: Routledge, 2018)

Purvis, June, 'Did Militancy Help or Hinder the Granting of Women's Suffrage in Britain?', *Women's History Review*, vol. 28, no. 7 (2019), pp. 1200–34

Purvis, June, *Emmeline Pankhurst: A Biography* (London & New York: Routledge, 2003)

Purvis, June, 'Emmeline Pankhurst (1858–1928), Suffragette Leader and Single Parent in Edwardian Britain', *Women's History Review*, vol. 20, no. 1 (2011), pp. 87–108

Purvis, June, 'The Prison Experiences of the Suffragettes in Edwardian Britain', *Women's History Review*, vol. 4, no. 1 (1995), pp. 103–33

Purvis, June, 'The Women's Party of Great Britain (1917–19): A Forgotten Episode in British Women's Political History', *Women's History Review*, vol. 25, no. 4 (2016), pp. 638–51

Raeburn, Antonia, *The Militant Suffragettes* (London: Michael Joseph, 1973)

Rankin, Nicholas, *Telegram from Guernica: The Extraordinary Life of George Steer, War Correspondent* (London: Faber & Faber, 2003)

Raw, Louise, *Striking a Light: The Bryant and May Matchwomen and their Place in History* (London: Bloomsbury, 2009)

Rebel Ireland: 'Thoughts on Easter Week, 1916' by E. Sylvia Pankhurst; 'Scenes from the Rebellion' by Patricia Lynch; 'The First Sinn Fein Member of Parliament' by May O'Callaghan (London: The Workers' Socialist Federation, 1919)

Reed, John, *Ten Days that Shook the World* (London: Penguin, 1977)

Robins, Elizabeth, *The Convert* (New York: Macmillan, 1913)

Robinson, Jane, *Hearts and Minds: The Untold Story of the Great Pilgrimage and How Women Won the Vote* (London: Doubleday, 2018)

Roe, Jill, *Her Brilliant Career: The Life of Stella Miles Franklin* (Cambridge, Mass.: Belknap Press, 2009)

Rogers, J. A., *The Real Facts about Ethiopia* (Mansfield Centre, Conn.: Martino Publishing, 2015)

Romero, Patricia, *E. Sylvia Pankhurst: Portrait of a Radical* (New Haven & London: Yale University Press, 1990)

Rose, Jacqueline, Mothers: *An Essay on Love and Cruelty* (London: Faber & Faber, 2018)

Rowbotham, Sheila, *Dreamers of a New Day: Women Who Invented the Twentieth Century* (London: Verso, 2010)

Rowbotham, Sheila, *Hidden from History: 300 Years of Women's Oppression and the Fight against It* (London: Pluto Press, 1973)

Schreiner, Olive, *Story of an African Farm* (1883) (Oxford: Oxford University Press, 2008)

Segal, Lynn, *Radical Happiness* (London: Verso, 2017)

Service, Robert, *Lenin: A Biography* (London: Macmillan, 2000)

Shaw, George Bernard, *Saint Joan* (London: Penguin, 2001)

Shiach, Morag, ' "To Purify the Dialect of the Tribe": Modernism and Language Reform', *Modernism/modernity*, vol. 14, no. 1 (2007), pp. 21–34

Shipway, Mark, *Anti-Parliamentary Communism: The Movement for Workers' Councils in Britain, 1917–45* (London: Palgrave Macmillan, 1988)

Smith, H. L. (ed.), *British Feminism in the Twentieth Century* (Aldershot: Edward Elgar, 1990)

Smyth, Ethel, *Female Pipings in Eden* (London: Peter Davies, 1933)

Smyth, Ethel, *The Memoirs of Ethel Smyth*, ed. Ronald Crichton (London: Viking, 1987)

Sparham, Anna, *Soldiers & Suffragettes: The Photography of Christina Broom* (London: Philip Wilson Publishing and Museum of London, 2015)

Srivastava, Neelam, *Italian Colonialism and Resistances to Empire, 1930–1970* (Cambridge: Cambridge University Press, 2018)

Stewart, William, *J. Keir Hardie: A Biography* (London: Independent Labour Party, 1925)

Stone, Helena, 'The Soviet Government and Moonshine, 1917–1929', *Cahiers du Monde Russe et Soviétique*, vol. 27, no. 3/4 (July–December 1986), pp. 359–79

Stranger, Yves-Marie, *Ethiopia through Writers' Eyes* (London: Eland Publishing, 2016)

Stuart, Tristram, *The Bloodless Revolution: Radical Vegetarians and the Discovery of India* (London: HarperCollins, 2006)

Taylor, Rosemary, *In Letters of Gold: The Story of Sylvia Pankhurst and the East London Federation of the Suffragettes in Bow* (London: Stepney Books, 1993)

Togliatti, Palmiro, *Lectures on Fascism* (London: Lawrence & Wishart, 1976)

Vaninskaya, Anna, ' "My Mother, Drunk or Sober": G. K. Chesterton and Patriotic Anti-Imperialism', *History of European Ideas*, vol. 34, no. 4 (2008), pp. 535–47, DOI: 10.1016/j.histeuroideas.2008.07.001

Wainwright, Robert, *Miss Muriel Matters: The Fearless Suffragist Who Fought for Equality* (London: Allen & Unwin, 2017)

Waugh, Evelyn, *Waugh in Abyssinia* (Baton Rouge: Louisiana State University Press, 2007)

Wells, H. G., *Ann Veronica* (London: Virago, 1980)

Whitman, Walt, *Leaves of Grass* (Philadelphia: David McKay, 1891–2)

Williams, Val, *Women Photographers: The Other Observers, 1900 to the Present* (London: Virago, 1986)

Winslow, Barbara, 'Sylvia Pankhurst and the Great War', in Ian Bullock and Richard Pankhurst (eds), *Sylvia Pankhurst: From Artist to Anti-Fascist* (New York: St Martin's Press, 1992), pp. 86–120

Winslow, Barbara, *Sylvia Pankhurst: Sexual Politics & Political Activism* (London: Routledge, 1996)

Woolbert, Robert Gale, 'The Ethiopian People: Their Rights and Progress', *Foreign Affairs*, January 1947, https://www.foreignaffairs.com/reviews/capsule-review/1947-01-01/ethiopian-people-their-rights-and-progress

Woolf, Leonard, *Imperialism and Civilization* (London: Hogarth Press, 1928)

Wright, Patrick, 'Dropping their Eggs: The History of Bombing', *London Review of Books*, vol. 23, no. 16 (23 August 2001), https://www.lrb.co.uk/the-paper/v23/n16/patrick-wright/dropping-their-eggs

Zagladin, Vadim Valentinovich et al. (eds), *The International Working-Class Movement*, vol. 4: *The Socialist Revolution in Russia and the International Working Class (1917–23)* (Moscow: Progress Publishers, 1984)

Index

Acknowledgements

My early research for this biography was supported and enabled by a generous grant from The Authors' Foundation, for which I'm indebted to the Society of Authors and those who leave legacies to writing. I benefited from a visiting literary fellowship at Mansfield College, Oxford, where talks and responses to early draft papers helped me work out how to approach the composition of this book. I am enormously grateful to Helena Kennedy for my time there, and the conversations it produced, in particular with her and Sheila Rowbotham.

I visited many archives, libraries and museums in the course of my research. I am especially indebted to the International Institute of Social History in Amsterdam (IISG), part of the Royal Netherlands Academy of Arts and Sciences, which has become something of a second home. It is to the Dutch that the British owe thanks for the preservation of the greater part of Sylvia Pankhurst's vast personal archive. The IISG has recently invested in state-of-the-art digitization of the Sylvia Pankhurst Papers that now makes this precious archive available on open source as never before.

There are numerous Sylvia Pankhurst collections and holdings across the United Kingdom, maintained by wonderful people committed to her legacy, to all of whom I owe my thanks. In Manchester and Salford, I am forever grateful to The Pankhurst Centre, the Working Class Movement Library, People's History Museum and the University of Manchester Library. In London, the Women's Library housed by the London School of Economics, the National Archives, East End Women's Museum, Imperial War Museum and British Library are custodians of profoundly important Sylvia Pankhurst collections, where I was assisted by terrific archivists and librarians. My particular appreciation to the brilliant Meirian Jump at the Marx Memorial Library & Workers' School, and to the librarians at the Museum of London Library who so patiently helped me work my way through David Mitchell's labyrinthine storehouse of primary Pankhurst research. Many thanks to young feminist scholar Tania Shew for her bibliographical research that helped me plot my course.

I had the opportunity to try out segments of this work before a number of audiences who gave me extremely helpful feedback. My thanks in particular to those who invited, listened and responded at the TUC, Wolfson College, Oxford, the London School of Economics, National Portrait Gallery, Tolpuddle Radical History School, Gladstone Library, and the British Academy. I'm particularly grateful to Mary Davis, Fiona Smith, Isobel Armstrong, Maya Goodfellow, Lyndall Gordon, Hermione Lee, Les Kennedy, and Robert Service for their engagement. I have been enriched by glimpses of Joan Ashworth's fascinating film about Sylvia in development, and the dialogue that this exciting work has generated.

A great deal of thought and writing for this book took place at Gladstone's Library in Hawarden, where I was a Writer in Residence in 2015, and to which haven of inspiration, informed discussion and collegiality I often return. I am particularly grateful to Peter and Helen Francis, generous hosts who have become treasured friends. Britain's only Prime Ministerial library is an incredible place for writers to congregate and create. I spent the summer of 2016 with a wonderful group of international artists on a Cove Park Literary Residency, for another book in development. Nonetheless, the discussions on the shores of Loch Long – not least on the night of the Brexit referendum – contributed to this work as well. I cannot thank Polly, Julian and Lucy Clarke enough, and for sharing a love of boats as well as books.

I owe a huge debt to the generosity and solidarity of individual scholars, in particular John Callow, Katherine Connelly and Dana Mills. John shared discoveries about Sylvia that turned up in the course of his own research into other British socialists. His knowledgeable nudges in the right directions were the height of subtlety and support, and I am indebted to his work on Sylvia's friends and comrades, particularly William Gallacher. Katherine Connelly has been the quintessential learned comrade and stalwart friend to me and this book. Dana Mills has shared the journey from the start, contributing in so many significant ways, reeling in critical research with expertise and enthusiasm on tireless dancing feet. Her new works on *Rosa Luxemburg* and *Dance and Activism* form a choreography of conversation and community of thought with this book.

My heartfelt thanks to the Pankhurst family for their grace, forbearance and generosity. Sylvia's granddaughter, Helen Pankhurst, has been an invaluable help throughout. She introduced me to her brother Alula and their late mother Rita, and also shared her significant insights as a writer. Her first-hand knowledge, fact checking and sharing of new material are a testament to her feminist solidarity. Alula was unstintingly hospitable and informative in Addis. Rita was one of the most remarkable people that I have ever met.

I owe so much to Alexandra Pringle, as my publisher and champion of all women writers. Michael Fishwick is that rarest of beings: a great editor. We spent much of the winter of 2019 line-editing in the best tradition – old-school style – in his Bloomsbury office. He has that special gift of being able to read a writer's mind and is a joy and inspiration to work with. It takes a natural born rebel to know one. According to Tolstoy, the two most powerful warriors are time and patience. I had a third in Peter James. He caught infelicities of language, awkward repetitions, questions of chronology and errors of transcription in his meticulous manuscript editing. His exacting standards, sharp curiosity, wit and eloquence are in a league of their own. We worked together in the sudden new world of lockdown, and I am so grateful for his consummate professionalism amidst unprecedented challenges. I am very grateful to Lin Vasey for bringing fresh eyes and new perspectives – and a great deal of stamina – to Sylvia's large life.

Miranda Havelock-Allan has been the most miraculous picture editor. She did superb work in difficult times, tracking down images and liaising with a plethora of institutions who are also coping with the impact of Covid 19. Her excellent eye, aesthetic flair, unending patience, thoroughness and good humour make her the best and most reliable of colleagues.

None of us have ever before worked through a book production process under pandemic conditions. The nimble resilience and commitment of my publisher Bloomsbury have been exemplary. Enormous gratitude to marvellous managing editor Lauren Whybrow for becoming a General in Sylvia's Army. Thanks to Ruth Crafer for photographing women as we are. The brilliant Emma Ewbank has designed a jacket fit for a great graphic designer and artist, and thanks to Lilidh Kendrick who so adeptly managed its realisation. I am so lucky to have Hetty Touquet as Sylvia's ambassador for this book, along with Hannah Paget, Penny Liechti, and the whole team at Bloomsbury.

I owe the greatest debt of gratitude to the incomparable Sarah Chalfant and Alba Ziegler-Bailey at The Wylie Agency. Alba has also brought her skills as a historian to this book and I am deeply grateful for her wisdom and intellect. Thanks also to Jessica Bullock and everyone who supports me there.

None of it would have been possible without great colleagues and good friends. For sharing the journey over the years, my special thanks to: Zackie Achmat, Tahmima Anam, Meredith Anderson, Lisa Appignanesi, Jane Beese, Brian Box, Florri Burton, Paul Burston, Shami Chakrabarti, Morgan Cooper, Natasha Fairweather, Andrew Feinstein, Nathan Geffen, Mark Gevisser, Gav Gillibrand, Lennie Goodings, Colin Grant, Diane Gray-Smith, Ronnie Green, John Greyson, Ellie Hobhouse, Christian Hopper, Nadine Houghton, Adel Jabbar, Jude Kelly, Jack Lewis, Loring McAlpine, Fiona McMorrough, Samantha Meeson, Gillian Moore, Kate and Greg Mosse, Tania, Hanna and Bassem Nasir, Susheila Nasta, Susie Nicklin, Frances O'Grady, Margie Orford, John Owen, Ursula Owen, Nii Parkes, Maha Khan Phillips, Graham Reid, Janie and Jim Rodgers, Jacqueline Rose, Josie Rourke, Susanna Rustin, Deok Joo Rhee, Bee Rowlatt, Louise and Adam Shaljean, Lemn Sissay, Kamila Shamsie, Faizel Slamang, Gillian Slovo, Rick Stroud, Shirley Thompson and Jeanette Winterson.

Thank you, Karen Simmons, the best of friends, so close for so long, even when so far away. Susie Abulhawa, thank you for the solidarity during the hard graft and urging me onwards. Polly Clayden, you are a true Sylvian and sister, here finally is the outcome of all those conversations long ago in Muizenberg. Thank you Sarah Hickson, kindred nomad, but always there. Thank you Nathalie Handal, sister soul. Thank you Ali Smith for offering the right words when I needed them most. Thank you, Ann Grant for always believing in me, for the rock-solid support during the long haul, for being such a good reader and great fun. Deep gratitude to Ahdaf Soueif for enhancing my understanding of Sylvia's art and vision, by way of Coptic Angels, Khufu Ship and Umm Kulthum. Your own fearless example illuminates the mezzaterra from which Sylvia Pankhurst's legacy is so urgently calling.

Carmen Callil started it all. Our continuing conversation about Sylvia has shaped this book and been profound and sustaining. Thank you from the furious young feminist saved by the University of Virago. You never forget the courage of others and I never forget yours.

Thanks always to all my family, in particular to my big sister Karen Holmes and my little sister Gudi Pibernik, my aunt Ruth Jesinskis and all the Silén tribe. Gratitude also to my extended family, especially my godson Rufus Shaljean and the Plattners – Samantha, Willy, Maria Pia and Harald.

Thank you to my beloved mother Karin Pibernik, who has maintained her enthusiasm and support for the process of writing this book through the hardest of times. We will always miss Helmut, who faced death with courage, and life with the greatest sense of humour.

Jonathan Evans is an extraordinary reader. He is such a special person, with a heart and intellect that are simply unique. Principled, thoughtful and consistent in less than stable times and always looking for the reasoned argument buried by the noise. Thank you – once again – for making this possible, for all the understanding, inspiration, encouragement, wonderful debates and constant love and support. The world would be a kinder place if there were more like you. Thank you for sustaining me, day in, day out, and for keeping the ship on course in all weather.

This book is dedicated to two extraordinary sisters: Sarah Holmes & Ann Baskerville, with a lifetime of my gratitude, admiration and love.

About the Author

Rachel Holmes is the author of *Eleanor Marx: A Life*, *The Secret Life of Dr James Barry* and *The Hottentot Venus: The Life and Death of Sarah Baartman*.

Note on the Type

The text of this book is set Adobe Garamond. It is one of several versions of Garamond based on the designs of Claude Garamond. It is thought that Garamond based his font on Bembo, cut in 1495 by Francesco Griffo in collaboration with the Italian printer Aldus Manutius. Garamond types were first used in books printed in Paris around 1532. Many of the present-day versions of this type are based on the *Typi Academiae* of Jean Jannon cut in Sedan in 1615.

Claude Garamond was born in Paris in 1480. He learned how to cut type from his father and by the age of fifteen he was able to fashion steel punches the size of a pica with great precision. At the age of sixty he was commissioned by King Francis I to design a Greek alphabet, and for this he was given the honourable title of royal type founder. He died in 1561.